Consumer Bankers Association	www.cbanet.org
Conway Data, Inc.	www.conway.com
Countrywide Financial Corp.	www.countrywide.com
Credit Research Foundation	www.crfonline.org
Credit Union National Association	www.cuna.org
Dailyii.com	www.institutionalinvestor.com
DefaultRisk.com	www.defaultrisk.com
The Derivatives 'Zine	www.margrabe.com
Deutsche Bundesbank	www.bundesbank.de
Dresdner Bank	www.dresdner-bank.de
Dun & Bradstreet	www.dnb.com
Economagic.com	www.economagic.com
eFinancialCareers Ltd.	www.efinancialcareers.com
Equifax	www.equifax.com
European Banking Industry Committee	www.eubic.org
European Central Bank	www.ecb.int
Experian	www.experian.com
FairIsaac	www.fairisaac.com
FannieMae	www.fanniemae.com
Farin & Associates	www.cyfi.com
The Federal Deposit Insurance Corporation	www.fdic.gov
Federal Financial Institutions Examination Council	www.ffiec.gov
Federal Reserve Bank of Chicago	www.chicagofed.org
Federal Reserve Bank of Cleveland	www.clevelandfed.org
Federal Reserve Bank of Kansas City	www.kc.frb.org
Federal Reserve Bank of New York	www.ny.frb.org
Federal Reserve Bank of Richmond	www.richmondfed.org
Federal Reserve Bank of San Francisco	www.frbsf.org
Federal Reserve Bank of St. Louis	www.stlouisfed.org
Federal Reserve Discount Window	www.frbdiscountwindow.org
Federal Trade Commission	www.ftc.gov
Federally Insured Savings Network	www.fisn.com
FHLB Boston	www.fhlbboston.com
Finance Encyclopedia	www.finance-encyclopedia.com
Financial Institutions Center	http://fic.wharton.upenn.edu
Financial Jobs	www.financial-jobs.com
Financial Managers Society	www.fmsinc.org
Financial Pipeline	www.finpipe.com
Financial Security Assurance, Inc.	www.fsa.com
FindLaw	www.library.findlaw.com
Freddie Mac	www.freddiemac.com
FreeCreditDerivatives.com	www.freecreditderivatives.com
Futuresweb	www.futuresweb.com
GE Capital	www.gecapital.com
Global Islamic Banking Consulting	www.globalislamicbanking.com
GMAC Financial Services	www.gmacfs.com
Hedge Fund Center	www.hedgefundcenter.com
Home Loan Learning Center	www.homeloanlearningcenter.com
How to Advice	www.howtoadvice.com
HSBC	www.hsbcusa.com
HSH Associates	www.hsh.com
IBT	www.intbantec.com
iHireBanking LLC	www.ihirebanking.com

Welcome to the Educational Version of Market Insight!

www.mhhe.com/edumarketinsight

Check out your textbook's website for details on how this special offer enhances the value of your purchase!

1. To get started, use your web browser to go to
www.mhhe.com/edumarketinsight

2. Enter your site ID exactly as it appears below.

3. You may be prompted to enter the site ID for future use—please keep this card.

Your site ID is:

ua11n879

STANDARD
&POOR'S

ISBN: 978-0-07-304629-7
MHID: 0-07-304629-9

 McGraw-Hill
Irwin

Bank Management & Financial Services

The McGraw-Hill/Irwin Series in Finance, Insurance and Real Estate

Stephen A. Ross
*Franco Modigliani Professor of Finance
and Economics
Sloan School of Management
Massachusetts Institute of Technology
Consulting Editor*

FINANCIAL MANAGEMENT

Adair
Excel Applications for Corporate Finance
First Edition

Benninga and Sarig
Corporate Finance: A Valuation Approach

Block and Hirt
Foundations of Financial Management
Twelfth Edition

Brealey, Myers, and Allen
Principles of Corporate Finance
Eighth Edition

Brealey, Myers and Marcus
Fundamentals of Corporate Finance
Fifth Edition

Brooks
FinGame Online 4.0

Bruner
**Case Studies in Finance: Managing for
Corporate Value Creation**
Fifth Edition

Chew
**The New Corporate Finance: Where
Theory Meets Practice**
Third Edition

Chew and Gillan
**Corporate Governance at the Crossroads:
A Book of Readings**
First Edition

DeMello
Cases in Finance
Second Edition

Grinblatt and Titman
Financial Markets and Corporate Strategy
Second Edition

Helfert
**Techniques of Financial Analysis:
A Guide to Value Creation**
Eleventh Edition

Higgins
Analysis for Financial Management
Eighth Edition

Kester, Ruback, and Tufano
Case Problems in Finance
Twelfth Edition

Ross, Westerfield and Jaffe
Corporate Finance
Eighth Edition

Ross, Westerfield, Jaffe and Jordan
**Corporate Finance: Core Principles
and Applications**
First Edition

Ross, Westerfield and Jordan
Essentials of Corporate Finance
Fifth Edition

Ross, Westerfield and Jordan
Fundamentals of Corporate Finance
Eighth Edition

Shefrin
**Behavioral Corporate Finance: Decisions
That Create Value**
First Edition

White
**Financial Analysis with an Electronic
Calculator**
Sixth Edition

INVESTMENTS

Adair
Excel Applications for Investments
First Edition

Bodie, Kane and Marcus
Essentials of Investments
Sixth Edition

Bodie, Kane and Marcus
Investments
Seventh Edition

Hirt and Block
Fundamentals of Investment Management
Eighth Edition

Hirschey and Nofsinger
Investments: Analysis and Behavior
First Edition

Jordan and Miller
**Fundamentals of Investments: Valuation
and Management**
Fourth Edition

FINANCIAL INSTITUTIONS
AND MARKETS

Rose and Hudgins
Bank Management & Financial Services
Seventh Edition

Rose and Marquis
**Money and Capital Markets: Financial
Institutions and Instruments in a Global
Marketplace**
Ninth Edition

Saunders and Cornett
**Financial Institutions Management:
A Risk Management Approach**
Fifth Edition

Saunders and Cornett
**Financial Markets and Institutions: An
Introduction to the Risk Management
Approach**
Third Edition

INTERNATIONAL FINANCE

Eun and Resnick
International Financial Management
Fourth Edition

Kuemmerle
**Case Studies in International
Entrepreneurship: Managing and
Financing Ventures in the Global
Economy**
First Edition

REAL ESTATE

Brueggeman and Fisher
Real Estate Finance and Investments
Thirteenth Edition

Corgel, Ling and Smith
**Real Estate Perspectives: An Introduction
to Real Estate**
Fourth Edition

Ling and Archer
Real Estate Principles: A Value Approach
Second Edition

FINANCIAL PLANNING
AND INSURANCE

Allen, Melone, Rosenbloom and Mahoney
**Pension Planning: Pension,
Profit-Sharing, and Other Deferred
Compensation Plans**
Ninth Edition

Altfest
Personal Financial Planning
First Edition

Harrington and Niehaus
Risk Management and Insurance
Second Edition

Kapoor, Dlabay, and Hughes
**Focus on Personal Finance: An Active
Approach to Help You Develop Successful
Financial Skills**
First Edition

Kapoor, Dlabay, and Hughes
Personal Finance
Eighth Edition

Bank Management & Financial Services

Seventh Edition

Peter S. Rose
Texas A & M University

Sylvia C. Hudgins
Old Dominion University

McGraw-Hill
Irwin

Boston   Burr Ridge, IL   Dubuque, IA   Madison, WI   New York   San Francisco   St. Louis
Bangkok   Bogotá   Caracas   Kuala Lumpur   Lisbon   London   Madrid   Mexico City
Milan   Montreal   New Delhi   Santiago   Seoul   Singapore   Sydney   Taipei   Toronto

McGraw-Hill Irwin

BANK MANAGEMENT & FINANCIAL SERVICES
Published by McGraw-Hill/Irwin, a business unit of The McGraw-Hill Companies, Inc., 1221 Avenue of the
Americas, New York, NY, 10020. Copyright © 2008 by The McGraw-Hill Companies, Inc. All rights reserved.
No part of this publication may be reproduced or distributed in any form or by any means, or stored in a
database or retrieval system, without the prior written consent of The McGraw-Hill Companies, Inc.,
including, but not limited to, in any network or other electronic storage or transmission, or broadcast for
distance learning.
Some ancillaries, including electronic and print components, may not be available to customers outside the
United States.

This book is printed on acid-free paper.

1 2 3 4 5 6 7 8 9 0 QPD/QPD 0 9 8 7 6

ISBN: 978-0-07-304623-5
MHID: 0-07-304623-X

Editorial director: *Brent Gordon*
Executive editor: *Paul Ducham*
Editorial assistant: *Michelle Driscoll*
Executive marketing manager: *Dan Wiencek*
Media producer: *Jennifer Fisher*
Project manager: *Marlena Pechan*
Lead production supervisor: *Michael R. McCormick*
Lead designer: *Matthew Baldwin*
Cover design: *Studio Montage*
Lead media project manager: *Becky Szura*
Typeface: *10/12 Goudy*
Compositor: *Laserwords Private Limited, Chennai, India*
Printer: *Quebecor World Dubuque Inc.*

Library of Congress Cataloging-in-Publication Data

Rose, Peter S.
    Bank management & financial services / Peter S. Rose, Sylvia C. Hudgins.—7th ed.
       p. cm.
    Includes index.
    ISBN-13: 978-0-07-304623-5 (alk. paper)
    ISBN-10: 0-07-304623-X (alk. paper)
    1. Financial institutions—United States. 2. Bank management—United States. 3. Financial
services industry—United States. 4. Banks and banking, International. I. Hudgins, Sylvia
Conway, 1956– II. Title. III. Title: Bank management and financial services.
HG181.R65 2008
332.1068—dc22
                                                                                          2006018734

To my family.

—Peter S. Rose

To my mother, Bertha Watson Hudgins
(1920–2004).

—Sylvia C. Hudgins

Brief Contents

Contents

PART SIX
PROVIDING LOANS TO BUSINESSES AND CONSUMERS   511

Chapter 16
Lending Policies and Procedures   513

Chapter 17
Lending to Business Firms and Pricing Business Loans   543

Chapter 18
Consumer Loans, Credit Cards, and Real Estate Lending 583

PART SEVEN
MANAGING THE FUTURE IN A GLOBAL MARKETPLACE 621

Chapter 19
Acquisitions and Mergers in Financial-Services Management 623

Preface

Banks lie at the heart of the world's financial system. They represent the source we often visit to find a loan to purchase a new home or automobile, start a new business, or finance a college education. They execute our orders by check, plastic card, telephone, or electronic network to pay for the many goods and services we buy daily. They provide credit cards that offer a convenient record of how we spend our money and invite us to "buy now and pay later." They protect and manage our savings to help us prepare financially for a "rainy day," for help with college expenses, and for the retirement years when we hope to experience a different side of life. They advise us on the investments we make, help guide our businesses in raising funds in the capital markets, and create markets where old loans are sold to raise cash for making new loans.

But banks are not the only financial firms today that stand in the spotlight at the center ring of the financial system. In truth, for many of us it is no longer possible to separate banks from other financial firms. Whether it's a security broker or dealer, insurance company, credit union, family of mutual funds, finance company, or even retail stores like Target and J.C. Penny—all seem to offer many of the same financial services and advertise for our business in about the same way. Moreover, some of the biggest and best known of what we sometimes call "nonbank" institutions (such as Prudential, Met Life, State Farm, and Merrill Lynch) now own and operate their own banks, which in many cases are growing rapidly and recording solid profits. And knocking on the door is the world's biggest retailer, Wal-Mart, which seems to be venturing into financial services with one new service after another, including credit cards, money orders, and money transfers. Wal-Mart seems to be testing the waters of the financial marketplace and perhaps getting ready for the biggest splash of all, creating or acquiring a bank if they can gain federal and state approval.

There was a time—it seems like ages ago now—when, if we wanted to study banking, we might ignore these other financial institutions, fierce competitors though they are, and somehow pretend they weren't there. That time passed us by long ago and today compels us to explore the management principles and best practices not just of banks, but all the rest of the financial-services sector as well. The manager of any financial institution who ignores this highly competitive, kaleidoscopic financial-service environment won't be around the shop for long anymore. After all, consumers know which way the wind is blowing in the financial system and now are cruising the Internet to find the best deals and don't seem to care a whole lot whose name happens to be attached to the particular financial services they buy.

Of course, banks, insurance companies, security firms, and other financial-service providers have not taken these recent events lying down. The most aggressive are struggling to be ever bigger, more cost competitive and efficient, increasingly globalized, selling their wares by television, satellite, and the Web and reaching into every city and continent on the planet. Some observers say there is no room anymore for the "small fry" in financial services—the small bank, modest-size finance company, store-front insurance agency, etc., situated just down the street. Yet, strangely, thousands of these "small fry" financial firms are still with us and, in every year that passes, still more new small firms appear with their financial weapons in hand, ready to joust, often quite successfully, with the biggest financial companies around.

Thus, writing a book about financial-service institutions today is a daunting challenge. We have to present the principles of sound management and best practice, arming our readers with the knowledge they need to grapple with the biggest and the smallest financial-service providers, the narrow-focused boutiques and the highly service-diversified giants, the regulated and the unregulated financial providers, the familiar financial institutions and those not so well-known but just emerging to grab a piece of the financial-services pie. Sounds tough, doesn't it?

Yes, writing about and studying financial institutions *is* a tough job, but it's also adventurous and exciting! Financial services is an industry we ignore at our personal and professional peril. We must learn how to be comfortable with our knowledge of these firms and the services they offer because each of us as individuals and as professionals in our chosen field must rely upon their services as essentials that will shape our future.

Moreover, some of us may need to know even more about financial firms because they often represent an attractive *career* opportunity. After all, financial-service providers are becoming more and more creative, more and more sensitive about how to "sell" their products instead of just sitting there and waiting for a customer to walk in the door or key into their Web site. Securing a job and a career in this dynamic sector of the economy might be a fascinating and challenging alternative for you to explore. Hopefully this book will help you decide whether banking and financial services offers a real career opportunity that meets your needs and interests.

New and Continuing Trends Covered in the Seventh Edition

The great changes that are reshaping banking and financial services today are captured in all parts of this new seventh edition of *Bank Management & Financial Services*. Among the key trends to watch for as you progress through this new edition of the text are the following:

- Expanded coverage of the growing controversy over *the walls erected by the United States, Japan, and other nations separating banking and commerce in order to safeguard the public's funds* and *Wal-Mart's possible future expansion into banking and financial services* (see especially Chapters 1, 2, and 20).

- A more in-depth look at *nonbank financial institutions, especially investment banks, insurance companies, and finance companies* and their increasingly aggressive role within the financial system. *Investment banking,* in particular, has been given substantially greater prominence in this new edition with greater emphasis on the interaction between commercial and investment banking firms (particularly in Chapters 2, 3, and 14).

- Expanded coverage of the increasingly dominating role played today by *financial holding companies (FHCs),* bringing together banks, insurance companies, investment banks, and other financial firms under the same corporate umbrella. FHCs now hold the majority of assets reported by all American financial institutions (see especially Chapters 2, 3, and 14).

- Examination of the emergence of *virtual banks*—their strategies, services, and competitive limitations (particularly in Chapters 3 and 4).

- A more in-depth analysis of *Basel II* as the largest banks around the world come under new capital guidelines laid down by the recently revised *Basel Agreement* among leading nations, including an expanded discussion of value at risk (VaR), internal modeling, and stress testing (see especially Chapter 15).

- An exploration of newly recognized forms of risk in banking and financial services, including *operational risk, compliance and legal risk, reputational risk,* and *strategic risk* (particularly in Chapters 6 and 15).

- Expanded coverage of the *securitization process* and *credit derivatives*—devices aimed at reducing risk exposure and providing new sources of revenue for financial institutions (see especially Chapter 9).

- Expanded coverage of *international banking* and the critical roles played by *foreign central banks*, especially the *central banks of China, Japan,* and the *European Community,* where we take a close look at their similarities and differences with the Federal Reserve System in the United States (particularly in Chapters 2 and 20).

- The presentation of new information on *the use of futures and options contracts to track central bank monetary policy* and its possible impact on the management of financial institutions working to control interest rate risk (see especially Chapter 8).

- Exploration of the *banking industry structure* in other leading nations outside the United States, especially looking at the varied structure of banking and financial services inside China, Japan, and leading nations of Western Europe (particularly in Chapters 3 and 20).

- Expanded discussion of possible *simplification of the regulatory structure* of the United States, Great Britain, and other industrialized nations in an effort to more efficiently use regulatory resources and increase regulatory effectiveness in a financial marketplace increasingly characterized by much larger, but fewer, financial firms (see especially Chapters 2, 15, and 20).

- Examination of the new *Check 21 Act* and the dramatic changes going on inside the payments system, especially the rapid growth of electronic information and electronic money transfers and the increasingly widespread use of digital imaging and substitute checks (particularly in Chapters 2, 12, and 18).

- Exploration of the *FACT Act* and its emerging role in grappling with the vexing problem of *identity theft* plaguing many consumers seeking access to financial services and presenting financial institutions with significant financial losses and damage to their public credibility (see especially Chapters 2 and 18).

- Expanded coverage of the controversial issues surrounding *customer privacy* and *customer security,* including the search for new ways for financial institutions to perform *customer authentication* (particularly in Chapters 4, 14, and 18).

- Examination of the causes and possible consequences of the recently passed U.S. *Bankruptcy Abuse Prevention and Consumer Protection Act,* the first major change in the federal bankruptcy code in nearly 30 years (see especially Chapters 2 and 18).

- Discussion of the controversial *Bank Secrecy* and *Patriot Acts* in the United States and similar laws in Great Britain and their application to the financial services sector, including the costs that must be borne by financial institutions attempting to carry out the customer surveillance requirements of these laws (particularly in Chapter 2).

- Introduction to the new *FDIC Insurance Reform Act of 2005,* which calls for increasing federal insurance coverage on retirement deposits of various types and for the possible indexing of deposit insurance protection for the effects of inflation (see especially Chapters 2 and 12).

- Increased attention to *FICO credit scoring* and the crucial role *credit bureaus* play today in the consumer lending process (particularly in Chapter 18).

- Expanded coverage of the *real estate mortgage market* and the rapid development of newer and more controversial mortgage instruments, including *interest-only (option) home mortgage loans* that may place new home owners under significant financial stress (see especially Chapter 18).

- An in-depth look at the growing array of *fee income* sources among financial firms (particularly in Chapters 5 and 14).

- New or expanded coverage of several unique dimensions of today's financial-services environment, including the intense competition now under way between banking and *captive finance companies* (especially in Chapter 17), *economies of scope and the diversification of financial services* (particularly in Chapter 14), and the *identification of key information sources for international bankers* (especially in Chapter 20).

- An exploration of some of the most exotic financial instruments developed in recent years, including *option mortgages, equity-linked CDs, trust-preferred securities, equity-indexed annuities, dynasty trusts, exchange-traded funds,* and *range notes,* to name a few (see especially Chapters 10, 14, 15, and 18).

- An examination of the risks associated with *duration and interest-sensitive gaps* with special emphasis on the challenges facing *Fannie Mae (FNMA)* and *Freddie Mac (FHLMC)* in the residential mortgage market (particularly in Chapters 7, 8, and 9).

- Movement of the important chapter on *establishing new financial-service delivery channels* (which in earlier editions was Chapter 18) into Part One of the new edition (now Chapter 4), dealing with the *chartering of new banks,* the *expansion of branch offices, ATM-provided services, telephone services,* and *Internet-based services.* This is where we can learn about the most important service-delivery vehicles through which financial firms reach out to the public and provide those financial services most in demand (see especially Chapters 3 and 4).

- *Ethics* remains a key issue in the new edition along with the continuing controversy over the Sarbanes/Oxley Accounting Standards Act, and there are several boxes that take us on a tour of important ethical issues in finance (for example, in Chapters 2, 3, and 14).

- A new section at the conclusion of the final chapter that takes a glimpse at the *future of banking and the financial-services industry,* reviewing several of the key trends presented in earlier chapters and projecting how those ongoing trends may reshape the future of this vital industry and the future of us all (Chapter 20).

Pedagogical Features of the Seventh Edition: Enhancing Teaching and Learning

This new seventh edition is a combination of time-tested tools for more effective teaching and learning plus new features that enhance both teaching and learning. Among the new educational features of the seventh edition are:

- Many *new problems and newly revised problems, including Excel problems,* expanding upon the extensive set of exercises and problems from previous editions.
- *More URLs* in the margins of the textual material that point the reader to new informational Web site adventures in financial services.
- Retention and expansion in the new edition of the *factoids* and *filmtoids* that were so popular in the previous edition.
- Narrowing of box material to the most crucial topics, including informational boxes labeled *E-Banking and E-Commerce, Real Banks, Real Decisions, Insights and Issues,* and *Ethics in Banking and Financial Services.*

All chapters in the seventh edition, as in previous editions, have several key elements designed to help the reader. These include:

Part Openers which describe the material about to be presented in the chapters of each of the seven parts of the text and point out the significance of what is about to be learned.

Chapter Introductions that set the tone and list the most important topics that will be addressed in the book's chapters.

Key URLs which have been expanded in number and coverage and appear repeatedly in the text margins.

Factoids that present pertinent and interesting facts about items under discussion in the text and are designed to excite the interest of our readers.

Filmtoids which cite popular movies that have focused on the banking and financial services sector. (Some instructors apparently have shown portions of these films in class.)

Boxed Features which sharply focus on e-commerce, real-world management decision-making, various key issues affecting the financial-services sector, and ethical dilemmas faced by financial firms and their managers.

Concept Checks which are laced in at crucial points in each chapter's discussion to challenge the reader with questions and problems in order to make sure he or she has grasped the key points just read.

Chapter Summaries that concisely outline each chapter's key points and provide a useful tool not only to double-check the reader's sensitivity to chapter content but also to prepare for exams and other assignments.

Key Terms at the end of the chapters with the page numbers cited, showing where definitions and discussions of those terms may be found.

Problems and Projects that challenge the reader with numerous numerical problems (including Excel problems) to solve and pertinent issues to discuss. Many of these problems are either new or contain new data and facts for the user to experiment with.

Internet Exercises which ask the reader to "go digging" in the rich reservoir of the Worldwide Web to learn what resources are present to help amplify the understanding of each chapter, to gather information on significant financial-service issues, and employ Web-based data to help unravel problems and issues.

Real Numbers for Real Banks at the end of each chapter guides the reader into the extensive Web site of data on individual depository institutions and the banking system that is maintained by the Federal Deposit Insurance Corporation. This section asks the user to conduct an analysis, create exhibits and tables, and draw management-oriented conclusions from the data pulled from this most comprehensive Web site.

S&P Market Insight Challenge poses interesting issues for the reader to explore by extracting pertinent data from the huge S&P database of hundreds of financial and nonfinancial firms and analyzing the data that has been gathered in order to reach important conclusions.

Selected References arranged by topic at the conclusion of each chapter give the reader suggestions about where to go to find more reading material pertinent to the chapter's discussion in recently published articles and studies.

A **Dictionary of Banking and Financial-Service Terms** at the end of the book lists and defines the most important technical terms found throughout the book so that the reader can review and remember the terminology of the financial-services marketplace.

Supplementary Educational Materials

Readers of this text and those who teach have access to outstanding educational supplements. The most important of these supplements include:

- **Instructors Manual and Testbank,** which provides an outline of each chapter, makes available hundreds of questions to answer and problems to solve that assist instructors in putting lectures and exams together, and suggests learning devices to support the classroom experience.

- **PowerPoint Presentation System** to help structure classroom lectures and discussions and provide students with logically arranged and complete study notes. These slides contain numerous charts, graphs, and numerical examples as well as outlines of key points from each chapter. Those choosing the PowerPoint slides to organize and present material can rearrange and edit these slides to meet their particular educational requirements.

- **Text Web site, www.mhhe.com/rose7e**, is open to both students and their instructors. Periodically after the new edition appears the authors supply new chapter updates to the Web site in order to pass on to readers the newest developments in the field that surface between editions.

- **S&P Market Insight, Educational Version, www.mhhe.com/edumarketinsight,** is a large database consisting of hundreds of financial and nonfinancial corporations. This site draws together extensive information from the financial and operating statements of hundreds of large corporations and will aid readers in unraveling several problem and research assignments that are presented throughout the text, enabling them to check out individual companies and form groups of companies for comparative analysis. Many readers not only draw upon S&P's Market Insight for reports to class, but often compile important information when seeking employment after graduation and want to research the background of the companies they might work for.

The foregoing supplementary educational tools can help make each class and educational setting a place where people who really want to learn really do have plenty of opportunities to do so.

Grateful Acknowledgment to Those Who Have Contributed to This Book

As this text has gone through its various editions over the years the authors have benefited in many ways from the criticisms and creative ideas of professionals in the banking and financial-services field. These talented and dedicated people include:

Faud Abdullah
University of Nebraska–Omaha

Lyle L. Bowlin
University of Northern Iowa

Emile J. Brinkmann
University of Houston

Samuel Bulmash
Stockton College

Tony Cherin
San Diego State University

Edwin Cox
Boston University

David R. Durst
University of Akron

Jack Griggs
Abilene Christian University

James B. Kehr
Miami University

George W. Kutner
Marquette University

Young Kwak
Delaware State University

Nelson J. Lacey
University of Massachusetts–Amherst

Edward C. Lawrence
The University of Missouri–St. Louis

David G. Martin
Bloomsberg University

James E. McNulty
Florida Atlantic University

Iqbal Memon
Fort Lewis College

Armand Picou
University of Central Arkansas

Sudhir Singh
Frostberg State University

David Rand
Northwest Tech College in Ohio

David Stewart
Winston-Salem University

William Sackley
*University of North Carolina
at Wilmington*

Oliver G. Wood, Jr.
University of South Carolina

The authors wish to offer a special note of gratitude to those talented professionals who helped with their comments and suggestions in the building of this new seventh edition, including:

Ronnie Clayton
Jacksonville State University

William H. Lepley
University of Wisconsin–Green Bay

David T. Flynn
University of North Dakota–Grand Forks

Walt A. Nelson
Southwest Missouri State University

Scott Hein
Texas Tech University

Therese E. Pactwa
St. John's University

Marcos A. Kerbel
Florida International University

Cevdet Uruk
University of Memphis

George W. Kutner
Marquette University

Robert Wyatt
University of Northern Iowa

The authors also express their gratitude to Ann Gleason for her good work in preparing the PowerPoint slides and tackling the daunting task of preparing the *Instructor's Manual* and the all-important test bank. A note of gratitude also must be expressed to *The Canadian Banker* and the Canadian Bankers' Association for permission to use portions of earlier articles written by one of the authors.

We are also thankful for the high quality of work and advice provided by the professionals in editing and production at McGraw-Hill Higher Education. This must include a special note of thanksgiving and gratitude for the contributions of Steve Patterson, Paul Ducham, Michelle Driscoll, Dan Wiencek, Marlena Pechan, and Peter deLissovoy for the dedication and professionalism they demonstrated repeatedly and that is so essential to complete a book of this size and detail. Any demerits and deficiencies, however, belong to the authors.

A Note to Students and Other Readers of This Book

The banking and financial-services sector of a modern economy represents one of those topics about which few of us can afford to be ignorant. Our lifestyles and living standards often depend on the willingness of financial-service firms to extend us credit, protect and manage our savings, and make payments on our behalf to the businesses from whom we buy goods and services. However, the banking and financial-services sector is changing rapidly today—some experts call it a *revolution*—so we can no longer be content with only a casual, broad-brush understanding of what is happening and why.

This textbook, now in its seventh edition, is crafted with *you* in mind. It is designed specifically to help you dig deeply into this fascinating and often trouble-plagued segment of our economic system. The authors want to make it possible for you to master the ideas behind the management of these important institutions and to be able to confront head on the often confusing mix of risk, regulation, technological change, and competition that financial-service managers must face every day.

This text includes several learning aids that are designed to help you achieve mastery of this subject. In particular, the following learning aids stand out:

1. Each major part of the book begins with a *Part Opener* to help explain the goals and most important topics covered by the chapters in that part. In short, each Part Opener offers you a road map of what interesting issues lie ahead in the collection of chapters belonging to that portion of the book.

2. Each chapter opens with an *Introduction* to set the stage for what is to follow and to explain the overall importance of the subjects and issues to be presented.

3. Numerous references to the Internet appear in the margins of every chapter, labeled *Key URLs*—a place to go when you need to know more about the subject under discussion (perhaps to complete an assignment or just because you are curious).

4. Interesting facts and supporting background information appear in the margins under the labels *Factoids* and *Filmtoids*, with the former raising interesting questions and answering them on the spot and the latter asking if you have ever seen a particular Hollywood film that happens to address the topics you are reading about. The list includes some extremely popular films that you may be able to find in your neighborhood video store or from online movie sources.

5. You will confront *Concept Checks* in every chapter placed at critical points in order to pose questions and problems to help you determine if you feel comfortable with what you have read and have grasped what's going on.

6. Each chapter concludes with a bulleted *Summary* that lists the key points delivered by the chapter so you can get a quick refresher. Often these summaries are helpful when you are facing an exam or preparing a report.

7. Immediately after the Summary is a list of *Key Terms* designed to help you learn the language of banking and the financial-services marketplace. You will notice page numbers after each key term, making it possible for you to find the point within each

chapter where that particular term is defined and discussed. This can also be handy information when you are reviewing for an exam or wish to prepare a report.

8. A *Dictionary of Banking and Financial-Service Terms* lies at the back of the book, supplying definitions for a large number of key terms presented in the text. If you have been assigned a specific chapter or collection of chapters to read, you may want to double-check your understanding of the key terms by employing this dictionary.

9. Several kinds of problems and questions appear toward the end of each chapter (including new Excel problems). These are labeled *Problems and Projects, Internet Exercises, S&P Market Insight Challenge,* and *Real Numbers for Real Banks.* You are likely to find that these problems, in many different formats, can be especially useful in firming up what you have learned and in introducing additional ideas you would benefit from knowing. Your instructor may assign some of these problems to help strengthen what you know.

10. Boxed features called *Insights and Issues, Real Banks, Real Decisions, E-Banking and E-Commerce, Ethics in Banking and Financial Services,* and others appear throughout the text. Their function is to explore new ideas and raise thoughtful, sometimes controversial issues, offering you specific, relevant views of today's financial world.

Although this text provides you with many ideas and tools to help you along the road toward mastery of the subject, it is, like every book, locked in time. It supplies a snapshot of the world of banking and financial services at a particular moment in time. However, this is an industry in change and we must go beyond one book to keep up with the ever-unfolding financial scene. The authors' hope is to awaken your interest in this field and encourage you to go further. If *Bank Management & Financial Services* makes you eager to read and understand *more* about this very important sector of the economy it will have done its job.

The financial-services marketplace is one of those areas of study in which the effort you put into the subject is likely to pay big dividends down the road. You are likely to find a sense of accomplishment and fulfillment if you are willing to put the required effort and time into this important subject.

Indeed, there is an old piece of wisdom that contends: "chance favors the prepared mind." It may be an old idea, but it certainly holds true in this particular field. Mastery of this subject builds your confidence and determination and is likely to reward you greatly in the long run, no matter what twists and turns the future may bring to your life.

We extend our best wishes for your successful journey in the days, weeks, months, and years ahead. Our hope is that a rewarding journey for you begins this very day and ultimately reaches far beyond the boundaries of a single semester or term.

Peter S. Rose and Sylvia C. Hudgins

PART ONE

Introduction to the Business of Banking and Financial-Services Management

Opening this book launches us on an adventure, exploring one of the oldest and most important industries in the world. Banking and the financial-services industry encompasses some of the largest business firms ever created—behemoths such as Citibank, J. P. Morgan Chase, and Bank of America in the United States, Toronto-Dominion Bank in Canada, Deutsche Bank in Germany, and Barclays PLC in Great Britain. And let's not forget banking's huge nonbank competitors, including AXA, ING, Prudential, MetLife, GE Capital, GMAC, Fannie Mae, Freddie Mac, and scores of other financial-service giants that serve every major market around the globe. Yet, astonishingly, this industry also contains some of the smallest businesses to ever open their doors, such as Heritage Bank in Bozeman, Montana.

Whether big or small, however, banking and the financial-services industry has a profound effect on our lives, influencing the availability of jobs, the cost of living, the adequacy of our savings, and the quality of our existence.

However, banking and the financial-services industry as we know it today is rapidly becoming a quite different industry than in the past. For example, bank and nonbank financial firms are declining in numbers, *consolidating* into fewer but also much larger companies that may be more efficient and failure resistant. At the same time banks, insurance companies, security dealers, finance companies, and other financial firms are *converging* toward each other, each proliferating the number of services they offer to capture new markets. The result is that the boundaries between banking, insurance, security firms, finance companies, and other financial-service providers are becoming hopelessly blurred—customers, employees, and industry regulators often cannot tell the difference between them. Financial-service providers are aggressively invading each other's territories.

For example, if you are looking for a credit card today you can probably find what you are looking for not only at the neighborhood bank, but also from retailers such as Target and Wal-Mart, from leading security firms such as Fidelity and Merrill Lynch, and from major insurance companies such as Prudential and State Farm. If you are seeking a personal loan and your credit is good you likely have thousands of options, from credit card companies and credit unions to finance companies and security brokers, not to mention your friendly neighborhood bank. If you are computer oriented and want to access financial services over the Internet, virtual banks and scores of other financial-service vendors are waiting there for you, reflecting the fact that the entire financial-services sector is undergoing a vast wave of technological change. Instead of focusing just on banking today, as we used to do in the past, we must continually expand our focus to view banking within a far broader financial-services industry. Instead of using only a microscope we also need a telescope or we may miss something really important!

Hang on, then, because this rapidly changing industry is about to unfold before us. In this opening part of the text we explore the origins of financial-service providers, examine their range of services, tally up who the key competitors are, and see what career opportunities may be waiting out there for you if you find enjoyment and satisfaction in learning about the financial-services industry. We also explore the important roles played by government in regulating and supervising financial firms and discover how these firms are organized today and the service-delivery vehicles (such as branches, ATMs, cell phones, the Internet, etc.) they employ to attract and hold their customers.

We welcome you on this important journey and hope you find it fascinating and useful as you live for the present and plan for the future.

CHAPTER ONE

An Overview of Banks and the Financial-Services Sector

Key Topics in This Chapter

- Powerful Forces Reshaping the Industry
- What Is a Bank?
- The Financial System and Competing Financial-Service Institutions
- Old and New Services Offered to the Public
- Key Trends Affecting All Financial-Service Firms
- Appendix: Career Opportunities in Financial Services

1–1 Introduction

There is an old joke attributed to comedian Bob Hope that says "a bank is a financial institution where you can borrow money only if you can prove you don't need it." Although many of a bank's borrowing customers may get the impression that old joke is more truth than fiction, the real story is that banks today readily provide hundreds of different services to millions of people, businesses, and governments all over the world. And many of these financial services are vital to our personal well-being and the well-being of the communities and nations where we live.

Banks are the principal source of credit (loanable funds) for millions of individuals and families and for many units of government (school districts, cities, counties, etc.). Moreover, for small businesses ranging from grocery stores to automobile dealers, banks are often the major source of credit to stock shelves with merchandise or to fill a dealer's lot with new cars. When businesses and consumers must make payments for purchases of goods and services, more often than not they use bank-supplied checks, credit or debit cards, or electronic accounts accessible through a Web site. And when they need financial information and financial advice, it is the banker to whom they turn most frequently for advice and counsel. More than any other financial-service firm, banks have a reputation for public trust.

Worldwide, banks grant more installment loans to consumers (individuals and families) than any other financial-service provider. In most years, they are among the leading buyers of bonds and notes governments issue to finance public facilities, ranging from auditoriums and football stadiums to airports and highways. Banks are among the most important sources of short-term working capital for businesses and have become increasingly active in recent years in making long-term business loans to fund the purchase of new plant and equipment. The assets held by U.S. banks represent about one-fifth of the total assets and an even larger proportion of the earnings of all U.S.-based financial-service institutions. In other nations—for example, in Japan—banks hold half or more of all assets in the financial system. The difference is because in the United States, many important non-bank financial-service providers can and do compete to meet the needs of businesses, consumers, and governments.

Powerful Forces Are Reshaping Banking and Financial Services Today

As we begin our study of this important industry, we should keep in mind the great forces reshaping the whole financial-services sector. For example, most banks today are profitable—and, in fact, in several recent quarters they have posted record earnings—but their *market share* of the financial-services marketplace is falling significantly. As the former chairman of the Federal Deposit Insurance Corporation (FDIC) noted recently, in 1980 insured commercial banks and other depository financial institutions held more than 90 percent of Americans' money—a share that had dropped to only about 45 percent as the 21st century opened. Over the same time span, banks' and other depositories' share of U.S. credit market liabilities fell from about 45 percent of the grand total to only about 25 percent (as reported by Powell [6]).

The industry is also *consolidating* rapidly with substantially fewer, but much larger, banks and other financial firms. For example, the number of U.S. commercial banks fell from about 14,000 to fewer than 8,000 between 1980 and 2005. The number of separately incorporated commercial banks in the United States has now reached the lowest level in more than a century, and much the same pattern of industry consolidation appears around the globe in most financial-service industries.

Moreover, banking and the financial-services industry are rapidly *globalizing* and experiencing *intense competition* in marketplace after marketplace around the planet, not just between banks, but also involving security dealers, insurance companies, credit unions, finance companies, and thousands of other financial-service competitors. These financial heavyweights are all *converging* toward each other, offering parallel services and slugging it out for the public's attention. If consolidation, globalization, convergence, and competition were not enough to keep an industry in turmoil, banking and its financial-service neighbors are also undergoing a *technological revolution* as the management of information and the production and distribution of financial services become increasingly electronic. For example, thanks to the Check 21 Act passed in the United States in 2004, even the familiar "paper check" is gradually being replaced with electronic images. People increasingly are managing their deposit accounts through the use of personal computers, cell phones, and debit cards, and there are *virtual banks* around the world that offer their services exclusively through the Internet.

Clearly, if we are to understand banks and their financial-service competitors and see where they all are headed, we have our work cut out for us. But, then, you always wanted to tackle a big challenge, right?

1–2 What Is a Bank?

As important as banks are to the economy as a whole and to the local communities they call home, there is still much confusion about what exactly a **bank** is. A *bank* can be defined in terms of (1) the economic functions it serves, (2) the services it offers its customers, or (3) the legal basis for its existence.

Factoid
What nation has the greatest number of *commercial* banks?
Answer: The United States with about 7,800 commercial banks, followed by Germany with close to 2,500.

Certainly banks can be identified by the *functions* they perform in the economy. They are involved in transferring funds from savers to borrowers (financial intermediation) and in paying for goods and services.

Historically, banks have been recognized for the great range of financial services they offer—from checking accounts and savings plans to loans for businesses, consumers, and governments. However, bank service menus are expanding rapidly today to include investment banking (security underwriting), insurance protection, financial planning, advice for merging companies, the sale of risk-management services to businesses and consumers, and numerous other innovative services. Banks no longer limit their service offerings to traditional services but have increasingly become *general financial-service providers*.

Unfortunately in our quest to identify what a bank is, we will soon discover that not only are the functions and services of banks changing within the global financial system, but their principal competitors are going through great changes as well. Indeed, many financial-service institutions—including leading security dealers, investment bankers, brokerage firms, credit unions, thrift institutions, mutual funds, and insurance companies—are trying to be as similar to banks as possible in the services they offer. Examples include Merrill Lynch, Dreyfus Corporation, and Prudential Insurance—all of which own banks or banklike firms. Moreover, if this were not confusing enough, several industrial companies have stepped forward in recent decades in an effort to control a bank and offer loans, credit cards, savings plans, and other traditional banking services. Examples of these giant banking-market invaders include General Motors Acceptance Corporation (GMAC), GE Capital, and Ford Motor Credit, to name only a few. Even Wal-Mart, the world's largest retailer, recently has explored the possibility of acquiring an industrial bank in Utah in an effort to expand its financial-service offerings! American Express and Target already control banklike institutions.

Bankers have not taken this invasion of their turf lying down. They are demanding relief from traditional rules and lobbying for expanded authority to reach into new markets all around the globe. For example, with large U.S. banks lobbying heavily, the United States Congress passed the Financial Services Modernization Act of 1999 (known more popularly as the Gramm-Leach-Bliley or GLB Act after its Congressional sponsors), allowing U.S. banks to enter the securities and insurance industries and permitting nonbank financial holding companies to acquire and control banking firms.

To add to the prevailing uncertainty about what a bank is, over the years literally dozens of organizations have emerged from the competitive financial marketplace proudly bearing the label of *bank*. As Exhibit 1–1 shows, for example, there are savings banks, investment banks, mortgage banks, merchant banks, universal banks, and so on. In this text we will spend most of our time focused upon the most important of all banking institutions—the commercial bank—which serves both business and household customers all over the world. However, the management principles and concepts we will explore in the chapters that follow apply to many different kinds of "banks" as well as to other financial-service institutions that provide similar services.

While we are discussing the many different kinds of banks, we should mention an important distinction between banking types that will surface over and over again as we make our way through this text—*community banks* versus *money-center banks*. Money-center banks are giant industry leaders, spanning whole regions, nations, and continents, offering the widest possible menu of financial services, gobbling up smaller businesses, and facing tough competition from other giant financial firms around the globe. Community banks, on the other hand, are usually much smaller and service local communities, towns, and cities, offering a significantly narrower, but often more personalized, menu of financial services to the public. As we will see, community banks are declining in numbers, but they also are proving to be tough competitors in the local areas they choose to serve.

EXHIBIT 1–1
The Different Kinds of Financial-Service Firms Calling Themselves *Banks*

Name of Banking-Type Firm	Definition or Description
Commercial banks:	Sell deposits and make loans to businesses and individuals
Money center banks:	Are large commercial banks based in leading financial centers
Community banks:	Are smaller, locally focused commercial and savings banks
Savings banks:	Attract savings deposits and make loans to individuals and families
Cooperative banks:	Help farmers, ranchers, and consumers acquire goods and services
Mortgage banks:	Provide mortgage loans on new homes but do not sell deposits
Investment banks:	Underwrite issues of new securities by their corporate customers
Merchant banks:	Supply both debt and equity capital to businesses
Industrial banks:	State-chartered loan companies owned by financial or nonfinancial corporations
International banks:	Are commercial banks present in more than one nation
Wholesale banks:	Are larger commercial banks serving corporations and governments
Retail banks:	Are smaller banks serving primarily households and small businesses
Limited-purpose banks:	Offer a narrow menu of services, such as credit card companies and subprime lenders
Bankers' banks:	Supply services (e.g., check clearing and security trading) to banks
Minority banks:	Focus primarily on customers belonging to minority groups
National banks:	Function under a federal charter through the Comptroller of the Currency
State banks:	Function under charters issued by banking commissions in the various states
Insured banks:	Maintain deposits backed by federal deposit insurance plans (e.g., the FDIC)
Member banks:	Belong to the Federal Reserve System
Affiliated banks:	Are wholly or partially owned by a holding company
Virtual banks:	Offer their services only over the Internet.
Fringe banks:	Offer payday and title loans, cash checks, or operate as pawn shops and rent-to-own firms
Universal banks:	Offer virtually all financial services available in today's marketplace.

One final note in our search for the definition of *banks* concerns the *legal basis* for their existence. When the federal government of the United States decided that it would regulate and supervise banks more than a century ago, it had to define what was and what was not a bank for purposes of enforcing its rules. After all, if you plan to regulate banks you have to write down a specific description of what they are—otherwise, the regulated firms can easily escape their regulators, claiming they aren't really banks at all!

The government finally settled on the definition still used by many nations today: A *bank is any business offering deposits subject to withdrawal on demand* (such as by writing a check or making an electronic transfer of funds) *and making loans of a commercial or business nature* (such as granting credit to private businesses seeking to expand the inventory of goods on their shelves or purchase new equipment). Over a century later, during the 1980s, when hundreds of financial and nonfinancial institutions (such as J. C. Penney and Sears) were offering either, but not both, of these two key services and, therefore, were claiming exemption from being regulated as a bank, the U.S. Congress decided to take another swing at the challenge of defining banking. Congress then defined a *bank* as *any institution that could qualify for deposit insurance administered by the Federal Deposit Insurance Corporation (FDIC)*.

A clever move indeed! Under federal law in the United States a *bank* had come to be defined, not so much by its array of service offerings, but by the government agency insuring its deposits! Please stay tuned—this convoluted and complicated story undoubtedly will develop even more bizarre twists as the 21st century unfolds.

Key URLs
The Federal Deposit Insurance Corporation not only insures deposits, but provides large amounts of data on individual banks. See especially **www.fdic.gov** and **www.fdic.gov/bank/ index.html**.

A BRIEF HISTORY OF BANKING AND OTHER FINANCIAL-SERVICE FIRMS

As best we can tell from historical records, *banking* is the oldest of all financial-service professions. Where did these powerful financial institutions come from?

Linguistics (the science of language) and *etymology* (the study of word origins) tell us that the French word *banque* and the Italian *banca* were used centuries ago to refer to a "bench" or "money changer's table." This describes quite well what historians have observed about the first bankers offering their services more than 2,000 years ago. They were money changers, situated usually at a table in the commercial district, aiding travelers by exchanging foreign coins for local money or discounting commercial notes for a fee.

The earliest bankers pledged a lot of their own money to support these early ventures, but it wasn't long before the idea of attracting deposits and loaning out those same funds emerged. Loans were granted to shippers, landowners, and others at interest rates as low as 6 percent to as high as 48 percent a month for the riskiest ventures! Most of the early banks were Greek in origin.

The banking industry gradually spread from the classical civilizations of Greece and Rome into Europe. It encountered religious opposition during the Middle Ages primarily because loans to the poor often carried high interest rates. However, as the Middle Ages drew to a close and the Renaissance began in Europe, the bulk of loans and deposits involved wealthy customers, which helped to reduce religious objections.

The development of overland trade routes and improvements in navigation in the 15th, 16th, and 17th centuries gradually shifted the center of world commerce from the Mediterranean toward Europe and the British Isles. During this period, the seeds of the Industrial Revolution, which demanded a well-developed financial system, were planted. The adoption of mass production required an expansion in global trade to absorb industrial output, which in turn required new methods for making payments and obtaining credit. Banks that could deliver on these needs grew rapidly, led by such institutions as the Medici Bank in Italy and the Hochstetter Bank in Germany.

The early banks in Europe were places for the safekeeping of wealth (such as gold and silver) for a fee as people came to fear loss of their assets due to war, theft, or expropriation by government. Merchants shipping goods found it safer to place their payments of gold and silver in the nearest bank rather than risking loss to pirates or storms at sea. In England government efforts to seize private holdings resulted in people depositing their valuables in goldsmiths' shops, which issued tokens or certificates indicating the customer had made a deposit. Soon, goldsmith certificates began to circulate as money because they were more convenient and less risky to carry around than gold or other valuables. The goldsmiths also offered *certification of value* services—what we today call property appraisal. Customers would bring in their valuables to have an expert certify these items were real and not fakes.

When colonies were established in North and South America, Old World banking practices entered the New World. At first the colonists dealt primarily with established banks in the countries from which they had come. Later, state governments in the United States began chartering banking companies. The U.S. federal government became a major force in banking during the Civil War. The Office of the Comptroller of the Currency (OCC) was established in 1864, created by the U.S. Congress to charter *national banks*. This divided bank regulatory system, in which both the federal government and the states play key roles in the supervision of banking activity, has persisted in the United States to the present day.

Despite banking's long history and success, tough financial-service competitors have emerged over the past century or two, mostly from Europe, to challenge bankers at every turn. Among the oldest were life insurance companies—the first American company was chartered in Philadelphia in 1759. Property-casualty insurers emerged at roughly the same time, led by Lloyds of London in 1688, underwriting a wide range of risks to persons and property.

The 19th century ushered in a rash of new financial competitors, led by savings banks in Scotland in 1810. These institutions offered small savings deposits to individuals at a time when most commercial banks largely ignored this market segment. A similar firm, the savings and loan association, appeared in the midwestern United States during the 1830s, encouraging household saving and financing the construction of new homes. Credit unions were first chartered in Germany during the same era, providing savings accounts and low-cost credit to industrial workers.

Mutual funds—one of banking's most successful competitors—appeared in Belgium in 1822. These investment firms entered the United States in significant numbers during the 1920s, were devastated by the Great Depression of the 1930s, and rose again to grow rapidly. A closely related institution—the money market fund—surfaced in the 1970s to offer professional cash management services to households and institutions. These aggressive competitors attracted a huge volume of deposits away from banks and ultimately helped to bring about government deregulation of the banking industry. Finally, hedge funds appeared to offer investors a less regulated, more risky alternative to mutual funds. They grew explosively into the new century.

1–3 The Financial System and Competing Financial-Service Institutions

Roles of the Financial System

As we noted at the opening of this chapter, bankers face challenges from all sides today as they reach out to their financial-service customers. Banks are only one part of a vast financial system of markets and institutions that circles the globe. The primary purpose of this ever-changing financial system is to *encourage individuals and institutions to save and to transfer those savings to those individuals and institutions planning to invest in new projects.* This process of encouraging savings and transforming savings into investment spending causes the economy to grow, new jobs to be created, and living standards to rise.

But the financial system does more than simply transform savings into investment. It also provides a variety of supporting services essential to modern living. These include *payment services* that make commerce and markets possible (such as checks, credit cards, and interactive Web sites), *risk protection services* for those who save and venture to invest (including insurance policies and derivative contracts), *liquidity services* (making it possible to convert property into immediately available spending power), and *credit services* for those who need loans to supplement their income.

The Competitive Challenge for Banks

For many centuries banks were way out in front of other financial-service institutions in supplying savings and investment services, payment and risk protection services, liquidity, and loans. They dominated the financial system of decades past. But this is no longer as true today. Banking's financial market share generally has fallen as other financial institutions have moved in to fight for the same turf. In the United States of a century ago, for example, banks accounted for more than two-thirds of the assets of all financial-service providers. However, as Exhibit 1–2 illustrates, that share has fallen to only about one-fifth of the assets of the U.S. financial marketplace.

Some authorities in the financial-services field suggest this apparent loss of market share may imply that traditional banking is *dying*. (See, for example, Beim [2] and the counterargument by Kaufman and Mote [3].) Certainly as financial markets become more efficient and the largest customers find ways around banks to obtain the funds they need (such as by borrowing in the open market), traditional banks may become less necessary. Some experts argue that the reason we still have thousands of banks scattered around the globe—perhaps many more than we need—is that governments often subsidize the industry through cheap deposit insurance and low-cost loans. Still others argue that banking's market share is falling due to excessive government regulation, restricting the industry's ability to compete. Perhaps banking is being "regulated to death," which may hurt those customers who most heavily depend on banks for critical services—individuals and small businesses. Other experts counter that banking is *not* dying, but only *changing*—offering new services and changing its form—to reflect what today's market demands. Perhaps the traditional measures of the industry's importance (like total assets) no longer reflect how truly diverse and competitive bankers have become in the modern world.

Leading Competitors with Banks

Among the leading competitors with banks in wrestling for the loyalty of financial-service customers are such nonbank financial-service institutions as:

Savings associations: Specialize in selling savings deposits and granting home mortgage loans and other forms of credit to individuals and families, illustrated by such financial firms as Atlas Savings and Loan Association (**www.atlasbank.com**),

EXHIBIT 1–2

Comparative Size by Industry of Commercial Banks and Their Principal Financial-Service Competitors

Source: Board of Governors of the Federal Reserve System, *Flow of Funds Accounts of the United States*. First Quarter 2005, June 2005.

Financial-Service Institutions	Total Financial Assets Held in 2005 (bill.)*	Percent of All Financial Assets Held in 2005
Depository Institutions:		
Commercial banks**	8,713	20.1%
Savings institutions***	1,693	3.9
Credit unions	670	1.5
Nondeposit Financial Institutions:		
Life insurance companies	4,166	9.6
Property/casualty and other insurers	1,197	2.8
Private pension funds	4,286	9.9
State and local government retirement funds	2,040	4.7
Federal government retirement funds	71	0.2
Money market funds	1,841	4.2
Investment companies (mutual funds)	5,443	12.5
Finance companies	1,424	3.3
Mortgage companies	32	****
Real estate investment trusts	259	0.6
Security brokers and dealers	1,941	4.5
Other financial service providers (including government-sponsored enterprises, mortgage pools, payday lenders, etc.)	9,670	22.3
Totals	43,446	100.0%

Notes: Columns may not add to totals due to rounding error.
*Figures are for the first quarter of 2005.
**Commercial banking as recorded here includes U.S. chartered commercial banks, foreign banking offices in the United States, bank holding companies, and banks operating in United States affiliated areas.
***Savings institutions include savings and loan associations, mutual and federal savings banks, and cooperative banks.
****Figure is less than one-tenth of one percent.

Flatbush Savings and Loan Association (**www.flatbush.com**) of Brooklyn, New York, Washington Mutual (**www.wamu.com**), and American Federal Savings Bank (**www.americanfsb.com**).

Credit unions: Collect deposits from and make loans to their members as nonprofit associations of individuals sharing a common bond (such as the same employer), including such firms as American Credit Union of Milwaukee (**www.americancu.org**) and Chicago Post Office Employees Credit Union (**www.my-creditunion.com**).

Money market funds: Collect short-term, liquid funds from individuals and institutions and invest these monies in quality securities of short duration, including such firms as Franklin Templeton Tax-Free Money Fund (**www.franklintempleton.com**) and Scudder Tax-Free Money Fund (**www.scudder.com**).

Mutual funds (investment companies): Sell shares to the public representing an interest in a professionally managed pool of stocks, bonds, and other securities, including such financial firms as Fidelity (**www.fidelity.com**) and The Vanguard Group (**www.vanguard.com**).

Hedge funds: Sell shares mainly to upscale investors in a broad group of different kinds of assets (including nontraditional investments in commodities, real estate, loans to new and ailing companies, and other risky assets); for additional information see such firms as Magnum Group (**www.magnum.com**) and Turn Key Hedge Funds (**www.turnkeyhedgefunds.com**).

Security brokers and dealers: Buy and sell securities on behalf of their customers and for their own accounts, such as Merrill Lynch (**www.ml.com**) and Charles Schwab (**www.Schwab.com**).

Key URLs
To explore the character of the credit union industry see www.cuna.org and www.occu.org.

Key URLs
The nature and characteristics of money market funds and other mutual funds are explained at length in such sources as www.smartmoney.com, www.ici.org, www.morningstar.com, and www.marketwatch.com.

Key URLs
To learn more about security brokers and dealers see www.sec.gov or www.investorguide.com.

Key URL
You can explore the world of investment banking more fully at **www.wallstreetprep. com**.

Key URL
To discover more about hedge funds see the Security and Exchange Commission's Web site at **www.sec.gov/ answers/hedge.htm**.

Key URLs
To explore the life insurance and property/casualty insurance industries see especially **www.acli.com** and **www.iii.org**.

Key URLs
To learn more about finance companies see **www.nacm.org**, **www.hsbcusa.com**, and **www.capitalone.com**.

Investment banks: Provide professional advice to corporations and governments raising funds in the financial marketplace or seeking to make business acquisitions, including such prominent investment banking houses as Bear Stearns (**www.bearstearns.com**) and Morgan Stanley (**www.morganstanley.com**).

Finance companies: Offer loans to commercial enterprises (such as auto and appliance dealers) and to individuals and families using funds borrowed in the open market or from other financial institutions, including such well-known financial firms as Household Finance (**www.household.com**) and GMAC Financial Services (**www.gmacfs.com**).

Financial holding companies: (FHCs) Often include credit card companies, insurance and finance companies, and security broker/dealer firms under one corporate umbrella as highly diversified financial-service providers, including such leading financial conglomerates as GE Capital (**www.gecapital.com**) and UBS Warburg AG (**www.ubswarburg.com**).

Life and property/casualty insurance companies: Protect against risks to persons or property and manage the pension plans of businesses and the retirement funds of individuals, including such industry leaders as Prudential Insurance (**www.prudential. com**) and State Farm Insurance Companies (**www.statefarm.com**).

As suggested by Exhibit 1–3, all of these financial-service providers are converging in terms of the services they offer—rushing toward each other like colliding trains—and embracing each other's innovations. Moreover, recent changes in government rules, such as the U.S. Financial Services Modernization (Gramm-Leach-Bliley) Act of 1999, have allowed many of the financial firms listed above to offer the public one-stop shopping for financial services. To bankers the financial-services marketplace appears to be closing in from all sides as the list of aggressive competitors grows.

Thanks to more liberal government regulations, banks with quality management and adequate capital can now truly become conglomerate financial-service providers. The same is true for security firms, insurers, and other financially oriented companies that wish to acquire bank affiliates.

Thus, the historic legal barriers in the United States separating banking from other financial-service businesses have, like the walls of ancient Jericho, "come tumbling down." The challenge of differentiating banks from other financial-service providers is greater than ever before. However, inside the United States, Congress (like the governments of many other nations around the globe) has chosen to limit severely banks' association with industrial and manufacturing firms, fearing that allowing banking–industrial combinations of companies might snuff out competition, threaten bankers with new risks, and possibly weaken the safety net that protects depositors from loss when the banking system gets into trouble.

Concept Check

1–1. What is a *bank?* How does a bank differ from most other financial-service providers?

1–2. Under U.S. law what must a corporation do to qualify and be regulated as a *commercial bank?*

1–3. Why are some banks reaching out to become one-stop financial-service conglomerates? Is this a good idea, in your opinion?

1–4. Which businesses are banking's closest and toughest competitors? What services do they offer that compete directly with banks' services?

1–5. What is happening to banking's share of the financial marketplace and why? What kind of banking and financial system do you foresee for the future if present trends continue?

EXHIBIT 1–3   The Most Important Nonbank Competitors for Banks

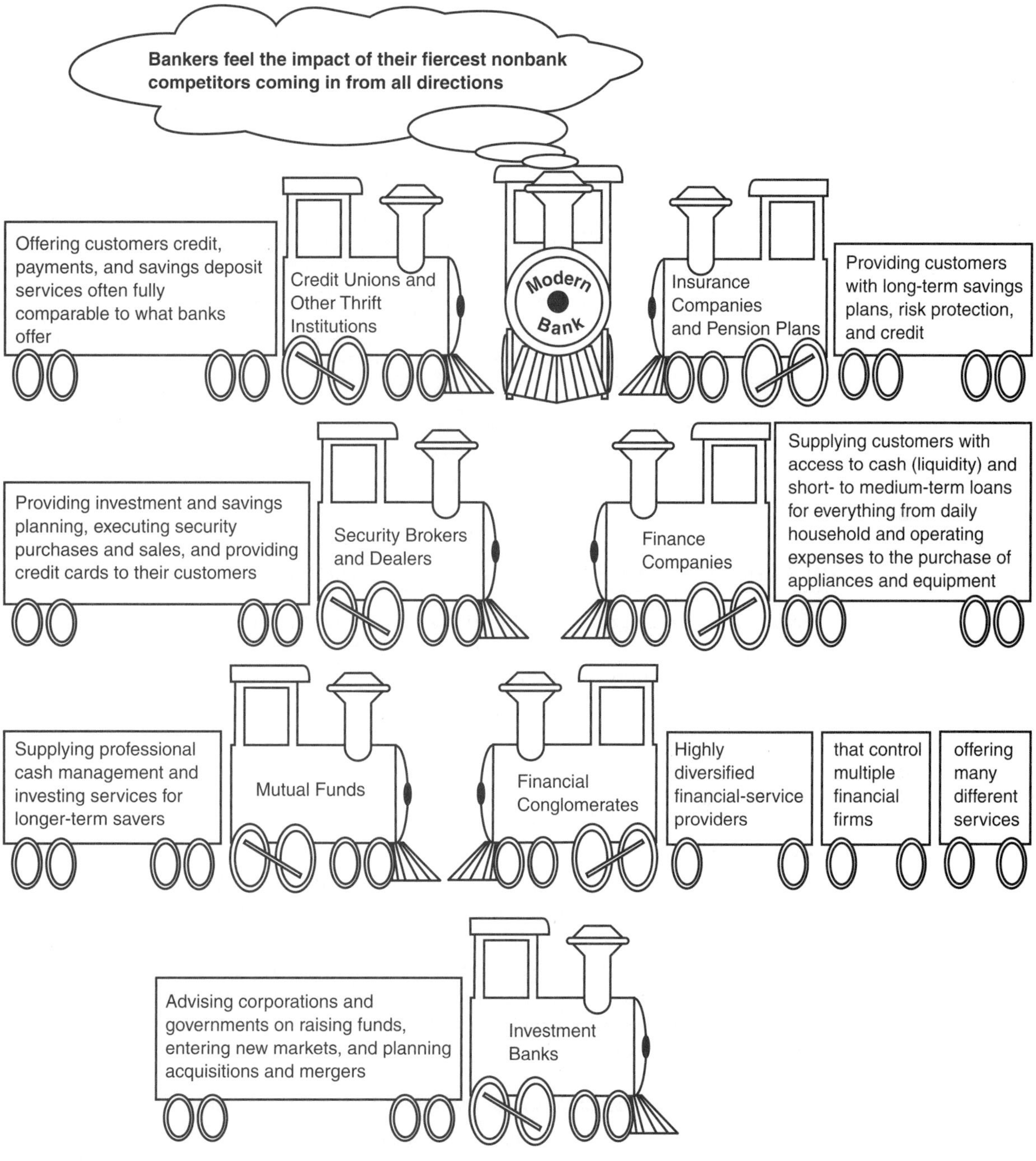

Bankers feel the impact of their fiercest nonbank competitors coming in from all directions

Offering customers credit, payments, and savings deposit services often fully comparable to what banks offer — **Credit Unions and Other Thrift Institutions**

Modern Bank

Insurance Companies and Pension Plans — Providing customers with long-term savings plans, risk protection, and credit

Providing investment and savings planning, executing security purchases and sales, and providing credit cards to their customers — **Security Brokers and Dealers**

Finance Companies — Supplying customers with access to cash (liquidity) and short- to medium-term loans for everything from daily household and operating expenses to the purchase of appliances and equipment

Supplying professional cash management and investing services for longer-term savers — **Mutual Funds**

Financial Conglomerates — Highly diversified financial-service providers / that control multiple financial firms / offering many different services

Advising corporations and governments on raising funds, entering new markets, and planning acquisitions and mergers — **Investment Banks**

The result of all these recent legal maneuverings is a state of confusion in the public's mind today over what is or is not a *bank*. The safest approach is probably to view these historic financial institutions in terms of the many key services—especially credit, savings, payments, financial advising, and risk protection services—they offer to the public. This multiplicity of services and functions has led to banks and their nearest competitors being labeled "financial department stores" and to such familiar advertising slogans as "Your Bank—a Full-Service Financial Institution."

TABLE 1–1
The Many Different Roles Banks and Their Closest Competitors Play in the Economy

The modern bank has had to adopt many roles to remain competitive and responsive to public needs. Banking's principal roles (and the roles performed by many of its competitors) today include:	
The intermediation role	Transforming savings received primarily from households into credit (loans) for business firms and others in order to make investments in new buildings, equipment, and other goods.
The payments role	Carrying out payments for goods and services on behalf of customers (such as by issuing and clearing checks and providing a conduit for electronic payments).
The guarantor role	Standing behind their customers to pay off customer debts when those customers are unable to pay (such as by issuing letters of credit).
The risk management role	Assisting customers in preparing financially for the risk of loss to property, persons, and financial assets.
The investment banking role	Assisting corporations and governments in marketing securities and raising new funds.
The savings/investment advisor role	Aiding customers in fulfilling their long-range goals for a better life by building and investing savings.
The safekeeping/certification of value role	Safeguarding a customer's valuables and certifying their true value.
The agency role	Acting on behalf of customers to manage and protect their property.
The policy role	Serving as a conduit for government policy in attempting to regulate the growth of the economy and pursue social goals.

1–4 Services Banks and Many of Their Closest Competitors Offer the Public

Banks, like their neighboring competitors, are financial-service providers. As such, they play a number of important roles in the economy. (See Table 1–1.) Their success hinges on their ability to identify the financial services the public demands, produce those services efficiently, and sell them at a competitive price. What services does the public demand from banks and their financial-service competitors today? In this section, we present an overview of both banking's traditional and its modern service menu.

Services Banks Have Offered throughout History

Carrying Out Currency Exchanges

History reveals that one of the first services banks offered was **currency exchange.** A banker stood ready to trade one form of coin or currency (such as dollars) for another (such as francs or pesos) in return for a service fee. Such exchanges have been important to travelers over the centuries, because the traveler's survival and comfort may depend on gaining access to local funds. In today's financial marketplace, trading in foreign currency is conducted primarily by the largest financial-service firms due to the risks involved and the expense required to carry out these transactions.

Discounting Commercial Notes and Making Business Loans

Early in history, bankers began **discounting commercial notes**—in effect, making loans to local merchants who sold the debts (accounts receivable) they held against their customers to a bank to raise cash quickly. It was a short step from discounting commercial notes to making *direct loans* for purchasing inventories of goods or for constructing new facilities—a service that today is provided by banks, finance companies, insurance firms, and other financial-service competitors.

Offering Savings Deposits

Making loans proved so profitable that banks began searching for ways to raise additional loanable funds. One of the earliest sources of these funds consisted of offering

THE ROLE OF BANKS AND OTHER FINANCIAL INTERMEDIARIES IN THEORY

Banks, along with insurance companies, mutual funds, finance companies, and similar financial-service providers, are *financial intermediaries.* The term *financial intermediary* simply means a business that interacts with two types of individuals and institutions in the economy: (1) *deficit-spending individuals and institutions,* whose current expenditures for consumption and investment exceed their current receipts of income and who, therefore, need to raise funds externally through borrowing or issuing stock; and (2) *surplus-spending individuals and institutions* whose current receipts of income exceed their current expenditures on goods and services so they have surplus funds that can be saved and invested. Intermediaries perform the indispensable task of acting as a *bridge* between these two groups, offering convenient financial services to surplus-spending units in order to attract funds and then allocating those funds to deficit spenders. In so doing, intermediaries accelerate economic growth by expanding the available pool of savings, lowering the risk of investments through diversification, and increasing the productivity of savings and investment.

Intermediation activities will take place (1) if there is a positive spread between the expected yields on loans that financial intermediaries make to deficit spenders and the expected cost of the funds intermediaries attract from surplus spenders; and (2) if there is a positive correlation between the yields on loans and other assets and the cost of attracting funds. If an intermediary's asset yields and its fund-raising costs are positively correlated, this will reduce uncertainty about its expected profits and allow it to expand.

An ongoing debate in finance concerns *why* financial intermediaries exist at all. What services do they provide that other businesses and individuals cannot provide for themselves?

This question has proven difficult to answer. Research evidence showing that our financial markets are reasonably efficient has accumulated in recent years. Funds and information flow readily to market participants, and the prices of assets seem to be determined in highly competitive markets. In a perfectly competitive and efficient financial system, in which all participants have equal and open access to the financial marketplace, no one participant can exercise control over prices, all pertinent information affecting the value of various assets is available to all, transactions costs are not significant impediments to trading, and all assets are available in denominations anyone can afford, *why* would banks and other financial-service firms be needed at all?

Most current theories explain the existence of financial intermediaries by pointing to *imperfections* in our financial system. For example, all assets are *not* perfectly divisible into small denominations that everyone can afford. To illustrate, marketable U.S. Treasury bonds—one of the most popular securities in the world—have minimum denominations of $1,000, which is beyond the reach of many small savers and investors. Financial intermediaries provide a valuable service in dividing up such instruments into smaller units that are readily affordable for millions of people.

Another contribution that intermediaries make is their willingness to accept risky loans from borrowers, while issuing low-risk securities to their depositors and other funds providers. These service providers engage in *risky arbitrage* across the financial markets and sell risk-management services as well.

Financial intermediaries satisfy the need for *liquidity.* Financial instruments are liquid if they can be sold quickly in a ready market with little risk of loss to the seller. Many households and businesses, for example, demand large precautionary balances of liquid funds to cover future cash needs. Intermediaries satisfy this customer need by offering high liquidity in the financial assets they provide, giving customers access to liquid funds precisely when they are needed.

Still another reason intermediaries have prospered is their *superior ability to evaluate information.* Pertinent data on financial investments is limited and costly. Some institutions know more than others or possess inside information that allows them to choose profitable investments while avoiding the losers. This uneven distribution of information and the talent to analyze it is known as *informational asymmetry.* Asymmetries reduce the efficiency of markets, but provide a profitable role for intermediaries that have the expertise to evaluate potential investments.

Yet another view of why financial institutions exist in modern society is called *delegated monitoring.* Most borrowers prefer to keep their financial records confidential. Lending institutions are able to attract borrowing customers because they pledge confidentiality. For example, a bank's depositors are not privileged to review the records of its borrowing customers. Depositors often have neither the time nor the skill to choose good loans over bad. They turn the monitoring process over to a financial intermediary. Thus a depository institution serves as an *agent* on behalf of its depositors, monitoring the financial condition of those customers who do receive loans to ensure that depositors will recover their funds. In return for monitoring, depositors pay a fee to the lender that is probably less than the cost they would incur if they monitored borrowers themselves.

By making a large volume of loans, lending institutions acting as delegated monitors can diversify and reduce their risk exposure, resulting in increased safety for savers' funds. Moreover, when a borrowing customer has received the stamp of approval of a lending institution it is easier and less costly for that customer to raise funds elsewhere. This signals the financial marketplace that the borrower is likely to repay his or her loans. This *signaling effect* seems to be strongest, not when a lending institution makes the first loan to a borrower, but when it renews a maturing loan.

savings deposits—interest-bearing funds left with depository institutions for a period of time. According to some historical records, banks in ancient Greece paid as high as 16 percent in annual interest to attract savings deposits from wealthy patrons and then made loans to ship owners sailing the Mediterranean Sea at loan rates double or triple the rate bankers were paying to their savings deposit customers. How's that for a nice profit spread?

Safekeeping of Valuables and Certification of Value

During the Middle Ages, banks and other merchants (often called "goldsmiths") began the practice of holding gold and other valuables owned by their customers inside secure vaults, thus reassuring customers of their safekeeping. These financial firms would assay the market value of their customers' valuables, especially gold and jewelry, and certify whether or not these "valuables" were worth what others had claimed.

Supporting Government Activities with Credit

During the Middle Ages and the early years of the Industrial Revolution, governments in Europe noted bankers' ability to mobilize large amounts of funds. Frequently banks were chartered under the proviso that they would purchase government bonds with a portion of the deposits they received. This lesson was not lost on the fledgling American government during the Revolutionary War. The Bank of North America, chartered by the Continental Congress in 1781, was set up to help fund the struggle to throw off British rule and make the United States a sovereign nation. Similarly, during the Civil War the U.S. Congress created a whole new federal banking system, agreeing to charter national banks provided these institutions purchased government bonds to help fund the war.

Offering Checking Accounts (Demand Deposits)

The Industrial Revolution ushered in new financial services and new service providers. Probably the most important of the new services developed during this period was the demand deposit—a checking account that permitted the depositor to write drafts in payment for goods and services that the bank or other service provider had to honor immediately. **Demand deposit services** proved to be one of the financial-service industry's most important offerings because it significantly improved the efficiency of the payments process, making transactions easier, faster, and safer. Today the checking account concept has been extended to the Internet, to the use of plastic debit cards that tap your checking account electronically, and to "smart cards" that electronically store spending power. Today payment-on-demand accounts are offered not only by banks, but also by savings associations, credit unions, securities firms, and other financial-service providers.

Offering Trust Services

For many years banks and a few of their competitors (such as insurance and trust companies) have managed the financial affairs and property of individuals and business firms in return for a fee. This property management function is known as **trust services.** Providers of this service typically act as trustees for wills, managing a deceased customer's estate by paying claims against that estate, keeping valuable assets safe, and seeing to it that legal heirs receive their rightful inheritance. In commercial trust departments, trust-service providers manage security portfolios and pension plans for businesses and act as agents for corporations issuing stocks and bonds.

Services Banks and Many of Their Financial-Service Competitors Have Offered More Recently

Granting Consumer Loans

Historically, banks did not actively pursue loan accounts from individuals and families, believing that the relatively small size of most consumer loans and their relatively high default rate would make such lending unprofitable. Accordingly, other financial-service providers—especially credit unions, savings and loans, and finance companies—soon moved in to focus on the consumer. Early in this century, however, bankers began to rely more heavily on consumers for deposits to help fund their large corporate loans. In addition, heavy competition for business deposits and loans caused bankers increasingly to turn to the consumer as a potentially more loyal customer. By the 1920s and 1930s several major banks, led by one of the forerunners of New York's Citibank and by the Bank of America, had established strong consumer loan departments. Following World War II, consumer loans were among the fastest-growing forms of bank credit. Their rate of growth has slowed recently, though, as bankers have run into stiff competition for consumer credit accounts from nonbank service providers.

Financial Advising

Filmtoid
What 2001 documentary recounts the creation of an Internet company, **GovWorks.com**, using more than $50 million in funds provided by venture capitalists? **Answer:** *Startup.com*.

Customers have long asked financial institutions for advice, particularly when it comes to the use of credit and the saving or investing of funds. Many service providers today offer a wide range of **financial advisory services,** from helping to prepare tax returns and financial plans for individuals to consulting about marketing opportunities at home and abroad for business customers.

Managing Cash

Over the years, financial institutions have found that some of the services they provide for themselves are also valuable for their customers. One of the most prominent is **cash management services,** in which a financial intermediary agrees to handle cash collections and disbursements for a business firm and to invest any temporary cash surpluses in interest-bearing assets until cash is needed to pay bills. Although banks tend to specialize mainly in business cash management services, many financial institutions are offering similar services to consumers.

Offering Equipment Leasing

Many banks and finance companies have moved aggressively to offer their business customers the option to purchase equipment through a lease arrangement in which the lending institution buys the equipment and rents it to the customer. These **equipment leasing services** benefit leasing institutions as well as their customers because, as the real owner of the leased equipment, the lessor can depreciate it for additional tax benefits.

Making Venture Capital Loans

Key URL
For more information on the venture capital industry see **www.nvca.org**.

Increasingly, banks, security dealers, and other financial conglomerates have become active in financing the start-up costs of new companies. Because of the added risk involved in such loans, this is generally done through a separate venture capital firm that raises money from investors to support young businesses in the hope of turning a profit when those firms are sold or go public.

Selling Insurance Policies

For many years bankers have sold credit life insurance to their customers receiving loans, guaranteeing repayment if borrowers die or become disabled. Moreover, during the 19th and early 20th centuries, many bankers sold insurance and provided financial advice to their customers, literally serving as the local community's all-around financial-service store. However, beginning with the Great Depression of the 1930s, U.S. banks were prohibited from acting as insurance agents or underwriting **insurance policies.** For example, banks in most cases couldn't provide automobile or homeowners' coverage or general life and health insurance protection. Congress acted out of fear that selling insurance would increase bank risk and lead to conflicts of interest in which customers asking for one service would be compelled to buy other services as well.

Leading Nonbank Financial Firms That Have Reached into Traditional Bank Service Markets

For several decades now bankers have watched as some of the world's most aggressive nonbank institutions have invaded banking's traditional marketplace. Among the most successful and aggressive of such companies are these:

Merrill Lynch & Co. (www.ml.com).* Merrill is one of the largest security trading and underwriting firms on the planet and serves as an adviser to corporations and governments on every continent. Beginning as an investment firm in 1885, Merrill now competes directly with banks in offering money market accounts and online banking services to both businesses and households. It was one of the first nonbank firms to adopt the holding company form and acquire or establish affiliates dealing in government securities, asset management, and the management of mutual funds. During the 1970s Merrill Lynch organized one of the largest of all money market funds and today also controls an industrial bank.

American Express Company (http://home.americanexpress.com).* American Express was one of the first credit card companies in the United States and now serves millions of households and business firms. It also owns an FDIC-insured industrial bank (American Express Centurion Bank) through which it offers home mortgage and home equity loans, savings deposits, checking and retirement accounts, and online bill paying. AEX is registered with the Federal Reserve Board as a financial holding company.

Household International (www.household.com).* Household is the largest finance company in the world, offering personal loans as well as financial assistance to businesses requiring inventory financing. Reaching over 50 million customers in Canada, the United States, and Great Britain, Household competes directly with banks in offering credit cards, auto financing, home mortgages, and credit life insurance. It also operates a joint venture with an insurance company to offer term life and auto insurance coverage. During 2002, Household International announced its acquisition by HSBC of London, one of the world's largest banks.

Countrywide Financial Corp. (www.countrywide.com). Countrywide is the largest home mortgage lender in the United States. Founded in New York in 1969, the company pioneered banklike branches (known as "country stores"), based initially in California and then spreading nationwide, subsequently forming a broker–dealer subsidiary, an insurance agency, and an online lending unit. Subsequently Countrywide bought Treasury Bank, NA, in Alexandria, Virginia.

*Indicates this financial firm is included in the Educational Version of S&P's Market Insight.

Many bankers arranged to have insurance companies sell policies to customers by renting space in bank lobbies. This picture of extreme separation between banking and insurance changed dramatically in 1999 when the U.S. Congress passed the Gramm-Leach-Bliley (GLB) Act and tore down the legal barriers between the two industries, allowing bank holding companies to acquire control of insurance companies and, conversely, permitting insurance companies to acquire banks. Today, these two industries are competing aggressively with each other, pursuing cross-industry mergers and acquisitions.

Selling Retirement Plans

Banks, trust departments, mutual funds, and insurance companies are active in managing the **retirement plans** that most businesses make available to their employees, investing incoming funds and dispensing payments to qualified recipients who have reached retirement or become disabled. Banks and other depository institutions sell retirement plans (such as IRAs and Keoghs) to individuals holding these deposits until the funds are needed for income after retirement.

Dealing in Securities: Offering Security Brokerage and Investment Banking Services

One of the biggest of all banking service targets in recent years, particularly in the United States, has been dealing in securities, executing buy and sell orders for security trading customers (referred to as **security brokerage services**) and marketing new securities to raise funds for corporations and other institutions (referred to as **security underwriting** or **investment banking** services). However, much of this security brokerage and security underwriting activity was prohibited in the United States due to the separation of commercial and investment banking by the Glass-Steagall Act, passed in 1933. With the passage of the Gramm-Leach-Bliley Act in the fall of 1999, however, banks are now permitted to affiliate with securities firms and security firms can acquire banks. Two venerable old industries, long separated by law, especially in the United States and Japan, are now like two out-of-control locomotives rushing toward each other, pursuing many of the same customers.

Offering Mutual Funds and Annuities

Many customers have come to demand *investment products* from their financial-service providers. Mutual fund investments and annuities that offer the prospect of higher yields than the returns often available on conventional bank deposits are among the most sought-after investment products. However, these product lines also tend to carry more risk than do bank deposits.

Annuities consist of long-term savings plans that promise the payment of a stream of income to the annuity holder beginning on a designated future date (e.g., at retirement). In contrast, *mutual funds* are professionally managed investment programs that acquire stocks, bonds, and other assets that appear to "fit" the funds' announced goals (such as to maximize current income or to achieve long-term capital appreciation). Recently many banking firms have organized special subsidiary organizations to market these services or entered into joint ventures with security brokers and insurance companies. In turn, many of bankers' key competitors, including insurance companies and security firms, have moved aggressively to expand their public offerings of fixed and variable annuity plans and broaden their menu of investment services in order to attract customers away from banks.

Offering Merchant Banking Services

U.S. financial-service providers are following in the footsteps of leading financial institutions all over the globe (for example, Barclays Bank of Great Britain and Deutsche Bank of Germany) in offering **merchant banking services** to larger corporations. These consist of the temporary purchase of corporate stock to aid the launching of a new business venture or to support the expansion of an existing company. Hence, a merchant banker becomes a temporary stockholder and bears the risk that the stock purchased may decline in value. In practice, merchant banking services often encompass the identification of possible merger targets for a corporate customer, providing that customer with strategic marketing advice.

Offering Risk Management and Hedging Services

Many observers see fundamental changes going on in the banking sector with larger banks (such as J. P. Morgan Chase and Citibank) moving away from a traditionally heavy emphasis on deposit-taking and loan-making toward *risk intermediation*—providing their customers with financial tools to combat risk exposure in return for substantial fees. The largest banks around the globe now dominate the risk-hedging field, either acting as dealers (i.e., serving as "market makers") in arranging for risk protection for the banks' customers from third parties or directly selling their customers the bank's own

Some Leading Retailing and Industrial Firms Reaching into the Banking and Financial-Services Sector

Banks and other financial-service firms have experienced a rising tide of competition from leading manufacturing, retailing, and other businesses in recent decades. These companies based outside the financial sector nevertheless have often been successful in capturing financial-service customers. Among the best known of such nonfinancial-based entities are these:

GE Capital (www.gecapital.com).* The predecessor of GE Capital was set up during the 1930s as a captive finance company of its parent, General Electric, to provide financing so that consumers and appliance and equipment dealers could afford GE products. The firm branched out as it grew to finance more than just GE products. Today it offers such diverse services as leasing airplanes, autos, and oil tankers; credit cards; equity investments; and insurance. If GE Capital were a bank it would rank in the top 10 of all U.S. banks. In 2002 GE announced that GE Capital would become four separate businesses—GE Commercial Finance, GE Consumer Finance, GE Equipment Management, and GE Insurance. General Electric also owns Monogram Credit Card Bank.

GMAC Financial Services (www.gmacfs.com). GMAC began in 1919 as a captive finance company, financing the vehicles produced by General Motors by lending to both dealers and consumers. Today GMAC Financial Services is a family of financial-service companies that not only finance purchases of motor vehicles, but extend home mortgage loans, provide real estate brokerage services, make commercial loans, sell insurance on homes and autos, and provide banking services through GMAC bank and a thrift institution.

Wal-Mart (www.wal-mart.com/financial-services).* The largest consumer retailer on the planet today, offering several financial services through its more than 3,500 stores, is Wal-Mart. Working largely through cooperative ventures with such companies as MoneyGram, Discover Card, and SunTrust, Wal-Mart cashes payroll checks, sells money orders, and provides wire transfers of funds to Mexico. It has allocated space to allow some banks to set up bank branch offices in nearly 1,000 of its superstores and applied for an industrial bank charter.

*Indicates this firm is included in the Educational Version of S&P's Market Insight.

risk-protection contracts (i.e., acting as "matched traders") in which bankers take on their customers' risk exposure and find creative ways to protect their own institutions from that exposure. As we will see later on, this popular financial service has led to phenomenal growth in such risk-hedging tools as swaps, options, and futures contracts.

Convenience: The Sum Total of All Banking and Financial Services

It should be clear from the list of services we have described that not only are banks and their financial-service competitors offering a wide array of comparable services today, but that service menu is growing rapidly. New service delivery methods like the Internet, cell phones, and smart cards with digital cash are expanding and whole new service lines are being launched every year. Viewed as a whole, the impressive array of services offered and the service delivery channels used by modern financial institutions add up to greater convenience for their customers, who can satisfy virtually all their financial-service needs at one location. Banks and some of their competitors have become the financial department stores of the modern era, working to unify banking, fiduciary, insurance, and security brokerage services under one roof—a trend often referred to as *universal banking* in the

TABLE 1–2
Some of the Leading
Financial-Service
Firms around the
Globe

Sources: Bank for International
Settlements, Bank of England,
Bank of Japan, and Board of
Governors of the Federal
Reserve System.

Leading Banking-Oriented Firms around the Globe	Leading Global Nonbank Service Providers, Security Dealers, Brokers, and Investment Bankers
Mizuho Financial Group Ltd., Japan*	Merrill Lynch, USA*
Mitsubishi Banking Corp., Japan*	Goldman Sachs, USA*
Deutsche Bank AG, Germany	Nomura Securities, Japan
UBS AG, Switzerland	Daiwa Securities, Japan
Citigroup, Inc., USA*	
HSBC Holdings PLC, Great Britain*	
Lloyds TSB, Great Britain	**Insurance Companies**
Industrial and Commercial Bank of China	Nippon Life Insurance
BNP Paribus Group, France	Axa/Equitable, Paris, France
Barclays PLC, London, Great Britain*	Metropolitan Life Insurance, USA*
Bank of Montreal, Canada	Prudential Insurance, USA
Canadian Imperial Bank of Commerce	
J. P. Morgan Chase & Company, USA*	
Bank of America Corp., USA*	**Finance Companies**
Agricultural Bank of China	Household International, USA*
Australian & N.Z. Banking Group	GE Capital, USA*

*This financial firm appears in the Educational Version of S&P's Market Insight.

United States and Great Britain, as *allfinanz* in Germany, and as *bancassurance* in France. Table 1–2 lists some of these financial department stores, including some of the very largest banks and competing nonbank financial firms in the world, while Table 1–3 lists the largest banks operating in the United States.

TABLE 1–3
The Largest Banks
Operating in the
United States
(Total assets as
reported for March
31, 2005)

Source: National Information
Center, Federal Reserve
System, Washington, D.C.

Bank Name	Location of Headquarters	Total Assets ($ bill.)
J. P. Morgan Chase Bank, N.A.	Columbus, Ohio	$983
Bank of America, NA	Charlotte, North Carolina	838
Citibank, N.A.	New York City, New York	685
Wachovia Bank, N.A.	Charlotte, North Carolina	455
Wells Fargo Bank, N.A.	Sioux Falls, South Dakota	367
Fleet National Bank	Providence, Rhode Island	213
U.S. Bank, N.A.	Cincinnati, Ohio	198
HSBC Bank USA, N.A.	Wilmington, Delaware	139
SunTrust Bank	Atlanta, Georgia	136
Chase Bank USA, N.A.	Newark, Delaware	89
State Street Bank and Trust Company	Boston, Massachusetts	88
KeyBank, N.A.	Cleveland, Ohio	85

Notes: The designation N.A. means National Association, indicating that the bank carrying this designation is a national bank chartered by the Office of the Comptroller of the Currency in Washington, D.C. as opposed to most other banks, which are chartered by their home states.

Concept Check

1–6. What different kinds of services do banks offer the public today? What services do their closest competitors offer?

1–7. What is a *financial department store?* A *universal bank?* Why do you think these institutions have

become so important in the modern financial system?

1–8. Why do banks and other financial intermediaries exist in modern society, according to the theory of finance?

1–5 Key Trends Affecting All Financial-Service Firms

The foregoing survey of financial services suggests that banks and many of their financial-service competitors are currently undergoing sweeping changes in function and form. In fact, the changes affecting the financial-services business today are so important that many industry analysts refer to these trends as a *revolution,* one that may well leave financial institutions of the next generation almost unrecognizable. What are the key *trends* reshaping banking and financial services today?

Service Proliferation

Leading financial firms have been rapidly expanding the menu of services they offer to their customers. This trend toward service proliferation has accelerated in recent years under the pressure of increasing competition from other financial firms, more knowledgeable and demanding customers, and shifting technology. The new services have opened up new sources of revenue—service fees (called *fee income*), which are likely to continue to grow relative to more traditional sources of financial-service revenue (such as the interest earned on loans).

Rising Competition

The level and intensity of competition in the financial-services field have grown as financial institutions have proliferated their service offerings. For example, the local bank offering business and consumer credit, savings and retirement plans, and financial counseling faces direct competition for all of these services today from other banks, thrift institutions like Washington Mutual, securities firms like Merrill Lynch, finance companies like GE Capital, and insurance companies and agencies like Prudential. This trend toward rising competition has acted as a spur to develop still more services for the future and to reduce operating costs.

Government Deregulation

Rising competition and the proliferation of financial services have been spurred on by government deregulation—a loosening of government control—of the financial services industry that began more than two decades ago and has spread around the globe. As we will see more fully in the chapters ahead, U.S. deregulation began with the lifting of government-imposed interest rate ceilings on savings deposits in an effort to give the public a fairer return on their savings. Almost simultaneously, the services many of banking's key competitors, such as savings and loans and credit unions, could offer were sharply expanded by legislation so they could remain competitive with banks. Such leading nations as Australia, Canada, Great Britain, and Japan have recently joined the deregulation movement, broadening the legal playing field for banks, security dealers, and other financial-service companies operating in a freer and more competitive marketplace.

An Increasingly Interest-Sensitive Mix of Funds

Government deregulation of the financial sector has made it possible for customers to earn higher and more flexible rates of return on their savings and payments accounts. Massive amounts of funds have flowed from older, low-yielding savings instruments and noninterest-bearing checking accounts into newer high-yielding accounts whose rates of return could be changed with market conditions. Thus, bankers and their closest competitors found themselves with an increasingly interest-sensitive mix of funds.

Financial-service managers have discovered that they are facing a better-educated, as well as more interest-sensitive, customer today, whose loyalty can more easily be lured away by aggressive competitors. Financial-service providers must now strive to be more competitive in the returns they offer on the public's money and more sensitive to changing public preferences with regard to how savings are allocated.

Technological Change and Automation

Banks and many of their most serious competitors (for example, insurance companies) have been faced with higher operating costs in recent years and, therefore, have turned increasingly to automation and the installation of sophisticated electronic systems to replace older, labor-based production and delivery systems. This move toward greater technological change is especially evident in the delivery of such services as dispensing payments and making credit available to qualified customers.

The most prominent examples of major technological innovations in financial services include automated teller machines (ATMs), cell phones, point of sale (POS) terminals, and debit cards. There are well over 300,000 ATMs in the United States today and a comparable number in Europe, giving customers 24-hour access to their accounts for cash withdrawals and deposits and to a widening menu of other services. Also accessible well beyond "bankers' hours" are POS terminals in stores and shopping centers that replace paper-based means of paying for goods and services with rapid computer entries. Even more rapidly growing are encoded debit cards that permit a customer to pay for purchases of goods and services with the swipe of a card through an electronic card reader, while in some parts of the world customers can pay for purchases simply by waving their cell phones, which contain embedded chips, over an electronic sensor at some merchants' cash registers.

Thus, banking and financial services now comprise a more capital-intensive, fixed-cost industry and a less labor-intensive, variable-cost industry than in the past. Some experts believe that traditional brick-and-mortar buildings and face-to-face meetings with customers eventually will become relics of the past, replaced almost entirely by electronic communication. Service production and delivery would then be fully automated. Technological advances such as these will significantly lower the per-unit costs associated with high-volume transactions, but they will tend to depersonalize financial services and result in further loss of jobs as capital equipment is substituted for labor. Recent experience suggests, however, that fully automated financial services for *all* customers may be a long time coming. A substantial proportion of customers still prefer personalized service and the opportunity to consult personally, one to one, with their financial advisor.

Consolidation and Geographic Expansion

Making efficient use of automation and other technological innovations requires a high volume of sales. So financial-service providers have had to expand their customer base by reaching into new and more distant markets and by increasing the number of service units sold. The result has been a dramatic increase in branching activity in order to provide multiple offices (i.e., points of contact) for customers, the formation of financial holding companies that bring smaller institutions into larger conglomerates offering multiple services in multiple markets, and mergers between some of the largest bank and nonbank financial firms, such as J. P. Morgan Chase with Bank One, Bank of America with Fleet Boston Financial Group and MBNA, and Deutsche Bank of Germany with Bankers Trust Company of New York.

The number of small, independently owned financial institutions is declining and the average size of individual banks, as well as securities firms, credit unions, finance companies, and insurance firms, has risen significantly. This *consolidation* of financial institutions has resulted in a decline in employment in the financial-services sector.

Convergence

Service proliferation and greater competitive rivalry among financial firms have led to a powerful trend, toward *convergence*, particularly on the part of the largest financial institutions. *Convergence* refers to the movement of businesses across industry lines so that a firm formerly offering only one product line ventures into other product lines to broaden its sales base. This phenomenon has been most evident among larger banks, insurance companies, and security broker/dealer firms that have eagerly climbed into each other's backyard. Clearly, competition intensifies in the wake of convergence as businesses previously separated into different industries now find their former industry boundaries no longer discourage new competitors. Under these more intense competitive pressures, weaker firms will fail or be merged into companies that are ever larger and offer more diverse services.

Globalization

Factoid

When in American history did the greatest number of banks fail? Between 1929 and 1933 when about one-third (approximately 9,000) of all U.S. banks failed or were merged out of existence.

The geographic expansion and consolidation of financial-service units have reached well beyond the boundaries of a single nation to encompass the whole planet—a trend called *globalization*. The largest financial firms in the world compete with each other for business on every continent. For example, huge banks headquartered in France (led by BNP Paribus), Germany (led by Deutsche Bank), Great Britain (led by HSBC), and the United States (led by Citigroup and J. P. Morgan Chase) have become heavyweight competitors in the global market for corporate and government loans. Deregulation has helped all these institutions compete more effectively and capture growing shares of the global market for financial services.

1–6 The Plan of This Book

The primary goal of this book is to provide the reader with a comprehensive understanding of the financial-services industry and the role of banking in that industry. Through its seven major parts we pursue this goal both by presenting an overview of the financial-services industry as a whole and by pointing the reader toward specific questions and issues that bankers and their principal competitors must resolve every day.

Part One, consisting of Chapters 1 through 4, provides an introduction to the world of banking and financial services and their functions in the global economy. We explore the principal services offered by banks and many of their closest competitors, and we examine the many ways financial firms are organized to bring together human skill, capital equipment, and natural resources to produce and deliver their services. Part One also explains how and why banks and other financial-service providers are regulated and who their principal regulators are. Part One concludes with an analysis of the different ways financial institutions deliver their services to the public, including the chartering of new financial firms, constructing branches, installing ATMs and point-of-sale terminals, expansion of call centers, and use of the Internet.

Part Two introduces readers to the financial statements of banks and their closest competitors. Chapter 5 explores the content of balance sheets and income/expense statements, while Chapter 6 examines measures of performance often used to gauge how well banks and their closest competitors are doing in serving their stockholders and the public. Among the most important performance indicators discussed are numerous measures of financial firm profitability and risk.

Part Three opens up the dynamic area of asset-liability management (ALM). Chapters 7, 8, and 9 describe how financial-service managers have changed their views about managing assets, liabilities, and capital and controlling risk in recent years. These chapters take a detailed look at the most important techniques for hedging against changing market interest rates, including financial futures, options, and swaps. Part Three also explores some of the newer tools to deal with credit risk and the use of off-balance-sheet financing techniques, including securitizations, loan sales, and credit derivatives.

Real Banks, Real Decisions

CONVERGENCE AND CONSOLIDATION IN FINANCIAL SERVICES SLOWS DOWN

Although financial institutions have continued to move closer to each other, heating up competition in the financial-services sector, the pace of convergence and consolidation in financial services appears to have slowed somewhat. As the 21st century opened, mergers were proceeding at about half the pace of the hectic 1990s. The formation of new financial holding companies, combining banking, insurance, and security services under one roof, paused and leveled out.

Perhaps most dramatic of all, the leading financial firm in the world—Citigroup—divested itself of Travelers Property and Casualty Insurance in 2001 (after acquiring the latter in 1998) and then subsequently announced its intention to sell to MetLife Insurance its Travelers Life and Annuity Insurance unit and to sell to GE its CitiCapital Transportation Financial Services affiliate. This was a big surprise because Citigroup, perhaps more than any other financial institution, has epitomized the expansion of "one-stop financial services shopping" around the world. And Citigroup is not alone. American Express recently announced plans to sell its Financial Advisers unit and move closer to being a pure credit card company, while J. P. Morgan Chase sold its life insurance and annuity underwriting business to Protective Life Corporation.

Why did these leading financial-service conglomerates take an apparent step backward from their highly publicized "one-stop" financial services strategies? Is the drive toward consolidation and convergence now reversing itself and returning to more traditional lines? After all, the financial-service giants named above had argued long and loud that one-stop shopping was the "wave of the future." They had contended that multiple-service firms would achieve greater efficiency in generating revenues and capture ample cost savings, while their customers would not only experience greater convenience, but also lower service fees. What customer wouldn't relish being able to go to *one location* and open a savings account, sign up for a new auto insurance policy, and purchase stocks and bonds for their retirement plan? Was this one-stop, financial-conglomerate strategy now falling apart?

Not likely, but the pace of financial-services diversification appears to have slowed. One reason: the economies of Europe and America have been growing more slowly in the current decade. Moreover, efforts to further deregulate financial-service firms slowed in the new century. Then, too, the cost savings from one-stop financial shopping have been much less than many financial firms anticipated. Moreover, many firms that tried to combine managing the public's assets and selling in-house investment products ran into conflict-of-interest problems. And new electronic shopping channels (especially the Internet) have encouraged more customers to "shop around" in search of the best deal rather than making all their purchases from one place. One thing *is* clear: *Change* in the financial-services industry often proceeds by fits and starts, due principally to the continual interaction between economic conditions, changing technology, and government regulation.

Part Four addresses two age-old problem areas for depository institutions and their closest competitors: managing a portfolio of investment securities and maintaining enough liquidity to meet daily cash needs. We examine the different types of investment securities typically acquired and review the factors that an investment officer must weigh in choosing what investment securities to buy or sell. This part of the book also takes a critical look at why depository institutions and their closest competitors must constantly struggle to ensure that they have access to cash precisely when and where they need it.

Part Five directs our attention to the funding side of the balance sheet—raising money to support the acquisition of assets and to meet operating expenses. We present the principal types of deposits and nondeposit investment products and review recent trends in the mix and pricing of deposits for their implications for managing banks and other financial firms today and tomorrow. Next, we explore all the important nondeposit sources of short-term funds—federal funds, security repurchase agreements, Eurodollars, and the like—and assess their impact on profitability and risk for banks and other financial firms. This part of the book also examines the increasing union of commercial banking, investment banking, and insurance industries in the United States and selected other areas of the world and the rise of bank sales of nondeposit investment products, including sales of securities, annuities, and insurance. We explore the implications of the newer product lines for financial-firm return and risk. The final source of funds we review is equity capital—the source of funding provided by a financial firm's owners.

Part Six takes up what many bankers and other financial-service managers regard as the essence of their business—granting credit to customers through the making of loans. The types of loans made by banks and their closest competitors, regulations applicable to the lending process, and procedures for evaluating and granting loans are all discussed. This portion of the text includes expanded information about credit card services—one of the most successful, but challenging, service areas for financial institutions today.

Finally, Part Seven tackles two of the most important strategic decisions that many financial firms have to make—acquiring or merging with other financial-service providers and following their customers into international markets. As the financial-services industry continues to consolidate and converge into larger units, managerial decisions about acquisitions, mergers, and global expansion become crucial to the long-run survival of many financial institutions. This final part of the book concludes with an overview of the future of the financial-services marketplace in the 21st century.

Concept Check

1–9. How have banking and the financial-services market changed in recent years? What powerful forces are shaping financial markets and institutions today? Which of these forces do you think will continue into the future?

1–10. Can you explain why many of the forces you named in the answer to the previous question have led to significant problems for the management of banks and other financial firms and for their stockholders?

1–11. What do you think the financial-services industry will look like 20 years from now? What are the implications of your projections for its management today?

Summary

In this opening chapter we have explored many of the roles played by modern banks and their financial-service competitors. We have examined how and why the financial-services marketplace is rapidly changing, becoming something new and different as we move forward into the future.

Among the most important points presented in this chapter were these:

- Banks—the oldest and most familiar of all financial institutions—have changed greatly since their origins centuries ago, evolving from moneychangers and money issuers to become the most important gatherers and dispensers of financial information in the economy.

- Banking is being pressured on all sides by key financial-service competitors—savings and loan associations and savings banks, credit unions, money market funds, investment banks, security brokers and dealers, investment companies (mutual funds), hedge funds, finance companies, insurance companies, and financial-service conglomerates.

- The leading nonbank businesses that compete with banks today in the financial sector offer many of the same services and, therefore, make it increasingly difficult to separate banks from other financial-service providers. Nevertheless, larger banks tend to offer the widest range of services of any financial-service firm today.

- The principal functions (and services) offered by banks and many of their financial-service competitors today include: (1) lending and investing money (the credit function); (2) making payments on behalf of customers to facilitate their purchases of goods and services (the payments function); (3) managing and protecting customers' cash and other forms of customer property (the cash management, risk management, and trust functions); and (4) assisting customers in raising new funds and investing those funds profitably (through the brokerage, investment banking, and savings functions).

- Major trends affecting the performance of financial firms today include: (1) widening service menus (i.e., greater product-line diversification); (2) the globalization of the financial marketplace and the spread of services worldwide (i.e., geographic diversification); (3) the easing or elimination of government rules affecting banks and other financial firms (i.e., deregulation); (4) the growing rivalry among banks themselves and with their closest financial-service competitors (i.e., intense competition); (5) the tendency for all financial firms increasingly to look alike, offering similar services (i.e., convergence); (6) the declining numbers and larger size of financial-service providers (i.e., consolidation); and (7) the increasing automation of financial-service production and delivery (i.e., technological change) in order to offer greater convenience for customers, reach wider markets, and promote cost savings.

Key Terms

bank, 4
savings associations, 8
credit unions, 9
money market funds, 9
mutual funds, 9
hedge funds, 9
security brokers and dealers, 9
investment banks, 10
finance companies, 10
financial holding companies, 10

life and property/casualty insurance companies, 10
currency exchange, 12
discounting commercial notes, 12
savings deposits, 14
demand deposit services, 14
trust services, 14
financial advisory services, 15
cash management services, 15

equipment leasing services, 15
insurance policies, 15
retirement plans, 16
security brokerage services, 17
security underwriting, 17
investment banking, 17
merchant banking services, 17

www.mhhe.com/rose7e

Problems and Projects

1. You have just been hired as the marketing officer for the new First National Bank of Vincent, a suburban banking institution that will soon be serving a local community of 120,000 people. The town is adjacent to a major metropolitan area with a total population of well over 1 million. Opening day for the newly chartered bank is just two months away, and the president and the board of directors are concerned that the new bank may not be able to attract enough depositors and good-quality loan customers to meet its growth and profit projections. (There are 18 other financial-service competitors in town, including two credit unions, three finance companies, four insurance agencies, and two security broker offices.) Your task is to recommend the various services the bank should offer initially to build an adequate customer base. You are asked to do the following:
   a. Make a list of the services the new bank could offer, according to current regulations.
   b. List the types of information you will need about the local community to help you decide which of many possible services are likely to have sufficient demand to make them profitable.
   c. Divide the possible services into two groups: those you think are essential to customers (which should be offered opening day) and those you believe can be offered later as the bank grows.

d. Briefly describe the kind of advertising campaign you would like to run to help the public see how your bank is different from all the other financial-service providers in the local area. Which services offered by nonbank service providers would be of most concern to the new bank's management?

2. Leading money center banks in the United States have accelerated their *investment banking* activities all over the globe in recent years, purchasing corporate debt securities and stock from their business customers and reselling those securities to investors in the open market. Is this a desirable move by banking organizations from a profit standpoint? From a risk standpoint? From the public interest point of view? How would you research these questions? If you were managing a corporation that had placed large deposits with a bank engaged in such activities, would you be concerned about the risk to your company's funds? Why or why not?

3. The term *bank* has been applied broadly over the years to include a diverse set of financial-service institutions, which offer different financial-service packages. Identify as many of the different kinds of banks as you can. How do the banks you have identified compare to the largest banking group of all—the commercial banks? Why do you think so many different financial firms have been called *banks?* How might this terminology confusion affect financial-service customers?

4. What advantages can you see to banks affiliating with insurance companies? How might such an affiliation benefit a bank? An insurer? Can you identify any possible disadvantages to such an affiliation? Can you cite any real-world examples of bank–insurer affiliations? How well do they appear to have worked out in practice?

5. Explain the difference between *consolidation* and *convergence*. Are these trends in banking and financial services related? Do they influence each other? How?

6. What is a *financial intermediary?* What are its key characteristics? Is a bank a type of financial intermediary? What other financial-services companies are financial intermediaries? What important roles within the financial system do financial intermediaries play?

7. Four main types of financial-service firms—depository institutions, investment banks, insurance companies, and finance/credit card companies—are in intense competition with one another today. Using Standard & Poor's Market Insight, Educational Version, available to users of this McGraw-Hill book, describe the principal similarities and differences among these four types of companies. You may find it helpful in answering this question to examine the files on Market Insight devoted to such financial firms as Bank of America (BAC), Bear Stearns Companies (BSC), American International Group (AIG), and Capital One Financial Corp (COF).

Internet Exercises

1. The beginning of this chapter addresses the question, "What is a bank?" (That is a tough question!) A number of Web sites also try to answer the very same question. Explore the following Web sites and try to develop an answer from two different perspectives:

   http://money.howstuffworks.com/bank1.htm

   http://law.freeadvice.com/financial_law/banking_law/bank.htm

   http://www.pacb.org/banks_and_banking/

   a. In the broadest sense, what constitutes a bank?

   b. In the narrowest sense, what constitutes a bank?

2. What services does the bank you use offer? Check out its Web site, either by surfing the Web using the bank's name and location or by checking the Federal Deposit Insurance Corporation's Web site for the bank's name, city, and state. How does your current bank seem to compare with neighboring banks in the range of services it offers? In the quality of its Web site? (See especially **www.fdic.gov**.)

3. In this chapter we discuss the changing character of the financial-services industry and the role of *consolidation*. Visit the Web site **http://www.financialservicesfacts.org/financial/** and look at consolidation for the financial-services industry. What do the numbers tell us? How have the numbers changed since 2000?

   a. Specifically, which sectors of the financial-services industry have increased the dollar amount of assets they control?

   b. In terms of market share based on the volume of assets held, which sectors have increased their shares (percentagewise) and which have decreased their shares?

4. As college students, we often want to know: How big is the job market? Visit the Web site **http://www.financialservicesfacts.org/financial/** and look at employment for the financial-services industry. Answer the following questions using the most recent data on this site.

   a. How many employees work at depository institutions? What is the share (percentage) of total financial-services employees?

   b. How many employees work in insurance? What is the share (percentage) of total financial-services employees?

   c. How many employees work in securities and commodities? What is the share (percentage) of total financial-services employees?

5. What kinds of jobs seem most plentiful in the banking industry today? Make a brief list of the most common job openings you find at various bank Web sites. Do any of these jobs interest you? (See, for example, **www.bankjobs.com**.)

6. According to the sources mentioned earlier on the World Wide Web, how did banking get its start and why do you think it has survived for so long? What major event occurred in 1934 that has affected banking, not only in the United States, but in many countries around the world ever since then? (See **www.factmonster.com/ipka/A080/059.html** and **www.fdic.gov**.)

7. In what ways do the following corporations resemble banks? How are they different from banks of about the same asset size?

   Charles Schwab Corporation (**www.schwab.com**)

   Household International (**www.hsbcusa.com**)

   GMAC Financial Services (**www.gmacfs.com**)

S&P Market Insight Challenge (www.mhhe.com/edumarketinsight).

STANDARD &POOR'S

1. GE Capital is a financial-services affiliate of General Electric. Reread the description of GE Capital in this chapter. Then, using the Educational Version of S&P's Market Insight, read and print the "Long Business Description" for GE. Describe any new developments concerning the company's financial-service affiliates. What is the most recent contribution of the financial-services affiliates to the total revenue received by the entire company? (This would be expressed as a percentage of total revenue.)

STANDARD &POOR'S

2. Table 1–2 in this chapter provides a list of the leading banking and nonbanking financial-service providers around the globe. The left-hand column lists *banks* and the right-hand column lists several *nonbank financial-service firms*. (Those firms found in the Educational Version of S&P's Market Insight are noted in the table.) Choose one banking-oriented firm from the left-hand column and one nonbank financial-service firm from the right-hand column. Using Market Insight, print out the "Long Business Description" for your two selected financial firms. Compare and contrast the business descriptions of the two financial-service firms. What are the implications for these firms of any differences you detect in their business descriptions?

REAL NUMBERS FOR REAL BANKS　　The Very First Assignment

Identification of a bank to follow throughout the semester (or perhaps for the rest of your life):

A. Choose a bank holding company (BHC) that is both among the 25 largest U.S. banking companies and in S&P's Market Insight. Do not choose National City Corporation because that BHC is used for examples throughout the text. (Your instructor may impose constraints to ensure that your class examines a significant number of institutions, rather than just a few.)

　The list of the 50 largest U.S. BHCs is found at **www.ffiec. gov/nic**. Click on the link "Top 50 BHCs/Banks" and choose from the top 25.

B. Having chosen a BHC, check to make sure that your banking company is covered by Standard & Poor's Market

Insight, Educational Version. (At last count, 21 of the 25 largest U.S. banking companies were included in Market Insight.) Using Market Insight, read and print the "Long Business Description" for your firm. Also, print and read the most recent S&P stock report. In Chapter 1 we discussed the traditional financial services that have been associated with commercial banking for decades and then the services that have recently been added to banks' financial-service offerings. What do the Market Insight descriptions for your chosen banking firm reveal regarding types of services?

C. In conclusion, write approximately one page on your chosen banking company and the focus of its operations.

Selected References

For a review of the history of banking and nonbank financial firms, see especially:

1. Kindleberger, Charles P. A *Financial History of Western Europe*. Boston: Allen and Unwin, 1984.

For a discussion of the changing role and market share of banking and its competitors, see, for example:

2. Beim, David U. "Why Are Banks Dying?" *The Columbia Journal of World Business*, Spring 1992, pp. 1–12.

3. Kaufman, George G., and Larry R. Mote. "Is Banking a Declining Industry? A Historical Perspective." *Economic Perspectives*, Federal Reserve Bank of Chicago, May/June 1994, pp. 2–12.

4. Kwan, Simon. "Banking Consolidation." *FRBSF Economic Letter*, Federal Reserve Bank of San Francisco, no. 2004-15 (June 2004), pp. 1–3.

5. Poposka, Klimantina, Mark D. Vaughan, and Timothy J. Yeager. "The Two Faces of Banking." *The Regional Economist*, Federal Reserve Bank of St. Louis, October 2004, pp. 10–11.

6. Powell, Donald E., Former Chairman of the Federal Deposit Insurance Corporation. "South America and Emerging Risks in Banking." Speech to the Florida Bankers Association, Orlando, Florida, October 23, 2002.

7. Rose, Peter S., and Milton H. Marquis. *Money and Capital Markets: Financial Institutions and Instruments in a Global Marketplace*. 9th ed. Burr Ridge, IL: McGraw-Hill/Irwin Press, 2006. See especially Chapters 4, 14, and 17.

For a review of the theory of banking and financial intermediation, see especially:

8. Rose, John T. "Commercial Banks as Financial Intermediaries and Current Trends in Banking: A Pedagogical Framework." *Financial Practice and Education* 3, no. 2 (Fall 1993), pp. 113–118.

Appendix

Career Opportunities in Financial Services

In this chapter, we have focused on the great importance of banks and nonbank financial-service firms in the functioning of the economy and financial system and on the many roles played by financial firms in dealing with the public. But banks and their financial competitors are more than just financial-service providers. They can also be the place for a satisfying professional career. What different kinds of professionals work inside most financial firms?

Key URLs
To see what kinds of jobs are available in the financial services field see **www.careers-in-finance.com/cb.htm** and **www.bankjob_search.com**.

Loan Officers   Many financial managers begin their careers accepting and analyzing loan applications submitted by business and household customers. Loan officers make initial contact with potential new customers and assist them in filing loan requests and in developing a service relationship with a lending institution. Loan officers are needed in such important financial institutions as banks, credit unions, finance companies, and savings associations.

Key URLs
For jobs in lending and credit analysis see, for example, **www.bankjobs.com** and **www.scottwatson.com**.

Credit Analysts   The credit analyst backstops the work of the loan officer by preparing detailed written assessments of each loan applicant's financial position and advises management on the wisdom of granting any particular loan. Credit analysts and loan officers need professional training in accounting, financial statement analysis, and business finance.

Managers of Operations   Managers in the operations division are responsible for processing checks and clearing other cash items on behalf of their customers, for maintaining the institution's computer facilities and electronic networks, for supervising the activities of tellers, for handling customer problems with services, for maintaining security systems to protect property, and for overseeing the operation of the personnel (human resources) department. Managers in the operations division need sound training in the principles of business management and in computers and management information systems, and they must have the ability to interact with large groups of people.

Branch Managers   When financial service providers operate large branch systems, many of these functions are supervised by the manager of each branch office. Branch managers lead each branch's effort to attract new accounts, calling on business firms and households in their local area. They also approve loan requests and resolve customer complaints. Branch managers must know how to motivate employees and how to represent their institution in the local community.

Key URL
For opportunities in branch management, operations, and systems management see, for example, **www.bankstaffers.com**.

Systems Analysts   These computer specialists work with officers and staff in all departments, translating their production and information needs into programming language. The systems analyst provides a vital link between managers and computer programmers in making the computer an effective problem-solving tool and an efficient channel for delivering customer services. Systems analysts need in-depth training in computer programming as well as courses emphasizing business problem solving.

Auditing and Control Personnel   Keeping abreast of the inflow of revenues and the outflow of expenses and tracking changes in the service provider's financial position are the responsibilities of auditors and accountants. These are some of the most important tasks within a financial institution because they help guard against losses from criminal activity and waste. Jobs as important as these require considerable training in accounting and auditing.

Trust Department Specialists   Specialists in a trust department aid companies in managing their employee retirement programs, issuing securities, maintaining business records, and investing funds. Consumers also receive help in managing their property and in building an estate for retirement. Men and women employed in trust departments usually possess a wide range of backgrounds in commercial and property law, real estate appraisal, securities investment strategies, and marketing.

Key URL
For jobs in trust departments see, for example, **www.ihirebanking.com**.

Tellers   One employee that many customers see and talk with at virtually all depository institutions is the teller—the individual who occupies a fixed station within a branch office or at a drive-in window, receiving deposits and dispensing cash and information. Tellers must sort and file deposit receipts and withdrawal

Key URL
For information about teller jobs see **www.bankjobs.com**.

slips, verify customer signatures, check account balances, and balance their own cash position at least once each day. Because of their pivotal role in communicating with customers, tellers must be friendly, accurate, and knowledgeable about other departments and the services they sell.

Security Analysts and Traders Security analysts and traders are usually found in a financial firm's bond department and in its trust department. All financial institutions have a pressing need for individuals skilled in evaluating the businesses and governments issuing securities that the institution might buy and in assessing financial market conditions. Such courses as economics, money and capital markets, and investment analysis are usually the best fields of study for a person interested in becoming a security analyst or security trader.

Key URL
For opportunities in marketing see, for example, **www.ritesite. com**.

Marketing Personnel With greater competition today, financial-service providers have an urgent need to develop new services and to more aggressively sell existing services—tasks that usually fall primarily to the marketing department. This important function requires an understanding of the problems involved in producing and selling services and a familiarity with service advertising techniques. Course work in economics, services marketing, statistics, and business management is especially helpful in this field.

Human Resources Managers A financial firm's performance in serving the public and its owners depends, more than anything else, on the talent, training, and dedication of its management and staff. The job of human resources managers is to find and hire people with superior skills and to train them to fill the roles needed by the institution. Many institutions provide internal management training programs directed by the human resources division or outsource this function to other providers. Human resources managers keep records on employee performance and counsel employees on ways to improve their performance and opportunities for promotion.

Key URLs
Investment banking career opportunities are often found at **www.efinancial careers.com** and **www.bankjobs.com**.

Investment Banking Specialists Banks are becoming increasingly involved in assisting their business customers with the issue of bonds and stock to raise new capital, and they frequently render advice on financial market opportunities and on business mergers and acquisitions. This is the dynamic, fast-paced field of investment banking, one of the highest-paid and most challenging areas in the financial marketplace. Investment banking personnel must have intensive training in accounting, economics, strategic planning, investments, and international finance.

Bank Examiners and Regulators Because banks are among the most heavily regulated of all business firms, there is an ongoing need for men and women to examine the financial condition and operating procedures of banks and their closest competitors and to prepare and enforce regulations. Regulatory agencies hire examiners from time to time, often by visiting college campuses or as a result of phone calls and letters from applicants. Examiners and regulators must have knowledge of accounting, business management, economics, and financial laws and regulations.

Key URLs
Information about possible employment at key bank regulatory agencies may be found, for example, at **www.federal.reserve. gov/careers** or at **www. fdic.gov/about/jobs**.

Regulatory Compliance Officers Compliance personnel must make sure the regulated financial firm is in compliance with state, national, and international rules. Training in business law, economics, and accounting is most useful.

Risk Management Specialists These professionals monitor each financial firm's exposure to a variety of risks (especially market, credit, and operational risks) and develop strategies to deal with that exposure. Training in economics, statistics, and accounting is especially important in this rapidly developing field.

In summary, with recent changes in services offered, technology, and regulation, the financial-services field can be an exciting and challenging career. However, finding a good job in this industry will *not* be easy. Hundreds of smaller financial institutions are being absorbed by larger ones, with subsequent reductions in staff. Nevertheless, if such a career path sounds interesting to you, there is no substitute for further study of the industry and its history, services, and problems. It is also important to visit with current personnel working in financially oriented businesses to learn more about the daily work environment. Only then can you be sure that financial services is really a good career path for you.

CHAPTER TWO

The Impact of Government Policy and Regulation on Banking and the Financial-Services Industry

Key Topics in This Chapter

- The Principal Reasons for Bank and Nonbank Financial-Services Regulation
- Major Bank and Nonbank Regulators and Laws
- The Riegle-Neal and Gramm-Leach-Bliley (GLB) Acts
- The Check 21, FACT, Patriot, Sarbanes-Oxley, and Bankruptcy Abuse Acts
- Key Regulatory Issues Left Unresolved
- The Central Banking System
- Organization and Structure of the Federal Reserve System and Leading Central Banks of Europe and Asia
- Financial-Services Industry Impact of Central Bank Policy Tools

2–1 Introduction

Some people fear financial institutions. They may be intimidated by the power and influence these institutions seem to possess. Thomas Jefferson, third President of the United States, once wrote: "I sincerely believe that banking establishments are more dangerous than standing armies." Partly out of such fears and concerns a complex web of laws and regulations has emerged.

This chapter is devoted to a study of the complex regulatory environment that governments around the world have created for financial-service firms in an effort to safeguard the public's savings, bring stability to the financial system, and prevent abuse of financial-service customers. Financial institutions must contend with some of the heaviest and most comprehensive rules applied to any industry. These government-imposed regulations are enforced by federal and state agencies that oversee the operations, service offerings, performance, and expansion of most financial-service firms.

Regulation is an ugly word to many people, especially to managers and stockholders, who often see the rules imposed upon them by governments as burdensome, costly, and unnecessarily damaging to innovation and efficiency. But the rules of the game are changing—more and more financial-service regulations are being set aside or weakened and the free marketplace, not government dictation, is increasingly being relied upon to shape and restrain what financial firms can do. One prominent example in the United States is the 1999 Gramm-Leach-Bliley (Financial Services Modernization) Act, which tore down the regulatory walls separating banking from security trading and underwriting and from the insurance industry, allowing these different types of financial firms to acquire each other, dramatically increasing financial-services competition.

In this chapter we examine the key regulatory agencies that supervise and examine banks and their closest competitors. The chapter concludes with a brief look at monetary policy and several of the most powerful financial institutions in the world, including the Federal Reserve System, the European Central Bank, the Bank of Japan, and the People's Bank of China.

2–2 Banking Regulation

First, we turn to one of the most government regulated of all industries—commercial banking. As bankers work to supply loans, accept deposits, and provide other financial services to their customers, they must do so within a climate of extensive federal and state rules designed primarily to protect the *public interest*.

A popular saying among bankers is that the letters FDIC (Federal Deposit Insurance Corporation) really mean Forever Demanding Increased Capital! To U.S. bankers, at least, the FDIC and the other regulatory agencies seem to be forever demanding something: more capital, more reports, more public service, and so on. No new bank can enter the industry without government approval (in the form of a charter to operate). The types of deposits and other financial instruments sold to the public to raise funds must be sanctioned by each institution's principal regulatory agency. The quality of loans and investments and the adequacy of capital are carefully reviewed by government examiners. For example, when a bank seeks to expand by constructing a new building, merging with another bank, setting up a branch office, or acquiring or starting another business, regulatory approval must first be obtained. Finally, the institution's owners cannot even choose to close its doors and leave the industry unless they obtain explicit approval from the government agency that granted the original charter of incorporation.

To encourage further thought concerning the process of regulatory governance, we can use an analogy between the regulation of financial firms and the experiences of youth. We were all children and teenagers before growing physically, mentally, and emotionally into adults. As children and teenagers, we liked to have fun; however, we pursued this objective within the constraints set by our parents, and some kids had more lenient parents than others. Financial firms like to maximize shareholders' wealth (shareholders are having fun when they are making money); however, they must operate within the constraints imposed by regulators. Moreover, banks are in essence the "kids" with the strictest parents on the block.

Pros and Cons of Strict Rules

Why are banks so closely regulated—more so than virtually any other financial-service firm? A number of reasons can be given for this heavy and costly burden of government supervision, some of them centuries old.

First, banks are among the leading repositories of the public's savings, especially the savings of individuals and families. While most of the public's savings are placed in relatively short-term, highly liquid deposits, banks also hold large amounts of long-term savings in retirement accounts. The loss of these funds due to bank failure or crime would be catastrophic to many individuals and families. However, many savers lack the financial expertise or depth of information needed to correctly evaluate the riskiness of a bank or other financial-service provider. Therefore, regulatory agencies are charged with the responsibility of gathering and evaluating the information needed to assess the true condition of banks and other financial firms to protect the public against loss. Cameras and guards patrol bank lobbies to reduce the risk of loss due to theft. Periodic examinations and audits are aimed at limiting losses from embezzlement, fraud, or mismanagement. Government agencies stand ready to loan funds to financial firms faced with unexpected shortfalls of spendable reserves so that the public's savings are protected.

Banks are especially closely watched because of their power to create money in the form of readily spendable deposits by making loans and investments. Changes in the volume of money created by banks and competing financial firms appear to be closely correlated with economic conditions, especially the growth of jobs and the presence or absence of inflation. However, the fact that banks and many of their nearest competitors create money, which impacts the vitality of the economy, is not necessarily a valid excuse for regulating them. As long as government policymakers can control a nation's money supply, the volume of money that individual financial firms create should be of no great concern to the regulatory authorities or to the public.

Banks and their closest competitors are also regulated because they provide individuals and businesses with loans that support consumption and investment spending. Regulatory authorities argue that the public has a keen interest in an adequate supply of credit flowing from the financial system. Moreover, where discrimination in granting credit is present, those individuals who are discriminated against face a significant obstacle to their personal well-being and an improved standard of living. This is especially true if access to credit is denied because of age, sex, race, national origin, or other irrelevant factors. Perhaps, however, the government could eliminate discrimination in providing services to the public simply by promoting more competition among providers of financial services, such as by vigorous enforcement of the antitrust laws, rather than through regulation.

Finally, banks, in particular, have a long history of involvement with federal, state, and local government. Early in the history of the industry governments relied upon cheap bank credit and the taxation of banks to finance armies and to supply the funds they were unwilling to raise through direct taxation of their citizens. More recently, governments have relied upon banks to assist in conducting economic policy, in collecting taxes, and in dispensing government payments. This reason for regulation has come under attack recently, however, because banks and their competitors probably would provide financial services to governments if it were profitable to do so, even in the absence of regulation.

In the United States, banks are regulated through a **dual banking system;** that is, *both* federal and state authorities have significant regulatory powers. This system was designed to give the states closer control over industries operating within their borders, but also, through federal regulation, to ensure that banks would be treated fairly by individual states and local communities as their activities expanded across state lines. The key bank regulatory agencies within the U.S. government are the Comptroller of the Currency, the Federal Reserve System, and the Federal Deposit Insurance Corporation. The Department of Justice and the Securities and Exchange Commission have important, but smaller, federal regulatory roles, while **state banking commissions** are the primary regulators of American banks at the state level, as shown in Table 2–1.

Key URL

News concerning bank regulation and bank compliance with current rules can be found at the American Bankers Association Web site at **www.aba.com/ compliance**.

Insights and Issues

The Impact of Regulation—The Arguments for Strict Rules versus Lenient Rules

Although the reasons for regulation are well known, the possible impacts of regulation on the banking and financial-services industry are in dispute. One of the earliest theories about regulation, developed by economist George Stigler [5], contends that firms in regulated

TABLE 2–1
Banking's Principal Regulatory Agencies and Their Responsibilities

Federal Reserve System
- Supervises and regularly examines all state-chartered member banks and bank holding companies operating in the United States and acts as the "umbrella supervisor" for financial holding companies (FHCs) that are now allowed to combine banking, insurance, and securities firms under common ownership.
- Imposes reserve requirements on deposits (Regulation D).
- Must approve all applications of member banks to merge, establish branches, or exercise trust powers.
- Charters and supervises international banking corporations operating in the United States and U.S. bank activities overseas.

Comptroller of the Currency
- Issues charters for new national banks.
- Supervises and regularly examines all national banks.
- Must approve all national bank applications for branch offices, trust powers, and acquisitions.

Federal Deposit Insurance Corporation
- Insures deposits of federally supervised depository institutions conforming to its regulations.
- Must approve all applications of insured depositories to establish branches, merge, or exercise trust powers.
- Requires all insured depository institutions to submit reports on their financial condition.

Department of Justice
- Must review and approve proposed mergers and holding company acquisitions for their effects on competition and file suit if competition would be significantly damaged by these proposed organizational changes.

Securities and Exchange Commission
- Must approve public offerings of debt and equity securities by banking and thrift companies and oversee the activities of bank securities affiliates.

State Boards or Commissions
- Issue charters for new depository institutions.
- Supervise and regularly examine all state-chartered banks and thrifts.

Key URLs

If you are interested in exploring regulatory agencies from your home state or other U.S. states, enter the state's name and the words "banking commission." See, for example, the New York and California state banking commissions at **www.banking.state.ny. us** and **www.csbs.org**.

industries actually seek out regulation because it brings benefits in the form of monopolistic rents due to the fact that regulations often block entry into the regulated industry. Thus, some financial firms may lose money if regulations are lifted because they will no longer enjoy protected monopoly rents that increase their earnings. Samuel Peltzman [4], on the other hand, contends that regulation shelters a firm from changes in demand and cost, lowering its risk. If true, this implies that lifting regulations would subject individual financial-service providers to greater risk and eventually result in more failures.

More recently, Edward Kane [3] has argued that regulations can increase customer confidence, which, in turn, may create greater customer loyalty toward regulated firms. Kane believes that regulators actually compete with each other in offering regulatory services in an attempt to broaden their influence among regulated firms and with the general public. Moreover, he argues that there is an ongoing struggle between regulated firms and the regulators, called the *regulatory dialectic*. This is much like the struggle between children (banks) and parents (regulators) over such rules as curfew and acceptable friends. Once regulations are set in place, financial-service managers will inevitably search to find ways around the new rules in order to reduce costs and allow innovation to occur. If they are successful in skirting existing rules, then *new* regulations will be created, encouraging financial managers to further innovate to relieve the burden of the new rules. Thus, the struggle between regulated firms and regulators goes on indefinitely. The regulated firms never really grow up. Kane also believes that regulations provide an incentive for less-regulated businesses to try to win customers away from more-regulated firms, something that appears to have happened in banking in recent years as mutual funds, financial conglomerates, and other less-regulated financial firms have stolen away many of banking's best customers.

Concept Check

2–1. What key areas or functions of a bank or other financial firm are regulated today?

2–2. What are the *reasons* for regulating each of these key areas or functions?

2–3 Major Banking Laws—Where and When the Rules Originated

One useful way to see the potent influence regulatory authorities exercise on the banking industry is to review some of the major laws from which federal and state regulatory agencies receive their authority and direction. See Table 2–2 for a summary of these U.S. laws and major regulatory events in the history of American banking. Table 2–3 lists the number of U.S. banks by their regulators.

Key URL

The supervision and examination of national banks is the primary responsibility of the Comptroller of the Currency in Washington, D.C., at **www.occ.treas.gov/ law.htm**.

Meet the "Parents": The Legislation That Created Today's Bank Regulators

National Currency and Bank Acts (1863–64)

The first major federal government laws in U.S. banking were the National Currency and Bank Acts, passed during the Civil War. These laws set up a system for chartering new national banks through a newly created bureau inside the U.S. Treasury Department, the Office of the **Comptroller of the Currency** (OCC). The Comptroller not only assesses the need for and charters new national banks, but also regularly examines those institutions. These examinations vary in frequency and intensity with the bank's financial condition. However, every national bank is examined by a team of federal examiners at least once every 12 to 18 months. In addition, the Comptroller's office must approve all applications for the establishment of new branch offices and any mergers where national banks are

TABLE 2–2
Summary of Major Banking Laws and Their Provisions

Laws limiting bank lending and loan risk: National Bank Act (1863–64) Federal Reserve Act (1913) Banking Act of 1933 (Glass-Steagall) **Laws restricting the services banks and other depository institutions can offer:** National Bank Act (1863–64) Banking Act of 1933 (Glass-Steagall) Competitive Equality in Banking Act (1987) FDIC Improvement Act (1991) **Laws expanding the services banks and other depositories can offer:** Depository Institutions Deregulation and Monetary Control Act (1980) Garn–St Germain Depository Institutions Act (1982) Gramm-Leach-Bliley Act (1999) **Laws prohibiting discrimination in offering financial services:** Equal Credit Opportunity Act (1974) Community Reinvestment Act (1977) **Laws mandating increased information to the consumer of financial services:** Consumer Credit Protection Act (Truth in Lending, 1968) Competitive Equality in Banking Act (1987) Truth in Savings Act (1991) Gramm-Leach-Bliley Act (1999) Fair and Accurate Transactions Act (2003)	**Laws requiring more accurate financial reporting:** Sarbanes-Oxley Act (2002) **Laws regulating branch banking:** Banking Act of 1933 (Glass-Steagall) Riegle-Neal Interstate Banking and Branching Efficiency Act (1994) **Laws regulating holding company activity:** Bank Holding Company Act of 1956 Riegle-Neal Interstate Banking and Branching Efficiency Act (1994) Gramm-Leach-Bliley Act (1999) **Laws regulating mergers:** Bank Merger Act (1960) Riegle-Neal Interstate Banking and Branching Efficiency Act (1994) **Laws assisting federal agencies in dealing with failing depository institutions:** Garn–St Germain Depository Institutions Act (1982) Competitive Equality in Banking Act (1987) Financial Institutions Reform, Recovery, and Enforcement Act (1989) Federal Deposit Insurance Corporation Improvement Act (1991) Federal Deposit Insurance Reform Act (2005) **Laws requiring the sharing of customer information with government:** Bank Secrecy Act (1970) USA Patriot Act (2001)

TABLE 2–3
Regulators of U.S. Insured Banks (Showing Numbers of U.S. Banks Covered by Deposit Insurance as of 2004 and 2005)

Source: Federal Deposit Insurance Corporation.

Factoid
What is the oldest U.S. federal banking agency?
Answer: The Comptroller of the Currency, established during the 1860s to charter and regulate U.S. national banks.

Types of U.S. Insured Banks	Number of U.S. Insured Banks (as of 7/22/05)	Number of Branch Offices of Insured Banks (as of 12/31/04)

Banks chartered by the federal government:
    U.S. insured banks with national (federal)
    charters issued by the Comptroller
    of the Currency
	1,864	38,683

Banks chartered by state governments:
    State-chartered member banks of the
    Federal Reserve System and insured by the
    Federal Deposit Insurance Corporation
	907	13,181

State-chartered nonmember banks
    insured by the Federal Deposit
    Insurance Corporation
	<u>4,778</u>	<u>19,310</u>

Total of All U.S. Insured Banks and Branches	7,549	71,174

Primary Federal Regulators of U.S. Insured Banks (as of March 31, 2005):	Number of U.S. Insured Banks under Direct Regulation
Federal Deposit Insurance Corporation (FDIC)	4,778
Office of the Comptroller of the Currency (OCC)	1,864
Board of Governors of the Federal Reserve System (BOG)	907

Notes: The number of insured banks subject to each of the three federal regulatory agencies listed immediately above may not exactly match the numbers shown in the top portion of the table due to shared jurisdictions and other special arrangements among the regulatory agencies. Moreover, the figures in the bottom half of the table are for March 31, 2005, while those in the top portion represent totals as of July 22, 2005.

involved. The Comptroller can close a national bank that is insolvent or in danger of imposing substantial losses on its depositors.

The Federal Reserve Act (1913)

A series of financial panics in the late 19th and early 20th centuries led to the creation of a second federal bank regulatory agency, the **Federal Reserve System** (the Fed). Its principal roles are to serve as a lender of last resort—providing temporary loans to depository institutions facing financial emergencies—and to help stabilize the financial markets and the economy in order to preserve public confidence. The Fed also was created to provide important services, including the establishment of a nationwide network to clear and collect checks (supplemented later by an electronic funds transfer network). The Federal Reserve's most important job today, however, is to control money and credit conditions to promote economic stability. This final task assigned to the Fed is known as *monetary policy,* a topic we will examine later in this chapter.

The Banking Act of 1933 (Glass-Steagall)

Between 1929 and 1933, more than 9,000 banks failed and many Americans lost confidence in the banking system. The legislative response to this disappointing performance was to enact stricter rules and regulations in the **Glass-Steagall Act.** If as children we brought home failing grades, our parents might react by revoking our TV privileges and supervising our homework more closely. Congress reacted in much the same manner. The Glass-Steagall Act defined the boundaries of commercial banking by providing constraints that were effective for more than 50 years. This legislation separated commercial banking from investment banking and insurance. The "kids" (banks) could no longer play with their friends—providers of insurance and investment banking services.

The most important part of the Glass-Steagall Act was Section 16, which prohibited national banks from investing in stock and from underwriting new issues of *ineligible securities* (especially corporate stocks and bonds). Several major New York banking firms split into separate entities—for example, J. P. Morgan, a commercial banking firm, split off from Morgan Stanley, an investment bank. Congress feared that underwriting privately issued securities (as opposed to underwriting government-guaranteed securities, which has been legal for many years) would increase the risk of bank failure. Moreover, banks might be able to coerce their customers into buying the securities they were underwriting as a condition for getting a loan (called *tying arrangements*).

Establishing the FDIC under the Glass-Steagall Act

One of the Glass-Steagall Act's most important legacies was quieting public fears over the soundness of the banking system. The **Federal Deposit Insurance Corporation** (FDIC) was created to guarantee the public's deposits up to a stipulated maximum amount (initially $2,500; today up to $100,000 per account holder for most kinds of deposits). Without question, the FDIC, since its inception in 1934, has helped to reduce the number of bank runs, though it has not prevented bank failures. In fact, it may have contributed to individual bank risk taking and failure in some instances. Each insured depository institution is required to pay the federal insurance system an insurance premium based upon its volume of insurance-eligible deposits and its risk exposure. The hope was that, over time, the FDIC's pool of insurance funds would grow large enough to handle a considerable number of failures. However, the federal insurance plan was never designed to handle a rash of failures like the hundreds that occurred in the United States during the 1980s. This is why the FDIC was forced to petition Congress for additional borrowing authority in 1991, when the U.S. insurance fund had become nearly insolvent.

Criticisms of the FDIC and Responses via New Legislation: The FDIC Improvement Act (1991)

The FDIC became the object of strong criticism during the 1980s and early 1990s. Faced with predictions from the U.S. General Accounting Office that failing-bank claims would soon render the deposit insurance fund insolvent, the House and Senate passed the **Federal Deposit Insurance Corporation Improvement Act** in 1991. This legislation permitted the FDIC to borrow from the Treasury to remain solvent, called for risk-based insurance premiums, and defined the actions to be taken when depository institutions fall short of meeting their capital requirements.

The debate leading to passage of the FDIC Improvement Act did not criticize the fundamental concept of deposit insurance, but it *did* criticize the way the insurance system had been administered through most of its history. Prior to 1993, the FDIC levied fixed insurance premiums on all deposits eligible for insurance coverage, regardless of the riskiness of an individual depository institution's balance sheet. This fixed-fee system led to a *moral hazard* problem: *it encouraged depository institutions to accept greater risk because the government was pledged to pay off their depositors if they failed.* Because all insured institutions paid an identical insurance fee (unlike most private insurance systems), more risky institutions were being supported by more conservative ones. The moral hazard problem created the need for regulation because it encouraged some institutions to take on greater risk than they otherwise would have had no low-cost federal insurance system been available.

Most depositors (except for the very largest) do not carefully monitor bank risk. Instead, they rely on the FDIC for protection. Because this results in subsidizing the riskiest depository institutions—encouraging them to gamble with their depositors' money—a definite need developed for a risk-scaled insurance system in which the riskiest banks paid the highest insurance premiums. In response, Congress in 1991 ordered the FDIC to develop a risk-sensitive fee schedule under which the riskiest banks pay the highest insurance premiums and face the most restrictive regulations. In 1993, the FDIC implemented premiums differentiated on the basis of risk. Nevertheless, the federal government today sells relatively cheap deposit insurance that may still encourage greater risk taking.

Congress also ordered the regulatory agencies to develop a new measurement scale for describing how well capitalized each depository institution is and to take "prompt corrective action" when an institution's capital begins to weaken, using such steps as slowing its growth, requiring the owners to raise additional capital, or replacing management. If steps such as these do not solve the problem, the government can seize a depository institution whose ratio of tangible capital to total risk-adjusted assets falls to 2 percent or below and sell it to a healthy institution.

Under the law, regulators have to examine all depository institutions over $100 million in assets on site at least once a year; for smaller banks, on-site examinations have to take place at least every 18 months. In a move toward "reregulating" the banking industry—bringing it under tighter control—federal agencies were required to develop new guidelines for the depository institutions they regulate regarding loan documentation, internal management controls, risk exposure, and salaries paid to employees. At the same time, in reaction to the debacle of the huge Bank of Credit and Commerce International (BCCI) of Luxembourg, which allegedly laundered drug money and illegally tried to secure control of U.S. banks, Congress ordered foreign banks to seek approval from the Federal Reserve Board before opening or closing any U.S. offices. They must apply for FDIC insurance coverage if they wish to accept domestic deposits under $100,000. Moreover, foreign bank offices can be closed if their home countries do not adequately supervise their activities, and the FDIC is restricted from fully reimbursing uninsured and foreign depositors if their banks fail.

In an interesting final twist the Federal Reserve was restrained from propping up failing banks with long-term loans unless the Fed, the FDIC, and the current presidential administration agree that all the depositors of a bank should be protected in order to avoid damage to public confidence in the financial system. Congress's intent here was to bring the force of "market discipline" to bear on depository institutions that have taken on too much risk and encourage problem institutions to solve their own problems without government help.

One popular (but as yet unadopted) proposal for revamping or replacing the current deposit insurance system includes turning over deposit insurance to the private sector (privatization). Presumably, a private insurer would be more aggressive in assessing the riskiness of individual depository institutions and would compel risky institutions buying its insurance plan to pay much greater insurance fees. However, privatization of the insurance system would not solve all the problems of trying to protect the public's deposits. For example, an effective private insurance system would be difficult to devise because, unlike most other forms of insured risk, where the appearance of one claim does not necessarily lead to other claims, depositors' risks can be highly intercorrelated. The failure of a single depository institution can result in thousands of claims. Moreover, the failure of one institution may lead to still other failures. If a state's or region's economy turns downward, hundreds of failures may occur almost simultaneously. Could private insurers correctly price or even withstand that kind of risk?

In its earlier history, the FDIC's principal task was to restore public confidence in the banking system and avoid panic on the part of the public. Today, the challenge is how to *price* deposit insurance fairly so that risk is managed and the government is not forced to use excessive amounts of taxpayer funds to support private risk taking by depository institutions.[1]

Raising the FDIC Insurance Limit?

As the 21st century opened, the FDIC found itself embroiled in another public debate: *Should the federal deposit insurance limit be raised?* The FDIC pointed out that the $100,000 limit of protection for depositors was set nearly three decades ago in 1980. In the interim, inflation in the cost of living had significantly reduced the real purchasing power of the FDIC's $100,000 insurance coverage limit. Accordingly, the FDIC and several other groups recommended a significant coverage hike, perhaps up to $200,000, along with an indexing of deposit insurance coverage to protect against inflation.

Proponents of the insurance hike pointed out that during the previous decade depository institutions had lost huge amounts of deposits to mutual funds, security brokers and dealers, retirement plans provided by insurance companies, and the like. Thus, it was argued, depository institutions needed a boost to make their deposits more attractive in the race for the public's savings.

Opponents of the insurance increase also made several good arguments. For example, the original purpose of the insurance program was to protect the smallest and most vulnerable depositors, and $100,000 seems to fulfill that purpose nicely (even with inflation taken into account). Moreover, the more deposits that are protected, the more likely it is that depository institutions will take advantage of a higher insurance limit and make high-risk loans that, if they pay off, reap substantial benefits for both stockholders and management (behavior we referred to earlier as *moral hazard*). On the other hand, if the risky loans are not

[1]The FDIC is unique in one interesting aspect: While many nations collect funds from healthy institutions to pay off the depositors of failed depository institutions only when failure occurs, the FDIC steadily collects funds over time to build up a reserve until these funds are needed to cover failures.

Some observers believe that the FDIC *may* need a larger reserve in the future due to ongoing consolidation in the banking industry. Instead of facing mainly small institutional failures, as in the past, the FDIC may face record losses in the future from the failure of one or more very large depository institutions.

repaid, the depository institution fails, but the government is there to rescue its depositors. With more risk taking, more depository institutions will probably fail, leaving a government insurance agency (and, ultimately, the taxpayers) to pick up the pieces and pay off the depositors.

The ongoing debate over increasing federal deposit insurance protection led to the introduction of a bill known as the Federal Deposit Insurance Reform Act (H.R. 4636) in the U.S. House of Representatives, calling for the first significant increase in deposit insurance coverage in more than 25 years. Smaller depository institutions favored an increase in deposit insurance protection in order to slow recent outflows of deposits toward the largest banks, while big banks generally opposed the bill, fearing it would result in higher insurance premiums and thereby raise their costs.

Finally, the Federal Deposit Insurance Reform Act became law on February 8, 2006, raising federal insurance limits from $100,000 to $250,000 for IRA-type retirement deposits and selected other self-directed retirement accounts and calling for a possible increase in deposit insurance protection over time to keep abreast of inflation. Specifically, the boards of the FDIC and the National Credit Union Administration (NCUA) are empowered to adjust the insurance coverage limit for inflation every five years, beginning in 2010, if that adjustment appears warranted. The new law also instituted a risk-based insurance premium system so that riskier banks will pay higher premiums, but depository institutions that built up the insurance fund in past years would receive premium credits to lower their future insurance costs. Moreover, dividend payments may be paid to depository institutions if the federal insurance fund grows to exceed certain levels. In addition, the new law merges the Bank Insurance Fund (BIF) and the Savings Association Insurance Fund (SAIF) into the Deposit Insurance Fund or DIF to cover the deposits of *all* federally supervised depository institutions.

Factoid
Which U.S. banking agencies use taxpayers' money to fund their operations?
Answer: None of them do; they collect fees from the banks supervised and some have earnings from their trading in securities.

Instilling Social Graces and Morals—Social Responsibility Laws

Key URL
The Federal Deposit Insurance Corporation has several of the finest banking sites on the World Wide Web, all of which can be directly or indirectly accessed through **www.fdic.gov**.

The 1960s and 1970s ushered in a concern with the impact banks and other depository institutions were having on the quality of life in the communities they served. Congress feared that banks were not adequately informing their customers of the terms under which loans were made and especially about the true cost of borrowing money. In 1968 Congress moved to improve the flow of information to the consumer of financial services by passing the Consumer Credit Protection Act (known as Truth in Lending), which required that lenders spell out the customer's rights and responsibilities under a loan agreement.

In 1974, Congress targeted possible discrimination in providing financial services to the public with passage of the Equal Credit Opportunity Act. Individuals and families could not be denied a loan merely because of their age, sex, race, national origin, or religious affiliation, or because they were recipients of public welfare. In 1977, Congress passed the Community Reinvestment Act (CRA), prohibiting U.S. banks from discriminating against customers residing within their trade territories merely on the basis of the neighborhood in which they lived. Government examiners must periodically evaluate each bank's performance in providing services to all segments of its trade area and assign an appropriate CRA numerical rating.

Further steps toward requiring fair and equitable treatment of customers and improving the flow of information from banks to consumers were taken in 1987 with passage of the Competitive Equality in Banking Act and in 1991 with the approval of the Truth in Savings Act. These federal laws required banks to more fully disclose their deposit service policies and the true rates of return offered on the public's savings.

Insights and Issues

HOW THE FDIC USUALLY RESOLVES THE FAILURE OF AN INSURED DEPOSITORY INSTITUTION

Most troubled situations are detected in a regular examination of a depository institution conducted by either federal or state agencies. If examiners find a serious problem, they ask management and the board of directors of the troubled institution to prepare a report, and a follow-up examination normally is scheduled several weeks or months later. If failure seems likely, FDIC examiners are called in to see if they concur that the troubled institution is about to fail.

The FDIC then must choose among several different methods to resolve each failure. The two most widely used methods are *deposit payoff* and *purchase and assumption*. A deposit payoff is used when the closed institution's offices are not to be reopened, often because there are no interested bidders and the FDIC perceives that the public has other convenient banking alternatives. With a payoff, all insured depositors receive checks from the FDIC for up to $100,000, while uninsured depositors and other creditors receive a pro rata share of any funds generated from the eventual liquidation of the troubled institution's assets. A purchase and assumption transaction, on the other hand, is employed if a healthy institution can be found to take over selected assets and the deposits of the failed institution.

When a purchase and assumption is employed, shortly before the bank's closing the FDIC will contact healthy depository institutions in an effort to solicit bids for the failing institution. Interested buyers will negotiate with FDIC officials on the value of the failing institution's "good" and "bad" assets and on which assets and debts the FDIC will retain for collection and which will become the responsibility of the buyer.

On a predetermined date the state or federal agency that issued the troubled institution's charter officially closes the troubled firm and its directors and officers meet with FDIC officials. After that meeting a press release is issued and local newspapers are contacted.

On the designated closing date the FDIC's liquidation team assembles at some agreed-upon location. When all team members are ready (and often just after the troubled firm's offices are closed for the day), the liquidation team will enter the failed depository and place signs on the doors indicating that it has been seized by the FDIC. The team will move swiftly to take inventory of all assets and determine what funds the depositors and other creditors are owed. In subsequent days the liquidators may move their operations to rented office space nearby so the closed institution's facilities can open for business under the control of its new owners.

Concept Check

2–3. What is the principal role of the Comptroller of the Currency?

2–4. What is the principal job performed by the FDIC?

2–5. What key roles does the Federal Reserve System perform in the banking and financial system?

2–6. What is the Glass-Steagall Act and why was it important in banking history?

2–7. Why did the federal insurance system run into serious problems in the 1980s and 1990s? Can the current federal insurance system be improved? In what ways?

2–8. How did the Equal Credit Opportunity Act and the Community Reinvestment Act address discrimination?

Legislation Aimed at Allowing Interstate Banking: Where Can the "Kids" Play?

Not until the 1990s was one of the most controversial subjects in the history of American banking—*interstate bank expansion*—finally resolved. Prior to the 1990s many states prohibited banking firms from entering their territory and setting up full-service branch offices. Banks interested in building an interstate banking network usually had to form holding companies and acquire banks in other states as *affiliates* of those holding companies—not the most efficient way to get the job done because it led to costly duplication of capital and management. Moreover, many states as well as the federal government for a time outlawed an out-of-state bank holding company from acquiring control of a bank unless state law specifically granted that privilege.

The Riegle-Neal Interstate Banking Law (1994)

In an effort to reduce the cost of duplicating companies and personnel in order to cross state lines and provide more convenient services to millions of Americans who cross state lines every day, both houses of Congress voted in August 1994 to approve a new law. The **Riegle-Neal Interstate Banking and Branching Efficiency Act** was signed into law by President Clinton in September 1994, repealing provisions of the McFadden Act of 1927 and Douglas amendments of 1970 that prevented full-service interstate banking nationwide. These provisions of the new law were among the most notable:

- Adequately capitalized and managed holding companies can acquire banks anywhere in the United States.

Factoid
One reason interstate banking laws were passed during the 1990s is that more than 60 million Americans were then crossing state lines daily on their way to work, school, or shopping. Moreover, there was a need to permit bank and thrift mergers across state lines to absorb failing depository institutions.

- Interstate bank holding companies may consolidate their affiliated banks acquired across state lines into full-service branch offices. However, branch offices established across state lines to take deposits from the public must also create an adequate volume of loans to support their local communities.[2]

- No single banking company can control more than 10 percent of all U.S. deposits or more than 30 percent of the deposits in a single state (unless a state waives this latter restriction).

Thus, for the first time in U.S. history, these new banking laws gave a wide spectrum of American banks the power to take deposits and follow their customers across state lines, perhaps eventually offering full-service banking nationwide. While the change undoubtedly enhanced banking convenience for some customers, some industry analysts feared that these new laws would increase the consolidation of the industry into the largest banks and threaten the survival of many smaller banks. We will return to these issues in Chapter 3.

Bank Expansion Abroad

While U.S. banks still face a few restrictions on their branching activity, even in the wake of the Riegle-Neal Interstate Banking Act, banks in most other industrialized countries usually do not face regulatory barriers to creating new branch offices. However, some nations, including Canada and member states of the European Community (EC), either limit foreign banks' branching into their territory (in the case of Canada) or reserve the right to treat foreign banks differently if they so choose. Within the European Community, EC-based banks may offer any services throughout the EC that are permitted by each bank's home country.

Moreover, each European home nation must regulate and supervise its own financial-service firms, no matter in what markets they operate inside the EC's boundaries, a principle of regulation known as *mutual recognition*. For example, banks chartered by an EC member nation receive, in effect, a single banking license to operate wherever they wish

---

[2]Concern that interstate banking firms entering a particular state and buying up its banks and branches might drain deposits from that state led the U.S. Congress to insert Section 109 in the Riegle-Neal Interstate Banking Act. This section prohibits a bank from establishing or acquiring branch offices outside its home state *primarily for deposit production.* The same prohibition applies to interstate acquisitions of banks by holding companies. Interstate acquirers are expected to make an adequate volume of loans available in those communities outside their home state that they have entered with deposit-taking facilities.

Several steps are taken annually to determine if an interstate banking firm is in compliance with Section 109. First, an interstate bank's statewide loan-to-deposit ratio is computed for each state it has entered and that ratio is then compared to the entered state's overall loan-to-deposit ratio for all banks based in that state. The regulatory agencies look to see if the interstate bank's loan-to-deposit ratio in a given state is *less than half* of that state's overall loan-to-deposit ratio for banks calling that state home. If it is, an investigation ensues to determine if the banking firm's interstate branches are "reasonably helping to meet the credit needs of the communities served." A banking firm failing this investigation is subject to penalties imposed by its principal federal regulator.

inside the European Community. However, because EC countries differ slightly in the activities in which each country allows its financial firms to engage, some regulatory arbitrage may exist in which financial-service firms migrate to those areas inside Europe (or, for that matter, to any place on the globe) that permit the greatest span of activities and impose the fewest restrictions against geographic expansion.

The Gramm-Leach-Bliley Act (1999): What Are Acceptable Activities for Playtime?

One of the most important banking laws of the 20th century in the United States was signed into law by President Bill Clinton in November 1999. Overturning long-standing provisions of the Glass-Steagall Act and the Bank Holding Company Act, the new Financial Services Modernization Act (more commonly known as the **Gramm-Leach-Bliley Act** or GLB) permitted well-managed and well-capitalized banking companies with satisfactory Community Reinvestment Act (CRA) ratings to affiliate with insurance and securities firms under common ownership. Conversely, securities and insurance companies could form financial holding companies (FHCs) that control one or more banks. Banks were permitted to sell insurance provided they conform to state insurance rules.

GLB permits banking-insurance-securities affiliations to take place either through (1) a financial holding company (FHC), with banks, insurance companies or agencies, and securities firms each operating as separate companies but controlled by the same stock-holding corporation (if approved by the Federal Reserve Board), or (2) through subsidiary firms owned by a bank (if approved by the bank's principal regulator).

GLB's purpose was to allow qualified U.S. financial-service companies the ability to diversify their service offerings and thereby reduce their overall business risk exposure. For example, if the banking industry happened to be in a recession with declining profits, the insurance or the securities business might be experiencing an economic boom with rising profits, thereby bringing greater overall stability to a fully diversified financial firm's cash flow and profitability.

Moreover, GLB seems to offer financial-service customers the prospect of "one-stop shopping," obtaining many, if not all, of their financial services from a single provider. While this type of *convergence* of different financial services may well increase customer convenience, some financial experts believe that competition may be reduced as well if larger financial-service providers continue to acquire smaller financial firms in greater numbers and merge them out of existence. In the long run the public may have fewer alternatives and could wind up paying higher fees.

One of the most controversial parts of GLB concerns *customer privacy*. GLB requires financial-service providers to disclose their policies regarding the sharing of their customers' private ("nonpublic") data with others. When customers open a new account, they must be told what the financial-service provider's customer privacy policies are and be informed at least once a year thereafter about the company's customer privacy rules.

GLB allows affiliates of the same financial-services company to share nonpublic customer information with each other. Customers cannot prevent this type of *internal* sharing of their personal information, but they are permitted to "opt out" of any private information sharing by financial-service providers with third parties, such as telemarketers. GLB states that customers must notify their financial-service firm if they do not want their personal information shared with "outsiders."

Although many customers appear to be concerned about protecting their privacy, many financial firms are fighting recent attempts that limit information sharing about customers. These companies point out that by sharing personal data, the financial firm can more efficiently design and market services that will benefit customers.

The Gramm-Leach-Bliley Act of 1999

(MODIFICATION AND REPEAL OF THE GLASS-STEAGALL ACT OF 1933)

- Commercial banks can affiliate with insurance companies and securities firms (either through the holding-company route or through a bank subsidiary structure), provided they are well capitalized and have regulatory approval from their principal federal supervisory agency.
- Protections must be put in place for consumers considering the purchase of insurance through a bank. Consumers must be reminded that nondeposit financial-service products, including insurance, mutual funds, and various types of securities, are *not* FDIC-insured and their purchase cannot be imposed by a lender as a requirement for obtaining a loan.
- Banks, insurance companies, security brokers, and other financial institutions must inform consumers about their *privacy policies* when accounts are opened and at least once a year thereafter, indicating whether consumers' nonpublic personal information can be shared with an affiliated firm or with outsiders. Customers are allowed to "opt out" of their financial institutions' plans for sharing customer information with unaffiliated parties.
- Fees to use an automated teller machine (ATM) must be clearly disclosed at the site where the machine is located so that customers can choose to cancel a transaction before they incur a fee.
- It is a federal crime punishable with up to five years in prison to use fraud or deception to steal someone else's "means of identification" (called *identify theft*) from a financial institution.

Factoid
What is the fastest growing financial crime in the United States?
Answer: *Identity theft*— a subject addressed with stiffer criminal penalties by the Identify Theft and Assumption Deterrence Act of 1998.

Moreover, some financial firms argue that they can make better decisions and more effectively control risk if they can share consumer data with others. For example, if an insurer knows that a customer is in poor health or is a careless driver and would not be a good credit risk, this information would be especially helpful to a lender who is part of the same company in deciding whether this customer should be granted a loan.

The USA Patriot and Bank Secrecy Acts: Fighting Terrorism and Money Laundering

Adverse political developments and news reports rocked the financial world as the 21st century began and gave rise to more financial-services regulation. Terrorists used commercial airliners to attack the World Trade Center in New York City and the Pentagon in Washington, D.C., with great loss of life on September 11, 2001. The U.S. Congress quickly responded with passage of the **USA Patriot Act** in the Fall of that same year. The Patriot Act made a series of amendments to the Bank Secrecy Act (passed originally in 1970 to combat money laundering) that required selected financial institutions to report "suspicious" activity on the part of their customers.

Among the numerous provisions of the Patriot and amended Bank Secrecy Acts are requirements that financial-service providers establish the *identity* of any customers opening new accounts or holding accounts whose terms are changed. This is usually accomplished, at minimum, by asking for a driver's license or other acceptable picture ID and obtaining the Social Security number of the customer. Service providers are also required to check the customer's ID against a government-supplied list of terrorist organizations and report to the U.S. Treasury any suspected terrorists or suspicious activity in a customer's account.

Recent evidence indicates that governments intend to enforce laws like the Patriot and Bank Secrecy Acts. For example, in the Fall of 2002 Western Union was fined $8 million for allegedly failing to fully comply with the requirements for reporting money transfers. In Great Britain, which has a similar law, The Royal Bank of Scotland, second largest in the British Isles, was fined the equivalent of about $1.2 million for allegedly not taking enough care to establish its customers' identities. More recently, Riggs National Bank in Washington, D.C. (now owned by PNC Financial Services), ABN

ETHICS IN BANKING AND FINANCIAL SERVICES

BANK SECRECY AND REPORTING SUSPICIOUS TRANSACTIONS

Recent anti–money laundering and antiterrorist legislation, especially the Bank Secrecy and USA Patriot Acts, have attempted to turn many financial-service institutions, particularly banks, security brokers, and investment advisers, into "front-line cops" in the battle to ferret out illegal or suspicious financial activities. For example, in the United States if a covered financial firm detects suspicious customer activity it must file a report with the Financial Crimes Enforcement Network, inside the U.S. Treasury Department. Moreover, every federally supervised financial firm must develop and deploy a Customer Identification Plan (CIP) that gives rise to screening computer software and office procedures to make sure each institution knows who its customers are and can spot suspicious financial activity that may facilitate terrorism.

Some bankers have expressed concern about these suspicious-activity reporting requirements. One problem is the high cost (often in the tens of millions of dollars for a money center bank) of installing computer software and launching employee training programs and the substantial expense of

hiring more accountants and lawyers to detect questionable customer account activity. Another problem centers on the vagueness of the new rules—for example, what exactly is "suspicious activity"? Bankers are usually trained to be bankers, not policemen. Because of uncertainty about what to look for and the threat of heavy fines many financial firms tend to "overreport"—turning in huge amounts of routine customer data to avoid being accused of "slacking" in their surveillance activities. (The Bank Secrecy Act requires any cash transaction of $10,000 or more to be reported to the government.) Other bankers are simply uncomfortable about eavesdropping on their customers' business and possibly, as a result of their suspicious-activity reports, setting in motion a "witch hunt."

For their part, regulators argue that these requirements are essential in a modern world where an act of terrorism seems to happen somewhere nearly every day. If bankers and other financial advisers have not been educated in the past to spot suspicious financial transactions, then, it is argued, they must become educated. Regulators contend that the cost of poor reporting and lax law enforcement threatens the safety of the public and the institutions that serve them.

AMRO operating in New York and Chicago, Banco Popular de Puerto Rico, and Arab Bank PLC were fined for not filing adequate reports of possible money-laundering activities by some of their international customers.

Telling the Truth and Not Stretching It—The Sarbanes-Oxley Accounting Standards Act (2002)

Key URLs
For further information about the USA Patriot, Bank Secrecy, and Sarbanes-Oxley Acts see www.fdic.gov, www.sec.gov, www.AICPA.org, and Sarbanes-Oxley.com.

On the heels of the terrorist attacks of 9/11 came disclosures in the financial press of widespread manipulation of corporate financial reports and questionable dealings among leading corporations (such as Enron), commercial and investment bankers, and public accounting firms to the detriment of employees and market investors. Faced with deteriorating public confidence the U.S. Congress moved quickly to pass the **Sarbanes-Oxley Accounting Standards Act** of 2002.

Sarbanes-Oxley created the Public Company Accounting Oversight Board to enforce higher standards in the accounting profession and to promote accurate and objective audits of the financial reports of public companies (including financial-service corporations). Publishing false or misleading information about the financial performance and condition of publicly owned corporations is prohibited. Moreover, top corporate officers must vouch for the accuracy of their companies' financial statements. Loans to senior management and directors (insiders) of a publicly owned lending institution are restricted to the same credit terms that regular customers of comparable risk receive. Extensive new regulations affecting the accounting practices of public companies are emerging in the wake of this new law. Beginning October 1, 2003, federal banking agencies acquired the power to bar accounting firms from auditing depository institutions if these firms displayed evidence of negligence, reckless behavior, or lack of professional qualifications.

2–4 The 21st Century Ushers In an Array of New Laws, Regulations, and Regulatory Strategies

The opening decade of the 21st century unfolded with a diverse set of new laws and new regulations to enforce them, creating opportunities for financial firms to reduce their operating costs, expand their revenues, and better serve their customers.

The FACT Act

In 2003 the Fair and Accurate Credit Transactions (FACT) Act was passed in an effort to head off the growing problem of *identity* (ID) *theft,* in which someone attempts to steal another person's identifying private information (such as a Social Security number) in an effort to gain access to the victim's bank account, credit cards, or other personal property. The U.S. Congress ordered the Federal Trade Commission to make it easier for individuals victimized by ID theft to file a theft report and required the nation's credit bureaus to help victims resolve the problem. Individuals and families are entitled to receive at least one free credit report each year to determine if they have been victimized by this form of fraud. Many financial institutions see the new law as helping to reduce their costs, including reimbursements to customers, due to ID theft.

Check 21

The following year the Check 21 Act became effective, reducing the need for banks to transport paper checks across the country—a costly and risky operation. Instead, Check 21 allows checking-account service providers to replace a paper check written by a customer with a "substitute check," containing the images of the front and back of the original check. Substitute checks can be transported electronically at a fraction of the cost of the old checking system.

New Bankruptcy Rules

In 2005 banking industry lobbyists fought successfully for passage of the Bankruptcy Abuse Prevention and Consumer Protection Act of 2005, tightening U.S. bankruptcy laws. The new law will tend to push higher-income borrowers into more costly forms of bankruptcy. More bankrupts will be forced to repay at least some of what they owe. Bankers favoring the new law argued that it would lower borrowing costs for the average customer and encourage individuals and businesses to be more cautious in their use of debt.

Federal Deposit Insurance Reform

With passage of the Federal Deposit Insurance Reform Act of 2005 the U.S. Congress expanded the safety net protecting the retirement savings of individual depositors, allowed federal regulators to periodically adjust deposit insurance coverage upward to fight inflation, and stabilized the flow of premium payments into a single insurance fund for all federally supervised bank and thrift institutions.[3]

New Regulatory Strategies in a New Century and Unresolved Regulatory Issues

As reflected in the above new laws, the nature of financial-services regulation began to change its focus in the new century. The 1990s had ushered in a period of extensive government *deregulation* of the financial sector with legal restrictions against geographic and

---

[3]See Chapters 12 and 18 for additional discussion of the Check 21, FACT, and FDIC Insurance Reform Acts and new bankruptcy rules.

service expansion drastically reduced, permitting regulated financial institutions to compete more effectively and respond more rapidly to changing market conditions.

For example, in 1980 the U.S. Congress passed the Depository Institutions Deregulation and Monetary Control Act (DIDMCA) that lifted U.S. government ceilings on deposit interest rates in favor of free-market interest rates. In 1982 the Garn–St Germain Depository Institutions Act made bank and nonbank depository institutions more alike in the services they could offer and allowed banks and thrift institutions to more fully compete with other financial institutions for the public's money. Passage of the Financial Institutions Reform, Recovery and Enforcement Act in 1989 allowed bank holding companies to acquire nonbank depository institutions and, if desired, convert them into branch offices.

With the opening of the new century, however, there emerged a changed emphasis in the field of government regulation. In particular, the regulation of *geography* and *services* became less important and the regulation of *capital* and *risk taking* became more important. Increasingly, government regulatory agencies expressed concern about whether banks and their competitors held sufficient capital (especially funds contributed by their owners) to absorb large and unpredictable losses.

Moreover, regulators began to take a more serious look at *market data* as a barometer of the strengths and weaknesses of individual financial institutions. For example, if a bank experiences a decline in the value of its stock or a rise in the interest cost attached to its senior debt instruments this could be a signal that this institution has taken on greater risk and needs closer scrutiny from regulators.

The new century has also brought greater regulatory interest in *public disclosure*. For example, can we find a way to safely provide greater information to the public about the prices and fees of financial services and about how well financial institutions are or are not protecting their customers' private information? Can we find a way to reveal the true financial condition and risk of regulated financial firms without creating misunderstanding and mindless panic in the public? The hope among regulators is that greater public disclosure will promote greater competition in the financial-services sector, reduce risk taking, and help customers make better decisions about purchasing and using financial services.

Unfortunately, even with all of these strides toward a new focus in regulation many key regulatory issues remain unresolved. For example:

- What should we do about the regulatory *safety net* set up to protect small depositors from loss, usually by providing government-sponsored deposit insurance? Doesn't this safety net encourage financial firms to take on added risk? How can we balance risk taking and depositor safety?

- If we allow financial firms to accept more risk and respond more rapidly to competitors by offering new services, how do we prevent taxpayers from being stuck with the bill when more of these deregulated financial firms fail and depositors demand their money back?

- How can we be sure that a conglomerate financial firm that includes a bank will not loot the bank in order to prop up its other businesses, causing the bank to fail and leaving it up to the government to pay off its depositors?

- As financial firms become bigger and more complex, how do we insure that government regulators can effectively oversee what these more complicated firms are doing? Can we train regulators to be as good as they need to be in a more complex financial marketplace?

- Will *functional regulation,* in which each different type of business owned by a complex financial firm is regulated by a different and specialized government agency,

Insights and Issues

BANKING AND COMMERCE: THE HOT REGULATORY ISSUE FOR THE 21ST CENTURY?

Many observers of the financial-services marketplace believe that the key regulatory issue in banking in the 21st century centers on *banking versus commerce*—how far will banks and nonfinancial industrial firms be able to go in invading each other's territory? How much overlap in ownership can we allow between financial and nonfinancial businesses and still adequately protect the public's savings?

Currently several legal barriers exist between banks and non-financial businesses, preventing their combining with each other. These barriers include such laws as the Bank Holding Company Act and the National Bank Act, which define what banks can and cannot do. For those companies that do find clever ways to slip through these barriers, Section 23 of the Federal Reserve Act limits transactions between bank and nonbank firms owned by the same company in order to protect banks from being looted by their nonbank affiliates. For example, bank transactions with an affiliated business cannot exceed 10 percent of the bank's capital or a maximum of 20 percent of a bank's capital for *all* its nonbank affiliates combined.

Even with such tough rules, however, serious holes have been punched in the legal barriers that prevent banks from affiliating with commercial and industrial firms over the years. For example, prior to passage of the Bank Holding Company Act (as amended in 1970) companies controlling a single bank could purchase or start virtually any other kind of business. After passage of this sweeping law, however, banking was confined essentially to the financial services sector with a couple of exceptions.

One of these exceptions centered around thrift institutions (such as savings and loans) that could get into the commercial sector by having a company acquire a single thrift and then add other businesses. Passage of the Gramm-Leach-Bliley Act of 1999 closed this *unitary thrift device*.

As the 21st century opened, still another crack in the barriers separating banking and commerce remained in the form of *industrial loan companies*. These state-chartered deposit and loan businesses are often affiliated with industrial firms and may provide credit to help finance the purchase of their parent company's products. Industrial loan companies raise funds by selling noncheckable deposits, and they can apply for FDIC insurance. These firms, centered mostly in California and Utah, currently play a fairly modest role in the financial sector, however, holding about $140 billion in assets compared to more than $8 trillion in total bank assets.

The banking-commerce issue remains a hot one as creative financial minds look for (and often find) clever ways to invade new turf despite existing barriers. For an excellent expanded discussion of this issue, see John R. Walter, "Banking and Commerce: Tear Down This Wall?" *Economic Quarterly,* Federal Reserve Bank of Richmond, 89, no. 2 (Spring 2003), pp. 7–31.

really work? For example, an investment bank belonging to a conglomerate financial firm may be regulated by the Securities and Exchange Commission, while the commercial bank that conglomerate also owns may be regulated by the Comptroller of the Currency. What if these regulators disagree? Can they cooperate effectively for the public benefit?

- With the financial-services industry consolidating and converging into fewer, but bigger, firms, can we get by with fewer regulators? Can we simplify the current regulatory structure and bring greater efficiency to the task?

- What about *mixing banking and commerce?* Should industrial firms be free to acquire or start financial firms and vice versa? For example, should a bank be able to sell cars and trucks alongside deposits and credit cards? Would this result in unfair competition? Would it create too much risk of bank failure? Should regulators be allowed to oversee industrial firms that are affiliated with financial firms in order to protect the latter?

- As financial firms reach their arms around the globe, what nation or nations should regulate their activities? What happens when nations disagree about financial-services regulation? What if a particular nation is a weak and ineffective regulator? Who should take up the slack? Shouldn't countries cooperate in financial-services regulation just as they do in the defense of their homelands?

All of the foregoing questions represent tough issues in public policy to which regulators must find answers in this new century of challenge and global expansion.

Epic Moments in the History of Modern Banking Regulation

1863–64—The U.S. government begins chartering and supervising national banks to expand the nation's supply of money and credit and to compete with state-chartered banks.

1913—The Federal Reserve Act is signed into law, setting up the Federal Reserve System to improve the payments mechanism, supervise banks, and regulate the supply of money and credit in the United States.

1933—The Glass-Steagall (Banking) Act creates the Federal Deposit Insurance Corporation (FDIC) and separates commercial and investment banking into different industries.

1934—The Securities and Exchange Act requires greater disclosure of information about securities sold to the public and creates the Securities and Exchange Commission (SEC) to prevent the use of deceptive information in the marketing of securities.

1935—The Banking Act expands the powers of the Board of Governors as the chief administrative body of the Federal Reserve System and establishes the Federal Open Market Committee as the Fed's principal monetary policy decision-making group.

1956—The Bank Holding Company Act requires corporations controlling two or more banks to register with the Federal Reserve Board and seek approval for any new business acquisitions.

1960—The Bank Merger Act requires federal approval for any mergers involving federally supervised banks and, in subsequent amendments, subjects bank mergers and acquisitions to the antitrust laws.

1970—Bank Holding Company Act is amended to include one-bank companies that must register with the Federal Reserve Board. Permissible nonbank businesses that bank holding companies can acquire must be "closely related to banking," such as finance companies and thrift institutions.

1977—Community Reinvestment Act (CRA) prevents banks from "redlining" certain neighborhoods, refusing to serve those areas.

1978—International Banking Act imposes federal regulation on foreign banks operating in the United States and requires FDIC insurance coverage for foreign banks selling retail deposits inside the United States.

1980—Deposit interest-rate ceilings are lifted and reserve requirements are imposed on all depository institutions offering checkable or nonpersonal time deposits under the terms of the Depository Institutions Deregulation and Monetary Control Act. Interest-bearing checking accounts are legalized nationwide for households and nonprofit institutions.

1982—With passage of the Garn–St Germain Depository Institutions Act, depositories may offer deposits competitive with money market fund share accounts, while nonbank thrift institutions are given new service powers that allow them to compete more fully with commercial banks.

1987—Competitive Equality in Banking Act is passed, allowing some bank and thrift mergers to take place across state lines and requiring public disclosure of checking account deposit policies. The Federal Reserve Board rules that bank holding companies can establish securities underwriting subsidiaries subject to limits on the revenues they generate.

1988—The Basel Agreement imposes common minimum capital requirements on banks in leading industrialized nations based on the riskiness of their assets.

1989—The Financial Institutions Reform, Recovery, and Enforcement Act (FIRREA) is enacted in order to resolve failures of hundreds of depository institutions and set up the Savings Association Insurance Fund (SAIF). FIRREA launches the Office of Thrift Supervision inside the U.S. Treasury Department to regulate nonbank depository institutions. U.S. tax payers wound up paying more than $500 billion to rescue the FDIC and resolve scores of bank and thrift failures.

1991—The FDIC Improvement Act mandates fees for deposit insurance based on risk exposure, grants the FDIC authority to borrow, and creates the Truth in Savings Act to require greater public disclosure of the terms associated with selling deposits.

(continued)

1994—The Riegle-Neal Interstate Banking and Branching Efficiency Act permits interstate full-service banking through acquisitions, mergers, and branching across state lines.

1999—The Gramm-Leach-Bliley Financial Services Modernization Act allows banks to create securities and insurance subsidiaries, and financial holding companies (FHCs) can set up banking, insurance, security, and merchant banking affiliates and engage in other "complementary" activities. Financial-service providers must protect the privacy of their customers and limit sharing private information with other businesses.

2000—The European Monetary Union allows European and foreign banks greater freedom to cross national borders. A new central bank, the ECB, can reshape money and credit policies in Europe, and the European Community adopts a common currency, the *euro*.

2001—The USA Patriot Act requires financial-service firms to collect and share information about customer identities with government agencies and to report suspicious activity.

2002—The Sarbanes-Oxley Accounting Standards Act requires publicly owned companies to strengthen their auditing practices and prohibits the publishing of false or misleading information about the financial condition or operations of a publicly held firm.

2003—The Fair and Accurate Credit Transactions (FACT) Act makes it easier for victims of identity theft to file fraud alerts, and the public can apply for a free credit report annually.

2004—The Check 21 Act makes it faster and less costly for banks to electronically transfer check images ("substitute checks") rather than ship paper checks themselves.

2005—The Bankruptcy Abuse Prevention and Consumer Protection Act requires more troubled business and household borrowers to repay at least some of their debts.

2006—The Federal Deposit Insurance Reform Act authorizes the FDIC to periodically increase deposit insurance coverage for inflation and merges bank and thrift insurance funds.

Concept Check

2–9. How does the FDIC deal with most failures?

2–10. What changes have occurred in U.S. banks' authority to cross state lines?

2–11. How have bank failures influenced recent legislation?

2–12. What changes in regulation did the Gramm-Leach-Bliley (Financial Services Modernization) Act bring about? Why?

2–13. What new regulatory issues remain to be resolved now that interstate banking is possible and security and insurance services are allowed to commingle with banking?

2–14. Why must we be concerned about *privacy* in the sharing and use of a financial-service customer's information? Can the financial system operate efficiently if sharing nonpublic information is forbidden? How far, in your opinion, should we go in regulating who gets access to private information?

2–15. Why were the Sarbanes-Oxley, Bank Secrecy, and USA Patriot Acts enacted in the United States? What impact are these new laws and their supporting regulations likely to have on the financial-services sector?

2–16. Explain how the FACT, Check 21, 2005 Bankruptcy, and FDIC Insurance Reform Acts are likely to affect the revenues and costs of financial firms and their service to customers.

2–5 The Regulation of Nonbank Financial-Service Firms Competing with Banks

Regulating the Thrift (Savings) Industry

While commercial banks rank at or near the top of the list in terms of government control over their businesses, several other financial intermediaries—most notably credit unions, savings associations and savings banks, and money market funds—are not far behind. These so-called *thrift* institutions together attract a large proportion of the public's savings and grant a rapidly growing portion of consumer (household) loans. As such, even though they are privately owned, the thrifts are deemed to be "vested with the public interest" and, therefore, often face close supervision and regulation.

Credit Unions

Key URLs
To find out more about credit unions, see the World Council of Credit Unions at **www.woccu.org** and the Credit Union National Association at **www.cuna.org**. For more about the regulation of credit unions see the National Credit Union Administration at **www.ncua.gov**.

These nonprofit associations of individuals accept savings and share draft (checkable) deposits from and make loans only to their members. Federal and state rules prescribe what is required to be a credit union member—you must share a "common bond" with other credit union members (such as working for the same employer). Credit union deposits may qualify for federal deposit insurance coverage up to $100,000 from the National Credit Union Share Insurance Fund (NCUSIF). During the 1930s the Federal Credit Union Act provided for federal as well as state chartering of qualified credit unions. Federal credit unions are supervised and examined by the **National Credit Union Administration** (NCUA). Several aspects of credit union activity are closely supervised to protect their members, including the services they are permitted to offer and how they allocate funds. Risk connected with granting loans to members must be counterbalanced by sizable investments in government securities, insured bank CDs, and other short-term money market instruments.

Savings and Loans and Savings Banks

Key URL
To further explore the characteristics and services of savings and loan associations and savings banks and the rules they are governed by, see the Office of Thrift Supervision at **www.ots.treas.gov**.

These depository institutions include state and federal savings and loans and savings banks, created to encourage family savings and the financing of new homes. Government deregulation of the industry during the 1980s led to a proliferation of new consumer services to mirror many of those offered by commercial banks. Moreover, savings associations, like commercial banks, face multiple regulators in an effort to protect the public's deposits. State-chartered associations are supervised and examined by state boards or commissions, whereas federally chartered savings associations fall under the jurisdiction of the **Office of Thrift Supervision**—a part of the U.S. Treasury Department. Deposits are insured by the Savings Association Insurance Fund (SAIF), administered by the FDIC, bringing savings-association balance sheets under FDIC supervision. Passage of the FDIC Reform Act of 2005 calls for a merger of the SAIF with the Bank Insurance Fund (BIF) to create a single fund of insurance reserves for both savings associations and banks.

Money Market Funds

Although many financial institutions regard government regulation as burdensome and costly, money market funds owe their existence to regulations limiting the rates of interest banks and thrifts could pay on deposits. Security brokers and dealers found a way to attract short-term savings away from depository institutions and invest in money market securities bearing higher interest rates. Investment assets must be dollar denominated, have remaining maturities of no more then 397 days, and a dollar-weighted average maturity of no more then 90 days. There is no federal deposit insurance program for money funds, but they are regulated by the **Securities and Exchange Commission** (SEC) with the goal of keeping money fund share prices fixed at $1.

Regulating Other Nonbank Financial Firms

Life and Property/Casualty Insurance Companies

Key URLs
For additional information about life and property casualty insurers and the regulations they face, see especially the American Council for Life Insurance (**www.acli.com**) and the Insurance Information Institute (**www.iii.com**).

These sellers of risk protection for persons and property are one of the few financial institutions regulated almost exclusively at the state level. **State insurance commissions** generally prescribe the types and content of insurance policies sold to the public, often set maximum premium rates the public must pay, license insurance agents, scrutinize insurer investments for the protection of policyholders, charter new companies, and liquidate failing ones.

Recently the federal government has become somewhat more involved in insurance company regulation. For example, when these firms sell equity or debt securities to the public, they need approval from the Securities and Exchange Commission—a situation that is happening more frequently as many mutual insurers (which are owned by their policyholders) are converting to stockholder-owned companies. Similarly, when insurers form holding companies to acquire commercial and investment banks or other federally regulated financial businesses, they may come under the Federal Reserve's review.

Finance Companies

These business and consumer lenders have been regulated at the state government level for many decades, and state commissions look especially closely at their treatment of individuals borrowing money. Although the depth of state regulation varies across the United States, most states focus upon the types and contents of loan agreements they offer the public, the interest rates they charge (with some states setting maximum loan rates), and the methods they use to repossess property or to recover funds from delinquent borrowers. Relatively light regulation has led to a recent explosion in the number of small-loan companies (such as payday lenders, pawn shops, and check-cashing firms) that generally charge the highest loan interest rates of any financial institution.

Mutual Funds

These investment companies, which sell shares in a pool of income-generating assets (especially stocks and bonds), have faced close federal and state regulation since the Great Depression of the 1930s when many failed. The U.S. Securities and Exchange Commission (SEC) requires these businesses to register with that agency, submit periodic financial reports, and provide investors with a prospectus that reveals the financial condition, recent performance, and objectives of each fund. Recently the SEC has cooperated closely with the FDIC in warning the public of the absence of federal deposit insurance behind these funds.

Security Brokers and Dealers and Investment Banks

Filmtoid
What 2001 romantic comedy begins with stockbroker Ryan Turner (played by Charlie Sheen) finding himself without a job and being investigated by the SEC for insider trading?
Answer: *Good Advice.*

A combination of federal and state supervision applies to these traders in financial instruments who buy and sell securities, underwrite new security issues, and give financial advice to corporations and governments. Security dealers and investment banks have been challenging commercial banks for big corporate customers for decades, but deregulation under the Gramm-Leach-Bliley Act of 1999 has encouraged commercial banks to fight back and win a growing share of the market for security trading and underwriting. The chief federal regulator is the SEC, which requires these firms to submit periodic reports, limits the volume of debt they take on, and investigates insider trading practices. Recent corporate scandals have redirected the SEC to look more closely at the accuracy and objectivity of the research and investment advice these companies pass on to their clients.

Key URLs
Important information about mutual funds, investment banks, and security brokers and dealers may be found at such key sites as the Investment Company Institute (**www.ici.com**) and the Securities and Exchange Commission (**www.sec.gov**).

Financial Conglomerates

These highly diversified companies, which may combine commercial and investment banking, insurance, security trading, and other services in *one* organization, have created something of a regulatory crisis because only parts of each firm may come under the purview of any one regulator, leaving room for highly risky ventures. Recently the state regulatory commissions (which oversee finance and insurance companies that may be part of a conglomerate), the SEC (responsible for regulating securities firms), and the Federal Reserve Board (which supervises bank holding companies) have been cooperating more extensively in sharing oversight of these complex financial firms.

Are Regulations Really Necessary in the Financial-Services Sector?

A great debate is raging today about whether *any* of the remaining regulations affecting financial-service institutions are really necessary. Perhaps, as a leading authority in this field, George Benston, suggests [1], "It is time we recognize that financial institutions are simply businesses with only a few special features that require regulation." He contends that depository institutions, for example, should be regulated no differently from any other corporation with no subsidies or other special privileges.

Why? Benston contends that the historical reasons for regulating the financial sector— taxation of monopolies in supplying money, prevention of centralized power, preservation of solvency to mitigate the adverse impact of financial firm failures on the economy, and the pursuit of social goals (such as ensuring an adequate supply of housing loans for families and preventing discrimination and unfair dealing)—are no longer relevant today. Moreover, regulations are *not* free: they impose real costs in the form of taxes on money users, production inefficiencies, and reduced competition.

In summary, the trend under way today all over the globe is to free financial-service firms from the rigid boundaries of regulation; however, much still remains to be done if we wish to enhance the benefits of free competition to financial institutions and the public they serve.

2–6 The Central Banking System: Its Impact on the Decisions and Policies of Financial Institutions

As we have seen in this chapter, law and government regulation exert a powerful impact on the behavior, organization, and performance of financial-service firms. But there is one other government-created institution that also significantly shapes the behavior and performance of financial firms through its money and credit policies. That institution is the *central bank,* including the central bank of the United States, the Federal Reserve System (the Fed). Like most central banks around the globe, the Fed has more impact on the day-to-day activities of financial-service providers, especially on their revenues and costs, than any other institution, public or private.

A central bank's primary job is **monetary policy,** which involves making sure the supply and cost of money and credit from the financial system contribute to the nation's economic goals. By controlling the growth of money and credit, the Fed and other central banks around the globe try to ensure that the economy grows at an adequate rate, unemployment is kept low, and inflation is held down.

In the United States the Fed is relatively free to pursue these goals because it does not depend on the government for its funding. Instead, the Fed raises its own funds from sales of its services and from securities trading, and it passes along most of its earnings (after making small additions to its capital and paying dividends to member banks holding Federal Reserve bank stock) to the U.S. Treasury.

The nations belonging to the new European Union also have a central bank, the **European Central Bank (ECB),** which is relatively free and independent of governmental control as it pursues its main goal of avoiding inflation. In contrast, the **Bank of Japan** (BOJ), the **People's Bank of China** (PBC), and central banks in other parts of Asia appear to be under close control of their governments, and several of these countries have experienced higher inflation rates, volatile currency prices, and other significant economic problems in recent years. Though the matter is still hotly disputed, recent research studies (e.g., Pollard [10] and Walsh [11]) suggest that more independent central banks have been able to come closer to their nation's desired level of economic performance (particularly better control of inflation).

Organizational Structure of the Federal Reserve System

To carry out the objectives noted above, many central banks have evolved into complex quasi-governmental bureaucracies with many divisions and responsibilities. For example, the center of authority and decision making within the Federal Reserve System is the **Board of Governors** in Washington, D.C. By law, this governing body must contain no more than seven persons, each selected by the president of the United States and confirmed by the Senate for terms not exceeding 14 years. The board chairman and vice chairman are appointed by the president from among the seven board members, each for four-year terms (though these appointments may be renewed).

Key URL
The central Web site for the Board of Governors of the Federal Reserve System is **www.federalreserve. gov.**

The board regulates and supervises the activities of the 12 district Reserve banks and their branch offices. It sets reserve requirements on deposits held by depository institutions, approves all changes in the discount (loan) rates posted by the 12 Reserve banks, and takes the lead within the system in determining open market policy to affect interest rates and the growth of money and credit.

The Federal Reserve Board members make up a majority of the voting members of the **Federal Open Market Committee (FOMC).** The other voting members are 5 of the 12 Federal Reserve bank presidents, who each serve one year in filling the five official voting seats on the FOMC (except for the president of the New York Federal Reserve Bank, who is a permanent voting member). While the FOMC's specific task is to set policies that guide the conduct of **open market operations (OMO)**—the buying and selling of securities by the Federal Reserve banks, this body actually looks at the whole range of Fed policies and actions to influence the economy and financial system.

Key URL
All 12 Federal Reserve banks have their own Web sites that can be accessed from **www.federalreserve. gov/otherfrb.htm.**

The Federal Reserve System is divided into 12 districts, with a **Federal Reserve Bank** chartered in each district to supervise and serve member banks. Among the key services the Federal Reserve banks offer to depository institutions in their districts are (1) issuing wire transfers of funds between depository institutions, (2) safe-keeping securities owned by depository institutions and their customers, (3) issuing new securities from the U.S. Treasury and selected other federal agencies, (4) making loans to qualified depository institutions through the "Discount Window" in each Federal Reserve bank, (5) dispensing supplies of currency and coin, (6) clearing and collecting checks and other cash items, and (7) providing information to keep financial-firm managers and the public informed about developments affecting the welfare of their institutions.

All banks chartered by the Comptroller of the Currency (national banks) and those few state banks willing to conform to the Fed's supervision and regulation are designated **member banks.** Member institutions must purchase stock (up to 6 percent of their paid-in capital and surplus) in the district Reserve bank and submit to comprehensive examinations by Fed staff. There are few unique privileges stemming from being a member bank of the Federal Reserve System, because Fed services are also available on the same terms to other depository institutions keeping reserve deposits at the Fed. Many bankers believe, however, that belonging to the system carries prestige and the aura of added safety, which helps member banks attract large deposits.

THE EUROPEAN CENTRAL BANK (ECB)

In January 1999, 11 member nations of the European Union launched a new monetary system based on a single currency, the euro, and surrendered leadership of their monetary policymaking to a single central bank, the ECB. This powerful central bank is taking leadership to control inflationary forces, promote a sounder European economy, and help stabilize the euro's value in international markets.

The ECB is similar in structure to the Federal Reserve System with a governing council (known as the Executive Board, composed of six members) and a policy-making council (similar to the Fed's Federal Open Market Committee). The ECB has a cooperative arrangement with each EC member nation's central bank (such as Germany's Bundesbank and the Bank of France), just as the Fed's Board of Governors works with the 12 Federal Reserve banks that make up the Federal Reserve System. The ECB is the centerpiece of the European System of Central Banks, which includes

- The national central bank (NCB) of each member nation, and
- The ECB, headquartered in Frankfurt, Germany.

The chief administrative body for the ECB is its Executive Board, consisting of a president, vice president, and four bank directors and appointed by the European Council, which consists of the heads of state of each member nation. The key policy-making group is the Governing Council, which includes all members of the ECB's Executive Board plus the leaders of the national Central Banks of each member nation, each leader appointed by its home nation.

Unlike the Federal Reserve System, which has multiple policy goals—including pursuing greater price stability, low unemployment, and sustainable economic growth—the ECB has a much simpler policy menu. Its central goal is to maintain *price stability*. Moreover, it has a relatively free hand in the pursuit of this goal with minimal interference from member states of the European Community. The principal policy tools of the ECB to help it achieve greater price stability are open market operations and reserve requirements.

Although it has a much simpler policy focus than the Federal Reserve, the ECB has no easy task. It must pursue price stability across different countries (with more nations from both Eastern and Western Europe to join in the future) having very different economies, political systems, and social and economic problems. The ECB is a "grand experiment" in economic policy cooperation. How well it will work in keeping the right balance of political and economic forces in Europe remains to be seen.

The Central Bank's Principal Task: Making and Implementing Monetary Policy

Key URLs

Compare the Federal Reserve System to other leading central banks around the globe, especially the European Central Bank at **www.ecb.int**, the Bank of Japan at **www.boj.or.jp/en/** and the People's Bank of China at **www.pbc.gov.cn/english/**.

A central bank's principal function is to conduct money and credit policy to promote sustainable growth in the economy and avoid severe inflation. To pursue these important objectives, most central banks use a variety of tools to affect the *legal reserves of the banking system*, the *interest rates charged on loans* made in the financial system, and relative *currency values* in the global foreign exchange markets.

By definition, *legal reserves* consist of assets held by a depository institution that qualify in meeting the reserve requirements imposed on an individual depository institution by central banking authorities. In the Unites States legal reserves consist of cash that depository institutions keep in their vaults and the deposits these institutions hold in their legal reserve accounts at the district Federal Reserve banks.

Each of a central bank's policy tools also affects the level and rate of change of interest rates. A central bank drives interest rates higher when it wants to reduce lending and borrowing in the economy and slow down the pace of economic activity; on the other hand, it lowers interest rates when it wishes to stimulate business and consumer borrowing. Central banks also can influence the demand for their home nation's currency by varying the level of interest rates and by altering the pace of domestic economic activity.

To influence the behavior of legal reserves, interest rates, and currency values, central banks usually employ one or more of three main tools: open market operations, the discount rate on loans to qualified financial institutions, and legal reserve requirements on various bank liabilities. For example, the Bank of England uses open market operations in the form of purchases of short-term government and commercial bills and makes discount loans. The Swiss National Bank conducts open market operations in the currency markets, while Germany's Bundesbank trades security repurchase agreements and sets its preferred interest (discount and Lombard) rates on short-term loans. In contrast, the Bank of Canada uses both open market operations and daily transfers of government deposits between private banks and the central bank to influence credit conditions. The fundamental point is that while different central banks may use different tools, nearly all focus upon the reserves of the banking system, interest rates, and, to some extent, currency prices as key operating targets to help achieve each nation's most cherished economic goals.

The Open Market Policy Tool of Central Banking

Among many leading nations today *open market operations (OMO)*, using a variety of different financial instruments, have become the principal tool of central bank monetary policy. For example, in the United States the Federal Reserve System, represented by the System Open Market Account (SOMA) Manager at the trading desk inside the Federal Reserve Bank of New York, buys and sells U.S. Treasury bills, bonds, and notes and selected federal agency securities. These transactions are conducted between the Fed's trading desk and selected *primary dealers* who meet the Fed's qualifications. OMO is considered to be the most important policy tool for many central banks because it can be used every day and, if a mistake is made or conditions change, its effects can be quickly reversed.

Key URL
For further information about the Federal Open Market Committee (FOMC) and open market operations (OMO), see **www.federalreserve. gov/fomc/**.

Central bank *sales* of securities tend to *decrease* the growth of deposits and loans within the financial system. When the Fed sells U.S. government securities, the dealers purchasing those securities authorize the Fed to deduct the dollar amount of the purchase from the reserve accounts dealers' banks hold at a district Federal Reserve bank. Banks and other depository institutions have less raw material for making loans and extending other types of credit. Interest rates tend to *rise*.

In contrast, central bank *purchases* of securities tend to *increase* the growth of deposits and loans. The Federal Reserve pays for its purchases of U.S. government securities simply by crediting the reserve deposits of the dealers' banks that are held at the district Federal Reserve banks. This means that the banks and dealers involved in the transaction have the proceeds of the securities' sale immediately available for their use. Interest rates tend to *fall*. (See Exhibit 2–1 for a list of several leading security dealers who are authorized to trade securities with the Federal Reserve.)

Key URL
To find out what it takes to become a primary dealer and trade with the Federal Reserve, see especially the Federal Reserve Bank of New York at **www.newyorkfed.org/ aboutthefed/fedpoint/ fed02.html**.

Today the Federal Reserve's Federal Open Market Committee (FOMC) targets the *federal funds rate* attached to overnight loans of reserves between depository institutions in order to achieve the Fed's monetary policy goals. Open market operations are carried out to hit the targeted funds rate, in the hope that changes in the federal funds rate will spread to other interest rates in the economy. An example of a recent federal funds rate target called for by the FOMC is shown in Exhibit 2–2.

Other Central Bank Policy Tools

Most central banks are an important source of *short-term loans* for depository institutions, especially the largest banks, which tend to borrow frequently to replenish their reserves.

EXHIBIT 2–1
Leading Primary Dealers Authorized to Trade Securities with the Federal Reserve in order to Assist with Monetary Policy

JP Morgan Securities, Inc.	Morgan Stanley & Co., Incorporated.
Lehman Brothers Inc.	Nomura Securities International, Inc.
Merrill Lynch Government Securities Inc.	UBS Securities LLC
Greenwich Capital Markets Inc.	Bank of America Securities LLC
Barclays Capital Inc.	Bear, Stearns and Company, Inc.
Citigroup Global Markets, Inc.	Credit Suisse First Boston LLC
Goldman Sachs & Co.	HSBC Securities (USA) Inc.
Mizuho Securities USA Inc.	ABN AMRO Bank NV, New York Branch
BNP Paribus Securities Corp.	CIBC World Markets Corp.
Countrywide Securities Corp.	Daiwa Securities America Inc.
Deutsche Bank Securities Inc.	Dresdner Kleinwort Wasserstein Securities

EXHIBIT 2–2

Example of a Federal Open Market Committee (FOMC) Statement, Setting a Target for the Federal Funds Rate to Be Achieved through Open Market Operations

The Federal Open Market Committee decided on March 22, 2005, to raise its target for the federal funds rate 25 basis points, to $2\frac{3}{4}$ percent.

The Committee believes that, even after this action, the stance of monetary policy remains accommodative and, coupled with underlying growth in productivity, is providing ongoing support to economic activity. Output evidently continues to grow at a solid pace despite the rise in energy prices, and labor market conditions continue to improve gradually. Though longer-term inflation expectations remain well-contained, pressures on inflation have picked up in recent months and pricing power is more evident. The rise in energy prices, however, has not notably fed through to core consumer prices.

The Committee perceives that, with appropriate monetary policy action, the upside and downside risks to the attainment of both sustainable growth and price stability should be kept roughly equal. With underlying inflation expected to be contained, the Committee believes that policy accommodation can be removed at a pace likely to be measured. Nonetheless, the Committee will respond to changes in economic prospects as needed to fulfill its obligation to maintain price stability.

Source: Board of Governors of the Federal Reserve System, *Federal Reserve Bulletin*, Spring 2005, p. 241.

For example U.S. banks place signed borrowing authorizations at the Federal Reserve bank in their district for this purpose. When the Fed loans reserves to borrowing institutions, the supply of legal reserves expands temporarily, which may cause loans and deposits to expand. Later, when these *discount window loans* are repaid, the borrowing institutions lose reserves and may be forced to curtail the growth of their deposits and loans. The loan rate charged by the Fed, the *discount rate*, is set by each Reserve bank's board of directors and must be approved by the Federal Reserve Board. In 2003 the Fed began setting the discount rate slightly above its target federal funds rate to promote greater stability.

Central banks also occasionally use *changes in reserve requirements* as a monetary policy tool. Institutions selling deposits (such as checking accounts) must place a small percentage of each dollar of those deposits in reserve, either in the form of vault cash or in a deposit at the central bank. Changes in the percentage of deposits and other funds sources that must be held in reserve can have a potent impact on credit expansion. Raising reserve requirements, for example, means that financial firms must set aside more of each incoming dollar of deposits into required reserves, and less money is available to support making new loans. Lowering reserve requirements, on the other hand, releases reserves for additional lending. Interest rates also tend to decline because financial institutions have more funds to loan. However, central banks usually change reserve requirements very infrequently because the impact can be so powerful and cannot easily be reversed and because banks are less dependent on deposits as a source of funds than in the past.

One other important policy tool the Federal Reserve, the Bank of Japan, and other central banks use to influence the economy and the behavior of financial firms is *moral suasion*. Through this policy tool the central bank tries to bring psychological pressure to bear on individuals and institutions to conform to its policies. Examples of moral suasion include central bank officials testifying before legislative committees to explain what the bank is doing and what its objectives are, letters and phone calls sent to those institutions that seem to be straying from central bank policies, and press releases urging the public to cooperate with central bank efforts to strengthen the economy.

A Final Note on Central Banking's Impact on Financial Firms

Clearly managers of financial firms must be fully aware of the impact of *both* government regulation and central bank monetary policy on their particular institutions. No financial institution's management can ignore the effects of these key government activities upon the value of a financial-service provider's assets, liabilities, and equity capital and upon the magnitude of its revenues and expenses.

Real Banks, Real Decisions

THE CENTRAL BANKS OF CHINA AND JAPAN

China's central bank, the People's Bank of China (PBC), was formed from the combination of three domestic banks in 1948 and was officially designated as that nation's central bank in 1995. Until recently the PBC was both China's principal regulator of financial institutions and the conduit for that nation's monetary policy. It was the chief supervisor of domestic and foreign financial institutions selling services inside China, issued charters for new financial firms, dissolved failing ones, and regulated the entry of foreign banks. However, several of these important regulatory functions were handed over to the China Bank Regulatory Commission in 2003, leaving to the PBC the principal roles of conducting *monetary policy,* issuing currency and coin, regulating interbank lending and the bond markets, supervising China's payments system, and serving as the government's bookkeeper.

The PBC's monetary policy goals include maintaining the stability of the nation's currency, promoting sustainable economic growth, and controlling inflation. It pursues these objectives using changes in deposit reserve requirements, central bank loans, and open market operations. The PBC's pursuit of monetary policy is supported by an advisory group, the Monetary Policy Committee (MPC), which meets at least quarterly and includes the PBC's Governor, the Chair of the China Bank Regulatory Commission, the Finance Minister, and other members of the Chinese government.

Considerably older is the Bank of Japan (BOJ), founded in 1882 and dedicated to ensuring price stability, a stable financial system, and sound economic development. The BOJ regulates the volume of money and interest rates through open market operations (using securities issued by the Japanese government and commercial bills), by providing emergency loans to institutions in trouble, and through the use of moral suasion to convince financial mangers to adhere to the BOJ's policies.

In addition to monetary policy the BOJ is responsible for issuing currency and coin, monitoring the nation's payments system, and conducting on-site examinations of financial-service firms. The BOJ receives and disburses Treasury funds and issues and redeems government securities. It may also intervene in the foreign exchange market on behalf of the Minister of Finance.

Concept Check

2–17. In what ways is the regulation of nonbank financial institutions different from the regulation of banks in the United States? How are they similar?

2–18. Which financial-service firms are regulated primarily at the federal level and which at the state level? Can you see problems in this type of regulatory structure?

2–19. Can you make a case for having only *one* regulatory agency for financial-service firms?

2–20. What is *monetary policy?*

2–21. What services does the Federal Reserve provide to depository institutions?

2–22. How does the Fed affect the banking and financial system through open market operations (OMO)? Why is OMO the preferred tool for many central banks around the globe?

2–23. What is a *primary dealer* and why are they important?

2–24. How can changes in the central bank loan (discount) rate and reserve requirements affect the operations of depository institutions? What happens to the legal reserves of the banking system when the Fed grants loans through the discount window? How about when these loans are repaid? What are the effects of an increase in reserve requirements?

2–25. How did the Federal Reserve change the policy and practice of the discount window recently? Why was this change made?

2–26. How do the structures of the European Central Bank (ECB), the Bank of Japan, and the People's Bank of China appear to be similar to the structure of the Federal Reserve System? How are these powerful and influential central banks different from one another?

Summary

What financial-service firms can do within the financial system is closely monitored by *regulation*—government oversight of the behavior and performance of financial firms. Indeed, financial-service institutions are among the most heavily regulated of all industries due, in part, to their key roles in attracting and protecting the public's savings, providing credit to a wide range of borrowers, and creating money to serve as the principal medium of exchange in a modern economy. The principal points in this chapter include:

- Financial-services regulations are created to implement federal and state laws by providing practical guidelines for financial firms' behavior and performance. Among the key laws that have had a powerful and lasting impact on the regulation of banks and competing financial institutions are the National Bank Act (which authorized federal chartering of banks), the Glass-Steagall Act (which separated commercial and investment banking), the Riegle-Neal Interstate Banking and Branching Efficiency Act (which allowed U.S. banking firms to branch across state lines), the Gramm-Leach-Bliley Act (which repealed restrictions against banks, security firms, and insurance companies affiliating with each other), the Sarbanes-Oxley Accounting Standards Act (which imposed new rules upon the financial accounting practices that financial firms and other publicly held businesses use), the Bank Secrecy and USA Patriot Acts, (which required selected financial-service providers to gather and report customer information to the government in order to prevent terrorism and money laundering), the Check 21 Act (which allows the conversion of paper checks into electronically transferable payment items), and the Fair and Accurate Credit Transactions (FACT) Act (which promised greater public access to credit bureau reports and made it easier for consumers to report and fight identity theft).

- Regulation of financial firms takes place in a *dual system* in the United States—*both* federal and state governments are involved in chartering, supervising, and examining selected financial-service companies.

- The key federal regulators of banks include the Federal Deposit Insurance Corporation (FDIC), the Federal Reserve System (FRS), and the Office of the Comptroller of the Currency (OCC). The OCC supervises and examines federally chartered (national) banks, while the FRS oversees state-chartered banks that have elected to join the Federal Reserve System. The FDIC regulates state-chartered banks that are *not* members of the Federal Reserve System. State regulation of banks is carried out in the 50 U.S. states by boards or commissions.

- Nonbank financial-service providers are regulated and supervised either at the state or federal government level or both. Examples include credit unions, savings associations, and security firms where state boards or commissions and federal agencies often share regulatory responsibility. In contrast, finance and insurance companies are supervised chiefly by state agencies. The chief federal regulatory agency for credit unions is the National Credit Union Administration (NCUA), while the Office of Thrift Supervision (OTS) oversees savings and loans and federally chartered savings banks. Security brokers, dealers, and investment banks are usually subject to supervision by the Securities and Exchange Commission (SEC) and state commissions.

- *Deregulation* of financial institutions is a new and powerful force reshaping financial firms and their regulators today in an effort to encourage increased competition and greater discipline from the marketplace. Even as deregulation has made progress around the world, key regulatory issues remain unresolved. For example, should banking and industrial companies be kept separate from each other to protect the safety of the public's funds? Do we need fewer regulators as the number of independently owned financial firms continues to fall?

www.mhhe.com/rose7e

- One of the most powerful of all financial institutions in the financial system is the *central bank*, which regulates money and credit conditions, (i.e., conducts *monetary policy*) using such tools as open market operations, short-term loans, and legal reserve requirements. Central banks have a powerful impact upon the profitability, growth, and viability of financial-service providers.

Key Terms

dual banking system, 33
state banking commissions, 33
Comptroller of the Currency, 35
Federal Reserve System, 37
Glass-Steagall Act, 37
Federal Deposit Insurance Corporation, 37
Federal Deposit Insurance Corporation Improvement Act, 38
Riegle-Neal Interstate Banking and Branching Efficiency Act, 42

Gramm-Leach-Bliley Act, 43
USA Patriot Act, 44
Sarbanes-Oxley Accounting Standards Act, 45
National Credit Union Administration, 51
Office of Thrift Supervision, 51
Securities and Exchange Commission, 52
state insurance commissions, 52

monetary policy, 53
European Central Bank (ECB), 54
People's Bank of China, 54
Bank of Japan, 54
Board of Governors, 54
Federal Open Market Committee (FOMC), 54
open market operations (OMO), 54
Federal Reserve Bank, 54
member banks, 54

Problems and Projects

1. For each of the actions described, explain which government agency or agencies a financial manager must deal with and what laws are involved:
   a. Chartering a new bank.
   b. Establishing new bank branch offices.
   c. Forming a bank or financial holding company. (FHC).
   d. Completing a bank merger.
   e. Making holding company acquisitions of nonbank businesses.

2. See if you can develop a good case *for* and *against* the regulation of financial institutions in the following areas:
   a. Restrictions on the number of new financial-service institutions allowed to enter the industry each year.
   b. Restrictions on which depository institutions are eligible for government-sponsored deposit insurance.
   c. Restrictions on the ability of financial firms to underwrite debt and equity securities issued by their business customers.
   d. Restrictions on the geographic expansion of banks and other financial firms, such as limits on branching and holding company acquisitions across state and international borders.
   e. Regulations on the failure process, defining when banks and other financial firms are to be allowed to fail and how their assets are to be liquidated.

3. Consider the issue of whether or not the government should provide a system of deposit insurance. Should it be wholly or partly subsidized by the taxpayers? What portion of the cost should be borne by depository institutions? by depositors? Should riskier depository institutions pay higher deposit insurance premiums? Explain how you would determine exactly how big an insurance premium each depository institution should pay each year.

4. The Trading Desk at the Federal Reserve Bank of New York elects to *sell* $100 million in U.S. government securities to its list of primary dealers. If other factors are held constant, what is likely to happen to the supply of legal reserves available? To deposits and loans? To interest rates?

5. Suppose the Federal Reserve's discount rate is 7 percent. This afternoon the Federal Reserve Board announces that it is approving the request of several of its Reserve banks to raise their discount rates to 7.5 percent. What will happen to other interest rates tomorrow morning? Carefully explain the reasoning behind your answer.

   Would the impact of the discount rate change described above be somewhat different if the Fed simultaneously sold $100 million in securities through its Trading Desk at the New York Fed?

6. Suppose the Fed *purchases* $500 million in government securities from a primary dealer. What will happen to the level of legal reserves in the banking system and by how much will they change?

7. If the Fed loans depository institutions $200 million in reserves from the discount windows of the Federal Reserve banks, by how much will the legal reserves of the banking system change? What happens when these loans are repaid by the borrowing institutions?

Internet Exercises

1. Does the banking commission or chief bank regulatory body in your home state have a Web site? What functions does this regulatory agency fulfill? Do they post job openings?

2. What U.S. banking laws have been important in shaping American history? (See **www.fdic.gov.**)

3. Have you ever wanted to be a bank examiner? What do bank examiners do? See if you can prepare a job description for a bank examiner. (See, for example, **www.federalreserve.gov.**)

4. One of the key financial regulators in Europe is Britain's Financial Services Authority. (See **www.fsa.gov.uk.**) What are its principal activities?

5. What does it take to become a central banker? What does the job entail and what kind of training do you think you should have (perhaps to become a member of the Federal Reserve Board)? (See **www.federalreserve.gov.**)

6. Can you describe the structure and mission of the European Central Bank (ECB)? The Bank of Japan? The People's Bank of China? Do any of these central banks resemble the structure of the Federal Reserve System? In what ways? (See especially **www.ecb.int**, **www.boj.or.jp/en/**, and **www.pbc.gov.com/english/.**)

7. Compare the federal regulatory agencies that oversee the activities and operations of credit unions, savings and loan associations and savings banks, and security brokers and dealers. In what ways are these regulatory agencies similar and in what ways do they seem to differ from each other? (See, for example, the Web sites **www.ncua.gov**, **www.ots.treas.gov**, and **www.sec.gov.**)

S&P Market Insight Challenge (www.mhhe.com/edumarketinsight)

STANDARD &POOR'S

1. Government regulations of financial-service companies continue to change and evolve. For timely information concerning changes in regulatory environments, utilize the Industry tab in S&P's Market Insight, Educational Version. The drop-down menu provides subindustry selections that may interest you, including Asset Management & Custody Banks, Consumer Finance, Diversified Banks, Diversified Capital Markets, Insurance Brokers, Investment Banking and Brokerage, Life and Health Insurance, Multi-line Insurance, Property & Casualty Insurance, Regional Banks, and Thrifts & Mortgage Finance. Once you select an industry, you will find S&P Industry Surveys

REAL NUMBERS FOR REAL BANKS — Assignment for Chapter 2

THE REGULATORY INFLUENCE ON YOUR BANKING COMPANY

In Chapter 2, we focus on the *regulations* that created and empower today's regulators, govern how and where financial institutions may operate, and what those operations may entail. For this segment of the project we will be developing a table (Excel sheet) of information, using some of the terminology from the regulations discussed in this chapter, and becoming familiar with the FDIC's Web site.

A. Go to the FDIC's Institution Directory at **www3.fdic.gov/ idasp/** and search for your bank holding company (BHC). When you find your BHC make a note of the "BHC ID" because you will be using this number in future assignments. We suggest including it in the name of this spreadsheet. If you click on the active bank holding company name link, you will also see a list of bank and thrift subsidiaries. (These are just the bank and thrift subsidiaries of the BHC and do not include nonbank subsidiaries.) List these individual institutions (subsidiaries) and their FDIC certificate numbers in the first column of your spread-sheet. The "class" column will

give you information concerning the regulator that chartered each institution, whether the institution is a member of the Federal Reserve, and which regulator has primary supervisory authority. Create columns B through D on your spreadsheet with this information—Column B defines state/federal charter; Column C defines member/nonmember of the Fed; and Column D identifies the primary federal regulator. (For a commercial bank this would be the OCC, Fed, or FDIC.)

B. Go to the FDIC's Institution Directory at **www3.fdic.gov/ idasp/** and do office searches using the certificate numbers you found. Collect the information on the number of offices in each state and any offshore offices.

What have we accomplished? We have begun to organize information and become familiar with the FDIC's Web site. (Make sure that you provide an appropriate title for the spreadsheet and label the columns.) In Chapter 3 we will be focusing on organization and structure and you will be able to relate your banking company to the industry as a whole. (We always have something to look forward to!)

STANDARD &POOR'S

that can be downloaded in Adobe Acrobat and are updated frequently. The S&P Industry Surveys include Banking, Investment Services, Financial Services Diversified, Insurance: Property and Casualty, Insurance: Life and Health, and Savings and Loans. Download two industry surveys and explore the first section, "Current Environment." Identify recent regulatory changes that appear to be affecting the current environments of the two industries and write a summary of these changes and their apparent effects.

2. Using the S&P Industry Surveys mentioned in the previous challenge problem explore the following issues: Which of the financial-service firms listed in the Educational Version of S&P's Market Insight appear to bear the heaviest level of government regulation, and which ones appear to be least government regulated? Why do you think these differences in the intensity of regulation exist? Which financial-service companies listed on Market Insight are regulated predominantly by the states? By the U.S. government? By foreign governments? Which are regulated at *both* federal and state levels? Do you think it makes a difference to the regulated firms?

Selected References

See the following for a discussion of the reasons for and against the regulation of financial institutions:

1. Benston, George G. "Federal Regulation of Banks: Analysis and Policy Recommendations." *Journal of Bank Research*, Winter 1983, pp. 216–44.
2. Berlin, Mitchell. "True Confessions: Should Banks Be Required to Disclose More?" *Business Review*, Federal Reserve Bank of Philadelphia, Fourth Quarter 2004, pp. 7–15.
3. Kane, Edward J. "Metamorphosis in Financial-Services Delivery and Production." In *Strategic Planning of Economic and Technological Change in the Federal Savings and Loan.* San Francisco: Federal Home Loan Bank Board, 1983, pp. 49–64.

4. Peltzman, Samuel. "Toward a More General Theory of Regulation." *Journal of Law and Economics*, August 1976, pp. 211–40.

5. Stigler, George J. "The Theory of Economic Regulation." *The Bell Journal of Economics and Management Science* II (1971), pp. 3–21.

For a review of the Gramm-Leach-Bliley Financial Services Modernization Act and other current regulatory issues, see the following:

6. Guzman, Mark G. "Slow but Steady Progress toward Financial Deregulation." *Southwest Economy*, Federal Reserve Bank of Dallas, no. 1 (January/February 2003), pp. 1, 6–9, and 12.

7. Harshman, Ellen, Fred C. Yeager, and Timothy J. Yeager. "The Door Is Open, but Banks Are Slow to Enter Insurance and Investment Areas." *The Regional Economist*, Federal Reserve Bank of St. Louis, October 2005.

8. Thomson, James B. "Raising the Deposit Insurance Limit: A Bad Idea Whose Time Has Come?" *Economic Commentary*, Federal Reserve Bank of Cleveland, April 15, 2000.

For a discussion of monetary policy and its impact on financial institutions, see the following:

9. Federal Reserve Bank of San Francisco. "U.S. Monetary Policy: An Introduction." *FRBSF Economic Letter*, Federal Reserve Bank of San Francisco, no. 2004-01 (January 16, 2004), parts 1–4.

10. Pollard, Patricia S. "Central Bank Independence and Economic Performance." *Review*, Federal Reserve Bank of St. Louis, July/August 1993, pp. 21–36.

11. Walsh, Carl E. "Is There a Cost to Having an Independent Central Bank?" *FRBSF Weekly Letter*, Federal Reserve Bank of San Francisco, February 4, 1994, pp. 1–2.

To learn more about central banking inside and outside the United States, see:

12. Pollard, Patricia. "A Look inside Two Central Banks: The European Central Bank and the Federal Reserve." *Review*, Federal Reserve Bank of St. Louis, January/February 2003, pp. 11–30.

13. Santomero, Anthony M. "Monetary Policy and Inflation Targeting in the United States." *Business Review*, Federal Reserve Bank of Philadelphia, Fourth Quarter 2004, pp. 1–6.

14. Spiegel, Mark M. "Easing Out of the Bank of Japan's Monetary Easing Policy." *FRBSF Economic Letter*, Federal Reserve Bank of San Francisco, no. 2004-33 (November 19, 2004).

The great debate over the separation of banking and commerce and whether the walls between these sectors should be removed is discussed in:

15. Walter, John R. "Banking and Commerce: Tear Down the Wall?" *Economic Quarterly*, Federal Reserve Bank of Richmond 89, no. 2 (Spring 2003), pp. 7–31.

www.mhhe.com/rose7e

The Organization and Structure of Banking and the Financial-Services Industry

Key Topics in This Chapter

- The Organization and Structure of the Commercial Banking Industry
- Internal Organization of the Banking Firm: Community and Money-Center Banks
- The Array of Organizational Structures in Banking: Unit, Branch, Holding Company and Electronic-Service Providers
- Interstate Banking and the Riegle-Neal Act
- Two Alternative Types of Banking Organizations as the 21st Century Opened: The Financial Holding Company and Bank Subsidiaries Model
- Mergers and Acquisition
- Banking Structure and Organization in Europe and Asia
- The Changing Organization and Structure of Banking's Principal Competitors
- Economies of Scale and Scope

3–1 Introduction

Chapter 1 of this text explored the many roles and services the modern bank and many of its financial-service competitors offer. In that chapter we viewed banks and other financial firms as providers of credit, channels for making payments, repositories of the public's savings, managers of business and household cash balances, trustees of customers' property, providers of risk protection, and brokers charged with carrying out purchases and sales of securities and other assets to fulfill their customers' wishes. Over the years, bankers and the managers of other financial institutions have evolved different **organizational forms** to perform these various roles and to supply the services their customers demand.

Truly, organizational form follows function, for banks and other financial firms usually are organized to carry out the roles assigned to them by the marketplace as efficiently as possible. Because larger institutions generally play a wider range of roles and offer more services, *size* is also a significant factor in determining how financial firms are organized. Indeed, the financial-services industry has the greatest disparity in size of firms of virtually any industry—from behemoths like J. P. Morgan Chase Bank, with offices all over the world and close to a trillion dollars in assets to manage, to the Big Sky Bank of Gallatin County, Montana, which, comparatively speaking, has relatively few assets to manage. Thus, banking today reminds us a bit of the hardware industry with giant Wal-Mart at one end of the size distribution and little Main Street Hardware at the other. Smaller firms need a market niche where they can claim a service advantage or, eventually, they may be driven from the industry.

However, a financial institution's role and size are not the only determinants of how it is organized or of how well it performs. As we saw in Chapter 2, law and regulation, too, have played a major role in shaping the performance and diversity of financial-service organizations around the globe. In this chapter we will see how changing public mobility and changing demand for financial services, the rise of hundreds of potent competitors for the financial-service customer's business, and changing rules of the game have dramatically changed the structure, size, and types of organizations dominating the financial-services industry over time.

3–2 The Organization and Structure of the Commercial Banking Industry

Advancing Size and Concentration of Assets

In our exploration of the impact of organization and structure on the performance of banks and their competitors we turn first to the leading financial-services industry, *commercial banking*—the dominant supplier of credit to businesses and the leading provider of deposits accessible by check and debit card in the global financial system.

The structure of the American banking industry is somewhat unique compared to most of the rest of the world. Most commercial banks in the United States are *small* by global standards. For example, as Exhibit 3–1 shows, almost half of all U.S. insured banking organizations—approximately 3,600 commercial banks—held total assets of less than $100 million each in 2005. However, these smallest financial institutions, numerous as they are, held only about 2 percent of total industry assets.

In contrast, the American banking industry also contains some of the largest financial-service organizations on the planet. For example, Citigroup and J. P. Morgan Chase, both based in New York City, and the Bank of America, based in Charlotte, North Carolina, hold sufficient assets—approximately a trillion dollars each—to rank these financial-service providers among the very largest businesses in the world.

Moreover, banking continues to be increasingly concentrated not in the smallest or mid-size range, but in the very largest of all financial firms. For example, the 10 largest American banks now control close to half of all industry assets, while the 100 largest U.S. banking organizations hold more than three-quarters of industrywide assets and their market share has risen year after year. Today a quarter of all domestic deposits are controlled by only three U.S. banking companies. In contrast, as Exhibit 3–2 illustrates, both small and medium-size banks have lost substantial market share to the biggest banks holding more than $25 billion in assets apiece.

Interestingly enough, not only industry assets but also profits tend to be concentrated in the largest financial firms. For example, most American banks that lost money at the opening of the 21st century were among the smallest banking organizations, holding less than 1 percent of industry assets.

Although banking globally has become more concentrated in the largest institutions, the concentration of bank assets and deposits at the local level—in the towns and cities where most people work—seems to have changed in a fairly limited way in recent years. There appear to have been relatively small changes in the average number of banks and in the percentage of assets under bank control in most cities and rural areas across America.

Factoid

What is the largest banking company in the United States and the fifth largest in the world (measured by total assets)?
Answer: Citigroup, Inc., based in New York City.

EXHIBIT 3–1

The Structure of the U.S. Commercial Banking Industry, March 31, 2005

Source: Federal Deposit Insurance Corporation.

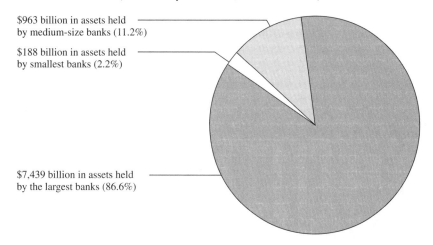

Assets Held by U.S. FDIC-insured Commercial Banks
(Total Industry Assets of $8,589 Billion in 2005)

$963 billion in assets held by medium-size banks (11.2%)

$188 billion in assets held by smallest banks (2.2%)

$7,439 billion in assets held by the largest banks (86.6%)

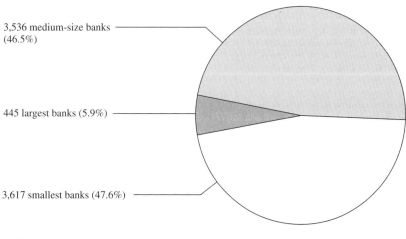

Number of U.S. FDIC-insured Banks
(Total of 7,598 Banks Operating in 2005)

3,536 medium-size banks (46.5%)

445 largest banks (5.9%)

3,617 smallest banks (47.6%)

☐ Smallest FDIC-insured banks with total assets of up to $100 million each

▨ Medium-size FDIC-insured banks with total assets of more than $100 million up to $1 billion

▨ Largest FDIC-insured banks with total assets of $1 billion or more

Key URL

If you are interested in tracking changes over time in the structure and organization of the U.S. banking industry, see especially **www.fdic.gov/ individual/index.html**.

In part, this moderate change in banking structure in many local towns and cities reflects the rise of local *competition* as more financial firms reach into local communities, sometimes from great distances away, using the rapidly exploding technology of information.

Is a Countertrend Now under Way?

However, before we get too set in our views about what's happening to the structure of banking in the United States and around the world, we need to recognize that a *new* trend *may*

EXHIBIT 3–2   Small and Medium-Size U.S. Banks Lose Market Share to the Largest Banking Institutions

Sources: Data: Call Report, FFIEC; Consumer Price Index for All Urban Consumers, Bureau of Labor Statistics. Graphical presentation: Jeffrey W. Gunther and Robert R. Moore. "Small Banks' Competitors Loom Large," *Southwest Economy*, Federal Reserve Bank of Dallas, January/February 2004, p. 9.

Small Banks Lose Market Share to Large Banks

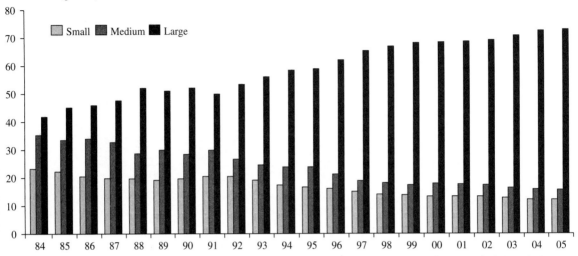

Notes: Small banks belong to organizations with less than $1 billion in commercial bank assets, medium-sized banks to those with $1 billion to $25 billion in bank assets, and large banks to those with more than $25 billion. Assets are measured in 2002 dollars. All data are year-end except 2005 data, which are as of June 30. The market share for each size group is that group's proportion of total bank assets.

be emerging. True, smaller banks continue to disappear and the biggest banks are gobbling up greater industry shares each year. But there are signs that this pattern of change may be slowing down. Indeed, as FDIC economists Jones and Critchfield [14] suggest in a new study, the long decline in the number of banking organizations may be nearing an end. Ultimately, they suggest, the number of banking organizations inside the United States may stabilize in perhaps 5 to 10 years.

Already the number of bank mergers has slowed substantially in the new century as the remaining desirable targets for acquisition have fallen off. The industry may be approaching a point where the number of mergers is approximately offset each year by the number of newly chartered banking firms. That is, those leaving the industry may be roughly counterbalanced by new start-ups. This suggests that, once industry stability is reached, there may still be thousands of small banks in operation along with a handful of money-center, globally reaching banks.

3–3 Internal Organization of the Banking Firm

Whether or not the above projections for the future of banking actually happen, the great differences in size across the industry that have appeared in recent years have led to marked differences in the way banks are organized internally and in the types and variety of financial services each bank sells in the markets it chooses to serve.

Community Banks and Other Community-Oriented Financial Firms

The influence of size upon internal organization can be seen most directly by looking at the "typical" organization chart supplied by the management of a small *community bank* with about $250 million in assets and located in a smaller city in the Midwest. (See Exhibit 3–3.) Like hundreds of financial firms serving smaller cities and towns,

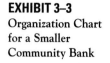

EXHIBIT 3–3
Organization Chart
for a Smaller
Community Bank

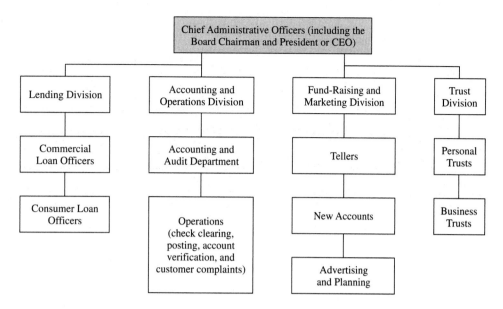

this bank is heavily committed to attracting smaller household deposits and to making household and small business loans.

A bank like this, devoted principally to the markets for smaller, locally based deposits and loans, is also often referred to as a *retail bank*. Financial firms of this type stand in sharp contrast to *wholesale banks*, like J. P. Morgan Chase and Citibank of New York, which concentrate mainly on serving commercial customers and making large corporate loans all over the globe.

The service operations of a community bank are usually monitored by a cashier and auditor working in the accounting department and by the vice presidents heading up the bank's loan, fund-raising, marketing, and trust departments. These officers report to the senior executives of the firm, consisting of the board chairman, the president (who usually runs the bank from day to day), and the senior vice president (who is usually responsible for long-range planning and for assisting heads of the various departments in solving their most pressing problems). Senior management, in turn, reports periodically to members of the **board of directors**—the committee selected by the **stockholders** (owners) to set policy and monitor performance.

The organization chart in Exhibit 3–3 is not complicated. Close contact between top management and the management and staff of each division is common. If smaller community banks have serious problems, they usually center on trying to find competent new managers to replace aging administrators and struggling to afford the cost of new equipment and keep pace with new regulations. Also, community banks are usually significantly impacted by changes in the health of the local economy. For example, many are closely tied to agriculture or to the condition of other locally based businesses, so when local sales are depressed, the bank itself often experiences slowed growth and its earnings may fall.

Community banks often present limited opportunities for advancement or for the development of new banking skills. Nevertheless, banks of this size and geographic location may represent attractive employment opportunities because they place the banker close to his or her customers and give bank employees the opportunity to see how their actions can have a real impact on the quality of life in local cities and towns. Unlike some larger institutions, community bankers usually know their customers well and are good at monitoring the ever-changing fortunes of households and small businesses.

Despite these favorable features of community banking, these institutions have been losing ground, both in numbers of institutions and in industry shares. For example, their

Key URL
For further information about community banks and their management, see America's Community Bankers at **www.acbankers.org**.

Key URL
If you would like to find out how the structure of banking is changing in your home town, see, for example, **www2. fdic.gov/idasp/main.asp**.

numbers (including commercial banks and thrift institutions combined) have fallen from close to 14,000 community banks in 1985 to just over 7,000 in 2005. Over the same time span their share of industry assets has dropped from about 26 percent to little more than 12 percent. In contrast, the industry share claimed by the 25 largest money-center banks in the United States rose from about 28 percent in 1985 to more than 60 percent in 2005.

Larger Banks—Money Center, Wholesale and Retail

Factoid
If you want to know how a particular bank is organized internally, try typing its name into your Web browser, which often calls up information on what departments the bank operates, what services it offers, and where its facilities are located.

In comparison to smaller community banks, the organization chart of a large (multibillion dollar) *money center bank*—located in a large city and wholesale or wholesale plus retail in its focus—typically looks far more complex than that of a smaller, community-oriented bank. A fairly typical organization chart from an eastern U.S. money-center bank with more than $25 billion in assets is shown in Exhibit 3–4. This bank is owned and controlled by a holding company whose stockholders elect a board of directors to oversee the bank and nonbank businesses allied with the same holding company. Selected members of the holding company's board of directors serve on the bank's board as well. The key problem in such an organization is often the *span of control*. Top management may be knowledgeable about banking practices but less well informed about the products and services offered by subsidiary companies. Moreover, because the bank itself offers so many different services in both domestic and foreign markets, serious problems may not surface for weeks or months. In recent years a number of the largest banks have moved toward the profit-center approach, in which each major department strives to maximize its contribution to profitability and closely monitors its own performance.

EXHIBIT 3–4 Organization Chart for a Money Center or Wholesale Bank Serving Domestic and International Markets

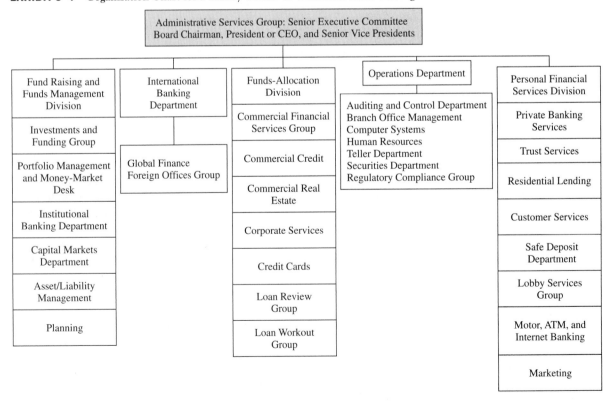

Key URL
Retail-oriented banks
are represented in the
industry by the
Consumer Bankers
Association at
www.cbanet.org.

The largest money-center banks possess some advantages over smaller, community-oriented institutions. Because the largest institutions serve many different markets with many different services, they are better diversified—both geographically and by product line—to withstand the risks of a fluctuating economy. These institutions are rarely dependent on the economic fortunes of a single industry or, in many cases, even a single nation. For example, such banking companies as Citigroup, J. P. Morgan Chase, and Deutschebank often receive half or more of their earnings from sources outside their home country. They also possess the important advantage of being able to raise huge amounts of financial capital at relatively low cost. As interstate banking spreads across the United States and global banking expands throughout Asia, Europe, and the Middle East, these banks should be well positioned because of their greater capacity to accept the risks of entering new markets and their potentially greater access to capital and managerial talent.

Trends in Organization

The tendency in recent years has been for most financial institutions to become *more complex* organizations over time. When a financial firm begins to grow, it usually adds new services and new facilities. With them come new departments and new divisions to help management more effectively focus and control the firm's resources.

Another significant factor influencing banking organizations today is the changing makeup of the skills bankers need to function effectively. For example, with the global spread of government deregulation and the resultant increase in the number of competitors in major markets, more and more financial firms have become *market driven* and *sales oriented*, more alert to the changing demands of their customers and also to the challenges competitors pose.

These newer activities require the appointment of management and staff who can devote more time to surveying customer service needs, developing new services, and modifying old service offerings to reflect changing customer needs. Similarly, as the technology of financial services production and delivery has shifted more toward computer-based systems and the Internet, financial firms have needed growing numbers of people with computer skills and the electronic equipment they work with. At the same time, automated book-keeping has reduced the time managers spend in routine operations, thus allowing greater opportunity for planning new services and thinking creatively about how to better serve customers.

Concept Check

3–1.   How would you describe the *size distribution* of American banks and the *concentration* of industry assets inside the United States? What is happening in general to the size distribution and concentration of banks in the United States and in other industrialized nations and why?

3–2.   Describe the typical organization of a smaller community bank and a larger money-center bank. What does each major division or administrative unit within the organization do?

3–3.   What trends are affecting the way banks and their competitors are organized today?

3–4 The Array of Organizational Structures and Types in the Banking Industry

There are so many different types of banks and other depository institutions in the financial system today that the distinctions between these different types of organizations often get very confusing. For example, as Exhibit 3–5 points out, most depository institutions are labeled "insured" because the great majority of American depositories have chosen to

EXHIBIT 3–5

U.S. Commercial Banks with Federal versus State Charters, Membership in the Federal Reserve System, and Deposit Insurance from the Federal Government (as of March 31, 2005)

Source: Board of Governors of the Federal Reserve System and the Federal Deposit Insurance Corporation.

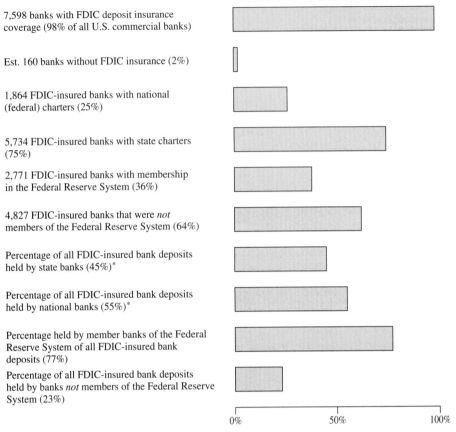

Percent of all FDIC-Insured Banks

7,598 banks with FDIC deposit insurance coverage (98% of all U.S. commercial banks)

Est. 160 banks without FDIC insurance (2%)

1,864 FDIC-insured banks with national (federal) charters (25%)

5,734 FDIC-insured banks with state charters (75%)

2,771 FDIC-insured banks with membership in the Federal Reserve System (36%)

4,827 FDIC-insured banks that were *not* members of the Federal Reserve System (64%)

Percentage of all FDIC-insured bank deposits held by state banks (45%)*

Percentage of all FDIC-insured bank deposits held by national banks (55%)*

Percentage held by member banks of the Federal Reserve System of all FDIC-insured bank deposits (77%)

Percentage of all FDIC-insured bank deposits held by banks *not* members of the Federal Reserve System (23%)

0%   50%   100%

Note: Figures are for June 2004.

apply for and receive federal insurance, mostly provided by the FDIC, to back their deposits and reassure the public.

Moreover, as Exhibit 3–5 also indicates, a majority of banks and other depositories in the United States are classified as "state chartered" because the financial-services commission of a particular state has issued them a charter of incorporation. The remaining institutions in the banking sector are labeled "national banks" because their charter has been issued by a federal government agency, the Comptroller of the Currency. Similarly, so-called "member banks" belong to the Federal Reserve System in the United States, although most American banks are *not* members of the Fed. State-chartered, nonmember banks are more numerous, but national and member banks tend to be larger and hold most of the public's deposits.

Are these the only ways we can classify modern depository institutions? Hardly! We can also classify them by their *corporate or organizational structure*. Their assets may be under the control of a single corporation or they may be structured as multiple corporations linked to each other through a common group of stockholders. They may sell all of their services through a single office or offer those services through multiple facilities scattered all over the region and around the globe. They may reach the public exclusively online, using computers and the telephone, or set up scores of neighborhood branch offices ("stores") to offer their customers a physical presence near their homes or offices. Let's look closely at the different types of organizational structures that have dominated the banking industry over the years.

Unit Banking Organizations

Unit banks, one of the oldest kinds, offer all of their services from *one office*, although some services (such as taking deposits, cashing checks, or paying bills) may be offered from limited-service facilities, such as drive-up windows and automated teller machines (ATMs) that are linked to the bank's computer system. These organizations are still common in U.S. banking today. For example, in 2004 just over 2,100 of the nation's commercial banks, about one-third, operated just one full-service office, compared to about 5,500 banks that had two or more full-service offices in operation.

One reason for the comparatively large number of unit banks is the rapid formation of *new* banks, even in an age of electronic banking and megamergers among industry leaders. About 15 percent of all community banks are less than 10 years old. Many customers still seem to prefer small banks, which get to know their customers well. Between 1980 and 2005, about 4,800 new banks were chartered in the United States, or an average of almost 200 per year—substantially more than the number of failing banks in most years, as Table 3–1 relates.

Most new banks start out as unit organizations, in part because their capital, management, and staff are severely limited until the bank can grow and attract additional resources and professional staff. However, most banks desire to create multiple service facilities—branch offices, electronic networks, Web sites, and other service outlets—to open up new markets and to diversify geographically in order to lower their overall risk

TABLE 3–1
Entry and Exit in
U.S. Banking

Source: Board of Governors of the Federal Reserve System and the Federal Deposit Insurance Corporation.

Year	Entry into the Industry — Newly Chartered Banks	Exit from the Industry — Failures of FDIC-Insured Banks	Exit from the Industry — Number of Unassisted Mergers and Acquisitions	Bank Branches — Opened	Bank Branches — Closed
1980	205	10	126	2,397	287
1981	198	7	210	2,326	364
1982	317	32	256	1,666	443
1983	361	45	314	1,320	567
1984	391	78	330	1,405	889
1985	331	116	336	1,480	617
1986	257	141	341	1,387	763
1987	219	186	543	1,117	960
1988	229	209	598	1,676	1,082
1989	192	206	411	1,825	758
1990	165	158	393	2,987	926
1991	106	105	447	2,788	1,456
1992	72	98	428	1,677	1,313
1993	61	62	481	1,499	1,215
1994	50	11	548	2,461	1,146
1995	102	6	609	2,367	1,319
1996	145	5	554	2,487	1,870
1997	188	1	601	NA	NA
1998	194	3	564	1,436	NA
1999	232	6	422	1,450	1,158
2000	192	6	456	1,286	NA
2001	129	3	360	1,010	NA
2002	91	10	217	1,285	1,137
2003	116	3	149	1,465	649
2004	126	3	236	2,078	666
2005	179	0	315	NA	NA

Key URL

One of the more interesting bankers' associations is the NBA or National Bankers Association—a trade group that serves to protect the interests of minority-owned banks, including those owned by African Americans, Native Americans, Hispanic Americans, and women. See especially **www.nationalbankers. org** for a fuller description.

exposure. Bankers know that relying on a single location from which to receive customers and income can be risky if the surrounding economy weakens and people and businesses move away to other market areas.

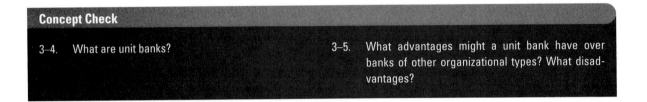

Branch Banking Organizations

As a unit bank grows larger in size it usually decides at some point to establish a **branch banking** organization, particularly if it serves a rapidly growing region and finds itself under pressure either to follow its business and household customers as they move into new locations or lose them to more conveniently located financial-service competitors. Branch banking organizations offer the full range of banking services from several locations, including a head office and one or more full-service branch offices. Such an organization is also likely to offer limited services through a supporting network of drive-in windows, ATMs, computers electronically linked to the bank's computers, point-of-sale terminals in stores and shopping centers, the Internet, and other advanced communications systems.

Senior management of a branch banking organization is usually located at the home office, though each full-service branch has its own management team with limited authority to make decisions on customer loan applications and other facets of daily operations. For example, a branch manager may be authorized to approve a customer loan of up to $100,000. Larger loan requests, however, must be referred to the home office for a final decision. Thus, some services and functions in a branch banking organization are highly centralized, whereas others are decentralized at the individual service facility level. Exhibit 3–6 displays a typical branch banking organization.

EXHIBIT 3–6
The Branch Banking Organization

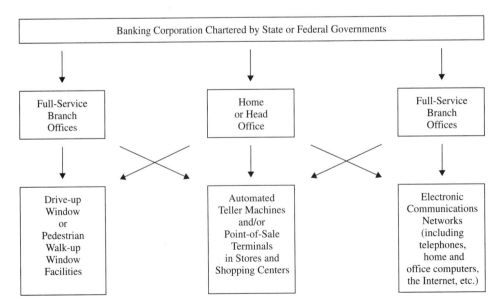

Branching's Expansion

Most branch banks in the United States are small compared to other banks around the globe. For example, as the 21st century opened there were about 5,500 branch banking organizations in the United States, operating close to 70,000 full-service branch office facilities. As Table 3–1 reminds us, while the number of U.S. banks declined over this last half-century from around 14,000 to about 7,500 today, the number of branch offices has soared from only about 3,000 to about 70,000 full-service offices, not counting more than 300,000 computer-terminal banking facilities scattered across the United States in thousands of stores, shopping centers, and lobbies, and at more than 3,000 service-providing Internet sites.

During the Great Depression of the 1930s, only one in five American banks, on average, operated a full-service branch office. By the beginning of the 21st century the average U.S. bank operated about ten full-service branch offices, although some of the nation's leading banks, like Bank America and J. P. Morgan Chase, operate hundreds of branch offices today. By and large, these limited numbers of U.S. branches per bank are small potatoes compared to banks in Canada, Great Britain, and Western Europe that often operate hundreds or thousands of branch outlets in addition to their computer terminal and Internet customer connections.

This wide disparity in national banking structures arises from differences in public attitudes toward branch banking. Early in the history of the United States, there was great fear of the power of branch banks to eliminate competition and charge their customers excessive prices for services. As a result, most states passed laws to limit branching activity. Unfortunately, this antibranching attitude may have allowed some banks, freed from the danger of outside entry by other banking organizations, to act as monopolies, raising prices and restricting output. Today, however, all 50 states and the District of Columbia permit some form of branch facilities.

Reasons behind Branching's Growth

The causes of the rapid growth in branch banking are many. One factor has been the exodus of population over the past several decades from cities to suburban communities, forcing many large downtown banks to either follow or lose their mobile customers. The result has been the expansion of branch offices and automated tellers, radiating out from downtown areas of major cities like the spokes of a wheel, with leading money-center banks at the hub of the branching wheel. Bank failures have also spawned branching activity as healthier banks have been allowed to take over sick ones and convert them into branch offices. Business growth, too, has fueled the spread of branch banking; the credit needs of rapidly growing corporations necessitate larger and more diversified banks that can reach into many local markets for small deposits and pool those funds into large-volume loans. Table 3–2 demonstrates how the concentration of U.S. banking facilities has shifted from main offices to branch offices over the past half century.

The passage of the Riegle-Neal Interstate Banking and Branching Efficiency Act in 1994 provided the basis for an expansion of new bank branch offices nationwide (i.e., interstate banking). However, in recent years new bank branch office expansion appears to have slowed somewhat and no single bank has yet established full-service branch offices in all 50 states. One reason is a recent rise in full-service office closings as the burgeoning cost of brick-and-mortar buildings has soared and some neighborhoods have declined and become less attractive to bankers. Then, too, the Internet and other electronic access media have taken over many routine financial transactions and there may be less need for extensive full-service branch offices. Finally, as we saw in Chapter 2, U.S. legislation in 1994 that allows branching anywhere in the country now permits bankers to buy *existing* branch networks in the most desirable communities, no matter where they are located, rather than always having to build new offices.

TABLE 3–2
Growth of
Commercial Bank
Branch Offices in the
United States

Source: Federal Deposit
Insurance Corporation.

Year	Number of Bank Home (Main) Offices	Number of Branch Offices	Total of All U.S. Bank Offices	Average Number of Branches per U.S. Bank
1934	14,146	2,985	17,131	0.21
1940	13,442	3,489	16,931	0.26
1952	13,439	5,486	18,925	0.41
1964	13,493	14,703	28,196	1.09
1970	13,511	21,810	35,321	1.61
1982*	14,451	39,784	54,235	2.75
1988	13,137	46,619	59,756	3.55
1993	10,960	52,868	63,828	4.82
1999	8,551	63,684	72,265	7.45
2001	8,096	64,938	73,034	8.02
2002	7,887	66,185	74,072	8.39
2003	7,769	67,390	75,159	9.67
2004	7,630	69,975	77,605	10.17

*Beginning in 1982 remote service facilities (ATMs) were not included in the count of total branches. At year-end 1981, there were approximately 3,000 remote service banking facilities.

Advantages and Disadvantages of Branch Banking

Branch banking organizations often buy out smaller banks, converting them into branches and concentrating the industry's assets into the hands of fewer firms. However, there is little or no evidence that this necessarily lessens competition. Customer convenience seems to improve because more services are available at every branch location and branching areas tend to have more offices per unit of population, reducing transactions costs for the average customer. However, some service fees seem to be higher in branching areas, especially when branch banks acquire smaller institutions and boost service charges after these acquisitions are made. However, the higher service fees may reflect greater knowledge on the part of larger banks concerning the true cost of each service.

Branch banks appear to be less prone to failure than banks without full-service branch offices. For example, Canada—where the typical bank operates hundreds of branches—experienced not a single bank failure during the Great Depression of the 1930s, whereas the United States—a nation of many small, frequently branchless banks—experienced thousands of failures.

Concept Check

3–6.   What is a branch banking organization?

3–7.   What trend in branch banking has been prominent in the United States in recent years?

3–8.   Do branch banks seem to perform differently than unit banks? In what ways? Can you explain any differences?

Electronic Branching—Web Sites and Electronic Networks: An Alternative or a Supplement to Traditional Bank Branch Offices?

As we saw in the preceding section, traditional brick-and-mortar bank branch offices continue to expand across the United States and in many other countries as well. Growing somewhat faster today, however, are what some experts call "electronic branches." These include Web sites offering **Internet banking services, automated teller machines (ATMs)** and ATM networks dispensing cash and accepting deposits, **point-of-sale (POS) terminals** in stores and shopping centers to facilitate payment for goods and services, and personal computers and telephone systems connecting the customer to his or her bank.[1] (See Exhibit 3–7.) Through many of these computer- and telephone-based delivery systems customers can check account balances, set up new accounts, move money between accounts, pay bills, request loans, and invest spare funds any hour of the day or night. Moreover, if you happen to be the holder of an electronic account, you do not necessarily have to change financial-service institutions when you move.

EXHIBIT 3–7 Electronic Banking Systems, Computer Networks, and Web Banking: An Effective Alternative to Full-Service Branches?

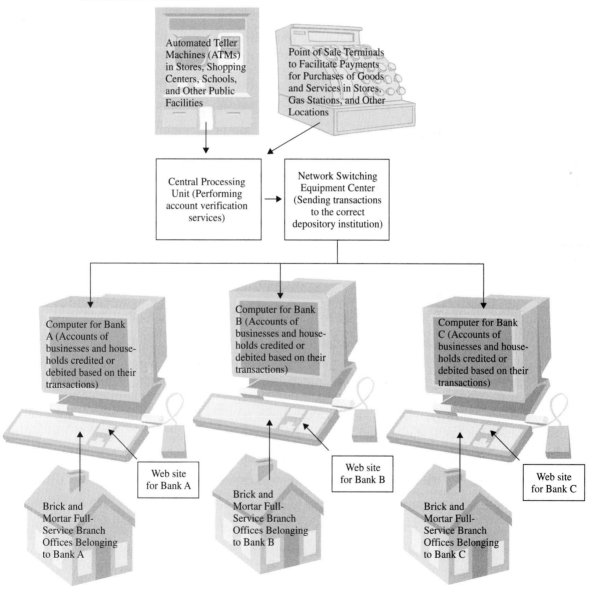

[1]The installation and use of these forms of "electronic branches" are discussed more fully in Chapter 4.

Most electronic branches seem to operate at far lower cost than do conventional brick-and-mortar branch offices, at least for routine transactions. For example, a deposit made through the Internet may be at least 10 times cheaper to execute than the same deposit made through a nearby ATM.

Many banks—especially **virtual banks** that provide their services exclusively through the Web—are moving today to pass these Web-generated cost savings along to their customers and gain a market advantage over depository institutions still relying heavily on neighborhood brick-and-mortar branch offices. However, despite significantly lower transactions costs, virtual banking firms have not yet demonstrated they can be consistently profitable. Part of the reason may be their tendency to advertise much lower customer fees than do many brick-and-mortar-oriented deposit institutions. Moreover, virtual banks have to combat the fact that customers often feel more secure if they know that their depository institution, besides being Web accessible, also has full-service branches where they can go to straighten out serious problems. However, this picture seems to be changing as millions of new Internet-connected customers continue to switch from older service-access channels toward instantly available online services.

Bank Holding Company Organizations

In earlier decades when governments prohibited or severely restricted branch banking, the *holding company* often became the most attractive organizational alternative inside the United States and in several other countries as well. A **bank holding company** is simply a corporation chartered for the purpose of holding the stock (equity shares) of at least one bank.

Many holding companies hold only a small minority of the outstanding shares of one or more banks, thereby escaping government regulation. However, if a holding company seeks to *control* a U.S. bank, it must seek approval from the Federal Reserve Board to become a registered bank holding company. Under the terms of the Bank Holding Company Act, control is assumed to exist if the holding company acquires 25 percent or more of the outstanding equity shares of at least one bank or can elect at least two directors of at least one bank. Once registered, the company must submit to periodic examinations by the Federal Reserve Board and receive approval from the Fed when it reaches out to acquire other businesses.

Why Holding Companies Have Grown

The growth of holding companies has been rapid in recent decades. As long ago as 1971 these organizations controlled banks holding about half of U.S. bank deposits. By 2004, the nearly 6,000 bank holding companies operating in the United States controlled in excess of 90 percent of the industry's assets. Just over 6,200 U.S. commercial banks were affiliated with bank holding companies as 2004 drew to a close. (A list of the 10 largest U.S. bank holding companies appears in Table 3–3.) The principal reasons for this rapid upsurge in bank holding company activity include their greater ease of access to capital markets in raising funds, their ability to use higher leverage (more debt capital relative to equity capital) than nonaffiliated banking firms, their tax advantages in being able to offset profits from one business with losses generated by other firms that are part of the same company, and their ability to expand into businesses outside banking.

One-Bank Holding Companies

Most registered bank holding companies in the United States are one-bank companies. By the beginning of the 21st century, about 5,000 of the roughly 6,000 bank holding companies in the United States controlled stock in just *one* bank.

E-BANKING AND E-COMMERCE

VIRTUAL BANKS

The rapid growth of Internet access and the millions of daily Web transactions by the public soon brought thousands of financial-service providers to the Internet. Most Web sites in the early years were *information-only sites*—for example, describing services offered or explaining how to reach the nearest branch office. As the 21st century began, however, the most rapidly growing financial-service Web sites were of the *transactions* variety where the customer could access basic services (e.g., checking account balances, transferring funds, and paying bills) and, in a growing number of cases, access extended services (including access to credit and the ability to make investments in securities).

Initially, most of these Web sites were established by conventional banks that also operated brick-and-mortar, full-service branch offices. More recently, however, a cadre of *virtual banks*

has emerged that do not operate conventional branches, but work exclusively over the Internet and through the ATMs of the banks. Some have qualified for FDIC deposit insurance and offer an expanding menu of services, though many remain unprofitable.

Some of the most prominent virtual banks are listed below along with their Web site addresses. You may want to explore how these banks are organized and what services they sell to the public.

E-Trade Bank (**www.etradebank.com**)

Netbank (**www.netbank.com**)

First Internet Bank of Indiana (**www.firstib.com**)

National Interbank (**www.nationalinterbank.com**)

Bank of Internet USA (**www.bankofinternet.com**)

Juniper Bank (**www.juniper.com**)

Key URL

Banks *not* affiliated with holding companies are represented in industry and legislative affairs by the Independent Community Bankers of America at **www.ibaa.org**.

However, these one-bank companies frequently owned and operated one or more nonbank businesses as well. Once a bank holding company registers with the Federal Reserve Board, any nonbank business activities it starts or acquires must first be approved by the Fed. These nonbank businesses must offer services "closely related to banking" that also yield "public benefits," such as improved availability of financial services or lower service prices. (See Table 3–4 for examples of nonbank businesses that registered holding companies are allowed to own and control.) Today, the principal advantage for bank holding companies entering nonbank lines of business is the prospect of diversifying sources of revenue and profits (and, therefore, reducing risk exposure).

TABLE 3–3
The 10 Largest Bank Holding Companies Operating in the United States (Total Assets as Reported on March 31, 2005)

Source: National Information Center, Federal Reserve System.

Bank Holding Company Name	Location of Headquarters	Total Assets ($Bill)
Citigroup, Inc. (www.citigroup.com)	New York City, New York	$1,490
Bank of America Corporation (www.BankofAmerica.com)	Charlotte, North Carolina	1,214
JPMorgan Chase & Co. (www.jpmorganchase.com)	New York City, New York	1,178
Wachovia Corporation (www.wachovia.com)	Charlotte, North Carolina	507
Wells Fargo & Company (www.wellsfargo.com)	San Francisco, California	435
Taunus Corporation (www.taunus.com)	New York City, New York	362
HSBC North America Holdings Inc. (www.hsbcusa.com)	Prospect Heights, Illinois	351
U.S. Bancorp (www.usbank.com)	Minneapolis, Minnesota	199
SunTrust Banks, Inc. (www.suntrust.com)	Atlanta, Georgia	165
Citizens Financial Group, Inc. (www.citizensbank.com)	Providence, Rhode Island	142

TABLE 3–4

The Most Important Nonbank Financially Related Businesses Registered Holding Companies Can Acquire under U.S. Banking Regulations

Finance Companies
Lend funds to businesses and households.

Mortgage Companies
Provide short-term credit to improve real property for residential or commercial use.

Data Processing Companies
Provide computer processing services and information transmission.

Factoring Companies
Purchase accounts receivable from businesses in exchange for supplying temporary financing.

Security Brokerage Firms
Execute customer buy and sell orders for securities, foreign exchange, financial futures, and option contracts.

Financial Advising
Advise institutions and high-net-worth individual customers on managing assets, mergers, reorganizations, raising capital, and feasibility studies.

Credit Insurance Underwriters
Supply insurance coverage to customers borrowing money to guarantee repayment of a loan.

Merchant Banking
Invest in corporate stock as well as loan money to help finance the start of new ventures or to support the expansion of existing businesses.

Investment Banking Firms
Purchase new U.S. government and municipal bonds and corporate stocks and bonds from issuers and offer these securities to buyers (permissible for well-managed and well-capitalized holding companies).

Trust Companies
Manage the property of businesses, individuals, and nonprofit organizations and place customers' securities with private investors.

Credit Card Companies
Provide short-term credit to individuals and businesses in order to support retail trade.

Leasing Companies
Purchase and lease assets for businesses and individuals needing the use of these assets.

Insurance Companies and Agencies
Sell or underwrite insurance polices to businesses and individuals in order to provide risk protection.

Real Estate Services
Supply real estate appraisals, arrange for the financing of real estate projects, and broker real properties.

Savings Associations
Offer savings deposit plans and housing-related credit, predominantly to individuals and families.

The holding company form permits the *de jure* (legal) separation between banks and nonbank businesses having greater risk, allowing these different firms to be owned by the same group of stockholders. Outside the United States, the holding company form is usually legal but not often used. Instead most industrialized countries allow banks themselves to offer more services or permit a bank to set up a subsidiary company under direct bank ownership and sell services that banks themselves are not allowed to offer.

Multibank Holding Companies

A minority of bank holding company organizations are **multibank holding companies.** Multibank companies number just under 900 but control close to 70 percent of the total assets of all U.S. banking organizations. Prior to the Riegle-Neal Act (1994), this form of banking organization appealed especially to bank stockholders and managers who wanted to set up an interstate banking organization composed of several formerly independent banking firms. One very dramatic effect of holding company expansion has been a sharp decline in the number of independently owned banking organizations.

A bank holding company that wishes to acquire 5 percent or more of the equity shares of an additional bank must seek approval from the Federal Reserve Board and demonstrate that such an acquisition will not significantly damage competition, will promote public convenience, and will better serve the public's need for financial services. Banks acquired by holding companies are referred to as **affiliated banks.** (See Exhibit 3–8.) Banks that are not owned by holding companies are known as *independent banks*.

EXHIBIT 3–8
The Multibank
Holding Company

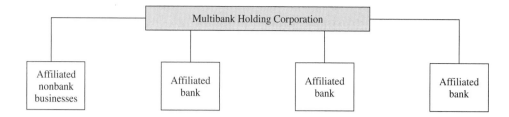

Advantages and Disadvantages of Holding Company Banking

Many of the advantages and disadvantages associated with branch banking have also been claimed by proponents and opponents of holding company banking. Thus, holding company banking has been blamed for reducing competition as it swallows up formerly independent banks, for overcharging customers, for ignoring the credit needs of smaller towns and cities, and for accepting too much risk. In contrast, supporters of the holding company movement claim greater efficiency, more services available to customers, lower probability of organizational failure, and higher and more stable profits.

If holding companies actually reduce competition, we might expect this to result in higher profits for holding company banks relative to other banks. There is, however, little convincing evidence that this has happened. But while individual banks may not benefit from acquisition by holding companies, the holding company as a whole tends to be more profitable than banking organizations that do *not* form holding companies. Moreover, the failure rate for holding company banks appears to be below that of comparable-size independent banks.

There is at least anecdotal evidence that multibank holding companies drain scarce capital from some communities and may sometimes weaken smaller towns and rural areas. For example, there may be a tendency in some small cities for local funds to be siphoned away in an effort to shore up troubled lead banks of major holding companies, meaning that less credit may be available for local community projects. Some customers of holding-company banks complain about the rapid turnover of bank personnel, the lack of personalized service, and long delays when local office managers were forced to refer questions to the company's home office.

As we saw earlier, holding companies have reached outside the banking business in recent years, acquiring or starting insurance companies, security underwriting firms, and other businesses. Have these nonbank acquisitions paid off? If added profitability was the goal, the results must be described as disappointing thus far. Frequently, acquiring companies have lacked sufficient experience with nonbank products to manage their nonbank firms successfully. However, not all nonbank business ventures of holding companies have been unprofitable. Certainly, the attractiveness of using nonbank firms as a vehicle for interstate expansion has declined somewhat with the continuing spread of full-service interstate banking across the United States.

Factoid
Which type of banking organization holds more than 90 percent of all U.S. banking assets?
Answer: Holding companies.

Concept Check

3–9.   What is a bank holding company?

3–10.   When must a holding company register with the Federal Reserve Board?

3–11.   What nonbank businesses are bank holding companies permitted to acquire under the law?

3–12.   Are there any significant advantages or disadvantages for holding companies or the public if these companies acquire banks or nonbank business ventures?

3–5 Interstate Banking and the Riegle-Neal Interstate Banking and Branching Efficiency Act of 1994

Many authorities today confidently predict that full-service interstate banking eventually will invade virtually every corner of the United States. We saw in Chapter 2 that the federal government took a giant step toward this goal when the U.S. Congress passed the Riegle-Neal Interstate Banking and Branching Efficiency Act of 1994—an action supported by most of the states. Riegle-Neal allows holding companies operating in the United States to acquire banks throughout the nation without needing any state's permission to do so and to establish branch offices across state lines in every state (except Montana, which opted out of interstate branching).

Why did the federal government enact and the states support interstate banking laws in 1994 after so many years of resistance, especially by community banks, to the very idea of interstate expansion? Multiple factors were at work:

- The need to bring in new capital to revive struggling local economies.
- The expansion of financial-service offerings by nonbank financial institutions that face few restrictions on their ability to expand nationwide.
- A strong desire on the part of the largest banks to geographically diversify their operations and open up new marketing opportunities.
- The belief among regulators that large banks may be more efficient and less prone to failure.
- Advances in the technology of financial-services delivery, permitting banks to serve customers over broader geographic areas.

Proponents of interstate banking believe that it will bring new capital into states that are rapidly growing and short of investment capital, result in greater convenience for the customer (especially if the customer is traveling or changing residence to another state), and stimulate competitive rivalry that will promote greater efficiency and lower prices for financial services. Interstate expansion may also bring greater stability by allowing individual banking organizations to further diversify their operations across different markets, offsetting losses that may arise in one market with gains in other markets.

Not everyone agrees, however. Some economists contend that interstate banking may lead to increases in market concentration as smaller banks are merged into larger interstate organizations, possibly leading to less competition and higher prices and to the draining of funds from local areas into distant financial centers. Indeed, on a nationwide basis concentration of resources in the largest banks has significantly increased. The top 100 U.S. banks held only about half of all U.S. domestic banking assets in 1980, but by 2000 their proportion of the nation's domestic banking assets had climbed to more than 70 percent. By 2005 the three largest U.S. banking companies controlled nearly a quarter of all domestic deposits and the largest domestic bank, Bank of America, accounted for nearly 10 percent of nationwide deposits. However, small banks seem to have little to fear from large interstate organizations if the former are willing to compete aggressively for their customers' business.

Doesn't this national concentration trend suggest possible damage to the consumer? Not necessarily. Many experts believe that those customers most likely to be hurt by a reduced number of competitors—the *potentially most damaged market*—are households and small businesses that trade for financial services mainly in smaller cities and towns. Interestingly enough, there has apparently been little change in the concentration of bank deposits at the local level in many metropolitan areas and rural counties. Therefore, it appears that in the interstate banking movement, thus far, many customers, particularly the smallest, have seen little change in their many alternatives for obtaining financial services.

Concentration in the United States, measured by the share of assets and deposits held by the largest banks in the system, is among the lowest in the world. For example, while the three largest banking organizations in the United States hold about a quarter of the U.S. banking industry's assets, in most other industrialized countries (such as Canada, France, Germany, the Netherlands, Spain, Sweden, and Switzerland), half or more of all banking assets rest in the hands of the three largest banking companies. No American bank yet has a banking franchise physically present in all 50 states.

Research on Interstate Banking

Recent research suggests that the actual benefits the public and bank stockholders can expect from the expansion of **full-service interstate banking** may be limited. For example, an interesting study by Goldberg and Hanweck [4] of the few early interstate banking organizations protected by grandfather provisions of federal law found that banks previously acquired across state lines did *not* gain on their in-state competitors. In fact, these older interstate-controlled banks actually lost market share over time and were, on average, no more profitable than were neighboring banks serving the same states. Moreover, studies by Rose [6, 7] of interstate bank acquisitions found that many of the banks acquired across state lines were in poor financial condition, which limited the growth and profitability of the interstate banking firms that acquired them.

Employees seem to have more opportunity for promotions in an expanding interstate banking organization. However, many of the largest interstate firms (for example, J. P. Morgan Chase and Bank of America) frequently have laid off substantial numbers of employees in acquired businesses in an effort to cut expenses and increase efficiency. On the other hand, some interstate firms have experienced an *increase* in the market value of their stock when laws were passed permitting interstate banking, suggesting that stock market investors regarded the trend toward nationwide banking as a positive event for the industry.

Key URL

The most important banking industry trade association, representing the industry as a whole, is the American Bankers Association at **www.aba.com**.

In theory at least, if an interstate organization can acquire banks in states where bank earnings have a negative or low-positive correlation with bank earnings in those states where the interstate company is already represented, a "portfolio effect" could occur. Earnings losses at banks in one group of states could offset profits earned at banks in other states, resulting in lower overall earnings risk for the interstate banking firm as a whole. However, research by Levonian [5] and Rose [8] suggests that reduction of bank earnings risk does not occur automatically simply because a banking organization crosses state lines. To achieve at least some reduction in earnings risk, interstate banks must expand into a number of different states (at least four) and different regions (at least two economically distinct regions of the nation). The bottom line is that *interstate banking organizations must be selective about which states they enter if risk reduction is an important consideration.*

3–6 Two Alternative Types of Banking Organizations Available as the 21st Century Opened: Financial Holding Companies (FHCs) and Bank Subsidiaries

In 1999 the landmark Gramm-Leach-Bliley (GLB) Act moved U.S. banking closer to the concept of *universal banking*, popular in Europe, in which banks merge with security and insurance firms and sell other financial products as well. To allow banks to offer selected nonbank financial services (especially selling or underwriting insurance and trading in or underwriting securities) the new law opened wide the door to two forms of banking organizations: the financial holding company and the bank subsidiaries type organization, as illustrated in Exhibit 3–9.

THE SUPER STORE NEXT DOOR

While depository institutions have been branching across the nation and forming holding companies to offer a bewildering array of new services, they have suddenly found themselves facing a potentially formidable foe from the retailing sector. Many financial firms have discovered recently that their toughest competitor of the future may not be the bank, finance company, or insurance agency next door but a "super store" giant that has been remarkably successful in reaching into hundreds of towns in every state and beyond. Wal-Mart—the world's biggest retailer—seems to be creeping into financial services, perhaps slowly at first but with an apparent momentum that few can safely ignore.

For example, in 2005 Wal-Mart submitted an application to the State of Utah, in an effort to establish an industrial bank—essentially a small finance company providing loans and savings accounts to industrial workers. Earlier Wal-Mart apparently had attempted to purchase an industrial bank in California and also reached across the Canadian border in an effort to partner with Toronto-Dominion Bank. However, these adventures seemed to hit a stone wall.

Undaunted, Wal-Mart found other promising pathways and today its financial-services division appears to be outgrowing many of its older lines of goods and services. It now sells money orders, wires money to distant locations (including Mexico), partners with Discover in a credit-card program, cashes payroll checks, and leases space to some local banks to operate branches in more than a thousand of its neighborhood stores.

Many smaller banks, in particular, are frightened by the prospect that the Wal-Mart store in their neighborhood will eventually walk right into nationwide, if not global, banking, operating a branch office in every town big enough to support a Wal-Mart retailing store. Just as Wal-Mart appears to have sunk some smaller grocery, hardware, and clothing stores with its bargain pricing and one-stop shopping convenience, many smaller financial firms see themselves as possibly its next victim. After all, what would be more convenient than accessing your savings and credit-card accounts in the same location where you buy bread, fishing tackle, and toys?

For its part Wal-Mart claims it is not seeking to establish a full-service bank right now, but rather wants a facility for processing the millions of checks, debit-card entries, electronic funds transfers, and money orders it handles each month. Some experts believe Wal-Mart will avoid a quick leap into full-service interstate branch banking because many of its customers may not trust banks. Only time will tell how this intriguing tale finally works itself out.

EXHIBIT 3–9
Two New Bank Organization Models

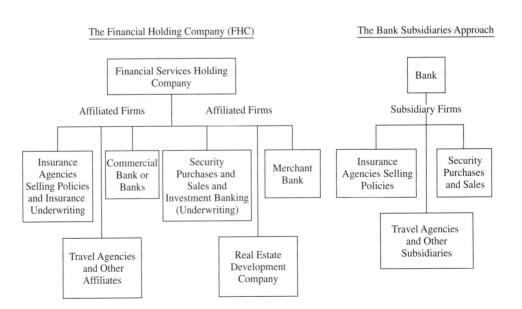

The Financial Holding Company (FHC)

The Bank Subsidiaries Approach

Under the terms of GLB *financial holding companies* (FHCs) are defined as a special type of holding company that may offer the broadest range of financial services. Moreover, the list of services FHCs are permitted to offer may be expanded in future years as a result of joint action by the U.S. Treasury Department and the Federal Reserve, provided any new service offerings appear to be "compatible" with banking and are "financial in nature." With the FHC approach each affiliated financial firm has its own capital and management and its own profits or losses separate from the profits or losses of other affiliates of the FHC. Thus, bank affiliates of an FHC have some protection against companywide losses.

GLB also empowered qualified banks to produce and market their services through a *bank subsidiaries* organizational structure. The bank in this organizational form controls one or more subsidiary companies that can offer insurance policies, security brokerage, and other permissible services. In this instance the profits and losses of each subsidiary impact the parent bank, however, which could increase that bank's risk exposure.

Currently, the FHC organizational form seems to have an advantage over the bank subsidiaries organizational approach because size limits are imposed upon how big bank subsidiaries may be allowed to grow and still be small enough to avoid threatening the soundness of the bank that owns them. Moreover, more financial services (including setting up merchant banks that make temporary equity investments in commercial ventures and owning companies that engage in real estate development) currently may be offered through FHCs, as Exhibit 3–9 suggests.

Key URLs
Educational organizations striving to teach bankers how to keep up with changing industry trends include the Bank Administration Institute at **www.bai.org** and the American Bankers Association at **www.aba.com**.

Despite these apparent advantages of forming an FHC the number of financial holding companies operating in the United States has expanded slowly. By year-end 2004 less than 500 domestic bank holding companies and fewer than 40 foreign banking organizations had achieved financial holding company status. These approved FHCs represented only about 10 percent of all registered U.S. bank holding companies but controlled the majority (more than 90 percent) of U.S. banking's assets. (See Table 3–5 for a list of the 10 largest FHCs approved by the Federal Reserve Board to operate inside the United States.)

Whereas earlier banking legislation gradually moved the American banking system toward greater *consolidation* into larger, but fewer banks, each serving a wider geographic area, the GLB Act promotes the *convergence* of different types of financial institutions, moving them on a collision course toward each other. More and more financial-service customers will be able to enjoy the option of one-stop financial-services shopping, buying more of their services through a single financial firm if they choose to do so.

Perhaps these most recent and powerful banking trends—greater geographic and product-line diversification through consolidation and convergence—will work together to reduce risk in financial services and, ultimately, better serve the customer. Only the passage of time

TABLE 3–5
Leading Financial Holding Companies (FHCs) Registered with the Federal Reserve Board

Source: Board of Governors of the Federal Reserve System.

ABN AMRO Holding, N.V. Amsterdam, the Netherlands (**www.abnamro.com**)	HSBC Holdings OLC London, England (**www.hsbc.com**)
Bank of America Corp. Charlotte, North Carolina (**www.BankofAmerica.com**)	JP Morgan Chase & Co. New York City, New York (**jpmorganchase.com**)
Barclays PLC London, England (**www.barclays.com**)	MetLife, Inc. New York City, New York (**www.metlife.com**)
Citigroup, Inc. New York City, New York (**www.citigroup.com**)	Rabobank Nederland Utrect, The Netherlands (**www.rabobank.nl/**)
Credit Suisse Group Zurich, Switzerland (**www.credit-suisse.com**)	Royal Bank of Canada Montreal, Canada (**www.rbcroyalbank.com**)

will tell us what real benefits and real burdens we may ultimately encounter as a result of the GLB Act and similar financial-services legislation around the globe.

3–7 Mergers and Acquisitions Reshaping the Structure and Organization of the Financial-Services Sector

The rise of branch banking, bank holding companies, and, most recently, financial holding companies (FHCs) has been fueled by multiple factors, including an expanding economy and a rapidly growing and more mobile population. Yet another powerful factor spurring these organizational types forward is their ability to carry out *mergers and acquisitions*. Internal growth is important in the financial-services field, but it has never been enough for the managers and stockholders of the largest financial firms. Bigger companies have pursued smaller financial-service providers and purchased their assets in great numbers.

For example, between 1994 and 2004 nearly 2,900 U.S. banks and close to 500 thrift institutions were acquired by commercial banking companies. A study by Pilloff [13], covering the 1994–2003 period, finds that depository institutions acquired in the United States alone accounted for more than $3 trillion in industry assets. In total, in excess of 47,000 offices of depository institutions were acquired by merger during the decade ending in 2003. In most cases the acquired depository institutions were small, measured at the median, with offices usually in only a single state and assets of just over $100 million apiece. Most of the acquired depository institutions were converted into branch offices or into affiliates and subsidiaries of the acquiring companies. Clearly, acquisitions and mergers have been a major force in recent decades in reshaping the structure and organization of banking and the financial-services sector.[2]

3–8 The Changing Organization and Structure of Banking's Principal Competitors

In the preceding sections of this chapter we have explored the great changes going on in the structure and organization of the banking industry. Propelled by powerful forces—including rising operating costs and rapidly changing technology—the banking industry of the future is likely to look quite different from what we see today.

Key URL
If you would like to learn more about one of banking's newest and fastest growing bank competitors, hedge funds, see especially **www.hedgefundcenter.com**.

But what about banking's principal *competitors*—the credit unions, savings associations, finance companies, insurance firms, security dealers, and financial conglomerates? Are they insulated from these same powerful forces for change? Is the structure of nonbank financial-service industries also changing in much the same way?

Indeed, virtually all of banking's top competitors are experiencing much the same changes as banks are undergoing. For example, *consolidation* (fewer, but much larger service providers) is occurring at a rapid pace, particularly among savings associations, finance companies, credit unions, security firms, and insurance companies, all of which are experiencing falling industry populations and the emergence of a handful of giant firms.

Convergence (with all financial firms coming to look alike, especially in the menu of services offered) has been sweeping through virtually all of banking's competitors. For example, finance companies, security firms, and insurance companies have greatly broadened their service menus to challenge banks in both business and consumer credit markets, in some cases buying banks to aid them in their financial services expansion. To illustrate, several leading insurance companies (including Met-Life, State Farm, and All-State) own banks in order to cross-sell banking and insurance services. At the same time, credit unions have moved to capture a growing share of such vital banking markets as checkable

[2]For a more complete discussion of mergers and acquisitions among financial firms, see especially Chapter 19.

Insights and Issues

THE STRUCTURE AND ORGANIZATION OF BANKS IN EUROPE AND ASIA

Most of the trends in structure and organization sweeping through U.S. banking are also reshaping the banking industries in Europe and Asia. Smaller banks are consolidating into larger ones, converging with securities, insurance, and other financial-service industries, and crossing national boundaries. However, the banking structures of Europe and Asia differ substantially from one nation to the next.

For example, the largest European banking industry lies in Germany, leading the continent in assets and numbers of banks. German banks fall into two broad groups: *private-sector banks,* among the largest, and *public-sector banks,* including Sparkassen (savings) banks, Landeshanken (wholesale business banks), and Co-operatives—all of which enjoy some governmental support, though that support is fading under the European Community. There are about 2,500 German banks operating close to 37,000 domestic branch offices and nearly 740 foreign branches. Yet, the numbers of German banks and domestic branch offices are falling and the industry is increasingly dominated by such institutions as Deutsche Bank AG, Commerzbank, Dresdner, and Deutsche Postbank.

France ranks second in number of banks and includes several large money center institutions: PNB Paribus, Societe Generali, and Credit Lyonnais, along with large numbers of smaller regional banks and cooperatives. In total, France is home to at least 500 banks with more than 25,000 branch offices. In contrast to the great diversity in Germany and France, Belgium's banking industry is dominated by five large *bancassurance* firms (including Fortis, Dexia, KBC, ING, and AXA) that offer a wide menu of services along with over 100 smaller institutions. Netherlands has a similar banking structure, led by ABN AMRO, ING, and Rabobank.

The British banking industry is dominated by half a dozen banking firms, including the Royal Bank of Scotland, Barclays, Halifax & Bank of Scotland, Lloyds TSB, Hongkong & Shanghai Banking Corp. (HSBC), and National Westminster, operating hundreds of branch offices and subsidiary companies devoted to security trading, commercial and consumer financing, and other services. A second tier of smaller, more domestically oriented British banks include Clydesdale, Yorkshire, Bristol & West, and Bradford & Bingley. British banking has been comparatively slow, however, to adopt an efficient Internet system.

Switzerland is home to two of the world's best-known banks—Credit Suisse and UBS—each operating extensive branch office systems. There are about 500 smaller banks licensed by the Swiss Banking Commission. Swiss banks offer sophisticated asset management and estate planning services for wealthier clients around the globe.

Italy's banking sector is led by half a dozen major banks that were owned by the state until the 1990s. The Italian banking sector subsequently was privatized and the majority of their shares offered to the public. However, the earlier state ownership has tended to slow the development of online banking in that nation relative to the rest of Europe. Among Italy's leading banking firms are Banca Sella, Banco di Roma, Banco di Napoli, and Banca Agricola Mantovana.

Banking in Asia is even more diverse. For example, the Chinese banking industry has a large, dominating government sector. However, privately owned banks are expanding and a number of foreign-owned banks have bought shares of Chinese banks in preparation for a larger future role within the Chinese system. At the apex of the Chinese system are four state-owned banks (including the Bank of China), each supporting different industries. There are also three policy-oriented banks—China Development Bank, the Export-Import Bank, and the Agricultural Development Bank—aimed at funding infrastructure growth and not-for-profit programs.

Banking at the local level is dominated by more than a hundred regional Chinese banks and more than 30,000 cooperatives, supporting small and medium-size businesses. About 200 foreign banks from at least 40 nations have representative offices on Chinese soil. China has been slow, however, to allow the integration of banking with security trading and insurance as is common in America and Europe.

The Japanese banking system is dominated by the big four financial group (including UFJ Group, Mizuho Bank, Mitsubishi Tokyo Financial Group, and Sumitomo-Mitsui Banking Corporation). It also encompasses more than a hundred smaller, domestic-oriented banking firms and a handful of pure Internet banks (e.g., Sony Bank). There are more than 70 foreign banks inside the country. Qualified banks are permitted to operate ancillary businesses, including security and insurance subsidiaries.

deposits, consumer installment credit, and small business loans, and several credit unions have recently converted to banks, taking advantage of a 1998 U.S. law.

In brief, the great structural and organizational changes we have examined in the pages of this chapter have "spilled over" onto nonbank financial firms. This dynamic structural and organizational revolution has occurred among nonbank firms for many of the same reasons it has happened to banks. But, whatever its causes, the *effects* are manifest around the world—intensifying financial-services competition, a widening gulf between the smallest and the largest firms in each industry, and greater exposure to the risks associated with larger and more cumbersome organizations striving to compete in a globally integrated financial marketplace.

3–9 Efficiency and Size: Do Bigger Financial Firms Operate at Lower Cost?

Key URLs
For further information on the changing organization and structure of banking around the world, see, for example, the Institute of International Bankers at **www.iib.org**, the Bank for International Settlements at **www.bis.org**, and the World Bank and International Monetary Fund at **http://jolis. worldbankimflib.org/ external.htm**.

Key URLs
To explore more fully what is happening to banking in Europe, especially since the formation of the European Community (EC), see, for example, the Centre for Economic Policy Research at **www.cepr.org** and the European Banking Industry Committee at **www.eubic.org**.

Key URLs
To examine recent trends in Chinese and Japanese banking see especially **www2. chinadaily.com**.and **www.zenginkyo.or.jp/en**.

As banks and their closest competitors have expanded from their origins as small unit (branchless) institutions into much larger corporate entities with many branch offices and holding-company affiliated firms, reaching across countries and continents with a growing menu of services, one question has emerged over and over again: *Do larger financial firms enjoy a cost advantage over smaller firms?* In other words, *Are bigger financial institutions simply more efficient than smaller ones?* If not, then why have some financial institutions (such as Citigroup and Deutsche Bank) become some of the largest businesses on the planet?

This is not an easy question to answer. There are two possible sources of cost savings due to growth in the *size* of financial firms. *Economies of scale*, if they exist, mean that doubling output of any one service or package of services will result in *less* than doubling production costs because of greater efficiencies in using the firm's resources to produce multiple units of the same service package. *Economies of scope* imply that a financial-service provider can save on operating costs when it expands the mix of its output because some resources, such as management and plant and equipment, are more efficiently used in jointly producing multiple services rather than just turning out one service. Fixed costs can be spread over a greater number of service outputs.

Efficiency in Producing Financial Services

The large majority of cost and efficiency studies in the financial sector have focused on the banking industry, not only because of its great importance within the financial system, but also because extensive cost data is readily available for some banks. A few cost studies have appeared for nonbank firms (especially credit unions, savings associations, and insurance companies) and their conclusions are, in most cases, broadly similar to the banking studies.

What do the studies tell us about costs and efficiency for big and small financial firms? Most recent research suggests that the average cost curve in the banking industry—the relationship between bank size (measured usually by total assets or total deposits) and the cost of production per unit of output—is roughly U-shaped, like that shown in Exhibit 3–10, but appears to have a fairly flat middle portion. This implies that a fairly wide range of banking firms lie close to being at maximally efficient size. However, smaller banks tend to produce a different menu of services than do larger banks. As a result, some cost studies have attempted to figure out the average costs for smaller banks separately from their cost calculations for larger banks. These studies suggest that smaller and middle-size banks tend to reach their lowest production costs somewhere between $100 million and $500 million in aggregate assets. Larger banks, on the other hand, tend to achieve an optimal (lowest-cost) size at somewhere between $2 and as high as $10 to $25 billion in assets.[3] Thus, there is evidence for at least moderate economies of scale in banking, though most studies find only weak evidence or none at all for economies of scope.

Studies of selected nonbank financial firms often reach conclusions that roughly parallel the results for banking firms. The U-shaped cost curve described above, with medium-size firms usually the most competitive costwise, also seems to prevail in the thrift industry (including savings and loans, savings banks, and credit unions). However, evidence suggests that the "U" in the cost curve for these near-bank firms is somewhat deeper and more pronounced (i.e., a greater operating cost advantage for midsize firms) than is true in the banking industry—a situation frequently attributed to somewhat narrower diversity of services among thrifts compared to the highly diverse service offerings of banks.

Of course, the problem with these findings is that they leave unresolved the question of why many financial-service firms around the world are much larger than *any* of the

---

[3]See, for example, the studies by Berger, Hunter, and Timme [1], Berger and Humphrey [2], and Wilcox [3].

EXHIBIT 3–10
The Most Efficient
Sizes for Banks

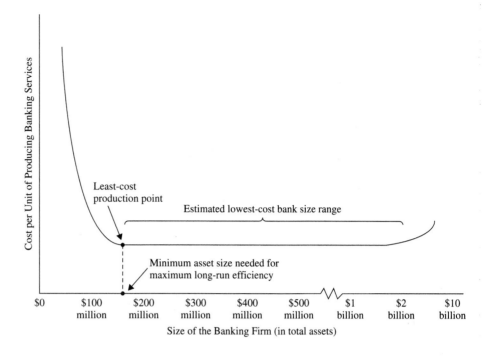

calculated optimal size levels. For example, when Chase Manhattan and J. P. Morgan merged recently, their combined assets were approaching a trillion dollars, and both banks claimed substantial "cost savings" flowing from their merger. Indeed, it may be true that the optimal operating size in banking and for selected other financial institutions is really a moving target, changing all the time and probably getting bigger as technology moves forward.[4]

For example, with banks increasingly producing and delivering services via computer, operating costs probably have fallen substantially. At the same time new laws and regulations have made it possible for financial-service companies to establish smaller branches inside retail stores, set up more limited-service facilities (such as ATMs and Web sites), and branch more freely across the nation. These lower-cost service delivery vehicles suggest that recent cost studies must be regarded with some suspicion unless, of course, larger banks are currently gaining something other than lower operating costs from their mergers and continuing growth. The larger institutions may reap greater operating revenues or bigger rewards for their managers at the expense of their stockholders.

One other important aspect of more recent cost studies asks a slightly different question than earlier studies: Is a financial-service firm, regardless of its size, operating as efficiently as it possibly can? This question raises an issue known to economists as *x-efficiency*. Given the size of a financial firm, is it operating near to or far away from its lowest possible operating cost? Another way of posing the same question is to ask if the financial firm is currently situated along what economists would label its *cost-efficient frontier*, with little or no waste. Research evidence to date is not encouraging, suggesting that most banks, for example, do not operate at their minimum possible cost. Rather, their degree of x-efficiency tends to be 20 to 25 percent greater in aggregate production costs than it should be under conditions of maximum efficiency.

---

[4]Some authorities suggest that while economies of scale tend to be modest for the whole financial firm, selected divisions within the individual firm (including the advertising department, employee training, and information systems) may provide substantial cost savings as a financial-service provider grows in size.

This latter finding implies that financial-service providers could gain more from lowering operating costs at their current size than they could from changing their scale of output (i.e., by shrinking or growing bigger). Thus, x-efficiencies seem to override economies of scale for many financial firms. To be sure, larger banks seem to operate closer to their low-cost point than do smaller banks, probably because the larger institutions operate in more intensely competitive markets.

Either way, however, we must remain cautious about cost studies. The financial-services business is changing rapidly in form and content. The statistical methodologies available today to carry out cost studies have serious limitations and tend to focus upon a single point in time rather than attempting to capture the dynamics of this ever-changing industry.

3–10 Financial Firm Goals: Their Impact on Operating Cost, Efficiency, and Performance

Filmtoid

What 1991 comedy casts Danny Devito as Lawrence Garfield—the disgruntled shareholder—who undertakes a hostile takeover when he feels the management of New England Wire and Cable is not making decisions in his best interest?
Answer: *Other People's Money.*

One of the reasons studies of financial-firm operating costs and efficiency are sometimes confusing in their results and implications may lie in the *motivations* of managers and owners (stockholders). For example, pursuing minimum operating costs and maximum efficiency makes some sense for financial firms that seek maximum profitability and earnings for their owners. However, for those financial firms wanting minimum risk exposure or the biggest market share, cost control and efficiency would appear to have a much lower priority.

Moreover, suppose the management of a financial firm decides that *benefits for managers* (and not the stockholders or the public) should be the primary objective of the company. In this case the *opposite* of cost control and efficiency—something called **expense preference** behavior—may come to shape the firm's performance.

Expense-Preference Behavior

Recent research finds evidence of considerable expense-preference behavior among the managers of some financial firms. These managers often appear to value fringe benefits, plush offices, and ample travel budgets over the pursuit of maximum returns for the stockholders. Such expense-preference behavior may show up in the form of staffs larger than required to maximize profits or excessively rapid growth, which causes expenses to get out of control. Some economists believe that expense-preference behavior is more likely in those institutions where management is dominant and the stockholders are not well organized. There, managers have more opportunity to enjoy a lavish lifestyle at the shareholder's expense.

Agency Theory

The concept of expense-preference behavior is part of a much larger view of how modern corporations operate, called **agency theory,** which analyzes relationships between a firm's owners (stockholders) and its managers, who legally are agents for the owners. Agency theory explores whether mechanisms exist in a given situation to compel managers to maximize the welfare of their firm's owners. For example, if a bank's owners do not have access to all the information its managers possess, they cannot fully evaluate how good management has been at making decisions. For many financial firms today, ownership is increasingly being spread out, and the dominance of individual stockholders in the industry appears to be decreasing. These trends may worsen any agency problems that may already be present.

One way to reduce costs from agency problems is to develop better systems for monitoring the behavior of managers and to put in place stronger incentives for managers to follow the wishes of owners. The latter *might* be accomplished by tying management salaries more closely to the firm's performance or giving management access to valuable benefits (such as stock options), though recent events suggest these steps may also encourage managers to take on greater risk. New research evidence (especially the Federal Reserve Bank of New York [11]) suggests, however, that banks (and perhaps other financial firms as well) are less likely than businesses in the manufacturing sector to tie management compensation to company performance and also less likely to offer stock options to management. This may be due to heavier regulation and greater use of leverage (i.e., higher debt-to-equity ratios) in the financial sector compared to the manufacturing sector.

Many experts believe that lower agency costs and better company performance depend upon the effectiveness of **corporate governance**—the relationships that exist among managers, the board of directors, and the stockholders and other stakeholders (such as creditors) of a corporation. (In financial institutions management, governance relationships tend to be more complicated due to the presence of regulators and depositors who often have different goals than stockholders and management may have.) Hopefully, better governance leads to better performance. Unfortunately, we cannot really validate this notion yet because we know very little to date about corporate governance in the financial sector. Research suggests that banking companies tend to have larger boards of directors and a higher proportion of outside directors than do manufacturing companies, due in part to the influence of regulations. This *may* mean that managers of financial firms are subject to greater monitoring and discipline than managers in other sectors of the economy, although there is some evidence that larger boards of directors also may lead to poorer firm performance.

In the long run, agency problems may be reduced by efficient labor and capital markets. Labor markets can reduce management's tendency to feather its own nest at the expense of the stockholders by rewarding better-performing managers with higher salaries and more job opportunities. Capital markets can help eliminate bad managers and poor performance with the threat of corporate takeovers (which could lead new owners to fire existing management) and by lowering the stock price of poorly managed firms. Because recent changes in laws and regulations in the financial sector have tended to allow more takeovers, we can entertain the hope that agency problems among financial firms will diminish over time as the financial-services industry faces more intense competition.

Concept Check

3–13. What did the Riegle-Neal Interstate Banking Act do? Why was it passed into law?

3–14. Can you see any advantages to allowing interstate banking? What about potential disadvantages?

3–15. How is the structure of the nonbank financial-services industry changing? How do the organizational and structural changes occurring today among nonbank financial-service firms parallel those experienced by the banking industry?

3–16. What relationship appears to exist between bank size, efficiency, and operating costs per unit of service produced and delivered? How about among nonbank financial-service providers?

3–17. Why is it so difficult to measure output and economies of scale and scope in the financial services industry?

How could this measurement problem affect any conclusions reached about firm size, efficiency, and expense behavior?

3–18. What is *expense-preference* behavior? How could it affect the performance of a financial firm?

3–19. Of what benefit is *agency theory* in helping us understand the consequences of changing control of a financial-services firm? How can control by management as opposed to control by stockholders affect the behavior and performance of a financial-services provider?

3–20. What is *corporate governance* and how might it be improved for the benefit of the owners and customers of financial firms?

Summary

This chapter has highlighted the different ways banks and other financial firms are organized to serve their customers. Among the key points in the chapter are the following:

- Financial-service firms have changed dramatically over time, often moving from relatively simple, single-office (unit) firms to more complex branching organizations with multiple offices to serve the public and ultimately financial holding companies that acquire the stock of one or more financial-service businesses.

- When a financial firm starts out, it must secure a *charter of incorporation* from either state or federal authorities. In the case of banks and their closest competitors a state charter may be obtained from a state board or commission, whereas at the federal level charters are issued for national (federal) banks from the Office of the Comptroller of the Currency (OCC) or, in the case of savings associations and credit unions, from the Office of Thrift Supervision (OTS) or the National Credit Union Administration (NCUA). Pursuing a federal charter usually results in stricter regulations and tougher standards, but may help attract larger customer accounts.

- Each organizational form adopted by a financial firm is usually a response to competitive pressures, to the demands of customers for better service, to the need to diversify geographically and by product line in order to reduce risk exposure, and to the pressure of government regulation.

- The rapid growth of today's financial-service firms also reflects a desire for a greater volume of service production and sales. With greater overall *size* comes the possibility of *economies of scale* (lower cost) in the production of each individual financial service and *economies of scope* (lower cost) in producing multiple services using the same organization and resources. These economies can lead to reduced production costs and a stronger competitive presence in the marketplace.

- In the United States one of the most dramatic changes in the banking industry of the past two decades has been the spread of interstate banking as state and federal laws (especially the Riegle-Neal Interstate Banking Act of 1994) paved the way for banking companies to purchase or start branch offices in different states, making possible nationwide banking for the first time in U.S. history. This interstate banking law reflects the need for banking firms to diversify into different geographic markets and the demands of the public for financial-service providers that can follow businesses and individuals as they move across the landscape.

- Another major change in law and regulation was the passage of the Gramm-Leach-Bliley (Financial Services Modernization) Act in 1999. This law permitted U.S. banks to affiliate with insurance firms, security firms, and selected other nonbank businesses. The GLB law has led to the formation of new organizational types—financial holding companies (FHCs) and bank subsidiaries are entering into product lines (such as security and insurance underwriting services for corporations) previously prohibited or restricted under federal law. GLB paves the way for well-managed financial firms to become one-stop financial-service providers.

- All of these sweeping changes in organization are contributing to fundamental changes in the production and delivery of services. Banks and their competitors are *consolidating*—resulting in fewer, but much larger surviving service providers—and *converging*—the survivors offer a wider menu of services that permit them to invade new industries and reach for possible risk-reducing benefits from product-line diversification.

- As the financial-services industry consolidates and converges, public and regulatory concern about firms' *operating efficiency* (to keep operating costs as low a possible) and *corporate governance* (the relationships between management, stockholders, and depositors) has increased. Perhaps the management of some financial firms today is focusing on the wrong target, striving to better management's position at the expense of stockholders and customers, creating *agency* problems and giving rise to *expense-preference behavior* where operating costs are higher than necessary.

- Finally, *consolidation* is intensifying as a few large financial firms come to dominate banking, insurance, security brokerage, and other key product lines, perhaps offering greater customer *convenience* but possibly also decreasing *competition* in some markets. Governments and the public will need to be vigilant in the years ahead to ensure that customer convenience is fully served, but not at the cost of decreasing competitive rivalry.

Key Terms

organizational forms, 65
board of directors, 69
stockholders, 69
unit banks, 73
branch banking, 74
Internet banking services, 77

automated teller machines (ATMs), 77
point-of-sale (POS) terminals, 77
virtual banks, 78
bank holding company, 78
multibank holding companies, 80

affiliated banks, 80
full-service interstate banking, 83
expense preference, 90
agency theory, 90
corporate governance, 91

Problems and Projects

1. Suppose you owned a bank holding company headquartered in California. According to the law, what other states could you enter and acquire banks through your holding company today?

2. Of the business activities listed here, which activities can be conducted through U.S.-regulated holding companies today?
   a. Data processing companies
   b. Office furniture sales
   c. Auto and truck leasing companies
   d. General life insurance and property-casualty insurance sales
   e. Savings and loan associations
   f. Mortgage companies
   g. General insurance underwriting activities
   h. Professional advertising services
   i. Underwriting of new common stock issues by nonfinancial corporations
   j. Real estate development companies
   k. Merchant banks

3. You are currently serving as president and chief executive officer of a unit bank that has been operating out of its present location for five years. Due to the rapid growth of households and businesses in the market area served by the bank and the challenges posed to your share of this market by several aggressive competitors, you want to become a branch bank by establishing satellite offices. Please answer the following questions:
   a. What laws and regulations have a bearing on where you might be able to locate the new facilities and what services you may offer?
   b. Based on the content of this chapter, what advantages would your branch be likely to have over the old unit bank? What disadvantages are likely to come with adding branch offices? Any ideas on how you might minimize these disadvantages?
   c. Would it be a good idea to form a holding company? Based on the material in this chapter, what advantages could a holding company bring to your bank? Disadvantages?

4. Suppose you are managing a medium-size branch banking organization (holding about $25 billion in assets) with all of its branch offices located within the same state. The board of directors has asked you to look into the possibility of the bank offering limited security trading and investment banking services as well as insurance sales. What laws open up the possibility of offering the foregoing services and under what circumstances may they be offered? What do you see as the principal benefits from and the principal stumbling blocks to successful pursuit of such a project?

5. First Security Trust National Bank of Boston is considering making aggressive entry into the People's Republic of China, possibly filing the necessary documents with the government in Beijing to establish future physical and electronic service facilities. What advantages might such a move bring to the management and shareholders of First Security? What potential drawbacks should be considered by the management and board of directors of this bank?

Internet Exercises

1. Suppose you want to determine whether the top 10 banks in the United States are capturing a growing share of the banking industry's resources. Where can you go on the Web to answer that question? What are the implications of the trend in banking concentration that you observe? Should the public be concerned? Why or why not? (See, for example, **www.fdic.gov**.)

2. What has been happening to the structure of banking in your home town? Which banks in your home town belong to holding companies? How can you figure this out? (See, in particular, **www.federalreserve.gov** and **www.fdic.gov**.)

3. How many U.S.-insured banks have failed in recent years? Where would you look on the Web for this information? Do these failures concern you or are they the sign of a relatively healthy industry? Please explain. (See, for example, **www.fdic.gov/bank/historical**.)

4. How are mergers changing the shape of banking? (Consider such sites as **www.snl.com** and **www.federalreserve.gov**.)

5. Several educational and trade associations service the banking industry in the United States and around the globe. Among the most active are the American Bankers Association (**www.aba.com**), the Bank Administration Institute (**www.bai.org**), and the Japanese Bankers Association (**www.zenginkyo.or.jp/en**). What are the principal goals of these institutions? What services do they offer?

6. Smaller banks in recent years have been under intense pressure from the aggressive competition posed by leading money-center banks, both domestic and foreign. In response bankers serving predominantly local areas have formed associations to represent their interests. What are the names, objectives, and services of these associations? (See especially America's Community Bankers at **www.acbankers.org** and Independent Community Bankers of America at **www.icba.org**.)

7. If you want to learn more about electronic banking and its future scope in the financial-services industry, where can you go on the Web to find out? (See, in particular, the ATM Industry Association at **www.atmia.com** and the American Bankers Association at **www.aba.com**.)

8. What kinds of services are offered by *virtual banks*? What advantages do they seem to have in competing against traditional banking organizations? What disadvantages? (See for example, **www.netbank.com** and **www.bankofinternet.com**.)

Assignment for Chapter 3

YOUR BANK'S CORPORATE ORGANIZATION, NETWORK OF BANKS AND BRANCHES AND THE HOLDING COMPANY STRUCTURE

A. Your bank was chosen from the largest 25 banking companies in America. It is a big bank, rather than a community bank. Some of the corporate offices of these banking companies are located in global money centers such as New York and others are not, such as Bank of America located in Charlotte, North Carolina. Some have focused on wholesale banking, whereas others are more retail oriented and then some balance their efforts in both retail and wholesale banking. In Chapter 3, we first examine the internal organization of your banking firm. To get a better feel for your bank's internal organization, go to your bank's primary Web site. (If you do not have this, review the assignment for Chapter 2.) Because we rarely find an explicit organization chart, we will look at the lists of boards of directors and senior management to provide some insights. This information is almost always provided in the Web pages "About the Company" and "Investor Relations" and is often titled "Officers and Directors." (If you have trouble locating this information, try exploring the site map of the banking company's Web site.) Think about the designated role of the board of directors. Write one paragraph characterizing the composition of this board. Then turn your attention to the officers and senior management. Their titles and bio-sketches provide some insights regarding the internal organization of the banking company. Try to characterize the internal organization in one paragraph.

B. You have the spreadsheet you created in Chapter 2's assignment. Often finance folks are asked to tell the story of the data. You are being given this task.

1. First focus on regulatory organization. Your banking company is a bank holding company (BHC) and, as such, it is registered and overseen by the Federal Reserve Board. Within your BHC, you have at least one institution (bank) chartered by either state or federal governments. How many bank/thrift subsidiaries does the BHC have and what are their charters? Are the individual institutions members of the Fed? How long have they been in operation? What about FDIC insurance? Write a page about your banking company with the focus on regulatory supervision. The above questions provide some structure for the coverage of your written comments.

2. Second, in this chapter we discussed unit and branch banking operations. Write a paragraph or so describing your banking company's use of branching by its affiliated institutions. Include the types of offices it operates and some reference to the number of offices.

C. As of 1999 the Gramm-Leach-Bliley (GLB) Act allowed banks to extend their nonbank financial services (particularly insurance and investment banking services). They can achieve this by utilizing the financial holding company (FHC) model or the bank subsidiaries model. Go to the Federal Reserve Web site at **www.federalreserve.gov/generalinfo/fhc/** and determine whether your banking company has registered as an FHC. Having completed Assignment 1 and Part A of this assignment, you have some idea about how much your bank has become involved in nonbanking financial services. Write a paragraph about how the GLB Act appears to have affected your bank's organization.

www.mhhe.com/rose7e

STANDARD &POOR'S

S&P Market Insight Challenge (www.mhhe.com/edumarketinsight)

1. As the organization and structure of individual financial firms change, the operations of entire industries change. For up-to-date information concerning recent changes in financially oriented industries please use the Industry tab in S&P's Market Insight, Educational Version. The drop-down menu provides subindustry selections that may be of interest, including such industry categories as Asset Management & Custody Banks, Consumer Finance, Diversified Banks, Diversified Capital Markets, Insurance Brokers, Investment Banking and Brokerage, Life and Health Insurance, Multi-Insurance, Property & Casualty Insurance, Regional Banks, and Thrifts & Mortgage Finance. For any of the foregoing financial-services industry categories, S&P Industry Surveys may be downloaded in Adobe Acrobat. These industry surveys cover such financial-service groups as Banking,

Investment Services, Financial Services Diversified, Insurance: Property and Casualty, Insurance: Life and Health, and Savings and Loans. Download the S&P Industry Survey for Banking and for one other financial-services industry. Then read the section titled "How the Industry Operates," focusing particularly upon organization and structure. Compare and contrast these two industries along the lines of organization and structure.

STANDARD &POOR'S

2. Of the nonfinancial companies listed on S&P's Market Insight, Educational Version, which appear to be most closely linked to banks and other financial firms (through holding companies, subsidiary relationships, or other organizational ties)? Please list the nonfinancial companies in the Market Insight list that seem most closely connected to banks and other financial-service providers. Why do you believe these close financial–nonfinancial ties exist for the firms you have listed but not for other nonfinancial companies? Are there advantages for the firms involved and for the public stemming from such financial–nonfinancial organizational ties?

Selected References

For a discussion of economies of scale and scope in financial services, please consult the following:

1. Berger, Allen N., W. C. Hunter, and S. G. Timme. "The Efficiency of Financial Institutions: A Review and Preview of Research Past, Present, and Future." *Journal of Banking and Finance* 17 (1993), pp. 221–49.

2. Berger, Alan N., and David B. Humphrey. "Efficiency of Financial Institutions: International Survey and Directions for Future Research." *European Journal of Operations Research* 98 (1997), pp. 175–212.

3. Wilcox, James A. "Economies of Scale and Continuing Consolidation of Credit Unions." *FRBSF Economic Letter*, Federal Reserve Bank of San Francisco, no. 2005-29 (November 4, 2005), pp. 1–3.

To explore the benefits and costs of interstate banking, see, in particular:

4. Goldberg, Lawrence G., and Gerald A. Hanweck. "What Can We Expect from Interstate Banking?" *Journal of Banking and Finance* 12 (1988), pp. 51–67.

5. Levonian, Mark E. "Interstate Banking and Risk." *FRBSF Economic Letter*, Federal Reserve Bank of San Francisco, July 22, 1994, pp. 1–2.

6. Rose, Peter S. "The Firms Acquired by Interstate banks: Testable Hypotheses and Consistent Evidence." *Journal of Business and Economic Perspectives* 15, no. 2 (1989), pp. 127–35.

7. ———. "The Banking Firms Making Interstate Acquisitions: Theory and Observable Motives." *Review of Business and Economic Research* 25, no. 1 (Fall 1989), pp. 1–18.

8. ———. "Diversification and Cost Effects of Interstate Banking." *The Financial Review* 33, no. 2 (May 1996).

For an examination of structure and organization measures and their potential impact on the behavior of financial institutions, see, for example:

9. Guzman, Mark G. "The Economic Impact of Bank Structure: A Review of Recent Literature." *Economic and Financial Review*, Federal Reserve Bank of Dallas, Second Quarter 2000, pp. 11–25.

For a discussion of the formation and impact of financial holding companies (FHCs), see especially:

10. Guzman, Mark G. "Slow but Steady Progress toward Financial Deregulation." *Southwest Economy*, Federal Reserve Bank of Dallas, January/February 2003, pp. 1, 6–9, and 12.

To learn more about corporate governance issues in banking and financial services, see especially:

11. Federal Reserve Bank of New York. "Corporate Governance: What Do We Know and What Is Different about Banks?" *Economic Policy Review*, Special Issue, April 2003, pp.1–142.

For an analysis of recent bank mergers and acquisitions, please review the following:

12. Rhoades, Stephen A. "Bank Mergers and Banking Structure in the United States, 1980–98." *Staff Study 174*, Board of Governors of the Federal Reserve System, August 2000.

13. Pilloff, Steven J. "Bank Merger Activity in the United States, 1994–2003." *Staff Study 176*, Board of Governors of the Federal Reserve System, May 2004.

For a discussion of the present and future of community banks, see especially:

14. Jones, Kenneth D., and Tim Critchfield. "The Declining Number of U.S. Banking Organizations: Will the Trend Continue?" *Future of Banking Study*, Federal Deposit Insurance Corporation, 2004.

15. Gunther, Jeffrey W., and Robert R. Moore. "Small Banks' Competitors Loom Large." *Southwest Economy*, Federal Reserve Bank of Dallas, January/February 2004.

To explore the nature and focus of Internet banks and other limited-purpose banking firms, see, for example:

16. Yom, Chiwon. "Limited-Purpose Banks: Their Specialties, Performance, and Prospects." *FDIC Banking Review* 17, no. 1 (2005), pp. 19–36.

For an overview of commercial banks, insurance companies, and investment banks entering each other's territory and the rise of universal banking, see:

17. Harshman, Ellen, Fred C. Yeager, and Timothy J. Yeager. "The Door Is Open, but Banks Are Slow to Enter Insurance and Investment Arenas." *The Regional Economist*, Federal Reserve Bank of St. Louis, October 2005, pp. 5–9.

www.mhhe.com/rose7e

CHAPTER FOUR

Establishing New Banks, Branches, ATMs, Telephone Services, and Web Sites

Key Topics in This Chapter

- Chartering New Financial-Service Institutions
- The Performance of New Banks
- Establishing Full-Service Branches
- In-Store Branching
- Establishing Limited-Service Facilities
- ATMs and Telephone Centers
- The Internet and Online Banking

4–1 Introduction

There is an old joke that claims drive-up windows were invented in order to permit cars to occasionally visit their true owner—the bank! While managers of financial institutions have developed many unique service-delivery facilities for many different reasons, checking up on the cars they finance is usually not one of them! Rather, financial-service facilities are usually established today for the *convenience* of customers.

For example, customers want to be able to access their checking and savings accounts and access loans at a time and place that conveniently answers their daily needs. For most of the history of financial-service providers, "convenience" has meant *location*. Businesses and consumers have preferred to buy the services supplied by a financial firm located in the same community or neighborhood rather than from a financial institution situated across town, in another state, or from another region or nation.

However, customers' views about what is "convenient" are changing rapidly with the growing use of the Internet, home and office computers, cell phones, automated tellers dispensing cash and accepting deposits, point-of-sale terminals in retail stores, and credit cards that grant access to an instant loan any time and any place without requiring lender approval of every purchase. These newer technologies for storing and transmitting financial information have eroded the significance of physical location (geography) as the main determinant of which financial firm a customer chooses today. In the modern world *timely access* to financial services, not just physical location, becomes the key indicator of customer convenience. For example, it may be faster and less troublesome to request a loan over the telephone or through an online application or via fax from hundreds of miles away than it is to visit a financial-service provider situated only blocks away, but reachable only by weaving your way through traffic and crowded parking lots, and open only during "regular business hours."

However, for some important financial services today—especially checking accounts, smaller savings deposits, safety deposit boxes, and consumer and small business loans—*physical presence* is still of considerable importance to many customers. This is especially true when something goes wrong with a service account. For example, when a customer discovers that his or her account is overdrawn, or if he or she suspects an account is being victimized by identity theft, or when the customer's estimate of an account balance does not agree with the institution's that holds that account, and checks begin to bounce, the presence of a nearby service facility may become important. Thus, for some financial services, and especially when special problems arise, the convenient physical location of a financial-service provider is still a valued commodity to many customers.

In deciding how they will respond to customers' changing demands for timely access to services, financial firms today have several options to choose from:

1. *Chartering new (de novo) financial institutions.*
2. *Establishing new full-service branch offices,* offering most or perhaps all the services that are also available from the home office.
3. *Setting up limited-service facilities,* including drive-up and walk-up teller windows, self-service terminals inside branch offices, automated teller machines, point-of-sale terminals in retail stores, cell phone connections, home and office computers linked to a financial institution's computer through the Internet, and other electronic media.

In the sections that follow we examine each of these options for delivering financial services *conveniently* to customers.

4–2 Chartering a New (*De Novo*) Financial-Service Institution

No one can start a major financial firm inside the United States (and in many other nations as well) without the express approval of federal or state authorities, and sometimes both. This is particularly true for depository institutions (such as banks, credit unions, and savings associations).

For example, in the case of banks, the public's need for a new (*de novo*) bank in a particular location must be demonstrated and the honesty and competence of its organizers and proposed management established. Sufficient protection against failure must be provided in the form of equity capital pledged by the founding stockholders. Usually they must supply enough start-up capital (in the $2 million to $10 million range) to cover several years (usually at least the initial three years) and show that the proposed new institution will achieve adequate levels of profitability.

Why is all of this required? Government chartering agencies believe that financial-service providers need special scrutiny for several reasons: (1) they hold the public's savings, and unregulated chartering activity might result in excessive numbers of poorly capitalized institutions that fail; (2) many financial firms are at the heart of the payments process to support trade and commerce, so their failure could disrupt business activity; and (3) they often create money (immediate spending power), which suggests that chartering too many might result in excessive money creation and inflation. Although there is considerable debate about the validity of these arguments, they constitute the key rationale for the elaborate structure of cradle-to-grave regulation and restrictions on entry that characterize most financial systems today.

4–3 The Bank Chartering Process in the United States

Key URLs

Federal charters for banks and thrift institutions are issued by the Office of the Comptroller of the Currency at **www.occ.treas.gov** and the Office of Thrift Supervision at **www.ots.treas.gov**.

Key URLs

The states have set up Web sites to help individuals and corporations apply for a state bank charter. For example, see Organizing a New State Bank in the State of New York Banking Department at **www.banking.state. ny.us**. See also the conference of State Bank Supervisors at **www.csbs.org**.

To understand more fully the process of chartering new financial firms let's take a close look at how new banks are chartered in the United States. Only the banking commissions in each of the 50 states and the **Office of the Comptroller of the Currency** (OCC)—a division of the Treasury Department—can issue a **charter of incorporation** to start a new U.S. bank. Generally speaking, federal standards for receiving a bank charter are more rigorous than the rules of the **state banking commissions.** However, organizers often seek a federal bank charter for the added prestige it conveys in the minds of customers, especially large depositors.

The choice between pursuing a federal or a state charter usually comes down to weighing the benefits and costs of each for the particular bank and location the organizers have in mind.[1] The key pros and cons include the following:

Benefits of Applying for a Federal (National) Bank Charter

- It brings added prestige due to stricter regulatory standards, which may help attract larger deposits.
- In times of trouble the technical assistance supplied to a struggling bank by national bank authorities may be of better quality, giving the troubled bank a better chance of long-run survival.
- Federal banking rules can pre-empt state laws.

Benefits of Applying for a State Bank Charter

- It is generally easier and less costly to secure a state charter and supervisory fees are usually lower.
- The bank need not join the Federal Reserve System.
- Some states allow a bank to lend a higher percentage of its capital to a single borrower.
- State-chartered banks may be able to offer certain services (e.g., real estate brokerage) that national banks may not be able to offer.

Concept Check

4–1. Why is the physical presence of a bank still important to many customers despite recent advances in long-distance communications technology?

4–2. Why is the creation (chartering) of new banks closely regulated? What about nonbank financial firms?

4–3. What do you see as the principal benefits and costs of government regulation of the number of financial-service charters issued?

4–4. Who charters new banks in the United States? New thrift institutions?

4–5. What key role does the FDIC play in the chartering process?

4–6. What are the advantages of having a national bank charter? A state bank charter?

---

[1] In March 2002 the FDIC, the OCC, and the Office of Thrift Supervision (OTS) issued a uniform application form—the "Interagency Charter and Federal Deposit Insurance Application"—to be used by financial institutions to apply for a national bank or federal savings association charter and for federal deposit insurance. The purpose of the new form is to simplify the chartering process, especially for federally chartered depository institutions. (See, for example, **www.fdic.gov**.)

4–4 Questions Regulators Usually Ask the Organizers of a New (*De Novo*) Bank

Factoid
In what region of the United States are most new banks chartered?
Answer: In the Southeast (including such states as Florida, North Carolina, and Georgia) and the West (including such states as California and Washington). Illinois and Texas also rank high in new charters.

It is instructive to look at the types of information chartering authorities may demand before approving or denying a charter application. These criteria may be used by organizers and chartering agencies to assess a new financial firm's prospects for success:

1. What are the population and geographic boundaries of the primary service area (PSA) from which the new financial firm is expected to generate most of its loans and deposits? The PSA must have enough businesses and households to ensure an adequate customer base for the new institution.

2. How many competing banks, savings and loans, credit unions, finance companies, and insurance companies are located within the service area of the proposed new financial institution? What are competitors' services, hours of operation, and distances from the proposed new institution? The more intense competition is, the more difficult it is for a new financial firm to attract customers.

3. What are the number, types, and sizes of businesses in the area? Many new financial-service providers depend heavily on the demands of businesses for commercial deposit services and for loans to stock their shelves with inventories and purchase equipment.

4. What are the traffic patterns in the proposed service area, adequacy of roads and highways, and geographic barriers to the flow of traffic? Most new financial-service firms are situated along major routes of travel for commuters going to work and to shopping and schools, providing greater customer convenience.

5. What is happening to population growth, incomes, types of occupations represented, educational levels, and the age distribution of residents in the proposed service area? The presence of well-educated residents in the service area implies higher incomes and greater use of financial services.

6. The organizers often are asked to describe the financial history of the community served, the frequency with which new financial firms have been added to the area, and their track record. The rapid growth of financial institutions in the service area and good profitability among these institutions suggests that the proposed new institution might also become profitable and experience growth.

Factoid
Does being "easy" in allowing new bank charters in your state result in more bank failures?
Answer: A study by De Young[2] at the Chicago Fed suggests liberal chartering states have no more failures, on average, than those with restrictive chartering policies. (See WP-00-09 at the Federal Reserve Bank of Chicago.)

7. Who is to own any stock issued? What amount of stock will be held by the organizers, directors, and officers? The chartering agency wants to be sure the new institution can raise adequate capital to support its future growth and protect the public, and it likes to see evidence of a broad base of support among area residents.

8. What is the experience of the organizers, senior management, and the board of directors of the new institution? Successful businesspeople on the board and staff will help attract new accounts.

9. What are the organizers' projections for deposits, loans, revenues, operating expenses, and net income for the first few years? The quality of these projections may shed light on how much the organizers of a proposed new financial firm know about the business.

Under the feasibility standard adopted by the Comptroller of the Currency [1] applicants for a national bank charter are required to submit a detailed *business plan*, which contains a description of the proposed national bank and its marketing, management, and financial plans. Such a plan normally covers at least three years and describes how the proposed new bank will organize its resources to achieve its goals.

The Comptroller's office looks for realistic assessment of market demand, the probable customer base, competition and economic conditions in the proposed institution's primary

Factoid
The FDIC requires new insured banks to maintain a ratio of Tier 1 (permanent equity) capital to assets of at least 8 percent for the first 3 years of their operation to provide an extra cushion against failure.

market area, and the risks inherent in the services to be offered to the public. A marketing plan must assess the prospects for achieving the organizers' projections for revenue, customer volume, and income. The organizers (a minimum of five persons) must also demonstrate that the new institution will hire skilled management and enlist qualified directors and that it will be adequately capitalized to cover all organizational expenses and have enough money to conduct operations once the doors are open.

An application to the Federal Deposit Insurance Corporation (FDIC) is filed at the same time a charter application is tendered to the Comptroller's office in order to expedite the new-bank formation process and avoid duplication of effort. The Federal Deposit Insurance Corporation Improvement Act of 1991 requires *all* depository institutions—including both new federally chartered and new state-chartered banks—to apply to the FDIC for insurance coverage.

Concept Check

4–7. What kinds of information must the organizers of new national banks provide the Comptroller of the Currency in order to get a charter? Why might this required information be important?

4–8. Why do you think the organizers of a new financial firm are usually expected to put together and submit to the chartering authority a detailed *business plan*, including marketing, management, and financial components?

4–5 Factors Weighing on the Decision to Seek a New Charter

Filmtoid
What 1998 romantic comedy, starring Meg Ryan and Tom Hanks, illustrates the effects of competition in a less-regulated market when a small owner-operated book store fails because it cannot compete in terms of price with the "large-box" book store? **Answer:** *You've Got Mail.*

Filing a charter application is a costly process. The organizers must carefully analyze their business prospects and answer several questions regarding external and internal factors that might affect the new institution's chances for success.

1. External factors the organizers should consider include:
   a. *The level of economic activity.* Is it high enough to generate sufficient service demand? Often measured by the volume of retail sales, personal income, bank debits (i.e., check volume), and number of households and businesses in the service area.
   b. *Growth of economic activity.* Is the market area growing fast enough to generate additional deposits and loans so that the new institution can grow to an efficient size? Often measured by trends in deposits and loans, retail sales, bank debits, population growth, construction activity, and school enrollments.
   c. *The need for a new financial firm.* Has the population grown or moved into new areas not currently receiving convenient financial services? Often measured by population per banking office, recent earnings and deposit growth, and the number and size of new residential construction projects.
   d. *The strength and character of competition in supplying financial services.* How many competing financial institutions are there and how aggressive are they in advertising their services? This is often measured by the number of offices relative to area population and the number of other financial institutions offering checkable accounts, savings plans, consumer loans, and business credit.

2. Internal factors the organizers should consider include:
   a. *Qualifications and contacts of the organizers.* Do the organizers have adequate depth of experience? Is their reputation in the community strong enough to attract customers?

Key URL
The Comptroller of the Currency provides a handy checklist of steps to be followed by the organizers of a new bank at **www.occ.treas. gov/corpbook/forms/ preopenchecklist- org.pdf**.

b. *Management quality.* Have the organizers been able to find a chief executive officer with adequate training and experience in management? Will the organizing group be able to find and pay competent management and staff to fill the new institution's key posts?

c. *Pledging of capital to cover the cost of filing a charter application and getting under way.* Is the net worth position of the organizers strong enough to meet the initial capitalization requirements imposed by regulation and cover consulting and legal fees? Because the chartering process covers many months and may wind up in court if competitiors file suits before the new firm is allowed to open, do the organizers have sufficient financial strength to see the project through to its completion?

4–6 Volume and Characteristics of New Bank Charters

Factoid
Are newly chartered banks more or less likely to fail than established banks?
Answer: A study by De Young [2] at the Federal Reserve Bank of Chicago suggests that, on average, they are less likely to fail during their first four years, more likely to fail for a time thereafter, and eventually have a failure rate matching that of established banks.

In view of all the foregoing issues and their associated costs and risks, it may come as no surprise that only a fraction of the businesspeople who consider starting a new financial firm ultimately submit formal applications for new charters. Yet, surprisingly, the number of new depository institutions being chartered in the United States recently has averaged well over a hundred per year, due, in part, to the displacement of many officers who lost their jobs when their former institutions were merged and decided to start a new competing institution. Then, too, there appears to be considerable public demand for more personalized service sometimes not available from large, established financial firms.

Clearly, merely getting charter approval does not end the challenges facing a new firm's organizers and management. Following charter approval, stock can be legally offered to the public through an *offering memorandum* that describes the charter's business plan, management, and terms of the stock sale. Corporate bylaws must be adopted, operating policies drafted, and bonding and insurance secured for employees.

Where are most new charteres located? For example, what types of markets do new banks serve? Analysis of charter approvals suggests that most new U.S. banks are chartered in relatively large urban areas where, presumably, expected rates of return on the organizers' investments are the highest. As population increases relative to the number of financial firms operating in a given state, increased numbers of new charters are issued. Presumably, many organizers view population growth as a proxy for growth in the demand for financial services. The faster *bank assets* grow, for example, the greater the probability of chartering new banks, presumably because the success of area banks leads new-bank organizers to expect success when their bank is chartered. In contrast, significant increases in the *bank concentration ratio* tend to reduce chartering activity. This suggests that some organizers fear having to take on a dominant financial firm in their chosen area. Still, no one has found convincing evidence that new financial firms are overwhelmed by their competition, nor can they be driven from most markets if they are willing to compete. Indeed, in recent years areas where there has been merger activity have been more likely to attract new charterings.

4–7 How Well Do New Charters Perform?

Launching a new financial firm entails risk. There is no guarantee the new institution will survive and prosper. Deregulation of the financial sector has brought scores of new competitors into traditional markets. Moreover, existing financial firms have a decided advantage over newly chartered institutions in their greater experience, size, and well-established reputations. How successful, in general, are new financial firms?

Research findings for the banking industry at least are generally optimistic. Most new financial firms grow at a moderate to rapid rate, attracting funds from their organizers, from business associates, and from customers dissatisfied with other financial-service providers. Increases in loan accounts tend to outstrip gains in deposits as customers denied loans by other lending institutions move quickly to sound out the credit policies of the new institution. Despite a track record of loan losses that generally exceed those of established banks, most new banks are profitable within two to three years after opening their doors.

In a review of new banks formed in Massachusetts, Shea [4] found that early monitoring and control of operating expenses are vital for a new bank to be successful. It must carve out a solid niche in the community that differentiates it from other financial service providers in the minds of customers.

Research also suggests that the early performance of a new bank is strongly tied to the experience, financial strength, and market contacts of those who put the organization together. Selby [3], for example, found that the volume of deposits generated by the first board of directors accounted for a major share of deposits brought in during the initial year of operation. This finding emphasizes the need to find organizers who have successfully operated other businesses. Moreover, the growth of income in the market, especially household after-tax income and business sales, appears to be positively related to new bank growth.

Numerous research studies have shown that chartering new banks has competitive effects that generally serve the public interest. Most such studies (e.g., McCall and Peterson [6]) have looked at small cities and rural communities in which a new competitor is suddenly chartered. Generally, existing banks in these smaller communities have stepped up their lending activities and become more active in attracting funds through deposit sales after a new financial firm has entered, suggesting that customers gained better service. Evidence on whether the prices of financial services were reduced is decidedly mixed, however. Most studies find *few* price effects from the entry of new competitors. Finally, a newly released study by Yom [5], prepared for the FDIC, summarizes the findings of several more recent new-bank research studies. Yom notes that:

- The most recently chartered banks show evidence of being "financially fragile" and more prone to failure than established banks.
- New banks tend to underperform established banks in profitability until they reach maturity (which may be as much as nine years after opening).
- One reason for new banks' tendency to underperform is that they appear to be more vulnerable to real estate crises because their loan portfolios are often heavily invested in riskier real estate loans.
- Today new banks are more closely supervised by government regulators than are established institutions and tend to be examined more frequently (one or more times per year).

Factoid

About four-fifths of new banks chartered each year in the United States are located in metropolitan areas, especially the fastest growing areas, and about one-fifth have received federal charters.

Concept Check

4–9. What are the key factors the organizers of a new financial firm should consider before deciding to seek a charter?

4–10. Where are most new banks chartered in the United States?

4–11. How well do most new banks perform for the public and for their owners?

E-BANKING AND E-COMMERCE

CHARTERING INTERNET BANKS

Both the federal government and many states authorize the banks they supervise to offer Internet services or even charter an Internet-only bank (a "virtual bank"). The concern of most regulators is that an application to offer Internet services or to form a new electronic bank (1) be backed by a sound business plan to help insure that the new venture succeeds (especially because many Internet ventures are not yet profitable); and (2) provide adequate safeguards for the bank's records and its customers' accounts from "hackers" attempting to invade the privacy of the bank and its customers.

A good example of the regulations that apply to Internet banks may be found at the Web site established by the Comptroller of the Currency (OCC) (**www.occ.treas.gov/corpbook/group4/public/pdf/internetnbc.pdf**).

The OCC allows Internet-only banks to receive charters as well as banks with more traditional facilities that also want a Web-based service delivery channel, provided the proposed Web service unit "may reasonably be expected to operate successfully and in a safe and sound manner."

Organizers of Internet banks must consist of a group of at least five people who will serve as the Internet bank's initial board of directors. These organizers must be U.S. citizens in good standing in the banking and business community. The OCC places no express limits on the electronic devices or facilities that may be used to deliver services, provided services are delivered in a "safe, sound, and secure way".

National banks may operate "information only" Web sites; "transactional" Web sites that enable customers to access their accounts, purchase goods and services, apply for loans, pay bills, and transfer funds; wireless service channels; and home and office banking through personal computers. A key issue for the future centers on which of these electronic approaches is likely to be profitable and, therefore, economically viable in the long run. At this point few of these different service delivery routes have convincingly demonstrated consistent profitability.

4–8 Establishing Full-Service Branch Offices: Choosing Locations and Designing New Branches

When an established financial institution wishes to enter new markets or when its valued customers move, an important vehicle for market entry in the modern era has been the creation of new **branch offices,** offering many, if not all, the services also available from the home office. Branches are usually much cheaper to establish than chartering whole new financial-service corporations. Less capital is required, the application for new branch offices is less detailed than usually required for a new corporate charter, and there is usually much less duplication of staff because a new branch doesn't normally require a full slate of officers and operations personnel as would a whole new corporation. Partly as a result, new bank branch offices, for example, have soared in recent years, reaching close to 70,000 by the end of 2004 (see Exhibit 4–1).

The location, design, and services offered by a branch office depend, first, upon the preferences of customers and, secondly, on the preferences of management and employees. Marketing research suggests that most customers rate an atmosphere of *confidentiality,* "*homeyness*", and *privacy* in carrying out their personal transactions as the most important features of new branch offices. And customers and employees seem also to rank *efficiency* high in describing the arrangement of an ideal branch office—service departments and workstations should be easily reachable for both customers and employees.

BancOne based in Chicago (now a part of J. P. Morgan Chase Corp.) has been an industry leader in testing out new ideas for the design of branch offices and other customer service facilities. When the customer enters one of its newer branches, he or she may be confronted with such eye-catching features as neon lights that highlight what financial services each department offers and direct customers' attention to merchandising graphics. To further ease customer anxiety, there may be an information desk near the entrance to help confused customers find the service counters that best meet their needs. Visually

EXHIBIT 4–1 Number of Insured Commercial Banks and Branch Offices, 1934–2004 (as of Year-End)

Source: Federal Deposit Insurance Corporation, *FDIC Statistics on Banking*, December 31, 2004, Washington, D.C., March 2005, p. A-2.

Number of U.S. Banking Offices

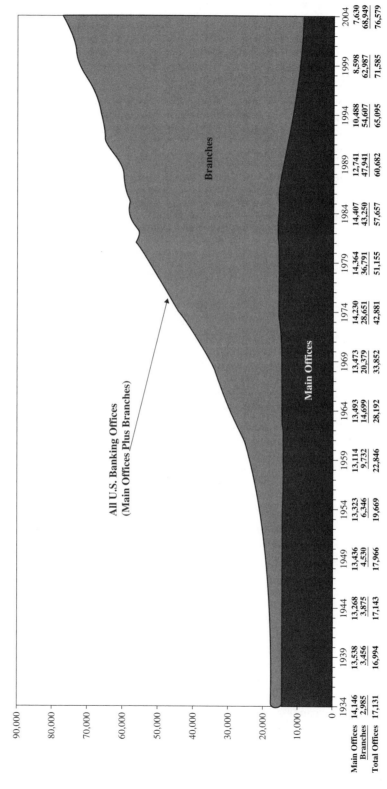

	1934	1939	1944	1949	1954	1959	1964	1969	1974	1979	1984	1989	1994	1999	2004
Main Offices	14,146	13,538	13,268	13,436	13,323	13,114	13,493	13,473	14,230	14,364	14,407	12,741	10,488	8,598	7,630
Branches	2,985	3,456	3,875	4,530	6,346	9,732	14,699	20,379	28,651	36,791	43,250	47,941	54,607	62,987	68,949
Total Offices	17,131	16,994	17,143	17,966	19,669	22,846	28,192	33,852	42,881	51,155	57,657	60,682	65,095	71,585	76,579

Note: Beginning in 1982, remote service facilities (ATMs) were not included in the count of total branches. (At the end of 1981, there were approximately 3,000 such facilities.) Includes U.S. Territories and Possessions.

107

attractive advertisements may confront customers waiting in the lobby to meet with financial-service representatives. More recently, BancOne developed both full-service branches, providing traditional services (such as loans and deposits), and specialized branches ("boutiques") that supply services specifically geared to their local area (such as savings and investment products for retired customers). Other branch-office innovators include Wells Fargo, Bank of America, Washington Mutual Inc., and Charter One Financial Inc. (Recent research at Washington Mutual Inc. suggests that branch offices for that company cost about $1 million each to open and reach the break-even point in as little as 18 months, on average.) The message of these recent innovations seems clear: Customers (particularly new customers) need guidance on where to go and what services are available inside each branch office. Otherwise, they may become frustrated and go elsewhere.

Desirable Sites for New Branches

Among the most desirable sites for full-service branch offices today are those with at least some of the following characteristics:

1. *Heavy traffic count* (for example, 30,000 to 40,000 cars per day), indicating a large flow of vehicular traffic (and potential customers) passing near the proposed site, but even at peak times (e.g., on Friday afternoons) customers must be able to easily see and access the office and its drive-up windows.

2. *Large numbers of retail shops and stores* present in the surrounding neighborhood, which usually generate a substantial volume of loan and deposit business.

3. *Populations that are of above-average age* (particularly those individuals 45 years of age and older) who often have substantial amounts of savings and need advice on how to invest those savings.

4. A surrounding area that encompasses *substantial numbers of business owners, managers, and professional men and women at work or in residence.*

5. A *steady or declining number of service facilities operated by financial-service competitors,* leaving a substantial volume of business that a new branch might be able to attract.

6. *Above-average population growth,* usually favorable to establishing a branch office in an area.

7. *Above-average population density* (i.e., a greater number of persons per square mile around the proposed site).

8. A *relatively high target ratio of population per branch*; measured by:

$$\text{Population per branch office} = \frac{\text{Total population in the area to be served}}{\text{Number of branch offices present in the area}} \qquad \textbf{(4–1)}$$

In the United States, for example, there is an average of about 4,000 people per branch office. However, some nations have even higher average population-per-branch ratios. For example, Austria and Germany count more than 10,000 people per bank branch, while Japan estimates more than 8,000 people per branch office. The larger the population served by each office, the more financial services are likely to be purchased, expanding revenues and enhancing operating efficiency.

Key URL
To discover what's happening in the design of new bank branches, see **www.intbantec. com/.**

9. *Above-average levels of household income,* with higher-income groups usually offering branch offices the opportunity to sell more services.

For offices designed primarily to attract *deposits,* key branch sites to look for usually include neighborhoods with relatively high median incomes, heavy concentrations of retail stores, older-than-average resident populations, and high proportions of homeowners rather than renters. On the other hand, financial firms seeking more *checking accounts* through their branches generally should enter neighborhoods with high levels of family income as well as areas where retail stores are concentrated. Higher levels of *savings deposits* are usually to be found in markets where there is an above-average proportion of older heads of households (including retired individuals) and a large proportion of residents who own their own homes.

For branches primarily created to generate *loan demand from household customers*, residential areas with a heavy proportion of young families and substantial new home construction, along with concentrations of retail stores and high traffic flow, are particularly desirable locations. In contrast, *commercial loan demand* is usually focused upon central city office locations where a lending institution's credit analysts and loan approval committees are normally housed.

Expected Rate of Return

The decision of whether or not to establish a branch office is a *capital-budgeting decision*, requiring a large initial cash outflow (cost) to fund the purchase or lease of property and to begin operations. Branches are usually created with the expectation that future net cash inflows (NCF) will be large enough to guarantee the financial firm an acceptable return, $E(r)$, on its invested capital. That is, management can estimate expected return from the opening of a new branch facility from this formula:

$$\text{Cash outflow to fund the establishment of a new branch office} = \frac{NCF_1}{[1 + E(r)]^1} + \frac{NCF_2}{[1 + E(r)]^2} + \cdots + \frac{NCF_n}{[1 + E(r)]^n} \quad \textbf{(4–2)}$$

where a new branch will be judged to be economically viable if its expected return, $E(r)$, equals or exceeds the minimum acceptable return (k) to the offering firm's stockholders; that is, $E(r) \geq k$. For example, if a new branch office is expected to cost \$3 million to acquire the site and install the necessary equipment to begin operations and to generate \$600,000 in annual cash inflow net of all operating expenses for 10 years, the branch's expected return will be found from:

$$\$3,000,000 = \frac{\$600,000}{[1 + E(r)]^1} + \frac{\$600,000}{[1 + E(r)]^2} + \cdots + \frac{\$600,000}{[1 + E(r)]^{10}}$$

Using a financial calculator, we find that the proposed branch's expected return, $E(r)$, is 15.1 percent.[2]

If the shareholders' minimum acceptable rate of return is 10 percent, this branch project appears to be economically viable. Of course, the return actually earned from the investment in each branch depends upon the demand for its services, the quality of its management and staff, and the cost in capital and other resources necessary to operate the branch.

Geographic Diversification

When considering possible locations for new branches, management should consider not only the expected rate of return from each new location, but also (*a*) the variance around that expected return, which is due mainly to fluctuations in economic conditions in the

---

[2]A financial calculator such as the Texas Instruments BAII Plus is used to calculate the expected return where N = 10, I/Y = ?, PV = –3,000,000, Pmt = 600,000, and FV = 0.

area served by the branch, and *(b)* the covariance of expected returns from the proposed new branch, existing branches, and other assets previously acquired by the offering institution. The impact of a new branch's expected return (R_B) on the offering institution's total return (R_T) from its existing branches and other assets (R_{OA}) can be found from

$$E(R_T) = W \times E(R_B) + (1 - W) \times E(R_{OA}) \qquad \textbf{(4–3)}$$

where W is the proportion of total resources to be invested in new branch B and $(1 - W)$ is the proportion of the offering institution's resources invested in all of its other assets (OA). The marginal impact of a new branch on overall risk, measured by the variance of total return (R_T), is

$$\sigma^2(R_T) = W^2\sigma^2(R_B) + (1 - W)^2\sigma^2(R_{OA}) + 2W(1 - W)\,COV(R_B, R_{OA}) \qquad \textbf{(4–4)}$$

where

$$COV(R_B, R_{OA}) = \rho_{B,OA} \times \sigma_B \times \sigma_{OA} \qquad \textbf{(4–5)}$$

with $\rho_{B,OA}$ representing the correlation coefficient between the expected return from the proposed new branch and the returns from other assets of the offering institution, σ_B the standard deviation of the proposed new branch's expected return, and σ_{OA} the standard deviation of return from other assets held by the financial firm.

To see the usefulness of these formulas, let's suppose management knows the following return and risk information about a proposed new branch office project:

$$E(R_B) = 15 \text{ percent} \qquad \sigma(R_B) = 3 \text{ percent}$$
$$E(R_{OA}) = 10 \text{ percent} \qquad \sigma(R_{OA}) = 3 \text{ percent}$$

Suppose the proposed new branch would represent 25 percent of total assets, meaning the other assets must represent the remaining 75 percent of all assets. That is,

$$W = 0.25$$
$$\text{and}$$
$$(1 - W) = 0.75$$

and the new branch's returns are *negatively* related to the returns from other assets, specifically

$$\rho_{B,A} = -0.40$$

Using Equation 4–3, this bank's expected return after investing in the new branch B would be

$$E(R_T) = 0.25\,(15 \text{ percent}) + 0.75\,(10 \text{ percent}) = 11.25 \text{ percent}$$

The total risk carried by the bank after adding the new branch would be

$$\sigma^2(R_T) = (0.25)^2\,(3 \text{ percent})^2 + (0.75)^2\,(3 \text{ percent})^2$$
$$+ 2(0.25)(0.75)(-0.40)(3 \text{ percent})(3 \text{ percent})$$

Then,

$$\sigma^2(R_T) = 4.28 \text{ percent}$$

or

$$\sigma(R_T) = 2.07 \text{ percent}$$

The foregoing calculations show us that not only would the proposed new branch increase this bank's total rate of return from all of its assets (increasing R_T from 10 percent to 11.25 percent) but the proposed new branch's negative return correlation with existing branch offices and other assets also lowers the bank's standard deviation of its total return from 3 percent to just over 2 percent, producing a **geographic diversification** *effect* that reduces overall risk exposure.

Thus, it is not always optimal for management to choose only those branch sites offering the highest expected returns. Risk and the covariance of a proposed new branch's expected return with the expected returns from other assets must also be considered. If two branches cost about the same to construct and generate about the same expected returns, management would most likely choose that branch location that is situated in a more stable local economy so that the variability about the branch's expected return is lower. Moreover, if two branch sites have similar construction costs, expected returns, and return variances, management is usually better off to select that site whose expected return has a low positive or even a negative covariance with the returns expected from the firm's other branches. Such a choice would tend to lower the overall risk from the institution's whole portfolio of service facilities and other assets.

Branch Regulation

Regulation in the United States recently has made it more difficult to close full-service branch offices of depository institutions. The FDIC Improvement Act of 1991, for example, requires a U.S. depository institution to notify its principal regulatory agency and its customers at least 90 days before a branch office is to be closed and to post a conspicuous notice of the plan to close at the branch site at least 30 days prior to closing. Moreover, the Community Reinvestment Act of 1977 requires depository institutions to make an effort to reach all segments of their communities with services, which often makes it difficult to receive permission to close a branch in neighborhoods where customer volume and deposits may be declining but there are few other financial-service outlets available.

The Changing Role of Financial-Service Branch Offices

Many analysts see the roles played by branch offices evolving in new directions today. For example, in the banking industry, where there is a strong *sales orientation*, branch offices represent the bank's "eyes and ears" in local areas that help the organization identify potentially the most profitable customers and link them to the most profitable services. Also, branches appear to offer the greatest opportunities for *cross-selling*, where each customer is offered a *package* of financial services that fully meets his or her needs. Most automated facilities do not appear to be as effective at cross-selling multiple services as full-service branch offices are.

This concept of making branches as *sales oriented* as possible explains why some branch offices today are specially configured to maximize sales opportunities. For example, the low-profit, but heavily used, teller stations may be placed at the rear of branch office lobbies so that customers going to the teller windows must pass by departments advertising other fee-generating services. Customers waiting in their cars at drive-up windows today are often confronted with signs advertising loans and other services and with loudspeakers that, over a backdrop of soft music, remind them of new service options. Moreover, branch office hours are sometimes set to match local customers' shopping and recreational schedules, including customer access to some branches on Sundays. Of course, the sales-oriented strategy of branching assumes that all employees in each branch office are trained to know about all services the firm offers and are taught to look for every opportunity to sell additional services to their customers.

Branch offices are coming to be viewed today less as mere deposit gatherers and more as sources of fee-generating service sales and for booking profitable assets. In a sense, financial-service branches are struggling today to become more like other retail stores, where the goal is to sell customers as many products as possible, while minimizing operating costs. Increasingly, this objective has meant the substitution of as much automation as possible in place of personnel and office space.

One of the keys to branch office profitability is to apply the latest information technology and thereby lower personnel costs, moving operations personnel and those who

Key URL
How long does it take to install an in-store bank branch? Normally at least two months. However, Bank of America has developed a special kit that can have one up and running in about three days! See especially **www.conway.com/sshig hlites/0697/511.htm.**

must review and approve customer loan requests—that is, those personnel not needed for direct selling to the customer—to a centrally located operations center. Customer self-service terminals are becoming more readily available so that customers themselves can readily obtain price quotations on new services, get copies of forms and legal documents, monitor their own accounts, and even schedule appointments with staff. However, automation on this scale demands that the financial-service branches of the future be much larger, perhaps averaging $75 million to $100 million in accounts served instead of the $10 million to $50 million size range prevalent today. In many cases this will require consolidation of smaller branches into fewer large branch offices with fewer and more productive employees serving customers.

In-Store Branching

A significant portion of financial-service branches in the future will be located inside supermarkets, shopping centers, and other retail establishments, selling not just loans and cashing checks, but also marketing fee-based services (such as credit and debit cards). Among the leaders in in-store banking are Bank of America, Wells Fargo, and Canadian Imperial Bank of Commerce. While these retail-oriented service facilities typically have only one or perhaps a handful of employees, their staff is usually trained to be highly *sales oriented*, making customers aware of the many other financial services they might need. Estimates vary, but the most frequently cited statistics suggest there are just under 7,000 of these special facilities, representing about 8 percent of all bank offices in the United States.

In-store branches typically are much less costly to build and maintain, costing as little as a fourth of the expenses often incurred in constructing and operating stand-alone branches, and tend to become profitable about 12 months earlier than stand-alone facilities. These sales-oriented service units often operate for longer hours (including weekends and holidays that may be more convenient for those with heavy weekday work schedules). Placed in a high-volume location (such as inside a Wal-Mart Super Store) these sites experience more traffic flow than conventional branches as customers pass by, perhaps intent on stocking up on groceries or purchasing clothing and hardware, but then discovering they can get their financial affairs in order at the same time. While there is evidence that fewer loans typically arise from in-store branches, deposit volume may be heavier at in-store sites because they frequently attract the store's own deposits and the personal accounts of its employees.

These store-branch environments present their own challenges, however. Indeed, construction of these branches appears to have slowed recently, perhaps because of the rise of the Internet and point-of-sale terminals as alternative customer-service channels. Some former market leaders in this area—for example, FleetBoston Corporation (acquired recently by Bank of America)—appear to have downsized their in-store programs. Others appear to be using in-store facilities as the initial "gate crasher" in order to open up a new market area and then establish a more solid presence later on.

In-store services may require more aggressive marketing strategies than banks normally are used to in order to get the customer, who is focused on bread, jewelry, and jeans, to get into "a banking frame of mind." Then, too, many financial transactions, such as designing a retirement plan, seem to require more personal attention and expertise than an in-store facility normally can provide.

Moreover, in-store branches normally have no drive-up windows and depend heavily upon close cooperation with store owners and employees (including joint advertising and sales promotion activities). It helps greatly if the store is willing to mention the financial-service facility in its advertising and, if public announcements are made periodically during store hours, to remind shoppers of the financial firm's physical presence in the store. For example, customers who open a new account may be offered free merchandise.

In a sort of "reverse approach" to in-store branching some financial firms have invited other vendors inside their own branch networks, hoping to increase the volume of customer traffic. For example, a couple of New York banking firms, Charter One Financial and North Fork Bancorp, experimented with branch facilities with Starbuck's coffee shops inside. Nevertheless, the frequency of in-person visits to branch offices appears to be declining due, in part, to the rapid growth of *limited service facilities*. We turn now to this latest avenue for marketing financial services and see why, today, limited-service facilities are soaring in popularity.

4–9 Establishing and Monitoring Automated Limited-Service Facilities

The high cost of chartering new financial firms and of setting up and operating full-service branch offices has led recently to a sharp expansion in *limited-service facilities*: point-of-sale (POS) terminals, automated teller machines (ATMs), telephone banking (including cell phones with imbedded financial accounts and customer call centers), and Internet-supplied services. Even though full-service branches still represent a very important channel through which financial firms communicate with their customers, electronic facilities and systems represent the most rapidly growing firm-customer link today. Online banking through the Internet to pay bills, check account balances, and transfer funds, in particular, has soared from about 4 million U.S. customers a decade ago to more than 30 million today. In truth, the most effective service delivery systems in use today appear to be *multichannel*—combining full-service branches and electronic, limited-service facilities within the same financial firm.

Point-of-Sale Terminals

Key URLs
To learn more about the operation and services of POS networks, see, for example, Interlink at **www.usa.visa.com/interlink/** and Merchant Connect at **www.merchantconnect.com**.

Computer facilities in stores that permit a customer to instantly pay for goods and services electronically by deducting the cost of each purchase directly from his or her account are known as **point-of-sale** (POS) **terminals.** The customer presents an encoded *debit card* to the store clerk who inserts it into a computer terminal connected to the financial firm's computer system. The customer's account is charged for the purchase and funds are automatically transferred to the store's deposit account.

Current point-of-sale networks are divided between *online* and *offline* POS systems. The latter accumulate all of a customer's transactions until day's end and then the total of all transactions is subtracted from the customer's account. In contrast, online systems deduct each purchase from the customer's account as that purchase is made. Costwise, financial firms would generally prefer offline POS systems, but online systems appear to reduce the frequency of customer overdrafts and, thus, may be less costly in the long run.

POS terminals are increasing rapidly all over the world. In the United States the number of POS terminals climbed during the 1990s from 50,000 to over 100,000 as the 21st century opened. The majority of the recently installed POS terminals have appeared in gasoline stations and supermarkets. Among the market leaders in this field are MasterCard and VISA, which sell their point-of-sale systems under the trade names MAESTRO and INTERLINK.

Customer resistance to POS usage appears to be fading, and their future growth is expected to continue to be rapid. Service providers must work to overcome several disadvantages for the customer, such as loss of checkbook float (because loss of funds occurs the same day), computer problems that can generate costly mistakes, and the absence of canceled checks or check images, which give customers handy written receipts for tax purposes. However, checking account fees are on the rise at a rate faster than inflation, which eventually may make POS terminals more economically *attractive* for more customers.

Automated Teller Machines (ATMs)

An **ATM** combines a computer terminal, recordkeeping system, and cash vault in one unit, permitting customers to enter a financial firm's bookkeeping system with either a plastic card containing a personal identification number (PIN) or by punching a special code number into a computer terminal linked to the financial firm's computerized records 24 hours a day. Once access is gained into the system, cash withdrawals may be made up to prespecified limits, and deposits, balance inquiries, and bill paying may take place. With ATMs taking over more routine services like cashing checks, the personnel of a financial-service provider have more time to sell other services and help those customers who have special service needs. The average ATM processes at least 200 transactions per day.

History of ATMs

Where did ATMs begin? The forerunner of all automated teller machines began operations at a branch office of Britain's Barclays Bank in 1967. This first automatic cash dispenser could only accommodate customer cash withdrawals, however; no other services were provided. Most bankers at the time expected that customers would use this automated device only when full-service offices were not open. One of the earliest visitors to Barclays new machine was U.S. entrepreneur B. J. Meredith. When Meredith's own firm showed no immediate interest in producing these new machines, he contacted his famous relative, Don Meredith, former professional football quarterback. Together with other investors, the Merediths set up a new firm, Docutel, Inc., to manufacture ATMs. Soon, depository institutions worldwide were asking for these new machines and competing manufacturers, such as Diebold and IBM, became active suppliers.

Key URLs
To learn more about ATMs and the issues that surround them, see, for example, **www.atmmagazine.com, www.atmsurcharges. com** and **www. bankrate.com/brm.**

ATM Services

Automated teller machines are among the most efficient providers of basic financial services, costing far less per transaction than human tellers, though they apparently are not quite as efficient as the Internet for certain simple transactions. A recent study by Humphrey, Willesson, Bergendahl, and Lindblom [16] of European payments systems finds that, as Europe moved away from paper to electronic transactions and made heavier use of ATMs, the number of ATM machines in Europe expanded sharply to more than 200,000 over the 1987–1999 period, while the number of less efficient brick-and-mortar branch offices leveled out. European banks saved more than $30 billion in operating costs over the same time period.

While ATMs are best known for providing customers with cash and accepting deposits and bill payments, many of these machines recently have lengthened their menus, issuing bus and train tickets, selling postage stamps, providing passes to athletic events and other forms of entertainment, and selling gift certificates. Some serve as a channel for making payments for purchases made at selected retail stores. Today ATMs are often shared by several financial firms in order to lower costs and are networked with thousands of other machines to offer customers access to their accounts while traveling. Though expensive to purchase and install, ATMs save on employee salaries, utility bills, and maintenance costs. Recent estimates suggest that an ATM costs an average of about $70,000 to $80,000 to purchase and install and about $1,500 per month to operate, while the cost of operating a full-service branch office averages at least a million dollars and often far more.

There may be as many as 370,000 ATMs in the United States and thousands more in Europe and Asia. Close to half of U.S. households possess at least one ATM access card. U.S. ATMs handle 5 to 6 billion financial transactions annually and bring in a billion or more dollars a year in industry revenues. Access fees are cheaper (averaging about 30 cents per cash withdrawal) and are waived in some instances if a customer uses an ATM owned by his or her depository institution. However, fees are more common and generally larger

Key URL
To learn more about ATM networks, see especially **www. atmscrip.com/ processing_networks. html**.

if you use another institution's ATM because most institutions charge each other an *interchange fee* (often 50 cents to about $2) that may be passed on to customers as surcharges.

If an ATM service fee *is* charged, customers must be informed of the charge in advance under the terms of the 1999 Gramm-Leach-Bliley Act. ATM service providers that do charge their customers user fees often employ *conditional pricing schedules*. For example, if the customer's account drops below $1,000, a fee of 25 to 50 cents may be assessed per transaction; for large depositors, however, machine access may be free.

Charging an ATM usage fee is highly controversial. Recently two of the largest ATM networks—PLUS and Cirrus—decided to let owners of ATMs that are part of their network charge noncustomers a surcharge for ATM use. Several regional systems also began to charge for their services. In part, the appearance of higher fees reflects today's pattern of ATM usage—about 80 percent of all ATM transactions consist of cash withdrawals and only about 10 percent represent incoming deposits. Moreover, ATM usage has slowed and, in some places, declined as more customers are bypassing these machines in favor of using credit and debit cards, on-site terminals, and the Internet.

ATM surcharge fees may put smaller financial firms that own few machines at a disadvantage, encouraging customers seeking to avoid service fees to transfer their accounts to the largest financial firms, which operate more machines in more locations. These fees may be especially damaging to low-income consumers who often have few branch offices in their neighborhoods but may have ATMs nearby.

Advantages and Disadvantages of ATMs

Factoid
Service fees from the use of ATMs normally are greatest when a customer uses the ATMs belonging to a depository institution other than his or her own. These out-of-network ATM fees currently are growing faster than the rate of inflation.

During the past two decades, many depository institutions have moved to lower their operating costs by adding ATMs onto their full-service branch offices and by simultaneously reducing the number of personnel and the amount of rented space inside each branch office. An important consideration in installing ATMs, however, is the amount of downtime they may experience. If no human tellers are available and the service provider has only one ATM on-site and it is not working, customers become frustrated and may take their business elsewhere. This is why many financial firms install multiple ATMs at the same site and replace old machines frequently.

Automated tellers rank high in resource efficiency: they call for only a limited commitment of resources, particularly staff. ATMs process more transactions per month than human tellers (a rough average of about 50 percent more) and do so at lower cost per transaction. On a per-transaction basis, the same transaction that costs an average of about 36 cents through an ATM costs over a dollar through a human teller. This is why some large banking firms (such as Bank One—now a part of J. P. Morgan Chase) have at times experimented with charging service fees if a customer uses a human teller for a transaction that could be handled more cheaply through an ATM.

However, automated tellers and other limited-service facilities do *not* rank high among those customers interested in personalized service (particularly older customers), nor do they rank high in their ability to sell peripheral services, such as enticing customers to take out a car loan or purchase a retirement plan. Depository institutions that put their ATMs outside or away from branch office lobbies often find that this move sharply diminishes their ability to sell other services. Moreover, many customers view limited-service facilities as less safe due to the frequent incidence of crime—robbery and even murder of customers in an effort to steal their cash or their personal identification numbers so that a thief can access the customer's account at will. ATMs frequently attract crime because most transactions carried out through these machines are cash withdrawals. Video and central station monitoring, along with privacy screens, extensive lighting systems, and built-in alarms, are popular methods today for increasing ATM safety and security.

Key URLs
What is the future of ATMs and their service polices? See such Web locations as **www.pulse-eft.com** and **www.atmmarketplace. com/futuretrends.htm.**

The Decision to Install a New ATM

How do service providers decide whether to add a new ATM to the services they currently offer? A common approach is to estimate the cash savings the new machine is likely to generate if customers use the ATM instead of writing a check or going to a human teller, translate the estimated volume of future savings into their present value, and then compare that estimated present value to the cash outlay required to purchase and install the new machine. For example, suppose ATMs cost $50,000 each and require another $30,000 to install. Suppose the total cash outlay will be $80,000 for a bank considering installing a new cash machine. After analyzing its check-processing costs, the bank estimates that it will save $1.00 for each check that is not written because customers will use the machine instead. Suppose the machine is expected to last for 10 years and handle 30,000 cash transactions per year. At $1.00 in savings per transaction, the total annual volume of savings should be approximately $30,000. The cost of capital to raise new funds to finance the ATM's purchase and installation is estimated to be 14 percent based upon the bank's risk exposure and expected future earnings. Therefore, we have:

$$\begin{array}{ccc} \text{Net} & \text{Present value}^3 \text{ of} & \\ \text{present} & \text{the stream of} & \text{The total} \\ \text{value of} & = \text{cash savings from} - \text{cash outlay} & \quad (4\text{–}6) \\ \text{the new ATM} & \text{the new ATM} & \text{for the} \\ & \text{discounted} & \text{new ATM} \\ & \text{at } 14\% & \end{array}$$

$$\$76,483 = \$156,483 - \$80,000$$

Because the new machine generates a net present value (NPV) of + $76,483 for the bank, thus adding value to that institution's balance sheet, management would be likely to proceed with this project.

In closing, however, we must note that ATMs are not necessarily profitable for all service providers. For example, because ATMs are available 24 hours a day, customers may use these machines more frequently and for smaller transactions than they would with a human teller. If the customer needs cash for a movie on Friday night and for dinner on Sunday, he or she may access an ATM Friday afternoon for $30 and then drive to the ATM again on Sunday for another $50 to pay for dinner. In contrast, customers may visit a human teller in the branch office lobby or drive-up center on Friday and withdraw $80 for the whole weekend. Moreover, customers show little hesitation to use ATMs for their cash withdrawals but then use a human teller when it's time to deposit a payroll check, thus requiring the financial firm to have *both* machines and human tellers available. Then, too, the widening use of surcharge fees for ATM use may cause some customers to reduce their usage of these machines in favor of human tellers, pushing up operating costs. A recent study conducted at the Federal Reserve [11] concluded that the cost of operating ATMs has exceeded the income they generate by more than $10,000 annually per machine.

Key URLs
To explore the expanding role of the Internet and online banking, see, in particular, **www.onlinebanking report.com, www. usdoj.gov/criminal/ frand/Internet.htm, www.banksecurity. com,** and **www. bankersonline.com/ roadmaps/roadmaps. html.**

4–10 Home and Office Banking

Giving customers continuous access to financial services—via telephone, computer terminal, TV screen, or other electronic device—from their home, workplace, or anywhere in between may be the ultimate endpoint in the long-term evolution of financial-service delivery. Someday, some experts predict, all financial transactions will arise from the customer's

---

[3] The present value of the stream of cash savings from the new ATM is calculated using a financial calculator where N = 10, I/Y = 14%, PV = ?, Pmt = –30,000, and FV = 0.

own location, be it at home, in an automobile or airplane, at the office, or in a shopping mall any hour of the day or night. When that day arrives the particular geographic location of the financial firm and its customers may mean little or nothing to either party.

Telephone Banking and Call Centers

Key URLs
For interesting examples of telephone banking services offered by major banks around the world, see especially, RBC Royal Bank of Canada at **www.rbcroyalbank.com /business/services/ banking_phone.html** and Barclays Personal Banking site at **www.personal.barclays. co.uk/goto/disability_ bankinghome**. Among key U.S. providers are Key Bank (**www.key.com**) of Cleveland and Pennsylvania's Sovereign Bank (**www.sovereignbank. com**).

Whatever the future may bring, the century-old *telephone* remains among the most popular means for putting customers in contact with financial firms today. Many financial-service providers have *call centers* to assist their customers in obtaining account information and carrying out transactions, avoiding walking or driving to a branch office or ATM. The most common telephone services allow a customer to obtain: (*a*) the current balance in his or her loan, deposit, or investment account; (*b*) verification of what transactions have passed through the customer's account; (*c*) how much interest has been paid or received on a customer's account; (*d*) how to move funds from one account to another (such as from savings to checking to cover overdrafts); (*e*) fax or downloadable copies of application forms and account statements; and (*f*) details on different services currently available.

Increasingly, call centers are being used not only to answer customers' questions, but also to cross-sell services and build customer relationships. Some financial experts believe that the telephone will be the key financial-service delivery channel well into the future because so many different services can be marketed, delivered, and verified at low cost via telephone. Moreover, as more *cell phones* appear and are linked technologically with the Internet and with credit and debit card accounts, the cell phone literally becomes a "portable bank." Pioneers in this field include several leading Japanese electronics firms whose cell phones carry "electronic wallets," storing cash and credit card account numbers, enabling the user to either spend stored cash or to charge purchases simply by waving his or her cell phone next to a device that picks up the phone's signal. Moreover, by combining cell networks with the power of the Internet to convey vast amounts of information at high speed, the cell phone and text-messaging technology seem to offer the potential to promote worldwide use of debit and credit card accounts and make purchases and payments from anywhere on the globe.

Internet Banking

Services Provided through the Internet

Key URL
For a discussion of different call center strategies, see, for example, Bank Systems & Technology Online at **www.banktech.com**.

Use of the Internet to carry out financial transactions is certainly one of the most promising avenues today for linking customers with financial-service providers. Through the Internet a customer can: (*a*) verify real-time account balances anytime from any location; (*b*) move funds instantly from one account to another; (*c*) confirm that deposits have been made, checks have cleared, and online transactions have taken place; (*d*) view and print images of checks that have passed through a customer's account; (*e*) place an order for new checks; (*f*) submit an application for loans and credit cards; and (*g*) carry out online bill paying.

What is so remarkable about the Internet is its apparent capacity for almost unlimited expansion as new customer service needs become evident. The "Net" is rapidly emerging as a device not only for communication, but also for entertainment, for conducting and storing transactions, for the acquisition of knowledge, and for sharing important business and personal information to support instant decision making. No wonder some experts have predicted that the expansion of Internet banking may eventually spell the doom for neighborhood brick-and-mortar branch offices with their huge resource demands.

Challenges in Providing Internet Services

However, despite all of these potential advantages of the "Net" financial-service managers have discovered there are some real limits to what the Internet can do, at least with current technology. While scores of Internet-only ("virtual") banks have appeared over the past decade, not all of these institutions have succeeded. For example, the managers of such virtual banks as National Interbank and Juniper Financial have discovered that not having a network of convenient neighborhood branch offices may prove to be a real business obstacle, especially in attracting household deposits.

Customers of many virtual banks have to mail in their deposits or drive to prearranged ATM locations to obtain the spendable cash they need. They sometimes complain about their inability to speak with "real live" service representatives in order to straighten out problems. Most online-only bankers have found they must compensate their customers when they don't have a network of neighborhood branch offices by promising higher interest rates on the electronic accounts they do attract.

By the beginning of the 21st century several online banks with no neighborhood branches began to look around for effective substitutes. One strategy has been to approach chain stores, such as Mail Boxes Etc., and ask to "piggyback" on their numerous neighborhood outlets. Others, such as ING Direct in Canada, have begun to build their own neighborhood locations. In ING's case a string of cafes was created in Canada, Europe, and the United States in order to offer customers food, drink, and comfortable surroundings and attract new investment accounts. The United States may, however, be the biggest challenge for the operators of virtual banks because it still possesses one of the world's lowest ratios of online banking customers relative to the total number of Internet shoppers.

The Net and Customer Privacy and Security

Probably the greatest challenge facing Internet services is the issue of customer safety and security. The net has proven especially vulnerable to fraud and identity theft in which sensitive private information about businesses and individuals is stolen by unauthorized persons and used to run up large credit card bills or to ravage the savings and reputation of victims. Moreover, following the deadly attacks of 9/11, banking authorities soon discovered how efficient the Net had become in moving money around the globe to finance terror.

So rapid has been the growth of Internet-based crimes that U.S. federal agencies published new guidelines for depository institutions in 2005 with the goal of combating account fraud, money laundering, the diversion of funds to terrorist organizations, and theft of credit-card and Social Security numbers and other forms of private data now protected under federal law. Recently members of the Federal Financial Institutions Examination Council (including the FDIC and the Federal Reserve Board) directed the depository institutions they supervise to assess their risk exposure from providing Internet services and to develop more effective risk-control procedures.

In a document entitled *Authentication in an Internet Banking Environment* [9] the U.S. federal banking agencies have focused upon how to effectively verify the identity (ID) of each financial-service customer and thereby reduce the risks associated with ID theft and other illegal acts. Current ID procedures require customers to present one or more *authentication factors* to gain access to their accounts. These authentication factors generally fall into three categories today:

1. Something a customer *knows* (such as a password or PIN)
2. Something a customer *has* (such as a smart card or password-generating token)
3. Something a customer *is* (such as his or her fingerprint or handprint)

Regulated financial firms have been asked to assess the risk they and their customers face from illegal manipulation of their accounts and, where the amount of risk exposure found justifies the step, to move beyond today's dominant *single-factor authentication* systems (in which customers are usually asked for a password, PIN, or Social Security number) toward *multi-factor authentication* systems (in which customers may be asked for a password initially, then perhaps for a card or token with encoded information, and then

E-BANKING AND E-COMMERCE

ACHs AND CHECKS: THE TIDE IS TURNING, BUT SLOWLY

Every day billions of dollars flow across the United States as businesses, households, and governments pay their bills and depository institutions collect those funds and route them into the correct accounts. Some institutions and individuals pay by check—still a popular route, though now accounting for less than half of the value of all payments made in the United States—and others by currency and coin, money orders, and credit and debit cards. A third route is *the direct deposit of funds electronically.* At work daily routing these "electronic dollars" to the accounts of their rightful owners is a nation-wide network of automated clearinghouses (ACHs).

ACHs permit businesses to electronically deposit their employees' paychecks and permit households and businesses to make regular payments on their mortgages and to pay utility bills and other recurring costs via computer, thereby avoiding checks and other, less-convenient payment methods. The hard fact to explain, however, is why electronic transactions have not completely taken over the American payments system. In Europe they nearly have (with some countries reporting that at least two-thirds of their payments move electronically). *Why is the American experience so different?*

For one thing, Americans are reluctant to give up their checkbooks, probably because the price usually charged for this service is below its true cost. Many depositories fear losing their checking account customers if they were to raise checkbook fees to cover all the costs of paying by check.

Another problem centers on the high cost of equipment to make electronic payments possible. Bankers, for example, cannot be sure an adequate volume of their customers will choose the electronic payments route after they have invested in the proper equipment, nor can they accurately predict how many other depository institutions will join them online, thereby making the service more valuable to customers. Thus, the success of such an investment depends not just on the institution making the investment, but on competitors and other outsiders (a phenomenon called "network externality"). In the United States, which has a more decentralized banking system than does Europe, the outcome of such an investment is more uncertain. Therefore, many U.S. financial firms have postponed offering full electronic services. (For further discussion, see especially Joanna Stavins, "Perspective on Payments," *Regional Review,* Federal Reserve Bank of Boston, First Quarter 2003, pp. 6–9.)

Factoid
U.S. customers using Web banking services totaled more than 25 million in 2003.

possibly must pass a fingerprint, voice-recognition, or other biometric test to gain access to their accounts). These tighter risk-control procedures are likely to be substantially more costly to Internet-service providers than what is in common use today and may provide a significant advantage for the largest financial institutions who can afford to install and maintain more complex customer ID procedures. Clearly, customer privacy and account security are major issues that will shape the future expansion of Internet-provided financial services.

4–11 Financial-Service Facilities of the Future

Despite continually advancing technology, most experts seem to agree that the total number of financial-service outlets industrywide will probably not decline significantly; indeed, the total of all financial-service facilities may continue to grow in the future if the population desiring to use these services continues to increase. However, the design and function of most financial-service facilities are likely to evolve into new configurations—more wholly or partially automated facilities with broader self-service capability and adjacent to other stores and shops. Future facilities will also likely include information-accessing equipment that is so portable that financial-service outlets will be able to visit or accompany the customer, wherever he or she goes, rather than requiring the customer to visit them.

The use of "digital cash" will permit customers to be their own financial-service branches for certain transactions. Customers will be able to carry a pocketsize computer terminal to register payments for goods and services and to transfer funds as needed or carry a "smart card," which is an electronic purse holding a specified amount of electronic money to spend. When all the customer's electronic money is spent on purchases of goods

Use of the Internet as a Financial-Service Delivery Medium

Increasingly, financial-service providers are establishing Web "branches." Many of these institutions sell selected services via their **Internet service sites,** such as bill paying, funds transfer, balance inquiries, and mortgage and consumer loans, and acquaint customers with other services that are available from the main office. Some financial firms include maps on their Web sites so customers can not only find where nearby offices are located but also what locations within each branch office offer certain services.

ADVANTAGES FOR FINANCIAL-SERVICE PROVIDERS

The Internet is a low-cost source of information and service delivery vehicle that can serve customers around the globe. The cost to establish and maintain a Web site is relatively low when compared to building, equipping, and staffing a traditional branch office. Online services are available 24 hours a day, 365 days a year, and usually offer consistently accurate transactions. Internet customers find the financial-service provider rather than the financial firm searching for customers. A final advantage is that customer use is measurable, and it's easier to get customer feedback on service quality, pricing, and problems than at a busy brick-and-mortar branch office.

DISADVANTAGES

Among the toughest problems are protecting customer privacy and heading off crime, such as by using private dial-ups, breaking transactions into small bundles, or using coded data so that thieves have a tougher time breaking in. As the Internet's popularity continues to grow, so does the threat of slowdowns and "hacker"-imposed system crashes. In addition, the Internet is not a warm and inviting medium through which a financial-services manager can easily get to know and recognize his or her clients. Many customers do not yet have compatible electronic systems, and the cost of being able to link up may be prohibitive to some. Finally, competition on the Internet is not limited by geography; thousands of financial-service providers are vying for each customer's accounts.

WAYS TO PROMOTE CUSTOMER INTERNET USE

Financial firms should use the Internet to emphasize safety, promote Web services, and revise their Web sites as often as possible to hold customer interest. They should survey customers frequently about quality, satisfaction, and availability of services and allow customers to download information about services and service facilities. The Web can promote customer dialogue to resolve problems through e-mail and telephone conversations.

Financial-service managers need to ask themselves several questions when planning to offer services via the Internet and in designing their Web sites. For example:

- Is the financial institution doing a good job describing its service offerings and explaining how a customer can access those services?
- Is the institution concerned enough about security and privacy to take significant steps to protect its customers?
- Does the institution provide a way for the public to get questions answered and problems solved?
- Does the financial firm identify someone specifically (by name) that the customer can contact with questions and problems?
- Does the service provider give the customer enough information to evaluate his or her current financial condition—data that would matter especially to large account holders and stockholders?
- Does the financial firm provide a way for job seekers to find out about career opportunities with the institution?
- Is the financial firm willing to invest in state-of-the-art Internet functionality to stay competitive in a marketplace of thousands of service providers?

and services, the card can be electronically "refilled" again with digital cash in order to support future purchases. But even with these service innovations, there is still likely to be a significant role for traditional full-service branch offices geared to the special service needs of the neighborhoods and communities they serve, helping customers plan for the future with the aid of a broad menu of service offerings and expert financial advice.

Whatever form future service facilities take, however, each branch office and limited-service facility will have to continually prove its worth in generating revenues and net earnings for financial firms. Service-providers of the future are likely to follow the lead of many retail stores in evaluating the success of their branch offices and limited-service facilities in terms of profits and costs per square foot. Future service facilities will have to combine a retail, sales-oriented environment with customer-friendly automation and still be flexible enough to deal with continuing product innovation. No longer can branches and limited-service facilities be just deposit gatherers; they must also be aggressive fee generators, selling credit, money management, and planning services to businesses and individuals as well as traditional savings plans. And the roles of branch managers will change as well; they must spend more time generating new business (i.e., becoming highly sales oriented) by calling regularly on prospective clients and building stronger links to their client base.

Key URLs
To learn more about Web site banking and its services, see such sites as **www.bankofamerica. com, www.sterlingbank. com,** and **www.bitsinfo. org.**

Concept Check

4–12. Why is the establishment of new branch offices usually favored over the chartering of new financial firms as a vehicle for delivering financial services?

4–13. What factors are often considered in evaluating possible sites for new branch offices?

4–14. What changes are occurring in the design of, and the roles played by, branch offices? Please explain why these changes are occurring.

4–15. What laws and regulations affect the creation of new bank and thrift branches and the closing of existing branches? What advantages and what problems can the closing of a branch office create?

4–16. What new and innovative sites have been selected for new branch offices in recent years? Why have these sites been chosen by some financial firms?

Do you have any ideas about other sites that you believe should be considered?

4–17. What are POS terminals and where are they usually located?

4–18. What services do ATMs provide? What are the principal limitations of ATMs as a service provider? Should ATMs carry fees? Why?

4–19. What are self-service terminals and what advantages do they have for financial institutions and their customers?

4–20. What financial services are currently available on the Internet? What problems have been encountered in trying to offer Internet services?

4–21. How can financial firms better promote their Internet service options?

Summary

In this chapter we examined the major types of service outlets financial firms use today to deliver services to the public. We examined these key points:

- *Convenience*—timely access to financial services—is a key factor in determining how customers choose which financial-service firm to use. Advances in communications technology allow customers to reach financial firms over great distances so that timely access today does not necessarily mean that service providers need to locate their service outlets in the same communities where their customers live and work.

- Nevertheless, for services where costly problems may occur (such as checking accounts) the nearby presence of the financial-service provider remains appealing to many customers, especially households and small businesses.

- The key types of financial-service outlets used today include (1) chartering new corporate service providers; (2) establishing new full-service branch offices; or (3) setting up limited-service facilities, such as automated teller machines, point-of-sale terminals, Internet service channels, telephone centers, and electronically coded cards. Each type of service facility has its own unique advantages and disadvantages and appeals to different customer groups.

- If a financial-service provider elects to charter a new corporation, applications must be submitted to federal or state regulatory authorities. In the case of commercial banks in the United States, the individual states and the Comptroller of the Currency in Washington, D.C., can issue charters of incorporation. For thrift institutions, both the states and the federal Office of Thrift Supervision can award charters to organizing groups.

- Newly chartered banks generally are profitable within two to three years and depend heavily on the local business contacts of the organizers, the expansion of population and income in their principal service area, and the intensity of competition.

- Less costly than chartering new financial firms is the creation of full-service branch offices, usually set up in areas of high traffic volume. Other key factors in locating service facilities are population density, retail and wholesale sales, and industrial development. Traditional branches are stand-alone facilities that provide most of the same services as a financial institution's home office. More recently, limited-service facilities, such as automated teller machines (ATMs), set up in prime shopping areas have helped to reduce operating costs from offering high-volume services.

- Internet sites generally operate at only a fraction of the cost of services provided through traditional brick-and-mortar branch offices. Unfortunately those facilities that are the cheapest to operate—for example, ATMs and Web sites—are often the least effective at cross-selling additional services and are more vulnerable to criminal activity. Whatever service facilities move to dominance in the future, these delivery vehicles are likely to be scrutinized more closely for performance and efficiency and configured for marketing multiple services more effectively.

Key Terms

Office of the Comptroller of the Currency, *101*	branch offices, *105*	point-of-sale terminals, *113*
charter of incorporation, *101*	geographic diversification, *110*	ATM, *114*
state banking commissions, *101*	in-store branches, *112*	Internet service sites, *120*

Problems and Projects

1. A group of businesspeople from the town of Mathews are considering filing an application with the state banking commission to charter a new bank. Due to a lack of current banking facilities within a 10-mile radius of the community, the organizing group estimates that the initial banking facility would cost about $3.2 million to build along with another $700,000 in other organizing expenses and would last for about 20 years. Total revenues are projected to be $510,000 the first year, while total operating expenses are projected to reach $180,000 in year 1. Revenues are expected to increase 6 percent annually after the first year, while expenses will grow an estimated 5 percent annually after year 1. If the organizers require a minimum of a 10 percent annual rate of return on their investment of capital in the proposed new bank, are they likely to proceed with their charter application given the above estimates?

2. Andover Savings Bank is considering the establishment of a new branch office at the corner of Lafayette and Connecticut Avenues. The savings association's economics

department projects annual operating revenues of $1.75 million from fee income generated by service sales and annual branch operating expenses of $880,000. The cost of procuring the property is $2.5 million and branch construction will total an estimated $2.32 million; the facility is expected to last 16 years. If the savings bank has a minimum acceptable rate of return on its invested capital of 12 percent, will Andover likely proceed with this branch office project?

3. Jackson Bank of Commerce estimates that building a new branch office in the newly developed Guidar residential township will yield an annual expected return of 13 percent with an estimated standard deviation of 5 percent. The bank's marketing department estimates that cash flows from the proposed Guidar branch will be mildly positively correlated (with a correlation coefficient of +0.37) with the bank's other sources of cash flow. The expected annual return from the bank's existing facilities and other assets is 10 percent with a standard deviation of 3 percent. The branch will represent just 10 percent of Jackson's total assets. Will the proposed branch increase Jackson's overall rate of return? Its overall risk?

4. The following statistics and estimates were compiled by First Saving Bank of Talbot regarding a proposed new branch office and the bank itself:

Branch office expected return	= 16%
Standard deviation of return	= 7%
Bank's overall expected return	= 10%
Standard deviation of bank's return	= 3%
Branch asset value as a percentage of total bank assets	= 15%
Correlation of net cash flows for branch and bank as a whole	= +0.27

What will happen to the Talbot bank's total expected return and overall risk if the proposed new branch project is adopted?

5. First National Bank of Yukon is considering installing three ATMs in its westside branch. The new machines are expected to cost $48,000 apiece. Installation costs will amount to about $16,000 per machine. Each machine has a projected useful life of 10 years. Due to rapid growth in the westside district, these three machines are expected to handle 180,000 cash transactions per year. On average, each cash transaction is expected to save 32 cents in check processing costs. If First National has a 12 percent cost of capital, should the bank proceed with this investment project?

6. First State Security Bank is planning to set up its own Web page to advertise its location and services on the Internet and to offer customers selected service options, such as paying recurring households bills, verifying account balances, and dispensing deposit account and loan application forms. What factors should First State take into account as it plans its own Web page and Internet service menu? How can the bank effectively differentiate itself from other banks currently present on the Internet? How might the bank be able to involve its own customers in designing its Web site and pricing its Internet service package?

Internet Exercises

1. If you need information about new charters for financial institutions, the place to look is the Web site of the chartering agency. For national banks, that would be the OCC at **www.occ.treas.gov** where you will find the Comptroller's Licensing Manual for Charters. Summarize the organizing group's role in seeking a charter for a new bank.

2. Suppose your bank is considering the construction of an in-store branch. Visit **www.int-bantec.com/** for information from a company that designs and installs such branches.

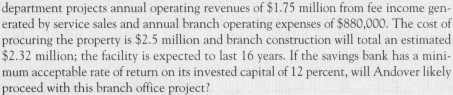

REAL NUMBERS FOR REAL BANKS — Assignment for Chapter 4

A LOOK AT YOUR BANK'S USE OF BRANCHES, ATMs AND OTHER SERVICE OUTLETS FOR EXPANSION

While the overall number of BHCs and banks is decreasing, the number of newly chartered banks, branch offices, and ATMs is on the rise. In this assignment we will assess the changing structure of the BHC you have followed since Chapter 1.

An Examination of New Offices

A. Go to the FDIC's Institution Directory at **http://www3.fdic.gov/idasp/** and do a search for your bank holding company (BHC) using the BHC ID. This search will produce a list of bank and thrift subsidiaries. If you click on the active certificate links, additional information will appear and you will be able to pull up a current list of offices for that bank. A list of all offices associated with that bank will appear, accompanied with information on location, codes identifying the type of office, and the date established. You will want to focus your attention on new offices established since January 1, 2000. Collect information on the type of office, location (city, state), and date established for all new offices of each bank within your bank holding company.

B. In aggregate, how many new offices has your BHC established? What are the types of offices it has created? (Note that the codes are defined using their active link.) Where are the new offices located?

C. Compose several paragraphs discussing your bank's expansion using different types of offices and evaluating its strategy. Note: Your bank may have established limited new offices if it has focused on expansion via mergers and acquisitions, the topic for Chapter 19.

Use the "view our portfolio" pull-down menu. What is the difference between an In-Store and Storefront branch?

3. If you want to stay abreast of the newest developments in the ATM field, visit **http://www.atmmarketplace.com**. If you are comparison shopping for ATMs for your institution, go to **www.atmmarketplace.com/buyersguide.php** and compare the features of three different ATMs. Print your comparison page.

4. Many U.S. banks and credit unions offer full Internet services. Visit **www.onlinebankingreport.com** and use the "Search Reports" box to find articles on Web banks. What did you learn from reading the articles on Web banks?

5. What should you do if you suspect you may have become the victim of Internet fraud? Visit **www.internetfraud.usdoj.gov**. This site also provides information on possible types of Internet fraud. Review one of the four general tips on possible Internet fraud schemes found at this site.

STANDARD &POOR'S

S&P Market Insight Challenge (www.mhhe.com/edumarketinsight)

While both banking and thrift industries are consolidating, charters for *new* depository institutions are still being issued. For up-to-date information concerning the profiles of these two industries, utilize the Industry tab in S&P's Market Insight. When you encounter the drop-down menu, you will see the subindustry groups labeled Diversified Banks, Regional Banks, and Thrifts & Mortgage Finance. By choosing these particular industry groupings, you will bring up the S&P Industry Survey covering banking and the survey devoted to savings and loans. Please download these surveys and read through the sections marked "Industry Profile" and "Industry Trends." What information were you able to collect on the number of new charters issued? What factors appear to influence the issuance of new charters in the banking and thrift field? Do you think the recent rapid growth of electronic service delivery channels (such as ATMs and the Internet) has affected chartering activity? In what ways?

Selected References

To understand more about how banks are chartered in the United States, see especially:

1. Comptroller of the Currency. *Comptroller's Licensing Manual.* Washington, D.C., January 2005.

For information on how well new banks perform, see the following studies:

2. De Young, Robert. "For How Long Are Newly Chartered Banks Financially Fragile?" *Working Paper Series*, Research Department, Federal Reserve Bank of Chicago, September 2000.
3. Selby, Edward. "The Role of Director Deposits in New Bank Growth." *Journal of Bank Research*, Spring 1981, pp. 60–61.
4. Shea, Maurice P., III. "New Commercial Banks in Massachusetts." *New England Business Review*, Federal Reserve Bank of Boston, September 1967, pp. 2–9.
5. Yom, Chiwon. "Recently Chartered Banks' Vulnerability to Real Estate Crisis." *FDIC Banking Review* 16, no. 3 (2004), pp. 1–15.

For a discussion of the reasons for and the impact of entry regulation in banking, see:

6. McCall, Allan S., and Manfred D. Peterson. "The Impact of De Novo Commercial Bank Entry." *Working Paper No. 76-7*, Federal Deposit Insurance Corporation, 1976.

To discover more about the challenges posed by Internet banking and electronic financial-service delivery, see, for example:

7. Board of Governors of the Federal Reserve System. *The Future of Retail Electronic Payments Systems: Industry Interviews and Analysis.* Staff Study 175, Washington, D.C., 2002.
8. Comptroller of the Currency. *The Internet and the National Bank Charter.* Washington, D.C., January 2001.
9. Federal Financial Institutions Examination Council. *Authentication in an Internet Banking Environment.* Washington, D.C., 2005 (**http://www.ffiec.gov**).
10. Stavins, Joanna. "Perspective on Payments." *Regional Review*, Federal Reserve Bank of Boston, First Quarter 2003, pp. 6–9.
11. Stefanadis, Chris. "Why Hasn't Electronic Bill Presentment and Payment Taken Off?" *Current Issues in Economics and Finance*, Federal Reserve Bank of New York, July/August 2002.
12. Wenninger, John. "The Emerging Role of Banks in E-Commerce." *Current Issues in Economics and Finance*, Federal Reserve Bank of New York, March 2000, pp. 1–5.

For the issues associated with full-service branching and branch site selection, see:

13. Rose, Peter S. "The Bank Branch: Which Way to the Future?" *The Canadian Banker* 43, no. 6 (December 1986), pp. 40–50.
14. Zdanowicz, John S. "Applying Portfolio Theory to Branch Selection." *Journal of Retail Banking* 13, no. 4 (Fall 1991), pp. 25–28.

For further discussion of ATMs and their impact on customers and depository institutions, see:

15. Hannan, Timothy H. "ATM Surcharge Bans and Bank Market Structure: The Case of Iowa and Its Neighbors." *Finance and Economics Discussion Series*, Board of Governors of the Federal Reserve System, no. 2005-46 (October 2005).

16. Humphrey, David; Magnus Willesson; Goran Bergendahl; and Ted Lindblom. "Cost Savings from Electronic Payments and ATMs in Europe." *Working Papers*, Research Department, Federal Reserve Bank of Philadelphia, August 2003.

17. Gowrisankaran, Gautam, and John Krainer. "Bank ATMs and ATM Surcharges." *FRBSF Economic Letter*, Federal Reserve Bank of San Francisco, December 16, 2005.

For an exploration of possible links between the adoption of Internet technology and bank performance, see:

18. Hernandez-Murillo, Ruben, and Deborah Roisman. "Point and Click or Mortar and Brick?" *The Regional Economist*, Federal Reserve Bank of St. Louis, October 2004, pp. 12–13.

To learn more about how federal and state rules influence the chartering of federal and state depository institutions, see especially:

19. Blair, Christine E., and Rose M. Kushmeider. "Challenges to the Dual Banking System: The Funding of Bank Supervision." *FDIC Banking Review*, Vol. 18 No. 1 (2006), pp. 1–22.

PART TWO

Financial Statements and Financial Firm Performance

In this part of the text we continue on our journey through the banking and financial-services industry by first examining the financial statements of banks and their principal competitors. Our principal focus is on *balance sheets* and *income/expense statements*. We want to understand how these financial reports are built and what they tell us about the nature and characteristics of banks and competing financial firms.

Moreover, in Part Two we go behind the financial statements themselves to explore the ways in which we can observe and evaluate the *performance* of leading financial firms. Our goal is to discover how important such performance measures as stock values, profitability, risk in its multiple dimensions, growth, and efficiency really are in evaluating how successful or unsuccessful a financial-service provider really is. We want to discover the links between the size and location of financial institutions and the regulatory environment that surrounds them and how well they perform in serving the public and in providing an adequate return to their owners.

We will remind ourselves repeatedly in this part of the text how important the level of performance of financial firms is to many different groups in our economy. The public relies on these institutions for vital services—for example, making payments for the goods and services we buy, storing and protecting our savings for future use, managing our investments, and providing us with credit to maintain our standard of living. If financial firms cannot provide these essential financial products efficiently, at low cost, at acceptable levels of risk, and with a competitive rate of return to their stakeholders, then both we as individuals and society as a whole may suffer. So important is this essential mission of financial-service providers that their performance and the content of their financial statements are scrutinized heavily all the time by government regulators, their largest customers, financial analysts on behalf of investors, and the public.

CHAPTER FIVE

The Financial Statements of Banks and Their Principal Competitors

Key Topics in this Chapter

- An Overview of the Balance Sheets and Income Statements of Banks and Other Financial Firms
- The Balance Sheet or Report of Condition
- Asset Items
- Liability Items
- Recent Expansion of Off-Balance Sheet Items
- The Problem of Book-Value Accounting and "Window Dressing"
- Components of the Income Statement: Revenues and Expenses

5–1 Introduction

The particular services that each financial firm chooses to offer and the overall size of each financial-service organization are reflected in its *financial statements*. Financial statements are literally a "road map" telling us where a financial firm has been in the past, where it is now, and, perhaps, where it is headed in the future. They are invaluable guideposts that can, if properly constructed and interpreted, signal success or signal disaster. Unfortunately, much the same problems with faulty and misleading financial statements that placed Enron and WorldCom in the headlines have also visited some financial-service providers, teaching us to be cautious in reading and interpreting the financial statements that financial companies routinely publish.

The two main financial statements that managers, customers (particularly large depositors not fully protected by deposit insurance), and the regulatory authorities rely upon are the *balance sheet (Report of Condition)* and the *income statement (Report of Income)*. We will examine these two important financial reports in depth in this chapter. Finally, we explore some of the similarities and some of the differences between bank financial statements and those of their closest financial competitors.

5–2 An Overview of Balance Sheets and Income Statements

The two most important financial statements for a *banking firm*—its balance sheet, or Report of Condition, and its income statement, or Report of Income—may be viewed as a list of financial inputs and outputs, as Table 5–1 shows. The Report of Condition shows the amount and composition of funds sources (financial inputs) drawn upon to finance lending and investing activities and how much has been allocated to loans, securities, and other funds uses (financial outputs) at any given point in time.

In contrast, the financial inputs and outputs on the Report of Income show how much it has cost to acquire funds and to generate revenues from the uses the bank or other financial firm has made of those funds. These costs include interest paid to depositors and other creditors of the institution, the expenses of hiring management and staff, overhead costs in acquiring and using office facilities, and taxes paid for government services. The Report of Income also shows the revenues (cash flow) generated by selling services to the public, including making loans and leases and servicing customer deposits. Finally, the Report of Income shows net earnings after all costs are deducted from the sum of all revenues, some of which will be reinvested in the business for future growth and some of which will flow to stockholders as dividends.

5–3 The Balance Sheet (Report of Condition)

The Principal Types of Accounts

A balance sheet, or **Report of Condition**, lists the assets, liabilities, and equity capital (owners' funds) held by or invested in a bank or other financial firm on any given date. Because financial institutions are simply business firms selling a particular kind of product, the basic balance sheet identity

$$\text{Assets} = \text{Liabilities} + \text{Equity capital} \qquad \text{(5–1)}$$

must be valid for banks and other financial-service providers.

In banking, the *assets* on the balance sheet are of four major types: cash in the vault and deposits held at other depository institutions (C), government and private interest-bearing securities purchased in the open market (S), loans and lease financings made available to customers (L), and miscellaneous assets (MA). *Liabilities* fall into two principal categories: deposits made by and owed to various customers (D) and nondeposit borrowings of funds in the money and capital markets (NDB). Finally, *equity capital* represents long-term funds the owners contribute (EC). (See Table 5–1.) Therefore, the bank's *balance sheet identity* can be written:

$$C + S + L + MA = D + NDB + EC \qquad \text{(5–2)}$$

Cash assets (C) are designed to meet a bank's need for *liquidity* (i.e., immediately spendable cash) in order to meet deposit withdrawals, customer demands for loans, and other unexpected or immediate cash needs. Security holdings (S) are a backup source of liquidity and provide another source of income. Loans (L) are made principally to supply income, while miscellaneous assets (MA) are usually dominated by fixed assets (plant and equipment) and investments in subsidiaries (if any). Deposits (D) are typically the main source of funding for banks, with nondeposit borrowings (NDB) carried out mainly to supplement deposits and provide the additional liquidity that cash assets and securities cannot provide. Finally, equity capital (EC) supplies the long-term, relatively stable base of financial support upon which the financial firm will rely to grow and to cover any extraordinary losses it incurs.

TABLE 5–1

Key Items on Bank
Financial Statements

The Balance Sheet (Report of Condition)	
Assets—Uses of Funds (includes financial outputs)	**Liabilities & Equity—Sources of Funds (includes financial inputs)**
Cash and deposits in other institutions (primary reserves) Securities for liquidity (secondary reserves) Securities for investment (the income-generating portion) Loans and leases Miscellaneous assets (buildings, equipment, etc.)	Deposits (demand, NOWs, money market, savings and time) Nondeposit borrowings Equity capital from shareholders (stock, surplus, and retained earnings)

Note: Total sources of funds must equal total uses of funds (Total assets = Total liabilities + Equity capital).

The Income Statement or The Statement of Earnings and Expenses (Report of Income)

Revenues (financial outputs from making use of funds and other resources to produce and sell services)
Interest income from loans and investments
Noninterest income (fee income from miscellaneous sources)

Expenses (financial inputs—the cost of acquiring funds and other resources needed for the sale of services)
Interest paid on deposits
Interest paid on nondeposit borrowings
Salaries and wages (employee compensation)
Provision for loan losses (allocations to reserves for loan losses)
Other expenses

Pretax net operating income (revenues – expenses listed above)
Taxes
Gains or losses from trading in securities

Net income (Pretax net operating income – taxes + securities gains – securities losses)

Note: Total revenues minus Total expenses equal Net earnings (Net income).

One useful way to view the balance sheet identity is to note that liabilities and equity capital represent *accumulated sources of funds*, which provide the needed spending power to acquire assets. A bank's assets, on the other hand, are its *accumulated uses of funds*, which are made to generate income for its stockholders, pay interest to its depositors, and compensate its employees for their labor and skill. Thus, the balance sheet identity can be pictured simply as:

Key URL

Key financial reports for all publicly traded companies are available through Edgar at **www.sec.gov**.

$$\begin{matrix} \text{Accumulated uses} \\ \text{of funds} \\ (\text{assets}) \end{matrix} = \begin{matrix} \text{Accumulated sources} \\ \text{of funds} \\ (\text{liabilities and equity capital}) \end{matrix} \qquad (5\text{–}3)$$

Clearly, each use of funds must be backed by a source of funds, so that accumulated uses of funds must equal accumulated sources of funds.

Of course, in the real world, balance sheets vary both in composition and complexity. For instance, if you visit the FDIC's Statistics for Depository Institutions (SDI) Web site, you can generate the Report of Condition for a bank or for an aggregation of all banks belonging to a holding company. On the other hand, you could go to the holding company's Web site or the Web site of the U.S. Securities and Exchange Commission (**www.sec.gov**) and access the balance sheet for the entire financial-services organization. These balance sheets are more complicated than the simple sources and uses statement we have just discussed because each item on the balance sheet contains several components.

If you are looking for the simple highlights of a balance sheet for an individual financial firm, a good place to start is Standard and Poor's Stock Report. In Table 5–2 you will

TABLE 5–2
Highlighted Bank
Balance Sheet Data
from S&P's Stock
Reports

Balance Sheet Data (million $)	J. P. Morgan Chase & Co. (12/31/2004)	National City Corp. (12/31/2004)
Money market assets	$ 390,168	$ 303
Investment securities	149,675	10,518
Commercial loans	170,676	40,847
Other loans	231,438	59,290
Total assets	1,157,248	139,280
Demand deposits	136,188	47,916
Time deposits	385,268	38,039
Long-term debt	105,718	28,444
Common equity	105,314	12,804

find many of the key balance sheet items just discussed as reported by S&P for two very large financial corporations—J. P. Morgan Chase and Co. and National City Corp. J. P. Morgan, one of the largest bank holding companies in the world with close to $1.2 trillion in assets at the close of 2004, is compared with National City Corp., which is among the largest domestic U.S. holding companies with assets of close to $140 billion. National City Corp. is used in several of this text's chapters to illustrate real world banking data.

In Table 5–3 you will find bank holding company data collected from the FDIC's SDI Web site for National City Corp. (Note that the balance sheet figures reported by the

TABLE 5–3
Report of Condition
(Balance Sheet) for
National City
Corporation

Financial data is from the FDIC Web site for the Bank Holding Company. The dollar amounts represent combined amounts for all FDIC-insured bank and thrift subsidiaries, and do *not* reflect nondeposit subsidiaries or parent companies.

National City Corporation
(Note: Dollar figures in thousands)

Date	12/31/2004	12/31/2003
Total assets	**$144,802,221**	**$131,683,868**
Cash and due from depository institutions	8,744,393	12,098,574
Investment securities	8,221,252	6,224,870
Federal funds sold and reverse repurchase agreements	2,474,898	8,393,385
Gross loans and leases	113,181,843	96,223,410
(less) Loan loss allowance	1,187,909	1,125,330
Trading account assets	268,983	216,154
Bank premises and fixed assets	1,254,640	1,045,266
Other real estate owned	89,362	97,865
Goodwill and other intangibles	5,051,313	2,264,972
All other assets	6,703,446	6,244,702
Total liabilities and capital	**$144,802,221**	**$131,683,868**
Total liabilities	**130,924,661**	**122,080,582**
Total deposits	90,491,765	73,499,065
Federal funds purchased and repurchase agreements	8,127,367	14,956,262
Trading liabilities	0	0
Other borrowed funds	25,721,773	26,602,895
Subordinated debt	2,306,409	2,079,955
All other liabilities	4,277,347	4,942,405
Total equity capital	**$ 13,877,560**	**$ 9,603,286**
Perpetual preferred stock	0	0
Common stock	329,984	277,324
Surplus	7,269,528	3,375,913
Undivided profits	6,278,048	5,950,049

Key URLs
The most complete sources for viewing the financial statements of individual banks in the United States are at **www2.fdic.gov/sdi** and **www.ffiec.gov/nic/**.

FDIC for National City Corp. differ somewhat from the figures presented in Standard and Poor's Stock Report, reflecting in part differences in the components of the National City Corp. holding company that are included in each report.) Let's take a closer look at the principal components of this banking firm's Report of Condition.

Assets of the Banking Firm

Cash and Due from Depository Institutions   The first asset item normally listed on a banking firm's Report of Condition is *cash and due from depository institutions*. This item includes cash held in the bank's vault, any deposits placed with other depository institutions (usually called *correspondent deposits*), cash items in the process of collection (mainly uncollected checks), and the banking firm's reserve account held with the Federal Reserve bank in the region. The cash and due from depository institutions is also referred to as *primary reserves*. This means that these assets are the first line of defense against customer deposit withdrawals and the first source of funds to look to when a customer comes in with a loan request. Normally, banks strive to keep the size of this account as low as possible, because cash balances earn little or no interest income. Note that the $8,744 million in cash and due from other depository institutions listed in Table 5–3 for National City Corporation represented just over 6 percent of its total assets of $144,802 million as of December 31, 2004.

Investment Securities: The Liquid Portion   A second line of defense to meet demands for cash is liquid security holdings, often called *secondary reserves* or referenced on regulatory reports as "available for sale." These typically include holdings of short-term government securities and privately issued money market securities, including interest-bearing time deposits held with other banking firms and commercial paper. Secondary reserves occupy the middle ground between cash assets and loans, earning some income but held mainly for the ease with which they can be converted into cash on short notice. In Table 5–3, some portion of the $8,221 million shown as investment securities held by this banking firm will serve as a secondary reserve to help deal with liquidity needs.

Investment Securities: The Income-Generating Portion   Bonds, notes, and other securities held primarily for their expected rate of return or yield are known simply as *investment securities*. (These are called held-to-maturity securities on regulatory reports.) Frequently investments are divided into *taxable securities*—for example, U.S. government bonds and notes, securities issued by various federal agencies (such as the Federal National Mortgage Association or Fannie Mae), and corporate bonds and notes—and *tax-exempt securities*, which consist principally of state and local government (municipal) bonds. The latter generate interest income that is exempt from federal income taxes.

Investment securities may be recorded on the books of a banking firm at their original cost or at market value, whichever is lower. Of course, if interest rates rise after the securities are purchased, their market value will be less than their original cost (book value). Therefore, banks that record securities on their balance sheets at cost often include a parenthetical note giving the securities' current market value. Accounting rules for banking firms are changing— the trend is toward replacing original or historical cost figures with current market values.

Trading Account Assets   Securities purchased to provide short-term profits from short-term price movements are not included in "Securities" on the Report of Condition. They are reported as trading account assets. In Table 5–3, about $269 million is reported for National City Corporation. If the banking firm serves as a security dealer, the securities acquired for resale are included here. The amount recorded in the trading account is valued at market.

Federal Funds Sold and Reverse Repurchase Agreements   A type of loan account listed as a separate item on the Report of Condition is *federal funds sold and reverse repurchase agreements*. This item includes mainly temporary loans (usually extended overnight, with the funds returned the next day) made to other depository institutions, securities dealers, or even major industrial corporations. The funds for these temporary loans often come from the reserves a bank has on deposit with the Federal Reserve Bank in its district—hence the name *federal funds*. Some of these temporary credits are extended in the form of reverse re-purchase (resale) agreements (RPs) in which the banking firm acquires temporary title to securities owned by the borrower and holds those securities as collateral until the loan is paid off (normally after only a few days).

Loans and Leases   By far the largest asset item is *loans and leases*, which generally ac-count for half to almost three-quarters of the total value of all bank assets. A bank's loan account typically is broken down into several groups of similar type loans. For example, one commonly used breakdown is by the *purpose* for borrowing money. In this case, we may see listed on a banking firm's balance sheet the following loan types:

1. Commercial and industrial (or business) loans.
2. Consumer (or household) loans; on regulatory reports these are referenced as Loans to Individuals.
3. Real estate (or property-based) loans.
4. Financial institutions loans (such as loans made to other depository institutions as well as to nonbank financial institutions).
5. Foreign (or international) loans (extended to foreign governments and institutions).
6. Agricultural production loans (or farm loans, extended primarily to farmers and ranch-ers to harvest crops and raise livestock).
7. Security loans (to aid investors and dealers in their trading activities).
8. Leases (usually consisting of the bank buying equipment for business firms and making that equipment available for the firms' use for a stipulated period of time in return for a series of rental payments—the functional equivalent of a regular loan).

As we will see in Chapter 16, bank loans can be broken down in other ways, too, such as by maturity (i.e., short-term versus long-term), by collateral (i.e., secured versus unse-cured), or by their pricing terms (i.e., floating-rate versus fixed-rate loans).

The two loan figures—gross loans and leases and net loans and leases—nearly always appear on bank balance sheets. The larger of the two, *gross loans and leases,* is the sum of all outstanding IOUs owed to the banking firm. In Table 5–3 gross loans and leases amounted to $113,182 million in the most recent year, or about 78 percent of total assets.

Loan Losses   However, loan losses, both current and projected, are deducted from the amount of this total (gross) loan figure. Under current U.S. tax law, depository institutions are allowed to build up a reserve for future loan losses, called the *allowance for loan losses* (ALL), from their flow of income based on their recent loan-loss experience. The ALL, which is a contra-asset account, represents an accumulated reserve against which loans de-clared to be uncollectible can be charged off. This means that bad loans normally do not affect current income. Rather, when a loan is considered uncollectible, the accounting de-partment will write (charge) it off the books by reducing the ALL account by the amount of the uncollectible loan while simultaneously decreasing the asset account for gross loans.

For example, suppose a bank granted a $10 million loan to a property development company to build a shopping center and the company subsequently went out of business.

Factoid
Did you know that the total financial assets of the commercial banking industry operating in the United States in 2005, totaling more than $9.3 trillion, was more than three times the financial assets held by the entire thrift industry (including savings and loan associations, savings banks, and credit unions combined)?

Another Way of Classifying Banks: By the Types of Assets They Hold

Recently the Federal Deposit Insurance Corporation and other regulatory agencies have been grouping depository institutions (DIs) by the make-up of their assets. The table below illustrates the different types of U.S. DIs grouped by the types of assets they hold (Asset Concentrations):

Type of Bank	Definition	Number of U.S. DIs in 2005
International	Assets over $10 billion with more than 25% of assets in foreign offices	5
Agricultural	Over 25% of total loans and leases in agricultural loans and real estate loans secured by farmland	1730
Credit Card	Credit-card loans and securitized receivables over 50% of assets plus securitized receivables	34
Commercial Lenders	Commercial and industrial loans and loans secured by commercial real estate over 25% of total assets	4424
Mortgage Lenders	Residential mortgage loans and mortgage-backed securities over 50% of total assets	990
Consumer Lenders	Loans to individuals (including residential mortgages and credit-card loans) over 50% of total assets	132
Other Specialized	Assets under $1 billion and loans and leases less than 40% of total assets	465
All Other	Significant lending activity with no identified asset concentrations	1146
Total of All U.S. Insured Depository Institutions, First Quarter 2005		8975

Source: Federal Deposit Insurance Corporation, *Quarterly Banking Profile*, First Quarter 2005.

Key URL
The National Information Center, which supplies financial reports for bank holding companies, banks, savings and loan associations, credit unions, and international banking organizations, is reachable at **www.ffiec.gov/nic/pubweb/nicweb/nichome.aspx**.

If the bank could reasonably expect to collect only $1 million of the original $10 million owed, the unpaid $9 million would be subtracted from total (gross) loans and from the ALL account.

The allowance for possible loan losses is built up gradually over time by annual deductions from current income. These deductions appear on the banking firm's income and expense statement (or Report of Income) as a noncash expense item called the *provision for loan losses* (PLL). For example, suppose a banking firm anticipated loan losses this year of $1 million and held $100 million already in its ALL account. It would take a noncash charge against its current revenues, entering $1 million in the provision for loan-loss account (PLL) on its Report of Income. Thus:

Amount reported on the income and expense statement

Annual provision for loan-loss expense (PLL) = $1 million, a noncash expense item deducted from current revenues

↓ Then adjust the banking firm's balance sheet, in its ALL account, as follows:

Allowance for loan losses (ALL) = $100 million + $1 million (from PLL on the current income and expense statement)

= $101 million

Now suppose the bank subsequently discovers that its truly worthless loans, which must be written off, total only $500,000. Then we would have:

Beginning balance in the allowance for loan loss account (ALL)	= $100 million
+	
This year's provision for loan losses (PLL)	= +$1 million
= Adjusted allowance for loan losses (ALL)	= $101 million
− Actual charge-offs of worthless loans	−$500,000
= Net allowance for loan losses (ALL) after all charge-offs	= $100.5 million

At about the same time suppose that management discovers it has been able to recover some of the funds (say $1.5 million) that it had previously charged off as losses on earlier loans. Often this belated cash inflow arises because the banking firm was able to take possession of and then sell the collateral that a borrower had pledged behind his or her defaulted loan. These so-called *recoveries*, then, are added back to the allowance for loan-loss account (ALL) as follows:

Net allowance for loan losses (ALL) after all charge-offs	= $100.5 million
+ Recoveries from previously charged-off loans	= + $1.5 million
= Ending balance in the allowance for loan loss account (ALL)	= $102.0 million

If writing off a large loan reduces the balance in the ALL account too much, management will be called upon (often by examiners representing its principal regulatory agency) to increase the annual PPL deduction (which will lower its current net income) in order to restore the ALL to a safer level. Additions to ALL are usually made as the loan portfolio grows in size, when any sizable loan is judged to be completely or partially uncollectible, or when an unexpected loan default occurs that has not already been reserved. The required accounting entries simply increase the contra-asset ALL and the expense account PLL. The total amount in the loan-loss reserve (ALL) as of the date of the Report of Condition is then deducted from gross loans to help derive the account entry called *net loans* on the banking firm's balance sheet—a measure of the net realizable value of all loans outstanding.

Specific and General Reserves Many financial firms divide the ALL account into two parts: specific reserves and general reserves. *Specific reserves* are set aside to cover a particular loan or loans expected to be a problem or that represent above-average risk. Management may simply designate a portion of the reserves already in the ALL account as specific reserves or add more reserves to cover specific loan problems. The remaining reserves in the loan-loss account are called *general reserves*. This division of loan-loss reserves helps managers better understand their institutions need for protection against current or future loan defaults. (See especially Walter [9] and O'Toole [6].)

Reserves for loan losses are determined by management; however, they are influenced by tax laws and government regulations. The Tax Reform Act of 1986 mandated that only loans actually declared worthless could be expensed through the loan-loss provision (PLL) expense item for large banking companies (with assets over $500 million) for tax purposes. This has motivated a backward-looking rather than a forward-looking process. In Chapter 15, we will see that total loan loss reserves (the ALL account) are counted as Supplemental capital up to 1.25 percent of a bank's total risk-weighted assets. However, retained earnings (undivided profits) are counted fully as permanent capital. This difference in regulatory treatment encourages management to build retained earnings at the cost of the

ALL account. Thus the dollar amount expensed through PLL and allocated to the ALL account on the balance sheet is influenced by tax laws and government regulations.

International Loan Reserves   The largest U.S. banks that make international loans to lesser-developed countries are required to set aside *allocated transfer-risk reserves* (ATRs). ATRs were created to help American banks deal with possible losses on loans made to lesser-developed countries. Like the ALL account, the ATR total is deducted from gross loans to help determine net loans. These international-related reserve requirements are established by the Intercountry Exposure Review Committee (ICERC), which consists of representatives from the Federal Deposit Insurance Corporation, the Federal Reserve System, and the Comptroller of the Currency.

Unearned Discount Income   This item consists of interest income on loans received from customers, but not yet earned under the accrual method of accounting banks use today. For example, if a customer receives a loan and pays all or some portion of the interest up front, the banking firm cannot record that interest payment as earned income because the customer involved has not yet had use of the loan for any length of time. Over the life of the loan, the bank will gradually earn the interest income and will transfer the necessary amounts from unearned discount to the interest income account.

Nonperforming (noncurrent) Loans   Banks have another loan category on their books called *nonperforming (noncurrent) loans*, which are credits that no longer accrue interest income or that have had to be restructured to accommodate a borrower's changed circumstances. A loan is placed in the nonperforming category when any scheduled loan repayment is past due for more than 90 days. Once a loan is classified as "nonperforming," any accrued interest recorded on the books, but not actually received, must be deducted from loan revenues. The bank is then forbidden to record any additional interest income from the loan until a cash payment actually comes in.

Key URL
To view the services offered and the recent financial history of the Bank of America, one of the best known and largest banks in the United States, see **www.bankofamerica .com**.

Bank Premises and Fixed Assets   Bank assets also include the net (adjusted for depreciation) value of buildings and equipment. A banking firm usually devotes only a small percentage (less than 2 percent) of its assets to the institution's physical plant—that is, the fixed assets represented by buildings and equipment needed to carry on daily operations. In Table 5–3 National City Corporation has less than 1 percent of its assets ($1,255 million) devoted to premises and fixed assets. Indeed, the great majority of a bank's assets are financial claims (loans and investment securities) rather than fixed assets. However, fixed assets typically generate fixed operating costs in the form of depreciation expenses, property taxes, and so on, which provide *operating leverage*, enabling the institution to boost its operating earnings if it can increase its sales volume high enough and earn more from using its fixed assets than those assets cost. But with so few fixed assets relative to other assets, banks cannot rely heavily on operating leverage to increase their earnings; they must instead rely mainly upon *financial leverage*—the use of borrowed funds—to boost their earnings and remain competitive with other industries in attracting capital.

Other Real Estate Owned (OREO)   This asset category includes direct and indirect investments in real estate. When bankers speak of OREOs, they are not talking about two chocolate cookies with sweet white cream in the middle! The principal component of OREO is commercial and residential properties obtained to compensate for nonperforming loans. While "kids" may want as many Oreos as possible, bankers like to keep the OREO account small by lending funds to borrowers who will make payments in a timely fashion.

Goodwill and Other Intangible Assets   Most banking firms have some purchased assets lacking physical substance. *Goodwill* occurs when a firm acquires another firm and pays more than the market value of its net assets (assets less liabilities). Other intangible assets include mortgage servicing rights and purchased credit card relationships. In Table 5–3, we note that Goodwill and Other Intangible Assets at National City Corporation account for 3.49 percent of that bank's assets.

All Other Assets   This group of assets accounts for just under 5 percent of National City's assets in Table 5–3. This account includes investments in subsidiary firms, customers' liability on acceptances outstanding, income earned but not collected on loans, net deferred tax assets, excess residential mortgage servicing fees receivable, and all other assets.

Liabilities of the Banking Firm

Deposits   The principal liability of any bank is its *deposits*, representing financial claims held by businesses, households, and governments against the banking firm. In the event a bank is liquidated, the proceeds from the sale of its assets must first be used to pay off the claims of its depositors (along with the IRS!). Other creditors and the stockholders receive whatever funds remain. There are five major types of deposits:

1. *Noninterest-bearing demand deposits*, or regular checking accounts, generally permit unlimited check writing. But, under federal regulations, they cannot pay any explicit interest rate (though many banks offer to pay postage costs and offer other "free" services that yield the demand deposit customer an implicit rate of return).
2. *Savings deposits* generally bear the lowest rate of interest offered to depositors but may be of any denomination (though most depository institutions impose a minimum size requirement) and permit the customer to withdraw at will.
3. *NOW accounts*, which can be held by individuals and nonprofit institutions, bear interest and permit drafts (checks) to be written against each account to pay third parties.
4. *Money market deposit accounts* (MMDAs) can pay whatever interest rate the offering institution feels is competitive and have limited check-writing privileges attached. No minimum denomination or maturity is required by law, though depository institutions must reserve the right to require seven days' notice before any withdrawals are made.
5. *Time deposits* (mainly certificates of deposit, or CDs) usually carry a fixed maturity (term) and a stipulated interest rate but may be of any denomination, maturity, and yield agreed upon by the offering institution and its depositor. Included are large ($100,000-plus) *negotiable CDs*—interest-bearing deposits that depository institutions use to raise money from their most well-to-do customers.

The bulk of deposits are held by individuals and business firms. However, governments (federal, state, and local) also hold substantial deposit accounts, known as *public fund deposits*. Any time a school district sells bonds to construct a new school building, for example, the proceeds of the bond issue will flow into its deposit in a local depository institution. Similarly, when the U.S. Treasury collects taxes or sells securities to raise funds, the proceeds normally flow initially into public deposits that the Treasury has established in thousands of depository institutions across the United States. Major banks also draw upon their foreign branch offices for deposits and record the amounts received from abroad simply as *deposits at foreign branches*.

Clearly, as Table 5–3 suggests, many banking firms are heavily dependent upon their deposits, which today often support between 70 and 80 percent of their total assets. In the case of the bank we are analyzing, total deposits of $90,492 million funded 62 percent of its assets in the most recent year. Because these financial claims of the public are often volatile and because they are so large relative to the owners' capital (equity) investment in the banking firm, the average depository institution has considerable exposure to failure risk. It must continually stand ready (be liquid) to meet deposit withdrawals. These twin pressures of risk and liquidity force bankers to exercise caution in their choices of loans and other assets. Failure to do so threatens the institution with collapse under the weight of depositors' claims.

Borrowings from Nondeposit Sources   Although deposits typically represent the largest portion of funds sources, sizable amounts of funds also stem from miscellaneous liability accounts. All other factors held equal, the larger the depository institution, the greater use it tends to make of *nondeposit sources of funds*. One reason borrowings from nondeposit funds sources have grown rapidly in recent years is that there are no reserve requirements or insurance fees on most of these funds, which lowers the cost of nondeposit funding. Also, borrowings in the money market usually can be arranged in a few minutes and the funds wired immediately to the depository institution that needs them. One drawback, however, is that interest rates on nondeposit funds are highly volatile. If there is even a hint of financial problems at an institution trying to borrow from these sources, its borrowing costs can rise rapidly, or money market lenders may simply refuse to extend it any more credit.

The most important nondeposit funding source for most depository institutions, typically, is represented by *federal funds purchased and repurchase agreements*. This account tracks temporary borrowings in the money market, mainly from reserves loaned by other institutions (federal funds purchased) or from repurchase agreements in which the financial firm has borrowed funds collateralized by some of its own securities from another institution. Other borrowed funds that may be drawn upon include short-term borrowings such as *borrowing reserves from the discount windows of the Federal Reserve banks, issuing commercial paper,* or *borrowing in the Eurocurrency market from multinational banks.* In the worldwide banking system, *Eurocurrency borrowings* (i.e., transferable time deposits denominated in a variety of currencies) represent the principal source of short-term borrowings by banks. Many banks also issue *long-term debt,* including real estate mortgages, for the purpose of constructing new office facilities or modernizing plant and equipment. Subordinated debt (notes and debentures) are yet another source of funds that are identified on the Report of Condition. This category includes *limited-life preferred stock* (that is, preferred stock that eventually matures) and any noncollateralized borrowings. The *other liabilities* account serves as a catch-all of miscellaneous amounts owed, such as a deferred tax liability and obligations to pay off investors who hold bankers' acceptances.

Equity Capital for the Banking Firm   The equity capital accounts on a depository institution's Report of Condition represent the owners' (stockholders') share of the business. Every new financial firm begins with a minimum amount of owners' capital and then borrows funds from the public to "lever up" its operations. In fact, financial institutions are among the most heavily leveraged (debt-financed) of all businesses. Their capital accounts normally represent less than 10 percent of the value of their total assets. In the case of the bank whose balance sheet appears in Table 5–3, the *stockholders' equity capital* of $13,878 million in the most recent year accounted for less than 10 percent of its total assets.

Bank capital accounts typically include many of the same items that other business corporations display on their balance sheets. They list the total par (face) value of *common stock outstanding.* When that stock is sold for more than its par value, the excess market value of the stock flows into a *surplus* account. Few banking firms issue *preferred stock,*

E-BANKING AND E-COMMERCE

THE IMPACT OF DEPOSITORS' CHOICES AMONG ELECTRONIC BANKING FACILITIES ON BANK FINANCIAL STATEMENTS

Electronic banking facilities, including automated teller machines (ATMs), point-of-sale (POS) terminals, and telephone and online banking connections, continue to grow. Customers expect these electronic conveniences today and the managers of financial firms continue to invest in new electronic technology. According to the EFT Data Book the number of ATMs increased by just over 3 percent between March 2003 and 2004. However, during this same period ATM monthly transactions volume grew less than 2 percent and the average volume of transactions per ATM decreased. Depositors appear to be using ATMs less frequently, on average, but are using their debit cards at POS terminals in retail stores at a rapidly increasing rate. The volume of debit transactions at POS terminals increased a whopping 25 percent during the same period!

Will managers of depository institutions complain as their depositors increasingly substitute POS transactions for ATM transactions? Not likely. While most ATMs are purchased and operated by depository institutions, most POS terminals are owned and operated by merchants. The purchase of new ATMs increases a depository institution's investment in the asset account labeled "Bank Premises and Fixed Assets" on the Report of Condition. In contrast, the expansion of new POS terminals usually requires no investment on the part of a depository institution. The value of Bank Premises and Fixed Assets relative to total industry assets has been declining through most of the past decade. For example, in 1996 the ratio of premises and fixed assets to total bank assets stood at 1.41 percent but then fell steadily to only 1.02 percent of all banking assets in June of 2005.

The income from fees charged when ATMs are used or that may arise from POS transactions is included in the "Other Noninterest Income" account found on a depository institution's Report of Income. The volume of "Other Noninterest Income" relative to total industry assets generally has been decreasing in volume, falling from 0.82 percent of all bank assets in 2001 to 0.74 percent in 2005. The foregoing changes in accounting entries on the balance sheet and income statement reflect the efforts of depositors to minimize the cost of their financial transactions.

which guarantees its holders an annual dividend before common stockholders receive any dividend payments. *Perpetual preferred stock* is part of equity capital, while *limited-life preferred stock* is usually listed as debt capital. Preferred stock is generally viewed in the banking community as expensive to issue, principally because the annual dividend is not tax deductible, and a drain on the earnings that normally would flow to stockholders, though the largest bank holding companies have issued substantial amounts of preferred shares in recent years.

Usually, the largest item in the capital account is *retained earnings* (undivided profits), which represent accumulated net income left over each year after payment of stockholder dividends. There may also be a *contingency reserve* held as protection against unforeseen losses and *treasury stock* that has been retired.

Comparative Balance Sheet Ratios for Different Size Banks

The items discussed previously generally appear on all bank balance sheets, regardless of size. But the relative importance of each balance sheet item varies greatly with bank size. A good illustration of how bank size affects the mix of balance sheet items is shown in Table 5–4. For example, larger banks tend to trade securities for short-term profits while smaller, community-oriented banks do not. Smaller banks hold more investment securities and loans relative to assets than larger depository institutions. Smaller community banks rely more heavily on deposits to support their assets than do larger depository institutions, while larger institutions make heavier use of money market borrowings (such as the purchase of Eurocurrencies or federal funds). Clearly, the analyst examining a bank's financial condition must consider the *size* of the institution and compare it to other institutions of the same size and serving a similar market.

TABLE 5–4
The Composition of Bank Balance Statements (Percentage Mix of Sources and Uses of Funds for Year-End 2004)

Source: Federal Deposit Insurance Corporation.

Assets, Liabilities, and Equity Capital Items	Percentage of Total Assets for:			
	All U.S. Insured Banks	U.S. Banks with Less than $100 Million in Total Assets	U.S. Banks with $100 Million to $1 Billion in Total Assets	U.S. Banks with More than $1 Billion in Total Assets
Total assets	**100.00%**	**100.00%**	**100.00%**	**100.00%**
Cash and due from depository institutions	4.61	5.29	3.75	4.70
Interest-bearing balances	1.83	1.67	0.85	1.96
Securities	18.44	24.74	22.08	17.80
Federal funds sold and reverse repurchase agreements	4.58	4.63	2.60	4.84
Net loans and leases	57.43	60.81	66.39	56.16
Loan loss allowance	0.87	0.89	0.94	0.87
Trading account assets	5.99	0.00*	0.01	6.93
Bank premises and fixed assets	1.03	1.86	1.84	0.90
Other real estate owned	0.05	0.15	0.12	0.03
Goodwill and other intangibles	3.27	0.34	0.72	3.68
All other assets	4.61	2.18	2.50	4.95
Total liabilities and capital	**100.00%**	**100.00%**	**100.00%**	**100.00%**
Total liabilities	**89.89**	**88.48**	**90.01**	**89.92**
Total deposits	66.48	83.69	80.85	64.14
Interest-bearing deposits	53.96	69.60	67.27	51.81
Federal funds purchased and repurchase agreements	6.87	0.91	2.53	7.59
Trading liabilities	3.33	0.00*	0.00*	3.86
Other borrowed funds	8.75	3.28	5.74	9.29
Subordinated debt	1.31	0.01	0.08	1.50
All other liabilities	3.15	0.60	0.79	3.52
Equity capital	10.11	11.52	9.99	10.08

*Less than 0.005 percent. Totals may not exactly equal 100% due to rounding.

Recent Expansion of Off-Balance-Sheet Items in Banking

The balance sheet, although a good place to start, does not tell the whole story about a financial firm. For more of the story we must turn to "off-balance-sheet items" that will be explored in greater detail in Chapters 8 and 9. Financial firms offer their customers a number of fee-based services that normally do not show up on the balance sheet. Prominent examples of these off-balance-sheet items include:

1. *Unused commitments*, in which a lender receives a fee to lend up to a certain amount of money over a defined period of time; however, these funds have not yet been transferred from lender to borrower.

2. *Standby credit agreements*, in which a financial firm receives a fee to guarantee repayment of a loan that a customer has received from another lender.

3. *Derivative contracts*, in which a financial institution has the potential to make a profit or incur a loss on an asset that it presently does not own. This category includes futures contracts, options, and swaps that can be used to hedge credit risk, interest rate risk, or foreign exchange risk.

The problem with these off-balance-sheet transactions is that they often expose a financial firm to considerable risk that conventional financial reports simply won't pick up. Unauthorized trading in derivatives has created notorious losses for financial institutions

Factoid
Other than commercial banks what financial-service industry holds the most deposits received from the public?
Answer: Savings and loans and savings banks at more than $1 trillion in early 2005.

Filmtoid
What 1999 British drama tells the story of how one trader's risk exposure resulted in losses that closed the doors of England's oldest merchant bank, Barings?
Answer: *Rogue Trader.*

around the world. For example, in 1995 Nicholas Leeson's estimated losses from trading futures contracts amounted to $1.4 billion and led to the collapse of Barings—Great Britain's 242-year-old merchant bank.

Off-balance-sheet items have grown so rapidly that they exceed total bank assets many times over, as illustrated in Table 5–5. These contingent contracts are heavily concentrated in the largest banks where their nominal value recently was more than 13 times the volume of these banks' on-balance-sheet assets. For the largest banking firms—those institutions holding more than a billion dollars in assets—approximately 93 percent of their off-balance-sheet items arose from derivatives carrying a notional value of more than $88 billion. (Warning!! Do not give too much relevance to the *notional* value of derivative contracts for it is the gains or losses associated with these contracts that are important, not their face amount. Off-balance-sheet activities can be used to either increase or decrease a financial firm's risk exposure.)

The Financial Accounting Standard's Board (FASB) Statement No. 133—Accounting for Derivative Instruments and Hedging Activities—is designed to make derivatives more publicly visible on corporate financial statements and to capture the impact of hedging transactions on corporate earnings. Gains or losses on derivative contracts must be marked to market value as they accrue, which affects a financial firm's Report of Income and may increase the volatility of its earnings. Moreover, heavily regulated financial firms must connect their use of hedging contracts to actual risk exposures in their operations (thereby curbing speculative use of derivatives).

Factoid
What has been the leading source of new funds for U.S. banks thus far during the 21st century?
Answer: Savings deposits, particularly Money Market Deposit Accounts.

The Problem of Book-Value Accounting

A broader public confidence issue concerns how bankers and other financial-firm managers have recorded the value of their assets and liabilities for, literally, generations. The banking industry, for example, has followed the practice of recording assets and liabilities

TABLE 5–5 Off-Balance-Sheet Items Reported by U.S. Banks

Source: Federal Deposit Insurance Corporation.

Off-Balance-Sheet Items	Total Off-Balance-Sheet Items Reported by U.S. Banks Arranged by Size Group (in Billions of Dollars) on December 31, 2004			
	Total Volume in Billions of Dollars at All U.S. Insured Banks	U.S. Insured Banks under $100 Million in Total Assets	U.S. Insured Banks $100 Million to $1 Billion in Total Assets	U.S. Insured Banks $1 Billion or More in Total Assets
Total unused commitments	$ 5,813.68	$ 69.88	$272.39	$ 5,471.41
Standby letters of credit and foreign office guarantees	409.90	0.51	6.90	402.50
(Amount conveyed to others)	−72.20	−0.01	−0.40	−71.79
Commercial letters of credit	28.37	0.08	0.88	27.41
Securities lent	1,165.31	0.05	0.88	1,164.38
Derivatives				
Notional amount of credit derivatives	2,346.69	0.00*	0.06	2,346.63
Interest rate contracts	75,518.57	0.06	6.35	75,512.17
Foreign exchange rate contracts	9,025.42	0.00*	0.03	9,025.39
Contracts on other commodities and equities	1,400.81	0.03	0.26	1,400.52
All other off-balance sheet liabilities	49.34	0.19	1.57	47.58
Total off-balance-sheet items	95,685.90	70.80	288.91	95,326.20
Total assets (on-balance sheet)	8,413.08	189.04	953.40	7,270.64
Off-balance-sheet items ÷ On-balance sheet assets	1137.35%	37.45%	30.30%	1311.11%

*Less than $50 million

at their *original cost* on the day they are posted or received. This accounting practice, known as *book-value, historical,* or *original cost accounting,* has come under attack in recent years. The book-value accounting method assumes that all balance-sheet items will be held to maturity. It does not reflect the impact on a balance sheet of changing interest rates and changing default risk, which affect both the value and cash flows associated with loans, security holdings, and debt.

While we usually say that most assets are valued at historical or original cost, the traditional bank accounting procedure should really be called *amortized cost.* For example, if a loan's principal is gradually paid off over time, a bank will deduct from the original face value of the loan the amount of any repayments of loan principal, thus reflecting the fact that the amount owed by the borrowing customer is being amortized downward over time as loan payments are received. Similarly, if a security is acquired at a discounted price below its par (face) value, the spread between the security's original discounted value and its value at maturity will be amortized upward over time as additional income until the security reaches maturity.

For example, if market interest rates on government bonds maturing in one year are currently at 10 percent, a $1,000 par-value bond promising an annual interest (coupon) rate of 10 percent would sell at a current market price of $1,000. However, if market interest rates rise to 12 percent, the value of the bond must fall to about $980 so that the investment return from this asset is also about 12 percent.

Similarly, changes in the default risk exposure of borrowers will affect the market value of loans. Clearly, if some loans are less likely to be repaid than was true when they were granted, their market value must be lower. For example, a $1,000 loan for a year granted to a borrower at a loan rate of 10 percent must fall in market value if the borrower's financial situation deteriorates. If interest rates applicable to other borrowers in the same higher risk class stand at 12 percent, the $1,000, one-year loan will decline to about $980 in market value. Recording assets at their original (or historical) cost and never changing that number to reflect current market conditions does not give depositors, stockholders, and other investors interested in buying the stock or debt of a financial firm a true picture of the firm's real financial condition. Investors could easily be deceived.

Under the historical or book-value accounting system, interest rate changes do not affect the value of a bank's capital because they do not affect the value of its assets and liabilities recorded at cost. Moreover, only realized capital gains and losses affect the book values shown on a bank's balance sheet. Banks can increase their current income and their capital, for example, by selling assets that have risen in value while ignoring the impact of any losses in value experienced by other assets still on the books.

In the summer of 1992, FASB issued Rule 115, which focuses primarily upon investments in marketable securities, probably the easiest balance sheet item to value at market. The FASB asked banks to divide their security holdings into two broad groups: those they planned to hold to maturity and those that may be traded before they reach maturity. Securities that a bank plans to hold to maturity could be valued at their original cost while tradable securities would be valued at their current market price. At the same time the Securities and Exchange Commission (SEC) asked leading banks that were actively trading securities to put any securities they expected to sell into a balance sheet account labeled *assets held for sale.* These reclassified assets must be valued at cost or market, whichever is lower at the time. FASB and the SEC seem determined to eradicate "gains trading," a practice in which managers sell securities that have appreciated in order to reap a capital gain, but hold onto those securities whose prices have declined and continue to value these lower-priced instruments at their higher historical cost.

Currently, for regulatory purposes you will find securities identified as *held-to-maturity* or *available-for-sale* on the Report of Condition. The available-for-sale securities are reported at their fair market value. When we examine the schedule for securities held by a banking company, we find that both the amortized cost and the market value are often reported.

Auditing: Assuring Reliability of Financial Statements

U.S. banks (especially those holding $500 million or more in assets) are required to file with the FDIC and with the federal or state agency that chartered them financial statements audited by an independent public accountant within 90 days of the end of each fiscal year. Along with audited financial statements each depository institution must also submit a statement concerning the effectiveness of its internal controls and its compliance with safety and soundness laws. Moreover, an audit committee consisting entirely of outside directors must review and evaluate the annual audit with management and with an independent public accountant.

Larger U.S. banks, with $3 billion or more in assets, must meet even more stringent requirements for setting up outside audit committees, including requiring at least two audit committee members to have prior banking experience, prohibiting the most significant customers from serving on such a committee, and mandating that audit committees must have access to legal counsel that is independent of bank management. These tough reporting rules are designed to prevent the FDIC's insurance reserves from being drained away by bank failures.

Even tougher accounting and reporting rules emerged in 2002 in the wake of the collapse of energy-trader Enron and dozens of reports of corporate fraud. The Sarbanes-Oxley Accounting Standards Act mandates that CEOs and CFOs of publicly traded corporations certify the accuracy of their institutions' financial reports. The publication of false or misleading information may be punished with heavy fines and even jail sentences. Internal auditing and audit committees of each institution's board of directors are granted greater authority and independence in assessing the accuracy and quality of their institutions' accounting and financial reporting practices.

Concept Check

5–1. What are the principal accounts that appear on a bank's balance sheet (Report of Condition)?

5–2. Which accounts are most important and which are least important on the asset side of a bank's balance sheet?

5–3. What accounts are most important on the liability side of a balance sheet?

5–4. What are the essential differences among demand deposits, savings deposits, and time deposits?

5–5. What are primary reserves and secondary reserves and what are they supposed to do?

5–6. Suppose that a bank holds cash in its vault of $1.4 million, short-term government securities of

$12.4 million, privately issued money market instruments of $5.2 million, deposits at the Federal Reserve banks of $20.1 million, cash items in the process of collection of $0.6 million, and deposits placed with other banks of $16.4 million. How much in primary reserves does this bank hold? In secondary reserves?

5–7. What are off-balance-sheet items and why are they important to some financial firms?

5–8. Why are bank accounting practices under attack right now? In what ways could financial institutions improve their accounting methods?

5–4 Components of the Income Statement (Report of Income)

An income statement, or **Report of Income,** indicates the amount of revenue received and expenses incurred over a specific period of time. There is usually a close correlation between the size of the principal items on a bank's balance sheet (Report of Condition)

and its income statement. After all, assets on the balance sheet usually account for the majority of operating revenues, while liabilities generate many of a bank's operating expenses.

The principal source of bank revenue generally is the interest income generated by *earning assets*—mainly loans and investments. Additional revenue is provided by the *fees* charged for specific services (such as ATM usage). The major expenses incurred in generating this revenue include interest paid out to depositors; interest owed on nondeposit borrowings; the cost of equity capital; salaries, wages, and benefits paid to employees; overhead expenses associated with the physical plant; funds set aside for possible loan losses; and taxes owed.

The difference between all revenues and expenses is *net income*. Thus:

$$\text{Net income} = \text{Total revenue items} - \text{Total expense items} \qquad \textbf{(5–4)}$$

where:

Revenue Items

↓

Cash assets × average yield on cash assets

   +

security investments × average yield on security investments

   +

loans outstanding × average yield on loans

   +

miscellaneous assets × average yield on miscellaneous assets

   +

income from fiduciary activities + fee income + trading account gains

Minus (−) Expense Items

↓

Total deposits × average interest cost on deposits

   +

nondeposit borrowings × average interest cost on nondeposit borrowings

   +

owners' capital × average cost of owners' capital

   +

employee salaries, wages, and benefits expense

   +

overhead expense

   +

provision for possible loan losses

   +

miscellaneous expenses

   +

taxes owed

The previous chart on revenue and expense items reminds us that financial firms interested in increasing their net earnings (income) have a number of options available to achieve this goal: (1) increase the net yield on each asset held; (2) redistribute earning assets toward those assets that carry higher yields; (3) increase the volume of services that provide fee income; (4) increase the fees associated with various services; (5) shift their funding sources toward less-costly borrowings; (6) find ways to reduce their employee, overhead, loan-loss, and miscellaneous operating expenses; or (7) reduce their taxes owed through improved tax management practices.

Of course, management does not have full control of all of these items that affect net income. The yields earned on various assets, the revenues generated by sales of services, and the interest rates that must be paid to attract deposits and nondeposit borrowings are determined by demand and supply forces in the marketplace. Over the long run, the public will be the principal factor shaping what types of loans the financial-service provider will be able to make and what services it will be able to sell in its market area. Within the broad boundaries allowed by competition, regulation, and the pressures exerted by public demand, however, management decisions are still a major factor in determining the particular mix of loans, securities, cash, and liabilities each financial firm holds and the size and composition of its revenues and expenses.

Financial Flows and Stocks

Income statements are a record of *financial flows* over time, in contrast to the balance sheet, which is a statement of *stocks* of assets, liabilities, and equity held at any given point in time. Therefore, we can represent the income statement as a report of *financial outflows* (expenses) and *financial inflows* (revenues).

Of course, actual income reports are usually more complicated than this simple statement because each item may have several component accounts. Most bank income statements, for example, closely resemble the income statement shown in Table 5–6 for National City Corporation, the bank whose balance sheet we examined earlier. Table 5–6

TABLE 5–6
Report of Income
(Income Statement)
for National City
Corporation

Financial data is from the FDIC Web site for the bank holding company. (The dollar amounts represent combined amounts for all FDIC-insured bank and thrift subsidiaries, and do *not* reflect nondeposit subsidiaries or parent companies.) Note: all figures are expressed in thousands of dollars.

Report of Income	2004	2003	
Total interest income	$6,317,502	$6,193,817 }	Financial inflows
Total interest expense	1,848,517	1,777,250 }	Financial outflows
Net interest income	4,468,985	4,416,567	
Provision for loan and lease losses	322,920	638,193 }	Noncash financial outflows
Total noninterest income	3,960,662	3,187,461	
Fiduciary activities	258,113	250,551	
Service charges on deposit accounts	642,961	557,751	
Trading account gains and fees	3,586	37,993	Financial inflows
Additional noninterest income	3,056,002	2,341,166	
Total noninterest expense	4,278,510	3,683,345	
Salaries and employee benefits	2,214,989	1,926,225	
Premises and equipment expense	551,965	375,746	Financial outflows
Additional noninterest expense	1,511,556	1,381,374	
Pretax net operating income	3,828,217	3,282,490	
Securities gains (losses)	15,365	7,713 }	Financial inflows
Applicable income taxes	1,384,300	1,148,490 }	Financial outflows
Income before extraordinary items	2,459,282	2,141,713	
Extraordinary gains—net	0	0 }	Financial inflows
Net income	2,459,282	2,141,713	

is divided into four main sections: (1) interest income, (2) interest expenses, (3) noninterest income, and (4) noninterest expenses.

Interest Income

Not surprisingly, interest earned from loans and security investments accounts for the majority of revenues for most depository institutions and for many other lenders as well. In the case of the bank—National City Corp.—that we have been following, its $6,318 million in loan and investment revenues represented 61 percent of its total interest and noninterest income. It must be noted, however, that the relative importance of interest revenues versus noninterest revenues (*fee income*) is changing rapidly, with fee income today growing faster than interest income on loans and investments as financial-service managers work hard to develop more fee-based services.

Interest Expenses

The number one expense item for a depository institution normally is *interest on deposits*. For the banking company we have been following interest on deposits accounted for almost 60 percent of this bank's total interest costs. Another important interest expense item is the interest owed on short-term borrowings in the money market—mainly borrowings of federal funds (reserves) from other depository institutions and borrowings backstopped by security repurchase agreements—plus any long-term borrowings that have taken place (including mortgages on the financial firm's property and subordinated notes and debentures outstanding).

Net Interest Income

Total interest expenses are subtracted from total interest income to yield *net interest income*. This important item is often referred to as the *interest margin*, the gap between the interest income the financial firm receives on loans and securities and the interest cost of its borrowed funds. It is usually a key determinant of profitability. When the interest margin falls, the stockholders of financial firms will usually see a decline in their bottom line—net after-tax earnings—and the dividends their stockholders receive on each share of stock held may decrease as well.

Loan-Loss Expense

As we saw earlier in this chapter, another expense item that banks and selected other financial institutions can deduct from current income is known as the *provision for loan and lease losses*. This provision account is really a *noncash expense*, created by simple bookkeeping entry. Its purpose is to shelter a portion of current earnings from taxes to help prepare for bad loans. The annual loan-loss provision is deducted from current revenues before taxes are applied to earnings.

Under today's tax laws, U.S. banks calculate their loan-loss deductions using either the *experience method* (in which the amount of deductible loan-loss expense would be the product of the average ratio of net loan charge-offs to total loans in the most recent six years times the current total of outstanding loans) or the *specific charge-off method*, which allows them to add to loan-loss reserves from pretax income each year no more than the amount of those loans actually written off as uncollectible. Expensing worthless loans usually must occur in the year that troubled loans are judged to be worthless. The largest banking companies are required to use the specific charge-off method.

Noninterest Income

Sources of income other than interest revenues from loans and investments are called *noninterest income* (or *fee income*). The financial reports that banks are required to submit to regulatory authorities apportion this income source into four broad categories, as noted in the nearby box. The breakdown includes: (1) fees earned from fiduciary activities (such as trust services); (2) service charges on deposit accounts; (3) trading account gains and fees; and (4) additional noninterest income (including revenues from investment banking, security brokerage, and insurance services). Recently financial-service providers have focused intently on noninterest income as a key target for future expansion.

Trust services—the management of property owned by customers (such as cash, securities, land, and buildings)—are among the oldest fee-generating, nondeposit products offered by financial institutions. For most of banking's history trust departments were not particularly profitable due to the space and high-price talent required. However, with increasing public acceptance of charging fees for services rendered, trust departments have become an increasingly popular source of noninterest income.

While trust department fees have been around for many years, the fees associated with investment banking and insurance services represent relatively new revenue opportunities flowing from passage of the Gramm-Leach-Bliley (GLB) Act and are explored further in Chapter 14. By more aggressively selling services other than loans, financial firms have opened up a promising new channel for boosting the bottom line on their income statements, diversifying their revenue sources, and better insulating their institutions from fluctuations in market interest rates. The $3,961 million of noninterest income reported by National City Corp. in Table 5–6 represented almost 40 percent of that bank's total revenue. More than three-quarters of National City's noninterest income came from a category called "Additional Noninterest Income" which brings together some of the newest sources of fee income for banks.

Noninterest Expenses

The key noninterest expense item for most financial institutions is *wages, salaries, and employee benefits*, which has been a rising expense item in recent years as leading financial firms have pursued top-quality college graduates to head their management teams and lured experienced senior management away from competitors. The costs of maintaining a financial institution's properties and rental fees on office space show up in the *premises and equipment expense*. The cost of furniture and equipment also appears under the noninterest expense category, along with numerous small expense items such as legal fees, office supplies, and repair costs.

Net Operating Income and Net Income

The sum of *net interest income* (interest income − interest expense) and *net noninterest income* (noninterest income − noninterest expense) is called *pretax net operating income*. Applicable federal and state income tax rates are applied to pretax net operating income plus *securities gains or losses* to derive *income before extraordinary items*.

Securities gains (losses) are usually small, but can be substantial for some financial firms. For example, banks purchase, sell, or redeem securities during the year, and this activity often results in gains or losses above or below the original cost (book value) of the securities. Regulators require that banks report securities gains or losses as a separate item; however, other income statements may record these gains or losses as a component of noninterest income. A bank can use these gains or losses to help smooth out its net income from year to year. If earnings from loans decline, securities gains may offset all or part of the decline. In contrast, when loan revenues (which are fully taxable) are high, securities losses can be used to reduce taxable income.

Another method for stabilizing the earnings of financial institutions consists of *nonrecurring sales of assets*. These one-time-only (*extraordinary income or loss*) transactions often

Principal Types of Noninterest ("Fee") Income Received by Many Financial Firms Today

FIDUCIARY ACTIVITIES

Income from services rendered by the financial firm's trust department or by any of its consolidated subsidiaries acting in any fiduciary capacity, such as:

1. Fees for managing and protecting a customer's property.
2. Fees for recordkeeping for corporate security transactions and dispensing interest and dividend payments.
3. Fees for managing corporate and individual pension and retirement plans.

SERVICE CHARGES ON DEPOSIT ACCOUNTS

Service charges on deposit accounts held in domestic offices, such as:

1. Checking account maintenance fees.
2. Checking account overdraft fees.
3. Fees for writing excessive checks.
4. Savings account overdraft fees.
5. Fees for stopping payment of checks.

TRADING ACCOUNT GAINS AND FEES

Net gains and losses from trading cash instruments and off-balance-sheet derivative contracts (including commodity contracts) that have been recognized during the accounting period.

ADDITIONAL NONINTEREST INCOME

Includes the following noninterest income sources:

1. Investment banking, advisory, brokerage, and underwriting.
2. Venture capital revenue.
3. Net servicing fees.
4. Net securitization income.
5. Insurance commission fees and income.
6. Net gains (losses) on sales of loans.
7. Net gains (losses) on sales of real estate owned.
8. Net gains (losses) on sales of other assets (excluding securities).

Note: Categories and definitions, in part, are borrowed from SDI at **www.FDIC.gov**.

involve the sale of financial assets, such as common stock, or real property pledged as collateral behind a loan upon which the lender has foreclosed. A financial firm may also sell real estate or subsidiary firms that it owns. Such transactions frequently have a substantial effect on current earnings, particularly if a lender sells property it acquired in a loan foreclosure. Such property is usually carried on the lender's books at minimal market value, but its sale price may turn out to be substantially higher.

The key bottom-line item on any financial firm's income statement is *net income*, which the firm's board of directors usually divides into two categories. Some portion of net income may flow to the stockholders in the form of *cash dividends*. Another portion (usually the larger part) will go into *retained earnings* (also called *undivided profits*) in order to provide a

Concept Check

5–9.   What accounts make up the Report of Income (income statement) of a bank?

5–10. In rank order, what are the most important revenue and expense items on a Report of Income?

5–11. What is the relationship between the provision for loan losses on a bank's Report of Income and the allowance for loan losses on its Report of Condition?

5–12. Suppose a bank has an allowance for loan losses of $1.25 million at the beginning of the year, charges current income for a $250,000 provision for loan losses, charges off worthless loans of $150,000, and recovers $50,000 on loans previously charged off. What will be the balance in the allowance for loan losses at year-end?

TABLE 5–7   The Composition of Bank Income Statements (Percentage of Total Assets Measured as of Year-End 2004)

Source: Federal Deposit Insurance Corporation.

Income and Expense Items	Percentage of Total Assets for:			
	All U.S. Insured Banks	U.S. Banks with Less than $100 Million in Total Assets	U.S. Banks with $100 Million to $1 Billion in Total Assets	U.S. Banks with $1 Billion or More in Total Assets
Total interest income	4.13%	4.99%	5.00%	3.99%
Domestic office loans	2.86	3.98	4.10	2.67
Foreign office loans	0.25	0.00*	0.00*	0.29
Lease financing receivables	0.09	0.01	0.02	0.10
Balances due from depository institutions	0.04	0.04	0.02	0.04
Securities	0.68	0.88	0.80	0.66
Trading accounts	0.12	0.00*	0.00*	0.13
Federal funds sold	0.06	0.06	0.03	0.06
Other interest income	0.04	0.02	0.03	0.04
Total interest expense	1.16	1.30	1.32	1.14
Domestic office deposits	0.59	1.17	1.10	0.50
Foreign office deposits	0.16	0.00*	0.00*	0.18
Federal funds purchased	0.11	0.01	0.03	0.13
Trading liabilities and other borrowed money	0.25	0.11	0.18	0.26
Subordinated notes and debentures	0.06	0.00*	0.00*	0.06
Net interest income	2.97	3.69	3.68	2.85
Provision for loan and lease losses	0.31	0.21	0.25	0.32
Total noninterest income	2.19	0.91	1.34	2.33
Fiduciary activities	0.27	0.08	0.19	0.28
Service charges on deposit accounts	0.38	0.41	0.41	0.37
Trading account gains and fees	0.11	0.00*	0.00*	0.13
Additional noninterest income	1.42	0.42	0.74	1.54
Total noninterest expense	3.06	3.21	3.15	3.05
Salaries and employee benefits	1.32	1.73	1.59	1.27
Premises and equipment expense	0.38	0.43	0.40	0.38
Additional noninterest expense	1.36	1.05	1.16	1.40
Pretax net operating income	1.78	1.18	1.62	1.82
Securities gains (losses)	0.04	0.01	0.01	0.05
Applicable income taxes	0.58	0.24	0.42	0.61
Income before extraordinary items	1.24	0.95	1.22	1.25
Extraordinary gains—net	0.00*	0.00*	0.00*	0.00*
Net income	1.24	0.95	1.22	1.25

*Less than 0.005 percent.

ETHICS IN BANKING AND FINANCIAL SERVICES

THE COSMETICS OF "WINDOW DRESSING" AND "CREATIVE ACCOUNTING"

Some financial institutions are notorious for creating "better-looking" financial statements. The "window dressing" of balance sheets and income statements can occur at any time, but is most common at the end of a calendar quarter and especially at the end of a fiscal year.

For example, managers may decide they want their firm to look "bigger," giving it an apparent increase in market share. This is often accomplished by the firm borrowing in the money market using federal funds, repurchase agreements, certificates of deposit, or Eurocurrency deposits just prior to the end of the quarter or year and reversing the transaction a few hours or few days later.

Alternatively, management may decide they want their financial firm to look "financially stronger." Recently, Ashikaga Bank of Japan sued its management for alleged window dressing of its year-end financial statements created in order to generate inflated profits, permitting the bank to declare a dividend to those who held its preferred stock.

Security dealers often engage in a similar practice called "painting the tape," which consists of temporarily buying or selling securities that have a relatively thin market and, therefore, tend to be more volatile in price. A few sales or purchases can have a significant impact on price in such a market. Thus, such a transaction may dress up the firm's financial statement at the end of the quarter and be reversed shortly thereafter. Other financial firms may elect to temporarily sell off some of their worst-performing assets so the shareholders won't complain. Within minutes, the transaction can be undone.

More than just a harmless game, window dressing, painting the tape, or, more commonly, "creative accounting" can do real harm to investors and to the efficiency of the financial marketplace. Activities of this sort work to conceal the true financial condition of the firms involved. Financial decision making may be flawed because investors must work with poor quality information. Regulators like the Securities and Exchange Commission and the Federal Reserve System discourage such activity whenever they find evidence that financial statements contain misleading information.

---

larger capital base to support future growth. We note in Table 5–6 that the bank we are studying in this chapter reported net income of $2,459 million for the year just ended.

Comparative Income Statement Ratios for Different-Size Financial Firms

Like bank balance sheets, income statements usually contain much the same items for both large and small financial firms, but the relative importance of individual income and expense items varies substantially with the size of a bank or other financial institution. For example, as shown in Table 5–7, larger banks receive more of their total income from noninterest fees (e.g., service charges and commissions) than do small banks, while smaller banks rely more heavily on deposits than on money market borrowings for their funding and, thus, pay out relatively more deposit interest per dollar of assets than many larger banks. Any meaningful analysis of an individual financial institution's income statement requires comparisons with other financial firms of comparable size and location.

5–5 The Financial Statements of Leading Nonbank Financial Firms: A Comparison to Bank Statements

Key URLs
For regulatory financial reports of savings associations, go to **www2.fdic.gov/ call_tfr_rpts/** and for credit unions visit **www.ncua.gov**.

While the balance sheet, income statement, and other financial reports of banks are unique, the statements of nonbank financial firms have, in recent years, come closer and closer to what we see on bank statements. This is particularly true of *thrift institutions*—including credit unions and savings associations. Like banks, the thrifts' balance sheet is dominated by loans (especially home mortgage loans and consumer installment loans), deposits from customers, and borrowings in the money market. Also paralleling the banking sector, the thrifts' income statements are heavily tilted toward revenue from loans and by the interest they must pay on deposits and money market borrowings.

Key URLs
To learn more about commercial bank similarities and differences with their major competitors in the insurance and securities industries, see **www.acli.com**, **www.iii.org**, and **www.ici.org**.

As we move away from the thrift group into such financial-service industries as finance companies, life and property/casualty insurers, mutual funds, and security brokers and dealers, the financial statements include sources and uses of funds unique to the functions of these industries and to their often unusual accounting practices. For example, *finance company* balance sheets, like those of banks, are dominated by loans, but these credit assets are usually labeled "accounts receivable" and include business, consumer, and real estate receivables, reflecting loans made to these customer segments. Moreover, on the sources of funds side, finance company financial statements show heavy reliance, not on deposits for funding, but on borrowings from the money market and from parent companies in those cases where a finance company is controlled by a larger firm (e.g., as GE Capital is controlled by General Electric).

Life and property/casualty insurance companies also make loans, especially to the business sector. But these usually show up on insurance company balance sheets in the form of holdings of bonds, stocks, mortgages, and other securities, many of which are purchased in the open market. Key sources of funds for insurers include policyholder premium payments to buy insurance protection, returns from investments, and borrowings in the money and capital markets. Most of the insurance industry's profits come from the investments they make, not policyholder premiums.

In contrast, *mutual funds* hold primarily corporate stocks, bonds, asset-backed securities, and money market instruments that are financed principally by their net sales of shares to the public and from occasional borrowings. *Security dealers and brokers* tend to hold a similar range of investments in stocks and bonds, financing these acquisitions by borrowings in the money and capital markets and equity capital contributed by their owners. The dealers also generate large amounts of revenue from buying and selling securities for their customers, by charging underwriting commissions to businesses needing assistance with new security offerings, and by assessing customers fees for financial advice. Increasingly, banks are offering the same services, and their consolidated financial reports look very much like those of these tough nonbank competitors.

5–6 An Overview of Key Features of Financial Statements and Their Consequences

We have explored a substantial number of details about the content of bank financial statements and the comparable statements of some of their closest competitors in this chapter. Table 5–8 provides a useful overview of the key features of bank and closely related institutions' financial statements and their consequences for managers and the public.

Concept Check

5–13. Who are banking's chief competitors in the financial-services marketplace?

5–14. How do the financial statements of major nonbank financial firms resemble or differ from bank financial statements? Why do these differences or similarities exist?

5–15. What major trends are changing the content of the financial statements prepared by financial firms?

5–16. What are the key features or characteristics of the financial statements of banks and similar financial firms? What are the consequences of these statement features for managers of financial-service providers and for the public?

TABLE 5–8

Features and
Consequences of the
Financial Statements
of Banks and Similar
Financial Firms

Key Features of the Financial Statements of Banks and Similar Financial Institutions	Consequences for the Managers of Banks and Similar Financial Institutions
• Heavy dependence on borrowed funds supplied by others (including deposits and nondeposit borrowings); thus, many financial firms make heavy use of financial leverage (debt) in an effort to boost their stockholders' earnings.	• The earnings and the very existence of financial institutions are exposed to significant risk if those borrowings cannot be repaid when due. Thus, financial firms must hold a significant proportion of high-quality and readily marketable assets to meet their debt obligations.
• Most revenues stem from interest and dividends on loans and securities. The largest expense item is often the interest cost of borrowed funds, followed by personnel costs.	• Management must choose loans and investments carefully to avoid a high proportion of earning assets that fail to pay out as planned, damaging expected revenue flows. Because revenues and expenses are sensitive to changing interest rates, management must be competent at protecting against losses due to interest-rate movements by using interest-rate hedging techniques.
• The greatest proportion of assets is devoted to financial assets (principally loans and securities). A relatively small proportion of assets is devoted to plant and equipment (fixed assets); thus, financial institutions tend to make very limited use of operating leverage.	• With only limited resources devoted to fixed assets and, therefore, few fixed costs stemming from plant and equipment, financial firms' earnings are less sensitive to fluctuations in sales volume (operating revenues) than those of many other businesses, but this also limits potential earnings. (Banking, for example, tends to be a moderately profitable industry.)

Summary

This chapter presents us with an overview of the types and content of bank financial statements, which provide us with vital information that managers, investors, regulators, and other interested parties can use to assess each firm's performance. The reader also is given a glimpse at how selected nonbank financial-service firms' financial statements compare with those issued by banks. Several key points emerge in the course of the chapter:

- The two most important financial statements issued by depository institutions are the balance sheet or Report of Condition and the income and expense statement or Report of Income.

- Bank balance sheets report the value of assets held (usually broken down into such categories as cash assets, investment securities, loans, and miscellaneous assets), liabilities outstanding (including deposits and nondeposit borrowings), and capital or stockholders' equity. The values recorded on the balance sheet are measured at a single moment in time (such as the last day of the quarter or year).

- In contrast, the income and expense statement or Report of Income includes key sources of revenue and operating expenses. Revenue sources for banks and closely related financial firms typically include loan and investment income and revenue from the sale of fee-generating services. Major sources of operating expense include interest payments on borrowed funds, employee wages, salaries and benefits, taxes, and miscellaneous expenses.

- The financial statements of nonbank financial firms (including thrift institutions, finance companies, life and property/casualty insurers, and security firms) are increasingly coming to resemble bank financial statements and vice versa as these different industries rush toward each other. Among the common features are heavy use of financial leverage (debt) to finance their operations, the dominance of financial assets over real (physical) assets, and the concentration of revenues from making loans and assisting businesses in selling their securities. For most financial firms the key expense is usually interest expense on borrowings, followed by personnel costs.

www.mhhe.com/rose7e

• By carefully reading the financial statements of banks and their competitors, we learn more about the services these institutions provide and how their financial condition changes with time. These statements, when accurately prepared, provide indispensable information to managers, owners, creditors, and regulators of financial-service providers. Unfortunately, some financial institutions engage in "window dressing" and other forms of data manipulation, which can send misleading information to their shareholders, creditors, customers, and the regulatory community.

Key Terms

Report of Condition, *130*   Report of Income, *144*

Problems and Projects

eXcel

1. Jasper National Bank has just submitted its Report of Condition to the FDIC. Please fill in the missing items from its statement shown below (all figures in millions of dollars):

Report of Condition	
Total assets	**$1,400**
Cash and due from depository institutions	87
Securities	___
Federal funds sold and reverse repurchase agreements	24
Gross loans and leases	1,131
Loan loss allowance	___
Net loans and leases	1,131
Trading account assets	2
Bank premises and fixed assets	12
Other real estate owned	2
Goodwill and other intangibles	5
All other assets	67
Total liabilities and capital	**$1,400**
Total liabilities	___
Total deposits	904
Federal funds purchased and repurchase agreements	81
Trading liabilities	0
Other borrowed funds	25
Subordinated debt	___
All other liabilities	42
Total equity capital	**$138**
Perpetual preferred stock	0
Common stock	3
Surplus	___
Undivided profits	62

eXcel

2. Along with the Report of condition submitted above, Jasper has also prepared a Report of Income for the FDIC. Please fill in the missing items from its statement shown below (all figures in millions of dollars):

Report of Income	
Total interest income	$63
Total interest expense	18
Net interest income	___
Provision for loan and lease losses	3
Total noninterest income	39
Fiduciary activities	2
Service charges on deposit accounts	6
Trading account gains and fees	___
Additional noninterest income	30
Total noninterest expense	42
Salaries and employee benefits	___

(continued)

Premises and equipment expense	5
Additional noninterest expense	15
Pretax net operating income	____
Securities gains (losses)	1
Applicable income taxes	13
Income before extraordinary items	____
Extraordinary gains—net	0
Net income	____

eXcel

3. If you know the following figures:

Total interest income	$290	Provision for loan losses	$10
Total interest expenses	205	Income taxes	15
Total noninterest income	27	Dividends to common stockholders	11
Total noninterest expenses	40		

Please calculate these items:

Net interest income	____	Total operating revenues	____
Net noninterest income	____	Total operating expenses	____
Pretax net operating income	____	Increases in bank's undivided profits	____
Net income after taxes	____		

eXcel

4. If you know the following figures:

Gross loans	$300	Trading-account securities	$2
Allowance for loan losses	15	Other real estate owned	4
Federal funds sold	26	Goodwill and other intangibles	3
Common stock	12	Total liabilities	380
Surplus	19	Preferred stock	3
Total equity capital	49	Nondeposit borrowings	20
Cash and due from banks	9	Bank premises and equipment, net	29
Miscellaneous assets	38		
Bank premises and equipment, gross	34		

Please calculate these items:

Total assets	____	Investment securities	____
Net loans	____	Depreciation	____
Undivided profits	____	Total deposits	____

5. The Hokie High Bank has Gross Loans of $550 million with an ALL account of $30 million. Two years ago the bank made a loan for $10 million to finance the Hokie Hotel. One million in principal was repaid before the borrowers defaulted on the loan. The Loan Committee at Hokie High Bank believes the Hotel will sell at auction for $7 million and they want to charge off the remainder immediately.

   a. The dollar figure for Net Loans before the charge-off is _____?

   b. After the charge-off, what are the dollar figures for Gross Loans, ALL, and Net Loans assuming no other transactions?

   c. If the Hokie Hotel sells at auction for $8 million, how will this affect the pertinent balance sheet accounts?

6. For each of the following transactions, which items on a bank's statement of income and expenses (Report of Income) would be affected?

   a. Office supplies are purchased so the bank will have enough deposit slips and other necessary forms for customer and employee use next week.

   b. The bank sets aside funds to he contributed through its monthly payroll to the employee pension plan in the name of all its eligible employees.

   c. The bank posts the amount of interest earned on the savings account of one of its customers.

   d. Management expects that among a series of real estate loans recently granted the default rate will probably be close to 3 percent.

www.mhhe.com/rose7e

e. Mr. and Mrs. Harold Jones just purchased a safety deposit box to hold their stock certificates and wills.

f. The bank collects $1 million in interest payments from loans it made earlier this year to Intel Composition Corp.

g. Hal Jones's checking account is charged $30 for two of Hal's checks that were returned for insufficient funds.

h. The bank earns $5 million in interest on the government securities it has held since the middle of last year.

i. The bank has to pay its $5,000 monthly utility bill today to the local electric company.

j. A sale of government securities has just netted the bank a $290,000 capital gain (net of taxes).

7. For each of the transactions described here, which of at least two accounts on a bank's balance sheet (Report of Condition) would be affected by each transaction?

a. Sally Mayfield has just opened a time deposit in the amount of $6,000 and these funds are immediately loaned to Robert Jones to purchase a used car.

b. Arthur Blode deposits his payroll check for $1,000 in the bank and the bank invests the funds in a government security.

c. The bank sells a new issue of common stock for $100,000 to investors living in its community and the proceeds of that sale are spent on the installation of new ATMs.

d. Jane Gavel withdraws her checking account balance of $2,500 from the bank and moves her deposit to a credit union; the bank employs the funds received from Mr. Alan James, who has just paid off his home equity loan, to provide Ms. Gavel with the funds she withdrew.

e. The bank purchases a bulldozer from Ace Manufacturing Company for $750,000 and leases it to Cespan Construction Company.

f. Signet National Bank makes a loan of reserves in the amount of $5 million to Quesan State Bank and the funds are returned the next day.

g. The bank declares its outstanding loan of $1 million to Deprina Corp. to be uncollectible.

8. Out-of-Sync Bank is developing a list of off-balance-sheet items for its call report. Please fill in the missing items from its statement shown below. Using Table 5–5, describe how Out-of-Sync compares with other banks in the same size category regarding its off-balance sheet activities.

Off-balance-sheet items for Out-of-Sync Bank (in millions of $)	
Total unused commitments	$ 5,000
Standby letters of credit and foreign office guarantees	350
(Amount conveyed to others)	−70
Commercial letters of credit	25
Securities lent	1,000
Derivatives (total)	79,000
Notional amount of credit derivatives	2,000
Interest rate contracts	_____
Foreign exchange rate contracts	9,000
Contracts on other commodities and equities	1,200
All other off-balance sheet liabilities	49
Total off-balance-sheet items	_____
Total assets (on-balance sheet)	8,600
Off-balance-sheet items divided by on-balance sheet assets	_____

9. See if you can determine the amount of Rosebush State Bank's current net income after taxes from the figures below (stated in millions of dollars) and the amount of its retained

earnings from current income that it will be able to reinvest in the bank. (Be sure to arrange all the figures given in correct sequence to derive the bank's Report of Income.)

Effective tax rate	30%
Interest and fees on loans	$75
Employee wages, salaries, and benefits	13
Interest and dividends earned on government bonds and notes	9
Provision for loan losses	8
Overhead expenses	3
Service charges paid by depositors	5
Security gains	3
Interest paid on federal funds purchased	9
Payment of dividends of $2 per share on 1 million outstanding shares to be made to common stockholders	
Interest paid to customers holding time and savings deposits	34
Trust department fees	3

10. Which of these account items or entries would normally occur on a bank's balance sheet (Report of Condition) and which on a bank's income and expense statement (Report of Income)?

Federal funds sold	Deposits due to banks
Retained earnings	Leases of business equipment
Credit card loans	to customers
Utility expense	Interest received on credit card loans
Vault cash	Employee benefits
Allowance for loan losses	Savings deposits
Depreciation on plant and equipment	Provision for loan losses
Commercial and industrial loans	Service charges on deposits
Repayments of credit card loans	Undivided profits
Common stock	Mortgage owed on the bank's buildings
Interest paid on money market deposits	Other real estate owned
Securities gains or losses	

eXcel

11. You were informed that a bank's latest income and expense statement contained the following figures (in $ millions):

Net interest income	$800
Net noninterest income	−300
Net income before income taxes	484
Increases in bank's undivided profits	100

Suppose you also were told that the bank's total interest income is twice as large as its total interest expense and its noninterest income is three-fourths of its noninterest expense. Imagine that its provision for loan losses equals 1 percent of its total interest income, while its taxes generally amount to 30 percent of its net income before income taxes. Calculate the following items for this bank's income and expense statement:

Total interest income	_____
Total interest expenses	_____
Total noninterest income	_____
Total noninterest expenses	_____
Provision for loan losses	_____
Income taxes	_____
Dividends paid to common stockholders	_____

12. Why do the financial statements issued by banks and by nonbank financial-service providers look increasingly similar today? Which nonbank financial firms have balance sheets and income statements that closely resemble those of commercial banks (especially community banks)?

www.mhhe.com/rose7e

13. What principal types of assets and funds sources do nonbank thrifts (including savings banks, savings and loans, and credit unions) draw upon? Where does the bulk of their revenue come from and what are their principal expense items?

14. How are the balance sheets and income statements of finance companies, insurers, and securities firms similar to those of banks, and in what ways are they different? What might explain the differences you observe?

Internet Exercises

1. The regulators' Web sites provide a wealth of information for bank holding companies (BHCs). The FDIC's Statistics for Depository Institutions (SDI) site (**www2.fdic.gov/sdi/**) is the source of National City's Report of Condition and Report of Income presented in Tables 5–3 and 5–6. The data for bank holding companies provided at the FDIC's site represent combined amounts for all FDIC insured bank and thrift subsidiaries, and do not reflect nondeposit subsidiaries or parent companies. Visit SDI and search for information for Wachovia Corporation. What are the dollar amounts of Total assets, Total liabilities, Total deposits, Net interest income, and Net income for the most recent year-end?

   More comprehensive holding company information can be found at the National Information Center's (NIC's) Web site maintained by the Federal Financial Institutions Examination Council (FFIEC). Go to **www.ffiec.gov/nicpubweb/nicweb/nichome.aspx** and collect the most recent year-end data for Wachovia. What are the dollar amounts of Total assets, Total liabilities, Total deposits (you will need to sum the different types of deposits), Net interest income, and Net income? You will see that there is more information available at this site, but it is a little more challenging to sort through. You are interested in the Schedule HC—Consolidated Balance Sheet and Schedule HI—Consolidated Income Statement. Compare and contrast the information found for Wachovia at both Web sites.

2. Data for individual banks are available at the same regulatory Web sites referenced in Internet Exercise 1. Use SDI and the NIC to collect the most recent year-end data for Wachovia Bank (you want the bank located in Charlotte, North Carolina). What are the dollar amounts of Total assets, Total liabilities, Total deposits, Net interest income, and Net income? At the NIC Web site, you are interested in the Schedule RC—Balance Sheet and Schedule RI—Income Statement. Compare and contrast the information found for Wachovia at both Web sites.

3. The Report of Condition has information about the sources and uses of funds. Go to SDI (**www2.fdic.gov/sdi/**) and pull up the Assets and Liabilities for the Bank of America's most recent year-end. Access the bank holding company information.

   a. Using the link for Other Real Estate Owned (OREO), identify and describe the dollar composition of this item.

   b. Using the link for Goodwill and Other Intangibles, identify and describe the dollar composition of this item.

4. The Report of Income has information about revenues and expenses. Net interest income is the difference between the Interest revenue and Interest expense. Using SDI (**www2.fdic.gov/sdi/**) pull up the annual Income and Expense for the most recent year-end for Bank of America—the bank holding company.

   a. Using the link for Total interest income, identify and describe the dollar composition of this item.

   b. Using the link for Total interest expense, identify and describe the dollar composition of this item.

5. Noninterest income and Expenses are detailed in the Report of Income. Using SDI (**www2.fdic.gov/sdi/**) pull up the annual Income and Expense for Bank of America's most recent year-end.

   a. What components are combined to create the dollar amount of Noninterest income? You will need to use the links for Trading account gains and fees and Additional noninterest income to describe the dollar composition of this item.

   b. What components are combined to create the dollar amount of Noninterest expense? You will need to use the link for Additional noninterest expense to describe the dollar composition of this item.

6. What similarities do you see between the balance sheets and income statements of smaller community banks versus major money center banks? What are the principal differences? For comparison purposes view the most recent financial reports of one or more community banks in your hometown or local area and compare them to the financial reports filed most recently by such industry leaders as J. P. Morgan Chase and Citigroup. You can find data for all FDIC insured institutions at SDI (**www2.fdic.gov/sdi/**) and you can always search the institutions' own Web sites.

7. Consulting the Web sites posted by Atlantic Commercial Credit Corporation (**www.atlanticcommercial.com**), Goldman Sachs (**www.gs.com**), State Farm Insurance Companies (**www.statefarm.com**) and Wells Fargo Bank (**www.wellsfargo.com**), what differences do you observe between the financial reports of the finance company, Atlantic Commercial Credit Corporation; the security dealer, Goldman Sachs; the insurance industry leader, State Farm Insurance Companies; and one of the leaders of the domestic U.S. banking industry, Wells Fargo? Are there any important similarities among the financial statements of these different financial-service providers?

S&P Market Insight Challenge (www.mhhe.com/edumarketinsight)

STANDARD &POOR'S

1. Becoming familiar with the names and types of banks makes the study of banking a little more interesting. In the S&P Industry Survey on Banking, banks are currently categorized as Diversified Banks, Regional Banks, and Other Companies with Significant Commercial Banking Operations. For up-to-date information concerning the size and profitability of banks, use the industry tab in S&P's Market Insight and select either Diversified Banks or Regional Banks from the drop-down menu. Upon selecting one of these subindustries, you will find a recent S&P Industry Survey on Banking. Download the Banking Survey and view the Comparative Company Analysis at the back. Focus on the most recent year's data and answer the following questions, providing the relevant dollar amounts in each category, that is, Diversified Banks, Regional Banks, and Other Companies with Significant Commercial Banking Operations: (1) Which company has the highest operating revenues? (2) The highest net income? (3) The largest asset total? (4) The most loans? (5) The largest volume of deposits?

STANDARD &POOR'S

2. Examine the most recent highlights for balance sheets and income statements provided by S&P's Market Insight for a large bank holding company (such as Bank of America or J. P. Morgan Chase). (Hint: Remember that Table 1–2 in Chapter 1 has a list of leading banking firms with those appearing on Market Insight clearly marked.) Do the same for a leading manufacturing firm or nonfinancial service provider listed on Market Insight (such as Ford Motor Company or United Airlines). You will find highlights from the balance sheets and income statements by using the company tab and accessing the most recent S&P Stock Report. How do these bank and nonbank balance sheets and income statements compare with each other? What major differences do you observe and why?

REAL NUMBERS FOR REAL BANKS
Assignment for Chapter 5

FIRST LOOK AT YOUR BHC'S FINANCIAL STATEMENTS

In Chapter 5, we focus most heavily on the financial statements for banking companies. As you read this chapter, you progress through a lengthy, yet interesting, discussion of the items found on the Report of Condition (balance sheet) and the Report of Income (income statement). In the chapter you find financial statements providing dollar amounts and then comparative financial statements where the ratios of items-to-assets are presented. The data was collected from Statistics for Depository Institutions at the FDIC's Web site (**www3.fdic.gov/sdi/**) and organized into tables using Excel. You will first create financial statements using dollar figures collected from SDI for your banking company for year-to-year comparisons and you will then create financial statements for your banking company and its Peer Group using the ratios of items-to-assets.

A. Create a spreadsheet using Excel for dollar amounts that appears as follows:

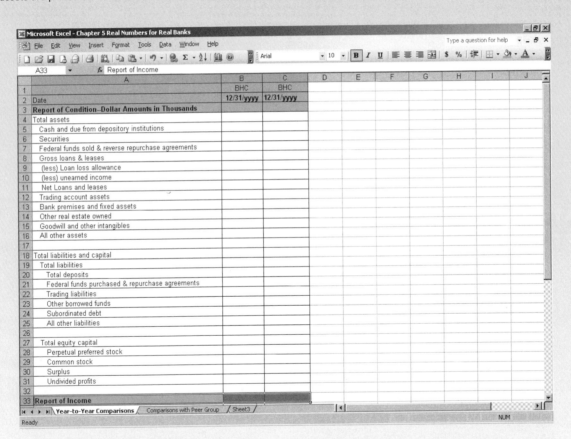

To fill in the dollar amounts for the Year-to-Year Comparisons spreadsheet, go to **www3.fdic.gov/sdi** and enter SDI. You will create a report with two columns and you are presented with two pull-down menus. From the first pull-down menu, select "Bank Holding Company," then enter your company's BHC number and select the report date for the most recent year-end. From the second pull-down menu, repeat the process, only you will select reports for December, one year prior. Follow the cues to generate a report selecting to "View" in "Dollars" for the

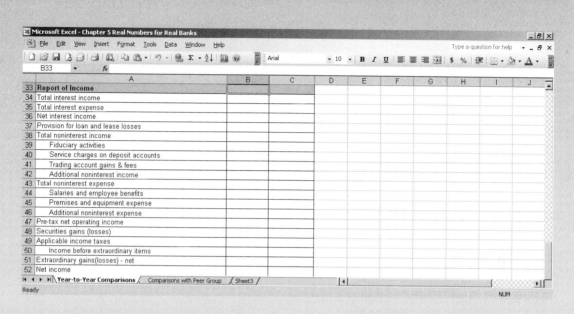

first spreadsheet. For the Report of Condition you will be able to enter most data directly from the Assets and Liabilities report generated at the FDIC Web site; however, you will have to explore the Net Loans and Leases link to get Gross Loans and Leases and Unearned Income. For the Report of Income, you will find the information you need in Income and Expense.

B. Create a second worksheet in the same workbook, but collect data in "Percent of Assets" rather than in dollars. This will be useful for comparative analysis and you will connect data both for your BHC and a group of peer banks. To fill in the percentages of total assets, return to **www3.fdic.gov/sdi** and enter SDI. This time, you will create a report with four columns and you are presented with four pull-down menus. From the first pull-down menu, select "Bank Holding Company," then enter your company's BHC number and select the report date for the most recent year-end. From the second pull-down menu, choose "Standard Peer Group" and select "All Commercial Banks with assets greater than 10 Billion" for the most recent year-end. You will repeat this process using the last two pull-down menus, only you will select reports for December, one year prior. Follow the cues to generate a report selecting to "View" in "Percent of Assets"

and enter the same items as in Part A. By working with these statements, you will be familiarizing yourself with real-world financial statements and developing the language to talk with finance professionals from all types of financial institutions.

C. To develop an understanding of the relationships on the Reports of Condition and Income and to double-check for data collection errors, we will use our formula functions to calculate total assets, total liabilities and capital, total liabilities, total equity capital, net interest income, pretax net operating income, income before extraordinary items, and net income, using the spreadsheet developed in Part A. First Step: copy Columns B and C to Columns D and E. Second Step: clear the values in the cells containing total assets (i.e., Cells D4 and E4), total liabilities and capital, total liabilities, total equity capital, net interest income, pretax net operating income, income before extraordinary items, and net income. Then use the formula functions in Excel to create entries for the empty cells. For example, the formula for total liabilities used in Column D would be =SUM(B20:B25). If the formulas and entries are correct, you will get the same numerical values as in columns B and C and you can be reassured that you are developing an understanding of the financial statements of banks and similar financial firms.

www.mhhe.com/rose7e

Selected References

See the following for an overview of the components of financial statements prepared by banks and their closest competitors:

1. Badenhausen, Kurt. "Borrowing Trouble." *Forbes,* April 11, 2005, p. 80.

2. Bies, Susan Schmidt. "Fair Value Accounting." *Federal Reserve Bulletin,* Winter 2005, pp. 26–29.

3. Ennis, Huberto M. "Some Recent Trends in Commercial Banking." *Economic Quarterly,* Federal Reserve Bank of Richmond, volume 90/2 (Spring 2004), pp. 41–61.

4. Gosnell, David. "The EFT Networks' Mixed Results." *Credit Card Management,* October 2004, pp. 38–40.

5. Klee, Elizabeth C., and Fabio M. Natalucci. "Profits and Balance Sheet Developments at U.S. Commercial Banks in 2004." *Federal Reserve Bulletin,* Spring 2005, pp. 143–74.

6. O'Toole, Randy. "Recent Developments in Loan Loss Provisioning at U.S. Commercial Banks." *FRBSF Economic Letter,* Federal Reserve Bank of San Francisco, no. 97-21 (July 25, 1997).

7. Shaffer, Sherrill. "Marking Banks to Market." *Business Review,* Federal Reserve Bank of Philadelphia, July/August 1992, pp. 13–22.

8. Spieker, Ronald L. "Bank Branch Growth Has Been Steady—Will It Continue?" *Future of Banking Study,* Federal Deposit Insurance Corporation, Draft FOB 2004.

9. Walter, John R. "Loan-Loss Reserves." *Economic Review,* Federal Reserve Bank of Richmond, July/August 1991, pp. 20–30.

CHAPTER SIX

Measuring and Evaluating the Performance of Banks and Their Principal Competitors

Key Topics in This Chapter

- Stock Values and Profitability Ratios
- Measuring Credit, Liquidity, and Other Risks
- Measuring Operating Efficiency
- Performance of Competing Financial Firms
- Size and Location Effects
- The UBPR and Comparing Performance

6–1 Introduction

Humorist and poet Ogden Nash once wrote, "Bankers are just like anybody else, except richer." It turns out that statement may or may not be true; a lot depends upon how successful bankers and other financial-service managers are as performers in the financial marketplace. Indeed, in today's world, bankers and their competitors are under great pressure to *perform* well all the time.

What do we mean by the word *perform* when it comes to financial firms? In this case *performance* refers to how adequately a financial firm meets the needs of its stockholders (owners), employees, depositors and other creditors, and borrowing customers. At the same time, financial firms must find a way to keep government regulators satisfied that their operating policies, loans, and investments are sound, protecting the public interest. The success or lack of success of these institutions in meeting the expectations of others is usually revealed by a careful study of their financial statements.

Why are financial statements under such heavy scrutiny today? One key reason is that banks and other financial institutions now depend heavily upon the open market to raise the funds they need, selling stocks, bonds, and short-term IOUs (including deposits). Entry into the open market to raise money means that a financial firm's financial statements will be gone over "with a fine tooth comb" by stock and bond market investors, credit rating agencies (such as Moody's and Standard & Poor's), regulators, and scores of other people and institutions.

This development has placed the management of banks and many of their competitors under great pressure to set and meet the institution's performance goals or suffer serious financial and reputational losses. In 2002 J. P. Morgan Chase, the second largest banking company in the United States, became a prominent example. The firm's credit rating came under review and, for a time, it faced rising borrowing costs as major depositors and other creditors reacted negatively to the bank's potential loan losses and the adverse publicity from its alleged involvement with Enron Corporation and other troubled companies. Subsequently, J. P. Morgan Chase's position strengthened and improved.

At the same time, as we saw in Chapters 1–4, competition for traditional loan and deposit customers has increased dramatically. Credit unions, money market funds, insurance companies, brokerage firms and security dealers, and even chain stores are fighting for a bigger slice of nearly every credit or deposit market. Bankers have been called upon to continually reevaluate their loan and deposit policies, review their plans for growth and expansion, and assess their returns and risk exposure in light of this new competitive environment.

In this chapter we take a detailed look at the most widely used indicators of the quality and quantity of bank performance and at some performance indicators used to measure banking's principal competitors. The chapter centers on the most important dimensions of performance—*profitability* and *risk*. After all, financial institutions are simply businesses organized to maximize the value of the shareholders' wealth invested in the firm at an acceptable level of risk. The objectives of maximum (or at least satisfactory) profitability with a level of risk acceptable to the institution's owners is not easy to achieve, as recent institutional failures around the globe suggest. Aggressive pursuit of such an objective requires a financial firm to be continually on the lookout for new opportunities for revenue growth, greater efficiency, and more effective planning and control. The pages that follow examine the most important measures of return and risk for banks and some of their toughest competitors.

6–2 Evaluating Performance

How can we use financial statements, particularly the Report of Condition (balance sheet) and Report of Income (income statement), to evaluate how well a financial firm is performing? What do we look at to help decide if a financial institution is facing serious problems that its management should deal with?

Determining Long-Range Objectives

The first step in analyzing financial statements is to decide what objectives the bank or other financial firm is seeking. Performance must be directed toward *specific objectives*. A fair evaluation of any financial firm's performance should start by evaluating whether it has been able to achieve the objectives its management and stockholders have chosen.

Certainly many financial institutions have their own unique objectives. Some wish to grow faster and achieve some long-range growth objective. Others seem to prefer the quiet life, minimizing risk and conveying the image of a sound institution, but with modest rewards for their shareholders.

Maximizing the Value of the Firm: A Key Objective for Nearly All Financial-Service Institutions

While all of the foregoing goals have something to recommend them, increasingly financial-service corporations are finding they must pay close attention to the *value of their stock*. Indeed, the basic principles of financial management, as that science is practiced today, suggest strongly that attempting to maximize a corporation's stock value is the key objective that should have priority over all others. If the stock fails to rise in value commensurate with stockholder expectations, current investors may seek to unload their shares and the financial institution will have difficulty raising new capital to support its future growth. Clearly, then, management should pursue the objective of maximizing the value of the financial firm's stock.

What will cause a financial firm's stock to *rise* in value? Each institution's stock price is a function of the

$$\frac{\text{Value of}}{\text{stock}} = \frac{\text{Expected stream of future stockholder dividends}}{\text{Discount factor (based on the minimum required market rate of return on equity capital given each financial firm's perceived level of risk)}} = \sum_{t=0}^{\infty} \frac{E(D_t)}{(1 + r)^t} \qquad \textbf{(6–1)}$$

Key URLs

The most comprehensive sites on the World Wide Web for the financial statements of individual banks and for the industry as a whole are **www2.fdic.gov/sdi** and **www.ffiec.gov/ nicpubweb/nicweb/ nichome.aspx**.

where $E(D_t)$ represents stockholder dividends expected to be paid in future periods, discounted by a minimum acceptable rate of return (r) tied to the financial firm's perceived level of risk. The minimum acceptable rate of return, r, is sometimes referred to as an institution's *cost of capital* and has two main components: (1) the risk-free rate of interest (often proxied by the current yield on government bonds) and (2) the equity risk premium (which is designed to compensate an investor for accepting the risk of investing in a financial firm's stock rather than in risk-free securities).

The value of the financial firm's stock will tend to *rise* in any of the following situations:

1. The value of the stream of future stockholder dividends is expected to increase, due perhaps to recent growth in some of the markets served or perhaps because of profitable acquisitions the organization has made.
2. The financial organization's perceived level of risk falls, due perhaps to an increase in equity capital, a decrease in its loan losses, or the perception of investors that the institution is less risky overall (perhaps because it has further diversified its service offerings and expanded the number of markets it serves) and, therefore, has a lower equity risk premium.
3. Market interest rates decrease, reducing shareholders' acceptable rates of return via the risk-free rate of interest component of all market interest rates.
4. Expected dividend increases are combined with declining risk, as perceived by investors.

Research evidence over the years has found the stock values of financial institutions to be especially sensitive to changes in market interest rates, currency exchange rates, and the strength or weakness of the economy that each serves. Clearly, management can work to achieve policies that increase future earnings, reduce risk, or pursue a combination of both actions in order to raise its company's stock price.

The formula for the determinants of a financial firm's stock price presented in Equation (6–1) assumes that the stock may pay dividends of varying amounts over time. However, if the dividends paid to stockholders are expected to grow at a constant rate over time, perhaps reflecting steady growth in earnings, the stock price equation can be greatly simplified into the form

$$P_o = D_1/(r - g) \qquad \textbf{(6–2)}$$

where D_1 is the expected dividend on stock in period 1, r is the rate of discount reflecting the perceived level of risk attached to investing in the stock, g is the expected constant growth rate at which stock dividends will grow each year, and r must be greater than g.

For example, suppose that a bank is expected to pay a dividend of $5 per share in period 1, dividends are expected to grow 6 percent a year thereafter, and the appropriate discount rate to reflect shareholder risk is 10 percent. Then the bank's stock price must be valued at

$$P_o = \$5/(0.10 - 0.06) = \$125 \text{ per share}$$

The two stock-price formulas discussed above assume the financial firm will pay dividends indefinitely into the future. Most capital-market investors have a limited time horizon, however, and plan to sell the stock at the end of their planned investment horizon. In this case the current value of a financial corporation's stock is determined from

$$P_o = \frac{D_1}{(1 + r)^1} + \frac{D_2}{(1 + r)^2} + \cdots + \frac{D_n}{(1 + r)^n} + \frac{P_n}{(1 + r)^n} \quad \textbf{(6–3)}$$

where we assume the investor will hold the stock for n periods, receiving the stream of dividends D_1 D_2, ..., D_n, and sell the stock for price P_n at the end of the planned investment horizon. For example, suppose investors expect a bank to pay a $5 dividend at the end of period 1, $10 at the end of period 2, and then plan to sell the stock for a price of $150 per share. If the relevant discount rate to capture risk is 10 percent, the current value of the bank's stock should approach:

$$P_o = \frac{\$5}{(1 + 0.10)^1} + \frac{\$10}{(1 + 0.10)^2} + \frac{\$150}{(1 + 0.10)^2} = \$136.78 \text{ per share}^{[1]}$$

Concept Check

6–1. Why should banks and other corporate financial firms be concerned about their level of profitability and exposure to risk?

6–2. What individuals or groups are likely to be interested in these dimensions of performance for a financial institution?

6–3. What factors influence the stock price of a financial-service corporation?

6–4. Suppose that a bank is expected to pay an annual dividend of $4 per share on its stock in the current period and dividends are expected to grow 5 percent a year every year, and the minimum required return to equity capital based on the bank's perceived level of risk is 10 percent. Can you estimate the current value of the bank's stock?

Profitability Ratios: A Surrogate for Stock Values

While the behavior of a stock's price is, in theory, the best indicator of a financial firm's performance because it reflects the market's evaluation of that firm, this indicator is often not available for smaller banks and other relatively small financial-service corporations because the stock issued by smaller institutions is frequently not actively traded in international or national markets. This fact forces the financial analyst to fall back on surrogates for market-value indicators in the form of various *profitability ratios*.

---

[1] A financial calculator can be used to help solve the above equation for stock price per share where N = 2, I/Y = 10, PV = (?), Pmt = 5, FV = 155.

E-BANKING AND E-COMMERCE

FINANCIAL FIRMS IMPROVE PERFORMANCE BY OUTSOURCING

Financial firms utilize *information* handled by computers for nearly every service they offer. As electronic data processing of financial information becomes more and more integral to the functions of financial-service firms, their managers can realize cost advantages from *outsourcing*—transferring tasks from inside the financial firm itself to outside firms specializing in information technology, known as *vendors*. Often the vendors are centered in distant locations, such as China, India, and Costa Rica.

Institutions like Wachovia Bank, Bank of America, and Germany's Deutsche Bank have become leaders in the adoption of outsourcing designed to reduce the cost of operations. By outsourcing computer facilities and people, these leading financial-service firms hope to save money and time while improving overall accuracy. Savings on personnel and equipment are obvious benefits, but outsourcing also improves efficiency by eliminating "dead time" when a financial firm's computer equipment and staff are not being fully utilized. Through outsourcing, financial institutions are basically "renting" the facilities and employees of the vendor on an "as needed" basis.

Factoid

Contrary to popular opinion, the largest banks in the industry are not always the most profitable. The same is true for the smallest banks. The highest ROAs and ROEs often lie among medium-size institutions.

Key Profitability Ratios

Among the most important ratio measures of **profitability** used today are the following:

$$\text{Return on equity capital} \atop (\text{ROE}) = \frac{\text{Net income}}{\text{Total equity capital}} \qquad (6\text{--}4)$$

$$\text{Return on assets} \atop (\text{ROA}) = \frac{\text{Net income}}{\text{Total assets}} \qquad (6\text{--}5)$$

$$\text{Net interest margin} = \frac{\left(\begin{array}{c} \text{Interest income} \\ - \text{ Interest expense} \end{array} \right)}{\text{Total assets}^2} \qquad (6\text{--}6)$$

$$\text{Net noninterest} \atop \text{margin} = \frac{\left(\begin{array}{c} \text{Noninterest revenues} \\ - \text{ Noninterest expenses} \end{array} \right)}{\text{Total assets}^2} \qquad (6\text{--}7)$$

$$\text{Net operating margin} = \frac{\left(\begin{array}{c} \text{Total operating revenues} \\ - \text{ Total operating expenses} \end{array} \right)}{\text{Total assets}} \qquad (6\text{--}8)$$

$$\text{Earnings per share} \atop \text{of stock (EPS)} = \frac{\text{Net income}}{\text{Common equity shares outstanding}} \qquad (6\text{--}9)$$

Like all financial ratios, each of these profitability measures often varies substantially over time and from market to market.

Interpreting Profitability Ratios

Each of the foregoing ratios looks at a slightly different aspect of profitability. Thus, return on assets **(ROA)** is primarily an indicator of *managerial efficiency*; it indicates how capable management has been in converting assets into net earnings. Return on equity **(ROE)**, on the other hand, is a measure of the *rate of return flowing to shareholders*. It approximates the

---

[2]Many authorities prefer to use total *earning assets* in the denominator of the net interest margin and noninterest margin. Earning assets are those generating interest or fee income, principally loans and security investments. The reasoning is that net interest income as well as net noninterest income should be compared, not to all assets, but rather to those assets that account for the majority of all income.

net benefit that the stockholders have received from investing their capital in the financial firm (i.e., placing their funds at risk in the hope of earning a suitable profit).

The net operating margin, net interest margin, and net noninterest margin are **efficiency** measures as well as profitability measures, indicating how well management and staff have been able to keep the growth of revenues (which come primarily from loans, investments, and service fees) ahead of rising costs (principally the interest on deposits and other borrowings and employee salaries and benefits). The **net interest margin** measures how large a spread between interest revenues and interest costs management has been able to achieve by close control over earning assets and pursuit of the cheapest sources of funding. The **net non-interest margin**, in contrast, measures the amount of noninterest revenues stemming from service fees the financial firm has been able to collect relative to the amount of noninterest costs incurred (including salaries and wages, repair and maintenance of facilities, and loan-loss expenses). Typically, the net noninterest margin is *negative:* Noninterest costs generally outstrip fee income, though fee income has been rising rapidly in recent years as a percentage of all revenues.

Another traditional measure of earnings efficiency is the *earnings spread*, or simply the *spread*, calculated as follows:

$$\frac{\text{Earnings}}{\text{spread}} = \frac{\text{Total interest income}}{\text{Total earning assets}} - \frac{\text{Total interest expense}}{\text{Total interest-bearing liabilities}} \quad \textbf{(6–10)}$$

The spread measures the effectiveness of a financial firm's intermediation function in borrowing and lending money and also the intensity of competition in the firm's market area. Greater competition tends to squeeze the difference between average asset yields and average liability costs. If other factors are held constant, the spread will decline as competition increases, forcing management to try to find other ways (such as generating fee income from new services) to make up for an eroding earnings spread.

Concept Check

6–5. What is return on equity capital and what aspect of performance is it supposed to measure? Can you see how this performance measure might be useful to the managers of financial firms?

6–6. Suppose a bank reports that its net income for the current year is $51 million, its assets total $1,144 million, and its liabilities amount to $926 million. What is its return on equity capital? Is the ROE you have calculated good or bad? What information do you need to answer this last question?

6–7. What is the return on assets (ROA), and why is it important? Might the ROA measure be important to banking's key competitors?

6–8. A bank estimates that its total revenues will amount to $155 million and its total expenses (including taxes) will equal $107 million this year. Its liabilities total $4,960 million while its equity capital amounts to $52 million. What is the bank's return on assets? Is this ROA high or low? How could you find out?

6–9. Why do the managers of financial firms often pay close attention today to the net interest margin and noninterest margin? To the earnings spread?

6–10. Suppose a banker tells you that his bank in the year just completed had total interest expenses on all borrowings of $12 million and noninterest expenses of $5 million, while interest income from earning assets totaled $16 million and noninterest revenues totaled $2 million. Suppose further that assets amounted to $480 million, of which earning assets represented 85 percent of that total while total interest-bearing liabilities amounted to 75 percent of total assets. See if you can determine this bank's net interest and noninterest margins and its earnings base and earnings spread for the most recent year.

Useful Profitability Formulas for Banks and Other Financial-Service Companies

In analyzing how well any given financial-service firm is performing, it is often useful to break down some of these profitability ratios into their key components. For example, it is easy to see that ROE and ROA, two of the most popular profitability measures in use today, are closely related. Both use the same numerator: *net income*. Therefore, these two profit indicators can be linked directly:

$$ROE = ROA \times \frac{\text{Total assets}}{\text{Total equity capital}} \qquad (6\text{--}11)$$

Or, in other words:

$$\frac{\text{Net income}}{\text{Total equity capital}} = \frac{\text{Net income}}{\text{Total assets}} \times \frac{\text{Total assets}}{\text{Total equity capital}} \qquad (6\text{--}12)$$

But we note that net income is equal to total revenues minus operating expenses and taxes. Therefore,

$$ROE = \frac{\text{Total revenues} - \text{Total operating expenses} - \text{Taxes}}{\text{Total assets}} \times \frac{\text{Total assets}}{\text{Total equity capital}} \qquad (6\text{--}13)$$

The relationships in Equations (6–12) and (6–13) remind us that the return to a financial firm's shareholders is highly sensitive to how its assets are financed—whether more debt or more owners' capital is used. Even a financial institution with a low ROA can achieve a relatively high ROE through heavy use of debt (leverage) and minimal use of owners' capital.

In fact, the ROE–ROA relationship illustrates quite clearly the fundamental trade-off the managers of financial-service firms face between risk and return. For example, a bank whose ROA is projected to be 1 percent this year will need $10 in assets for each $1 in capital to achieve a 10 percent ROE. That is, following Equation (6–11):

$$ROE = ROA \times \frac{\text{Total assets}}{\text{Total equity capital}}$$
$$= \frac{0.01 \times \$10 \times 100}{\$1} = 10 \text{ percent}$$

If, however, the bank's ROA is expected to fall to 0.5 percent, a 10 percent ROE is attainable only if each $1 of capital supports $20 in assets. In other words:

$$ROE = \frac{0.005 \times \$20 \times 100}{\$1} = 10 \text{ percent}$$

Indeed, we could construct a risk-return trade-off table like the one following that will tell us how much leverage (debt relative to equity) must be used to achieve a financial institution's desired rate of return to its stockholders. For example, the trade-off table on page 170 indicates that a financial firm with a 5-to-1 assets-to-capital ratio can expect (*a*) a 2.5 percent ROE if ROA is 0.5 percent and (*b*) a 10 percent ROE if ROA is 2 percent. In contrast, with a 20 to 1 assets-to-capital ratio a financial firm can achieve a 10 percent ROE simply by earning a modest 0.5 percent ROA.

Clearly, as earnings efficiency represented by ROA declines, the firm must take on more risk in the form of higher leverage to have any chance of achieving its desired rate of return to its shareholders (ROE).

Risk-Return Trade-Offs for Return on Assets (ROA) and Return on Equity (ROE)

Ratio of Total Assets to Total Equity Capital Accounts	ROE with an ROA of:			
	0.5%	1.0%	1.5%	2.0%
5:1	2.5%	5.0%	7.5%	10.0%
10:1	5.0	10.0	15.0	20.0
15:1	7.5	15.0	22.5	30.0
20:1	10.0	20.0	30.0	40.0

Breaking Down Equity Returns for Closer Analysis

Another highly useful profitability formula focusing upon ROE is this one:

$$\text{ROE} = \frac{\text{Net income}}{\text{Total operating revenue}} \times \frac{\text{Total operating revenue}}{\text{Total assets}}$$

$$\times \frac{\text{Total assets}}{\text{Total equity capital}} \qquad (6\text{–}14)$$

or

$$\text{ROE} = \text{Net profit margin} \times \text{Asset utilization ratio} \times \text{Equity multiplier}$$

where:

$$\text{The } \textbf{net profit margin} \text{ (NPM)} = \frac{\text{Net income}}{\text{Total operating revenues}} \qquad (6\text{–}15)$$

$$\text{The degree of } \textbf{asset utilization} \text{ (AU)} = \frac{\text{Total operating revenues}}{\text{Total assets}} \qquad (6\text{–}16)$$

$$\text{The } \textbf{equity multiplier} \text{ (EM)} = \frac{\text{Total assets}}{\text{Total equity capital}} \qquad (6\text{–}17)$$

Each component of this simple equation is a telltale indicator of a different aspect of a financial firm's operations. (See Exhibit 6–1.)

For example:

The net profit margin (NPM)	reflects ⟶	effectiveness of expense management (cost control) and service pricing policies.
The degree of asset utilization (AU)	reflects ⟶	portfolio management policies, especially the mix and yield on assets.
The equity multiplier (EM)	reflects ⟶	leverage or financing policies: the sources chosen to fund the financial institution (debt or equity).

If any of these ratios begins to decline, management needs to pay close attention and assess the reasons behind that change. For example, of these three financial ratios the equity multiplier (EM), or assets to equity ratio, is normally the largest, averaging about 15X or larger for most banks. Bigger banks often operate with multipliers of 20X or more. The multiplier is a

EXHIBIT 6–1 Elements that Determine the Rate of Return Earned on the Stockholders' Investment (ROE) in a Financial Firm

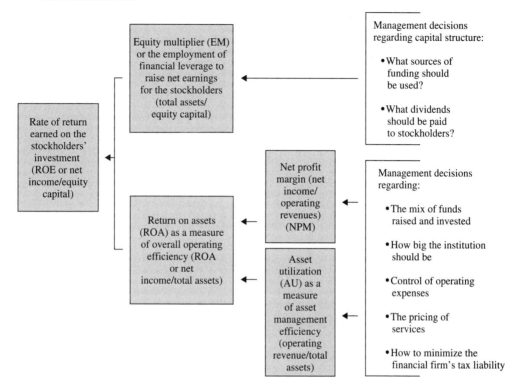

Factoid
In the years since World War II the number of U.S. banks failing annually has averaged less than 1 or 2 percent of the industry population.

direct measure of financial leverage—how many dollars of assets must be supported by each dollar of equity (owners') capital and how much of the financial firm's resources, therefore, must rest on debt. Because equity must absorb losses on assets, the larger the multiplier, the more exposed to failure risk the financial institution is. However, the larger the multiplier, the greater the potential for high returns for the stockholders.

The net profit margin (NPM), or the ratio of net income to total revenues, is also subject to some degree of management control and direction. It reminds us that financial-service corporations can increase their earnings and the returns to their stockholders by successfully controlling expenses and maximizing revenues. Similarly, by carefully allocating assets to the highest-yielding loans and investments while avoiding excessive risk, management can raise the average yield on assets (AU, or asset utilization).

An interesting case in point is the recent track record of average ROE for all FDIC-insured depository institutions between 1992 and 2005, shown in Table 6–1. Careful perusal of the figures in this table reveals very attractive ROEs for FDIC-insured depository institutions covering more than a decade. The lowest earnings over this period for depository institutions, as measured by ROE, were a very acceptable 12.21 percent in 1992. The average ROE for the industry gradually increased over the years, reaching 15.04 percent in 2003 before falling back slightly.

What created such healthy ROEs between 1992 and 2005? Table 6–1 shows clearly that the primary cause was the industry's net profit margin (NPM), which surged upward (particularly noninterest revenues or fee income). Operating revenues expanded significantly faster than operating expenses. The industry's expanding net profit margin more than offset decreases in its asset utilization (AU) ratio and equity multiplier (EM).

TABLE 6–1
Components of
Return on Equity
(ROE) for All FDIC-
Insured Institutions
(1992–2005)

Source: Federal Deposit
Insurance Corporation.

Year	Return on Equity Capital (ROE)	=	Net Profit Margin (NPM) (Net After-Tax Income/Total Revenues)	X	Asset Utilization (AU) (Total Revenues/ Total Assets)	X	Equity Multiplier (EM) (Total Assets/ Total Equity Capital)
2005*	12.68%	=	18.89%	×	6.93%	×	9.63x
2004	13.27	=	19.81	×	6.51	×	9.72x
2003	15.04	=	19.86	×	6.95	×	10.93x
2002	14.11	=	17.10	×	7.60	×	10.87x
2000	13.53	=	12.02	×	9.48	×	11.78x
1998	13.51	=	12.73	×	9.11	×	11.74x
1996	13.31	=	12.21	×	9.01	×	12.17x
1994	13.33	=	12.59	×	8.34	×	12.80x
1992	12.21	=	9.55	×	9.11	×	13.42x

*Figures for 2005 are for first half only.

Why did these latter two ratios (AU and EM) decline? The industry's asset utilization (AU) ratio fell mainly because market interest rates stayed low and were declining much of the time. The equity multiplier (EM) fell because equity capital increased due to record profits and encouragement from government regulators that depository institutions use more equity and less debt to finance their purchases of assets. Regulators urged depository institutions to increase their capital in hopes of protecting depositors and preserving the government's deposit insurance reserves. At the same time banks managed to slow their asset growth by making much heavier use of off-balance-sheet transactions (as we saw in Chapter 5) and by increasing revenues from the sale of fee-based services rather than booking so many new assets.

A slight variation on this simple ROE model produces an efficiency equation useful for diagnosing problems in four different areas in the management of financial-service firms:

$$ROE = \frac{\text{Net income}}{\text{Pretax}\atop\text{net operating}\atop\text{income}} \times \frac{\text{Pretax}\atop\text{net operating}\atop\text{income}}{\text{Total operating}\atop\text{revenue}}$$

$$\times \frac{\text{Total operating}\atop\text{revenue}}{\text{Total assets}} \times \frac{\text{Total assets}}{\text{Total equity capital}} \qquad \textbf{(6–18)}$$

or:

$$ROE = \underset{\text{efficiency}}{\text{management}} \times \underset{\text{efficiency}}{\text{control}} \times \underset{\text{efficiency}}{\text{management}} \times \underset{\text{efficiency}}{\text{management}} \qquad \textbf{(6–19)}$$
$$\quad\;\; \text{Tax} \qquad\;\; \text{Expense} \qquad \text{Asset} \qquad\;\; \text{Funds}$$

In this case we have merely split the net profit margin (NPM) into two parts: (1) a tax-management efficiency ratio, reflecting the use of security gains or losses and other tax-management tools (such as buying tax-exempt bonds) to minimize tax exposure, and (2) the ratio of before-tax income to total revenue as an indicator of how many dollars of

ETHICS IN BANKING AND FINANCIAL SERVICES

QUESTIONABLE ACCOUNTING PRACTICES CAN TURN BANK PERFORMANCE SOUR

In 2001 Superior Bank of Chicago—a federal savings bank—failed and was taken over by the Federal Deposit Insurance Corporation (FDIC). This failed banking firm provides a classic example of how misleading accounting practices that inflate asset values and revenues and deflate liabilities and expenses can hurt a financial institution's performance and ultimately bring it down.

In 2002 the FDIC, acting as receiver and liquidator, filed suit against the public accounting firm of Ernst and Young LLP, claiming that the firm's auditors detected flawed accounting practices at Superior Bank, but did not report their findings until months later. Allegedly, this delay on the part of the outside auditors prevented regulators from acting quickly to minimize losses to the government's insurance fund.

Ernst and Young allegedly had both an auditor–client and a consultant–client relationship with Superior. The FDIC charged that this dual relationship compromised the auditors' judgment and discouraged them from "blowing the whistle" on the bank's accounting problems. The delay in reporting overvaluation of the bank's mortgage-related assets allegedly caused the FDIC's loss to eventually balloon to about three-quarters of a billion dollars. The Sarbanes-Oxley Accounting Standards Act of 2002 now restricts combined auditing and consulting relationships in order to promote auditor objectivity and independence. However, that law was passed *after* the Superior Bank failure occurred.

In short, strong performance on the part of financial-service providers depends on honest reporting that fairly values current and expected revenues, operating costs, assets, and liabilities so that both insiders and outsiders get a clear picture of how well a financial firm is performing and where it seems to be headed.

Source: Federal Deposit Insurance Corporation.

revenue survive after operating expenses are removed—a measure of operating efficiency and expense control. For example, suppose a bank's Report of Condition and Report of Income show the following figures:

$$\text{Net income} = \$1.0 \text{ million}$$
$$\text{Pretax net operating income} = \$1.3 \text{ million}$$
$$\text{Total operating revenue} = \$39.3 \text{ million}$$
$$\text{Total assets} = \$122.0 \text{ million}$$
$$\text{Total equity capital} = \$7.3 \text{ million}$$

Its ROE must be

$$\text{ROE} = \frac{\$1.0 \text{ mil}}{\$1.3 \text{ mil}} \times \frac{\$1.3 \text{ mil}}{\$39.3 \text{ mil}} \times \frac{\$39.3 \text{ mil}}{\$122.0 \text{ mil}} \times \frac{\$122.0 \text{ mil}}{\$7.3 \text{ mil}}$$
$$\text{ROE} = 0.769 \times 0.033 \times 0.322 \times 16.71 = 0.137, \text{ or } 13.7 \text{ percent}$$

Clearly, when any one of these four ratios begins to drop, management needs to reevaluate the financial firm's efficiency in that area. In the banking example shown above, if the ratio of net income to pretax net operating income falls from 0.769 to 0.610 next year, management will want to look closely at how well the bank's tax exposure is being monitored and controlled. If pretax net operating income to operating revenue drops from 0.033 to 0.025 in the coming year, the bank's effectiveness in controlling operating expenses needs to be reviewed. And if the ratio of operating revenues to assets plummets from 0.322 to 0.270, a careful reexamination of asset portfolio policies is warranted to see if the decline in asset yields is due to factors within management's control.

Breakdown Analysis of the Return on Assets

We can also divide a financial firm's return on assets (ROA) into its component parts, as shown in Table 6–2. Actually, ROA is based on three simple component ratios:

Components of ROA

$$\text{Net interest margin} = \frac{(\text{Interest income} - \text{Interest expense})}{\text{Total assets}} \quad \textbf{(6–20)}$$

PLUS

$$\text{Net noninterest margin} = \frac{(\text{Noninterest income}) - \text{Noninterest expense})}{\text{Total assets}}$$

LESS

$$\text{Special transactions affecting its net income} = \frac{\text{Provision for loan losses} \pm \text{securities gains (or losses)} + \text{taxes} - \text{extraordinary net gains}}{\text{Total assets}}$$

EQUALS

$$\text{Return on assets (ROA,) or the ability of management to generate income from assets)} = \frac{\text{Net income}}{\text{Total assets}}$$

Such a breakdown of the components of return on assets (ROA) can be very helpful in explaining some of the recent changes that financial-service providers have experienced in their financial position. For example, as shown in Table 6–3, the average ROA for all FDIC-insured institutions between 1992 and 2005 rose from 0.87 percent in 1992 to a high of 1.38 percent in 2003 before leveling out in 2004 and 2005.

Why did ROA for 1992–2003 keep getting better and better? Better control over expenses, led by advances in automation and mergers that eliminated many overlapping facilities, along with an expanding economy, which propelled upward the public's demand for financial services, resulted in a rapid expansion of fee (noninterest) income and loan revenues. All this occurred in the face of falling market interest rates, which

TABLE 6–2
Calculation Return on Assets (ROA)

Gross interest income ÷ Total assets	← Income from holding assets
− *Interest expense ÷ Total assets*	← Supply cost of funds for holding assets
= Net interest margin ÷ Total assets	← Return earned because the lending institution's credit quality is better than its customers' credit quality
+ Noninterest income ÷ Total assets	← Income from handling customer transactions
− Noninterest expenses ÷ Total assets	← Cost of operations
− Provision for loan losses ÷ Total assets	← *Accrual expense*
= Pretax net operating income ÷ Total assets	← Return on assets before taxes
− *Income taxes ÷ Total assets**	← The financial firm's share of the cost of government services
= Income before extraordinary items ÷ Total assets	← Net income from recurring sources of revenue
+ Extraordinary net gains ÷ Total assets	← Nonrecurring sources of income or loss
= Net income ÷ Total assets (or ROA)	← Earnings left over for the stockholders after all costs are met

*Both income and taxes applicable to income need to be adjusted for any tax-exempt earnings received. One can restate such income on a fully tax-equivalent basis by multiplying the amount of tax-exempt income by the expression $1 \div (1 - t)$ where t is the firm's tax bracket rate.

TABLE 6–3
Components of
Return on Assets
(ROA) for All FDIC
Insured Depository
Institutions
(1992–2005)

Source: Federal Deposit
Insurance Corporation.

Income Statement Items	2005*	2003	2002	2000	1998	1996	1994	1992
Total interest income/ Total assets	4.79%	4.63%	5.32%	7.17%	6.97%	7.14%	6.64%	7.49%
– Total interest expense/ Total assets	1.73	1.40	1.90	3.87	3.56	3.56	2.99	3.77
= Net interest income/ Total assets	3.06	3.22	3.43	3.30	3.41	3.58	3.65	3.72
– Provision for loan and lease losses/Total assets	0.25	0.43	0.64	0.45	0.39	0.35	0.28	0.70
+ Total noninterest income/ Total assets	2.13	2.32	2.27	2.32	2.14	1.87	1.70	1.62
– Total noninterest expense/ Total assets	3.05	3.20	3.27	3.39	3.51	3.45	3.46	3.51
= Pretax net operating income/ Total assets	1.89	1.92	1.80	1.77	1.66	1.64	1.61	1.12
+ Securities gains(losses)/ Total assets	0.06	0.13	0.15	–0.02	0.09	0.04	–0.01	0.14
– Applicable income taxes/ Total assets	0.64	0.67	0.64	0.61	0.60	0.58	0.54	0.41
= Income before extraordinary items/Total assets	1.31	1.37	1.30	1.14	1.15	1.10	1.06	0.85
+ Extraordinary gains (net)/ Total assets	0.00**	0.00**	0.00**	0.00**	0.01	0.00**	–0.01	0.02
= Net income/Total assets	1.31	1.38	1.30	1.14	1.16	1.10	1.05	0.87

Notes: Figures may not add exactly to totals due to rounding and the exclusion of extraordinary items.
*2005 figures are for first half of year only.
**Less than 0.005 percent.

lowered banking's ratio of gross interest income to total assets and reduced its net interest margin. The decline in banks' net interest earnings was more than made up for, however, by dramatic increases in their fee income and improved loan quality as reflected in somewhat smaller loan-loss expenses. By 2003 the industry's ROA, averaging 1.38 percent, represented the biggest average rate of return on bank assets since the FDIC began its operations in 1934.

Concept Check

6–11. What are the principal components of ROE and what does each of these components measure?

6–12. Suppose a bank has an ROA of 0.80 percent and an equity multiplier of 12×. What is its ROE? Suppose this bank's ROA falls to 0.60 percent. What size equity multiplier must it have to hold its ROE unchanged?

6–13. Suppose a bank reports net income of $12, pretax net income of $15, operating revenues of $100, assets of $600, and $50 in equity capital. What is the bank's ROE? Tax-management efficiency indicator?

Expense control efficiency indicator? Asset management efficiency indicator? Funds management efficiency indicator?

6–14. What are the most important components of ROA and what aspects of a financial institution's performance do they reflect?

6–15. If a bank has a net interest margin of 2.50%, a noninterest margin of –1.85%, and a ratio of provision for loan losses, taxes, security gains, and extraordinary items of –0.47%, what is its ROA?

What a Breakdown of Profitability Measures Can Tell Us

Clearly, breaking down profitability measures into their respective components tells us much about the causes of earnings difficulties and suggests where management needs to look for possible cures for any earnings problems that surface. The foregoing analysis reminds us that achieving superior profitability for a financial institution depends upon several crucial factors:

1. Careful use of financial leverage (or the proportion of assets financed by debt as opposed to equity capital).
2. Careful use of operating leverage from fixed assets (or the proportion of fixed-cost inputs used to boost operating earnings as output grows).
3. Careful control of operating expenses so that more dollars of sales revenue become net income.
4. Careful management of the asset portfolio to meet liquidity needs while seeking the highest returns from any assets acquired.
5. Careful control of exposure to risk so that losses don't overwhelm income and equity capital.

Measuring Risk in Banking and Financial Services[3]

Risk to the manager of a financial institution or to a regulator supervising a financial institution means the perceived uncertainty associated with a particular event. For example, will the customer renew his or her loan? Will deposits and other sources of funds grow next month? Will the financial firm's stock price rise and its earnings increase? Are interest rates going to rise or fall next week, and will a financial institution lose income or value if they do?

Bankers, for example are usually interested in achieving high stock values and high profitability, but none can fail to pay attention to the risks they are accepting to achieve these goals. Earnings may decline unexpectedly due to factors inside or outside the financial firm, such as changes in economic conditions, competition, or laws and regulations. For example, recent increases in competition have tended to narrow the spread between earnings on assets and the cost of raising funds. Thus, stockholders always face the possibility of a decline in their earnings per share of stock, which could cause the bank's stock price to fall, eroding its resources for future growth.

Among the more popular measures of *overall risk* for a financial firm are the following:

- Standard deviation (σ) or variance (σ^2) of stock prices.
- Standard deviation or variance of net income.
- Standard deviation or variance of return on equity (ROE) and return on assets (ROA).

The higher the standard deviation or variance of the above measures, the greater the overall risk. Risk can be broken down into a number of components and even referenced using different terms as illustrated by the different risk matrices used currently by U.S. federal regulatory agencies and summarized below.

Risk Matrices Used by Selected U.S. Regulatory Agencies

Federal Reserve System	Comptroller of the Currency	National Credit Union Administration
Credit	Credit	Credit
Liquidity	Liquidity	Liquidity
Market	Interest Rate	Interest Rate
Operational	Transaction	Transactional
Legal	Compliance	Compliance
Reputation	Reputation	Reputation
	Strategic	Strategic

[3]This section is based, in part, on Peter S. Rose's article in the *Canadian Banker* [3] and is used with permission.

Insights and Issues

HOW TOP-EARNING BANKS GET THAT WAY

A number of research studies have examined top-earning firms in the banking industry in an effort to answer a simple question: *What distinguishes a bank with above-average profitability from banks that are only average performers?* How did top-earning banks get that way?

Bank size is clearly one factor. The top-earning banks in the industry, at least as measured by their ROA and ROE, are often medium-size or larger institutions that seem to benefit from lower overall operating costs and greater operating efficiency.

Expense control stands out as the most important discriminator between top performers and the also-rans. For example, high-profit banks manage their operating expenses better, generally posting lower average interest costs, and especially lower personnel expenses and overhead. Their ratios of operating expenses to operating revenues tend to be significantly below the expense-to-revenue ratios of low-profit institutions.

The *deposit structure* also appears to influence profit performance. Top-earning banks often hold more demand deposits than other banks; these checkable deposits pay little or no interest and carry customer service fees that bring in more revenues. Relatedly, many highly profitable banks hold a large volume of *core deposits*—smaller denomination deposits from individuals and small businesses that pay low interest rates and are more loyal to the bank than larger deposit accounts.

Employee productivity tends to be higher among top earners. For example, banks with the best profits seem to generate and manage more assets and income per employee and pay their more productive employees higher salaries.

Leverage (lower equity capital and greater use of debt) also emerges as a profit motivator. Top-earning banks, for example, generally economize on using high-cost owners' capital and rely on the *earnings-leveraging effects of cheaper debt*.

The *expansion of fee income* has become a key element in strategies to increase profits in recent years. Government deregulation has put added pressure on financial institutions to charge fees for many formerly "free" services and develop new fee-generating services.

Growth in assets, deposits, and loans seems to play a role because top-earning banks seem to grow faster than average, possibly reflecting the presence of more aggressive management or greater customer acceptance of their services. However, growth should not become a substitute for profits. Top-earning banks seem to recognize that growth can be overdone, resulting in uncontrolled expansion that increases operating expenses faster than revenues. Moderate growth is usually a better route to high profits.

For further information on the characteristics of high-profit banks see especially Elizabeth C. Klee and Fabio M. Natalucci, "Profits and Balance Sheet Developments at U.S. Commercial Banks in 2004," *Federal Reserve Bulletin*, Spring 2005, pp. 143–74.

Each of these forms of risk can threaten a financial firm's day-to-day performance and its solvency and long-run survival. Let's examine now several of the most important types of risk encountered daily by financial institutions.

Credit Risk

The probability that some of a financial institution's assets, especially its loans, will decline in value and perhaps become worthless is known as **credit risk.** Because financial firms tend to hold little owners' capital relative to the aggregate value of their assets, only a small percentage of total loans needs to turn bad to push them to the brink of failure. The following are four of the most widely used indicators of credit risk:

- The ratio of nonperforming assets to total loans and leases.
- The ratio of net charge-offs of loans to total loans and leases.
- The ratio of the annual provision for loan losses to total loans and leases or to equity capital.
- The ratio of allowance for loan losses to total loans and leases or to equity capital.
- The ratio of nonperforming assets to equity capital.

Nonperforming assets are income-generating assets, including loans, that are past due for 90 days or more. *Charge-offs*, on the other hand, are loans that have been declared worthless and written off the lender's books. If some of these loans ultimately generate income, the amounts recovered are deducted from gross charge-offs to yield net charge-offs. As these ratios rise, exposure to credit risk grows, and failure of a lending institution may be just around the corner. The final two credit risk indicator ratios reveal the extent to which a lender is preparing for loan losses by building up its loan-loss reserves (the allowance for loan losses) through annual charges against current income (the provision for loan losses).

Another popular and long-standing credit risk measure is:

- The ratio of total loans to total deposits.

As this ratio grows, examiners representing the regulatory community may become more concerned because loans are usually among the riskiest of all assets for depository institutions, and, therefore, deposits must be carefully protected. A rise in bad loans or declining market values of otherwise good loans relative to the amount of deposits creates greater depositor risk.

Liquidity Risk

Financial-service managers are also concerned about the danger of not having sufficient cash and borrowing capacity to meet customer withdrawals, loan demand, and other cash needs. Faced with **liquidity risk** a financial institution may be forced to borrow emergency funds at excessive cost to cover its immediate cash needs, reducing its earnings. Very few financial firms ever actually run out of cash because of the ease with which liquid funds can be borrowed from other institutions. In fact, so rare is such an event that when a small Montana bank in the early 1980s had to refuse to cash checks for a few hours due to a temporary "cash-out," there was a federal investigation of the incident!

Somewhat more common is a shortage of liquidity due to unexpectedly heavy deposit withdrawals, which forces a depository institution to borrow funds at an elevated interest rate, higher than the interest rates other institutions are paying for similar borrowings. For example, significant decline in its liquidity position often forces a bank to pay higher interest rates to attract negotiable money market CDs, which are sold in million-dollar units and therefore are largely unprotected by deposit insurance. One useful measure of liquidity risk exposure is the ratio of

- Purchased funds (including Eurodollars, federal funds, security RPs, large CDs, and commercial paper) to total assets.

Heavier use of purchased funds increases the chances of a liquidity crunch in the event deposit withdrawals rise or loan quality declines. Other indicators of exposure to liquidity risk include the ratios of

- Cash and due from balances held at other depository institutions to total assets.
- Cash assets and government securities to total assets.

Cash assets include vault cash held on the financial firm's premises, deposits held with the central bank in the region, deposits held with other depository institutions to compensate them for clearing checks and other interbank services, and cash items in the process of collection (mainly uncollected checks). Standard remedies for reducing a financial institution's exposure to liquidity risk include increasing the proportion of funds committed to cash and readily marketable assets, such as government securities, or using longer-term liabilities to fund the institution's operations.

Market Risk

In market-oriented economies, where most of the world's leading financial institutions offer their services today, the market values of assets, liabilities, and net worth of financial-service providers are constantly in a state of flux due to uncertainties concerning market rates or prices. **Market risk** is composed of both *price risk* and *interest rate risk*.

Price Risk

Especially sensitive to these market-value movements are bond portfolios and stockholders' equity (net worth), which can dive suddenly as market prices move against a financial firm. Among the most important indicators of price risk in financial institutions' management are

- The ratio of book-value assets to the estimated market value of those same assets.
- The ratio of book-value equity capital to the market value of equity capital.
- The market value of bonds and other fixed-income assets held relative to their value as recorded on a financial institution's books.
- The market value of common and preferred stock per share, reflecting investor perceptions of a financial institution's risk exposure and earnings potential.

Interest Rate Risk

Movements in market interest rates can also have potent effects on the margin of revenues over costs for both banks and their competitors. For example, rising interest rates can lower the margin of profit if the structure of a financial institution's assets and liabilities is such that interest expenses on borrowed money increase more rapidly than interest revenues on loans and security investments.

The impact of changing interest rates on a financial institution's margin of profit is called **interest rate risk.** Among the most widely used measures of interest-rate risk exposure are these:

- The ratio of interest-sensitive assets to interest-sensitive liabilities: when interest-sensitive assets exceed interest-sensitive liabilities in a particular maturity range, a financial firm is vulnerable to losses from falling interest rates. In contrast, when rate-sensitive liabilities exceed rate-sensitive assets, losses are likely to be incurred if market interest rates rise.
- For a depository institution, the ratio of uninsured deposits to total deposits, where uninsured deposits are usually government and corporate deposits that exceed the amount covered by insurance and are usually so highly sensitive to changing interest rates that they will be withdrawn if yields offered by competitors rise even slightly higher.

With more volatile market interest rates in recent years, bankers and their competitors have developed several new ways to defend their earnings margins against interest-rate changes, including interest-rate swaps, options, and financial futures contracts. We will examine these and other risk-management tools in Chapters 7, 8, and 9.

Operational (Transactional) Risk

Operational risk refers to uncertainty regarding a financial firm's earnings due to failures in computer systems, errors, misconduct by employees, floods, lightning strikes, and similar events. The broad group of actions included in this risk definition often decrease earnings due to unexpected operating expenses. Some analysts say that *operational risk* is the risk of loss due to anything other than credit or market risk. Others say it includes *legal* and *compliance risk*, but not *reputation* or *strategic risk*. The consolidation and convergence of financial firms and the complexity of today's financial-services technology has made operational risk a broad risk category that needs to be addressed by both managers of financial firms and government regulators.

As technology has improved, computer hardware and software systems have become essential to the daily operations of most financial firms. If computer systems involve a patchwork of old programs, requiring employee intervention to reconcile and create reports, then operational risk may be high. While the failure of a new computer system may be less likely, heavy reliance by the institution's personnel and customers on such systems creates vulnerability for any financial firm.

Today, acts of terrorism such as 9/11 and natural disasters such as hurricanes, earthquakes, and tsunamis can lead to great loss for any financial firm. These natural and not-so-natural disasters may close financial institutions for extended periods and interrupt their service to customers. Foregone income from such disasters is unpredictable, resulting in unexpected operating expenses and greater variability in earnings.

Financial fraud provides the plots for great movies, such as *Rogue Trader, The Bank*, and *Boiler Room*, and the basis for many "60 Minutes" episodes. It's about money, stealing, and the ultimate failure of some at-risk institutions. A financial firm's owners, employees, customers, or outsiders may violate the law and perpetrate fraud, forgery, theft, misrepresentation, or other illegal acts, sometimes leading to devastating losses to otherwise well-managed financial institutions.

Key URLs

Many of the types of risk discussed in this section have been developed and refined by the Bank for International Settlements at **www.bis.org** and by a related entity, the Basel Committee on International Capital Standards, at **www.bis.org/publ/bcbs/ 107.htm**, which is explored in detail in Chapter 15.

Legal and Compliance Risks

Legal risk creates variability in earnings resulting from actions taken by our legal system. Unenforceable contracts, lawsuits, or adverse judgments may reduce a financial firm's revenues and increase its expenses. Lawyers are never cheap and fines can be expensive! In a broader sense **compliance risk** reaches beyond violations of the legal system and includes violations of rules and regulations. For example, if a depository institution fails to hold adequate capital, costly corrective actions must be taken to avoid its closure. These corrective actions are laid out in capital adequacy regulations and are examined in more detail in Chapter 15.

Reputation Risk

Negative publicity, whether true or not, can affect a financial firm's earnings by dissuading customers from using the services of the institution, just as positive publicity may serve to promote a financial firm's services and products. **Reputation risk** is the uncertainty associated with public opinion. The very nature of a financial firm's business requires maintaining the confidence of its customers and creditors.

Strategic Risk

Variations in earnings due to adverse business decisions, improper implementation of decisions, or lack of responsiveness to industry changes are parts of what is called **strategic risk.** This risk category can be characterized as the *human element* in making bad long-range management decisions that reflect poor timing, lack of foresight, lack of persistence, and lack of determination to be successful.

Capital Risk

The impact of all the risks examined above can affect a financial firm's long-run survival, often referred to as its **capital risk.** Because variability in capital stems from other types of risk it is often not considered separately by government regulatory agencies. However, risks to the capital that underlies every financial firm captures the all-important risk of insolvency or ultimate failure.

For example, if a bank takes on an excessive number of bad loans or if a large portion of its security portfolio declines in market value, generating serious capital losses when sold, then its equity capital account, which is designed to absorb such losses, may be overwhelmed. If investors and depositors become aware of the problem and begin to withdraw their funds, regulators may have no choice but to declare the institution insolvent and close its doors.

The failure of a financial-service corporation may leave its stockholders with none of the capital they committed to the institution. Moreover, in the case of depository institutions, depositors not covered by insurance also risk losing a substantial portion of their funds. For this reason, the prices and yields on capital stock and on large uninsured deposits can serve as an early warning sign of solvency problems. When investors believe that a financial firm has an increased chance of failing, the market value of its capital stock usually begins to fall and it must post higher interest rates on its borrowings in order to attract needed funds. Economists call this phenomenon *market discipline:* interest rates and security prices in the financial marketplace move against the troubled firm, forcing it to make crucial adjustments in policies and performance in order to calm investors' worst fears. This suggests that capital risk can be measured approximately by such factors as

- The interest rate spread between market yields on debt issues (such as capital notes and CDs issued by depository institutions) and the market yields on government securities of the same maturity. An increase in that spread indicates that investors in the market expect increased risk of loss from purchasing and holding a financial institution's debt.
- The ratio of stock price per share to annual earnings per share. This ratio often falls if investors come to believe that a financial firm is undercapitalized relative to the risks it has taken on.
- The ratio of equity capital (net worth) to total assets, where a decline in equity funding relative to assets may indicate increased risk exposure for shareholders and debtholders.
- The ratio of purchased funds to total liabilities. Purchased funds usually include uninsured deposits and borrowings in the money market from banks, nonbank corporations, and governmental units that fall due within one year.
- The ratio of equity capital to risk assets, reflecting how well the current level of a financial institution's capital covers potential losses from those assets most likely to decline in value.

Risk assets consist mainly of loans and securities and exclude cash, plant and equipment, and miscellaneous assets. Some authorities also exclude holdings of short-term government securities from risk assets because the market values of these securities tend to be stable and there is always a ready resale market for them. Concern in the regulatory community over the risk exposure of depository institutions has resulted in heavy pressure on their management to increase capital. As we saw earlier in this chapter, capital, at least in the banking industry, has moved significantly higher relative to the industry's assets and liabilities in recent years.

Concept Check

6–16. To what different kinds of risk are banks and their financial-service competitors subjected today?

6–17. What items on a bank's balance sheet and income statement can be used to measure its risk exposure? To what other financial institutions do these risk measures seem to apply?

6–18. A bank reports that the total amount of its net loans and leases outstanding is $936 million, its assets total $1,324 million, its equity capital amounts to $110 million, and it holds $1,150 million in deposits, all expressed in book value. The esti-mated market values of the bank's total assets and equity capital are $1,443 million and $130 million, respectively. The bank's stock is currently valued at $60 per share with annual per-share earnings of $2.50. Uninsured deposits amount to $243 million and money-market borrowings total $132 million, while nonperforming loans currently amount to $43 million and the bank just charged off $21 million in loans. Calculate as many of the risk measures as you can from the foregoing data.

Other Goals in Banking and Financial-Services Management

In an effort to maximize profitability and the value of the shareholders' investment in a financial institution, many financial firms recognize the need for greater *efficiency* in their operations. This usually means reducing operating expenses and increasing the productivity of their employees through the use of automated equipment and improved employee training. The government deregulation movement has forced depository institutions, for example, to pay higher interest costs for their funds and encouraged management to reduce noninterest costs, especially employee salaries and benefits and overhead costs. Among the most revealing measures of operating efficiency and employee productivity for a financial institution are its

$$\text{Operating efficiency ratio} = \frac{\text{Total operating expenses}}{\text{Total operating revenues}} \qquad \textbf{(6–21)}$$

$$\text{Employee productivity ratio} = \frac{\text{Net operating income}}{\text{Number of full-time-equivalent employees}}$$

Factoid
Which banks tend to be most efficient in controlling costs and revenues? **Answer:** Usually medium-size and larger institutions (over $100 million in assets).

Not all financial firms pursue high profitability, maximum stock values, increased growth, or greater efficiency as key goals, however. There is considerable evidence that some institutions prefer greater *market power* in the markets they serve, not only because it gives them increased control over prices and customer relationships, but also because a financial-service provider with greater market influence can enjoy a more "quiet life," or face less risk of losing earnings or market share. Several recent studies have found, for example, that some banks in this situation display expense preference behavior: They spend more on salaries and wages of management and staff, enjoy more fringe benefits, or build larger and more sumptuous offices. Unfortunately for the stockholders of these institutions, a preference for expenses sacrifices profits and limits potential gains in stock values.

6–3 Performance Indicators among Banking's Key Competitors

Factoid
In recent years FDIC-insured savings associations (savings and loans and savings banks) have had lower assets and equity returns than insured commercial banks, but not by much. For example, for all of 2004 commercial banks reported an average ROA of 1.31 percent versus 1.17 percent for savings associations and an average ROE of 13.80 percent versus 10.87 percent for savings associations. Why do you think these differences exist?

Many of the performance indicators discussed in the foregoing sections apply equally well for measuring the performance of both banks and their nonbank competitors. This is especially true of those nonbank financial institutions that are private, profit-making corporations, including stockholder-owned thrift institutions, insurance companies, finance and credit-card companies, security broker and dealer firms, and mutual funds.

Among the key bank performance indicators that often are equally applicable to privately owned, profit-making nonbank financial firms are these:

Prices on common and preferred stock	Return on equity capital (ROE)
Return on assets (ROA)	Net operating margin
Net interest margin	Equity multiplier
Asset utilization ratio	Cash accounts to total assets
Nonperforming assets to equity capital ratio	Interest-sensitive assets to interest-sensitive liabilities
Book-value assets to market-value assets	Interest-rate spread between yields on the financial firm's debt and market yields on government securities
Equity capital to risk-exposed assets	
Earnings per share of stock	

Some performance indicators are unique to each nonbank financial-service industry. For example, among insurance companies, key performance measures include the growth of net premiums written (a measure of total sales) and the size of life and pension reserves (their chief liabilities) relative to total assets. Insurers also pay close attention to an efficiency measure—the combined ratio of claims paid out plus operating expenses relative to premiums earned from policyholders.

Among mutual funds, key performance markers include the growth of net sales (i.e., gross sales of shares less share redemptions by the public), service fees relative to average assets, and the rate of return on funds invested. In contrast, finance and credit-card companies often pay close attention to the growth of their outstanding debt and their gross receivables (a measure of total loans extended to customers). Finally, among competing depository institutions, such as credit unions and mutual savings associations, key performance measures include total loans to members relative to capital reserves (a measure of risk), home mortgage loans to total assets (a rapidly growing credit service), and the number of actual members (customers) relative to potential members (customers).

No financial institution can safely ignore its level of performance today relative to its past performance and relative to its competitors. Even if some financial-service institutions don't seem to care about their performance, both the public and the regulatory community clearly do.

6–4 The Impact of Size on Performance

When the performance of one financial firm is compared to that of another, *size*—often measured by total assets or, in the case of a depository institution, total deposits—becomes a critical factor. Most of the performance ratios presented in this chapter are highly sensitive to the size group in which a financial institution finds itself.

Thus, "size bias" is especially evident in the banking industry. For example, as Table 6–4 shows, key earnings and risk measures change dramatically as we move from the smallest banks (those in the table with assets of less than $100 million) to the largest banking firms (with assets exceeding $10 billion). For example, the most profitable banks in terms of ROA were banks with more than $1 billion in assets and less than $10 billion in assets, while the largest equity returns (ROE) were obtained by the very largest banks with more than $10 billion in assets in 2005.

On the other hand, middle-size and large banks with assets ranging from $100 million to $10 billion in total assets often display the most favorable net operating margins and the best operating efficiency (often with the lowest operating-expense-to-revenue ratio). Similarly, the largest banks generally report the highest (least negative) noninterest margins because they charge fees for so many of their services. Smaller and medium-size banks frequently display larger net interest margins and, therefore, greater spreads between interest revenue and interest costs because most of their deposits are small-denomination accounts with lower average interest costs. Moreover, a larger proportion of small and medium-size banks' loans tend to be higher-interest consumer loans.

In terms of balance-sheet ratios, many of which reflect the various kinds of risk exposure banks face, the smallest banks usually report higher ratios of equity capital to assets. Some bank analysts argue that larger banks can get by with lower capital-to-asset cushions because they are more diversified across many different markets and have more risk-hedging tools at their disposal. Smaller banks appear to be more liquid, as reflected in their lower ratios of net loans to deposits, because loans are often among a bank's least liquid assets. The biggest banks also appear to carry greater credit risk as revealed by their higher loan-loss (net charge-offs to total loans and leases) ratios.

TABLE 6–4 Important Performance Indicators Related to the Size and Location of FDIC-Insured Banks (2005)*

Source: Federal Deposit Insurance Corporation.

	Average for All FDIC-Insured Institutions	Average for All FDIC-Insured Banks	Banks Arrayed by Total Assets in the Size Range			
			Under $100 Million	$100 Million to $1 Billion	$1 Billion to $10 Billion	Greater than $10 Billion
Return on assets (ROA)	1.31%	1.34%	1.05%	1.33%	1.41%	1.34%
Return on equity (ROE)	12.68	13.12	8.84	13.15	13.09	13.26
Net operating income to assets	1.27	1.32	1.05	1.32	1.41	1.32
Net interest margin	3.51	3.59	4.23	4.25	3.89	3.42
Net noninterest margin	−1.05	−1.01	−2.60	−2.09	−1.35	−0.74
Efficiency ratio	57.35	57.36	68.74	61.67	56.80	56.56
Credit loss provision to net charge-offs	92.44	91.34	183.09	148.82	115.34	85.47
Net charge-offs to loans	0.44	0.50	0.16	0.20	0.26	0.60
Loss allowance to loans	1.23	1.38	1.43	1.32	1.31	1.40
Noncurrent assets plus other real estate owned to assets	0.48	0.50	0.72	0.56	0.45	0.49
Net loans and leases to deposits	92.74	87.29	74.21	83.22	92.01	87.76
Equity capital to assets	10.38	10.23	11.87	10.13	10.87	10.10
Yield on earning assets	5.50	5.52	5.89	6.05	5.70	5.40
Cost of funding earning assets	1.99	1.94	1.66	1.80	1.82	1.99
Noninterest income to earning assets	2.45	2.69	1.02	1.46	2.15	3.02

Notes: Data for all U.S. commercial banking and savings institutions whose deposits are FDIC insured.
*Figures shown are for the first 2 quarters of 2005 and are annualized.

Size, Location, and Regulatory Bias in Analyzing the Performance of Banks and Competing Financial Institutions

As we saw in the preceding section, the *size* of a financial institution (often measured by its assets, deposits, or equity capital) can have a highly significant impact on profitability and other performance measures. For example, when we compare the performance of one financial firm with another, it is best to compare institutions of similar size. One reason is that similar-size financial firms tend to offer the same or similar services, so you can be a bit more confident that your performance comparisons have some validity.

To conduct even more valid performance comparisons, we should also compare financial firms serving the same or similar market areas. Performance is usually greatly influenced by whether a financial-service provider operates in a major financial center, smaller city, or rural area. The best performance comparison of all is to choose institutions of similar size serving the *same* market area. Unfortunately, in some smaller communities it may be difficult, if not impossible, to find another financial firm comparable in size. The financial analyst will then usually look for another community with a similar-size financial institution, preferably a community with comparable businesses and households because the character of a financial firm's customer base significantly impacts how it performs.

Finally, where possible, it's a good idea to compare financial institutions subject to *similar regulations* and regulatory agencies. For example, in the banking community each regulator has a somewhat different set of rules banks must follow, and these government-imposed rules can have a profound impact on performance. This is why comparison of financial firms in different countries is often so difficult and must be done with great caution.

Even in the United States, with so many different regulatory agencies, analysts often stress the importance of comparing member banks of the Federal Reserve System against other member banks of the Federal Reserve System. Similarly, the performance of national

CREDIT RATINGS BY THOMSON'S BANKWATCH, INC.

One of the most widely respected private institutions that rates the credit quality of financial institutions is Thomson's BankWatch, Inc. Thomson's rates both short-term debt and long-term obligations (debt and preferred stock), assessing the likelihood that the institutions issuing these obligations may not be able to pay.

BankWatch's credit ratings are among the most widely followed risk indicators anywhere, particularly by large depositors and those who purchase the stock and capital notes of financial firms.

Examples of Thomson's BankWatch ratings of credit worthiness include these:

Short-Term Ratings

TBW-1: Very high likelihood of timely repayment of principal and interest.
TBW-2: Strong likelihood of timely repayment of principal and interest.
TBW-3: Adequate capacity to service principal and interest in a timely way.
TBW-4: Noninvestment grade and speculative in nature.

Long-Term Ratings

AAA: Extremely high capacity to repay.
AA: Strong ability to repay.
A: Relatively strong ability to repay.
BBB: Lowest investment grade rating with an acceptable capacity to repay.
BB: Likelihood of default just above investment grade with some significant uncertainties affecting the capacity to repay.
B: Higher degree of uncertainty and greater likelihood of default than for higher-rated issues
CCC: High likelihood of default.
CC: Subordinated to CCC obligations with less risk protection.
D: Defaulted obligation.

Note: The long-term credit ratings may be marked with a + or a – depending upon whether the rated institution appears to lie nearer the top or nearer the bottom of each rating category.

Key URLs

If you wanted to compare the overall profitability of the insurance industry to that of the banking industry, where would you look? The data supplied by the American Council of Life Insurance at **www.acli.org** and by the Insurance Information Institute at **www.iii.org** would be helpful.

banks, where possible, should be compared against that of other national banks, and state-chartered institutions should be compared against other state-licensed institutions. If a financial firm is an affiliate of a holding company, it can be revealing to compare its performance with other holding company affiliates rather than with independently owned institutions. There is an old saying about avoiding comparing apples and oranges because of their obvious differences; the same is true in the financial-services field. No two financial firms are ever exactly alike in size, location, service menu, or customer base. The performance analyst must make his or her best effort to find the most comparable institutions—and then proceed with caution.

Using Financial Ratios and Other Analytical Tools to Track Bank Performance—The UBPR

Compared to other financial institutions, more information is available about banks than any other type of financial firm. Through the cooperative effort of four federal banking agencies—the Federal Reserve System, the Federal Deposit Insurance Corporation, the Office of Thrift Supervision, and the Office of the Comptroller of the Currency—the Uniform Bank Performance Report (UBPR) provides key information for financial analysts. The **UBPR**, which is sent quarterly to all federally supervised banks, reports each bank's assets, liabilities, capital, revenues, and expenses.

Supplementary items in the UBPR include breakdowns of loan and lease commitments, analysis of problem loans and loan losses, and a profile of each bank's exposure to risk and its sources of capital. Bankers can also obtain *peer group reports*, which allow them to compare their bank with other institutions of comparable size; *average reports*, which provide mean ratio values for each peer group; and *state reports*, which permit comparisons between an individual bank and the combined financial statements of all banks in a given state. An important added feature is that a banker can acquire the UBPR report for any

TABLE 6–5 The Assets Section from the Balance Sheet for National City Bank

Source: Uniform Bank Performance Reports (**www.ffiec.gov**).

Items (dollar amounts in thousands)	12/31/2004	12/31/2003	$ Change	Percentage Change
Assets				
1. Real estate loans	$24,625,884	$21,209,496	$3,416,388	16.11%
2. Commercial loans	9,271,907	8,672,817	599,090	6.91
3. Individual loans	7,851,544	7,912,526	−60,982	−0.77
4. Agricultural loans	25,317	6,369	18,948	297.50
5. Other loans and leases in domestic offices	212,112	276,387	−64,275	−23.26
6. Loans and leases in foreign offices	272,417	234,689	37,728	16.08
7. Gross loans and leases	42,259,181	38,312,284	3,946,897	10.30
8. Less: Unearned Income	27,130	25,738	1,392	5.41
9. Less: Loan and lease loss allowance	514,318	592,394	−78,076	−13.18
10. Net loans and leases	41,717,733	37,694,152	4,023,581	10.67
11. U.S. Treasury and agency securities	1,087,363	1,324,272	−236,909	−17.89
12. Municipal securities	86,420	20,293	66,127	325.86
13. Foreign debt securities	85	78	7	8.97
14. All other securities	984,143	1,232,536	−248,393	−20.15
15. Interest-bearing bank balances	2,811,741	12,372	2,799,369	22626.65
16. Federal funds sold and resale agreements	1,103,067	463,760	639,307	137.85
17. Trading account assets	193,987	210,932	−16,945	−8.03
18. Total investments	6,266,806	3,264,243	3,002,563	91.98
19. Total earning assets	47,984,539	40,958,395	7,026,144	17.15
20. Noninterest-bearing cash and deposits due from other banks	1,792,763	1,646,705	146,058	8.87
21. Premises, fixed assets, capital leases	558,058	511,519	46,539	9.10
22. Other real estate owned	5,643	6,902	−1,259	−18.24
23. Investments in unconsolidated subsidiaries	0	0	0	
24. Acceptances and Other assets	2,633,913	3,152,501	−518,588	−16.45
25. Total assets	$52,974,916	$46,276,022	$6,698,894	14.48%
Memoranda:				
26. Noninvestment other real estate owned	5,643	6,902	−1,259	−18.24
27. Loans held for sale	23,731	749,899	−726,168	−96.84
28. Held-to-maturity securities	0	0	0	
29. Available-for-sale securities	2,158,011	2,577,179	−419,168	−16.26

other federally supervised bank, thus enabling comparison of banks in the same market area subject to the same environmental conditions.

To get a better picture of the type of information in the UBPR, we present an example based on the 2004 and 2003 UBPRs of the lead bank for National City Corporation, National City Bank (NCB). In Chapter 5, we examined the aggregate numbers for all the banks in this holding company, using data found at the FDIC's Web site. The financial statements we see in this analysis, however, are focused on a single bank. The format of the UBPR is more detailed and extensive, but similar to the financial statements presented in Chapter 5.

NCB is a large national bank located in Cleveland, Ohio, with total assets exceeding $52 billion on December 31, 2004. How well or how poorly has NCB performed in recent years? We will examine this bank's financials for 2003 and 2004 in order to provide insights regarding this question. To put this analysis in context, we should recall that the U.S. central bank, the Federal Reserve System, reduced short-term interest rates 13 times from 2001 to 2003 as they tried to stimulate a sluggish economy. The 10-year Treasury bond yield dropped to a 45-year low in June of 2003. The lowered interest rates and disappointing stock returns inspired consumers to invest in real estate, which increased the prices of homes and other properties while increasing the demand for real estate loans. As the economy slowly recovered from the business recession of 2001, the Federal Reserve began to slowly increase interest rates in 2004. In a period characterized by low, but volatile interest rates, investors and lenders talked about whether a real estate bubble was about to burst!

Tables 6–5 through 6–9, taken from UBPR reports for 2004 and 2003, are used to assess the performance of NCB. Tables 6–5 and 6–6 indicate the principal assets, liabilities, and capital items held by this bank and show how these items and their components have increased or decreased in volume since the same time a year earlier. In terms of growth, NCB's assets increased by more than $6.6 billion for an annual growth rate close to 14.5 percent (Table 6–5, line 25). If we examine the asset items having the largest dollar increases, we find that net loans and leases (item 10) increased by $4.02 billion (10.67 percent) and total investments (item 18) increased by $3 billion (91.98 percent). The sources of funds supporting this growth included a $3.21 billion rise (13.01 percent) in total deposits (Table 6–6, item 9) and a dramatic $4.88 billion increase (169.73 percent) in other borrowings with maturities greater than one year (item 14).

Table 6–5 indicates that NCB focuses on traditional banking services with $41.7 billion in net loans and leases (item 10). In 2004 NCB increased its real estate loans (item 1) by 16.11 percent or $3.4 billion, while the balances in most other loan categories (items 2–5) increased or decreased by smaller dollar amounts. Essentially, NCB provided what customers wanted—financing for housing at a time when prices in the stock market were declining and securities (i.e., government and private bonds) were offering historically low returns. The increased proportion of real estate loans would most likely increase the average maturity of the bank's loan portfolio and also increase its interest-rate risk exposure, a concept introduced earlier in this chapter and discussed in detail in Part Three of this book.

NCB's deposit growth and its growth in nondeposit liabilities more than covered the growth in its loan portfolio. In Table 6–6 we see that deposits in foreign offices (item 8) increased significantly, up more than 53 percent, while core deposits (item 6) increased a mere 2.87 percent. Core deposits are the sum of items 1–5 in Table 6–6, representing stable funds that are less likely to be removed from the bank. Core deposits also tend to be

TABLE 6–6   The Liabilities and Capital Section from the Balance Sheet for National City Bank

Source: Uniform Bank Performance Reports (**www.ffiec.gov**).

Items (dollar amounts in thousands)	12/31/2004	12/31/2003	$ Change	Percentage Change
Liabilities and Capital				
1. Demand deposits	$3,873,889	$4,348,224	−$474,335	−10.91%
2. All NOW and ATS accounts	270,253	189,433	80,820	42.66
3. Money market deposit accounts	9,087,746	8,219,768	867,978	10.56
4. Other savings deposits	4,611,592	4,652,219	−40,627	−0.87
5. Time deposits under $100,000	2,797,895	2,655,344	142,551	5.37
6. Core deposits	**20,641,375**	**20,064,988**	**576,387**	**2.87**
7. Time deposits of $100,000 or more	1,934,527	1,149,764	784,763	68.25
8. Deposits in foreign offices	5,343,291	3,490,673	1,852,618	53.07
9. Total deposits	**27,919,193**	**24,705,425**	**3,213,768**	**13.01**
10. Federal funds purchased and REPOs	2,820,675	4,139,388	−1,318,713	−31.86
11. FHL borrowing with maturities less than 1 year	245,006	22	244,984	1113563.64
12. FHL borrowing with maturities greater than 1 year	1,281,709	1,122,701	159,008	14.16
13. Other borrowings with maturities less than 1 year	6,274,512	6,888,395	−613,883	−8.91
14. Other borrowings with maturities greater than 1 year	7,761,259	2,881,257	4,880,002	169.37
15. Acceptances and other liabilities	1,475,244	2,201,346	−726,102	−32.98
16. Total liabilities (including mortgages)	**47,777,598**	**41,938,534**	**5,839,064**	**13.92**
17. Subordinated notes and debentures	1,413,606	1,434,585	−20,979	−1.46
18. All common and preferred capital	3,783,712	2,902,903	880,809	30.34
19. Total liabilities and capital	**52,974,916**	**46,276,022**	**6,698,894**	**14.48**

among the least expensive sources of funds. Overall, total deposits (item 9) increased by 13.01 percent or $3.2 billion. As interest rates began to rise, NCB increased its borrowings with maturities greater than one year (item 14) which soared upward by nearly $5 billion. As market interest rates increased the growth in core deposits subsided and NCB apparently worked to lock in longer-term nondeposit borrowings.

NCB reported substantial growth in security investments, driven by a sharp advance (137.85 percent) in Federal funds sold and resale agreements (Table 6–5, item 16) and a very large gain in interest-bearing bank balances (item 15). NCB apparently increased the liquidity of its investment portfolio by changing its composition while nearly doubling the overall size of that portfolio. Liquidity choices on the asset side of the balance sheet teamed up with increases in long-term nondeposit borrowings as sources of bank funds to help this large banking firm get ready for rising market interest rates.

Table 6–7 shows the composition of assets and liabilities held by NCB, using averages across the four quarters of the year, and presents analogous information for a peer group of banks. The *peer group* used for NCB consists of all national banks with average assets in excess of $3 billion, including the largest 170 banks in 2004 and biggest 163 banks in 2003. The changes in assets and liabilities that we discussed in Tables 6–5 and 6–6 are based on year-end numbers whereas the percentages in Table 6–7 represent averages that tend to reduce the effects of seasonality and window dressing. From this point on, our discussion will focus on *average* data for NCB and its peers.

For NCB we see relatively small changes in asset composition in Table 6–7. Net loans and leases as a percentage of average assets (line 4) increased from 78.41 percent at the end of 2003 to 81.34 percent as 2004 ended—a 3.74 percent increase in net loans and leases relative to average assets. However, in both years larger percentages of assets were accounted for by loans at NCB than was true for its peer group who reported ratios of net loans and leases to average assets of only 58.47 percent in 2003 and 58.91 percent in 2004. Because loans often represent the highest-yielding assets a bank can hold, NCB's higher loan-asset ratio would be expected to produce relatively higher earnings than the average earnings for the peer group.

NCB has slightly decreased its holdings of liquid assets (short-term securities and cash assets). If we sum the percentages for items 5, 6, 7, 9, and 11 in Table 6–7, we find that interest-bearing liquid assets and cash assets accounted for 13.25 percent of assets in 2003 and 11.61 percent of assets in 2004. In contrast, the peer group has about twice the portion of liquid assets relative to total assets. In 2003 and 2004, liquid assets accounted for 28.11 percent and 27.17 percent of assets at peer institutions. Could NCB's management be accepting greater liquidity risk (i.e., the possibility of a cash-out) than is warranted? Banks, like other firms, want to have enough liquid assets to meet their needs without oppressing profitability with excessive funds invested in relatively low-yielding instruments. Their needs for funds are usually derived from their customers' needs for funds where the customer draws down loan commitments (off-balance-sheet items that become on-balance-sheet assets) or withdraws deposits.

On the sources of funds side, we note from Table 6–7 that NCB holds a significantly smaller proportion of core deposits (item 22) than the peer group of banks. Core deposits, as reported in the UBPR, include demand deposits, negotiable order of withdrawal (NOW) accounts, regular savings deposits, money market deposits, and time deposits of less than $100,000. The difference is derived for the most part from money market deposit accounts (MMDAs) (in item 19). The cost of MMDAs is comparable to the cost of many nondeposit sources of funds. Given that their checkable deposits are comparable—NCB has 8.48 percent (sum of items 17 and 18) and the peer group reports 8.56 percent—the lower proportion of core deposits does not necessarily indicate excessive funding costs.

TABLE 6–7 Percentage Composition of Assets and Liabilities for National City Bank and Its Peer Group (all figures are percentages of average total assets)

Source: Uniform Bank Performance Reports (**www.ffiec.gov**).

	NCB 12/31/04	Peer 12/31/04	NCB 12/31/03	Peer 12/31/03
Assets: Percentage of average assets				
1. Total loans	82.50%	58.22%	79.65%	57.68%
2. Lease financing receivables	0.01	1.03	0.02	1.19
3. Less: Loan and lease loss allowance	1.17	0.80	1.26	0.86
4. Net loans and leases	**81.34**	**58.91**	**78.41**	**58.47**
5. Interest-bearing bank balances	1.18	0.76	0.03	0.87
6. Federal funds sold and resale agreements	1.85	2.37	2.19	2.61
7. Trading account assets	0.53	0.34	0.63	0.39
8. Held-to-maturity securities	0.00	2.01	0.00*	1.45
9. Available-for-sale securities	4.62	21.02	6.55	21.11
10. Total earning assets	**89.52**	**90.08**	**87.81**	**89.84**
11. Noninterest-bearing cash and deposits due from other banks	3.43	2.68	3.85	3.13
12. Premises, fixed assets, capital leases	1.06	1.09	1.03	1.08
13. Other real estate owned	0.01	0.05	0.02	0.05
14. Acceptances and other assets	5.98	5.82	7.29	5.49
15. Subtotal	**10.48**	**9.92**	**12.19**	**10.16**
16. Total assets	**100.00**	**100.00**	**100.00**	**100.00**
Liabilities				
17. Demand deposits	8.05	6.65	9.28	6.59
18. All NOW and ATS accounts	0.43	1.91	0.42	1.81
19. Money market deposit accounts	17.91	24.34	19.34	22.00
20. Other savings deposits	9.38	8.42	9.83	8.73
21. Time deposits under $100,000	5.30	8.36	6.40	9.59
22. Core deposits	**41.07**	**54.67**	**45.27**	**53.93**
23. Time deposits of $100,000 or more	2.80	8.99	3.95	9.02
24. Deposits in foreign offices	9.86	1.94	4.75	2.04
25. Total deposits	**53.73**	**68.35**	**53.97**	**67.82**
26. Federal funds purchased and REPOs	8.12	8.00	10.83	8.16
27. Total federal home loan borrowings	2.62	4.63	2.34	4.81
28. Total other borrowings	21.97	2.64	17.77	2.84
29. Memo:Short-term noncore funding	**22.47**	**22.84**	**26.39**	**22.85**
30. Acceptances and other liabilities	4.03	2.10	5.46	2.46
31. Total liabilities (including mortgages)	**90.46**	**89.83**	**90.36**	**90.24**
32. Subordinated notes and debentures	2.90	0.62	3.14	0.71
33. All common and preferred capital	6.64	9.39	6.50	8.93
34. Total liabilities and capital	**99.99**	**100.00**	**99.99**	**100.00**

* Figure is less than 0.05 percent.

When we look at nondeposit liabilities, we see that total other borrowings are significantly higher for NCB than for the peer group. To some extent, NCB has substituted nondeposit borrowings for money market deposits compared to its peers.

Turning to NCB's statement of earnings and expenses (Table 6–8), we must recall the changing interest rate environment from the beginning of 2003 to the conclusion of 2004. Interest rates hit bottom in 2003 and then began to rise slowly. The federal funds rate dropped below 1 percent in December 2003 and then climbed to 2.28 percent by year-end 2004. The 30-year home mortgage interest rate dropped to a low of 5.23 percent in June 2003, rose to a high of 6.29 percent in June 2004, and ended that year at 5.71 percent. While total interest income (item 16) increased by 11.56 percent—a favorable result—total interest expenses also increased. In an ideal world we would like income to

TABLE 6–8 National City Bank Income Statement (Revenues and Expenses)

Source: Uniform Bank Performance Reports (**www.ffiec.gov**).

Items (dollar amounts in thousands)	12/31/2004	12/31/2003	Percentage Change
1. Interest and fees on loans	$2,170,542	$1,927,084	12.63%
2. Income from lease financing	102	86	18.60
3. Tax-exempt	2,071	1,998	3.65
4. Estimated tax benefit	976	909	7.37
5. Income on loans and leases (tax-equivalent basis)	**2,171,620**	**1,928,079**	**12.63**
6. Income from U.S. Treasury and agency securities	2,333	7,812	−70.14
7. Mortgage-backed securities (MBS) income	73,379	69,222	6.01
8. Estimated tax benefit	13	11	18.18
9. Income from all other securities	35,919	50,196	−28.44
10. Tax-exempt securities income	27	25	8.00
11. Investment income (tax-equivalent basis)	**111,644**	**127,241**	**−12.26**
12. Interest on due from other banks	4,968	493	907.71
13. Interest on federal funds sold and resales	19,225	15,239	26.16
14. Trading account income	5,393	1,688	219.49
15. Other interest income	4,310	4,351	−0.94
16. Total interest income (tax-equivalent basis)	**2,317,160**	**2,077,091**	**11.56**
17. Interest on deposits in foreign offices	88,743	33,449	165.31
18. Interest on time deposits over $100,000	36,021	43,248	−16.71
19. Interest on all other deposits	156,541	188,654	−17.02
20. Interest on federal funds purchased & repurchase agreements	61,140	64,926	−5.83
21. Interest on trading liabilities and other borrowings	208,472	162,851	28.01
22. Interest on mortgages and leases for other property & equipment	0	0	0.00
23. Interest on subordinated notes and debentures	34,627	25,019	38.40
24. Total interest expense	**585,544**	**518,147**	**13.01**
25. Net interest income (tax-equivalent basis)	**1,731,616**	**1,558,944**	**11.08**
26. Noninterest income	802,999	783,373	2.51
27. Adjusted operating income (tax-equivalent basis)	**2,534,615**	**2,342,317**	**8.21**
28. Noninterest expense	1,243,716	1,160,735	7.15
29. Provision: Loan and lease losses	147,147	422,562	−65.18
30. Pretax operating income (tax-equivalent basis)	**1,143,752**	**759,020**	**50.69**
31. Realized gains/losses on held-to-maturity securities	0	0	0.00
32. Realized gains/losses on available-for-sale securities	5,992	3,639	64.66
33. Pretax net operating income (tax-equivalent basis)	**1,149,744**	**762,659**	**50.75**
34. Applicable income taxes	421,806	208,817	102.00
35. Current tax equivalent adjustments	989	920	7.50
36. Other tax-equivalent adjustments	0	0	0.00
37. Applicable income taxes (tax-equivalent basis)	422,795	209,737	101.58
38. Net operating income	**726,949**	**552,922**	**31.47**
39. Net extraordinary items	0	0	0.00
40. Net income	**726,949**	**552,922**	**31.47**
41. Cash dividends declared	150,000	300,000	−50.00
42. Retained earnings (addition to)	**576,949**	**252,922**	**128.11**

go up and expenses to go down. This ideal situation is similar to the famous directive to investors to "Buy Low and Sell High"—simplistic in theory but hard to apply, especially when we are talking about interest income and expenses and both items are correlated with market interest rates. (We will soon be exploring the effects of these correlations in Chapter 7.) Most interest income items (items 1 through 15 in Table 6–8) increased and, while the signs were mixed for individual interest expense items (items 17–23), the overall effect was an increase in NCB's total interest expenses (item 24).

NCB's net interest income (item 25) increased by 11.08 percent during the year. When net interest income is measured relative to average total assets, the net interest margin (NIM) increases slightly as illustrated by the following:

$$\frac{\begin{array}{c}\text{Interest income} \\ \text{from loans and} \\ \text{security investments}\end{array} - \begin{array}{c}\text{Interest expense on} \\ \text{borrowed funds}\end{array}}{\text{Average assets}} = \text{Net interest margin}^4$$

$$\begin{array}{cc} 2004 & 2003 \\ \dfrac{\$1,731,616}{\$48,025,306} = 3.61\% & \dfrac{\$1,558,944}{\$44,445,794} = 3.51\% \end{array}$$

As Table 6–9 illustrates, NCB's 3.61 percent net interest margin (NIM) is above the average for its peer group of banks, which reported net interest margins of only 3.23 percent in both 2003 and 2004. Certainly staying in front of one's peers is positive. Management should be happy that the NIM gap between NCB and its peer group is expanding, indicating relative improvement in NCB's spread between all its interest revenues and all its interest expenses.

NCB's *net operating margin* (line 10 in Table 6–9)—the gap between its total operating revenues and total operating expenses—has changed as follows:

$$\frac{\text{Net operating income}}{\text{Average assets}} = \text{Net operating margin}^5$$

$$\begin{array}{cc} 2004 & 2003 \\ \dfrac{\$726,949}{\$48,025,306} = 1.51\% & \dfrac{\$552,922}{\$44,445,794} = 1.24\% \end{array}$$

Once again, NCB's net operating margin is above that of its peer group, 1.51 percent versus 1.31 percent in 2004 and that is "good." The margin between NCB and its peers has

TABLE 6–9

Relative Income
Statement and Margin
Analysis for National
City Bank and Its
Peer Group (all
figures are
percentages of average
total assets)

Source: Uniform Bank
Performance Reports
(www.ffiec.gov).

	NCB 2004	Peer Group 2004	NCB 2003	Peer Group 2003
1. Total interest income (tax-equivalent basis)	4.82%	4.46%	4.67%	4.57%
2. Less: Interest expense	1.22	1.20	1.17	1.29
3. **Equals: Net interest income (tax-equivalent basis)**	**3.61**	**3.23**	**3.51**	**3.23**
4. Plus: Noninterest income	1.67	1.73	1.76	1.83
5. Minus: Noninterest expense	2.59	2.89	2.61	2.95
6. Minus: Provision for loan and lease losses	0.31	0.14	0.95	0.27
7. **Equals: Pretax operating income (tax-equivalent basis)**	**2.38**	**1.97**	**1.71**	**1.89**
8. Plus: realized gains/losses on securities	0.01	0.02	0.01	0.05
9. **Equals: Pretax net operating income (tax-equivalent basis)**	**2.39**	**2.00**	**1.72**	**1.95**
10. **Net operating income**	**1.51**	**1.31**	**1.24**	**1.28**
11. **Adjusted net operating income**	**1.43**	**1.29**	**1.37**	**1.29**
12. Net income adjusted for Subchapter S status		1.31		1.28
13. **Net income**	**1.51**	**1.31**	**1.24**	**1.28**

[4]The numbers in the numerator are taken from Table 6–8, items 16 and 24. The denominator is average assets based on quarterly totals for 2004 of $48,025,306 thousand and for 2003 of $44,445,794 thousand.

[5]The numerator is based on item 38 in Table 6–8 and the denominator is average assets as provided in footnote 4.

increased significantly: while NCB's net operating margin rose by a whopping 21.77 percent, the peer group's comparable ratio increased by only 2.34 percent. By this measure NCB outshines its peer group of banking firms.

However, NCB's stockholders will probably be most concerned about the earnings per share (EPS) of stock that they hold. National City Corporation (the bank holding company) had 605,996,120 shares outstanding in 2003 and 646,749,650 shares of stock in 2004 (according to its annual report submitted to the SEC and accessible using the student version of S&P's Market Insights and the associated Edgar link). Using this data we can calculate the EPS on a bank basis (using net income from NCB). Its EPS changed as follows between year-end 2003 and 2004:

$$\text{EPS} = \frac{\text{Net income}}{\text{Common equity shares outstanding}}$$

2004	2003
$\dfrac{\$726,949,000}{646,749,650} = \$1.12 \text{ per share}$	$\dfrac{\$552,922,000}{605,996,120} = \$0.91 \text{ per share}$

The bank experienced a significant jump in stockholders' earnings per share. Remember this calculation is based on the net income for the lead bank divided by the number of shares of National City Corporation, the bank holding company. Hence, caution in interpreting these results is important. Keeping this in mind, management would certainly like to see this trend continue.

As we move further down the income and expense statement in Table 6–8 we see that, while net interest income increased by 11.08 percent in 2004, net income (item 40) increased by a remarkable 31.47 percent! This was due to a small 2.51 percent increase in noninterest income (item 26), a 64.66 percent increase in realized gains on available-for-sale securities (item 32), and a 65.18 percent decrease in the provision for loan and lease losses (item 29). With a bank that focuses substantially on lending like NCB, changes in the Report of Income's provision for loan and lease losses (item 29) and the related loan and lease allowance for losses account (item 9 in Table 6–5) contained in the Report of Condition may provide some insights into the quality of the bank's loan portfolio. (Note: If you are a bit confused about what these accounts represent, please review the discussion in Chapter 5.)

NCB's loan-loss provision expense of $147,147 thousand was just over a third of the loss provision for the previous year. The loan-loss allowance account decreased 13.18 percent to $514,318 thousand. This tells us that the annual loan-loss expense was less than the actual volume of net charge-offs, resulting in a smaller allowance account on NCB's Report of Condition. According to Table 6–7 the loan and lease loss allowance to average assets (item 3) went from 1.26 percent in 2003 to 1.17 percent in 2004. Management appears to be cashing in on the low loan losses that were characteristic of this time period.

How did NCB do relative to its peer group with regard to income and expenses? Table 6–9 provides a glimpse of an answer for this question. NCB improved its performance in 2004. It outperformed its peer group on interest income (item 1) and noninterest expense (item 5) in both 2003 and 2004. *Outperformed* means NCB's interest income was higher as a percentage of its average assets and its noninterest expenses were lower as a percentage of its average assets than comparable banks. The lower noninterest expense indicates that management has succeeded in controlling overhead costs relative to its peer group. Overall, the successes regarding interest income and noninterest expenses illustrated in the upper portion of Table 6–9 led to both higher net operating income (item 10) and higher net income (item 13) relative to average total assets for NCB versus its peer group of banks in 2004.

NCB looks good relative to its peers and the profitability ratios are getting better. ROA increased by 21.77 percent. We can explore NCB's earnings further using Equations (6–11), (6–14), and (6–18) discussed earlier in this chapter. Equation (6–11) provides the following breakdown using quarterly average figures for Report of Condition items:

$$\text{ROE} = \text{ROA} \times \frac{\text{Average assets}}{\text{Average equity capital}}$$

NCB's ROE in 2004:[6]

$$\text{ROE} = 0.0151 \times 15.06$$
$$= 0.2280 \text{ or } 22.80\%$$

NCB's ROE in 2003:[6]

$$\text{ROE} = 0.0124 \times 15.38$$
$$= 0.1914 \text{ or } 19.14\%$$

Clearly, NCB's ROE increased because its ROA—a measure of managerial efficiency—improved. At the same time NCB's use of leverage (i.e., the proportion of its assets supported by debt) decreased. Management and the board of directors expanded the amount of equity capital through increased profits and reductions in stock dividend payments. The dollar amount of dividends declared in 2004 was half the 2003 dividend declaration and this tended to lower the equity multiplier.

We can expand this analysis a bit further using Equation (6–14) for ROE:

$$\text{ROE} = \frac{\text{Net income}}{\text{Total operating revenue}} \times \frac{\text{Total operating revenue}}{\text{Average assets}}$$

$$\times \frac{\text{Average assets}}{\text{Average equity capital}}$$

NCB's ROE in 2004:[7]

$$\text{ROE} = \frac{\$726,949}{\$3,120,159} \times \frac{\$3,120,159}{\$48,025,306} \times \frac{\$48,025,306}{\$3,188,880}$$

$$= 0.2330 \times 0.0650 \times 15.06$$

$$= 0.2280 \text{ or } 22.80\%$$

NCB's ROE in 2003.[7]

$$\text{ROE} = \frac{\$552,922}{\$2,860,464} \times \frac{\$2,860,464}{\$44,445,794} \times \frac{\$44,445,794}{\$2,888,977}$$

$$= 0.1933 \times 0.0644 \times 15.38$$

$$= 0.1914 \text{ or } 19.14\%$$

What factors in these earnings relationships caused NCB's return to its stockholders (ROE) to rise? The key factors were: (1) NCB's rising net profit margin, which increased by 20.54 percent, and (2) the nearly 1 percent rise in NCB's asset utilization ratio (operating

---

[6]ROA is item 13 from Table 6–9 and for balance sheet items we use average assets as reported in the UBPR and derive average equity capital from item 33 in Table 6–7. For 2004 average equity capital equaled 6.64 percent of average assets where average assets were $48,025,306.

[7]Total operating revenue is item 16 plus item 26 from Table 6–8.

revenues to average assets). These positive effects were mitigated to some extent by the 2.08 percent decline in the equity multiplier from 15.38 times to 15.06 times.

Analysis of ROE using Equation (6–18) emphasizes NCB's record of expense control as illustrated by its rising net profit margin and improved asset management efficiency. The relevant equation is:

$$ROE = \frac{\text{Net income}}{\text{Pretax net operating income}} \times \frac{\text{Pretax net operating income}}{\text{Total operating revenues}}$$

$$\times \frac{\text{Total operating revenues}}{\text{Average assets}} \times \frac{\text{Average assets}}{\text{Average equity capital}}$$

NCB's ROE in 2004:[8]

$$ROE = \frac{\$726,949}{\$1,149,744} \times \frac{\$1,149,744}{\$3,120,159} \times \frac{\$3,120,159}{\$48,025,306} \times \frac{\$48,025,306}{\$3,188,880}$$

$$= 0.6323 \times 0.3685 \times 0.0650 \times 15.06$$

$$= 0.2280 \text{ or } 22.80\%$$

NCB's ROE in 2003:[8]

$$ROE = \frac{\$552,922}{\$762,659} \times \frac{\$762,659}{\$2,860,464} \times \frac{\$2,860,464}{\$44,445,794} \times \frac{\$44,445,794}{\$2,888,977}$$

$$= 0.7250 \times 0.2666 \times 0.0644 \times 15.38$$

$$= 0.1914 \text{ or } 19.14\%$$

A glance at the breakdown of ROE above shows a decline in tax-management efficiency with net income to pretax operating income decreasing from 72.50 percent in 2003 to 63.23 percent in 2004. For every dollar of pretax operating income NCB paid out about 27 cents in taxes in 2003, which rose further to nearly 37 cents in 2004. On a brighter note, however, the measure of expense-control efficiency (pretax net operating income to total operating revenue) advanced by more than 38 percent, pointing to improved expense control.

In conclusion, we have utilized the tools developed in this chapter and NCB's UBPR to get a better picture of the operations and management of this bank. NCB appears to be more focused on the traditional business of lending than is the average large bank today. Its operations have generated higher revenues and lower expenses than its peers and this performance superiority generally broadened between 2003 and 2004.

[8]Pretax net operating income is item 33 from Table 6–8.

Summary

The principal focus of this chapter has been on how well banks and other financial firms perform in serving their customers and in providing acceptable returns to their owners. We have also noted that many of the measures of financial-firm performance provide key insights regarding the interindustry competition today between banks, thrift institutions, security brokers and dealers, mutual funds, finance companies, and insurance firms. Increasingly, bankers and their competitors are being forced to assess their performance over time, analyze the reasons for any performance problems that appear, and find ways to strengthen their performance in the future.

Among the key points made in the chapter are these:

- The two key dimensions of performance among financial-service firms are *profitability* and *risk*. Satisfactory profits and adequate risk controls preserve capital, providing a basis for a financial firm's survival and future growth.

- For the largest profit-oriented financial institutions the market value of their stock (equities) is usually the best overall indicator of profitability and risk exposure.

- For smaller financial firms whose stock is not actively traded every day a number of key *profitability ratios* (such as return on assets, return on equity capital, net interest margin, noninterest margin, and earnings spread) become important performance measures and significant managerial targets.

- Pursuit of profitability must always be tempered with concern for *risk exposure*, including the management and control of credit or default risk, liquidity or cash-out risk, market risk to the value of assets and liabilities held, interest-rate risk, operational risk, legal and compliance risks, reputation risk, strategic risk, and capital risk. The latter risk measure focuses upon the probability of ultimate failure if a financial firm is undercapitalized relative to the risks it faces.

- Increasingly financial-service firms are adding operating *efficiency* to their list of performance criteria, focusing upon measures of expense control and the productivity of employees in managing assets, revenues, and income.

- The chapter concludes with a discussion of the Uniform Bank Performance Report (UBPR) available from the Federal Financial Institutions Examination Council. This financial report on individual FDIC-insured commercial and savings banks has become one of the most widely used performance summaries available to bankers, regulators, customers, and the general public.

Key Terms

profitability, *167*
ROA, *167*
ROE, *167*
efficiency, *168*
net interest margin, *168*
net noninterest,
margin, *168*

net profit margin, *170*
asset utilization, *170*
equity multiplier, *170*
credit risk, *177*
liquidity risk, *178*
market risk, *178*
interest rate risk, *179*

operational risk, *179*
legal risk, *180*
compliance risk, *180*
reputation risk, *180*
strategic risk, *180*
capital risk, *180*
UBPR, *185*

Problems and Projects

1. An investor holds the stock of First National Bank of Imoh and expects to receive a dividend of $12 per share at the end of the year. Stock analysts have recently predicted that the bank's dividends will grow at approximately 3 percent a year indefinitely into the future. If this is true, and if the appropriate risk-adjusted cost of capital (discount rate) for the bank is 15 percent, what should be the current price per share of Imoh's stock?

2. Suppose that stockbrokers have projected that Poquoson Bank and Trust Company will pay a dividend of $3 per share on its common stock at the end of the year; a dividend of $4.50 per share is expected for the next year, and $6 per share in the following year. The risk-adjusted cost of capital for banks in Poquoson's risk class is 17 percent. If an investor holding Poquoson's stock plans to hold that stock for only three years and hopes to sell it at a price of $55 per share, what should the value of the bank's stock be in today's market?

3. Depositors Savings Association has a ratio of equity capital to total assets of 7.5 percent. In contrast, Newton Savings reports an equity-capital-to-asset ratio of 6 percent.

What is the value of the equity multiplier for each of these institutions? Suppose that both institutions have an ROA of 0.85 percent. What must each institution's return on equity capital be? What do your calculations tell you about the benefits of having as little equity capital as regulations or the marketplace will allow?

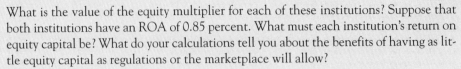

4. The latest report of condition and income and expense statement for Galloping Merchants National Bank are as shown in the following tables:

Galloping Merchants National Bank

Income and Expense Statement (Report of Income)

Interest and fees on loans	$65
Interest and dividends on securities	12
Total interest income	
Interest paid on deposits	49
Interest paid on nondeposit borrowings	6
Total interest expense	
Net interest income	
Provision for loan losses	2
Noninterest income and fees	7
Noninterest expenses:	
Salaries and employee benefits	12*
Overhead expenses	5
Other noninterest expenses	3
Total noninterest expenses	
Pretax operating income	
Securities gains (or losses)	1
Pretax net operating income	
Taxes	1
Net operating income	
Net extraordinary items	(−1)
Net income	

*Note: the bank currently has 40 FTE employees.

Galloping Merchants National Bank

Report of Condition

Assets		Liabilities	
Cash and deposits due from banks	$100	Demand deposits	$190
Investment securities	150	Savings deposits	180
Federal funds sold	10	Time deposits	470
Net loans	670	Federal funds purchased	60
(Allowance for loan losses = 25)		Total liabilities	900
(Unearned income on loans = 5)		Equity capital	
Plant and equipment	50	Common stock	20
Total assets	980	Surplus	25
		Retained earnings	35
		Total capital	80
Total earning assets	830	Interest-bearing deposits	650

Fill in the missing items on the income and expense statement. Using these statements, calculate the following performance measures:

ROE	Asset utilization
ROA	Equity multiplier
Net interest margin	Tax management efficiency

Net noninterest margin	Expense control efficiency
Net operating margin	Asset management efficiency
Earnings spread	Funds management efficiency
Net profit margin	Operating efficiency ratio

What strengths and weaknesses are you able to detect in Galloping Merchants' performance?

5. The following information is for Shallow National Bank:

Interest income	$ 2,100.00
Interest expense	1,400.00
Total assets	30,000.00
Security losses or gains	21.00
Earning assets	25,000.00
Total liabilities	27,000.00
Taxes paid	16.00
Shares of comon stock outstanding	5,000
Noninterest income	$ 700.00
Noninterest expense	900.00
Provision for loan losses	100.00

Please calculate:

ROE	_____
ROA	_____
Net interest margin	_____
Earnings per share	_____
Net noninterest margin	_____
Net operating margin	_____

Alternative scenarios:

a. Suppose interest income, interest expenses, noninterest income, and noninterest expenses each increase by 5 percent while all other revenue and expense items shown in the preceding table remain unchanged. What will happen to Shallow's ROE, ROA, and earnings per share?

b. On the other hand, suppose Shallow's interest income and expenses as well as its noninterest income and expenses decline by 5 percent, again with all other factors held constant. How would the bank's ROE, ROA, and per-share earnings change?

6. Blue and White National Bank holds total assets of $1.69 billion and equity capital of $139 million and has just posted an ROA of 1.10 percent. What is the bank's ROE?

Alternative scenarios:

a. Suppose Blue and White Bank finds its ROA climbing by 50 percent, with assets and equity capital unchanged. What will happen to its ROE? Why?

b. On the other hand, suppose the bank's ROA drops by 50 percent. If total assets and equity capital hold their present positions, what change will occur in ROE?

c. If ROA at Blue and White National remains fixed at 0.0076 but both total assets and equity double, how does ROE change? Why?

d. How would a decline in total assets and equity by half (with ROA still at 0.0076) affect the bank's ROE?

www.mhhe.com/rose7e

7. Monarch State Bank reports total operating revenues of $135 million, with total operating expenses of $121 million, and owes taxes of $2 million. It has total assets of $1.00 billion and total liabilities of $900 million. What is the bank's ROE?

Alternative scenarios:

a. How will the ROE for Monarch State Bank change if total operating expenses, taxes, and total operating revenues each grow by 10 percent while assets and liabilities remain fixed?

b. Suppose Monarch State's total assets and total liabilities increase by 10 percent, but its revenues and expenses (including taxes) are unchanged. How will the bank's ROE change?

c. Can you determine what will happen to ROE if both operating revenues and expenses (including taxes) decline by 10 percent, with the bank's total assets and liabilities held constant?

d. What does ROE become if Monarch State's assets and liabilities decrease by 10 percent, while its operating revenues, taxes, and operating expenses do not change?

8. Suppose a stockholder-owned thrift institution is projected to achieve a 1.25 percent ROA during the coming year. What must its ratio of total assets to equity capital be if it is to achieve its target ROE of 12 percent? If ROA unexpectedly falls to 0.75 percent, what assets-to-capital ratio must it then have to reach a 12 percent ROE?

9. Saylor County National Bank presents us with these figures for the year just concluded. Please determine the net profit margin, equity multiplier, asset utilization ratio, and ROE.

Net income	$ 18.00
Total operating revenues	125.00
Total assets	1,500.00
Total equity capital accounts	155.00

10. Lochiel Commonwealth Bank and Trust Company has experienced the following trends over the past five years (all figures in millions of dollars):

Year	Net Income After-Tax	Total Operating Revenues	Total Assets	Total Equity Capital
1	$2.70	$26.50	$293.00	$18.00
2	3.50	30.10	382.00	20.00
3	4.10	39.80	474.00	22.00
4	4.80	47.50	508.00	25.00
5	5.70	55.90	599.00	28.00

Determine the figures for ROE, profit margin, asset utilization, and equity multiplier for this bank. Are any adverse trends evident? Where would you recommend that management look to deal with the bank's emerging problem(s)?

11. Wilmington Hills State Bank has just submitted its Report of Condition and Report of Income to its principal supervisory agency. The bank reported net income before taxes and securities transactions of $27 million and taxes of $6 million. If its total operating

revenues were $780 million, its total assets $2.1 billion, and its equity capital $125 million, determine the following for Wilmington:

a. Tax management efficiency ratio.

b. Expense control efficiency ratio.

c. Asset management efficiency ratio.

d. Funds management efficiency ratio.

e. ROE.

Alternative scenarios:

a. Suppose Wilmington Hills State Bank experienced a 20 percent rise in net before-tax income, with its tax obligation, operating revenues, assets, and equity unchanged. What would happen to ROE and its components?

b. If total assets climb by 20 percent, what will happen to Wilmington's efficiency ratio and ROE?

c. What effect would a 20 percent higher level of equity capital have upon Wilmington's ROE and its components?

12. Using this information for Lochness International Bank and Trust Company (all figures in millions), calculate the bank's net interest margin, noninterest margin, and ROA.

Interest income	$65
Interest expense	48
Provision for loan losses	3
Security gains (or losses)	2
Noninterest expense	8
Noninterest income	5
Extraordinary net gains	1
Total assets	986

13. Valley Savings reported these figures (in millions) on its income statement for the past five years. Calculate the institution's ROA in each year. Are there any adverse trends? Any favorable trends? What seems to be happening to this institution?

	Current Year	One Year Ago	Two Years Ago	Three Years Ago	Four Years Ago
Gross interest income	$40	$41	$38	$35	$33
Interest expenses	24	23	20	18	15
Noninterest income	4	4	3	2	1
Noninterest expense	8	7	7	6	5
Provision for loan losses	2	1	1	0	0
Income taxes owed	1	1	0	1	0
Net securities gains (losses)	−2	−1	0	1	2
Total assets	385	360	331	319	293

14. An analysis of the UBPR reports on NCB was presented in this chapter. We examined a wide variety of profitability measures for that bank, including ROA, ROE, net profit margin, net interest and operating margins, and asset utilization. However, the various measures of earnings risk, credit risk, liquidity risk, market risk (price risk and interest rate risk), and capital risk were not discussed in detail. Using the data in Tables 6–5 through 6–9, calculate each of these dimensions of risk for NCB for the most recent two years and discuss how the bank's risk exposure appears to be changing over time. What steps would you recommend to management to deal with any risk exposure problems you observe?

Internet Exercises

1. You have been asked to compare the growth rate in assets and deposits of several banks that are regarded as takeover targets for your growth-oriented company. These banks include:

   Amsouth Bank (**www.amsouth.com**)

   BB&T (**www.bbt.com**)

   SunTrust Banks (**www.suntrust.com**)

   Using the above company Web sites and other appropriate sites, determine which of these banks seems to be growing faster and why. Which would you recommend as a possible takeover target and why?

2. A guest speaker visiting your class contends that Bank of America is one of the most profitable banks of its size in the United States. Your instructor says that's really not true; it tends to be a middle-of-the-road performer. Check these claims out on the Web (for example, at **www.bankofamerica.com** and **www.fdic.gov**). Who is right and what makes you think so?

3. The Uniform Bank Performance Reports (UBPRs) provide detailed financial performance data on all federally supervised U.S. banks. Using the Web site of the Federal Financial Institutions Examination Council (at **www.ffiec.gov**), see if you can determine what happened to the earnings and credit risk exposure of Wachovia Corp. (**www.wachovia.com**) and Wells Fargo Bank (**www.wellsfargo.com**) in the most recent year for which data is available.

S&P Market Insight Challenge (www.mhhe.com/edumarketinsight)

STANDARD &POOR'S

1. You can depend on S&P Industry Surveys concluding with sections on "How to Analyze a Company" and a "Comparative Company Analysis." To access these surveys use the Industry tab, and the drop-down menu supplies several subfinancial-service industry selections, such as Asset Management & Custody Banks, Consumer Finance, Diversified Banks, Diversified Capital Markets, Insurance Brokers, Investment Banking and Brokerage, Life & Health Insurance, Multiline Insurance, Property & Casualty Insurance, Regional Banks, and Thrifts & Mortgage Finance. Once an industry has been selected you will find downloadable S&P Industry Surveys, covering such key financial-services sectors as Banking, Investment Services, Financial Services Diversified, Insurance: Property and Casualty, Insurance: Life and Health, and Savings and Loans. Please download S&P Industry Surveys for two of these financial sectors and review the How to Analyze and Comparative Company Analysis write-ups on each. In each category of financial firms found in the Comparative Company Analysis, identify the firm with the highest return on equity capital (ROE). How do the ROEs compare across categories and subindustries? Are there any other performance measures that could be compared across financial-service sectors?

STANDARD &POOR'S

2. Today banks, securities firms, insurance companies, and finance/credit-card businesses are battling for many of the same customers and for many of the same sources of capital to support their growth and expansion. As a result there is keen interest today in the comparative financial performance of firms in these four competing industries. Using S&P's Market Insight, Educational Version, see if you can determine which of these financial-service industries are outperforming the others in terms of returns on equity capital and risk exposure. You may find it useful to select certain firms from the Market Insight file to compare performances across these industries. For example, you can compare the financial statements of such companies as MetLife Insurance Inc. (MET), Capital One Financial Group (COF), Goldman Sachs Group (GS), and FleetBoston Financial Corp. (FBF).

REAL NUMBERS FOR REAL BANKS

Assignment for Chapter 6

EVALUATION OF YOUR BANK'S PROFITABILITY

Part One: A Performance Comparison to Peers

In Chapter 6 we focus on the evaluation of financial statements. Key profitability ratios are introduced and ROE and ROA are broken down into component ratios to aid interpretation. We used the UBPR for National City Bank, the lead bank of National City Corporation, to illustrate trends (comparison of December 2004 with December 2003 bank data) and for comparative analysis (comparison of bank data with peer group data). You will be evaluating your BHC by (1) calculating percentage changes using your dollar data and interpreting this information; (2) comparing your BHC with the group of peer banks using the percentages-to-total assets data; and (3) utilizing the profitability ratios discussed in this chapter to evaluate management's performance.

A. Open your Excel Workbook and go to the spreadsheet containing dollar amounts for Year-to-Year Comparisons. Delete any numbers in columns D and E. Refer to Tables 6–5, 6–6, and 6–8 as examples for what you are about to do. Calculate the dollar changes in Column D and the Percentage Changes

in Column E for each item. Write one paragraph discussing the percentage changes in Total Assets, Total Liabilities, and Total Equity Capital.

B. The spreadsheet containing items expressed as percentages of assets developed for Comparisons with the Peer Group in Chapter 5's Real Numbers for Real Banks assignment is very similar to the data provided for NCB in Tables 6–7 and 6–9.

   a. Write one paragraph comparing the asset composition for your BHC with that of the peer group.

   b. Write one paragraph comparing the sources of funds composition for your BHC with that of the peer group.

   c. Write one paragraph comparing the components of income and expenses for your BHC with that of the peer group.

Part Two: A Breakdown of Returns

A. Open the Year-to-Year Comparisons spreadsheet. Immediately below the income and expense data, add the rows illustrated below:

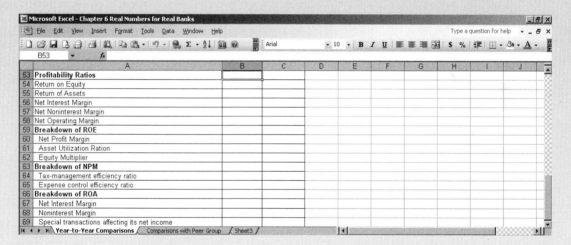

B. Calculate the ratios for the most recent year in Column B and then for the prior year in column C using the formula functions in Excel and the data in Rows 1 through 52 to create the entries. For example, the formula for ROE entered in cell B54 would be: "=B52/B26".

C. In rows 54 through 58, calculate the key profitability ratios from Equations (6–4) through (6–8) in the chapter. Write one paragraph comparing profitability across years.

D. Rows 59 through 62 provide the framework for a breakdown of equity returns using Equations (6–14) through (6–17) in this chapter. Write one paragraph discussing the

change in ROE using this breakdown. Incorporate the basic equation and interpret the information for your bank.

E. Rows 63 through 65 call for a breakdown of the net profit margin, as illustrated by Equation (6–18). Write one paragraph discussing the components of the net profit margin for your bank and the implications of the changes occurring across the years.

F. Rows 66 through 69 provide the framework for a breakdown of ROA (Equation [6–20] in this chapter). Write one paragraph discussing the change in ROA and its components for your bank.

www.mhhe.com/rose7e

Selected References

For an explanation of measuring and evaluating risk in banking and financial services, see the following studies:

1. Gilbert, R. Alton, Andrew P. Meyer, and Mark D. Vaughn. "How Healthy Is the Banking System? Funneling Financial Data into Failure Probability." *Regional Economist*, Federal Reserve Bank of St. Louis, April 2001, pp. 12–13.

2. Kristad, Jeffrey, and Pat Donnelly. "An Examiner's View of Operational Risk." *Bank News*, July 31, 2001, pp. 25–27.

3. Rose, Peter S. "Risk—Taking the Temperature and Finding a Cure." *The Canadian Banker*, November/December, 1987, pp. 54–63.

4. Wright, David M., and James Houpt. "An Analysis of Commercial Bank Exposure to Interest Rate Risk." *Federal Reserve Bulletin*, February 1996, pp. 116–28.

For information on how to read bank financial statements and make comparisons among different institutions, see the following:

5. Federal Financial Institutions Examination Council. *A User's Guide for the Uniform Bank Performance Report*. Washington, D.C., 2002.

6. Gilbert, R. Alton, and Gregory E. Sierra. "The Financial Condition of U.S. Banks: How Different Are Community Banks?" *Review*, Federal Reserve Bank of St. Louis, January/February 2003, pp. 43–56.

7. Gunther, Jeffrey W., and Robert R. Moore. "Financial Statements and Reality: Do Troubled Banks Tell All?" *Economic and Financial Review*, Federal Reserve Bank of Dallas, Third Quarter 2000, pp. 30–35.

8. Klee, Elizabeth C., and Fabio M. Natalucci. "Profits and Balance Sheet Developments at U.S. Commercial Banks in 2004." *Federal Reserve Bulletin*, Spring 2005, pp. 143–74.

9. Wetmore, Jill L., and John R. Brick. "The Basis Risk Component of Commercial Bank Stock Returns." *Journal of Economics and Business* 50 (1998), pp. 67–76.

www.mhhe.com/rose7e

Appendix

Improving the Performance of Financial Firms through Knowledge: Sources of Information on the Financial-Services Industry

Chapter 6 focused on how to measure the performance of banks and some of their closest competitors in today's financial marketplace. However, mere measurement of the dimensions of performance is not enough. Managers must have the tools and the knowledge necessary to improve performance over time. The chapters that follow this one will provide many of the tools needed for successful management of a financial institution, but managers will always need more information than textbooks can provide. Their problems and solutions may be highly technical and will shift over time, often at a faster pace than the one at which textbooks are written. The same difficulty confronts regulators and customers. They must often reach far afield to gather vital information in order to evaluate their financial-service providers and get the best service from them.

Where do the managers of financial institutions find the information they need? One good source is the professional schools in many regions of the nation. Among the most popular of these is the Stonier Graduate School of Banking sponsored by the American Bankers Association. Other professional schools are often devoted to specific problem areas, such as marketing, consumer lending, and commercial lending. Each offers educational materials and often supplies homework problems to solve.

Beyond the professional schools, selected industry trade associations annually publish a prodigious volume of written studies and management guidelines for wrestling with important performance problems, such as developing and promoting new services, working out problem assets, designing a financial plan, and so on. Among the most popular trade associations publishing problem-solving information in the financial-services field are:

- The American Bankers Association at **www.aba.com**.
- Bank Administration Institute at **www.bai.org**.
- Risk Management Association (RMA), Association of Risk Management and Lending Professionals at **www.rmahq.org**.
- America's Community Bankers at **www.acbankers.org**.
- Credit Union National Association (CUNA) at **www.cuna.org**.
- American Council of Life Insurance (ACLI) at **www.acli.org**.
- Investment Company Institute (ICI) at **www.ici.org**.

- Insurance Information Institute (III) at **www.iii.org**.

In addition to the material provided by these and numerous other trade associations, dozens of journals and books are released each year by book publishing houses, magazine publishers, and government agencies. Among the most important of these recurring sources are the following:

General Information on Banking and Competing Financial-Service Industries

- *ABA Banking Journal* (published by the American Bankers Association at **www.banking.com**).
- *Risk Management and Lending Professionals Journal* (published by the Risk Management Association at **www.rmahq.org**).
- *The Canadian Banker* (published by the Canadian Bankers Association at **www.cba.ca**).
- *ABA Bank Marketing Magazine* at **www.aba.com/MarketingNetwork**.

Sources of Data on Individual Banks and Competing Financial Firms

- Uniform Bank Performance Reports (UBPR) (published quarterly by the Federal Financial Institutions Examination Council at **www.fiec.gov**).
- Historical Bank Condition and Income Reports (available from the National Technical Information Service at **www.ntis.org**).
- *American Banker Online* (banking industry newspaper published by the American Bankers Association at **www.americanbanker.com**).
- *The Wall Street Journal* (published by Dow Jones & Co., Inc., and online at **www.wsj.com**).

Economic and Financial Trends Affecting Banking and the Financial Services Sector

- *Survey of Current Business* (published by the U.S. Department of Commerce at **www.bea.gov/bea/pubs.htm**).
- *Federal Reserve Bulletin* (published by the Board of Governors of the Federal Reserve System and available at **www.federalreserve.gov/pubs/bulletin**).
- *National Economic Trends and Monetary Trends* (all published by the Federal Reserve Bank of St. Louis at **www.stls.frb.org**).

Books and Journals Focusing on Laws and Regulations and International Developments Affecting Banks and Other Financial-Service Providers

- *International Economic Conditions* (published by the Federal Reserve Bank of St. Louis at **www.stls.frb.org**).
- *The Economist* (London) (available by subscription; information may be found at **www.economist.com**).

Key Regulatory Agencies

- Office of the Comptroller of the Currency (OCC) at **www.occ.treas.gov**.
- Board of Governors of the Federal Reserve System at **www.federalreserve.gov**.
- Federal Deposit Insurance Corporation (FDIC) at **www.fdic.gov**.
- Office of Thrift Supervision at **www.ots.treas.gov**.

Basic Education in Banking and Financial Services for Both Bankers and Their Customers

- Consumer Action at **www.consumeraction.org**.

- Federal Reserve System at **www.federalreserve.gov**.
- Federal Reserve Bank of Minneapolis at **www.minneapolisfed.org**.

Industry Directories

Directories for many industries give lists of businesses in an industry by name, city, state, and country of location. Some of the more complete directories provide essential avenues of contact for directory users, such as the names of key officers within a firm and the company's mailing address, telephone number, and e-mail address. More detailed directories have abbreviated financial statements of the firms listed and may even have a historical sketch about each firm. One common use of these directories is to pursue possible employment opportunities. Among the better-known industry directories are these:

- *The Bankers Almanac* at **www.bankersalmanac.com**.
- *Investment Bankers Directory* at **www.chicagobusiness.com**.
- *International Insurance Directory* (also described at **www.insurance-network.com**).
- *Directory of Savings and Loans* at **www.abbycon.com/financial**.

PART THREE

Asset-Liability Management Techniques and Hedging Against Risk

Interest rates—the prices charged for obtaining credit—are one of the most important variables that the managers of financial firms must work with every day. Adverse movements in market interest rates can erode a financial institution's profitability and wipe out all, or a substantial portion of, the stockholders' investment in the institution. Banks' sensitivity to interest rate movements is especially intense because of the mismatch between their volatile short-term liabilities (principally deposits) and their longer-term assets (especially loans and securities). However, banks are not the only financial institutions carrying heavy interest-rate sensitivity; so do insurance companies, security dealers and most other financial-service providers, who face the risk of significant losses should changing market interest rates drive up their borrowing costs and lower the value and net returns on their assets.

Especially troublesome is the fact that the managers of financial firms do *not* control interest rates—these rates are determined in national and international markets. Financial-service providers must learn how to manage well no matter how high or low interest rates happen to be and no matter how those rates change from day to day. The critical forces driving market interest rates include the demands of thousands of borrowers, the actions of thousands of suppliers of savings, and the forces of inflation, credit risk, liquidity risk, maturity or term risk, and scores of other factors. Due to the tremendous number of factors shaping interest rates in the financial marketplace, they are difficult—indeed, virtually impossible—to forecast. However, sometimes financial managers attempt to do so and get themselves into serious trouble.

Consider an example: Japan's huge money center banks recently bought into interest-rate swap contracts to the tune of more than 40 trillion yen. Swaps are sophisticated risk-management contracts that can be tricky, but in this case could be very profitable provided longer-term market interest rates stayed low. The danger, of course, was that market interest rates might refuse to stay low and, instead, rise substantially, resulting in significant losses to the financial firms involved. This risky situation was all the more serious because Japanese bankers found themselves struggling at the same time with big losses from troubled loans. Some of their biggest customers couldn't repay what they had borrowed due to a weak domestic economy and the ravages of deflation.

The Japanese situation teaches us that the managers of financial firms must avoid speculating on movements in market interest rates and, instead, learn how to properly use interest-rate hedging tools, including such useful weapons as gap analysis, duration, financial futures and options, and interest-rate swaps. They must be conscious all the time of their institutions' exposure to interest-rate risk from their growing off-balance-sheet activities (such as loan securitizations, standby credits, and credit derivatives).

Hedging tools and off-balance-sheet activities are explored in depth in this part of the book. Here is where we learn that managers must know about so much more than just one or a few departments operating within their financial firms. The important management technique known as asset-liability management (ALM) teaches us that every department, division, and activity within a financial firm affects its overall performance. Competent financial-service managers must learn how to take into account in their decisions the situation and performance of those departments that are raising funds and those that are using funds. Only then can a financial-services manager hope to deal effectively with changing market interest rates and other risk factors that impact a financial institution's performance and its ultimate survival.

CHAPTER SEVEN

Asset-Liability Management: Determining and Measuring Interest Rates and Controlling Interest-Sensitive and Duration Gaps

Key Topics in This Chapter

- Asset, Liability, and Funds Management
- Market Rates and Interest-Rate Risk
- The Goals of Interest-Rate Hedging
- Interest-Sensitive Gap Management
- Duration Gap Management
- Limitations of Hedging Techniques

7–1 Introduction

Financial institutions today are often highly complex organizations, offering multiple financial services through multiple departments and divisions, each staffed by specialists in making different kinds of financial decisions.[1] Thus, different groups of individuals inside each modern financial firm usually make the decisions about which customers are to receive credit, which securities should be added to or subtracted from the financial institution's portfolio, which terms should be offered to the public on loans, investment advice, and other services, and which sources of capital the institution should draw upon.

[1]Portions of this chapter are based upon Peter S. Rose's article in *The Canadian Banker* [6] and are used with the permission of the publisher.

Key URL
www.ALMprofessional.com is a Web site devoted to articles and discussions about ALM tools.

Yet, all of the foregoing management decisions are intimately linked to each other. For example, decisions on which customer credit requests should be fulfilled are closely related to the ability of the financial firm to raise funds in order to support the requested new loans. Similarly, the amount of risk that a financial firm accepts in its portfolio is closely related to the adequacy and composition of its capital (net worth), which protects its stockholders, depositors, and other creditors against loss. Even as a financial institution takes on more risk it must protect the value of its net worth from erosion, which could result in ultimate failure.

In a well-managed financial institution all of these diverse management decisions must be coordinated across the whole institution in order to insure that they do not clash with each other, leading to inconsistent actions that damage earnings and net worth. Today financial-service managers have learned to look at their asset and liability portfolios as an *integrated whole*, considering how their institution's whole portfolio contributes to the firm's broad goals of adequate profitability and acceptable risk. This type of coordinated and integrated decision making is known as **asset-liability management** (ALM). The collection of managerial techniques that we call asset-liability management provides financial institutions with defensive weapons to handle such challenging events as business cycles and seasonal pressures and with offensive weapons to shape portfolios of assets and liabilities in ways that promote each institution's goals. The key purpose of this chapter is to give the reader a picture of how this integrated approach to managing assets, liabilities, and equity really works.

7–2 Asset-Liability Management Strategies

Asset Management Strategy

Financial institutions have not always possessed a completely integrated view of their assets and liabilities. For example, through most of the history of banking, bankers tended to take their sources of funds—liabilities and equity—largely for granted. This **asset management** view held that the amount and kinds of deposits a depository institution held and the volume of other borrowed funds it was able to attract were largely determined by its customers. Under this view, the public determined the relative amounts of checkable deposits, savings accounts, and other sources of funds available to depository institutions. The key decision area for management was not deposits and other borrowings but assets. The financial manager could exercise control only over the allocation of incoming funds by deciding who was to receive the scarce quantity of loans available and what the terms on those loans would be. Indeed, there was some logic behind this asset management approach because, prior to government deregulation, the types of deposits, the rates offered, and the nondeposit sources of funds depository institutions could draw upon were closely regulated. Managers had only limited discretion in reshaping their sources of funds.

Liability Management Strategy

Recent decades have ushered in dramatic changes in asset-liability management strategies. Confronted with fluctuating interest rates and intense competition for funds, bankers and many of their competitors began to devote greater attention to opening up new sources of funding and monitoring the mix and cost of their deposit and nondeposit liabilities. The new strategy was called **liability management.** Its goal was simply to gain control over funds sources comparable to the control financial managers had long exercised over their assets. The key control lever was *price*—the interest rate and other terms offered on deposits and other borrowings to achieve the volume, mix, and cost desired. For example,

EXHIBIT 7–1 Asset-Liability Management in Banking and Financial Services

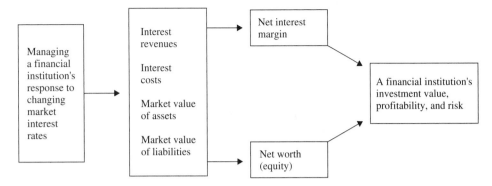

a lender faced with heavy loan demand that exceeded its available funds could simply raise the offer rate on its borrowings relative to its competitors, and funds would flow in. On the other hand, a depository institution flush with funds but with few profitable outlets for those funds could leave its offer rate unchanged or even lower that price, letting competitors outbid it for whatever funds were available in the marketplace. Exhibit 7–1 charts the goals of asset-liability management.

Funds Management Strategy

The maturing of liability management techniques, coupled with more volatile interest rates and greater risk, eventually gave birth to the **funds management** approach, which dominates today. This view is a more balanced approach to asset-liability management that stresses several key objectives:

1. Management should exercise as much control as possible over the volume, mix, and return or cost of *both* assets and liabilities in order to achieve the financial institution's goals.
2. Management's control over assets must be coordinated with its control over liabilities so that asset management and liability management are internally consistent and do not pull against each other. Effective coordination in managing assets and liabilities will help to maximize the spread between revenues and costs and control risk exposure.
3. Revenues and costs arise from both sides of the balance sheet (i.e., from both asset and liability accounts). Management policies need to be developed that maximize returns and minimize costs from supplying services.

Thus, the traditional view that all income received by financial firms must come from loans and investments has given way to the notion that financial institutions today sell a *bundle of financial services*—credit, payments, savings, financial advice, and the like—that should each be priced to cover their cost of production. *Income* from managing the liability side of the balance sheet can help achieve profitability goals as much as revenues generated from managing loans and other assets.

Concept Check

7–1. What do the following terms mean: *asset management? liability management? funds management?*

7–2. What factors have motivated financial institutions to develop funds management techniques in recent years?

7–3 Interest Rate Risk: One of the Greatest Asset-Liability Management Challenges

No financial manager can completely avoid one of the toughest and potentially most damaging forms of risk that all financial institutions must face—**interest rate risk.** When interest rates change in the financial marketplace, the sources of revenue that financial institutions receive—especially interest income on loans and securities—and their most important source of expenses—interest cost on borrowings—must also change. Moreover, changing market interest rates also change the market value of assets and liabilities, thereby changing each financial institution's net worth—that is, the value of the owner's investment in the firm. Thus, changing market interest rates impact both the balance sheet and the statement of income and expenses of financial firms.

Forces Determining Interest Rates

The problem with interest rates is that although they are critical to most financial institutions, the managers of these firms simply cannot control either the level of or the trend in market rates of interest. The rate of interest on any particular loan or security is ultimately determined by the financial marketplace where suppliers of loanable funds (credit) interact with demanders of loanable funds (credit) and the interest rate (price of credit) tends to settle at the point where the quantities of loanable funds demanded and supplied are equal, as shown in Exhibit 7–2.

In granting loans, financial institutions are on the *supply* side of the loanable funds (credit) market, but each lending institution is only one supplier of credit in an international market for loanable funds that includes many thousands of lenders. Similarly, depository institutions come into the financial marketplace as demanders of loanable funds (credit) when they offer deposit services to the public or issue nondeposit IOUs to raise funds for lending and investing. But, again, each financial institution, no matter how large it is, is only *one* demander of loanable funds in a market containing thousands of borrowers.

Thus, whether financial firms are on the supply side or the demand side of the loanable funds (credit) market at any given moment (and financial intermediaries are usually on *both* sides of the credit market simultaneously), they cannot determine the level, or be sure about the trend, of market interest rates. Rather, the individual institution can only react to the level of and trend in interest rates in a way that best allows it to achieve its goals. In other words, most financial managers must be *price takers*, not price makers, and must accept interest rates as a given and plan accordingly.

EXHIBIT 7–2
Determination of the Rate of Interest in the Financial Marketplace

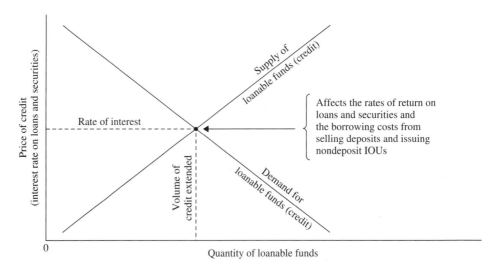

As market interest rates move, financial firms typically face at least two major kinds of interest rate risk—price risk and reinvestment risk. *Price risk* arises when market interest rates rise, causing the market values of most bonds and fixed-rate loans to fall. If a financial institution wishes to sell these financial instruments in a rising rate period, it must be prepared to accept capital losses. *Reinvestment risk* rears its head when market interest rates fall, forcing a financial firm to invest incoming funds in lower-yielding earning assets, lowering its expected future income. A big part of managing assets and liabilities consists of finding ways to deal effectively with these two forms of risk.

The Measurement of Interest Rates

When we use the term *interest rates* exactly what do we mean? How are interest rates measured?

Most of us understand what interest rates are because we have borrowed money at one time or another and know that interest rates are the *price of credit*, demanded by lenders as compensation for the use of borrowed funds. In simplest terms the interest rate is a ratio of the fees we must pay to obtain credit divided by the amount of credit obtained. However, over the years a bewildering array of interest-rate measures have been developed as we will see in future pages of this book.

One of the most popular rate measures is the **yield to maturity (YTM),** which is the discount rate that equalizes the current market value of a loan or security with the expected stream of future income payments that the loan or security will generate. In terms of a formula, the yield to maturity may be found from

$$\begin{matrix}\text{Current market price} \\ \text{of a loan or security}\end{matrix} = \frac{\begin{matrix}\text{Expected cash flow} \\ \text{in Period 1}\end{matrix}}{(1 + \text{YTM})^1} + \frac{\begin{matrix}\text{Expected cash flow} \\ \text{in Period 2}\end{matrix}}{(1 + \text{YTM})^2} \quad \text{(7–1)}$$

$$+ \cdots + \frac{\begin{matrix}\text{Expected cash flow} \\ \text{in Period n}\end{matrix}}{(1 + \text{YTM})^n} + \frac{\begin{matrix}\text{Sale or redemption} \\ \text{price of security} \\ \text{or loan in Period n}\end{matrix}}{(1 + \text{YTM})^n}$$

For example, a bond purchased today at a price of $950 and promising an interest payment of $100 each year over the next three years, when it will be redeemed by the bond's issuer for $1,000, will have a promised interest rate, measured by the yield to maturity, determined by:

$$\$950 = \frac{\$100}{(1 + \text{YTM})^1} + \frac{\$100}{(1 + \text{YTM})^2} + \frac{\$100}{(1 + \text{YTM})^3} + \frac{\$1000}{(1 + \text{YTM})^3}$$

This bond's YTM is determined to be 12.10 percent.[2]

Another popular interest rate measure is the **bank discount rate,** which is often quoted on short-term loans and money market securities (such as Treasury bills). The formula for calculating the discount rate (DR) is as follows:

$$\text{DR} = \left(\frac{100 - \text{Purchase price on loan or security}}{100} \right) \quad \text{(7–2)}$$

$$\times \frac{360}{\begin{matrix}\text{Number of days to} \\ \text{maturity}\end{matrix}}$$

---

[2]Financial calculators and spreadsheets such as Excel will give this yield to maturity figure directly after entering the bond's purchase price, promised interest payments, sales or redemption price, and number of time periods covered. (Note: the YTM for bonds is equivalent to the APR for loans.)

Key URL
For help in calculating
YTM, discount rates,
and bond prices see
especially the
calculators provided at
**www.investopedia.com/
calculator/.**

For example, suppose a money market security can be purchased for a price of $96 and has a face value of $100 to be paid at maturity. If the security matures in 90 days, its interest rate measured by the bank DR must be

$$DR = \frac{(100 - 96)}{100} \times \frac{360}{90} = 0.16, \text{ or } 16 \text{ percent}$$

We note that this interest rate measure ignores the effect of compounding of interest and is based on a 360-day year, unlike the yield to maturity measure, which assumes a 365-day year and assumes as well that interest income is compounded at the calculated YTM.

In addition, the DR uses the *face value* of a financial instrument to calculate its yield or rate of return, a simple approach that makes calculations easier but is theoretically incorrect. The purchase price of a financial instrument, rather than its face amount, is a much better base to use in calculating the instrument's true rate of return.

To convert a DR to the equivalent yield to maturity we can use the formula:

$$\text{YTM equivalent yield} = \frac{(100 - \text{Purchase price})}{\text{Purchase price}} \times \frac{365}{\text{Days to maturity}} \quad \textbf{(7–3)}$$

For the money market security discussed previously, its equivalent yield to maturity would be

$$\text{YTM equivalent} = \frac{(100 - 96)}{96} \times \frac{365}{90} = 0.1690, \text{ or } 16.90 \text{ percent}$$

While the two interest rate measures listed above are very popular, we should keep in mind that there are literally dozens of other measures of "the interest rate," many of which we will encounter in later chapters of this book.

The Components of Interest Rates

Filmtoid
What 2001 Australian
drama finds the head of
Centabank enthralled
with a computer
program that forecasts
interest rate movements
in the world's money
markets?
Answer: *The Bank.*

Over the years many financial managers have tried to forecast future movements in market interest rates as an aid to combating interest rate risk. However, the fact that interest rates are determined by the interactions of thousands of credit suppliers and demanders makes consistently accurate rate forecasting virtually impossible. Adding to the forecasting problem is the fact that any particular interest rate attached to a loan or security is composed of multiple elements or building blocks, including

$$\begin{matrix} \text{Nominal} \\ \text{(published)} \\ \text{market} \\ \text{interest rate} \\ \text{on a risky} \\ \text{loan or} \\ \text{security} \end{matrix} = \begin{matrix} \text{Risk-free real} \\ \text{interest rate} \\ \text{(such as the} \\ \text{inflation-adjusted} \\ \text{return on} \\ \text{government bonds)} \end{matrix} + \begin{matrix} \text{Risk premiums to compensate} \\ \text{lenders who accept risky} \\ \text{IOUs for their default (credit)} \\ \text{risk, inflation risk, term or} \\ \text{maturity risk, liquidity} \\ \text{risk, call risk, and so on} \end{matrix} \quad \textbf{(7–4)}$$

Not only does the *risk-free real interest rate* change over time with shifts in the demand and supply for loanable funds, but the perceptions of lenders and borrowers in the financial marketplace concerning each of the *risk premiums* that make up any particular market interest rate on a risky loan or security also change over time, causing market interest rates to move up or down, often erratically.

Risk Premiums

To cite some examples, when the economy goes into a recession with declining business sales and rising unemployment, many lenders will conclude that some businesses will fail and some individuals will lose their jobs, increasing the risk of borrower default. The *default-risk premium* component of the interest rate charged a risky borrower will increase, raising the borrower's loan rate (all other factors held constant). Similarly, an announcement of rising prices on goods and services may trigger lenders to expect a trend toward higher inflation, reducing the purchasing power of their loan income unless they demand from borrowers a higher *inflation-risk premium* to compensate for their projected loss in purchasing power. Many loan and security interest rates also contain a premium for *liquidity risk*, because some of these financial instruments are more difficult to sell quickly at a favorable price to another lender, and for *call risk*, which arises when a borrower has the right to pay off a loan early, reducing the lender's expected rate of return.

Yield Curves

Another key component of each interest rate is the *maturity*, or *term*, *premium*. Longer-term loans and securities often carry higher market interest rates than shorter-term loans and securities due to maturity risk because of greater opportunities for loss over the life of a longer-term loan. The graphic picture of how interest rates vary with different maturities of loans viewed at a single point in time (and assuming that all other factors, such as credit risk, are held constant) is called a *yield curve*.

Exhibit 7–3 charts three different U.S. Treasury security yield curves plotted in October of 2004, October 2005, and for the week ending September 30, 2005. The maturities of Treasury securities (in months and years) are plotted along the horizontal axis and their yields to maturity (YTMs) appear along the vertical axis.

Yield curves are constantly changing shape because the yields of the financial instruments included in each curve change every day. For example, we notice in Exhibit 7–3 that the steeply upward-sloping yield curve prevailing in October of 2004 had become a flatter, less precipitous yield curve one year later. Moreover, different yields change at different speeds with short-term interest rates tending to rise or fall faster than long-term

EXHIBIT 7–3
Yield Curves for U.S. Treasury Securities (October 2004 and 2005)

Source: Federal Reserve Bank of St. Louis, *Monetary Trends*.

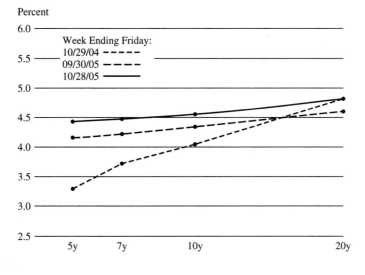

Treasury Yield Curve

interest rates. For example, in the yield curves shown in Exhibit 7–3 long-term interest rates (along the right-hand portion of the yield curve) had moved downward by about a quarter of a percentage point during 2005, while short-term interest rates (along the left-hand portion of the curve) increased about a percentage point over the same time period.

The relative changes in short-term interest rates versus long-term interest rates vary greatly over time. This is very evident in the picture presented in Exhibit 7–4, which plots the 3-month U.S. Treasury bill rate compared to the 10-year Treasury bond rate. We notice, for example, that in periods of recession (the shaded areas in Exhibit 7–4), with the economy struggling, short-term interest rates tend to fall relative to long-term interest rates and the gap between the two tends to widen. In contrast, a period of economic prosperity usually begins with a fairly wide gap between long- and short-term interest rates, but that interest-rate gap tends to narrow and sometimes becomes negative.

In summary, yield curves will display an *upward* slope (i.e., a rising yield curve) when long-term interest rates exceed short-term interest rates. This often happens when all interest rates are rising but short-term rates have started from a lower level than long-term rates. Yield curves can also slope *downward* (i.e., a negative yield curve), with short-term interest rates higher than long-term interest rates. Finally, *horizontal* yield curves prevail when long-term interest rates and short-term rates are at approximately the same level so that investors receive the same yield to maturity no matter what maturity of security they buy.

The Maturity Gap and the Yield Curve

Typically managers of financial institutions that focus on lending fare somewhat better with an *upward-sloping yield curve*, where longer-term interest rates are higher than shorter-term interest rates, than they do under a horizontal or downward-sloping yield curve. The upward-sloping yield curve is usually more favorable for the profitability of lending institutions because their loans and security holdings on the asset side of their balance sheet tend to have longer maturities than their sources of funds (liabilities).

Thus, most lending institutions experience a positive **maturity gap** between the average maturity of their assets and the average maturity of their liabilities. If the yield curve is upward sloping, then revenues from longer-term assets will outstrip expenses from shorter-term liabilities. The result will normally be a *positive* net interest margin (interest revenues

Key URLs

If you want to keep track of interest rates from day to day and week to week where would you look? See, for example, **www.bloomberg.com/ markets/rates**; **http://money.cnn.com/ pf/informa**, as well as **www.federalreserve. gov/releases/h.15/ current**.

EXHIBIT 7–4
Spread between Short-Term and Long-Term Interest Rates (based on 3-month and 10-year U.S. Treasury yields)

Source: Federal Reserve Bank of St. Louis, FRED.

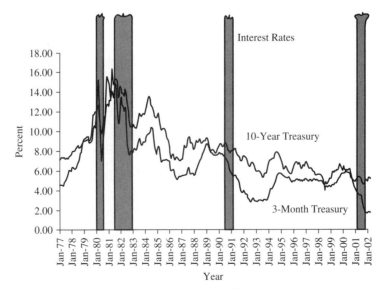

Note: Shaded areas reflect periods of economic recession in the U.S. economy.

greater than interest expenses), which tends to generate higher earnings. In contrast, a relatively flat (horizontal) or negatively sloped yield curve often generates a small or even negative net interest margin, putting downward pressure on the earnings of financial firms that borrow short and lend long.

Responses to Interest Rate Risk

Factoid
As the 21st century opened and market interest rates fell to record lows, interest-rate risk threatened to severely impact the net asset values of what major competitor of banks?
Answer: Money market funds, which were often forced to lower their fees in order to avoid reducing the net value of their assets below the accepted market standard of $1.00 per share.

As we noted at the outset, changes in market interest rates can damage a financial firm's profitability by increasing its cost of funds, lowering its returns from earning assets, and reducing the value of the owners' investment (net worth or equity capital). Moreover, recent decades have ushered in a period of volatile interest rates, confronting financial managers with a more unpredictable environment to work in. A dramatic example of the huge losses associated with interest-rate risk exposure occurred some years ago in Minnesota when First Bank System, Inc., of Minneapolis bought unusually large quantities of government bonds. First Bank's management had forecast a decline in interest rates. Unfortunately, bond prices fell as interest rates rose, and First Bank reported a loss of about $500 million, resulting in the sale of its headquarters building (see Bailey [2]).

In recent decades managers of financial institutions have aggressively sought ways to insulate their asset and liability portfolios and their profits from the ravages of changing interest rates. For example, many banks now conduct their asset-liability management strategies under the guidance of an *asset-liability committee*, which often meets daily. Such a committee not only chooses strategies to deal with interest rate risk but also participates in both short- and long-range planning, in preparing strategies to handle the institution's liquidity needs, and in dealing with other management issues.

7–4 One of the Goals of Interest Rate Hedging

In dealing with interest rate risk, one important goal is to insulate *profits*—net income—from the damaging effects of fluctuating interest rates. No matter which way interest rates go, managers of financial institutions want stable profits that achieve the level of profitability desired.

To accomplish this particular goal, management must concentrate on those elements of the institution's portfolio of assets and liabilities that are most sensitive to interest rate movements. Normally this includes loans and investments on the asset side of the balance sheet—earning assets—and borrowings on the liability side. In order to protect profits against adverse interest rate changes, then, management seeks to hold fixed the financial firm's **net interest margin** (NIM), expressed as follows:

$$\text{NIM} = \frac{\begin{pmatrix} \text{Interest income} & & \text{Interest expense on} \\ \text{from loans} & - & \text{deposits and other} \\ \text{and investments} & & \text{borrowed funds} \end{pmatrix}}{\text{Total earning assets}} \quad \textbf{(7–5)}$$

$$= \frac{\text{Net interest income}}{\text{Total earning assets}}$$

For example, suppose a large international bank records $4 billion in interest revenues from its loans and security investments and $2.6 billion in interest expenses paid out to attract borrowed funds. If this bank holds $40 billion in earning assets, its net interest margin is

$$\text{NIM} = \frac{(\$4 \text{ billion} - \$2.6 \text{ billion})}{\$40 \text{ billion}} \times 100 = 3.50 \text{ percent}$$

Note how narrow this net interest margin (which is fairly close to the average for the banking industry) is at just 3.5 percent, which is not this bank's profit from borrowing and lending funds because we have not considered noninterest expenses (such as employee salaries and overhead expenses). Once these expenses are also deducted, the manager of this bank generally has very little margin for error against interest rate risk. If management does find this 3.5 percent net interest margin acceptable, it will probably use a variety of interest-rate risk hedging methods to protect this NIM value, thereby helping to stabilize net earnings.

If the interest cost of borrowed funds rises faster than income from loans and securities, a financial firm's NIM will be squeezed, with adverse effects on profits.[3] If interest rates fall and cause income from loans and securities to decline faster than interest costs on borrowings, the NIM will again be squeezed. In other words, yield curves do not usually move in parallel fashion over time, so that the spread between borrowing costs and interest revenues is never constant. Management must struggle continuously to find ways to ensure that borrowing costs do not rise significantly relative to interest income and threaten the margin of a financial institution.

Concept Check

7–3. What forces cause interest rates to change? What kinds of risk do financial firms face when interest rates change?

7–4. What makes it so difficult to correctly forecast interest rate changes?

7–5. What is the yield curve and why is it important to know about its shape or slope?

7–6. What is it that a lending institution wishes to protect from adverse movements in interest rates?

7–7. What is the goal of *hedging?*

7–8. First National Bank of Bannerville has posted interest revenues of $63 million and interest costs from all of its borrowings of $42 million. If this bank possesses $700 million in total earning assets, what is First National's net interest margin? Suppose the bank's interest revenues and interest costs double, while its earning assets increase by 50 percent. What will happen to its net interest margin?

Interest-Sensitive Gap Management

Among the most popular interest rate hedging strategies in use today is **interest-sensitive gap management.** Gap management techniques require management to perform an analysis of the maturities and repricing opportunities associated with interest-bearing assets and with interest-bearing liabilities. If management feels its institution is excessively exposed to interest rate risk, it will try to match as closely as possible the volume of assets that can be repriced as interest rates change with the volume of liabilities whose rates can also be adjusted with market conditions during the same time period.

For example, a financial firm can hedge itself against interest rate changes—no matter which way rates move—by making sure for each time period that the

$$\text{Dollar amount of repriceable (interest-sensitive) assets} = \text{Dollar amount of repriceable (interest-sensitive) liabilities} \quad \textbf{(7–6)}$$

[3]In recent years, as noted by Alden Toevs [7], the net interest income of U.S. banks has accounted for about 60 to 80 percent of their net earnings. Toevs also found evidence of a substantial increase in the volatility of net interest income over time, encouraging managers of financial institutions to find better methods for managing interest-rate risk. One interesting management strategy that became prominent near the close of the 20th century and into the new century has been to de-emphasize interest rate–related sources of revenue and to emphasize noninterest rate–related revenue sources (fee income).

In this case, the revenue from earning assets will change in the same direction and by approximately the same proportion as the interest cost of liabilities.

What is a repriceable asset? A repriceable liability? The most familiar examples of repriceable assets are loans that are about to mature or are coming up for renewal. If interest rates have risen since these loans were first made, the lender will renew them only if it can get an expected yield that approximates the higher yields currently expected on other financial instruments of comparable quality. Similarly, loans that are maturing will provide the lender with funds to reinvest in new loans at today's interest rates, so they represent repriceable assets as well. Repriceable liabilities include a depository institution's CDs about to mature or be renewed, where the financial firm and its customers must negotiate new deposit interest rates to capture current market conditions; floating-rate deposits whose yields move automatically with market interest rates; and money-market borrowings whose rates are often adjusted daily to reflect the latest market developments.

What happens when the amount of repriceable assets does *not* equal the amount of repriceable liabilities? Clearly, a *gap* exists between these interest-sensitive assets and interest-sensitive liabilities. The gap is the portion of the balance sheet affected by interest rate risk:

$$\text{Interest-sensitive gap} = \text{Interest-sensitive assets} - \text{Interest-sensitive liabilities} \quad \textbf{(7–7)}$$

Examples of Repriceable Assets and Liabilities and Nonrepriceable Assets and Liabilities

Repriceable Assets	Repriceable Liabilities	Nonrepriceable Assets	Nonrepriceable Liabilities
Short-term securities issued by governments and private borrowers (about to mature) Short-term loans made to borrowing customers (about to mature) Variable-rate loans and securities	Borrowings from the money market (such as federal funds or RP borrowings) Short-term savings accounts Money-market deposits (whose interest rates are adjustable every few days)	Cash in the vault and deposits at the Central Bank (legal reserves) Long-term loans made at a fixed interest rate Long-term securities carrying fixed rates Buildings and equipment	Demand deposits (which pay no interest rate or a fixed interest rate) Long-term savings and retirement accounts Equity capital provided by the financial institution's owners

If interest-sensitive assets in each planning period (day, week, month, etc.) exceed the volume of interest-sensitive liabilities subject to repricing, the financial firm is said to have a *positive gap* and to be *asset sensitive*. Thus:

$$\text{Asset-sensitive (positive) gap} = \text{Interest-sensitive assets} - \text{Interest-sensitive liabilities} > 0 \quad \textbf{(7–8)}$$

For example, a bank with interest-sensitive assets of $500 million and interest-sensitive liabilities of $400 million is asset sensitive with a positive gap of $100 million. If interest rates rise, this bank's net interest margin will increase because the interest revenue generated by assets will increase more than the cost of borrowed funds. Other things being equal, this financial firm will experience an increase in its net interest income. On the other hand, if interest rates fall when the bank is asset sensitive, this bank's NIM will decline as interest revenues from assets drop by more than interest expenses associated with liabilities. The financial firm with a positive gap will lose net interest income if interest rates fall.

In the opposite situation, suppose an interest-sensitive bank's liabilities are larger than its interest-sensitive assets. This bank then has a *negative gap* and is said to be *liability sensitive*. Thus:

$$\text{Liability-sensitive (negative) gap} = \text{Interest-sensitive assets} - \text{Interest-sensitive liabilities} < 0 \qquad \textbf{(7–9)}$$

A financial institution holding interest-sensitive assets of $150 million and interest-sensitive liabilities of $200 million is liability sensitive, with a negative gap of $50 million. Rising interest rates will lower this institution's net interest margin, because the rising cost associated with interest-sensitive liabilities will exceed increases in interest revenue from interest-sensitive assets. Falling interest rates will generate a higher interest margin and probably greater earnings as well, because borrowing costs will decline by more than interest revenues.

Actually, there are several ways to measure the interest-sensitive gap (IS GAP). One method is called simply the Dollar IS GAP. For example, as we saw above, if interest-sensitive assets (ISA) are $150 million and interest-sensitive liabilities (ISL) are $200 million, then the Dollar IS GAP = ISA – ISL = $150 million – $200 million = –$50 million. Clearly, an institution whose Dollar IS GAP is positive is asset sensitive, while a negative Dollar IS GAP describes a liability-sensitive condition.

An Asset-Sensitive Financial Firm Has:	A Liability-Sensitive Financial Firm Has:
Positive Dollar IS GAP	Negative Dollar IS GAP
Positive Relative IS GAP	Negative Relative IS GAP
Interest Sensitivity Ratio greater than one	Interest Sensitivity Ratio less than one

We can also form the Relative IS GAP ratio:

$$\text{Relative IS GAP} = \frac{\text{IS GAP}}{\substack{\text{Size of financial institution}\\ \text{(measured, for example,}\\ \text{by total assets)}}} = \frac{-\$50 \text{ million}}{\$150 \text{ million}} = -0.33 \qquad \textbf{(7–10)}$$

A Relative IS GAP greater than zero means the institution is asset sensitive, while a negative Relative IS GAP describes a liability-sensitive financial firm. Finally, we can simply compare the ratio of ISA to ISL, sometimes called the Interest Sensitivity Ratio (ISR). Based on the figures in our previous example,

$$\text{Interest Sensitivity Ratio (ISR)} = \frac{\text{ISA}}{\text{ISL}} = \frac{\$150 \text{ million}}{\$200 \text{ million}} = 0.75 \qquad \textbf{(7–11)}$$

In this instance an ISR of less than 1 tells us we are looking at a liability-sensitive institution, while an ISR greater than unity points to an asset-sensitive institution.

Only if interest-sensitive assets and liabilities are *equal* is a financial institution relatively insulated from interest rate risk. In this case, interest revenues from assets and funding costs will change at the same rate. The interest-sensitive gap is *zero*, and the net interest margin is protected regardless of which way interest rates go. As a practical matter, however, a zero gap does not eliminate all interest rate risk because the interest rates attached to assets and liabilities are not perfectly correlated in the real world. Loan interest rates, for example, tend to lag behind interest rates on many money market borrowings. So interest revenues often tend to grow more slowly than interest expenses during economic expansions, while interest expenses tend to fall more rapidly than interest revenues during economic downturns.

Gapping methods used today vary greatly in complexity and form. All methods, however, require financial managers to make some important decisions:

1. Management must choose the time period during which the net interest margin (NIM) is to be managed (e.g., six months or one year) to achieve some desired value and the length of subperiods ("maturity buckets") into which the planning period is to be divided.
2. Management must choose a target level for the net interest margin—that is, whether to freeze the margin roughly where it is or perhaps increase the NIM.
3. If management wishes to increase the NIM, it must either develop a correct interest rate forecast or find ways to reallocate earning assets and liabilities to increase the spread between interest revenues and interest expenses.
4. Management must determine the volume of interest-sensitive assets and interest-sensitive liabilities it wants the financial firm to hold.

Computer-Based Techniques

Many institutions use computer-based techniques in which their assets and liabilities are classified as due or repriceable today, during the coming week, in the next 30 days, and so on. Management tries to match interest-sensitive assets with interest-sensitive liabilities in each of these *maturity buckets* in order to improve the chances of achieving the financial firm's earnings goals. For example, a bank's latest computer run might reveal the following:

Maturity Buckets	Interest-Sensitive Assets	Interest-Sensitive Liabilities	(dollars in millions)	
			Size of Gap	Cumulative Gap
1 day (next 24 hours)	$ 40	$ 30	+10	+10
Day 2–day 7	120	160	–40	–30
Day 8–day 30	85	65	+20	–10
Day 31–day 90	280	250	+30	+20
Day 91–day 120	455	395	+60	+80
•	•	•	•	•
•	•	•	•	•
•	•	•	•	•

It is obvious from the table above that the *time period* over which the gap is measured is crucial to understanding this bank's true interest-sensitive position. For example, within the next 24 hours, the bank in this example has a positive gap; its earnings will benefit if interest rates rise between today and tomorrow. However, a forecast of rising money market interest rates over the next week would be bad news because the cumulative gap for the next seven days is negative, which will result in interest expenses rising by more than interest revenues. If the interest rate increase is expected to be substantial, management should consider taking countermeasures to protect earnings. These might include selling longer-term CDs right away or using futures contracts to earn a profit that will help offset the margin losses that rising interest rates will almost surely bring in the coming week. Looking over the remainder of the table, it is clear the bank will fare much better over the next several months if market interest rates rise, because its cumulative gap eventually turns positive again.

The foregoing example reminds us that the net interest margin of a financial-service provider is influenced by multiple factors:

1. Changes in the level of interest rates, up or down.
2. Changes in the spread between asset yields and liability costs (often reflected in the changing shape of the *yield curve* between long-term rates and short-term rates).

E-BANKING AND E-COMMERCE

COMPUTER SOFTWARE AND DATABASE SYSTEMS SYNCHRONIZE ASSET-LIABILITY MANAGEMENT WITH BALANCE-SHEET FORECASTING

There is no question that financial institutions carry powerful interest-rate risk and, unmediated, that risk can lead to serious losses in income and in the value of the financial firm. As potent as interest-rate risk is for most financial institutions, however, it should not be analyzed in isolation, but in the context of other risks across the whole financial firm.

Today computer software, databases, and hardware capabilities allow financial firms to synchronize asset-liability management with balance-sheet forecasting. And that is just what many of the largest financial firms are doing. Technology providers such as Boston-based BancWare and Chicago-based Quantitative Risk Management provide the software and systems that calculate interest-rate risk exposure in conjunction with forecasting simulations.

For example, in 2005, SunTrust Banks made the transition from a standard personal computer–based system to a new SQL (Structured Query Language) server–based system. Because of technological improvements SunTrust's new system apparently runs simulations in a fraction of the time required under their older network, supplies management with intricate calculations of value-at-risk (VaR), and provides complex earnings-at-risk estimates.

In short, interest-rate risk is a powerful force shaping the performance of financial firms. However, it is not the only important risk facing the financial-services industry and must be balanced against other risks impacting the industry at the same time. The latest technology allows financial firms to simultaneously model risks and examine balance-sheet dynamics across the whole firm. For further information about these challenges and trends, see, for example, Vicki Gerson, "Starting on the Same Page," *Bank Systems and Technology* 42, no. 4, p. 42.

3. Changes in the volume of interest-bearing (earning) assets a financial institution holds as it expands or shrinks the overall scale of its activities.
4. Changes in the volume of interest-bearing liabilities that are used to fund earning assets as a financial institution grows or shrinks in size.
5. Changes in the mix of assets and liabilities that management draws upon as it shifts between floating and fixed-rate assets and liabilities, between shorter and longer maturity assets and liabilities, and between assets bearing higher versus lower expected yields (e.g., a shift from less cash to more loans or from higher-yielding consumer and real estate loans to lower-yielding commercial loans).

Table 7–1 provides a more detailed example of interest-sensitive gap management techniques as they are applied to asset and liability data for an individual bank. In it, management has arrayed (with the help of a computer) the amount of all the bank's assets and liabilities, grouped by the future time period when those assets and liabilities will reach maturity or their interest rates will be subject to repricing. Note that this bank is liability sensitive during the coming week and over the next 90 days and then becomes asset sensitive in later periods. Consciously or unconsciously, management has positioned this institution for falling interest rates over the next three months and for rising interest rates over the longer horizon.

At the bottom of Table 7–1, we calculate this financial firm's net interest income and net interest margin to see how they will change if interest rates rise. Net interest income can be derived from the following formula:

$$\begin{aligned}
\text{Net interest income} &= \text{Total interest income} - \text{Total interest cost} \\
&= \text{Average interest yield on rate-sensitive assets} \times \text{Volume of rate-sensitive} \\
&\quad \text{assets} + \text{Average interest yield on fixed (non-rate-sensitive) assets} \times \text{Volume} \\
&\quad \text{of fixed assets} - \text{Average interest cost on rate-sensitive liabilities} \\
&\quad \times \text{Volume of interest-sensitive liabilities} - \text{Average interest cost on fixed} \\
&\quad \text{(non-rate-sensitive) liabilities} \times \text{Volume of fixed} \\
&\quad \text{(non-rate-sensitive) liabilities}
\end{aligned}$$

(7–12)

For example, suppose the yields on rate-sensitive and fixed assets average 10 percent and 11 percent, respectively, while rate-sensitive and non-rate-sensitive liabilities cost an average of 8 percent and 9 percent, respectively. During the coming week the bank holds $1,700 million in rate-sensitive assets (out of an asset total of $4,100 million) and $1,800 million in rate-sensitive liabilities. Suppose, too, that these annualized interest rates remain steady. Then this institution's net interest income on an annualized basis will be

$$0.10 \times \$1,700 + 0.11 \times [4,100 - 1,700] - 0.08 \times \$1,800 - 0.09$$
$$\times [4,100 - 1,800] = \$83 \text{ million}$$

However, if the market interest rate on rate-sensitive assets rises to 12 percent and the interest rate on rate-sensitive liabilities rises to 10 percent during the first week, this liability-sensitive institution will have an annualized net interest income of only

$$0.12 \times \$1,700 + 0.11 \times [4,100 - 1,700] - 0.10 \times \$1,800 - 0.09$$
$$\times [4,100 - 1,800] = \$81 \text{ million}$$

Therefore, this bank will lose $2 million in net interest income on an annualized basis if market interest rates rise in the coming week. Management must decide whether to accept that risk or to counter it with hedging strategies or tools.

A useful overall measure of interest rate risk exposure is the *cumulative gap*, which is the total difference in dollars between those assets and liabilities that can be repriced over a designated period of time. For example, suppose that a bank has $100 million in earning assets and $200 million in liabilities subject to an interest rate change each month over the next six months. Then its cumulative gap must be −$600 million—that is, ($100 million in earning assets per month × 6) − ($200 million in liabilities per month × 6) = −$600 million. The cumulative gap concept is useful because, given any specific change in market interest rates, we can calculate approximately how net interest income will be affected by an interest rate change. The key relationship is this:

$$\begin{array}{c} \text{Change in} \\ \text{net interest} \\ \text{income} \end{array} = \begin{array}{c} \text{Overall change in} \\ \text{interest rate} \\ \text{(in percentage points)} \end{array} \times \begin{array}{c} \text{Size of the} \\ \text{cumulative gap} \\ \text{(in dollars)} \end{array} \quad \textbf{(7–13)}$$

For example, suppose market interest rates suddenly rise by 1 full percentage point. Then the bank in the example given above will suffer a net interest income loss of approximately

$$(+0.01) \times (-\$600 \text{ million}) = -\$6 \text{ million}$$

Aggressive Interest-Sensitive GAP Management	Expected Changes in Interest Rates (Management's Forecast)	Best Interest-Sensitive GAP Position to Be in:	Aggressive Management's Most Likely Action
	Rising market interest rates	Positive IS GAP	Increase interest-sensitive assets Decrease interest-sensitive liabilities
	Falling market interest rates	Negative IS GAP	Decrease interest-sensitive assets Increase interest-sensitive liabilities

If management anticipates an increase in interest rates, it may be able to head off this pending loss of income by shifting some assets and liabilities to reduce the size of the cumulative gap or by using hedging instruments (such as financial futures contracts, to be

TABLE 7–1 Sample Interest-Sensitivity Analysis (GAP management) for a Bank

Asset and Liability Items	One Week	Next 8–30 Days	Next 31–90 Days	Next 91–360 Days	More than One Year	Total for All Assets, Liabilities, and Net Worth on the Bank's Balance Sheet
	Volume of Asset and Liability Items Maturing or Subject to Repricing within the Following Maturity Buckets (in millions of dollars)					
Assets						
Cash and deposits owned	$ 100	—	—	—	—	$ 100
Marketable securities	200	$ 50	$ 80	$110	$ 460	900
Business loans	750	150	220	170	210	1,500
Real estate loans	500	80	80	70	170	900
Consumer loans	100	20	20	70	90	300
Farm loans	50	10	40	60	40	200
Buildings and equipment	—	—	—	—	200	200
Total repriceable (interest-sensitive) assets	**$1,700**	**$310**	**$440**	**$480**	**$1,170**	**$4,100**
Liabilities and Net Worth						
Checkable deposits	$ 800	$100	—	—	—	$ 900
Savings accounts	50	50	—	—	—	100
Money market deposits	550	150	—	—	—	700
Long-term time deposits	100	200	450	150	300	1,200
Short-term borrowings	300	100	—	—	—	400
Other liabilities	—	—	—	—	100	100
Net worth	—	—	—	—	700	700
Total repriceable (interest-sensitive) liabilities and net worth	**$1,800**	**$600**	**$450**	**$150**	**$1,100**	**$4,100**
Interest-sensitive gap (repriceable assets – repriceable liabilities)	–$100	–$290	–$ 10	+$330	+$70	
Cumulative gap	–$100	–$390	–$400	–$ 70	–0	
Ratio of interest-sensitive assets to interest-sensitive liabilities	**94.4%**	**51.7%**	**97.8%**	**320%**	**106.4%**	
This bank is	liability sensitive	liability sensitive	liability sensitive	asset sensitive	asset sensitive	
The bank's net interest margin will be squeezed if	Interest rates rise	Interest rates rise	Interest rates rise	Interest rates fall	Interest rates fall	

discussed in Chapter 8). In general, financial institutions with a negative cumulative gap will benefit from falling interest rates but lose net interest income when interest rates rise. Institutions with a positive cumulative gap will benefit if interest rates rise, but lose net interest income if market interest rates decline.

Some financial firms shade their interest-sensitive gaps toward either asset sensitivity or liability sensitivity, depending on their degree of confidence in their own interest rate forecasts. This is often referred to as *aggressive GAP management*. For example, if management firmly believes interest rates are going to fall over the current planning horizon, it will probably allow interest-sensitive liabilities to climb above interest-sensitive assets. If interest rates do fall as predicted, liability costs will drop by more than revenues and the institution's NIM will grow. Similarly, a confident forecast of higher interest rates will trigger many financial firms to become asset sensitive, knowing that if rates do rise, interest revenues will rise by more than interest expenses. Of course, such an aggressive strategy creates greater risk. Consistently correct interest rate forecasting is impossible; most financial managers have learned to rely on hedging against, not forecasting, changes in market interest rates. Interest rates that move in the wrong direction can magnify losses. (See Table 7–2.)

TABLE 7–1 *Continued*

Suppose that interest yields on interest-sensitive assets currently average 10%, while interest-sensitive liabilities have an average cost of 8%. In contrast, fixed assets yield 11% and fixed liabilities cost 9%. If interest rates stay at these levels, the bank's net interest income and net interest margin measured on an annualized basis will be as follows:

	One Week	Next 8–30 Days	Next 31–90 Days	Next 91–360 Days	More than One Year
Total interest income on an annualized basis	$0.10 \times \$1,700$ $+0.11 \times$ $[4,100 - 1,700]$	$0.10 \times \$310$ $+0.11 \times$ $[4,100 - 310]$	$0.10 \times \$440$ $+0.11 \times$ $[4,100 - 440]$	$0.10 \times \$480$ $+0.11 \times$ $[4,100 - 480]$	$0.10 \times \$1,170$ $+0.11 \times$ $[4,100 - 1,170]$
Total interest costs on an annualized basis	$-0.08 \times \$1,800$ $-0.09 \times$ $[4,100 - 1,800]$	$-0.08 \times$ $\$600 - 0.09 \times$ $[4,100 - 600]$	$-0.08 \times$ $\$450 - 0.09 \times$ $[4,100 - 45]$	$-0.08 \times$ $\$150 - 0.09 \times$ $[4,100 - 150]$	$-0.08 \times$ $\$1,100 - 0.09 \times$ $[4,100 - 1,100]$
Annualized net interest income	$= \$83$	$= \$84.9$	$= \$82.10$	$= \$80.20$	$= \$81.30$
Annualized net interest margin	$\$83 \div 4,100$ $= 2.02\%$	$\$84.9 \div 4,100$ $= 2.07\%$	$\$82.10 \div 4,100$ $= 2.00\%$	$\$78.7 \div 4,100$ $= 1.92\%$	$\$81.3 \div 4,100$ $= 1.98\%$

Suppose the interest rates attached to rate-sensitive assets and liabilities rise two full percentage points on an annualized basis to 12% and 10%, respectively.

	One Week	Next 8–30 Days	Next 31–90 Days	Next 91–360 Days	More than One Year
Total interest income on an annualized basis	$0.12 \times \$1,700$ $+0.11 \times [4,100 -$ $1,700] - 0.10 \times$	$0.12 \times \$310$ $+0.11 \times$ $[4,100 - 310]$	$0.12 \times \$440$ $+0.11 \times$ $[4,100 - 440]$	$0.12 \times \$480$ $+0.11 \times$ $+[4,100 - 480]$	$0.12 \times \$1,170$ $+0.11 \times$ $[4,100 - 1,170]$
Total interest cost on an annualized basis	$\$1,800 - 0.09 \times$ $[4,100 - 1,800]$	-0.10×600 -0.09 $\times [4,100 - 600]$	-0.10×450 -0.09 $\times [4,100 - 450]$	-0.10×150 -0.09 $[4,100 - 150]$	-0.10 $\times 1,100$ $-0.09 \, [4,100$ $-1,100]$
Annualized net interest income	$= \$81$	$= \$79.10$	$= \$81.90$	$= \$85.30$	$= \$82.70$
Annualized net interest margin	$\$81 \div 4,100$ $= 1.98\%$	$\$79.1 \div 4,100$ $= 1.93\%$	$\$81.9 \div 4,100$ $= 2.00\%$	$\$85.3 \div 4,100$ $= 2.08\%$	$\$82.7 \div 4,100$ $= 2.02\%$

We note by comparing annualized interest income and margins for each time period (maturity bucket) that this bank's net interest income and margin will fall if it is liability sensitive when interest rates go up. When the bank is asset sensitive and market interest rates rise, the net interest income and margin increase.

Many financial-service managers have chosen to adopt a purely defensive GAP management strategy:

Defensive Interest-Sensitive GAP Management

Set interest-sensitive GAP as close to zero as possible to reduce the expected volatility of net interest income

While interest-sensitive gap management works beautifully in theory, practical problems in its implementation always leave financial institutions with at least *some* interest-rate risk exposure. For example, interest rates paid on liabilities (which often are predominantly short term) tend to move faster than interest rates earned on assets (many of which are long term). Then, too, changes in interest rates attached to assets and liabilities do not necessarily move at the same speed as do interest rates in the open market. In the case of a bank, for example, deposit interest rates typically lag loan interest rates.

TABLE 7–2
Eliminating an
Interest-Sensitive
Gap

		Possible Management Responses
With Positive Gap	**The Risk**	
Interest-sensitive assets > interest-sensitive liabilities (asset sensitive)	Losses if interest rates fall because the net interest margin will be reduced.	1. Do nothing (perhaps interest rates will rise or be stable).
		2. Extend asset maturities or shorten liability maturities.
		3. Increase interest-sensitive liabilities or reduce interest-sensitive assets.
		Possible Management Responses
With Negative Gap	**The Risk**	
Interest-sensitive assets < interest-sensitive liabilities (liability sensitive)	Losses if interest rates rise because the net interest margin will be . reduced	1. Do nothing (perhaps interest rates will fall or be stable).
		2. Shorten asset maturities or lengthen liability maturities
		3. Decrease interest-sensitive liabilities or increase interest-sensitive assets.

Some financial institutions have developed a *weighted* interest-sensitive gap approach that takes into account the tendency of interest rates to vary in speed and magnitude relative to each other and with the up and down cycle of business activity. The interest rates attached to assets of various kinds often change by different amounts and at different speeds than many of the interest rates attached to liabilities—a phenomenon called *basis risk*.

The Weighted Interest-Sensitive Gap: Dealing with Basis Risk

	Original Balance Sheet Entries		Interest-Rate Sensivity Weight		Balance Sheet Refigured to Reflect Interest Rate Sensitivities
Asset items sensitive to interest rate movements:					
Federal funds loans	$ 50	×	1.0	=	$ 50.00
Government securities and other investments	25	×	1.3	=	32.50
Loans and leases	125	×	1.5	=	187.50
Total rate-sensitive assets	$200				$270.00
Liability items sensitive to interest rate movements:					
Interest-bearing deposits	$159	×	0.86	=	$137.00
Other borrowings in the money market	64	×	0.91	=	58.00
Total rate-sensitive liabilities	$223				$195.00
The interest-sensitive GAP	–$23				+$75

How net interest income would change if the federal funds rate in the money market increases by 2 percentage points:

	Original Balance Sheet	Refigured Balanced Sheet
Predicted movement in net interest income	–$0.46 (=–$23 × .02)	+$1.50 (= +$75 × .02)

Concept Check

7–9. Can you explain the concept of *gap management?*

7–10. When is a financial firm asset sensitive? Liability sensitive?

7–11. Commerce National Bank reports interest-sensitive assets of $870 million and interest-sensitive liabilities of $625 million during the coming month. Is the bank asset sensitive or liability sensitive? What is likely to happen to the bank's net interest margin if interest rates rise? If they fall?

7–12. People's Savings Bank, a thrift institution, has a cumulative gap for the coming year of +$135 million and interest rates are expected to fall by two and a half percentage points. Can you calculate the expected change in net interest income that this thrift institution might experience? What

change will occur in net interest income if interest rates rise by one and a quarter percentage points?

7–13. How do you measure the dollar interest-sensitive gap? The relative interest-sensitive gap? What is the interest sensitivity ratio?

7–14. Suppose Carroll Bank and Trust reports interest-sensitive assets of $570 million and interest-sensitive liabilities of $685 million. What is the bank's dollar interest-sensitive gap? Its relative interest-sensitive gap and interest-sensitivity ratio?

7–15. Explain the concept of *weighted interest-sensitive gap.* How can this concept aid management in measuring a financial institution's real interest-sensitive gap risk exposure?

Key URL

Bank examiners today have access to a variety of tools to assess a depository institution's risk exposure from changing market interest rates. One of the best known is the Federal Reserve's Economic Value Model (EVM). See especially **http://research.stlouis fed.org/publications**.

For example, suppose a bank has the current amount and distribution of interest-sensitive assets and liabilities shown in the table at the bottom of page 224 with rate-sensitive assets totaling $200 million and rate-sensitive liabilities amounting to $223 million, yielding an interest-sensitive GAP of –$23 on its present balance sheet. Its federal funds loans generally carry interest rates set in the open market, so these loans have an interest rate sensitivity weight of 1.0—that is, we assume the bank's fed funds rate tracks market rates one for one. In this bank's investment security portfolio, however, suppose there are some riskier, somewhat more rate-volatile investments than most of the security interest rates reported daily in the financial press. Therefore, its average security yield moves up and down by somewhat more than the interest rate on federal funds loans; here the interest-rate sensitivity weight is estimated to be 1.3. Loans and leases are the most rate-volatile of all with an interest-rate sensitivity weight half again as volatile as federal funds rates at an estimated 1.5. On the liability side, deposit interest rates and some money-market borrowings (such as borrowing from the central bank) may change more slowly than market interest rates. In this example, we assume deposits have a rate-sensitive weight of 0.86 and money-market borrowings are slightly more volatile at 0.91, close to but still less than the volatility of federal funds interest rates.

We can simply multiply each of the rate-sensitive balance-sheet items by its appropriate interest-rate sensitivity indicator, which acts as a weight. More rate-volatile assets and liabilities will weigh more heavily in the refigured (weighted) balance sheet we are constructing in the previous table. Notice that after multiplying by the interest rate weights we have created, the new weighted balance sheet has rate-sensitive assets of $270 and rate-sensitive liabilities of $195. Instead of a negative (liability-sensitive) interest rate gap of –$23, we now have a positive (asset-sensitive) rate gap of +$75.

Thus, this institution's interest-sensitive gap has changed direction and, instead of being hurt by rising market interest rates, for example, this financial firm would actually benefit from higher market interest rates. Suppose the federal funds interest rate rose by 2 percentage points (+.02). Instead of declining by –$0.46, this bank's net interest income increases by $1.50. Clearly, management would have an entirely different reaction to a forecast of rising interest rates with the new weighted balance sheet than it would have with its original, conventionally constructed balance sheet. Indeed, when it comes to assessing interest rate risk, things are not always as they appear!

Key URLs
If you want to learn more about asset-liability management techniques see such useful Web sites as **www.fmsinc.org/cms** and **www.nexus generations.com/courses. htm**.

Moreover, the point at which certain assets and liabilities can be repriced is not always easy to identify. And the choice of planning periods over which to balance interest-sensitive assets and liabilities is highly arbitrary. Some items always fall between the cracks in setting planning periods, and they could cause trouble if interest rates move against the financial firm. Wise asset-liability managers use several different lengths of planning periods ("maturity buckets") in measuring their possible exposure to changing market interest rates.

Finally, interest-sensitive gap management does *not* consider the impact of changing interest rates on the owners' (stockholders') position in the financial firm as represented by the institution's *net worth*. Managers choosing to pursue an aggressive interest-rate sensitive gap policy may be able to expand their institution's net interest margin, but at the cost of increasing the volatility of net earnings and reducing the value of the stockholders' investment (net worth). Effective asset-liability management demands that financial managers work to achieve desirable levels of both net interest income and net worth.

Duration Gap Management

In the preceding sections of this chapter we examined a key management tool—*interest-sensitive gap management*—that enables managers of financial institutions to combat the possibility of losses to their institution's *net interest margin* or spread due to changes in market interest rates. Unfortunately, changing interest rates can also do serious damage to another aspect of a financial firm's performance—its *net worth*, the value of the stockholders' investment in a financial institution. Just because the net interest margin is protected against interest-rate risk doesn't mean an institution's net worth is also sheltered from loss. This requires the application of yet another managerial tool—**duration gap management.** We turn now to look at the concept of duration and its many valuable uses.

7–5 The Concept of Duration

Duration is a value- and time-weighted measure of maturity that considers the timing of all cash inflows from earning assets and all cash outflows associated with liabilities. It measures the average maturity of a promised stream of future cash payments (such as the payment streams that a financial firm expects to receive from its loans and security investments or the stream of interest payments it must pay out to its depositors). In effect, duration measures the average time needed to recover the funds committed to an investment.

The standard formula for calculating the duration (D) of an individual financial instrument, such as a loan, security, deposit, or nondeposit borrowing, is

$$D = \frac{\sum_{t=1}^{n} \text{Expected CF in Period t} \times \text{Period t}/(1 + \text{YTM})^t}{\sum_{t=1}^{n} \frac{\text{Expected CF in Period t}}{(1 + \text{YTM})^t}} \qquad \textbf{(7–14)}$$

Key URL
For assistance in calculating regular and modified duration, see, in particular, the calculators available from the Web site at **www.investopedia.com/ calculator/**.

D stands for the instrument's duration in years and fractions of a year; t represents the period of time in which each flow of cash off the instrument, such as interest or dividend income, is to be received; CF indicates the volume of each expected flow of cash in each time period (t); and YTM is the instrument's current yield to maturity. We note that the denominator of the above formula is equivalent to the instrument's current market value (price). So, the duration formula can be abbreviated to this form:

$$D = \frac{\sum_{t=1}^{n} \text{Expected CF} \times \text{Period t}/(1 + \text{YTM})^t}{\text{Current Market Value or Price}} \qquad \textbf{(7–15)}$$

For example, suppose that a bank grants a loan to one of its customers for a term of five years. The customer promises the bank an annual interest payment of 10 percent (that is, $100 per year). The face (par) value of the loan is $1,000, which is also its current market value (price) because the loan's current yield to maturity is 10 percent. What is this loan's duration? The formula with the proper figures entered would be this:

$$D_{Loan} = \frac{\sum_{t=1}^{5} \$100 \times t/(1 + .10)^t + \$1,000 \times 5/(1 + .10)^5}{\$1,000}$$

$$D_{Loan} = \frac{\$4,169.87}{\$1,000}$$

$$D_{Loan} = 4.17 \text{ years}$$

We can calculate duration of this loan a little more simply by setting up the table below to figure the components of the formula. As before, the duration of the loan is $4,169.87/$1,000.00, or 4.17 years.

We recognize from Chapter 5 that the net worth (NW) of any business or household is equal to the value of its assets less the value of its liabilities:

$$NW = A - L \qquad\qquad \textbf{(7–16)}$$

As market interest rates change, the value of both a financial institution's assets and liabilities will change, resulting in a change in its net worth (the owner's investment in the institution):

	Period of Expected Cash Flow	Expected Cash Flow from Loan	Present Value of Expected Cash Flows (at 10% YTM in this case)	Time Period Cash Is to Be Received (t)	Present Value of Expected Cash Flows × t
Expected	1	$ 100	$ 90.91	1	$ 90.91
interest	2	100	82.64	2	165.29
income	3	100	75.13	3	225.39
from loan	4	100	68.30	4	273.21
	5	100	62.09	5	310.46
Repayment of loan principal	5	1,000	620.92	5	3,104.61
		Price or Denominator of Formula = $1,000.00		PV of Cash Flows × t = $4,169.87	

$$\Delta NW = \Delta A - \Delta L \qquad\qquad \textbf{(7–17)}$$

Portfolio theory teaches us that

A. A rise in market rates of interest will cause the market value (price) of both fixed-rate assets and liabilities to decline.

B. The longer the maturity of a financial firm's assets and liabilities, the more they will tend to decline in market value (price) when market interest rates rise.

Thus, a change in net worth due to changing interest rates will vary depending upon the relative maturities of a financial institution's assets and liabilities. Because duration is a measure of maturity, a financial firm with longer-duration assets than liabilities will suffer a greater decline in net worth when market interest rates rise than a financial institution whose asset duration is relatively short term or one that matches the duration of its liabilities with the duration of its assets. By equating asset and liability durations, management can balance the average maturity of expected cash inflows from assets with the average maturity of expected cash outflows associated with liabilities. Thus, duration analysis can be used to stabilize, or *immunize*, the market value of a financial institution's net worth (NW).

The important feature of duration from a risk management point of view is that it measures the sensitivity of the market value of financial instruments to changes in interest rates. The percentage change in the market price of an asset or a liability is equal to its duration times the relative change in interest rates attached to that particular asset or liability. That is,

$$\frac{\Delta P}{P} \approx -D \times \frac{\Delta i}{(1 + i)} \qquad \textbf{(7–18)}$$

where $\Delta P \div P$ represents the percentage change in market price and $\Delta i \div (1 + i)$ is the relative change in interest rates associated with the asset or liability. D represents duration, and the negative sign attached to it reminds us that market prices and interest rates on financial instruments move in opposite directions. For example, consider a bond held by a savings institution that carries a duration of four years and a current market value (price) of $1,000. Market interest rates attached to comparable bonds are about 10 percent currently, but recent forecasts suggest that market rates may rise to 11 percent. If this forecast turns out to be correct, what percentage change will occur in the bond's market value? The answer is:

$$\frac{\Delta P}{P} = -4 \text{ years} \times (0.01)/(1 + 0.10) = -0.0364 \text{ or } -3.64 \text{ percent}$$

Equation (7–18) tells us that the interest-rate risk of financial instruments is directly proportional to their durations. A financial instrument whose duration is 2 will be twice as risky (in terms of price volatility) as one with a duration of 1.

The relationship between an asset's change in price and its change in yield or interest rate is captured by another term in finance related to duration—**convexity.** Convexity increases with the duration of an asset. The concept of convexity for interest-bearing assets tells us that the rate of change in any interest-bearing asset's price (value) for a given change in its interest rate or yield varies according to the prevailing level of interest rates or yields. For example, an interest-bearing asset's price change is greater at low interest rates or yields than it is at high interest rates or yields. To express this idea another way, price risk is greater at lower interest rates or yields than at higher interest rates or yields.

As an illustration, suppose the interest rate or yield attached to a 30-year bond held by a financial institution decreases from 6.5 percent to 6 percent. Then, this bond's price will rise by about 8 points (i.e., by about $8 per $1,000 in face value). In contrast, suppose the bond's interest rate or yield falls from 10 percent to 9.5 percent; then its market price will rise by just slightly more than 4 points (about $4 per $1,000 in face value). Moreover, if we hold the maturity and yield of an asset constant, the convexity of that asset will fall as the asset's promised return (or coupon rate) rises. Financial managers using asset-liability management techniques to protect the value of their assets must keep in mind that asset values change differently according to their duration, their promised (coupon) rates of return, and the prevailing level of market interest rates.

7–6 Using Duration to Hedge against Interest Rate Risk

A financial-service provider interested in fully hedging against interest rate fluctuations wants to choose assets and liabilities such that

$$\text{The dollar-weighted duration of the asset portfolio} \approx \text{The dollar-weighted duration of liabilities} \qquad \textbf{(7–19)}$$

so that the **duration gap** is as close to zero as possible (see Table 7–3):

$$\text{Duration gap} = \begin{array}{c}\text{Dollar-weighted}\\ \text{duration}\\ \text{of asset}\\ \text{portfolio}\end{array} - \begin{array}{c}\text{Dollar-weighted}\\ \text{duration}\\ \text{of liability}\\ \text{portfolio}\end{array} \qquad \textbf{(7–20)}$$

Because the dollar volume of assets usually exceeds the dollar volume of liabilities (otherwise the financial firm would be insolvent!), a financial institution seeking to minimize the effects of interest rate fluctuations would need to adjust for *leverage*:

$$\begin{array}{c}\text{Leverage-}\\ \text{adjusted}\\ \text{duration}\\ \text{gap}\end{array} = \begin{array}{c}\text{Dollar-weighted}\\ \text{duration}\\ \text{of asset}\\ \text{portfolio}\end{array} - \begin{array}{c}\text{Dollar-weighted}\\ \text{duration of}\\ \text{liabilities}\\ \text{portfolio}\end{array} \times \frac{\text{Total liabilities}}{\text{Total assets}} \quad \textbf{(7–21)}$$

Equation (7–21) tells us that the value of liabilities must change by slightly more than the value of assets to eliminate a financial firm's overall interest-rate risk exposure.

The larger the leverage-adjusted duration gap, the more sensitive will be the net worth (equity capital) of a financial institution to a change in market interest rates. For example, if we have a positive leverage-adjusted duration gap, a parallel change in all market interest rates will result in the value of liabilities changing by less (up or down) than the value of assets. In this case, a rise in interest rates will tend to lower the market value of net worth as asset values fall further than the value of liabilities. The owner's equity in the institution will decline in market value terms. On the other hand, if a financial firm has a negative leverage-adjusted duration gap, then a parallel change in all interest rates will generate a larger change in liability values than asset values. If interest rates fall, liabilities

TABLE 7–3
Use of Duration
Analysis to Hedge
Interest Rate
Movements

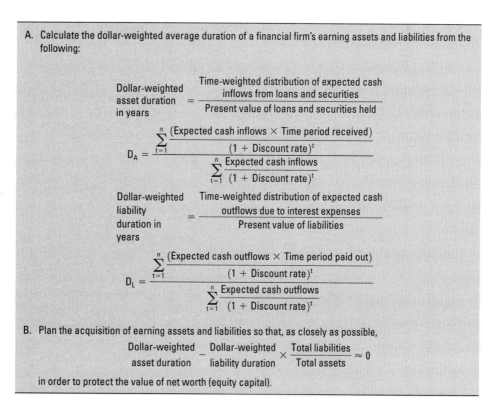

A. Calculate the dollar-weighted average duration of a financial firm's earning assets and liabilities from the following:

$$\frac{\text{Dollar-weighted}}{\text{asset duration}} = \frac{\text{Time-weighted distribution of expected cash inflows from loans and securities}}{\text{Present value of loans and securities held}}$$

$$D_A = \frac{\sum_{t=1}^{n}\frac{(\text{Expected cash inflows} \times \text{Time period received})}{(1 + \text{Discount rate})^t}}{\sum_{t=1}^{n}\frac{\text{Expected cash inflows}}{(1 + \text{Discount rate})^t}}$$

$$\frac{\text{Dollar-weighted}}{\text{liability duration in years}} = \frac{\text{Time-weighted distribution of expected cash outflows due to interest expenses}}{\text{Present value of liabilities}}$$

$$D_L = \frac{\sum_{t=1}^{n}\frac{(\text{Expected cash outflows} \times \text{Time period paid out})}{(1 + \text{Discount rate})^t}}{\sum_{t=1}^{n}\frac{\text{Expected cash outflows}}{(1 + \text{Discount rate})^t}}$$

B. Plan the acquisition of earning assets and liabilities so that, as closely as possible,

$$\frac{\text{Dollar-weighted}}{\text{asset duration}} - \frac{\text{Dollar-weighted}}{\text{liability duration}} \times \frac{\text{Total liabilities}}{\text{Total assets}} \approx 0$$

in order to protect the value of net worth (equity capital).

will increase more in value than assets and net worth will decline. Should interest rates rise, however, liability values will decrease faster than asset values and the net worth position will increase in value.

We can calculate the change in the market value of a financial institution's net worth if we know its dollar-weighted average asset duration, its dollar-weighted average liability duration, the original rate of discount applied to the institution's cash flows, and how interest rates have changed during the period we are concerned about. The relevant formula is based upon the balance-sheet relationship we discussed earlier in Equation (7–17):

$$\Delta NW = \Delta A - \Delta L$$

Because $\Delta A/A$ is approximately equal to the product of asset duration times the change in interest rates $\left[-D_A \times \dfrac{\Delta i}{(1 + i)} \right]$ and $\Delta L/L$ is approximately equal to liability duration times the change in interest rates $\left[-D_L \times \dfrac{\Delta i}{(1 + i)} \right]$, it follows that:

$$\Delta NW = \left[-D_A \times \frac{\Delta i}{(1 + i)} \times A \right] - \left[-D_L \times \frac{\Delta i}{(1 + i)} \times L \right] \quad \textbf{(7–22)}$$

In words,

$$
\begin{aligned}
\text{Change in value} \atop \text{of net worth}
&=
\left[
\begin{array}{c}
-\text{Average} \\ \text{duration} \\ \text{of assets}
\end{array}
\times
\frac{\text{Change in}\ \text{interest rate}}{\substack{(1 + \text{Original} \\ \text{discount rate})}}
\times
\begin{array}{c}
\text{Total} \\ \text{assets}
\end{array}
\right] \\[2em]
&\quad -
\left[
\begin{array}{c}
-\text{Average} \\ \text{duration} \\ \text{of liabilities}
\end{array}
\times
\frac{\text{Change in}\ \text{interest rates}}{\substack{(1 + \text{Original} \\ \text{discount rate})}}
\times
\begin{array}{c}
\text{Total} \\ \text{liabilities}
\end{array}
\right]
\end{aligned}
\quad \textbf{(7–23)}
$$

For example, suppose that a bank has an average duration in its assets of three years, an average liability duration of two years, total liabilities of $100 million, and total assets of $120 million. Interest rates were originally 10 percent, but suddenly they rise to 12 percent.

In this example:

$$
\begin{aligned}
\text{Change in the} \atop \text{value of} \atop \text{net worth}
&=
\left[-3 \times \frac{+0.02}{(1 + 0.10)} \times \$120\ \text{million} \right] \\[1em]
&\quad - \left[-2 \times \frac{+0.02}{(1 + 0.10)} \times \$100\ \text{million} \right] = -\$2.91\ \text{million.}
\end{aligned}
$$

Clearly, this bank faces a substantial decline in the value of its net worth unless it can hedge itself against the projected loss due to rising interest rates.

Let's consider an example of how duration can be calculated and used to hedge a financial firm's asset and liability portfolio. We take advantage of the fact that the duration of a portfolio of assets and of a portfolio of liabilities equals the value-weighted average of the duration of each instrument in the portfolio. We can start by (1) calculating the duration of each loan, deposit, and the like; (2) weighting each of these durations by the market values of the instruments involved; and (3) adding all the value-weighted durations together to derive the duration of a financial institution's entire portfolio.

For example, suppose management of a bank finds that it holds a U.S. Treasury $1,000 par bond with 10 years to final maturity, bearing a 10 percent coupon rate with a current price of $900. Based on the formula shown in Equation (7–15), this bond's duration is 7.49 years.

Suppose this bank holds $90 million of these Treasury bonds, each with a duration of 7.49 years. The bank also holds other assets with durations and market values as follows:

Assets Held	Actual or Estimated Market Values of Assets	Asset Durations
Commercial loans	$100 million	0.60 years
Consumer loans	50 million	1.20 years
Real estate loans	40 million	2.25 years
Municipal bonds	20 million	1.50 years

Weighting each asset duration by its associated dollar volume, we calculate the duration of the asset portfolio as follows:

$$\text{Dollar-weighted asset portfolio duration} = \frac{\sum_{i=1}^{n} \begin{matrix}\text{Duration of} \\ \text{each asset in} \\ \text{the portfolio}\end{matrix} \times \begin{matrix}\text{Market value} \\ \text{of each asset} \\ \text{in the portfolio}\end{matrix}}{\begin{matrix}\text{Total market value} \\ \text{of all assets}\end{matrix}} \quad (7\text{--}24)$$

$$= \frac{\begin{pmatrix}7.49 \text{ years} \times \$90 \text{ million in Treasury bonds} \\ + 0.60 \text{ years} \times \$100 \text{ million in commercial loans} \\ + 1.20 \text{ years} \times \$50 \text{ million in consumer loans} \\ + 2.25 \text{ years} \times \$40 \text{ million in real estate loans} \\ + 1.50 \text{ years} \times \$20 \text{ million in municipal bonds}\end{pmatrix}}{\begin{pmatrix}\$90 \text{ million} + \$100 \text{ million} + \$50 \text{ million} \\ + \$40 \text{ million} + \$20 \text{ million}\end{pmatrix}}$$

$$= \frac{\$914.10 \text{ million}}{\$300 \text{ million}}$$

$$= 3.047 \text{ years}$$

Duration is a measure of *average maturity*, which for this bank's portfolio of assets is about three years. The bank can hedge against the damaging effects of rising deposit interest rates by making sure the dollar-weighted average duration of its liabilities is also approximately three years.[4] In this way the present value of bank assets will balance the present value of liabilities, approximately insulating the bank from losses due to fluctuating interest rates.

The calculation of duration for liabilities proceeds in the same way as asset durations are calculated. For example, suppose this same bank has $100 million in negotiable CDs outstanding on which it must pay its customers a 6 percent annual yield over the next two calendar years. The duration of these CDs will be determined by the distribution of cash payments made over the next two years in present-value terms.

[4]As noted earlier, we must adjust the duration of the liability portfolio by the value of the ratio of total liabilities to total assets because asset volume typically exceeds the volume of liabilities. For example, suppose the bank described in the example above has an asset duration of three years and its total assets are $100 million while total liabilities are $92 million. Then management will want to achieve an approximate average duration for liabilities of 3.261 years (or asset duration × total assets ÷ total liabilities = 3 years × $100 million ÷ $92 million = 3.261 years).

DURATION GAP MANAGEMENT AT THE WORLD'S LARGEST MORTGAGE BANK

The world's leading mortgage banking institution—the Federal National Mortgage Association (FNMA), better known as *Fannie Mae*—reports its *duration gap* on a monthly basis. Fannie is a crucial institution supporting the U.S. housing market. It issues notes and bonds to raise new capital and then uses the proceeds to purchase residential mortgages from private lenders and to package home loans into pools that support the issuance of mortgage-backed securities. Fannie has contributed significantly to making more families eligible to receive loans to purchase new homes.

As market interest rates plummeted early in the 21st century and the volume of home mortgage financings soared, FNMA experienced a significant shift in the average maturity of its assets and liabilities. Lengthening liabilities and shorter-term assets generated a *negative duration gap* of about 14 months at the close of 2002. Fannie's assets were rolling over into cash more than a year sooner than its liabilities. If market interest rates had continued to fall, the value of Fannie's net worth would also have continued to decline as longer-term liabilities increased in value relative to shorter-term assets. Investors in the financial markets reacted negatively to FNMA's announcement of a widening negative duration gap and its stock price fell for a time.

Fannie strives to maintain a duration gap between negative 6 months and positive 6 months. By October of 2002 Fannie Mae had its duration gap in line with this objective—a negative 6 months. By 2005 its monthly duration gaps fell within the −1 month to + 1 month range. (Fannie publishes its duration gap calculations in its *Monthly Summary*, published by FNMA's Office of Investor Relations, and on its Web site at **www.fanniemae.com**.)

Thus:

$$\text{Duration of negotiable CDs} = \frac{\dfrac{\$6 \times 1}{(1.06)^1} + \dfrac{\$6 \times 2}{(1.06)^2} + \dfrac{\$100 \times 2}{(1.06)^2}}{\$100} = 1.943 \text{ years}$$

We would go through the same calculation for the remaining liabilities in this example, as illustrated in Table 7–4. This institution has an average liability duration of 2.669 years, substantially *less* than the average duration of its asset portfolio, which is 3.047 years. Because the average maturity of its liabilities is shorter than the average maturity of its assets, this financial firm's net worth will decrease if interest rates rise and increase if interest rates fall. Clearly, management has positioned this institution in the hope that interest rates will fall in the period ahead. If there is a substantial probability interest rates will rise, management may want to hedge against damage from rising interest rates by lengthening the average maturity of its liabilities, shortening the average maturity of its assets, or employing hedging tools (such as financial futures or swaps, as discussed in the next chapter) to cover this duration gap.

In summary, the impact of changing market interest rates on net worth is indicated by entries in the following table:

If the Financial Institution's Leverage-Adjusted Duration Gap Is:	And If Interest Rates:	The Financial Institution's Net Worth Will:
Positive $\left(D_A > D_L \times \dfrac{\text{Liabilities}}{\text{Assets}} \right)$	Rise	Decrease
	Fall	Increase
Negative $\left(D_A < D_L \times \dfrac{\text{Liabilities}}{\text{Assets}} \right)$	Rise	Increase
	Fall	Decrease
Zero $\left(D_A = D_L \times \dfrac{\text{Liabilities}}{\text{Assets}} \right)$	Rise	No Change
	Fall	No Change

TABLE 7–4   Calculating the Duration of a Bank's Assets and Liabilities (dollars in millions)

Composition of Assets (uses of funds)	Market Value of Assets	Interest Rate Attached to Each Category of Assets	Average Duration of Each Category of Assets (in years)	Composition of Liabilities and Equity Capital (sources of funds)	Market Value of Liabilities	Interest Rate Attached to Each Liability Category	Average Duration of Each Liability Category (in years)
U.S. Treasury Securities	$ 90	10.00%	7.490	Negotiable CDs	$100	6.00%	1.943
Municipal bonds	20	6.00	1.500	Other time deposits	125	7.20	2.750
Commercial loans	100	12.00	0.600	Subordinated notes	50	9.00	3.918
Consumer loans	50	15.00	1.200	Total liabilities	275		
				Stockholders' equity capital			
Real estate loans	40	13.00	2.250		25		
			Average in Years				Average in Years
Total	$300		3.047	Total	$300		2.669

$$\text{Duration of assets} = \frac{\$90}{\$300} \times 7.49 + \frac{\$20}{\$300} \times 1.50 + \frac{\$100}{\$300} \times 0.60 + \frac{\$50}{\$300} \times 1.20 + \frac{\$40}{\$300} \times 2.25$$

$$= 3.047 \text{ years}$$

$$\text{Duration of liabilities} = \frac{\$100}{\$275} \times 1.943 + \frac{\$125}{\$275} \times 2.750 + \frac{\$50}{\$275} \times 3.198 = 2.669 \text{ years}$$

$$\frac{\text{Current leverage-adjusted}}{\text{duration gap}} = \frac{\text{Average asset}}{\text{duration}} - \frac{\text{Average liability}}{\text{duration}} \times \frac{\text{Total liabilities}}{\text{Total assets}}$$

$$= 3.047 \text{ years} - 2.669 \text{ years} \times \frac{\$275}{\$300} = +0.60 \text{ years}$$

Management Interpretation

The positive duration gap of +0.60 years means that the bank's net worth will decline if interest rates rise and increase if interest rates fall. Management may be anticipating a decrease in the level of interest rates. If there is significant risk of rising market interest rates, however, the asset-liability management committee will want to use hedging tools to reduce the exposure of net worth to interest rate risk. How much will the value of this bank's net worth change for any given change in interest rates? The appropriate formula is as follows:

$$\frac{\text{Change in value}}{\text{of net worth}} = -D_A \cdot \frac{\Delta r}{(1 + r)} \cdot A - \left[-D_L \cdot \frac{\Delta r}{(1 + r)} \cdot L \right],$$

where A is total assets, D_A the average duration of assets, r the initial interest rate, Δr the change in interest rates, L total liabilities, and D_L the average duration of liabilities.

Example: Suppose interest rates on both assets and liabilities *rise* from 8 to 10 percent. Then filling in the asset and liability figures from the table above gives this result:

$$\frac{\text{Change in}}{\text{value of}}_{\text{net worth}} = -3.047 \text{ years} \times \frac{(+0.02)}{(1 + 0.08)} \times \$300 \text{ million} - \left[-2.669 \text{ years} \times \frac{(+0.02)}{(1 + 0.08)} \times \$275 \text{ million} \right]$$

$$= -\$16.93 \text{ million} + \$13.59 \text{ million} = -\$3.34 \text{ million}$$

This institution's net worth would fall by approximately $3.34 million if interest rates increase by 2 percentage points.

(continued)

TABLE 7–4 *Continued*

Suppose interest rates *fall* from 8 percent to 6 percent. What would happen to the value of the above institution's net worth? Again, substituting in the same formula:

$$\text{Change in value of net worth} = -3.047 \text{ years} \times \frac{(-0.02)}{(1 + 0.08)} \times \$300 \text{ million}$$

$$- \left[-2.669 \text{ years} \times \frac{(-0.02)}{(1 + .08)} \times \$275 \text{ million} \right]$$

$$= \$16.93 \text{ million} - \$13.59 \text{ million} = +\$3.34 \text{ million}.$$

In this instance, the value of net worth would *rise* by about $3.34 million if all interest rates fell by 2 percentage points.

The above formula reminds us that the impact of interest rate changes on the market value of net worth depends upon three crucial size factors:

A. The size of the duration gap $(D_A - D_L)$, with a larger duration gap indicating greater exposure of a financial firm to interest rate risk.
B. The size of a financial institution (A and L), with larger institutions experiencing a greater change in net worth for any given change in interest rates.
C. The size of the change in interest rates, with larger rate changes generating greater interest-rate risk exposure.

Management can reduce a financial firm's exposure to interest rate risk by closing up the firm's duration gap (changing D_A, D_L, or both) or by changing the relative amounts of assets and liabilities (A and L) outstanding.

For example, suppose in the previous example the leverage-adjusted duration gap, instead of being + 0.60 years, is *zero*. If the average duration of assets (D_A) is 3.047 years (and assets and liabilities equal $300 and $275 million respectively) this would mean the institution's average liability duration (D_L) must be as follows:

$$\text{Current leverage-adjusted duration gap} = \text{Average asset duration } (\bar{D}_A) - \text{Average liability duration } (\bar{D}_L) \times \frac{\text{Total liabilities}}{\text{Total assets}}$$

or,

$$0 = 3.047 - \text{Average liability duration } (\bar{D}_L) \times \frac{\$275}{\$300}$$

Then:

$$\text{Average liability duration } (\bar{D}_L) = 3.324 \text{ years}$$

Suppose, once again, market interest rates all rise from 8 percent to 10 percent. Then the change in the value of net worth would be as shown below:

$$\text{Change in value of net worth} = -3.047 \text{ years} \times \frac{(-0.02)}{(1 + 0.08)} \times \$300 \text{ million} - \left[-3.324 \text{ years} \times \frac{(+0.02)}{(1 + 0.08)} \times \$275 \text{ million} \right]$$

$$= -\$16.93 \text{ million} + \$16.93 \text{ million} = 0$$

As expected, with asset and liability durations perfectly balanced (and adjusted for differences in the amounts of total assets versus total liabilities), the change in net worth must be *zero*. Net worth doesn't move despite the rise in market interest rates.

It shouldn't surprise us to discover that if market interest rates drop from, say, 8 percent to 6 percent, net worth will also not change if asset and liability durations are perfectly balanced. Thus:

$$\text{Change in value of net worth} = -3.047 \text{ years} \times \frac{(-0.02)}{(1 + 0.08)} \times \$300 \text{ million} - \left[-3.324 \text{ years} \times \frac{(-0.02)}{(1 + .08)} \times \$275 \text{ million} \right]$$

$$= +\$16.93 \text{ million} - \$16.93 \text{ million} = 0$$

The change in the value of the financial firm's net worth must be zero because assets and liabilities, adjusted for the difference in their dollar amounts, exhibit a similar response to interest rate movements.

In the final case, with a leverage-adjusted duration gap of zero, the financial firm is *immunized* against changes in the value of its net worth. Changes in the market values of assets and liabilities will simply offset each other and net worth will remain where it is.

Of course, more aggressive financial-service managers may not like the seemingly "wimpy" strategy of **portfolio immunization** (duration gap = 0). They may be willing to take some chances to maximize the shareholders' position. For example,

Expected Change in Interest Rates	Management Action	Possible Outcome
Rates will rise	Reduce D_A and increase D_L (moving closer to a negative duration gap).	Net worth increases (if management's rate forecast is correct).
Rates will fall	Increase D_A and reduce D_L (moving closer to a positive duration gap).	Net worth increases (if management's rate forecast is correct).

7–7 The Limitations of Duration Gap Management

While duration is simple to interpret, it has several limitations. For one thing, finding assets and liabilities of the same duration that fit into a financial-service institution's portfolio is often a frustrating task. It would be much easier if the maturity of a loan or security equaled its duration; however, for financial instruments paying out gradually over time, duration is *always* less than calendar maturity. Only in the case of instruments like zero-coupon securities, single-payment loans, and Treasury bills does the duration of a financial instrument equal its calendar maturity. The more frequently a financial instrument pays interest or pays off principal, the shorter is its duration. One useful fact is that the shorter the maturity of an instrument, the closer the match between its maturity and its duration is likely to be.

Some accounts held by depository institutions, such as checkable deposits and passbook savings accounts, may have a pattern of cash flows that is not well defined, making the calculation of duration difficult. Moreover, customer prepayments distort the expected cash flows from loans and so do customer defaults (credit risk) when expected cash flows do not happen. Moreover, duration gap models assume that a linear relationship exists between the market values (prices) of assets and liabilities and interest rates, which is not strictly true.

A related problem with duration analysis revolves around the concept of *convexity*. Duration gap analysis tends to be reasonably effective at handling interest rate risk problems if the yield curve (i.e., the maturity structure of interest rates) changes by relatively small amounts and moves in parallel steps with short-term and long-term interest rates changing by about the same proportion over time. However, if there are major changes in interest rates and different interest rates move at different speeds, the accuracy and effectiveness of duration gap management decreases somewhat. Moreover, yield curves in the real world typically do *not* change in parallel fashion—short-term interest rates tend to move over a wider range than long-term interest rates, for example—and a *big* change in market interest rates (say, one or two percentage points) can result in a distorted reading of how much interest rate risk a financial manager is really facing. Duration itself can shift as market interest rates move, and the durations of different financial instruments can change at differing speeds with the passage of time.

Fortunately, recent research suggests that duration balancing can still be effective, even with moderate violations of the technique's underlying assumptions. We need to remember, too, that duration gap analysis helps a financial manager better manage the value of a financial firm to its shareholders (i.e., its net worth). In this age of mergers and continuing financial-services industry consolidation, the duration gap concept remains a valuable managerial tool despite its limitations.

Concept Check

7–16. What is *duration?*

7–17. How is a financial institution's *duration gap* determined?

7–18. What are the advantages of using duration as an asset-liability management tool as opposed to interest-sensitive gap analysis?

7–19. How can you tell if you are fully hedged using duration gap analysis?

7–20. What are the principal limitations of duration gap analysis? Can you think of some way of reducing the impact of these limitations?

7–21. Suppose that a thrift institution has an average asset duration of 2.5 years and an average liability duration of 3.0 years. If the thrift holds total assets of $560 million and total liabilities of $467 million, does it have a significant leverage-adjusted duration gap? If interest rates rise, what will happen to the value of its net worth?

7–22. Stilwater Bank and Trust Company has an average asset duration of 3.25 years and an average liability duration of 1.75 years. Its liabilities amount to $485 million, while its assets total $512 million. Suppose that interest rates were 7 percent and then rise to 8 percent. What will happen to the value of the Stilwater bank's net worth as a result of a decline in interest rates?

Summary

The managers of financial-service companies focus heavily today on the *management of risk*—attempting to control their exposure to loss due to changes in market rates of interest, the inability or unwillingness of borrowers to repay their loans, regulatory changes, and other risk-laden factors. Successful risk management requires effective tools that provide managers with the weapons they need to achieve their institution's goals. In this chapter several of the most important risk management tools for financial firms were discussed. The most important points in the chapter include:

- Early in the history of banking managers focused principally upon the tool of *asset management*—emphasizing control and selection of assets, such as loans and security investments, to achieve institutional goals because liabilities were assumed to be dominated by customer decisions and government rules.

- Later, *liability management* tools emerged in which managers discovered they could achieve a measure of control over the liabilities on their balance sheet by changing interest rates and other terms offered to the public relative to the terms offered by competitors.

- More recently, many financial firms have practiced *funds management*, discovering how to *coordinate* the management of *both* assets and liabilities in order to achieve institutional goals, especially those related to profitability and risk.

- One of the strongest risk factors financial-service managers have to deal with every day is *interest rate risk*. Managers cannot control market interest rates, but instead they must learn how to react to interest-rate changes in order to control their risk exposure and achieve their objectives.

- One of the most popular tools for handling interest-rate risk exposure is *interest-sensitive gap management*, which focuses upon protecting or maximizing each financial firm's *net interest margin* or spread between interest revenues and interest costs. For example, a financial firm's assets and liabilities may be divided using computer software into those items that are *interest-rate sensitive* (that is, whose revenue or expense flow changes with movements in market interest rates) and those that are not rate sensitive. Managers determine for any given time period (maturity bucket) whether their institution is *asset sensitive* (with an excess of interest-rate sensitive assets) or *liability sensitive* (with more rate-sensitive liabilities than rate-sensitive assets). These interest-sensitive gaps are then compared with the financial firm's interest rate forecast, and management takes appropriate action (such as the use of futures contracts or the shifting of asset and/or liability portfolios) in order to protect the firm's net interest margin.

- Managers soon discovered that interest-sensitive gap management didn't necessarily protect a financial firm's *net worth*—value of shareholders' investment in the institution. This job required the development of *duration gap management*.

- Based on the concept of *duration*—a value- and time-weighted measure of maturity— the managers of financial institutions learned how to assess their exposure to loss in net worth from relative changes in the value of assets and liabilities when market interest rates change. This technique points to the importance of avoiding large gaps between the average duration of a financial firm's asset portfolio compared to the average duration of its portfolio of liabilities.

- Finally, financial-service managers have discovered that *risk* in all of its forms—interest rate risk, market risk, default risk, regulatory risk, and so on—cannot be eliminated. Rather it must be *managed* properly if the financial firm is to survive and prosper.

Key Terms

asset-liability management, *208*
asset management, *208*
liability management, *208*
funds management, *209*
interest rate risk, *210*
yield to maturity (YTM), *211*

bank discount rate, *211*
maturity gap, *214*
net interest margin, *215*
interest-sensitive gap management, *216*
duration gap management, *226*

duration, *226*
convexity, *228*
duration gap, *229*
portfolio immunization, *235*

Problems and Projects

e**X**cel

1. A government bond is currently selling for $900 and pays $75 per year in interest for nine years when it matures. If the redemption value of this bond is $1,000, what is its yield to maturity if purchased today for $900?

e**X**cel

2. Suppose the government bond described in Problem 1 above is held for three years and then the savings institution acquiring the bond decides to sell it at a price of $1,020. Can you figure out the average annual yield the savings institution will have earned for its three-year investment in the bond?

e**X**cel

3. U.S. Treasury bills are available for purchase this week at the following prices (based upon $100 par value) and with the indicated maturities:
   a. $98.25, 182 days
   b. $97.25, 270 days
   c. $99.25, 91 days

   Calculate the bank discount rate (DR) on each bill if it is held to maturity. What is the equivalent yield to maturity (sometimes called the bond-equivalent or coupon-equivalent yield) on each of these Treasury bills?

e**X**cel

4. The First State Bank of Gregsville reports a net interest margin of 2.5 percent in its most recent financial report, with total interest revenue of $88 million and total interest costs of $72 million. What volume of earning assets must the bank hold? Suppose the bank's interest revenues rise by 8 percent and its interest costs and earning assets increase 9 percent. What will happen to Gregsville's net interest margin?

e**X**cel

5. If a bank's net interest margin, which was 2.50 percent, increases 70 percent and its total assets, which stood originally at $545 million, rise by 40 percent, what change will occur in the bank's net interest income?

6. The cumulative interest rate gap of Gemstone Federal Savings and Loan increases 60 percent from an initial figure of $40 million. If market interest rates rise by 25 percent from an initial level of 6 percent, what changes will occur in this thrift's net interest income?

7. Old Misers State Bank has recorded the following financial data for the past three years (dollars in millions):

	Current Year	Previous Year	Two Years Ago
Interest revenues	$ 88.00	$ 84.00	$ 80.00
Interest expenses	79.00	77.00	74.00
Loans (excluding nonperforming loans)	415.00	400.00	390.00
Investments	239.00	197.00	174.00
Total deposits	487.00	472.00	467.00
Money market borrowings	143.00	118.00	96.00

What has been happening to the bank's net interest margin? What do you think caused the changes you have observed? Do you have any recommendations for Old Misers' management team?

8. The First National Bank of Sylvania finds that its asset and liability portfolio contains the following distribution of maturities and repricing opportunities:

Dollar Volume of Assets and Liabilities Maturing or Subject to Repricing Within:			
	Coming Week	Next 8–30 Days	Next 31–90 Days	More than 90 Days
---	---	---	---	---
Loans	$210.00	$100.00	$175.00	$225.00
Securities	30.00	20.00	30.00	25.00
Interest-sensitive assets				
Transaction deposits	$250.00	$ 0.00	$ 0.00	$ 0.00
Time accounts	100.00	84.00	196.00	100.00
Money market borrowings	36.00	20.00	0.00	0.00
Interest-sensitive liabilities				

When and by how much is the bank exposed to interest rate risk? For each maturity or repricing interval, what changes in interest rates will be beneficial to the bank and which will be damaging, given its current portfolio position?

9. First National Bank of Fluffy Clouds currently has the following interest-sensitive assets and liabilities on its balance sheet with the interest-rate sensitivity weights noted.

Interest-Sensitive Assets	$ Amount	Rate Sensitivity Index
Federal fund loans	$ 50.00	1.00
Security holdings	50.00	1.15
Loans and leases	230.00	1.35

Interest-Sensitive Liabilities	$ Amount	Rate Sensitivity Index
Interest-bearing deposits	$250.00	0.79
Money-market borrowings	85.00	0.98

What is the bank's current interest-sensitive gap? Adjusting for these various interest-rate sensitivity weights what is the bank's weighted interest-sensitive gap? Suppose the federal funds interest rate increases or decreases one percentage point. How will the bank's net interest income be affected (*a*) given its current balance sheet makeup and (*b*) reflecting its weighted balance sheet adjusted for the foregoing rate-sensitivity indexes?

10. Mountaintop Savings Association has interest-sensitive assets of $300 million, interest-sensitive liabilities of $175 million, and total assets of $500 million. What is the bank's dollar interest-sensitive gap? What is Mountaintop's relative interest-sensitive gap? What is the value of its interest sensitivity ratio? Is it asset sensitive or liability sensitive? Under what scenario for market interest rates will Mountaintop experience a gain in net interest income? A loss in net interest income?

11. Casio Merchants and Trust Bank, N.A., has a portfolio of loans and securities expected to generate cash inflows for the bank as follows:

Expected Cash Inflows of Principal and Interest Payments	Annual Period in Which Cash Receipts Are Expected
$1,385,421	Current year
746,872	Two years from today
341,555	Three years from today
62,482	Four years from today
9,871	Five years from today

Deposits and money market borrowings are expected to require the following cash outflows:

Expected Cash Outflows of Principal and Interest Payments	Annual Period during Which Cash Payments Must Be Made
$1,427,886	Current year
831,454	Two years from today
123,897	Three years from today
1,005	Four years from today
—	Five years from today

If the discount rate applicable to the previous cash flows is 8 percent, what is the duration of Casio's portfolio of earning assets and of its deposits and money market borrowings? What will happen to the bank's total returns, assuming all other factors are held constant, if interest rates rise? If interest rates fall? Given the size of the duration gap you have calculated, in what type of hedging should Casio engage? Please be specific about the hedging transactions that are needed and their expected effects.

12. Given the cash inflow and outflow figures in Problem 11 for Casio Merchants and Trust Bank, N.A., suppose that interest rates began at a level of 8 percent and then suddenly rise to 9 percent. If the bank has total assets of $125 million, and total liabilities of $110 million, by how much would the value of Casio's net worth change as a result of this movement in interest rates? Suppose, on the other hand, that interest rates decline from 8 percent to 7 percent. What happens to the value of Casio's net worth in this case and by how much in dollars does it change? What is the size of its duration gap?

eXcel

13. Watson Thrift Association reports an average asset duration of 5 years and an average liability duration of 4.25 years. In its latest financial report, the association recorded total assets of $1.8 billion and total liabilities of $1.5 billion. If interest rates began at 7 percent and then suddenly climbed to 9 percent, what change will occur in the value of Watson's net worth? By how much would Watson's net worth change if, instead of rising, interest rates fell from 7 percent to 5 percent?

eXcel

14. A bank holds a bond in its investment portfolio whose duration is 13.5 years. Its current market price is $1,020. While market interest rates are currently at 8 percent for comparable quality securities, a decrease in interest rates to 7.25 percent is expected in the coming weeks. What change (in percentage terms) will this bond's price experience if market interest rates change as anticipated?

eXcel

15. A savings bank's weighted average asset duration is seven years. Its total liabilities amount to $900 million, while its assets total 1 billion dollars. What is the dollar-weighted duration of the bank's liability portfolio if it has a zero leverage-adjusted duration gap?

eXcel

16. New Phase National Bank holds assets and liabilities whose average durations and dollar amounts are as shown in this table:

Asset and Liability Items	Avg. Duration (years)	Dollar Amount (millions)
Investment-grade bonds	10.00	$ 50.00
Commercial loans	4.00	400.00
Consumer loans	7.00	250.00
Deposits	1.10	600.00
Nondeposit borrowings	0.10	20.00

What is the weighted-average duration of New Phase's asset portfolio and liability portfolio? What is its leverage-adjusted duration gap?

eXcel

17. A government bond currently carries a yield to maturity of 8 percent and a market price of $1,080. If the bond promises to pay $100 in interest annually for five years, what is its current duration?

eXcel

18. Dewey National Bank holds $15 million in government bonds having a duration of six years. If interest rates suddenly rise from 6 percent to 7 percent, what percentage change should occur in the bonds' market price?

Internet Exercises

1. At **www.ALMprofessional.com** you will find a network devoted to articles and discussions of the asset-liability management field. Visit the site and find an article entitled: "Principles for the Management of Interest Rate Risk." What are the major sources of interest rate risk according to this article?

2. If a new model applying ALM techniques to a bank's risk exposure is developed, you would most likely find a discussion of that new ALM model at **www.ALMprofessional.com**. What models are presently found at this Web site?

3. If you want to find a useful definition for *duration*, use a search engine to explore the Web. Provide one definition of duration and the Web site where it was found.

4. See if you can find the meaning of *modified duration* on the Web. Where did you find it and what did you find?

5. Duration gap management is a powerful analytical tool for protecting net worth of a financial institution from damage due to shifting interest rates. Asset-liability managers have found this tool surprisingly resilient and robust even when its basic assumptions are not fully met. Go to **www.aba.com** and do a quick search for "duration gap." What did you find?

REAL NUMBERS FOR REAL BANKS   Assignment for Chapter 7

YOUR BANK'S INTEREST RATE SENSITIVITY

In Chapter 7 the focus is interest-rate risk management. Regulatory agencies began to collect relevant information in the 1980s when large numbers of thrifts failed due to their interest-rate risk exposure at a time when market rates were increasing both in level and volatility. You will find Interest Rate Risk Analysis or Interest Sensitivity Reports included in both the UBPR (introduced in Chapter 6) and the Uniform Bank Holding Company Performance Report (UBHCPR). Both reports are available at **www.ffiec.gov**. This is one area where measurement within banks and BHCs is more sophisticated than the measures used by regulatory agencies. For instance, to date, none of the regulatory agencies require their financial institutions to submit measures of the duration gap.

Part One: NIM: A Comparison to Peers

A. Open your Excel Workbook and access the spreadsheet with Comparisons with Peer Group. On line 36, you find net interest income (NII) as a percentage of total assets (TA). This is one calculation of NIM. You may have noticed from a footnote in Chapter 6 that sometimes NIM is calculated using total assets as the denominator and sometimes total earning assets (TEA) are used as the denominator as illustrated in Equation (7–5). To transform the first measure of NIM (NII/TAA) to the second measure using TEA, we need to collect one more item from the FDIC's Web site. Using the directions in Chapter 6's assignment, go to the FDIC's Statistics for Depository Institutions, **www3.fdic.gov/sdi/**, and collect from the Memoranda Section of Assets and Liabilities the Earning Assets as a percentage of Total Assets for Your Bank Holding Company and its Peer Group for the two periods. We will add this information to this spreadsheet to calculate NIM (NII/TEA) as follows:

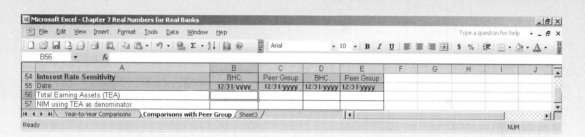

B. Use your formula functions to generate the percentages in row 57. For instance, cell **B57 = B36/B56**.

C. Once you have collected the data on NIM, write one paragraph discussing interest rate sensitivity for your bank

(continued)

STANDARD &POOR'S

S&P Market Insight Challenge (www.mhhe.com/edumarketinsight)

1. Changing market interest rates affect the profitability of many financial-service firms. For up-to-date information concerning the current interest-rate environment, use the Industry tab from S&P's Market Insight, Educational Version database. Several subindustry categories should appear, including Consumer Finance, Diversified Banks, Diversified Capital Markets, Regional Banks, and Thrifts and Mortgage Finance. Once an industry group has been chosen you can download one or more S&P Industry Surveys using Adobe Acrobat. The Industry Surveys associated with the above categories include Banking, Financial Services Diversified, and Savings and Loans. Please download these particular surveys and read the information on Interest Rates in the Key Industry Ratios and Statistics section. Write a paragraph concerning recent developments in short-term market interest rates and a paragraph covering long-term interest rates.

relative to the peer group across the two time periods based on the NIM. Discuss what is revealed by the variation of NIM across time. Review the discussion of NIM in this chapter for further direction.

Part Two: Interest-Sensitive Gaps and Ratios

While the FDIC's Web site is powerful in providing basic data concerning assets, liabilities, equity, income, and expenses for individual banks and the banking component of BHCs, it does not provide any reports on interest sensitivity. For individual banks such information is available in the UBPR, and for BHCs information is available in the BHCPR. (Note that this data is for the entire BHC and not an aggregation of the

chartered bank and thrifts that we have used to this point.) We will access the BHCPR and create a report for the most recent year-end. You will use information from this report to calculate one-year interest-sensitive gaps (Equation [7–7]) and one-year interest-sensitive ratios (Equation [7–11]) for the two most recent years.

A. Using the BHCPR created for your BHC please fill in rows 73 and 74. You will find Net assets repriceable in one-year-to-total assets in the Liquidity and Funding Section and the dollar amount of Average Assets on page 1 of the report. We will add your information to the spreadsheet as follows:

	A	B	C	D	E	F	G	H	I	J
71	Interest-sensitivity data from UBHCPR--Liquidity and Funding	BHC	BHC							
72	Date	12/31/yyyy	12/31/yyyy							
73	Net assets repriceable in 1 year (interest sensitivity ratio)									
74	Average assets (found top of Page 1 BHCPR)									
75	Interest-sensitive gap									

B. Having acquired the above information, you have the interest sensitivity ratio in row 73 and you will calculate the interest-sensitive gap by multiplying the interest sensitivity ratio by average assets.

C. Write one paragraph discussing the interest rate risk exposure for your BHC. Is it asset or liability sensitive at

the conclusion of each year? What are the implications of the changes occurring across the years? Using Equation (7–13), discuss the effects on net interest income if market interest rates increase or decrease by one full percentage point.

STANDARD &POOR'S

2. Select three banks listed in S&P's Market Insight, Educational Version. Which bank appears to have the greatest exposure to interest rate risk? Why do you think so? What damages could these banking firms incur on their income and expense statements? Their balance sheets? What does this chapter suggest might be appropriate remedies to help reduce the possible damages you have described?

Selected References

To examine the nature and impact of interest-rate movements, see, for example:

1. Wu, Tao. "What Makes the Yield Curve Move." *FRBSF Economic Letter*, Federal Reserve Bank of San Francisco, no. 2003-15 (June 6, 2003), pp. 1–3.

To explore the need for asset-liability management techniques and their potential effectiveness and importance, see especially:

2. Bailey, Jess. "Minnesota Bank Begins to Shed Its U.S. Bonds." *The Wall Street Journal*, December 20, 1988, p. 3.

3. Gerson, Vicki. "Starting on the Same Page." *Bank Systems and Technology* 42, issue #4, p. 42.

4. Lopez, Jose A. "Supervising Interest Rate Risk Management." *FRBSF Economic Letter*, Federal Reserve Bank of San Francisco, no. 2004-26 (September 17, 2004), pp. 1–3.

5. Sienna, Gregory E., and Timothy J. Yeager. "What Does the Federal Reserve's Economic Value Model Tell Us about Interest-Rate Risk at U.S. Community Banks?" *Review*, Federal Reserve Bank of St. Louis, November/December 2004, pp. 45–60.

To learn more about gap management techniques, see these studies:

6. Rose, Peter S. "Defensive Banking in a Volatile Economy—Hedging Loan and Deposit Interest Rates." *The Canadian Banker* 93, no. 2 (April 1986), pp. 52–59.

7. Toevs, Alden L. "Gap Management: Managing Interest-Rate Risk in Banks and Thrifts." *Economic Review*, Federal Reserve Bank of San Francisco, no. 2 (Spring 1983), pp. 20–35.

For an excellent collection of historical data on interest rates, especially rates attached to U.S. Treasury securities, federal funds, prime bank loans, and Federal Reserve discount rates, see:

8. Federal Reserve Bank of Dallas, *Selected Interest Rates*, December 2005.

CHAPTER EIGHT

Using Financial Futures, Options, Swaps, and Other Hedging Tools in Asset-Liability Management

Key Topics in This Chapter

- The Use of Derivatives
- Financial Futures Contracts: Purpose and Mechanics
- Short and Long Hedges
- Interest-Rate Options: Types of Contracts and Mechanics
- Interest-Rate Swaps
- Regulations and Accounting Rules
- Caps, Floors, and Collars

8–1 Introduction

The American humorist James Thurber once wrote: "A pinch of probably is worth a pound of perhaps." Financial-service managers have learned how to live in a new kind of world today—a world, not of perhapses, but of *probabilities*. A world of *calculated risk* rather than one of simple uncertainty.

What is the probability that interest rates will rise or fall tomorrow? What is the probability that the expected outcome for market interest rates simply won't materialize? How can a financial firm protect itself if "probably" turns out to be wrong?

In the preceding chapter we introduced one of the most important topics in the field of financial-services management—the concept of risk and the risk-management tool known as *asset-liability management* (ALM). As we saw in Chapter 7, the tools of asset-liability management are designed principally to control the threat of significant losses due to unexpected changes in interest rates in the financial markets. Asset-liability managers are especially concerned about stabilizing their institution's *net interest margin*—the spread between its interest revenues and interest expenses—and about protecting a financial firm's *net worth*—the value of the stockholders' investment in the institution. This chapter explores several of the most widely used weapons for dealing with a financial firm's exposure to interest rate risk—financial futures contracts, interest-rate options, interest-rate swaps, and the use of interest-rate caps, collars, and floors.

As we enter this important chapter we should keep a few key points in mind. First, the asset-liability management tools we explore here are useful across a broad range of financial-service providers sensitive to the risk of changes in market interest rates. In fact, one of the most vulnerable financial industries as the 21st century began was the life insurance business, which soon began to wish it had made even heavier use of risk-management tools such as futures and options. Some of the largest life insurers in Asia (especially China and Japan), Western Europe, and the United States had promised their customers high-interest yields on their savings, only to be confronted subsequently with record low market interest rates that made it close to impossible to deliver on some of their promises.

Second, many of the risk management tools we study in this part of the book not only are used by banks and other financial firms to cover their own interest rate risk, but also are sold to customers who need risk protection and generate important *fee income* for the providers. Finally, we need to be aware that most of the financial instruments we will be discussing are *derivatives*—that is, they derive their value from the value and terms of underlying instruments such as Treasury bills and bonds and Eurodollar deposits. Not only do derivatives help financial managers deal with interest rate and other risks, but they also present some of their own risks and challenges for the managers of financial institutions.[1]

8–2 Uses of Derivative Contracts

Due to their high exposure to interest rate risk, banks are among the heaviest users of derivative contracts. Moreover, due to the presence of heavy regulation of this industry, bank usage of these hedging instruments is among the best documented of all financial firms. According to a report by the Office of the Comptroller of the Currency,[2] approximately 10 percent of all banks surveyed reportedly employ the use of derivative contracts. As of the second quarter of 2005, 769 banks operating in the United States held derivatives having a combined notional (face) value of $96.2 trillion. The dollar amount of derivatives employed by banks in the United States has increased almost 500 percent over the preceding 10 years. Exhibit 8–1, derived from the Comptroller's report, illustrates the growth of derivative contracts by type of contract for all banks over the period from the fourth quarter of 1991 through the second quarter of 2005. In this chapter we focus on futures, options, and swap contracts and then examine the possible uses of credit derivatives—the newest of derivative contracts—in Chapter 9.

Recent information supplied by the Comptroller of the Currency, the Federal Reserve Board, and other regulatory agencies reveals that the bulk of trading in derivatives is centered in the very largest banks. For example, the Comptroller's survey discussed above disclosed that the 25 largest U.S. banking companies accounted for more

[1]Portions of this chapter are based on Peter S. Rose's article in *The Canadian Banker* [4] and are used with the permission of the publisher.
[2]See especially the Web site posted by the Office of the Comptroller of the Currency (**www.occ.treas.gov**), which contains the "OCC Bank Derivatives Report, Second Quarter 2005."

EXHIBIT 8–1
Derivative Contracts by Product, All U.S. Commercial Banks, 1991–2005 II. Most Recent Quarters

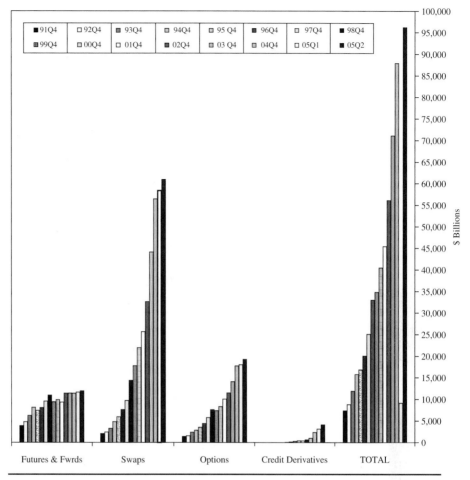

Derivative Contracts by Product ($ Billions)*

	91Q4 $	92Q4 $	93Q4 $	94Q4 $	95Q4 $	96Q4 $	97Q4 $	98Q4 $	99Q4 $	00Q4 $	01Q4 $	02Q4 $	03Q4 $	04Q4 $	05Q1 $	05Q2 $
Futures & Fwrds	3,876	4,780	6,229	8,109	7,399	8,041	9,550	10,918	9,390	9,877	9,313	11,374	11,393	11,373	11,634	11,918
Swaps	2,071	2,417	3,260	4,823	5,945	7,601	9,705	14,345	17,779	21,949	25,645	32,613	44,083	56,411	58,330	60,912
Options	1,393	1,568	2,384	2,841	3,516	4,393	5,754	7,592	7,361	8,292	10,032	11,452	14,605	17,750	18,027	19,265
Credit Derivatives							55	144	287	426	395	635	1,001	2,347	3,124	4,105
TOTAL	7,339	8,764	11,873	15,774	16,861	20,035	25,064	32,999	34,817	40,453	45,386	56,074	71,082	87,880	91,115	96,200

*In billions of dollars; notional amount of futures, total exchange traded options, total over-the-counter options, total forwards, and total swaps. Note that data after 1994 do not include spot fx in the total notional amount of derivatives.
Credit derivatives were reported for the first time in the first quarter of 1997. Currently, the call report does not differentiate credit derivatives by product and thus they have been added as a separate category. As of 1997, credit derivatives have been included in the sum of total derivatives in this chart.
Note: numbers may not add due to rounding.
Data Source: Call Reports assembled by the Office of the Comptroller of the Currency, Washington, D.C.

than 99 percent of derivatives activity. For these banks, most of their contracts are to service their customers with only about 3 percent being used for their own risk-management activity. We now turn to explore how futures, options, swaps, and other derivatives aid in the control of interest-rate risk exposure for banks and other financial-service providers.

8–3 Financial Futures Contracts: Promises of Future Security Trades at a Set Price

In Chapter 7, we explored the nature of *gaps* between assets and liabilities that are exposed to interest rate risk. For example, we developed the concept of an interest-sensitive gap:

$$\text{Interest-sensitive gap} = \text{Interest-sensitive assets} - \text{Interest-sensitive liabilities} \quad \textbf{(8–1)}$$

or

$$\text{IS GAP} = \text{ISA} - \text{ISL}$$

where interest-sensitive assets and liabilities are those items on a balance sheet whose associated interest rates can be changed, up or down, during a given interval of time. As we saw earlier, for example, a bank that is *asset sensitive* (i.e., interest-sensitive assets exceed interest-sensitive liabilities) will suffer a decline in its net interest margin if market interest rates fall. On the other hand, a financial firm that is *liability sensitive* (i.e., interest-sensitive liabilities are greater than interest-sensitive assets) will experience a decrease in its net interest margin when market interest rates rise.

The preceding chapter developed one other measure of the difference between risk-exposed assets and liabilities—the leverage-adjusted *duration gap*, which measures the difference in weighted-average maturity between a financial institution's assets and its liabilities. Specifically:

$$\text{Duration gap} = \text{Average (dollar-weighted) duration of assets} - \text{Average (dollar-weighted) duration of liabilities} \times \frac{\text{Total liabilities}}{\text{Total assets}} \quad \textbf{(8–2)}$$

or

$$\text{DG} = D_A - D_L \times \frac{\text{TL}}{\text{TA}}$$

For example, a financial firm whose asset portfolio has an average duration longer than the average duration of its liabilities has a positive duration gap. A rise in market interest rates will cause the value of the firm's assets to decline faster than its liabilities, reducing the institution's net worth. On the other hand, if a financial firm has a negative duration gap, falling interest rates will cause the value of its liabilities to rise faster than the value of its asset portfolio; its net worth will decline, lowering the value of the stockholders' investment. One of the most popular methods for neutralizing these gap risks is to buy and sell financial futures contracts.

Background on Futures

Key URLs
Among the more interesting Web sites dealing with the terminology and use of futures contracts are **www.cbot.com**, **www.cme.com**, and **www.futuresweb.com**.

A **financial futures** contract is an agreement reached today between a buyer and a seller that calls for delivery of a particular security in exchange for cash at some future date.

Financial futures trade in futures markets and are usually accounted for as off-balance-sheet items in the financial statements of financial-service firms. To put this in perspective, in our financial markets there are both *cash* (or *spot*) markets and *futures* markets. In cash markets, financial assets are exchanged between buyers and sellers. Sellers of financial assets remove the assets from their balance sheet and account for the losses/gains on their income statements. Buyers of financial assets add the item purchased to their balance sheet. In cash markets, buyers and sellers exchange the financial asset for cash at the time the price is set. In futures markets buyers and sellers exchange a contract calling for delivery of the underlying financial asset at a specified date in the future. When the contract is created, neither

Some of the World's Leading Futures and Options Exchanges

Chicago Board of Trade (CBT)
Chicago Board Options Exchange
New York Futures Exchange (NYFE)
Singapore Exchange Ltd (SGX)
Chicago Mercantile Exchange (CME)
Euronext.Liffe Eurex
Sydney Futures Exchange (SFE)
Toronto Futures Exchange (TFE)
South African Futures Exchange (SAFEX)

the buyer nor the seller is making a purchase or sale at that point in time, only an agreement for the future.

When an investor buys or sells futures contracts at a designated price, it must deposit an *initial margin*. The initial margin is a minimum dollar amount per contract specified by the exchange where the trading occurs. This deposit may be in cash or in the form of a security, such as a Treasury bill. The initial margin is the investor's equity in the position when he or she buys (or sells) the contract. At the end of the first trading day, the settlement price for that day (a price determined by the exchange, based on trades that day) is compared with the price at which the trade occurred. If the price has increased, the buyer of the contract has profited while the seller has lost an equal amount. Each trader's account is *marked-to-market*. This means the equity account of the buyer increases by the change in price, while the seller's equity position decreases by the same amount. When a trader's equity position falls below the maintenance margin (the minimum specified by the exchange) the trader must deposit additional funds to the equity account to maintain his or her position, or the futures position is closed out within 24 hours. If profits have accrued, the excess margin may be withdrawn. The mark-to-market process takes place at the end of each trading day. This mechanism allows traders to take a position with a minimum investment of funds.

Purpose of Financial Futures Trading

The financial futures markets are designed to shift the risk of interest-rate fluctuations from risk-averse investors, such as banks and insurance companies, to speculators willing to accept and possibly profit from such risks. Futures contracts are traded on organized exchanges (such as the Chicago Board of Trade, the Chicago Mercantile Exchange, or the London Financial Futures Exchange).

On the exchange floor, *floor brokers* execute orders received from the public to buy or sell these contacts at the best prices available. For example, when a financial institution contacts an exchange broker and offers to *sell* futures contracts (i.e., the institution wishes to "go short" in futures), this means it is promising to deliver the securities underlying the contract to the buyer of those contracts on a stipulated date at a predetermined price. Conversely, a financial institution may enter the futures market as a *buyer* of contracts (i.e., the institution chooses to "go long" in futures), agreeing to accept delivery of the underlying securities named in each contract or to pay cash to the exchange clearinghouse the day the contracts mature, based on their price at that time.

Futures contracts are also traded over the counter (OTC), without the involvement of an exchange, which is often less costly for traders. However, over-the-counter futures trades generally are more risky because there is no exchange that guarantees the settlement of

Key URL
For up-to-date comprehensive futures and options quotes visit **www.wsj.com/free**.

each contract if one or the other party to the contract defaults. Moreover, liquidity risk is usually less for exchange-traded futures and other financial instruments because of the presence of substantial numbers of speculators and specialists on the exchanges who are always ready to make a market for the instruments traded there.

Exhibit 8–2 contains the quotes for interest-rate futures contracts traded on American exchanges. The quotes are from the November 22, 2005, edition of *The Wall Street Journal* for trades made on November 21 of that year. A description of the most popular financial futures contracts is given below:[3]

1. The U.S. *Treasury bond futures contract* calls for the delivery of a $100,000-denomination bond (measured at its par value) carrying a minimum maturity of 15 years and a promised (coupon) rate of return of 6 percent.[4] To trade a Treasury bond futures contract, the buyer and seller must deposit the margin specified by the Chicago Board of Trade. For the hedger, the initial margin and the maintenance margin are $1,150 per contract, whereas for the speculator the initial margin is higher at $1,553 per contract.

   Exhibit 8–2 provides quotes for the December 2005 and March 2006 Treasury bond contracts. These are the months each contract will expire and delivery will be made if the futures contract has not been offset prior to delivery. If we look at the "Mr06" contract, we see that the first trade (OPEN) on November 21, 2005, took place at 112 6/32nds (percent of par value). (Note that Treasury bond quotes are in 32nds rather than decimals.) An increase in price of 1/32nd is equivalent to $31.25 in profits or losses per contract depending on whether the trader has a short or long position. The price agreed upon by the buyer and seller is $112,187.50 for the first contract initiated on November 21, 2005. The highest quote for a March 2006 contract on November 21, 2005, was 112-25 or 112 25/32nds, while the lower quote was 112-05 or 112 5/32nds.

EXHIBIT 8–2
Interest-Rate Futures

Source: *The Wall Street Journal*, November 22, 2005, p. C10. Reprinted by permission of *The Wall Street Journal*, © 2002 Dow Jones & Company, Inc. All Rights Reserved Worldwide.

	OPEN	HIGH	LOW	SETTLE	CHG	LIFETIME HIGH	LIFETIME LOW	OPEN INT
Interest Rate Futures								
Treasury Bonds (CBT) -$100,000; pts 32nds of 100%								
Dec	112-17	113-02	112-14	112-26	11	119-17	106-08	579,274
Mr06	112-06	112-25	112-05	112-18	12	118-19	110-01	56,292
Treasury Notes (CBT) -$100,000; pts 32nds of 100%								
Dec	108-245	109-040	108-225	109-005	9.0	113-205	106-260	1,617,097
Mr06	108-190	108-310	108-180	108-280	9.5	112-300	106-220	170,501
5 Yr. Treasury Notes (CBT)-$100,000; pts 32nds of 100%								
Dec	106-030	106-095	106-010	106-075	5.5	108-295	105-115	1,156,284
Mr06	105-295	106-045	105-285	106-030	6.0	108-240	105-060	245,321
2 Yr. Treasury Notes (CBT)-$200,000; pts 32nds of 100%								
Dec	102-210	102-232	102-197	102-227	2.2	103-208	102-097	338,039
Mr06	102-177	102-205	102-170	102-200	2.2	102-205	102-100	18,408
30 Day Federal Funds (CBT) $5,000,000; 100 - daily avg.								
Nov	96.000	96.005	96.00	96.000	—	96.590	95.980	95,622
Dec	95.835	95.840	95.835	95.840	—	96.955	95.830	88,583

	OPEN	HIGH	LOW	SETTLE	CHG	YIELD	CHG	OPEN INT
1 Month Libor (CME)-$3,000,000; pts of 100%								
Dec	95.6075	95.6075	95.5950	95.6100	.0050	4.3900	−.0050	10,977
Eurodollar (CME)-$1,000,000; pts of 100%								
Dec	95.4900	95.5000	95.4875	95.4950	.0050	4.5050	−.0050	1,253,935
Mr06	95.2000	95.2450	95.1900	95.2350	.0350	4.7650	−.0350	1,221,798
June	95.1150	95.1750	95.1100	95.1650	.0450	4.8350	−.0450	1,312,276
Dec	95.1900	95.2550	95.1850	95.2400	.0450	4.7600	−.0450	1,003,815

[3]The initial and maintenance margins were applicable as of January 2003 and were obtained from the Web sites of the CBOT and CME.

[4]If a contract is not offset prior to delivery, the seller has some freedom regarding the Treasury bond that is delivered to the buyer of the futures contract. Bonds whose coupon rates lie above or below the 6 percent standard and have at least 15 years until maturity are deliverable to the buyer. The price the buyer pays the seller is adjusted by a prespecified conversion factor depending on the coupon rate and maturity of the delivered bond.

The settlement price (SETTLE) determined by the clearinghouse and used to mark-to-market equity accounts was 112-18. The column following the SETTLE is labeled CHG and means that the settlement price increased 12 points since the prior trading day (November 18, 2005). Hence, on November 18, 2005, the settlement price was 112-06. The next two columns give the lifetime high (118-19) and low (110-01) prices for the contract calling for the delivery of Treasury bonds in March 2006. The last column, on the far right of the table, identifies the open interest as 56,292 T-bond futures contracts. This is the number of contracts that has been established and not yet offset or exercised.

2. Futures contracts on *three-month Eurodollar time deposits* are traded in million-dollar units at exchanges in Chicago (The Chicago Mercantile Exchange), London, Tokyo, Singapore, and elsewhere around the globe, offering investors the opportunity to hedge against market interest rate changes. Currently this is the most actively traded futures contract in the world and is based on the Eurodollar CD, which pays the London Interbank Offer Rate (LIBOR) for a three-month $1 million offshore deposit. To trade Eurodollar CD futures, hedgers must provide an initial margin and a maintenance margin of $700 per contract, whereas for speculators the initial margin is $945.

   Exhibit 8–2 provides the opening, high, low, and settlement quotes for four Eurodollar futures contracts extending out to one year. However, if you go to **wsj.com/free** you will find complete futures prices going out more than six years. Prices for Eurodollar contracts are quoted using the IMM Index, which is 100 minus the yield on a bank discount basis. (As we saw in Chapter 7, this means the yield is calculated using the convention of a 360-day year.) The (SETTLE) IMM index of 95.2350 for the March 2006 (Mr06) contract is consistent with an annualized discount yield of 4.7650 percent (or 100 − 95.2350).

   While a Treasury bond contract is a futures contract based on the price of the underlying bond, the Eurodollar futures contract is based on an interest rate. The convention for quoting Eurodollar futures contracts is derived from the methodology for pricing futures on Treasury bills—a contract that has recently lost popularity as the Eurodollar contract has gained popularity. The change in the settlement IMM index (CHG) on November 21, 2005, as compared to November 18, 2005, was 0.035. From this information we can infer that the SETTLE for November 18 was 95.2000.

   If you were "long" one March 2006 Eurodollar contract, then you realized a 3.5 index point gain or $87.50 in profits ($25 × 3.5) on November 21, 2005. (Note that every basis point or index point change translates to $25 in profits or losses.) Likewise, if you were "short" the March 2006 contract, then $87.50 would be deducted from your equity account for each contract that you held at the close of trading on the Chicago Mercantile Exchange on November 21, 2005. At the close of trading on November 21, the number of March 2006 Eurodollar contracts that had been established and not yet offset was 1,221,798. If a Eurodollar futures position is not offset before expiration, it is settled in cash based on the actual 90-day rate on Eurodollar deposits. (Note that, unlike Treasury bills, Eurodollar deposits are *not* quoted as a bank discount rate [DR].)

3. The 30-day *Federal funds futures contracts* are traded at the Chicago Board of Trade in units of $5 million with an index price equal to 100 less the Fed funds futures interest rate. This is essentially the same as the IMM Index the Chicago Mercantile Exchange uses for Treasury bill futures and Eurodollar futures. The quotes from *The Wall Street Journal* provide index information for the opening, high, low, and settlement prices for that trading day (November 21, 2005) and the index information for the highs and lows over the life of the particular contract. The initial and maintenance margins for hedgers are $400 per contract, with speculators having an initial

margin requirement of $540 per contract. These contracts are settled in cash, based on the monthly average of the daily interest rate quoted by Fed funds brokers.

4. The *one-month LIBOR futures contract* is traded in $3 million units on the Chicago Mercantile Exchange and quotes are in the form of an IMM index. The initial and maintenance margins for hedgers are $350 per contract, while speculators must provide an initial margin of $473. These contracts are settled in cash rather than through actual delivery of Eurodeposits.[5]

Today's selling price on a futures contract presumably reflects what investors in the market expect cash prices to be on the day delivery of the securities underlying the contract must be made. A futures hedge against interest rate changes generally requires a financial institution to take an *opposite* position in the futures market from its current position in the cash (immediate delivery) market. Thus, a financial firm planning to buy bonds ("go long") in the cash market today may try to protect the bonds' value by selling bond contracts ("go short") in the futures market. Then if bond prices fall in the cash market there will be an offsetting profit in the futures market, minimizing the loss due to changing interest rates. While financial institutions make heavy use today of financial futures in their security dealer operations and in bond portfolio management, futures contracts can also be used to protect returns and costs on loans, deposits, money market borrowings, and other financial assets.

The Short Hedge in Futures

Let us illustrate how the *short hedge* in financial futures works. Suppose market interest rates are expected to rise, boosting the cost of selling deposits or the cost of borrowing in the money market and lowering the value of any bonds or fixed-rate loans that a financial institution may hold or expect to buy. In this instance a short hedge in financial futures can be used.

This hedge would be structured to create profits from futures transactions in order to offset losses experienced on a financial institution's balance sheet if interest rates do rise. The asset-liability manager will sell futures contracts calling for the future delivery of the underlying securities, choosing contracts expiring around the time new borrowings will occur, when a fixed-rate loan is made, or when bonds are added to a financial firm's portfolio. Later, as borrowings and loans approach maturity or securities are sold and before the first futures contract matures, a like amount of futures contracts will be purchased on a futures exchange. If market interest rates have risen significantly, the interest cost of borrowings will increase and the value of any fixed-rate loans and securities held will decline.

For instance, suppose the securities portfolio of a bank contains $10 million in 6 percent, 15-year bonds and market yields increase from 6 percent to 6.5 percent. The market value of these bonds decreases from $10 million to $9,525,452.07—a loss in the cash market of $474,547.73. However, this loss will be approximately offset by a price gain on the futures contracts. Moreover, if the bank makes an offsetting sale and purchase of the *same* futures contracts on a futures exchange, it then has no obligation either to deliver or to take delivery of the securities named in the contracts. The clearinghouse that keeps

---

[5]Other traded interest-rate futures contracts include a $100,000 denomination Treasury note contract, two-year and five-year T-note contracts (with $100,000 and $500,000 denominations respectively), a Municipal Bond Index contract, 30-year U.S. Treasury bond and 30-day Federal funds contracts, and 10-year and 5-year interest-rate swap contracts, all traded on the Chicago Board of Trade (CBT). Added to these are several foreign-related contracts on non-U.S. financial instruments, including Euroyen deposits; British sterling accounts; the long-gilt British bond; EuroSwiss deposits; and various foreign government bonds. The appearance of euro deposit and currency units in the European Community (EC) has also spawned a three-month Euribor contract traded in units of 1 million euros on the London International Futures Exchange and another three-month Euribor contract (also with a face value of 1 million euros) bought and sold on France's Marche a Termine International (MATIF).

records for each futures exchange will simply cancel the two offsetting transactions. (See the Insights and Issues box: "Hedging Deposit Costs with Financial Futures" for an example of how depository institutions can protect themselves from rising deposit rates using futures contracts.)

The Long Hedge in Futures

We turn now to describe the *long hedge* in futures. While most financial institutions are generally more concerned about the potentially damaging effects of rising interest rates, there are times when a financial firm wishes to hedge itself against falling interest rates. Usually this occurs when a *cash inflow* is expected in the near future.

For example, suppose management expects to receive a sizable inflow of deposits a few weeks or months from today but forecasts lower interest rates by that time. This sounds favorable from a cost-of-funds point of view, but it is not favorable for the future growth of revenues. If management takes no action and the forecast turns out to be true, the financial institution will suffer an *opportunity loss* (i.e., reduced potential earnings) because those expected deposits will have to be invested in loans and securities bearing lower yields or having increased prices. For instance, if the institution was going to buy $1 million (par value) of 15-year, 6 percent bonds and interest rates dropped from 6 percent to 5.5 percent, the price of these bonds would increase from $1 million to $1,050,623.25, forcing the institution to pay a higher price to acquire the bonds. To offset this opportunity loss, management can use a *long hedge:* Futures contracts can be purchased today and then sold in like amount at approximately the same time deposits come flowing in. The result will be a profit on the futures contracts if interest rates do decline because those contracts will rise in value.

Using Long and Short Hedges to Protect Income and Value

Table 8–1 provides examples of other short and long hedges using financial futures. In general, the three most typical interest-rate hedging problems most financial firms face are (1) protecting the value of securities and fixed-rate loans from losses due to rising interest rates, (2) avoiding a rise in borrowing costs, and (3) avoiding a fall in the interest returns expected from loans and security holdings. In most cases, the appropriate hedging strategy using financial futures is:

Avoiding higher borrowing costs and declining asset values $\rightarrow$	Use a short (or selling) hedge: sell futures and then cancel with a subsequent purchase of similar futures contracts
Avoiding lower than expected yields from loans and security investments $\rightarrow$	Use a long (or buying) hedge: buy futures and then cancel with a subsequent sale of similar contracts

Where the financial institution faces a positive interest-sensitive gap (interest-sensitive assets > interest-sensitive liabilities), it can protect against loss due to falling interest rates by covering the gap with a long hedge (buy and then sell futures) of approximately the same dollar amount as the gap. On the other hand, if the institution is confronted with a negative interest-sensitive gap (interest-sensitive liabilities > interest-sensitive assets), it can avoid unacceptable losses from rising market interest rates by covering with a short hedge (sell and then buy futures) approximately matching the amount of the gap.

Active trading in futures contracts for a wide variety of assets now takes place on exchanges worldwide. One distinct advantage of this method of hedging against changes in interest rates is that only a *fraction* of the value of a futures contract must be pledged as collateral in the form of initial and maintenance margins, due to the daily mark-to-market process.

TABLE 8–1

Examples of Popular
Financial Futures
Transactions Used by
Financial Institutions

The Short, or Selling, Hedge to Protect against Rising Interest Rates

Fearing *rising* interest rates over the next several months, which will lower the value of its bonds, the management of a financial firm takes the following steps:

Today—contracts are *sold* through a futures exchange to another investor, with the firm promising to deliver a specific dollar amount of securities (such as Treasury bonds) at a set price six months from today.

Six months in the future—contracts in the same denominations are *purchased* through the same futures exchange, according to which the firm promises to take delivery of the same or similar securities at a future date at a set price.

Results—the two contracts are canceled out by the futures exchange clearinghouse ("zero out"), so the firm no longer has a commitment to sell or take delivery of securities—the position has been offset.

However, if interest rates rise over the life of the first futures contracts that are sold, security prices will fall. When the financial firm then purchases future contracts at the end of the six-month period, they will be obtainable for a lower price than when it sold the same futures contracts six months earlier. Therefore, a *profit* will be made on futures trading, which will offset some or all of the *loss* in the value of any bonds still held.

The Long, or Buying, Hedge to Protect against Falling Interest Rates

Suppose an economist has just predicted *lower* interest rates over the next six months, and management of a financial firm fears a decline in profits as interest rates on loans fall relative to deposit rates and other operating costs. Moreover, incoming funds must be invested in lower-yielding assets, thus incurring an opportunity loss for the firm. Management elects to do the following:

Today—contracts are *purchased* through a futures exchange, committing the firm to take delivery of a specific amount of securities (such as federal funds or Eurodollar deposits) at a set price six months from today.

Six months in the future—contracts are *sold* on the same futures exchange, committing the financial firm to deliver the same amount of securities at a set price on the same future date.

Results—the two contracts are canceled by the clearinghouse, so the firm is not obligated to either make or take delivery of the securities involved. The position has been offset.

However, if interest rates do fall while futures contracts are in force, security prices must rise. Therefore the firm will be able to sell futures contracts for a higher price than it paid for them six months earlier. The resulting *profit* from trading in financial futures will offset some or all the *loss* in revenue due to lower interest rates on loans.

Moreover, brokers commissions for trading futures are relatively low. Thus, traders of financial futures can hedge large amounts of borrowings, loans, and other assets with only a small outlay of cash.

Basis Risk

However, there are some limitations to financial futures as interest rate hedging devices, among them a special form of risk known as *basis risk*. *Basis* is the difference in interest rates or prices between the cash (immediate-delivery) market and the futures (postponed-delivery) market. Thus

$$\text{Basis} = \text{Cash-market price (or interest rate)} - \text{Futures market price (or interest rate)} \tag{8–3}$$

where both are measured at the same moment in time. For example, suppose 10-year U.S. government bonds are selling today in the cash market for \$95 per \$100 bond while futures contracts on the same bonds calling for delivery in six months are trading today at a price of \$87. Then the current basis must be

$$\$95 - \$87 = \$8 \text{ per contract}$$

If the basis changes between the opening and closing of a futures position, the result can be significant loss, which subtracts from any gains a trader might make in the cash market. Fortunately, basis risk is usually less than interest rate risk in the cash market, so hedging reduces (but usually does not completely eliminate) overall risk exposure.

The dollar return from a hedge is the sum of changes in prices in the cash market and changes in prices in the futures market. Let's take a look at the essence of basis risk for both a short and a long hedge.

Basis Risk with a Short Hedge

For instance, if you are concerned about the interest-rate risk exposure for bonds in a financial institution's securities portfolio, then you fear increasing interest rates that would decrease the value of those bonds. The change in the cash market prices ($C_t - C_0$) would be negative. You have a long position in the cash market. To hedge this possible increase in market interest rates, you could take a *short position* in the futures market. If your concerns are realized, then your dollar return is the sum of the loss in the cash market ($C_t - C_0$) and the gain in the futures market ($F_0 - F_t$). In a short position, you sell at F_0 and buy at F_t; hence, your gain (loss) is calculated as the sell price minus the buy price:

$$\text{\$ Return from a combined cash and futures position} = (C_t - C_0) + (F_0 - F_t) \tag{8-4}$$

This can be rearranged as:

$$\text{\$ Return from a combined cash and futures position} = (C_t - F_t) - (C_0 - F_0) \tag{8-5}$$

Thus, with a short hedge in futures,

$$\text{Dollar return} = \text{Basis at termination of hedge} - \text{Basis at initiation of hedge} \tag{8-6}$$

Basis Risk with a Long Hedge

Increasing interest rates are often the concern of the managers of financial institutions. However, declining interest rates can also weigh on profitability.

If you have concerns about declining interest rates, you could create a long hedge. For instance, you anticipate an inflow of cash in three months that will be used to purchase bonds at that time. In opportunity terms, you have essentially "gone short" in these bonds. To hedge the decrease in interest rates, you could take a *long position* in the futures market. Your dollar return is the sum of the loss (gain) in the cash market ($C_0 - C_t$) and the gain (loss) in the futures market ($F_t - F_0$).

$$\text{\$ Return from a combined cash and futures position} = (C_0 - C_t) + (F_t - F_0) \tag{8-7}$$

This can be rearranged as:

$$\text{\$ Return from a combined cash and futures position} = (C_0 - F_0) - (C_t - F_t) \tag{8-8}$$

$$\text{Dollar return} = \text{Basis at initiation of hedge} - \text{Basis at termination of hedge} \tag{8-9}$$

Insights and Issues

HEDGING DEPOSIT COSTS WITH FINANCIAL FUTURES

The Problem

Suppose the management of a depository institution is expecting a *rise* in market interest rates over the next three months. Currently deposits can be sold to customers at a promised interest rate of 10 percent. However, management is fearful that deposit interest rates may rise at least one-half of a percentage point (50 basis points) in the next three months, eroding the profit margin of loan revenues over deposit costs.

For example, if a depository institution needed to raise $100 million from sales of deposits over the next 90 days, its marginal cost of issuing the new deposits at a 10 percent annual rate would be as follows:

$$\begin{array}{c}\text{Amount of new} \\ \text{deposits to be} \\ \text{issued}\end{array} \times \begin{array}{c}\text{Annual} \\ \text{interest rate}\end{array} \times \frac{\text{Maturity of deposit in days}}{360}$$

$$= \begin{array}{c}\text{Marginal} \\ \text{deposit interest} \\ \text{cost}\end{array}$$

$$\$100 \text{ million} \times 0.10 \times 90 \div 360 = \$2,500,000$$

However, if deposit interest rates climb to 10.50 percent, the marginal deposit cost becomes

$$\$100 \text{ million} \times 0.1050 \times 90 \div 360 = \$2,625,000$$

Amount of added fund-raising costs (and potential loss in profit) = $2,625,000 − $2,500,000 = $125,000.

An Offsetting Financial Futures Transaction

To counteract the potential profit loss of $125,000, management might select the following financial futures transaction:

Today: Sell 100 90-day Eurodollar futures contracts trading at an IMM Index of 91.5.

Price per $100 = 100 − ((100-IMM Index) × 90 ÷ 360)

Price per $100 = 100 − (8.5 × 90 ÷ 360) = 97.875

100 contracts = $97,875,000

Within next 90 days: Buy 100 90-day Eurodollar futures contracts trading on the day of purchase at an IMM Index of 91.

Price per $100 = 100 − (9 × 90 ÷ 360) = 97.75

100 contracts = $97,750,000

Profit on the completion of sale and purchase of futures = $125,000

Result: Higher deposit cost has been offset by a gain in futures.

With an effective hedge, the positive or negative returns earned in the cash market will be approximately offset by the profit or loss from futures trading. The real risk the user faces from hedging with futures stems from the movement in basis that may occur over the life of a futures contract because cash and futures prices are not perfectly synchronized with each other. Futures market prices and market interest rates may change more or less than cash-market prices or rates, resulting in gains or losses for the trade as illustrated above.

The sensitivity of the market price of a financial futures contract depends, in part, upon the duration of the security to be delivered under the futures contract. (See Chapter 7 for a discussion of calculating duration for individual securities.) That is,

$$\frac{\text{Change in futures price}}{\text{Initial futures price}} = - \left[\begin{array}{c}\text{Duration of the} \\ \text{underlying security} \\ \text{named in the} \\ \text{futures contract}\end{array} \right] \times \left[\frac{\begin{array}{c}\text{Change expected in} \\ \text{interest rates}\end{array}}{\begin{array}{c}1 + \text{Original} \\ \text{interest rate}\end{array}} \right] \quad \textbf{(8–10)}$$

or

$$\frac{F_t - F_0}{F_0} = -D \times \frac{\Delta i}{(1 + i)}$$

If we rewrite this equation slightly we get an expression for the gain or loss from the use of financial futures:

$$\begin{bmatrix} \text{Positive or negative} \\ \text{change in futures} \\ \text{position value} \end{bmatrix} = -\begin{bmatrix} \text{Duration of the} \\ \text{underlying security} \\ \text{named in the} \\ \text{futures contract(s)} \end{bmatrix} \times \begin{bmatrix} \text{Initial} \\ \text{futures} \\ \text{price} \end{bmatrix}$$

$$\times \begin{bmatrix} \text{Number} \\ \text{of futures} \\ \text{contracts} \end{bmatrix} \times \begin{bmatrix} \dfrac{\text{Change expected in}}{\text{interest rates}} \\ \dfrac{}{1 + \text{Original}} \\ \text{interest rate} \end{bmatrix} \qquad \textbf{(8-11)}$$

or

$$(F_t - F_0) = -D \times F_0 \times N \times \frac{\Delta i}{(1 + i)}$$

The negative sign in Equation (8–11) clearly shows that when interest rates rise, the market value (price) of futures contracts must fall.

For example, suppose a $100,000 par value Treasury bond futures contract is traded at a price of $99,700 initially but then interest rates on T-bonds increase a full percentage point from 7 to 8 percent. If the T-bond has a duration of nine years, then the change in the value of one T-bond futures contract would be

$$\begin{bmatrix} \text{Change in} \\ \text{market value of} \\ \text{a T-bond futures contract} \end{bmatrix} = -9 \text{ years} \times \$99,700$$

$$\times \frac{+0.01}{1 \times (1 + 0.07)} = -\$8,385.98$$

In this case the one percentage point rise in interest rates lowered the price of a $100,000 futures contract for Treasury bonds by almost $8,386.

Exhibit 8–3 summarizes how trading in futures contracts can help protect a financial-service provider against loss due to interest rate risk. The *long hedge* in futures consists of first buying futures contracts (at price F_0) and, then, if interest rates fall, selling comparable contracts (in which case the futures price moves toward F_t). The decline in interest rates will generate a gross profit of $F_t - F_0 > 0$, less, of course, any taxes or broker commissions that have to be paid to carry out the long-hedge transaction. In contrast, the *short hedge* consists of first selling futures contracts (at price F_0) and, then, if interest rates rise, buying comparable futures contracts (whose price may move to F_n). The rise in interest rates will generate a profit of $F_0 - F_n > 0$, net of any tax obligations created or traders' commissions. These profitable trades can be used to help offset any losses resulting from a decline in the market value of a financial institution's assets or a decline in its net worth or in its net interest income due to adverse changes in market interest rates.

EXHIBIT 8–3

Trade-Off Diagrams
for Financial Futures
Contracts

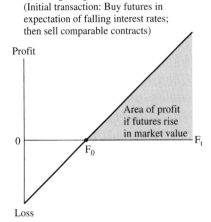

The Long Hedge in Financial Futures
(Initial transaction: Buy futures in
expectation of falling interest rates;
then sell comparable contracts)

Purpose: Protect against falling yields on
assets (such as current loans and future
loans and investments in securities).

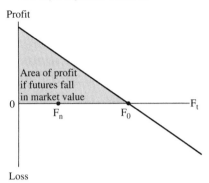

The Short Hedge in Financial Futures
(Initial transaction: Sell futures in
expectation of rising interest rates;
then buy comparable contracts)

Purpose: Protect against rising deposit
and other borrowing costs and falling
market values of assets (such as
security investments and loans).

Number of Futures Contracts Needed

How many futures contracts does a financial firm need to cover a given size risk exposure?
The objective is to offset the loss in net worth due to changes in market interest rates with
gains from trades in the futures market. From Chapter 7, we quantify the change in net
worth from an increase in interest rates as follows:

$$
\begin{aligned}
\text{Change} \\
\text{in net} \\
\text{worth}
\end{aligned}
= -\left(D_{assets} - \frac{\text{Total liabilities}}{\text{Total assets}} \times D_{liabilities} \right)
$$

$$
\times \left(\begin{array}{c} \text{Total} \\ \text{assets} \end{array} \right) \times \left(\dfrac{\begin{array}{c}\text{Change expected}\\ \text{in interest rates}\end{array}}{1 + \begin{array}{c}\text{original}\\ \text{interest rate}\end{array}} \right)
$$

(8–12)

or

$$
\Delta \, NW = -\left(D_A - \frac{TL}{TA} \times D_L \right) \times TA \times \frac{\Delta i}{(1 + i)}
$$

where, for example, a bank may have an average asset duration represented by D_A and the
average duration of the bank's liabilities is labeled D_L. (See Chapter 7 for a description of
how to calculate the average duration of a financial institution's assets and liabilities.) If
we set the change in net worth equal to the change in the futures position value (Equation [8–12]), we can solve for the number of futures contracts needed to fully hedge a
financial firm's overall interest-rate risk exposure and protect its net worth:

$$
\begin{array}{c}\text{Number of}\\ \text{futures}\\ \text{contracts}\\ \text{needed}\end{array} = \frac{\left(D_{assets} - \dfrac{\text{Total liability}}{\text{Total assets}} \times D_{liabilities} \right) \times \text{Total assets}}{\begin{array}{c}\text{Duration of the}\\ \text{underlying security}\\ \text{named in the}\\ \text{futures contract}\end{array} \times \begin{array}{c}\text{Price of the}\\ \text{futures}\\ \text{contract}\end{array}}
$$

(8–13)

or

$$N = \frac{(D_A - TL/TA \times D_L) \times TA}{D \times F_0}$$

For example, suppose a bank has an average asset duration of four years, an average liability duration of two years, total assets of $500 million, and total liabilities of $460 million. Suppose, too, that the bank plans to trade in Treasury bond futures contracts. The T-bonds named in the futures contracts have a duration of nine years and the T-bonds' current price is $99,700 per $100,000 contract. Then this institution would need about

$$N = \frac{\left(4 \text{ years} - \dfrac{\$460 \text{ million}}{\$500 \text{ million}} \times 2 \text{ years}\right) \times \$500 \text{ million}}{9 \text{ years} \times \$99,700}$$

$$\approx 1,200 \text{ contracts}$$

We note that this financial firm has a positive duration gap of +2.16 years (or 4 years − $460/$500 million × 2 years), indicating that its assets have a longer average maturity than its liabilities. Then if market interest rates rise, its assets will decline in value by more than its liabilities, reducing the stockholders' investment (net worth). To protect against an interest rate rise, this institution would probably want to adopt a short hedge in T-bond futures contracts, selling about 1,200 of these contracts initially. An interest rate decline, on the other hand, usually would call for a long hedge, purchasing contracts on T-bonds or other securities.

Concept Check

8–1. What are *financial futures* contracts? Which financial institutions use futures and other derivatives for risk management?

8–2. How can financial futures help financial service firms deal with interest-rate risk?

8–3. What is a long hedge in financial futures? A short hedge?

8–4. What futures transactions would most likely be used in a period of rising interest rates? Falling interest rates?

8–5. How do you interpret the quotes for financial futures in *The Wall Street Journal?*

8–6. A futures contract on Eurodollar deposits is currently selling at an interest yield of 4 percent, while yields on 3-month Eurodollar deposits currently stand at 4.60 percent. What is the *basis* for the Eurodollar futures contracts?

8–7. Suppose a bank wishes to sell $150 million in new deposits next month. Interest rates today on comparable deposits stand at 8 percent but are expected to rise to 8.25 percent next month. Concerned about the possible rise in borrowing costs, management wishes to use a futures contract. What type of contract would you recommend? If the bank does not cover the interest-rate risk involved, how much in lost potential profits could the bank experience?

8–8. What kind of futures hedge would be appropriate in each of the following situations?

   a.   A financial firm fears that rising deposit interest rates will result in losses on fixed-rate loans.

   b.   A financial firm holds a large block of floating-rate loans and market interest rates are falling.

   c.   A projected rise in market rates of interest threatens the value of a firm's bond portfolio.

8–4 Interest-Rate Options

The **interest-rate option** grants a holder of securities the right to either (1) place (put) those instruments with another investor at a prespecified exercise price before the option expires or (2) take delivery of securities (call) from another investor at a prespecified price before the option's expiration date. In the put option, the option writer must stand ready to accept delivery of securities from the option buyer if the latter requests. In the call option, the option writer must stand ready to deliver securities to the option buyer upon request. The fee that the buyer must pay for the privilege of being able to put securities to or call securities away from the option writer is known as the *option premium.*

How do options differ from futures contracts? Unlike futures, options do not obligate any party to deliver securities. They grant the *right* to deliver or take delivery, but not the obligation to do so. The option buyer can (1) exercise the option, (2) sell the option to another buyer, or (3) simply allow the option to expire. Interest-rate options are traded mostly in over-the-counter markets where the exercise date and price can be tailored to the needs of the option buyer. For standardized exchange-traded interest-rate options, the most activity occurs using options on futures, which is referred to as the *futures options market.*

Key URL
The employment of option trades by mortgage-lending institutions is discussed at **www.freddiemac.com**.

The buyer of a *call* futures option has the right, but not the obligation, to take a long position in the futures market at the exercise (strike) price any time prior to expiration of the options contract. The buyer of a put futures option has the right, but not the obligation, to take a short position in the futures market at the exercise (strike) price any time prior to expiration of the option. The futures price is highly correlated with the underlying cash price; hence, futures on options can be used to hedge interest rate risk. For example, the buyer of a T-bond futures option at the Chicago Board of Trade is granted the right for a long position (call) or short position (put) in a T-bond futures contract at the exercise (strike) price until the option expires. If interest rates rise, *put* (sell) options are most likely to be exercised. If interest rates fall, holders of *call* (buy) options will be more inclined to exercise their option right and demand delivery of bond futures at the agreed-upon *strike price.* The reason is that falling interest rates can push bond prices higher than the strike price specified in the option contract. (See Tables 8–2 and 8–3.)

Exchange-traded futures options are generally set to expire in March, June, September, or December to conform to most futures contracts. The option on a futures contract expires on or just a few days before the first delivery date of the futures contract. The exceptions to this rule are the serial contracts for the nearest expiration month. For example, if it is currently January and the nearest expiration month in the futures market is March, futures options trades may expire in January and February, in addition to the March futures options. This is exemplified in Exhibit 8–4.

The exchange's clearinghouse normally guarantees fulfillment of any option agreements traded on that exchange just as the exchange also stands behind any exchange-traded futures contracts. Interest-rate options offer the buyer added leverage—control of large amounts of financial capital with a limited investment and limited risk. The maximum loss to the option buyer is the premium paid to acquire the option.

Exhibit 8–4 shows quotes for options on futures found on December 14, 2005, posted on *The Wall Street Journal's* Web site, **wsj.com/free**. The information provided by these quotes is for two of the most popular futures options contracts traded today.

1. *U.S. Treasury bond futures options* grant the options buyer the right to a short position (put) or a long position (call) involving one T-bond futures contract for each option. In Exhibit 8–4, the premiums for eight strike prices ranging from 109 to 116 are quoted. Three months—January, March, and June—are listed for both the call and put premiums at the Chicago Board of Trade. These options apply to the nearest T-bond futures contract. The T-bond futures options contract expires just a few days prior to the first delivery date of the underlying futures contract for March, June, September, and December.

   The premium quote for the March call is 3-24 for a strike (exercise) price of 109. This means that you would pay 3 and 24/64ths (percent of par value) or \$3,375 as a premium to have the right to a long position in the T-bond futures contract at

TABLE 8–2
Put Options to Offset
Rising Interest Rates

Key URL
For additional
information about
Eurodollar futures and
option contracts, see
especially the contracts
offered by the Chicago
Mercantile Exchange
(CME) as described at
www.cme.com/clearing.

Put Option

Buyer receives from an option writer the right to sell and deliver securities, loans, or futures contracts to the writer at an agreed-upon *strike price* up to a specified date in return for paying a fee (*premium*) to the option writer. If interest rates *rise*, the market value of the optioned securities, loans, or futures contracts will fall. Exercise of the put results in a gain for the buyer.

Example of a Put Option Transaction: A bank plans to issue $150 million in new 180-day interest-bearing deposits (CDs) at the end of the week but is concerned that CD rates in the market, which now stand at 6.5 percent (annual yield), will rise to 7 percent. An increase in deposit interest rates of this magnitude will result in an additional $375,000 in interest costs on the $150 million in new CDs, possibly eroding any potential profits from lending and investing the funds provided by issuing the CDs. In order to reduce the potential loss from these higher borrowing costs, the bank's asset-liability manager decides to buy put options on Eurodollar deposit futures traded at the Chicago Mercantile Exchange. For a strike price of 9500 the quoted premium for the put option is .50, which is (50 × $25) or $1,250. If interest rates rise as predicted, the market index of the Eurodollar futures will fall below 95.00, perhaps to 94.00. If the market index drops far enough, the put option will be exercised because it is now "in the money" since the futures contract named in the put option has fallen in value below its strike price (9500). The bank's asset-liability manager can exercise a put option, receiving a short position in the futures market at 95.00 and then offset the short position by buying a futures contract at the current index of 94.00. The profit from exercising the option is $2,500 (100 × $25) per contract.

The bank's before-tax profit on this put option transaction could be found from:

$$\text{Before-tax profit on put option} = \left[\text{Option strike price} - \left(\frac{\text{Futures market}}{\text{price}} \times 100\right)\right] \times 25 - \text{Option premium} \quad (8\text{--}14)$$

The before-tax profit on each million-dollar Eurodollar futures contract would be:

$$\text{Before-tax profit on put} = [9500 - (94.00 \times 100)] \times \$25.00 - \$1,255$$

$$= \$1,250 \text{ per contract.}$$

The $1,250 option profit per futures contract will at least partially offset the higher borrowing costs should interest rates rise.

If you bought 150 puts, you would have partially offset the additional $375,000 in interest costs by $187,500 in futures option profits.

If interest rates don't rise, the option will likely remain "out of the money" and the bank will lose money equal to the option premium. However, if interest rates do not rise, the bank will not face higher borrowing costs and, therefore, has no need of the option. Put options can also be used to protect the value of bonds and loans against rising interest rates.

$109,000. If in March, when this call option expires, the futures price is above the strike price of 109, then the option will be exercised. For instance, if the futures price is 112, then the buyer of the option would exercise that option, resulting in a long position for one March T-bond futures contract. The exerciser would have his or her equity account immediately marked-to-market for a gain of $3,000. The exerciser will have to meet the margin requirements of the futures exchange or offset his position in futures immediately.

2. *Eurodollar futures options* give the buyer the right to deliver (put) or accept delivery (call) of one Eurodollar deposit futures contract for every option exercised. In Exhibit 8–4, seven strike prices are quoted in the first column ranging from 9500 to 9575 in 12 or 13 basis point intervals for three call options and three put options on the March Eurodollars futures contract. The March puts and calls expire on the same day as the March Eurodollar futures contract. Both the futures contracts and the options on futures trade at the Chicago Mercantile Exchange.

TABLE 8–3
Call Options to Offset
Falling Interest Rates

Call Option

Buyer receives the right from an option writer to buy and take delivery of securities, loans, or futures contracts at a mutually agreeable *strike price* on or before a specific expiration date in return for paying a *premium* to the writer. If interest rates *fall,* the market value of the optioned securities, loans, or contracts must rise. Exercising the call option gives the buyer a gain.

Example of a Call Option Transaction: A financial firm plans to purchase $50 million in Treasury bonds in a few days and hopes to earn an interest return of 8 percent. The firm's investment officer fears a drop in market interest rates before she is ready to buy, so she asks a security dealer to write a call option on Treasury bonds at a strike price of $95,000 for each $100,000 bond. The investment officer had to pay the dealer a premium of $500 to write this call option. If market interest rates fall as predicted, the T-bonds' market price may climb up to $97,000 per $100,000 bond, permitting the investment officer to demand delivery of the bonds at the cheaper price of $95,000. The call option would then be "in the money" because the securities' market price is above the option's strike price of $95,000.

What profit could be earned from this call option transaction? On a before-tax basis the profit formula for a call option is

$$\begin{matrix} \text{Before-tax} \\ \text{profit} \\ \text{on call} \\ \text{option} \end{matrix} = \text{Security market price} - \text{Strike price} - \text{Option premium} \qquad \textbf{(8–15)}$$

The before-tax profit on each $100,000 bond would be:

$$\begin{matrix} \text{Before-tax} \\ \text{profit on call} \end{matrix} = \$97,000 - \$95,000 - \$500 = \$1,500 \text{ per bond}$$

The projected profit per bond will at least partially offset any loss in interest return experienced on the bonds traded in the cash market if interest rates fall. If interest rates rise instead of fall, the option would likely have dropped "out of the money" as Treasury bond prices fell below the strike price. In this case the T-bond option would likely expire unused and the firm would suffer a loss equal to the option premium. However, the rise in interest rates would permit the firm to come closer to achieving its desired interest return on any newly purchased T-bonds. A call option could also be used to help combat falling interest returns on loans.

The premium quote for the March put is 0.50. As with the underlying futures contract, one basis point or index point is equivalent to $25; hence a quote of .50 is indicative of a premium of $1250 (50 basis points × $25.00). For $1,250, you can purchase the

EXHIBIT 8–4
Futures Options
Prices

Source: *The Wall Street Journal,*
December 14, 2005. Reprinted
by permission of *The Wall Street
Journal,* © 2005 Dow Jones &
Company, Inc. All Rights
Reserved Worldwide. See
wsj.com/free.

For Tuesday, December 13, 2005

REUTERS ▸All prices are settlement prices. Volume and open interest are from the previous trading day.

US TREASURY BONDS (CBOT)
$100,000,pts & 64ths of 100 pct

Strike Price	Calls			Puts		
	Jan	Mar	Jun	Jan	Mar	Jun
109	2-58	3-24	3-63	0-02	0-33	1-19
110	1-61	2-40	3-19	0-05	0-49	1-41
111	1-06	1-63	2-45	0-14	1-07	2-02
112	0-30	1-27	2-12	0-38	1-35	2-33
113	0-10	0-63	1-47	1-18	2-07	3-02
114	0-03	0-41	1-23	2-11	2-49	3-41
115	0-01	0-26	1-03	3-09	3-33	4-23
116	0-01	0-16	0-51	4-08	4-22	5-07
Volume		**Calls**	5,012	**Puts**	5,773	
Open Interest		**Calls**	290,779	**Puts**	253,698	

EURODOLLARS (CME)
$1 million,pts of 100 pct.

Strike Price	Calls			Puts		
	Dec	Jan	Mar	Dec	Jan	Mar
9500	49.25	22.00	22.25	-	-	0.50
9512	36.75	10.00	11.75	-	0.50	2.25
9525	24.25	3.25	6.25	-	6.25	9.25
9537	11.75	1.00	2.75	-	16.50	18.00
9550	0.50	0.50	1.50	1.25	28.50	29.25
9562	-	0.25	1.00	13.25	-	41.25
9575	-	-	0.75	25.75	53.00	53.50
9587	-	-	0.50	38.25	-	-
9600	-	-	0.25	50.75	-	78.00
Volume		**Calls**	115,573	**Puts**	132,278	
Open Interest		**Calls**	9,661,050	**Puts**	7,812,448	

right to a short position for one Eurodollar futures contract. Your exercise (strike price) is 95.00 in IMM index terms. If you hold your put until expiration and the final settlement IMM index is 94.25 then you will receive $1,875 (75 basis points × $25.00) at the time the put is exercised. (Recall that Eurodollar futures contracts are settled in cash.)

In addition to those futures options that trade on the Chicago Board of Trade, the Chicago Mercantile Exchange, and other exchanges around the world, all types of interest-rate options can be tailored specifically to a financial institution's needs in the over-the-counter-market.

Most options today are used by money center banks. They appear to be directed at two principal uses:

1. Protecting a security portfolio through the use of put options to insulate against falling security prices (rising interest rates); however, there is no delivery obligation under an option contract so the user can benefit from keeping his or her securities if interest rates fall and security prices rise.

2. Hedging against positive or negative gaps between interest-sensitive assets and interest sensitive liabilities; for example, put options can be used to offset losses from a negative gap (interest-sensitive liabilities > interest-sensitive assets) when interest rates rise, while call options can be used to offset a positive gap (interest-sensitive assets > interest-sensitive liabilities) when interest rates fall.

Financial institutions can both buy and sell (write) options, but regulated financial institutions are most often buyers of puts and calls rather than writers. The reason is the much greater risk faced by option writers compared to that faced by option buyers; an option seller's potential profit is limited to the premium charged the buyer, but the potential loss if interest rates move against the seller is much greater. Regulations in the United States prohibit banks and selected other regulated firms from writing put and call options in some high-risk areas and generally require any options purchased to be directly linked to specific risk exposures.

Exhibits 8–5 and 8–6 provide us with a convenient summary of how financial firms can profit or at least protect their current position through the careful use of options. For

EXHIBIT 8–5

Payoff Diagrams for Put and Call Options Purchased by a Financial Institution

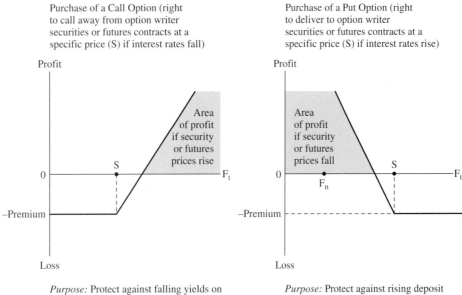

Purchase of a Call Option (right to call away from option writer securities or futures contracts at a specific price (S) if interest rates fall)

Purchase of a Put Option (right to deliver to option writer securities or futures contracts at a specific price (S) if interest rates rise)

Purpose: Protect against falling yields on assets (such as current and future loans and investments in securities).

Purpose: Protect against rising deposit and other borrowing costs and falling market values of assets (such as security investments and loans).

EXHIBIT 8–6

Payoff Diagrams for
Put and Call Options
Written by a
Financial Firm

Financial Firm Sells Call Option to a
Buyer (giving the buyer the right to
call away securities or futures contracts
at price (S) if interest rates rise)

Financial Firm Sells Put Option to a
Buyer (giving the buyer the right to
deliver securities or futures contracts
at the price (S) if interest rates fall)

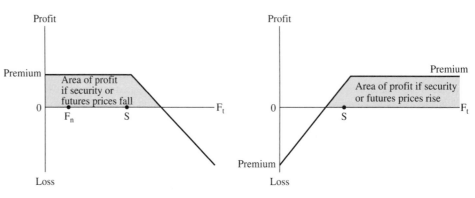

Purpose: Protect against rising deposit and
other borrowing costs and falling market
values of assets (such as security
investments and loans).

Purpose: Protect against falling yields on
assets (such as current loans and future
loans and investments in securities).

Key URLs

For additional
information about how
trading in futures and
option contracts is
regulated, see especially
the Commodity Futures
Trading Commission at
www.cftc.gov and
**www.riskglossary.com/
link/united_states
_financial_regulation.
htm**.

example, a bank concerned about possible losses in net earnings due to falling market interest rates may elect to purchase a call option from an option writer, such as a securities dealer. The call option grants the bank the right to demand delivery of securities or futures contracts at price S (as shown in the left panel of Exhibit 8–5). If interest rates do fall, the securities or futures contracts will rise in price toward F_t, opening up the opportunity for profit equal to $F_t - S$ (less the premium that must be paid to buy the call option and any taxes that may be owed). Conversely, as the right panel in Exhibit 8–5 suggests, an expectation of rising interest rates may lead management to purchase a put option on securities or futures contracts. The upward movement in interest rates will perhaps be large enough to send market prices down to F_n, below strike price S. The bank will purchase the securities or futures contracts mentioned in the put option at current price F_n and deliver them to the writer of the option at price S, pocketing the difference $S - F_n$ (less the premium charged by the option writer and any tax payments due).

Banks and their competitors can also be option writers, offering to sell calls or puts to option buyers. For example, as illustrated in Exhibit 8–6, suppose a bank sells a call option to another institution and the option carries a strike price of S. As shown in the left panel of Exhibit 8–6, if interest rates rise, the call option's market value may fall to F_n and the option will have no value to the buyer. It will go unused and the bank will pocket the option's premium as a profit to help offset any damaging losses due to a trend of rising market interest rates. On the other hand, a financial manager fearful of losses because of falling interest rates may find another institution interested in purchasing a put option at strike price S. If market interest rates do, in fact, decline, the market price of the securities or futures contracts mentioned in the option will rise, and the put will be of no value to its buyer. The option writer will simply pocket the option's premium, helping to offset any losses that might occur due to falling interest rates.

8–5 Regulations and Accounting Rules for Bank Futures and Options Trading

All three federal banking agencies in the United States have guidelines for the risk management of financial derivatives, of which financial futures and options are an important part. For instance, the Office of the Comptroller of the Currency (OCC) has a 186-page

Real Banks, Real Decisions

TRACKING MONETARY POLICY USING FUTURES AND OPTIONS

Two of the most popular futures and options contracts today center on the trading of *Federal funds*—overnight loans of reserves, primarily between banks. The current Fed funds futures and options contracts are both traded at the Chicago Board of Trade (CBOT). These particular contracts seem to provide an unbiased estimate of what the market as a whole is thinking about the likely future course of market interest rates in the months ahead. This appears to be true because the central bank—in this case, the Federal Reserve System— has a powerful impact on the direction and magnitude of interest-rate movements. Therefore, knowledge of the market's consensus opinion about the future course of central bank policy is critical to the interest-rate hedging and asset-liability management process.

In 1988 CBOT opened public trading of Federal funds futures contracts in $5 million denominations, priced at 100 minus the average overnight Fed funds rate for the contract delivery month. The funds rate attached to this contract provides a low-cost forecast of what the Federal Open Market Committee (FOMC), the Federal Reserve's principal policy-making body, is expected to do, on average, in setting future Fed funds interest rate targets. Suppose the current funds rate stands at 4 percent (i.e., the current futures contract is priced at $96 on a $100 basis), but the same contract for delivery next month is currently priced at 4.25 percent ($95.75 on a $100 basis). Then the "average" forecast in the market is that the Federal Reserve will raise the target funds rate by 0.25 percent (i.e., 25 basis points) in the month ahead. If the Fed does make such a move all short-term interest rates are likely to rise as well (unless this projected move is already fully priced in the market).

During 2003 CBOT took a further step with the creation of options contracts on Fed funds futures. These newer contracts seem to provide greater accuracy in market forecasts of the expected Fed funds rate, especially just before the next regularly scheduled FOMC meeting. For example, the current price of the options contract expiring next month may indicate that the market has assigned a probability of 25 percent that the Fed will lift the target funds rate 25 basis points and a 75 percent probability the target rate will remain unchanged following next month's FOMC meeting. With contracts available for a sequence of months out to two years several possible paths for future Federal funds rates can be constructed over time.

Managers of financial institutions, armed with these forecasts, can assess whether or not the marketplace's opinion about the future course of interest rates matches their own and decide accordingly whether and how much they wish to protect against possible adverse interest-rate movements using futures, options, and other hedging tools. (See especially Kwan [7] in the list of references at the end of this chapter and **CBOT.com**.)

document, "Risk Management of Financial Derivatives: Comptrollers Handbook," outlining the necessary elements for such a system. The regulators expect a bank's board of directors to provide oversight while senior management is responsible for the development of an appropriate risk-management system. The risk-management system is to be comprised of

1. Policies and procedures to control financial risk taking.
2. Risk measurement and reporting systems.
3. Independent oversight and control processes.

The OCC requires banks to measure and set limits with regards to nine different aspects of risk associated with derivatives. These risks include strategic risk, reputation risk, price risk, interest-rate risk, liquidity risk, foreign exchange risk, credit risk, transaction risk, and compliance risk.

Debilitating losses due to derivative activities of hedge funds and companies such as Enron point to the need for comprehensive accounting guidelines for derivatives. In 1998 the Financial Accounting Standards Board (FASB) introduced Statement 133 (FAS 133) "Accounting for Derivative Instruments and Hedging Activities." This statement became applicable to all publicly traded firms in the year 2000.

FAS 133 requires that all derivatives be recorded on the balance sheet as assets or liabilities at their fair value. With regard to interest rate risk, FAS 133 recognized two types of hedges: a *fair value hedge* and a *cash flow hedge*. Of course, the proper accounting treatment is based on the type of hedge. The objective of a fair value hedge is to offset losses due to changes in the value of an asset or liability. The change in the fair value of the derivative (i.e., the change in the underlying price of the futures contract) plus the change in the fair value of the hedged item must be reflected on the income statement.

Cash flow hedges try to reduce the risk associated with future cash flows (interest on loans or interest payments on debt). For cash flow hedges, the change in the fair value of the derivative (for futures, the change in the underlying price) is divided into the effective portion and the ineffective portion. The effective portion must be claimed on the balance sheet as equity, identified as Other Comprehensive Income. Meanwhile, the ineffective portion must be reported on the income statement. This derivatives regulation can have a significant impact on the earnings of financial firms by compelling them to reveal the potential profit or loss from their current holdings of futures and options contracts and other derivatives.

Concept Check

8–9. Explain what is involved in a *put option*.

8–10. What is a *call option*?

8–11. What is an option on a futures contract?

8–12. What information do T-bond and Eurodollar futures option quotes contain?

8–13. Suppose market interest rates were expected to rise. What type of option would normally be used?

8–14. If market interest rates were expected to fall, what type of option would a financial institution's manager be likely to employ?

8–15. What rules and regulations have recently been imposed on the use of futures, options, and other derivatives? What does the Financial Accounting Standards Board (FASB) require publicly traded firms to do in accounting for derivative transactions?

8–6 Interest-Rate Swaps

Early in the 1980s, an interest-rate hedging device was developed in the Eurobond market that enables borrowers of funds, including financial institutions, to aid each other by exchanging some of the most favorable features of their loans. For example, a borrower may be small or have a relatively low credit rating so that it cannot go into the open market and sell bonds at the lowest fixed rates of interest. This borrower may be forced to use short-term credit and accept relatively high-cost, variable-rate loans. Another borrower, in contrast, may have a very high credit rating and be able to borrow long term in the open market at a relatively low fixed interest rate. However, the highly rated borrower (which is often a large bank) may desire a more flexible short-term loan if the interest rate can be made low enough. These two borrowers, often with the help of a security dealer or other intermediary, can simply agree to *swap interest payments*, tapping the best features of each other's borrowings. (See Exhibit 8–7.)

An **interest-rate swap,** then, is a way to change a borrowing institution's exposure to interest-rate fluctuations and achieve lower borrowing costs. Swap participants can convert from fixed to floating interest rates or from floating to fixed interest rates and more closely match the maturities of their liabilities to the maturities of their assets. In addition, a financial intermediary arranging a swap for its customers earns fee income (usually

EXHIBIT 8–7
The Interest-Rate
Swap

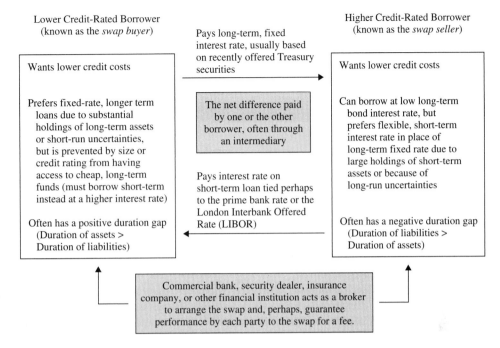

Lower Credit-Rated Borrower
(known as the *swap buyer*)

Wants lower credit costs

Prefers fixed-rate, longer term
loans due to substantial
holdings of long-term assets
or short-run uncertainties,
but is prevented by size or
credit rating from having
access to cheap, long-term
funds (must borrow short-term
instead at a higher interest rate)

Often has a positive duration gap
(Duration of assets >
Duration of liabilities)

Pays long-term, fixed
interest rate, usually based
on recently offered Treasury
securities

The net difference paid
by one or the other
borrower, often through
an intermediary

Pays interest rate on
short-term loan tied perhaps
to the prime bank rate or the
London Interbank Offered
Rate (LIBOR)

Higher Credit-Rated Borrower
(known as the *swap seller*)

Wants lower credit costs

Can borrow at low long-term
bond interest rate, but
prefers flexible, short-term
interest rate in place of
long-term fixed rate due to
large holdings of short-term
assets or because of
long-run uncertainties

Often has a negative duration gap
(Duration of liabilities >
Duration of assets)

Commercial bank, security dealer, insurance
company, or other financial institution acts as a broker
to arrange the swap and, perhaps, guarantee
performance by each party to the swap for a fee.

amounting to 0.25 to 0.50 percent of the amount involved) for serving as an intermediary and may earn additional fees if it agrees to guarantee a swap agreement against default.

Under the terms of an agreement called a *quality swap*, a borrower with a lower credit rating (perhaps with a credit rating of A) enters into an agreement to exchange interest payments with a borrower having a higher credit rating (perhaps with a top-quality rating of AAA). In this case the lower credit-rated borrower agrees to pay the higher credit-rated borrower's fixed long-term borrowing cost. In effect, the lower credit-rated borrower receives a long-term loan from the financial markets at a much lower effective interest cost than the lower-rated borrower could obtain without the swap agreement. At the same time, the borrower with the higher credit rating covers all or a portion of the lower-rated borrower's short-term floating loan rate, thus converting a fixed long-term interest rate into a more flexible and possibly cheaper short-term interest rate.

In summary, the higher credit-rated borrower gets a long-term fixed-rate loan, but pays a floating interest rate to the lower credit-rated borrower. The lower credit-rated borrower gets a short-term, floating rate loan, but pays a fixed interest rate to the higher credit-rated borrower. Often the lower-rated borrower, such as a thrift institution or insurance company, has longer duration assets than liabilities, while the higher-rated borrower may have longer duration liabilities than assets (such as a bank). Through the swap agreement just described, each party achieves cash outflows in the form of interest costs on liabilities that more closely match the interest revenues generated by its assets.

The most popular short-term, floating rates used in interest rate swaps today include the London Interbank Offered Rate (LIBOR) on Eurodollar deposits, Treasury bill and bond rates, the prime bank rate, the Federal funds rate, and interest rates on CDs issued by depository institutions. Each swap partner simply borrows in that market in which it has the greatest comparative cost advantage, and then the two parties exchange interest payments owed on the funds they have each borrowed. In total, the cost of borrowing is lower after a swap is arranged, even though one of the parties (the borrower with the highest credit rating) can usually borrow more cheaply in *both* short-term and long-term markets than the borrower with the lower credit rating.

Factoid
Most derivatives
(measured by their
notional value) used by
depository institutions
are traded on organized
exchanges, like the
Chicago Board of
Trade. True or false?
Answer: False; on
average about four-fifths
are over-the-counter
(OTC) contracts.

Key URL
For an excellent glossary of derivatives terminology, including the terms associated with swaps, see **www.finpipe.com**.

Notice that neither firm lends money to the other. The principal amount of the loans, usually called the *notional* amount, is *not* exchanged.[6] Each party to the swap must still pay off its own debt. In fact, only the *net* amount of interest due usually flows to one or the other party to the swap, depending on how high short-term interest rates in the market rise relative to long-term interest rates on each interest-due date. The swap itself normally will not show up on a swap participant's balance sheet, though it can reduce interest-rate risk associated with the assets and liabilities on that balance sheet.[7]

As noted earlier, swaps are often employed to deal with asset-liability maturity mismatches. For example, as shown in Exhibit 8–7, one firm may have short-term assets with flexible yields and long-term liabilities carrying fixed interest rates. Such a firm fears that a decline in market interest rates will reduce its earnings. In contrast, a company having long-term assets with fixed rates of return, but facing shorter-term liabilities, fears rising interest rates. These two firms are likely candidates for a swap. The one with long-term fixed-rate assets can agree to take over the interest payments of the one with long-term fixed-rate liabilities, and vice versa.

A financial firm can use swaps to alter the effective duration of its assets and liabilities. It can shorten asset duration by swapping out a fixed interest-rate income stream in favor of a variable interest-rate income stream. If the duration of liabilities is too short the financial firm can swap out a variable interest-rate expense in favor of a fixed interest-rate expense. Thus, interest-rate swaps can help immunize a portfolio by moving closer to a balance between asset and liability durations.

Why use swaps for these problem situations? Wouldn't refinancing outstanding debt or perhaps using financial futures accomplish the same thing? In principle, yes, but practical problems frequently favor swaps. For example, retiring old debt and issuing new securities with more favorable characteristics can be expensive and risky. New borrowing may have to take place in an environment of higher interest rates. Underwriting costs, registration fees, time delays, and regulations often severely limit how far any business firm can go in attempting to restructure its balance sheet. Financial futures also present problems for hedgers because of their rigid maturity dates (they usually fall due within a few weeks or months) and the limited number of financial instruments they cover.

In contrast, swaps can be negotiated to cover virtually *any* period of time or borrowing instrument desired, though most fall into the 3-year to 10-year range. They are also easy to carry out, usually negotiated and agreed to over the telephone or via e-mail through a broker or dealer. Several large American and British banks have developed a communications network to make swap trading relatively easy. Another key innovation was the development of *master swap agreements,* which spell out the rights and responsibilities of each swap partner, thereby simplifying the negotiation of an agreement and improving the liquidity and smoothness of the international swap market.

Reverse swaps can also be arranged, in which a new swap agreement offsets the effects of an existing swap contract. Many swap agreements today contain termination options, allowing either party to end the agreement for a fee. Other swaps carry interest-rate ceilings (caps), interest-rate minimums (floors), or both ceilings and floors (collars), which limit the risk of large changes in interest-rate payments. There may also be escape clauses

---

[6]Swaps in which the notional amount is constant are called *bullet swaps.* In *amortizing* swaps, notional amount declines over time, and in *accruing* swaps, notional principal accumulates during their term. *Seasonal* swaps have notional principals that vary according to the seasonal cash flow patterns the swap parties experience.

[7]If a financial institution agrees to guarantee a swap agreement negotiated between two of its customers or if it participates in a swap with another firm, it usually marks the transaction down as a contingent liability. Because such arrangements may become real liabilities for a financial firm, many financial analysts seek out information on any outstanding swaps in evaluating individual financial-service firms as possible investments for their clients.

and "swaptions," which are options for one or both parties to make certain changes in the agreement, take out a new option, or cancel an existing swap agreement.

On the negative side, swaps may carry substantial brokerage fees, credit risk, basis risk, and interest rate risk. With *credit risk,* either or both parties to a swap may go bankrupt or fail to honor their half of the swap agreement (though the loss would be limited to promised net interest payments, not repayment of loan principal). Moreover, a third party with a top credit rating, such as a bank or security dealer, may be willing to *guarantee* the agreed-upon interest payments through a letter of credit if the swap partner seeking the guarantee pays a suitable fee (for example: 10 to 50 basis points). The most heavily used intermediaries in arranging and guaranteeing swap contracts include the largest U.S., Canadian, Japanese, and European banks and securities firms (such as J. P. Morgan Chase, Merrill Lynch, and Salomon Brothers). Sometimes the lower-rated swap partner may be asked to post collateral to strengthen the contract. Indeed, the posting of collateral appears to be increasing in this market, even among high-credit-quality participants.

In fairness to swaps, we should note that actual defaults are rare.[8] Credit quality is relatively high, with swap partners usually carrying credit ratings of A or higher. If a swap partner is rated BBB or lower it may be impossible to find a counterparty to agree to the swap or the low-rated partner may be required to agree to a *credit trigger clause,* which allows the other partner to terminate the contract should the lower-rated borrower's credit rating deteriorate.

One element that significantly reduces the potential damage if a swap partner does default on its obligation to pay is called *netting.* Remember that on each payment due date the parties exchange only the *net* difference between the interest payments each owes the other. This amount is much smaller than either the fixed or floating interest payment itself and would be the actual amount subject to default. Moreover, when a financial intermediary is involved in several swap contracts with another party, it will often calculate only the *net* amount owed across all swap contracts, which further reduces the actual amount of credit risk.

Basis risk arises because the particular interest rates that define the terms of a swap, such as a long-term bond rate and a floating short-term rate like LIBOR, are not exactly the same interest rates as those attached to all the assets and liabilities that either or both swap partners hold. This means that as a swap's reference interest rate changes, it may not change in exactly the same proportion as the interest rates attached to the swap buyer's and seller's various assets and liabilities. Thus, an interest-rate swap cannot hedge away all interest-rate risk for both parties to the agreement; some risk exposure must remain in any real-world situation.

Indeed, swaps may carry substantial *interest rate risk.* For example, if the yield curve slopes upward, the swap buyer, who pays the fixed interest rate, normally would expect to pay a greater amount of net interest cost during the early years of a swap contract and to receive greater amounts of net interest income from the swap seller, who pays the floating interest rate, toward the end of the swap contract. This could encourage the seller to default on the swap agreement near the end of the contract, possibly forcing the swap buyer to negotiate a new agreement with a new partner under less-favorable conditions. Swap dealers, which account for most contracts in the market, work to limit their interest-rate risk exposure by setting up offsetting swap contracts with a variety of partners.

---

[8]In addition to conventional interest-rate swaps, financial intermediaries today engage in several other types of swaps, including commodity swaps, equity swaps, and currency swaps. *Commodity* swaps are designed to hedge against price fluctuations in oil, natural gas, copper, and selected other commodities where one party fears rising prices and the other fears falling prices. *Equity* swaps are designed to convert the interest flows on debt into cash flows related to the behavior of a stock index, which allows swap partners to benefit from favorable movements in stock prices. *Currency* swaps are discussed in Chapter 20.

Key URLs

The use of interest-rate swaps by financial firms may be explored further using such sites as **www.snl.com,** **www.scotiacapital.com,** and **www.aei.org.**

Key URL

For information and data on the extent of the swap market, visit the International Swaps and Derivatives Association's Web site at **www.isda.org.**

Insights and Issues

AN EXAMPLE OF A SWAP TRANSACTION

This example shows how two businesses can each save on borrowing costs by agreeing to swap interest payments with each other. The savings arise principally because interest rate spreads, often called *quality spreads,* are normally much wider in the long-term credit market than in the short-term credit market.

Parties to the Swap	Fixed Interest Rates Parties Must Pay if They Issue Long-Term Bonds	Floating Interest Rates Parties Must Pay if They Receive a Short-Term Loan	Potential Interest Rate Savings of Each Borrower
A lower credit-rated borrower	11.50%	Prime + 1.75%	0.50%
A higher credit-rated borrower	9.00	Prime interest rate	0.25%
Difference in interest rates due to differences in borrowers' credit ratings (*quality spread*)	2.50%	1.75%	0.75%

FINANCING METHODS USED

Suppose higher-rated borrower issues long-term bonds at 9 percent, while the lower-rated borrower gets a loan at prime plus 1.75 percent. They then swap interest payments.

A swap transaction might be arranged in which the lower-rated borrower agrees to pay the higher-rated borrower's 9 percent interest cost, thus saving 2.5 percent in long-term borrowing costs because it would have had to pay 11.5 percent for long-term credit. The higher-rated borrower pays the lower-rated borrower's prime interest rate minus 0.25 percent, thus saving the higher-rated borrower, who normally would borrow at prime, a quarter of a percentage point (−0.25 percent) on a short-term loan. Notice that the lower credit-rated borrower saves a *net* interest rate of 0.50 percent (that is, 2.50 percentage points saved on the long-term rate minus the 2 percent additional it must pay above the amount of the prime rate less 0.25 percent contributed by the higher-rated borrower). Thus:

Low credit-rated borrower pays	9 percent (fixed rate)
High credit-rated borrower pays	Prime rate less 0.25 percent (floating rate)
Low credit-rated borrower saves	[(11.5 percent − 9 percent) − (1.75 percent more than the prime rate + 0.25 percent less than the prime rate)] = 0.50 percent
High credit-rated borrower saves	0.25 percent (below the prime rate)

The lower-rated borrower may also agree to pay the underwriting costs associated with the higher-rated borrower's issue of long-term bonds so that both ultimately wind up with roughly equal savings of about 0.5 percent.

Clearly, *both* parties save as a result of this swap. They also benefit from a closer matching of cash inflows and outflows from their respective portfolios of assets and liabilities.

Some authorities argue, however, that these savings are illusory, that an efficient financial marketplace will rapidly eliminate such arbitrage opportunities between long-term and short-term markets except for possible market imperfections. Others contend that the supposed savings from a swap are counterbalanced by the surrender of valuable options by the swap parties, who, were it not for the swap, could refinance their loans if interest rates move in a favorable direction. However, they must honor the terms of a swap contract regardless of how interest rates subsequently behave unless they can work out a revised contract.

In general, if short-term market interest rates are expected to fall and stay low, this will be a plus for the short-term rate payer and a disadvantage to the long-term rate payer whose swap rate will consistently be higher. The fixed-rate paying partner will have to pay out the difference between short-term and long-term interest rates whenever a payment is owed. On the other hand, if the yield curve becomes negatively sloped, the long-term fixed-rate payer may benefit if the short-term rate rises above the long-term fixed swap rate. In the latter case the short-rate payer must now pay out a stream of interest payments to the swap partner as long as the short-term (variable) interest rate stays above the fixed interest rate.

The Interest-Rate Swap Yield Curve

Recently the Federal Reserve Board began reporting a series of interest rates for swap contracts of varying maturities from 1 year to 30 years. Collected under the auspices of the International Swaps and Derivatives Association, Inc., the reported rates represent the interest rates that a fixed-rate partner to a swap would pay based on swap rates collected by survey at 11 A.M. each business day. Each swap agreement in the survey assumes that the variable-rate partner would pay the fixed-rate partner the prevailing three-month London Interbank Offer Rate (LIBOR).

An example of the fixed interest rates attached to swaps of varying maturities as reported for December 16, 2005.

Maturity of Swap Contract Reported in Survey	Prevailing Interest Rate Paid by Fixed-Rate Swap Partner in Return for Receiving the 3-Month LIBOR Rate
1 year	4.81%
2 years	4.81
3 years	4.82
4 years	4.84
5 years	4.86
7 years	4.91
10 years	4.97
30 years	5.16

At the time these interest rates were obtained, the variable-rate party in each of these swap contracts was paying a money market interest rate at or close to 4.48 percent. Two key points stand out from this data source:

1. The long-term rate payer, at least at the beginning of the swap, paid the higher interest rate compared to the short-term rate payer.
2. The swap yield curve generally slopes upward, suggesting that the longer the term of a swap contract, the higher the fixed interest rate tends to be.

What accounts for these differences in swap interest rates? The key factor tends to be risk—the risk of changing market interest rates and shifts in the term structure of interest rates (the yield curve).

For example, if short-term market interest rates are expected to remain relatively low, it will benefit the short-term rate payer and be a disadvantage to the long-term rate payer whose swap rate will consistently be higher. In this instance the fixed-rate-paying partner will have to pay out the difference between short-term and long-term interest rates whenever a payment is due. On the other hand, if the yield curve gets flatter or becomes negatively sloped, the long-term fixed-rate payer may benefit if the short-term (variable) rate rises above the long-term fixed rate. In the latter case the short-rate payer must now pay out a stream of interest payments to the swap partner as long as the short-term (variable) interest rate stays above the fixed interest rate. Clearly, *shifting interest-rate expectations can play a key role in the attractiveness of swaps to either or both swap partners*.

For more information on the interest-rate swap yield curve, see especially the International Swaps and Derivatives Association at **www.isda.org** and the Federal Reserve Board, Statistical Release H.15 at **www.federalreserve.gov**.

The swap market's growth has been truly phenomenal. Starting from zero in the early 1980s, outstanding swap contracts denominated in U.S. dollars and measured by their notional (face) value exceded $60 trillion in 2005. Further testimony to the swap market's rapid growth is provided by the substantial breadth of market participants today. Among the most important are depository institutions; insurance companies; finance companies;

nonfinancial corporations; dealers in government, corporate, and asset-backed securities; hedge funds; and government-related enterprises, including U.S. federal agencies (such as Fannie Mae) and the World Bank.

Concept Check

8–16. What is the purpose of an interest-rate swap?

8–17. What are the principal advantages and disadvantages of interest-rate swaps?

8–18. How can a financial institution get itself out of an interest-rate swap agreement?

8–7 Caps, Floors, and Collars

Finally, among the most familiar hedging devices developed by lending institutions for themselves and their customers are interest-rate caps, floors, and collars.

Interest-Rate Caps

An **interest-rate cap** protects its holder against rising market interest rates. In return for paying an up-front premium, borrowers are assured that institutions lending them money cannot increase their loan rate above the level of the cap. Alternatively, the borrower may purchase an interest-rate cap from a third party, with that party promising to reimburse borrowers for any additional interest they owe their creditors beyond the cap. If a lending institution sells a rate cap to one of its borrowing customers, it takes on interest rate risk from that customer but earns a fee (premium) as compensation for added risk taking. If a lender takes on a large volume of cap agreements it can reduce its overall risk exposure by using another hedging device, such as an interest-rate swap.

Consider the following example: A bank purchases a cap of 11 percent from an insurance company on its borrowings of $100 million in the Eurodollar market for one year. Suppose interest rates in this market rise to 12 percent for the year. Then the financial institution selling the cap will reimburse the bank purchasing the cap the additional 1 percent in interest costs due to the recent rise in interest rates. In terms of dollars, the bank will receive a rebate of

$$\left(\begin{array}{c} \text{Market} \\ \text{interest rate} \end{array} - \begin{array}{c} \text{Cap} \\ \text{rate} \end{array} \right) \times \begin{array}{c} \text{Amount} \\ \text{borrowed} \end{array} = (12 \text{ percent} - 11 \text{ percent}) \quad \text{(8–16)}$$

$$\times \ \$100 \text{ million} = \$1 \text{ million}$$

for one year. Thus, the bank's effective borrowing rate can float over time but it will never exceed 11 percent. Financial firms buy interest rate caps when conditions arise that could generate losses, such as when a financial institution finds itself funding fixed-rate assets with floating-rate liabilities, possesses longer-term assets than liabilities, or perhaps holds a large portfolio of bonds that will drop in value when market interest rates rise.

Interest-Rate Floors

Financial-service providers can also lose earnings in periods of falling interest rates, especially when rates on floating-rate loans decline. For example, a lending institution can insist on establishing an **interest-rate floor** under its loans so that, no matter how far loan rates tumble, it is guaranteed some minimum rate of return.

Another popular use of interest-rate floors arises when a financial firm sells an interest rate floor to its customers who hold securities but are concerned that the yields on those securities might fall to unacceptable levels. For example, a bank's customer may hold a 90-day negotiable CD promising 6.75 percent but anticipates selling the CD some time within the 90-day period. Suppose the customer does not want to see the CD's yield drop below 6.25 percent. In this instance, the customer's bank may sell its client a rate floor of 6.25 percent, agreeing to pay the customer the difference between the floor rate and the actual CD rate if interest rates fall too far in the days ahead.

How can financial institutions benefit from trading in interest-rate floors? To cite one example, suppose a bank extending a $10 million floating-rate loan to one of its corporate customers for a year at prime insists on a minimum (floor) interest rate on this loan of 7 percent. If the prime rate drops below the floor to 6 percent for one year, the customer will pay not only the 6 percent prime rate (or $10 million × 0.06 = $600,000 in interest) but also pay out an interest rebate to the lender of

$$\left(\begin{matrix}\text{Floor} \\ \text{rate}\end{matrix} - \begin{matrix}\text{Current loan} \\ \text{interest rate}\end{matrix}\right) \times \begin{matrix}\text{Amount} \\ \text{borrowed}\end{matrix} = (7\% - 6\%) \times \$10 \text{ million} \tag{8-17}$$
$$= \$100,000$$

Through this hedging device the lender is guaranteed, assuming the borrower doesn't default, a minimum return of 7 percent on its loan. Financial intermediaries use interest-rate floors most often when their liabilities have longer maturities than their assets or when they are funding floating-rate assets with fixed-rate debt.

Interest-Rate Collars

Lending institutions and their borrowing customers also make heavy use of the **interest-rate collar,** which combines in one agreement a rate floor and a rate cap. Many banks, security firms, and other institutions sell collars as a separate fee-based service for the loans they make to their customers. For example, a customer who has just received a $100 million loan may ask the lender for a collar on the loan's prime rate between 11 percent and 7 percent. In this instance, the lender will pay its customer's added interest cost if prime rises above 11 percent, while the customer reimburses the lender if prime drops below 7 percent. In effect, the collar's purchaser pays a premium for a rate cap while receiving a premium for accepting a rate floor. The net premium paid for the collar can be positive or negative, depending upon the outlook for interest rates and the risk aversion of borrower and lender at the time of the agreement.

Normally, caps, collars, and floors range in maturity from a few weeks out to as long as 10 years. Most such agreements are tied to interest rates on government securities, commercial paper, prime-rated loans, or Eurodollar deposits (LIBOR). Lenders often make heavy use of collars to protect their earnings when interest rates appear to be unusually volatile and there is considerable uncertainty about the direction in which market rates may move.

Caps, collars, and floors are simply special types of options designed to deal with interest rate risk exposure from assets and liabilities held by lending institutions and their customers. Sales of caps, collars, and floors to customers have generated a large volume of fee income (up-front revenues) in recent years, but these special options carry both credit risk (when the party is obligated to pay defaults) and interest rate risk that must be carefully weighed by financial managers when making the decision to sell or use these rate-hedging tools.

Concept Check

8–19. How can financial-service providers make use of interest-rate *caps, floors,* and *collars* to generate revenue and help manage interest-rate risk?

8–20. Suppose a bank enters into an agreement to make a $10 million, three-year floating-rate loan to one of its best corporate customers at an initial rate of 8 percent. The bank and its customer agree to a cap and a floor arrangement in which the customer reimburses the bank if the floating loan rate drops below 6 percent and the bank reimburses the customer if the floating loan rate rises above 10 percent. Suppose that at the beginning of the loan's second year, the floating loan rate drops to 5 percent for a year and then, at the beginning of the third year, the loan rate increases to 12 percent for the year. What rebates must each party to the agreement pay?

Summary

In this chapter we have focused upon major types of *derivatives*—financial futures contracts; options; swaps; and interest-rate caps, collars, and floors—designed to deal with the exposure of financial institutions to losses due to changing market interest rates. The key points which surfaced in this chapter include these:

- *Financial futures contracts* are agreements to deliver or take delivery of financial instruments, such as bonds, bills, and deposits, at a stipulated price on a specific future date. This brand of derivatives has grown rapidly in recent years because of their relatively low cost and ready availability in a variety of types and maturities.

- *Option contracts* give their holders the right to deliver (put) or to take delivery of (call) specified financial instruments at a prespecified (strike) price on or before a stipulated future date. Options are widely traded on organized exchanges and can be particularly effective when the managers of financial institutions wish to have downside risk protection but do not want to restrict potential gains should market interest rates move in a favorable direction.

- *Interest-rate swaps* are agreements between parties to exchange interest payments so that each participating institution can achieve a better match of its cash inflows and outflows. Swaps also can help lower interest costs because each party to the agreement normally borrows in that credit market offering the greatest cost advantage.

- *Interest-rate caps* place an upper limit on a borrower's loan rate, while *interest-rate floors* protect a lender from declining loan yields should market interest rates fall too far. *Collars* combine caps and floors, freezing loan rates or security yields within the limits spelled out by the accompanying contractual agreement.

- Derivative usage is heavily centered in the largest financial firms, including banks, security firms, and insurance companies. This size bias in the employment of interest-rate hedging tools stems from the huge market risk exposures leading financial firms experience, as well as the highly technical skills required to use derivatives successfully as an asset-liability management tool. Moreover, it is the biggest banks, security dealers, and insurance firms that most corporations and governments turn to when they require effective risk protection.

Key Terms

financial futures, *248*
interest-rate option, *259*
interest-rate swap, *266*
interest-rate cap, *272*
interest-rate floor, *273*
interest-rate collar, *273*

Problems and Projects

1. You hedged your bank's exposure to declining interest rates by buying one March Treasury bond futures contract at the opening price on November 21, 2005 (see Exhibit 8–2). It is now Monday, January 9, and you discover that on Friday, January 6, March T-bond futures opened at 113-17 and settled at 113-16.

   a. What is the profit or loss on your long position as of settlement on January 3?

   b. If you deposited the required initial margin on 11/21 and have not touched the equity account since making that cash deposit, what is your equity account balance?

2. Use the quotes of Eurodollar futures contracts traded on the Chicago Mercantile Exchange on December 20, 2005, to answer the following questions:

	Open	High	Low	Settle	Chg	Yield	Chg	Open Int
Eurodollar (CME)-$1,000,000; pts of 100%								
Jan	95.3900	95.3950	95.3850	95.3870	−.0080	4.6130	+.0080	18,442
Feb	95.3000	95.3000	95.2950	95.3000	−.0100	4.7000	+.0100	3,741
Mar	95.2350	95.2400	95.2100	95.2200	−.0150	4.7800	+.0150	1,214,372
June	95.1750	95.1750	95.1300	95.1400	−.0350	4.8600	+.0350	1,272,562
Sept	95.1750	95.1800	95.1250	95.1400	−.0400	4.8600	+.0400	1,080,754
Dec	95.2200	95.2200	95.1600	95.1750	−.0450	4.8250	+.0450	979,425
Mr07	95.2650	95.2650	95.2000	95.2100	−.0500	4.7900	+.0500	863,266

Source: **wsj.com/free**, December 21, 2005.

   a. What is the annualized discount yield based on the low IMM index for the nearest June contract?

   b. If your bank took a short position at the high price for the day for 15 contracts, what would be the dollar gain or loss at settlement on December 20, 2005?

   c. If you deposited the initial required hedging margin in your equity account upon taking the position described in *b*, what would be the marked-to-market value of your equity account at settlement?

3. What kind of futures or options hedges would be called for in the following situations?

   a. Market interest rates are expected to increase and First National Bank's asset and liability managers expect to liquidate a portion of their bond portfolio to meet depositors' demands for funds in the upcoming quarter.

   b. Silsbee Savings Bank has interest-sensitive assets of $79 million and interest-sensitive liabilities of $88 million over the next 30 days and market interest rates are expected to rise.

   c. A survey of Tuskee Bank's corporate loan customers this month (January) indicates that on balance, this group of firms will need to draw $165 million from their credit lines in February and March, which is $65 million more than the bank's management has forecasted and prepared for. The bank's economist has predicted a significant increase in money market interest rates over the next 60 days.

   d. Monarch National Bank has interest-sensitive assets greater than interest-sensitive liabilities by $24 million. If interest rates fall (as suggested by data from the Federal Reserve Board), the bank's net interest margin may be squeezed due to the decrease in loan and security revenue.

e. Caufield Thrift Association finds that its assets have an average duration of 1.5 years and its liabilities have an average duration of 1.1 years. The ratio of liabilities to assets is .90. Interest rates are expected to increase by 50 basis points during the next six months.

4. Your bank needs to borrow $300 million by selling time deposits with 180-day maturities. If interest rates on comparable deposits are currently at 4 percent, what is the cost of issuing these deposits? Suppose interest rates rise to 5 percent. What then will be the cost of these deposits? What position and types of futures contracts could be used to deal with this cost increase?

5. In response to the above scenario, management sells 300 90-day Eurodollar time deposit futures contracts trading at an IMM Index of 98. Interest rates rise as anticipated and your bank offsets its position by buying 300 contracts at an IMM index of 96.98. What type of hedge is this? What before-tax profit or loss is realized from the futures position?

6. It is March and Cavalier Financial Services Corporation is concerned about what an increase in interest rates will do to the value of its bond portfolio. The portfolio currently has a market value of $101.1 million and Cavalier's management intends to liquidate $1.1 million in bonds in June to fund additional corporate loans. If interest rates increase to 6 percent, the bond will sell for $1 million with a loss of $100,000. Cavalier's management sells 10 June Treasury bond contracts at 109-05 in March. Interest rates do increase, and in June Cavalier's management offsets its position by buying 10 June Treasury bond contracts at 100-03.

   a. What is the dollar gain/loss to Cavalier from the combined cash and futures market operations described above?

   b. What is the basis at the initiation of the hedge?

   c. What is the basis at the termination of the hedge?

   d. Illustrate how the dollar return is related to the change in the basis from initiation to termination.

7. By what amount will the market value of a Treasury bond futures contract change if interest rates rise from 5 to 6 percent? The underlying Treasury bond has a duration of 10.48 years and the Treasury bond futures contract is currently being quoted at 113-06. (Remember that Treasury bonds are quoted in 32nds.)

8. Trojan National Bank reports that its assets have a duration of 8 years and its liabilities average 3 years in duration. To hedge this duration gap, management plans to employ Treasury bond futures, which are currently quoted at 112-17 and have a duration of 10.36 years. Trojan's latest financial report shows total assets of $120 million and liabilities of $97 million. Approximately how many futures contracts will the bank need to cover its overall exposure?

9. You hedged your bank's exposure to declining interest rates by buying one March call on Treasury bond futures at the premium quoted on December 13, 2005 (see Exhibit 8–4).

   a. How much did you pay for the call in dollars if you chose the strike price of 110? (Remember that option premiums are quoted in 64ths.)

   b. Using the following information for trades on December 21, 2005, if you sold the call on 12/21/05 due to a change in circumstances would you have reaped a profit or loss? Determine the amount of the profit/loss.

For Wednesday, December 21, 2005

All prices are settlement prices. Volume and open interest are from the previous trading day.

US TREASURY BONDS (CBOT)

$100,000,pts & 64ths of 100 pct

	Calls			Puts		
Strike Price	Jan	Mar	Jun	Jan	Mar	Jun
109	3-46	3-62	4-31	0-01	0-17	0-60
110	2-46	3-08	3-47	0-01	0-27	1-12
111	1-46	2-23	3-05	0-01	0-42	1-34
112	0-47	1-46	2-31	0-02	1-00	1-60
113	0-04	1-11	1-63	0-22	1-29	2-26
114	0-01	0-49	1-35	1-19	2-03	2-62
115	0-01	0-30	1-11	2-18	2-47	3-38
116	0-01	0-18	0-56	3-18	3-35	4-18

Source: **wsj.com/free,** December 21, 2005.

10. Refer to the information given for Problem 9. You hedged your bank's exposure to increasing interest rates by buying one March put on Treasury bond futures at the premium quoted on December 13, 2005 (see Exhibit 8–4).

    a. How much did you pay for the put in dollars if you chose the strike price of 110? (Remember that premiums are quoted in 64ths.)

    b. Using the above information for trades on December 21, 2005, if you sold the put on 12/21/05 due to a change in circumstances would you have reaped a profit or loss? Determine the amount of the profit/loss.

11. You hedged your thrift institution's exposure to declining interest rates by buying one March call on Eurodollar deposit futures at the premium quoted on December 13, 2005 (see Exhibit 8–4).

    a. How much did you pay for the call in dollars if you chose the strike price of 9,525? (Remember that premiums are quoted in IMM Index terms.)

    b. If March arrives and Eurodollar Deposit Futures have a settlement index at expiration of 96.00, what is your profit or loss? (Remember to include the premium paid for the call option.)

12. You hedged your bank's exposure to increasing interest rates by buying one March put on Eurodollar deposit futures at the premium quoted on December 13, 2005 (see Exhibit 8–4).

    a. How much did you pay for the put in dollars if you chose the strike price of 9,550? (Remember that premiums are quoted in IMM Index terms.)

    b. If March arrives and Eurodollar Deposit Futures have a settlement index at expiration of 96.00, what is your profit or loss? (Remember to include the premium paid for the call option.)

13. A bank is considering the use of options to deal with a serious funding cost problem. Deposit interest rates have been rising for six months, currently averaging 5 percent, and are expected to climb as high as 6.75 percent over the next 90 days. The bank plans to issue $60 million in new money market deposits in about 90 days. It can buy put or call options on 90-day Eurodollar time deposit futures contracts for a quoted premium of .31 or $775.00 for each million-dollar contract. The strike price is quoted

as 9,500. We expect the futures to trade at an index of 93.50 within 90 days. What kind of option should the bank buy? What before-tax profit could the bank earn for each option under the terms described?

14. Hokie Savings Bank wants to purchase a portfolio of home mortgage loans with an expected average return of 8.5 percent. The bank's management is concerned that interest rates will drop and the cost of the portfolio will increase from the current price of $50 million. In six months when the funds become available to purchase the loan portfolio, market interest rates are expected to be in the 7.5 percent range. Treasury bond options are available today at a quoted price of $79,000 (per $100,000 contract), upon payment of a $700 premium, and are forecast to rise to a market value of $87,000 per contract. What before-tax profits could the bank earn per contract on this transaction? How many options should Hokie buy?

15. A savings and loan's credit rating has just slipped, and half of its assets are long-term mortgages. It offers to swap interest payments with a money center bank in a $100 million deal. The bank can borrow short term at LIBOR (8.05 percent) and long term at 8.95 percent. The S&L must pay LIBOR plus 1.5 percent on short-term debt and 10.75 percent on long-term debt. Show how these parties could put together a swap deal that benefits both of them about equally.

16. A bank plans to borrow $55 million in the money market at a current interest rate of 4.5 percent. However, the borrowing rate will float with market conditions. To protect itself, the bank has purchased an interest-rate cap of 5 percent to cover this borrowing. If money market interest rates on these funds sources suddenly rise to 5.5 percent as the borrowing begins, how much interest in total will the bank owe and how much of an interest rebate will it receive, assuming the borrowing is for only one month?

17. Suppose that Jasper Savings Association has recently granted a loan of $2.4 million to Fairhills Farms at prime plus 0.5 percent for six months. In return for granting Fairhills an interest-rate cap of 8 percent on its loan, this thrift has received from this customer a floor rate on the loan of 6 percent. Suppose that, as the loan is about to start, the prime rate declines to 5.25 percent and remains there for the duration of the loan. How much (in dollars) will Fairhills Farms have to pay in total interest on this six-month loan? How much in interest rebates will Fairhills have to pay due to the fall in the prime rate?

Internet Exercises

1. Bank trading in futures and options is subject to strict regulations. You can find out about the rules and regulatory supervision of banks (BHCs) in the Federal Reserve's *Trading and Capital-Markets Activity Manual*, found at **www.federalreserve.gov/board-docs/supmanual/trading/trading.pdf**. Using the index locate "Regulation, Compliance with." After reading this page, discuss which banking regulations and regulators are involved with futures, options, and swap activities.

2. All three federal banking regulators have guidelines for the risk management of financial derivatives (futures and options). In this chapter we have provided some of the details from the *Comptrollers Handbook for National Banks*. Go to the FDIC's Web site **www.fdic.gov/regulations/laws/rules/** and click on the index link and then look under *D* for *derivatives*. Under the heading of Risk Management, click on the link for FDIC Statement of Policy, which will provide the Supervisory Policy Statement on Investment Securities and End-User Derivatives Activities. Print and read the eight pages of this statement. In terms of managing the specific risks involved in investment activities, compare and contrast the types of risks listed in this statement with those identified by the OCC and listed in the chapter's discussion.

REAL NUMBERS FOR REAL BANKS

Assignment for Chapter 8

YOUR BANK'S USE OF INTEREST-RATE DERIVATIVE CONTRACTS

Chapter 8 explores how financial firms can use interest-rate derivatives to hedge interest-rate risk and increase noninterest income (fee income). The derivative contracts discussed in this chapter include interest-rate futures, options, options on futures, swaps, caps, floors, and collars. Early in the chapter, data provided from the Office of the Comptroller of the Currency (OCC) illustrates that the largest banks account for the bulk of trading activity. Your banking company was selected from the largest 25 banking companies in the United States. This assignment is designed to explore your bank's usage of derivative contracts, how its usage compares to other large banks, and the composition of its interest-rate derivatives portfolio.

For this assignment, you will once again access data at **www3.fdic.gov/sdi/main.asp** for your BHC (the bank and thrift chartered component) and its peer group of banks with more than $10 billion in assets. Follow the directions in Chapter 5's assignment for collecting data as a percentage of assets. In Report Selection use the pull-down menu to select Derivatives and view this in Percent of Assets. For Interest Rate Contracts, you are interested in Items 6–10. This includes all the interest-rate derivatives discussed here in Chapter 8 plus a few more. Caps, floors, and collars are part of the Purchased and Written Option Contract categories. Enter the percentage information for Interest Rate Contracts as an addition to the spreadsheet for comparisons with the Peer Group.

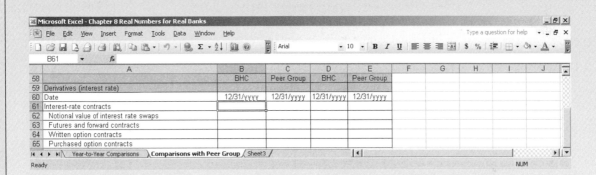

YOUR BHC'S USE OF DERIVATIVE CONTRACTS ACROSS PERIODS

A. Compare columns of row 61. How has the use of derivative contracts changed across periods? Is your bank more or less involved than the group of comparable institutions?

B. Use the chart function in Excel and the data by columns in rows 62 through 63 to create four pie charts illustrating the break-down of the type of interest-rate contracts held by your BHC and its peer group. Your pie charts should include titles and labels. For instance, what follows is a pie chart for National City Corp for 12/31/04.

C. Utilizing the above information, write approximately one page about your bank's usage of interest-rate derivatives

and how it compares to its peers. Use your pie charts as graphics and incorporate them in the discussion. The pie chart below was included by creating a text box and copying the Excel spreadsheet into the text box.

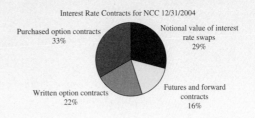

3. The *Federal Reserve's Trading and Capital-Markets Activity Manual* found at **www.federalreserve.gov/boarddocs/supmanual/trading/trading.pdf** includes the section, "Instrument Profiles." Read the descriptions of options (section 4330), financial futures (section 4320), and swaps (section 4325). Compare and contrast the risks associated with these instruments based on the Federal Reserve document.

www.mhhe.com/rose7e

4. What do the following terms mean in financial futures and options trading?

Basis	Daily trading limit
Carrying charge	Limit order
Clearing margin	Managed futures
Convergence	Market order

(To answer this question, see especially the Knowledge Center of the Chicago Board of Trade at **www.cbot.com.**)

5. If you want to become more familiar with swaps and other derivatives, visit **www.finpipe.com** and click on the Derivatives link. Explore the swap links. Discuss the example provided for a firm using an interest-rate swap to hedge changing interest rates.

S&P Market Insight Challenge (www.mhhe.com/edumarketinsight)

1. The S&P Industry Survey on Banking discusses banking's role in the derivatives market. For an up-to-date description use the Industry tab in S&P's Market Insight. The drop-down menu provides subindustry selections for Diversified Banks and Regional Banks. Upon selecting one of these subindustries, you will find a recent downloadable S&P Industry Survey on Banking. View the section, "How to Analyze a Bank," looking particularly at derivatives. Describe the advantages and the risks associated with derivative usage by banks and other financial-service providers.

2. Which financial firms in the Market Insight group appear to make the heaviest use of financial futures? Interest-rate options? Interest-rate swaps? Why and how can you tell? What industries do these firms represent?

Selected References

To learn more about the use of financial futures and option contracts in risk management, see the following:

1. Ackert, Lucy. "Derivative Securities Use Grows as Banks Strive to Hedge Risks." *Financial Update*, Federal Reserve Bank of Atlanta, January–March 1999, pp. 8–9.
2. Nosal, Ed, and Tan Wang. "Arbitrage: The Key to Pricing Options." *Economic Commentary*, Federal Reserve Bank of Cleveland, January 1, 2004, pp. 1–3.
3. Sundaresan, Suresh. *Fixed Income Markets and Their Derivatives*. Cincinnati: Southwestern College Publishing, 2002.
4. Rose, Peter S. "Defensive Banking in a Volatile Economy: Hedging Loan and Deposit Interest Rates." *The Canadian Banker* 93, no. 2 (April 1986), pp. 52–59.

For a review of the controversy over the alleged benefits and costs of derivative usage, see especially:

5. Gunther, Jeffrey W., and Thomas F. Siems. "Debunking Derivatives Delirium." *Southwest Economy*, Federal Reserve Bank of Dallas, March/April 2003, pp. 1, 5–9.

To understand more about the growing use of derivatives to track central bank monetary policy, see, for example:

6. Carlson, John B., William R. Melick, and Erkin Y. Sabinoz. "An Option for Anticipating Fed Action." *Economic Commentary*, Federal Reserve Bank of Cleveland, September 1, 2003.
7. Kwan, Simon. "Gauging the Market's Expectations about Monetary Policy." *FRBSF Economic Letter*, Federal Reserve Bank of San Francisco, no. 2004-28, October 8, 2004, pp. 1–3.

Risk Management Using Asset-Backed Securities, Loan Sales, Credit Standbys, and Credit Derivatives

Key Topics in This Chapter

- The Securitization Process
- Securitization's Impact and Risks
- Sales of Loans: Nature and Risks
- Standby Credits: Pricing and Risks
- Credit Derivatives and CDOs
- Benefits and Risks of Credit Derivatives

9–1 Introduction

The managers of financial firms have actively sought out newer, more efficient, and less costly ways to deal with *risk*. This is one of the most innovative areas of financial institutions' management today as talented young professionals continually enter the field with remarkable new risk-management ideas and tools. And thank goodness for all the creative and innovative risk-management weapons that have appeared and are still unfolding! For, as we saw in Chapter 6, financial firms face an incredible variety of different risk exposures. Indeed, financial-service managers often say they feel literally "surrounded" by risk.[1]

For example, as we discussed in Chapter 7, interest rates change and both interest revenues and interest expenses of the financial firm are immediately affected, as is the value of many of its assets, especially in its securities portfolio, and the value of the stockholders' investment in the firm. Borrowing customers may default on their loans, confronting lenders with serious credit losses and diminishing their expected earnings. Added to these problems are the demands of the regulatory community to strengthen capital—the most

---

[1]Portions of this chapter are taken from Peter S. Rose's article focusing on off-balance-sheet financing in *The Canadian Banker* [9] and are used with permission.

expensive source of funds for most financial-service institutions—in order to protect the financial firm against interest rate risk, credit risk, and other forms of risk exposure. Bankers and the managers of other financial firms have actively sought out newer, more efficient, and less costly ways to deal with these kinds of risks.

Key URL
To explore more fully the use of derivative instruments and other off-balance-sheet items and the regulatory rules that surround them, see especially,
www.fdic.gov.

In earlier chapters in Part Three we explored the workings of such risk-management tools as interest sensitivity analysis, duration gap management, financial futures and options contracts, interest-rate swaps, and interest-rate caps, floors, and collars. However, the foregoing tools focus principally upon combating interest rate risk—fending off damage to each financial firm as market interest rates change. True, that kind of protection is very important, but other costs and risks also have to be dealt with if you are going to successfully manage a financial institution today, including credit risk and the burden of having to raise new capital to meet the funding needs of your customers and satisfy regulatory standards. These management problem areas have spawned whole new weapons to help bankers and other financial-service managers do their job, including such devices as securitizing loans, selling loans off balance sheets, issuing standby letters of credit, and participating in credit derivative contracts.

Not only have these newer tools helped financial managers control risk more effectively, but they have also opened up new sources of fee income and helped serve customers better. Among the leaders in this field are such innovative companies as J. P. Morgan Chase in the banking industry, Bear Stearns in the securities field, and Prudential Inc. from the insurance industry. We take a close look at each of these risk-management, fee-generating tools in the sections that follow.

9–2 Securitizing Loans and Other Assets

The growth in securitizations of loans and other assets has been truly awesome, particularly among the largest, billion-dollar-plus banks and thrift institutions. The securitization of mortgage loans placed in pools or trusts with government agency sponsorship—the largest, but not the only segment of the asset-securitization market—reached more than $6 trillion in 2005, from just under $4 trillion five years earlier. What has led to such rapid growth? What are securitizations and why are they so popular among banks and other financial-service firms?

Securitization of loans and other assets is a simple idea for raising new funds and reducing risk exposure—so simple, in fact, that one wonders why it was not fully developed until the 1970s and 1980s. Securitizing assets requires a lending institution to set aside a group of income-earning assets, such as home mortgages or credit card loans, and to sell securities (financial claims) against those assets in the open market. As the assets pay out—for example, as borrowing customers repay the principal and interest owed on their loans—that income flows to the holders of the securities. In effect, loans are transformed into publicly traded securities. Thus, securitization is using the security markets to fund a portion of a lender's loan portfolio, allocate capital more efficiently, diversify funds sources, and lower the cost of fund raising. For its part, the securitizing institution receives back the money it originally expended to acquire the assets and uses those funds to acquire new assets or to cover operating expenses.

The bank or other lender whose loans are securitized is called the *originator* and those loans are passed on to an *issuer*, who is usually designated a *special purpose entity* (SPE). (See Exhibit 9–1.) The SPE usually is completely separate from the originator to help ensure that, if the originating lender goes bankrupt, this event will not affect the credit status of the pooled loans, making the pool and its cash flow "bankruptcy remote."

A *credit rating agency*, such as Moody's, Standard & Poor's, or Fitch, rates the securities to be sold so that investors have a better idea what the new securities are likely to be

EXHIBIT 9–1
Key Players in the
Securitization Process

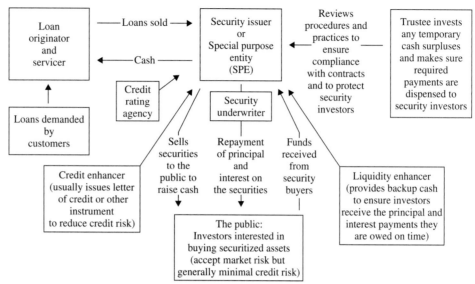

worth. The issuer then sells securities in the money and capital markets, often with the aid of a *security underwriter* (investment banker). A *trustee* is appointed to ensure that the issuer fulfills all the requirements of the transfer of loans to the pool and provides all the services promised to investors. A *servicer* (who is often also the loan originator) collects payments on the securitized loans and passes those payments along to the trustee, who ultimately makes sure that investors who hold loan-backed securities receive the proper payments on time.

Investors in the securities normally receive added assurance they will be repaid in the form of guarantees against default issued by a *credit enhancer* and guarantees against running short of cash issued by a *liquidity enhancer*. Enhancers may be internal (such as dividing the issued securities into risk classes or setting aside a cash reserve to cover loan defaults) or external (in the form of a letter of credit or credit swap). These enhancements can raise the credit rating of the securitization transaction beyond that attached to the underlying assets.

Pooling loans through securitization helps to diversify a lender's credit risk exposure and reduces the need to monitor each individual loan's payment stream. Securitization creates liquid assets out of what are often illiquid, expensive-to-sell assets and transforms these assets into new sources of funds for lenders and attractive investments for investors in the money and capital markets.

Securitizations permit lenders subject to economic downturns in their local areas to, in effect, hold a more geographically diversified loan portfolio, perhaps countering local losses with higher returns available from loans originating from different geographic areas with more buoyant economies.

Securitization is also a tool for managing interest rate risk. By choosing what loans to package and move off the balance sheet and by using securitization as an alternative source of funds it can be easier for any individual financial firm to adjust its asset portfolio so that the maturity (duration) of its assets more closely approximates the maturity (duration) of its liabilities.

Moreover, a lending institution can earn added fee income by agreeing to *service* the packaged loans. Usually this means monitoring borrowers' performance in repaying their loans, collecting payments due, and making sure adequate collateral is posted to protect

Key URLs
For additional information on securitization and other sources of fee income and risk management tools, see, for example, **www.investorwords. com, www.mortgage 101.com,** and **www.finpipe.com.**

holders of securities issued against those loans. While the lender may continue to service any assets pledged, it can remove those assets from its balance sheet, eliminating the risk of loss if the loans are not repaid or if interest-rate movements lower their value.[2] A lender may also secure additional earnings based on the spread between the interest rate being earned on the securitized assets and the interest rate paid to security holders, which usually is lower. Moreover, taxes may be reduced because of the deductibility of the interest expense incurred when assets are securitized and there is no regulatory tax in the form of deposit reserve requirements. However, the assets packaged to back any securities issued must be uniform in quality and purpose and carry investment features (such as high expected yields or ready marketability) that are attractive to investors.

As the foregoing paragraph suggests, securitization of loans creates numerous opportunities for revenue for a lender choosing this fund-raising alternative. A lender can benefit from the normal positive interest-rate spread between the average yield on the packaged loans and the coupon (promised) rate on the securities issued against those loans, capturing *residual income*. Many financial firms have also gained added income by selling guarantees to protect investors who hold loan-backed securities and by advising institutions securitizing their loans on the correct procedures.

Here is an illustration of a securitization transaction and the "cash flow waterfall" it might generate:

Expected gross portfolio yield on the pooled loans
(as a percent of the total value of the securitized loans) 20%

Promised fees and payments on these securitized loans might include the following (expressed as a percent of the total value of the securitized loans):

- Coupon rate promised to investors who buy
  the securities issued against the pool of loans 7%
- Default (charge-off) rate on the pooled loans—often
  covered by a government or private guarantee
  (enhancement) or the placement of some revenues
  generated by the pooled loans in a special reserve
  to ensure security holders against default 4%
- Fees to compensate a servicing institution for
  collecting payments from the loans in the pool
  and for monitoring the performance of the pooled loans 2%
- Fees paid for advising on how to set up the
  securitized pool of loans and security underwriting 1%
- Fees paid for providing a liquidity facility
  (enhancement) to cover any temporary shortfalls
  in cash needed to pay security investors 1%
- Residual income for the security seller, trust,
  or credit enhancer (left over after payment of servicing
  fees, expected losses, and the coupon rate promised
  to investors)—often called "the excess spread" 5%
- Sum of all fees, promised payments, and the excess spread 20%

---

[2]This step—removing loans in the securitized pool from the lender's balance sheet—can be a real plus from a regulatory point of view. Regulations generally limit the proportion of a lender's assets committed to loans in order to control risk exposure. A lender with a relatively high loan-asset ratio can bundle a group of loans and move them off its books to make the institution look financially stronger. Total assets decline while capital remains the same, so the lender's protective capital-to-assets ratio improves.

EXHIBIT 9–2
The Home Mortgage
Loan-Backed
Securities Market

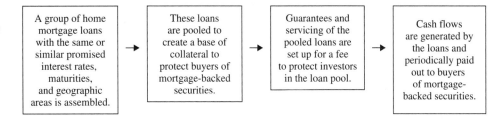

| A group of home mortgage loans with the same or similar promised interest rates, maturities, and geographic areas is assembled. | → | These loans are pooled to create a base of collateral to protect buyers of mortgage-backed securities. | → | Guarantees and servicing of the pooled loans are set up for a fee to protect investors in the loan pool. | → | Cash flows are generated by the loans and periodically paid out to buyers of mortgage-backed securities. |

The Beginnings of Securitization—The Home Mortgage Market

The concept of securitization began in the residential mortgage market of the United States. (See Exhibit 9–2.) In this huge home loan marketplace, three Government-Sponsored Enterprises (GSEs)—the Government National Mortgage Association (GNMA), the Federal National Mortgage Association (FNMA), and the Federal Home Loan Mortgage Corporation (FHLMC)—have worked to greatly improve the salability of residential mortgage loans. For example, GNMA sponsors a mortgage loan-backed securities program under which banks, thrifts, and other lenders can pool their home mortgages that are insured against default by the Federal Housing Administration (FHA), Veterans Administration (VA), and the Farmers Home Administration (FMHA) and issue securities against the pooled loans. GNMA insures the interest and principal payments owed to holders of those securities it sponsors. While GNMA guarantees the issuance of securities by private lenders, FNMA creates its own mortgage-backed securities, which it sells to individuals and major institutional investors like banks, insurance companies, and pension plans, using the proceeds of these sales to purchase packages of both conventional and government-insured home mortgage loans from lending institutions.

CMOs

For its part, FHLMC purchases pools of both conventional and government-insured home mortgage loans from private lending institutions and pays for these by issuing FHLMC-guaranteed mortgage-backed securities. Beginning in the 1980s with the cooperation of First Boston Corporation (later a part of Credit Suisse), a major security dealer, FHLMC developed a new mortgage-backed instrument—the collateralized mortgage obligation (CMO)—in which investors are offered different classes of mortgage-backed securities with different expected cash flow patterns. CMOs typically are created from a multistep process in which home mortgage loans are first pooled together, and then GNMA-guaranteed securities are issued against the mortgage pool that are purchased by investors. These securities are placed in a trust account off the lender's balance sheet and several different classes of CMOs are issued as claims against the security pool in order to raise new funds. As issuer of CMOs the lender hopes to make a profit by packaging the loan-backed securities in a form that appeals to many different types of investors. Each class (tranche) of CMOs promises a different coupon rate of return to investors and carries a different maturity and risk that some of the mortgage loans in the underlying pool will be paid off early, reducing the investor's expected yield.[3] (See Exhibit 9–3.)

With a CMO the different tiers (tranches) in which securities are issued receive the interest payments to which they are entitled, but all loan principal payments flow first to securities issued in the top tier until these top-tier instruments are fully retired. Subsequently

[3]See Chapter 10 for a discussion of *prepayment risk* and its implications for investors in loan-backed securities, such as CMOs and pass-throughs.

EXHIBIT 9–3
The Structure of
Collateralized
Mortgage Obligations
(CMOs)

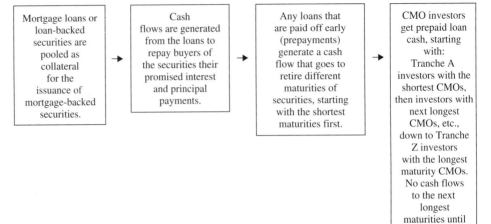

Mortgage loans or loan-backed securities are pooled as collateral for the issuance of mortgage-backed securities. → Cash flows are generated from the loans to repay buyers of the securities their promised interest and principal payments. → Any loans that are paid off early (prepayments) generate a cash flow that goes to retire different maturities of securities, starting with the shortest maturities first. → CMO investors get prepaid loan cash, starting with: Tranche A investors with the shortest CMOs, then investors with next longest CMOs, etc., down to Tranche Z investors with the longest maturity CMOs. No cash flows to the next longest maturities until all holders of shorter maturities are paid off.

Key URLs
To learn more about loan securitizations see especially **www.securitization.net** and **www.fdic.gov**.

received principal payments then go to investors who purchased securities belonging to the next tier until all securities in that tier are paid out, and so on until the point is reached where all CMO tiers are finally paid off. The upper tiers of a CMO carry shorter maturities, which reduces their reinvestment risk exposure. In contrast, the lower tiers carry lengthier maturities, and, hence, have more prepayment protection and promise higher expected returns.

Certain CMO instruments include a special Z tranche carrying the highest degree of risk exposure because this particular tranche generates no principal or interest payments until all other CMO tiers are paid off. Among the more exotic CMOs developed recently are floaters (whose rate of return is related to a particular interest rate index), superfloaters (which yield a multiple change in return based upon a particular interest rate index), and so-called "jump Z tranches" that may suddenly catapult to first place among the tiers of a CMO depending upon events in the market. These and other complex loan-backed instruments in recent years have become so complicated that even sophisticated traders have stumbled at times with sizable losses.

Home Equity Loans

During the 1990s a new market for home equity loan-backed securities grew rapidly. *Home equity loans* permit home owners to borrow against the residual value of their residence— that is, the difference between the current market value of their home and the amount of the mortgage loan against that property. Bonds backed by pools of home equity loans often carry higher yields than other loan-backed securities because of their substantial prepayment risk when interest rates fall and some homeowners elect to pay off their home equity loans early. Competition in this market has become intense among banks and other lending institutions trying to attract as many home equity borrowers as possible, increasing the risk of home-equity-backed securities for investors buying them.

Key URLs
To learn more about the legal aspects and structure of securitizations, see, for example, **www.realcorporate lawyer.com**.

Loan-Backed Bonds

Yet another securitization device to help raise funds has appeared in recent years in the form of *loan-backed bonds*. Lenders can set aside a group of loans on their balance sheet, issue bonds, and pledge the loans as collateral to backstop the bonds. Unlike CMOs and similar loan-backed instruments, which allow lenders to remove loans from their balance sheets, loan-backed bonds usually stay on the lender's balance sheet as liabilities. Moreover, while the loans backing these bonds provide collateral for borrowing (so that if the bond-issuing institution fails, the bondholders will have a priority claim against the pledged loans), the cash flow from the pooled loans is not the sole source of cash to pay the bonds' interest and principal. Rather, monies owed on loan-backed bonds can come from *any* revenues generated by the issuing financial firm. Because the market value of the loans pledged as collateral is normally greater in amount than the volume of bonds issued, loan-backed bonds may actually carry higher credit ratings than the issuing institution itself.

What does a lending institution gain from issuing loan-backed bonds? First, the cost of raising funds may go down because investors consider the bonds to have low default risk due to the greater dollar value of the loans that back the bonds. In fact, in the case of depository institutions it is often cheaper to issue such bonds than it is to sell large-denomination deposits that are not fully covered by government deposit insurance, suggesting that some institutions can replace uninsured deposits with bonds backed by selected assets. Moreover, the bonds generally have longer maturities than deposits, so a depository institution can extend the maturity of the liability side of its balance sheet by issuing loan-backed bonds, perhaps to better match the longer maturities (durations) of its assets. Unfortunately, a portion of this double benefit from loan-backed bonds stems from a depository institution's ability to sell insured deposits at low interest rates because of government-supplied deposit insurance, resulting in a moral hazard problem in which the tax-paying public may wind up stuck with losses.

Key URLs
One of the most rapidly growing segments of the securitization industry has been the creation of massive pools of home equity loans. See especially Lehman Brothers Holdings, Inc., at **www.lehman.com** and Asset-Backed Securities by Phillip L. Zweig at **www.econlib.org/library/ enc/assetbacked securities.html.**

Of course, there are some disadvantages from issuing loan-backed bonds. For example, any loans pledged behind these bonds must be held on a lender's balance sheet until the bonds reach maturity, which decreases the overall liquidity of a loan portfolio. Moreover, with these loans remaining on its balance sheet the lender must meet regulatory-imposed capital requirements to back the loans. At the same time, since a depository institution must hold more loans as collateral than the amount of bonds it issues, more deposits and other borrowings must be used to make up the difference, increasing the amount of liabilities taken on.

Examples of Other Assets That Have Been Securitized

In addition to securitized home mortgages there are many other examples of securitized assets. For example, in October 1986, First Boston Corp. (later a part of Credit Suisse), one of the world's leading investment banking firms, announced plans to sell $3.2 billion of securities backed by low-interest automobile loans granted originally by General Motors Acceptance Corporation (GMAC). One unusual twist was the tiered structure of this security offering, which consisted of a combination of short-term, medium-term, and long-term bonds, each with a different priority of claim to the income from the packaged auto loans (labeled *CARs*, or certificates of automobile receivables). A subsidiary of First Boston actually owned the loans after purchasing them from GMAC; therefore, investors acquiring the associated bonds were not given recourse to either First Boston or GMAC in the event some of the loans defaulted. However, GMAC did promise to repurchase up to 5 percent of the loans securitized in order to cover any loans that turned sour.

Another prominent example of securitized loans is the market for participations in discounted debt issued by less-developed countries (LDCs) and syndicated Euroloans. These international loans, extended mainly to governments and multinational companies, sometimes have not paid out as planned. In addition, many domestic securitizations have arisen out of adverse loan-loss situations faced by lenders that have been battered by losses on credit-card, real estate, and other loans and see securitization as a way to clean up their portfolios. With fewer risky and nonperforming loans on the books a lender looks financially stronger and may be able to lower its borrowing costs.

In the United States, loan-backed securities have been issued against an ever-widening range of loans, including commercial mortgages, Small Business Administration loans,

ETHICS IN BANKING AND FINANCIAL SERVICES

ETHICAL CONTROVERSIES SWIRLING AROUND FANNIE MAE AND FREDDIE MAC

In Chapter 7 we explored the consequences of interest-rate risk for the two best-known mortgage banks in the world—FNMA or Fannie Mae and FHLMC or Freddie Mac—which are the biggest private-sector guarantors of mortgage-backed securities. Unfortunately, interest-rate risk is not the only risk faced by Fannie and Freddie. They are now confronted with a swarm of ethical issues that *may* threaten their political survival.

These two giants—big enough to rank among the top 10 U.S. financial institutions—make markets for the sale of home loans and issue billions of dollars in guarantees for mortgage-backed securities. Compared to most private financial institutions Fannie and Freddie get by with little equity capital from their stockholders because they *seem* to carry the unofficial backing of the United States Government. Many investors assume Fannie and Freddie would be rescued if their failure seemed imminent. These agencies have made use of this implicit backing by borrowing heavily to finance their market-making activities, expanding their combined portfolio upward by close to a trillion and a half dollars.

The ethics of allowing a government-sponsored enterprise (GSE) to grow so fast that it pushes out of the market some privately owned mortgage institutions has aroused great controversy in recent years. The huge size and risk exposure of Fannie and Freddie have recently created concerns for the future stability of the credit markets. Moreover, these powerful agencies have come under fire for accounting irregularities, operating inefficiencies, and allegedly charging excessive fees for their services.

Fannie and Freddie have fought back. They contend that their purchasing huge quantities of home loans and guaranteeing repayment of billions in mortgage-backed securities have made possible home ownership for millions of Americans, encouraging lenders to extend long-term, fixed-rate mortgages that home buyers can afford. Moreover, these GSEs claim they have strengthened the U.S. economy by attracting thousands of foreign investors into the dollar-denominated securitization market.

The Office of Federal Housing Enterprise Oversight (OFHEO), which oversees Fannie and Freddie, recently asked these agencies to strengthen their capital and moderate their growth. OFHEO also launched an investigation into Fannie's and Freddie's accounting methods, focusing especially on how they value mortgage-backed securities, set fees, and determine salaries for their top executives. If Fannie's and Freddie's growth were slowed and their huge share of the roughly $9 trillion U.S. home-mortgage market began to decline, then such industry leaders as Bank of America, Countrywide Mortgage, and Washington Mutual would probably rush in to take up the slack. One financial firm's misfortune could become another's gain!

---

mobile home loans, credit-card receivables, truck leases, and computer leases. (The commercial mortgage-backed securities (CMBS) market, pooling loans against shopping malls, office towers, hotels, and other business structures, has been especially dynamic of late and has posted an exceptional default rate of only about 1 percent.) A new dimension was added to the market in the late 1980s when banks and other intermediaries began to help their corporate customers securitize credit and lease receivables and issue asset-backed commercial paper in order to provide these customers with low-cost, stable funding sources.

Securitization is *not* a funds source available to all lenders. Recent estimates suggest that the minimum-size loan-backed securities offering likely to be successful is at least $50 million. However, smaller institutions are often active investors in these securities, and it is possible for several small lenders to pool their loans and jointly issue securities.

Loan-backed securities closely resemble traditional bonds, promising a fixed interest rate payable monthly, quarterly, or semiannually. These securities often carry various forms of **credit enhancement** to give buyers the impression they are low-risk investments. These credit enhancers may include a credit letter from another financial institution willing to guarantee repayment or a dedicated cash reserve, created from the excess returns earned by the securitized loans over the amount of interest paid to security holders, in order to cover losses.

Innovation has crept into the securitization market in recent years. One interesting example lies in the insurance industry, responding to recent policyholder claims associated

Principal Types of Asset-backed Securities Often Created Today

Residential Mortgage-Backed Securities (GSE-backed Mortgage Pools and Private Mortgage Pass-Throughs and CMOs)

Commercial Mortgage-Backed Securities (CMBS)

Home Equity Loan-Backed Securities

Certificates of Credit Card Receivables (CCRs)

Certificates of Auto Receivables (CARs)

Mobile Home Loan-Backed Securities

Small Business Administration (SBA) Loan-Backed Securities

Securities Backed by Truck Lease Receivables

Securities Backed by Computer Lease Receivables

Asset-Backed Commercial Paper (ABCP) (Supported by Trade Receivables)

Participations in International Loans

Catastrophe-Linked Securities (Cat Bonds)

Miscellaneous Asset-Backed Instruments (including such assets as equipment loans, default swap contracts, lottery receivables, and second mortgages)

with such disasters as hurricanes and earthquakes. *Catastrophe-linked securities* ("cat bonds") have been developed to shift risk from insurers to the financial markets. In this case an SPE is created to issue securities designed to cover losses above a given threshold amount from different kinds of disasters (such as Hurricane Katrina). The proceeds of the security issue may be invested in high-quality fixed-income instruments (such as U.S. Treasury securities) in order to generate sufficient cash to cover excess losses or serve as a source of repayment for the "cat bonds."

A final trend in the securitization and loan-backed securities market that must be borne in mind is its continuing *international expansion* today. This market owes most of its origins to the United States, but it exploded on the international scene as the 1990s progressed and the 21st century opened. Nowhere was this more the case than in the European Community, where new groups of investors and new loan-backed security issuers appeared in droves, freely adopting innovations from the U.S. market and hiring away securitization specialists from U.S. companies. More recently many Asian lenders have also entered the securitization marketplace.

The Impact of Securitization upon Lending Institutions

Securitization is likely to affect the management of lending institutions in several different ways. Certainly it raises the level of competition for the best-quality loans between lending institutions. Securitization may also raise the level of competition among lenders trying to attract deposits because knowledgeable depositors may find that they can get a better yield by purchasing loan-backed securities than by buying deposits. Securitization has made it possible for many corporations to bypass traditional lenders and, instead, seek credit in the open market through securities sales, thereby reducing lenders' loan revenues.

However, lenders have been able to benefit indirectly from securitizations conducted by their corporate customers by providing, for a fee, *credit letters* (discussed later in this chapter) to enhance the credit rating of corporations selling their securities in the public market. Moreover, lenders can generate added fee income by providing backup liquidity in case the securitizing company runs short of cash and by acting as underwriters for *new* asset-backed security issues. Lenders also find they can use securitization to assist a good corporate customer in finding financing without having to make any direct loans to that customer, which would inflate the lender's risky assets. Overall, securitization allows a lender to originate a greater volume of loans at lower cost in terms of deposit insurance fees and reserve requirements and at lower credit, interest-rate, and liquidity risk with greater diversity of funding sources.

Regulators' Concerns about Securitization

Despite its many advantages for lenders, securitization has increased regulators' concerns about the soundness and safety of individual lenders and the financial system. In some instances the rapid growth of asset securitizations has led to sloppy management practices and a lack of adequate risk controls. Regulators today are looking more closely at the risk of (*a*) having to come up with large amounts of liquidity in a hurry to make payments to investors holding asset-backed securities and cover bad loans; (*b*) the risk of agreeing to serve as an underwriter for asset-backed securities that cannot be sold; (*c*) the risk of acting as a credit enhancer and underestimating the need for loan-loss reserves; (*d*) the risk that unqualified trustees will fail to protect investors in asset-backed instruments; and (*e*) the risk of loan servicers being unable to satisfactorily monitor loan performance and collect monies owed to lenders and investors. Regulators today are also focusing on the impact of securitization on the remaining portfolio of loans that are *not* securitized, looking for possible deterioration in loan portfolio quality.

Concept Check

9–1.   What does *securitization* of assets mean?

9–2.   What kinds of assets are most amenable to the securitization process?

9–3.   What advantages does securitization offer lending institutions?

9–4.   What risks of securitization should the managers of lending institutions be aware of?

9–5.   Suppose that a bank securitizes a package of its loans that bear a gross annual interest yield of 13 percent. The securities issued against the loan package promise interested investors an annualized yield of 8.25 percent. The expected default rate on the packaged loans is 3.5 percent. The bank agrees to pay an annual fee of 0.35 percent to a security dealer to cover the cost of underwriting and advisory services and a fee of 0.25 percent to Arunson Mortgage Servicing Corporation to process the expected payments generated by the packaged loans. If the above items represent all the costs associated with this securitization can you calculate the percentage amount of *residual income* the bank expects to earn from this particular transaction?

9–3 Sales of Loans to Raise Funds and Reduce Risk

Filmtoid
What 1993 made-for-HBO movie finds investment bankers scurrying for funds to support the leveraged buyout of RJR Nabisco?
Answer: *Barbarians at the Gate.*

Not only can loans be used as collateral for issuing securities to raise new funds, but the loans themselves can be sold in their entirety to a new owner. **Loan sales** are carried out today by banks, security dealers, and other financial firms of widely varying sizes. Included among the principal buyers of loans are banks (including foreign banking firms seeking a foothold in the domestic market), insurance companies, pension funds, nonfinancial corporations, mutual funds (including vulture and hedge funds that choose to concentrate on purchasing troubled loans), and security dealers (such as Goldman Sachs and Merrill Lynch). Among the leading sellers of these loans are Deutsche Bank, J. P. Morgan Chase, the Bank of America, and ING Bank of the Netherlands. (See Exhibit 9–4.)

EXHIBIT 9–4

The Impact of Loan Sales

Source: Peter S. Rose, "New Benefits, New Pitfalls," *The Canadian Banker*, September/October 1988.

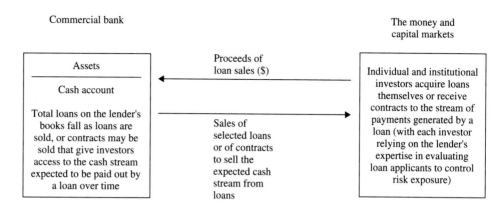

Most loans sold in the open market by banks usually mature within 90 days and may be either new loans or loans that have been on the seller's books for some time. The loan sale market received a boost during the 1980s when a wave of corporate buyouts led to the creation of thousands of loans to fund *highly leveraged transactions* (HLTs). The market for such loans in the United States expanded more than tenfold during the 1980s, but then fell in the 1990s and grew moderately in the new century as some corporate buyouts cooled off and federal regulatory agencies tightened their rules regarding the acceptability of such loans. Generally, HLT-related loans are secured by the assets of the borrowing company and, typically, are long-term, covering in some cases up to eight years. In contrast, most other loans sold carry maturities of only a few weeks or months, are generally extended to borrowers with investment-grade credit ratings, and carry interest rates that usually are connected to short-term corporate loan rates (such as the prime rate).

Typically, the seller retains **servicing rights** on the sold loans, enabling the selling institution to generate fee income (often one-quarter or three-eighths of a percentage point of the amount of the loans sold) by collecting interest and principal payments from borrowers and passing the proceeds along to loan buyers. Servicing institutions also monitor the performance of borrowers and act on behalf of loan buyers to make sure borrowers are adhering to the terms of their loans.

Most loans are purchased in million-dollar units by investors that already operate in the loan marketplace and have special knowledge of the debtor. During the 1990s a multibillion-dollar market for floating-rate corporate loans arose as some insurance companies and mutual funds that had purchased ordinary bonds in the past switched some of their money into corporate loans. These salable loans appear to have several advantages over bonds for many investors due to their strict loan covenants, floating interest rates, and array of both short and long maturities.

Two of the most popular types of loan sales are: (*a*) **participation loans** and (*b*) **assignments.** In a participation loan the purchaser is an outsider (i.e., not a partner) to the loan contract between lender and borrower. Only if there are significant alterations in the terms of the original loan can the buyer of a participation exercise any influence over the terms of the loan contract. Thus, the buyer of a participation faces substantial risk: the loan seller may fail or the borrower may fail. This means that the buyer of a loan participation must watch both borrower and seller closely. As a result of these limitations many loan sales today are by *assignment*. Under an assignment, ownership of a loan is transferred to the buyer, who thereby acquires a direct claim against the borrower. This means that, in some cases, the borrower has to agree to the sale of his or her loan before an assignment can be made.

A third type of loan sale is the **loan strip.** Loans strips are short-dated pieces of a longer-term loan and often mature in a few days or weeks. The buyer of a strip is entitled to a fraction of the expected income from a loan. With strips, the selling institution retains the risk of borrower default and may have to put up some of its own funds to support the loan until it reaches maturity.

Reasons Behind Loan Sales

There are many reasons why some lenders have turned to loan sales as an important method for funding their operations. One reason is the opportunity loan sales provide for getting rid of lower-yielding assets in order to make room for higher-yielding assets when interest rates rise. Moreover, selling loans and replacing them with more marketable assets can increase a lender's liquidity, better preparing the institution for deposit withdrawals or other cash needs. Loan sales remove both credit risk and interest-rate risk from the lender's balance sheet and may generate fee income up front. Then, too, selling loans off the balance sheet slows the growth of assets, which helps management maintain a better balance between growth of capital and the acceptance of risk in the lending function. In this way loan sales help lenders please regulators, who have put considerable pressure on heavily regulated institutions to get rid of their riskiest assets and strengthen their capital in recent years. A few studies (e.g., Hassan [7]), suggest that investors in the capital markets generally view loan sales as a way to reduce risk for the selling institution, helping to lower its cost of capital and diversify its asset portfolio. Buyers purchasing these loans receive help in diversifying their loan portfolio, acquiring loans from new regions outside their traditional trade areas. Diversification of this sort can lower risk exposure and result in lower borrowing costs for the loan buyer.

The development of the loan sales market may have profound implications for the future of lending institutions. The growth of this market means that banks, for example, can make some loans without taking in deposits and cover deposit withdrawals merely by selling loans. Moreover, depository institutions may have less need for deposit insurance or for borrowing from their central bank. Because loan sales are so similar to issuing securities, this financing device blurs the distinction between financial intermediaries, like banks and finance companies, that make loans and other financial institutions that trade securities.

The Risks in Loan Sales

Loan sales are another form of investment banking, in which the seller trades on his or her superior ability to evaluate the creditworthiness of a borrower and sells that expertise (represented by the content of the loan contract) to another investor. Investors may be willing to purchase loans that a bank or other trusted lender originates because they have confidence in the seller's ability to identify good-quality borrowers and write an advantageous loan contract. Nevertheless, loan sales as a source of funds for lenders are not without their problems. For example, the best-quality loans are most likely to find a ready resale market. But if the seller isn't careful, it will find itself selling off its soundest loans, leaving its portfolio heavily stocked with poor-quality loans. This development is likely to trigger the attention of regulators, and the lending institution may find itself facing demands from regulatory agencies to strengthen its capital.

Moreover, a sold loan can turn sour just as easily as a direct loan from the originating lender to its own customer. Indeed, the seller may have done a poor job of evaluating the borrower's financial condition. Buying an existing loan, therefore, obligates the purchasing institution to review the financial condition of *both* the seller and the borrower.

In some instances, the seller will agree to give the loan purchaser *recourse* to the seller for all or a portion of those sold loans that become delinquent. In effect, the purchaser gets a *put option*, allowing him or her to sell a troubled loan back to its originator. This arrangement forces buyer and seller to share the risk of loan default. Recourse agreements are not common in today's loan market, however, in part because some federal regulations require a lender selling loans with recourse to hold reserves behind those loans and to count them as part of its assets when determining the lender's required level of capital. However, many lenders seem to feel obligated to reacquire the troubled loans they sold to a customer, even if there is no legal requirement to do so, to protect an established customer relationship.

Finally, lending institutions must recognize that raising funds by selling loans is likely to be affected by a strong *cyclical* factor. In some years, particularly when the economy is expanding rapidly, there may be an abundance of salable loans, while in other years the volume of salable loans may decline significantly. Indeed, the loan sales market declined sharply in the closing years of the 20th century and continued depressed as the new century opened. More businesses have been bypassing traditional lenders for the loans they need, leading to a decrease in the availability of quality loans that are the easiest to sell. Moreover, corporate merger and acquisition activity has slowed and other sources of funds have opened up through deregulation. However, some authorities expect a future rebound in loan sales due to tougher capital-adequacy requirements, which may encourage banks, in particular, to continue to sell off selected loans and lower their capital requirements. Also, there has been a continuing swing among many international banks (such as Deutsche Bank of Germany and J.P. Morgan Chase) toward more market trading in place of traditional lending, causing these institutions to sell off more loans on their balance sheets.

Concept Check

9–6. What advantages do *sales of loans* have for lending institutions trying to raise funds?

9–7. Are there any disadvantages to using loan sales as a significant source of funding for banks and other financial institutions?

9–8. What is *loan servicing?*

9–9. How can loan servicing be used to increase income?

9–4 Standby Credit Letters to Reduce the Risk of Nonpayment or Nonperformance

One of the most rapidly growing of all risk-focused markets in recent years has been the market for **financial guarantees**—instruments used to enhance the credit standing of a borrower to help insure lenders against default and to reduce the borrower's financing costs. Financial guarantees are designed to ensure the timely repayment of the principal and interest from a loan even if the borrower goes bankrupt or cannot perform a contractual obligation. One of the most popular guarantees in the banking and insurance communities is the **standby letter of credit (SLC).** The growth of standby letters has been substantial in recent years, although this remains a large-bank market. Well over 90 percent of SLCs issued by U.S.-insured commercial banks come from those banking firms above a billion dollars in assets each.

SLCs may include (1) *performance guarantees,* in which a financial firm guarantees that a building or other project will be completed on time, or (2) *default guarantees,* under which a financial institution pledges the repayment of defaulted notes when borrowers cannot pay. These standbys enable borrowing customers to get the credit they require at lower cost and on more flexible terms. In order to sell SLCs successfully, however, the service provider must have a higher credit rating than its customer.

A standby credit letter is a **contingent obligation** of the letter's issuer. The issuing firm, in return for a fee, agrees to *guarantee* the credit of its customer or to guarantee the fulfillment of a contract made by its customer with a third party. The key advantages to a financial institution issuing SLCs are the following:

1. Letters of credit earn a fee for providing the service (usually around 0.5 percent to 1 percent of the amount of credit involved).
2. They aid a customer, who can usually borrow more cheaply when armed with the guarantee, without using up the guaranteeing institution's scarce reserves.
3. Such guarantees usually can be issued at relatively low cost because the issuer may already know the financial condition of its standby credit customer (e.g. when that customer applied for his or her last loan).
4. The probability usually is low that the issuer of an SLC will ever be called upon to pay.

Standbys have grown in recent years for several reasons:

1. The rapid growth of *direct finance* worldwide, with borrowers selling their securities directly to investors rather than going to traditional lenders. Direct financing has increased investor concerns about borrower defaults and resulted in increased demand for SLCs.
2. The risk of economic fluctuations (recessions, inflation, etc.) has led to demand for risk-reducing devices.
3. The opportunity standbys offer lenders to use their credit evaluation skills to earn additional fee income without the immediate commitment of funds.
4. The relatively low cost of issuing SLCs—unlike selling deposits, they carry zero reserve requirements and no insurance fees.

The Structure of SLCs

SLCs contain three essential elements: (1) a commitment from the **issuer** (often a bank or insurance company today), (2) an **account party** (for whom the letter is issued), and (3) a **beneficiary** (usually a lender concerned about the safety of funds committed to the account party). The key feature of SLCs is that they are usually *not* listed on the issuer's or the beneficiary's balance sheet. This is because a standby is only a *contingent liability*. In most cases, it will expire unexercised. Delivery of funds to the beneficiary can occur only if something unexpected happens to the account party (such as bankruptcy or nonperformance). Moreover, the beneficiary can claim funds from the issuer only if the beneficiary meets *all* the conditions laid down in the SLC. If any of those conditions are not met, the issuer is not obligated to pay. (See Exhibit 9–5.)

The Value and Pricing of Standby Letters

Under the terms of an SLC, the issuer of the letter will pay any interest or principal to the beneficiary that is left unpaid by its customer, the account party. In effect, the issuer agrees

EXHIBIT 9–5

The Nature of a Standby Credit Agreement (SLC)

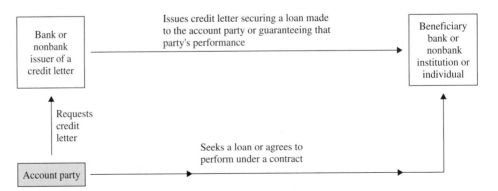

for a fee to take on a risk that, in the absence of the SLC, would be carried fully by the beneficiary. Therefore, the beneficiary may be willing to lend the account party more money or provide the same amount of funds at a lower interest rate than if there were no standby.

In general, an account party will seek an SLC if the issuer's fee for providing the guarantee is less than the value assigned to the guarantee by the beneficiary. Thus, if P is the price of the standby, NL is the cost of a nonguaranteed loan, and GL is the cost of a loan backed by a standby guarantee, then a borrower is likely to seek an SLC if

$$P < (NL - GL) \qquad\qquad \textbf{(9–1)}$$

For example, suppose a borrower can get a nonguaranteed loan at an interest cost of 7.50 percent, but is told that a quality SLC would reduce the loan's interest cost to 6.75 percent. If a bank offers the borrower a standby for 0.50 percent of the loan's face value, it will pay the borrower to get the guarantee because the savings on the loan of (7.50 percent – 6.75 percent) or 0.75 percent exceeds the 0.50 percent guarantee fee.

In turn, the value to the beneficiary of an SLC is a function of the credit ratings of issuer and account party and the information cost of assessing their credit standing. Beneficiaries will value highly the guarantee of an issuer with a superior credit rating. Account parties will be less likely to seek out a weak institution to issue a credit letter, because such a guarantee gives them little bargaining power. If the cost of obtaining relevant information about the condition of the guaranteeing institution or about the account party is high, the beneficiary also may find little or no value in an SLC.

Sources of Risk with Standbys

Standby credits carry several forms of risk exposure for the institution (beneficiary) relying upon them. For example, the issuing institution may not be able to cover its commitment, resulting in default. Also, some jurisdictions have held that an issuing institution cannot be forced to pay off on an SLC if doing so would force it to violate regulations (e.g., if the amount to be paid exceeds a bank's legal lending limit).

Beneficiaries relying on standbys received from other institutions must take care that such agreements are fully documented so they know how to file a valid claim for payment. A beneficiary cannot legally obtain reimbursement from the issuer unless *all* of the conditions required for successful presentation of a credit letter are met. In some bankruptcy court jurisdictions it has been held that any payments made upon presentation of a valid SLC are "preference items" under the federal bankruptcy code and, therefore, must be returned to the account party if bankruptcy is declared.

There also may be substantial interest rate and liquidity risks. If the issuer is compelled to pay under a credit letter without prior notice, it may be forced to raise substantial amounts of funds at unfavorable interest rates. Managers can use various devices to reduce risk exposure from standbys they have issued, such as

1. Frequently renegotiating the terms of any loans extended to customers who have SLCs so that loan terms are continually adjusted to the customer's changing circumstances and there is less need for beneficiaries to press for collection.
2. Diversifying SLCs issued by region and by industry to avoid concentration of risk exposure.
3. Selling participations in standbys in order to share risk with other lending institutions.

Regulatory Concerns about SLCs

Recent rapid growth of contingent obligations like SLCs has raised the specter of more institutional failures if more standbys than expected are presented for collection. For example, many regulators fear that investors in bank securities, including holders of uninsured deposits, may be lulled to sleep (i.e., will tend to underprice bank risk) if a bank books fewer loans but at the same time takes on a large volume of SLCs. Unfortunately, there is ample incentive for lenders to take on more standbys due to their relatively low production costs and the added leverage they generate because no cash reserves are required, at least at the beginning of the agreement.

Examiners and regulatory agencies are working to keep risk exposure from standbys under control. Several new regulatory rules are in use today. For example, in the banking community,

1. Banks must apply the same credit standards for approving SLCs as they do for approving direct loans.
2. Banks must count standbys as loans when assessing how risk-exposed the institution is to a single credit customer.
3. Since the adoption of international capital agreements between the United States and other leading nations (discussed in Chapter 15), banks have been required to post capital behind most standbys as though these contingent agreements were loans.

Research Studies on Standbys, Loan Sales, and Securitizations

Several studies have addressed the issue of the relative riskiness of direct loans versus standbys, loan sales, and securitizations for lenders. For example, Bennett [1] observed that direct loans carry substantially higher market risk premiums than do SLCs. This supports the idea that investors as a whole believe standbys carry significantly less risk than loans themselves. One reason may be that SLCs are usually requested by prime-quality borrowers. Another factor may be the market's expectation that most standbys will never be presented for collection. Apparently issuing SLCs has essentially *no* impact on the deposit costs of banks.

More recently, Hassan [2] finds evidence from option-pricing models that stockholders and creditors view off-balance-sheet SLCs as reducing bank risk by increasing the diversification of assets. Hassan argues that imposing capital requirements on standbys, therefore, may not be appropriate because, if properly used, they can reduce risk for the issuers of these letters. Moreover, various researchers have argued that standbys, loan sales, and securitizations are principally *defensive* reactions by financial firm managers to regulation. These off-balance-sheet activities can be viewed simply as attempts to increase financial leverage, thereby augmenting stockholder returns. Contingent obligations are being substituted for regular assets and deposits whenever regulation increases the cost of more traditional intermediation activities.

But according to James [3], for example, regulation is not the only motivation for loan sales, standbys, and other nontraditional fund-raising devices. These transactions are better viewed as substitutes for collateralized debt because depository institutions are prohibited from selling collateralized deposits (with the exception of government deposits where specific assets are pledged to protect these deposits). Both regulations and the cost of deposit insurance can be incentives for banks, for example, to pursue off-balance-sheet activities. However, if these new instruments increase the value of financial firms (i.e., raise their stock prices), it might be a mistake to severely restrict them by government regulation.

Concept Check

9–10. What are *standby credit letters?* Why have they grown so rapidly in recent years?

9–11. Who are the principal parties to a standby credit agreement?

9–12. What risks accompany a standby credit letter for *(a)* the issuer and *(b)* the beneficiary?

9–13. How can a lending institution mitigate the risks inherent in issuing standby credit letters?

9–5 Credit Derivatives: Contracts for Reducing Credit Risk Exposure on the Balance Sheet

Securitizing assets, selling loans, and issuing standby credits can help to reduce not only interest-rate risk exposure but also exposure to *credit risk*. Often, however, it is more efficient to reduce credit risk with a comparatively new financial instrument—the **credit derivative**—an over-the-counter agreement offering protection against loss when default occurs on a loan, bond, or other debt instrument.

The credit derivative market today is one of the fastest growing in the world. For example, according to the International Swaps and Derivatives Association the notional (face) value of credit default swaps—the biggest share of the credit derivatives market—topped $8 trillion by the end of 2004, increasing about nine-fold in only three years! So rapid has been the growth of these instruments that recordkeeping, especially tracking contract assignments and settlements, often lags well behind actual events in the marketplace, possibly increasing market volatility and risk exposure.

Banks generally lead the credit derivatives market, followed by security firms, insurance companies, and hedge funds. Banks and security firms use credit derivatives to protect their own portfolios of corporate IOUs and, acting as dealers, also sell this form of risk protection to their largest customers.

Credit Swaps

Key URLs:
One of the most controversial institutions in the credit derivatives market is hedge funds that value these credit agreements and buy and sell them in large volume. For an overview of this aspect of the credit derivatives market see **www.Hedge-Funds. big.com, www. credit-deriv.com/,** and **http://money. cnn.com**.

One prominent example of a credit derivative is the **credit swap,** where two lenders agree to exchange a portion of their customers' loan repayments. For example, Banks A and B may find a dealer, such as a large insurance company, that agrees to draw up a credit swap contract between the two banks. Bank A then transmits an amount (perhaps $100 million) in interest and principal payments that it collects from its credit customers to the dealer. Bank B also sends all or a portion of the loan payments its customers make to the same dealer. The dealer will ultimately pass these payments along to the other bank that signed the swap contract. (See Exhibit 9–6.) Usually the dealer levies a fee for the service of bringing these two swap partners together and may also guarantee each swap partner's performance for an additional charge.

What is the advantage for each partner in such an agreement? In the example shown below each bank is granted the opportunity to further spread out the risk in its loan portfolio, especially if the lenders involved are located in different market areas. Because each lender's portfolio may come from a different market, a credit swap permits each institution to broaden the number of markets from which it collects loan revenues and principal, thus reducing each institution's dependence on one or a narrow set of market areas.

A popular variation on the credit swap just described—a *total return swap*—may involve a financial institution (dealer) that guarantees the swap parties a specific rate of return on their credit assets. For example, a swap dealer may guarantee Bank A a return on its business loans that is 3 percentage points higher than the long-term government bond rate. In this instance Bank A would have exchanged the risky return from a portion of its loans for a much more stable rate of reward based upon the return from a government security.

EXHIBIT 9–6
Example of a Credit Swap

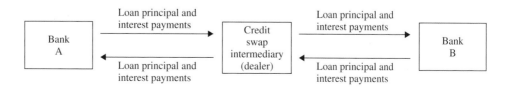

Key URLs
The recent rapid
expansion of credit
derivative contracts
worldwide has also
resulted in a rapid
increase in new Web
sites devoted to this
instrument, including
www.credit-deriv.com,
www.margrabe.com,
www.statestreet.com,
and **www.vankam**
pen.com.

Factoid
Who are the leading
institutions trading in
the credit derivatives
market today?
Answer: The leading
traders in credit
derivatives include J.P.
Morgan Chase,
Deutsche Bank, Morgan
Stanley, Goldman
Sachs Group, and
Citigroup.

Another example of a total return swap might rest upon a loan that Bank A has recently made to one of its commercial customers. Bank A then agrees to pay Bank B the total return earned on the loan (including interest and principal payments plus any increase [appreciation] in the loan's market value that occurs). Bank B, for its part, agrees to pay A the London InterBank Offer Rate (LIBOR) plus a small interest rate spread and to compensate A for any depreciation that occurs in the loan's market value. In essence, Bank B bears the credit risk associated with Bank A's loan just as though it actually owned Bank A's loan, even though it is not the owner. This swap may terminate early if the borrower defaults on the loan. (See Exhibit 9–7.)

Credit Options

Another popular credit risk derivative today is the **credit option,** which guards against losses in the value of a credit asset or helps to offset higher borrowing costs that may occur due to changes in credit ratings. For example, a depository institution worried about default on a large $100 million loan it has just made might approach an options dealer about an option contract that pays off if the loan declines significantly in value or turns bad. If the borrowing customer pays off as promised, the lender collects the loan revenue it expected to gather and the option issued by the dealer (option-writer) goes unused. The lender involved will, of course, lose the premium it paid to the dealer writing the option. Many financial institutions will take out similar credit options to protect the value of securities held in their investment portfolios should the securities' issuer fail to pay or should the securities decline significantly in value due to a change in credit standing. (See Exhibit 9–8.)

Another type of credit option can be used to hedge against a rise in borrowing costs due to a change in the borrower's default risk or credit rating. For example, a bank holding company may fear that its credit rating will be lowered just before it plans to issue some bonds to raise new capital. This would force the banking firm to pay a higher interest rate for its borrowed funds. One possible solution is for the banking company to purchase a call option on the default-risk interest-rate spread prevailing in the market for debt securities similar in quality to its own securities at the time it needs to borrow money. The credit risk option would have a *base rate spread* and would pay off if the market's default-risk rate spread over riskless securities climbs upward beyond the base rate spread specified in the option.

For example, suppose the banking company expected to pay a borrowing cost that was one percentage point over the 10-year government bond rate. In this instance, the base rate spread is one percentage point. If the banking firm's credit rating were lowered or a recession in the economy occurred, the default risk rate spread the bank must pay might balloon upward from one percentage point to perhaps two percentage points above the government bond rate. The call option becomes profitable if this happens and helps cover

EXHIBIT 9–7
Example of a Total
Return Swap

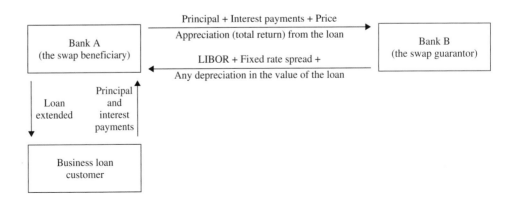

EXHIBIT 9–8
Example of a Credit
Option

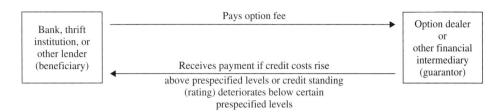

Key URLs
One of the most
common uses recently
of credit-default swaps
has been to protect
investors in
securitizations of sub-
prime home mortgage
loans. To learn more
about this particular use
of the credit derivative
market, see especially,
www.securitization.net
and **www.frbsf.org/
publications/economics/
letter**.

the borrower's higher borrowing costs, in effect lowering the default risk interest rate spread back to the neighborhood of one percentage point over the 10-year government bond rate. On the other hand, if default risk rate spreads fall (perhaps due to a rise in the bank's credit rating or a strengthening in the economy), this option will not be profitable and the bank will lose the option premium it paid.

Credit Default Swaps (CDSs)

Related to the credit option is the **credit default swap** (CDS), usually aimed at lenders able to handle comparatively limited declines in value, but wanting insurance against serious losses. In this case a lender may seek out a dealer willing to write a put option on a portfolio of bonds, loans, or other assets. Suppose, for example, that a bank has recently made 100 million-dollar commercial real estate loans to support the building of several investment projects in various cities. Fearing that several of these 100 loans might turn sour because of weakening economic conditions, it purchases a put option that pays off if more than two of these commercial real estate loans default. Thus, for each commercial real estate loan that fails to pay out above the bad-loan threshold of two, the lender will receive $1 million less the resale value of the building used to secure the loan.

In another example of a credit default swap, a lender may seek out a guarantor institution to unload the risk on one of its loans in case of default. For example, suppose Bank A swaps the credit risk from a five-year, $100 million construction loan to Bank B. Typically, A will pay B a fee based upon the loan's par or face value (for example, 1/2 percent of $100 million, or $500,000). For its part, B agrees to pay A a stipulated amount of money or a fixed percentage of the value of the loan *only if default occurs*. There may be a *materiality threshold*—a minimum amount of loss required before any payment occurs. If the swap ends in an actual default, the amount owed is normally the face value of the loan less the current market value of the defaulted asset. (See Exhibit 9–9.)

Factoid
What U.S. bank is one
of the world's leaders in
the market for
structuring credit
derivatives?
Answer: J. P. Morgan
Chase with a staff of
about 200 working on
structuring credit
derivatives worldwide.

EXHIBIT 9–9
Example of a Credit
Default Swap

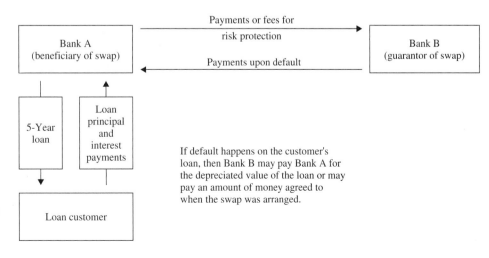

Key URLs
For added information
about credit default
swaps, see especially,
www.markit.com,
**www.FreeCreditDeriva
tives.com**, and
www.credit-deriv.com.

Credit-Linked Notes

Another credit derivative instrument, *credit-linked notes*, fuses together a normal debt instrument, such as a bond, plus a credit option contract to give a borrower greater payment flexibility. A credit-linked note grants its issuer the privilege of lowering the amount of loan repayments it must make if some significant factor changes. For example, suppose a finance company borrows through a bond issue in order to support a group of real estate loans it intends to make and agrees to pay the investors buying these bonds a 10 percent annual coupon payment (e.g., $100 a year for each $1,000 par-value bond). However, the credit-linked note agreement carries the stipulation that if defaults on the loans made with the borrowed funds rise significantly (perhaps above 7 percent of all the loans outstanding), then the note-issuing lender will only have to pay a 7 percent coupon rate (e.g., $70 a year per $1,000 bond). Therefore, the lender has taken on credit-related insurance from investors who bought into its bond issue.

Collateralized Debt Obligations (CDOs)

As the economy weakened early in the new century, coupled with worries about global terrorism, concern over credit risk soared in the financial markets. Not surprisingly, credit derivatives became more popular as risk-hedging devices and their outstanding volume skyrocketed. This strong demand led to innovation as important new types of credit derivatives appeared. Initially the most popular were **collateralized debt obligations** or **CDOs.**

CDOs may contain pools of high-yield corporate bonds, stock, commercial mortgages, or other financial instruments contributed by businesses interested in strengthening their balance sheets and raising new funds. Notes (claims) of varying grade are sold to investors seeking income from the pooled assets. The claims sold are divided into *tranches* similar to those created for the securitization of home mortgages, from the most risky tranche offering the highest potential return to the least risky tranche with lowest expected returns.

Some CDO pools contain debt and other financial instruments from dozens of companies in order to boost potential returns and diversify away much of the risk. The collateral contributed must be sufficient to cover expected debt-service payments to investors. Among the greatest challenges presented by CDOs is making estimates of their true credit risk exposure should some of the underlying assets go bad. To aid investors in this market both Moody's and Standard and Poor's assign credit ratings to larger CDOs.

Most recently regular CDOs have been surpassed by an explosion in **synthetic CDOs,** expanding five times over to more than $2 trillion within the last four years. These instruments rest on pools of credit derivatives (especially credit default swaps) that mainly ensure against defaults on corporate bonds. Thus, creators of synthetic CDOs do not have to buy and pool actual bonds, but can create synthetic instruments and generate revenues from selling and trading them. Among the leading providers of synthetic CDOs today are J. P. Morgan Chase & Co., Bank of America, Deutsche Bank AG, and Citibank of New York.

Risks Associated with Credit Derivatives

Credit derivatives are not without risk, though they can do much to protect a lender's loan, investment, or borrowing risk exposure. A partner to each swap or option may fail to perform, in which case a new swap partner has to be found to hedge its credit risk exposure. Courts may rule that credit risk agreements are not legal or are improperly drawn and parties to the derivative contract may lose all or a portion of its risk protection. A good example of the possibility of losing some or all of a credit derivative's risk protection in a legal battle occurred in 2003 when the Royal Bank of Canada was sued by Rabobank of the Netherlands, the latter seeking to avoid reimbursing Royal Bank under a total return swap after Enron Corporation collapsed. The relative newness surrounding these more exotic derivatives has left many legal issues in this field unresolved. In the case of Royal Bank, it settled for less than half of the amount claimed under its total return swap with Rabobank.

Major issues also remain for banks and other heavily regulated institutions that employ credit derivatives today. These contracts are largely unregulated right now, but they could become subject to regulation at any time. Capital regulations for these instruments are currently being closely studied by regulatory agencies, and no one knows for sure how regulators' attitudes toward these instruments might change with time. Many unknowns plague this relatively new risk-management arena.

Concept Check

9–14. Why were *credit derivatives* developed? What advantages do they have over loan sales and securitizations, if any?

9–15. What is a *credit swap?* For what kinds of situations was it developed?

9–16. What is a *total return swap?* What advantages does it offer the swap beneficiary institution?

9–17. How do *credit options* work? What circumstances result in the option contract paying off?

9–18. When is a *credit default swap* useful? Why?

9–19. Of what use are *credit-linked notes?*

9–20. What are CDOs? How do they differ from other credit derivatives?

9–21. What risks do credit derivatives pose for financial institutions using them? In your opinion what should regulators do about the recent rapid growth of this market, if anything?

Summary

This chapter has explored some of the newer sources of funding and risk management that many leading financial-service providers draw upon today. Among the key management tools explored in the chapter were the following:

- *Securitizing assets* in which loans are packaged into pools and moved off the balance sheet into a special purpose account, and securities are issued against the loan pool, providing new capital and freeing up space on a financial institution's balance sheet for stronger or higher-yielding assets.

- *Selling loans* or pieces of loans to other investors, such as insurance companies, mutual funds, and foreign banks, thus sharing the loans' risk exposure and raising new funds.

- *Issuing standby credit letters*, which help a borrowing customer raise funds more cheaply by pledging to guarantee the customer's loan, while helping the financial institution issuing the standby (usually a bank or insurance company) because it does not have to give up scarce funds in order to support the customer's loan request.

- *Utilizing credit derivatives*, which are contracts involving lenders who wish to slough off some of the default risk in their loan portfolios and investors who are willing to bear that risk and hope the derivatives will subsequently rise in value.

The foregoing tools have promised a number of advantages and some possible disadvantages for institutions that use them:

- Greater flexibility in managing assets in order to achieve a more balanced, more liquid, and more risk-resistant portfolio for financial firms skilled in the use of these tools.

- Making more efficient use of a financial institution's capital and avoiding having to sell financial instruments to raise new capital when market conditions are unfavorable.

www.mhhe.com/rose7e

- Generating new sources of income for a financial firm from helping customers more efficiently raise funds and deal with risk exposures.
- Presenting their own risks for financial firms, however, because of the greater skills required in their design and trading and their uncertain reception in the regulatory community, which is increasingly concerned about speculative activity in these highly specialized markets.

Key Terms	securitization, *282*	financial guarantees, *293*	credit derivative, *297*
	credit enhancement, *288*	standby letter of credit	credit swap, *297*
	loan sales, *290*	(SLC), *293*	credit option, *298*
	servicing rights, *291*	contingent obligation, *293*	credit default swap, *299*
	participation loans, *291*	issuer, *294*	collateralized debt
	assignments, *291*	account party, *294*	obligation (CDO), *300*
	loan strip, *291*	beneficiary, *294*	synthetic CDOs, *300*

Problems and Projects

1. Giant National Bank has placed a group of 10,000 consumer loans bearing an average expected gross annual yield of 8 percent in a package to be securitized. The investment bank advising Giant estimates that the securities will sell at a slight discount from par that results in a net interest cost to the issuer of 9 percent. Based on recent experience with similar types of loans, the bank expects 3 percent of the packaged loans to default without any recovery for the lender and has agreed to set aside a cash reserve to cover this anticipated loss. Underwriting and advisory services provided by the investment banking firm will cost 0.5 percent. Giant will also seek a liquidity facility, costing 0.5 percent, and a credit guarantee if actual loan defaults should exceed the expected loan default rate, costing 0.6 percent. Please calculate *residual income* for Giant from this loan securitization.

2. Colburn Corporation is requesting a loan for repair of some assembly line equipment in the amount of $7 million. The nine-month loan is priced by Farmers Financial Corporation at a 7.25 percent rate of interest. However, the finance company tells Colburn that if it obtains a suitable credit guarantee the loan will be priced at 7 percent. Quinmark Bank agrees to sell Colburn a standby credit guarantee for $10,000. Is Colburn likely to buy the standby credit guarantee Quinmark has offered? Please explain.

3. The Monarch Bank Corp. has placed $100 million of GNMA-guaranteed securities in a trust account off the balance sheet. A CMO with four tranches has just been issued by Monarch using the GNMAs as collateral. Each tranche has a face value of $25 million and makes monthly payments. The annual coupon rates are 4 percent for Tranche A, 5 percent for Tranche B, 6 percent for Tranche C, and 7 percent for Tranche D.

   a. Which tranche has the shortest maturity and which tranche has the most prepayment protection?

   b. Every month principal and interest are paid on the outstanding mortgages and some mortgages are paid in full. These payments are passed through to Monarch and the trustee uses the funds to pay coupons to CMO bondholders. What are the coupon payments owed for each tranche for the first month?

   c. If scheduled mortgage payments and early prepayments bring in $1 million, how much will be used to retire the principal of CMO bondholders and which tranche will be affected?

   d. Why does Tranche D have a higher expected return?

4. First Security National Bank has been approached by a long-standing customer, United Safeco Industries, for a $30 million *term loan* for five years to purchase new stamping machines that would further automate the company's assembly line in the manufacture of metal toys and containers. The company also plans to use at least half the loan proceeds to facilitate its buyout of Calem Corp., which imports and partially assembles video recorders and cameras. Additional funds for the buyout will come from a corporate bond issue that will be underwritten by an investment banking firm not affiliated with First Security.

   The problem the bank's commercial credit division faces in assessing this customer's loan request is a management decision reached several weeks ago that the bank should gradually work down its leveraged buyout loan portfolio due to a significant rise in nonperforming credits. Moreover, the prospect of sharply higher interest rates has caused the bank to revamp its loan policy toward more short-term loans (under one year) and fewer term (over one year) loans. Senior management has indicated it will no longer approve loans that require a commitment of the bank's resources beyond a term of three years, except in special cases.

   Does First Security have any *service option* in the form of off-balance-sheet instruments that could help this customer while avoiding committing $30 million in reserves for a five-year loan? What would you recommend that management do to keep United Safeco happy with its current banking relationship? Could First Security earn any fee income if it pursued your idea?

   Suppose the current interest rate on Eurodollar deposits (three-month maturities) in London is 8.40 percent, while federal funds and six-month CDs are trading in the United States at 8.55 percent and 8.21 percent, respectively. Term loans to comparable-quality corporate borrowers are trading at one-eighth to one-quarter percentage point above the three-month Eurodollar rate or one-quarter to one-half point over the secondary-market CD rate. Is there a way First Security could earn at least as much fee income by providing United Safeco with support services as it could from making the loan the company has asked for (after all loan costs are taken into account)? Please explain how the customer could benefit even if the bank does not make the loan requested.

5. What type of credit derivative contract would you recommend for each of these situations:

   a. A bank plans to issue a group of bonds backed by a pool of credit card loans but fears that the default rate on these credit card loans will rise well above 6 percent of the portfolio—the default rate it has projected. The bank wants to lower the interest cost on the bonds in case the loan default rate rises too high.

   b. A commercial finance company is about to make a $50 million project loan to develop a new gas field and is concerned about the risks involved if petroleum geologists' estimates of the field's potential yield turn out to be much too high and the field developer cannot repay.

   c. A bank holding company plans to offer new bonds in the open market next month, but knows that the company's credit rating is being reevaluated by credit-rating agencies. The holding company wants to avoid paying sharply higher credit costs if its rating is lowered by the investigating agencies.

   d. A mortgage company is concerned about possible excess volatility in its cash flow off a group of commercial real estate loans supporting the building of several apartment complexes. Moreover, many of these loans were made at fixed interest rates, and the company's economics department has forecast a substantial rise in capital market interest rates. The company's management would prefer a more stable cash flow emerging from this group of loans if it could find a way to achieve it.

e. First National Bank of Ashton serves a relatively limited geographic area centered upon a moderate-size metropolitan area. It would like to diversify its loan income but does not wish to make loans in other market areas due to its lack of familiarity with loan markets outside the region it has served for many years. Is there a derivative contract that could help the bank achieve the loan portfolio diversification it seeks?

Internet Exercises

1. Using the National Information Center, identify the four largest BHCs in the top 50 at **www.ffiec.gov/nicpubweb/nicweb/nichome.aspx**. Then go to Statistics on Depository Institutions (SDI) at the FDIC's Web site (**http://www3.fdic.gov/sdi/**) and, after looking up the BHC identification numbers for the four largest BHCs, compare the notional amount of credit derivatives as a percentage of total assets for each using the most recent year-end data. What is the difference between the bank acting as a guarantor and the bank acting as a beneficiary? This information is available in "Derivatives: report."

2. Using the same institutions and the same Web sites as in the previous exercise, compare the credit standbys-to-total assets for the four BHCs. This information is found in the Letters of Credit report.

3. As a stock analyst following the banking industry, you are especially concerned about the growth of off-balance-sheet activities among large institutions. Your argument is that these off-balance-sheet financial tools have, in fact, increased rather than decreased bank risk in many cases. Using the data at **http://www3.fdic.gov/sdi/**, compare the percentages obtained in Exercises 1 and 2 with data for the same institutions 10 years earlier.

4. The market for credit derivatives is one of the most rapidly growing financial markets in the world. What factors seem to explain this rapid expansion? (See **www.finpipe.com** and search for: Credit Derivatives—Effect on the Stability of Financial Markets.)

STANDARD &POOR'S

S&P Market Insight Challenge (www.mhhe.com/edumarketinsight)

1. In the S&P Industry Survey entitled "Financial Services: Diversified," *securitization* is a key measure of financial performance for consumer finance companies. For an up-to-date description of how consumer finance companies use securitization use the Industry tab in Market Insight and through the drop-down menu select the subindustry Consumer Finance. You will encounter a recent S&P Industry survey on Financial Services: Diversified. Please download this survey and review the section entitled "How to Analyze a Financial Services Company" with a particular focus on securitization activity. What does securitization mean for a consumer finance company? What are its advantages and disadvantages?

STANDARD &POOR'S

2. The largest banks and thrift institutions are heavy users of the risk-management devices discussed in this chapter, including securitization, loan sales, standby credits, and credit derivatives. Using the most recent financial reports of and news stories about bank and thrift institutions found in S&P's Market Insight, see if you can determine the extent to which the largest banks and thrifts are utilizing each of the risk-management devices discussed in this chapter. Measured by dollar volume, which of these financial instruments are most heavily used and why? For what specific purposes? Do you think this scale of usage is proper given the risks and costs discussed in this chapter?

REAL NUMBERS FOR REAL BANKS

Assignment for Chapter 9

YOUR BANK'S USE OF ASSET SECURITIZATION AND LOAN SALES AS RISK-MANAGEMENT TOOLS AND FEE INCOME GENERATORS

Chapter 9 describes a number of off-balance-sheet activities (asset-backed securities, loan sales, standby letters of credit, and credit derivatives) that can be used for risk management and fee generation. Some financial institutions have used asset securitization and loan sales to focus on loan brokerage where the institutions (1) make loans, (2) remove the loans from their balance sheets by either securitizing or selling the loans, and then (3) use the cash generated in the transfer to repeat the cycle time and time again. This process can generate income at the time of the loan transfer and over the lives of the loans if the institution continues to service the loans it created and sold or securitized. In this assignment we will examine to what degree your bank's income is generated using this means.

Part One: Gathering the Data
For this part, we will visit the FDIC's Web site located at **www3.fdic.gov/sdi/** where you will use SDI to create a four-column report of your bank's information and the peer group information across years. This is familiar because you have been here before. For Report Selection use the pull-down menu to choose Additional Noninterest Income and view this in Percentages of Total Assets. Collect the percentage information and enter in the spreadsheet for comparisons with the peer group.

Extend this portion of the spreadsheet to columns F, G, H, and I, where you will calculate each item as a percentage of

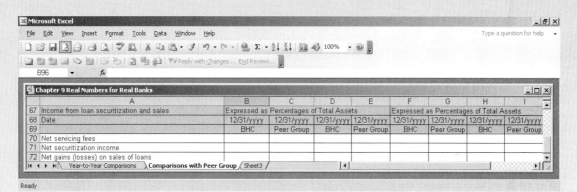

Total Operating Income (Interest Income plus Noninterest Income). To calculate these ratios from the data you have collected, divide each entry in columns B–E (rows 70–72) by Total Operating Income/Total Assets. Note this is equivalent to Item/Total Assets × Total Assets/Total Operating Income = Item/Total Operating Income. (A little algebra makes life worth living.) For example the formula for cell F70 would be B70/(B34+B38) and the formula for cell I72 would be E72/(E34+E38).

Part Two: Analyzing the Data for Interpretation
A. Compare the columns of rows 70–72, which have been standardized for size by using the Percentages of Total Assets. Is your bank involved in loan brokerage and to what degree?

B. Write one or two paragraphs interpreting your data and discussing your bank's involvement in loan securitization and sales relative to other large institutions (its peer group). How has income from these activities contributed to total operating income? What inferences can you make concerning the potential effects on risk exposure? You could incorporate tables using the Excel spreadsheets and reference these in your discussion.

Selected References

For an exploration of the off-balance-sheet activities of large money center banks, see especially:

1. Bennett, Barbara. "Off-Balance Sheet Risk in Banking: The Case of Standby Letters of Credit." *Review*, Federal Reserve Bank of San Francisco, no. 1 (1986), pp. 19–29.
2. Hassan, M. Kabir. "The Off-Balance-Sheet Banking Risk of Large U.S. Commercial Banks." *The Quarterly Review of Economics and Finance*, 33, no. 1 (Spring 1993), pp. 51–69.

www.mhhe.com/rose7e

3. James, Christopher. "Off-Balance-Sheet Banking." *Economic Review*, Federal Reserve Bank of San Francisco, no. 4 (Fall 1987), pp. 21–36.

To examine the techniques of securitization and the huge market for asset securitizations, see, in particular:

4. Elul, Ronel. "The Economics of Asset Securitization." *Business Review*, Federal Reserve Bank of Philadelphia, Third Quarter 2005, pp. 16–25.
5. Ergungor, O. Emre. "Securitization." *Economic Commentary*, Federal Reserve Bank of Cleveland, August 15, 2003, pp. 1–4.
6. Office of the Comptroller of the Currency. "Asset Securitization." In the *Comptroller's Handbook*. Washington, D.C., November 1997.

To understand more completely the potential impact on bank safety of off-balance sheet transactions, see, for example:

7. Hassan, M. Kabir. "Capital Market Tests of Risk Exposure of Loan Sales Activities of Large U.S. Commercial Banks." *Quarterly Journal of Business and Economics*, 32, no. 1 (Winter 1993), pp. 27–49.
8. Klee, Elizabeth C., and Fabio Natalucci. "Profits and Balance Sheet Developments at U.S. Commercial Banks in 2004." *Federal Reserve Bulletin*, Spring 2005, pp. 143–174.
9. Rose, Peter S. "The Search for Safety in an Uncertain Market." *The Canadian Banker* 97, no.1 (January/February 1990).

To learn more about devices, such as credit derivatives, designed to reduce credit risk, see:

10. Lopez, Jose A. "Recent Policy Issues Regarding Credit Risk Transfer." *FRBSF Economic Letter*, Federal Reserve Bank of San Francisco, no. 2005-34 (December 2, 2005), pp. 1–3.

For a discussion of the possible impacts of loan sales on financial firms selling their loans, see, for example:

11. Rose, Peter S. "New Benefits, New Pitfalls." *The Canadian Banker*, September/October 1988.

To learn more about collateralized debt obligations (CDOs) see especially:

12. Haughney, Christine. "Real Estate Bonds Gain Popularity." *The Wall Street Journal*, March 14, 2006.

PART FOUR

Managing the Investment Portfolios and Liquidity Positions of Banks and Their Principal Competitors

The managers of financial firms are not so very different from you and me really—they sometimes spend more cash than they have on hand, take on more debt than they can afford, or accept more risk in the assets they acquire than they really should.

For example, during the 1980s a small-town bank in the state of Montana, just a few miles from the Canadian border, suddenly ran out of cash—only small coins remained in its cash drawers. This is a relatively rare event—so rare that government investigators inquired into the situation. Fortunately, however, for the curious customers and worried employees, the bank's president hopped in his car and drove several hundred miles to pick up some much needed cash, stuffing it in his trunk for the long ride home!

This little bank is not alone. More recently, numerous financial firms stuffed their asset portfolios with investment securities they should have evaluated more closely and wound up taking losses they had not considered possible. In a period of relatively low market interest rates, for example, many investment officers bought interest-bearing securities backed by pools of home mortgage and credit-card loans. With the economy softening, market interest rates headed toward record lows, and thousands of homeowners took advantage of this situation to refinance their mortgages, retiring the older, higher-yielding loans upon which the value of these investment securities rested. The cash flow off these loan-backed investments soon sagged and their market values plummeted. At the same time a sluggish economy led to rising defaults on credit-card-backed securities, reducing their investment value as well.

We tend to think of the cash position of a financial firm and its investment portfolio, composed of marketable securities like Treasury notes and bonds, as a stodgy old place, neither exciting nor trendy. How wrong we can be! Really, the liquidity (cash position) of a financial firm and its portfolio of investments are all about *managing risk*. Investment securities help balance the greater risk financial firms generally take on in their portfolios of loans, generating relatively steady income even if the loan portfolio is in trouble. Liquidity managers, for their part, keep a watchful eye on the cash available to their institutions in order to make sure liquid funds are available precisely when they are needed.

Because most depository institutions—banks, credit unions, and savings associations— have extensive short-term deposits and large amounts of other short-term borrowings supporting assets that often carry far longer maturities, managing the cash position, like managing the investment portfolio, is one of the most important areas within these institutions. Moreover, rules and regulations in this area are constantly changing, new financial instruments (such as trust-preferred securities and equity-linked CDs) are constantly appearing to tempt investment managers, and new tax laws often show up over the horizon affecting what investment securities a financial manager should buy or dispose of. So hang on for a while! You may find Part Four of this book far more important and more interesting than you ever dreamed.

CHAPTER TEN

The Investment Function in Banking and Financial Services Management

Key Topics in This Chapter

- Nature and Functions of Investments
- Investment Securities Available: Advantages and Disadvantages
- Measuring Expected Returns
- Taxes, Credit, and Interest-Rate Risks
- Liquidity, Prepayment, and Other Risks
- Investment Maturity Strategies
- Maturity Management Tools

10–1 Introduction

An investments officer of a large money center bank was overheard to say: "There's no way I can win! I'm either buying bonds when their prices are the highest or selling bonds when their prices are the lowest. Who would want this job?" In this chapter we will discover what that officer really meant.

To begin our journey, we need to keep in mind that the primary function of most banks and other depository institutions is *not* to buy and sell bonds, but rather to make loans to businesses and individuals. After all, loans support business investment and consumer spending in local communities. Such loans ultimately provide jobs and income to thousands of community residents.

Yet buying and selling bonds has its place because not all of a financial firm's funds can be allocated to loans. For one thing, some loans are *illiquid*—they cannot easily be sold or securitized prior to maturity if a lending institution needs cash in a hurry. Another problem is that loans are among the riskiest assets, generally carrying the highest customer default rates of any form of credit. Moreover, for small and medium-size depository institutions, at least, the majority of loans tend to come from the local area. Therefore, a significant drop in local economic activity can weaken the quality of the average lender's loan portfolio, though the widespread use of securitization, loan sales, and credit derivatives (discussed in

EXHIBIT 10–1   Investments: The Crossroads Account on a Depository Institution's Balance Sheet

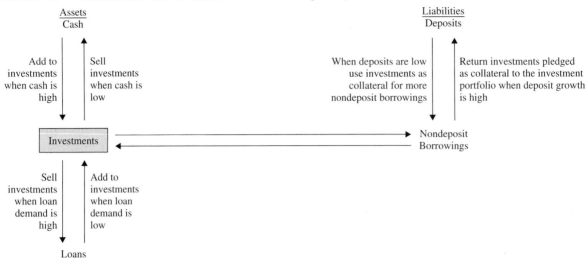

Chapter 9) has helped to insulate somewhat many lenders serving local areas. Then, too, loan income is usually taxable for commercial banks and selected other financial institutions, necessitating the search for tax shelters in years when earnings from loans are high.

For all these reasons depository institutions, for example, have learned to devote a significant portion of their asset portfolios—usually somewhere between a fifth to a third of all assets—to another major category of earning asset: *investments in securities that are under the management of investments officers*. Moreover, several nonbank financial-service providers—insurance companies, pension funds, and mutual funds, for example—often devote an even bigger portion of their assets to investment securities. These instruments typically include government bonds and notes; corporate bonds, notes, and commercial paper; asset-backed securities arising from lending activity; domestic and Eurocurrency deposits; and certain kinds of common and preferred stock where permitted by law.

As we will see as this chapter unfolds, these security holdings perform a number of vital functions in the asset portfolios of financial firms, providing income, liquidity, diversification, and shelter for at least a portion of earnings from taxation. Investments also tend to stabilize earnings, providing supplemental income when other sources of revenue are in decline. See Exhibit 10–1 and Table 10–1 for a summary of the principal roles investment portfolios play on the balance sheets of many financial firms.

10–2 Investment Instruments Available to Financial Firms

The number of financial instruments available for financial institutions to add to their securities portfolio is both large and growing. Moreover, each financial instrument has different characteristics with regard to expected yields, risk, sensitivity to inflation, and sensitivity to shifting government policies and economic conditions. To examine the different investment vehicles available, it is useful to divide them into two broad groups: (1) **money market instruments,** which reach maturity within one year and are noted for their low risk and ready marketability, and (2) **capital market instruments,** which have remaining maturities beyond one year and are generally noted for their higher expected rate of return and capital gains potential. See Table 10–2 for a summary of the advantages and disadvantages of the principal types of investment securities available.

TABLE 10–1
Functions of the
Investment Security
Portfolio

Investment security portfolios help to

a. *Stabilize income*, so that revenues level out over the business cycle—when loan revenues fall, income from investment securities may rise.
b. *Offset credit risk exposure in the loan portfolio.* High-quality securities can be purchased and held to balance out the risk from loans.
c. *Provide geographic diversification.* Securities often come from different regions than the sources of loans, helping diversify a financial firm's sources of income.
d. *Provide a backup source of liquidity,* because securities can be sold to raise needed cash or used as collateral for borrowing additional funds.
e. *Reduce tax exposure,* especially in offsetting taxable loan revenues.
f. *Serve as collateral* (pledged assets) to secure federal, state, and local government deposits held by a depository institution.
g. *Help hedge* against losses due to changing interest rates.
h. *Provide flexibility* in a financial firm's asset portfolio because investment securities, unlike many loans, can be bought or sold quickly to restructure assets.
i. *Dress up the balance sheet* and make a financial institution look financially stronger due to the high quality of most marketable securities.

Federal regulations stress the need for every regulated institution to develop a *written* investment policy giving specific guidelines on:

a. The quality or degree of default risk exposure the institution is willing to accept.
b. The desired maturity range and degree of marketability sought for all securities purchased.
c. The goals sought for its investment portfolio.
d. The degree of portfolio diversification to reduce risk the institution wishes to achieve with its investment portfolio.

Key URLs
If an investments officer wishes to gather risk/return data on specific financial instruments that might be bought or sold, the following Web sites might be especially helpful: **www. multexinvestor. com, www.wsrn.com, www.investinginbonds. com, www. municipalbonds.com, www.riskgrades.com/ retail/myportfolio,** and **www.publicdebt.treas. gov.**

Some authorities refer to investments as the *crossroads account*. Investments held by depository institutions literally stand between cash, loans, and deposits. When cash is low, some investments will be sold in order to raise more cash. On the other hand, if cash is too high, some of the excess cash will be placed in investment securities. If loan demand is weak, investments will rise in order to provide more earning assets and maintain profitability. But, if loan demand is strong, some investments will be sold to accommodate the heavy loan demand. Finally, when deposits are not growing fast enough, some investment securities will be used as collateral to borrow nondeposit funds. No other account on the balance sheet occupies such a critical intersection position as do investments.

10–3 Popular Money Market Investment Instruments

Treasury Bills

One of the most popular of all short-term investments is the **U.S. Treasury bill**—a debt obligation of the United States government that, by law, must mature within one year from date of issue. T-bills are issued in weekly and monthly auctions and are particularly attractive to financial firms because of their high degree of *safety.* Bills are supported by the taxing power of the federal government, their market prices are relatively stable, and they are readily marketable. Moreover, T-bills can serve as collateral for attracting loans from other institutions. Bills are issued and traded at a discount from their par (face) value. Thus, the investor's return consists purely of price appreciation as the bill approaches maturity. The rate of return (yield) on T-bills is figured by the bank discount method, which uses each bill's par value at maturity as the basis for calculating its return and is based on a 360-day year, as we discussed in Chapter 7.

TABLE 10–2 Key Advantages and Disadvantages of Popular Investment Securities Often Purchased by Banks and Other Financial Firms

Money Market Instruments

	Treasury Bills	Short-Term Treasury Notes and Bonds	Federal Agency Securities	Certificates of Deposit	International Eurocurrency Deposits	Bankers' Acceptances	Commercial Paper	Short-Term Municipal Obligations
Key advantages:	Safety and high liquidity; Good collateral for borrowing; Can pledge behind government deposits	Safety; Good resale market; Good collateral for borrowing; Offer yields usually higher than bill yields	Safety; Good to average resale market; Good collateral for borrowing; Higher yields than on U.S government securities	Insured to $100,000; Yields higher than on T-bills; Large denominations often marketable through dealers	Low risk; Higher yields than on many domestic CDs	Low risk due to multiple credit guarantees	Low risk due to high quality of borrowers	Tax-exempt interest income
Key disadvantages:	Low yields relative to other financial instruments; Taxable income	More price risk than T-bills; Taxable gains and income	Less marketable than Treasury securities; Taxable gains and income	Limited resale market on longer-term CDs; Taxable income	Volatile interest rates; Taxable income	Limited availability at specific maturities; Issued in odd denominations; Taxable income	Volatile market; Poor resale market; Taxable income	Limited resale market; Taxable capital gains

Capital Market Instruments

	Treasury Notes and Bonds	Municipal (State and Local Government) Bonds	Corporate Notes and Bonds	Asset-Backed Securities
Key advantages:	Safety; Good resale market; Good collateral for borrowing; May be pledged behind government deposits	Tax-exempt interest income; High credit quality; Liquidity and marketability of selected securities	Higher pretax yields than on government securities; Aid in locking in long-term rates of return	Higher pretax yields than on Treasury securities; Safety; Adequate resale market; Good collateral for borrowing
Key disadvantages:	Low yields relative to long-term private securities; Taxable gains and income; Limited supply of longest-term issues	Volatile market; Some issues have limited resale potential; Taxable capital gains	Limited resale market; Inflexible terms; Taxable gains and income	Less marketable and more unstable in price than Treasury securities; Taxable gains and income

Short-Term Treasury Notes and Bonds

At the time they are issued, **Treasury notes** and **Treasury bonds** have relatively long original maturities: 1 to 10 years for notes and over 10 years for bonds. However, when these securities come within one year of maturity, they are considered money market instruments. While T-notes and bonds are more sensitive to interest rate risk and less marketable than T-bills, their expected returns (yields) are usually higher than for bills with greater potential for capital gains. T-notes and bonds are *coupon instruments*, which means they promise investors a fixed rate of return, though the expected return may fall below or climb above the promised coupon rate due to fluctuations in their market price.

All negotiable Treasury Department securities are issued by electronic book entry, with no registered or engraved certificates issued. This system, known as Treasury Direct, provides owners of U.S. Treasury securities with a statement showing the bills, notes, and bonds they hold. Any interest and principal payments earned are deposited directly into the owners' checking or savings account. This approach means not only greater convenience in purchasing and selling Treasury securities but also increased protection against theft.

Federal Agency Securities

Marketable notes and bonds sold by agencies owned by or sponsored by the federal government are known as **federal agency securities.** Familiar examples include securities issued by the Federal National Mortgage Association (Fannie Mae), the Farm Credit System (FCS), the Federal Land Banks (FLBs), the Federal Home Loan Mortgage Corporation (Freddie Mac), and the Student Loan Marketing Association (Sallie Mae). Most of these securities are not formally guaranteed by the federal government, though many financial analysts believe Congress would move to rescue any agency in trouble. This implied government support keeps agency yields close to those on Treasury securities (often less than half a percentage point) and contributes to the high liquidity of many agency securities. Interest income on agency-issued notes is federally taxable and, in most cases, subject to state and local taxation as well.

Certificates of Deposit

A **certificate of deposit (CD)** is simply an interest-bearing receipt for the deposit of funds in a depository institution. Thus, the primary role of CDs is to provide depository institutions with an additional source of funds. Banks often buy the CDs issued by other depository institutions, regarding them as an attractive, lower-risk investment. CDs carry a fixed term and there is a federally imposed penalty for early withdrawal. Depository institutions issue both small *consumer-oriented CDs*, ranging in denomination from $500 to $100,000, and large *business-oriented* or *institution-oriented CDs* (often called *jumbos* or *negotiable CDs*) with denominations over $100,000 (though only the first $100,000 is federally insured). CDs have negotiated interest rates that, while normally fixed, may be allowed to fluctuate with market conditions. Security dealers make an active secondary market for $100,000-plus CDs maturing within six months.

International Eurocurrency Deposits

The 1950s in Western Europe ushered in the development of high-quality international bank deposits, sold in million-dollar units and denominated in a currency other than the home currency of the country in which they are deposited. *Eurocurrency deposits* are time deposits of fixed maturity issued by the world's largest banks headquartered in financial centers around the globe, though the heart of the Eurocurrency market is in London. Most of these international deposits are of short maturity—30, 60, or 90 days—to correspond with the funding requirements of international trade. They are *not* insured, and due to their perceived higher credit risk and greater sensitivity to foreign economic and political developments, they often carry slightly higher market yields than domestic time deposits issued by comparable-size U.S. banks. (For a detailed discussion of the role and creation of Eurocurrency deposits, see Chapter 13.)

Bankers' Acceptances

Because they represent a bank's promise to pay the holder a designated amount of money on a designated future date, **bankers' acceptances** are considered to be among the safest of all money market instruments. Most acceptances arise from a financial firm's decision to guarantee the credit of one of its customers who is exporting, importing, or storing goods or purchasing currency. In legal language, the financial firm issuing the credit guarantee agrees to be the *primary obligor*, committed to paying off the customer's debt regardless of what happens subsequently, in return for a fee. Through acceptances the issuing institution supplies its name and credit standing so that its customer will be able to obtain credit from someone else more easily and at lower cost.

The holder of the acceptance on its maturity date may be a financial institution or other money market investor attracted by its safety and active resale market. Because acceptances have a resale market, they may be traded from one investor to another before reaching maturity. If the current holder sells the acceptances, this does not erase the issuer's obligation to pay off its outstanding acceptances at maturity. However, by selling an acceptance, the holder adds to its reserves and transfers interest rate risk to another investor. The acceptance is a discount instrument and, therefore, is always sold at a price below par before it reaches maturity. The investor's expected return comes solely from the prospect that the acceptance will rise in price as it gets closer to maturity. Rates of return on acceptances generally lie close to the yields on Eurocurrency deposits and Treasury bills. Another important advantage of acceptances is that they may qualify for discounting (borrowing) at the Federal Reserve Banks, provided they are *eligible* acceptances. To be eligible as collateral for borrowing from the Fed, the acceptance must be denominated in dollars, normally cannot exceed six months to maturity, and must arise from the export or import of goods or from the storage of marketable commodities.

Commercial Paper

Many smaller banks, money market funds, and other financial firms find **commercial paper**—short-term, unsecured IOUs offered by major corporations—an attractive investment that is safer than most types of loans. Commercial paper sold in the United States is of relatively short maturity—the bulk of it matures in 90 days or less—and generally is issued by borrowers with the highest credit ratings. In Europe and Japan the paper market has attracted participation by major international banks, finance companies, and other lending institutions. European paper generally carries longer maturities and higher interest rates than U.S. paper due to its greater perceived credit risk; however, there is a more active resale market for Europaper than for most U.S. paper issues whose market has weakened in recent years. Most commercial paper is issued at a discount from par, though some paper bearing a promised rate of return (coupon) is also issued.

Short-Term Municipal Obligations

State and local governments—including counties, cities, and special districts—issue a wide variety of short-term debt instruments to cover temporary cash shortages. Two of the most common are tax-anticipation notes (TANs), issued in lieu of expected future tax revenues, and revenue-anticipation notes (RANs), issued to cover expenses from special projects, such as the construction of a toll bridge or a highway in lieu of expected revenues from those projects. All interest earned on municipal notes is exempt from federal income taxation, so they may be attractive to investors bearing relatively high income tax rates, such as wealthy individuals and banks. However, as we will see later, the tax savings associated with municipals has been sharply limited for U.S. banks in recent years, reducing their attractiveness relative to federal and privately issued securities. At the same time, some state and local governments have encountered serious financial problems that have weakened the credit quality of their notes, forcing investing institutions to take a closer look at the quality of the municipals they choose to buy.

10–4 Popular Capital Market Investment Instruments

Treasury Notes and Bonds

Among the safest and most liquid assets that investing institutions can buy are U.S. Treasury notes and bonds. T-notes are available in a wide variety of maturities (ranging from 1 year to 10 years when issued) and in large volume. T-bonds (with original maturities of more than 10 years) are traded in a more limited market with wider price fluctuations than is usually the case with T-notes. Treasury bonds and notes carry higher expected returns than T-bills, but present an investing institution with greater price and liquidity risk. They are issued normally in denominations of $1,000, $5,000, $10,000, $100,000, and $1 million. Paralleling the U.S. Treasury bond market in recent years has been the Eurozone government bond market, valued at about 90 percent of the $5 trillion U.S. government market.

Municipal Notes and Bonds

Long-term debt obligations issued by states, cities, and other local governmental units are known collectively as **municipal bonds.** As with short-term municipal notes, interest on the majority of these bonds is exempt from federal income tax provided they are issued to fund public, rather than private, projects. Capital gains on municipals are fully taxable, however, except for bonds sold at a discounted price, where the gain from purchase price to par value is considered a portion of the investor's tax-exempt interest earnings.

Investing institutions often submit competitive bids for, or purchase after private negotiation, the debt issued by local cities, counties, and school districts as a way of demonstrating support for their communities and to attract other business. They also purchase municipals from security dealers for reasons strictly related to after-tax return and risk because most municipals have high credit ratings. Unfortunately, municipals are often not very liquid—few issues trade on any given day.

Many different types of municipal bonds are issued today, but the majority fall into one of two categories: (1) *general obligation (GO) bonds,* backed by the full faith and credit of the issuing government, which means they may be paid from any available source of revenue (including the levying of additional taxes); and (2) *revenue bonds,* which can be used to fund long-term revenue-raising projects and are payable only from certain stipulated sources of funds. U.S. banks have long possessed the authority to deal in and underwrite general obligation (GO) municipal bonds, but for many years they faced restrictions on directly underwriting revenue bonds until this power was extended by the Gramm-Leach-Bliley Act in 1999.

Corporate Notes and Bonds

Long-term debt securities issued by corporations are usually called **corporate notes** when they mature within five years or **corporate bonds** when they carry longer maturities. There are many different varieties, depending on the types of security pledged (e.g., mortgages versus debentures), purpose of issue, and terms of issue. Corporate notes and bonds generally

Factoid
Which U.S. Treasury security is the most popular (measured by volume outstanding)— Treasury bills, notes, or bonds?
Answer: T-notes(with an original maturity of 1 to 10 years), followed by T-bills. (See, for example, **www. treas.gov.**)

are more attractive to insurance companies and pension funds than to banks because of their higher credit risk relative to government securities and their more limited resale market. However, they usually offer significantly higher yields than government securities of comparable maturity. Moreover, their yield spread over government securities widens when investors become more concerned about corporate credit quality.

Concept Check

10–1. Why do banks and other institutions choose to devote a significant portion of their assets to investment securities?

10–2. What key roles do investments play in the management of a bank or other depository institution?

10–3. What are the principal money market and capital market instruments available to institutions today? What are their most important characteristics?

10–5 Investment Instruments Developed More Recently

The range of investment opportunities for investing institutions has expanded in recent years. Many new securities have been developed; some of these are variations on traditional notes and bonds, while others represent entirely new investment vehicles. Examples include structured notes, securitized assets, and stripped securities.

Structured Notes

In their search to protect themselves against shifting interest rates, many investing institutions added *structured notes* to their portfolios during the 1990s. Most of these notes arose from security dealers who assembled pools of federal agency securities and offered investments officers a packaged investment whose interest yield could be reset periodically based on what happened to a reference rate, such as a U.S. Treasury bond rate. A guaranteed floor rate and cap rate may be added in which the investment return could not drop below a stated (floor) level or rise above some maximum (cap) level. Some structured notes carry multiple coupon (promised) rates that periodically are given a boost ("step-up") to give investors a higher yield; others carry adjustable coupon (promised) rates determined by formula. The complexity of these notes has resulted in substantial losses for some investing institutions, not from credit risk since few of these notes are actually defaulted upon, but from interest rate risk.

Securitized Assets

In recent years hybrid securities based upon pools of loans have been one of the most rapidly growing investment vehicles. These **securitized assets** are backed by selected loans of uniform type and quality, such as FHA- and VA-insured home mortgages and credit card loans.[1] The most popular securitized assets that depository institutions buy as investments today are based upon home mortgage loans.

There are at least three main types of mortgage-backed securitized assets: (1) pass-through securities, (2) collateralized mortgage obligations (CMOs), and (3) mortgage-backed bonds. *Pass-through securities* arise when a lender pools a group of similar home mortgages appearing on its balance sheet, removes them from that balance sheet into an account controlled by a legal trustee, and issues securities using the mortgage loans as collateral. As the mortgage loan pool generates principal and interest payments, these payments are "passed through" to

---

[1] See Chapter 9 for a discussion of how financial firms use securitized assets to raise new funds and to restructure their sources and uses of funds.

investors holding the mortgage-backed securities. Repayment of principal and interest on the calendar dates promised may be guaranteed by the Government National Mortgage Association (Ginnie Mae), an agency of the U.S. government, in return for a small fee (for example: 6 basis points or 0.06 percent of the total amount of loans placed in the pool).

The Federal National Mortgage Association (Fannie Mae), which was chartered by but is legally separate from the U.S. government, also helps create pass-throughs by purchasing packages of mortgage loans from lending institutions. While GNMA aids in the creation of mortgage-loan-backed securities for government-insured home loans, FNMA securitizes both conventional (noninsured) and government-insured home mortgages. Investors who acquire pass-throughs issued against pools of government-insured home mortgages are protected against default on those securities because the Federal Housing and Veterans Administrations ensure that the pooled loans will be repaid even if the homeowner abandons his or her home. Moreover, GNMA and FNMA may add their own guarantees of timely repayment of principal and interest.

In 1983 another government-sponsored agency, the Federal Home Loan Mortgage Corporation (Freddie Mac), now legally separate from the U.S. government, developed the *collateralized mortgage obligation* (CMO)—a pass-through security divided into multiple classes (tranches), each with a different promised (coupon) rate and level of risk exposure. CMOs arise either from the securitizing of mortgage loans themselves or from securitizing pass-through securities.

Closely related to CMOs are REMICs—Real Estate Mortgage Investment Conduits—that also partition the cash flow from a pool of mortgage loans or mortgage-backed securities into multiple maturity classes in order to help reduce the cash-flow uncertainty of investors. As we will see later in this chapter, the principal risk to an investor buying these securities is *prepayment risk* because some borrowers pay off their home mortgages early or default on their loans, meaning the holder may receive diminished income.

A third type of mortgage-related security is the **mortgage-backed bond.** Unlike pass-throughs and CMOs where mortgage loans are removed from the balance sheet, mortgage-backed bonds (MBBs) and the mortgage loans backing them stay on the issuer's balance sheet. The financial institution issuing these bonds will separate the mortgage loans held on its balance sheet from its other assets and pledge those loans as collateral to support the MBBs. A trustee acting on behalf of the mortgage bondholders keeps track of the dedicated loans and checks periodically to be sure that the market value of the loans is greater than what is owed on the bonds.

Pass-throughs, CMOs, and other securitized assets have been among the most rapidly growing financial instruments in recent years. Several factors appear to account for the popularity of these asset-backed investments:

1. Guarantees from government agencies (in the case of home-mortgage-related securities) or from private institutions (such as banks or insurance companies pledging to back credit card loans).
2. The higher average yields available on securitized assets than on most government securities.
3. The lack of good-quality assets of other kinds in some markets around the globe.
4. The superior liquidity and marketability of securities backed by loans compared to the liquidity and marketability of loans themselves.

Stripped Securities

Key URLs
For a close look at the rules for bank investments in securities markets, see **www.occ.treas.gov, www.thecommunity banker.com, www. bondmarkets.com**, and **www.fdic.gov/ regulations/resources**.

In the early 1980s, security dealers developed a hybrid instrument known as the **stripped security**—a claim against either the principal or interest payments associated with a debt security, such as a Treasury bond. Dealers create stripped securities by separating the principal and interest payments from an underlying debt security and selling separate claims to these two promised income streams. Claims against only the principal payments are called *PO (principal-only) securities*, while claims against only the stream of promised interest payments are referred to as *IO (interest-only) securities*.

Stripped securities often display markedly different behavior from the underlying securities from which they come. In particular, stripped securities offer interest-rate hedging possibilities to help protect an investment portfolio against loss from interest-rate changes. The securities whose interest and principal payments are most likely to be stripped today include U.S. Treasury notes and bonds and mortgage-backed securities. Both PO and IO bond strips are really *zero coupon bonds* with no periodic interest payments; they therefore carry zero reinvestment risk. Each stripped security is sold at a discount from par, so the investor's rate of return is based solely on the security's price appreciation. Because bonds normally pay interest twice a year, an investor can lock in a fixed rate of return for a holding period as short as six months or as long as several years up to the maturity of the original bond. POs tend to be *more* price sensitive to interest-rate changes than regular bonds, whereas IOs tend to be *less* price sensitive than the original bonds.

10–6 Investment Securities Held by Banks

We have examined the principal investment opportunities available to investing institutions, but which of these investments do *banks* actually prefer? Table 10–3 provides an overview of investment securities held by all U.S.-insured banks as of year-end 2004. Clearly just a few types of securities dominate bank investment portfolios:

1. Obligations of the U.S. government and of various federal agencies such as the Federal National Mortgage Association (FNMA), the Federal Home Loan Mortgage Corporation (FHLMC), and the Government National Mortgage Association (GNMA).
2. State and local government obligations (municipals).
3. Nonmortgage-related asset-backed securities (such as obligations backed by credit card and automobile loans).

Federal-government-related IOUs account for about 65 percent of the U.S. commercial bank investment total, counting various types of U.S. government and federal agency–guaranteed mortgage-backed instruments. In fact, mortgage-loan-backed securities account for close to half of all U.S. bank investment holdings (with the heaviest concentrations of these mortgage-related instruments held by the largest banks in the industry) due to their ready marketability and comparatively high yields. Nongovernment-guaranteed asset-backed securities (such as instruments backed by auto and credit-card loans) fall into a distant second place followed by holdings of tax-exempt state and local government IOUs.

Key URL
To determine how one bank's investment portfolio compares to another's, an investments officer could consult the Federal Deposit Insurance Corporation's Statistics on Depository Institutions at **www3.fdic.gov/sdi**.

As reflected in Table 10–3, we see that banks hold relatively few private-sector securities, such as corporate bonds, notes, and commercial paper or corporate stock. They would prefer to make direct loans to customers rather than to buy their securities because the yield is often lower on investment securities than on loans and because purchasing securities usually generates no new deposits for a bank.

Table 10–3 also tells us that management targets most bank-held investments for eventual resale rather than planning to hold them until they reach maturity. These investments will generally be sold when a financial firm needs cash to cover customer withdrawals of funds, to make loans, or to take advantage of more lucrative investment opportunities. About a third of the U.S. commercial-bank investment portfolio consists of *trading account securities*, and the largest banks perform the role of dealers by purchasing investments and reselling them to customers.

TABLE 10–3 Investment Securities That FDIC-Insured U.S. Banks Hold (year-end 2004; billions of dollars at all U.S.-insured banks)

Source: Federal Deposit Insurance Corporation, *Statistics on Banking*, 2004.

Types of Securities Held	All FDIC-Insured U.S. Commercial Banks	Percent of all Investment Holdings	Percent Held at Banks with Total Assets of		
			Smallest Banks Less than $100 Mill.	Medium-Size Banks $100 Mill. to $1 Bill.	Largest Banks $1 Billion or More
U.S. Treasury securities	$ 63,838	4.1%	4.4%	3.6%	4.2%
U.S. government obligations: U.S. government issued non-mortgage-backed securities	10,845	0.7	0.6	0.5	0.7
U.S. government enterprise issued nonmortgage-backed securities	259,076	16.7	50.9	37.2	12.1
Mortgage-backed pass-through securities issued by FNMA and FHLMC	548,652	35.4	13.8	19.3	38.8
Mortgage-backed pass-through securities issued by GNMA	43,494	2.8	3.1	3.5	2.7
Collateralized mortgage obligations (CMOs and REMICs)	159,928	10.3	4.9	10.1	10.5
All U.S. government obligations	1,021,995	65.9	73.3	70.6	69.0
Securities issued by states and political subdivisions (municipals)	111,908	7.2	18.7	19.5	4.8
Asset-backed securities (including credit-card, home equity, auto, and commercial loan-backed securities)	69,335	4.5	0.0*	0.3	5.3
Other domestic debt securities	168,939	10.9	2.9	4.8	12.2
Foreign debt securities	99,781	6.4	0.0*	0.1	7.7
Equity securities	15,491	1.0	0.8	1.1	1.0
Total investment securities	$1,551,286	100.0%	100.0%	100.0%	100.0%
Memo items: Total investments to total assets	–	18.2%	24.7%	20.9%	17.7%
Investment securities held to maturity (amortized cost) as a percent of total debt securities held	–	8.3%	16.8%	13.6%	7.0%
Investment securities available for sale (fair value) as a percent of total debt securities held	–	91.7%	83.2%	86.4%	93.0%
Pledged securities as a percent of all investments	–	49.8%	37.3%	45.5%	50.9%
Mortgage-backed securities as a percent of all investments	–	56.5%	22.1%	34.2%	61.4%
Structured notes as a percent of all investments (fair value)	–	1.3%	6.4%	4.6%	0.6%
Assets held in trading accounts as a percent of all investments	–	32.5%	0.0%*	0.0%*	39.0%

Note: * indicates figure is less than 0.05 percent.

Factoid
After loans, what is the greatest source of revenue for most banks around the world?
Answer: Interest and dividends on investment securities.

As might be expected, the smallest banks tend to invest more heavily in government securities than do the largest. The smaller institutions tend to be more heavily exposed to risk of loss from economic problems in their local areas and, therefore, tend to use the lowest-risk securities to offset the high risk often inherent in their loans. In contrast, the largest banks tend to be more heavily invested in foreign securities and private debt and equity obligations, especially corporate bonds and commercial paper, all of which tend to carry greater risk exposure than government securities.

In total, investment securities represent just under a fifth of all U.S. bank assets nationwide. But this proportion of total bank assets varies with size and location. Banks operating in areas with weak loan demand usually hold significantly greater percentages of investment securities relative to their total assets. Moreover, as Table 10–3 suggests, size also plays a key role. The smallest size group of banks holds nearly a quarter of its assets in the form of investments, while the largest multi-billion-dollar banks hold only about 18 percent of their assets in investment securities, reflecting the relatively heavy loan demand most large banks face. In contrast, loans often represent over half of all bank assets and a majority of bank revenues come from loans; no surprise, loans generally carry significantly higher average yields than investments. But as we have already seen, the investment portfolio is expected to do several jobs in addition to generating income, such as tax sheltering, and reducing risk exposure.

Concept Check

10–4. What types of investment securities do banks seem to prefer the most? Can you explain why?

10–5. What are securitized assets? Why have they grown so rapidly in recent years?

10–6. What special risks do securitized assets present to institutions investing in them?

10–7. What are structured notes and stripped securities? What unusual features do they contain?

10–7 Factors Affecting Choice of Investment Securities

The investments officer of a financial firm must consider several factors in deciding which investment securities to buy, sell, or hold. The principal factors bearing on which investments are chosen include:

1. Expected rate of return
2. Tax exposure
3. Interest rate risk
4. Credit or default risk
5. Business risk
6. Liquidity risk
7. Call risk
8. Prepayment risk
9. Inflation risk
10. Pledging requirements

Filmtoid
What 1987 film busted Michael Douglas's and Charlie Sheen's characters for insider trading when the expected rates of return in the market were not enough to satisfy their greed?
Answer: *Wall Street*.

We will briefly review each of these factors.

Expected Rate of Return

The investments officer must determine the total rate of return that can reasonably be expected from each security, including the interest payments promised and possible capital gains or losses. For most investments, this requires the investments manager to calculate the **yield to maturity (YTM)** if a security is to be held to maturity or the planned **holding period yield (HPY)** between point of purchase and point of sale.

As we saw in Chapter 7, *the yield to maturity formula determines the rate of discount (or yield) on a loan or security that equalizes the market price of the loan or security with its expected stream of cash flows (interest and principal).* To illustrate how the YTM formula can be useful to an investments officer, suppose the officer is considering purchasing a $1,000 par-value Treasury note that promises an 8 percent coupon rate (or $1,000 × 0.08 = $80) and is slated to mature in five years. If the T-note's current price is $900, we have

$$\$900 = \frac{\$80}{(1 + \text{YTM})^1} + \frac{\$80}{(1 + \text{YTM})^2} + \cdots + \frac{\$80}{(1 + \text{YTM})^5}$$
$$+ \frac{\$1,000}{(1 + \text{YTM})^5} \qquad \textbf{(10–1)}$$

Key URL
There are many Web site calculators that can be employed to determine the yield to maturity (YTM) or holding period yield (HPY) for any given investment. See, for example, **www.investopedia.com/calculator**.

Solving using a financial calculator or software reveals that the yield to maturity (YTM) is 10.74 percent. The calculated YTM should be compared with the expected yields on other loans and investments to determine where the best possible return lies.

However, many financial firms frequently do not hold all their investments to maturity. Some must be sold off early to accommodate new loan demand or to cover deposit withdrawals. To deal with this situation, the investments officer needs to calculate the holding period yield (HPY). *The HPY is simply the rate of return (discount factor) that equates a security's purchase price with the stream of income expected until it is sold to another investor.* For example, suppose the 8 percent T-note described above and currently priced at $900 was sold at the end of two years for $950. Its holding period yield could be found from

$$\$900 = \frac{\$80}{(1 + \text{HPY})^1} + \frac{\$80}{(1 + \text{HPY})^2} + \frac{\$950}{(1 + \text{HPY})^2} \qquad \textbf{(10–2)}$$

In this case, the note's HPY would be 11.51 percent.[2]

Tax Exposure

Interest and capital gains income from most investments held by U.S. banks are taxed as *ordinary income* for tax purposes, just as are the wages and salaries earned by U.S. citizens. Because of their relatively high tax exposure, banks are more interested in the *after-tax rate of return* on loans and securities than in their before-tax return. This situation contrasts with such institutions as credit unions and mutual funds, which are generally tax-exempt.

The Tax Status of State and Local Government Bonds

For banks in the upper tax brackets, tax-exempt state and local government (municipal) bonds and notes have been attractive from time to time, depending upon their status in tax law.

For example, suppose that Aaa-rated corporate bonds are carrying an average gross yield to maturity of 7 percent, the prime rate on top-quality corporate loans is 6 percent, and Aaa-rated municipal bonds have a 5.5 percent gross yield to maturity. The investments officer for a financial firm subject to the corporate income tax could compare each of these potential yields using this formula:

$$\text{Before-tax gross yield} \times (1 - \text{Firm's marginal income tax rate}) \qquad \textbf{(10–3)}$$
$$= \text{After-tax gross yield}$$

---

[2]Using a financial calculator such as the TI BA II Plus™, N = 2, i=?, PV = −900, Pmt = 80, FV = 950. Solving for the interest rate (HPY) gives i = 11.51%.

This comparison yields the following expected after-tax gross returns for a taxed financial firm in the top 35 percent federal income tax bracket:

$$\frac{\text{Aaa-rated corporate bonds}}{7.00 \text{ percent} \times (1 - 0.35) = 4.55 \text{ percent}}$$

$$\frac{\text{Prime-rated loans}}{6 \text{ percent} \times (1 - 0.35) = 3.90 \text{ percent}}$$

$$\frac{\text{Aaa-rated municipal bonds}}{5.50 \text{ percent} \times (1 - 0) = 5.50 \text{ percent before and after taxes}}$$

Under the assumptions given, the municipal bond is the most attractive investment in gross yield. However, other considerations do enter into this decision, such as the need to attract other customer accounts, management's desire to keep good loan customers, and recent changes in tax laws.

Note that Equation (10–3) above permits an investments officer to calculate what is called the tax-equivalent yield (TEY) from a municipal bond or other tax-exempt security. The TEY indicates what before-tax rate of return on a taxable investment provides an investor with the same after-tax return as a tax-exempt investment would. The TEY can usually be found using the following relationship:

$$\text{TEY} = \frac{\text{After-tax return on a tax-exempt investment}}{(1 - \text{Investing firm's marginal tax rate})} \qquad \textbf{(10–4)}$$

In the numerical example above the Aaa-rated corporate bond and the prime-rated loans would have to have a before-tax yield of 8.46 percent to match the Aaa-municipal bond's after-tax yield of 5.50 percent.

The Impact of Changes in Tax Laws

Tax reform in the United States has had a major impact on the relative attractiveness of state and local government bonds as investments for banks. Prior to federal tax reform legislation during the 1980s, banks held close to 30 percent of all state and local government debt outstanding. But their share of the municipal market has fallen substantially since that time, due to (1) declining tax advantages, (2) lower corporate tax rates, and (3) fewer qualified tax-exempt securities.

Bank Qualified Bonds

Before 1986 the federal tax code allowed significant tax deductions for interest expenses incurred when banks borrow funds to buy municipal securities. Today banks buying *bank qualified bonds*—those issued by smaller local governments (governments issuing no more than $10 million of public securities per year)—are allowed to deduct 80 percent of any interest paid to fund these bond purchases. This tax advantage is *not* available for nonbank-qualified bonds.

Prior to the 1986 Tax Reform Act the highest corporate tax bracket was 46 percent. Today the top bracket is 35 percent for corporations earning more than $10 million in annual taxable income or 34 percent otherwise. Lower tax brackets reduce the tax savings associated with the tax-exemption feature.[3]

---

[3]Under current federal law, U.S. banks must calculate their income taxes in two different ways—using a normal tax rate schedule (maximum 35 percent tax rate) and using an alternative minimum tax rate of 20 percent, and then must pay the greater of the two different amounts. Interest income from municipals has to be added in to determine each bank's alternative minimum tax, making municipal income subject to at least some taxation.

Real Banks, Real Decisions

CRISIS IN THE INVESTMENTS MARKET: WHAT THE 9/11 TERRORIST ATTACKS DID TO THE DELIVERY OF SECURITIES TO INVESTORS

The market for investment securities is one of the largest markets in the world. Trillions of dollars change hands daily and both payments and the delivery of securities purchased generally occur on time. Now consider what happened following the terrorist attacks on September 11, 2001. Within hours the system for delivering U.S. Treasury securities—the most popular financial investment in the world—began to unravel. Many sellers of Treasuries were unable to meet their promises to deliver securities and some buyers couldn't execute payments for them on the scheduled date. These *settlement fails* soared from an average of less than $2 billion a day before the terrorist attacks to as much as $190 billion a day immediately following the attacks.

The settlement fails occurred initially because some communications systems linking dealers, banks, and their customers were destroyed or damaged when the twin towers of the World Trade Center collapsed. Moreover, several key institutions experienced destruction of their records. A severe shortage of certain Treasury securities developed, and the usual remedy for such shortages—borrowing securities through special collateral repurchase agreements—became as costly as failure to deliver what was promised.

Fortunately, two critical government agencies reacted quickly. The Federal Reserve poured liquid funds into the banking system so that emergency money was available. The U.S. Treasury, even though it didn't need to borrow additional funds at the time, announced the reopening of a key security issue—the 10-year T-note that was currently "on the run." The Treasury's same day ("snap") auction expanded the supply of these particular notes by 50 percent, which helped to make borrowing these securities a superior alternative to failing to settle.

An excellent article prepared by two staff officers at the Federal Reserve Bank of New York, Michael J. Fleming and Kenneth D. Garbade [7] offers some proposals for the future, should a tragedy of comparable magnitude happen again. These proposals include setting up an expanded government facility that would be able to lend securities experiencing excess demand. Indeed, in the wake of 9/11 the Federal Reserve expanded its program, set up originally in 1969, to lend Treasury securities from its huge system open market account to dealers facing settlement problems.

Fewer state and local bonds qualify for tax exemption today. If 10 percent or more of the proceeds of a municipal bond issue is used to benefit a private individual or business, it is considered a private activity issue and fully taxable. In addition, Congress placed ceilings on the amount of industrial development bonds (IDBs) local governments could issue to provide new facilities or tax breaks in order to attract new industry. These laws reduced the supply of tax-exempt securities for investors to purchase and contributed to the lower proportion of municipals found in the securities portfolios of many taxed financial institutions.

To evaluate the attractiveness of municipals, financial firms calculate the net after-tax returns and/or the tax-equivalent yields to enable comparisons with other investment alternatives. The net after-tax return of bank-qualified municipals is calculated as follows:

$$\begin{matrix} \text{Net after-tax} \\ \text{return on} \\ \text{municipals} \\ \text{(in percent)} \end{matrix} = \begin{bmatrix} \begin{matrix} \text{Nominal return} \\ \text{on municipals} \\ \text{after taxes} \\ \text{(in percent)} \end{matrix} - \begin{matrix} \text{Interest expense incurred} \\ \text{in acquiring the} \\ \text{municipals} \\ \text{(in percent)} \end{matrix} \end{bmatrix}$$

$$+ \begin{matrix} \text{Tax advantage} \\ \text{of a} \\ \text{qualified bond} \end{matrix} \qquad \textbf{(10–5)}$$

where the tax advantage of a qualified bond is determined like this:

$$\begin{matrix} \text{Tax advantage} \\ \text{of} \\ \text{qualified} \\ \text{bond} \end{matrix} = \begin{bmatrix} \begin{matrix} \text{The bank's} \\ \text{marginal} \\ \text{income} \\ \text{tax rate} \\ \text{(in percent)} \end{matrix} \times \begin{matrix} \text{Percentage of} \\ \text{interest expense} \\ \text{that is still} \\ \text{tax deductible} \\ \text{(if any)} \end{matrix} \times \begin{matrix} \text{Interest} \\ \text{expense of} \\ \text{acquiring the} \\ \text{municipals} \\ \text{(in percent)} \end{matrix} \end{bmatrix} \quad \textbf{(10–6)}$$

Suppose a bank purchases a bank-qualified bond from a small city, county, or school district and the bond carries a nominal (published) gross rate of return of 7 percent. Assume also that the bank had to borrow the funds needed to make this purchase at an interest rate of 6.5 percent and is in the top (35 percent) income tax bracket. Because this bond comes from a small local government that qualifies for special tax treatment under the 1986 Tax Reform Act, the bond's net annual after-tax return to the bank (after all funding costs and taxes) must be:

$$\begin{matrix} \text{Net after-tax return} \\ \text{on a qualified} \\ \text{municipal security} \end{matrix} \begin{matrix} = (7.0 - 6.50) + (0.35 \times 0.80 \times 6.50) \\ \\ = 0.50 \text{ percent} + 1.82 \text{ percent} \\ = 2.32 \text{ percent} \end{matrix} \quad \textbf{(10–7)}$$

The investments officer would want to compare this calculated net after-tax return to the net returns after taxes available from other securities and loans, both taxable and tax-exempt. If the municipal bond described previously had come from a larger state or local government not eligible for special treatment under the Tax Reform Act, *none* of the interest expense would have been tax deductible and the net tax advantage to the bank purchasing the nonqualified bonds would be zero.

The Tax Swapping Tool

The size of a lender's revenue from loans in any given year plays a key role in how its investments are handled. In years when loan revenues are high, it is often beneficial to engage in tax swapping. In a **tax swap,** the lending institution sells lower-yielding securities at a loss in order to reduce its current taxable income, while simultaneously purchasing new high-yielding securities in order to boost future returns on its investment portfolio.

Tax considerations in choosing securities to buy or sell tend to be more important for larger lending institutions than for smaller ones. Usually larger lending institutions are in the top income-tax bracket and have the most to gain from security portfolio trades that minimize their tax exposure. The portfolio manager tries to estimate the institution's projected net taxable income under alternative portfolio choices.

This involves, among other things, estimating how much tax-exempt income the taxed lending institution can use. No financial firm can use unlimited amounts of tax-exempt income. For depository institutions, at least, some taxable income will be necessary to offset the allowable annual deduction for possible loan losses (ALL). However, once these conditions are met, the basic decision between purchasing tax-exempt securities or purchasing taxable securities and loans comes down to the relative after-tax returns of the two.

The Portfolio Shifting Tool

Lending institutions also do a great deal of **portfolio shifting** in their holdings of investment securities, with both taxes and higher returns in mind. Financial firms, for example, often sell off selected securities at a loss in order to offset large amounts of loan income,

Insights and Issues

RISKY AND COMPLEX INVESTMENTS ON THE RISE: RANGE NOTES, BANK OFFICER LIFE INSURANCE (BOLI), EQUITY-LINKED CDS, AND TRUST-PREFERRED SECURITIES

In recent years many financial firms have had the tendency to accept greater risk and complexity in their investment portfolios. New instruments have appeared that are intended to do more than just provide liquidity and income. Prominent examples include range notes, bank officer life insurance (BOLI), equity-linked CDs, and trust-preferred securities.

Range notes are callable securities that promise relatively high coupon interest rates contingent on which way the market moves. These notes pay out interest provided an agreed-upon market index stays within a specified range. If the market index moves outside the designated range, there is no payoff. For example, a range note might call for paying its holder interest only if the interest rate on Euro-currency deposits stays between 2 and 4 percent.

Some financial firms have purchased *life insurance on their officers and directors (BOLI)*, with the purchasing firm designated as beneficiary. As long as the purchaser continues to pay annual premiums, the BOLI is recorded as an asset on its books. If the officer or director dies during the policy's term the purchasing institution receiving the funds has several options, including donating the proceeds to charity and securing a tax deduction.

Equity-linked CDs contain features of both debt and stock. They promise guaranteed interest income and provide an embedded option, offering an additional bonus based on a market index (most often Standard & Poor's 500 stock index). For example, a bull CD with an embedded call option scores additional returns if the market index rises above a designated strike price. Alternatively, a bear CD contains a put option that pays off only if the market index falls below the strike price.

Finally, *trust-preferred securities* are created with the help of an investment banker who sets up a special purpose entity (SPE) that issues preferred shares. In return, the participating institution issues long-term debentures to support the new stock. Multiple possible payoffs include that the debentures are considered to be new capital, the interest paid out is tax deductible, and the risk of shareholder dilution is reduced.

Regulatory agencies have expressed concern in recent years that many such investments carry considerable credit and liquidity risk. Regulators insist that purchasing institutions do a careful *prepurchase analysis* of these investments and employ *stress testing* to determine what their possible risk exposure would be under different market conditions. (See, for example, **www.fdic.gov, www.emis.de/journals, www.wib.org,** and **www.aba.com**.)

thereby reducing their tax liability. They may also shift their portfolios simply to substitute new, higher-yielding securities for old security holdings whose yields are well below current market levels. The result may be to take substantial short-run losses in return for the prospect of higher long-run profits.

For example, the investments officer of First National Bank may be considering the following shift in its municipal bond portfolio:

Find a buyer for $10 million in 10-year New York City bonds bearing a 7 percent coupon rate that the bank currently holds.	→ Current market price Value recorded on the bank's balance sheet Annual interest income	= $9.5 million = $10 million = $0.7 million
Then acquire $10 million in 10-year Orange County (City of Los Angeles) bonds bearing a 9 percent coupon rate to add to the bank's investment portfolio.	→ Current market price Annual interest income	= $10 million = $0.9 million

Clearly, this bank takes an immediate $500,000 loss before taxes ($10 million – $9.5 million) on selling the 7 percent New York City bonds. But if First National is in the 35 percent tax bracket, its immediate loss after taxes becomes only $500,000 × (1 – 0.35), or $325,000. Moreover, it has swapped this loss for an additional $200,000 annually in tax exempt income for 10 years. This portfolio shift is probably worth the immediate loss the bank must absorb from its current earnings. Moreover, if the bank has high taxable income from loans, that near-term loss can be used to lower current taxable income and perhaps even increase this year's after-tax profits.

Interest Rate Risk

Changing interest rates create real risk for investments officers and their institutions. Rising interest rates lower the market value of previously issued bonds and notes, with the longest-term issues generally suffering the greatest losses. Moreover, periods of rising interest rates are often marked by surging loan demand. Because a lender's first priority is usually to make loans, many investments must be sold off to generate cash for lending at the very time their prices are headed downward. Such sales frequently result in substantial capital losses, which the lender hopes to counteract by a combination of tax benefits and the relatively higher yields available on loans. On the other hand, as noted back in the opening paragraph of this chapter, investments officers often find themselves purchasing investment securities when interest rates and loan demand are declining and, therefore, the prices the investments officer must pay for desired investments are headed upward. A growing number of tools to hedge (counteract) **interest rate risk** have appeared in recent years, including financial futures, options, interest-rate swaps, gap management, and duration, as we saw earlier in Chapters 7–9.

Credit or Default Risk

The investments made by banks and their closest competitors are closely regulated due to the **credit risk** displayed by many securities, especially those issued by private corporations and some governments. The risk that the security issuer may default on the principal or interest owed has led to regulatory controls that prohibit the acquisition of speculative securities—those rated below Baa by Moody's or BBB on Standard & Poor's bond-rating schedule. (See Table 10–4 for definitions of the various credit rating symbols used.) U.S. banks generally are

TABLE 10–4   Default Risk Ratings on Marketable Investment Securities

Investment securities sold by corporations and state and local governments must be assigned credit ratings that assess their probability of default before they can be successfully marketed. The two most popular private security rating companies are Moody's Investor Service and Standard & Poor's Corporation. Their credit quality rating symbols have served as general guides for assessing credit quality for decades:

Credit Quality of Securities	Rating Symbols		
	Moody's Rating Category	Standard & Poor's Rating Category	
Best quality/smallest investment risk	Aaa	AAA	Investment quality or
High grade or high quality	Aa	AA	investment grade/
Upper medium grade	A	A	considered acceptable
Medium grade	Baa	BBB	for most banks and
Medium grade with some			other closely regulated
speculative elements	Ba	BB	financial firms
Lower medium grade	B	B	Speculative quality and
Poor standing/may be in default	Caa	CCC	junk bonds/not considered
Speculative/often in default	Ca	CC	suitable for banks and
Lowest-grade speculative securities/			other closely regulated
poor prospects	C	C	financial firms
Defaulted securities and securities		DDD	
issued by bankrupt firms	Not rated	DD	
		D	

Most depository institutions are limited to investment-grade securities—that is, they must purchase securities rated AAA to BBB (by Standard & Poor's) or Aaa to Baa (by Moody's). Unrated securities may also be acquired, but the regulated institution must be able to demonstrate they are of investment-grade quality.

allowed to buy only *investment-grade securities,* rated at least Baa or BBB, in order to protect depositors against excessive risk. Moreover, banks through their securities affiliates or through the formation of a financial holding company are permitted to underwrite government and privately issued securities (including corporate bonds, notes, and stock). (See Chapters 1, 2, 3, and 4 for a review of legislative, regulatory, and court decisions that have significantly expanded the security underwriting powers of banking organizations in recent years.)

In 1997 Moody's Investors Service announced significant modification of its credit rating system for bonds issued by state and local (municipal) governments. Specifically, securities in selected categories (such as Aa, A, and Baa) have a 2 or 3 numerical modifier added to their rating to differentiate securities slightly different in quality that carry similar letter grades. In 1981 Moody's added the number 1 to the letter grades attached to some A- and B-rated municipals. Now, with the numbers 2 and 3 also added to some letter grades, an investments officer is alerted that a 1 means the security in question ranks at the upper end of its letter rating category, while a 2 implies the issue lies in the middle range and a 3 suggests the security in question lies at the low end of the letter grade category. These 1, 2, and 3 numerical modifiers were also added to corporate bond ratings from Aa to B. The table below provides a picture of these more refined credit ratings:

Moody's Investor Service's Credit Rating Symbols for State and Local Government Securities		
Aaa	Baa1	Caa
Aa1	Baa2	Ca
Aa2	Baa3	C
Aa3	Ba1	
A1	Ba2	
A2	Ba3	
A3	B1	
	B2	
	B3	

The above rating modifiers reflect growing concern about recent trends in the municipal market, especially increased credit risk and volatility.

There has been a fluctuating but general uptrend in municipal defaults over the past three decades. In 1991 a record 258 municipal bond defaults occurred, involving about $5 billion in defaulted IOUs. While the number of defaulted issues annually has since fallen somewhat, many state and local governments are under stress today due to declining federal monies to support local welfare, health (including medicaid), education, and other programs; rising needs for street, sewer, and other infrastructure repairs; higher energy costs; and taxpayer resistance to higher taxes. Moreover, with many local areas opposing new taxes and spending programs, many state and local governments have turned to more risky revenue bonds to supplement their financing options.

As we saw in the preceding chapter, many lending institutions have developed new methods for dealing with credit risk in their investments and loans in recent years. Credit options and swaps can be used to protect the expected yield on investment securities. For example, investments officers may be able to find another financial institution willing to swap an uncertain return on securities held for a lower but more certain return based upon a standard reference rate, such as the market yield on Treasury bonds. Credit options are also available in today's markets that help to hedge the value of a corporate bond, for example. If the bond issuer defaults, the option holder receives a payoff from the credit option that at least partially offsets the loss. Investments officers can also use credit options to protect the market value of a bond in case its credit rating is lowered.

Business Risk

Financial institutions of all sizes face significant risk that the economy of the market area they serve may turn down, with falling sales and rising unemployment. These adverse developments, often called **business risk**, can be reflected quickly in the loan portfolio, where delinquent loans may rise as borrowers struggle to generate enough cash flow to pay the lender. Because business risk is always present, many financial institutions rely heavily on their security portfolios to offset the impact of this form of risk on their loan portfolios. This usually means that many investment securities purchased will come from borrowers located outside the principal market for loans. For example, a bank located in Dallas or Kansas City will probably purchase a substantial quantity of municipal bonds from cities and other local governments outside the Midwest (e.g., Los Angeles or New York debt securities). Examiners often encourage out-of-market security purchases to balance risk exposure in the loan portfolio.

Liquidity Risk

Financial institutions must be ever mindful of the possibility they will be required to sell investment securities in advance of their maturity due to liquidity needs and be subjected to **liquidity risk.** Thus, a key issue that a portfolio manager must face in selecting a security for investment purposes is *the breadth and depth of its resale market*. Liquid securities are, by definition, those investments that have a ready market, relatively stable price over time, and high probability of recovering the original amount invested (i.e., the risk to the principal value is low). Treasury securities are generally the most liquid and have the most active resale markets, followed by federal agency securities, municipals, and mortgage-backed securities. Unfortunately, the purchase of a large volume of liquid, readily marketable securities tends to lower the average yield from a financial institution's earning assets and reduce its profitability. Thus, management faces a trade-off between profitability and liquidity that must be reevaluated daily as market interest rates and exposure to liquidity risk change.

Call Risk

Many corporations and some governments that issue securities reserve the right to call in those instruments in advance of maturity and pay them off. Because such calls usually take place when market interest rates have declined (and the borrower can issue new securities bearing lower interest costs), the financial firm investing in callable securities runs the risk of an earnings loss because it must reinvest its recovered funds at lower interest rates. Investments officers generally try to minimize this **call risk** by purchasing callable instruments bearing longer call deferments (so that a call cannot occur for several years) or simply by avoiding the purchase of callable securities. Fortunately for investments officers, call privileges attached to bonds have been declining significantly in recent years due to the availability of other tools to manage interest-rate risk (though call privileges are quite common today in the $2 trillion market for municipal bonds).

Prepayment Risk

A form of risk specific to asset-backed securities is **prepayment risk.** This form of risk arises because the realized interest and principal payments (cash flow) from a pool of securitized loans, such as GNMA or FNMA pass-throughs, collateralized mortgage obligations (CMOs), or securitized packages of auto or credit card loans, may be quite different from the cash flows expected originally. Indeed, having to price the prepayment option associated with asset-backed securities distinguishes these investments from any other investments.

For example, consider what can happen to the planned interest and principal payments from a pool of home mortgage loans that serve as collateral for the issuance of mortgage-backed securities. Variations in cash flow to holders of the securities backed by these loans can arise from

A. *Loan refinancings*, which tend to accelerate when market interest rates fall (in this case, borrowers may realize they will save on loan payments if they replace their existing loans with new lower-rate loans).
B. *Turnover of the assets behind the loans* (in this case borrowers may sell out and move away or some borrowers may not be able to meet their required loan payments and default on their loans).

In either or both of these cases some loans will be terminated or paid off ahead of schedule, generating smaller long-term cash flows than expected that can lower the expected rate of return from loan-backed securities.

The pace at which loans that underlie asset-backed securities are terminated or paid off depends heavily upon the interest rate spread between current interest rates on similar type loans and the interest rates attached to loans in the securitized pool. When market interest rates drop below the rates attached to loans in the pool far enough to cover refinancing costs, more borrowers will call in their loans and pay them off early. This means that the market value of a loan-backed security depends not only upon the promised cash flows it will generate, but also on the projected prepayments and loan defaults that occur—that is,

$$\text{Market value (price) of a loan-backed security} = \frac{\text{Expected cash flows adjusted for any prepayments or defaults of existing loans in the pool in Period 1}}{(1 + y/m)^1} + \cdots + \frac{\text{Expected cash flows adjusted for any prepayments or defaults of existing loans in the pool in Period n} \times m}{(1 + y/m)^{n \times m}} \quad (10\text{–}8)$$

where n is the number of years required for the last of the loans in the pool to be paid off or retired, m represents the number of times during the year interest and principal must be paid to holders of the loan-backed securities, and y is the expected yield to maturity from these securities.

In order to properly value an asset-backed security, the investments officer needs to make some reasonable assumptions about what volume of loans might be prepaid or terminated while his or her institution is holding the security. In making estimates of loan prepayment behavior, the officer must consider such factors as expected market interest rates, future changes in the shape of the yield curve, the impact of seasonal factors (e.g., most homes are bought and sold in the spring of each year), the condition of the economy, and how old the loans in the pool are (because new loans are less likely to be repaid than older loans).

One commonly employed way of making loan prepayment estimates is to use the prepayment model developed by the Public Securities Association (PSA), which calculates an average loan prepayment rate based upon past experience. The so-called PSA model assumes, for example, that insured home mortgages will prepay at an annual rate of 0.2 percent the first month and the prepayment rate will grow by 0.2 percent each month for the first 30 months. Loan prepayments are then assumed to level off at a 6 percent annual rate for the remainder of the loan pool's life. When an investments officer adopts the PSA model without any modifications, he or she is said to be assuming a 100 percent PSA repayment

Key URLs
To learn more about PSA models in estimating prepayments for loan-backed securities, see, for example, **www.investopedia.com/terms/p/psa.asp** and **http://financial-dictionary.thefree dictionary.com**

rate. However, the investments officer may decide to alter the PSA model to 75 percent PSA or some other percentage multiplier based upon his or her knowledge of the nature of loans in the pool, such as their geographic location, distribution of maturities, or the average age of borrowers.

It must be noted that while prepayment of securitized loans tends to accelerate in periods of falling interest rates, this is not always an adverse development for investors in asset-backed securities. For example, as prepayments accelerate, an investing institution recovers its invested cash at a faster rate, which can be a favorable development if it has other profitable uses for those funds. Moreover, lower interest rates increase the present value of all projected cash flows from a loan-backed security so that its market value could rise. The investments officer must compare these potential benefits to the potential losses from falling interest payments in the form of lower reinvestment rates and lost future income from loans that are prepaid. In general, asset-backed securities will fall in value when interest rates decline if the expected loss of interest income from prepaid loans and reduced reinvestment earnings exceeds the expected benefits that arise from recovering cash more quickly from prepaid loans.

Inflation Risk

Key URLs
To explore the recent growth of the loan-backed securities market and bank activity in that market see especially
www.dresdner-bank. com/index.html and **www.fanniemae.com.**

Investing institutions must be alert to the possibility that the purchasing power of interest income and repaid principal from a security or loan will be eroded by rising prices for goods and services. Inflation can also erode the value of the stockholders' investment in a financial firm—its *net worth*. Some protection against **inflation risk** is provided by short-term securities and those with variable interest rates, which usually grant the investments officer greater flexibility in responding to any flare-up in inflationary pressures.

One recently developed inflation risk hedge that may aid some financial firms is the United States Treasury Department's TIPS—Treasury Inflation-Protected Securities. Beginning in January 1997 the Treasury began issuing 5-, 10-, and 30-year inflation-adjusted marketable notes and later announced the offering of inflation-protected savings bonds for the small investor. Both the coupon rate and the principal (face) value of a TIPS are adjusted annually to match changes in the consumer price index (CPI). Thus, the spread between the market yield on noninflation-adjusted Treasury notes or bonds and the yield on TIPS of the same maturity provides an index of expected inflation as viewed by the average investor in the marketplace. If expected inflation rises, TIPS tend to become more valuable to investors.

Key URLs
Additional information on TIPS is available at **www.Inflation-Linked.com** and **www.publicdebt.treas. gov/sec/seciis.htm.**

Many financial institutions have not been particularly enthusiastic about TIPS recently for a variety of reasons. With inflation proceeding at a relatively moderate pace in the United States, the market yield on TIPS has been relatively modest as well. Then, too, other inflation hedges are available, such as real estate and selected stocks, with the potential for somewhat greater returns. Moreover, TIPS do not protect investors from all the effects of inflation, such as moving into higher tax brackets, and they carry market risk as do regular bonds.

Concept Check

10–8. How is the expected yield on most bonds determined?

10–9. If a government bond is expected to mature in two years and has a current price of $950, what is the bond's YTM if it has a par value of $1,000 and a promised coupon rate of 10 percent? Suppose this bond is sold one year after purchase for a price of $970. What would this investor's holding period yield be?

10–10. What forms of risk affect investments?

10–11. How has the tax exposure of various U.S. bank security investments changed in recent years?

Concept Check

10–12. Suppose a corporate bond an investments officer would like to purchase for her bank has a before-tax yield of 8.98 percent and the bank is in the 35 percent federal income tax bracket. What is the bond's after-tax gross yield? What after-tax rate of return must a prospective loan generate to be competitive with the corporate bond? Does a loan have some advantages for a lending institution that a corporate bond would not have?

10–13. What is the net after-tax return on a qualified municipal security whose nominal gross return is 6 percent, the cost of borrowed funds is 5 percent, and the financial firm holding the bond is in the 35 percent tax bracket? What is the tax-equivalent yield (TEY) on this tax-exempt security?

10–14. Spiro Savings Bank currently holds a government bond valued on the day of its purchase at $5 million, with a promised interest yield of 6 percent, whose current market value is $3.9 million. Comparable quality bonds are available today for a promised yield of 8 percent. What are the advantages to Spiro Savings from selling the government bond bearing a 6 percent promised yield and buying some 8 percent bonds?

10–15. What is tax swapping? What is portfolio shifting? Give an example of each.

10–16. Why do depository institutions face pledging requirements when they accept government deposits?

10–17. What types of securities are used to meet collateralization requirements?

Pledging Requirements

Depository institutions in the United States cannot accept deposits from federal, state, and local governments unless they post collateral acceptable to these governmental units in order to safeguard public funds. The first $100,000 of these public deposits is covered by federal deposit insurance; the rest must be backed up by holdings of Treasury and federal agency securities valued at par. Some municipal bonds (provided they are at least A-rated) can also be used to secure the federal government's deposits in depository institutions, but these securities must be valued at a discount from par (usually 80 to 90 percent of their face value) in order to give governmental depositors an added cushion of safety. State and local government deposit **pledging** requirements differ widely from state to state, though most allow a combination of federal and municipal securities to meet government pledging requirements. Sometimes the government owning the deposit requires that the pledged securities be placed with a trustee not affiliated with the institution receiving the deposit.

Pledging requirements also exist for selected other liabilities. For example, when a bank borrows from the discount window of the Federal Reserve bank in its district, it must pledge either federal securities or other collateral acceptable to the Fed. If a financial institution uses repurchase agreements (RPs) to raise money, it must pledge some of its securities (usually Treasury and federal agency issues) as collateral in order to receive funds at the low RP rate.

10–8 Investment Maturity Strategies

Once the investments officer chooses the type of securities he or she believes a financial firm should hold, there remains the question of how to distribute those security holdings over time. That is, what *maturities* of securities should the investing institution hold? Should it purchase mainly short-term bills and notes, or only long-term bonds, or perhaps some combination of the two? Several maturity distribution strategies have been developed over the years, each with its own unique set of advantages and disadvantages. (See Exhibits 10–2 and 10–3.)

EXHIBIT 10–2

Alternative Maturity
Strategies for
Managing Investment
Portfolios

STRATEGY: Divide
investment portfolio
equally among all
maturities acceptable
to the investing institution.
ADVANTAGES: Reduces
investment income
fluctuations/requires
little management
expertise.

The Ladder or Spaced-Maturity Policy

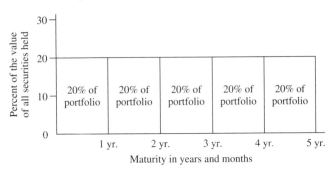

STRATEGY: All
security investments
are short-term.
ADVANTAGES:
Strengthens the
financial firm's
liquidity position
and avoids large
capital losses if
market interest
rates rise.

The Front-End Load Maturity Policy

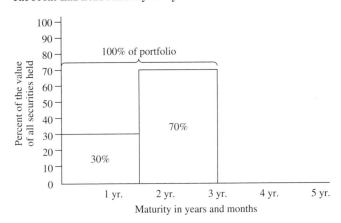

STRATEGY: All
security investments
are long-term.
ADVANTAGES:
Maximizes
income potential
from security
investments if
market interest
rates fall.

The Back-End Load Maturity Policy

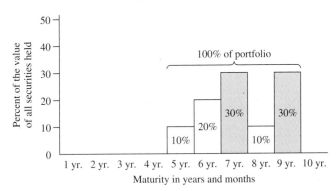

The Ladder, or Spaced-Maturity, Policy

One popular approach to the maturity problem, particularly among smaller institutions, is to choose some maximum acceptable maturity and then invest in an equal proportion of securities in each of several maturity intervals until the maximum acceptable maturity is reached.

For example, suppose management decided that it did not want to purchase any bonds or notes with maturities longer than five years. It might then decide to invest 20 percent of the firm's investment portfolio in securities one year or less from maturity, another 20 percent in securities maturing within two years but no less than one year, another 20 percent in the interval of two to three years, and so forth, until the

EXHIBIT 10–3
Additional Maturity
Strategies for
Managing Investment
Portfolios

STRATEGY:
Security holdings
are divided between
short-term and
long-term.
ADVANTAGES:
Helps to meet
liquidity needs with
short-term securities
and to achieve earnings
goals due to higher
potential earnings from
the long-term portion
of the portfolio.

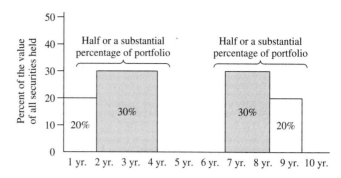

The Barbell Investment Portfolio Strategy

STRATEGY:
Change the mix of
investment maturities
as the interest-rate
outlook changes.
ADVANTAGES:
Maximizes the
potential for earnings
(and also for losses).

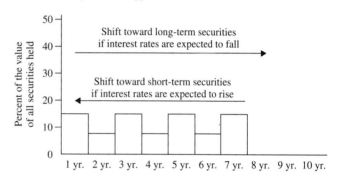

The Rate-Expectations Approach

five-year point is reached. This strategy certainly does *not* maximize investment income, but it has the advantage of reducing income fluctuations and requires little expertise to carry out. Moreover, this ladder approach tends to build in investment flexibility. Because some securities are always rolling over into cash, the firm can take advantage of any promising opportunities that may appear.

The Front-End Load Maturity Policy

Another popular strategy is to purchase only short-term securities and place all investments within a brief interval of time. For example, the investments officer may decide to invest 100 percent of his or her institution's funds not needed for loans or cash reserves in securities three years or less from maturity. This approach stresses using the investment portfolio primarily as a source of *liquidity* rather than a source of income.

The Back-End Load Maturity Policy

An opposite approach would stress the investment portfolio as a source of *income*. An investing institution following the *back-end load* approach might decide to invest only in bonds in the 5- to 10-year maturity range. This institution would probably rely heavily on borrowing in the money market to help meet its liquidity requirements.

The Barbell Strategy

A combination of the front-end and back-end load approaches is the *barbell strategy,* in which an investing institution places most of its funds in a short-term portfolio of highly liquid securities at one extreme and in a long-term portfolio of bonds at the other extreme, with minimal investment holdings in intermediate maturities. The short-term portfolio provides liquidity, while the long-term portfolio is designed to generate income.

The Rate Expectations Approach

The most aggressive of all maturity strategies is one that continually shifts maturities of securities in line with current forecasts of interest rates and the economy. This *total performance*, or *rate expectation*, approach calls for shifting investments toward the short end of the maturity spectrum when interest rates are expected to rise and toward the long end when falling interest rates are expected. Such an approach offers the potential for large capital gains, but also raises the specter of substantial losses. It requires in-depth knowledge of market forces, presents greater risk if expectations turn out to be wrong, and carries greater transactions costs because it may require frequent security trading and switching.

Banks, for example, often trade some of their unpledged security holdings whenever there is the prospect of significant gains in expected returns or the opportunity to reduce asset risk without significant loss in expected yield. They are particularly aggressive when loan revenues are down and the sale of securities whose market value has risen will boost net income and shareholder returns. However, because losses on security trades reduce before-tax income, portfolio managers do not like to take such losses unless they can demonstrate to the board of directors that the loss will be more than made up by higher expected returns on new assets acquired from the proceeds of the security sale. In general, investing institutions are inclined to trade securities if (*a*) their expected after-tax returns can be raised through effective tax management strategies; (*b*) higher yields can be locked in at the long-term end of the yield curve when the forecast is for falling interest rates; (*c*) the trade would contribute to an overall improvement in asset quality that would enable the institution to better weather an economic downturn; or (*d*) the investment portfolio can be moved toward higher-grade securities without an appreciable loss in expected return (especially if problems are developing in the loan portfolio).

10–9 Maturity Management Tools

In choosing among various maturities of investments to acquire, investments officers need to consider carefully the use of two key maturity management tools—the *yield curve* and *duration*. These tools help the investments officer understand more fully the consequences and potential impact upon earnings and risk from any particular maturity mix of securities he or she chooses.

The Yield Curve

As we saw in Chapter 7, the **yield curve** is simply a picture of how market interest rates differ across loans and securities of varying term or time to maturity. Each yield curve, such as the one drawn in Exhibit 10–4, assumes that all interest rates (or yields) included along the curve are measured at the same time and that all other rate-determining forces are held fixed. While the curve in Exhibit 10–4 slopes upward as we move to the right, yield curves may also slope downward or be horizontal, indicating that short- and long-term interest rates at that particular moment are about the same.

Yield curve shapes have critical implications for the decisions an investments officer must make. For example, the yield curve contains an *implicit forecast of future interest rate changes*. Positively sloped yield curves reflect the average expectation in the market that future short-term interest rates will be higher than they are today. In this case, investors expect to see an upward interest-rate movement, and they often translate this expectation into action by shifting their investment holdings away from longer-term securities (which will incur greater capital losses when market interest rates do rise). Conversely, a downward-sloping yield curve points to investor expectations of declining short-term interest rates in the period ahead. The investments officer will consider lengthening portfolio

EXHIBIT 10–4
The Yield Curve

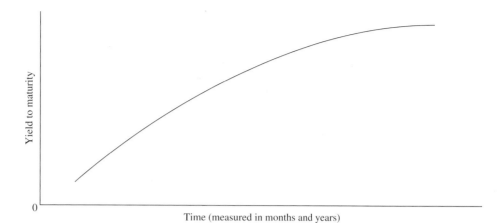

maturity because falling interest rates offer the prospect of substantial capital gains income from longer-term investments.

Yield curves also provide the investments officer with a clue about *overpriced and underpriced securities*. Because the prevailing yield curve indicates what the yield to maturity *should* be for each maturity, a security whose yield lies above the curve represents a tempting *buy* situation; its yield is temporarily too high (and, therefore, its price is too low). On the other hand, a security whose yield lies below the curve represents a possible *sell* or "don't buy" situation because its yield is too low for its maturity (and, thus, its price is too high).

In the long run, yield curves send signals about *what stage of the business cycle the economy presently occupies*. They generally rise in economic expansions and fall in recessions.

The yield curve is also useful because it tells the investments officer something important about the *current trade-offs between greater returns and greater risks*. The yield curve's shape determines how much additional yield the investments officer can earn by replacing shorter-term securities with longer-term issues, or vice versa. For example, a steeply sloped positive yield curve that rises 100 basis points between 2-year and 10-year maturity bonds indicates that the investments officer can pick up one percentage point in extra yield (less broker or dealer commissions and any tax liability incurred) by switching from 2-year bonds to 10-year bonds. However, 10-year bonds are generally more volatile in price than 2-year bonds, so the investments officer must be willing to accept greater risk of a capital loss on the 10-year bonds if interest rates rise. Longer-term bonds often have a thinner market in case cash must be raised quickly. The investments officer can measure along the curve what gain in yield will result from maturity extension and compare that gain against the likelihood a financial firm will face a liquidity crisis ("cash out") or suffer capital losses if interest rates go in an unexpected direction.

Likewise, yield curves provide the investments officer with a measure of how much might be earned at the moment by *pursuing the carry trade*. The officer can borrow funds at the shortest end of the curve (such as borrowing short-term money using the safest and most liquid investment securities in the financial firm's portfolio as collateral) and then invest the borrowed funds in income-generating assets farther out along the curve. For example, the officer may borrow funds for 30 days at 4 percent and use that money to invest in five-year government bonds yielding 6 percent. The difference between these two rates of return is called *carry income* and tends to be greatest when the yield curve has a steep upward slope.

If the yield curve does have a sufficiently strong positive slope, an investing institution may also be able to score significant gains with a maneuver known as *riding the yield curve*. The investments officer looks for a situation in which some securities are soon to approach maturity and their prices have risen significantly while their yields to maturity have fallen. If the yield curve's slope is steep enough to more than cover transactions costs, the investing institution can sell those securities, scoring a capital gain due to the recent rise in their prices, and reinvest the proceeds of that sale in longer-term securities carrying higher rates of return. If the riding maneuver works (i.e., the slope of the yield curve does not fall), the investing institution will reap both higher current income and greater future returns.

Duration

While the yield curve presents the investments officer with valuable information and occasionally the opportunity for substantial gains, it has several limitations, such as uncertainty over exactly how and why the curve appears the way it does at any particular moment and the possibility of a change in the curve's shape at any time, Moreover, the yield curve counts only clock time, not the timing of cash flows expected from a security. The most critical information for the investments officer is usually not how long any particular security will be around but, rather, *when* it will generate cash and *how much* cash will be generated each month, quarter, or year that the security is held.

The need for this kind of information gave rise to the concept of **duration**—a present value–weighted measure of maturity of an individual security or portfolio of securities. Duration measures the average amount of time it takes for all of the cash flows from a security to reach the investor who holds it.

Equation (7–15) in Chapter 7 illustrates how to calculate the duration of an investment. For example consider the 5-year Treasury note discussed earlier in this chapter which has a par value of $1,000, has a current market price of $900, pays $80 per year in interest, and carries a yield to maturity of 10.73 percent. Its duration must be:

$$D = \frac{\left[\frac{\$80 \times 1}{(1 + 0.1073)^1} + \frac{\$80 \times 2}{(1 + 0.1073)^2} + \frac{\$80 \times 3}{(1 + 0.1073)^3} + \frac{\$80 \times 4}{(1 + 0.1073)^4} + \frac{\$1,080 \times 5}{(1 + 0.1073)^5} \right]}{\$900} = 4.26 \text{ years} \qquad \textbf{(10–9)}$$

Thus, this Treasury note will pay itself out in present value terms in 4.26 years (or about 4 years and 3 months), which is its *average* maturity considering the amount and timing of all of its expected cash flows of principal and interest.

We recall from Equation (7–18) in Chapter 7 that the percentage change in the price of an investment security is equal to the negative of its duration times the change in interest rates divided by one plus the initial interest rate or yield.[4] To illustrate how this relationship can provide the investments officer with valuable information, consider the Treasury note whose duration we just calculated to be 4.26 years. Suppose market interest rates rose from the note's current yield of 10.73 percent to 12 percent, a change in yield of 1.27 percentage points. The approximate change in the T-note's price then would be:

$$\text{Percentage change in security's price} = -4.26 \times \left(\frac{0.0127}{1 + 0.1073} \right) \times 100\% = -4.89\% \qquad \textbf{(10–10)}$$

---

[4]The formula described in this sentence (and presented in Chapter 7) applies if a security pays interest once each year. If interest is paid more than once each year the appropriate formula is this:

$$\text{Percentage change in price} = -\text{Duration} \times \left[\frac{\text{Change in interest rate}}{1 + (1/m)(\text{Initial rate})} \right]$$

where m is the number of times during a year that the security pays interest. For example, most bonds pay interest semiannually, in which case m = 2.

In this instance, a rise in interest rates of just over one percentage point produces almost a 5 percent decline in the security's price. The investments officer must decide how much chance there is that interest rates will rise, whether this kind of price sensitivity is acceptable, and whether other investments would better suit the institution's current needs.

Duration also suggests a way to minimize damage to an investing institution's earnings that changes in market interest rates may cause. That is, *duration gives the investments officer a tool to reduce his or her institution's exposure to interest rate risk*. It suggests a formula for minimizing interest rate risk:

$$\begin{matrix}\text{Duration of} \\ \text{an individual} \\ \text{security or a} \\ \text{security portfolio}\end{matrix} = \begin{matrix}\text{Length of the investor's} \\ \text{planned holding period} \\ \text{for a security or a} \\ \text{security portfolio}\end{matrix} \qquad \textbf{(10–11)}$$

For example, suppose a bank is interested in buying Treasury notes because loan demand currently is weak. However, the investments officer is concerned that he or she may be required to sell those securities at this time next year in order to make profitable loans. Faced with this prospect and determined to minimize interest rate risk, the officer could choose those notes with a duration of one year. The effect of this step is to immunize the securities purchased from loss of return, no matter which way interest rates go.

Duration works to immunize a security or portfolio of securities against interest rate changes because two key forms of risk—*interest rate risk* and *reinvestment risk*—offset each other when duration is set equal to the investing institution's planned holding period. If interest rates rise after the securities are purchased, their market price will decline, but the investments officer can reinvest the cash flow those securities are generating at higher market rates. Similarly, if interest rates fall, the institution will be forced to reinvest at lower interest rates but, correspondingly, the prices of those securities will have risen. The net result is to approximately *freeze the total return from investment security holdings*. Capital gains or losses are counterbalanced by falling or rising reinvestment yields when duration matches the investing institution's planned holding period.

Concept Check

10–18. What factors affect a financial-service institution's decision regarding the different maturities of securities it should hold?

10–19. What maturity strategies do financial firms employ in managing their portfolios?

10–20. Bacone National Bank has structured its investment portfolio, which extends out to four-year maturities, so that it holds about $11 million each in one-year, two-year, three-year, and four-year securities. In contrast, Dunham National Bank and Trust holds $36 million in one- and two-year securities and about $30 million in 8- to 10-year maturities. What maturity strategy is each bank following? Why do you believe that each of these banks has adopted the particular strategy it has as reflected in the maturity structure of its portfolio?

10–21. How can the yield curve and duration help an investments officer choose which securities to acquire or sell?

10–22. A bond currently sells for $950 based on a par value of $1,000 and promises $100 in interest for three years before being retired. Yields to maturity on comparable-quality securities are currently at 12 percent. What is the bond's duration? Suppose interest rates in the market fall to 10 percent. What will be the approximate percent change in the bond's price?

Summary

This chapter has focused on *investments* in the banking and financial-services field. What is involved in making investments and why are they important?

- For most financial-service firms, *investments* refer to the buying and selling of marketable securities, such as government bonds and notes, federal agency securities, asset-backed notes and bonds, municipal (state and local government) bonds, domestic certificates of deposit and Eurocurrency deposits, and corporate securities (including commercial paper, corporate bonds, and corporate stock).

- Investments fulfill multiple roles in the management of a financial firm. These roles include (*a*) supplementing income from loans and stabilizing total income; (*b*) supplying extra liquidity when cash is low; (*c*) serving as collateral for borrowings; (*d*) reducing tax exposure; (*e*) offsetting risks inherent in other parts of the balance sheet, such as in the loan portfolio; (*f*) dressing up the balance sheet to attract customers and capital; (*g*) helping to hedge against interest rate risk; and (*h*) providing greater flexibility in the management of assets and liabilities.

- Some experts refer to investments as the *crossroads account* because the investment portfolio interacts in crucial ways with most other parts of a financial firm's balance sheet, especially its cash account, loan portfolio, and liabilities.

- The *investments officer* must choose what kinds of investments best contribute to the goals established for each institution's investment portfolio and for the financial firm as a whole. In lending-type institutions, such as banks, finance companies, and credit unions, the investment portfolio normally plays "second fiddle" to the loan portfolio and the investments officer is often charged with the responsibility of backstopping loans—providing more income when loan demand is weak and more cash when loan demand is high.

- In choosing which investments to hold, investments officers must weigh multiple factors: (*a*) the goal or purpose of the investment portfolio within each institution; (*b*) expected rates of return (yields) available on different financial instruments; (*c*) the financial firm's tax exposure and how any investment security might affect its tax obligations; (*d*) the risks associated with changing market interest rates and the changing maturity structure of rates (interest rate risk), with possible default by issuers of securities (credit risk), with the possible need for cash at any time (liquidity risk), with the impact of inflation and business cycle risk upon the demand for financial services, and with the prepayment of loans pledged behind asset-backed securities that can reduce their expected returns (prepayment risk).

- An additional factor that investments officers must consider is the *maturity* or *duration* of different investment securities. Maturity refers to the term structure of interest rates, often represented by the *yield curve*. Yield curves convey information about the market's outlook for interest rates and graphically illustrate the trade-off between risk and return that confronts the investments officer. Duration, on the other hand, provides a picture of the time distribution of expected cash flows from investments and can be used to help reduce interest rate risk.

- Most financial firms appear to have a preferred range of maturities and durations for the investments they make, with depository institutions tending to focus upon comparatively short and midrange maturities or durations, and many of their competitors, such as insurance companies and pension funds, tending to reach heavily into the longest maturities or durations of investments available. Investment decisions about the desired maturity structure or duration of the investment portfolio affect that portfolio's sensitivity to risk and its capacity for generating income.

- Investments officers have one of the toughest jobs inside a financial firm, with multiple tasks to perform and multiple factors to weigh each time they buy or sell investment instruments. Often investments officers working for a lending institution feel they "cannot win" because they may be compelled to *sell* securities for cash when loan demand is high, but security prices are falling, and to *buy* securities to generate income when loan demand is low, but, unfortunately, security prices are high. Sometimes it's a thankless task!

Key Terms

money market instruments, *310*

capital market instruments, *310*

U.S. Treasury bill, *311*

Treasury notes, *313*

Treasury bonds, *313*

federal agency securities, *313*

certificate of deposit (CD), *313*

bankers' acceptances, *314*

commercial paper, *314*

municipal bonds, *315*

corporate notes, *315*

corporate bonds, *315*

securitized assets, *316*

mortgage-backed bond, *317*

stripped security, *317*

yield to maturity (YTM), *320*

holding period yield (HPY), *320*

tax swap, *324*

portfolio shifting, *324*

interest rate risk, *326*

credit risk, *326*

business risk, *328*

liquidity risk, *328*

call risk, *328*

prepayment risk, *328*

inflation risk, *330*

pledging, *331*

yield curve, *334*

duration, *336*

Problems and Projects

1. A 10-year U.S. Treasury bond with a par value of $1,000 is currently selling for $1,015 from various security dealers. The bond carries a 7 percent coupon rate. If purchased today and held to maturity, what is its expected yield to maturity?

2. A municipal bond is selling today for $1,036.80 and has a $1,000 face (par) value. Its yield to maturity is 6 percent, and the bond promises its holders $65 per year in interest for the next 10 years before it matures. What is the bond's duration?

3. Calculate the yield to maturity of a 10-year U.S. government bond that is selling for $1,050 in today's market and carries an 8 percent coupon rate with interest paid semiannually.

4. A corporate bond being seriously considered for purchase by First Security Savings Bank will mature 20 years from today and promises a 12 percent interest payment once a year. Recent inflation in the economy has driven the yield to maturity on this bond to 15 percent, and it carries a face value of $1,000. Calculate this bond's duration.

5. Tiger National Bank regularly purchases municipal bonds issued by small rural school districts in its region of the state. At the moment, the bank is considering purchasing an $8 million general obligation issue from the Youngstown school district, the only bond issue that district plans this year. The bonds, which mature in 15 years, carry a nominal annual rate of return of 7.75 percent. Tiger, which is in the top corporate tax bracket of 35 percent, must pay an average interest rate of 7.38 percent to borrow the funds needed to purchase the municipals. Would you recommend purchasing these bonds?

   a. Calculate the net after-tax return on this bank-qualified municipal security. What is the tax advantage for being a qualified bond?

   b. What is the tax-equivalent yield for this bank-qualified municipal security?

6. Tiger National Bank also purchases municipal bonds issued by the city of Cleveland. Currently the bank is considering a nonqualified general obligation municipal issue. The bonds, which mature in 10 years, provide a nominal annual rate of return of 8.1 percent. Tiger National Bank has the same cost of funds and tax rate as stated in the previous problem.

a. Calculate the net after-tax return on this nonqualified municipal security.

b. What is the tax-equivalent yield for this nonqualified municipal security?

c. Discuss the pro's and con's of purchasing the nonqualified rather than the bank-qualified municipal described in the previous problem.

7. Lakeway Thrift Savings and Trust is interested in doing some investment portfolio shifting. This institution has had a good year thus far, with strong loan demand; its loan revenue has increased by 16 percent over last year's level. Lakeway is subject to the 35 percent corporate income tax rate. The investments officer has several options in the form of bonds that have been held for some time in its portfolio:

a. Selling $4 million in 12-year City of Dallas bonds with a coupon rate of 7.5 percent and purchasing $4 million in bonds from Bexar County (also with 12-year maturities) with a coupon of 8 percent and issued at par. The Dallas bonds have a current market value of $3,750,000 but are listed at par on the institution's books.

b. Selling $4 million in 12-year U.S. Treasury bonds that carry a coupon rate of 12 percent and are recorded at par, which was the price when the institution purchased them. The market value of these bonds has risen to $4,330,000.

Which of these two portfolio shifts would you recommend? Is there a good reason for not selling these Treasury bonds? What other information is needed to make the best decision? Please explain.

8. Current market yields on U.S. government securities are distributed by maturity as follows:

$$
\begin{array}{ll}
\text{3-month Treasury bills} & = 7.69 \text{ percent} \\
\text{6-month Treasury bills} & = 7.49 \text{ percent} \\
\text{1-year Treasury notes} & = 7.77 \text{ percent} \\
\text{2-year Treasury notes} & = 7.80 \text{ percent} \\
\text{3-year Treasury notes} & = 7.80 \text{ percent} \\
\text{5-year Treasury notes} & = 7.81 \text{ percent} \\
\text{7-year Treasury notes} & = 7.86 \text{ percent} \\
\text{10-year Treasury bonds} & = 7.87 \text{ percent} \\
\text{30-year Treasury bonds} & = 7.90 \text{ percent}
\end{array}
$$

Draw a *yield curve* for these securities. What shape does the curve have? What significance might this yield curve have for an investing institution with 75 percent of its investment portfolio in 7-year to 30-year U.S. Treasury bonds and 25 percent in U.S. government bills and notes with maturities under one year? What would you recommend to management?

9. A bond possesses a duration of 5.82 years. Suppose that market interest rates on comparable bonds were 7 percent this morning, but have now shifted upward to 7.5 percent. What percentage change in the bond's value occurred when interest rates moved 0.5 percent higher?

10. The investments officer for Sillistine Savings is concerned about interest rate risk lowering the value of the institution's bonds. A check of the bond portfolio reveals an average duration of 4.5 years. How could this bond portfolio be altered in order to minimize interest rate risk within the next year?

11. A bank's economics department has just forecast accelerated growth in the economy, with GDP expected to grow at a 4.5 percent annual growth rate for at least the next two years. What are the implications of this economic forecast for an investments officer? What types of securities should the officer think most seriously about adding

to the investment portfolio? Why? Suppose the bank holds a security portfolio similar to that described in Table 10–3 for all insured U.S. banks. Which types of securities might the investments officer want to think seriously about selling if the projected economic expansion takes place? What losses might occur and how could these losses be minimized?

12. Contrary to the exuberant economic forecast described in Problem 11, suppose a bank's economics department is forecasting a significant recession in economic activity. Output and employment are projected to decline significantly over the next 18 months. What are the implications of this forecast for an investment portfolio manager? What is the outlook for interest rates and inflation under the foregoing assumptions? What types of investment securities would you recommend as good additions to the portfolio during the period covered by the recession forecast and why? What other kinds of information would you like to have about the bank's current balance sheet and earnings report in order to help you make the best quality decisions regarding the investment portfolio?

13. Arrington Hills Savings Bank, a $3.5 billion asset institution, holds the investment portfolio outlined in the following table. This savings bank serves a rapidly growing money center into which substantial numbers of businesses are relocating their corporate headquarters. Suburban areas around the city are also growing rapidly as large numbers of business owners and managers along with retired professionals are purchasing new homes. Would you recommend any changes in the makeup of this investment portfolio? Please explain why.

Types of Securities Held	Percent of Total Portfolio	Types of Securities Held	Percent of Total Portfolio
U.S. Treasury securities	38.7%	Securities available	
Federal agency securities	35.2	for sale	45.6%
State and local government		Securities with maturities:	
obligations	15.5	Under one year	11.3
Domestic debt securities	5.1		
Foreign debt securities	4.9	One to five years	37.9
Equities	0.6	Over five years	50.8

Internet Exercises

1. As the investments officer for Bank of America, you have been informed by a member of that bank's board of directors that the investment policies you have followed over the past year have been substandard relative to your competitors, including Citigroup, Wells Fargo, and J.P. Morgan Chase. You protest and observe that all financial institutions have faced a tough market and, in your opinion, your bank has done exceptionally well. Challenged, your CEO asks you to prepare a brief memo with comparative investment facts, defending your bank's relative investment performance against the other BHCs mentioned. Use the FDIC's Statistics on Depository Institutions at **www3.fdic.gov/sdi** to develop a reply. What conclusion did you reach after examining your bank's relative investment performance over the last complete calendar year?

2. A number of Web sites are available to help in evaluating the merits and demerits of different types of securities that banks are allowed to hold in their investment portfolios. See **www.bondmarket.com** and **www.investinginbonds.com**. Find one additional Web site on your own and compare and contrast the usefulness of these three Web sites.

3. If you want a summary of regulations applying to bank and thrift security portfolios, you would turn to the regulators' Web sites. The Federal Reserve's *Trading and Capital-Markets*

Assignment for Chapter 10

YOUR BANK'S INVESTMENT FUNCTION: AN EXAMINATION OF THE SECURITIES PORTFOLIO

Chapter 10 explores how the investments officer manages a financial firm's securities portfolio and describes the portfolio's purpose and composition. A significant portion of the chapter outlines and describes the different types of money market and capital market instruments found in the securities portfolio. Part One of this assignment examines the types of securities in your bank's portfolio and asks you to make some inferences about factors that played a role in the selection of securities for that portfolio. The possible factors are discussed midchapter. Part Two of this assignment examines the maturity structure of your bank's securities portfolio. This topic is covered in the latter part of the chapter. Chapter 10's assignment is designed to focus on the issues of importance to investments officers in large commercial banks or similar competing institutions.

Part One: The Composition of Your Bank's Securities Portfolio—Trend and Comparative Analysis

A. **Data Collection:** For this part, you will once again access data at the FDIC's Web site located at **www3.fdic.gov/sdi** for your BHC. Use SDI to create a four-column report of your bank's information and the peer group information across years. In this part of the assignment for Report Selection use the pull-down menu to select Securities and view this in Percentages of Total Assets. For the size of the securities portfolio relative to total assets, see Item 1—the components of the securities portfolio are listed as Items 4–10. Enter the percentage information for these items as an addition to the spreadsheet for comparisons with the peer group as follows:

	A	B	C	D	E	F	G	H	I
75	Composition of Securities Portfolio	BHC	Peer Group	BHC	Peer Group				
76	Date	12/31/yyyy	12/31/yyyy	12/31/yyyy	12/31/yyyy				
77	Securities								
78	U.S. Treasury securities								
79	U.S. government obligations								
80	Securities issued by states and political subdivisions								
81	Asset-backed securities								
82	Other domestic debt securities								
83	Foreign debt securities								
84	Equity securities								

Year-to-Year Comparisons \ Comparisons with Peer Group / Sheet3

B. Compare columns of row 77. How has the relative size of your bank's securities portfolio-to-total assets ratio changed across periods? Does your BHC have more or less liquidity than the group of comparable institutions?

C. Use the Chart function in Excel and the data by columns in rows 78 through 84 to create four pie charts illustrating the profile of securities held by your BHC and its peer group.

With these pie charts provide titles, labels, and percentages. If you save these as separate sheets, they do not clutter the spreadsheets that you use most frequently, yet they are available to insert in Word documents. To give you an example, the Charts for NCC and its peer group would appear as follows:

Activity Manual found at **www.federalreserve.gov/boarddocs/supmanual/trading/trading.pdf** has a section on "Capital Market Activities." Read and briefly outline the first two pages on "Limitations and Restrictions on Securities Holdings." See if you can find similar information for thrifts at **www.ots.treas.gov**.

STANDARD &POOR'S

S&P Market Insight Challenge (www.mhhe.com/edumarketinsight)

1. In the S&P Industry Survey on Banking, commercial banks' earning assets are categorized as loans and securities. For a timely description of the banking industry's use of investment securities, click on the Industry tab in S&P's Market Insight, Educational

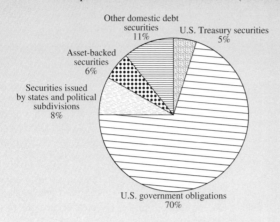

Composition of Securities Portfolio for NCC (12/31/2004)

- Other domestic debt securities 11%
- U.S. Treasury securities 5%
- Asset-backed securities 6%
- Securities issued by states and political subdivisions 8%
- U.S. government obligations 70%

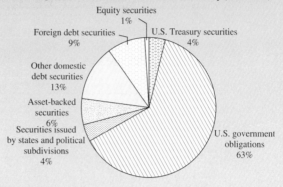

Composition of Securities Portfolio for Peer Group (12/31/2004)

- Equity securities 1%
- Foreign debt securities 9%
- U.S. Treasury securities 4%
- Other domestic debt securities 13%
- Asset-backed securities 6%
- Securities issued by states and political subdivisions 4%
- U.S. government obligations 63%

D. Utilizing the above information, write approximately one page about your bank's securities portfolio and how it compares to its peers. Use your pie charts as graphics and incorporate them in the discussion. Provide inferences concerning the factors (e.g., expected rate of return, tax exposure, interest rate risk) affecting the choice of investment securities.

Part Two: Investment Maturity Strategies

A. **Data Collection:** The chapter concludes with a discussion of investment maturity strategies. The SDI at **www3. fdic.gov/sdi** contains maturity data for debt securities for banks and BHCs. You will follow the process used to collect data for Part One; however, this time you will focus on the dollar year-end information for your BHC only. You will collect information in the two-column format. For Report Selection, use the pull-down menu to select Total Debt Securities and view this in Dollars. For maturity and repricing data for debt securities (all securities but equities), you are interested in Items 6–10. This includes a

breakdown by maturity of (1) mortgage pass-throughs backed by closed-end first lien 1–4 residential mortgages, (2) CMOs, REMICs, and stripped MBs, and (3) other debt securities. Groups 1 and 3 are partitioned into six maturity periods, whereas Group 2, given the prepayment risk, has its expected average life partitioned into two more general categories. Our objective is to aggregate the data for all the debt securities based on maturities and enter our dollar sums in the spreadsheet for year-to-year comparisons as illustrated below. For simplification we will include CMOs, REMICs, and stripped MBs with expected average lives of three years or less in the aggregation for row 82 and CMOs, REMICs, and stripped MBs with expected average lives of more than three years in row 84. Enter the aggregated data using dollar information for Debt Securities as an addition to Spreadsheet One as follows: For Example, Cell B80 would be the sum of mortgage pass-throughs and other debt securities with maturity and repricing of three months or less.

(continued)

STANDARD
&POOR'S

Version, using the drop-down menu to select one of the subindustry categories, Diversified Banks or Regional Banks. Download the S&P Industry Survey on Banking and review the section "How the Industry Operates." Describe the importance of investment securities to earnings. What does the typical bank's investment portfolio contain? What is the most recent total amount of investment securities held in all FDIC-insured commercial banks?

2. This chapter reminds us of the importance of investment securities in the asset portfolios of banks and closely related nonbank financial firms. The leading banks whose financial reports are represented in S&P's Market Insight tend to be heavy investors in

www.mhhe.com/rose7e

REAL NUMBERS FOR REAL BANKS — Assignment for Chapter 10 *(continued)*

	A	B	C
77	Maturity and repricing data for debt securities	BHC	BHC
78	Date	12/31/yyyy	12/31/yyyy
79	Total debt securities		
80	Three months or less		
81	Over 3 months through 12 months		
82	Over 1 year through 3 years		
83	Over 3 years through 5 years		
84	Over 5 years through 15 years		
85	Over 15 years		

B. Use the Chart function in Excel and the data by columns in rows 80 through 85 of spreadsheet labeled year-to-year comparison to create two bar charts that graphically portray the maturity characteristics of your bank's securities portfolio. With these bar charts provide titles and labels and save for insertion in Word documents. To give you an example, one chart for NCC appears as follows:

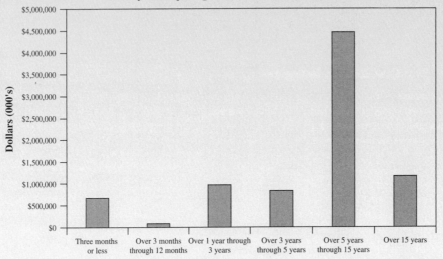

Maturity and Repricing Data for NCC Debt Securities (12/31/2004)

C. Interpreting the above information, write one paragraph about your bank's maturity strategy and how it has changed between the two year-ends. Use your bar charts as graphics and incorporate them in the discussion. Tie your discussion to the types of strategies discussed in the latter part of Chapter 10.

marketable securities. Why? See if you can determine the percentage of total assets that investment securities represent for the Market Insight–listed banks. Which banks show the highest proportion of investment security holdings (relative to total assets)? The lowest proportion? What factors would help explain these differences?

Selected References

See below for a discussion of securitization, security stripping, and other investment instruments:

1. Becketti, Sean. "The Role of Stripped Securities in Portfolio Management." *Economic Review*, Federal Reserve Bank of Kansas City, May 1988, pp. 20–31.

2. Dupont, Dominique, and Brian Sack. "The Treasury Securities Market: Overview and Recent Developments." *Federal Reserve Bulletin* 85, no. 12 (1999), pp. 785–806.

3. Smith, Stephen D. "Analyzing Risk and Return for Mortgage-Backed Securities." *Economic Review*, Federal Reserve Bank of Richmond, January/February 1991, pp. 2–10.

The following review yield to maturity, yield curves, and other investment yield measures:

4. Poole, William. "Understanding the Term Structure of Interest Rates." *Review*, Federal Reserve Bank of St. Louis, September/October 2005, pp. 589–595.

5. Rose, Peter S., and Milton H. Marquis. *Money and Capital Markets: Financial Institutions and Instruments in a Global Marketplace*, 9th ed. Burr Ridge, IL: McGraw-Hill/Irwin, 2005. (See especially Chapter 6, "Measuring and Calculating Interest Rates and Financial Asset Prices.")

For a discussion of investment strategies and regulatory rules involving many securities purchased by banks and other financial institutions, see these sources:

6. Office of the Comptroller of the Currency. *Investment Securities*. Comptroller's Handbook, Section 203, Washington, D.C., March 1990.

7. Fleming, Michael J., and Kenneth Garbade. "When the Back Office Moved to the Front Burner: Settlement Fails in the Treasury Market After 9/11." *Economic Policy Review*, Federal Reserve Bank of New York, November 2002, pp. 35–58.

8. Kopcke, Richard W., and Ralph C. Kimball. "Inflation-Indexed Bonds: The Dog That Didn't Bark." *New England Economic Review*, Federal Reserve Bank of Boston, January/February 1999, pp. 3–24.

9. Sundaresan, Suresh M. *Fixed Income Markets and Their Derivatives*. Cincinnati, OH: Southwestern Publishing, 1997.

For a description of key investment securities markets see the following:

10. Carlstrom, Charles T., and Timothy S. Fuerst. "Expected Inflation and TIPS." *Economic Commentary*, Federal Reserve Bank of Cleveland, November 2004, pp. 1–4.

11. Sack, Brian, and Robert Elsasser. "Treasury Inflation-Indexed Debt: A Review of the U.S. Experience." *Economic Policy Review*, Federal Reserve Bank of New York, May 2004, pp. 47–63.

www.mhhe.com/rose7e

CHAPTER ELEVEN

Liquidity and Reserve Management: Strategies and Policies

Key Topics in This Chapter

- Sources of Demand for and Supply of Liquidity
- Why Financial Firms Have Liquidity Problems
- Liquidity Management Strategies
- Estimating Liquidity Needs
- The Impact of Market Discipline
- Legal Reserves and Money Management

11–1 Introduction

Not long ago, as noted in a recent article from the Federal Reserve Bank of St. Louis [8], a savings bank headquartered in the northeastern United States experienced a real liquidity crisis. Acting on rumors of a possible embezzlement of funds, some worried depositors launched an old-fashioned "run" on the bank. Flooding into the institution's Philadelphia and New York City branches, some frightened customers yanked out close to 13 percent of the savings bank's deposits in less than a week, sending management scrambling to find enough cash to meet the demands of concerned depositors. While the bank appeared to weather the storm in time, the event reminds us of at least two things: (1) how much financial institutions depend upon public confidence to survive and prosper, and (2) how quickly the essential item called "liquidity" can be eroded when the public, even temporarily, loses its confidence in one or more financial institutions.

One of the most important tasks the management of any financial institution faces is ensuring adequate **liquidity** at all times, no matter what emergencies may appear. A financial firm is considered to be "liquid" if it has ready access to immediately spendable funds at reasonable cost at precisely the time those funds are needed. This suggests that a liquid financial firm either has the right amount of immediately spendable funds on hand when they are required or can raise liquid funds in timely fashion by borrowing or selling assets.

Indeed, lack of adequate liquidity can be one of the *first* signs that a financial institution is in trouble. For example, a troubled bank that is losing deposits will likely be forced to dispose of some of its safer, more liquid assets. Other lending institutions may become increasingly reluctant to lend the troubled firm any new funds without additional security or the promise of a higher rate of interest, which may reduce the earnings of the beleaguered institution and threaten it with failure.

The cash shortages that some financial-service providers experience make clear that liquidity needs cannot be ignored. A financial firm can be closed if it cannot raise sufficient liquidity even though, technically, it may still be solvent. For example, during the 1990s, the Federal Reserve forced the closure of the $10 billion Southeast Bank of Miami because it couldn't come up with enough liquidity to repay the loans it had received from the Fed. Moreover, the competence of liquidity managers is an important barometer of management's overall effectiveness in achieving any institution's goals. So, let's begin our journey and see how important quality liquidity management is to the success of a financial firm.

11–2 The Demand for and Supply of Liquidity

A financial institution's need for liquidity—immediately spendable funds—can be viewed within a demand–supply framework. What activities give rise to the demand for liquidity? And what sources can be relied upon to supply adequate liquidity?

For depository institutions, the most pressing demands for spendable funds generally come from two sources: (1) customers withdrawing money from their accounts, and (2) credit requests from customers the institution wishes to keep, either in the form of new loan requests or drawings upon existing credit lines. Other sources of liquidity demand include paying off previous borrowings, such as loans the institution may have received from other financial firms or from the central bank (e.g., the Federal Reserve System). Similarly, payment of income taxes or cash dividends to stockholders periodically gives rise to a demand for immediately spendable cash. (See Table 11–1.)

To meet the foregoing demands for liquidity, financial firms can draw upon several potential sources of supply. The most important source for a depository institution normally is receipt of new customer deposits. These deposit inflows tend to be heavy the first of each month as business payrolls are dispensed, and they may reach a secondary peak toward the middle of each month as bills are paid. Another important element in the supply of liquidity comes from customers repaying their loans and from sales of assets, especially marketable securities, from the investment portfolio. Liquidity also flows in from revenues (fee income) generated by selling nondeposit services and from borrowings in the money market.

These various sources of liquidity demand and supply come together to determine each financial firm's **net liquidity position** at any moment in time. That net liquidity position (L) at time t is:

Supplies of Liquidity Flowing into the Financial Firm

$$
\begin{array}{c}
\text{A financial firm's} \\
\text{net liquidity} \\
\text{position} \\
(L_t)
\end{array}
=
\begin{array}{c}
\text{Incoming} \\
\text{deposits} \\
\text{(inflows)}
\end{array}
+
\begin{array}{c}
\text{Revenues from} \\
\text{the sale of} \\
\text{nondeposit} \\
\text{services}
\end{array}
+
\begin{array}{c}
\text{Customer} \\
\text{loan} \\
\text{repayments}
\end{array}
+
\begin{array}{c}
\text{Sales of} \\
\text{assets}
\end{array}
+
\begin{array}{c}
\text{Borrowings} \\
\text{from the} \\
\text{money} \\
\text{market}
\end{array}
$$

– Demands on the Financial Firm for Liquidity **(11–1)**

$$
\begin{array}{c}
\text{Deposit} \\
- \text{withdrawals} \\
\text{(outflows)}
\end{array}
-
\begin{array}{c}
\text{Volume of} \\
\text{acceptable} \\
\text{loan requests}
\end{array}
-
\begin{array}{c}
\text{Repayments} \\
\text{of} \\
\text{borrowings}
\end{array}
-
\begin{array}{c}
\text{Other} \\
\text{operating} \\
\text{expenses}
\end{array}
-
\begin{array}{c}
\text{Dividend} \\
\text{payments} \\
\text{to} \\
\text{stockholders}
\end{array}
$$

TABLE 11–1
Sources of Demand and Supply for Liquidity for a Depository Institution

Supplies of Liquid Funds Typically Come From:	Demands for Liquidity Typically Arise From:
Incoming customer deposits	Customer deposit withdrawals
Revenues from the sale of nondeposit services	Credit requests from quality loan customers
Customer loan repayments	Repayment of nondeposit borrowings
Sales of assets	Operating expenses and taxes incurred in
Borrowings from the money market	producing and selling services
	Payment of stockholder cash dividends

Key URL
Data on the liquidity positions of individual depository institutions may be found in the FDIC's Statistics for Depository Institutions at **www3.fdic.gov/sdi** if you specify each institution's name, city and state, certificate number, or bank holding company (BHC) number.

Factoid
Did you know that a serious liquidity crisis inside the United States in 1907, which followed several other liquidity crises in the 19th century, led to the creation of the U.S. central bank, the Federal Reserve System, to prevent liquidity problems in the future?

When the demand for liquidity exceeds its supply (i.e., $L_t < 0$), management must prepare for a *liquidity deficit*, deciding when and where to raise additional funds. On the other hand, if at any point in time the supply of liquidity exceeds all liquidity demands (i.e., $L_t > 0$), management must prepare for a *liquidity surplus*, deciding when and where to profitably invest surplus liquid funds until they are needed to cover future cash needs.

Liquidity has a critical time dimension. Some liquidity needs are *immediate* or nearly so. For example, in the case of a depository institution several large CDs may be due to mature tomorrow, and the customers may have indicated they plan to withdraw these deposits rather than simply rolling them over into new deposits. Sources of funds that can be accessed immediately must be used to meet these near-term liquidity pressures.

Longer-term liquidity demands arise from seasonal, cyclical, and trend factors. For example, liquid funds are generally in greater demand during the fall and summer coincident with school, holidays, and travel plans. Anticipating these longer-term liquidity needs managers can draw upon a wider array of funds sources than is true for immediate liquidity needs, such as selling off accumulated liquid assets, aggressively advertising the institution's current menu of services, or negotiating long-term borrowings of reserves from other financial firms. Of course, not all demands for liquidity need to be met by selling assets or borrowing new money. For example, just the right amount of new deposits may flow in or loan repayments from borrowing customers may occur close to the date new funds are needed. Timing is critical to liquidity management: Financial managers must plan carefully how, when, and where liquid funds can be raised.

Most liquidity problems arise from outside the financial firm as a result of the activities of customers. In effect, customers' liquidity problems gravitate toward their liquidity suppliers. If a business is short liquid reserves, for example, it will ask for a loan or draw down its account balances, either of which may require the firm's financial institution to come up with additional funds. A dramatic example of this phenomenon occurred in the wake of the worldwide stock market crash in October 1987. Investors who had borrowed heavily to buy stock on margin were forced to come up with additional funds to secure their stock loans. They went to their lending institutions in huge numbers, turning a liquidity crisis in the capital market into a liquidity crisis for lenders.

The essence of liquidity management problems for financial institutions may be described in two succinct statements:

1. *Rarely are demands for liquidity equal to the supply of liquidity at any particular moment in time.* The financial firm must continually deal with either a liquidity deficit or a liquidity surplus.
2. *There is a trade-off between liquidity and profitability.* The more resources are tied up in readiness to meet demands for liquidity, the lower is that financial firm's expected profitability (other factors held constant).

Thus, ensuring adequate liquidity is a never-ending problem for management that will always have significant implications for the financial firm's performance.

Moreover, resolving liquidity problems subjects a financial institution to costs, including the interest cost on borrowed funds, the transactions cost of time and money in finding adequate liquid funds, and an *opportunity cost* in the form of future earnings that must be forgone when earning assets are sold in order to meet liquidity needs. Clearly, management must weigh these costs against the immediacy of the institution's liquidity needs. If a financial firm winds up with excess liquidity, its management must be prepared to invest those excess funds immediately to avoid incurring an opportunity cost from idle funds not generating earnings.

From a slightly different vantage point, we could say that the management of liquidity is subject to the risks that interest rates will change *(interest rate risk)* and that liquid funds will not be available in the volume needed *(availability risk)*. If market interest rates rise, assets that the financial firm plans to sell to raise liquid funds will decline in value, and some must be sold at a loss. Not only will fewer liquid funds be raised from the sale of those assets, but the losses incurred will reduce earnings as well. Then, too, raising liquid funds by borrowing will cost more as interest rates rise, and some forms of borrowed liquidity may no longer be available. If lenders perceive a financial institution to be more risky than before, it will be forced to pay higher interest rates to borrow liquidity, and some lenders will simply refuse to make liquid funds available at all.

11–3 Why Financial Firms Often Face Significant Liquidity Problems

It should be clear from the foregoing discussion that most financial institutions face major liquidity problems. This significant exposure to liquidity pressures arises from several sources.

For example, depository institutions borrow large amounts of short-term cash from individuals and businesses and from other lending institutions and then turn around and make long-term credit available to their borrowing customers. Thus, depository institutions typically face an *imbalance* between the maturity dates attached to their assets and the maturity dates of their liabilities. Rarely will incoming cash flows from assets exactly match the cash flowing out to cover liabilities.

A problem related to the maturity mismatch situation is that most depository institutions hold an unusually high proportion of liabilities subject to immediate payment, especially demand deposits and money market borrowings. They must stand ready to meet immediate cash demands that can be substantial at times, especially near the end of a week, near the first of each month, and during certain seasons of the year.

Another source of liquidity problems is sensitivity to changes in market interest rates. When interest rates rise, for example, some customers will withdraw their funds in search of higher returns elsewhere. Many loan customers may postpone new loan requests or speed up their drawings on those credit lines that carry lower interest rates. Thus, changing market interest rates affect both customer demand for deposits and customer demand for loans, each of which has a potent impact on a depository institution's liquidity position. Moreover, movements in market interest rates affect the market values of assets the financial firm may need to sell in order to raise additional funds, and they directly affect the cost of borrowing in the money market.

Beyond these factors, financial firms must give high priority to meeting demands for liquidity. To fail in this area may severely damage public confidence in the institution. We can imagine the reaction of a bank's customers, for example, if the teller windows and ATMs had to be closed one morning because the bank was temporarily out of cash and could not cash checks or meet deposit withdrawals (as happened to a bank in Montana several years ago, prompting a federal investigation, as we discussed in the opener to Part Four). One of the most important tasks of a liquidity manager is to keep close contact with

Concept Check

11–1. What are the principal sources of *liquidity demand* for a financial firm?

11–2. What are the principal sources from which the *supply of liquidity* comes?

11–3. Suppose that a bank faces the following cash inflows and outflows during the coming week: (a) deposit withdrawals are expected to total $33 million, (b) customer loan repayments are expected to amount to $108 million, (c) operating expenses demanding cash payment will probably approach $51 million, (d) acceptable new loan requests should reach $294 million, (e) sales of bank assets are projected to be $18 million, (f) new deposits should total $670 million, (g) borrowings from the money market are expected to be about $43 million, (h) nondeposit service fees should amount to $27 million, (i) previous bank borrowings totaling $23 million are scheduled to be repaid, and (j) a dividend payment to bank stockholders of $140 million is scheduled. What is this bank's projected net liquidity position for the coming week?

11–4. When is a financial institution *adequately liquid*?

11–5. Why do financial firms face significant liquidity management problems?

the largest funds-supplying customers and the holders of large unused credit lines to determine if and when withdrawals will be made and to make sure adequate funds will be available when demand for funds occurs.

11–4 Strategies for Liquidity Managers

Over the years, experienced liquidity managers have developed several strategies for dealing with liquidity problems: (1) providing liquidity from assets (asset liquidity management), (2) relying on borrowed liquidity to meet cash demands (liability management), and (3) balanced (asset and liability) liquidity management.

Asset Liquidity Management (or Asset Conversion) Strategies

The oldest approach to meeting liquidity needs is known as **asset conversion.** In its purest form, this strategy calls for storing liquidity in assets, predominantly in cash and marketable securities. When liquidity is needed, selected assets are converted into cash until all demands for cash are met.

What is a **liquid asset?** It must have three characteristics:

1. A liquid asset has a *ready market* so it can be converted into cash without delay.
2. It has a reasonably *stable price* so that, no matter how quickly the asset must be sold or how large the sale is, the market is deep enough to absorb the sale without a significant decline in price.
3. It is *reversible*, meaning the seller can recover his or her original investment (principal) with little risk of loss.

Among the most popular liquid assets are Treasury bills, federal funds loans, certificates of deposit, municipal bonds, federal agency securities, bankers' acceptances, and Eurocurrency loans. (See the box entitled "Storing Liquidity in Assets—The Principal Options" for brief descriptions of these liquid assets.) Although a financial firm can strengthen its liquidity position by holding more liquid assets, it will not necessarily be a liquid institution if it does so, because each institution's liquidity position is also influenced by the demands for liquidity made against it. Remember: A financial firm is liquid only if it has access, at reasonable cost, to liquid funds in exactly the amounts required at precisely the time they are needed.

Key URLs
To find out how the Federal Reserve System dealt with the 9/11 terrorist attacks and helped to stabilize the U.S. financial system, see especially **www.clevelandfed.org** and **www.ny.frb.org/research/search.html**.

Storing Liquidity in Assets— The Principal Options

The principal options open to liquidity managers for holdings of liquid assets that can be sold when additional cash is needed are

1. *Treasury bills*—direct obligations of the United States government or of foreign governments issued at a discount and redeemed at par (face value) when they reach maturity; T-bills have original maturities of 3, 6, and 12 months, with an active resale market through security dealers.

2. *Federal funds loans to other institutions*—loans of reserves held by depository institutions with short (often overnight) maturities.

3. *Purchase of liquid securities under a repurchase agreement (RP)*—using high quality securities as collateral to raise new funds.

4. *Placing correspondent deposits with various depository institutions*—these interbank deposits can be borrowed or loaned in minutes by telephone or by wire.

5. *Municipal bonds and notes*—debt securities issued by state and local governments that range in maturity from a few days to several years.

6. *Federal agency securities*—short- and long-term debt instruments sold by federally sponsored agencies such as FNMA (Fannie Mae) or FHLMC (Freddie Mac).

7. *Negotiable certificates of deposit*—investing in short-term CDs until they mature and can be converted into cash without penalty.

8. *Eurocurrency loans*—the lending of deposits accepted by bank offices located outside a particular currency's home country for periods stretching from a few days to a few months.

Filmtoid
What 1980s thriller, starring Kris Kristofferson and Jane Fonda, aligned murder with the liquidity problems of Borough National Bank created by Arab withdrawals of Eurodeposits?
Answer: *Rollover.*

Asset conversion strategy is used mainly by smaller financial institutions that find it a less risky approach to liquidity management than relying on borrowings. But it is *not* a costless approach to liquidity management. First, selling assets means loss of future earnings those assets would have generated had they not been sold off. Thus, there is an **opportunity cost** to storing liquidity in assets when those assets must be sold. Most asset sales also involve transactions costs (commissions) paid to security brokers. Moreover, the assets in question may need to be sold in a market experiencing declining prices, increasing the risk of substantial losses. Management must take care that assets with the least profit potential are sold *first* in order to minimize the opportunity cost of future earnings forgone. Selling assets to raise liquidity also tends to weaken the appearance of the balance sheet because the assets sold are often low-risk government securities that give the impression the financial firm is financially strong. Finally, liquid assets generally carry the lowest rates of return of all assets. Investing in liquid assets means forgoing higher returns on other assets that might be acquired.

Borrowed Liquidity (Liability) Management Strategies

For several decades now the largest banks around the world have chosen to raise more of their liquid funds through borrowings in the money market. This borrowed liquidity strategy—called *purchased liquidity* or **liability management**—in its purest form calls for borrowing immediately spendable funds to cover all anticipated demands for liquidity. Today many different types of financial institutions use this liquidity management strategy.

Borrowing liquid funds has a number of advantages. A financial firm can choose to borrow only when it actually needs funds, unlike storing liquidity in assets where a storehouse of liquid assets must be held at all times, lowering potential returns. Then, too, using borrowed funds permits a financial institution to leave the volume and composition of its

Borrowing Liquidity— The Principal Options

When a liquidity deficit arises, the financial firm can borrow funds from:

1. *Federal funds borrowings*—reserves from other lenders that can be accessed immediately.
2. *Selling liquid, low-risk securities under a repurchase agreement (RP)* to financial institutions having temporary surpluses of funds. RPs generally carry a fixed rate of interest and maturity, though continuing-contract RPs remain in force until either the borrower or lender terminates the loan.
3. *Issuing jumbo ($100,000+) negotiable CDs* to major corporations, governmental units, and wealthy individuals for periods ranging from a few days to several months.
4. *Issuing Eurocurrency deposits* to multinational banks and other corporations at interest rates determined by the demand and supply for these short-term international deposits.
5. *Securing advances from the Federal Home Loan Bank (FHLB) system,* which provides loans to institutions lending in the real-estate-backed loan market.
6. *Borrowing reserves from the discount window of the central bank* (such as the Federal Reserve or the Bank of Japan)—usually available within a matter of minutes provided the borrowing institution has collateral on hand and a signed borrowing authorization.

asset portfolio unchanged if it is satisfied with the assets it currently holds. In contrast, selling assets to provide liquidity for liability-derived demands, such as deposit withdrawals, shrinks the size of a financial firm as its asset holdings decline. Finally, as we saw in Chapter 7, liability management comes with its own *control lever*—the interest rate offered to borrow funds. If the borrowing institution needs more funds, it merely raises its *offer rate* until the requisite amount of funds flow in. If fewer funds are required, the financial firm's offer rate may be lowered.

The principal sources of borrowed liquidity for a depository institution include jumbo ($100,000+) negotiable CDs, federal funds borrowings, repurchase agreements (in which securities are sold temporarily with an agreement to buy them back), Eurocurrency borrowings, advances from the Federal Home Loan Banks, and borrowings at the discount window of the central bank in each nation or region. (See the box entitled "Borrowing Liquidity—The Principal Options" for a description of these instruments.) Liability management techniques are used most extensively by the largest banks that often borrow close to 100 percent of their liquidity needs.

Borrowing liquidity is the most risky approach to solving liquidity problems (but also carries the highest expected return) because of the volatility of interest rates and the rapidity with which the availability of credit can change. Often financial-service providers must purchase liquidity when it is most difficult to do so, both in cost and availability. Borrowing cost is always uncertain, which adds greater uncertainty to earnings. Moreover, a financial firm that gets into trouble is usually most in need of borrowed liquidity, particularly because knowledge of its difficulties spreads and customers begin to withdraw their funds. At the same time, other financial firms become less willing to lend to the troubled institution due to the risk involved.

Balanced Liquidity Management Strategies

Due to the risks inherent in relying on borrowed liquidity and the costs of storing liquidity in assets, most financial firms compromise by using *both* asset and liability management. Under a **balanced liquidity management** strategy, some of the expected demands for liquidity are stored in assets (principally holdings of marketable securities), while other anticipated liquidity needs are backstopped by advanced arrangements for lines of credit from potential suppliers of funds. Unexpected cash needs are typically met from near-term borrowings. Longer-term liquidity needs can be planned for and the funds to meet these needs can be parked in short-term and medium-term assets that will provide cash as those liquidity needs arise.

Concept Check

11–6. What are the principal differences among *asset liquidity management, liability management,* and *balanced liquidity management?*

11–7. What guidelines should management keep in mind when it manages a financial firm's liquidity position?

Guidelines for Liquidity Managers

Over the years, liquidity managers have developed several rules that often guide their activities. First, the liquidity manager must keep track of the activities of *all* departments using and/or supplying funds while coordinating his or her department's activities with theirs. Whenever the loan department grants a new credit line to a customer, for example, the liquidity manager must prepare for possible drawings against that line. If the savings account division expects to receive several large deposits in the next few days, this information should also be passed on to the liquidity manager.

Second, the liquidity manager should know in *advance,* wherever possible, when the biggest credit or funds-supplying customers plan to withdraw their funds or add funds to their accounts. This allows the manager to plan ahead to deal more effectively with emerging liquidity surpluses and deficits.

Third, the liquidity manager must make sure the financial firm's priorities and objectives for liquidity management are clear. For example, in the past, a depository institution's liquidity position was often assigned top priority when it came to allocating funds. A typical assumption was that a depository institution had little or no control over its sources of funds—those were determined by the public—but the institution could control its uses of funds. In addition, because the law may require depository institutions to set aside liquid funds at the central bank to cover reserve requirements and because the depository must be ready at all times to handle deposit withdrawals, liquidity management and the diverting of sufficient funds into liquid assets were given the highest priority. Today, liquidity management has generally been relegated to a supporting role compared to most financial firms' number one priority—making loans and supplying fee-generating services to all qualified customers in order to maximize returns.

Fourth, liquidity needs must be analyzed *on a continuing basis* to avoid both excess and deficit liquidity positions. Excess liquidity that is not reinvested the same day it occurs results in lost income, while liquidity deficits must be dealt with quickly to avoid dire emergencies where the hurried borrowing of funds or sale of assets results in excessive losses for the financial firm involved.

11–5 Estimating Liquidity Needs

Several methods have been developed in recent years for estimating a financial institution's liquidity requirements: the *sources and uses of funds approach,* the *structure of funds approach,* the *liquidity indicator approach,* and the *market signals* (or *discipline*) *approach.* Each method rests on specific assumptions and yields only an approximation of actual liquidity requirements. This is why a liquidity manager must always be ready to fine-tune estimates of liquidity requirements as new information becomes available. In fact, most financial firms make sure their liquidity reserves include both a *planned component*, consisting of the reserves called for by the latest forecast, and a *protective component*, consisting of an extra margin of liquid reserves over those dictated by the most recent forecast. The protective liquidity component may be large or small, depending on management's philosophy and attitude toward risk—that is, how much chance of running a "cash-out" management wishes to accept.

Let us turn now to the most popular methods for estimating a financial institution's liquidity needs. For illustrative purposes, we will focus on the problem of estimating a bank's liquidity needs because banks typically face the greatest liquidity management challenges of any financial firm. However, the principles we will explore apply to other financial-service providers as well.

The Sources and Uses of Funds Approach

The **sources and uses of funds method** for estimating liquidity needs begins with two simple facts:

1. In the case of a bank, for example, liquidity *rises* as deposits increase and loans decrease.
2. Alternatively, liquidity *declines* when deposits decrease and loans increase.

Whenever sources and uses of liquidity do not match, there is a **liquidity gap,** measured by the size of the difference between sources and uses of funds. When sources of liquidity (e.g., increasing deposits or decreasing loans) exceed uses of liquidity (e.g., decreasing deposits or increasing loans), the financial firm will have a *positive liquidity gap* (surplus). Its surplus liquid funds must be quickly invested in earning assets until they are needed to cover future cash needs. On the other hand, when uses exceed sources, a financial institution faces a *negative liquidity gap* (deficit). It now must raise funds from the cheapest and most timely sources available.

The key steps in the sources and uses of funds approach, using a bank as an example, are:

1. Loans and deposits must be forecast for a given liquidity planning period.
2. The estimated change in loans and deposits must be calculated for that same period.
3. The liquidity manager must estimate the net liquid funds' surplus or deficit for the planning period by comparing the estimated change in loans (or other uses of funds) to the estimated change in deposits (or other funds sources).

Banks, for example, use a wide variety of statistical techniques, supplemented by management's judgment and experience, to prepare forecasts of deposits and loans. For example, a bank's economics department or its liquidity managers might develop the following forecasting models:

$$
\begin{aligned}
&\begin{array}{l}\text{Estimated}\\ \text{change in total}\\ \text{loans for the}\\ \text{coming period}\end{array}
\begin{array}{l}\text{is a}\\ \text{function}\\ \text{of}\end{array}
\left[\left(\begin{array}{c}\text{projected growth in the}\\ \text{economy}\\ \text{(for example, the}\\ \text{growth of gross domestic}\\ \text{product (GDP) or}\\ \text{(business sales)}\end{array}\right),\left(\begin{array}{c}\text{projected}\\ \text{quarterly}\\ \text{corporate}\\ \text{earnings}\end{array}\right),\right.\\
\\
&\left.\left(\begin{array}{c}\text{current rate of}\\ \text{growth in the}\\ \text{nation's money}\\ \text{supply}\end{array}\right),\left(\begin{array}{c}\text{projected prime}\\ \text{loan rate}\\ \text{minus the}\\ \text{commercial}\\ \text{paper rate}\end{array}\right),\text{and}\left(\begin{array}{c}\text{estimated}\\ \text{rate of}\\ \text{inflation}\end{array}\right)\right]
\end{aligned}
\tag{11–2}
$$

Factoid
Did you know that robberies of cash from banks have been on the rise again in recent years due, in part, to banking offices that stress customer convenience and easy access rather than security? Does this seem to make sense as a business decision? Why?

$$\begin{matrix} \text{Estimated} \\ \text{change in total} \\ \text{deposits for} \\ \text{the coming} \\ \text{period} \end{matrix} \quad \begin{matrix} \text{is a} \\ \text{function} \\ \text{of} \end{matrix} \left[\begin{pmatrix} \text{projected growth} \\ \text{in personal income} \\ \text{in the economy} \end{pmatrix}, \begin{pmatrix} \text{estimated} \\ \text{increase in} \\ \text{retail sales} \end{pmatrix}, \right.$$

$$\left. \begin{pmatrix} \text{current rate of} \\ \text{growth of the} \\ \text{nation's money} \\ \text{supply} \end{pmatrix}, \begin{pmatrix} \text{projected yield on} \\ \text{money market} \\ \text{deposits} \end{pmatrix}, \text{and} \begin{pmatrix} \text{estimated rate} \\ \text{of inflation} \end{pmatrix} \right]$$

Using the forecasts of loans and deposits generated by the foregoing relationships, management could then estimate the bank's need for liquidity by calculating as follows:

$$\begin{matrix} \text{Estimated liquidity} \\ \text{deficit} (-) \text{ or surplus} (+) \\ \text{for the coming period} \end{matrix} = \begin{matrix} \text{Estimated change in} \\ \text{deposits} \end{matrix} - \begin{matrix} \text{Estimated} \\ \text{change in} \\ \text{loans} \end{matrix} \quad \textbf{(11–3)}$$

A somewhat simpler approach for estimating future deposits (or other funds sources) and loans (or other funds uses) is to divide the forecast of future deposit and loan growth into three components:

1. A *trend component*, estimated by constructing a trend (constant-growth) line using as reference points year-end, quarterly, or monthly deposit and loan totals established over at least the last 10 years (or some other base period sufficiently long to define a trend growth rate).

2. A *seasonal component*, measuring how deposits (or other funds sources) and loans (or other funds uses) are expected to behave in any given week or month due to seasonal factors, as compared to the most recent year-end deposit or loan level.

3. A *cyclical component*, representing positive or negative deviations from a bank's total expected deposits and loans (measured by the sum of trend and seasonal components), depending upon the strength or weakness of the economy in the current year.

For example, suppose we are managing liquidity for a bank whose trend growth rate in deposits over the past decade has averaged 10 percent a year. Loan growth has been slightly less rapid, averaging 8 percent a year for the past 10 years. Our bank's total deposits stood at $1,200 million and total loans outstanding reached $800 million at the most recent year-end. Table 11–2 presents a forecast of weekly deposit and loan totals for the first six weeks of the new year. Each weekly loan and deposit *trend* figure shown in column 1 accounts for a one-week portion of the projected 10 percent annual increase in deposits and the expected 8 percent annual increase in loans. To derive the appropriate *seasonal* element shown in column 2, we compare the ratio for the average (trend) deposit and loan figure for each week of the year to the average deposit and loan level during the final week of the year for each of the past 10 years. We assume the seasonal ratio of the current week's level to the preceding year-end level applies in the current year in the same way as it did for all past years, so we simply add or subtract the calculated seasonal element to the trend element.

The *cyclical* element, given in column 3, compares the sum of the estimated trend and seasonal elements with the actual level of deposits and loans the previous year. The dollar gap between these two numbers is presumed to result from cyclical forces, and we assume that roughly the same cyclical pressures that prevailed last year apply to the current year. Finally, column 4 reports estimated *total* deposits and loans, consisting of the sum of trend (column 1), seasonal (column 2), and cyclical components (column 3).

TABLE 11–2

Forecasting Deposits and Loans with the Sources and Uses of Funds Approach (figures in millions of dollars)

Deposit Forecast for	Trend Estimate for Deposits	Seasonal Element*	Cyclical Element**	Estimated Total Deposits
January, Week 1	$1,210	−4	−6	$1,200
January, Week 2	1,212	−54	−58	1,100
January, Week 3	1,214	−121	−93	1,000
January, Week 4	1,216	−165	−101	950
February, Week 1	1,218	+70	−38	1,250
February, Week 2	1,220	+32	−52	1,200

Loan Forecast for	Trend Estimate for Loans	Seasonal Element*	Cyclical Element**	Estimated Total Loans
January, Week 1	$799	+6	−5	$ 800
January, Week 2	800	+59	−9	850
January, Week 3	801	+174	−25	950
January, Week 4	802	+166	+32	1,000
February, Week 1	803	+27	−80	750
February, Week 2	804	+98	−2	900

*The seasonal element compares the average level of deposits and loans for each week over the past 10 years to the average level of deposits and loans for the final week of December over the preceding 10 years.

**The cyclical element reflects the difference between the expected deposit and loan levels in each week during the preceding year (measured by the trend and seasonal elements) and the actual volume of total deposits and total loans the bank posted that week.

Table 11–3 shows how we can take estimated deposit and loan figures, such as those given in column 4 of Table 11–2, and use them to estimate expected liquidity deficits and surpluses in the period ahead. In this instance, the liquidity manager has estimated liquidity needs for the next six weeks. Columns 1 and 2 in Table 11–3 merely repeat the estimated total deposit and total loan figures from column 4 in Table 11–2. Columns 3 and 4 in Table 11–3 calculate the *change* in total deposits and total loans from one week to the next. Column 5 shows differences between change in loans and change in deposits each week. When deposits fall and loans rise, a liquidity deficit is more likely to occur. When deposits grow and loans decline, a liquidity surplus is more likely.

As Table 11–3 reveals, our bank has a projected liquidity *deficit* over the next three weeks—$150 million next week, $200 million the third week, and $100 million in the fourth week—because its loans are growing while its deposit levels are declining. Due to a forecast of rising deposits and falling loans in the fifth week, a liquidity surplus of $550 million is expected, followed by a $200 million liquidity deficit in week 6. What liquidity management decisions must be made over the six-week period shown in Table 11–3? The liquidity manager must prepare to raise new funds in weeks 2, 3, 4, and 6 from the cheapest and most reliable funds sources and to profitably invest the expected funds surplus in week 5.

TABLE 11–3 Forecasting Liquidity Deficits and Surpluses with the Sources and Uses of Funds Approach (figures in millions of dollars)

Time Period	Estimated Total Deposits	Estimated Total Loans	Estimated Deposit Change	Estimated Loan Change	Estimated Liquidity Deficit (−) or Surplus (+)
January, Week 1	$1,200	$ 800	$___	$___	$___
January, Week 2	1,100	850	−100	+50	−150
January, Week 3	1,000	950	−100	+100	−200
January, Week 4	950	1,000	−50	+50	−100
February, Week 1	1,250	750	+300	−250	+550
February, Week 2	1,200	900	−50	+150	−200

Management can now begin planning which sources of liquid funds to draw upon, first evaluating the bank's stock of liquid assets to see which assets are likely to be available for use and then determining if adequate sources of borrowed funds are also likely to be available. For example, the bank probably has already set up lines of credit for borrowing from its principal correspondent banks and wants to be sure these credit lines are still adequate to meet the projected amount of borrowing needed.

The Structure of Funds Approach

Another approach to estimating a financial firm's liquidity requirements is the **structure of funds method.** Once again we will illustrate this liquidity estimation procedure using some figures provided by a bank that frequently faces substantial liquidity demands. In the first step in the structure of funds approach, deposits and other funds sources are divided into categories based upon their estimated probability of being withdrawn and, therefore, lost to the financial firm. As an illustration, we might divide a bank's deposit and nondeposit liabilities into three categories:

1. *"Hot money" liabilities* (often called volatile liabilities)—deposits and other borrowed funds (such as federal funds) that are very interest sensitive or that management is sure will be withdrawn during the current period.
2. *Vulnerable funds*—customer deposits of which a substantial portion, perhaps 25 to 30 percent, will probably be withdrawn sometime during the current time period.
3. *Stable funds* (often called *core deposits* or *core liabilities*)—funds that management considers unlikely to be removed (except for a minor percentage of the total).

Second, the liquidity manager must set aside liquid funds according to some desired *operating rule* for each of these funds sources. For example, the manager may decide to set up a 95 percent liquid reserve behind all hot money funds (less any required legal reserves held behind hot money deposits). This liquidity reserve might consist of holdings of immediately spendable deposits in correspondent banks plus investments in Treasury bills and repurchase agreements where the committed funds can be recovered in a matter of minutes or hours.

A common rule of thumb for vulnerable deposit and nondeposit liabilities is to hold a fixed percentage of their total amount—say, 30 percent—in liquid reserves. For stable (core) funds sources, a banker may decide to place a small proportion—perhaps 15 percent or less—of their total in liquid reserves. Thus, the liquidity reserve behind deposit and nondeposit liabilities would be:

$$
\begin{aligned}
\text{Liability liquidity reserve} = {}& 0.95 \times (\text{Hot money deposits and nondeposit funds} \\
& - \text{Legal reserves held}) + 0.30 \\
& \times (\text{Vulnerable deposit and nondeposit funds} \quad \textbf{(11--4)} \\
& - \text{Legal reserves held}) + 0.15 \\
& \times (\text{Stable deposits and nondeposit funds} \\
& - \text{Legal reserves held})
\end{aligned}
$$

In the case of loans, a bank or other lending institution must be ready at all times to make good loans—that is, to meet the legitimate credit needs of those customers who satisfy the lender's loan quality standards. The bank in this example must have sufficient liquid reserves on hand because, once a loan is made, the borrowing customer will spend the proceeds immediately and those funds will flow out to other depository institutions. However, this bank does not want to turn down any good loan, because loan customers bring in new deposits and normally are the principal source of earnings from interest and fees.

Indeed, a substantial body of current thinking suggests that any lending institution should make *all* good loans, counting on its ability to borrow liquid funds, if necessary, to cover any pressing cash needs. Under today's concept of *relationship banking*, once the customer is sold a loan, the lender can then proceed to sell that customer other services, establishing a multidimensional relationship that will bring in additional fee income and increase the customer's dependence on (and, therefore, loyalty to) the lending institution. This reasoning suggests that management must try to estimate the maximum possible figure for total loans and hold in liquid reserves or borrowing capacity the full amount (100 percent) of the difference between the actual amount of loans outstanding and the maximum potential for total loans.

Combining both loan and deposit liquidity requirements, this bank's *total liquidity requirement* would be:

Total liquidity requirement = Deposit and nondeposit liability liquidity requirement and loan liquidity requirement

$$
\begin{aligned}
&= 0.95 \times (\text{Hot money funds} \\
&\quad - \text{Required legal reserves held} \\
&\quad \text{behind hot money deposits}) \\
&\quad + 0.30 \times (\text{Vulnerable deposits and} \\
&\quad \text{nondeposit funds} - \text{Required legal} \\
&\quad \text{reserves}) + 0.15 \times (\text{Stable deposits} \\
&\quad \text{and nondeposit funds} - \text{Required legal} \\
&\quad \text{reserves}) + 1.00 \times (\text{Potential loans} \\
&\quad \text{outstanding} - \text{Actual loans outstanding})
\end{aligned}
\qquad \textbf{(11–5)}
$$

Admittedly, the deposit and loan liquidity requirements that make up the above equation are *subjective* estimates that rely heavily on management's judgment, experience, and attitude toward risk.

A numerical example of this liquidity management method is shown in Table 11–4. First National Bank has broken down its deposit and nondeposit liabilities into hot money, vulnerable funds, and stable (core) funds, amounting to $25 million, $24 million, and $100 million, respectively. The bank's loans total $135 million currently, but recently have been as high as $140 million, and loans are projected to grow at a 10 percent annual rate. Thus, within the coming year, total loans might reach as high as $154 million, or $140 million + (0.10 × $140 million), which would be $19 million higher than they are now. Applying the percentages of deposits that management wishes to hold in liquid reserves, we find the bank needs more than $60 million in total liquidity, consisting of both liquid assets and borrowing capacity.

TABLE 11–4
Estimating Liquidity Needs with the Structure of Funds Method

A. First National Bank finds that its current deposits and nondeposit liabilities break down as follows:

Hot money	$ 25 million
Vulnerable funds (including the largest deposit and nondeposit liability accounts)	$ 24 million
Stable (core) funds	$100 million

First National's management wants to keep a 95% reserve behind its hot money deposits (less the 3% legal reserve requirement behind many of these deposits) and nondeposit liabilities, a 30% liquidity reserve in back of its vulnerable deposits and borrowings (less required reserves), and a 15% liquidity reserve behind its core deposit and nondeposit funds (less required reserves).

B. First National Bank's loans total $135 million but recently have been as high as $140 million, with a trend growth rate of about 10 percent a year. The bank wishes to be ready at all times to honor customer demands for all those loans that meet its quality standards.

C. The bank's total liquidity requirement is:

Deposit/Nondeposit Funds plus Loans

0.95 ($25 million − 0.03 × $25 million)
+0.30 ($24 million − 0.03 × $24 million)
+0.15 ($100 million − 0.03 × $100 million)
+$140 million × 0.10 + ($140 − $135 million)
= $23.04 million + $6.98 million + $14.55 million + $19 million
= $63.57 million (held in liquid assets and additional borrowing capacity)

Real Banks, Real Decisions

LIQUIDITY SHORTAGES IN THE WAKE OF THE SEPTEMBER 11, 2001, TERRORIST ATTACKS

The terrorist attacks of 9/11 in New York City assaulted the financial system as well as the twin towers of the World Trade Center. Banks with facilities for making payments located in or near the World Trade Center experienced temporary, intense shortages of funds due to their inability to collect and record payments they were owed and to dispense payments they were obligated to make. The problems banks near "ground zero" in Lower Manhattan faced soon spread to outlying financial firms in domino fashion. Banks whose electronic communications systems were destroyed or damaged couldn't make timely payment of their obligations to other institutions that, in turn, could not make good on their own promises to pay. Within hours many financial firms faced a full-blown *liquidity crisis*.

One of the first signs of trouble was a sharp reduction in the movement of funds through Fed Wire—the Federal Reserve's electronic funds transfer network—as banks hit hardest by the attacks stopped transferring reserves to other institutions because they could not be sure they themselves would receive the incoming funds they expected. Several banks that borrowed reserves from other institutions on September 10 were unable to return the borrowed funds on the 11th. Moreover, many financial firms near ground zero were unable to communicate with their customers to explain what was happening. Nor could they update their records or make deliveries of securities they had promised to their clients.

Within hours, however, the system began to recover and was approaching near-normal operating levels by September 14. Why did recovery from such a serious liquidity crisis come about so quickly? The Federal Reserve—the proverbial "lender of last resort"—stepped in aggressively. At 10:00 A.M. on September 11, the Fed announced that loans from its discount window would be available. At the same time, the Fed temporarily suspended penalties against banks running overdrafts and cranked up its open market operations to pour new funds into the money market. Discount window loans jumped from a daily average of about $100 million to more than $45 billion on September 12, while the Fed's open-market trading desk accelerated its trading activity from a relatively normal $3.5 billion a day to about $38 billion that same day. The Fed's quick reaction along with the determination of many bankers to restore communications links to their customers soon quelled the liquidity crisis. (See especially Champ [2].)

Many financial firms like to use *probabilities* in deciding how much liquidity to hold. Under this refinement of the structure of funds approach, the liquidity manager will want to define the best and the worst possible liquidity positions his or her financial institution might find itself in and assign probabilities to each. For example,

1. *The worst possible liquidity position.* Suppose deposit growth at the bank we have been following falls below management's expectations, so that actual deposit totals sometimes go below the lowest points on the bank's historical minimum deposit growth track. Moreover, suppose loan demand rises significantly above management's expectations, so that loan demand sometimes goes beyond the high points of the bank's loan growth track. In this instance, the bank would face maximum pressure on its available liquid reserves because deposit growth would not likely be able to fund all the loans customers were demanding. In this worst situation the liquidity manager would have to prepare for a sizable *liquidity deficit* and develop a plan for raising substantial amounts of new funds.

2. *The best possible liquidity position.* Suppose deposit growth turns out to be above management's expectations, so that it touches the highest points in the bank's deposit growth record. Moreover, suppose loan demand turns out to be below management's expectations, so that loan demand grows along a minimum path that touches the low points in the bank's loan growth track. In this case, the bank would face minimum pressure on its liquid reserves because deposit growth probably could fund nearly all the

quality loans that walk in the door. In this "best" situation, it is likely that a *liquidity surplus* will develop. The liquidity manager must have a plan for investing these surplus funds in order to maximize the bank's return.

Of course, neither the worst nor the best possible outcome is likely for both deposit and loan growth. The most likely outcome lies somewhere between these extremes. Many financial firms like to calculate their *expected liquidity requirement*, based on the probabilities they assign to different possible outcomes. For example, suppose the liquidity manager of the bank we have been following considers the institution's liquidity situation next week as likely to fall into one of three possible situations:

Possible Liquidity Outcomes for Next Week	Estimated Average Volume of Deposits Next Week (millions)	Estimated Average Volume of Loans Next Week (millions)	Estimated Liquidity Surplus or Deficit Position Next Week (millions)	Probability Assigned by Management to Each Possible Outcome
Best possible liquidity position (maximum deposits, minimum loans)	$170	$110	+$60	15%
Liquidity position bearing the highest probability	$150	$140	+$10	60%
Worst possible liquidity position (minimum deposits, maximum loans)	$130	$150	−$20	25%

Thus, management sees the worst possible situation next week as one characterized by a $20 million liquidity deficit, but this least desirable outcome is assigned a probability of only 25 percent. Similarly, the best possible outcome would be a $60 million liquidity surplus. However, this is judged to have only a 15 percent probability of occurring. More likely is the middle ground—a $10 million liquidity surplus—with a management-estimated probability of 60 percent.

What, then, is the bank's expected liquidity requirement? We can find the answer from:

$$
\begin{aligned}
\text{Expected liquidity requirement} &= \text{Probability of Outcome A} \times \left(\begin{array}{c}\text{Estimated liquidity}\\ \text{surplus or}\\ \text{deficit in}\\ \text{Outcome A}\end{array}\right) \\
&+ \text{Probability of Outcome B} \times \left(\begin{array}{c}\text{Estimated liquidity}\\ \text{surplus or}\\ \text{deficit in}\\ \text{Outcome B}\end{array}\right) \\
&+ \cdots + \cdots
\end{aligned}
\tag{11–6}
$$

for all possible outcomes, subject to the restriction that the sum of all probabilities assigned by management must be 1.

Using this formula, this bank's expected liquidity requirement must be:

$$\begin{array}{l} \text{Expected} \\ \text{liquidity} \\ \text{requirement} \end{array} = \begin{array}{l} 0.15 \times (+\$60 \text{ million}) + 0.60 \times (+\$10 \text{ million}) \\ \qquad + 0.25 \times (-\$20 \text{ million}) \end{array}$$

$$= +\$10 \text{ million}$$

On average, management should plan for a $10 million liquidity surplus next week and begin now to review the options for investing this expected surplus. Of course, management would also do well to have a contingency plan in case the worst possible outcome occurs.

Liquidity Indicator Approach

Many financial-service institutions estimate their liquidity needs based upon experience and industry averages. This often means using certain **liquidity indicators.** For example, for depository institutions the following liquidity indicator ratios are useful:

1. *Cash position indicator:* Cash and deposits due from depository institutions ÷ total assets, where a greater proportion of cash implies the institution is in a stronger position to handle immediate cash needs.

2. *Liquid securities indicator:* U.S. government securities ÷ total assets, which compares the most marketable securities an institution can hold with the overall size of its asset portfolio; the greater the proportion of government securities, the more liquid the depository institution's position tends to be.

3. *Net federal funds and repurchase agreements position:* (Federal funds sold and reverse repurchase agreements – Federal funds purchased and repurchase agreements) ÷ total assets, which measures the comparative importance of overnight loans relative to overnight borrowings of reserves; liquidity tends to increase when this ratio rises.

4. *Capacity ratio:* Net loans and leases ÷ total assets, which is really a negative liquidity indicator because loans and leases are often the most illiquid of assets.

5. *Pledged securities ratio:* Pledged securities ÷ total security holdings, also a negative liquidity indicator because the greater the proportion of securities pledged to back government deposits, the fewer securities are available to sell when liquidity needs arise.[1]

6. *Hot money ratio:* Money market (short-term) assets ÷ volatile liabilities = (Cash and due from deposits held at other depository institutions + holdings of short-term securities + Federal funds loans + reverse repurchase agreements) ÷ (large CDs + Eurocurrency deposits + Federal funds borrowings + repurchase agreements), a ratio that reflects whether the institution has roughly balanced the volatile liabilities it has issued with the money market assets it holds that could be sold quickly to cover those liabilities.

7. *Deposit brokerage index:* Brokered deposits ÷ total deposits, where brokered deposits consist of packages of funds (usually $100,000 or less to gain the advantage of deposit insurance) placed by securities brokers for their customers with institutions paying the highest yields. Brokered deposits are interest sensitive and may be quickly withdrawn; the more a depository institution holds, the greater the chance of a liquidity crisis.

8. *Core deposit ratio:* Core deposits ÷ total assets, where core deposits include total deposits less all deposits over $100,000. Core deposits are primarily small-denomination checking and savings accounts that are considered unlikely to be withdrawn on short notice and so carry lower liquidity requirements.

9. *Deposit composition ratio:* Demand deposits ÷ time deposits, where demand deposits are subject to immediate withdrawal via check writing, while time deposits have fixed

---

[1] See Chapter 10 for a discussion of the nature and use of pledged securities.

maturities with penalties for early withdrawal. This ratio measures how stable a funding base each institution possesses; a decline suggests greater deposit stability and a lesser need for liquidity.

10. *Loan commitments ratio:* Unused loan commitments ÷ total assets, which measures the volume of promises a lender has made to its customers to provide credit up to a prespecified amount over a given time period. These commitments will not appear on the lender's balance sheet until a loan is actually "taken down" (i.e., drawn upon) by the borrower. Thus, with loan commitments there is risk as to the exact amount and timing when some portion of loan commitments become actual loans. The lender must be prepared with sufficient liquidity to accommodate a variety of "take-down" scenarios that borrowers may demand. A rise in this ratio implies greater future liquidity needs.

Table 11–5 indicates recent trends in a few of these liquidity indicators among U.S.-insured banks. In general, most liquidity indicators appear to show a recent *decline* in liquidity, especially those indicators that track holdings of liquid assets. We note too that the last indicator ratio suggests that loan commitments have been rising relative to industry assets, possibly leading to bigger future liquidity demands.

One reason for the apparent decline in industry liquidity is *consolidation*—smaller depository institutions being absorbed by larger institutions. With fewer, but much larger, depositories in the industry, chances are greater that money withdrawn from one customer's account will wind up in the account of another customer of the *same* bank. Thus, from the vantage point of the whole institution daily transactions more frequently "net out" with no overall change in a depository's cash position.

Some analysts argue that the continuing shift in deposit accounts toward longer-maturity deposits that tend to be more stable and experience fewer unexpected customer withdrawals has lowered industry liquidity needs. Another important factor is the recent decline in legal reserve requirements imposed by the Federal Reserve and other central banks around the world, thus lowering legal cash needs. Moreover, there are more ways to raise liquidity today and advancing technology has made it easier to anticipate liquidity needs and prepare for them. Finally, the appearance of a more stable economy may have dampened the need for large holdings of liquid reserves.

The first five liquidity indicators discussed above focus principally upon *assets* or *stored liquidity*. The last five focus mainly upon liabilities or on future commitments to lend money and are aimed mainly at forms of *purchased liquidity*. These indicators tend to be highly sensitive to season of the year and stage of the business cycle. For example,

TABLE 11–5
Recent Trends in Liquidity Indicators for FDIC-Insured U.S. Banks

Source: Federal Deposit Insurance Corporation (www.fdic.gov).

Selected Liquidity Indicators	1985	1989	1993	1996	2001	2003	2005*
Cash Position Indicator: Cash and deposits due from depository institutions ÷ total assets	12.5%	10.6%	6.3%	7.3%	6.0%	4.6%	4.4%
Net Federal Funds Position: (Federal funds sold − Federal funds purchased) ÷ total assets	−3.3	−3.9	−3.4	−3.4	−2.8	−1.2	−2.9
Capacity Ratio: Net loans and leases ÷ total assets	58.9	60.7	56.6	60.2	58.2	58.6	58.0
Deposit Composition Ratio: Demand deposits ÷ time deposits	68.4	44.8	52.4	58.2	44.4	42.2	36.6
Loan Commitments Ratio: Unused loan commitments ÷ total assets	NA	NA	NA	33.1	49.9	70.9	66.9

Notes: *Indicates that figures shown in the 2005 column are for June 30, 2005. NA indicates the missing figures are not available.

liquidity indicators often decline in boom periods under pressure from rising loan demand, only to rise again during the ensuing business recession.

We must also note that using industrywide averages for each liquidity indicator can be misleading. Each financial institution's liquidity position must be judged relative to peer institutions of similar size operating in similar markets. Moreover, liquidity managers usually focus on *changes* in their institution's liquidity indicators rather than on the level of each indicator. They want to know whether liquidity is rising or falling and why.

The Ultimate Standard for Assessing Liquidity Needs: Signals from the Marketplace

Many analysts believe there is one ultimately sound method for assessing a financial institution's liquidity needs and how well it is fulfilling them. This method centers on *the discipline of the financial marketplace*. No financial-service provider can tell for sure if it has sufficient liquidity until it has passed the *market's test*.

For example, liquidity managers should closely monitor the following market signals:

1. *Public confidence.* Is there evidence the institution is losing money because individuals and institutions believe there is some danger it will be unable to pay its obligations?

2. *Stock price behavior.* Is the corporation's stock price falling because investors perceive the institution has an actual or pending liquidity crisis?

3. *Risk premiums on CDs and other borrowings.* Is there evidence the institution is paying higher interest rates on its offerings of time and savings deposits (especially on large negotiable CDs) and money market borrowings than other institutions of similar size and location? In other words, is the market imposing a *risk premium* in the form of higher borrowing costs because it believes the institution is headed for a liquidity crisis?

Concept Check

11–8. How does the sources and uses of funds approach help a manager estimate a financial institution's need for liquidity?

11–9. Suppose that a bank estimates its total deposits for the next six months in millions of dollars will be, respectively, $112, $132, $121, $147, $151, and $139, while its loans (also in millions of dollars) will total an estimated $87, $95, $102, $113, $101, and $124, respectively, over the same six months. Under the sources and uses of funds approach, when does this bank face liquidity deficits, if any?

11–10. What steps are needed to carry out the structure of funds approach to liquidity management?

11–11. Suppose that a thrift institution's liquidity division estimates that it holds $19 million in hot money deposits and other IOUs against which it will hold an 80 percent liquidity reserve, $54 million in vulnerable funds against which it plans to hold a 25 percent liquidity reserve, and $112 million in stable or core funds against which it will hold a 5 percent liquidity reserve. The thrift expects its loans to grow 8 percent annually; its loans currently total $117 million but have recently reached $132 million. If reserve requirements on liabilities currently stand at 3 percent, what is this depository institution's total liquidity requirement?

11–12. What is the liquidity indicator approach to liquidity management?

11–13. First National Bank posts the following balance sheet entries on today's date: Net loans and leases, $3,502 million; cash and deposits held at other banks, $633 million; Federal funds sold, $48 million; U.S. government securities, $185 million; Federal funds purchased, $62 million; demand deposits, $988 million; time deposits, $2,627 million; and total assets, $4,446 million. How many liquidity indicators can you calculate from these figures?

11–14. How can the discipline of the marketplace be used as a guide for making liquidity management decisions?

4. *Loss sales of assets.* Has the institution recently been forced to sell assets in a hurry, with significant losses, in order to meet demands for liquidity? Is this a rare event or has it become a frequent occurrence?

5. *Meeting commitments to credit customers.* Has the institution been able to honor all potentially profitable requests for loans from its valued customers? Or have liquidity pressures compelled management to turn down some otherwise acceptable credit applications?

6. *Borrowings from the central bank.* Has the institution been forced to borrow in larger volume and more frequently from the central bank in its home territory (such as the Federal Reserve or Bank of Japan) lately? Have central bank officials begun to question the institution's borrowings?

If the answer to any of the foregoing questions is *yes*, management needs to take a close look at its liquidity management policies and practices to determine whether changes are needed.

11–6 Legal Reserves and Money Position Management

The Money Position Manager

Management of a financial institution's liquidity position can be a harrowing job, requiring quick decisions that may have long-run consequences for profitability. Nowhere is this more evident than in the job of **money position manager.**

Most large depository institutions have designated an officer of the firm as *money position manager.* Smaller banks and thrifts often hand this job over to larger depositories with which they have a correspondent relationship (that is, that hold deposits to help clear checks and meet other liquidity needs).

Legal Reserves

The manager of the money position is responsible for ensuring that the institution maintains an adequate level of **legal reserves**—assets the law and central bank regulation say must be held in support of the institution's deposits. In the United States, only two kinds of assets can be used for this purpose: (1) *cash in the vault;* and (2) *deposits held in a reserve account at the Federal Reserve bank in the region* (or, for smaller depository institutions, deposits held with a Fed-approved institution that passes reserves through to the Fed). Incidentally, the smallest U.S. depository institutions (those holding $7.8 million or less in reservable deposits in 2005–6) are generally exempt from legal reserve requirements. This exemption amount is adjusted annually to help reduce the impact of inflation on deposit growth. Legal reserve requirements apply to all qualified depository institutions, including commercial and savings banks, savings and loan associations, credit unions, and agencies and branches of foreign banks that offer transaction deposits or nonpersonal (business) time deposits or borrow through Eurocurrency liabilities.

Regulations on Calculating Legal Reserve Requirements

Reserve Computation

Exhibit 11–1 illustrates the timing associated with calculating reserve requirements and maintaining reserves that the Federal Reserve has set up for institutions holding deposits and other liabilities subject to legal reserve requirements. As the exhibit shows, under the current system of accounting for legal reserves—called **lagged reserve accounting (LRA)**—the daily average amount of deposits and other reservable liabilities are computed using information gathered over a two-week period stretching from a Tuesday to a Monday two

EXHIBIT 11–1
Federal Reserve Rules
for Calculating a
Weekly Reporting
Bank's Required
Legal Reserves

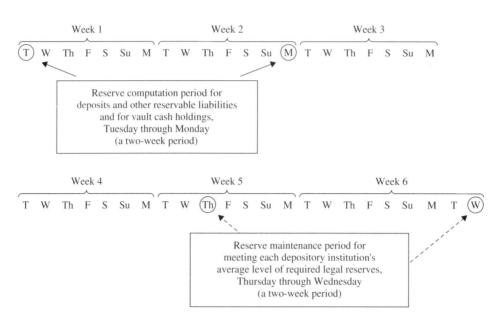

Federal Reserve rules for calculating and maintaining required legal reserves
(Regulation D):

weeks later. This interval of time is known as the **reserve computation period.** The daily average amount of *vault cash* each depository institution holds is also figured over the same two-week computation period. Exhibit 11–1 illustrates one computation cycle. For large institutions another cycle begins immediately.[2]

Reserve Maintenance

After the money position manager calculates daily average deposits and the institution's required legal reserves, he or she must maintain that required legal reserve on deposit with the Federal Reserve bank in the region (less the amount of daily average vault cash held), on average, over a 14-day period stretching from a Thursday to a Wednesday. This is known as the **reserve maintenance period.** Notice from Exhibit 11–1 that this period begins 30 days after the beginning of the reserve computation period for deposits and other reservable liabilities. Using LRA, the money position manager has a 16-day lag following the computation period and preceding the maintenance period. This period provides time for money position management planning.

Reserve Requirements

How much money must be held in legal reserves? That answer depends upon the volume and mix of each institution's deposits and also on the particular time period, since the amount of deposits subject to legal reserve requirements changes each year. For transaction deposits—

[2]The process used for calculating legal reserve requirements described here applies to the largest U.S. depository institutions, known as *weekly reporters,* that must report their cash positions to the Federal Reserve banks on a weekly basis. The more numerous, but smaller U.S. banks and qualifying thrift institutions are known as *quarterly reporters.* This latter group of institutions have their daily average deposit balances figured over a seven-day computation period beginning on the third Tuesday in the months of March, June, September, and December, each representing one-quarter of the calendar year. These smaller U.S. depository institutions, then, must settle their reserve position at the required level weekly based on a legal reserve requirement determined once each quarter of the year. In contrast, the largest U.S. depositories must meet (settle) their legal reserve requirement over successive two-week periods (biweekly).

checking accounts, NOWs, and other deposits that can be used to make payments—the reserve requirement in 2005–6 was 3 percent of the end-of-the-day daily average amount held over a two-week period, from $7.8 million to $48.3 million. Transaction deposits over $48.3 million held at the same depository institution carried a 10 percent reserve requirement.

The $48.3 million figure, known as the *reserve tranche*, is changed once each year based upon the annual rate of U.S. deposit growth. Under the dictates of the Depository Institutions Deregulation and Monetary Control Act of 1980, the Federal Reserve Board must calculate the June-to-June annual growth rate of all deposits subject to legal reserve requirements. The dollar cut-off point above which reserve requirements on transaction deposits become 10 percent instead of 3 percent is then adjusted by 80 percent of the calculated annual deposit growth rate. This annual legal reserve adjustment is designed to offset the impact of inflation, which over time would tend to push depository institutions into higher reserve requirement categories.

Calculating Required Reserves

The largest depository institutions must hold the largest percentage of legal reserves, reflecting their great importance as funds managers for themselves and for hundreds of smaller financial institutions. However, whether large or small, the total required legal reserves of each depository institution are figured by the same method. Each reservable liability item is multiplied by the stipulated reserve requirement percentage to derive each depository's total legal reserve requirement. Thus:

$$
\begin{aligned}
\text{Total required legal reserves} = {}& \text{Reserve requirement on transaction deposits} \\
& \times \text{Daily average amount of net transaction} \\
& \text{deposits over the computation period} \\
& + \text{Reserve requirement on nontransaction} \quad \textbf{(11–7)} \\
& \text{reservable liabilities} \times \text{Daily average} \\
& \text{amount of nontransaction reservable liabilities} \\
& \text{over the computation period.}[3]
\end{aligned}
$$

A sample calculation of a U.S. bank's total required legal reserves is shown in Table 11–6.

Once a depository institution determines its required reserve amount, it compares this figure to its actual daily average holdings of legal reserve assets—vault cash and its reserve deposit at the central bank. If total legal reserves held are greater than required reserves, the depository institution has *excess reserves*. Management will move quickly to invest the excess because excess reserves pay no interest.

If, on the other hand, the calculated required reserve figure exceeds the amount of legal reserves actually held on a daily average basis, the depository institution has a *reserve deficit*. The law requires the institution to cover this deficit by acquiring additional legal reserves. Actually, current regulations allow a depository institution to run up to a 4 percent deficit from its required daily average reserve position, provided this shortfall is balanced out by a corresponding excess the next reserve maintenance period.

Penalty for a Reserve Deficit

Any deficit above 4 percent may be assessed an interest penalty equal to the Federal Reserve's discount (primary credit) rate at the beginning of the month plus 2 percentage

---

[3] *Net transaction deposits* include the sum total of all deposits on which a depositor is permitted to make withdrawals by check, telephone, or other transferable instrument minus any cash items in the process of collection, and deposits held with other depository institutions. Nonpersonal (business) time deposits and Eurocurrency liabilities also may, from time to time, be subject to legal reserve requirements. Nonpersonal time deposits include savings deposits, CDs, and other time accounts held by a customer who is not a natural person (i.e., not an individual, family, or sole proprietorship). Eurocurrency liabilities are mainly the sum of net borrowings from foreign offices.

TABLE 11–6
Sample Calculation of
Legal Reserve
Requirements in the
United States

Source: Board of Governors of
the Federal Reserve System.

Key URLs
To learn more about
U.S. legal reserve
requirements under
Regulation D, see
**www.federalreserve.
gov/regulations/default.
htm.** For information
about the reserve
requirements of the
European Central Bank,
see **www.ecb.int.** For
the rules applied by
other central banks
enter each central
bank's name in your
search engine.

The applicable percentage reserve requirements imposed by the Federal Reserve Board on banks selling deposits in the United States are as follows:*

The first $7.8 million of net transaction deposits are subject to a 0 percent legal reserve requirement (known as the "exemption amount"). The volume of net transaction deposits over $7.8 million up to $48.3 million carries a 3 percent reserve requirement (known as the "low reserve tranche"), while the amount over $48.3 million is subject to a 10 percent reserve requirement. Nontransaction reserveable liabilities (including nonpersonal time deposits and Eurocurrency liabilities) are subject to a 0 percent reserve requirement.**

First National's net transaction deposits averaged $100 million over the 14-day reserve computation period while its nontransaction reserveable liabilities had a daily average of $200 million over the same period.

Then First National's daily average required legal reserve level = $0.0 × $7.8 million + 0.03 × ($48.3 million – $7.8 million) + 0.10 × ($100 million – $48.3 million) = $6.385 million.

First National held a daily average of $5 million in vault cash over the required two-week computation period. Therefore, it must hold at the Federal Reserve Bank in its district the following amount, on average, over its two-week reserve maintenance period:

$$\begin{matrix} \text{Daily average level} \\ \text{of required legal} \\ \text{reserves to hold on} \\ \text{deposit at the Fed} \end{matrix} = \begin{matrix} \text{Total} \\ \text{required} \\ \text{legal} \\ \text{reserves} \end{matrix} - \begin{matrix} \text{Daily} \\ \text{average} \\ \text{vault} \\ \text{cash holdings} \end{matrix} = \$6.385 \text{ million} - \$5.00 \text{ million} = \$1.385 \text{ million}$$

Federal Reserve officials today differentiate between so-called *bound* and *nonbound* depository institutions. Bound institutions' required reserves are larger than their vault cash holdings, meaning that they must hold additional reserves beyond the amount of their vault cash at the Federal Reserve Bank in their district. Nonbound institutions hold more vault cash than their required reserves and therefore are not required to hold legal reserves at the Fed. As reserve requirements have been lowered in recent years, the number of nonbound depositories has increased.

*As of October 2005.
**Net transaction deposits are gross demand deposits less cash items in process of collection and deposits due from other banks. The percentage reserve requirement on nonpersonal time deposits with an original maturity of less than 18 months and on Eurocurrency liabilities was reduced to zero in 1991. Nonpersonal time deposits 18 months or longer to maturity were assigned a zero reserve requirement in 1983.

points (measured as an annual rate), which is applied to the amount of the deficiency. Increased surveillance costs may also be assessed if repeated reserve deficits lead regulators to monitor the bank's operations more closely, possibly damaging its efficiency.

Clearing Balances

In addition to holding a legal reserve account at the central bank, many depository institutions also hold a **clearing balance** with the Fed to cover any checks or other debit items drawn against them. In the United States any depository institution using the Federal Reserve's check-clearing facilities must maintain a minimum-size clearing balance—an amount set by agreement between each institution and its district Federal Reserve bank, based on its estimated check-clearing needs and recent overdrafts.

Clearing balance rules work much like legal reserve requirements, with depository institutions required to maintain a minimum daily average amount in their clearing account over the same two-week maintenance period as applies to legal reserves. When they fall more than 2 percent below the minimum balance required, they must provide additional funds to bring the balance up to the promised level. If a clearing balance has an excess amount in it, this can act as an extra cushion of reserves to help a depository institution avoid a deficit in its legal reserve account.

A depository institution earns credit from holding a clearing balance that it can apply to help cover the cost of using Fed services (such as the collection of checks or making use of Fed Wire, the Federal Reserve's electronic wire transfer service). The amount of credit earned from holding a Fed clearing balance depends on the size of the average account balance and the level of the Federal funds interest rate over the relevant period. For example, suppose a bank had a clearing balance averaging $1 million during a particular two-week maintenance period and the Federal funds interest rate over this same period averaged 5.50 percent. Then it would earn a Federal Reserve credit of

$$\text{Average clearing balance} \times \text{Annualized Fed funds rate} \times 14 \text{ days/360 days}$$
$$= \$1,000,000 \times .055 \times .0389 = \$2,138.89 \qquad \textbf{(11–8)}$$

Assuming a 360-day year for ease of computation, this bank could apply up to $2,138.89 to offset any fees charged the bank for its use of Federal Reserve services.

Factors Influencing the Money Position

A depository institution's money position is influenced by a long list of factors, some of which are included in the following table. Among the most important are the volume of checks and other drafts cleared each day, the amount of currency and coin shipments back and forth between each depository and the central bank's vault, purchases and sales of government securities, and borrowing and lending in the Federal funds (interbank) market. Some of these factors are largely *controllable* by management, while others are essentially *noncontrollable*, and management needs to anticipate and react quickly to them.

Factoid
The oldest kind of sweep account offered by depository institutions is business-oriented sweep programs that convert business checking accounts, usually overnight, into interest-bearing savings deposits or off-balance-sheet interest-bearing investments.

Controllable Factors Increasing Legal Reserves	Controllable Factors Decreasing Legal Reserves
• Selling securities.	• Purchasing securities.
• Receiving interest payments on securities.	• Making interest payments to investors holding the bank's securities.
• Borrowing reserves from the Federal Reserve bank.	• Repaying a loan from the Federal Reserve bank.
• Purchasing Federal funds from other banks.	• Selling Federal funds to other institutions in need of reserves.
• Selling securities under a repurchase agreement (RP).	• Security purchases under a repurchase agreement (RP).
• Selling new CDs, Eurocurrency deposits, or other deposits to customers.	• Receiving currency and coin shipments from the Federal Reserve bank.

Noncontrollable Factors Increasing Legal Reserves	Noncontrollable Factors Decreasing Legal Reserves
• Surplus position at the local clearinghouse due to receiving more deposited checks in its favor than checks drawn against it.	• Deficit position at the local clearinghouse due to more checks drawn against the bank than in its favor.
• Credit from cash letters sent to the Fed, listing drafts received by the bank.	• Calls of funds from the bank's tax and loan account by the U.S. Treasury.
• Deposits made by the U.S. Treasury into a tax and loan account held at the bank.	• Debits received from the Federal Reserve bank for checks drawn against the bank's reserve account.
• Credit received from the Federal Reserve bank for checks previously sent for collection (deferred availability items).	• Withdrawal of large deposit accounts, often immediately by wire.

In recent years the volume of legal reserves held at the Federal Reserve by depository institutions operating in the United States has declined sharply. Today, for example, legal reserves held by depository institutions at all 12 Federal Reserve banks are less than half their volume in the mid-1990s. The decline in legal reserves is largely due to the development of **sweep accounts**—a customer service that results in bankers shifting their customers' deposited funds out of low-yielding accounts that carry reserve requirements (currently checkable or transaction accounts), usually overnight, into repurchase agreements, shares in money market funds, and savings accounts (not currently bearing reserve requirements). Such sweeps yield an advantage to the offering depository institution because they lower its overall cost of funds, while still preserving depositor access to his or her checking account and the ability to make payments or execute withdrawals.

These sweep arrangements have ballooned in size to cover well over $500 billion in deposit balances, substantially lowering total required reserves of depository institutions. Sweep activities have been aided by access to online sites made available from the Federal Reserve banks that track on a real-time basis any large dollar payments flowing into or out of reserve accounts, allowing money managers to better plan what happens to their legal reserve positions on a daily basis. Today the sweep accounts depository institutions offer include *retail sweeps,* involving checking and savings accounts of individuals and families, and *business sweeps,* where commercial checkable deposit balances are changed overnight into commercial savings deposits or moved off depository institutions' balance sheets into interest-bearing investments and then quickly returned.

The key goal of money position management is to keep legal reserves at the required level, with no excess reserves and no reserve deficit large enough to incur a penalty. If a depository institution has an *excess* reserve position, it will sell Federal funds to other depositories short of legal reserves, or if the excess appears to be longer lasting, purchase securities or make new loans. If the depository institution has a legal reserve *deficit,* it will usually purchase Federal funds or borrow from the Federal Reserve bank in its district. If the deficit appears to be especially large or long lasting, the institution may sell some of its marketable securities and cut back on its lending.

An Example

Table 11–7 illustrates how a bank, for example, can keep track of its reserve position on a daily basis. This example also illustrates the money desk manager's principal problem—trying to keep track of the many transactions each day that will affect this particular bank's legal reserves. In this example, the money desk manager had estimated that his bank needed to average $500 million per day in its reserve account at the district Reserve bank. However, at the end of the first day (Thursday) of the new reserve maintenance period, it had a $550 million reserve position. The money manager tried to take advantage of this excess reserve position the next day (Friday) by purchasing $100 million in Treasury securities. The result was a reserve deficit of $130 million, much deeper than expected, due in part to an $80 million *adverse clearing balance* (that is, this bank had more checks presented for deduction from its customers' deposits than it received from other depository institutions for crediting to its own customers' accounts).

To help offset this steep decline in its reserve account, the money manager borrowed $50 million from the Federal Reserve bank's discount window on Friday afternoon. This helped a little because Friday's reserve position counts for Saturday and Sunday as well, when most depository institutions are closed, so the $130 million reserve deficit on Friday resulted in a $390 million (3 × $130 million) cumulative reserve deficit for the whole weekend. If the money desk manager had not borrowed the $50 million from the Fed, the deficit would have been $180 million for Friday and thus $540 million (3 × $180 million) for the entire weekend.

The bank depicted in Table 11–7 continued to operate below its required daily average legal reserve of $500 million through the next Friday of the reserve maintenance period, when a fateful decision was made. The money manager decided to borrow $100 million in Federal funds, but at the same time to sell $50 million in Federal funds to other depository institutions. Unfortunately, the manager did not realize until day's end on Friday that the bank had suffered a $70 million adverse clearing balance due to numerous checks written by its depositors that came back for collection. On balance, the bank's reserve deficit

Key URLs

For more information on sweep accounts, see especially **www. research.stlouisfed.org/ aggreg/swdata.html** and **www.treasurystrategies. com.**

Factoid

Two of the most important regulations focusing on the management of reserves and liquidity for depository institutions are Regulations Q and D of the Federal Reserve Board. Q impacts the interest rates depository institutions are allowed to pay on deposits, while D sets out the rules for calculating and meeting legal reserve requirements in the United States.

TABLE 11–7 An Example: Daily Schedule for Evaluating a Bank's Money Position (all figures in millions of dollars)

Days in the Reserve Maintenance Period	Required Daily Average Balance at the Fed	Daily Adjustments to the Bank's Balance Held at the Federal Reserve Bank								Closing Daily Average Balance at the Federal Reserve Bank	Excess or Deficit in Legal Reserve Position	Cumulative Excess or Deficit in Legal Reserves	Cumulative Closing Balance at the Fed
		Federal Funds Transactions		Fed's Discount Window		Treasury Securities		Check Clearing					
		Purchases (+)	Sales (−)	Borrow (+)	Repay (−)	Redeem (+)	Purchase (−)	Credit (+)	Debit (−)				
Carryover excess (+) or deficit (−) in legal reserves from previous period:											0		
Thursday	$ 500	+50	−25		−25			+50		$550	+50	+50	$ 550
Friday	500			+50			−100		−80	370	−130	−80	920
Saturday	500			+50			−100		−80	370	−130	−210	1,290
Sunday	500			+50			−100		−80	370	−130	−340	1,660
Monday	500		−25		−50			+40		465	−35	−375	2,125
Tuesday	500	+50							−25	525	+25	−350	2,650
Wednesday	500					+50			−60	490	−10	−360	3,140
Thursday	500							+10		510	+10	−350	3,650
Friday	500	+100	−50						−70	480	−20	−370	4,130
Saturday	500	+100	−50						−70	480	−20	−390	4,610
Sunday	500	+100	−50						−70	480	−20	−410	5,090
Monday	500	+250					−25	+15		740	+240	−170	5,830
Tuesday	500	+100								600	+100	−70	6,430
Wednesday	500	+70								570	+70	0	7,000
Cumulative	$7,000												
Daily average	$ 500												

increased another $10 million, for a closing balance on Friday of $480 million. Once again, because Friday's balance carried over for Saturday and Sunday, the money desk manager faced a cumulative reserve deficit of $410 million on Monday morning, with only that day plus Tuesday and Wednesday to offset the deficit before the reserve maintenance period ended.

As we noted earlier, Federal Reserve regulations require a depository institution to be within 4 percent of its required daily average reserve level or pay a penalty on the amount of the deficit. Trying to avoid this penalty, the bank money manager swung into high gear, borrowing $250 million in Federal funds on Monday and $100 million on Tuesday. Over two days this injected $350 million in new reserves. With an additional borrowing of $70 million in the Federal funds market on Wednesday, the last day of the reserve maintenance period (known as "bank settlement day"), the bank in our example ended the period with a zero cumulative reserve deficit.

Use of the Federal Funds Market

In the foregoing example, the money position manager had a large reserve deficit to cover in a hurry. This manager elected to borrow heavily in the **Federal funds market**—usually one of the cheapest places to borrow reserves, but also frequently volatile.

The effective interest rate on Federal funds changes minute by minute so money position managers must stay abreast of both the level and upward or downward movements in the effective daily Fed funds rate. One factor that aids the manager in anticipating changes in the funds market is the fact that the Federal Reserve sets a target Fed funds rate and intervenes periodically to move the current funds rate closer to its target. As Exhibit 11–2 indicates, the effective daily funds rate hovers close to the Fed's target (intended) Fed funds rate, generally within a few basis points of that target. The most volatile day in terms of trying to anticipate which way and by how much the funds rate will move is during *bank settlement day* (usually a Wednesday), when many depository institutions may find themselves short of required reserves with the door (i.e., the reserve maintenance period) about to slam shut on them at day's end!

EXHIBIT 11–2

Movements in the Effective Federal Funds Rate, Its Target (the Intended Federal Funds) Rate, and the Discount Rate Applying to Depository Institutions Seeking Loans of Reserves from the Federal Reserve Banks

Source: Federal Reserve Bank of Cleveland, *Economic Trends*, April 2005, p. 5.

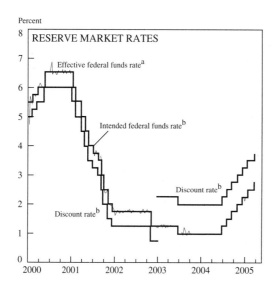

a. Weekly average of daily figures.
b. Daily observations.

Other Options besides Fed Funds

While the Federal funds market is usually the most popular route for solving immediate shortages of reserves, the money position manager usually has a fairly wide range of options to draw upon from both the asset (stored liquidity) and liability (purchased liquidity) sides of the balance sheet. These include selling liquid securities the institution may already hold, drawing upon any excess correspondent balances placed with other depository institutions, entering into repurchase agreements for temporary borrowing, selling new time deposits to the largest customers, and borrowing in the Eurocurrency market. The money position manager's job is to find the best options in terms of cost, risk, and other factors.

Bank Size and Borrowing and Lending Reserves for the Money Position

Recent research on money position management suggests that smaller depository institutions tend to have frequent reserve surpluses, particularly when loan demand is low in their market areas, and, therefore, are interested in lending these surpluses out to larger institutions. If smaller depositories do have reserve deficits, these normally occur late in the reserve maintenance period. In contrast, the largest depository institutions tend to have reserve needs day after day and find themselves on the borrowing side of the money market most of the time.

Overdraft Penalties

Depository institutions operating inside the U.S. financial system run the risk of modest penalties if they run an intraday overdraft and possibly a stiffer penalty if overnight overdrafts occur in their reserves. Avoiding intraday and overnight overdrafts is not easy for most institutions because they have only partial control over the amount and timing of inflows and outflows of funds from their reserves. Because of possible overdraft penalties, many financial institutions hold "precautionary balances" (extra supplies of reserves) to help prevent overdrafting of their reserve account.

11–7 Factors in Choosing among the Different Sources of Reserves

In choosing which source of reserves to draw upon to cover a legal reserve deficit, money position managers must carefully consider several aspects of their institution's need for liquid funds:

1. *Immediacy of need.* If a reserve deficit comes due within minutes or hours, the money position manager will normally tap the Federal funds market for an overnight loan or contact the central bank for a loan from its discount window. In contrast, a depository institution can meet its nonimmediate reserve needs by selling deposits or assets, which may require more time to arrange than immediately available borrowings normally do.

2. *Duration of need.* If the liquidity deficit is expected to last for only a few hours, the Federal funds market or the central bank's discount window is normally the preferred source of funds. Liquidity shortages lasting days, weeks, or months, on the other hand, are often covered with sales of assets or longer-term borrowings.

3. *Access to the market for liquid funds.* Not all depository institutions have access to all funds markets. For example, smaller depositories cannot, as a practical matter, draw upon the Eurocurrency market or sell commercial paper. Liquidity managers must restrict their range of choices to those their institution can access quickly.

11–15. What is *money position* management?

11–16. What is the principal *goal* of money position management?

11–17. Exactly how is a depository institution's legal reserve requirement determined?

11–18. First National Bank finds that its net transaction deposits average $140 million over the latest reserve computation period. Using the reserve requirement ratios imposed by the Federal Reserve as given in the textbook, what is the bank's total required legal reserve?

11–19. A U.S. savings bank has a daily average reserve balance at the Federal Reserve bank in its district of $25 million during the latest reserve maintenance period. Its vault cash holdings averaged $1 million and the savings bank's total transaction deposits (net of interbank deposits and cash items in collection) averaged $200 million daily over the latest reserve maintenance period. Does this depository institution currently

have a legal reserve deficiency? How would you recommend that its management respond to the current situation?

11–20. What factors should a money position manager consider in meeting a deficit in a depository institution's legal reserve account?

11–21. What are clearing balances? Of what benefit can clearing balances be to a depository that uses the Federal Reserve System's check-clearing network?

11–22. Suppose a bank maintains an average clearing balance of $5 million during a period in which the Federal funds rate averages 6 percent. How much would this bank have available in credits at the Federal Reserve Bank in its district to help offset the charges assessed against the bank for using Federal Reserve services?

11–23. What are *sweep accounts?* Why have they led to a significant decline in the total legal reserves held at the Federal Reserve banks by depository institutions operating in the United States?

4. *Relative costs and risks of alternative sources of funds.* The cost of each source of reserves changes daily, and the availability of surplus liquidity is also highly uncertain. Other things being equal, the liquidity manager will draw on the cheapest source of reliable funds, maintaining constant contact with the money and capital markets to be aware of how interest rates and credit conditions are changing.

5. *The interest rate outlook.* When planning to deal with a future liquidity deficit, the liquidity manager wants to draw upon those funds sources whose interest rates are expected to be the lowest. As we saw earlier in Chapter 8 new futures and options contracts, especially the Fed funds futures and options contracts and the Eurodollar futures contracts traded on the Chicago Mercantile Exchange and Chicago Board of Trade, have greatly assisted liquidity managers in forecasting the most likely scenario for future borrowing costs. These contracts provide estimates of the probability that market interest rates will be higher or lower in the days and weeks ahead.

6. *Outlook for central bank monetary policy.* Closely connected to the outlook for interest rates is the outlook for changes in central bank monetary policy which shapes the direction and intensity of credit conditions in the money market. For example, a more restrictive monetary policy implies higher borrowing costs and reduced credit availability for liquidity managers. The Federal funds and Eurodollar futures and options contracts mentioned above and in Chapter 8 have proven to be especially useful to liquidity managers in gauging what changes in central bank policies affecting interest rates are most likely down the road.

7. *Rules and regulations applicable to a liquidity source.* Most sources of liquidity cannot be used indiscriminately; the user must conform to the rules. For example, borrowing reserves from a central bank frequently requires the borrowing institution to provide collateral behind the loan. In the United States and Europe two key liquidity sources—the

Federal funds and Eurocurrency markets—close down near the end of the trading day, forcing borrowing institutions that are in danger of overdrafting their accounts to quickly arrange for their funding needs before the door closes or look for cash elsewhere.

The liquidity manager must carefully weigh each of these factors in order to make a rational choice among alternative sources of reserves.

11–8 Central Bank Reserve Requirements around the Globe

We should note that not all central banks impose legal reserve requirements on the depository institutions they regulate. For example, the Bank of England has not established official reserve requirements for its banks and there is a trend among central banks around the globe to eliminate, suspend, or at least make less use of the reserve requirement tool, in part because it is so difficult to control. A notable exception is the European Central Bank (ECB), whose reserve requirements are often a binding constraint on European banks, with the latter frequently accessing the additional liquidity they need to meet these cash requirements by participating in the ECB's weekly auction of liquid funds.

Finally, it is important to recognize that even if central banks imposed no reserve requirements at all, the managers of depository institutions would still have a demand for cash reserves. All depository institutions at one time or another need immediately available funds to handle customer withdrawals, meet new loan demand, and satisfy other emergency cash needs. Capable liquidity managers are indispensable in the modern world.

Summary

Managing the *liquidity* position for a financial institution can be one of the most challenging jobs in the financial sector. In this chapter we reviewed several fundamental principles of liquidity management and looked at several of the liquidity manager's best tools. Key points in the chapter include:

- A *liquid* financial firm is one that can raise cash in the amount required at reasonable cost precisely when the need for liquidity arises.

- Among depository institutions the two most common needs for cash arise when depositors withdraw their funds and when requests for loans come in the door.

- Liquidity needs are generally met either by selling assets (i.e., converting *stored liquidity* into cash) or by borrowing in the money market (i.e., using *purchased liquidity*) or by a combination of these two approaches.

- Managers of financial firms have developed several different methods to estimate what their institution's true liquidity needs are likely to be. One of these estimation methods is the *sources and uses of funds method* in which total sources and uses of funds are projected over a desired planning horizon and liquidity deficits and surpluses are calculated from the difference between funds sources and funds uses.

- Another popular liquidity estimation technique is the *structure of funds method*. This requires each financial firm to classify its funds uses and sources according to their probability of withdrawal or loss. Assigning probabilities of withdrawal or loss makes it possible to give a quantitative estimate of future liquidity needs.

- Still another liquidity estimation approach focuses on *liquidity indicators*, in which selected financial ratios measuring a financial firm's liquidity position on both sides of its balance sheet are calculated with the liquidity manager looking for any evidence of adverse trends in liquidity.

- Financial institutions today can draw upon multiple sources of liquid assets and borrowed liquidity. Key sources of liquidity on the asset side of the balance sheet include correspondent balances held with depository institutions and sales of highly liquid money market instruments. Important borrowed liquidity sources include borrowing from the central bank's discount window, purchasing Federal funds, employing repurchase agreements (RPs), and issuing CDs or Eurocurrency deposits.

- One of the most challenging areas of funds management among depository institutions centers upon the *money position manager* who oversees the institution's *legal reserve account.* These legal reserves include vault cash held on a depository institution's premises and a deposit kept with the central bank, which must be managed to achieve a target level of legal reserves over each reserve maintenance period. Failure to hold adequate legal reserves can incur monetary penalties and greater surveillance by regulatory authorities.

- Liquidity and money position managers choose their sources of liquidity based on several key factors, including (1) immediacy of need; (2) duration of need; (3) market access; (4) relative costs and risks; (5) the outlook for market interest rates; (6) the outlook for central bank monetary policy and (7) government regulations.

Key Terms

liquidity, *347*
net liquidity position, *348*
asset conversion, *351*
liquid asset, *351*
opportunity cost, *352*
liability management, *352*
balanced liquidity management, *353*
sources and uses of funds method, *355*

liquidity gap, *355*
structure of funds method, *358*
liquidity indicators, *362*
money position manager, *365*
legal reserves, *365*
lagged reserve accounting (LRA), *365*

reserve computation period, *366*
reserve maintenance period, *366*
clearing balance, *368*
sweep account, *369*
Federal funds market, *372*

Problems and Projects

1. Clear Hills State Bank estimates that over the next 24 hours the following cash inflows and outflows will occur (all figures in millions of dollars):

Deposit withdrawals	$ 68	Sales of bank assets	16
Deposit inflows	87	Stockholder dividend payments	178
Scheduled loan repayments	89	Revenues from sale of nondeposit services	95
Acceptable loan requests	32	Repayments of bank borrowings	67
Borrowings from the money market	61	Operating expenses	45

What is this bank's projected net liquidity position in the next 24 hours? From what sources can the bank cover its liquidity needs?

2. Hillpeak Savings is projecting a net liquidity surplus of $2 million next week partially as a result of expected quality loan demand of $24 million, necessary repayments of previous borrowings of $15 million, disbursements to cover operating expenses of $18 million, planned stockholder dividend payments of $5 million, expected deposit inflows of $26 million, revenues from nondeposit service sales of $18 million, scheduled repayments of previously made customer loans of $23 million, asset sales of $10 million, and money market borrowings of $11 million. How much must Hillpeak's expected deposit withdrawals be for the coming week?

3. First National Bank of Los Alamos has forecast its checkable deposits, time and savings deposits, and commercial and household loans over the next eight months. The resulting estimates (in millions) are shown below. Use the sources and uses of funds approach to indicate which months are likely to result in liquidity deficits and which in liquidity surpluses if these forecasts turn out to be true. Explain carefully what you would do to deal with each month's projected liquidity position.

	Checkable Deposits	Time and Savings Deposits	Commercial Loans	Consumer Loans
January	$111	$543	$682	$137
February	102	527	657	148
March	98	508	688	153
April	91	491	699	161
May	101	475	708	165
June	87	489	691	170
July	84	516	699	172
August	99	510	672	156

4. Jefferson Security Savings is attempting to determine its liquidity requirements today (the last day in August) for the month of September. September is usually a month of heavy loan demand due to the beginning of the school term and the buildup of business inventories of goods and services for the fall season and winter. This thrift institution has analyzed its deposit accounts thoroughly and classified them as explained below.

Management has elected to hold a 75 percent reserve in liquid assets or borrowing capacity for each dollar of hot money deposits, a 20 percent reserve behind vulnerable deposits, and a 5 percent reserve for its holdings of core funds. The estimated reserve requirements on most deposits are 3 percent, except that savings deposits carry a zero percent reserve requirement and all checkable deposits above $48.3 million carry a 10 percent reserve requirement. Jefferson currently has total loans outstanding of $2,389 million, which two weeks ago were as high as $2,567 million. Its loans' mean annual growth rate over the past three years has been about 8 percent. Carefully prepare low and high estimates for Jefferson's total liquidity requirement for September.

Millions of Dollars	Checkable Deposits	Savings Deposits	Nonpersonal Time Deposits
Hot money funds	$132	$____	$782
Vulnerable funds	207	52	540
Stable (core) funds	821	285	72

5. Using the following financial information for Watson National Bank, calculate as many of the *liquidity indicators* discussed in this chapter for Watson as you can. Do you detect any significant liquidity trends? Which trends should management investigate?

	Most Recent Year	Previous Year
Assets:		
Cash and due from depository institutions	$ 358,000	$ 379,000
U.S. Treasury securities	178,000	127,000
Other securities	343,000	358,000
Pledged securities	223,000	202,000

(continued)

www.mhhe.com/rose7e

	Most Recent Year	Previous Year
Assets (continued):		
Federal funds sold and reverse repurchase agreements	$ 131,000	$ 139,000
Loans and leases net	1,948,000	1,728,000
Total assets	3,001,000	2,941,000
Liabilities:		
Demand deposits	456,000	511,000
Savings deposits	721,000	715,000
Time deposits	853,000	744,000
Total Deposits	2,130,000	2,070,000
Core deposits	644,000	630,000
Brokered deposits	37,000	12,000
Federal funds purchased and repurchase agreements	237,000	248,000
Other money market borrowings	16,000	84,000

6. The Bank of Your Dreams has a simple balance sheet. The figures are in millions of dollars as follows:

Assets		Liabilities and Equity	
Cash	$ 100	Deposits	$4,000
Securities	1,000	Other liabilities	500
Loans	4,000	Equity	600
Total assets	5,100	Total liabilities and equity	5,100

Although the balance sheet is simple, the bank's manager encounters a liquidity challenge when depositors withdraw $500 million.

a. If the asset conversion method is used and securities are sold to cover the deposit drain, what happens to the size of Bank of Your Dreams?

b. If liability management is used to cover the deposit drain, what happens to the size of Bank of Your Dreams?

7. The liquidity manager for the Bank of Your Dreams needs cash to meet some unanticipated loan demand. The loan officer has $600 million in loans that he/she wants to make. Use the simplified balance sheet provided in the previous problem to answer the following questions:

a. If asset conversion is used and securities are sold to provide money for the loans, what happens to the size of Bank of Your Dreams?

b. If liability management is used to provide funds for the loans, what happens to the size of the Bank of Your Dreams?

8. Suppose Abigail Savings Bank's liquidity manager estimates that the bank will experience a $430 million liquidity deficit next month with a probability of 10 percent, a $300 million liquidity deficit with a probability of 40 percent, a $230 million liquidity surplus with a probability of 30 percent, and a $425 million liquidity surplus bearing a probability of 20 percent. What is this savings bank's *expected liquidity requirement?* What should management do?

9. First Savings of Pierce, Iowa, reported transaction deposits of $75 million (the daily average for the latest two-week reserve computation period). Its nonpersonal time deposits over the most recent reserve computation period averaged $37 million daily, while vault cash averaged $0.978 million over the vault-cash computation period. Assuming that reserve requirements on transaction deposits are 3 percent for deposits over $7.8 million and up to $48.3 million and 10 percent for all transaction deposits

over $48.3 million while time deposits carry a 3 percent required reserve, calculate this savings institution's required daily average reserve balance at the Federal Reserve Bank in the district.

10. Elton Harbor Bank has a cumulative legal reserve deficit of $44 million at the Federal Reserve bank in the district as of the close of business this Tuesday. The bank must cover this deficit by the close of business tomorrow (Wednesday).

    Charles Tilby, the bank's money desk supervisor, examines the current distribution of money market and long-term interest rates and discovers the following:

Money Market Instruments	Current Market Yield
Federal funds	8.46%
Borrowing from the central bank's discount window	7.00
Commercial paper (one-month maturity)	8.40
Bankers' acceptances (three-month maturity)	8.12
Certificates of deposit (one-month maturity)	8.35
Eurodollar deposits (three-month maturity)	8.38
U.S. Treasury bills (three-month maturity)	7.60
U.S. Treasury notes and bonds (one-year maturity)	7.64
U.S. Treasury notes and bonds (five-year maturity)	7.75
U.S. Treasury notes and bonds (10-year maturity)	7.83

One week ago, the bank borrowed $20 million from the Federal Reserve's discount window, which it paid back yesterday. The bank had a $5 million reserve deficit during the previous reserve maintenance period. From the bank's standpoint, which sources of reserves appear to be the most promising? Which source would you recommend to cover the bank's reserve deficit? Why?

11. Poquoson Building and Loan Association estimates the following information regarding this institution's reserve position at the Federal Reserve for the reserve maintenance period that begins today (Thursday):

Calculated required daily average balance at the Federal Reserve bank	=	$750 million
A loan received from the Fed's discount window a week ago that comes due on Friday (day 9)	=	$ 70 million
Planned purchases of U.S. Treasury securities on behalf of the association and its customers:		
Tomorrow (Friday)	=	$ 80 million
Next Wednesday (day 7)	=	$ 35 million
Next Friday (day 9)	=	$ 18 million

Poquoson also had a closing reserve deficit in the preceding reserve maintenance period of $5 million. What problems are likely to emerge as this savings association tries to manage its reserve position over the next two weeks? Relying on the Federal funds market and loans from the Federal Reserve's discount window as tools to manage its reserve position, carefully construct a pro forma daily worksheet for this association's money position over the next two weeks. Insert your planned adjustments in discount window borrowing and Federal funds purchases and sales over the period to show how you plan to manage Poquoson's reserve position and hit your desired reserve target.

Check-clearing estimates over the next 14 days are as follows:

Day	Credit Balance in Millions (+)	Debit Balance in Millions (−)
1	+10	
2		−60
3	Closed	
4	Closed	
5		−40
6		−25
7	+30	
8		−45
9		−5
10	Closed	
11	Closed	
12	+20	
13		−70
14	+10	

12. R, W, & B Savings Bank and Trust Co. has calculated its daily average deposits and vault cash holdings for the most recent two-week computation period as follows:

Net transaction deposits	= $ 81,655,474
Nonpersonal time deposits under 18 months to maturity	= $147,643,589
Eurocurrency liabilities	= $ 5,840,210
Daily average balance in vault cash	= $ 1,002,031

Suppose the reserve requirements posted by the Board of Governors of the Federal Reserve System are as follows:

Net transaction accounts:	
$7.8 to $48.3 million	3%
More than $48.3 million	10%
Nonpersonal time deposits:	
Less than 18 months	3%
18 months or more	0%
Eurocurrency liabilities—all types	3%

What is this savings bank's total required level of legal reserves? How much must the bank hold on a daily average basis with the Federal Reserve bank in its district?

13. Frost Street National Bank currently holds $750 million in transaction deposits subject to reserve requirements but has managed to enter into sweep account arrangements with its transaction deposit customers affecting $150 million of their deposits. Given the current legal reserve requirements applying to transaction deposits (as mentioned in this chapter), by how much would Frost Street's total legal reserves decrease as a result of these new sweep account arrangements, which stipulate that transaction deposit balances covered by the sweep agreements will be moved overnight into savings deposits?

14. Jasper Savings Association maintains a clearing account at the Federal Reserve Bank and agrees to keep a minimum balance of $22 million in its clearing account. Over the two-week reserve maintenance period ending today Jasper managed to keep an average clearing account balance of $24 million. If the Federal funds interest rate has averaged 3.75 percent over this particular maintenance period, what maximum amount would

REAL NUMBERS FOR REAL BANKS

Assignment for Chapter 11

YOUR BANK'S LIQUIDITY REQUIREMENT: AN EXAMINATION OF ITS LIQUIDITY INDICATORS

Chapter 11 describes liquidity and reserve management. Within the chapter we explore how liquidity managers evaluate their institution's liquidity needs. Four methodologies are described: (1) the sources and uses of funds approach, (2) the structure of funds approach, (3) the liquidity indicator approach, and (4) signals from the marketplace. In this assignment we will calculate and interpret several of the ratios associated with the liquidity indicators approach. By comparing these ratios across time and with a group of contemporary banks, we will examine the liquidity needs of your BHC. In doing so, you will familiarize yourself with some new terms and tools associated with real data. This assignment involves some data exploration that is best described as a financial analyst's "treasure hunt."

Application of the Liquidity Indicator Approach: Trend and Comparative Analysis

A. **Data Collection:** To calculate these liquidity ratios, we will use some data collected in prior assignments and revisit the Statistics for Depository Institutions Web site (**www3.fdic. gov/sdi/**) to gather more information for your BHC and its peer group. Use SDI to create a four-column report of your bank's information and the peer group information across years. In this part of the assignment, for Report Selection you will access a number of different reports. We suggest that you continue to collect percentage information to calculate your liquidity indicators. The additional information you need to collect before calculating the indicators is denoted by **. All data is available in SDI by the name given next to the **. As you collect the information, enter the percentages for items marked ** in Columns B–E as an addition to the spreadsheet used for comparisons with Peer Group.

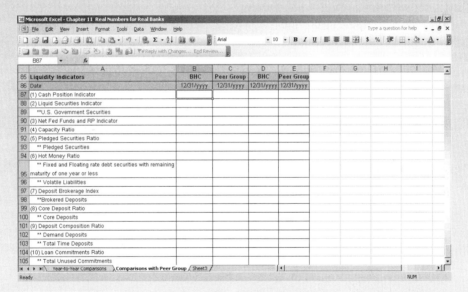

B. Having collected the additional data needed, use the newly collected and previously collected data to calculate the liquidity indicators. For instance, the percentage data you have can be used to calculate the pledged securities ratio. The formula to enter for Cell B92 is B93/B6.

C. Compare the set of liquidity ratios for your BHC across years. Write one or two paragraphs describing changes you observe between the two years.

D. Compare and contrast the set of liquidity ratios for the peer group in Columns C and E to your BHC's ratios in Columns B and D. Write one or two paragraphs describing your BHC's use of asset and liability management compared to that of the Peer Group.

Jasper have available in the form of Federal Reserve credit to help offset any fees the Federal Reserve bank might charge this association for using Federal Reserve services?

Internet Exercises

1. Evaluate the cash assets, including legal reserves, held by the Bank of America and Citigroup. How has their liquidity position changed recently? One Web site that provides this information for all the depository institutions in a bank holding company (BHC) is **www3.fdic.gov/sdi/.** You are particularly interested in the items identified as "Cash and Due from Depository Institutions."

2. With reference to the BHCs mentioned in exercise 1, what was their ratio of cash and due from depository institutions to total assets at last year's year-end? Do you notice any significant trends in their liquidity position that you think have also affected the banking industry as a whole? Examine the ratios for all FDIC-insured banks. This can also be accomplished at **www3.fdic.gov/sdi/.**

3. In describing reserve management, we referenced some numbers that change every year based on U.S. bank deposit growth. The reservable liabilities exemption determines which banks are exempt from legal reserve requirements, and the low reserve tranche is used in calculating reserve requirements. Go to **www.federalreserve.gov/regulations/default.htm** and explore information concerning Regulation D. Find and report the low reserve tranche adjustment and the reservable liabilities exemption adjustment that are being used this year.

S&P Market Insight Challenge (www.mhhe.com/edumarketinsight)

1. In the S&P Industry Survey entitled "Banking," *liquidity* is a key measure of financial condition for banking firms. For an up-to-date description of how banks measure liquidity, use the Industry tab in Standard & Poor's Market Insight and the drop-down menu to select Diversified Banks or Regional Banks. Upon selecting one of these subindustries, you will find the S&P Industry Survey on Banking. Please download this survey and view the section, "How to Analyze a Bank." Describe what it means to be "liquid." When is a bank "loaned up," and how does this relate to liquidity?

2. Of all the businesses represented in S&P's Market Insight, banks and thrift institutions typically face the most critical liquidity problems. Examining closely the most recent financial reports of such institutions as Barclays PLC, J. P. Morgan Chase & Company, Washington Mutual, and other leading depositories, can you see any significant trends in liquidity among these institutions? Is liquidity in this industry really declining, as some financial experts claim, or have depository institutions simply discovered new ways to manage cash and raise additional liquidity? Are structural changes under way in the industry that might explain its recent liquidity trends?

Selected References

The following studies discuss the instruments often used to manage the liquidity positions of financial institutions and their customers:

1. Bartolini, Leonardo, Svenja Gudell, Spence Hilton, and Krista Schwarz. "Intraday Trading in the Overnight Federal Funds Market." *Current Issues in Economics and Finance*, Federal Reserve Bank of New York 11, no. 11 (November 2005), pp. 1–7.

2. Champ, Bruce. "Open and Operating: Providing Liquidity to Avoid a Crisis." *Economic Commentary*, Federal Reserve Bank of Cleveland, February 15, 2003.

3. Fleming, Michael J., and Kenneth D. Garbade. "Repurchase Agreements with Negative Interest Rates." *Current Issues in Economics and Finance*, Federal Reserve Bank of New York 10, no. 5 (April 2004), pp. 1–7.

4. Hilton, Spence. "Trends in Federal Funds Rate Volatility." *Current Issues in Economics and Finance*, Federal Reserve Bank of New York 11, no. 7 (July 2005), pp. 1–7.

For a review of the rules for meeting Federal Reserve deposit reserve requirements, see the following:

5. Cyree, Ken B., Mark D. Griffiths, and Drew B. Winters. "On the Pervasive Effects of Federal Reserve Settlement Regulations." *Review*, Federal Reserve Bank of St. Louis, March/April 2003, pp. 27–46.

6. Hein, Scott E., and Jonathan D. Stewart. "Reserve Requirements: A Modern Perspective." *Economic Review*, Federal Reserve Bank of Atlanta, Fourth Quarter 2002, pp. 41–52.

For an examination of market discipline as a force in the liquidity management of financial firms, see especially:

7. Krainer, John, and Jose A. Lopez. "How Might Financial Information Be Used for Supervisory Purposes?" *FRBSF Economic Review*, Federal Reserve Bank of San Francisco, 2003, pp. 29–45.

8. Stackhouse, Julie L., and Mark D. Vaughan. "Navigating the Brave New World of Bank Liquidity." *The Regional Economist*, Federal Reserve Bank of St. Louis, July 2003, pp. 12–13.

PART FIVE

Managing Sources of Funds for Banks and Their Principal Competitors

To fund their operations and grow financial institutions have learned to seek out multiple sources of funds, including checkable accounts and savings deposits sold to the public and nondeposit borrowings from other financial firms and even from industrial corporations. They have also unearthed new funds sources that add to revenues and, ultimately, to earnings, such as fees for providing investment banking services, brokerage commissions for executing the purchase or sale of stocks, bonds, and mutual funds on behalf of their customers, sales revenue and underwriting profits from providing insurance policies, fees for managing their customers' property (trust services), and numerous other sources of fee income. Finally, the owners of financial firms are always expected to contribute some of their own funds (equity capital) to reduce risk and provide protection for depositors and others who hold claims against a financial firm.

This broadening of funds sources for most financial institutions reflects multiple forces at work within the financial system. First, it would be foolhardy to rely upon only one or two sources of incoming funds that may dry up or increase sharply in cost. Managers of financial firms need to diversify their sources of funding, just as they diversify their assets, in order to reduce risk, provide a firmer base for growth, and protect their profits.

Moreover, *competition* has spurred the development of multiple sources of funding. Banks, money market funds, stock and bond mutual funds, security broker/dealer firms, and other financial-service companies have been bidding against each other for money for decades, striving to offer the best yields to funds-providing customers and thereby wrest financial capital away from their competitors to permit expansion and grow profits. Presumably customers benefit from this competition among financial firms, earning more on their savings. This phenomenon was especially evident just before the new century began when billions of dollars left depository institutions for a time and flowed into the stock market and the managers of these institutions had to scramble to find other ways to survive and grow.

Access to both old and new funds sources depends heavily upon the *condition of the economy*. For example, if the economy dives into a recession and unemployment rises, deposits supplied by the public may slow drastically and new sources of money must be uncovered. Rapid economic expansion, in contrast, often ushers in a wealth of new savings to support financial firms as incomes rise and people become more conscious of the need to save. Not only do financial institutions impact the economy by offering vital services, but the economy impacts them as well, opening up or closing down various funds sources and challenging their managers to find new sources of capital.

As financial firms have reached out in many different directions for the funds they need, these institutions have become more aware of how the particular mix of funding they choose affects in a significant way their operating costs, personnel needs, liquidity (cash) risk, and exposure to loss from changing market interest rates. Accordingly, the concept of *liability management* emerged in the financial-services industry, reminding its managers that their sources of funding need to be as closely managed as they manage the asset side of their balance sheets.

In Part Five of the book we explore several critical topics for financial firms raising money. For example, how should a financial firm determine the cost of each funding source it hopes to draw upon? How can we measure the impact of various funding sources on a financial institution's risk exposure and capital requirements? And why is the funding base of a financial institution (especially its owners' capital) such a critical determinant of its ability to expand today and in the future? This is an important topic area for the successful management of any financial institution. We can't just skip over it as some experts in the field seem inclined to do.

CHAPTER TWELVE

Managing and Pricing Deposit Services

Key Topics in This Chapter

- Types of Deposit Accounts Offered
- The Changing Mix of Deposits and Deposit Costs
- Pricing Deposit Services and Deposit Interest Rates
- Conditional Deposit Pricing
- Rules for Deposit Insurance Coverage
- Disclosure of Deposit Terms
- Lifeline Banking

12–1 Introduction

Barney Kilgore, one of the most famous presidents in the history of Dow Jones & Company and publisher of *The Wall Street Journal*, once cautioned his staff: "Don't write banking stories for bankers. Write for the bank's customers. There are a hell of a lot more depositors than bankers." Kilgore was a wise man, indeed. For every banker in this world there are thousands upon thousands of depositors. Deposit accounts are the number one source of funds at most (but not all) banks.

Deposits are a key element in defining what a banking firm really does and what critical roles it really plays in the economy. The ability of management and staff to attract transaction (checkable) and savings deposits from businesses and consumers is an important measure of a depository institution's acceptance by the public. Moreover, deposits provide much of the raw material for making loans and, thus, may represent the ultimate source of profits and growth for a depository institution. Important indicators of management's effectiveness are whether or not funds deposited by the public have been raised at the lowest possible cost and whether sufficient deposits are available to fund all those loans and projects management of a bank or thrift wishes to pursue.[1]

This last point highlights two key issues that every depository institution must deal with in managing the public's deposits: (1) Where can funds be raised at lowest possible cost? and (2) How can management ensure that the institution always has enough deposits to support the volume of loans and other investments and services the public demands? Neither question is easy to answer, especially in today's competitive marketplace. Both the cost and amount of deposits that depository institutions sell to the public

---

[1]Portions of this chapter are based on an article by Peter S. Rose in *The Canadian Banker* [5] and are used with permission of the publisher.

are heavily influenced by the pricing schedules and competitive maneuverings of other financial institutions offering similar services, such as share accounts in money market mutual funds and credit unions, cash management accounts offered by brokerage firms and insurance companies, and interest-bearing investment accounts offered by many security firms. Innovation in the form of new types of deposits, new service delivery methods (increasingly electronic in design), and new pricing schemes is accelerating today. Financial-service managers who fail to stay abreast of changes in their competitors' deposit pricing and marketing programs stand to lose both customers and profits.

In this chapter we explore the types of deposits that depository institutions sell to the public. We also examine how deposits are priced, the methods for determining their cost to the offering institution, and the impact of government regulation on the deposit function.

12–2 Types of Deposits Offered by Banks and Other Depository Institutions

The number and range of deposit services offered by depository institutions are impressive indeed and often confusing for customers. Like a Baskin-Robbins ice cream store, deposit plans designed to attract customer funds today come in 31 flavors and more, each plan having features intended to closely match business and household needs for saving money and making payments for goods and services.

Transaction (Payments or Demand) Deposits

Factoid

In 2003 for the first time in the history of the United States payments made by checks written against transaction deposit accounts were smaller in number than electronic payments, due principally to the explosive growth of debit cards.

One of the oldest services offered by depository institutions has centered on making *payments* on behalf of customers. This **transaction,** or *demand*, **deposit** service requires financial-service providers to honor immediately any withdrawals made either in person by the customer or by a third party designated by the customer to be the recipient of funds withdrawn. Transaction deposits include *regular noninterest-bearing demand deposits* that do not earn an explicit interest payment but provide the customer with payment services, safekeeping of funds, and recordkeeping for any transactions carried out by check, card, or via an electronic network, and *interest-bearing demand deposits* that provide all of the foregoing services and pay interest to the depositor as well.

Noninterest-Bearing Transaction Deposits

Interest payments have been prohibited on regular checking accounts in the United States since passage of the Glass-Steagall Act of 1933. Congress feared at the time that paying interest on immediately withdrawable deposits endangered bank safety—a proposition that researchers have subsequently found to have little support. However, demand (transaction) deposits are among the most volatile and least predictable of a depository institution's sources of funds, with the shortest potential maturity, because they can be withdrawn without prior notice. Most noninterest-bearing demand deposits are held by business firms.

Interest-Bearing Transaction Deposits

Many consumers today have moved their funds into other types of transaction deposits that pay at least some interest. Beginning in New England during the 1970s, hybrid checking–savings deposits began to appear in the form of *negotiable order of withdrawal* **(NOW) accounts.** NOWs are interest-bearing savings deposits that give the offering depository institution the right to insist on prior notice before the customer withdraws funds. Because this notice requirement is rarely exercised, the NOW can be used just like a checking (transaction) account to pay for purchases of goods and services. NOWs were permitted nationwide beginning in 1981 as a result of passage of the Depository Institutions Deregulation Act of 1980. However, they can be held only by individuals and nonprofit institutions. When NOWs became legal nationwide, the U.S. Congress also sanctioned the offering of automatic transfers (ATS), which permit the customer to preauthorize a depository institution to move funds from a savings account to a transaction account in order to cover overdrafts. The net effect was to pay interest on transaction balances roughly equal to the interest earned on a savings account.

Key URLs

Among the best sources for the current deposit interest rates offered by many banks and thrift institutions are **www.bankrate.com,** **www.imoneynet.com,** **www.fisn.com,** and **www.bankcd.com.**

Two other important interest-bearing transaction accounts were created in the United States in 1982 with passage of the Garn–St Germain Depository Institutions Act. Banks and thrift institutions could offer deposits competitive with the share accounts offered by money market funds that carried higher, unregulated interest rates and were backed by a pool of high-quality securities. The result was the appearance of **money market deposit accounts** (MMDAs) and **Super NOWs** (SNOWs), offering flexible money market interest rates but accessible via check or preauthorized draft to pay for goods and services.

MMDAs are short-maturity deposits that may have a term of only a few days, weeks, or months, and the offering institution can pay any interest rate that is competitive enough to attract and hold the customer's deposit. Up to six preauthorized drafts per month are allowed, but only three withdrawals may be made by writing checks. There is no limit to the personal withdrawals the customer may make (though service providers reserve the right to set maximum amounts and frequencies for personal withdrawals). Unlike NOWs, MMDAs can be held by businesses as well as individuals.

Super NOWs were authorized at about the same time as MMDAs, but they may be held only by individuals and nonprofit institutions. The number of checks the depositor may write is not limited by regulation. However, offering institutions post lower yields on SNOWs than on MMDAs because the former can be drafted more frequently by customers. Incidentally, federal regulatory authorities classify MMDAs today not as transaction (payments) deposits, but as savings deposits. They are included in this section on transaction accounts because they carry check-writing privileges.

Nontransaction (Savings or Thrift) Deposits

Savings deposits, or **thrift deposits,** are designed to attract funds from customers who wish to set aside money in anticipation of future expenditures or financial emergencies. These deposits generally pay significantly higher interest rates than transaction deposits do. While their interest cost is higher, thrift deposits are generally less costly to process and manage.

Key URLs

Issues in the deposit field often show up in such sources as the Financial Institutions Center at **fic.wharton.upenn.edu/ fic/,** Bank Security Publications at **www. banksecurity.com** and the Electronic Funds Transfer Services (EFTS) site maintained by the Federal Trade Commission at **www. ftc.gov/bcp/online/ pubs/credit/elbank.htm**.

Just as depository institutions for decades offered only one basic transaction deposit— the regular checking account—so it was with savings plans. **Passbook savings deposits** were sold to household customers in small denominations (frequently a passbook deposit could be opened for as little as $5), and withdrawal privileges were unlimited. While legally a depository institution could insist on receiving prior notice of a planned withdrawal from a passbook savings deposit, few institutions have insisted on this technicality because of the low interest rate paid on these accounts and because passbook deposits tend to be stable anyway, with little sensitivity to changes in interest rates. Individuals, nonprofit organizations, and governments can hold savings deposits, as can business firms, but in the United States businesses cannot place more than $150,000 in such a deposit.

Some institutions offer *statement savings deposits,* evidenced only by computer entry. The customer can get monthly printouts showing deposits, withdrawals, interest earned, and the balance in the account. Many depository institutions, however, still offer the more traditional passbook savings deposit, where the customer is given a booklet showing the account's balance, interest earnings, deposits, and withdrawals, as well as the rules that bind both depository institution and depositor.

For many years, wealthier individuals and businesses have been offered **time deposits,** which carry fixed maturity dates (usually covering 30, 60, 90, 180 or 360 days) with fixed interest rates. More recently, time deposits have been issued with interest rates adjusted periodically (such as every 90 days, known as a *leg* or *roll period*). Time deposits must carry a minimum maturity of seven days and cannot be withdrawn before that.

Time deposits come in a wide variety of types and terms. However, the most popular of all time deposits are *CDs—certificates of deposit*. CDs may be issued in *negotiable* form—the $100,000-plus instruments purchased principally by corporations and wealthy individuals that may be bought and sold any number of times prior to reaching their maturity—or in *nonnegotiable* form—smaller denomination accounts that cannot be traded prior to maturity and are usually acquired by individuals. Innovation has entered the CD marketplace recently with the development of *bump-up* CDs (allowing a depositor to switch to a higher interest rate if market interest rates rise); *step-up* CDs (permitting periodic upward adjustments in promised interest rates); and *liquid* CDs (allowing the depositor to withdraw some of his or her funds without a withdrawal penalty).

In 1981, with passage of the Economic Recovery Tax Act, Congress opened the door to yet another deposit instrument—*retirement savings accounts*. Wage earners and salaried individuals were granted the right to make limited contributions each year, tax free, to an *individual retirement account* (IRA), offered by depository institutions, brokerage firms, insurance companies, and mutual funds, or by employers with qualified pension or profit-sharing plans. There was ample precedent for the creation of IRAs; in 1962, Congress had authorized financial institutions to sell *Keogh plan* retirement deposits, available to self-employed persons. Unfortunately for depository institutions and their customers interested in IRAs, the Tax Reform Act of 1986 restricted the tax deductibility of additions to an IRA account, which reduced their growth rate somewhat, though Keogh deposits retained full tax benefits.

Then, in August 1997 the U.S. Congress, in an effort to encourage saving for retirement, purchases of new homes, and childrens' education, modified the rules for IRA accounts, allowing individuals with higher incomes to make annual tax-deductible contributions to their retirement accounts and families to set up new education savings accounts that could grow tax free until needed to cover college tuition and other qualified educational expenses. Finally, the Tax Relief Act of 1997 created the *Roth IRA,* which allows individuals to make nontax-deductible contributions to a savings fund that can grow tax free and also pay no tax on their investment earnings when withdrawn.

Today depository institutions in the United States hold about a quarter of all IRA and Keogh retirement accounts outstanding, ranking second only to mutual funds. The great appeal for the managers of depository institutions is the high degree of stability of IRA and Keogh deposits—financial managers can generally rely on having these funds around for several years. Moreover, many IRAs and Keoghs carry fixed interest rates—an advantage if market interest rates are rising—allowing depository institutions to earn higher returns on their loans and investments that more than cover the interest costs associated with IRAs and Keoghs. (These retirement accounts were made more attractive to the public in 2006 when the U.S. Congress voted to increase FDIC insurance coverage to $250,000 for qualified retirement-plan deposits.)

12–3 Interest Rates Offered on Different Types of Deposits

Each of the different types of deposits we have discussed typically carries a different rate of interest. In general, the longer the maturity of a deposit, the greater the yield that must be offered to depositors because of the time value of money and the frequent upward slope of the yield curve. For example, NOW accounts and savings deposits are subject to immediate withdrawal by the customer; accordingly, their offer rate to customers is among the lowest of all deposits. In contrast, negotiable CDs and deposits of a year or longer to maturity often carry the highest interest rates that depositories offer.

The size and perceived risk exposure of offering institutions also play an important role in shaping deposit interest rates. For example, banks in New York and London, due to their greater size and strength, are able to offer deposits at the lowest average interest rates, while deposit rates posted by other institutions are generally scaled upward from that level. Other key factors are the marketing philosophy and goals of the offering institution. Depository institutions that choose to compete for deposits aggressively will post higher offer rates to bid deposits away from their competitors.

The Composition of Deposits

The largest of all depository institutions are *commercial banks*, whose nearly $6 trillion in deposits in 2005 exceeded the total deposits held by all nonbank depository institutions (including thrifts and credit unions) by a ratio of four to one. By examining recent trends in bank deposits we can get a pretty good idea of recent changes in the mix of deposits at all types of depository institutions in recent years.

In recent years, banks have been most able to sell *time and savings deposits—*interest-bearing thrift accounts—to the public. As Table 12–1 shows, time and savings deposits represented more than four-fifths of the total deposits held by all U.S.-insured commercial banks in 2005. Not surprisingly, then, interest-bearing deposits and nontransaction deposits, both of which include time and savings deposits, have captured the majority share of all deposit accounts. In contrast, regular demand deposits, which generally pay no interest and make up the majority of transaction and noninterest-bearing deposits, have declined significantly to just over 10 percent of total deposits inside the United States.

Indeed, as Gerdes et al.[3] have observed, the volume of checks paid in the United States fell from close to 50 billion in 1995 to only about 40 billion in 2005 due mainly to the rise of electronic payments media, including credit and debit cards, Web-based payments systems, and electronic wire transfers. However, most authorities argue that checks written against demand (transaction) deposits will continue to be important in the American payments system, though in parts of Europe (particularly in Finland, Germany, and the Netherlands) electronic payments are rapidly taking over.

Bankers, if left to decide for themselves about the best mix of deposits, would generally prefer a high proportion of transaction deposits (including regular checking or demand accounts) and low-yielding time and savings deposits. These accounts are among the least expensive of all sources of funds and often include a substantial percentage of **core deposits**—a stable base of deposited funds that is not highly sensitive to market interest rates (i.e., bears a low interest-rate elasticity) and tends to remain with a depository institution. While many core deposits (such as small savings accounts) can be withdrawn

TABLE 12–1
The Changing Composition of Deposits in the United States

Source: Federal Deposit Insurance Corporation.

Deposit Type or Category	Percentages for All U.S. Insured Banks					
	1983	1987	1993	1998	2001	2005**
Noninterest-bearing deposits	37.9%	20.5%	20.8%	19.5%	19.9%	22.9%
Interest-bearing deposits	62.1	79.5	79.2	80.5	80.1	77.1
Total deposits	100.0%	100.0%	100.0%	100.0%	100.0%	100.0%
Transaction deposits	31.9%	32.3%	33.4%	24.3%	21.2%	15.5%
Nontransaction deposits	68.1	67.7	66.6	75.7	78.8	84.5
Total domestic office deposits	100.0%	100.0%	100.0%	100.0%	100.0%	100.0%
Demand deposits	25.4%	22.9%	20.2%	18.9%	19.0%	11.3%
Savings deposits*	30.2	36.2	41.2	43.5	48.0	57.9
Time deposits	44.4	40.9	38.6	37.6	33.0	30.8
Total domestic office deposits	100.0%	100.0%	100.0%	100.0%	100.0%	100.0%

Notes: *The savings deposit figures include money market deposit accounts (MMDAs).
**Figures for 2005 are as of June 30, 2005. Components may not add to totals due to rounding error.

immediately, they have an effective maturity often spanning years. Thus, the availability of a large block of core deposits increases the duration of a depository institution's liabilities and makes that institution less vulnerable to swings in interest rates. The presence of substantial amounts of core deposits in smaller banks helps explain why large banks in recent years have acquired so many smaller banking firms—to gain access to a more stable, less-expensive deposit base. However, the combination of inflation, deregulation, stiff competition, and better-educated customers has resulted in a dramatic shift in the mix of deposits that depository institutions are able to sell.

Operating costs for institutions offering deposit services have soared in recent years. For example, interest payments on deposits (both foreign and domestic) for all insured U.S. commercial banks amounted to about $10 billion in 1970, but had jumped to about $70 billion by 2005. At the same time new, higher-yielding deposits proved to be more interest sensitive than older, less-expensive deposits, thus putting pressure on management to pay competitive interest rates on their deposits. Depository institutions that didn't keep up with market interest rates had to be prepared for extra liquidity demands—substantial deposit withdrawals and fluctuating deposit levels. Faced with substantial interest cost pressures, many bankers have pushed hard to reduce their noninterest expenses (e.g., by automating their operations and reducing the number of employees on the payroll).

The Ownership of Deposits

The dominant holder of bank deposits inside the United States is the private sector—individuals, partnerships, and corporations (IPC), accounting for about four-fifths or more of all U.S. deposits. The next largest deposit owner is state and local governments (about 4 percent of the total), representing the funds accumulated by counties, cities, and other local units of government. These deposits are often highly volatile, rising sharply when tax collections roll in or bonds are sold, and falling precipitously when local government payrolls must be met or construction begins on a new public building. Many institutions accept state and local deposits as a service to their communities even though these deposits frequently are not highly profitable.

Factoid
The more rapid the turnover of population in a given market area, the more intensive tends to be competition among depository institutions in the sale of deposit services and the more favorable loan and deposit interest rates tend to be, unless the relocation of depositors doesn't require a change of depository institution.

Banks also hold comparatively small amounts of U.S. government deposits. In fact, the U.S. Treasury keeps most of its operating funds in domestic banking institutions in *Treasury Tax and Loan (TT&L) Accounts.* When taxes are collected from the public or Treasury securities are sold to investors, the government usually directs these funds into TT&L deposits first, in order to minimize the impact of government operations on the financial system. The Treasury then makes periodic withdrawals (directing the money into its accounts at the Federal Reserve banks) when it needs to make expenditures. Today the Treasury pays fees to depository institutions to help lower the cost of handling government deposits and receives interest income on many of the balances held with depository institutions.

Another deposit category of substantial size held by U.S. banks is deposits held by foreign governments, businesses, and individuals, many of which are received in offshore offices. Foreign-owned deposits rose rapidly during the 1960s and 1970s, climbing to nearly one-fifth of total U.S. bank deposits in 1980, reflecting the rapid growth in world trade and investments by U.S. businesses abroad. However, foreign-owned deposits then declined as a proportion of U.S. bank funds as domestic interest rates proved to be significantly cheaper. Moreover, international crises, the tragedy of 9/11, and a stronger economy at home encouraged American banks to scale down their overseas expansion plans. However, as the 21st century unfolded, foreign deposits began to grow again due to the availability of higher-yielding foreign investments and the rapid growth of several foreign economies (especially in Asia).

The final major deposit ownership category is deposits of other banks, which include *correspondent deposits*, representing funds that depository institutions hold with each other

E-BANKING AND E-COMMERCE

THE PASSAGE OF CHECK 21 AND SUBSTITUTE CHECKS

Paper checks are being processed faster these days and more people and businesses are bypassing checks and going electronic. In past years depositors used to count on "float" time between the moment they wrote a check and the time when funds were actually removed from their checking account. Today, however, funds often get moved out of one account into another the same day.

A good example is the process known as *electronic check conversion.* Used by many merchants and utility companies today, the electronic conversion process takes the information from the check you have just written and electronically debits your account, often on the spot. The check you have written is not sent through the normal clearing process. Indeed, some merchants stamp "void" on your check and give it back to you once they have electronically transferred the information it contains. Moreover, more depository institutions are *not* returning checks to their depositors today nor are they sending the original checks to other depositories.

Effective October 28, 2004, the Check 21 Act became law, permitting depository institutions to electronically transfer check *images* instead of checks themselves, replacing originals with *substitute checks.* These are photographed copies of the front and back of the original and can now be processed as though they were originals. The front will say: "This is a legal copy of your check. You can use it the same way you would use the original check." Thus, substitute checks provide proof that you paid a bill just as would be the case if you had the original check.

Check 21 carries a number of benefits for depositors and depository institutions. It protects depositors against loss from substitute checks. The account holder can contact his or her depository institution to request a refund when the use of substitute checks has led to an account error that cost the depositor money. Check 21 also benefits depository institutions by sharply reducing the cost of check clearing, especially in doing away with the necessity of flying or driving bundles of checks around the country. (For further information on Check 21 and the rights and obligations of depositors and depository institutions, see especially **www.federalreserve.gov/check 21**).

to pay for correspondent services. For example, large metropolitan banks provide data processing and computerized recordkeeping, investment counseling, participations in loans, and the clearing and collection of checks and other drafts for smaller urban and outlying depository institutions. An institution that holds deposits received from other depositories will record them as a liability on its balance sheet under the label *deposits due to banks and other depository institutions*. The institution that owns such deposits will record them as assets under the label *deposits due from banks and other depository institutions*.

The Cost of Different Deposit Accounts

Other factors held constant, the managers of depository institutions would prefer to raise funds by selling those types of deposits that cost the least amount of money or, when revenues generated by the use of deposited funds are considered, generate the greatest net revenue after all expenses. If a depository institution can raise all of its capital from sales of the cheapest deposits and then turn around and purchase the highest-yielding assets, it will maximize its spread and, possibly, its net income. But what are the cheapest deposits? And which deposits generate the highest net revenues?

Research based upon cost-accounting techniques suggests that *checkable* (demand or transaction) *deposits*—including regular checking accounts and special checkbook deposits (which usually pay no interest) and interest-bearing checking accounts—are typically among the cheapest deposits that depositories sell. While check processing and account maintenance are major expense items, the absence of interest payments on many demand (transaction) deposit accounts and the low interest rate on other checkable accounts help keep their cost down relative to the cost of time and savings deposits and other sources of funds.

Moreover, check-processing costs should move substantially lower in the period ahead as *check imaging* becomes more widely used. Paper checks are rapidly being supplanted by electronic images, permitting greater storage capacity and faster retrieval, cutting costs and improving customer service. Especially popular in the new century have been *automatic bill-paying services*, including online bill payment services offered by depository institutions and direct electronic debits that you authorize out of your bank account and are carried out by a credit-card company or other merchant to whom you owe money. Increasingly it is becoming possible to pay almost every bill without cutting a check or visiting a list of Web sites. Funds are simply automatically "yanked out" of your deposit account on the same day each month.

In fact, so significant has been the recent decline in paper check volume that the Federal Reserve System announced in 2003 that it was reducing the number of check processing regions in the United States from 44 to 32. This trend has gotten a favorable reception from financial institutions hoping to reduce operating costs. However, check writing has generated substantial fee income for most offering institutions in the past—a key source of revenue that will have to be replaced with new sources of revenue as the global financial system goes more and more automated and electronic.

Thrift deposits—particularly money market accounts, time deposits, and savings accounts—generally rank second to demand deposits as the least costly deposits. Savings deposits are relatively cheap because of the low interest rate they tend to carry—one of the lowest annual interest yields (APY) offered—and, in many cases, the absence of monthly statements for depositors. However, many passbook savings accounts have substantial deposit and withdrawal activity; some savers attempt to use them as checking (transaction) accounts. Depository institutions often discourage rapid turnover in their savings deposits by limiting withdrawals and charging activity fees.

While demand (checking or transaction) deposits have about the same gross expenses per dollar of deposit as time (thrift) deposits do, the higher service fees levied against transaction-account customers help to lower the net cost of checkable deposits (after service revenues are netted out) below the net cost of most time (thrift) accounts. When we give each type of deposit credit for the earnings it generates through the making of loans and investments, checkable (demand) deposits appear to be substantially more profitable than time deposits for the average depository institution. On average, checking-account service fees offset about one-third of a transaction account's cost. In contrast, service fees on time (thrift) deposits usually make only a negligible contribution to offsetting their cost. Moreover, interest expense per dollar of time deposits averages about triple the interest expense associated with each dollar of demand (transaction) deposits.

To be sure, demand (transaction) deposits incur much greater operating expenses due to the high employee and equipment costs associated with processing checks and recording deposits, while these "activity expenses" are far less for thrift (time) deposits. The critical difference in terms of their profitability to depository institutions is the service fees most checkable (transaction) accounts generate. This fact helps explain why depository institutions are more aggressively pricing their checkable deposits today, asking depositors to pay a bigger share of the activity costs they create when they write checks and transfer funds electronically.

If checkable (demand) deposits tend to be more profitable, what particular types of these transaction accounts yield the greatest profits? Interest-bearing checking accounts generate about twice the volume of net returns (after earnings from loan and investment portfolios are added in) that regular (noninterest-bearing) demand accounts generate. Special checking accounts, which charge the customer a fee for each transaction but generally require low or no minimum balances, tend to be the least profitable of all demand deposits principally because they tend to generate a small volume of investable funds at most depository institutions.

Business transaction accounts, generally speaking, are considerably more profitable than personal checking accounts. One reason is the lack of a significant interest expense with commercial deposits. Moreover, the average size of a personal transaction account normally is less than one-third the average size of a commercial account, so a depository institution receives

Real Banks, Real Decisions

WHO OFFERS THE HIGHEST DEPOSIT INTEREST RATES AND WHY?

Customers interested in purchasing the highest-yielding interest-bearing deposits and the managers of depository institutions interested in discovering what deposit interest yields their competitors are offering can consult daily newspapers or go online to key Web sites—for example, The BanxQuote Bank Center at **www.wsj.com** or **www.banx.com** and **Bankrate.com.**

Among the key types of deposit rate information available are these:

- The average yields offered by major depositories in leading states (e.g., California, Florida, Illinois, Texas, and New York) on money market deposits, savings deposits, and certificates of deposit (CDs) out to 5 years to maturity.
- The average yields (APY) offered on CDs purchased through security brokers who search the marketplace every day for the highest yields available on large deposits (usually close to $100,000 in size).
- A list of those depository institutions around the United States offering the highest yields (APYs) on retail deposits (typically $500 to $25,000 minimum denomination) and jumbo CDs (usually carrying an opening balance of $100,000).

Among the depository institutions offering the highest deposit yields are usually leading credit card and household lenders, such as GMAC Bank and Countrywide Bank, along with several virtual (Internet) banks, including E* Trade Bank and VirtualBank of Palm Beach, Florida.

Why are the foregoing institutions generally among the leaders in offering the public the highest deposit interest rates? One reason is they expect to earn relatively high returns on their consumer and credit card loans, giving them an ample margin over deposit costs.

In the case of Internet-based banking institutions these unique electronic firms must attract the public away from more traditional institutions and often provide few services, so they must offer exceptional deposit rates to attract the funds they need. Moreover, virtual banks typically have relatively low fixed (overhead) costs, allowing these firms to bid higher for the public's deposits.

On the negative side, however, virtual banks have not been as successful in attracting customers as have traditional depository institutions in recent years. Indeed, the most successful firms at attracting customer deposits recently have been *multichannel depository institutions*—offering both traditional and online services through the same institution—indicating that many customers are more likely to use the online services of financial firms that also are accessible in person through traditional branch offices and automated teller machines.

substantially more investable funds from commercial demand deposits. However, competition posed by foreign financial-service firms for commercial transaction accounts has become so intense that profit margins on these accounts tend to be razor thin in today's market.

Concept Check

12–1. What are the major types of deposit plans depository institutions offer today?

12–2. What are *core deposits* and why are they so important today?

12–3. How has the composition of deposits changed in recent years?

12–4. What are the consequences for the management and performance of depository institutions resulting from recent changes in deposit composition?

12–5. Which deposits are the least costly for depository institutions? The most costly?

12–6. First State Bank of Pine is considering a change of marketing strategy in an effort to lower its cost of funding and to maximize profitability. The new strategy calls for aggressive advertising of new commercial transaction accounts and interest-bearing household checking accounts and for de-emphasizing regular and special transaction accounts. What are the possible advantages and possible weaknesses of this new marketing strategy?

While the managers of depository institutions would prefer to sell only the cheapest deposits to the public, it is predominantly *public preference* that determines which types of deposits will be created. Depository institutions that do not wish to conform to customer preferences will simply be outbid for deposits by those who do. At the same time, deregulation of the financial markets has made it possible for more kinds of financial-service firms to respond to the public's deposit preferences.

12–4 Pricing Deposit-Related Services

Factoid
Several deposit-related fees charged by depository institutions have increased faster than inflation in recent years. These more rapidly rising bank fees include charges for checks returned for insufficient funds, stop-payment orders, ATM-usage fees, and overdraft fees.

We have examined the different types of deposit plans offered today and how the composition of deposits has been changing over time. An equally important issue remains: How should depository institutions price their deposit services in order to attract new funds and make a profit?

In pricing deposit services, management is caught between the horns of an old dilemma. It needs to pay a high enough interest return to customers to attract and hold their funds, but must avoid paying an interest rate that is so costly it erodes any potential profit margin from using customer funds. In fact, in a financial marketplace that approaches perfect competition, the individual depository institution has little control over its prices in the long run. It is the *marketplace*, not the individual financial firm, that ultimately sets all prices. In such a market, management must decide if it wishes to attract more deposits and hold all those it currently has by offering depositors at least the market-determined price, or whether it is willing to lose funds by offering customers terms different from what the market requires.

12–5 Pricing Deposits at Cost Plus Profit Margin

The idea of charging the customer for the full cost of deposit-related services is relatively new. In fact, until a couple of decades ago the notion that customers should receive most deposit-related services *free of charge* was hailed as a wise innovation—one that responded to the growing challenge posed by other financial intermediaries that were invading traditional deposit markets. Many managers soon found reason to question the wisdom of this new marketing strategy, however, because they were flooded with numerous low-balance, high-activity accounts that ballooned their operating costs.

Key URL
Each year under law the Federal Reserve Board must conduct a survey of retail fees charged by depository institutions on deposits and other services. For an example of recent survey data on service fees, see **www.federalreserve.gov/boarddocs/rptcongress/**.

The development of interest-bearing checkable deposits (particularly NOWs) offered financial managers the opportunity to reconsider the pricing of deposit services. Unfortunately, many of the early entrants into this new market moved aggressively to capture a major share of the customers through *below-cost pricing*. Customer charges were set below the true level of operating and overhead costs associated with providing deposit services. The result was a substantially increased rate of return to the customer, known as the *implicit interest rate*—the difference between the true cost of supplying fund-raising services and the service charges actually assessed the customer.

In the United States, variations in the implicit interest rate paid to the customer were the principal way most banks competed for deposits over the 50 years stretching from the Great Depression to the beginning of the 1980s. This was due to the presence of regulatory ceilings on deposit interest rates, beginning in 1933 with passage of the Glass-Steagall Act. These legal interest rate ceilings were designed to protect depository institutions from "excessive" interest rate competition for deposits, which could allegedly cause them to fail. Prevented from offering higher explicit interest rates, U.S. depositories competed instead by offering free bank-by-mail services, gifts ranging from teddy bears to toasters, and convenient neighborhood branch offices.

Unfortunately, such forms of *nonprice competition* tended to distort the allocation of scarce resources in the financial sector. Congress finally responded to these problems with passage of the Depository Institutions Deregulation Act of 1980, a federal law that called for a gradual phaseout of federal limits on the interest rates depositories could offer their customers. Today, the responsibility for setting deposit prices in the United States (and in other leading industrialized nations as well) has been transferred from public regulators to private decision makers—that is, to depository institutions and their customers.

Deregulation has brought more frequent use of *unbundled service pricing* as greater competition has raised the average real cost of a deposit for deposit-service providers. This means that deposits are usually priced separately from other services. And each deposit service is often priced high enough to recover all or most of the cost of providing that service, using the following **cost-plus pricing** formula:

$$
\begin{matrix}
\text{Unit price} \\
\text{charged the} \\
\text{customer for each} \\
\text{deposit service}
\end{matrix}
=
\begin{matrix}
\text{Operating} \\
\text{expense} \\
\text{per unit of} \\
\text{deposit service}
\end{matrix}
+
\begin{matrix}
\text{Estimated overhead} \\
\text{expense allocated} \\
\text{to the deposit-} \\
\text{service function}
\end{matrix}
+
\begin{matrix}
\text{Planned} \\
\text{profit margin} \\
\text{from each} \\
\text{service unit sold}
\end{matrix}
\quad \textbf{(12–1)}
$$

Tying deposit pricing to the cost of deposit-service production, as Equation (12–1) above does, has encouraged deposit providers to match prices and costs more closely and eliminate many formerly free services. In the United States, for example, more depositories are now levying fees for excessive withdrawals, customer balance inquiries, bounced checks, stop-payment orders, and ATM usages, as well as raising required minimum deposit balances. The results of these trends have generally been favorable to depository institutions, with increases in service fee income generally outstripping losses from angry customers closing their accounts.

Estimating Deposit Service Costs

Cost-plus pricing demands an accurate calculation of the cost of each deposit service. How can this be done? One popular approach is to base deposit prices on the estimated cost of raising funds. This requires management to: (1) calculate the cost rate of each source of funds (adjusted for reserves required by the central bank, deposit insurance fees, and float); (2) multiply each cost rate by the relative proportion of all funds coming from that particular source; and (3) sum all resulting products to derive the weighted average cost of all funds raised. This *pooled-funds cost approach* is based on the assumption that it is not the cost of each type of deposit that matters, but rather the weighted average cost of *all* funding sources for each depository institution.

An Example of Pooled-Funds Costing

Let's consider an example of the pooled-funds cost approach. Suppose a depository institution has raised a total of $400 million, including $100 million in checkable deposits, $200 million in time and savings deposits, $50 million borrowed from the money market, and $50 million from its owners in the form of equity capital. Suppose that interest and noninterest costs spent to attract the checkable deposits total 10 percent of the amount of these deposits, while thrift deposits and money market borrowings each cost 11 percent of funds raised in interest and noninterest expenses. Owners' equity is the most expensive funding source for most institutions; assume that equity capital costs an estimated 22 percent of any new equity raised. Suppose reserve requirements, deposit insurance fees, and uncollected balances (float) reduce the amount of money actually available for investing in interest-bearing assets by 15 percent for checkbook deposits, 5 percent for thrift

Insights and Issues

SUMMARY OF DEPOSIT INSURANCE COVERAGE PROVIDED BY THE FDIC

A major reason depository institutions are able to sell deposits at relatively low rates of interest compared to interest rates offered on other financial instruments is because of government-supplied deposit insurance. The **Federal Deposit Insurance Corporation (FDIC)** was established in 1934 to insure deposits and protect the nation's money supply in those cases where depository institutions having FDIC membership failed. Insured depository institutions must display an official sign at each teller station, indicating they hold an FDIC membership certificate.

FDIC insurance covers only those deposits payable in the United States, though the depositor does *not* have to be a U.S. resident to receive FDIC protection. All types of deposits normally are covered up to $100,000 for each single account holder, though Congress recently empowered the FDIC to increase future insurance coverage in order to keep up with inflation. Savings deposits, checking accounts, NOW accounts, Christmas Club accounts, time deposits, cashiers' checks, money orders, officers' checks, and any outstanding drafts normally are protected by federal insurance. Certified checks, letters of credit, and travelers' checks for which an insured depository institution is primarily liable also are insured if these are issued in exchange for money or in return for a charge against a deposit. On the other hand, U.S. government securities, shares in mutual funds, safe deposit boxes, and funds stolen from an insured depository institution are *not* covered by FDIC insurance. Depository institutions generally carry private insurance against such losses.

Deposits placed in separate financial institutions (including different parts of the same holding company) are insured separately, each eligible for full insurance coverage. However, deposits held in more than one branch office of the *same* depository institution are added together to determine the total amount of insurance protection available. In this case the individual depositor may receive no more than $100,000 in total insurance protection. If two formerly independent institutions merge, for example, and a depositor holds $100,000 in each of these two merging institutions, the total protection afforded this depositor would then be a maximum of $100,000, not $200,000, as it was before the merger. However, the FDIC normally allows a grace period so that, for a short time, a depositor with large deposits in two institutions that merge can receive expanded coverage up to $200,000 until arrangements can be made to transfer some of the depositor's funds to other institutions.

Insurance coverage may also be increased at a single institution by placing funds under *different categories of legal ownership.* For example, a depositor with $100,000 in a savings deposit and another $100,000 in a time deposit might achieve greater insurance coverage by making one of these two accounts a joint ownership account with his or her spouse. Also, if a family is composed of husband and wife plus one child, for example, each family member could own an account and each pair of family members (e.g., husband and wife, husband and child, and wife and child) could also hold joint accounts, resulting in insurance coverage up to $600,000 in total. Only natural persons, not corporations or partnerships, can set up insurance-eligible joint accounts, however.

Each co-owner of a joint account is assumed to have equal right of withdrawal and is also assumed to own an *equal share* of a joint account unless otherwise stated in the account record. No one person's total insured interest in all joint accounts at the same insured depository institution can exceed $100,000. For example,

---

deposits, and 2 percent for borrowings in the money market. Therefore, this institution's weighted average before-tax cost of funds would be:

$$
\begin{aligned}
&(\text{Checkbook deposits} \div \text{Total funds raised}) \\
&\quad \times \left(\frac{\text{Interest and noninterest fund-raising costs}}{100 \text{ percent} - \text{Percentage reserve requirements and float}}\right) \\
&+ (\text{Time and savings deposits} \div \text{Total funds raised}) \\
&\quad \times \left(\frac{\text{Interest and noninterest fund-raising costs}}{100 \text{ percent} - \text{Percentage reserve requirements and float}}\right) \\
&+ (\text{Owner's capital} \div \text{Total funds raised}) \\
&\quad \times (\text{Interest and noninterest costs} \div 100 \text{ percent}) \\
&= \$100 \text{ million} \div \$400 \text{ million} \times 10 \text{ percent} \div (100 \text{ percent} - 15 \text{ percent}) \\
&+ \$200 \text{ million} \div \$400 \text{ million} \times 11 \text{ percent} \div (100 \text{ percent} - 5 \text{ percent}) \\
&+ \$50 \text{ million} \div \$400 \text{ million} \times 11 \text{ percent} \div (100 \text{ percent} - 2 \text{ percent}) \\
&+ \$50 \text{ million} \div \$400 \text{ million} \times 22 \text{ percent} \div 100 \text{ percent} \\
&= 0.1288, \text{ or } 12.88 \text{ percent of funds raised}
\end{aligned}
$$

(12–2)

In this example management will want to make sure it earns at least a before-tax rate of return of 12.88 percent on its asset portfolio. If this particular institution can earn more

suppose Mr. Jones has a joint account with Mrs. Jones amounting to $120,000. Then each is presumed to have a $60,000 share and each would have FDIC insurance coverage of $60,000 unless the deposit record shows that, for example, Mrs. Jones owns $100,000 of the $120,000 balance. In this instance Mrs. Jones would receive the full $100,000 in insurance protection and Mr. Jones would be covered for a maximum of $20,000.

After December 1993, IRA and Keogh retirement deposits became separately insured from nonretirement deposits. All retirement accounts are added together for a maximum amount of insurance protection of $100,000, though a recent vote by the U.S. Congress raised the amount of insurance protection on certain retirement deposits to $250,000. Deposits belonging to pension and profit-sharing plans receive "pass-through insurance" provided the individual participants' beneficial interests are ascertainable and the depository institution involved is at least "adequately capitalized" and eligible to take deposits placed by brokers on behalf of their customers.

Funds deposited by a corporation, partnership, or unincorporated business or association are insured up to the maximum allowed by law and are insured separately from the personal accounts of the company's stockholders, partners, or members. Funds deposited by a sole proprietor are considered to be personal funds, however, and are added to any other single-owner accounts the individual business owner has, and are protected only up to $100,000.

The amount of insurance premiums that each FDIC-insured depository institution must pay is determined by the volume of deposits it receives from the public and by the insurance rate category in which each institution falls. Under the current risk-based deposit insurance system mandated by the FDIC Improvement Act

of 1991 more risky depository institutions must pay higher insurance premiums. The degree of risk exposure is determined by the interplay of two factors: (1) the adequacy of capital maintained by each depository institution, and (2) the risk class in which the institution is judged to be according to its regulatory supervisors. Well-capitalized, A-rated depositories pay the lowest deposit insurance fee per each $100 of deposit they hold, while undercapitalized, C-rated institutions pay the greatest insurance fees.

Twice each year the board of directors of the FDIC must decide what deposit insurance rates to assess each insured institution. If the federal insurance fund falls below $1.25 in reserves per $100 in covered deposits (known as the Designated Reserve Ratio [DRR]), the FDIC will raise its insurance assessment fees. When the amount of reserves exceeds the $1.25 per $100 standard, fees may be lowered or eliminated.

In February 2006 the Federal Deposit Insurance Reform Act was signed into law and will eventually change some of the foregoing insurance rules. For example, beginning in 2010 the boards of the FDIC and the National Credit Union Administration are authorized to increase the insurance limit every five years in order to protect against *inflation*, provided this step seems warranted. Moreover, the 1.25 percent required DRR mentioned above—sometimes referred to as the "hard" target—may be altered at the FDIC's discretion to form a "soft" target—that is, the FDIC has the authority to allow the DRR to range between 1.15 and 1.50 percent of all insured deposits. Thus, as a result of the new reform law the FDIC will have more flexibility in deciding when it needs to change insurance fees and the amount of depositor insurance protection that it provides.

Source: Federal Deposit Insurance Corporation.

from its loans and investments than 12.88 percent before taxes, the extra return (less taxes) will flow to the stockholders in the form of increased dividends and into retained earnings to strengthen capital.

The pooled-funds cost approach provides managers with a way to calculate the effects of any change in deposit terms. For example, management can experiment with alternative deposit terms (interest rates, fees, and minimum balance requirements) for any deposit plan offered and estimate their impact on funding costs. Of course, managers cannot safely price deposits without knowing how low customer balances can go and still be profitable. Overly generous pricing terms can set in motion substantial account shifting by customers, leading to a sharp increase in the cost of funds without significantly increasing total funds available.

12–6 Using Marginal Cost to Set Interest Rates on Deposits

Many financial analysts argue that, whenever possible, *marginal cost*—the added cost of bringing in new funds—and not historical average cost, should be used to help price funds sources for a financial-service institution. The reason is that frequent changes in interest rates will make *historical average cost* a treacherous standard for pricing. For example, if interest rates are declining, the added (marginal) cost of raising new money may fall well below the historical average cost over all funds raised. Some loans and investments that looked unprofitable

Key URLs
To learn more about FDIC deposit insurance rules, see especially, **www2.fdic.gov/edie** and the FDIC's new Learning Bank site, **www.fdic.gov/about/learn/learning/index.html**.

when compared to historical cost will now look profitable when measured against the lower marginal interest cost we must pay today. Conversely, if interest rates are on the rise, the marginal cost of today's new money may substantially exceed the historical cost of funds. If management books new assets based on historical cost, they may turn out to be unprofitable when measured against the higher marginal cost of raising new funds in today's market.

Economist James E. McNulty [10] has suggested a way to use the marginal, or new money, cost idea to help a depository institution set the interest rates it will offer on new deposit accounts. To understand this marginal cost pricing method, suppose a bank expects to raise $25 million in new deposits by offering its depositors an interest rate of 7 percent. Management estimates that if the bank offers a 7.50 percent interest rate, it can raise $50 million in new deposit money. At 8 percent, $75 million is expected to flow in, while a posted deposit rate of 8.5 percent will bring in a projected $100 million. Finally, if the bank promises an estimated 9 percent yield, management projects that $125 million in new funds will result from both new deposits and existing deposits that customers will keep in the bank to take advantage of the higher rates offered. Let's assume as well that management believes it can invest the new deposit money at a yield of 10 percent. This investment yield represents *marginal revenue*, the added operating revenue the bank will generate by making new investments from new deposits. Given these facts, what deposit interest rate should the bank offer its customers?

Key URL
To track the deposit growth of any FDIC-insured depository institution go to **www3.fdic.gov/sdi/**.

As Table 12–2 shows, we need to know at least two crucial items to answer this question: the *marginal cost* of moving the deposit rate from one level to another and the *marginal cost rate*, expressed as a percentage of the volume of additional funds coming into the bank. Once we know the marginal cost rate, we can compare it to the expected additional revenue (marginal revenue) the bank expects to earn from investing its new deposits. The items we need are:

$$\text{Marginal cost} = \text{Change in total cost} = \text{New interest rate} \times \text{Total funds}$$
$$\text{raised at new rate} - \text{Old interest rate} \times \text{Total funds raised at old rate} \quad \textbf{(12–3)}$$

and

$$\text{Marginal cost rate} = \frac{\text{Change in total cost}}{\text{Additional funds raised}} \quad \textbf{(12–4)}$$

TABLE 12–2 Using Marginal Cost to Choose the Interest Rate to Offer Customers on Deposits

Example of a Bank Attempting to Raise New Funds							
Expected Amounts of Deposits That Will Flow In	Average Interest the Bank Will Pay on New Funds	Total Interest Cost of New Funds Raised	Marginal Cost of New Deposit Money	Marginal Cost as a Percentage of New Funds Attracted (marginal cost rate)	Expected Marginal Revenue (return) from Investing the New Funds	Difference between Marginal Revenue and Marginal Cost Rate	Total Profits Earned (after interest cost)
$ 25	7.0%	$ 1.75	$1.75	7.0%	10.0%	+3%	$0.75
50	7.5	3.75	2.00	8.0	10.0	+2%	1.25
75	8.0	6.00	2.25	9.0	10.0	+1%	1.50
100	8.5	8.50	2.50	10.0	10.0	+0	1.50
125	9.0	11.25	2.75	11.0	10.0	−1%	1.25

Note: Figures in millions except percentages.

For example, if the bank raises its offer rate on new deposits from 7 percent to 7.5 percent, Table 12–2 shows the marginal cost of this change: Change in total cost = $50 million × 7.5 percent − $25 million × 7 percent = $3.75 million − $1.75 million = $2.00 million. The marginal cost rate, then, is the change in total cost divided by the additional funds raised, or

$$\frac{\$2 \text{ million}}{\$25 \text{ million}} = 8 \text{ percent}$$

Notice that the marginal cost rate at 8 percent is substantially above the average deposit cost of 7.5 percent. This happens because the bank must not only pay a rate of 7.5 percent to attract the second $25 million, but it must also pay out the same 7.5 percent rate to those depositors who were willing to contribute the first $25 million at only 7 percent.

Because the bank expects to earn 10 percent on these new funds, marginal revenue exceeds marginal cost by 2 percent at a deposit interest cost of 8 percent. Clearly, the new deposits will add more to revenue than they will to cost. The bank is justified (assuming its projections are right) in offering a deposit rate at least as high as 7.5 percent. Its total profit will equal the difference between total revenue ($50 million × 10 percent = $5 million) and total cost ($50 million × 7.5 percent = $3.75 million), for a profit of $1.25 million.

Scanning down Table 12–2, we note that the bank continues to improve its total profits, with marginal revenue exceeding marginal cost, up to a deposit interest rate of 8.5 percent. At that rate the bank raises an estimated $100 million in new money at a marginal cost rate of 10 percent, matching its expected marginal revenue of 10 percent.

There, total profit tops out at $1.5 million. It would *not* pay the bank to go beyond this point, however. For example, if it offers a deposit rate of 9 percent, the marginal cost rate balloons upward to 11 percent, which exceeds marginal revenue by a full percentage point. Attracting new deposits at a 9 percent offer rate adds more to cost than to revenue. Note, too, that total profits at a 9 percent deposit rate fall back to $1.25 million. The 8.5 percent deposit rate is clearly the *best* choice, given all the assumptions and forecasts made.

The marginal cost approach provides valuable information to the managers of depository institutions, not only about setting deposit interest rates, but also about deciding just how far the institution should go in expanding its deposit base before the added cost of deposit growth catches up with additional revenues, and total profits begin to decline. When profits start to fall, management needs either to find new sources of funding with lower marginal costs, or to identify new assets promising greater marginal revenues, or both.

Conditional Pricing

The appearance of interest-bearing checking accounts in the New England states during the 1970s led to fierce competition for customer transaction deposits among depository institutions across the United States. Out of that boiling competitive cauldron came widespread use of **conditional pricing,** where a depository sets up a schedule of fees in which the customer pays a low fee or no fee if the deposit balance remains *above* some minimum level, but faces a higher fee if the average balance falls *below* that minimum. Thus, the customer pays a price *conditional* on how he or she uses the deposit.

Conditional pricing techniques vary deposit prices based on one or more of these factors:

1. The number of transactions passing through the account (e.g., number of checks written, deposits made, wire transfers, stop-payment orders, or notices of insufficient funds issued).
2. The average balance held in the account over a designated period (usually per month).
3. The maturity of the deposit in days, weeks, or months.

The customer selects the deposit plan that results in the lowest fees possible and/or the maximum yields, given the number of checks he or she plans to write, or charges planned to be made, the number of deposits and withdrawals expected, and the planned average

Insights and Issues

THE TRUTH IN SAVINGS ACT

In November 1991, the U.S. Congress passed the **Truth in Savings Act,** which requires depository institutions to make greater disclosure of the interest rates and other terms attached to the deposits they sell the public. On September 14, 1992, the Federal Reserve Board issued Regulation DD to spell out the rules that depositories must follow to conform with this law.

The Fed's regulation stipulates that consumers must be fully informed of the terms on deposit plans *before* they open a new account. A depository institution must disclose the minimum balance required to open the account, how much must be kept on deposit to avoid paying fees or obtain the promised yield, how the balance in each account is figured, when interest actually begins to accrue, any penalties for early withdrawal, options available at maturity, reinvestment and disbursement options, advance notice of the approaching end of the deposit's term if it has a fixed maturity, and any bonuses available.

When a consumer asks for the current interest rate the offering institution must provide that customer with the interest rate offered within the most recent seven calendar days and also provide a telephone number so consumers can call and get the latest offered rate if interest rates have changed. On fixed-rate accounts offering institutions must disclose to customers for what period of time the fixed rate will be in effect. On variable-rate deposits institutions must warn consumers that interest rates can change, how frequently interest rates can change, how a variable interest rate is determined, and specify if there are limits on how far deposit rates can move over time. For all interest-bearing accounts the depository must disclose the frequency with which interest is compounded and credited, both in writing and in advertising.

If a customer decides to renew a deposit that would not be automatically renewed on its own, the renewed deposit is considered a *new* account, requiring full disclosure of fees and other terms. Customers must also be told if their account is automatically renewed and, if not, what will happen to their funds (e.g., will they be placed in a noninterest-bearing account?) if the customer does not remember to renew his or her deposit. (Generally, customers must receive at least 10 days' advance notice of the approaching maturity date for deposits over one year to maturity that are not automatically renewed.) If a change is made in fees or other terms of a deposit that could reduce a depositor's yield, a 30-day advance notice of the terms must be sent to the depositor.

Depository institutions must include information in each statement sent to their customers on the amount of interest earnings received, along with the annual percentage yield earned. The *annual percentage yield* (or *APY*) must be calculated using:

$$\text{APY earned} = 100[(1 + \text{Interest earned/Average account balance})^{(365/\text{Days in period})} - 1]$$

where the account balance is the average daily balance kept in the deposit for the period covered by each account statement. Customers must be informed of the impact of early withdrawals on their account's expected APY.

For example, suppose a depositor had $1,500 in an interest-bearing account for the first 15 days and $500 in the account for the remaining 15 days of a 30-day period. The average daily balance in this case is $1,000, or [($1,500 × 15 days + $500 × 15 days)/30 days]. Suppose the account has been credited with $5.25 in interest for the latest 30-day period. Then the APY earned is:

$$\text{APY} = 100[(1 + 5.25/1000)^{365/30} - 1] = 6.58 \text{ percent}$$

In determining the balance on which interest earnings are figured, the depository institution must use the *full* amount of the principal in the deposit for each day, rather than counting only the minimum balance that was in the account on one day during the statement period. Methods that do not pay interest on the full principal balance are prohibited. In 1994 Congress passed the Riegle Community Development and Regulatory Improvement Act of 1994, which narrowed the scope of deposit plans covered by the Truth in Savings Act to those accounts held by individuals for a personal, family, or household purpose.

balance. Of course, the depository institution must also be acceptable to the customer from the standpoint of safety, convenience, and service availability.

Economist Constance Dunham [9] has classified checking account conditional price schedules into three broad categories: (1) flat-rate pricing, (2) free pricing, and (3) conditionally free pricing. In *flat-rate pricing,* the depositor's cost is a fixed charge per check, per time period, or both. Thus, there may be a monthly account maintenance fee of $2, and each check written or charge drawn against that account may cost the customer 10 cents, regardless of the level of account activity.

Free pricing, on the other hand, refers to the absence of a monthly account maintenance fee or per-transaction charge. Of course, the word *free* can be misleading. Even if a deposit-service provider does not charge an explicit fee for deposit services, the customer may incur an implicit fee in the form of lost income (opportunity cost) because the effective

Insights and Issues

HOW U.S. DEPOSITORY INSTITUTIONS SHOULD DISCLOSE THE TERMS ON THEIR DEPOSIT SERVICES TO CUSTOMERS

In order to help institutions selling deposit services in the United States conform to the Truth in Savings Act the Federal Reserve Board provides managers with examples of proper disclosure forms to use to inform customers of the terms being quoted on their deposits. For example, the Fed has provided an example of a proper disclosure form for certificates of deposit as shown below.

Sample Disclosure Form for XYZ Savings Bank One-Year Certificate of Deposit

Rate Information The interest rate for your account is *5.20%* with an annual percentage yield of *5.34%*. You will be paid this rate until the maturity date of the certificate. Your certificate will mature on September 30, 2007. The annual percentage yield assumes interest remains on deposit until maturity. A withdrawal will reduce earnings.

Interest will be compounded daily and credited to your account on the last day of each month. Interest begins to accrue on the business day you deposit any noncash item (for example, checks).

Minimum Balance Requirements You must deposit $1,000 to open this account. You must maintain a minimum balance of $1,000 in your account every day to obtain the annual percentage yield listed above.

Balance Computation Method We use the daily balance method to calculate the interest on your account. This method applies a daily periodic rate to the principal in the account each day.

Transaction Limitations After the account is opened, you may not make deposits into or withdrawals from the account until the maturity date.

Early Withdrawal Penalty If you withdraw any principal before the maturity date, a penalty equal to three months' interest will be charged to your account.

Renewal Policy This account will be automatically renewed at maturity. You have a grace period of ten (10) calendar days after the maturity date to withdraw the funds without being charged a penalty.

Both the Truth in Savings Act and the Federal Reserve's Regulation DD stipulate that advertising of deposit terms may not be *misleading.* If interest rates are quoted in an advertisement, the institution must tell the public what the other relevant terms of the deposit are, such as the minimum balance needed to earn the advertised yield and whether any fees charged could reduce the depositor's overall yield.

The Federal Reserve has recently developed sample advertisements to guide managers in making sure that advertising contains all the essential information the consumer needs. For example, the sample advertisement form for CDs shown below was developed recently by the Federal Reserve Board.

The sample advertisement illustrates the basic requirements for legitimate advertising of deposits under the Truth in Savings Act: (*a*) deposit rates must be quoted as annual percentage yields (APY), (*b*) the dates and minimum balance required must be explicit, and (*c*) the depositor must be warned of penalties or fees that could reduce the yield.

Bank XYZ Always Offers You Competitive CD Rates!!

Certificate of Deposit	Annual Percentage Yield (APY)
5-year	6.31%
4-year	6.07%
3-year	5.72%
2-year	5.25%
1-year	4.54%
6-month	4.34%
90-day	4.21%
	APYs are offered on accounts from 5/9/07 through 5/18/12

The minimum balance to open an account and obtain the APY is $1,000. A penalty may be imposed for early withdrawal.
For more information call: (202) 123-1234

interest rate paid may be less than the going rate on investments of comparable risk. Many depository institutions have found free pricing decidedly unprofitable because it tends to attract many small, highly active deposits that earn positive returns for the offering institution only when market interest rates are very high.

Conditionally free deposits have come to replace both flat-rate and free deposit pricing systems in many financial-service markets. Conditionally free pricing favors large-denomination deposits because services are free if the account balance stays above some minimum figure. One of the advantages of this pricing method is that the customer, not the offering institution, chooses which deposit plan is preferable. This self-selection process is a form of *market signaling* that can give the depository institution valuable data

Factoid
Who cares most about
the location of a
depository institution—
high-income or low-
income consumers?
Recent research suggests
that low-income
consumers care more
about location in
choosing an institution
to hold their deposit,
while high-income
customers appear to be
more influenced by the
size of the financial firm
holding their account.

Key URLs
A recently introduced
Internet technology
called *aggregation* allows
consumers to monitor
their checking and
savings accounts, their
other financial
investments, personal
borrowings, and recent
online purchases
through a single Web
site. See, for example,
**www.bankofamerica.
com** and **corporate.
yodlee.com**.

on the behavior and cost of its deposits. Conditionally free pricing also allows the offering institution to divide its deposit market into high-balance, low-activity accounts and low-balance, high-activity accounts.

As an example of the use of *conditional pricing* techniques for deposits, the fees for regular checking accounts and savings accounts posted recently by two banks in the United States are given in Exhibit 12–1.

We note that Bank A in Exhibit 12–1 appears to favor high-balance, low-activity checking deposits, while Bank B is more lenient toward smaller checking accounts. For example, Bank A begins assessing a checking-account service fee when the customer's balance falls below $600, while Bank B charges no fees for checking-account services until the customer's account balance drops below $500. Moreover, Bank A assesses significantly higher service fees on low-balance checking accounts than does Bank B—$5 to $10 per month versus $3.50 per month. On the other hand, Bank A allows unlimited check writing from its regular accounts, while B assesses a fee if more than 10 checks or withdrawals occur in any month. Similarly, Bank A assesses a $3 per month service fee if a customer's savings account dips below $200, while Bank B charges only a $2 fee if the customer's savings balance drops below $100.

These price differences reflect differences in the philosophy of the management and owners of these two banks and the types of customers each bank is seeking to attract. Bank A is located in an affluent neighborhood of homes and offices and is patronized primarily by high-income individuals and businesses who usually keep high deposit balances, but also make many charges and write many checks. Bank B, on the other hand, is located across the street from a large university and actively solicits student deposits, which tend to have relatively low balances. Bank B's pricing schedules are set up to accept low-balance deposits, but the bank also recognizes that it needs to discourage excessive charges and check writing by numerous small depositors, which would run up costs. It does so by charging higher per-check fees than Bank A. In these two instances we can see that deposit pricing policy is sensitive to at least two factors:

1. *The types of customers each depository institution plans to serve*—each institution establishes price schedules that appeal to the needs of individuals and businesses representing a significant portion of its market area.
2. *The cost that serving different types of depositors will present to the offering institution*—most institutions today price deposit plans in such a way as to cover all or at least a significant portion of anticipated service costs.

EXHIBIT 12–1

Example of the Use of
Conditional Deposit
Pricing by Two U.S.
Banks Serving the
Same Market Area

Bank A		Bank B	
Regular checking account:		*Regular checking account:*	
Minimum opening balance	$100	Minimum opening balance	$100
If minimum daily balance is		If minimum daily balance is	
$600 or more	No fee	$500 or more	No fee
$300 to $599	$5.00 per mo.	Less than $500	$3.50 per mo.
Less than $300	$10.00 per mo.		
If the depositor's collected monthly		If checks written or ATM	
balance averages $1,500, there is no fee		transactions (debits)	
No limit on number of checks written		exceed 10 per month and	
		balance is below $500	$0.15 per debit
Regular savings account:		*Regular savings account:*	
Minimum opening balance	$100	Minimum opening balance	$100
Service fees:		Service fees:	
If balance falls below $200	$3.00 per mo.	If balance falls below $100	$2.00 per mo.
Balance of $200 or more	No fee	Balance above $100	No fee
Fee for more than two		Fee for more than three	
withdrawals per month	$2.00	withdrawals per month	$2.00

12–7 Pricing Based on the Total Customer Relationship and Choosing a Depository

Related to the idea of targeting the best customers for special treatment is the notion of pricing deposits according to the *number of services the customer uses*. Customers who purchase two or more services may be granted lower deposit fees compared to the fees charged customers having only a limited relationship to the offering institution. The idea is that selling a customer multiple services increases the customer's dependence on the institution and makes it harder for that customer to go elsewhere. In theory at least, **relationship pricing** promotes greater customer loyalty and makes the customer less sensitive to the prices posted on services offered by competing financial firms.

The Role That Pricing and Other Factors Play When Customers Choose a Depository Institution to Hold Their Accounts

Factoid
There is research evidence today that the interest rates banks pay on deposits and the account fees they charge for deposit services do influence which depository institution a customer chooses to hold his or her account. Interestingly, rural financial-service markets appear to be more responsive to interest rates and fees than do urban markets, on average.

To be sure, deposit pricing is important to financial firms offering this service. But how important is it to the customer? Are interest rates and fees the most critical factors a customer considers when choosing an institution to hold his or her deposit account? The correct answer appears to be *no*.

Households and businesses consider multiple factors, not just price, in deciding where to place their deposits, recent studies conducted at the Federal Reserve Board, the University of Michigan, and elsewhere suggest. As shown in Table 12–3, these studies contend that households generally rank *convenience, service availability*, and *safety* above price in choosing which financial firm will hold their transaction account. Moreover, *familiarity*, which may represent not only *name recognition* but also safety, ranks above the interest rate paid as an important factor in how individuals and families choose a depository institution to hold their savings account.

Indeed, surveys indicate that household customers tend to be extremely loyal to their depository institutions—about a third reported *never* changing their principal bank of deposit. When an institutional affiliation is changed, it appears to be due mainly to customer relocation, though once a move occurs many customers seem to pay greater attention to competing institutions and the relative advantages and disadvantages they offer as well as pricing. Three-quarters of the households surveyed recently by the University of

TABLE 12–3 Factors in Household and Business Customers' Choice of a Financial Firm for Their Deposit Accounts (ranked from most important to least important)

Source: Based on studies by the Federal Reserve Board, *Survey of Consumer Finances*.

In Choosing a Financial Firm to Hold Their Checking Transaction Accounts, Households Consider	In Choosing a Financial Firm to Hold Their Savings Deposits, Households Consider	In Choosing a Financial Firm to Supply Their Deposits and Other Services, Business Firms Consider
1. Convenient location.	1. Familiarity.	1. Financial health of lending institution.
2. Availability of many other services.	2. Interest rate paid.	2. Whether bank will be a reliable source of credit in the future.
3. Safety.	3. Transactional convenience (not location).	3. Quality of bank officers.
4. Low fees and low minimum balance.	4. Location.	4. Whether loans are competitively priced.
5. High deposit interest rates.	5. Availability of payroll deduction.	5. Quality of financial advice given.
	6. Fees charged.	6. Whether cash management and operations services are provided.

Concept Check

12–7. Describe the essential differences between the following deposit pricing methods in use today: cost-plus pricing, conditional pricing, and relationship pricing.

12–8. A bank determines from an analysis of its cost-accounting figures that for each $500 minimum-balance checking account it sells, account processing and other operating costs will average $4.87 per month and overhead expenses will run an average of $1.21 per month. The bank hopes to achieve a profit margin over these particular costs of 10 percent of total monthly costs. What monthly fee should it charge a customer who opens one of these checking accounts?

12–9. To price deposits successfully, service providers must know their costs. How are these costs determined using the historical average cost approach? The marginal cost of funds approach? What are the advantages and disadvantages of each approach?

12–10. How can the historical average cost and marginal cost of funds approaches be used to help select assets (such as loans) that a depository institution might wish to acquire?

12–11. What factors do household depositors rank most highly in choosing a financial firm for their checking account? Their savings account? What about business firms?

12–12. What does the 1991 Truth in Savings Act require financial firms selling deposits inside the United States to tell their customers?

12–13. Use the APY formula required by the Truth in Savings Act for the following calculation. Suppose that a customer holds a savings deposit in a savings bank for a year. The balance in the account stood at $2,000 for 180 days and $100 for the remaining days in the year. If the Savings bank paid this depositor $8.50 in interest earnings for the year, what APY did this customer receive?

Factoid
Recent research suggests that at least half of all households and small businesses hold their primary checking account at a depository institution situated within three miles of their location.

Michigan's Survey Research Center cited *location* as the primary reason for staying with the financial firm they first chose.

Business firms, on the other hand, prefer to leave their deposits with financial institutions that will be reliable sources of credit and, relatedly, are in good financial shape. They also rate highly the quality of officers and the quality of advice they receive from financial-service managers. Recent research suggests that financial-service providers need to do a better job of letting their customers know about the cost pressures they face today and why they need to charge fully and fairly for any services customers use.

12–8 Basic (Lifeline) Banking: Key Services for Low-Income Customers

Our overview in this chapter would not be complete without a brief look at a controversial social issue—**basic (lifeline) banking.** Should every adult citizen be guaranteed access to certain basic financial services, such as a checking account or personal loan? Is there a basic minimum level of financial service to which everyone is entitled? Can an individual today really function—secure adequate shelter, food, education, a job, and health care—without access to certain key financial services?

Some authorities refer to this issue as *lifeline banking* because it originated in the controversy surrounding electric, gas, and telephone services. Many people believe that these services are so essential for health and comfort that they should be provided at reduced prices to those who could not otherwise afford them. The basic, or lifeline, banking issue catapulted to nationwide attention during the 1980s and 1990s when several consumer groups, such as the Consumers Union and AARP, first studied the problem and campaigned actively for resolution of the issue. Some depositories have been picketed and formal complaints have been lodged with federal and state regulatory agencies.

The dimensions of the lifeline banking issue have been hinted at in several recent consumer surveys (see, for example, Good [6]). For example, recent studies by the Federal

Reserve indicate that about 15 percent of U.S. households have no checking accounts and about 12 percent hold neither checking nor savings accounts. Other estimates suggest there may be more than 10 million "unbanked" people in the United States and much higher numbers abroad. Most of these people are among the lowest-income groups, have little formal education, often live in households headed by single parents, and lack trust of the banking system. Many of these individuals appear to be turning increasingly to high-cost "fringe" financial institutions (such as pawnshops, title and payday lenders, and check-cashing firms) for the financial services they need.

Many members of the unbanked population represent potentially profitable customers for traditional financial-service providers. Among the financial services most in demand are *wire transfers* or *remittances* of money sent to loved ones elsewhere. For example, thousands of documented and undocumented workers regularly wire billions of dollars annually from the United States to families and friends in Latin America. It has been estimated that the wire-transfer market generates well over $100 billion in business annually for financial firms.

One of the most serious problems individuals outside the financial mainstream face is lack of access to a *deposit account*. Many of these potential deposit customers do not have Social Security numbers or other acceptable ID required to open an account under current U.S. law (especially the USA Patriot Act). Others who can submit acceptable ID find most conventional deposits too expensive to meet their needs.

Without a checking or savings account, few people can get approval for *credit* because most lending institutions prefer to make loans to those customers who keep deposits with them. Yet access to credit is essential for most families to secure adequate housing, medical care, and other important services. Several depository institutions have responded to this problem with *basic deposit plans* that allow users to cash some checks (such as Social Security checks), make a limited number of personal withdrawals or write a small number of checks (such as 10 free checks or charges per month), or earn interest on even the smallest balances. As yet, few laws compel financial institutions to offer basic services, except in selected states—for example, Illinois, Massachusetts, Minnesota, Pennsylvania, and Rhode Island—though many states have debated such legislation.

Another component was added to this dilemma when the U.S. Congress passed the Debt Collection Improvement Act in 1996 and, when the U.S. Treasury launched its Electronic Funds Transfer program in 1999. Both events required that government payments, such as paychecks and Social Security checks, eventually be delivered via *electronic* means. This, of course, implies that some sort of deposit account be available in the recipient's name in which these funds can be placed.

What, if anything, should government do? Even if new legislation is not forthcoming, do financial institutions have a responsibility to serve *all* customers within their communities? These are not easy questions to answer. Most financial-service providers are privately owned corporations responsible to their stockholders to earn competitive returns on invested capital. Providing financial services at prices so low they do not cover production costs interferes with that important goal.

However, the issue of lifeline banking may not be that simple because many financial firms are not treated in public policy like other private firms. For example, entry into the banking industry is regulated, with federal and state regulatory agencies compelled by law to consider "public convenience and needs" in permitting new banks to be established. Moreover, the Community Reinvestment Act of 1977 requires regulatory agencies to consider whether a covered financial organization applying to set up new branch offices or merge with another institution has really made an "affirmative effort" to serve all segments of the communities in which it operates.

This most recent legal requirement to fully serve the local community *may* include the responsibility to offer lifeline financial services. Moreover, depository institutions receive important aid from the government that grants them a competitive advantage over other financial institutions. One of the most important of these aids is *deposit insurance*, in which the government guarantees most of the deposits these institutions sell. If depository institutions benefit from insurance backed ultimately by the public's taxes, do they have a public responsibility to offer some services that are accessible to all? If yes, how should they decide which customers should have access to low-price services? Should they insist on imposing a means test on customers? Someone must bear the cost of producing services. Who should bear the cost of lifeline services? Answers to these questions are not readily apparent, but one thing is certain: These issues are *not* likely to go away.

Concept Check

12–14. What is *lifeline banking?* What pressures does it impose on the managers of banks and other financial institutions?

12–15. Should lifeline banking be offered to low-income customers? Why or why not?

Summary

Deposits are the vital input for banks and their closest competitors, the thrift institutions—the principal source of financial capital to fund loans and security investments and help generate profits to support long-term growth. The most important points this chapter has brought forward include:

• In managing their deposits managers of depository institutions must grapple with two key questions centered upon *cost* and *volume*. Which types of deposits will help minimize the cost of fund-raising? How can a depository institution raise sufficient deposits to meet its fund-raising needs?

• The principal types of deposits offered by depository institutions today include (1) *transaction* (or *payments*) accounts, which customers use primarily to pay for purchases of goods and services; and (2) *nontransaction* (*savings* or *thrift*) deposits, which are held primarily as savings to prepare for future emergencies and for the expected yield they promise. Transaction deposits include regular checking accounts, which often bear no interest return, and interest-bearing transaction deposits (such as NOWs), which pay a low yield and, in some cases, limit the number of checks or other drafts that can be written against the account. Nontransaction deposits include certificates of deposit (CDs), savings accounts, and money market accounts.

• Transaction deposits often are among the most profitable deposit services because of their nonexistent or low interest rates and the higher service fees these accounts usually carry. In contrast, nontransaction, or thrift, deposits generally have the advantage of a more stable funding base that allows a depository institution to reach for longer-term and higher-yielding assets. However, many nontransaction deposits carry relatively high interest costs, reducing potential profits.

• Unfortunately for many depository institutions today, deposit composition is shifting toward more costly nontransaction and interest-bearing transaction accounts, forcing their managers to become more sensitive to cost of production and the pricing of deposit services.

• Recent government deregulation of the financial-services industry has encouraged financial-service managers to think creatively about their deposit pricing policies—the interest rates and fees they post when offering deposit services. The key deposit-pricing models in use today fall into four broad categories: (1) cost-plus deposit pricing; (2) marginal cost pricing; (3) conditional pricing; and (4) relationship pricing.

- The most popular of these deposit-pricing methods today is *conditional pricing*. In this case the interest rate the customer may earn and the fees he or she may be asked to pay are conditional on the intensity of use of deposit services and the balance in the account. In contrast, the *cost-plus* pricing method calls for estimating all operating and overhead costs incurred in providing each service and adds a margin for profit. Under *marginal cost pricing*, the offering institution will set its price at a level just sufficient to attract *new* funds and still earn a profit on the last dollar of *new* funds raised. Finally, *relationship pricing* calls for assessing lower fees or promising more generous yields to those customers who buy the most services and are the most loyal.

- Recently new rules have entered the deposit market. The Truth in Savings Act requires U.S. banks and thrift institutions to make full and timely disclosure of the terms under which each deposit service is offered. This includes information on minimum-balance requirements, how deposit balances are determined, what yield is promised, what the depositor must do to earn the promised return, and any penalties or fees that might be assessed. A 30-day notice of any planned changes in deposit terms must be sent to the customer.

- Finally, one of the most controversial issues in modern banking—*lifeline banking*—continues to be debated in and outside the deposit-services industry. Banks, thrifts, and their competitors have been asked in several states to offer low-cost financial services, especially deposits and loans, for those customers unable to afford conventional services. Some banking institutions have responded positively with limited-service, low-cost accounts, while others argue that most financial firms are profit-making corporations that must pay close attention to the potential profitability and cost of each new service.

Key Terms

transaction deposit, *388*
NOW accounts, *388*
money market deposit accounts, *389*
Super NOWs, *389*
thrift deposits, *389*
passbook savings deposits, *389*

time deposits, *389*
core deposits, *391*
cost-plus pricing, *397*
Federal Deposit Insurance Corporation (FDIC), *398*
conditional pricing, *401*

Truth in Savings Act, *402*
relationship pricing, *405*
basic (lifeline) banking, *406*

Problems and Projects

1. Exeter National Bank reports the following figures in its current Report of Condition:

Assets (millions)		Liabilities (millions)	
Cash and interbank deposits	$ 50	Core deposits	$ 50
Short-term security investments	15	Large negotiable CDs	150
Total loans, gross	375	Deposits placed by brokers	65
Long-term securities	150	Other deposits	140
Other assets	10	Money market liabilities	95
Total assets	$600	Other liabilities	70
		Equity capital	30
		Total liabilities and equity capital	$600

a. Evaluate the funding mix of deposits and nondeposit sources of funds employed by Exeter. Given the mix of its assets, do you see any potential problems? What changes would you like to see management of this bank make? Why?

b. Suppose market interest rates are projected to rise significantly. Does Exeter appear to face significant losses due to liquidity risk? Due to interest rate risk? Please be as specific as possible.

2. Kalewood Savings Bank has experienced recent changes in the composition of its deposits (see the following table; all figures in millions of dollars). What changes have recently occurred in Kalewood's deposit mix? Do these changes suggest possible problems for management in trying to increase profitability and stabilize earnings?

Types of Deposits Held	This Year	One Year Ago	Two Years Ago	Three Years Ago
Regular and special checking accounts	$235	$294	$337	$378
Interest-bearing checking accounts	392	358	329	287
Regular (passbook) savings deposits	501	596	646	709
Money market deposit accounts	863	812	749	725
Retirement deposits	650	603	542	498
CDs under $100,000	327	298	261	244
CDs $100,000 and over	606	587	522	495

3. First Metrocentre Bank posts the following schedule of fees for its household and small business transaction accounts:

- For average monthly account balances over $1,500, there is no monthly maintenance fee and no charge per check or other draft.
- For average monthly account balances of $1,000 to $1,500, a $2 monthly maintenance fee is assessed and there is a 10¢ charge per check or charge cleared.
- For average monthly account balances of less than $1,000, a $4 monthly maintenance fee is assessed and there is a 15¢ per check or per charge fee.

What form of deposit pricing is this? What is First Metrocentre trying to accomplish with its pricing schedule? Can you foresee any problems with this pricing plan?

4. Diamond Pit Savings Association finds that it can attract the following amounts of deposits if it offers new depositors and those rolling over their maturing CDs the interest rates indicated below:

Expected Volume of New Deposits	Rate of Interest Offered Depositors
$10 million	5.00%
15 million	5.25
20 million	5.50
26 million	5.75
28 million	6.00

Management anticipates being able to invest any new deposits raised in loans yielding 7 percent. How far should this thrift institution go in raising its deposit interest rate in order to maximize total profits (excluding interest costs)?

5. Gold Brick Bank plans to launch a new deposit campaign next week in hopes of bringing in from $100 million to $600 million in new deposit money, which it expects to invest at a 7.75 percent yield. Management believes that an offer rate on new deposits of 5.75 percent would attract $100 million in new deposits and rollover funds. To attract $200 million, the bank would probably be forced to offer 6.25 percent. Gold

Brick's forecast suggests that $300 million might be available at 6.8 percent, $400 million at 7.25 percent, $500 million at 7.5 percent, and $600 million at 7.65 percent. What volume of deposits should the institution try to attract to ensure that marginal cost does not exceed marginal revenue?

6. Bender Savings Bank finds that its basic transaction account, which requires a $400 minimum balance, costs this savings bank an average of $2.65 per month in servicing costs (including labor and computer time) and $1.18 per month in overhead expenses. The savings bank also tries to build in a $0.50 per month profit margin on these accounts. What monthly fee should the bank charge each customer?

   Further analysis of customer accounts reveals that for each $100 above the $400 minimum in average balance maintained in its transaction accounts, Bender Savings saves about 5 percent in operating expenses with each account. For a customer who consistently maintains an average balance of $1,000 per month, how much should the bank charge in order to protect its profit margin?

7. Chris Orange maintains a savings deposit with Santa Paribe Credit Union. This past year Chris received $13.64 in interest earnings from his savings account. His savings deposit had the following average balance each month:

January	$400	July	$350
February	250	August	425
March	300	September	550
April	150	October	600
May	225	November	625
June	300	December	300

What was the annual percentage yield (APY) earned on Chris's savings account?

8. The National Bank of Taraville quotes an APY of 5 percent on a one-year money market CD sold to one of the small businesses in town. The firm posted a balance of $2,500 for the first 90 days of the year, $3,000 over the next 180 days, and $5,000 for the remainder of the year. How much in total interest earnings did this small business customer receive for the year?

Internet Exercises

1. Your education has paid off. You have stepped five years into the future and are reviewing your bank accounts. The money has just piled up. You have a joint account with your fianceé containing $175,000 to be used for your first home. You have a joint account with your mother containing $125,000, and you have an account in your own name with $55,000 for the necessities of life. All three accounts are at the Monarch National Bank. Go to the following FDIC Web site **www2.fdic.gov/edie** and have Edie determine the insurance coverage for the $355,000. How much is uninsured? Can you describe the rules determining coverage?

2. How has the composition of deposits changed at your favorite local depository institution over the past 10 years? You can find this deposit information for banks and savings institutions at the FDIC's Web site. Utilize the link Statistics on Depository Institutions at **www3.fdic.gov/sdi.** Using the points made in this chapter, explain why your local institution's mix of deposits is changing the way it is. How can depository institution managers influence the trends occurring in the composition of their deposits?

3. Which depository institutions currently quote the highest interest rates on checking accounts? Savings accounts? Money market deposits? Three- and six-months CDs? Visit **www.fisn.com, www.bankcd.com,** and **www.banx.com** for the answers.

**REAL NUMBERS
FOR REAL BANKS**   Assignment for Chapter 12

YOUR BANK'S DEPOSITS: VOLATILITY AND COST

Chapter 12 examines the major source of funds for depository institutions—*deposits*. The importance of attracting and maintaining deposits as a stable and low-cost source of funds cannot be overstated. This chapter begins by describing the different types of deposits, then explains why a depository institution's management is concerned with cost, volatility (risk of withdrawals), and the trade-off between the two. In this assignment, you will be comparing the character of your bank's deposits across time and with its peer group of banks to glean information concerning the cost and stability of this source of funds. Chapter 12's assignment is designed to develop your deposit-related vocabulary and to emphasize the importance of being able to attract funds in the form of deposits, which is unique to banks and thrift institutions.

The Character and Cost of Your Bank's Deposits— Trend and Comparative Analysis

A. **Data Collection:** Once again the FDIC's Web site located at **www3.fdic.gov/sdi/** will provide access to the data needed for your analysis. Use Statistics on Depository Institutions (SDI) to create a four-column report of your bank's information and peer group information across years. In this part of the assignment, for Report Selection use the pull-down menu to select Total Deposits and view this in Percentages of Total Assets. To assess the overall importance of deposits as a source of funding, focus on total deposits to total assets. From the Total Deposits report you will collect information to break down deposits in several ways: (1) total deposits into domestic deposits versus foreign; (2) total deposits into interest-bearing deposits versus noninterest-bearing deposits; and (3) domestic deposits into their basic types. All the data for rows 109–123 is available from the Total Deposits report; however, you will have to derive NOW accounts in Row 120 by subtracting demand deposits from transaction deposits. Finally we will go to the Interest Expense report and gather information on the proportion of interest paid for foreign and domestic deposits to total assets. Enter the percentage information for these items as an addition to the spreadsheet for comparisons with the peer group as follows:

B. Having collected all the data for Rows 109–125, you will calculate the entries for Rows 126 and 127. For example, the entry for Cell B126 is created using the formula function B124/B113.

C. Compare the columns of row 109. How has the reliance on deposits as a source of funds changed across periods? Has your bank relied more or less on depositors than the average bank in the peer group?

D. Use the chart function in Excel and the data by columns in rows 119 through 123 to create a group of four bar charts illustrating the types of domestic deposits supporting assets for your BHC and its peer group. You will be able to select the block and create the chart with just a few clicks of the mouse, saving it as a separate spreadsheet. Remember to provide titles, labels, and percentages; otherwise, we have something reminiscent of abstract art. To give you an example, the chart containing information for NCC and its peer group would appear as shown below. (Note that if you have access to a color printer you will not have to transform graphics to be effective in black and white as we have done below.)

E. Utilizing the information below, write approximately one page about your bank's use of deposits as a source of funds and how it compares to its peers. Use your bar charts as a graphic and incorporate tables from your Excel spreadsheets as references for the discussion. Provide inferences concerning interest costs and deposit volatility (withdrawal risk) based on the data you have to interpret.

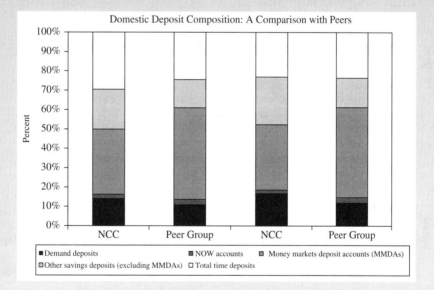

4. Compare your local depository institution's interest rates on six-month and one-year certificates of deposit (check newspaper ads, call its customer service line, or visit its Web site) with the best rates on these same savings instruments offered by depository institutions quoting the highest deposit interest rates in the United States. (See Web sites listed in Exercise 3.) Why do you think there are such large interest-rate differences between your local institution and those posting the highest interest rates?

S&P Market Insight Challenge (www.mhhe.com/edumarketinsight)

1. Deposits are normally the most important source of funds for depository institutions. For an up-to-date view of deposit growth use the Industry tab in Standard & Poor's Market Insight and employ the drop-down menu to select among the subindustry categories: Diversified Banks, Regional Banks, and Thrifts & Mortgage Finance. By selecting these subindustry groups, you will be able to access the S&P Industry Surveys on Banking and on Savings and Loans. Download both surveys and read the sections "Industry Trends" and "How the Industry Operates." Using this information describe recent trends in deposit availability and deposit growth for banks and thrifts.

2. The proportion of deposits versus other sources of funding that individual depository institutions draw upon varies greatly from institution to institution. To prove this to yourself, take advantage of the information S&P's Market Insight provides and try to determine the percentage of total assets represented by deposits at each of the leading banks the Web site covers. Which banks, in particular, have the highest deposit-to-asset ratios? Which report the lowest deposit-to-asset ratios? Can you explain these differences? Do you see any significant trends in deposit mix going on? What do they imply for management of the banks involved?

Selected References

For a discussion of recent trends in deposit services, see these sources:

1. Board of Governors of the Federal Reserve System. *Consumer Guide to Check 21 and Substitute Checks*, Washington, DC, 2004.
2. Federal Deposit Insurance Corporation. "Bank CDs: New Options, More Flexibility in Stashing Your Cash." *FDIC Consumer News*, Summer 2005, pp. 7, 10.
3. Gerdes, Geoffrey R., Jack K. Walton II, May X. Liu, and Darrel W. Parke. "Trends in the Use of Payment Instruments in the United States." *Federal Reserve Bulletin*, Spring 2005, pp. 180–201.
4. Santomero, Anthony M. "The Changing Patterns of Payments in the United States." *Business Review*, Federal Reserve Bank of Philadelphia, Third Quarter, 2005, pp. 1–8.
5. Rose, Peter S. "Pricing Deposits in an Era of Competition and Change." *The Canadian Banker* 93, no. 1 (February 1986), pp. 44–51.

For a discussion of the controversy over lifeline banking services, see:

6. Good, Barbara A. "Bringing the Unbanked Aboard." *Economic Commentary*, Federal Reserve Bank of Cleveland, January 15, 1999.

For a discussion of the role of depositors in disciplining bank risk taking and bank behavior, see especially:

7. Thompson, James B. "Raising the Deposit Insurance Limit: A Bad Idea Whose Time Has Come?" *Economic Commentary*, Federal Reserve Bank of Cleveland, April 15, 2000.
8. Vaughn, Mark D., and David C. Wheelock. "Deposit Insurance Reform: Is It Déjà Vu All Over Again?" *The Regional Economist*, Federal Reserve Bank of St. Louis, October 2002, pp. 5–9.

For a discussion of deposit pricing techniques, see these studies:

9. Dunham, Constance. "Unraveling the Complexity of NOW Account Pricing." *New England Economic Review*, Federal Reserve Bank of Boston, May/June 1983, pp. 30–45.

10. McNulty, James E. "Do You Know the True Cost of Your Deposits?" *Review*, Federal Home Loan Bank of Atlanta, October 1986, pp. 1–6.

For a discussion of recent trends in deposit service availability and service fees, see:

11. Anderson, Richard G. "Retail Sweep Programs and Money Demand." *Monetary Trends*, Federal Reserve Bank of St. Louis, November 2002.

12. Hannan, Timothy H. "Retail Fees of Depository Institutions, 1994–99." *Federal Reserve Bulletin*, January 2001, pp. 1–11.

For a discussion of the impact of the Truth in Savings Act on the cost of bank regulatory compliance, see:

13. Elliehausen, Gregory, and Barbara R. Lowrey. *The Cost of Implementing Consumer Financial Regulation: An Analysis of the Experience with the Truth in Savings Act.* Staff Study No. 170, Board of Governors of the Federal Reserve System, December 1997.

CHAPTER THIRTEEN

Managing Nondeposit Liabilities and Other Sources of Borrowed Funds

Key Topics in This Chapter

- Liability Management
- Customer Relationship Doctrine
- Alternative Nondeposit Funds Sources
- Measuring the Funds Gap
- Choosing among Different Funds Sources
- Determining the Overall Cost of Funds

13–1 Introduction

The traditional source of funds for depository institutions is the *deposit account*—both checking and savings deposits sold to individuals, businesses, and governments. Thus, the public's demand for deposits supplies much of the raw material for lending and investing and, ultimately, for the profits these institutions earn. But what does management do to find new money when deposit volume is inadequate to support all the loans and investments these institutions would like to make?

In Chapter 9 we found part of the answer to this question—services like standby credit letters and credit guarantees may be sold to bring in customer fees and loans may be securitized or sold outright to attract new funds in order to make new loans. Chapter 10 provided another part of the answer—when deposits don't bring in enough money some security investments, previously acquired, may be sold to generate more cash. In the present chapter we explore yet another important nondeposit source of funding—selling IOUs in the money and capital markets for periods of time that may stretch from overnight to several years.

13–2 Liability Management and the Customer Relationship Doctrine[1]

Managers of lending institutions learned over the years that turning down a profitable loan request with the excuse, "we don't have enough deposits or other funds sources to support

[1]Portions of this chapter are based on an article by Peter S. Rose in *The Canadian Banker* [6] and are used with permission.

Filmtoid
What 2003 drama casts
Philip Seymour
Hoffman as an assistant
bank manager with
authority over sources
and uses of funds at the
bank who cannot resist
the allure of Atlantic
City?
Answer: *Owning
Mahowny.*

the loan," is not well received by their customers. Denial of a credit request often means the immediate loss of a customer account and perhaps the loss of any future business from the disappointed customer. On the other hand, granting a loan request—even when deposits and other cash flows are inadequate—usually brings in both new deposits and the demand for other financial services as well. And the benefits may reach far beyond the borrowing customer alone. For example, a loan made to a business firm often brings in personal accounts from the firm's owners and employees.

The financial community learned long ago the importance of the **customer relationship doctrine**. This doctrine proclaims that the *first* priority of a lending institution is to make loans to all those customers from whom the lender expects to receive positive net earnings. Thus, lending decisions often *precede* funding decisions; all loans and investments whose returns exceed their costs and whose quality meets the lending institution's credit standards should be made. If enough deposits are not immediately available to cover these loans and investments, then management should seek out the lowest-cost source of borrowed funds available to meet its customers' credit needs.

Key URL
To learn more about
liability management,
see, for example, ALM
professional at
**www.almprofessional
.com.**

During the 1960s and 1970s, the customer relationship doctrine spawned the liquidity management strategy known as **liability management,** introduced in Chapters 7 and 11. Liability management consists of *buying funds*, mainly from other financial institutions, in order to cover good-quality credit requests and satisfy any legal reserve requirements on deposits and other borrowings that law or regulation may require. As we saw in Chapter 11, a lending institution may acquire funds by borrowing short term in the domestic Federal funds market, borrowing abroad through the Eurocurrency market, selling money market or jumbo ($100,000+) negotiable CDs to customers, securing a loan from the central bank or other government agency, negotiating security repurchase agreements with individuals and institutions having temporary surpluses of funds, issuing commercial paper through a subsidiary part of the same holding company, or even selling debentures (long-term debt) to raise capital for the long haul.

Table 13–1 illustrates the basic idea behind liability management. In this instance, one of a lender's business customers has requested a new loan amounting to $100 million. However, the deposit division reports that only $50 million in new deposits are expected today. If management wishes to fully meet the loan request of $100 million, it must find another $50 million from nondeposit sources. Some quick work by the lender's money market division, which called correspondent banks inside the United States and in London and negotiated with nonbank institutions with temporary cash surpluses, resulted in

TABLE 13–1
Sample Use of
Nondeposit Funds
Sources to
Supplement Deposits
and Make Loans

First National Bank and Trust Company Balance Sheet (Report of Condition)	
Assets	**Liabilities and Equity**
Loans: New loans to be made, $100,000,000	Funding sources found to support the new loans: Newly deposited funds expected today $ 50,000,000
	Nondeposit funds sources:
	Federal funds purchased 19,000,000
	Borrowings of Eurodollars abroad 20,000,000
	Securities sold under agreements to repurchase (RPs) 3,000,000
	Borrowings from a nonbank subsidiary of the bank's holding company that sold commercial paper in the money market +8,000,000
	Total new deposit and nondeposit funds raised to cover the new loans $100,000,000

Insights and Issues

raising the entire $50 million by borrowing domestic Federal funds, borrowing funds from a subsidiary part of the same holding company that sold notes (commercial paper) in the open market, selling investment securities under a security repurchase agreement, and borrowing Eurodollars from branch offices abroad.

Unfortunately, the money market division cannot rest on their laurels. They know that most of the $50 million just raised will be available only until tomorrow when many of the borrowed funds must be returned to their owners. These departing borrowed funds will need to be replaced quickly to continue to support the new loan. Customers who receive loans spend their funds quickly (otherwise, why get a loan?) by writing checks and wiring funds to other financial institutions. This lender, therefore, must find sufficient new funds to honor all those outgoing checks and wire transfers of funds that its borrowing customers initiate.

Clearly, liability management is an essential tool lenders need to sustain the growth of their lending programs. However, liability management also poses real challenges for financial-service managers, who must keep abreast of the market every day to make sure their institution is fully funded. Moreover, liability management is an *interest-sensitive* approach to raising funds. If interest rates rise and the lender is unwilling to pay those higher rates, funds borrowed from the money market will be gone in minutes. Money-market suppliers of funds typically have a highly elastic response to changes in market interest rates.

Yet, viewed from another perspective, funds raised by the use of liability management techniques are *flexible*: the borrower can decide exactly how much he or she needs and for how long and usually find a source of funds that meets those requirements. In contrast, when deposits are sold to raise funds, it is the depositor who decides how much and how long funds will be left with each financial firm. With liability management institutions in need of more funds to cover expanding loan commitments or deficiencies in legal reserves can simply raise their offer rate in order to reduce their volume of money market borrowing.

Thus, the hallmarks of liability management are (1) *buying funds* by selling liabilities in the money market and (2) *using price* (the interest rate offered) as the control lever to regulate the volume and timing of incoming funds. We should note, however, that individual firms cannot set the price they ultimately pay for borrowed funds. Rather it is the competitive marketplace that performs that job.

Key URL

To find out what kinds of nondeposit borrowings U.S. depository institutions are drawing upon see especially **www.fdic.gov**, typing in each institution's name and location.

13–3 Alternative Nondeposit Sources of Funds

As Table 13–2 suggests, the dollar usage of nondeposit sources of funds has fluctuated in recent years, but generally it has risen to provide a bigger share of funds for depository institutions. While smaller banks and thrift institutions usually rely most heavily on deposits for their funding needs, leading depository institutions around the globe have come to regard the nondeposit funds market as a key source of short-term money to meet both loan demand and unexpected cash emergencies.

Table 13–3 shows the relationship between the size of banks and thrifts and their affinity for nondeposit borrowing. Clearly, the smallest-size banks and thrift institutions (each under $100 million in assets) support only a small share (between 4 and 6 percent) of their assets by nondeposit borrowings. Among the largest depository institutions (over $1 billion in assets), however, nondeposit borrowings covered over 20 percent of large commercial bank assets and more than a quarter of the assets of the largest thrift institutions.

Overall, nondeposit borrowings have often outstripped the growth of traditional deposits, as Table 13–2 suggests, in part because of the greater flexibility of nondeposit borrowings, which are less regulated, and the loss of some deposits in recent years to competing financial institutions, such as mutual funds, insurance companies, hedge funds, and pension funds, that are competing aggressively today to attract the public's savings. In the sections that follow we examine the most popular nondeposit funds sources that financial firms use today.

Federal Funds Market ("Fed Funds")

The most popular domestic source of borrowed reserves among depository institutions is the **Federal funds market.** Originally, Fed funds consisted exclusively of deposits U.S. banks held at the Federal Reserve banks. These deposits are owned by depository institutions and are held at the Fed primarily to satisfy legal reserve requirements, clear checks, and pay for purchases of government securities. These Federal Reserve balances can be transferred from

TABLE 13–2   Recent Growth in Nondeposit Sources of Borrowed Funds at FDIC-Insured Banks and Thrifts

Sources: Board of Governors of the Federal Reserve System and Federal Deposit Insurance Corporation.

Nondeposit Sources of Borrowed Funds	Billions of Dollars at Year-End:								
	1990	1992	1994	1996	1998	2000	2002	2004	2005*
Money market negotiable (jumbo) CDs ($100,000+)	$ 431.8	$ 366.5	$ 344.9	$ 476.9	$ 671.4	$ 821.3	$ 814.0	$1,067.1	$1,204.1
Eurodollar borrowings from own foreign offices	168.0	160.4	185.9	177.3	148.8	194.3	231.5	382.6	419.7
Federal funds borrowings and security RPs	180.1	149.9	221.1	199.8	206.1	235.5	476.8	479.3	504.4
Commercial paper issued**	420.8	406.5	443.7	601.2	936.2	1,275.8	1,194.0	1,268.2	1,467.3
Borrowings from the Federal Reserve Banks	0.3	0.1	0.5	0.2	0.1	0.2	0.1	0.1	0.1
Total nondeposit funds raised by U.S.-insured banks and thrifts	$1,201.0	$1,083.4	$1,196.1	$1,455.4	$1,962.5	2,527.1	2,716.4	3,197.3	3,595.6
Total deposits of FDIC-insured depository institutions	$3,637.3	$3,527.1	$3,611.6	$3,925.2	$4,386.1	$4,914.8	$5,568.7	6,584.2	6,820.9
Ratio of nondeposit funds to total deposits for all FDIC-insured banks and thrifts	33%	31%	33%	37%	45%	51%	49%	49%	53%

Notes: *Figures for 2005 are through the second quarter or through September. **Includes all finance-company paper issued directly to investors by banks and other financial-service providers.

TABLE 13–3

The Relationship between the Size of Depository Institutions and Their Use of Nondeposit Borrowings (2005 figures for FDIC-insured banks and thrifts)

Source: Federal Deposit Insurance Corporation.

Size Group and Type of Depository Institution	Percent of Assets Supported by Nondeposit Borrowings
The largest U.S. commercial banks (over $1 billion in assets)	22%
The smallest U.S. commercial banks (under $100 million in assets)	4
The largest U.S. nonbank thrift institutions (over $1 billion in assets)	27%
The smallest U.S. nonbank thrift institutions (under $100 million in assets)	6

Notes: Thrift institutions include savings and loan associations and savings banks insured by the Federal Deposit Insurance Corporation.

one institution to another in seconds through the Fed's wire transfer network (Fedwire), linking all Federal Reserve banks. Today, however, correspondent deposits that depository institutions hold with each other also can be moved around the banking system the same day a request is made. The same is true of large collected demand deposit balances that securities dealers and governments own. All three of these types of deposits make up the raw material traded in the market for Federal funds. In technical terms, Fed funds are simply short-term borrowings of *immediately available money*.

It did not take financial institutions long to realize the potential source of profits inherent in these *same-day monies*. Because reserves deposited with the Federal Reserve banks and most demand deposits held by business firms pay no interest, bank and nonbank firms have a strong economic incentive to lend excess reserves or any demand deposit balances not needed to cover immediate cash needs. Moreover, there are no legal reserve requirements on Fed funds borrowings currently and few regulatory controls—features that have stimulated the growth of the market and helped keep the cost of borrowing down. Financial firms in need of immediate funds can negotiate a loan with a holder of surplus interbank deposits or reserves at the Fed, promising to return the borrowed funds the next day if need be.

The main use of the Fed funds market today is still the traditional one: a mechanism that allows depository institutions short of reserves to meet their legal reserve requirements or to satisfy loan demand by tapping immediately usable funds from other institutions possessing temporarily idle funds. Fed funds are also used to supplement deposit growth and give lenders a relatively safe outlet for temporary cash surpluses on which interest can be earned (even for a loan lasting only a few hours). Moreover, the Fed funds market serves as a conduit for the policy initiatives of the Federal Reserve System designed to control the growth of money and credit and stabilize the economy.

By performing all of these functions, the Fed funds market efficiently distributes reserves throughout the financial system to areas of greatest need. To help suppliers and demanders of Fed funds find each other, funds brokers soon appeared to trade Fed funds in return for commissions. Large correspondent banks, known as *accommodating banks*, play a role similar to that of funds brokers for smaller depository institutions in their region. An accommodating bank buys and sells Fed funds simultaneously in order to make a market for the reserves of its customer institutions, even though the accommodating bank itself may have no need for extra funds at the moment.

The procedure for borrowing and lending Fed funds is a simple one. Borrowing and lending institutions communicate either directly with each other or indirectly through a correspondent bank or funds broker. Once borrowing and lending institutions agree on the terms of a Fed funds loan, the lending institution arranges to transfer reserves from a deposit it holds, either at the Federal Reserve bank in its district or with a correspondent bank, into a deposit controlled by the borrowing institution. This may be accomplished by wiring Fed funds if the borrowing and lending institutions are in different regions of the country. If lender and borrower hold reserve deposits with the same Federal Reserve bank or with the same correspondent bank, the lending institution simply asks that bank to

Key URLs

If you would like to study the Federal funds market in greater detail, see **www.finance-encyclopedia.com** and **www.federalreserve.gov/fomc/fundsrate.htm**.

transfer funds from its reserve account to the borrower's reserve account—a series of book-keeping entries accomplished in seconds via computer. When the loan comes due, the funds are automatically transferred back to the lending institution's reserve account. (See Table 13–4 for a description of the bookkeeping entries involved.) The interest owed may also be transferred at this time, or the borrower may simply send a check to the lender to cover any interest owed.

TABLE 13–4 The Mechanics of Borrowing and Lending Federal Funds (in millions of dollars)

Step 1. Lending Reserve Balances Held at the Federal Reserve Banks

Lender's Balance Sheet

Assets		Liabilities and Net Worth
Federal funds sold (loaned)	+100	
Reserves on deposit at the Fed	−100	

Borrower's Balance Sheet

Assets		Liabilities and Net Worth	
Reserves on deposit at the Fed	+100	Federal funds purchased (borrowed)	+100

Step 2. Borrower Uses the Funds It Obtains to Make Loans

Borrower's Balance Sheet

Assets		Liabilities and Net Worth
Reserves on deposit at the Fed	−100	
Loans	+100	

Step 3. Repaying the Loan of Fed Funds

Lender's Balance Sheet

Assets		Liabilities and Net Worth
Reserves on deposit at the Fed	+100	
Federal funds sold (loaned)	−100	

Borrower's Balance Sheet

Assets		Liabilities and Net Worth	
Reserves on deposit at the Fed	−100	Federal funds purchased	−100

Step 4. Lending Fed Funds by a Respondent (usually smaller) Depository Institution to a Correspondent (usually larger) Depository Institution

Lender's (respondent's) Balance Sheet

Assets		Liabilities and Net Worth
Deposits held with correspondent	−100	
Federal funds loaned	+100	

Borrower's (correspondent's) Balance Sheet

Assets		Liabilities and Net Worth	
		Federal funds purchased	+100
		Respondent's deposit	−100

(continued)

TABLE 13–4 The Mechanics of Borrowing and Lending Federal Funds (*concluded*)

Step 5. The Corespondent Institution May Use the Fed Funds Borrowed to Meet Its Own Reserve Needs or Loan Those Funds to Another Institution (usually located in a major money center where credit demands are heavy)

Correspondent Lender's Balance Sheet		Money Center Borrower's Balance Sheet	
Assets	Liabilities and Net Worth	Assets	Liabilities and Net Worth
Reserves −100		Reserves +100	Federal funds purchased +100
Federal funds loaned +100			

Step 6. Repaying the Loan to the Respondent Institution

Respondent Institution		Correspondent Institution	
Assets	Liabilities and Net Worth	Assets	Liabilities and Net Worth
Deposits held with correspondent +100			Federal funds purchased −100
Federal funds loaned −100			Respondent's bank deposit +100

Key URL
For a look at the rapidly developing Fed funds futures market, see **www.cbot.com/** and explore "Interest Rate Product Information" in the Chicago Board of Trade's (CBOT's) Knowledge Center.

The interest rate on a Fed funds loan is subject to negotiation between borrowing and lending institutions. While the interest rate attached to each Fed funds loan may differ from the rate on any other loan, most of these loans use the *effective interest rate* prevailing each day—a rate of interest posted by Fed funds brokers and major accommodating banks operating at the center of the funds marketplace. In recent years, tiered Fed funds rates (i.e., interest-rate schedules) have appeared at various times, with borrowing institutions in trouble paying higher interest rates or simply being shut out of the market completely.

The Fed funds market uses three types of loan agreements: (1) overnight loans, (2) term loans, and (3) continuing contracts. *Overnight loans* are unwritten agreements, negotiated via wire or telephone, with the borrowed funds returned the next day. Normally these loans are not secured by specific collateral, though where borrower and lender do not know each other well or there is doubt about the borrower's credit standing, the borrower may be required to place selected government securities in a custody account in the name of the lender until the loan is repaid. *Term loans* are longer-term Fed funds contracts lasting several days, weeks, or months, often accompanied by a written contract. *Continuing contracts* are automatically renewed each day unless either borrower or lender decides to end this agreement. Most continuing contracts are made between smaller respondent institutions and their larger correspondents, with the correspondent automatically investing the smaller institution's deposits held with it in Fed funds loans until told to do otherwise.

Repurchase Agreements as a Source of Funds

Key URLs
Additional information about RPs may be found at **www.richmondfed.org/publications/**, **www.riskglossary.com/articles/repo.htm**, and **www.finance-encyclopedia.com**.

Repurchase agreements (RPs) are very similar to Fed funds transactions and are often viewed as collateralized Fed funds transactions. In a Fed funds transaction, the seller (lender) is exposed to credit risk via the uncertainty that the borrowing institution may not have the funds to repay. If the purchaser of Fed funds were to provide collateral in the form of marketable securities, credit risk would be reduced. The reduction in credit risk is exemplified in the lower cost of RPs when compared to Fed funds rates. Most RPs are transacted across the Fed Wire system, just as are Fed funds transactions. RPs may take a bit longer to transact because the seller of funds (the lender) must be satisfied with the quality and quantity of securities provided as collateral.[2]

RPs get their name from the process involved—the institution purchasing funds (the borrower) is temporarily exchanging securities for cash. They involve the temporary sale of high-quality, easily liquidated assets, such as Treasury bills, accompanied by an agreement to buy back those assets on a specific future date at a predetermined price. (See Table 13–5.) An RP transaction is often for overnight funds; however, it may be extended for months.

The interest cost for both Fed funds and repurchase agreements can be calculated from the following formula:

$$\frac{\text{Interest}}{\text{cost of RP}} = \frac{\text{Amount}}{\text{borrowed}} \times \frac{\text{Current}}{\text{RP rate}} \times \frac{\text{Number of days in RP borrowing}}{360 \text{ days}} \quad \textbf{(13–1)}$$

For example, suppose a bank borrows $50 million through an RP transaction collateralized by government bonds for three days and the current RP rate in the market is 6 percent. Then this bank's total interest cost would be:

$$\frac{\text{Interest}}{\text{cost of RP}} = \$50,000,000 \times 0.06 \times \frac{3}{360} = \$24,995$$

A major innovation occurred in the RP market with the invention of *General Collateral Finance (GCF) RPs* in 1998 under the leadership of the Bank of New York, J. P. Morgan Chase, and the Fixed Income Clearing Corporation (FICC). What is a GCF RP? How does it differ from the traditional RP?

TABLE 13–5 Raising Loanable Funds through a Repurchase Agreement Involving the Borrower's Securities (in millions of dollars)

Step 1. Bank Sells Some of Its Securities under an RP Agreement

Commercial Bank				Temporary Buyer of the Bank's Securities		
Assets		Liabilities and Net Worth		Assets		Liabilities and Net Worth
Securities	−100			Securities	+100	
Reserves	+100			Cash account	−100	

Step 2. The RP Agreement Ends and the Securities Are Returned

Commercial Bank				Temporary Buyer of the Bank's Securities		
Assets		Liabilities and Net Worth		Assets		Liabilities and Net Worth
Securities	+100			Securities	−100	
Reserves	−100			Cash account	+100	

[2]As a result of losses on RPs associated with the collapse of two government securities dealers in 1985, Congress passed the Government Securities Act, which requires dealers in U.S. government securities to report their activities and requires borrowers and lenders to put their RP contracts in writing, specifying the nature and location of collateral.

Conventional (fixed-collateral) repurchase agreements designate specific securities to serve as collateral for a loan, with the lender taking possession of those particular instruments until the loan matures. In contrast, the general-collateral GCF RP permits low-cost *collateral substitution*. Borrower and lender can agree upon a variety of securities, any of which may serve as loan collateral. This agreed-upon array of eligible collateral might include, for example, any obligation of the U.S. Treasury or a federal agency. Thus, the same securities pledged at the beginning do not have to be delivered at the end of a loan. Moreover, GCF RPs are settled on the books of the FICC, which allows *netting* of obligations between lenders, borrowers, and brokers so that less money and securities must be transferred. Finally, GCF RPs are reversed early in the morning and settled late each day, giving borrowers greater flexibility during daylight hours in deciding what to do with collateral securities. Overall, GCF RPs make more efficient use of collateral, lower transactions cost, and help make the RP market more liquid, helping to explain their explosive growth. (For further discussion of this important RP innovation, see especially Fleming and Garbade [2].)

Concept Check

13–1.   What is *liability management?*

13–2.   What advantages and risks does the pursuit of liability management bring to a borrowing institution?

13–3.   What is the *customer relationship doctrine,* and what are its implications for fund-raising by lending institutions?

13–4.   For what kinds of funding situations are Federal funds best suited?

13–5.   Chequers State Bank loans $50 million from its reserve account at the Federal Reserve Bank of Philadelphia to First National Bank of Smithville, located in the New York Federal Reserve Bank's district, for 24 hours, with the funds returned the next day. Can you show the correct accounting entries for making this loan and for the return of the loaned funds?

13–6.   Hillside Savings Association has an excess balance of $35 million in a deposit at its principal correspondent, Sterling City Bank, and instructs the latter institution to loan the funds today to another institution, returning them to its correspondent deposit the next business day. Sterling loans the $35 million to Imperial Security National Bank for 24 hours. Can you show the proper accounting entries for the extension of this loan and for the recovery of the loaned funds by Hillside Savings?

13–7.   Compare and contrast Fed funds transactions with RPs.

13–8.   What are the principal advantages to the borrower of funds under an RP agreement?

Borrowing from the Federal Reserve Bank

For a depository institution with immediate reserve needs, a viable alternative to Fed funds and RPs is negotiating a loan from a central bank for a short period of time. For example, depository institutions operating in the United States may be eligible for loans granted by the Federal Reserve Bank in their particular region. The Fed will make the loan through its **discount window** by crediting the borrowing institution's reserve account. (See Table 13–6 for an overview of the typical accounting entries associated with a discount window loan.)

Each loan made by the Federal Reserve Banks must be backed by collateral acceptable to the Fed. Most depository institutions keep U.S. government securities in the vaults of the Federal Reserve banks for this purpose. The Fed will also accept certain federal agency securities, high-grade commercial paper, and other assets judged satisfactory by the Fed.

Real Banks, Real Decisions

CHARGING U.S. DEPOSITORY INSTITUTIONS A "LOMBARD RATE"? WHAT'S THAT?

The Federal Reserve's recent changes in the rules (Regulation A) governing its discount window loans bring this aspect of U.S. central banking much closer to what central banks in Europe do.

Before 2003 the Federal Reserve's discount rate was frequently the lowest interest rate in the money market and often below the Fed funds interest rate. With the discount rate so low, many depository institutions were tempted to borrow from the Fed and relend the money in the Fed funds market. Some did!

Today the U.S. primary-credit discount rate is now set one percentage point *higher* than the Fed funds interest rate on overnight loans, which the Federal Reserve is using as a target to stabilize the economy. Setting the Fed's discount rate above market mirrors the "Lombard" credit facilities used by several European central banks. (Incidentally, the term *Lombard* owes its origin to a German word for *collateralized loan.* One of the earliest users of above-market loan rates for banks in need of funds was the Bundesbank, Germany's central bank.) Today these Lombard loan rates are employed by the European Central Bank (ECB) and the central banks of Austria, Belgium, France, Germany, Italy, and Sweden. Similar lending rules were adopted recently by the Bank of Canada and the Bank of Japan.

With the discount or Lombard rate set *above* market levels for similar loans, central banks are less inclined to restrict borrowing from the discount window and less concerned about what borrowers do with the money. Moreover, recent evidence suggests that an above-market Lombard rate tends to act as a ceiling on overnight borrowing rates and should serve as an effective ceiling for the U.S. Fed funds interest rate in the years ahead.

Three types of loans are available from the Fed's discount window:

1. **Primary credit**—loans available for short terms (usually overnight but occasionally extending over a few weeks) to depository institutions in sound financial condition. Primary credit normally carries an interest rate one percentage point above the Federal Reserve's target Fed funds interest rate. Users of primary credit do not have to show (as

TABLE 13–6
Borrowing Reserves from the Federal Reserve Bank in the District (in millions of dollars)

Securing a Loan from a Federal Reserve Bank			
Borrowing Depository Institution		**Federal Reserve Bank**	
Assets	Liabilities and Net Worth	Assets	Liabilities and Net Worth
Reserves on deposit at the Federal Reserve Bank +100	Notes Payable +100	Loan and advances +100	Bank reserve accounts +100

Repaying a Loan from a Federal Reserve Bank			
Borrowing Depository Institution		**Federal Reserve Bank**	
Assets	Liabilities and Net Worth	Assets	Liabilities and Net Worth
Reserves on deposit at the Federal Reserve bank −100	Notes Payable −100	Loan and advances −100	Bank reserve accounts −100

Key URLs

For further information about borrowing from the Federal Reserve's discount window, see **www.kc.frb.org/CRM/DiscountWindow/Discountwindow.htm**, **www.clevelandfed.org/DiscountWindow**, and **www.frbdiscount window.org**.

they did in the past) that they have exhausted other sources of funds before asking the Fed for a loan. Moreover, the borrowing institution is no longer prohibited from borrowing from the Fed and then loaning that money to other depository institutions in the Fed funds market.

2. **Secondary credit**—loans available at a higher interest rate to depository institutions not qualifying for primary credit. These loans are subject to monitoring by the Federal Reserve banks to make sure the borrower is not taking on excessive risk. The interest rate on secondary credit normally is set 50 basis points above the primary credit rate and 150 basis points above the Fed funds rate. Such a loan can be used to help resolve financial problems, to strengthen the borrowing institution's ability to find additional funds from private-market sources, and to reduce its debt to the Fed. However, secondary credit cannot be used to fund the expansion of a borrowing institution's assets.

3. **Seasonal credit**—loans covering longer periods than primary credit for small and medium-sized depository institutions experiencing seasonal (intrayear) swings in their deposits and loans (such as those swings experienced by farm banks during planting and harvesting time). The seasonal credit interest rate is set at the average level of the effective Fed funds rate and the secondary market rate on 90-day certificates of deposit.

Each type of discount-window loan carries its own loan rate, with secondary credit generally posting the highest interest rate and seasonal credit the lowest. For example, in December 2005 the Federal Reserve's discount window loan rates were 5.25 percent for primary credit, 5.75 percent for secondary credit, and 4.20 percent for seasonal credit.

Key URLs

You can learn more about FHLB advances from such Web sites as **www.fhlbboston.com/** and **www.stlouisfed.org/publications**.

In 1991 the U.S. Congress passed the FDIC Improvement Act, which places limits on how far the Federal Reserve banks can go in supporting a troubled depository institution with loans. Generally speaking, undercapitalized institutions cannot be granted discount window loans for more than 60 days in each 120-day period. Long-term Fed support is only permissible if the borrowing institution is a "viable entity." If the Fed exceeds these limitations, it could be held liable to the FDIC for any losses incurred by the insurance fund should the troubled institution ultimately fail.

Advances from the Federal Home Loan Banks

Recently another government agency—the Federal Home Loan Bank (FHLB) System—has been lending huge amounts of money to scores of home mortgage lenders. The FHLB System, composed of 12 regional banks, was created by federal charter in 1932 in order to extend cash advances to depository institutions experiencing runs by anxious depositors. By allowing these troubled institutions to use the home mortgages they held in their portfolios as collateral for emergency loans, the FHLB improved the liquidity of home mortgages and encouraged more lenders to provide credit to the housing market.

In recent years the number of financial institutions eligible to borrow from the FHLB has increased dramatically, especially among smaller community banks and thrift institutions. By 2003 nearly 6,000 commercial banks, more than 1,300 thrift institutions, over 700 credit unions, and close to 80 insurance companies had FHLB loans, amounting collectively to more than $500 billion. (See especially Maloney and Thomson [5].) Managers of mortgage-lending institutions are attracted to FHLB loans because they represent a stable source of funding at below-market interest rates. Fully collateralized by home mortgages the maturities of FHLB loans range from overnight to more than 20 years, bearing either fixed or variable interest rates. The system's federal charter enables it to borrow money cheaply and pass those savings along to member institutions who also hold FHLB stock and receive dividends on that stock. Should a borrowing institution fail, the FHLB, legally, is first in line (even ahead of the FDIC) in recovering its funds.

Development and Sale of Large Negotiable CDs

The concept of liability management and short-term borrowing to supplement deposit growth was given a significant boost early in the 1960s with the development of a new kind of deposit, the **negotiable CD.** This funding source is really a *hybrid* account: legally, it is a deposit, but, in practical terms, the negotiable CD is just another form of IOU issued to tap temporary surplus funds held by large corporations, wealthy individuals, and governments. A CD is an interest-bearing receipt evidencing the deposit of funds in the accepting depository institution for a specified time period at a specified interest rate or specified formula for calculating the interest rate.

There are four main types of negotiable CDs today. *Domestic* CDs are issued by U.S. institutions inside the territory of the United States. Dollar-denominated CDs issued by banks outside the United States are known as *EuroCDs*. The largest foreign banks active in the United States (such as Deutsche Bank and HSBC) sell CDs through their U.S. branches, called *Yankee* CDs. Finally, nonbank savings institutions sell *thrift* CDs.

During the 1960s, faced with slow growth in checkbook deposits held by their largest customers because these customers had found other higher-yielding outlets for their cash surpluses, U.S. money center banks began to search the market for new sources of funds. First National City Bank of New York (now Citibank), one of the most innovative financial firms in the world, was the first to develop the large ($100,000+) negotiable CD in 1961. Citigroup designed this marketable deposit to compete for funds with government bills and other well-known money market instruments. It was made large enough—generally sold in multiples of $1 million—to appeal to major corporations holding large quantities of liquid funds. Negotiable CDs would be confined to short maturities, ranging from seven days to one or two years in most cases, but concentrated mainly in the one- to six-month maturity range for the convenience of the majority of CD buyers. And the new instrument would be *negotiable*—able to be sold in the secondary market any number of times before reaching maturity—in order to provide corporate customers with liquidity in case their cash surpluses proved to be smaller or less stable than originally forecast. To make the sale of negotiable CDs in advance of their maturity easier, they were issued in *bearer* form. Moreover, several dealers agreed to make a market in negotiable CDs carrying maturities of six months or less.

The negotiable CD was an almost instant success. Large-denomination CDs grew from zero in the early 1960s to nearly $100 billion by the end of the 1960s and then surged upward during the high interest rate period of the 1970s and early 1980s. By the summer of 2005, time accounts of $100,000+ at U.S. banks totaled more than a trillion dollars. Thrift institutions issued close to $200 billion of these large CDs. As with all liability management instruments, management can control the quantity of CDs outstanding simply by varying the yield offered to CD customers.

Interest rates on *fixed-rate* CDs, which represent the majority of all large negotiable CDs issued, are quoted on an interest-bearing basis, and the rate is computed assuming a 360-day year. For example, suppose a depository institution promises an 8 percent annual interest rate to the buyer of a $100,000 six-month (180-day) CD. The depositor will have the following at the end of six months:

$$\text{Amount due CD customer} = \text{Principal} + \text{Principal} \times \frac{\text{Days to maturity}}{360 \text{ days}} \times \text{Annual rate of interest}$$

Key URLs
For a closer look at the market for negotiable CDs, see such Web sites as **www.richmondfed.org/publications** and **www.investopedia.com.**

$$= \$100,000 + \$100,000 \times \frac{180}{360} \times 0.08 \qquad \textbf{(13–2)}$$
$$= \$100,000 + \$4,000$$
$$= \$104,000$$

CDs that have maturities over one year normally pay interest to the depositor every six months. *Variable-rate* CDs have their interest rates reset after a designated period of time (called a *leg* or *roll* period). The new rate is based on a mutually accepted reference interest rate, such as the London Interbank Offer Rate (LIBOR) attached to borrowings of Eurodollar deposits or the average interest rate prevailing on prime-quality CDs traded in the secondary market.

The net result of CD sales to customers is often a simple transfer of funds from one deposit to another within the same depository institution, particularly from checkable deposits into CDs. The selling institution gains loanable funds even from this simple transfer because, in the United States at least, legal reserve requirements are currently zero for CDs, while checking accounts at the largest depository institutions carry a reserve requirement of 10 percent. Also, deposit stability is likely to be greater for the receiving depository institution because the CD has a set maturity and normally will not be withdrawn until maturity. In contrast, checkable (demand) deposits can be withdrawn at any time. However, the sensitive interest rates attached to the largest negotiable CDs mean that depository institutions making heavy use of these instruments must work harder to combat more volatile earnings, including aggressive use of rate-hedging techniques, discussed in Chapters 7–9.

The Eurocurrency Deposit Market

The development of the U.S. negotiable CD market came on the heels of another deposit market that began in Europe in the 1950s—the **Eurocurrency deposit** market. Eurocurrency deposits were developed originally in Western Europe to provide liquid funds that could be swapped among multinational banks or loaned to the banks' largest customers. Most such international borrowing and lending has occurred in the Eurodollar market.

Eurodollars are dollar-denominated deposits placed in bank offices outside the United States. Because they are denominated on the receiving banks' books in dollars rather than in the currency of the home country and consist of bookkeeping entries in the form of *time deposits*, they are *not* spendable on the street like currency.[3]

The banks accepting these deposits may be foreign banks, branches of U.S. banks overseas, or international banking facilities (IBFs) set up on U.S. soil but devoted to foreign transactions on behalf of a parent U.S. bank. The heart of the worldwide Eurodollar market is in London, where British banks compete with scores of American and other foreign banks for euro deposits. The Eurocurrency market is the largest unregulated financial marketplace in the world.

A domestic financial firm can tap the Euromarket for funds by contacting one of the major international banks that borrow and lend Eurocurrencies every day. The largest U.S. banks also use their own overseas branches to tap this market. When one of these branches lends a Eurodeposit to its home office in the United States, the home office records the deposit in an account labeled *liabilities to foreign branches*. When a U.S. financial firm borrows Eurodeposits from a bank operating overseas, the transaction takes place through the correspondent banking system. The lending bank will instruct a U.S. correspondent bank

---

[3]In general, whenever a deposit is accepted by a bank denominated in the units of a currency other than the home currency, that deposit is known as a *Eurocurrency deposit*. While the Eurocurrency market began in Europe (hence the prefix *Euro*), it reaches worldwide today.

Key URLs

For more information about the Eurocurrency deposit markets, see **www.ny.frb.org/ education/index.html** and **www. investopedia.com**.

where it has a deposit to transfer funds in the amount of the Eurocurrency loan to the correspondent account of the borrowing institution. These borrowed funds will be quickly loaned to qualified borrowers or, perhaps, used to meet a reserve deficit. Later, when the loan falls due, the entries on the books of correspondent banks are reversed. This process of borrowing and lending Eurodollars is traced out in Table 13–7.

Most Eurodollar deposits are *fixed-rate time deposits*. Beginning in the 1970s, however, floating-rate CDs (FRCDs) and floating-rate notes (FRNs) were introduced in an effort to protect banks and their Eurodepositors from the risk of fluctuating interest rates. FRCDs

TABLE 13–7   U.S. Bank Borrowing Eurodollars from Foreign Banks (in millions of dollars)

Step 1. The Loan Is Made to a U.S. Bank from the Eurodollar Market

U.S. Bank Borrowing Eurodollars		U.S. Bank Serving as Correspondent to Foreign Bank		Foreign Bank Lending Eurodollars	
Assets	Liabilities	Assets	Liabilities	Assets	Liabilities
Deposits held at other banks +100	Deposits due to foreign bank +100 (Eurodollars borrowed)		Deposits due to foreign bank −100 Deposits of U.S. correspondent bank doing the borrowing +100 (Eurodollars borrowed)	Deposits at U.S. correspondent bank −100 Eurodollar loan to U.S. bank +100	

Step 2. The Loan Is Repaid by the Borrowing U.S. Bank

U.S. Bank Borrowing Eurodollars		U.S. Bank Serving as Correspondent to Foreign Bank		Foreign Bank Lending Eurodollars	
Assets	Liabilities	Assets	Liabilities	Assets	Liabilities
Deposits held at other banks −100	Deposits due to foreign bank −100 (Eurodollars borrowed)		Deposits due to foreign bank +100 Deposits of U.S. correspondent bank doing the borrowing −100 (Eurodollars borrowed)	Deposits at U.S. correspondent bank +100 Eurodollar loan to U.S. bank −100	

and FRNs tend to be medium term to long term, stretching from 1 year to as long as 20 years. The offer rates on these longer-term negotiable deposits are adjusted, usually every three to six months, based upon interest rate movements in the interbank Eurodollar market. The majority of Eurodollar deposits mature within six months; however, some are as short as overnight. Most are interbank liabilities whose interest yield is tied closely to LIBOR—the interest rate money center banks quote each other for the loan of short-term Eurodollar deposits. Large-denomination EuroCDs issued in the interbank market are called *tap CDs*, while smaller-denomination EuroCDs sold to a wide range of investors are called *tranche CDs*. As with domestic CDs, there is an active resale market for these deposits.

Major banks and their large corporate customers practice arbitrage between the Eurodollar and American CD markets. For example, if domestic CD rates were to drop significantly below Eurodollar interest rates on deposits of comparable maturity, a bank or its corporate customers could borrow in the domestic CD market and lend those funds offshore in the Euromarket. Similarly, an interest rate spread in the opposite direction might well lead to increased Eurodollar borrowings, with the proceeds flowing into CD markets inside the United States.

Commercial Paper Market

Late in the 1960s, large banks and finance companies faced with intense demand for loans found a new source of loanable funds—the **commercial paper market.** Commercial paper consists of short-term notes, with maturities ranging from three or four days to nine months, issued by well-known companies to raise working capital. The notes are generally sold at a discount from their face value through security dealers or through direct contact between the issuing company and interested investors.

A substantial portion of this paper—often called *industrial paper*—is designed to finance the purchase of inventories of goods or raw materials and to meet other immediate cash needs of nonfinancial companies. Another form of commercial paper—usually called *finance paper*—is issued mainly by finance companies (such as GE Capital Corporation) and the affiliates of financial holding companies (such as HSBC Finance Corporation). The proceeds from issuing finance paper can be used to purchase loans off the books of other financial firms in the same organization, giving these institutions additional funds to make new loans. Table 13–8 summarizes the process of indirect borrowing through commercial paper issued by affiliated firms.

Long-Term Nondeposit Funds Sources

The nondeposit sources of funds discussed to this point are mainly short-term borrowings. The loans involved range from hours to days, occasionally stretching into weeks or months with term Fed funds contracts, commercial paper, and similar funding instruments. However, many financial firms also tap longer-term nondeposit funds stretching well beyond one year. Examples include *mortgages* issued to fund the construction of buildings and *capital notes and debentures*, which usually range from 5 to 12 years in maturity and are used to supplement equity (owners') capital. Capital notes and debentures are discussed in greater detail in Chapter 15.

These longer-term nondeposit funds sources have remained relatively modest over the years due to regulatory restrictions and the augmented risks associated with long-term borrowing. Also, because most assets and liabilities held by depository institutions are short- to medium-term, issuing long-term indebtedness creates a significant maturity mismatch. Nevertheless, the favorable leveraging effects of such debt have made it attractive to large banking organizations and selected other financial firms in recent years.

Key URLs

Want to learn more about the commercial paper market? See the Web sites at **www.investopedia. com** and **http:// beginnersinvest.about. com.**

Key URLs

You can explore the nature of finance company roles and structure through such sites as **www. gecapital.com** and **www.hsbcusa.com/ hsbc_finance.**

Concept Check

13–9. What are the advantages of borrowing from the Federal Reserve banks or other central bank? Are there any disadvantages? What is the difference between primary, secondary, and seasonal credit? What is a Lombard rate and why might such a rate be useful in achieving monetary policy goals?

13–10. How is a discount window loan from the Federal Reserve secured? Is collateral really necessary for these kinds of loans?

13–11. Posner State Bank borrows $10 million in primary credit from the Federal Reserve Bank of Cleveland. Can you show the correct entries for granting and repaying this loan?

13–12. Which institutions are allowed to borrow from the Federal Home Loan Banks? Why is this source so popular for many institutions?

13–13. Why were negotiable CDs developed?

13–14. What are the advantages and disadvantages of CDs as a funding source?

13–15. Suppose a customer purchases a $1 million 90-day CD, carrying a promised 6 percent annualized yield. How much in interest income will the customer earn when this 90-day instrument matures?

What total volume of funds will be available to the depositor at the end of 90 days?

13–16. Where do Eurodollars come from?

13–17. How does a bank gain access to funds from the Eurocurrency markets?

13–18. Suppose that J. P. Morgan Chase Bank in New York elects to borrow $250 million from Barclays Bank in London and loans the borrowed funds for a week to a security dealer, and then returns the borrowed funds. Can you trace through the resulting accounting entries?

13–19. What is *commercial paper?* What types of organizations issue such paper?

13–20. Suppose that the finance company affiliate of Citigroup issues $325 million in 90-day commercial paper to interested investors and uses the proceeds to purchase loans from Citibank. What accounting entries should be made on the balance sheets of Citibank and Citigroup's finance company affiliate?

13–21. What long-term nondeposit funds sources do banks and some of their closest competitors draw upon today? How do these interest costs differ from those costs associated with most money market borrowings?

TABLE 13–8 Commercial Paper Borrowing by a Holding Company That Channels the Borrowed Funds to One of Its Affiliated Lending Institutions (in millions of dollars)

Step 1. Commercial Paper Is Sold by an Affiliated Corporation in the Money Market

Lending Institution		Affiliated Corporation	
Assets	Liabilities and Net Worth	Assets	Liabilities and Net Worth
		Cash account +100	Commercial paper +100

Step 2. The Affiliated Corporation Purchases Loans from Lenders That Are Part of the Same Organization

Lending Institution		Affiliated Corporation	
Assets	Liabilities and Net Worth	Assets	Liabilities and Net Worth
Loans −100 Reserves +100		Cash account −100 Loans purchased from lending institution +100	

Key URLs

For a further look at debentures and other types of long-term debt issued by banks and other depository institutions, see especially **www.frbsf. org/publications/ economics/letter/index. php** and **www. fanniemae.com**.

Because of the long-term nature of these funding sources, they tend to be a sensitive barometer of the perceived risk exposure (particularly the risk of default) of their issuing institutions. In 1990, for example, when there were fears of major bank defaults, the capital notes of troubled Southeast Banking Corp. and the Bank of Boston carried annual yields of close to 20 percent, while notes issued by the Bank of New England were trading at a discount equal to only about one-fifth of their face value. By June 2005 more than $100 billion in capital notes and debentures (subordinated to the claims of depositors) had been issued by all U.S. insured commercial banks.

13–4 Choosing among Alternative Nondeposit Sources

With so many different nondeposit funds sources to draw upon, managers of financial firms must make choices among them. In using nondeposit funds, funds managers must answer the following key questions:

1. How much in total must be borrowed from these sources to meet funding needs?
2. Which nondeposit sources are best, given the borrowing institution's goals, at any given moment in time?

Measuring a Financial Firm's Total Need for Nondeposit Funds: The Available Funds Gap

The demand for nondeposit funds is determined basically by the size of the *gap* between the institution's total credit demands and its deposits and other available monies. Managers responsible for the asset side of the institution's balance sheet must choose which of a wide variety of customer credit requests they will meet by adding direct loans and investment securities to the institution's asset portfolio. Management must be prepared to meet, not only today's credit requests, but all those it can reasonably anticipate in the future. This means that projections of current and anticipated credit demands must be based on knowledge of the current and probable future funding needs of each institution's customers, especially its largest borrowers. Such projections should not be wild guesses; they should be based on information gathered from frequent contacts between the financial firm's officers and both its existing and potential customers.

The second decision that must be made is how much in deposits and other available funds is likely to be attracted in order to finance the desired volume of loans and security investments. Projections must be made of customer deposits and withdrawals, with special attention to the largest customers. Deposit projections must take into account current and future economic conditions, interest rates, and the cash flow requirements of the largest customers.

The difference between current and projected outflows and inflows of funds yields an estimate of each institution's **available funds gap.** Thus,

$$\text{Available funds gap (AFG)} = \begin{array}{l} \text{Current and projected loans and} \\ \text{investments the lending institution} \\ \text{desires to make} - \text{Current and expected} \\ \text{deposit inflows and other available funds} \end{array} \quad \textbf{(13–3)}$$

For example, suppose a commercial bank has new loan requests that meet its quality standards of $150 million; it wishes to purchase $75 million in new Treasury securities being issued this week and expects drawings on credit lines from its best corporate customers of

$135 million. Deposits and other customer funds received today total $185 million, and those expected in the coming week will bring in another $100 million. This bank's estimated available funds gap (AFG) for the coming week will be as follows (in millions of dollars):

$$\text{AFG} = (\$150 + \$75 + \$135) - (\$185 + \$100)$$
$$= \$360 - \$285$$
$$= \$75$$

Most institutions will add a small amount to this available funds gap estimate to cover unexpected credit demands or unanticipated shortfalls in deposits and other inflowing funds. Various nondeposit funds sources then may be tapped to cover the estimated funds gap.

Nondeposit Funding Sources: Factors to Consider

Which nondeposit sources will management use to cover a projected available funds gap? The answer to that question depends largely upon five factors:

1. The *relative costs* of raising funds from each source.
2. The *risk* (volatility and dependability) of each funding source.
3. The *length of time* (maturity or term) for which funds are needed.
4. The *size of the institution* that requires more funds.
5. *Regulations* limiting the use of alternative funds sources.

Relative Costs

Managers of financial institutions practicing liability management must constantly be aware of the going market interest rates attached to different sources of borrowed funds. Major lenders post daily interest rates at which they are willing to commit funds to other financial firms in need of additional reserves. In general, managers would prefer to borrow from the cheapest sources of funds, although other factors do play a role.

A sample of interest rates on money market borrowings, averaged over selected years, is shown in Table 13–9. Note that the various funds sources vary significantly in *price*—the interest rate the borrowing institution must pay for use of the money. Usually the cheapest short-term borrowed funds source is the prevailing *effective interest rate on Federal funds*

TABLE 13–9   **Money Market Interest Rates Attached to Nondeposit Borrowings and Large ($100,000+) CDs**

Source: Board of Governors of the Federal Reserve System.

Sources of Borrowed Funds	Interest Rate Averages Quoted for the Years:						
	1994	1996	1998	2000	2002	2004	2005**
Federal funds borrowings	4.47%	5.30%	5.35%	6.24%	1.34%	1.35%	3.62%
Borrowings from the Federal Reserve banks*	3.76	5.00	4.98	5.50	1.25	2.34	4.59
Selling commercial paper (1-month, directly placed)	4.65	5.43	n.a.	6.27	1.68	1.41	3.69
Issuing negotiable CDs (secondary market, 1-month)	4.60	5.35	5.49	6.35	1.39	1.45	3.74
Selling Eurodollar deposits (3-month maturities)	4.80	5.38	5.44	6.45	1.39	1.55	3.85

Notes: *Averages for the year as posted by the Federal Reserve banks. Beginning in 2003 the quoted discount rate on loans from the Federal Reserve banks is the primary credit rate, initially set at 100 basis points above the Fed's target Federal funds interest rate.
**2005 figures are for September 2005.

loaned overnight to borrowing institutions. In most cases the interest rates attached to domestic CDs and Eurocurrency deposits are slightly higher than the Fed funds rate. Commercial paper (short-term unsecured notes) normally may be issued at interest rates slightly above the Fed funds and CD rates, depending upon their maturity and time of issue. Today the discount rate attached to loans from the Federal Reserve banks (known as the primary credit rate) is generally among the highest short-term borrowing rates because this form of Federal Reserve credit is generally priced a percentage point above the central bank's target for the Fed funds rate.

Although low compared to most other borrowing rates, the effective Fed funds rate prevailing in the marketplace tends to be volatile, fluctuating around the central bank's target (intended) Fed funds rate, rising or falling several times each day. The key advantage of Fed funds is their ready availability through a simple phone call or online computer request. Moreover, their maturities often are flexible and may be as short as a few hours or last as long as several months. The key disadvantage of Fed funds, as we noted above, is their volatile market interest rate—its often wide fluctuations (especially during the last or settlement day that depository institutions are trying to meet their legal reserve requirements) that make planning difficult.

In contrast, market interest rates on negotiable CDs and commercial paper are usually somewhat more stable, but generally hover close to and slightly above the Fed funds rate due to their longer average maturity (with loans usually ranging from three or four days to several months) and because of the marketing costs spent in finding buyers for these instruments. CDs and commercial paper usually are less popular in the short run than Fed funds and borrowings from the central bank's discount window when a depository institution needs money right away. Instead, the CD and commercial paper borrowing avenues are usually better for longer-term funding needs that stretch over several days or weeks. This is also generally the case with Eurocurrency deposits.

The rate of interest is usually the principal expense in borrowing nondeposit funds. However, *noninterest* costs cannot be ignored in calculating the true cost of borrowing nondeposit funds, including the time spent by management and staff to find the best funds sources each time new money is needed. A good formula for doing cost comparisons among alternative sources of funds is:

Factoids
What interest rate attached to nondeposit borrowings tends to be among the lowest?
Answer: The effective Federal funds rate is often the lowest borrowing rate for depository institutions.
Is the Fed funds interest rate usually the absolute lowest in the money market? **Answer:** No, the interest rate on the shortest-term U.S. Treasury bills is often slightly lower than the Fed funds rate.

$$\text{Effective cost rate on deposit and nondeposit sources of funds} = \frac{\substack{\text{Current interest} \\ \text{cost on amounts} \\ \text{borrowed}} + \substack{\text{Noninterest costs} \\ \text{incurred} \\ \text{to access these funds}}}{\substack{\text{Net investable funds raised} \\ \text{from this source}}} \quad \textbf{(13–4)}$$

where

$$\text{Current interest cost on amounts borrowed} = \substack{\text{Prevailing interest} \\ \text{rate in the money} \\ \text{market}} \times \substack{\text{Amount of funds} \\ \text{borrowed}} \quad \textbf{(13–5)}$$

$$\text{Noninterest costs to access funds} = \substack{\text{Estimated cost} \\ \text{rate representing} \\ \text{staff time, facilities,} \\ \text{and transaction costs}} \times \substack{\text{Amount of funds} \\ \text{borrowed}} \quad \textbf{(13–6)}$$

$$\begin{array}{c} \text{Net investable funds} \\ \text{raised} \end{array} = \begin{array}{c} \text{Total amount borrowed less legal reserve} \\ \text{requirements (if any), deposit insurance} \\ \text{assessments (if any), and funds placed} \\ \text{in nonearning assets} \end{array} \qquad \textbf{(13–7)}$$

Note that the cost associated with attracting each funds source is compared to the net amount of funds raised after deductions are made for reserve requirements (if any), insurance fees, and that portion of borrowed funds diverted into such nonearning assets as excess cash reserves or fixed assets. We use *net investable funds* as the borrowing base because we wish to compare the dollar cost that must be paid out to attract borrowed funds relative to the dollar amount of those funds that can actually be used to acquire earning assets and cover the cost of fund-raising.

Let's see how the above formulas might be used to estimate the cost of borrowing funds. Suppose that Fed funds are currently trading at an interest rate of 6.0 percent. Moreover, management estimates that the marginal noninterest cost, in the form of personnel expenses and transactions fees, from raising additional monies in the Fed funds market is 0.25 percent. Suppose that a depository institution will need $25 million to fund the loans it plans to make today, of which only $24 million can be fully invested due to other immediate cash demands. Then the effective annualized cost rate for Fed funds today would be calculated as follows:

$$\begin{array}{c} \text{Current interest cost} \\ \text{on federal funds} \end{array} = 0.06 \times \$25 \text{ million} = \$1.5 \text{ million}$$

$$\begin{array}{c} \text{Noninterest cost to} \\ \text{access Federal funds} \end{array} = 0.0025 \times \$25 \text{ million} = \$0.063 \text{ million}$$

$$\begin{array}{c} \text{Net investable} \\ \text{funds raised} \end{array} = \$25 \text{ million} - \$1 \text{ million} = \$24 \text{ million}$$

Therefore, the effective annualized Fed funds cost rate is

$$\frac{\$1.5 \text{ million} + \$0.063 \text{ million}}{\$24 \text{ million}} = 0.0651 \text{ or } 6.51 \text{ percent}$$

The depository institution in the above example would have to earn a net annualized return of at least 6.51 percent on the loans and investments it plans to make with these borrowed Fed funds just to break even.

Suppose management decides to consider borrowing funds by issuing negotiable CDs that carry a current interest rate of 7.00 percent. Moreover, raising CD money costs 0.75 percent in noninterest costs. Then the annualized cost rate incurred from selling CDs would be as follows:

$$\begin{array}{c} \text{Effective CD} \\ \text{cost rate} \end{array} = \frac{(0.07 \times \$25 \text{ million} + \$0.0075 \times \$25 \text{ million})}{\$24 \text{ million}}$$

$$= \frac{\$1.75 \text{ million} + \$0.1875 \text{ million}}{\$24 \text{ million}}$$

$$= 0.0807 \text{ or } 8.07 \text{ percent}$$

An additional expense associated with selling CDs to raise money is the *deposit insurance fee*. In the United States this fee varies with the risk and capitalization of each depository institution whose deposits are insured by the Federal Deposit Insurance Corporation. In recent years the insurance fee has often been at or near zero due to the fact that the

FDIC's insurance reserve has grown because of the relatively few failures and exceeded the level required by federal law of $1.25 in reserves for every $100 in insured deposits.

However, let's assume that the current FDIC insurance fee is $0.0027 per dollar of deposits—a fee sometimes charged the riskiest insured depository institutions in the U.S. system. (We should note as well that the FDIC requires an insured depository institution to pay this fee not just on the first $100,000 in a customer's deposit account but on the full face amount of each deposit received from the public.) Thus, the total insurance cost for the riskiest depository institutions on the $25 million we are talking about raising through selling CDs would be

$$\begin{array}{c} \text{Total deposits} \\ \text{received from} \\ \text{the public} \end{array} \times \begin{array}{c} \text{Insurance fee} \\ \text{per dollar} \end{array} = \$25 \text{ million} \times 0.0027 \qquad \textbf{(13–8)}$$

$$= \$67{,}500 \text{ or } \$0.0675 \text{ million}$$

If we deduct this fee from the new amount of CDs actually available for use, we get this:

$$\begin{array}{c} \text{Effective CD} \\ \text{cost rate} \end{array} = \frac{\$1.9375 \text{ million}}{\$24 \text{ million} - \$0.0675 \text{ million}}$$

$$= \frac{\$1.9375 \text{ million}}{\$23{,}925 \text{ million}} = 0.0810 \text{ or } 8.10 \text{ percent}$$

Clearly, issuing CDs would be more expensive in the above example than borrowing Fed funds. However, CDs have the advantage of being available for several days or weeks, whereas Fed funds loans must often be repaid in 24 hours.

Nondeposit sources of funds generally are moderate in cost compared to other funding sources. Nondeposit funds tend to be more expensive than checkable deposits but less expensive than thrift (time and savings) deposits. We must add a note of caution here, however, because the costs and the profits associated with nondeposit funds tend to be more volatile from year to year than the cost and profitability of deposits. Nondeposit funds do have the advantage of *quick availability* compared to most types of deposits, but they are clearly not as stable a funding source for most institutions as time and savings deposits.

The Risk Factor

The managers of financial institutions must consider at least two types of risk when selecting among different nondeposit sources. The first is **interest rate risk**—the volatility of credit costs. All the interest rates shown in Table 13–9, except most central banks' discount rates, are determined by demand and supply forces in the open market and therefore are subject to erratic fluctuations. The shorter the term of the loan, the more volatile the prevailing market interest rate tends to be. Thus, most Fed funds loans are overnight and, not surprisingly, this market interest rate tends to be the most volatile of all.

Management must also consider **credit availability risk.** There is no guarantee in any credit market that lenders will be willing and able to accommodate every borrower. When general credit conditions are tight, lenders may have limited funds to loan and may ration credit, confining loans only to their soundest and most loyal customers. Sometimes a financial firm may appear so risky to money market lenders they will deny credit or make the price so high that its earnings will suffer. Experience has shown that the negotiable CD, Eurodollar, and commercial paper markets are especially sensitive to credit availability risks. Funds managers must be prepared to switch to alternative sources of credit and, if necessary, pay more for any funds they receive.

Figuring the Overall Cost of Funds

In our discussion of determining how much each source of borrowed funds costs, we looked at each funding source separately. However, borrowing institutions draw simultaneously on not one, but many different funds sources, including deposits, nondeposit borrowings, and owner's equity capital. Can we find a method for determining the cost of funding that brings together all the sources of funding normally in use?

The answer is *yes*. Here we examine two of the most popular overall funds cost methods—the historical average cost approach and the pooled-funds approach.

THE HISTORICAL AVERAGE COST APPROACH

This approach for determining how much funds cost looks at the past. It asks what funds the financial firm has raised to date and what they cost.

Sources of Funds Drawn Upon	Average Amount of Funds Raised (millions)	Average Rate of Interest Incurred	Total Interest Paid for Each Funds Source (millions)
Noninterest-bearing demand deposits	$ 100	0%	$ 0
Interest-bearing transaction deposits	200	7%	14
Savings accounts	100	5%	5
Time deposits	500	8%	40
Money market borrowings	100	6%	6
Total funds raised = $1,000		All interest costs = $65	

Then the average interest cost of deposits and money market borrowings is:

$$\text{Weighted average interest expense} = \frac{\text{All interest paid}}{\text{Total funds raised}} = \frac{\$65}{\$1,000} = 6.5 \text{ percent}$$

But other operating costs, such as salaries and overhead, are incurred to attract deposits. If these are an estimated $10 million, we have

$$\begin{array}{l}\text{Break-even cost} \\ \text{rate on borrowed} \\ \text{funds invested} \\ \text{in earning assets}\end{array} = \frac{\begin{array}{c}\text{Interest + Other} \\ \text{operating costs}\end{array}}{\text{All earning assets}} = \frac{\$65 + 10}{\$750} = 10 \text{ percent}$$

This cost rate is called *break-even* because the borrowing institution must earn at least this rate on its earning assets (primarily loans and securities) just to meet the total operating costs of raising borrowed funds. But what about the borrowing institution's stockholders and their required rate of return (assumed here to be 12 percent after taxes)?

$$\begin{array}{l}\text{Weighted} \\ \text{average} \\ \text{overall} \\ \text{cost of} \\ \text{capital}\end{array} = \begin{array}{l}\text{Break-even} \\ \text{cost on} \\ \text{borrowed} \\ \text{funds}\end{array} + \begin{array}{c}\text{Before-tax cost of the} \\ \text{stockholders'} \\ \text{investment} \\ \text{in the} \\ \text{borrowing institution}\end{array}$$

$$= \begin{array}{l}\text{Break-even} \\ \text{cost}\end{array} + \frac{\begin{array}{c}\text{After-tax cost of} \\ \text{stockholders'} \\ \text{investment}\end{array}}{(1 - \text{Tax rate})} \times \frac{\text{Stockholders'} \\ \text{investment}}{\text{Earning assets}}$$

$$= 10 \text{ percent} + \frac{12 \text{ percent}}{(1 - 0.35)} \times \frac{100}{750} = 10 \text{ percent} + 2.5 \text{ percent}$$

$$= 12.5 \text{ percent}$$

Thus, 12.5 percent is the lowest rate of return over all fund-raising costs the borrowing institution can afford to earn on its assets if its equity shareholders invest $100 million in the institution.

THE POOLED-FUNDS APPROACH

This method of costing borrowed funds looks at the future: What minimum rate of return must be earned on any future loans and security investments just to cover the cost of all new funds raised? Suppose our estimate for future funding sources and costs is as follows:

Profitable New Deposits and Nondeposit Borrowings	Dollars of New Deposit and Nondeposit Borrowings (millions)	Portion of New Borrowings That Will Be Placed in New Earning Assets	Dollar Amount That Can Be Placed in Earning Assets (millions)	Interest Expense and Other Operating Expenses of Borrowing Relative to Amounts Raised	All Operating Expenses Incurred (millions)
Interest-bearing transaction deposits	$100	50%	$50	8%	$8
Time deposits	100	60%	60	9%	9
New stockholders' investment in the institution	100	90%	90	13%	13
Total	$300		$200		$30

The overall cost of new deposits and other borrowing sources must be

$$\frac{\text{Pooled deposit and nondeposit funds expense}}{} = \frac{\text{All expected operating expenses}}{\text{All new funds expected}} = \frac{\$30 \text{ million}}{\$300 \text{ million}} = 10 \text{ percent}$$

But because only two-thirds of these expected new funds ($200 million out of $300 million raised) will actually be available to acquire earning assets,

$$\frac{\text{Hurdle rate of return over all earning assets}}{} = \frac{\text{All expected operating costs}}{\text{Dollars available to place in earning assets}} = \frac{\$30 \text{ million}}{\$200 \text{ million}} = 15 \text{ percent}$$

Thus, the borrowing financial firm in the example above must earn *at least* 15 percent (before taxes), on average, on all the new funds it invests to fully meet its expected fund-raising costs.

The Length of Time Funds Are Needed

As we have seen, some funds sources may be difficult to access immediately (such as commercial paper and long-term debt capital). A manager in need of loanable funds this afternoon would be inclined to borrow in the Fed funds market. However, if funds are not needed for a few days, selling longer-term debt becomes a more viable option. Thus, the term, or maturity, of the funds need plays a key role as well.

The Size of the Borrowing Institution

The standard trading unit for most money market loans is $1 million—a denomination that often exceeds the borrowing requirements of the smallest financial institutions. For example, Eurodollar borrowings are in multiples of $1 million and usually are available only to money-center commercial banks with the highest credit ratings. Large negotiable CDs from the largest depository institutions are preferred by most investors because there is an active secondary market for prime-rated CDs. Smaller depository institutions may not have the credit standing to be able to sell the largest negotiable CDs. The same is true of commercial paper. In contrast, the central bank's discount window and the Fed funds market can make relatively small denomination loans that are suitable for smaller depository institutions.

Regulations

Federal and state regulations may limit the amount, frequency, and use of borrowed funds. For example, in the United States CDs must be issued with maturities of at least seven days. The Federal Reserve banks may limit borrowings from the discount window, particularly by depository institutions that appear to display significant risk of failure. Other forms of borrowing may be subjected to legal reserve requirements by action of the Federal Reserve Board. For example, during the late 1960s and early 1970s, when the Federal Reserve was attempting to fight inflation with tight-money policies, it imposed legal reserve requirements for a time on Fed funds borrowings and repurchase agreements, and on commercial paper issued to purchase assets from affiliated lending institutions. While these particular requirements are not currently in force, it seems clear that in times of national emergency, government policy-makers would move swiftly to impose new controls, affecting both the costs and risks associated with nondeposit borrowings.

Concept Check

13–22. What is the *available funds gap*?

13–23. Suppose J. P. Morgan Chase Bank of New York discovers that projected new loan demand next week should total $325 million and customers holding confirmed credit lines plan to draw down $510 million in funds to cover their cash needs next week, while new deposits next week are projected to equal $680 million. The bank also plans to acquire $420 million in corporate and government bonds next week. What is the bank's projected available funds gap?

13–24. What factors must the manager of a financial institution weigh in choosing among the various nondeposit sources of funding available today?

Summary   Although the principal funding source for many banks and thrift institutions is *deposits*, nearly all depository institutions today supplement the funds they attract through sales of deposits with nondeposit borrowings in the money and capital markets. In this chapter we explore the most important nondeposit funds sources and the factors that bear on the managerial decision about which source or sources of funds to draw upon. The key points in the chapter include:

- Today's heavy use of nondeposit borrowings by depository institutions arose with the development of *liability management*, which calls upon managers of financial institutions to actively manage their liabilities as well as their assets on the balance sheet and to use *interest rates* as the control lever. For example, when funds are short relative to an institution's need for them, additional funds usually can be attracted by raising the offer rate.

- The use of nondeposit borrowings as a key source of funds was given a boost by the emergence of the *customer relationship doctrine*. This managerial strategy calls for putting the goal of satisfying the credit requests of all quality customers at the top of management's list, wherever possible. If deposits are inadequate to fund all quality loan requests, other sources of funds, including borrowings in the money and capital markets, should be used. Thus, the lending decision comes first, followed by the funding decision.

- One of the key sources of nondeposit funds today is the *Federal funds market*, where immediately available reserves are traded between financial institutions and usually returned within 24 hours. Borrowing from selected government agencies—in the United States, the *discount windows of the Federal Reserve banks* and *advances from the Federal Home Loan Banks*—has also grown rapidly in recent years and more lenient regulations have made this borrowing process easier.

- Other key funds sources include selling *negotiable jumbo ($100,000+) CDs* (mainly to corporate customers), borrowing *Eurocurrency deposits* from international banks offshore, issuing *commercial paper* in the open market through an affiliate or subsidiary corporation, executing *repurchase agreements* where loans collateralized by top-quality assets are made available to borrowing institutions for a few hours or days, and *longer-term borrowings in the capital markets* through the issuance of subordinated debentures and other forms of longer-term debt.

- Before tapping nondeposit borrowings, however, the managers of financial firms must estimate their funding requirements. One such estimate for a depository institution comes from the *available funds gap*, which is the spread between the current and expected volume of loans and investments and the current and expected volume of deposits and other funds sources.

- The particular nondeposit funds source(s) chosen by management usually rests upon such factors as (1) the relative cost of each nondeposit funding source; (2) the risk or dependability of each funds source; (3) the length of time funds will be needed; (4) the size of the borrowing institution and its funding needs; and (5) the content of government regulations affecting the fund-raising process.

- Among the most important government regulations bearing on the use of nondeposit funds are legal reserve requirements imposed by several central banks around the world (requiring minimum amounts of liquidity on the balance sheets of depository institutions) and rules dictating the required content of contractual agreements when funds are loaned by one financial institution to another.

Key Terms

customer relationship doctrine, *418*
liability management, *418*
Federal funds market, *420*
repurchase agreements (RPs), *423*

discount window, *425*
negotiable CD, *428*
Eurocurrency deposit, *429*
commercial paper market, *431*
available funds gap, *433*

interest rate risk, *437*
credit availability risk, *437*

Problems and Projects

1. Robertson State Bank decides to loan a portion of its reserves in the amount of $70 million held at the Federal Reserve Bank to Tenison National Security Bank for 24 hours. For its part, Tenison plans to make a 24-hour loan to a security dealer before it must return the funds to Robertson State Bank. Please show the proper accounting entries for these transactions.

2. Masoner Savings, headquartered in a small community, holds most of its correspondent deposits with Flagg Metrocenter Bank, a money center institution. When Masoner has a cash surplus in its correspondent deposit, Flagg automatically invests the surplus in Fed funds loans to other money center banks. A check of Masoner's records this morning reveals a temporary surplus of $11 million for 48 hours. Flagg will loan this surplus for two business days to Secoro Central City Bank, which is in need of additional reserves. Please show the correct balance sheet entries to carry out this loan and to pay off the loan when its term ends.

3. Relgade National Bank secures primary credit from the Federal Reserve Bank of San Francisco in the amount of $32 million for a term of seven days. Please show the proper entries for granting this loan and then paying off the loan.

4. Jason Corporation purchases a 45-day negotiable CD with a $5 million denomination from Payson Bank and Trust, bearing a 5.25 percent annual yield. How much in interest will the bank have to pay when this CD matures? What amount *in total* will the bank have to pay back to Itec at the end of 45 days?

5. Happy Valley Bank borrows $125 million overnight through a repurchase agreement (RP) collateralized by Treasury bills. The current RP rate is 3.65 percent. How much will the bank pay in interest cost due to this borrowing?

6. Lavendar Bank of New York expects new deposit inflows next month of $330 million and deposit withdrawals of $425 million. The bank's economics department has projected that new loan demand will reach $460 million and customers with approved credit lines will need $125 million in cash. The bank will sell $480 million in securities, but plans to add $75 million in new securities to its portfolio. What is its projected available funds gap?

7. Washington Mutual borrowed $150 million in Fed funds from J. P. Morgan Chase Bank in New York City for 24 hours to fund a 30-day loan. The prevailing Fed funds rate on loans of this maturity stood at 7.85 percent when these two institutions agreed on the loan. The funds loaned by Morgan were in the reserve deposit that the bank keeps at the Federal Reserve Bank of New York. When the loan to Washington Mutual was repaid the next day, J. P. Morgan used $50 million of the returned funds to cover its own reserve needs and loaned $100 million in Fed funds to Texas Savings, Houston, for a two-day period at the prevailing Fed funds rate of 7.92 percent. With respect to these transactions, (*a*) construct T-account entries similar to those you encountered in this chapter, showing the original Fed funds loan and its repayment on the books of J. P. Morgan, Washington Mutual, and Texas Savings; and (*b*) calculate the total interest income earned by Morgan on both Fed funds loans.

8. Bank Three of Florida issues a three-month (90-day) negotiable CD in the amount of $20 million to ABC Insurance Company at a negotiated annual interest rate of 4.75 percent (360-day basis). Calculate the value of this CD account on the day it matures and the amount of interest income ABC will earn. What interest return will ABC Insurance earn in a 365-day year?

9. Banks and other lending affiliates within the holding company of Interstate National Banc are reporting heavy loan demand this week from companies in the southeastern United States that are planning a significant expansion of inventories and facilities before the beginning of the fall season. The holding company and its lead bank plan to raise $850 million in short-term funds this week, of which about $835 million will be

used to meet these new loan requests. Fed funds are currently trading at 4.50 percent, negotiable CDs are trading in New York at 4.69 percent, and Eurodollar borrowings are available in London at all maturities under one year at 4.47 percent. One-month maturities of directly placed commercial paper carry market rates of 4.65 percent, while the primary credit discount rate of the Federal Reserve Bank of Richmond is currently set at 5.50 percent—a source that Interstate has used in each of the past two weeks. Noninterest costs are estimated at 0.25 percent for Fed funds, discount window borrowings, and CDs; 0.35 percent for Eurodollar borrowings; and 0.50 percent for commercial paper. Calculate the effective cost rate of each of these sources of funds for Interstate and make a management decision on what sources to use. Be prepared to defend your decision.

10. Surfs-Up Security Savings is considering the problem of trying to raise $80 million in money market funds to cover a loan request from one of its largest corporate customers, which needs a six-week loan. Money market interest rates are currently at the levels indicated below:

Federal funds, average for week just concluded	**4.50%**
Discount window of the Federal Reserve bank	**5.50**
CDs (prime rated, secondary market):	
One month	**3.85**
Three months	**3.89**
Six months	**3.98**
Eurodollar deposits (three months)	**4.58**
Commercial paper (directly placed):	
One month	**4.53**
Three months	**4.57**

Unfortunately, Surfs-Up's economics department is forecasting a substantial rise in money market interest rates over the next six weeks. What would you recommend to its funds management department regarding how and where to raise the money needed? Be sure to consider such cost factors as legal reserve requirements, regulations, and what happens to the relative attractiveness of each funding source if interest rates rise continually over the period of the proposed loan.

Alternative scenario:

What if Surfs-Up's economists are wrong and money market rates *decline* significantly over the next six weeks? How would your recommendation to the funds management department change on how and where to raise the funds needed?

11. Monarch Bank and Trust has received $800 million in total funding, consisting of $200 million in checkable deposit accounts, $400 million in time and savings deposits, $100 million in money market borrowings, and $100 million in stockholders' equity. Interest costs on time and savings deposits are 3.75 percent, on average, while noninterest costs of raising these particular deposits equal approximately .75 percent of their dollar volume. Interest costs on checkable deposits average only .75 percent because many of these deposits pay no interest, but noninterest costs of raising checkable accounts are about 3 percent of their dollar total. Money market borrowings cost Monarch an average of 4.25 percent in interest costs and .25 percent in noninterest costs. Management estimates the cost of stockholders' equity capital at 16 percent before taxes. (The bank is currently in the 35-percent corporate tax bracket.) When

www.mhhe.com/rose7e

reserve requirements are added in, along with uncollected dollar balances, these factors are estimated to contribute another 0.75 percent to the cost of securing checkable deposits and .50 percent to the cost of acquiring time and savings deposits. Reserve requirements (on Eurodeposits only) and collection delays add an estimated .25 percent to the cost of the money market borrowings.

   a. Calculate Monarch's weighted average interest cost on total funds raised, figured on a before-tax basis.

   b. If the bank's earning assets total $700 million, what is its break-even cost rate?

   c. What is Monarch's overall historical weighted average cost of capital?

12. Aspiration Savings Association is considering funding a package of new loans in the amount of $400 million. Aspiration has projected that it must raise $450 million in order to have $400 million available to make new loans. It expects to raise $325 million of the total by selling time deposits at an average interest rate of 3.75 percent. Noninterest costs from selling time deposits will add an estimated 0.45 percent in operating expenses. Aspiration expects another $125 million to come from noninterest-bearing transaction deposits, whose noninterest costs are expected to be 5.25 percent of the total amount of these deposits. What is the Association's projected pooled-funds marginal cost? What hurdle rate must it achieve on its earning assets?

Internet Exercises

1. In terms of size, which banks in the U.S. financial system seem to rely most heavily on deposits as a source of funding and which on nondeposit borrowings and liability management? To provide an example for the numbers reported in Table 13–3, go to the FDIC's Institution Directory at **http://www3.fdic.gov/idasp/** and search by city and state to find a small bank holding company (BHC) located in your hometown or somewhere you enjoy visiting. Write down the BHC ID of your selected bank. Then go to **www3.fdic.gov/sdi/** to compare your small BHC with two larger BHCs—Bank of America (BHC ID 1073757) and J. P. Morgan Chase (BHC ID 1039502). Compare and contrast Deposits/Total Assets and Liabilities/Total Assets for the three BHCs to illustrate your point.

    If you need some help maneuvering around this site to create a report, read on. The process to create a report requires that you "Select the Number of Columns." You want to select "3" to develop the format to collect data for the most recent report. This provides three pull-down menus, each labeled Select One. In the columns select Bank Holding Company from the menu and go on to type in the BHC ID #. After defining the three columns click on Next. At this point, you focus on Report Selection, choosing to View and to do calculations in Percentages. Then you get to identify the information you want to collect before creating the report by clicking Next. You will find deposit and liability information in the Assets and Liabilities report.

2. You are interested in borrowing from the discount window of the Federal Reserve Bank in your area. Go to **www.frbdiscountwindow.org/** and find out the current interest rates at your FRB. What are they?

3. As a home mortgage lender, you are interested in borrowing from a Federal Home Loan Bank. First determine which district you are in and then go to the bank in that district and find the interest rates on FHLB advances. The following site will get you started: **www.fhlbanks.com**.

4. In this chapter you have been introduced to a number of instruments used for liability management. Repurchase agreements are always a challenge. To learn a little more about these instruments go to **http://www.ny.frb.org/cfcbsweb/Fleming.Bk_w.pdf**. Who are the major participants in the RP market?

5. You have been introduced to the Eurodollar market. To learn more about this market go to **http://www.richmondfed.org/publications/economic-research/instruments_of _the_money-market**. For market participants, what are the three basic sources of risk associated with holding Eurodollars?

S&P Market Insight Challenge (www.mhhe.com/edumarketinsight)

STANDARD
&POOR'S

1. The S&P Industry Survey "Banking" discusses the Federal Reserve's influence over the cost and availability of nondeposit funds sources. For a description of how the Fed's actions increase or decrease the money supply and affect the cost of funds to financial firms use the Industry tab in Standard & Poor's Market Insight, Educational Version. The drop-down menu provides subindustry selections among Diversified Banks and Regional Banks. After selecting one of these subindustry groupings you will find a recent S&P Industry Survey on Banking. Please download the banking survey and examine the section, "How the Industry Operates." Now describe the Federal Reserve System's influence on nondeposit liabilities.

STANDARD
&POOR'S

2. Nondeposit borrowings in the Fed funds market and from other money market sources have become more important among depository institutions in recent years. You can get an idea of the magnitude of this change by examining the most recent financial statements of depository institutions represented on the Web site of S&P's Market Insight. Why do you think that major depository institutions are drawing so heavily upon nondeposit liabilities today? Are there significant advantages in doing so? Significant risks?

REAL NUMBERS FOR REAL BANKS   Assignment for Chapter 13

YOUR BANK'S USE OF LIABILITY MANAGEMENT: A STEP BEYOND DEPOSITS

Liability management was first mentioned in Chapters 7 and 11 and further developed with the focus on sources of funds in Chapter 13. After deposits, where do bank managers go for funding? To the financial markets or, in the United States, to the Federal Reserve banks and Federal Home Loan banks. These types of nondeposit borrowing are described in detail in this chapter. We will first look at liabilities to see what they reveal about our BHC's composition of sources of funds. Then we will explore the risk ratings for any implications concerning the market's evaluation of the BHC's risk exposure.

Part One: Collecting the Data

We have already collected most of the data available to examine nondeposit sources of funds. In the spreadsheet used for comparisons with the peer group, Rows 21–25 are the nondeposit sources of funds. We add negotiable CDs and Eurodollar deposits to the nondeposit sources and we have the materials most often used in liability management. We will once again visit the FDIC's SDI Web site located at **www3.fdic.gov/sdi/** to collect two items from the Memoranda section of the Assets and Liabilities report that may provide further insights for your particular BHC and the peer group of large banks (more than $10 billion in assets). You will create the four-column report for your bank and the peer group across the two years. Access the Assets and Liabilities report using the pull-down menus and collect the percentage information for the two items listed below. Once again, you will enter the percentages as an extension of the information in the designated cells.

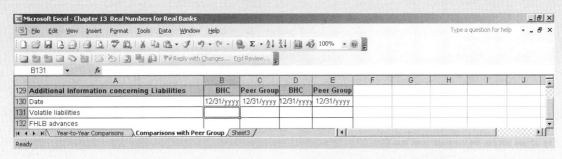

www.mhhe.com/rose7e

REAL NUMBERS FOR REAL BANKS

Assignment for Chapter 13 *(continued)*

Part Two: Analyzing the Data for Interpretation

A. Volatile liabilities include large-denomination time deposits, foreign-office deposits, Federal funds purchased, securities sold under agreements to repurchase, and other borrowings. These are the risk-sensitive sources used in liability management. You can compare the columns of row 131 to get a sense of the proper answers to the following questions: (1) Is your BHC increasing its reliance on liability management? (2) Is your bank using liability management more than its peers?

B. Once you have looked at the big picture using the aggregated measure of volatile liabilities to total assets, observe the comparative and trend differences of its components, especially FHLB advances, Federal funds purchased, and securities sold under agreements to repurchase as a proportion of total assets.

C. Write several paragraphs discussing your BHC's use of liability management from year to year and in comparison to its contemporaries.

Part Three: The Risk Associated with Your Banks' (BHC's) Marketable Liabilities: A Look at the Debt Ratings for Your Bank

A. Visit the Web site of an international ratings agency that covers financial institutions at **www.fitchibca.com**. Once there, read the definitions of the ratings that Fitch provides at **www.fitchibca.com/corporate/ratings/definitions/index.cfm.**

B. Then find your BHC and any subsidiaries (banks) that have issued liabilities by going back to **www.fitchibca.com** and clicking on the Financial Institutions-Banks link, followed by the Issuer List link. Once you arrive at the Issuer List, search for the banks and BHC you have been following this semester. Then click on the Active Name link to acquire information about outstanding issues and their ratings.

C. Summarize and interpret the above information in one or two paragraphs describing the types of issues outstanding and the associated risk for the holders of these issues. Can you develop any rationales for the amount of volatile liabilities given the ratings?

Selected References

For a fuller explanation of recent developments in nondeposit funding sources, see:

1. Bennett, Paul, and Spence Hilton. "Falling Reserve Balances and the Federal Funds Rate." *Current Issues in Economics and Finance,* Federal Reserve Bank of New York 3, no. 5 (April 1997), pp. 1–6.

2. Fleming, Michael J., and Kenneth D. Garbade. "The Repurchase Agreement Refined: The GCF Repo." *Current Issues in Economics and Finance,* Federal Reserve Bank of New York 9, no. 6 (June 2003), pp. 1–7.

3. Fleming, Michael J., and Kenneth D. Garbade. "Repurchase Agreements with Negative Interest Rates." *Current Issues in Economics and Finance,* Federal Reserve Bank of New York 10, no. 5 (April 2004), pp. 1–7.

4. Madigan, Brian F., and William R. Nelson. "Proposed Revision to the Federal Reserve's Discount Window Lending Programs." *Federal Reserve Bulletin,* July 2002, pp. 313–319.

5. Maloney, Daniel K., and James B. Thomson. "The Evolving Role of the Federal Home Loan Banks in Mortgage Markets." *Economic Commentary,* Federal Reserve Bank of Cleveland, June 2003, pp. 1–4.

6. Rose, Peter S. "The Quest for New Funds: New Dimensions in a New Market." *The Canadian Banker* 94, no. 5 (September/October 1987), pp. 436–455.

7. Stevens, Ed. "The New Discount Window." *Economic Commentary,* Federal Reserve Bank of Cleveland, May 15, 2003, pp. 1–4.

www.mhhe.com/rose7e

CHAPTER FOURTEEN

Investment Banking, Insurance, and Other Sources of Fee Income

Key Topics in This Chapter

- The Ongoing Search for Fee Income
- Investment Banking Services
- Mutual Funds and Other Investment Products
- Trust Services and Insurance Products
- Benefits of Product-Line Diversification
- Economies of Scope and Scale
- Information Flows and Customer Privacy

14–1 Introduction

Banks and many of their competitors have faced an increasingly intense struggle in recent years to attract all the funds needed to make loans and investments and boost their revenues. Unfortunately, the struggle to attract deposits has sometimes been frustrated by the changing attitudes of the public regarding how and where they wish to place their savings and by intense competition among bank and nonbank depository institutions, such as credit unions and savings associations. Scores of depository institutions have found that deposit markets are not always friendly to them when they need more funds.

This is especially true when stock and bond prices are rising and customers may be shifting large amounts of their financial resources from bank deposits to investments in securities, as happened, for example, during much of the 1990s. Of course, security prices don't always rise; indeed, the opening of the 21st century demonstrated this painfully when stock values plummeted, leading to a resurgence in the growth of new deposits. However, whenever deposit growth does slow, financial-service managers frequently are forced to pursue *new* sources of funds and *new* ways to generate revenue.

One of the most fertile fields for growth in future revenue on the part of financial firms appears to be **fee income**—revenues derived from charging customers for the particular services they use. Examples abound, including monthly service charges on transaction accounts, commissions for providing insurance coverage for homes and businesses, membership fees for accepting and using a particular credit card, fees for providing financial advice to individuals and corporations, and so on.

Fee income is among the most rapidly growing sources of revenue for depository institutions and selected other service providers. Some of this revenue comes from the sale of traditional services, such as charges associated with the use of checking and savings accounts, fees for the use of an automated teller machine (ATM), and commitment fees to extend a loan in the future when the customer needs it. Indeed, much to the anger of some customers, fees on many traditional services, particularly deposits, not only have been multiplying, but, on average, are often rising faster than the rate of inflation!

More recently much of the fee income has come from nontraditional services—newer services that, traditionally, were not offered by an ordinary commercial bank, credit union, or other familiar financial firm for many years. Examples include commissions and fees from supplying corporations and governments with investment banking services, commissions and fees from the sale of investment products (including buying or selling stocks, bonds and shares in mutual funds on behalf of customers), fees for managing a customer's property through an affiliated trust company or trust department, and commissions and fees from the sale of insurance products (including life, health, and property/casualty insurance policies) and from insurance underwriting. This expansion of nontraditional services and the revenues they generate is part of the consolidation and convergence of financial-service industries that has been going on now for several years, as we saw earlier in Chapter 1. Larger financial firms today can reach across industry boundaries to grab new fee-based service ideas and then take on the risks of offering these new services to their customers.

In some instances these nontraditional services appear to have a low correlation with more traditional revenue sources, thereby potentially helping to lower the overall risk of the offering institution. For example, if revenue from loans and deposits is falling because of a dip in the economy, perhaps revenues from the sale of bonds, mutual funds, and insurance policies may be rising. On balance, profits and income may not falter (or, at least, may decline by less) even in tough times. In brief, the drive among competing financial firms to generate more fee income as an increasingly important revenue source springs from several sources:

- A desire to supplement traditional sources of funds (such as deposits) when these sources are inadequate.
- An attempt to lower production costs by offering multiple services using the same facilities and resources (economies of scope).
- An effort to offset these higher production costs by asking customers to absorb a larger share of the cost of both old and new financial services.
- A desire to reduce overall risk to the financial-service provider's cash flow by finding new sources of revenue not highly correlated with revenues from sales of traditional services.
- A goal to promote cross-selling of traditional and new services in order to further enhance revenue and net income.

We turn now to look at several of these recently popular sources of revenue (fee income) for banks and some of their more aggressive competitors.

14–2 Sales of Investment Banking Services

Although banks and their closest competitors have not been as successful with some of the fee-income services they have recently offered as they had hoped, one service that has been successful, particularly when the economy is expanding, is **investment banking.**

Traditional and New Sources of Fee Income

TRADITIONAL SOURCES OF FEE INCOME FOR MOST BANKING FIRMS

- Service charges on checking accounts, savings deposits and for customer use of automated teller machines (ATMs), including fees for insufficient funds (NSF) and excessive withdrawals.
- Credit card service fees, including card membership fees, late-payment fees, etc.
- Commitment fees for making credit available over a designated time period.
- Fees for use of safe deposit boxes to keep customers' valuables secure.
- Rental of bank property to individuals and businesses.

NEWER SOURCES OF FEE INCOME FOR MANY BANKING FIRMS

- Commissions and fees from investment banking (security underwriting) services provided for corporations and governments.
- Brokerage commissions for aiding customers in purchasing and selling stocks, bonds, mutual funds, and other assets.
- Fiduciary income—trust service fees for managing the assets of individuals and businesses.
- Commissions for the sale of insurance-related products to businesses and individuals, including insurance policies, pension programs, and annuity plans.
- Servicing fees that arise from securitizing and selling loans, including monitoring borrowers' compliance with the terms of the loans they receive and keeping records of payments received.

Factoid
Which depository institutions are most likely to charge service fees and usually charge the highest fees—smaller or larger institutions?
Answer: The largest, often because they know their costs better.

Filmtoid
What 1996 comedy finds Whoopi Goldberg dressed in a man's suit to gain respect and create a market for her investment banking advice?
Answer: *The Associate.*

Acting under the authority of the Gramm-Leach-Bliley (GLB) Financial Services Modernization Act and earlier rulings by the Federal Reserve Board, many leading U.S. banking firms have recently either acquired or formed their own investment banking affiliates in order to serve corporations and governments around the world. Examples include Citigroup's acquisition of Salomon Brothers Smith Barney and Chase Manhattan's purchase of Hambrecht & Quist. The leading investment banks in the world today include Citigroup, J. P. Morgan Chase, Morgan Stanley, Merrill Lynch, Goldman Sachs, Credit Suisse, Bear Stearns, UBS, Lehman Brothers, Nomura Securities, Deutsche Bank, and Banc of America Securities. More than 50 of the roughly 600 financial holding companies (FHCs) approved to operate in the United States control investment banking subsidiaries.

Key Investment Banking Services

Investment bankers (IBs) are financial advisers to corporations, governments, and other large institutions. IBs provide critical advice and direction to their clients on such important issues as:

1. Should we (the IB's clients) attempt to raise new capital? If so, how much, where, and how do we go about this fund-raising task?

2. Should our company enter new market areas at home or abroad? If so, how can we best accomplish this market-expansion strategy?

3. Does our company need to acquire or merge with other firms? If so, how? And when is the best time to do so?

4. Should we sell our company to another firm? If so, what is our company worth? And how do we find the right buyer?

Traditionally, the best-known and often the most profitable investment banking service is *security underwriting*—the purchase for resale of new stocks, bonds, and other

Leading Investment Banks Underwriting New Issues of Bonds and Stocks in Markets around the World

Citigroup (citigroup.com)

Morgan Stanley (morganstanley.com)

Goldman Sachs (gs.com)

Merrill Lynch (ml.com)

J. P. Morgan Chase (jpmorgan.com)

Credit Suisse First Boston (csfb.com)

Bear, Stearns & Company (bearstearns.com)

United Bank of Switzerland (UBS) (ubs.com)

Lehman Brothers (lehman.com)

Nomura Securities (nomura.com)

Deutsche Bank AG (deutsche-bank.com)

Banc of America Securities (bofasceurities.com)

financial instruments in the money and capital markets on behalf of clients who need to raise new money. Among the most profitable and, recently, most controversial of these underwriting services has been the volatile initial public offering (IPO) market in which scores of formerly privately held companies have gone public by offering new shares of stock, often leading to large speculative gains or losses during the first few hours of the sale.

Investment banking is substantially more risky (but also more profitable, on average) than commercial banking. IBs must estimate, in advance, the probable value of the new securities they plan to purchase from their clients when the day arrives that those new securities must be offered to the public. Their hope is that the market price will move higher from the first day of sale—a hoped-for outcome that clearly may be spoiled by such random events as terrorism, war, and changes in government policy and regulation. If the IB misestimates and the market price plunges as the sale begins, the IB will be forced to absorb the resulting loss, which may mount into the hundreds of millions of dollars. Conversely, a strong rise in market price as the new security sale begins can magnify the IB's expected profits.

In addition to possible capital gains on security trading, IBs also charge fees and commissions for various services. For example, in making markets for IPOs recently, some investment banks have charged underwriting fees ranging up to 4 percent of the amount of the securities brought to market for sale. Thus, a relatively small $25 million offering of stock from a newly formed corporation might net the assisting IB a fee of a million dollars or more.

Because of abrupt changes in market conditions and fierce competition IB profits are volatile—far more volatile than the profits of most commercial banks. There isn't much job security in the IB field either. IB employees are usually highly skilled and at times in great demand but also face unemployment if market conditions deteriorate. They frequently leave the IB firm that hired them in order to join another firm. For example, Goldman Sachs, Merrill Lynch, and Morgan Stanley experienced significant turnover in their management staffs as the 21st century began.

Linkages between Commercial and Investment Banking

Research studies suggest that investment banking revenue and profitability are positively, but not highly, correlated with commercial banking revenues and profitability. Thus, there may be some significant *product-line diversification effects* (discussed later in this chapter) that help limit overall risk for a commercial banking company also engaging in IB activity

Investment Banking Revenue

THE PRINCIPAL TYPES OF SECURITIES UNDERWRITTEN BY INVESTMENT BANKS IN ORDER TO EARN COMMISSIONS AND FEES

Government and federal agency securities

Investment-grade corporate bonds

Convertible corporate bonds and stock

Common and preferred stock

Corporate junk bonds

Asset-backed securities

ADDITIONAL SOURCES OF INVESTMENT BANKING REVENUES

Advising clients regarding corporate acquisitions and mergers

Creating and trading derivatives for profit and risk reduction

Brokering loan sales

Setting up special purpose entities to support and monitor loan securitizations

Stock and bond trading for the IB and its clients

Currency and commodity trading for the IB and its clients

Issuing credit and liquidity enhancements for clients

Developing business plans for expansion into new markets

or from an IB controlling a commercial bank. Moreover, IB services complement traditional lending services, allowing commercial banking firms to offer *both* conventional loans and security underwriting to customers seeking to raise new funds.

One hallmark of this complementary IB–commercial banking relationship emerged after passage of the Gramm-Leach-Bliley (GLB) Act in 1999, with commercial banks rapidly rising to the top of IB activity in the junk (low-credit-rated) bond market. As the 21st century unfolded, the securities trading units of such prominent commercial banking companies as Bank of America, J. P. Morgan Chase, Citigroup, and Deutsche Bank led the IB industry in selling higher-yield, more risky bonds for many of the same corporate clients to whom they granted regular business loans. Then, too, there may be economies of scale in information gathering about clients; that is, commercial bank loan officers and investment bankers may share some information with each other about clients requesting both conventional loans and security underwriting services.

Possible Advantages and Disadvantages of Linking Commercial and Investment Banking

Key URLs

If you are interested in a career in investment banking, see especially **www.careers-in-finance.com**. Some companies offer to teach you how to be an investment banker. See, for example, **www.wallstreetprep.com**.

As we saw in Chapter 2, offering both commercial and investment banking services through the same financial-services firm was prohibited following passage of the Glass-Steagall Act in 1933. Only gradually, beginning in the 1980s, did this new service activity become available to the commercial banking community through a series of rulings by the Federal Reserve Board. With the passage of the GLB Act in the fall of 1999, the full range of IB services was opened up for adequately capitalized and well-managed commercial banking firms.

The earlier prohibition against the two industries combining was fueled by the Depression-era U.S. Congress's belief that such a combination would pose several significant costs and risks, including

- Possibly forcing customers seeking loans to buy the securities the IB was trying to sell as a condition for getting a loan (i.e., tying contracts).
- Increasing the risk exposure of affiliated commercial banking firms due to the inherently volatile and cyclical behavior of IB activity, resulting in more bank failures.

Executives of the largest U.S. banks and other industry leaders countered these arguments successfully in the 1990s by pointing out that combined commercial banking–investment banking operations were readily available outside the United States and, as a result, foreign banking firms were capturing U.S. customers. They also argued that allowing commercial banks into investment banking would increase competition and lower client fees.

It is not yet clear, however, that the benefits alleged from this new service dimension for commercial banking have been completely satisfied, though commercial banks have transformed the investment banking industry, acquiring some of its largest firms and consolidating smaller IBs into larger ones that are international in scope. Several of the most important investment banks today—such as Citigroup, J. P. Morgan Chase, Bank of America, Deutsche Bank, and UBS—are financial-service companies that encompass a huge commercial bank at the center of their operations. However, IB services are still highly sensitive to fluctuations in the economy, often dropping off sharply in recessions. For example, between 2000 and 2002, security firms in the United States wiped out the jobs of more than 30,000 employees due to fewer merger deals and declining issues of new securities amidst an economic slowdown.

Moreover, allegations about some banks forcing their loan customers to sign "tying contracts"—compelling these customers to purchase IB-offered securities that they didn't need or possibly couldn't afford—as a condition for getting a loan surfaced as the new century began. Other allegations soon appeared regarding possible "spinning" activity—that is, some IBs may have given the directors and officers of favorite corporate clients special deals on purchasing certain IPO shares not available to other security buyers.

Key Issues for Investment Banks of the Future

IBs today are wrestling with the question of what kind of financial firm they need to be in the future? What mix of services should they be offering to achieve high and sustained profitability?

For example, as 2005 unfolded, Morgan Stanley—one of the oldest, largest, and most respected of all IBs—found itself struggling with its tri-part business structure. Morgan operated not only an IB but also controlled a credit card company, Discover, and a retail brokerage house, Dean Witter. The company's management believed that linking the traditional underwriting of securities with the subsequent sale of those underwritten securities to the public through brokers at Dean Witter should be a money-maker. Management also liked the high profit margins in the credit card business and reasoned that many of Morgan Stanley's and Dean Witter's clients might be persuaded to sign up for the Discover credit card program. Unfortunately, this combination of financial firms and products proved to be disappointing, leading to considerable speculation about Morgan Stanley possibly selling off some of its non-IB affiliated firms.

Meanwhile, Merrill Lynch, one of the world's largest IBs, has been pursuing BlackRock Inc., a leading money manager for thousands of clients around the globe. The purpose of this proposed combination is to bring together money management services with IB products in order to sell mutual funds and other investments to both large and small investors around the globe.

By and large, the commercial bank-investment bank combinations have worked reasonably well of late as have banking firms combined with high-volume credit card operations (at least those who have successfully controlled credit card fraud and production expenses). It is not clear, however, that these particular combinations of financial firms will consistently turn out well in the future as the financial marketplace continues to undergo significant change and innovation.

ETHICS IN BANKING AND FINANCIAL SERVICES

ETHICS PROBLEMS IN THE INVESTMENT BANKING INDUSTRY

Hundreds of millions of dollars in fines have been levied against investment banking firms as a result of ethical breakdowns in this industry, causing many IBs to take a second look at their business practices. Among the most serious allegations are that some security firms have published distorted and false research information to get their customers to purchase securities the IBs most wanted to sell. Excessively optimistic research reports appear to have "sold" thousands of customers who ultimately got burned when more objective information appeared in the market.

A related problem in industry ethics emerged when lawsuits were filed by many investors who believed they had been misled into buying the stocks and debt securities of troubled companies without being forewarned by the underwriter. Several leading IB firms were charged with helping businesses on the brink of failure—for example, Enron, WorldCom and Parma let SpA—sell their overvalued securities to the public and conceal fraud. A series of suits recovered several billion dollars in damages from the IBs involved.

Under law and industry practice a "Chinese wall," preventing the transfer of insider information about clients, is supposed to exist between an IB's security underwriting and client advising department or division and the internal unit where proprietary trading of stocks and bonds takes place. The security trading department is not supposed to benefit from what the advisory and underwriting staffs have learned about a customer. Recently a dramatic controversy emerged in Australia over the alleged sharing of information between underwriters and stock traders working for Citigroup concerning a client Citigroup was already advising about a possible corporate takeover. Australian regulators quickly launched an investigation.

A major challenge also exists for the U.S. Securities and Exchange Commission (SEC) about how to set up effective firewalls that separate security sales functions from underwriting, advisory, and research functions inside IBs in a way that restores public confidence in the fundamental honesty of the investment banking and security trading businesses. A related issue to be resolved in the future centers on the question of whether IBs have a duty to uncover the problems of their clients and who must receive the information they uncover. Their clients? The public? The regulatory agencies?

14–3 Selling Investment Products to Consumers

In recent years many of the largest business and household depositors have moved their funds out of deposits at banks and thrift institutions into **investment products**—stocks, bonds, mutual funds, annuities, and similar financial instruments that seemed to promise better returns than are available on many conventional deposits. As the new century began many depositors also withdrew their money to invest in real estate in an effort to keep up with inflation. Moreover, the passing years have ushered in growing public concern over the lack of adequate savings for the retirement years, given today's longer average life spans. Then, too, yield curves have tended to be positively sloped in recent years, suggesting that longer-term assets, such as stocks, bonds, and real estate might ultimately deliver higher returns than relatively short-term deposits and build personal savings faster.

Accordingly, the public has made massive adjustments in their asset portfolios in recent years. For example, between 1993 and 2005, checkable deposits and time and savings accounts at U.S. depository institutions rose from about $3 trillion to just over $6 trillion, a respectable gain of about 88 percent. However, the checkable deposit total held by banks actually *fell* over this same period even as savings deposits rose. Far more remarkable was the rapid expansion of several nondeposit investment products. For example, the public's holdings of shares in mutual funds soared more than 400 percent. Household investments in individual stocks climbed by nearly 100 percent, while retirement (pension) plan volume more than tripled.

The willingness of traditional bank customers to convert many of their conservative investments in deposits, most of which normally are protected by federal deposit insurance,

Key URL
To learn more about recent trends in the service fees charged by depository institutions in recent years, see especially **www.federal.reserve.gov/boarddocs/RptCongress**.

into uninsured stocks, mutual funds, annuities, and other investment and insurance products surprised and shocked many members of the banking community. Banks quickly began to develop investment and insurance products and to offer financial planning services, hoping to win back some of the lost deposits or, at least, to get their customers to carry out their purchases and sales of investment and insurance products through a depository institution rather than through other competitors.

Mutual Fund Investment Products

The most popular of the investment products sold by depository institutions recently have been shares in **mutual funds**. First set up in Great Britain in the 19th century, mutual funds came to the United States in the 1920s. By the opening of the 21st century, these investment companies served more than 90 million shareholders.

Each share in a mutual fund permits an investor to receive a *pro rata* share of any dividends or other forms of income generated by a pool of stocks, bonds, or other securities the fund holds. If a mutual fund is liquidated, each investor receives a portion of the net asset value (NAV) of the fund after its liabilities are paid off, based on the number of shares each investor holds. Each fund has an announced investment objective, such as capital growth or the maximization of current income, and in the United States must register with the Securities and Exchange Commission (SEC) and provide investors with a prospectus describing its purpose, recent performance, and makeup. These investment pools have few employees. Instead, a board of directors, representing the stockholders, hires outside firms to provide most of the management expertise and labor needed to operate the fund.

Key URLs

To uncover more information about mutual funds, see www.mfea.com and www.ici.org.

Mutual funds have been attractive to many individuals and institutional investors because their long-run yields appear to be relatively high and most funds are well diversified, spreading the investor's risk exposure across many different types of stocks, bonds, and other financial instruments. These investment companies are highly innovative, developing many new types of funds in recent years, and are highly competitive with each other, recently pushing their commissions and fees significantly lower in order to attract more customers to this nearly 8 trillion-dollar industry.

Among the more popular mutual funds today are exchange-traded funds (ETFs) and hedge funds. *Exchange-traded funds* behave like index-tracking mutual funds but, unlike conventional funds, ETFs trade all day on stock exchanges, allowing mutual-fund-oriented investors to "play the market." Among the leading institutions offering ETFs are Barclays Global Investors and State Street Global Advisors.

Key URLs:

To learn more about Exchange-Traded Funds see www.etfconnect. com, www.morningstar. com, and http://finance. yahoo.com/etf. Hedge Funds may be explored at www.hedgeworld. com and www. hedgefundcenter.com.

Hedge funds, on the other hand, are private investment partnerships whose shares are offered primarily to wealthy individuals and major institutions and often make high-stakes bets (supported by substantial borrowing) on the direction the market will take. Increasingly these funds are supplying venture capital for business start-ups and loans to established companies as well as trading currencies and derivatives. Offered by such leading financial firms as Barclays, Canadian Imperial Bank of Commerce, Goldman Sachs, and other financial-service companies, hedge fund assets have more than doubled since 2000, reaching nearly a trillion dollars in the most recent year.

Mutual funds offer the advantage of having a professional money manager who monitors the performance of each security held by the fund and constantly looks for profitable trading opportunities. For many small investors, who have neither the expertise nor time to constantly watch the market, access to professional money management services can be a significant advantage. However, some authorities argue that mutual funds often engage in too much daily manipulation of security portfolios, running up their costs and reducing returns. Moreover, the sharp downturn in the stock market early in the 21st century sent many investors pulling their money out of mutual funds, with a substantial portion of these scurrying back to traditional deposits. It also led to a substantial pullback in the number of financial-service providers that chose to offer investments in mutual funds and other services related to buying and selling securities.

Passage of the Gramm-Leach-Bliley Act of 1999 granted banks, security firms, and insurance companies the right to apply to the Federal Reserve Board to become financial holding companies (FHCs) and thereby sponsor and distribute shares in all types of mutual funds. Most banks are involved in the mutual fund business in at least two different ways. First, larger banking firms may offer *proprietary funds* through one of their affiliated companies. In this case the banking firm's staff will advise the fund about trading opportunities and will buy and sell shares at the request of its customers. Examples include Mellon Bank's Dreyfus Corporation with its extensive family of mutual funds and Wachovia's Evergreen Funds. Banking firms are permitted to (1) offer investment advice, normally the greatest source of fee income; (2) serve as transfer agent and custodian for mutual fund shares, keeping records of who owns shares and who is entitled to receive fund reports and earnings; and (3) execute the transactions dictated by the fund's investment adviser.

Alternatively, banking firms may offer *nonproprietary funds*. In this case the offering institution acts as broker for an unaffiliated mutual fund or group of funds but does not act as an investment advisor. Nonproprietary funds are organized, distributed, and managed by an unaffiliated company that may, however, rent lobby space inside a bank's branch offices or sell its shares through a broker who is related to the offering institution in some way. Usually the institution involved receives a commission for any sales of shares in nonproprietary funds passing through its offices.

Some experts argue that proprietary funds have the advantage of providing a relatively continuous stream of income to a bank or other service provider, while fee income generated by sales of nonproprietary funds may fluctuate and is often quite small. Some banks merely advertise access to nonproprietary funds without earning substantial fees from their sales. Nevertheless, advertising the availability of nonproprietary funds may serve to bring in new customers and lead to selling them other services.

Certainly institutions that offer their customers access to mutual funds and other investments can benefit from offering these products. There is at least the possibility of earning substantial fee income and some of that income may be less sensitive to interest-rate movements than are more traditional services, such as deposits and loans. In addition, many financial-service providers appear to gain added prestige from offering their own (proprietary) mutual funds. Some CEOs argue that offering this service positions the offering institution well for the future, particularly with respect to those customers planning for their retirement and accumulating large amounts of savings.

Annuity Investment Products

A somewhat different investment product, **annuities,** often associated with insurance companies, comes in either fixed or variable form. *Fixed annuities* promise a customer who contributes a lump sum of savings a fixed rate of return over the life of the annuity contract. The fixed-rate annuity generates a continuous, level income stream to the customer or to his or her beneficiaries. Usually the customer pays no taxes on the annuity until he or she actually begins to receive the promised stream of income. *Variable annuities*, on the other hand, allow investors to invest a lump sum of money in a basket of stocks, mutual funds, or other investments under a tax-deferred agreement, but there is no promise of a guaranteed rate of return. The customer can usually add more funds to the variable annuity contract as time goes by and then at some designated future point receive a stream of income payments whose amount is based upon the accumulated market value in the contract. If the prices of assets placed in the annuity's fund have declined in value, the customer (annuitant) may receive less income than expected. On the other hand, the annuitant may receive a larger income stream if the value of accumulated assets has risen.

Factoid
If you deposit in your bank account a check that you received from someone else and it proves to be uncollectible, are you likely to be charged a fee on such a returned item?
Answer: In the United States, yes; more than half of U.S. banks charge such a fee, which averages about $7. Does this seem OK to you? Why?

Recently a new type of annuity contract has appeared, labeled the *equity-index annuity*, combining the features of *both* fixed and variable annuities. Investors buying equity-index annuities receive the benefits of buying stocks (principally the prospect of greater capital appreciation in order to keep up with inflation) with the promise that the principal amount of their investment will be protected. Thus, if the market (measured by such stock indexes as the S&P 500 or the Dow Jones Industrial Average) moves downward, the contract holder is still guaranteed a minimum return. This new contract, offered by about 40 leading insurance companies, is particularly attractive to investors approaching retirement. In addition, MetLife and Prudential are setting up new deferred annuity contracts that switch to become income annuities at retirement with a variety of interest rates attached, aimed principally at baby boomers soon to retire who, otherwise, may have no pension income (except for Social Security payments).

One advantage for banks and other providers selling this financial service is that variable annuities often carry substantial annual fees. An annuity is the reverse of life insurance; instead of hedging against dying too soon, annuities are a hedge against living too long and outlasting one's savings. Recently insurance companies have been working with depository institutions to create proprietary variable annuities carrying the depository institution's label.

Selling Investment Products

More than a thousand banking organizations—roughly a fifth of the U.S. banking industry—were selling third-party or proprietary mutual funds and/or annuity plans as the new century began. Most of these sales (better than 90 percent) were made by multibillion-dollar banks, the industry's largest institutions. Unfortunately, not all of these product-line innovations have been particularly successful. For example, mutual fund and annuity sales recently have accounted for less than 5 percent of total bank fee income.

Somewhat more successful have been sales of shares in low-risk money market (short-term) mutual funds rather than sales of shares in longer-term stock and bond mutual funds, due, in part, to the close affinity between money market fund shares and money market deposits. U.S. banks' share of equity and bond funds sales reached a high of about 8 percent of all mutual fund sales in 1994 and has generally fallen since that time.

In part, these disappointing sales of many investment products may be due to the record profits earned by the banking industry in recent years. With their earnings at record levels banks have felt less pressure to push hard on their investment products' sales. Bank sales fees also tend to be on the high side. At the same time regulators have placed sales of mutual funds and other investment products under intense scrutiny, while regulations applying to deposits, particularly deposit insurance fees and reserve requirements, have recently been lowered, making it more attractive and less costly to sell traditional deposits rather than many of the newer and more exotic investment products. Then, too, start-up costs of mutual funds are high and the minimum-size fund needed to be competitive may be $100 million or more in assets, larger than many funds created in recent years.

Some banks have found other ways to profit from sales of investment products today by serving as recordkeepers and processors for purchases and sales. Among the most famous of these institutions are the Bank of New York and the State Street Bank of Boston, which provide such services as transferring the ownership of securities bought and sold, managing foreign stocks purchased by U.S. investors, and accounting for mutual fund sales of new shares and the redemption of already issued fund shares.

Real Banks, Real Decisions

One of the best-known fee-focused banking companies in the world is State Street Corporation (**www.statestreet.com**) in Boston. Years ago State Street phased out much of its traditional lending program and came to focus instead on fee-based services for the bulk of its income. Currently this bank has offices in more than 20 nations scattered around the globe.

State Street offers *asset management* (including the management of assets for other banks, pension plans, and mutual funds), *custodian services* (keeping track of the ownership of securities and delivering financial reports and dividends to security holders), and *foreign exchange trading and risk management* on behalf of its larger corporate customers—to name just a few of State Street's wide array of financial-service offerings. In terms of earnings, State Street is one of the most consistently profitable banks in the world, due in part to its emphasis on fee income rather than interest-sensitive loans as is true of most other banks. State Street continues to expand its operations on the international front. Recently, for example, it announced the purchase of Deutsche Bank's custodian business, which would make it the largest recordkeeping and servicing agent for institutional investors on the planet.

Risks and Rules for Selling Investment Products

Several problems and risks are associated with sales of investment products. For one thing, their value is market determined and their performance can turn out to be highly disappointing, angering customers who may hold a bank offering the service to a higher standard of performance than it would a securities broker or dealer. Moreover, some depository institutions have become embroiled in costly lawsuits filed by disappointed customers who allege they were misled about the risks associated with investment products. Banks may run into *compliance* problems if they fail to properly register their investment products with the Securities Exchange Commission or fail to comply with all the rules laid down by regulatory agencies, state commissions, and other legal bodies that monitor this market.

Current U.S. regulations require that customers must be told orally (and sign a document indicating they were so informed) that investment products are

1. Not insured by the Federal Deposit Insurance Corporation (FDIC).
2. Not a deposit or other obligation of a depository institution and not guaranteed by the offering institution.
3. Subject to investment risks, including possible loss of principal.

These and other regulatory rules must be conspicuously displayed inside offices of depository institutions where investment products are sold. Moreover, these products must be sold in an area that is separate from the area where deposits are taken from the public. The managers of depository institutions must demonstrate to regulators that they are closely monitoring their investment products' sales practices, policing themselves in order to avoid serious problems that may adversely affect the public's confidence. They must have blanket bond insurance coverage and make only those sales recommendations to customers that are "suitable" for each customer's situation. Finally, the names chosen for in-house mutual funds cannot be similar to the names of the banking firms sponsoring these funds because this might lead to confusion on the part of the public about the safety of investment products compared to the safety of federally insured deposits. On balance, these costly regulations and closer public scrutiny of investments products sales practices have caused some banking units (such as Citigroup and AmSouth Corp.) to reduce their emphasis on the funds management and marketing business.

14–1.   What services are provided by *investment banks* (IBs)? Who are their principal clients?

14–2.   Why were U.S. commercial banks forbidden to offer investment banking services for several decades? How did this affect the ability of U.S. banks to compete for underwriting business?

14–3.   What advantages do commercial banks with investment banking affiliates appear to have over competitors that do not offer investment banking services? Possible disadvantages?

14–4.   What are *investment products?* What advantages might they bring to an institution choosing to offer these services?

14–5.   What risks do investment products pose for the institutions that sell them? How might these risks be minimized?

14–4 Trust Services as a Source of Fee Income

Trust services—the management of property owned by customers, such as securities, land, buildings, and other assets—are among the oldest nondeposit services that banks and some of their closest competitors offer. There is evidence that offering professional trust services, including safeguarding and generating earnings from the prudent management of a customer's assets, goes back to the origins of the financial-services industry.

What is less well known to the public is the close tie between deposit taking by banks and the offering of trust services. A bank operating a trust department can be a major source of new deposits. Of course, not all banks have trust powers, which must be applied for from the bank's chartering agency or principal regulator, but most medium and large-size banks and some thrift institutions do operate trust departments. Trust personnel are *not* permitted to share client information on those customers they serve with personnel in other parts of the financial firm.

Trust departments often generate large deposits because they manage property for their customers, which usually include business firms, units of government, individuals and families, charities, and foundations. A trust officer—either instructed by a customer or on his or her own initiative—may place certain monies in a checking or a time deposit account for future use, such as to pay bills or to seek a more favorable rate of return for the trust client. Deposits placed in a bank by a trust department must be *fully secured*. Like any other deposit, they are covered by deposit insurance up to the legal insurance limit, but any amount over the insurance limit must be protected by investment-grade securities the bank holds while the deposit is present in the institution.

Some aspects of the trust business stretch back to the Middle Ages when wealthy individuals (trustors) often chose to turn their property over to a manager (trustee), who would protect the use of that property for the benefit of its owners. State-chartered U.S. banks have been allowed to provide trust services for many years, while national banks were granted the right to seek trust powers with passage of the Federal Reserve Act in 1913. For most of banking's history, trust departments were regarded as a needed service area for the benefit of customers, but trust operations were usually regarded as unprofitable due to the large space and the highly skilled personnel required—usually a combination of portfolio managers, lawyers, and professional accountants. However, with the advent of government deregulation of the financial system and the increasing tendency of banks to levy fees for their services, trust departments became increasingly popular as a source of fee income. For example, trust departments typically levy asset management (trustee) fees based upon the value of a customer's assets they are called upon to manage and for filing tax reports. These fees are popular with financial-service managers today because they are often less sensitive to fluctuations in market interest rates than are other revenue sources.

Trust departments function in a great variety of roles. They routinely serve as executors or administrators of wills, identifying, inventorying, and protecting the property (estate) of a deceased person, ensuring that any unpaid bills are met and that the heirs of the deceased receive the income and assets to which they are entitled. Trust departments act as *agents* for corporations that need to service their security issues, such as by issuing new stock, paying stockholder dividends, and issuing or retiring bonds. Trust personnel often manage the retirement plans of both businesses and individuals. They also serve as guardians of assets held for the benefit of minors or act on behalf of adults judged to be legally incompetent to manage their own affairs.

In fulfilling these many roles, trust departments promulgate basic trust agreements—contracts that grant a trust officer legal authority on behalf of a customer to invest funds, pay bills, and dispense income to persons or institutions with valid claims against the trust's assets. Many different types of trusts are permitted under the laws of different states, though the types and procedures vary so that anyone desiring to enter into a trust agreement must consult state trust codes. More complex trust arrangements often require the services of an outside attorney as well.

Among the more popular kinds of trusts are *living trusts* (or grantor revocable trusts), which allow trust officers to act on behalf of a living customer without a court order, generally help to avoid expensive probate proceedings if the property owner dies or becomes legally incompetent, and may be revoked or amended by the customer as desired. There are *testamentary trusts,* which arise under a probated will and are often used to save on estate taxes. If properly drawn, a testamentary trust can sometimes be used to protect a customer's property from the claims of creditors or beneficiaries who may make unreasonable demands that might prematurely exhaust the trust's assets. Other common trust agreements include *irrevocable trusts,* which allow wealth to be passed free of gift and estate taxes or may be used to allocate funds arising from court settlements or private contracts; *charitable trusts,* which support worthwhile causes, such as medical research, the arts, and care of the needy; and *indenture trusts,* which usually collect, hold, and manage assets to back an issue of securities by a corporation and then are employed to retire the securities on behalf of the issuing company when their term ends.

In the wake of a political squabble over taxing estates in the United States, many financial planners began urging their clients to set up *dynasty trusts,* where permitted by state law, to avoid paying federal estate and generation-skipping taxes. The trustor uses this device to transfer assets to the care of a trustee on behalf of his or her beneficiaries (such as the trustor's grandchildren). The assets in such a perpetual trust may be protected from bankruptcy proceedings or divorce or from lawsuits launched against the trustor by creditors and may pass tax-free from generation to generation. However, the future of dynasty trusts is uncertain at the present time as governmental authorities consider further changes in estate tax rules.

Clearly, trust departments play a remarkable set of roles that are often unseen by the public. However, their activities usually center upon establishing a *fiduciary relationship* with a customer, protecting that customer's property, making asset management decisions, planning a customer's estate and ensuring that estate property is passed in timely fashion to those entitled to its benefits and assisting businesses in raising and managing funds and in providing retirement benefits to employees. Trust departments must follow the terms of a trust or agency agreement and any court orders that have been issued. They are expected to be competent and diligent in their fiduciary and agency activities and are legally liable for losses due to negligence or failure to act as a prudent decision maker would. Trust departments have come to play vital and sometimes highly profitable roles in modern banks, including attracting a considerable volume of new deposits. Moreover, many banks use their trust departments to set up mutual funds that provide their customers with multiple investment options and permit a financial-service provider to achieve an efficient size fund more quickly.

Key URLs

To learn more about the trust services of leading banking firms, see especially Wells Fargo & Co. at **www.wellsfargo.com/com/corporatetrust**, the Bank of New York at **www.bankofny.com**, LaSalle Bank at **www.lasallebank.com/trust/**, and Wachovia Bank at **www.wachovia.com**.

Key URLs

You can explore many of the more interesting types of trusts at such Web sites as **www.wsba.org**, **http:/contracts.onecle.com**, and **www.quizlaw.com**.

Historically, trust departments have been regarded as relatively staid and slow-moving activities. However, there has been a resurgence of trust activity in recent years as these units assist corporations with employee stock option plans (ESOPs), provide escrow agency and document custodial services, supply corporate asset management needs, and serve as a conduit and recordkeeper for debt and equity securities offerings. Corporate trust departments at such leading banks as Wells Fargo, Wachovia, HSBC, and the Bank of New York have played leading roles in creating a global marketplace for loan-backed security issues. This is one case where a nontraditional product line, *investment banking,* has helped to create demand for another product line, *trust services,* particularly for corporate customers seeking to protect assets, control risk, and expand their capital base as a platform for future growth.

14–5 Sales of Insurance-Related Products

Not only have leading commercial bankers around the globe made heavy inroads into the investment banking business and into the field of brokering securities and annuities for their customers, but they also have begun to aggressively invade the insurance (risk management) business. One of the most famous of such banking–insurance alliances in modern history took place in the United States in 1998 when Citicorp, headquartered on the East Coast of the United States and considered one of the most innovative banks in the world, and Travelers Insurance Company, on America's West Coast, came together as a single corporate unit to cross-sell each other's products across the United States and around the globe (though Citicorp and Travelers began to part company in 2002).

Citicorp and Travelers were by no means alone in their efforts to cross-sell financial services. Bankers and insurance executives in North America, Europe, and Asia have moved closer together to share in the hoped-for benefits of the convergence of two important financial-service industries. Banks have acquired insurance companies or developed their own insurance products, while insurers have acquired or launched banks. For example, in the United States alone over the past decade close to 20 leading insurance companies have acquired or established bank affiliates, including such industry leaders as Allstate (which operates Allstate Bank) and MetLife, Inc. (which controls MetLife Bank NA). Some large companies operate extensive insurance agency networks that can sell banking products as well, though most insurance-company-controlled banking firms are "virtual banks," selling services through the Internet and by mail. Banks too can use their branches to sell insurance; indeed, over 100 banks today sell their own insurance products in the United States. However, the rate of growth in banking-insurance alliances appears to have slowed somewhat of late, due in part to the wide gap between the relatively high profitability of many banks and the relatively low profitability of many insurers.

While convergences between insurers and other financial-service providers have slowed recently the *consolidation* of the insurance industry itself—insurance companies merging into bigger and bigger insurance entities—is thriving. A handful of industry leaders—Prudential Financial Inc., Axa, Allianz AG, American International Group Inc., Swiss Re, Lincoln National, and St. Paul Travelers—are buying out their competitors and emerging as global players. They seek lower production and marketing costs, diversification of risk exposure beyond one or two countries, and opening up greater revenue potential from what they see as "underinsured" markets (especially in Europe and Asia).

Types of Insurance Products Sold Today

Whether offered through a traditional insurance company or through some sort of banking-insurance convergence, what are the principal insurance products sold today? Certainly the most familiar insurance product to most people is **life insurance policies.** These insurance contracts protect individuals, families, and businesses against loss in the event of death and may also include a savings account component to prepare the policyholder or his beneficiaries for future financial needs.

In addition to marketing regular life insurance policies insurers (along with their banking competitors) can set up **life insurance underwriters** who hope to generate underwriting profits from managing insurable risks and collecting more in insurance premiums and income from investments than they must pay out in insurance claims. Life insurance companies also frequently sell health insurance policies and retirement plans to individuals and businesses in return for premiums and commissions from customers.

Bankers and many of their financial-service competitors today also sell **property/casualty insurance policies,** not only through branch offices, but also through separately incorporated insurance agencies. Property/casualty insurers and insurance agents sell policies to their customers that cover a wide array of business and personal risks. For example, these policies deal with such risks as driving an automobile, operating a boat or ship, industrial accidents, illness and medical care costs, negligence or fraud in operating a business, damages to or negligence associated with owning a home, and protecting against losses due to changing interest rates and defaults on credit extended to others. **Property/casualty insurance underwriters** accept the risks involved in protecting lives and property from accidents, negligence, and other adverse events in the hope of earning more in premiums charged and from investments they make than the claims brought against them by policyholders.

Key URL
In most cases insurance companies in the U.S. are regulated at the state level through state insurance commissions. See, for example, the National Association of Insurance Commissioners at **www.naic.org/**.

Rules Covering Insurance Sales by Federally Insured Depository Institutions

As bankers and many of their competitors have poured into the insurance products' business, concern over the possibility that customers may be misled or misinformed has greatly increased. For example, the public may conclude wrongly that insurance products offered by a depository institution are covered by government-sponsored deposit insurance in case the customer suffers a loss. This concern in the United States led the key U.S. federal banking agencies—the Federal Reserve System, the Federal Deposit Insurance Corporation, the Comptroller of the Currency, and the Office of Thrift Supervision—to issue consumer protection rules beginning in October 2001.

These rules call for mandatory public disclosures on the part of depository institutions selling insurance products that stipulate

Key URLs
One of the most controversial pieces of federal legislation affecting the insurance industry was passage of the Terrorism Risk Insurance Act (TRIA) following the tragedy of 9/11. For a discussion of the TRIA and its possible implications for the future see, for example, **www.treas. gov/trip** and **www.iii. org/media/hottopics/ insurance/terrorism**.

1. An insurance product or annuity is *not* a deposit or other obligation of a depository institution or its affiliate.
2. An insurance product or annuity sold by a depository institution in the United States is *not* insured by the FDIC, any other agency of the U.S. government, the depository institution, or its affiliates.
3. Insurance products or annuities may involve investment risk and possible loss of value.
4. U.S. depository institutions cannot base granting loans on the customer's purchase of an insurance product or annuity from a depository institution or any of its affiliates or on the customer's agreement not to obtain an insurance product or annuity from an unaffiliated entity.

Such disclosures to individuals and families must be made both orally and in writing before completion of the sale of an insurance product. Moreover, the proposed new U.S. rule requires written acknowledgment from the customer that these disclosures were received from the offering depository institution. Where practicable, a depository institution must keep insurance product sales activities physically separated from those areas

ETHICS IN BANKING AND FINANCIAL SERVICES

ETHICS PROBLEMS IN THE INSURANCE INDUSTRY

Scandals surfaced in the insurance industry as the 21st century opened. One of the most publicized centered around American International Group Inc. (AIG), one of the world's largest property-casualty insurance companies. Government investigators began looking at allegations of questionable accounting practices that may have distorted some of AIG's financial reports. While the adverse publicity soon led to declining stock prices, some investors saw good prospects for future recovery as AIG and other insurers continued to explore expansion opportunities in China and other underinsured global markets.

A similar problem with the validity of insurers' financial reports emerged in connection with the use of "finite risk" contracts. These multiyear, present-value-based contractual agreements are often supplied by reinsurance firms to backstop the underwriting risks taken on by regular insurance companies. Reinsurers provide an extra cushion of protection for insurers in case the latter are confronted with unexpectedly heavy claims from their policyholders, such as occurred after the 9/11 tragedy. To the extent that "finite risk" contracts actually transfer some risk from original insurers to reinsurance companies the original insurance providers appear to gain increased balance-sheet strength. However, if there is little actual transfer of risk, insurers may experience few risk-reducing benefits. Federal and state regulators have been working recently to determine if some of these "finite risk" agreements have been improperly used, misleading some insurance-company stockholders and clients.

within a federally insured depository institution where retail deposits are routinely accepted from the public. Finally, employees who sell insurance-related products must be qualified and licensed as required by each state's insurance authorities.

14–6 The Alleged Benefits of Financial-Services Diversification

Key URLs

For further exploration of finite risk contracts and other devices recently employed by the insurance industry to help stabilize the industry's financial performance, see, for example, **www.iii.org** and **www.risktransfer magazine.com**.

As we saw in Chapter 1, when two or more different industry types—such as commercial banks, investment banks, and insurance companies—merge with each other, this strategic move is called **convergence.** One of the possible (but by no means guaranteed) benefits of industry convergence is the relatively *low correlation* that may exist between cash flows or revenues generated by the sale of traditional industry products (such as loans and deposits) versus the sale of nontraditional products (such as banks selling automobile insurance coverage and mutual funds).

For example, Rose's study [6] of numerous bank and nonbank industries found low positive and even negative correlations in cash flows between the banking industry and such financial-service industries as business and personal finance companies, security and commodity brokers and dealers, life and property/casualty insurers and insurance agencies, and real estate firms. Because streams of revenue from different product lines may move in different directions at different times, the overall impact of combining these different industries and products under one roof may be to stabilize combined cash flows and profitability. The risk of failure might also be reduced.

This potential consequence of the convergence of two or more financial-service industries is called the **product-line diversification effect.** Offering different services with different cash-flow variances over time tends to lower the overall risk of the financial firm.[1]

---

[1]As we saw in Chapter 4, there is a also a *geographic diversification effect,* which can lead to reduced cash-flow risk for a financial firm serving several different geographic markets with different economic characteristics. If one market is declining, other markets served may be on the rise, helping to stabilize overall cash flow and profitability. We need to keep in mind, however, that merely because a financial firm may be able to take advantage of product-line and/or geographic diversification, this does not guarantee that its overall risk exposure must necessarily decline. For example, management, feeling it is safer because of geographic or product-line diversification effects, may take other steps, such as accepting more risky loans or reducing capital, that actually wind up making the institution even more risky than before.

An Example of the Product-Line Diversification Effect Reducing Risk

Let us briefly illustrate what could happen to overall institutional risk by combining traditional and nontraditional financial services in one organization. For example, suppose a banking company decides to add insurance services to its existing product menu. It expects to earn a 12 percent average return from sales of its traditional banking products and a 20 percent return from selling or underwriting insurance services. These two service lines are judged to be about equally risky in the variance of their cash flows (with a standard deviation of about 5 percent each), but the banking firm expects to receive 20 percent of its revenues from insurance sales and 80 percent from sales of traditional banking products. Suppose that cash flows from the two sets of services are *negatively* correlated over time with a correlation coefficient of –0.50.

What would happen to the bank's overall return from sales of traditional and nontraditional products in this case? Portfolio theory suggests the following would happen to bank returns if the above assumptions turn out to be true:

$$
\begin{aligned}
\text{Expected return from the overall service menu } (E(r)) =\ &\text{Proportion of revenue from traditional services } (R_{TS}) \times \text{Expected return from traditional services } (E(r_{TS})) \\
+\ &\text{Proportion of revenue from nontraditional services } (R_{NS}) \times \text{Expected return from nontraditional services } (E(r_{NS}))
\end{aligned}
$$

(14–1)

or

$$
E(r) = R_{TS} \times E(r_{TS}) + R_{NS} \times E(r_{NS})
$$

In this example using the figures given previously,

$$
E(r) = 0.80(12 \text{ percent}) + 0.20(20 \text{ percent}) = 13.6 \text{ percent}
$$

That return is a *higher* overall return than the bank would receive just from selling its traditional products, where the expected return is only 12 percent.

And what happens to the *risk* of return for this bank? The key relationship is:

$$
\begin{aligned}
\text{Variance of overall return from selling traditional and nontraditional services } (\sigma_r^2) =\ &\text{Squared proportion of revenue from traditional services } (R_{TS}^2) \times \text{Variance of revenue from traditional services } (\sigma_{TS}^2) + \text{Squared proportion of revenue from nontraditional services } (R_{NS}^2) \\
&\times \text{Variance of revenue from nontraditional services } (\sigma_{NS}^2) + 2 \times \text{Proportion of revenue from traditional services } (R_{TS}) \times (1 - \text{Proportion of revenue from nontraditional services } (R_{NS})) \\
&\times \text{Correlation of returns between traditional and nontraditional services } (\rho_{TS,\,NS}) \times \text{Standard deviation of return from traditional services } (\sigma_{TS}) \times \text{Standard deviation of return from nontraditional services } (\sigma_{NS})
\end{aligned}
$$

(14–2)

or

$$\sigma_r^2 = R_{TS}^2 \times \sigma_{TS}^2 + R_{NS}^2 \times \sigma_{NS}^2 + 2 \times R_{TS}(1 - R_{NS}) \times \rho_{TS, NS} \times \sigma_{TS} \times \sigma_{NS}$$

In this instance, using the figures from the example above,

$$\sigma_r^2 = \begin{array}{l} (0.80)^2(0.05)^2 + (0.20)^2(0.05)^2 \\ + 2(0.80)(0.20)(-0.50)(0.05)(0.05) \end{array}$$

$$= 13 \text{ percent}$$

so the overall standard deviation from selling traditional and nontraditional services must be:

$$\sigma_r = \sqrt{13 \text{ percent}} = 3.06 \text{ percent}$$

Thus, in this simple illustration offering both traditional and nontraditional banking services serves to *lower* the bank's standard deviation of its overall return—a measure of the riskiness of the overall rate of return—from an average of 5 percent to about 3 percent.

While this looks like a win–win situation—higher returns and lower overall risk with nontraditional products sold alongside traditional ones—not everyone agrees that this result will occur in the real world. In fact, a recent study by Stiroh [7] from the Federal Reserve Bank of New York argues that cash flows or revenues from nontraditional products have become more volatile and more highly correlated with interest revenues from sales of traditional loans and investments, reducing any potential diversification benefits. Moreover, the same study finds evidence that noninterest revenue sources (particularly revenues generated by trading securities) often carry greater risk and lower risk-adjusted returns than do traditional interest-rate related sources of income. In short, the evidence on the real benefits, if any, of combining traditional and nontraditional financial services within a single financial firm remains mixed; the jury is still out on the real magnitude of the growth, profitability, and risk-reducing gains from the modern trend toward financial-services convergence. Further evidence of this uncertainty about the future of financial convergence appeared most recently when J.P. Morgan Chase & Co. announced the proposed sale of Protective Life Corp., its life insurance and annuity underwriting unit as well as its online brokerage services business.

Potential Economies of Scale and Scope

Other potential benefits from offering multiple services, besides reduction of risk through diversification, include *economies of scale* and *economies of scope*. As we saw in Chapter 3, **economies of scale** emerge as a financial firm grows in *size* (usually measured by its total assets). The cost of production per unit of output tends to fall as a smaller firm grows into a larger one due to greater efficiency and the spreading of a greater volume of output over the firm's fixed costs (especially the costs associated with plant and equipment). Unfortunately, economies of scale studies suggest that many financial firms quickly use up their gains from lower costs. Few cost benefits appear once many financial firms reach even modest size.

Economies of scope, in contrast, refer to a situation in which the *joint costs* of producing two or more services in one firm are *less* than the combined cost of producing each of these services through separate firms. For example, if a single financial firm produces two

Potential Advantages of Combining Commercial Banking, Trust Services Management, Investment Banking, and Insurance Sales and Underwriting under the Same Financial Holding Company (FHC)

Financial Holding Company (FHC)			
Commercial Banking	**Trust Services Management**	**Investment Banking**	**Insurance Sales and Underwriting**
Extending loans at interest Providing credit guarantees, payments services, liquidity and savings plans	Managing property Managing pension plans Recordkeeping and safekeeping Distributing new securities and interest and dividend payments on existing securities	Assisting clients with acquisitions and mergers Raising debt and equity capital for government and corporate clients (security underwriting) Brokering securities for clients	Providing risk management services for persons and property, pension plan management, cash management services and long-term savings plans

The *potential* advantages of combining these financial-service activities under one corporate umbrella include supplementing traditional sources of funds and revenue with new funds and revenue sources, lowering the cost of service production and delivery through economies of scale (greater volume) and economies of scope (more intensive use of existing management and other productive resources), increased earnings stability, and reduced risk of failure through greater product-line and geographic diversification.

services (S_1 and S_2), instead of producing only one service (S_1), using the same resources, its cost of production (C) *may* be lower as shown below:

$$\underset{C(S_1, S_2)}{\substack{\text{Joint cost of producing} \\ \text{services 1 and 2 by the} \\ \text{same financial firm}}} < \underset{C(S_1, 0)}{\substack{\text{Cost of producing} \\ \text{service 1} \\ \text{by financial firm 1}}} + \underset{C(0, S_2)}{\substack{\text{Cost of producing} \\ \text{service 2} \\ \text{by financial firm 2}}} \qquad \textbf{(14–3)}$$

These cost savings from one firm producing *multiple* services *may* be lower because some inputs (such as advertising, management, computer and office facilities) are *shared*. Expanding the number of financial services offered *may* result in more intensive use of resources, reducing overall costs and widening a multiservice firm's profit margin.

We must be cautious, however, about believing that economies of scale and scope can bring significant cost benefits to multiservice financial firms. Research evidence, thus far, finds only weak support for scale and scope economies in most financial-service industries, with the possible exception of credit unions, mutual funds, security brokers, and some insurance companies. In the case of banks scale economies tend to be almost exhausted by the time a bank reaches $2 to $10 billion in assets—a middle-size bank in today's world—and scope economies are difficult to detect at all (as noted, for example, by Berger and Humphrey [8] and Clark [9]). So, it is not yet clear that the emergence of megasize, multiple-service financial firms has helped very much in lowering cost of production for many services. However, *revenues* may expand and become more stable when a financial firm expands its service menu.

14–7 Information Flows within the Financial Firm

As banks and many of their competitors have evolved into more widely diversified financial-service firms offering investment, insurance, and other new services, they have become more and more like pure information-gathering, information-processing, and information-dispersing businesses. Financial service-providers can use the same customer data over and over again to generate revenue or cash flow, minimizing information costs per unit of service at the same time. Financial institutions are in a unique position in the economy to serve as a collection point for customer data and as an information processor and interpreter. By supplying credit insurance, and other information-based services that many customers regard as essential, financial firms generate valuable customer data that may be useful to a wide range of other businesses trying to deepen and expand their customer bases.

For example, nonbank businesses, whether affiliated with banks or not, may seek to access bank-generated customer data and use it to enhance their own cash flow and market share. Indeed, some economists argue today that these potential information economies are literally the driving forces behind the mergers and acquisitions that are reshaping financial-service industries today. Some financial firms see an inherent advantage in being affiliated with a bank, especially if it is too costly to attempt to purchase vital customer information from an independent provider.

As the 20th century drew to a close, several governments around the world, including federal and state governments inside the United States, decided that information gathering, processing, and especially information dispensing by financial firms might well become a source of either "good" or "evil" for the public. For example, financial firms with a wider array of bank and nonbank services to sell could use their customers' data files to generate more revenue productivity at low cost and become highly profitable, giving them a key economic advantage over other firms but also offering great potential for damage to their customers.

For example, suppose that medical data supplied by a customer who is applying for life or health insurance coverage is shared with a bank where that customer is requesting a new home loan. Suppose the customer has a serious medical problem and is denied insurance coverage. Denial of access to that one service could easily lead to denial of access to other financial services as well. The bank where the same customer applied for a home loan might use the adverse medical information uncovered by the insurance company to deny that loan. Moreover, this same adverse information might be shared with other firms, resulting in the customer in question being "blacklisted" by many other service providers. Competition for a customer's business could be blunted by what is, in effect, coordinated and cooperative discrimination.

This very real possibility of personal damage from sharing data and the parallel problem of the outright invasion of personal privacy by businesses led to great controversy when the United States passed the Gramm-Leach-Bliley Act in 1999. As we recall from our earlier discussion of this law in Chapters 2 and 3, the act allowed financial-service companies to share customer information among their affiliated firms and also with independently owned third parties provided customers did not expressly say "no" to (or "opt out" of) having their personal data distributed to others.

EXHIBIT 14–1

Key Items That Must Be Included in a Financial Firm's Privacy Policy and Be Sent to Its Customers at Least Once a Year

What kinds of information about customers the financial firm may share with other firms (e.g., the customer's income, marital status, credit history and credit rating, employment history, etc.).

What kinds of companies the customer's private information may be shared with (e.g., mortgage bankers, insurance agents, retailers, direct marketers, etc.).

What the customer can do to "opt out" of information sharing and tell the financial firm not to share his or her private data (e.g., by providing the customer a toll-free number to call, a Web site address to contact, or a special form to complete and send in to the firm).

A warning that some private information (such as data needed to carry out a transaction requested by the customer) can be shared even if the customer might wish otherwise.

Factoid

In 2003 the FACT Act was passed in the United States, giving consumers a better chance of heading off ID theft, correcting their credit reports, and limiting marketing solicitations. FACT and its subsequent regulations (including Regulations B, V, and FF) limits creditors' ability to obtain and use private medical information. However, there are exceptions, such as if a consumer supplies such information voluntarily.

Subsequently, as the 21st century opened federal banking and thrift agencies (including the Federal Reserve System, Comptroller of the Currency, Federal Deposit Insurance Corporation, and Office of Thrift Supervision) prepared new regulations to give customers a real chance to opt out of or at least limit the sharing of personal information. The first step was to draft regulations to protect **customer privacy** in sharing a customer's private data between unrelated financial-service providers. This first set of new rules stipulated that when a customer applies to open a new account or access a new service he or she must be informed of the service provider's customer privacy policies. Moreover, at least once a year the customer must be reminded about the content of those privacy policies (see Exhibit 14–1).

If a customer objects to having his or her private data shared with other, unrelated businesses, such as telephone marketers, the service provider must tell the customer how to opt out of data sharing. If the customer fails to notify the service provider of his or her objections to sharing personal data, then the financial service firm can go ahead and share at least some of customer's private information with others, even with outsiders.

Concept Check

14–6. What exactly are *trust services*?

14–7. How do trust services generate fee income and often deposits as well for banks and other financial institutions offering this service?

14–8. What types of *insurance products* do banks and a number of their competitors sell today? What advantages could these products offer depository institutions choosing to sell insurance services? Can you see any possible disadvantages?

14–9. What is *convergence? Product-line diversification? Economies of scale and scope?* Why might they be of considerable importance for banks and other financial-service firms?

14–10. How can financial-service customers limit the sharing of their private data by different financial-service firms? In what ways could customer information sharing be useful for financial institutions and for their customers? What possible dangers does information sharing present?

Summary

In this chapter we have examined several of the newer services that many banks and non-bank financial firms have begun to offer in recent years, and we explored the reasons for this newest form of product-line (service) diversification among financial institutions. The most important points in the chapter include:

- Banks and a number of their strongest competitors are reaching beyond traditional industry boundaries to offer nontraditional products, such as life insurance, property/casualty insurance, investment banking, and brokerage of stocks, bonds, shares in mutual funds, and other securities. These services have provided new sources of *fee income.* They have also provided *product-line* (service) *diversification* to possibly lower risk and *economies of scale and scope,* in which management, facilities, and other business resources are used more intensively and perhaps more efficiently to generate revenue and income.

- Among the most important of the newer services offered by commercial banks and other service providers is *investment banking*—providing advice to businesses, governments, and other institutions interested in expansion into new markets, pursuing mergers and acquisitions, or offering new debt and equity securities in the financial marketplace. When the economy is expanding, investment banking can be among the most profitable of all financial services.

- Beginning in the 1990s hundreds of depository institutions began offering *investment products,* including the buying and selling of stocks, bonds, shares in mutual funds, and other financial instruments on behalf of their customers, generating commission and fee income in the process. Sales of these services also tend to soften the impact of the loss of deposits when customers are attracted away from depository institutions by perceived higher yields in the markets for stocks, bonds, and other investments.

- *Trust services*—the management of a customer's property and financial interests—are offered today primarily by banks, insurance companies, and trust companies. Trust departments provide a wide array of household and business trust services, including preparing wills and estate plans and managing the property of an individual or family, assisting companies with the management of their employee pension plans, aiding corporations selling securities to the public (including keeping records of the ownership of any securities issued and dispensing payments on behalf of corporate clients), and numerous other specialized financial services. Trust services generate fee income and often attract new funds to service-providing institutions.

- *Sales of insurance policies* and *the underwriting of insurance risks* have been added to the service menus of many larger financial institutions, particularly since passage of the Gramm-Leach-Bliley Act in 1999, allowing the formation of financial holding companies (FHCs). Sales of life insurance and property/casualty insurance policies to cover the financial risks of death, ill health, retirement, acts of negligence, and damage to personal and business property have generated substantial fees and commissions for financial firms offering these services. Larger banking organizations have also recently expanded into insurance underwriting in search of profits from investing and managing policyholder funds.

- As financial firms have expanded into nontraditional product lines they have become premier information-gathering and information-processing businesses, collecting and disseminating extensive personal or inside data about their customers. This information function helps financial firms devise new services more closely matched to each customer's service needs. However, it also carries risks to the customer whose private data may be shared with other businesses. Passage of the Gramm-Leach-Bliley Act of 1999 and other laws grant customers the opportunity to "opt out" of certain information sharing by banks and other financial firms.

Key Terms

Problems and Projects

1. Suppose the management of the First National Bank of New York decides that it needs to expand its fee-income generating services. Among the services the bank is considering adding to its service menu are *investment banking, the brokering of mutual funds, stocks, bonds, and annuities, sales of life and casualty insurance policies, and offering personal and commercial trust services.*

   a. Based on what you read in this chapter, list as many potential *advantages* as you can that might come to First National as a result of adding these services to its menu.

   b. What potential *disadvantages* might the bank encounter from selling these fee-generating services?

   c. Are there *risks* to the bank from developing and offering services such as these? If so, can you think of ways to lower the bank's risk exposure from offering these new services?

   d. What might happen to the size and volatility of revenues, expenses, and profitability from selling fee-based services like those mentioned above?

2. A commercial bank decides to expand its service menu to include the underwriting of new security offerings (i.e. investment banking) as well as offering traditional lending and deposit services. It discovers that the expected return and risk associated with these two sets of service offerings are as follows:

Expected return from traditional banking services	10%
Expected return from security underwriting	15%
Standard deviation of return from traditional banking services	3%
Standard deviation of return from security underwriting services	6%
Correlation of returns between traditional banking and security underwriting services	+0.25
Proportion of revenues expected to be derived from:	
Traditional banking services	85%
Security underwriting services	15%

Please calculate the effects of the new service on the banking company's overall return and risk.

3. Based on what you learned from reading this chapter and from studies you uncovered on the Web which of the financial firms listed below are most likely to benefit from *economies of scale or scope* and which will probably *not* benefit significantly from these economies based on the information given?

   a. A new bank offering traditional banking services (principally deposits and loans) was chartered earlier this year, gaining $50 million in assets within the first six months.

   b. A community bank with about $250 million in assets provides traditional banking services but also operates a small trust department for the convenience of families and small businesses.

c. A financial holding company (FHC) with about $2 billion in assets offers a full range of banking and investment services, giving customers access to a family of mutual funds.

d. A bank holding company with just over $10 billion in assets also operates a security brokerage subsidiary, trading in stocks and bonds for its customers.

e. A financial holding company (FHC) with $750 billion in assets controls a commercial bank, investment banking house, chain of insurance agency offices, and finance company and supplies commercial and consumer trust services through its recently expanded trust department.

Internet Exercises

1. One of the most adventurous of financial-service offerings in recent years has been the marketing of stock and bond mutual funds through banking companies. You will find offerings of mutual funds on many financial institutions' Web sites. For instance, visit **www.wachovia.com**; click the link for the Investing Center and explore the types of investments. One group of mutual funds offered by Wachovia is managed by a subsidiary. What is the name of the subsidiary? Visit the subsidiary's Web site and see what types of funds it manages.

2. If you want to evaluate mutual funds, explore **www.morningstar.com**. Go to the Morningstar Web site; click the Funds button and then the Mutual Fund Quickrank link. What are the top five bond funds when measured by a five-year annualized total return? What are the top five U.S. stock funds when measured by a five-year annualized total return? How do the returns compare?

3. Banking and insurance companies have invaded each other's territory and share information. To gather more information about this growing trend toward convergence among banking and insurance firms, visit **www.financialservicesfacts.org/financial**. What percentage of bank holding companies report insurance brokerage and underwriting fee income? How have insurance companies entered banking? What does this reveal to you?

4. If you are like millions of other financial-service customers, concerned about what financial-service companies may do with your private data, visit the Federal Trade Commission at **www.ftc.gov** and explore current regulations concerning privacy. Go to **www.ftc.gov/privacy/privacyinitiatives/glbact.html** and summarize the financial privacy rule and the safeguards rule.

5. If, like millions of other financial-service customers, you are concerned about what your financial institution's privacy policy is, visit its Web site. You should find their privacy policy posted. Read the policy and print out a copy. Are you pleased with their privacy policy? What concerns do you have?

S&P Market Insight Challenge (www.mhhe.com/edumarketinsight)

STANDARD & POOR'S

1. Investment banking and security brokerage activities are important sources of fee income for many financial-service businesses. In the S&P Industry Survey entitled "Investment Services," investment banking and brokerage services are classified by revenue source. For an up-to-date description of these particular revenue sources, click the Industry tab in S&P's Market Insight. The drop-down menu supplies the subindustry category of Investment Banking and Brokerage. Upon choosing this particular subindustry group, you will find a recent downloadable S&P Industry Survey on Investment Services. Download this survey and view the section, "How the Industry Operates," identifying and describing each source of revenue associated with investment banking and security brokerage.

REAL NUMBERS FOR REAL BANKS   **Assignment for Chapter 14**

YOUR BANK'S GENERATION OF FEE INCOME

After the passage of the Gramm-Leach-Bliley Act in 1999, financial holding companies (FHCs) were created and many institutions that wanted to broaden their activities and sources of income registered with the Federal Reserve. (In Chapter 3's assignment you determined whether your banking company is registered as a financial holding company.) The Gramm-Leach-Bliley Act also gave banks the go-ahead to expand beyond traditional banking activities within the individual banks. Chapter 14 describes the following nontraditional banking activities that can be used to generate noninterest fee income for financial institutions: (1) investment banking, (2) security trading, (3) insurance underwriting and sales, and (4) trust (fiduciary) activities. In this assignment, we will focus on the types of noninterest income generated by your bank's service activities.

Part One: Collecting the Data

First we will copy rows 38–41 to rows 136–139. Then we will go to the FDIC's SDI Web site located at **www3.fdic.gov/sdi/** and collect information from the "Additional Noninterest Income" report for a comparative examination of the fee income generated by your bank compared to that of the peer group across two years. Access the report using the pull-down menus and collect the percentage information for the items listed in rows 140 to 145. You will need to sum data to provide entries marked with * and **.

Part Two: Analyzing the Data for Interpretation

Utilize columns F, G, H, and I to calculate noninterest income as a percentage of total operating income (interest income plus noninterest income). For example, the formula for cell F136 would be B136/(B34 + B38) and the formula for cell I136 would be E136/(E34 + E38).

	A	B	C	D	E	F	G	H	I	J
			Percentage of Assets			Percentage of Total Operating Income				
133	Breakdown of Fee (Noninterest) Income	BHC	Peer Group	BHC	Peer Group	BHC	Peer Group	BHC	Peer Group	
135	Date	12/31/yyyy	12/31/yyyy	12/31/yyyy	12/31/yyyy	12/31/yyyy	12/31/yyyy	12/31/yyyy	12/31/yyyy	
136	Total noninterest income									
137	Fiduciary activities									
138	Service charges on deposit accounts									
139	Trading account gains & fees									
140	Investment banking, advisory, brokerage, and underwriting fees and commissions									
141	Venture capital revenue									
142	Net servicing and securitization income*									
143	Insurance commission fees and income									
144	Net gains* (losses) on sales of assets (excluding securities)**									
145	Other noninterest income									

*Is a sum of net servicing fees and net securitization income.
**Is a sum of net gains (losses) on sales of loans, net gains (losses) on sales of other real estate owned, and net gains (losses) on sales of other assets (excluding securities).

A. Is noninterest income a significant component of total operating income? Is it more important for your bank than for the peer group? Has this changed across the years? Write one paragraph addressing these issues.

(continued)

 **STANDARD &POOR'S**

2. Using the S&P's Investment Services Industry Survey (see above challenge for access directions) read the section on Industry Trends. How have firms moved across industry lines? Do these cross-industry affiliations carry any significant advantages for the companies involved?

www.mhhe.com/rose7e

REAL NUMBERS FOR REAL BANKS

Assignment for Chapter 14 *(continued)*

B. Use the chart function in Excel and the data by columns in rows 137 through 145 to create a group of four bar charts illustrating components of noninterest income for your BHC and its peer group over the two-year period. You will be able to select the block and create a single chart to be saved as one separate spreadsheet with just a few clicks of the mouse. To illustrate what you want to create, the chart containing information for NCC and its peer group would appear as shown below. (Note: if you have access to a color printer you will not have to transform graphics to be effective in black and white as we have done below):

C. Write one or two paragraphs interpreting your data and discussing your bank's generation of fee income relative to other large institutions (peer group) across the two-year period. What types of activities have contributed to the fee income generated by your bank? What inferences can you make concerning the potential effects on risk exposure? You may want to incorporate tables using the Excel spreadsheets and reference these in your discussion.

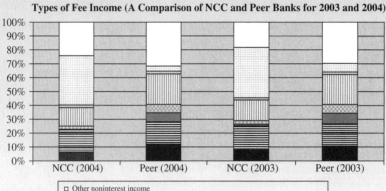

Types of Fee Income (A Comparison of NCC and Peer Banks for 2003 and 2004)

- □ Other noninterest income
- □ Net gains* (losses) on sales of assets (excluding securities)**
- □ Insurance commission fees and income
- □ Net servicing and securitization income*
- ■ Venture capital revenue
- □ Investment banking, advisory, brokerage, and underwriting fees and commissions
- ■ Trading account gains & fees
- ▣ Service charges on deposit accounts
- ■ Fiduciary activities

Selected References

For a discussion of fees frequently charged for banking services, see:

1. Hannan, Timothy H. "Retail Fees of Depository Institutions, 1997–2001." *Federal Reserve Bulletin*, September 2002, pp. 405–413.

For a discussion of the nature and types of investment banking services, see especially:

2. Hayes, Samuel L. III, and Philip M. Hubbard. *Investment Banking*. Boston: Harvard Business School Press, 1990.
3. Harshman, Ellen, Fred C. Yeager, and Timothy J. Yeager. "The Door Is Open, But Banks Are Slow to Enter Insurance and Investment Areas." *The Regional Economist*, Federal Reserve Bank of St. Louis, October 2005, pp. 5–9.

For a discussion of convergence trends among commercial banks, investment banks, and insurance companies and the effects of product-line diversification, see, in particular:

4. Carlson, John B., Edward Pelz, and Erkin Y. Sahonoz. "Mutual Funds, Fee Transparency and Competition." *Economic Commentary*, Federal Reserve Bank of Cleveland, March 1, 2004, pp. 1–3.

5. Guzman, Mark G. "Slow But Steady Progress Toward Financial Deregulation." *Southwest Economy*, Federal Reserve Bank of Dallas, no. 1 (January/February 2003), pp. 1, 6–9, and 12.

6. Rose, Peter S. "Diversification of the Banking Firm." *The Financial Review* 24, no. 2 (May 1989), pp. 251–280.

7. Stiroh, Kevin J. "Diversification in Banking: Is Noninterest Income the Answer?" *Staff Report No. 154*, Federal Reserve Bank of New York, 2002.

For an exploration of economies of scale and scope, see the following:

8. Berger, A. N., and David H. Humphrey. "Efficiency of Financial Institutions: International Survey and Directions for Future Research." *European Journal of Operations Research* 98 (1997), pp. 175–212.

9. Clark, Jeffrey A. "Economies of Scale and Scope at Depository Financial Institutions: Review of the Literature." *Economic Review*, Federal Reserve Bank of Kansas City, September/October 1988, pp. 16–33.

For a discussion of customer privacy and consumer information issues in offering financial services, see:

10. Lacker, Jeffrey M. "The Economics of Financial Privacy: To Opt Out or Opt In." *Economic Quarterly*, Federal Reserve Bank of Richmond 88 (Summer 2002), pp. 16–25.

CHAPTER FIFTEEN

The Management of Capital

Key Topics in This Chapter

- The Many Tasks of Capital
- Capital and Risk Exposures
- Types of Capital In Use
- Capital as the Centerpiece of Regulation
- Basel I and Basel II
- Planning to Meet Capital Needs

15–1 Introduction

In a book like this one all topics are important, all have a bearing upon the profitability and viability of financial firms. But some topics are clearly more important than others. *Capital* is one of those. Raising sufficient capital and retaining enough capital to protect the interests of customers, employees, owners, and the general public is one of the great challenges in the management of a financial-service provider.

What is **capital?** For bankers and many of their competitors the word *capital* has a special meaning. It refers principally to the funds contributed by the owners of a financial firm. In the case of a bank this means the *stockholders*—investors in the common and preferred stock that a financial firm has issued. In the case of banking's closest competitors, the thrift institutions, the "owners" may be stockholders if the thrift is a corporation or may be its customers in the case of a credit union or mutual savings bank. (For a customer-owned financial firm, capital consists of an accumulation of reinvested profits.)

What is it that the *owners* contribute? Their money—a portion of their wealth—is placed at the financial firm's disposal in the hope of earning a competitive rate of return on those contributed funds. Sometimes that desired rate of return on the wealth contributed by the owners emerges and sometimes it doesn't. Indeed, if the financial-firm fails, the owners may lose everything they invested. Thus, capital consists mainly of owners' funds placed at risk in the pursuit of a rate of return commensurate with the risks accepted by the owners.

What form does the owners' investment in a financial institution take? As we will see later in this chapter, some of the owners' capital contribution takes the form of *purchases of stock*. Another important component consists of *annual earnings that the owners reinvest in the financial firm*, building up its reserves in the hope that management will profitability invest those *retained earnings*, increasing the owners' future returns.

Why is capital so important in financial-services management? Capital performs such indispensable functions as supplying resources to start a new financial firm, creating a base of resources for future growth, providing a cushion of protection against risk, and promoting public confidence in the long-term viability of a financial firm. Moreover, capital has become the centerpiece of supervision and regulation today—the lever that regulators can pull whenever the alarm bell sounds in an effort to prevent the collapse of a financial firm. Indeed, it is difficult to name anything else on the balance sheet of a financial institution that performs so many vital tasks. *Yes, capital is important.*

15–2 The Many Tasks Capital Performs

The capital accounts play several vital roles in supporting the daily operations and ensuring the long-run viability of financial firms. In the first place, capital provides a cushion against the risk of failure by absorbing financial and operating losses until management can address the institution's problems and restore its profitability.

Second, capital provides the funds needed to charter, organize, and operate a financial firm before other sources of funds come flowing in. A new institution needs start-up funding to acquire land, build or lease facilities, purchase equipment, and hire officers and staff even before opening day.

Third, capital promotes public confidence and reassures creditors concerning an institution's financial strength. Capital must also be strong enough to reassure borrowers that a lending institution will be able to meet their credit needs even if the economy turns down.

Fourth, capital provides funds for the organization's growth and the development of new services and facilities. Most financial-service providers eventually outgrow the facilities they start with. An infusion of additional capital will permit a financial firm to expand into larger quarters or build additional branch offices in order to keep pace with its expanding market and follow its customers.

Fifth, capital serves as a regulator of growth, helping to ensure that growth is sustainable in the long run. Both the regulatory authorities and the financial markets require that capital increases roughly in line with the growth of risky assets. Thus, the cushion to absorb losses is supposed to increase along with a financial institution's growing risk exposure. For example, a bank that expands its loans and deposits too fast will start receiving signals from the market and the regulatory community that its growth must be slowed or additional capital must be added.

Relatively recent research evidence suggests that capital has played a key role in the rapid growth of mergers among financial firms. For example, Peek and Rosengren [5] of the Federal Reserve Bank of Boston find evidence that hundreds of smaller banks have disappeared via merger because of burgeoning growth in large business loans (over $1 million each), which can only be made by bigger lenders with stronger capital positions. Both banks' internal loan policies and federal regulations limit the maximum size of not fully secured loans made to a single borrower to no more than 15 percent of a bank's unimpaired capital and surplus, while fully collateralized loans are limited to no more than 25 percent of a federally chartered bank's unimpaired capital and surplus. Lenders whose capital fails to grow fast enough find themselves losing market share in the competition for the largest borrowing customers.

Finally, capital regulation has become an increasingly important tool to limit how much risk exposure financial firms can accept. In this role capital not only tends to promote public confidence in the financial system but also serves to protect the government's deposit insurance system ("safety net") from serious losses.

15–3 Capital and Risk

Capital and risk are intimately related to each other. Capital itself is mainly the funds contributed by the owners of a financial-firm that have been placed in the firm at the *owners' risk*—the risk that the institution will earn a less-than-satisfactory return on owners' funds or may even fail, with the stockholders recovering little or nothing. Thus, the risks facing the owners are substantial.

Key Risks in Banking and Financial Institutions' Management

Credit Risk

There is, first of all, *credit risk*. For example, financial intermediaries make loans and take on securities that are nothing more than promises to pay. When borrowing customers fail to make some or all of their promised payments, these defaulted loans and securities result in losses that can eventually erode capital. Because owners' capital is usually no more than 10 percent of the volume of loans and risky securities (often much less than that), it doesn't take too many defaults before capital simply becomes inadequate to absorb further losses. At this point, the financial firm fails and will close unless the regulatory authorities elect to keep it afloat until a buyer can be found.

Liquidity Risk

Depository institutions encounter substantial *liquidity risk*—the danger of running out of cash when cash is needed to cover deposit withdrawals and to meet credit requests from good customers. For example, if a bank cannot raise cash in timely fashion, it is likely to lose many of its customers and suffer a loss in earnings for its owners. If the cash shortage persists, it may lead to runs by depositors and ultimate collapse. The inability to meet liquidity needs at reasonable cost is often a prime signal that a financial institution is in trouble.

Interest Rate Risk

Financial intermediaries also encounter risk to their *spread*—the danger that revenues from earning assets will decline or that interest expenses will rise, squeezing the spread between revenues and expenses and thereby reducing net income. Changes in the spread are usually related to either *portfolio management decisions* (i.e., changes in the composition of assets and liabilities) or to *interest rate risk*—the probability that fluctuating interest rates will result in significant appreciation or depreciation in the value of and return from the institution's assets. In recent years financial firms have found ways to reduce their interest rate risk exposure, but such risks have not been completely eliminated—nor can they be.

Operational Risk

Financial-service providers also face **operational risk** due to weather damage, aging or faulty computer systems, breakdowns in quality control, inefficiencies in producing and delivering services, natural disasters, terrorist acts, errors in judgment by management, and fluctuations in the economy that impact the demand for each financial service. These changes can adversely affect revenue flows, operating costs, and the value of the owner's investment in the institution (e.g., its stock price).

Exchange Risk

Larger banks and securities firms face **exchange risk** from their dealings in foreign currency. The world's most tradable currencies float with changing market conditions today. Institutions trading in these currencies for themselves and their customers continually run the risk of adverse price movements on both the buying and selling sides of this market.

Filmtoid
What 1977 comedy revolves around two bank officers, played by Burgess Meredith and Richard Basehart, covering up employee embezzlement in the face of an on-site examination by regulators?
Answer: *The Great Bank Hoax.*

Crime Risk

Finally, all financial firms encounter significant **crime risk.** Fraud or embezzlement by employees or directors can severely weaken a financial institution and, in some instances, lead to its failure. In fact, the Federal Deposit Insurance Corporation lists fraud and embezzlement from insiders as one of the prime causes of recent bank closings. Moreover, the large amounts of money that banks keep in their vaults often prove to be an irresistible attraction to outsiders. As outlaw Jesse James was reputed to have said when asked why he robbed banks, "because that's where the money is."

Robberies of depository institutions approached record levels during the 1970s and 1980s. These thefts were frequently a by-product of bankers' efforts to make their lobbies, drive-up windows, and teller machines more accessible to the public. While the 1990s began an ongoing decline in the daily rate at which robberies were occurring, the extent and intensity of crime remain high by historical standards. The focus of robberies has shifted somewhat with changes in technology; theft from ATMs and from patrons using electronic networks has become one of the most problematic aspects of crime risk among financial institutions today.

Concept Check

15–1. What does the term *capital* mean as it applies to financial institutions?

15–2. What crucial roles does capital play in the management and viability of a financial firm?

15–3. What are the links between capital and risk exposure among financial-service providers?

Defenses against Risk

Of course, financial firms are not devoid of protection against these many risks. In fact, there are several rings of defense that owners can rely upon to protect their institution's financial position.

Quality Management

One of these defenses is *quality management*—the ability of top-notch managers to move swiftly to deal with problems before they overwhelm a financial firm.

Diversification

Diversification of a financial institution's sources and uses of funds also has risk-reducing benefits. For example, managers of financial firms generally strive to achieve two types of risk-reducing diversification: portfolio and geographic. **Portfolio diversification** means spreading out credit accounts and deposits among a wide variety of customers, including large and small business accounts, different industries, and households with a variety of sources of income and collateral. **Geographic diversification** refers to seeking out customers located in different communities or countries, which presumably will experience somewhat different economic conditions. These forms of diversification are most effective in reducing the risk of loss when cash flows from different groups of customers move in different patterns over time. Thus, declines in cash flow from one customer segment may be at least partially offset by increases in cash flow from other customer segments.

Deposit Insurance

Still another line of defense against risks is *deposit insurance*. The Federal Deposit Insurance Corporation, established in the United States in 1934 and today protecting depositors holding up to $100,000 in any federally insured depository institution, was designed to promote and preserve public confidence. While it has not stopped depository institutions from failing, the FDIC appears to have stopped runs on neighboring institutions when any one of them fails. Moreover, its power to examine depositories, issue cease and desist orders, levy civil money penalties, and seek criminal prosecution of violators of federal laws inhibits much risk taking by management and shareholders. This is why most industrialized countries today have some form of deposit insurance system.

Owners' Capital

When all else fails, it is *owners' capital* (net worth) that forms the ultimate defense against risk. Owners' capital absorbs losses from bad loans, poor securities investments, crime, and management misjudgment so that a financial firm can keep operating until its problems are corrected and its losses are recovered. Only when losses are so large they overwhelm not only all the other defenses but also the owners' capital will the institution be forced to close its doors. Owners' capital is the last line of defense against failure. Thus, the greater the risk of failure, from whatever source, the more capital a financial institution should hold.

15–4 Types of Capital in Use

Several different types of capital are in use in the industry today:

1. **Common stock,** measured by the par (face) value of common equity shares outstanding, which pay a variable return depending on whether the issuing institution's board of directors votes to pay a dividend.

2. **Preferred stock,** measured by the par value of any shares outstanding that promise to pay a fixed rate of return (dividend rate); preferred stock may be perpetual, have only limited life, or be issued as trust preferred stock.

3. **Surplus,** representing the excess amount above each share of stock's par value paid in by the institution's shareholders.

4. **Undivided profits,** representing the net earnings that have been retained in the business rather than being paid out as dividends.

5. **Equity reserves,** representing funds set aside for contingencies, such as legal action against the institution, as well as providing a reserve for dividends expected to be paid but not yet declared and a sinking fund to retire stock or debt in the future.

6. **Subordinated debentures,** representing long-term debt capital contributed by outside investors, whose claims legally follow (i.e., are subordinated to) the claims of depositors; these debt instruments may carry a convertibility feature, permitting their future exchange for shares of stock.

7. **Minority interest in consolidated subsidiaries,** where the financial firm holds ownership shares in other businesses.

8. **Equity commitment notes,** which are debt securities repayable from the sale of stock.

Relative Importance of Different Sources of Capital

To get some idea of the relative importance of the different kinds of capital we examine the capital account for all U.S.-insured banks. Table 15–1 shows these various sources of capital are by no means equal in importance. First, the *surplus* market value of all common and preferred stock above the stock's face or par value represents the largest proportion of U.S. bank capital, accounting for just over 50 percent of all long-term debt and equity capital. Close behind is *undivided profits* (retained earnings) and capital reserves, representing a third of U.S. banks' capitalization. The remainder is divided up among all other types of capital, including *long-term debt* (subordinated notes and debentures) at close to 12 percent and the *par value of common stock* at almost 5 percent.

TABLE 15–1   Capital Accounts of FDIC-Insured U.S. Commercial Banks, June 30, 2005

Source: Federal Deposit Insurance Corporation.

Forms of Capital	All U.S. FDIC-Insured Commercial Banks		Percent of Capital by Bank Size Group:		
	Amount of Capital in $ Billions	Percent of Total	Small	Medium	Large
Long-term debt capital:					
Subordinated notes and debentures	$ 114.8	11.4%	0.0%*	0.7%	13.0%
Equity capital:					
Common stock, par value	31.4	3.1	14.8	8.4	2.2
Perpetual preferred stock, par value	7.1	0.7	0.1	0.2	0.8
Surplus	513.5	51.0	41.6	40.9	52.3
Undivided profits and capital reserves	340.3	33.8	43.5	49.8	31.8
Total equity capital	$ 892.3	88.6%	99.9	99.3	87.1
Total long-term debt and equity capital	$1007.1	100.0%	100.0%	100.0%	100.0%
Ratio of Total Debt and Equity Capital to Total Bank Assets	....	11.5%	11.9%	10.2%	11.7%

Notes: *Small* banks have less than $100 million in total assets; *medium* banks range from $100 million to $1 billion in total assets; and *large* banks are over a billion dollars in total assets. *indicates a figure less than 0.5 percent. Figures may not add to column totals due to rounding error.

Preferred stock is relatively insignificant—about 1 percent of the U.S. banking industry's capital—though preferred has increased in importance in recent years among larger banks and bank holding companies around the world. Preferred stock often carries floating dividend rates and a redeemability feature that allows management to call in outstanding shares and pay off shareholders when it is financially advantageous to do so. However, bank preferred stock has been slow to win the confidence of some investors, in part because of bad experiences during the Great Depression of the 1930s when many troubled banks sold preferred shares just to stay afloat.

A unique form of preferred stock that emerged recently is *trust preferred stock*. This hybrid form of equity capital is issued to investors through a trust company, and the funds raised are loaned to the financial firm using this capital-raising device. Thus, trust-issued preferred stock generates dividends that are tax deductible for the issuing institution. As with other forms of preferred, the issuer can miss making dividend payments and still avoid bankruptcy. Moreover, this unique form of stock is considered to be part of the core (or Tier 1) capital that a bank must hold to satisfy regulations (especially the Basel Agreement on Bank Capital discussed later in this chapter), making trust preferred stock cheaper than many conventional types of common and preferred stocks. With all of the foregoing advantages, it's no wonder that many banks (especially the largest ones) have some trust preferred stock outstanding. However, a 2003 ruling by the Financial Accounting Standards Board (FASB) reduced the advantages of trust preferred stock for some issuing firms, requiring these companies to classify these shares as debt and their payments to investors as interest payments rather than stock dividends.

Subordinated notes and debentures are a relatively small component of bank capital but a growing source of long-term funding for banks and other intermediaries. Regulations require that these capital notes be subordinated to the claims of general creditors of a bank, including the depositors. Thus, if a bank closes and its assets are liquidated, the depositors have first claim on the proceeds and investors in debentures have a secondary claim. However, subordinated debtholders have a prior claim over common and preferred stockholders against earnings and assets.

Bank holding companies have issued substantial quantities of subordinated debt in recent years (especially to pension and mutual funds and insurance companies). Frequently, such notes are callable shortly after issue and carry either fixed or floating interest rates (often tied to interest rates on government securities or short-term Eurodollar deposits). One advantage of subordinated debt from a regulatory viewpoint is that it provides a form of *market discipline*. Because federal insurance does not cover debt subordinated to deposits, investors in subordinated notes will demand higher yields on their securities due to the issuing firm's acceptance of more risk. Holders of subordinated debt tend to be more risk sensitive than depositors and will therefore monitor financial firm behavior more closely, possibly reducing the incidence of failure. Subordinated notes and debentures generally can be issued successfully only by larger financial institutions whose credit standing is trusted by securities investors. Many securities dealers simply refuse to handle small debt issues because of the cost and risk involved.

The composition of capital is markedly different for the largest versus the smallest financial firms. The smallest banks, for example, rely most heavily upon *retained earnings* (undivided profits) to build their capital positions and issue minuscule amounts of long-term debt (subordinated notes and debentures). In contrast, the biggest banks rely principally upon the surplus value of their stock sold in the financial marketplace, as well as retained earnings, and also issue significant amounts of long-term debt capital. These differences reflect, in part, the greater ability of the biggest institutions to sell their capital instruments in the open market and attract thousands of investors, while the smallest institutions, having only limited access to the financial markets, must depend principally upon their ability to generate adequate income and retain a significant portion of those earnings in order to build an acceptable capital cushion.

Nevertheless, it is generally the smallest banks that maintain the thickest cushion of capital relative to their asset size. For example, in 2005, the smallest American banks (each holding less than $100 million in aggregate assets) posted an overall ratio of total equity and debt capital to total assets of 11.9 percent, compared to a 10.2 percent capital-to-asset ratio for medium-size banks (with assets totaling $100 million to $1 billion) and 11.7 percent for the largest FDIC-insured banks (whose asset holdings each exceed $1 billion). Many authorities in the field believe that the smallest financial firms should maintain larger capital-to-asset ratios because these smallest institutions are less well diversified, both geographically and by product line, and, therefore, run a greater risk of failing. Greater failure risk, in turn, poses a larger risk of loss to the government insurance fund that protects the public's deposits.

Factoid

The largest source of capital for commercial banks is *surplus*—the excess value of bank stock at the time it was issued above its par value. What is the largest component of capital among thrift institutions, banking's most important competitor?
Answer: Retained earnings.

Concept Check

15–4. What forms of capital are in use today? What are the key differences between the different types of capital?

15–5. Measured by volume and percentage of total capital, what are the most important and least important forms of capital held by U.S.-insured banks? Why do you think this is so?

15–6. How do small banks differ from large banks in the composition of their capital accounts and in the total volume of capital they hold relative to their assets? Why do you think these differences exist?

15–5 One of the Great Issues in the History of Banking: How Much Capital Is Really Needed?

How much capital a financial firm should hold has been one of the most controversial issues in the history of the banking industry. Banks are at the center of the financial system. If they fail because of a perceived shortage of capital, those failures could threaten the stability of the whole financial system. Much of this historic controversy has evolved around two questions, applicable to just about all financial institutions:

1. Who should set capital standards, the market or regulatory agencies?
2. What is a reasonable standard for the proper amount of capital?

Regulatory Approach to Evaluating Capital Needs

Reasons for Capital Regulation

The capital position of banks has been regulated for generations—longer than any other financial firm. Banks must meet minimum capital requirements before they can be chartered, and they must hold at least the minimum required level of capital throughout their corporate life. Regulatory agencies also indicate the forms of capital that are acceptable. As Wall [6] notes, the fundamental purposes of regulating capital are threefold:

1. To limit the risk of failures.
2. To preserve public confidence.
3. To limit losses to the federal government arising from deposit insurance claims.

The underlying assumption is that the private marketplace cannot accomplish all three of these objectives simultaneously because the market does not correctly price the impact of failures on the banking system's stability, nor is the market likely to accurately price the cost of bank failure to the deposit insurance fund.

Banks are unique in that they hold an unusually large proportion of short-term liabilities (especially transaction deposits) that can be withdrawn immediately when public confidence falls. Few banks are in a position to liquidate their asset portfolios immediately when threatened with massive customer withdrawals. Moreover, the managers of individual banks do not consider the possible external effects of their risk taking on other financial institutions, which may be dragged down by the collapse of neighboring institutions.

Large bank failures are a special problem, as Wall [6] observes. The failure of a big bank attracts significant media attention, causing depositors to raise questions about the soundness of *their* banks. Moreover, the largest banking organizations generally have a high proportion of nondeposit liabilities and large-denomination deposits that are not adequately covered by insurance. The failure of a large bank can have a greater impact on the government's deposit insurance fund than the failures of numerous small insured depository institutions.

One of the damaging side effects of government-funded deposit insurance is that it lowers the normal level of vigilance among depositors over bank safety and risk taking. Feeling fully protected, most depositors do not monitor the risk of the financial institutions they patronize, nor do they penalize those that take on excessive risk by moving their funds to lower-risk institutions. This "moral hazard" feature of government-sponsored insurance encourages insured depository institutions to drive their capital-to-deposit ratios lower, thus exposing government insurance funds to even greater risk of loss.

Research Evidence

Considerable research has been conducted in recent years on the issue of whether the private marketplace or government regulatory agencies exert a bigger effect on bank risk taking and capital decisions. The results of these studies are varied, but most find that the private marketplace is probably more important than government regulation in the long run in determining the amount and type of capital financial firms must hold. However, recently government regulation appears to have become nearly as important as the private marketplace by tightening capital regulations and imposing minimum capital requirements.

The financial markets do seem to react to the differential risk positions of banks by downgrading the debt and equity securities offered by riskier banking companies. However, as Eisenbeis and Gilbert [2] note, we are not at all sure market disciplining works as well for small and medium-size insured depository institutions whose capital instruments are not as actively traded in the open market. Nor is it clear that the risk premiums the market imposes on lower-quality bank securities (in the form of lower prices and higher interest rates) are really large enough to discipline bank risk taking. Also, while the market may make efficient use of all the information it possesses, some of the most pertinent information needed to assess a bank's true level of risk exposure is hidden from the market and is known only to government regulators.

Is a bank's capital-to-assets ratio significantly related to its probability of failure? Most research studies find little connection between capital ratios and the incidence of failure. For example, Santomero and Vinso [1] found that increased capital does not materially lower a bank's failure risk. Many banks would still fail even if their capital were doubled or tripled—a conclusion backed up by a study in New England by Peek and Rosengren [5], which found that four-fifths of banks failing there in the 1980s and 1990s were classified by examiners as "well capitalized" before they failed. It is by no means certain that imposing higher capital requirements will reduce banking risk. As Wall [6] observes, financial firms confronted with higher capital requirements may take on more risk in other aspects of their operations in order to keep from earning lower returns.

Factoid
True or false—the amount of capital a bank holds has proven to be a good predictor of its chances to fail?
Answer: False—banks that subsequently fail appear to have about as much capital, on average, as those who don't fail. Earnings and expenses appear to be better indicators of failure or survival.

Concept Check

15–7. What is the rationale for having the government set capital standards for financial institutions as opposed to letting the private marketplace set those standards?

15–8. What evidence does recent research provide on the role of the private marketplace in determining capital standards?

15–9. According to recent research, does capital prevent a financial institution from failing?

15–6 The Basel Agreement on International Capital Standards: A Historic Contract among Leading Nations

While research evidence on the benefits and costs of imposing capital requirements on financial-service firms continues, the regulatory community has taken important steps in recent years to strengthen government's role in assessing how much capital banks and their closest competitors really need and in making sure they comply with government-imposed capital standards.

In 1988 the Federal Reserve Board, representing the United States, and representatives from other leading countries (including Belgium, Canada, France, Germany, Italy, Japan, the Netherlands, Spain, Sweden, Switzerland, the United Kingdom, and Luxembourg) announced agreement on new capital standards—usually referred to as the **Basel Agreement** for the city in Switzerland where this agreement was reached. The new Basel standards were to be applied uniformly to all banking institutions in their respective countries (with modifications for varying local conditions), even though the original guidelines were intended only for "internationally active" banks.

Key URL
For a summary of the contents of the original Basel Agreement of 1988 see the Bank for International Settlements at **www.bis.org**.

Formally approved in July 1988, the Basel capital rules were designed to encourage leading banks around the world to keep their capital positions strong, reduce inequalities in capital requirements among different countries to promote fair competition, and catch up with recent rapid changes in financial services and financial innovation (such as the enormous expansion of off-balance-sheet commitments banks have made in recent years). The new capital requirements were phased in gradually to allow bankers time to adjust. The full set of initial Basel standards went into effect in January 1993, though adjustments and modifications continued to be made in subsequent years, particularly in allowing or denying new capital instruments to be added, in changing the relative weights attached to various bank assets and types of capital, and in adjusting for different types of risk exposure. The Federal Reserve Board announced that Basel's capital guidelines would also apply, with small modifications, to the state-chartered member banks it examines regularly and to bank holding companies.

Basel I

The original Basel capital standards are known today as **Basel I**. Under the terms of Basel I, the various sources of capital are divided into two tiers:

> **Tier 1** (core) **capital** includes common stock and surplus, undivided profits (retained earnings), qualifying noncumulative perpetual preferred stock, minority interest in the equity accounts of consolidated subsidiaries, and selected identifiable intangible assets less goodwill and other intangible assets.[1]
>
> **Tier 2** (supplemental) **capital** includes the allowance (reserves) for loan and lease losses, subordinated debt capital instruments, mandatory convertible debt, intermediate-term preferred stock, cumulative perpetual preferred stock with unpaid dividends, and equity notes and other long-term capital instruments that combine both debt and equity features.

To determine each bank's *total regulatory capital*, regulators must deduct from the sum of Tier 1 and Tier 2 capital several additional items, including investments in unconsolidated subsidiaries, capital securities held by the bank that were issued by other depository institutions and are held under a reciprocity agreement, activities pursued by savings and loan associations that may have been acquired by a banking organization but are not permissible for national banks, and any other deductions that regulatory supervisors may demand.

---

[1] Banks are allowed to record an intangible asset known as *goodwill* on their balance sheets, which arises when the stock of a business is purchased for cash at a price that exceeds the firm's book value. The goodwill that an established firm has attracted by providing good service to its customers helps explain the extra market value that firm has as a going concern over its book value. Most regulatory agencies do *not* allow goodwill to count as bank capital. However, *identifiable intangible assets*—intangibles other than goodwill—are allowed to be counted as part of a bank's capital. One important identifiable intangible asset today is *mortgage servicing rights* (MSRSs), in which a lending institution can earn income by collecting and distributing loan payments and monitoring borrower compliance with the terms of loans. Still another prominent identifiable intangible today is *purchased credit card relationships* (PCCRs). A financial firm buying into a credit card program acquires access to a new group of potential customers who may need future cash advances and other services that will generate profits in the future.

In February 1993 the Federal Reserve Board announced that purchased mortgage servicing rights (PMSRs) and PCCRs would be counted as qualifying intangible assets—a recognized part of bank capital—provided they do not exceed 50 percent of Tier 1 capital. Later, in 1997, federal regulators proposed that the limitation on the amount of mortgage servicing rights when combined with purchased credit card relationships (PCCRSs) be increased from 50 percent to 100 percent of Tier 1 capital. However, an added requirement was that PCCRs not exceed 25 percent of Tier 1 capital. Any amounts of PMSRs or PCCRs above the maximum allowable amount must be deducted from core capital.

Basel I stipulated that for a bank to qualify as adequately capitalized it must have:

1. A ratio of core capital (Tier 1) to total risk-weighted assets of at least 4 percent.
2. A ratio of total capital (the sum of Tier 1 and Tier 2 capital) to total risk-weighted assets of at least 8 percent, with the amount of Tier 2 capital limited to 100 percent of Tier 1 capital.[2]

Calculating Risk-Weighted Assets under Basel I

If a bank must compare its Tier 1 and Tier 2 capital to its total risk-weighted assets in order to determine if it is adequately capitalized, what exactly are *risk-weighted assets* as defined in Basel I?

Each asset item on a bank's balance sheet and each off-balance-sheet commitment it has made are multiplied by a *risk-weighting factor* designed to reflect its credit risk exposure. Among the most closely watched off-balance-sheet items are standby letters of credit and the long-term, legally binding credit commitments banks often make to their customers.

Here is an example of how bankers may calculate their minimum required level of capital under Basel I. Suppose a bank has $6,000 in total capital, $100,000 in total assets, and the following on-balance-sheet and off-balance-sheet (OBS) items:

On-Balance-Sheet Items (Assets):	
Cash	$ 5,000
U.S. Treasury securities	20,000
Deposit balances held at domestic banks	5,000
Loans secured by first liens on 1- to 4-family residential properties	5,000
Loans to private corporations	65,000
Total balance sheet assets	$100,000
Off-Balance-Sheet (OBS) Items:	
Standby letters of credit backing municipal and corporate borrowings	$ 10,000
Long-term, legally binding credit commitments to private companies	20,000
Total off-balance-sheet items	$ 30,000

This bank's total capital to total balance-sheet assets ratio would be

$$\$6,000 \div \$100,000 = 6.00 \text{ percent}$$

However, the international capital standards are based upon risk-weighted assets, not total assets. To compute this bank's risk-weighted assets under Basel I, we proceed as follows:

1. Compute the *credit-equivalent amount* of each off-balance-sheet (OBS) item. This figure is supposed to translate each OBS item into the equivalent amount of a direct loan considered to be of equal risk to the bank.

To learn more about the history of the Basel Agreement and the many issues it has raised in recent years you may wish to consult such sources as *Regulation Magazine* at **www.cato.org/pubs/regulation/index.html** and the International Monetary Fund's Working Papers at **www.imf.org/external/pubs/cat/wp.cfm**.

Key URLs

---

[2]The international capital standard permits subordinated debt with an original average maturity of at least five years to count toward required supplemental capital (Tier 2). The combined maximum amount of subordinated debt and intermediate-term preferred stock that qualifies as Tier 2 capital is limited to 50 percent of Tier 1 capital (net of goodwill and any other intangibles required to be deducted). Allowance for loan and lease losses also counts as supplemental capital, provided the loan-loss reserves are *general* (not specific) reserves and do not exceed 1.25 percent of risk-weighted assets. The components of Tier 2 capital are subject to the discretion of bank regulators in each nation covered by the Basel Agreement.

Off-Balance-Sheet (OBS) Items	Face Value	Conversion Factor		Credit Equivalent Amount
Standby letters of credit (SLCs) backing municipal and corporate borrowings, asset sales with recourse and repurchase agreements, and forward asset purchases	$10,000	× 1.00	=	$10,000
Long-term credit commitments made to private corporations	$20,000	× 0.50	=	$10,000

2. Multiply each balance sheet item and the credit-equivalent amount of each OBS item by its *risk weight*, as determined by regulatory authorities. The weights given to each item in the bank's portfolio include 0 percent for cash and government securities; 20 percent for deposits held at other banks and certain standby credit letters; 50 percent for home mortgage loans; and 100 percent for corporate loans, long-term credit commitments, and all other claims on the private sector as well as bank premises and other fixed assets.

In the case of the bank we are using as an example, it would have the following risk-weighted assets:

0 Percent
Risk-Weighting Category

Cash	$ 5,000
U.S. Treasury securities	20,000
	$25,000 × 0 = $ 0

20 Percent
Risk-Weighting Category

Deposits at domestic banks	$ 5,000
Credit-equivalent amounts of	10,000
SLCs backing municipal and corporate borrowings	$15,000 × 0.20 = $ 3,000

50 Percent
Risk-Weighting Category

Mortgage loans secured by first liens on 1- to 4-family residential properties	$ 5,000 × 0.50 = $ 2,500

100 Percent
Risk-Weighting Category

Loans to private corporations	$65,000
Credit-equivalent amounts of	10,000
long-term credit commitments to private corporations	$75,000 × 1.00 = $75,000
Total risk-weighted assets held by this bank	$80,500

Calculating the Capital-to-Risk-Weighted Assets Ratio under Basel I

Once we know a bank's total risk-weighted assets and the total amount of its capital (Tier 1 + Tier 2) we can determine its capital adequacy ratio as required under the Basel I Agreement. The key formula is:

$$\text{Capital adequacy ratio under the Basel I Agreement on International Capital Standards} = \frac{\text{Total regulatory capital (or Tier 1 + Tier 2 Capital)}}{\text{Total risk-weighted assets}} \quad \textbf{(15–1)}$$

Factoid
At the center of the debate and discussion of the Basel Agreement is the Bank for International Settlements (BIS), headquartered in Basel, Switzerland, which assists central banks in their transactions with each other and serves as a forum for international financial issues. The BIS was established in 1930 and is the oldest international financial organization in the world.

For the bank whose risk-weighted assets we just calculated above at \$80,500, which currently has \$6,000 in total regulatory capital, its capital adequacy ratio would be as follows:

$$\frac{\text{Total regulatory capital}}{\text{Total risk-weighted assets}} = \frac{\$6,000}{\$80,500} = 0.0745, \text{ or } 7.45 \text{ percent}$$

Note that this bank's total-regulatory-capital-to-risk-weighted assets ratio of 7.45 percent is more than the required minimum for Tier 1 capital of 4 percent but *below* the combined Tier 1 plus Tier 2 capital requirement of 8 percent. Therefore, this institution would have to raise new capital or reduce risky assets to comply with the standards of Basel I.

Capital Requirements Attached to Derivatives

Recently, the Basel I capital standards were adjusted to take account of the risk exposure banks face today from *derivatives*—futures, options, interest rate and currency swaps, interest rate cap and floor contracts, and other instruments designed to hedge against changing currency prices, interest rates, and positions in commodities. Many of these instruments expose a bank to *counterparty risk*—the danger that a customer will fail to pay or to perform, forcing the bank to find a replacement contract with another party that may be less satisfactory.

One significant factor that limits risk exposure in many of these cases is that many futures and option contracts are traded on organized exchanges, such as the London International Financial Futures Exchange or the Chicago Mercantile Exchange, that guarantee the performance of each party to these contracts. Thus, if a customer fails to deliver under an exchange-traded futures or options contract, the exchange involved will make delivery in full. In these instances banks would not normally be expected to post capital behind such exchange-traded contracts.

For other types of contracts, however, Basel I required bankers, first, to convert each risk-exposed contract into its credit-equivalent amount as though it were a risky asset listed on the balance sheet. Then, the credit-equivalent amount of each interest rate or currency contract is multiplied by a prespecified risk weight. Recent research suggests that interest rate contracts display considerably less risk exposure than do foreign-currency contracts. Accordingly, Basel I credit-conversion factors for interest-rate derivatives were set far lower than for contracts tied to the value of foreign currencies. For example, interest rate contracts with a maturity of one year or less were assigned a 0 credit-conversion factor, while rate contracts over one year carry a credit conversion factor of only 0.005 or 0.5 percent. In contrast, currency-based contracts one year or less to maturity carry a credit-conversion factor of 0.01 or 1 percent and those with maturities over one year have been assigned a credit-conversion factor of 0.05 or 5 percent.

In determining the credit-equivalent amounts of these off-balance-sheet contracts, Basel I requires a banker to divide each contract's risk exposure into two categories: (1) potential market risk exposure and (2) current market risk exposure. *Potential market risk exposure* refers to the danger of loss at some future time if the customer who entered into a market-based contract with the bank fails to perform. In contrast, the *current market risk exposure* is designed to measure the risk of loss should a customer default today on its contract, which would compel the bank to replace the failed contract with a new one. Basel I required bankers to determine the current market value for a contract that is similar to the contract they have actually made with a customer in order to figure out the latter's replacement cost. Future cash flows expected under current contracts must be discounted back to their present values using today's interest rates, currency, or commodity prices to determine the value of such a contract in today's market.

Once the replacement cost of a contract is determined, the estimated potential market risk exposure amount is then added to the estimated current market risk exposure amount to derive the total credit-equivalent amount of each contract. This total is multiplied by the correct risk weight, which in most cases is 50 percent, or 0.50, to find the equivalent amount of risk-weighted bank assets represented by each contract. We then add this risk-weighted amount to all of a bank's other risk-weighted assets to derive its total on-balance-sheet and off-balance-sheet risk-weighted assets. As we saw in the preceding section, with Basel I the total of all risk-weighted assets is then divided into each bank's total regulatory capital (Tier 1 plus Tier 2) to determine if it is adequately capitalized.

For example, consider the bank whose risk-weighted assets we previously calculated to be $80,500. Suppose this bank has also entered into a $100,000 five-year interest rate swap agreement with one of its customers and a $50,000 three-year currency swap agreement with another customer. First, we multiply the face amount (notional value) of these two contracts by the appropriate credit conversion factor for each instrument—in this case, by 0.005 for the interest rate swap contract and by 0.05 for the currency swap contract—in order to find the bank's potential market risk exposure from each instrument. Second, we add the estimated replacement cost if suddenly the bank has to substitute new swap contracts at today's prices and interest rates for the original contracts. Let's assume these replacement costs amounted to $2,500 for the interest rate contract and $1,500 for the currency contract. Then:

Interest Rate and Currency Contracts under Basel I	Face Amount of Contract		Conversion Factor for Potential Market Risk Exposure		Potential Market Risk Exposure		Current Market Risk Exposure (replacement cost)		Credit-Equivalent Volume of Interest Rate and Currency Contracts
Five-year interest rate swap contract	$100,000	×	0.005	=	$500	+	$2,500	=	$3,000
Three-year currency swap contract	$50,000	×	0.05	=	$2,500	+	$1,500	=	$4,000
							Total	=	$7,000

The total credit-equivalent amount of these contracts is $7,000.

The final step is to multiply this total by the correct risk weight, which is 50 percent, or 0.50. This step yields:

Insights and Issues

EXAMPLES OF RISK WEIGHTS APPLIED TO BANK ASSETS AND OFF-BALANCE-SHEET ITEMS UNDER THE BASEL I AGREEMENT

A. Credit Risk Categories for Bank Assets on the Balance Sheet

Credit Risk Weights Used in the Calculation of a Bank's Risk-Weighted Assets (percent of amount of each asset)	Assumed Amount of Credit Risk Exposure from Each Category of Bank Assets	Examples of Types of Bank Assets in Each Credit-Risk Category
0%	Zero credit risk	Cash; deposits at the Federal Reserve Banks; U.S. Treasury bills, notes, and bonds of all maturities; Government National Mortgage Association (GNMA) mortgage-backed securities; and debt securities issued by governments of the world's leading industrial countries.
20	Low credit risk	Interbank (correspondent) deposits, general obligation bonds and notes issued by states and local governments, securities issued or backed by U.S. government agencies, and mortgage-backed securities issued or guaranteed by the Federal National Mortgage Association (FNMA) or by the Federal Home Loan Mortgage Corporation (FHLMC).
50	Moderate credit risk	Residential mortgage loans and revenue bonds issued by state and local government units or agencies.
100	Highest credit risk	Commercial and industrial (business) loans, credit card loans, real property, investments in bank subsidiary companies, and all other assets not listed previously.

(continued)

$$\begin{array}{c}\text{Credit-equivalent} \\ \text{volume of interest-rate} \\ \text{and currency contracts}\end{array} \times \begin{array}{c}\text{Credit risk} \\ \text{weight}\end{array} = \begin{array}{c}\text{Volume of risk-weighted} \\ \text{assets represented by} \\ \text{off-balance-sheet} \\ \text{interest-rate and currency} \\ \text{contracts}\end{array} \quad \textbf{(15–2)}$$

$$\$7,000 \quad \times \quad 0.50 \quad = \quad \$3,500$$

To make use of this result let's return to our previous example. Recall that the bank we examined earlier held total regulatory capital of $6,000, and total risk-weighted assets of $80,500. Its total risk-weighted assets included total on-balance-sheet assets of $68,500 and off-balance-sheet standby credit letters and corporate loan commitments of $12,000. We now must add to these other assets the $3,500 in risk-weighted currency

Insights and Issues (continued)

B. Credit Risk Categories for Off-Balance-Sheet Items

Conversion Factor for Converting Off-Balance-Sheet Items into Equivalent Amounts of On-Balance-Sheet Assets	Credit Risk Weights (percent)	Assumed Amount of Credit Risk	Examples of Types of Off-Balance-Sheet Items in Each Credit-Risk Category
0	0%	Zero or lowest credit risk	Loan commitments with less than one year to go.
0.20	20	Low credit risk	Standby credit letters backing the issue of state and local government general obligation bonds.
0.20	100	Modest credit risk	Trade-based commercial letters of credit and bankers' acceptances.
0.50	100	Moderate credit risk	Standby credit letters guaranteeing a customer's future performance and unused bank loan commitments longer than a year.
1.00	100	Highest credit risk	Standby credit letters issued to back repayment of commercial paper.

C. Credit Risk Categories for Derivatives and Other Market-Based Contracts Not Shown on a Bank's Balance Sheet

Conversion Factor for Converting Interest Rate and Currency Contracts into Equivalent Amounts of On-Balance-Sheet Assets	Credit Risk Weights (percent)	Assumed Amount of Credit Risk	Categories or Types of Off-Balance-Sheet Currency and Interest-Rate Contracts
0	50%	Lowest credit risk	Interest-rate contracts one year or less to maturity.
0.005	50	Modest credit risk	Interest-rate contracts over one year to maturity.
0.01	50	Moderate credit risk	Currency contracts one year or less to maturity.
0.05	50	Highest credit risk	Currency contracts over one year to maturity.

Source: Board of Governors of the Federal Reserve System.

and interest rate contracts that we just determined. In this case the bank's ratio of total regulatory capital to risk-weighted assets would be:

$$
\begin{aligned}
\text{Total regulatory capital} \div \text{Total risk-weighted assets} &= \frac{\text{Total (Tier 1 + Tier 2) capital}}{\text{Risk-weighted on-balance-sheet assets} + \text{Risk-weighted off-balance-sheet assets}} \\[2mm]
&= \frac{\$6,000}{(\$68,500 + \$12,000 + \$3,500)} \\[2mm]
&= \frac{\$6,000}{\$84,000} = 0.0714, \text{ or } 7.14 \text{ percent}
\end{aligned}
$$

(15–3)

We note that this bank is now *substantially below* the minimum total regulatory capital requirement of 8 percent of total risk-weighted assets. This capital-deficient bank will probably be compelled to dispose of some of its risky assets and to raise new capital through retained earnings or, perhaps, through sales of stock to bring its capital position up to the levels stipulated by Basel I. Notice, too, that we have only taken *credit risk* into account in the calculation of capital adequacy. We have not even considered the possibility of declines in the market value of assets on bank balance sheets due to increasing interest rates or falling currency or commodity prices. If regulators detect an excessive amount of risk exposure from these market forces, the bank would be asked to post even more capital than the $6,000 it already holds. In this instance this financial firm would face an even deeper capital deficiency than we calculated above and would be placed under considerable regulatory pressure to improve its capital position.

Bank Capital Standards and Market Risk

One of the most glaring holes in the original Basel Agreement was its failure to deal with *market risk*. The risk weights on bank assets were designed primarily to take account of *credit risk*—the danger that a borrowing customer might default on his or her loan. But banks also face significant *market risk*—the losses a bank may suffer due to adverse changes in interest rates, security prices, and currency and commodity prices. For example, banks are leading traders in foreign securities and overseas business property and can be severely damaged financially when foreign currency prices change (usually referred to as *exchange rate* or *currency risk*). In an effort to deal with these and other forms of market risk, the Basel Committee on Banking Supervision released new proposals during the 1990s that would require banks facing greater exposure to market risk to hold larger amounts of capital.

Market Risk and Value at Risk (VaR) Models

In January 1996 the Basel Committee formally approved a modification to the rules, permitting the largest banks to conduct internal risk measurement, and estimate the amount of capital necessary to cover *market risk*. Two years later regulators imposed capital requirements on the market risk exposure of the trading positions of the largest banks (those with trading accounts of more than $1 billion or that represent at least 10 percent of their total assets). Of particular concern was the potential loss to bank earnings and net worth (capital) if the market value of their asset portfolios were to fall significantly.

Value at Risk (VaR)

Revised Basel rules began to allow the largest banks in the world to use their own preferred methods to determine the maximum loss they might sustain over a designated period of time—known as **value at risk (VaR) models.** These models are complex computer algorithms used to determine the maximum amount a bank might lose over a specific time period. They attempt to measure the market risk of a portfolio of assets whose value may decline due to adverse movements in interest rates, stock prices, currency values, or commodity prices.

Key URLs
Greater detail on the use of VaR modeling to assess market risk may be found at **www.riskmetrics.com** and **www.barcap.com**.

For example, suppose a bank estimates that its portfolio's daily average value at risk is $100 million over a 10-day interval with a 99 percent level of confidence. Then, if this VaR estimate of $100 million is correct, losses in portfolio value greater than $100 million should occur less than 1 percent of the time. More precisely, the bank's management anticipates losing at most $100 million for 99 out of 100 10-day intervals.

An analysis of the bank's historical distribution of losses in its trading portfolio will indicate whether this estimate is reasonable or not. Management would want to compare the estimated future loss to the bank's current level of equity capital to make sure the institution is sufficiently capitalized in order to avoid failure. If management determines that its VaR estimates are rising, the bank must consider either increasing the amount of regulatory-defined capital it holds in order to absorb the rising level of risk or take steps to reduce its risk exposure.

The central elements of the VaR method under Basel's rules must include:

1. An estimate of the maximum loss in a bank's portfolio value that could occur at a specified level of risk over intervals of 10 business days.
2. A statement of the confidence level management attaches to its estimate of the probability of loss. Under current rules this must be 99 percent (in a one-tailed test).
3. An estimate of the time period over which the assets in question could be liquidated should the market deteriorate (for example, 24 hours for the most liquid assets and perhaps two weeks for less liquid assets).
4. A statement of the historical period management uses to help develop forecasts of market value and market rates of interest (under current regulations this period must cover at least one year).

Limitations and Challenges of VaR and Internal Modeling

While a possible step forward, VaR estimates and internal modeling to determine each bank's market risk exposure and the amount of capital it needs are *not* perfect—this approach has several potential glitches that could challenge bankers and regulators in the period ahead. For example, inaccurate VaR estimates can expose a bank to excessive risk for which it may be ill-prepared (i.e., its capital position may turn out not to be large enough to cover the actual losses the bank faces). Moreover, the portfolios of the largest banks are so huge and complex with thousands of risk factors it may be impossible to consistently forecast VaRs accurately. This may explain why some banks today appear to make very conservative VaR estimates, which increases the amount of capital they must hold.

Key URLs
Research on the risk exposures of banks and other financial firms and the possible role of *market discipline* in shaping capital requirements may be found at **www.frbsf. org./publications** and **http://ideas.repec.org.**

One potentially useful stipulation to promote accuracy is "backtesting," which evaluates a bank's past forecasting performance and slaps on a higher capital requirement if it has a track record of frequent inaccuracies, thus encouraging bankers to develop better estimating models. Even if an individual bank is a good forecaster, however, there may still be trouble in the system due to *systemic risk*—that is, market losses may occur at several banks simultaneously due to the interdependence of the financial system, magnifying each bank's risk exposure and possibly presenting regulators with a major crisis.

Basel II: A New Capital Accord Unfolding

Why Basel II Appears to Be Needed

Soon after the first Basel Agreement was adopted, work began on the next "edition" of the international bank capital accord, known today as **Basel II.** Of special concern to bankers, regulatory agencies, and industry analysts was how to correct the obvious weaknesses of Basel I, particularly its insensitivity to *innovation* in the financial marketplace, something that is happening all the time.

Smart bankers have found ways around many of Basel I's restrictions. For example, many of the largest banks have used *capital arbitrage* to increase their profitability and minimize their required levels of capital. These banking firms discovered that the broad asset risk categories in Basel I actually encompass many different levels of risk exposure. For example, business loans and credit card loans were placed in the same risk category with the same weight, even though credit card loans are often far riskier. However, because risk weights were the same for *all* assets in the same risk category, a bank could simply sell off lower-risk assets and acquire more risky (but higher-yielding) assets without increasing its capital requirement. Thus, instead of making banks *less* risky, some parts of Basel I seemed to be encouraging them to become *more* risky.

Moreover, Basel I represents a "one size fits all" approach to capital regulation. It failed to recognize that no two banks are alike in terms of their risk profiles. Different banks have different risk exposure and, therefore, should use different models to estimate risk and be subject to different capital requirements.

On June 26, 2004, international bank supervisors agreed on a revised framework for the world's largest banks to calculate their capital requirements. The new framework will apply initially only to about 20 of the largest U.S. banks plus a handful of leading foreign banks. The remaining 7,000-plus U.S. banks as well as smaller banks abroad will be guided, at least for a time, by rules paralleling the requirements of Basel I. Under current plans Basel II will be gradually phased in for the largest banks starting in 2008. Bankers are encouraged to gradually adjust their policies and procedures so they will be ready for the new capital accord when the official start takes place.

Basel II sets up a system in which capital requirements are more sensitive to risk and protect against more types of risk than has been true under Basel I. Basel II attempts to ensure that, consistently, low-risk assets require less capital than high-risk assets, whereas the reverse was often the case with Basel I. However, for the majority of banks Basel I seems to be working reasonably well and frees up smaller banks from having to undertake the complex calculations of probable loss for the wide range of asset categories typically found in each bank's portfolio.

While most banks will not be required, at least initially, to meet the standards of Basel II, *all* banks will likely be affected by Basel II due to *competition*. The biggest banks that use the most advanced risk-calculation techniques allowed under Basel II will, in many cases, be able to hold *less capital per dollar of risky assets* than is true for many smaller banks using the older Basel I approach. This would tend to give Basel II banks a competitive advantage in granting certain kinds of loans to borrowers (such as residential mortgage loans) at lower cost and may even result in smaller banks still using Basel I to take on more risk.

Some experts believe the advent of Basel II may *consolidate* the banking industry even further in favor of the biggest banks. Stockholders, depositors, credit rating agencies, and other industry observers may conclude that Basel II banks are better able to determine true risk exposure and better able to manage risk than smaller Basel I banks. Moreover, Basel II banks may be able to conduct risk analysis more cheaply than smaller Basel I banks, which may eventually force some Basel-I size banks to sell out to the huge international banks governed by Basel II. Eventually, *all* banks may be required to follow the guidelines of Basel II and, therefore, Basel I banks will have to play "catch up" with industry leaders. The ultimate hope of regulators and the public is that Basel II's approach to determining minimum capital requirements based upon advanced risk-measurement techniques will significantly reduce the chances of instability in the global financial system.

Pillars of Basel II

The three "pillars" of Basel II are:

1. *Minimum capital requirements* for each bank are based on its own estimated risk exposure from credit, market and operational risks.
2. *Supervisory review* of each bank's risk-assessment procedures and the adequacy of its capital will be done to ensure they are "reasonable."
3. *Greater public disclosure* of each bank's true financial condition so that market discipline can become a powerful force compelling excessively risky banks to lower their risk exposure.

Internal Risk Assessment

Basel II represents a revolutionary change in regulatory philosophy. Banks will be permitted to measure their own risk exposure and determine how much capital they will need to meet that exposure, subject, of course, to review by the regulators to make sure those measurements are "reasonable." Moreover, participating banks are required to carry out their own repeated *stress testing,* using an internal-rating-based (IRB) approach, to ensure they are prepared for the possibly damaging impacts of ever-changing market conditions.

The hope is that allowing each bank to assess its own risks and determine its own unique capital needs will promote greater flexibility in responding to changing market conditions and continuing innovation in the financial-services industry. Hopefully, Basel II will counteract one of the great weaknesses of the original Basel Accord—rigid rules that simply couldn't keep up with the ability of the largest financial institutions to develop new services and new methods. The fundamental goal of Basel II is to create a better alignment of capital regulations with the risks international banks actually face in the modern world.

Key URLs
To gather more information about the development of Basel II's new capital rules, consult such sources as **www.bundesbank.de/index** and **www.bis.org/.**

Operational Risk

One of the key innovations associated with Basel II is requiring banks to hold capital to deal with *operational risk* in addition to credit and market risks. This type of risk exposure includes losses from employee fraud, product flaws, accounting errors, computer breakdowns, terrorism, and natural disasters (such as storms and earthquakes) that may damage a bank's physical assets and reduce its ability to communicate with customers. To lower their capital requirement, bankers must demonstrate they are using effective measures to reduce operational risk, including adequate insurance coverage, backup service capability, effective internal audits, quality contingency plans, and effective management information systems. Banks subject to Basel II will be asked to estimate the probability of adverse operating events and the potential losses these may generate.

Basel II and Credit Risk Models

Key URLs
To learn more about credit risk models see **www.defaultrisk.com** and **www.moodyskmv.com.**

Paralleling the development of VaR models to estimate market risk exposure has been the rapid rise of **credit risk models** under the leadership of such organizations as Credit Metrics and J. P. Morgan Chase. These computer algorithms attempt to measure a lender's exposure to default by its borrowing customers or to credit downgradings that result in lowering the value of some of the lender's loans. Such changes tend to reduce the resale value of loans and the probability of full recovery of monies owed the lender.

The fundamental purpose of credit risk models is to ask and answer the question: *If an adverse situation develops in the future, what magnitude of losses (loan defaults and declining loan values) can be expected?* While there are many different risk models in use today, most generate credit risk estimates based upon: (*a*) borrower credit ratings; (*b*) the probability those credit ratings will change; (*c*) the probable amount of recovery should some loans default; and (*d*) the possibility of changing interest-rate spreads between riskier and less risky loans.

This is a challenging exercise, even more difficult than assessing a lending institution's market risk. Statistical credit risk models must take into account the degree of concentration of loans extended to a few large borrowers and variations in loan portfolio diversification across a wide range of borrowers with markedly different credit ratings. Moreover, when they occur, loan losses can come in bunches (joint defaults), often due to a weakening economy. Management must be prepared for extreme credit losses during some periods, but only minimal losses during other periods.

Then, too, the statistical distribution of loan defaults is not normal, but heavily skewed with low probabilities of large losses and high probabilities of only modest returns. (Most loans, after all, have only limited upside earnings potential because borrowers will repay no more than they have promised to repay.) Regardless of the difficulties involved, however, credit risk models provide a quantitative basis for estimating how much *capital* is necessary to cover potential loan losses and still protect the solvency of the lending institution.

A COMPARISON OF THE CHANGING RULES FOR INTERNATIONAL REGULATION OF BANK CAPITAL

Features of Basel I Rules (as formally adopted in 1988):

- Identified the principal types of capital acceptable to regulators (including Tier 1 or core capital and Tier 2 or supplemental capital) and was the first capital standard to account for risk exposure from off-balance-sheet (OBS) transactions.

- Focused primarily upon credit risk inherent in the assets on a bank's balance sheet and among off-balance-sheet items (such as derivative contracts and credit commitments), with market risk exposure from changing interest rates, currency, and commodity prices added later.

- Determined individual banks' capital requirements using the same formula and the same set of risk weights (a "one size fits all" approach).

- Applied the same minimum capital requirements to all banks (including a 4 percent minimum ratio of Tier 1 capital to risk-weighted assets and an 8 percent minimum ratio of Tier 1 plus Tier 2 capital to risk-weighted assets).

Features of Basel II Rules (scheduled for future implementation):

- Provides for greater sensitivity to arbitrage and innovation in the financial marketplace, which demands more flexible capital rules than Basel I allowed.

- Recognizes that different banks have different risk exposures, may have to employ different methods to assess their own unique risk exposures, and may be subject to different capital requirements (including different rules for large versus small banking firms).

- Broadens the types of risk considered in determining capital requirements and establishes minimum capital requirements for credit, market, and operational risks. Basel II is substantially more risk sensitive than Basel I.

- Requires each bank to develop in-house risk-management models and stress tests for assessing its risk exposure (VaR or value at risk) under a variety of different marketplace scenarios.

- Requires each bank to determine its own capital requirements based on its own calculated risk exposure, subject to review for "reasonableness" by regulatory authorities.

- Promotes greater public disclosure of each bank's true financial condition so that greater market discipline will be applied to banks perceived to be taking on excessive risk.

Credit risk models are likely to be used more heavily in the future when Basel II is in full force. Under Basel I, minimum capital requirements remain the same for most types of loans regardless of credit rating. Under Basel II, however, minimum capital requirements may vary significantly with credit quality. One example that the FDIC cited recently (see FDIC News Release PR-3-2003) shows a AAA-rated commercial loan under Basel II bearing a projected minimum capital requirement as low as $0.37 or as high as $4.45 per $100 loaned. If the loan is BBB rated, however, its minimum capital requirement may range from as low as $1.01 to as high as $14.13. In contrast, Basel I's minimum capital requirement for such a loan remains fixed at $8 per $100. Clearly, Basel II is much more sensitive to credit risk than its predecessor.

A Dual (Large-Bank, Small-Bank) Set of Rules

Basel II will operate under one set of capital rules for the handful of largest multinational banks and another set for the much more numerous smaller banking firms. Regulators are especially concerned that smaller banks could be overwhelmed by the heavy burdens of gathering risk-exposure information and performing complicated risk calculations. Then, too, if Basel II results in *lowering* the capital requirements of many of the world's largest banks, this "bifurcated" system could create a competitive disadvantage for smaller banking firms. It is expected that smaller institutions will be able to continue to use simpler and more standardized approaches in determining their capital requirements and risk exposures, paralleling the rules under Basel I.

Problems Accompanying the Implementation of Basel II

The Basel II plan is by no means perfect at this stage. Major questions and issues remain to be resolved. First, the technology of risk measurement still has a long way to go. For example, some forms of risk (such as operational risk) have *no generally accepted measurement scale*. In these instances we don't know exactly how to calculate the amount of risk exposure present and how that exposure may be changing over time.

Then, too, there is the complex issue of *risk aggregation*. How do we add up the different forms of risk exposure in order to get an accurate picture of a bank's *total* risk exposure? Clearly, the different forms of risk considered in Basel II must be quantified in some way so we can combine them into one corporate risk index that guides us in figuring out how much regulatory capital each bank needs to have.

Moreover, what should we do about the *business cycle*? It is likely that most banks will face greater risk exposure in the middle of an economic recession than they will in a period of economic expansion. This implies that most banks will need greater amounts of capital when the economy is down. But how much? Is it possible that some forms of risk will be rising and while others are falling over the course of the business cycle?

Finally, some financial experts have expressed concern about *improving regulator competence*. As the technology of advanced risk-management models moves forward, regulators must be trained to keep up so they can assess the effectiveness of the different risk models and procedures each bank has adopted. The regulatory community must change along with changes in the financial-services industry.

Concept Check

15–10. What are the most popular financial ratios regulators use to assess the adequacy of bank capital today?

15–11. What is the difference between core (or Tier 1) capital and supplemental (or Tier 2) capital?

15–12. A bank reports the following items on its latest balance sheet: allowance for loan and lease losses, $42 million; undivided profits, $81 million; subordinated debt capital, $3 million; common stock and surplus, $27 million; equity notes, $2 million; minority interest in subsidiaries, $4 million; mandatory convertible debt, $5 million; identifiable intangible assets, $3 million; and noncumulative perpetual preferred stock, $5 million. How much does the bank hold in Tier 1 capital? In Tier 2 capital? Does the bank have too much Tier 2 capital?

15–13. What changes in the regulation of bank capital were brought into being by the Basel Agreement? What is Basel I? Basel II?

15–14. First National Bank reports the following items on its balance sheet: cash, $200 million; U.S. government securities, $150 million; residential real estate loans, $300 million; and corporate loans, $350 million. Its off-balance-sheet items include standby credit letters, $20 million, and long-term credit commitments to corporations, $160 million. What are First National's total risk-weighted assets? If the bank reports Tier 1 capital of $30 million and Tier 2 capital of $20 million, does it have a capital deficiency?

15–15. How is the Basel Agreement likely to affect a bank's choices among assets it would like to acquire?

15–16. What are the most significant differences between Basel I and Basel II? Explain the importance of the concepts of internal risk assessment, VaR, and market discipline.

15–7 Changing Capital Standards Inside the United States

Inside the United States, regulatory agencies stress the need for strong capital positions before they will approve the offering of new services or the establishment or acquisition of new offices or subsidiary firms. Strongly capitalized banks will be allowed to venture into new fields (such as investment banking or insurance underwriting) and expand geographically. Banks with weak capital face more regulatory pressure and will be restricted in their activities until they improve their capital positions. The underlying rationale for "capital-based supervision" is that financial firms will be less likely to fail or take on excessive risk if their owners are forced to place more of their own money at risk. In effect, the more capital backing a financial firm's activities, the more its stockholders will likely exercise quality control over its operations. However, there are limits on how much capital regulators can demand. Demanding too much capital throttles back a financial firm's ability to lend funds profitably in order to support economic growth and tends to lower the overall return on equity (ROE), making the firm less attractive to investors and making it more difficult to raise new capital in the future.

Several new capital rules created recently by U.S. regulatory agencies were mandated by the FDIC Improvement Act passed by Congress in November 1991. This law requires federal regulators to take Prompt Corrective Action (PCA) when an insured depository institution's capital falls below acceptable levels. Section 131 of the act allows regulators to impose tougher restrictions on an insured depository institution as its capital level declines, such as prohibiting the payment of management fees or stockholder dividends. If an institution's ratio of tangible equity capital to total assets drops to 2 percent or less, a depository institution is considered "critically undercapitalized," and it can be placed in conservatorship or receivership within 90 days unless the institution's principal regulator and the FDIC determine that it would be in the interest of the public to allow the troubled institution to continue under present ownership and management. To avoid seizure, a depository institution must have a positive net worth and demonstrate that it is actually improving its condition.

In the fall of 1992 the FDIC and the other federal regulators created five capital-adequacy categories for depository institutions for purposes of implementing prompt corrective action when a bank or thrift becomes inadequately capitalized. These five categories describe how well capitalized each depository institution is:

A. *Well capitalized*—a U.S. depository institution in this category has a ratio of capital to risk-weighted assets of at least 10 percent, a ratio of Tier 1 (or core) capital to risk-weighted assets of at least 6 percent, and a leverage ratio (Tier 1 capital to average assets) of at least 5 percent. A well-capitalized institution faces *no* significant regulatory restrictions on its expansion.

B. *Adequately capitalized*—a U.S. depository institution in this group has a minimum ratio of capital to risk-weighted assets of at least 8 percent, a ratio of Tier 1 capital to risk-weighted assets of at least 4 percent, and a leverage ratio of at least 4 percent. Such an institution cannot accept broker-placed deposits without regulatory approval.

C. *Undercapitalized*—a U.S. depository institution that fails to meet one or more of the capital minimums for an adequately capitalized institution is considered undercapitalized and is subject to a variety of mandatory or discretionary regulatory restrictions, including limits on the dividends and management fees it is allowed to pay, on access to the Federal Reserve's discount window, on its maximum asset growth rate, on the expansion of its facilities or services, or on any proposed merger unless approval is obtained in advance from federal regulators. Such a depository institution is subject to increased monitoring and must pursue a plan for capital recovery.

D. *Significantly undercapitalized*—a U.S. depository institution belonging to this group possesses a ratio of total capital to risk-weighted assets of less than 6 percent, a Tier 1 capital to risk-weighted assets ratio of under 3 percent, and a leverage ratio average of less than 3 percent. A depository institution in this category is subject to all the restrictions faced by undercapitalized institutions plus other restrictions, such as mandatory prohibitions on paying bonuses and raises to senior officers without regulator approval, limits on deposit interest rates that may be paid, and, in some cases, mandatory merger.

Key URLs
To learn more about the capital requirements of U.S. depository institutions see especially the following Web sites: **www.fdic.gov, www.occ.treas.gov, www.ots.treas.gov,** and **www.federalreserve.gov/regulations/default.htm**.

E. *Critically undercapitalized*—this category applies to those U.S. depository institutions whose ratio of tangible equity capital to total assets is 2 percent or less (where tangible equity includes common equity capital and cumulative perpetual preferred stock minus most forms of intangible assets). Depository institutions in this lowest capital group face all the restrictions applying to undercapitalized institutions plus required regulator approval for such transactions as granting loans to highly leveraged borrowers, making changes in their charter or bylaws, paying above-market interest rates on deposits, changing their accounting methods, or paying excessive compensation or bonuses to consultants or staff. A critically undercapitalized institution may be prevented from paying principal and interest on its subordinated debt and will be placed in conservatorship or receivership if its capital level is not increased within a prescribed time limit. U.S. federal banking agencies plan to retain both the current Prompt Corrective Action (PCA) and leverage capital requirements discussed above as part of the U.S. domestic implementation of Basel II.

In recent years the FDIC has analyzed the financial reports of federally insured depository institutions and found that over 90 percent fall in either the *well-capitalized* or *adequately capitalized* groups. Regulators have repeatedly concluded that the American banking system must be in reasonably good shape. Unfortunately, this conclusion usually is based upon the book values of assets and capital, not on market values, and could turn out to be an exaggeration of the industry's true condition. Only time will tell.

15–8 Planning to Meet Capital Needs

Facing regulatory pressures to maintain adequate capital, financial institutions are increasingly recognizing the need to plan for their long-range capital needs and to raise new capital as they grow from both internal and external sources.

Raising Capital Internally

In most years, the principal source of capital is from *earnings kept inside* rather than paid out to stockholders. Internally generated capital has the advantage of not having to depend on the open market for funds, thus avoiding flotation costs. Not only is internal capital generally less expensive to raise, but it also does not threaten existing stockholders with loss of control—that is, it avoids dilution of their share of ownership and their earnings per share of stock held. For example, if a financial firm chooses to sell stock, some shares may be sold to new stockholders, who will then be entitled to share in any future earnings and to vote on policies. However, internal capital has the disadvantage of being fully taxable and is significantly affected by changing interest rates and economic conditions not controllable by management.

Dividend Policy

Relying on the growth of earnings to meet capital needs means that a decision must be made concerning the amount of earnings retained in the business versus the amount paid out to stockholders in the form of dividends. That is, the board of directors and management must agree on the appropriate *retention ratio*—current retained earnings divided by current after-tax net income—which then determines the *dividend payout ratio*—current dividends to stockholders divided by current after-tax income.

The retention ratio is of great importance to management. A retention ratio set too low (and, therefore, a dividend payout ratio set too high) results in slower growth of internal capital, which may increase failure risk and retard the expansion of assets. A retention ratio set too high (and, therefore, a dividend payout ratio set too low) can result in a cut in the stockholders' dividend income. Other factors held constant, such a cut would reduce the market value of stock issued by a financial institution. The optimal dividend policy is one that maximizes the value of the stockholders' investment. New stockholders will be attracted and existing stockholders retained if the rate of return on owners' equity capital at least equals returns generated by other investments of comparable risk.

It is important for management to achieve a *stable* dividend track record. If the financial institution's dividend payout ratio is kept relatively constant, interested investors will perceive less risk in their dividend payments and the institution will look more attractive to investors. As a study of banks by Keen [4] suggests, stock prices typically drop quickly after a dividend cut is announced. This not only disappoints current stockholders but also discourages potential buyers of equity shares, making it more difficult to raise new capital in the future.

How Fast Must Internally Generated Funds Grow?

A key factor affecting management's decision about an appropriate retention ratio and dividend payout ratio is how fast the financial firm can allow its assets to grow so that its existing ratio of capital assets is protected from erosion. In other words, how fast must earnings grow to keep the capital-to-assets ratio protected if the financial firm continues paying the same dividend rate to its stockholders?

The following formula helps management and the board of directors answer such questions:

Internal capital growth rate, or Retained earnings

$$\div \text{ Equity capital} = \text{ROE} \times \text{Retention ratio} \tag{15–4}$$

$$= \frac{\text{Net income}}{\text{Equity capital}} \times \frac{\text{Retained earnings}}{\text{Net income}}$$

The reader will recall the ROE relationship discussed in Chapter 6:

$$\text{ROE} = \text{Profit margin} \times \text{Asset utilization} \times \text{Equity multiplier} \tag{15–5}$$

Then it must be true that

$$\frac{\text{Retained earnings}}{\text{Equity capital}} = \frac{\text{Net income}}{\text{Operating revenue}} \times \frac{\text{Operating revenue}}{\text{Total assets}}$$

$$\times \frac{\text{Total assets}}{\text{Equity capital}} \times \frac{\text{Retained earnings}}{\text{Net income}} \tag{15–6}$$

This formula shows that if we want to increase internally generated capital, we must increase earnings (through a higher profit margin, asset utilization ratio, and/or equity multiplier) or increase the earnings retention ratio, or both.

To illustrate the use of this formula, imagine that management has forecast a return on equity (ROE) of 10 percent for this year and plans to pay the stockholders 50 percent of any net earnings generated. How fast can assets grow without reducing the current ratio of total capital to total assets? Equation (15–4) above yields

$$\text{ICGR} = \text{ROE} \times \text{Retention ratio} = 0.10 \times 0.50 = 5 \text{ percent}$$

Thus, assets cannot grow more than 5 percent under the assumptions made. Otherwise, the capital-to-assets ratio will fall. If it falls far enough, the regulatory authorities will insist that capital be increased.

To take one more example, suppose assets are forecast to grow 10 percent this year. What options are open to management in terms of an earnings rate, measured by ROE, and an earnings retention ratio if the current ratio of capital to total assets is to be preserved? There are, of course, numerous possibilities that the formula above will generate, as revealed in the following table. For example, if management can boost return on equity to 20 percent, it can pay out 50 percent of its net after-tax income, retain the other 50 percent, and still protect its current capital-to-assets ratio. With an ROE of 10 percent, however, management must retain *all* of its current earnings. It should also be clear that if ROE falls below 10 percent, the capital-to-assets ratio must decline as well, even if it retains all current income. In this instance, management may find regulators insisting on raising more capital from outside to offset a poor earnings record.

Example: If assets are expected to grow at a 10 percent rate this year, what combination of return on equity and retention rate for earnings will preserve its current capital-to-assets ratio?

$$\text{Forecasted asset growth rate of 10 percent} = \text{ROE} \times \text{Retention ratio}$$

0.10	= 0.20 ×	0.50
0.10	= 0.15 ×	0.67
0.10	= 0.10 ×	1.00

Raising Capital Externally

If a financial firm does need to raise capital from outside sources, it has several options: (1) selling common stock, (2) selling preferred stock, (3) issuing debt capital, (4) selling assets, (5) leasing certain fixed assets, especially buildings and (6) swapping stock for debt securities. Which alternative management chooses will depend primarily on the impact each source would have on returns to stockholders, usually measured by earnings per share (EPS). Other key factors to consider are the institution's risk exposure, the impact on control by existing stockholders, the state of the market for the assets or securities being sold, and regulations.

Issuing Common Stock

The sale of equity shares is generally the most expensive way to raise external capital, considering flotation costs and the greater risk to earnings that stockholders face compared to debtholders. Unless current stockholders can absorb all the new shares, a new stock issue may dilute control and EPS unless the institution can earn more on funds raised than their cost of issue. Issuing stock also reduces the degree of leverage a financial firm can employ. The offsetting advantage, however, is that increasing ownership shares tends to increase future borrowing capacity.

Issuing Preferred Stock

The sale of preferred stock is, like the sale of common stock, generally among the more expensive sources of capital. Because preferred shareholders have a prior claim on earnings over holders of common equity, dividends to common stockholders may be lower after preferred shares are issued. However, preferred stock has an advantage over debt in the form of greater flexibility (because dividends need not be paid), and newly issued preferred shares add future borrowing capacity. Moreover, as we saw earlier in this chapter, new hybrid forms of preferred shares (such as trust preferred stock) have appeared recently that carry lower cost.

Issuing Subordinated Notes and Debentures

The advantage of issuing new debt capital is the generation of increased financial leverage to boost EPS if more can be earned from the use of borrowed funds than their cost.

Moreover, interest payments on debt securities are tax deductible. However, debt adds to failure and earnings risk and may make it more difficult to sell stock in the future.

Selling Assets and Leasing Facilities

Occasionally, financial-service providers sell all or a portion of their office facilities and lease back from the new owner space to carry on their operations. Recent examples include Bank of America and Barclays PLC selling and then leasing back bank branches and other offices. Such a transaction usually creates a substantial inflow of cash and a sizable addition to net worth strengthening the selling institution's capital position.

The most successful sale-and-leaseback transactions have occurred where inflation and economic growth have significantly increased current property values over the book value of the property recorded on the balance sheet. When faster write-offs of commercial real estate are possible, the economic incentive from selling and leasing back property can be most attractive. However, this potentially attractive feature was dimmed a bit in 1986 with passage of the Tax Reform bill. This law lengthened real estate depreciation requirements for most structures, thus requiring management to evaluate their real estate transactions more in terms of economic benefits rather than tax benefits. However, the leasing institution usually receives substantial amounts of cash at low cost, increasing earnings.

Many depository institutions in recent years have *sold assets* to improve their capital-to-assets ratios. They have also frequently slowed the growth of more risky assets and redistributed some of their assets toward lower-risk investments so that their risk-weighted assets decline. A related strategy is to avoid booking loans, thereby avoiding an increase in assets and capital requirements, by referring loan customers to alternative sources of outside funds, such as securitizations or standby credit agreements (as described, for example, in Chapter 9).

Swapping Stock for Debt Securities

In recent years a number of banking organizations have undertaken stock-for-debt swaps. For example, a bank may have $2 million in subordinated debentures on its balance sheet, issued at an interest cost of 8 percent. Following conventional practice, these bonds are recorded at their issue price (book value). If interest rates have risen recently, say to 10 percent, these notes may now have a *market value* of just $1 million. By selling new stock in the amount of $1 million and buying back the notes at their current market price, the bank is able to remove a $2 million debt from its balance sheet. From the regulators' perspective, the swapping institution has strengthened its capital and saved the cost of future interest payments on the notes. Moreover, most debt issues have a sinking fund requirement, which requires annual payments into the fund to retire the bonds. These future cash outlays are no longer needed after a stock-for-debt swap is completed.

Choosing the Best Alternative for Raising Outside Capital

The choice of which method to use in raising outside capital should be made on the basis of a careful financial analysis of the alternatives and their effects on a financial firm's earnings per share. Table 15–2 gives an example of a bank that needs to raise $20 million in external capital. The institution currently has 8 million shares of common stock outstanding at a $4-per-share par value and has assets of close to $1 billion, with $60 million in equity capital. If this bank can generate total revenue of about $100 million and hold operating expenses to no more than $80 million, it should have about $10.8 million in earnings left after taxes. If management elects to raise the needed $20 million in new capital by issuing 2 million new equity shares, each at a net price of $10, the common stockholders will receive $1.30 in earnings per share.

TABLE 15–2

Methods of Raising External Capital for a Financial Firm

Income or Expense Item	Sell Common Stock at $10 per Share	Sell Preferred Stock Promising an 8 Percent Dividend at $20 per Share	Sell Capital Notes with a 10 Percent Coupon Rate
Estimated revenues	$ 100 million	$ 100 million	$ 100 million
Estimated operating expenses	80	80	80
Net revenues	20	20	20
Interest expense on capital notes	—	—	2
Estimated before-tax net income	20	20	18
Estimated income taxes (35%)	7	7	6.3
Estimated after-tax net income	13	13	11.7
Preferred stock dividends	—	1.6	—
Net income available to common stockholders	$13 million	$11.4 million	$11.7 million
Earnings per share of common stock	$1.30 (10 million shares)	$1.43 (8 million shares)	$1.46 (8 million shares)

Note: Initially the issuing institution has 8 million shares of common stock outstanding, with a $4-per-share par value.

Is the issue of common stock the *best* alternative for this institution? Not if its goal is to maximize earnings per share. For example, management finds that it could issue preferred stock, bearing an 8 percent dividend, at $20 per share. If the board of directors elects to declare an annual dividend on these preferred shares, this will drain $1.6 million ($20 million × 0.08) each year from earnings that would normally flow to the common stockholders. But it will still leave $11.6 million for holders of the 8 million in common shares, or a dividend rate of $1.43 per share. Thus, the preferred stock route would yield the common stockholders $0.13 more in dividends per share than would the issue of additional common stock.

Management also discovers that it could sell $20 million in debt capital notes bearing a 10 percent coupon rate. While the issuing institution must pay $2 million in interest annually on these notes, this still leaves almost $12 million left over after all expenses (including taxes). When distributed among the 8 million common shares, this will yield $1.46 per share. Clearly, the best of the three capital-raising options in this example is *issuing debt capital*. Moreover, the capital notes carry no voting power, so the current stockholders retain control.

Concept Check

15–17. What steps should be part of any plan for meeting a long-range need for capital?

15–18. How does dividend policy affect the need for capital?

15–19. What is the ICGR and why is it important to the management of a financial firm?

15–20. Suppose that a bank has a return on equity capital of 12 percent and that its retention ratio is 35 percent. How fast can this bank's assets grow without reducing its current ratio of capital to assets?

Suppose that the bank's earnings (measured by ROE) drop unexpectedly to only two-thirds of the expected 12 percent figure. What would happen to the bank's ICGR?

15–21. What are the principal sources of external capital for a financial institution?

15–22. What factors should management consider in choosing among the various sources of external capital?

Summary

In the history of banking and financial institutions there are few more controversial issues than those surrounding *capital*. A long-standing debate among bankers, regulators, and financial analysts concerns how much and what types of capital should be held. Not only the definition and concept of capital but also our views on the proper role for capital in controlling the behavior of financial firms are changing. Among the key points in this chapter are the following:

- The term *capital* in the financial-services field refers to the funds contributed by the *owners*—money invested in a financial firm and placed at risk in the hope of earning a competitive return. Banks are corporations and their owners are shareholders—investors in common and preferred stock, while for some other financial firms, such as credit unions and mutual savings banks, the owners are customers who invest their deposits in the institution and capital is an accumulation of reinvested profits.

- Capital consists principally of common and preferred stock, surplus (the excess value of stock over its par value), reserves for contingencies, undivided profits, equity reserves, minority interest in consolidated subsidiaries, and equity commitment notes. Most financial firms don't have all of these types of instruments in their capital account. The most important capital sources include stock, surplus, undivided profits, and equity reserves. However, increasingly in recent years depository institutions have issued long-term debt subordinated to the claims of depositors, which is also recognized as capital by most regulatory agencies.

- Capital is the ultimate line of defense against failure, giving the financial firm time to respond to the various kinds of risks it faces and return to profitability again. Capital also supplies long-term money to get a new financial institution started, provide a base for future growth, and promote public confidence in each financial firm and in the financial system.

- The volume of capital a regulated financial institution holds and the makeup of its capital account are determined by both *regulation* and the *financial marketplace*. Because not all the information on the true condition of regulated financial firms is normally released to the public, the private marketplace alone may not be completely reliable as an effective regulator in promoting the public interest, creating a role for government regulation of each institution's capital account.

- Capital requirements today are set by regulatory agencies and, for banks in more than 100 nations today, under rules laid out in the Basel Agreement on International Bank Capital Standards—one of the first successful efforts in history to impose common rules on banks from many different countries. These government agencies set minimum capital requirements and assess the capital adequacy of the financial firms they regulate.

- Capital regulation aimed primarily at the largest international banks formally began in 1988 with a multinational agreement known as Basel I. This set of international rules requires many of the largest banks to separate their on-balance-sheet and off-balance-sheet assets and commitments into risk categories and to multiply each asset by its appropriate risk weight to determine total risk-weighted assets. The ratio of total regulatory capital relative to total risk-weighted assets and off-balance-sheet commitments is a key indicator of the strength of each bank's capital position.

- Weaknesses in Basel I, especially its inability to respond to change and innovation in the financial marketplace, have led to a Basel II agreement to be phased in. This new approach to capital regulation will require the world's largest banking firms to conduct a continuing internal assessment of their risk exposures, including stress testing, and to calculate their required level of capital. Thus, each participating bank will have its own

www.mhhe.com/rose7e

unique capital requirements based on its own unique risk profile. Smaller banks will use a simpler, standardized approach to determining their minimum capital requirements similar to the rules of Basel I.

- Financial firms in need of additional capital have several different sources to draw upon, including internal and external sources of funds. The principal internal source is retained earnings. The principal external sources include (*a*) selling common stock; (*b*) selling preferred stock; (*c*) issuing capital notes; (*d*) selling assets; (*e*) leasing fixed assets; and (*f*) swapping stock for debt.

- Choosing among the various sources of capital requires the management of a financial institution to consider the relative cost and risk of each capital source, the institution's overall risk exposure, the potential impact of each source on returns to shareholders, government regulations, and the demands of investors in the private marketplace.

Key Terms

capital, 475	surplus, 479	Basel Agreement, 483
operational risk, 477	undivided profits, 479	Basel I, 484
exchange risk, 477	equity reserves, 479	Tier 1 capital, 484
crime risk, 478	subordinated	Tier 2 capital, 484
portfolio	debentures, 479	value at risk (VaR)
diversification, 478	minority interest in	models, 491
geographic	consolidated	Basel II, 492
diversification, 478	subsidiaries, 479	credit risk models, 494
common stock, 479	equity commitment	internal capital growth
preferred stock, 479	notes, 479	rate, 499

Problems and Projects

1. Carter Savings Association has forecast the following performance ratios for the year ahead. How fast can Carter allow its assets to grow without reducing its ratio of equity capital to total assets, assuming its performance holds steady over the period?

Profit margin of net income over operating revenue	8.30%
Asset utilization (operating revenue ÷ assets)	9.25%
Equity multiplier	15.22X
Net earnings retention ratio	45.00%

2. Using the formulas developed in this chapter and in Chapter 6 and the information that follows, calculate the ratios of total capital to total assets for the banking firms listed below. What relationship among these banks' return on assets, return on equity capital, and capital-to-assets ratios did you observe? What implications or recommendations would you draw for the management of each of these institutions?

Name of Bank	Net Income ÷ Total Assets (or ROA)	Net Income ÷ Total Equity Capital (or ROE)
First National Bank of Hopkins	1.6%	15%
Safety National Bank	1.3%	13%
Ilsher State Bank	0.95%	10%
Mercantile Bank and Trust Company	0.83%	9%
Lakeside National Trust	−0.43%	−5%

3. Using the following information for Sun-up National Bank, calculate that bank's ratio of total-capital-to-risk-weighted assets under the terms of the Basel I Agreement. Does the bank have sufficient capital?

On-Balance-Sheet Items (Assets)		Off-Balance-Sheet Items	
Cash	$ 3.5 million	Standby letters of credit	
U.S. Treasury securities	25.6	backing municipals and	
Deposit balances due from		corporate borrowing	$18.1 million
other banks	4.0	Long-term binding	
Loans secured by first lines		commitments to	
on residential property		corporate customers	40.2 million
(1- to 4-family dwellings)	19.7	Total off-balance-	
Loans to corporations	105.3	sheet items	$58.3 million
Total assets	$158.1 million	Total capital	$11.8 million

4. Top-of-the Mountain Savings has been told by examiners that it needs to raise an additional $8 million in long-term capital. Its outstanding common equity shares total 7.5 million, each bearing a par value of $1. This thrift institution currently holds assets of nearly $2 billion, with $105 million in equity. During the coming year, the thrift's economist has forecast operating revenues of $175 million, of which operating expenses are $25 million plus 70% of operating revenues.

   Among the options for raising capital considered by management are (*a*) selling $8 million in common stock, or 320,000 shares at $25 per share; (*b*) selling $8 million in preferred stock bearing a 9 percent annual dividend yield at $12 per share; or (*c*) selling $8 million in 10-year capital notes with a 10 percent coupon rate. Which option would be of most benefit to the stockholders? (Assume a 34% tax rate.) What happens if operating revenues are more than expected ($200 million rather than $175 million)? What happens if there is a slower-than-expected volume of revenues (only $125 million instead of $175 million)? Please explain.

5. Please calculate New River National Bank's total risk-weighted assets, based on the following items that the bank reported on its latest balance sheet. Does the bank appear to have a capital deficiency?

Cash	$ 95 million
Domestic interbank deposits	240 million
U.S. government securities	320 million
Residential real estate loans	370 million
Commercial loans	520 million
Total assets	$1,545 million
Total liabilities	$1,440 million
Total capital	$ 105 million

Off-balance-sheet items include

Standby credit letters	
that back municipal borrowings	$ 95 million
Long-term loan commitments	
to private companies	190 million

6. Suppose New River National Bank, whose balance sheet is given in Problem 5, reports the forms of capital shown in the following table as of the date of its latest financial

www.mhhe.com/rose7e

statement. What is the total dollar volume of Tier 1 capital? Tier 2 capital? According to the data given in Problems 5 and 6, does New River have a capital deficiency?

Common stock (par value)	$ 8 million
Surplus	17 million
Undivided profits	35 million
Allowance for loan losses	25 million
Subordinated debt capital	15 million
Intermediate-term preferred stock	5 million

7. Please indicate which items appearing on the following financial statements would be classified under the terms of the Basel Agreement as (*a*) Tier 1 capital or (*b*) Tier 2 capital.

Allowance for loan and lease losses	Subordinated debt capital instruments with an original average maturity of at least five years
Subordinated debt under two years to maturity	Common stock
Intermediate-term preferred stock	Equity notes
Qualifying noncumulative perpetual preferred stock	Undivided profits
	Mandatory convertible debt
Cumulative perpetual preferred stock with unpaid dividends	Minority interest in the equity accounts of consolidated subsidiaries

8. Under the terms of the Basel I Agreement, what *risk weights* apply to the following on-balance-sheet and off-balance-sheet items?

Residential real estate loans	Credit card loans
Cash	Standby letters of credit for municipal bonds
Commercial loans	
U.S. Treasury securities	Long-term commitments to make corporate loans
Deposits held at other banks	
GNMA mortgage-backed securities	Currency derivative contracts
	Interest-rate derivative contracts
Standby credit letters for commercial paper	Short-term (under one year) loan commitments
Federal agency securities	Bank real property
Municipal general obligation bonds	Bankers' acceptances
Investments in subsidiaries	Municipal revenue bonds
FNMA or FHLMC issued or guaranteed securities	Reserves on deposit at the Federal Reserve banks

Internet Exercises

1. You are the CFO of a large corporation that is reevaluating the depository institutions it relies upon for financial services. Since your company will maintain deposits in excess of $100,000, you want to make sure that the institutions you rely upon are well capitalized. Compare the total capital to risk-weighted assets, the Tier 1 capital to risk-weighted assets, and the leverage ratio for the following four banks: Bank of America (BHC ID 1073757), J. P. Morgan Chase (BHC ID 1039502), National City

Corp (BHC ID 1069125), and Wachovia (BHC ID 1073551). This is easily accomplished at **www3.fdic.gov/sdi/** where you can create a report for the four BHCs.

If you need some help maneuvering within the FDIC's Statistics on Depository Institutions (SDI), read on. The process to create a report requires you to select the number of columns. You want to select "4" to develop the format to collect data for the most recent report. This provides four pull-down menus, each labeled Select One. In the columns select Bank Holding Company from the menu and go on to type in the BHC ID #. After defining the four columns click on Next. At this point you focus on Report Selection, choosing to view and do calculations in percentages. Then you get to identify the information you want to collect before creating the report by clicking Next. You will find the "Performance and Conditions" report to be quite helpful. Are all the institutions well capitalized? Which institution has the highest capital ratios?

2. You are moving to Philadelphia and two savings banks have been recommended by soon-to-be colleagues. They are Beneficial Mutual Savings Bank (OTS Docket # 15697) and United Savings Banks (OTS Docket # 28836). You thought you would compare their capital adequacy, which is easily accomplished at **www3.fdic.gov/sdi/** where you can create a report for the two savings associations. If you need some help creating a report using SDI continue reading. The process to create a report requires you to select the number of columns. You want to select "2" to develop the format to collect data for the most recent report. This provides two pull-down menus, each labeled Select One. In the columns select Single Institution from the menu and go on to type in the OTS Docket Number. After defining the two columns, click on Next. At this point you focus on Report Selection, choosing to view and do calculations in percentages. Then you get to identity the information you want to collect before creating the report by clicking Next. You will find the "Performance and Conditions" report to be helpful. What capital adequacy category is appropriate?

3. The Basel Agreement is always evolving. Visit **http://www.bis.org/publ/bcbsca.htm** to find out what the current state of the new agreement is. What are the key issues?

S&P Market Insight Challenge (www.mhhe.com/edumarketinsight)

STANDARD &POOR'S

1. Capital levels capture the abilities of depository institutions to sustain losses and are very important to regulatory agencies watching this industry. For an up-to-date view of capital levels in the banking and thrift industries, please use the Industry tab in S&P's Market Insight, Educational Version and the drop-down menu to select among the subindustry choices of Diversified Banks, Regional Banks, and Thrifts & Mortgage Finance. By choosing among these subgroups, you will be able to access the S&P Industry Survey on Banking and the Survey on Savings and Loans. Please download both surveys and explore the sections, "How to Analyze a Bank" and "How to Analyze a Savings and Loan Company," with particular focus on the capital adequacy issue. Compare and contrast the most recent capital levels posted by banks and thrift institutions.

STANDARD &POOR'S

2. One of the most important topics in this chapter centers around the Basel Agreement on standards for bank capital. Basel I established minimum capital requirements for all banks in participating countries based on Tier 1 and Tier 2 capital and the risk-weighted assets of each bank. Choose the banks listed in Market Insight. How well capitalized are these banks relative to Basel's requirements? Do you see any apparent weaknesses? Are there other facts you'd like to know before relying exclusively on the capital ratios you have just calculated to make a judgment?

REAL NUMBERS FOR REAL BANKS | Assignment for Chapter 15

YOUR BANK'S CAPITAL: THE CUSHION FOR LOSSES AND FUNDS FOR GROWTH

Chapter 15 describes the management of capital in a depository institution and the tasks capital performs. The regulators have capital adequacy requirements that depository institutions must meet to continue operations. This chapter describes how to calculate three different capital adequacy ratios that are then used to place an institution in one of five capital adequacy categories. Each category determines permissible activities. For instance, for a bank holding company to be certified as a financial holding company (FHC) as outlined in the Gramm-Leach-Bliley Act, all the banks within the holding company must be *well capitalized.*

Part One of this assignment examines the capital ratios in aggregate for the depository institutions in your BHC. Another role of capital is to support the growth of an institution. In this chapter we learn to calculate the internal capital growth rate (ICGR). The internal capital growth rate measures how fast the bank can allow its assets to grow without reducing its capital-to-assets ratio. In Part Two we will calculate ICGRs and discuss growth opportunities or limitations.

Data Collection: You will once again access data at the FDIC's Web site at **www3.fdic.gov/sdi/** for your BHC. Use SDI to create a two-column report of your bank's information—a column for each year. In this part of the assignment, for Report Selection use the pull-down menu to select the "Performance and Condition Ratios" report, where you will find the three capital ratios and your internal capital growth rate computed for you. (What a nice surprise, given the tedious process of calculating risk-weighted assets.) Enter this data in your year-to-year comparison spreadsheet as shown below:

	A	B	C
87	**Capital Adequacy and Growth**	BHC	BHC
88	Date	12/31/yyyy	12/31/yyyy
89	Core capital (leverage) ratio		
90	Tier 1 risk-based capital ratio		
91	Total risk-based capital ratio		
92	Retained earnings to average equity (ICGR)		
93	Growth of assets over the last year (calculated using total assets)		

Part One: Regulatory Capital Adequacy

A. Using the information in rows 89–91 determine the capital adequacy category of the aggregation of banks (BHC as defined by the FDIC's SDI) for each year.

B. Compare the columns of rows 89–91.

C. Write one paragraph about your bank's capital adequacy and any changes you have observed between the two years.

Part Two: Evaluating the Internal Capital Growth Rate

A. This chapter concludes with a discussion of raising capital internally and externally. You have the ICGR for your BHC. Using the year-end dollar amounts and your formula function calculate the growth in total assets for the most recent year-end and enter this in cell B93.

B. Write one paragraph interpreting the ICGRs and discussing your BHC's most recent growth in assets and the potential for future growth.

Selected References

For an analysis of the factors contributing to the failures of banks and other financial firms, see, for example:

1. Santomero, Anthony M., and Joseph D. Vinso. "Estimating the Probability of Failure for Commercial Banks and the Banking System." *Journal of Banking and Finance 1* (1977), pp. 185–205.

For an overview of the market's role in influencing bank capital positions, see:

2. Eisenbeis, Robert A., and Gary G. Gilbert. "Market Discipline and the Prevention of Bank Problems and Failure." *Issues in Bank Regulation* 3 (Winter 1985), pp. 16–23.

3. Federal Reserve Bank of New York. *Beyond Pillar 3 in International Banking Regulation: Disclosure and Market Discipline of Financial Firms.* Proceedings of a conference cosponsored by the Federal Reserve Bank of New York and the Jerome A. Chazen Institute of International Business at Columbia University, 10, no. 2 (September 2004).

4. Keen, Howard, Jr. "The Impact of a Dividend Cut Announcement on Bank Share Prices." *Journal of Bank Research*, Winter 1983, pp. 274–281.

For a discussion of capital adequacy standards, their effects, and recent changes, see the following:

5. Peek, Joe, and Eric Rosengren. "Have Borrower Concentration Limits Encouraged Bank Consolidation?" *New England Economic Review*, Federal Reserve Bank of Boston, January/February 1997, pp. 37–47.

6. Wall, Larry D. "Regulation of Bank Equity Capital." *Economic Review*, Federal Reserve Bank of Atlanta, November 1985, pp. 4–18.

For more information about Basel II and the issues it raises, see especially:

7. Basel Committee on Bank Supervision. *International Convergence of Capital Measurement and Capital Standards: A Revised Framework.* Bank for International Settlements, June 2004.

8. Lopez, Jose A. "What Is Operational Risk?" *FRBSF Economic Letter*, Federal Reserve Bank of San Francisco, no. 2002-02 (January 25, 2002).

9. Lopez, Jose A. "Disclosure as a Supervisory Tool: Pillar 3 of Basel II." *FRBSF Economic Letter*, Federal Reserve Bank of San Francisco, no. 2003-22 (August 1, 2003).

10. Santomero, Anthony M. "Process and Progress in Risk Management." *Business Review*, Federal Reserve Bank of Philadelphia, First Quarter 2003, pp. 1–5.

11. Emmons, William R., Vahe Lskavyan, and Timothy J. Yeager. "Basel II Will Trickle Down to Community Bankers, Consumers." *Regional Economist*, Federal Reserve Bank of St. Louis, April 2005.

For a detailed discussion of U.S. regulation of bank capital, known as PCA ("prompt corrective action"), see, in particular:

12. Shibut, Lynn, Tim Critchfield, and Sarah Bohn. "Differentiating among Critically Undercapitalized Banks and Thrifts." *FDIC Banking Review* 15, no. 2 (2003), pp. 1–38.

To learn more about credit risk modeling for financial firms, see especially:

13. Lopez, Jose A. "Stress Tests: Useful Complements to Financial Risk Models." *FRBSF Economic Letter*, Federal Reserve Bank of San Francisco, no. 2005-14 (June 24, 2005), pp. 1–3.

For further information about Value at Risk (VaR) and what it tells us, see for example:

14. Jorion, Philippe. "How Informative Are Value-at-Risk Disclosures?" *The Accounting Review* 77 (2003), pp. 911–931, **www.edhec-risk.com/site**.

www.mhhe.com/rose7e

PART SIX

Providing Loans to Businesses and Consumers

Lending money to customers is central to banking, as it is for many nonbank lenders, such as finance companies and credit unions. Loans are the principal asset of many business and consumer lending institutions, often their principal source of operating revenues, and their chief source of risk exposure. Lenders may fail for many reasons, but at or near the top of the list are the bad loans they sometimes make.

Making credit available to its customers often defines a lender's role in the marketplace it serves, whether that marketplace lies in a small town or covers the entire face of the globe. There is a critical interaction between the lending function and the economic welfare of communities. Credit provided by financial institutions fuels economic expansion. Experts in the field often note that you can usually tell quickly which communities are served by aggressive lenders—evidence of a commitment to economic growth through lending is usually evident in the form of new homes, new businesses, new schools, and the like.

As in other areas of the financial-services business today, however, *competition* presses in on all sides of the lending function. For example, bank business lending programs are challenged by aggressive nonbank business lenders (such as GE Capital and Commercial Credit) and by credit underwriters (like Merrill Lynch and Goldman Sachs). Bank household loan programs are challenged by the rapidly growing credit programs advertised by credit unions, savings associations, consumer finance companies (such as Household Finance), and credit card lenders (like Capital One).

Because of the risks involved lenders must monitor their loan portfolios all the time. They create management policies that spell out what types of loans are to be made and on what terms. Lending institutions often watch their ratio of total loans to total assets carefully, aware that increases in this ratio promise more revenues perhaps, but also more risk. They also keep a close eye on their ratio of loans to capital (net worth). In order to protect those who place their savings with lending institutions, government regulators often discourage rapid loan growth unless a financial firm's capital grows apace.

We will see in this part of the book that the lending business is changing in unprecedented, remarkable ways. More loans are finding their way into the resale market or into loan pools taken off lenders' balance sheets. This allows many lending institutions to avoid having to raise more expensive capital and makes them appear less risky, helping to hold down their cost of raising new money to make more loans. In the future more financial holding companies are likely to be engaged in some form of merchant banking, not only extending loans to their top business customers but also taking equity (ownership) positions in many of the firms to whom they lend.

Part Six of the text proceeds in careful steps. We look first at policies and procedures that help to shape a lender's portfolio in the desired direction and train loan officers in how to make good lending decisions. Then we turn to lending to businesses—the different types of business credit available today, how business loans should be evaluated to control risk, and how these credits can be priced to generate adequate lender revenue. Finally, we examine household lending—consumer installment loans, credit cards, and home mortgage loans—in order to determine how consumer loans should be made and to explore the extensive regulations that shape household lending in markets around the globe.

CHAPTER SIXTEEN

Lending Policies and Procedures

Key Topics in This Chapter

- Types of Loans Banks Make
- Factors Affecting the Mix of Loans Made
- Regulation of Lending
- Creating a Written Loan Policy
- Steps in the Lending Process
- Loan Review and Loan Workouts

16–1 Introduction

J. Paul Getty, once the richest man in the world, observed: "If you owe the bank $100, that's your problem. If you owe the bank $100 million, that's the bank's problem." To be sure, lending to businesses, governments, and individuals is one of the most important services banks and their competitors provide, and it is also among the riskiest.

However, risky or not, the principal reason many financial firms are issued charters of incorporation by state and national governments is to make loans to their customers.[1] Banks and other lenders are expected to support their local communities with an adequate supply of credit for all legitimate business and consumer financial needs and to price that credit reasonably in line with competitively determined market interest rates.

Indeed, making loans to fund consumption and investment spending is the principal economic function of banks and their closest competitors. How well a lender performs in fulfilling the lending function has a great deal to do with the economic health of its region, because loans support the growth of new businesses and jobs within the lender's trade territory. Moreover, loans frequently convey information to the marketplace about a borrower's credit quality, often enabling a borrower whose loan is approved to obtain more and somewhat cheaper funds from other sources as well.

Despite all the benefits of lending for both lenders and their customers, the lending process bears careful monitoring at all times. When a lender gets into serious financial trouble, its problems usually spring from loans that have become uncollectible due to mismanagement, illegal manipulation, misguided policies, or an unexpected economic downturn. No wonder, then, that when examiners appear at a regulated lending institution they conduct a thorough review of its loan portfolio. Usually this involves a detailed analysis of the documentation and collateral for the largest loans, a review of a sample of small loans, and an evaluation of loan policies to ensure they are sound and prudent in order to protect the public's funds.

[1] Portions of this chapter are based upon Peter S. Rose's article in *The Canadian Banker* [3] and are used with the permission of the publisher.

16–2 Types of Loans

What *types* of loans do banks and their closest competitors make? The answer, of course, is that banks make a wide variety of loans to a wide variety of customers for many different purposes—from purchasing automobiles and buying new furniture, taking dream vacations, or pursuing college educations to constructing homes and office buildings. Fortunately, we can bring some order to the diversity of lending by grouping loans according to their *purpose*—what customers plan to do with the proceeds of their loans. At least once each year, the Federal Reserve System, FDIC, and the Comptroller of the Currency require each U.S. bank to report the composition of its loan portfolio by purpose of loan on a report form known as Schedule A, attached to its balance sheet. Table 16–1 summarizes the major items reported on Schedule A for all U.S. banks as of June 30, 2005.

We note from Table 16–1 that loans may be divided into seven broad categories, delineated by their purposes:

Factoid

In the most recent years which financial institution has been the number one lender in the U.S. economy?
Answer: Commercial banks, followed by insurance companies, savings institutions, finance companies, and credit unions.

1. **Real estate loans** are secured by real property—land, buildings, and other structures—and include short-term loans for construction and land development and longer-term loans to finance the purchase of farmland, homes, apartments, commercial structures, and foreign properties.
2. **Financial institution loans** include credit to banks, insurance companies, finance companies, and other financial institutions.
3. **Agricultural loans** are extended to farms and ranches to assist in planting and harvesting crops and supporting the feeding and care of livestock.
4. **Commercial and industrial loans** are granted to businesses to cover purchasing inventories, paying taxes, and meeting payrolls.

TABLE 16–1

Loans Outstanding for All U.S.-Insured Banks as of June 30, 2005 (consolidated domestic and foreign offices)

Source: Federal Deposit Insurance Corporation.

Bank Loans Classified by Purpose	Amount for All FDIC-Insured U.S. Banks ($ billions)	Percentage of Loan Portfolio		
		Percentage of Total Loans for all FDIC-Insured U.S. Banks	Smallest U.S. Banks (less than $100 million in total assets)	Largest U.S. Banks (over $1 billion in total assets)
Real estate loans[a]	$2817.6	54.9%	62.8%	51.9%
Loans to depository institutions[b]	151.6	3.0	0.0*	3.5
Loans to finance agricultural production	48.2	0.1	10.3	0.4
Commercial and industrial loans[c]	980.3	19.1	16.0	19.7
Loans to individuals[d]	813.7	15.9	9.6	17.4
Miscellaneous loans[e]	231.4	4.5	0.9	4.0
Lease financing receivables	136.6	2.7	0.4	3.1
Total (gross) loans and leases shown on U.S. banks' balance sheet	$5132.1	100.0%	100.0%	100.0%

*Less than 0.05 percent.
[a]Construction and land development loans; loans to finance one- to four-family homes; multifamily residential property loans; nonfarm, nonresidential property loans; foreign real estate loans.
[b]Loans to commercial banks and other foreign and domestic depository institutions and acceptances of other banks.
[c]Credit to construct business plant and equipment; loans for business operating expenses; loans for other business uses, including international loans and acceptances.
[d]Loans to purchase automobiles; credit cards; mobile home loans; loans to purchase consumer goods; loans to repair and modernize residences; all other personal installment loans; single-payment loans; and other personal loans.
[e]Includes loans to foreign governments and state and local governments and acceptances of other banks. Columns may not add exactly to totals due to rounding error.

5. **Loans to individuals** include credit to finance the purchase of automobiles, mobile homes, appliances, and other retail goods, to repair and modernize homes, and to cover the cost of medical care and other personal expenses, and are either extended directly to individuals or indirectly through retail dealers.

6. *Miscellaneous loans* include all loans *not* listed above, including securities' loans.

7. *Lease financing receivables*, where the lender buys equipment or vehicles and leases them to its customers.

Of the loan categories shown, the largest in dollar volume is *real estate loans*, accounting for just over half of total bank loans. The next largest category is commercial and industrial (C&I) loans, representing about one-fifth of the total, followed by loans to individuals and families, accounting for about one-sixth of all loans federally insured banks make.

Factors Determining the Growth and Mix of Loans

While Table 16–1 indicates the relative amounts of different kinds of loans for the whole banking industry, the mix usually differs markedly from institution to institution. One of the key factors in shaping an individual lender's loan portfolio is the profile of *characteristics of the market area* it serves. Each lender must respond to the demands for credit arising from customers in its own market. For example, a lender serving a suburban community with large numbers of single-family homes and small retail stores will normally have mainly residential real estate loans, automobile loans, and credit for the purchase of home appliances and for meeting household expenses. In contrast, a lender situated in a central city surrounded by office buildings, department stores, and manufacturing establishments will typically devote the bulk of its loan portfolio to business loans designed to stock shelves with inventory, purchase equipment, and meet business payrolls.

Of course, lenders are not totally dependent on the local areas they serve for *all* the loans they acquire. They can purchase whole loans or pieces of loans from other lenders, share in loans with other lenders (known as *participations*), or even use credit derivatives to offset the economic volatility inherent in loans from their trade territory (as we saw in Chapter 9, for example). These steps can help reduce the risk of loss if the local areas served incur severe economic problems. However, most lenders are chartered to serve selected markets and, as a practical matter, most of their loan applications will come from these areas.

Lender size is also a key factor shaping the composition of a loan portfolio. For example, the volume of capital held by a depository institution determines its *legal lending limit* to a single borrower. Larger banks are often **wholesale lenders,** devoting the bulk of their credit portfolios to large-denomination loans to business firms. Smaller banks, on the other hand, tend to emphasize **retail credit,** in the form of smaller-denomination personal cash loans and home mortgage loans extended to individuals and families, as well as smaller business loans.

Table 16–1 reveals some of the differences between the largest and smallest U.S. banks in loan portfolio mix. The smallest banks (under $100 million in total assets) are more heavily committed to real estate and agricultural loans than the largest banking firms (over $1 billion in assets), which tend to be more heavily committed to commercial loans and loans to individuals. The *experience and expertise of management* in making different types of loans also shape the composition of a loan portfolio, as does the lending institution's *loan policy*, which prohibits loan officers from making certain kinds of loans.

We should also note that the composition of loans varies with the type of lending institution involved. For example, while commercial banks typically extend large numbers of commercial and industrial (business) loans, savings associations and credit unions tend to emphasize home mortgage and personal installment loans. In contrast, finance companies favor business inventory and equipment loans and also grant large amounts of household credit to purchase appliances, furniture, and automobiles.

Finally, loan mix at any particular lending institution depends heavily upon the *expected yield* that each loan offers compared to the yields on all other assets the lender could acquire. Other factors held equal, a lender would generally prefer to make loans bearing the highest expected returns after all expenses and the risk of loan losses are taken into account. Recent research suggests that gross yields (i.e., total revenue received divided by loan volume) typically have been exceptionally high for credit card loans, installment loans (mainly to households and smaller businesses), and real estate loans. However, when *net yields* (with expenses and loss rates deducted from revenues received) are calculated, real estate and commercial loans generally rank high relative to other loan types, helping to explain their popularity among many lenders.

Concept Check

16–1. In what ways does the lending function affect the economy of its community or region?

16–2. What are the principal types of loans made by banks?

16–3. What factors appear to influence the growth and mix of loans held by a lending institution?

16–4. A lender's cost accounting system reveals that its losses on real estate loans average 0.45 percent of loan volume and its operating expenses from making these loans average 1.85 percent of loan volume. If the gross yield on real estate loans is currently 8.80 percent, what is this lender's net yield on these loans?

Lender size appears to have a significant influence on the net yield from different kinds of loans. Smaller banks, for example, seem to average higher net returns from granting real estate and commercial loans, whereas larger banks appear to have a net yield advantage in making credit card loans. Of course, *customer size* as well as lender size can affect relative loan yields. For example, the largest banks make loans to the largest corporations where loan rates are relatively low due to generally lower risk and the force of competition; in contrast, small institutions lend money primarily to the smallest-size businesses, whose loan rates tend to be much higher than those attached to large corporate loans. Thus, it is not too surprising that the net yields on commercial loans tend to be higher among the smallest lending institutions.

As a general rule, a lending institution should make those types of loans for which it is the *most efficient producer*. The largest banks appear to have a cost advantage in making nearly all types of real estate and installment loans. Medium-size and large lenders are generally the lowest-cost producers of credit card loans. While the smallest lenders appear to have few cost advantages relative to larger institutions for almost any type of loan, these smaller lenders are frequently among the most effective at controlling loan losses, perhaps because they often have better knowledge of their customers.

16–3 Regulation of Lending

Lending institutions are among the most closely regulated of all financial-service institutions. Not surprisingly, the mix, quality, and yield of the loan portfolio are heavily influenced by the character and depth of *regulation*. Any loans made are subject to examination and review and many are restricted or even prohibited by law.

Key URLs
To discover more facts about the rules and regulations of lending see, for example, the Federal Financial Institutions Examination Council at **www.ffiec.gov/press. htm**, the Federal Deposit Insurance Corporation at **www.fdic.gov**, and the Federal Reserve System at **www. federalreserve.gov**.

For example, banks are frequently prohibited from making loans collateralized by their own stock. Real estate loans granted by a U.S. national bank cannot exceed that bank's capital and surplus or 70 percent of its total time and savings deposits, whichever is greater. A loan to a single customer normally cannot exceed 15 percent of a national bank's unimpaired capital and surplus account. The lending limit may be further increased to 25 percent of unimpaired capital and surplus if the loan amount exceeding the 15 percent limit is fully secured by marketable securities.

Loans to a bank's officers extended for purposes other than funding education or the purchase of a home or that are not fully backed by U.S. government securities or deposits are limited to the greater of 2.5 percent of the bank's capital and unimpaired surplus or $25,000, but cannot be more than $100,000. State-chartered banks face similar restrictions on insider loans in their home states and from the Federal Deposit Insurance Corporation. The Sarbanes-Oxley Act of 2002 requires that loans to insiders be priced at market value rather than being subsidized by the lending institution.

The Community Reinvestment Act (1977) requires banks and selected other lenders to make "an affirmative effort" to meet the credit needs of individuals and businesses in their trade territories so that no areas of the local community are discriminated against in seeking access to credit. Moreover, under the Equal Credit Opportunity Act (1974), no individual can be denied credit because of race, sex, religious affiliation, age, or receipt of public assistance. Disclosure laws require that the borrower be quoted the "true cost" of a loan, as reflected in the annual percentage interest rate (APR) and all required charges and fees for obtaining credit, *before* the loan agreement is signed.[2]

In the field of international lending, special regulations have appeared in recent years in an effort to reduce the risk exposure associated with granting loans overseas. In this field lenders often face significant political risk from foreign governments passing restrictive laws or seizing foreign-owned property, and substantial business risk due to lack of knowledge concerning foreign markets. U.S. law in the form of the International Lending and Supervision Act requires U.S. banks to make public any credit exposures to a single country that exceed 15 percent of their primary capital or 0.75 percent of their total assets, whichever is smaller. This law also imposes restrictions on the fees lenders may charge a troubled international borrower to restructure a loan.

The quality of a loan portfolio and the soundness of its policies are the areas federal and state regulators look at most closely when examining a lending institution. Under the Uniform Financial Institutions Rating System used by federal examiners, each banking firm is assigned a numerical rating based on the quality of its asset portfolio, including its loans. The examiner assigns one of these ratings:

1 = strong performance

2 = satisfactory performance

3 = fair performance

4 = marginal performance

5 = unsatisfactory performance

The better a bank's asset-quality rating, the less frequently it will be subject to examination by banking agencies, other factors held equal.

Examiners generally look at all loans above a designated minimum size and at a random sample of small loans. Loans that are performing well but have minor weaknesses because the lender has not followed its own loan policy or has failed to get full documentation from

---

[2]See Chapter 18 for a more detailed discussion of antidiscrimination and disclosure laws applying to bank loans to individuals and families.

Key URLs
Information about the regulation of lending around the world can be gathered from such sources as the Bank for International Settlements at **www. bis.org** and the libraries of the World Bank and the International Monetary Fund at **jolis.worldbankimflib. org/external.htm**.

the borrower are called *criticized loans*. Loans that appear to contain significant weaknesses or that represent what the examiner regards as a dangerous concentration of credit in one borrower or in one industry are called *scheduled loans*. A scheduled loan is a warning to management to monitor that credit carefully and to work toward reducing the lender's risk exposure from it.

When an examiner finds loans that carry an immediate risk of not paying out as planned, these credits are *adversely classified*. Typically, examiners will place adversely classified loans into one of three groupings: (1) *substandard loans*, where the loans' margin of protection is inadequate due to weaknesses in collateral or in the borrower's repayment abilities; (2) *doubtful loans*, which carry a strong probability of an uncollectible loss to the lending institution; and (3) *loss loans*, regarded as uncollectible and not suitable to be called bankable assets. A common procedure for examiners is to multiply the total of all substandard loans by 0.20, the total of all doubtful loans by 0.50, and the total of all loss loans by 1.00, then sum these weighted amounts and compare their grand total with the lender's sum of loan-loss allowances and equity capital. If the weighted sum of all adversely classified loans appears too large relative to loan-loss allowances and equity capital, examiners will demand changes in the lender's policies and procedures or, possibly, require additions to loan-loss allowances and capital. Financial institutions that disagree with examiner classifications of their loans can appeal these rulings.

Of course, the quality of loans is only one dimension of a lender's performance that is rated under the Uniform Financial Institutions Rating System. Numerical ratings are also assigned based on examiner judgment about capital adequacy, management quality, earnings record, liquidity position, and sensitivity to market risk exposure. All five dimensions of performance are combined into one overall numerical rating, referred to as the **CAMELS rating.** The letters in CAMELS are derived from

Capital adequacy	Earnings record
Asset quality	Liquidity position
Management quality	Sensitivity to market risk

Depository institutions whose overall CAMELS rating is toward the low, riskier end of the numerical scale—an overall rating of 4 or 5—tend to be examined more frequently than the highest-rated institutions, those with ratings of 1, 2, or 3.

One final note on the examination process today: Rapidly changing technology and the emergence of very large financial institutions appear to have weakened the effectiveness of traditional examination procedures. An added problem is that examinations tend to occur no more frequently than once a year and the decay in the quality of examination information over time can be rapid, especially among weakly performing or poorly managed lending institutions. Accordingly, regulators are beginning to turn more toward *market forces* as a better long-run approach to monitoring behavior and encouraging lenders to manage their institutions prudently. The new emerging emphasis in examination is to rely more heavily upon "private market discipline" in which such factors as borrowing costs, stock prices, and other market values are used as "signals" as to how well a lender is performing and to help examiners determine if they need to take a close look at how a lending institution is managing its loans and protecting the public's funds.[3]

---

[3]In order to more closely monitor the condition of depository institutions between regular examinations the regulatory agencies today use *off-site monitoring* systems. For example, the FDIC employs SCOR—the Statistical CAMELS Off-Site Rating—which forecasts future CAMELS ratings quarterly, based on 12 key financial ratios tracking equity capital, loan loss exposure, earnings, liquid assets, and loan totals. See especially Collier et al. [7].

Key URL

For an interesting source of information about trends in lending and loan policies, see the Senior Loan Officer Opinion Survey at **www.federalreserve. gov/boarddocs/SnLoan Survey**.

Establishing a Written Loan Policy

One of the most important ways a lending institution can make sure its loans meet regulatory standards and are profitable is to establish a *written loan policy*. Such a policy gives loan officers and management specific guidelines in making individual loan decisions and in shaping the overall loan portfolio. The actual makeup of a lender's loan portfolio should reflect what its loan policy says. Otherwise, the loan policy is not functioning effectively and should be either revised or more strongly enforced.

What should a written loan policy contain? The examinations manual, which the Federal Deposit Insurance Corporation gives to new examiners, suggests the most important elements of a well-written loan policy. These elements include:

1. A goal statement for the loan portfolio (i.e., statement of the characteristics of a good loan portfolio in terms of types, maturities, sizes, and quality of loans).
2. Specification of the lending authority given to each loan officer and loan committee (measuring the maximum amount and types of loan that each employee and committee can approve and what signatures of approval are required).
3. Lines of responsibility in making assignments and reporting information.
4. Operating procedures for soliciting, evaluating, and making decisions on customer loan applications.
5. The required documentation that is to accompany each loan application and what must be kept in the lender's files (financial statements, security agreements, etc.).
6. Lines of authority detailing who is responsible for maintaining and reviewing the institution's credit files.
7. Guidelines for taking, evaluating, and perfecting loan collateral.
8. Procedures for setting loan rates and fees and the terms for repayment of loans.
9. A statement of quality standards applicable to all loans.
10. A statement of the preferred upper limit for total loans outstanding (i.e., the maximum ratio of total loans to total assets allowed).
11. A description of the lending institution's principal trade area, from which most loans should come.
12. Procedures for detecting and working out problem loan situations.

Concept Check

16–5. Why is lending so closely regulated by state and federal authorities?

16–6. What is the CAMELS rating and how is it used?

16–7. What should a good written loan policy contain?

Key URLs

To learn more about how loan officers are educated see, for example, the Risk Management Association (RMA) at **www.rmahq.org**. If you are interested in a possible career in lending see especially **www. jobsinthemoney.com** and **www.bls.gov/oco/ cg/cgs027.htm**.

Other authorities would add to this list such items as specifying what loans the lender would prefer *not* to make, such as loans to support the construction of speculative housing or loans to support leveraged buyouts (LBOs) of companies by a small group of insiders who typically make heavy use of debt to finance the purchase, as well as a list of preferred loans (such as short-term business inventory loans that are self-liquidating).

A written loan policy carries a number of advantages for the lending institution adopting it. It communicates to employees what procedures they must follow and what their responsibilities are. It helps the lender move toward a loan portfolio that can successfully blend *multiple objectives*, such as promoting profitability, controlling risk exposure, and satisfying regulatory requirements. Any exceptions to the loan policy should be fully documented, and the reasons why a variance from the loan policy was permitted should be listed. While any loan policy must be flexible due to continuing changes in economic conditions and regulations, violations of loan policy should be infrequent events.

16–4 Steps in the Lending Process

1. Finding Prospective Loan Customers

Most loans to individuals arise from a direct request from a customer who approaches a member of the lender's staff and asks to fill out a loan application. Business loan requests, on the other hand, often arise from contacts the loan officers and sales representatives make as they solicit new accounts from firms operating in the lender's market area. Increasingly the lending game is becoming a *sales position*. Sometimes loan officers will call on the same company for months before the customer finally agrees to give the lending institution a try by filling out a loan application. Most loan department personnel fill out a customer contact report similar to the one shown in Table 16–2 when they visit a prospective customer's place of business. This report is updated after each subsequent visit, giving the next loan officer crucial information about a prospective client before any other personal contacts are made.

2. Evaluating a Prospective Customer's Character and Sincerity of Purpose

Once a customer decides to request a loan, an interview with a loan officer usually follows, giving the customer the opportunity to explain his or her credit needs. That interview is particularly important because it provides an opportunity for the loan officer to *assess the customer's character and sincerity of purpose*. If the customer appears to lack sincerity in acknowledging the need to adhere to the terms of a loan, this must be recorded as a strong factor weighing against approval of the loan request.

TABLE 16–2
Sample Customer Contact Report (results of previous calls on a customer)

Name of customer: _____

Address:_____ Telephone: ( ) _____

Lender personnel making most recent contact: _____

Names of employees making previous contacts with this customer: _____

Does this customer currently use any of our services? _____ Yes _____ No

Which ones? _____

Has the customer used any of our services in the past? _____

If a business firm, what officials with the customer's firm have we contacted?

_____

If an individual, what is the customer's occupation? _____

What line of business is the customer in? _____

Approximate annual sales: $ _____ Size of labor force: _____

Who provides financial services to this customer at present? _____

What problems does the customer have with his/her current financial service relationship?

_____

What financial services does this customer use at present? (Please check)

_____ Line of credit   _____ Funds transfers

_____ Term loan   _____ Cash management services

_____ Checkable deposits   _____ Other services

What services does this customer *not* use currently that might be useful to him or her?

_____

Describe the results of the most recent contact with this customer: _____

_____

Recommended steps to prepare for the next call (e.g., special information needed):

_____

3. Making Site Visits and Evaluating a Prospective Customer's Credit Record

If a business or mortgage loan is applied for, a loan officer often makes a *site visit* to assess the customer's location and the condition of the property and to ask clarifying questions. The loan officer may contact other creditors who have previously loaned money to this customer to see what their experience has been. Did the customer fully adhere to previous loan agreements and, where required, keep satisfactory deposit balances? A previous payment record often reveals much about the customer's character, sincerity of purpose, and sense of responsibility in making use of credit extended by a lending institution.

4. Evaluating a Prospective Customer's Financial Condition

If all is favorable to this point, the customer is asked to submit several crucial documents the lender needs in order to fully evaluate the loan request, including complete financial statements and, in the case of a corporation, board of directors' resolutions authorizing the negotiation of a loan with the lender. Once all documents are on file, the lender's credit analysis division conducts a thorough financial analysis of the applicant, aimed at determining whether the customer has sufficient cash flow and backup assets to repay the loan. The credit analysis division then prepares a brief summary and recommendation, which goes to the appropriate loan committee for approval. On larger loans, members of the credit analysis division may give an oral presentation and discussion will ensue between staff analysts and the loan committee over the strong and weak points of a loan request.

5. Assessing Possible Loan Collateral and Signing the Loan Agreement

If the loan committee approves the customer's request, the loan officer or the credit committee will usually check on the property or other assets to be pledged as collateral in order to ensure that the lending institution has immediate access to the collateral or can acquire title to the property involved if the loan agreement is defaulted. This is often referred to as *perfecting* the lender's claim to collateral. Once the loan officer and the loan committee are satisfied that both the loan and the proposed collateral are sound, the note and other documents that make up a loan agreement are prepared and signed by all parties to the agreement.

6. Monitoring Compliance with the Loan Agreement and Other Customer Service Needs

Is this the end of the process? Can the loan officer put the signed loan agreement on the shelf and forget about it? Hardly! The new agreement must be monitored continuously to ensure that the terms of the loan are being followed and that all required payments of principal and interest are being made as promised. For larger commercial credits, the loan officer will visit the customer's business periodically to check on the firm's progress and see what other services the customer may need. Usually a loan officer or other staff member enters information about a new loan customer in a computer file known as a *customer profile*. This file shows what services the customer is currently using and contains other information required by management to monitor a customer's progress and financial service needs.

16–5 Credit Analysis: What Makes a Good Loan?

The division or department responsible for analyzing and making recommendations on the fate of most loan applications is the *credit department*. Experience has shown that this department must satisfactorily answer three major questions regarding each loan application:

1. Is the borrower *creditworthy*? How do you know?
2. Can the loan agreement be properly *structured and documented* so the lending institution and those who supply it with funds are adequately protected and the borrower has a high probability of being able to service the loan without excessive strain?

3. Can the lender *perfect* its claim against the assets or earnings of the customer so that, in the event of default, the lender's funds can be recovered rapidly at low cost and with low risk?

Let's look at each of these three key issues in the "yes" or "no" decision a lending institution must make on every loan request.

1. Is the Borrower Creditworthy?

The question that must be dealt with before any other is whether or not the customer can *service the loan*—that is, pay out the credit when due, with a comfortable margin for error. This usually involves a detailed study of six aspects of a loan application: *character, capacity, cash, collateral, conditions*, and *control*. *All* must be satisfactory for the loan to be a good one from the lender's point of view. (See Table 16–3.)

Character

The loan officer must be convinced the customer has a well-defined *purpose* for requesting credit and a serious intention to repay. If the officer is not sure why the customer is requesting a loan, this purpose must be clarified to the lender's satisfaction. The loan officer must determine if the purpose is consistent with the lending institution's loan policy. Even with a good purpose, however, the loan officer must determine that the borrower has a responsible attitude toward using borrowed funds, is truthful in answering questions, and will make every effort to repay what is owed. Responsibility, truthfulness, serious purpose, and serious intention to repay all monies owed make up what a loan officer calls *character*. If the loan officer feels the customer is insincere in promising to use borrowed funds as planned and in repaying as agreed, the loan should *not* be made, for it will almost certainly become a problem credit.

Capacity

The loan officer must be sure that the customer has the authority to request a loan and the legal standing to sign a binding loan agreement. This customer characteristic is known as the *capacity* to borrow money. For example, in most areas a minor (e.g., under age 18 or 21) cannot legally be held responsible for a credit agreement; thus, the lender would have great difficulty collecting on such a loan. Similarly, the loan officer must be sure that the representative from a corporation asking for credit has proper authority from the company's board of directors to negotiate a loan and sign a credit agreement binding the company. Usually this can be determined by obtaining a copy of the resolution passed by a corporate customer's board of directors, authorizing the company to borrow money. Where a business partnership is involved, the loan officer must ask to see the firm's partnership agreement to determine which individuals are authorized to borrow for the firm. A loan agreement signed by unauthorized persons could prove to be uncollectible and, therefore, result in substantial losses for the lending institution.

Cash

This feature of any loan application centers on the question: Does the borrower have the ability to generate enough **cash**—in the form of *cash flow*—to repay the loan? In general, borrowing customers have only three sources to draw upon to repay their loans: (*a*) cash flows generated from sales or income, (*b*) the sale or liquidation of assets, or (*c*) funds raised by issuing debt or equity securities. Any of these sources may provide sufficient cash to repay a loan. However, lenders have a strong preference for *cash flow* as the principal source of loan repayment because asset sales can weaken a borrowing customer and make the lender's position as creditor less secure. Moreover, shortfalls in cash flow are common

TABLE 16–3 The Six Basic Cs of Lending

Source: Peter S. Rose, "Loans in a Troubled Economy," *The Canadian Banker* 90, no. 3 (June 1983), p. 55.

Character	Capacity	Cash	Collateral	Conditions	Control
Customer's past payment record	Identity of customer and guarantors	Take-home pay for an individual; the past earnings, dividends, and sales record for a business firm	Ownership of assets	Customer's current position in industry and expected market share	Applicable laws and regulations regarding the character and quality of acceptable loans
Experience of other lenders with this customer	Copies of Social Security cards, driver's licenses, corporate charters, resolutions, partnership agreements, and other legal documents	Adequacy of past and projected cash flows	Vulnerability of assets to obsolescence	Customer's performance vis-à-vis comparable firms in the same industry	Adequate documentation for examiners who may review the loan
Purpose of loan	Description of history, legal structure, owners, nature of operations, products, and principal customers and suppliers for a business borrower	Availability of liquid reserves	Liquidation value of assets	Competitive climate for customer's product	Signed acknowledgments and correctly prepared loan documents
Customer's track record in forecasting business or personal income		Turnover of payables, accounts receivable, and inventory	Degree of specialization in assets	Sensitivity of customer and industry to business cycles and changes in technology	Consistency of loan request with lender's written loan policy
Credit rating		Capital structure and leverage	Liens, encumbrances, and restrictions against property held	Labor market conditions in customer's industry or market area	Inputs from noncredit personnel (such as economists or political experts) on the external factors affecting loan repayment
Presence of cosigners or guarantors of the proposed loan		Expense controls	Leases and mortgages issued against property and equipment	Impact of inflation on customer's balance sheet and cash flow	
		Coverage ratios	Insurance coverage	Long-run industry or job outlook	
		Recent performance of borrower's stock and price-earnings (P/E) ratio	Guarantees and warranties issued to others	Regulations, political and environmental factors affecting the customer and/or his or her job, business, and industry	
		Management quality	Lender's relative position as creditor in placing a claim against borrower's assets		
		Recent accounting changes	Probable future financing needs		

indicators of failing businesses and troubled loan relationships. This is one reason current banking regulations require that the lender document the cash flow basis for approving a loan.

What is **cash flow?** In an accounting sense, it is usually defined as

$$\text{Cash flow} = \begin{array}{c}\text{Net Profits}\\\text{(or total}\\\text{revenues less}\\\text{all expenses)}\end{array} + \begin{array}{c}\text{Noncash Expenses}\\\text{(especially}\\\text{depreciation)}\end{array}$$

This is often called *traditional cash flow* and can be further broken down into:

$$\text{Cash flow} = \begin{array}{c}\text{Sales Revenues} - \text{Cost of Goods Sold} - \text{Selling, General and}\\\text{Administrative Expenses} - \text{Taxes Paid in Cash} + \text{Noncash Expenses}\end{array}$$

with all of the above items (except noncash expenses) figured on the basis of actual cash inflows and outflows instead of on an accrual basis.

For example, if a business firm has $100 million in annual sales revenue, reports $70 million in cost of goods sold, carries annual selling and administrative expenses of $15 million, pays annual taxes amounting to $5 million, and posts depreciation and other noncash expenses of $6 million, its projected annual cash flow would be $16 million. The lender must determine if this volume of annual cash flow will be sufficient to comfortably cover repayment of the loan as well as deal with any unexpected expenses.

In this slightly expanded format, traditional cash flow measures point to at least five major areas loan officers should look at carefully when lending money to business firms or other institutions. These are:

1. The level of and recent trends in sales revenue (which reflect the quality and public acceptance of products and services).
2. The level of and recent changes in cost of goods sold (including inventory costs).
3. The level of and recent trends in selling, general, and administrative expenses (including the compensation of management and employees).
4. Any tax payments made in cash.
5. The level of and recent trends in noncash expenses (led by depreciation expenses).

Adverse movements in *any* of these key sources and uses of cash demand inquiry and satisfactory resolution by a loan officer.

A more recent and, in some ways, more revealing approach to measuring cash flow is often called the *direct cash flow method* or sometimes *cash flow by origin*. It answers the simple but vital question: *Why is cash changing over time?* This method divides *cash flow* into its three principal sources:

1. *Net cash flow from operations* (the borrower's net income expressed on a cash rather than an accrual basis).
2. *Net cash flow from financing activity* (which tracks cash inflows and outflows associated with selling or repurchasing borrower-issued securities).
3. *Net cash flow from investing activities* (which examines outflows and inflows of cash resulting from the purchase and sale of the borrower's assets).

This method of figuring cash flow and its components can be extremely useful in ferreting out the recent sources of a borrower's cash flow. For example, most lenders would prefer that most incoming cash come from operations (sales of product or service). If, on the other hand, a substantial proportion of incoming cash arises instead from the sale of assets (investing activities) or from issuing debt (financing activities), the borrower may have even less opportunity to generate cash in the future, presenting any prospective lender with added risk exposure if a loan is granted.

Collateral

In assessing the *collateral* aspect of a loan request, the loan officer must ask, Does the borrower possess adequate net worth or own enough quality assets to provide adequate support for the loan? The loan officer is particularly sensitive to such features as the age, condition, and degree of specialization of the borrower's assets. Technology plays an important role here as well. If the borrower's assets are technologically obsolete, they will have limited value as collateral because of the difficulty of finding a buyer for those assets should the borrower's income falter.

Conditions

The loan officer and credit analyst must be aware of recent trends in the borrower's line of work or industry and how changing economic *conditions* might affect the loan. A loan can look very good on paper, only to have its value eroded by declining sales or income in a recession or by high interest rates occasioned by inflation. To assess industry and economic conditions, most lenders maintain files of information—newspaper clippings, magazine articles, and research reports—on the industries represented by their major borrowing customers.

Control

The last factor in assessing a borrower's creditworthy status is *control*. This factor centers on such questions as whether changes in law and regulation could adversely affect the borrower and whether the loan request meets the lender's and the regulatory authorities' standards for loan quality.

Factoid
Who is the number one originator of loans to households (consumers) in the United States? **Answer:** Commercial banks, followed by finance companies, credit unions, and savings institutions.

2. Can the Loan Agreement Be Properly Structured and Documented?

The six Cs of credit aid the loan officer and the credit analyst in answering the broad question: Is the borrower creditworthy? Once that question is answered, however, a second issue must be faced: Can the proposed loan agreement be *structured* and *documented* to satisfy the needs of both borrower and lender?

The loan officer is responsible not only to the borrowing customer but also to the depositors or other creditors as well as the stockholders and must seek to satisfy the demands of *all*. This requires, first, the drafting of a loan agreement that meets the borrower's need for funds with a comfortable repayment schedule. The borrower must be able to comfortably handle any required loan payments, because the lender's success depends fundamentally on the success of its customers. If a major borrower gets into trouble because of an inability to service a loan, the lending institution may find itself in serious trouble as well. Proper accommodation of a customer may involve lending more or less money than requested (because many customers do not know their own financial needs), over a longer or shorter period than requested. Thus, a loan officer must be a financial counselor to customers as well as a conduit for loan applications.

A properly structured loan agreement must also protect the lender and those the lender represents—principally depositors, other creditors, and stockholders—by imposing certain restrictions (covenants) on the borrower's activities when these activities could threaten recovery of the lender's funds. The process of recovering the lender's funds—when and where the lender can take action to get its funds returned—also must be carefully spelled out in any loan agreement.

3. Can the Lender Perfect Its Claim against the Borrower's Earnings and Any Assets That May Be Pledged as Collateral?

Reasons for Taking Collateral

While large corporations and other borrowers with impeccable credit ratings often borrow unsecured (with no specific collateral pledged behind their loans except their reputation and ability to generate earnings), most borrowers at one time or another will be asked to pledge some of their assets or to personally guarantee the repayment of their loans. Getting a pledge of certain borrower assets as collateral behind a loan really serves two purposes for a lender. If the borrower cannot pay, the pledge of collateral gives the lender the right to seize and sell those assets designated as loan collateral, using the proceeds of the sale to cover what the borrower did not pay back. Secondly, collateralization gives the lender a psychological advantage over the borrower. Because specific assets may be at stake (such as the customer's automobile or home), a borrower feels more obligated to work hard to repay his or her loan and avoid losing valuable assets. Thus, the third key question faced with many loan applications is, Can the lender *perfect* its claim against the assets or earnings of a borrowing customer?

The goal of a lender taking collateral is to precisely *define* which borrower assets are subject to seizure and sale and to *document* for all other creditors to see that the lender has a legal claim to those assets in the event of nonperformance on a loan. When a lender holds a claim against a borrower's assets that stands superior to the claims of other lenders and to the borrower's own claim, we say that lender's claim to collateral has been *perfected*. Lending institutions have learned that the procedures necessary for establishing a perfected claim on someone else's property differ depending on the nature of the assets pledged by the borrower and depending on the laws of the state or nation where the assets reside. For example, a different set of steps is necessary to perfect a claim if the lender has actual possession of the assets pledged (e.g., if the borrower pledges a deposit already held in the bank or lets the lender hold some of the customer's stocks and bonds) as opposed to the case where the borrower retains possession of the pledged assets (e.g., an automobile). Yet another procedure must be followed if the property pledged is real estate—land and buildings.

Key URLs

For an overview of modern loan risk evaluation techniques see, for example, **www.riskmetrics.com/ sitemap.html** and **www.defaultrisk.com**.

Common Types of Loan Collateral

Examples of the most popular assets pledged as collateral for loans include the following:

Accounts Receivable. The lender takes a security interest in the form of a stated percentage (usually somewhere between 40 and 90 percent) of the face amount of accounts receivable (sales on credit) shown on a business borrower's balance sheet. When the borrower's credit customers send in cash to retire their debts, these cash payments are applied to the balance of the borrower's loan. The lending institution may agree to lend still more money as new receivables arise from the borrower's subsequent sales to its customers, thus allowing the loan to continue as long as the borrower has need for credit and continues to generate an adequate volume of sales and credit repayments.

Factoring. A lender can purchase a borrower's accounts receivable based upon some percentage of their book value. The percentage figure used depends on the quality and age of the receivables. Moreover, because the lender takes over ownership of the receivables, it will inform the borrower's customers that they should send their payments to the purchasing institution. Usually the borrower promises to set aside funds in order to cover some or all of the losses that the lending institution may suffer from any unpaid receivables.

Inventory. In return for a loan, a lender may take a security interest against the current amount of inventory of goods or raw materials a business borrower owns. Usually a lending institution will advance only a percentage (30 to 80 percent is common) of the estimated market value of a borrower's inventory in order to leave a substantial cushion in case the inventory's value declines. The inventory pledged may be controlled completely by the borrower, using a so-called *floating lien* approach. Another option, often used for auto and truck dealers or sellers of home appliances, is called *floor planning*, in which the lender takes temporary ownership of any goods placed in inventory and the borrower sends payments or sales contracts to the lender as goods are sold.[4]

Real Property. Following a title search, appraisal, and land survey, a lending institution may take a security interest in land and/or improvements on land owned by the borrower and record its claim—a *mortgage*—with a government agency in order to warn other lenders that the property has already been pledged (i.e., has a lien against it) and to help defend the original lender's position against claims by others.

Concept Check

16–8. What are the typical steps followed in receiving a loan request from a customer?

16–9. What three major questions or issues must a lender consider in evaluating nearly all loan requests?

16–10. Explain the following terms: character, capacity, cash, collateral, conditions, and control.

16–11. Suppose a business borrower projects that it will experience net profits of $2.1 million, compared to $2.7 million the previous year, and will record depreciation and other noncash expenses of $0.7 million

this year versus $0.6 million last year. What is this firm's projected cash flow for this year? Is the firm's cash flow rising or falling? What are the implications for a lending institution thinking of loaning money to this firm? Suppose sales revenue rises by $0.5 million, cost of goods sold decreases by $0.3 million, while cash tax payments increase by $0.1 million and noncash expenses decrease by $0.2 million. What happens to the firm's cash flow? What would be the lender's likely reaction to these events?

For example, public notice of a mortgage against real estate may be filed with the county courthouse or tax assessor/collector in the county where the property resides. The lender may also take out title insurance and insist that the borrower purchase insurance to cover damage from floods and other hazards, with the lending institution receiving first claim on any insurance settlement made.

Personal Property. Lenders often take a security interest in automobiles, furniture and equipment, jewelry, securities and other forms of personal property a borrower owns. A *financing statement* may be filed with state or local government offices in those cases where the borrower keeps possession of any personal property pledged as collateral during the term of a loan. To be effective, the financing statement must be signed by both the borrower and an officer of the lending institution. On the other hand, a *pledge agreement* may be prepared (but will usually not be publicly filed) if the lender or its agent holds the pledged property, giving the lending institution the right to control that property until the loan is repaid in full. The various states in the United States have adopted the Uniform Commercial Code (UCC) which spells out how lenders can perfect liens and how borrowers should file collateral statements.

---

[4]Lenders seeking closer control over a borrower's inventory may employ *warehousing* in which the goods are stored and monitored by the lender or by an independent agent working to protect the lender's interest. (The warehouse site may be away from the borrower's place of business—a *field warehouse*.) As the inventory grows, warehouse receipts are issued to the lending institution, giving it a legal claim against the warehoused materials. The lender will make the borrower a loan equal to some agreed-upon percentage of the expected market value of the inventory covered by the warehouse receipts. When the public buys goods from the borrowing firm, the lender surrenders its claim so the company's product can be delivered to its customers. However, the customer's cash payments go straight to the lending institution to be applied to the loan's balance. Because of the potential for fraud or theft, loan officers may inspect a business borrower's inventory periodically to ensure the loan is well secured and that proper procedures for protecting and valuing inventory are being followed.

EXHIBIT 16–1
Safety Zones
Surrounding Funds
Loaned

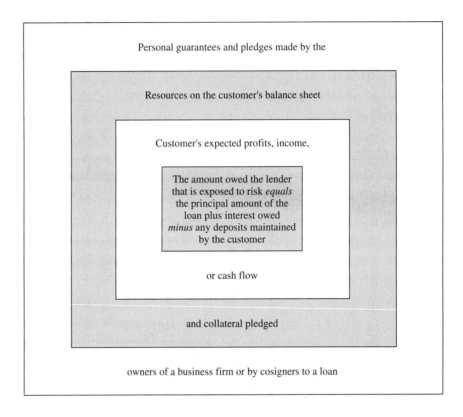

Personal guarantees and pledges made by the

Resources on the customer's balance sheet

Customer's expected profits, income,

The amount owed the lender that is exposed to risk *equals* the principal amount of the loan plus interest owed *minus* any deposits maintained by the customer

or cash flow

and collateral pledged

owners of a business firm or by cosigners to a loan

Typically financial statements that detail collateral associated with a loan are filed in one location, such as the secretary of state's office in the debtor's home state.

Personal Guarantees. A pledge of the stock, deposits, or other personal assets held by the major stockholders or owners of a company may be required as collateral to secure a business loan. Guarantees are often sought in lending to smaller businesses or to firms that have fallen on difficult times. Then, too, getting pledges of personal assets from the owners of a business firm gives the owners an additional reason to want their firm to prosper and repay their loan.

Other Safety Devices to Protect a Loan

Many loan officers argue that the collateral a customer pledges behind a loan is just one of the safety zones that a lending institution must wrap around the funds it has loaned for adequate protection. As Exhibit 16–1 indicates, most loan officers prefer to have at least two safety zones—ideally, three—around the funds they have placed at risk with the customer. The primary safety zone is income or cash flow—the preferred source from which the customer will repay the loan. The second consists of strength on the customer's balance sheet, in the form of assets that can be pledged as collateral or liquid assets that can be sold for cash in order to fill any gaps in the customer's cash flow. Finally, the outer safety zone consists of guarantees from a business firm's owners to support a loan to their firm or from third-party cosigners who pledge their personal assets to back another person's loan.

16–6 Sources of Information about Loan Customers

A lender often relies heavily on outside information to assess the character, financial position, and collateral of a loan customer (see Table 16–4). Such an analysis begins with a review of information the borrower supplies in the loan application. How much money is

TABLE 16–4
Sources of
Information
Frequently Used in
Loan Analysis and
Evaluation

Information about Consumers (Individuals and Families) Borrowing Money
Customer-supplied financial statements
Credit bureau reports on borrower credit history
Experience of other lenders with the borrower
Verification of employment with the consumer's employer
Verification of property ownership through local government records
The World Wide Web
Information about Businesses Borrowing Money
Financial reports supplied by the borrowing firm
Copies of boards of directors' resolutions or partnership agreements
Credit ratings supplied by Dun & Bradstreet, Moody's Investor Service, Standard & Poor's Corporation, Fitch, etc.
New York Times and *New York Times Index*
The Wall Street Journal, Fortune, and other business publications
Risk Management Associates (RMA) or Dun & Bradstreet industry averages
The World Wide Web
Information about Governments Borrowing Money
Governmental budget reports
Credit ratings assigned to government borrowers by Moody's, Standard & Poor's Corporation, etc.
The World Wide Web
Information about General Economic Conditions Affecting Borrowers
Local newspapers and the Chamber of Commerce
The Wall Street Journal, The Economist, and other general business publications
U.S. Department of Commerce
Central bank business data series (as in the *Federal Reserve Bulletin*)
The World Wide Web

being requested? For what purpose? What other obligations does the customer have? What assets might be used as collateral to back up the loan?

The lending institution may contact other lenders to determine their experience with this customer. Were all scheduled payments in previous loan agreements made on time? Were deposit balances kept at high enough levels? In the case of a household borrower one or more *credit bureaus* will be contacted to ascertain the customer's credit history. How much was borrowed previously and how well were those earlier loans handled? Is there any evidence of slow or delinquent payments? Has the customer ever declared bankruptcy?

Most business borrowers of any size carry credit ratings on their bonds and other debt securities and on the firm's overall credit record. Moody's and Standard & Poor's assigned credit ratings reflect the probability of default on bonds and shorter-term notes. Dun & Bradstreet provides overall credit ratings for several thousand corporations. It and other firms and organizations provide benchmark operating and financial ratios for whole industries so that the borrower's particular operating and financial ratios in any given year can be compared to industry standards.

One of the most widely consulted sources of data on business firm performance is Risk Management Associates, founded as RMA in Philadelphia in 1914 to exchange credit information among business lending institutions and to organize conferences and publish educational materials to help train loan officers and credit analysts. While RMA began in the United States, its members have now spread over much of the globe with especially active groups in Canada, Great Britain and Western Europe, Hong Kong, and Mexico. RMA publishes several respected journals and studies, including *Creative Considerations, Lending to Different Industries*, and the *RMA Journal*, to help inform and train credit decision makers.

Another popular RMA publication is its *Annual Statement Studies: Financial Ratio Benchmarks*, which provides financial performance data on businesses grouped by industry type and by size category. Loan officers who are members of RMA submit financial performance information based on data supplied by their borrowing business customers. RMA

Key URLs
Among the most important Web sites for financial data and analysis of firms and industries of particular use to loan officers are Dun and Bradstreet at **www.dnb.com** and RMA at **www.rmahq. org/** (see Annual Statement Studies link).

then groups this data and calculates average values for selected performance ratios. Among the ratios published by RMA and grouped by industry and firm size are

> Current assets to current liabilities (the current ratio).
>
> Current assets minus inventories to current liabilities (the quick ratio).
>
> Sales to accounts receivable.
>
> Cost of sales to inventory (the inventory turnover ratio).
>
> Earnings before interest and taxes to total interest payments (the interest coverage ratio).
>
> Fixed assets to net worth.
>
> Total debt to net worth (the leverage ratio).
>
> Profits before taxes to total assets and to tangible net worth.
>
> Total sales to net fixed assets and to total assets.

RMA also calculates common-size balance sheets (with all major asset and liability items expressed as a percentage of total assets) and common-size income statements (with profits and operating expense items expressed as a percentage of total sales) for different size groups of firms within an industry. Recently the association began publishing a second volume of its statement studies series called *Annual Statement Studies: Industry Default Probabilities and Cash Flow Measures*, which reports on the risk exposure of about 450 different industries, estimates default probabilities for one- and five-year intervals, and tracks at least four different measures of cash flow—a key element in any lending decision.

Finally, RMA has offered lenders a Windows-based version of its statement studies series, called eCompare2, which permits a credit analyst or loan officer to do a *spreadsheet analysis*—arraying the loan customer's financial statements and key financial and operating ratios over time relative to industry averages based upon data from more than 150,000 financial statements. eCompare2 enables a loan officer to counsel his or her borrowing customer, pointing out any apparent weaknesses in the customer's financial or operating situation compared to industry standards. It also reports on recent developments in each of more than 600 different industries. This credit analysis routine is also available to business firms planning to submit a loan request to a lending institution so business owners can personally evaluate their firm's financial condition from the lender's perspective.

A similar array of industry data is provided by Dun & Bradstreet Credit Services. This credit-rating agency collects information on several million firms in more than 800 different business lines. D&B prepares detailed financial reports on individual borrowing companies for its subscribers. For each firm reviewed, the D&B *Business Information Reports* provide a credit rating, a financial and management history of the firm, a summary of recent balance sheet and income and expense statement trends, its terms of trade, and the location and condition of the firm's facilities. D&B calculates key ratios measuring efficiency, profitability, and solvency, as well as common-size balance sheets and income statements (with each entry expressed as a percent of total assets or total net sales) for the medium-size, or typical, firm and for the uppermost and lowest quartiles of firms in each industry.

In evaluating a credit application, the loan officer must look beyond the customer to the economy of the local area for smaller loan requests and to the national or international economy for larger credit requests. Many loan customers are especially sensitive to the fluctuations in economic activity known as the *business cycle*. For example, auto dealers, producers of farm and other commodities, home builders, and security dealers and brokers face cyclically sensitive markets for their goods and services. This does not mean that lending institutions should not lend to such firms. Rather, they must be aware of the vulnerability of some of their borrowers to cyclical changes and structure loan terms to take care of such fluctuations in economic conditions. Moreover, for all business borrowers it is important to develop a forecast of future industry conditions. The loan officer must determine if the customer's projections for the future conform to the outlook for the industry as a whole. Any differences in outlook must be explained before a final decision is made about approving or denying a loan request.

16–7 Parts of a Typical Loan Agreement

The Note

When a lending institution grants a loan to one of its customers, such an extension of credit is accompanied by a *written contract* with several different parts. First, the **note,** signed by the borrower, specifies the principal amount of the loan. The face of the note will also indicate the interest rate attached to the principal amount and the terms under which repayment must take place (including the dates on which any installment payments are due).

Loan Commitment Agreement

In addition, larger business and home mortgage loans often are accompanied by **loan commitment agreements,** in which the lender promises to make credit available to the borrower over a designated future period up to a maximum amount in return for a commitment fee (usually expressed as a percentage—such as 0.5 percent—of the maximum amount of credit available). This practice is common in the extension of short-term business credit lines, where, for example, a business customer may draw against a maximum $1 million credit line as needed over a given period (such as six months).

Collateral

Loans may be either secured or unsecured. Secured loans contain a pledge of some of the borrower's property behind them (such as a home or an automobile) as **collateral** that may have to be sold if the borrower has no other way to repay the lender. Unsecured loans have no specific assets pledged behind them; these loans rest largely on the reputation and estimated earning power of the borrower. Secured loan agreements include a section describing any assets pledged as collateral to protect the lender's interest, along with an explanation of how and when the lending institution can take possession of the collateral in order to recover its funds. For example, an individual seeking an auto loan usually must sign a *chattel mortgage* agreement, which means that the borrower temporarily assigns the vehicle's title to the lender until the loan is paid off.

Covenants

Most formal loan agreements contain **restrictive covenants,** which are usually one of two types: *affirmative* or *negative*.

1. *Affirmative covenants* require the borrower to take certain actions, such as periodically filing financial statements with the lending institution, maintaining insurance coverage on the loan and on any collateral pledged, and maintaining specified levels of liquidity and equity.
2. *Negative covenants* restrict the borrower from doing certain things without the lender's approval, such as taking on new debt, acquiring additional fixed assets, participating in mergers, selling assets, or paying excessive dividends to stockholders.

Recently the use of loan covenants appears to be shrinking (especially for business loans), averaging only about 5 to 6 covenants per loan, due to intense competition among lenders, the sale of loans off lenders' balance sheets, and increased market volatility, making it harder for borrowers to meet performance targets.

Borrower Guaranties or Warranties

In most loan agreements, the borrower specifically *guarantees* or **warranties** that the information supplied in the loan application is true and correct. The borrower may also be required to pledge personal assets—a house, land, automobiles, and so on—behind a business loan or against a loan that is consigned by a third party. Whether collateral is posted or not, the loan agreement must identify who or what institution is responsible for the loan and obligated to make payment.

Events of Default

Key URL
For more information about loan accounting and disclosure of problem loans in an international setting, see especially **www.bis.org/publ**.

Finally, most loans contain a section listing **events of default,** specifying what actions or inactions by the borrower would represent a significant violation of the terms of the loan agreement and what actions the lender is legally authorized to take in order to secure recovery of its funds. The events-of-default section also clarifies who is responsible for collection costs, court costs, and attorney's fees that may arise from litigation of the loan agreement.

16–8 Loan Review

What happens to a loan agreement after it has been endorsed by the borrower and the lending institution? Should it be filed away and forgotten until the loan falls due and the borrower makes the final payment? Obviously that would be a foolish thing for any lender to do because the conditions under which each loan is made are constantly changing, affecting the borrower's financial strength and his or her ability to repay . Fluctuations in the economy weaken some businesses and increase the credit needs of others, while individuals may lose their jobs or contract serious health problems, imperiling their ability to repay any outstanding loans. The loan department must be sensitive to these developments and periodically review *all* loans until they reach maturity.

While most lenders today use a variety of different **loan review** procedures, a few general principles are followed by nearly all lending institutions. These include:

1. Carrying out reviews of all types of loans on a periodic basis—for example, routinely examining the largest loans outstanding every 30, 60, or 90 days, along with a random sample of smaller loans.

2. Structuring the loan review process carefully to make sure the most important features of each loan are checked, including

   a. The record of borrower payments to ensure that the customer is not falling behind the planned repayment schedule.

   b. The quality and condition of any collateral pledged behind the loan.

   c. The completeness of loan documentation to make sure the lender has access to any collateral pledged and possesses the full legal authority to take action against the borrower in the courts if necessary.

   d. An evaluation of whether the borrower's financial condition and forecasts have changed, which may have increased or decreased the borrower's need for credit.

   e. An assessment of whether the loan conforms to the lender's loan policies and to the standards applied to its loan portfolio by examiners from the regulatory agencies.

3. Reviewing the largest loans most frequently because default on these credit agreements could seriously affect the lender's own financial condition.

4. Conducting more frequent reviews of troubled loans, with the frequency of review increasing as the problems surrounding any particular loan increase.

5. Accelerating the loan review schedule if the economy slows down or if the industries in which the lending institution has made a substantial portion of its loans develop significant problems (e.g., the appearance of new competitors or shifts in technology that will demand new products and delivery methods).

Loan review is *not* a luxury but a *necessity* for a sound lending program. It not only helps management spot problem loans more quickly but also acts as a continuing check on whether loan officers are adhering to their institution's own loan policy. For this reason, and to promote objectivity in the loan review process, many of the largest lenders separate their loan review personnel from the loan department itself. Loan reviews also aid senior management and the lender's board of directors in assessing the institution's overall exposure to risk and its possible need for more capital in the future.

16–9 Handling Problem Loan Situations

Inevitably, despite the safeguards most lenders build into their loan programs, some loans will become *problem loans*. Usually this means the borrower has missed one or more promised payments or the collateral pledged behind a loan has declined significantly in value. While each problem loan situation is somewhat different, several features common to most such situations should warn a lending institution that troubles have set in (see Table 16–5):

1. Unusual or unexplained delays in receiving promised financial reports and payments or in communicating with bank personnel.

TABLE 16–5
Warning Signs of
Weak Loans and Poor
Lending Policies

Source: Federal Deposit
Insurance Corporation, *Bank
Examination Policies*,
Washington, D.C., selected
years.

The manual given to bank and thrift examiners by the FDIC discusses several telltale indicators of problem loans and poor lending policies:

Indicators of a Weak or Troubled Loan	Indicators of Inadequate or Poor Lending Policies
Irregular or delinquent loan payments	Poor selection of risks among borrowing customers
Frequent alterations in loan terms	Lending money contingent on possible future events (such as a merger)
Poor loan renewal record (little reduction of principal when the loan is renewed)	Lending money because a customer promises a large deposit
Unusually high loan rate (perhaps an attempt to compensate the lender for a high-risk loan)	Failure to specify a plan for loan liquidation
Unusual or unexpected buildup of the borrowing customer's accounts receivable and/or inventories	High proportion of loans outside the lender's trade territory
Rising debt-to-net-worth (leverage) ratio	Incomplete credit files
Missing documentation (especially missing financial statements)	Substantial self-dealing credits (loans to insiders—employees, directors, or stockholders)
Poor-quality collateral	Tendency to overreact to competition (making poor loans to keep customers from going to competing lending institutions)
Reliance on reappraisals of assets to increase the borrowing customer's net worth	Lending money to support speculative purchases
Absence of cash flow statements or projections	Lack of sensitivity to changing economic conditions
Customer reliance on nonrecurring sources of funds to meet loan payments (e.g., selling buildings or equipment)	

2. For business loans, any sudden change in methods used by the borrowing firm to account for depreciation, make pension plan contributions, value inventories, account for taxes, or recognize income.

3. For business loans, restructuring outstanding debt or eliminating dividends, or experiencing a change in the customer's credit rating.

4. Adverse changes in the price of a borrowing customer's stock.

5. Losses in one or more years, especially as measured by returns on the borrower's assets (ROA), or equity capital (ROE), or earnings before interest and taxes (EBIT).

6. Adverse changes in the borrower's capital structure (equity/debt ratio), liquidity (current ratio), or activity levels (e.g., the ratio of sales to inventory).

7. Deviations of actual sales, cash flow, or income from those projected when the loan was requested.

8. Unexpected or unexplained changes in customer deposit balances.

Factoid
What are the principal causes of failure among banks and thrift institutions?
Answer: Bad loans, management error, criminal activity, and adverse economic conditions.

What should a lender do when a loan is in trouble? Experts in **loan workouts**—the process of recovering funds from a problem loan situation—suggest the following steps:

1. Lenders must always keep the *goal* of loan workouts firmly in mind: to maximize the chances for full recovery of funds.

2. Rapid detection and reporting of any problems with a loan are essential; delay often worsens a problem loan situation.

3. The loan workout responsibility should be separate from the lending function to avoid possible conflicts of interest for the loan officer.

4. Loan workout specialists should confer with the troubled customer *quickly* on possible options, especially for cutting expenses, increasing cash flow, and improving management control. Precede this meeting with a preliminary analysis of the problem and its possible causes, noting any special workout problems (including the presence of competing creditors). Develop a preliminary plan of action after determining the lending institution's risk exposure and the sufficiency of loan documents, especially any claims against the customer's collateral other than that held by the lender.

5. Estimate what resources are available to collect the troubled loan, including the estimated liquidation values of assets and deposits.

6. Loan workout personnel should conduct a tax and litigation search to see if the borrower has other unpaid obligations.

7. For business borrowers, loan personnel must evaluate the quality, competence, and integrity of current management and visit the site to assess the borrower's property and operations.

8. Loan workout professionals must consider all reasonable alternatives for cleaning up the troubled loan, including making a new, temporary agreement if loan problems appear to be short-term in nature or finding a way to help the customer strengthen cash flow (such as reducing expenses or entering new markets) or to infuse new capital into the business. Other possibilities include finding additional collateral; securing endorsements or guarantees; reorganizing, merging, or liquidating the firm; or filing a bankruptcy petition.

Of course, the preferred option nearly always is to seek a *revised loan agreement* that gives both the lending institution and its customer the chance to restore normal operations. Indeed, loan experts often argue that even when a loan agreement is in serious trouble, the customer may not be. This means that a properly structured loan agreement rarely runs into irreparable problems. However, an improperly structured loan agreement can contribute to a borrower's financial problems and be a cause of loan default.

Concept Check

16–12. What sources of information are available today that loan officers and credit analysts can use in evaluating a customer loan application?

16–13. What are the principal parts of a loan agreement? What is each part designed to do?

16–14. What is *loan review?* How should a loan review be conducted?

16–15. What are some warning signs to management that a problem loan may be developing?

16–16. What steps should a lender go through in trying to resolve a problem loan situation?

Summary

This chapter has focused on lending policies and procedures and the many different types of loans that lenders offer their customers. It makes these key points:

- Making loans is the principal *economic function* of banks and other lending institutions. Loans support communities and nations by providing credit to finance the development of new businesses, sustain existing activities, and create jobs for individuals so that living standards can grow over time.

- Lending is also *risky*, because loan quality is affected by both external and internal factors. *External factors* include changes in the economy, natural disasters, and regulations imposed by government. *Internal factors* affecting loan risk include management errors, illegal manipulation, and weak or ineffective lending policies.

- The risk of loss in the lending function is at least partially controlled by (*a*) *government regulation* and (*b*) *internal policies and procedures*. Regulatory agencies such as the FDIC send out teams of examiners to investigate the lending policies and procedures and the quality of loans within each lending institution. Among depository institutions today a five-point CAMELS rating system is used to evaluate the performance and risk exposure of lenders based upon the quantity and quality of their capital, assets, management, earnings, liquidity, and sensitivity to market risk.

- Risk is also controlled by creating and following written policies and procedures for processing each credit request. Written loan policies should describe the types of loans the lender will and will not make, the desired terms for each type of loan, the necessary documentation before approval is granted, how collateral is to be evaluated, desired pricing techniques, and lines of authority for loan approvals.

- Lenders consider multiple factors in approving or denying each loan request: (1) *character* (including loan purpose and borrower honesty); (2) *capacity* (especially the legal authority of the borrower to sign a loan agreement); (3) *cash* (including the adequacy of income or cash flow); (4) *collateral* (including the quality and quantity of assets to backstop a loan); (5) *conditions* (including the state of the economy); and (6) *control* (including compliance with the lender's loan policy and regulations).

- Most lending decisions center around three key issues: (1) Is the borrower creditworthy and how do you know? (2) Can the loan agreement be properly structured to protect the lender and the public's funds? (3) Can a claim against the borrower's assets or earnings be perfected in the event of loan default?

- Finally, a sound lending program must make provision for the periodic review of all outstanding loans. When this *loan review* process turns up problem loans, they may be turned over to a *loan workout* specialist who must investigate the causes of the problem and work with the borrower to find a solution that maximizes chances for recovery of funds.

www.mhhe.com/rose7e

Key Terms

real estate loans, *514*
financial institution
loans, *514*
agricultural loans, *514*
commercial and industrial
loans, *514*
loans to individuals, *515*
wholesale lenders, *515*

retail credit, *515*
CAMELS rating, *518*
cash, *522*
cash flow, *524*
note, *531*
loan commitment
agreements, *531*
collateral, *531*

restrictive covenants, *531*
warranties, *532*
events of default, *532*
loan review, *532*
loan workouts, *534*

**Problems
and Projects**

1. The lending function of depository institutions is highly regulated and this chapter gives some examples of the structure of these regulations for national banks. In this problem you are asked to apply those regulations to Tea Rose National Bank (TRNB). Tea Rose has the following sources of funds: $200 million in capital and surplus, $100 million in demand deposits, $800 million in time and savings deposits, and $200 million in subordinated debt.

   a. What is the maximum dollar amount of real estate loans that TRNB can grant?

   b. What is the maximum dollar amount TRNB may lend to a single customer?

2. Aspiration Corporation, seeking renewal of its $12 million credit line, reports the data in the following table (in millions of dollars) to Hot Springs National Bank's loan department. Please calculate the firm's cash flow as defined earlier in this chapter. What trends do you observe and what are their implications for the decision to renew or not renew the firm's line of credit?

	20X1	20X2	20X3	20X4	Projections for Next Year
Cost of goods sold	$5.1	$5.5	$5.7	$6.0	$ 6.4
Selling and administrative expenses	8.0	8.2	8.3	8.6	8.9
Sales revenues	7.9	8.4	8.8	9.5	9.9
Depreciation and other noncash expenses	11.2	11.2	11.1	11.0	10.9
Taxes paid in cash	4.4	4.6	4.9	4.1	3.6

3. Rogers Manufacturing and Service Company holds a sizable inventory of dryers and washing machines, which it hopes to sell to retail dealers over the next six months. These appliances have a total estimated market value currently of $18,357,422. The firm also reports accounts receivable currently amounting to $10,452,876. Under the guidelines for taking collateral discussed in this chapter, what is the *minimum* size loan or credit line Rogers is likely to receive from its principal lender? What is the *maximum* size loan or credit line Rogers is likely to receive?

4. Under which of the *six Cs of credit* discussed in this chapter does each of the following pieces of information belong?

   a. First National Bank discovers there is already a lien against the fixed assets of one of its customers asking for a loan.

   b. Xron Corporation has asked for a type of loan its lender normally refuses to make.

   c. John Selman has an excellent credit rating.

   d. Smithe Manufacturing Company has achieved higher earnings each year for the past six years.

   e. Consumers Savings Association's auto loan officer asks a prospective customer, Harold Ikels, for his driver's license.

f. Merchants Center National Bank is concerned about extending a loan for another year to Corrin Motors because a recession is predicted in the economy.

g. Wes Velman needs an immediate cash loan and has gotten his brother, Charles, to volunteer to cosign the note should the loan be approved.

h. ABC Finance Company checks out Mary Earl's estimate of her monthly take-home pay with Mary's employer, Bryan Sims Doors and Windows.

i. Hillsoro Bank and Trust would like to make a loan to Pen-Tab Oil and Gas Company but fears a long-term decline in oil and gas prices.

j. First State Bank of Jackson seeks the opinion of an expert on the economic outlook in Mexico before granting a loan to a Mexican manufacturer of auto parts.

k. The history of Membres Manufacture and Distributing Company indicates the firm has been through several recent changes of ownership and there has been a substantial shift in its principal suppliers and customers in recent years.

l. Home and Office Savings Bank has decided to review the insurance coverages maintained by its borrowing customer, Plainsman Wholesale Distributors.

5. Butell Manufacturing has an outstanding $11 million loan with Citicenter Bank for the current year. As required in the loan agreement, Butell reports selected data items to the bank each month. Based on the following information, is there any indication of a developing *problem loan?* About what dimensions of the firm's performance should Citicenter Bank be concerned?

	Current Month	One Month Ago	Two Months Ago	Three Months Ago	Four Months Ago
Cash account (millions of dollars)	$33	$57	$51	$44	$43
Projected sales (millions of dollars)	$298	$ 295	$294	$291	$288
Stock price per share (monthly average)	$6.60	$6.50	$6.40	$6.25	$6.50
Capital structure (equity/debt ratio in percent)	32.8%	33.9%	34.6%	34.9%	35.7%
Liquidity ratio (current assets/ current liabilities)	1.10x	1.23x	1.35x	1.39x	1.25x
Earnings before interest and taxes (EBIT; in millions of dollars)	$15	$14	$13	$11	$13
Return on assets (ROA; percent)	3.32%	3.25%	2.98%	3.13%	3.11%
Sales revenue (millions of dollars)	$290	$289	$290	$289	$287

Butell has announced within the past 30 days that it is switching to new methods for calculating depreciation of its fixed assets and for valuing inventories. The firm's board of directors is planning to discuss at its next meeting a proposal to reduce stock dividends in the coming year.

6. Identify which of the following loan covenants are *affirmative* and which are *negative* covenants:

a. Nige Trading Corporation must pay no dividends to its shareholders above $3 per share without express lender approval.

b. HoneySmith Company pledges to fully insure its production line equipment against loss due to fire, theft, or adverse weather.

c. Soft-Tech Industries cannot take on new debt without notifying its principal lending institution first.

www.mhhe.com/rose7e

    d. PennCost Manufacturing must file comprehensive financial statements each month with its principal bank.

    e. Dolbe King Company must secure lender approval prior to increasing its stock of fixed assets.

    f. Crestwin Service Industries must keep a minimum current (liquidity) ratio of 1.5× under the terms of its loan agreement.

    g. Dew Dairy Products is considering approaching Selwin Farm Transport Company about a possible merger but must first receive lender approval.

7. Please identify which of the *six basic Cs of lending—character, capacity, cash, collateral, conditions*, and *control*—applies to each of the loan factors listed here:

Insurance coverage	Asset liquidation
Competitive climate for customer's product	Inflation outlook
	Adequate documentation
Credit rating	Changes in accounting standards
Corporate resolution	Written loan policy
Liquid reserves	Coverage ratios
Asset specialization	Purpose of loan
Driver's license	Laws and regulations that apply to the making of loans
Expected market share	
Economists' forecasts	Wages in the labor market
Business cycle	Changes in technology
Performance of comparable firms	Obsolescence
Guarantees/warranties	Liens
Expense controls	Management quality
Inventory turnover	Leverage
Projected cash flow	History of firm
Experience of other lenders	Customer identity
Social Security card	Payment record
Price-earnings ratio	Partnership agreement
Industry outlook	Accounts receivable turnover
Future financing needs	Accounts payable turnover

Internet Exercises

1. If you wanted to find out about regulations applying to bank lending, where would you look on the Web? Why do you think this area has become so important lately? (See, for example, **www.ffiec.gov.**)

2. If you wanted to find out more about the evaluation of loan portfolios during onsite examinations, the FDIC provides an online copy of its Division of Supervision Manual of Examination Policies at **www.fdic.gov/regulations/safety/manual.** Go to this site and find the link for Loan Appraisal and Classification, then answer the following question: What are "special mention" assets?

3. Are you interested in becoming a loan officer? A credit analyst? Go to the Bureau of Labor Statistics' site at **www.bls.gov/oco/cg/cgs027.htm** and read about the banking industry. What is the outlook for positions as loan officers and credit analysts? What could you expect in terms of earnings?

4. Suppose you were hired as a consultant by a lending institution's loan department to look at the quality of its controls designed to minimize credit risk. You know this lender is concerned

REAL NUMBERS FOR REAL BANKS — Assignment for Chapter 16

YOUR BANK'S LOAN PORTFOLIO: LOANS CLASSIFIED BY PURPOSE

Chapter 16 is an overview of lending with a focus on policies and procedures. Table 16–1 illustrates the composition of the industry's (all FDIC-insured U.S. banks) loan portfolio, highlighting the differences between small banks (less than $100 million in total assets) and large banks (more than $1 billion in total assets). In this assignment we will be doing a similar analysis for your banking company compared to the peer group of very large banks (more than $10 billion in total assets).

Trend and Comparative Analysis

A. Data Collection: We have collected information for gross loans and leases and net loans and leases. Now we will further break down gross loans and leases based on purpose. Use SDI to create a four-column report of your bank's information and the peer group information across years. For report selection, you will access the "Net Loans and Leases" report. We suggest that you continue to collect percentage information for ease of entry. Enter this data into the spreadsheet used for peer group comparisons.

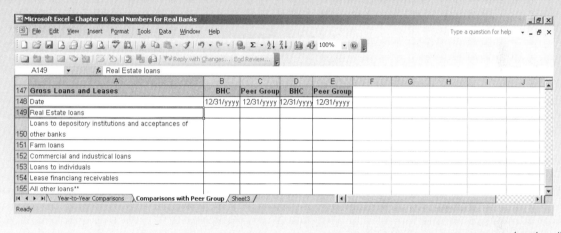

(continued)

www.mhhe.com/rose7e

that its principal government supervisory agency is going to take a hard look shortly at how the loan department is managed and the risks in its loan portfolio. Where on the Internet could you look to find some guidelines on how to control and manage credit risk? List two or three suggestions for credit risk control that you found at the Web site or sites you investigated. For example, you may wish to check **www.fdic.gov** and **www.bis.org**.

S&P Market Insight Challenge (www.mhhe.com/edumarketinsight)

STANDARD &POOR'S

1. The S&P Industry Survey covering the banking industry discusses commercial banks' earnings from loans. For a very recent description of the banking industry's loan portfolio click on the Industry tab in Standard & Poor's Market Insight and use the drop-down menu to select a subindustry group, such as diversified or regional banks. Upon choosing one of these groups, you will encounter a recent S&P Industry Survey on Banking. Download the survey and proceed to the section, "How the Industry Operates." What is the composition of the typical bank's loan portfolio? What is the amount of aggregate loans held by all FDIC-insured commercial banks?

STANDARD &POOR'S

2. Lending usually represents the greatest risk a banker can accept. Using the information in this chapter and in Chapters 5 and 6, develop a list of indicators of loan

REAL NUMBERS FOR REAL BANKS

Assignment for Chapter 16 *(continued)*

B. Use the chart function in Excel and the data by columns in rows 149 through 155 to create four pie charts illustrating the loan portfolio composition by purpose for the BHC you chose earlier and its peer group. Your pie charts should include titles and labels. For instance, the following are pie charts comparing National City Corp. and its peer group for 12/31/05.

NCC Loan Composition by Purpose (12/31/05)

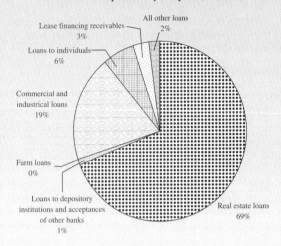

Peer Loan Composition by Purpose (12/31/05)

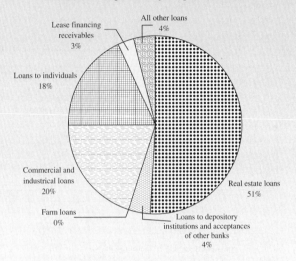

C. Interpreting the above information, write approximately one page about the composition of your bank's loan portfolio. Has the composition changed over time? How does the composition of your bank's loan portfolio compare to other very large banks (your peer group)? Use your pie charts as graphics and incorporate them in the discussion.

quality that could be used to assess the riskiness of an individual bank's loan portfolio. Now apply these loan quality indicators to the most recent loan portfolio information available for some of the banks contained in S&P's Market Insight. Which banks appear to have the strongest and the weakest loan quality? What are the implications of your findings for management of these institutions? How confident are you in the loan-quality indicators you developed?

Selected References

Methods used for assessing credit risk are described in:

1. Altman, Edward I., and Anthony Saunders. "Credit Risk Measurement: Developments over the Last 20 Years." *Journal of Banking and Finance* 21 (December 1997), pp. 1721–1742.

2. Treacy, William F., and Mark S. Carey. "Credit Risk Rating at Large U.S. Banks." *Federal Reserve Bulletin*, November 1998, pp. 897–921.

For a review of procedures for identifying and working out problem loans situations, see:

3. Rose, Peter S. "Loans in Trouble in a Troubled Economy." *The Canadian Banker* 90, no. 3 (June 1983), pp. 52–57.
4. Taylor, Jeremy D. "Understanding Industry Risk: Parts 1, 2, and 3." *Journal of Lending and Credit Risk Management*, August, September, and October 1996.

For an analysis of the impact of changing technology on lending, visit the following:

5. Rose, Peter S. "Lenders and the Internet." *Journal of Lending and Credit Risk Management*, June 1997, pp. 31–40.

For a more detailed review of bank examination and supervision of lending, see:

6. Hirtle, Beverly J., and Jose A. Lopez. "Supervisor Information and the Frequency of Bank Examinations." *Economic Policy Review*, Federal Reserve Bank of New York, April 1999, pp. 1–19.
7. Collier, Charles, Sean Forbush, David A. Nuxoll, and John O'Keefe. "The SCOR System of Off-Site Monitoring: Its Objectives, Functioning and Performance." *FDIC Banking Review*, Federal Deposit Insurance Corporation 15, no. 3 (2003), pp. 17–32.

CHAPTER SEVENTEEN

Lending to Business Firms and Pricing Business Loans

Key Topics in This Chapter

- Types of Business Loans: Short-Term and Long-Term
- Analyzing Business Loan Requests
- Collateral and Contingent Liabilities
- Sources and Uses of Business Funds
- Pricing Business Loans
- Customer Profitability Analysis

17–1 Introduction

The great American author and humorist Mark Twain once observed: "A banker is a fellow who lends his umbrella when the sun is shining and wants it back the minute it begins to rain." Many troubled businesses seeking credit in recent years might agree with Mark Twain. Indeed, securing the large amounts of credit that many businesses require can be a challenging task because bankers usually take a close look at business borrowers and their loan requests. Moreover, business loans—often called *commercial and industrial or C&I loans*—rank among the most important assets that banks and their closest competitors (such as finance companies like GE Capital and Commercial Credit Corporation) hold.

Indeed, a glance at the most recent balance sheet for all U.S. insured commercial banks combined reveals that close to a quarter of their loan portfolio is devoted to business or C&I loans. Moreover, this percentage of the total loan portfolio does not include many commercial real estate loans and loans to other financial institutions that banks make but classify elsewhere on their balance sheets. This is why any discussion of the methods and procedures used in analyzing and granting loans usually begins with a discussion of business lending.

In this chapter we look at the many different types of business loans that banks and other lending institutions typically make. We also explore the process for evaluating business loans based on an example from the energy industry. Finally, the chapter examines some of the most widely used techniques for pricing loans extended to business customers.

17–2 Brief History of Business Lending

Commercial and industrial (or business) loans represented the earliest form of lending that banks carried out in their more than 2,000-year history. Loans extended to ship owners, mining operators, goods manufacturers, and property owners dominated bankers' loan portfolios for centuries. Then, late in the 19th and early 20th centuries new competitors— particularly finance companies, life and property/casualty insurance firms, and some thrift institutions—entered the business lending field, placing downward pressure on the profit margins of many business lenders. In today's world, loan officers skilled in evaluating the credit requests of business firms rank among the most experienced and highest-paid people in the financial-services field, along with investment bankers (security underwriters), who also provide funds to the business sector.

17–3 Types of Business Loans

Banks, finance companies, and competing business lenders grant many different types of commercial loans. Among the most widely used forms of business credit are the following:

Key URL
To learn more about helpful procedures in applying for small business loans, see, in particular, **www. business.com/directory**.

Short-Term Business Loans	Long-Term Business Loans
• Self-liquidating inventory loans • Working capital loans • Interim construction financing • Security dealer financing • Retailer and equipment financing • Asset-based loans (accounts receivable financing, factoring, and inventory financing) • Syndicated loans	• Term loans to support the purchase of equipment, rolling stock, and structures • Revolving credit financing • Project loans • Loans to support acquisitions of other business firms

17–4 Short-Term Loans to Business Firms

Self-Liquidating Inventory Loans

Historically, commercial banks have been the leaders in extending short-term credit to businesses. In fact, until World War II banks granted mainly **self-liquidating loans** to business firms. These loans usually were used to finance the purchase of *inventory*—raw materials or finished goods to sell. Such loans take advantage of the normal *cash cycle* inside a business firm:

1. Cash (including borrowed cash) is spent to acquire inventories of raw materials and semifinished or finished goods.
2. Goods are produced or shelved and listed for sale.
3. Sales are made (often on credit).
4. The cash received (immediately or later from credit sales) is then used to repay the self-liquidating loan.

In this case, the term of the loan begins when cash is needed to purchase inventory and ends (perhaps in 60 to 90 days) when cash is available in the firm's account to write the lender a check for the balance of its loan.

While most lenders today make a far wider array of business loans than just simple self-liquidating credits, the short-term loan—frequently displaying many of the features of self-liquidation—continues to account for a significant share of all loans to business firms.

In fact, most business loans cover only a few weeks or months and are usually related closely to the borrower's need for short-term cash to finance purchases of inventory or cover production costs, the payment of taxes, interest payments on debt, and dividend payments to stockholders.

There is concern in the banking and commercial finance industries today that traditional inventory loans may be on the decline. Thanks to the development of just in time (JIT) and supply chain management techniques businesses can continuously monitor their inventory levels and more quickly replace missing items. Reflecting this trend, inventory-to-sales ratios recently have been declining in many industries. Thus, there appears to be less need for traditional inventory financing and many businesses are experiencing lower inventory financing costs. In the future, lenders will be forced to develop other services in order to replace potential losses in inventory-loan revenues as new software-driven technology speeds up ordering and shipment, allowing businesses to get by with leaner in-house stocks of goods and raw materials.

Working Capital Loans

Key URL
If you want to learn more about the regulations applicable to loans for small businesses and for minority groups (including loans made to minority-owned businesses) where can you go? See the educational pamphlets available at **www. federalreserve.gov**.

Working capital loans provide businesses with short-run credit, lasting from a few days to about one year. Working capital loans are most often used to fund the purchase of inventories in order to put goods on shelves or to purchase raw materials; thus, they come closest to the traditional self-liquidating loan described previously.

Frequently the working capital loan is designed to cover seasonal peaks in the business customer's production levels and credit needs. For example, a clothing manufacturer anticipating heavy demand in the fall for back-to-school clothes and winter wear will require short-term credit in the late spring and summer to purchase inventories of cloth and hire additional workers. The manufacturer's lender can set up a line of credit stretching from six to nine months, permitting that manufacturer to draw upon the credit line as needed over this period. The amount of the credit line is determined from the manufacturer's estimate of the maximum amount of funds that will be needed at any point during the six to nine-month term of the loan. Such loans are frequently renewed under the provision that the borrower pay off all or a significant portion of the loan before renewal is granted.

Normally, working capital loans are secured by accounts receivable or by pledges of inventory and carry a floating interest rate on the amounts actually borrowed against the approved credit line. A commitment fee is charged on the unused portion of the credit line and sometimes on the entire amount of funds made available. **Compensating deposit balances** may be required from the customer. These include required deposits whose minimum size is based on the size of the credit line (e.g., 1 to 5 percent of the credit line) and required deposits equal to a stipulated percentage of the total amount of credit actually used by the customer (e.g., 15 to 20 percent of actual drawings against the line).

Interim Construction Financing

A popular form of secured short-term lending is the **interim construction loan,** used to support the construction of homes, apartments, office buildings, shopping centers, and other permanent structures. Although the structures involved are permanent, the loans themselves are temporary. They provide builders with funds needed to hire workers, rent or lease construction equipment, purchase building materials, and develop land. But once the construction phase is over, this short-term loan usually is paid off with a longer-term mortgage loan issued by another lender, such as an insurance company or pension fund. In fact, many commercial lenders will not lend money to a property developer until that customer has secured a mortgage loan commitment to provide long-term financing of a project once its construction is completed. Recently, some lenders have issued "minipermanent" loans, providing funding for construction and the early operation of a project for as long as five to seven years.

Security Dealer Financing

Key URLs
Business loan officers
have a big job today
keeping up with
changing trends in the
nature and technology
of commercial credit.
The Web aids them
in this educational area
through such sites as
those maintained by the
Risk Management
Association (RMA) at
www.rmahq.org and
Quick Start at
www.quick-start.net.

Dealers in securities need short-term financing to purchase new securities and carry their existing portfolios of securities until they are sold to customers or reach maturity. Such loans normally are readily granted because of their high quality—often backed by pledging the dealer's holdings of government securities as collateral. Moreover, many loans to securities dealers are so short—overnight to a few days—that the lender can quickly recover its funds or make a new loan at a higher interest rate if credit markets have tightened up.

A related type of loan is extended to *investment banking firms* to support their underwriting of new corporate bonds, stocks, and government debt. Such issues of securities occur when investment bankers help their business clients finance a merger, assist in taking a company public so that its ownership shares can be purchased by any interested investor, or aid in launching a completely new venture. Once the investment banker is able to sell these new securities, the loan plus interest owed is repaid.

Banks and security firms also lend directly to businesses and individuals buying stocks, bonds, options, and other financial instruments. Margin requirements enforced in the United States by the Federal Reserve Board usually limit such loans to no more than *half* the amount of the security or securities being acquired (under Regulation U). However, in an effort to aid the market for small business capital, the Fed ruled in December 1997 that selected lenders could loan up to 100 percent of the purchase price of "small cap" stocks listed by NASDAQ.

Retailer and Equipment Financing

Business lenders support installment purchases of automobiles, home appliances, furniture, business equipment, and other durable goods by financing the receivables that dealers selling these goods take on when they write installment contracts to cover customer purchases. In turn, these contracts are reviewed by lending institutions with whom the dealers have established credit relationships. If they meet acceptable credit standards, the contracts are purchased by lenders at an interest rate that varies with the risk level of each borrower, the quality of collateral pledged, and the term of each loan.

In the case of dealers selling automobiles, business and electronic equipment, furniture, and other durable goods, lenders may agree to finance the dealer's whole inventory through *floor planning*. The lender agrees to extend credit to the dealer so he or she can place an order with a manufacturer to ship goods for resale. Many such loans are for 90-day terms initially and may be renewed for one or more 30-day periods. In return for the loan the dealer signs a security agreement, giving the lending institution a lien against the goods in the event of nonpayment. At the same time the manufacturer is authorized to ship goods to the dealer and to bill the lender for their value. Periodically, the lender will send an agent to check the goods on the dealer's floor to determine what is selling and what remains unsold. As goods are sold, the dealer sends a check to the lender for the manufacturer's invoice amount, known as a "pay-as-sold" agreement.

If the lender's agent visits the dealer and finds any items sold off for which the lender has not received payment (known as "sold out of trust"), payment will be requested immediately for those particular items. If the dealer fails to pay, the lender may be forced to repossess the remaining goods and return some or all of them to the manufacturer for credit. Floor planning agreements typically include a loan-loss reserve, built up from the interest earned as borrowers repay their loans, and is reduced if any loans are defaulted. Once the loan-loss reserve reaches a predetermined level, the dealer receives rebates for a portion of the interest earned on the installment contracts.

Insights and Issues

COMPETITION IN LENDING BETWEEN BANKS AND CAPTIVE FINANCE COMPANIES

Among the most aggressive competitors of banks in granting loans to businesses and individuals today are *finance companies.* Between 1999 and the first quarter of 2005 finance companies' total assets grew by 42 percent, just slightly more than U.S. banking's 41 percent asset growth over the same time period. However, finance company loans to individuals soared upward at more than twice the growth rate of consumer credit in the banking sector.

Especially active were the "captive finance companies" affiliated with large manufacturing companies. Among the most visible "captives" are such familiar names as General Motors Acceptance Corporation (GMAC), Ford Motor Credit, and GE Capital, which, among other activities, provide customer financing to promote the sales of their manufacturing parents' products. Many of the captives have become giant firms—for example, GE Capital has sufficient assets to rank it among the top 10 U.S. banks.

Why have these aggressive business and consumer lenders been so successful in competing with bankers in recent years?

Some experts point to the heavy burden of federal and state regulation banks must carry that may retard their growth. Others point to the fact that captives can package together the purchasing and financing of their parents' products, linking manufacturing and finance in ways banks cannot do. Indeed, the United States has erected a high wall separating banking from manufacturing out of fear that allowing these two industries to amalgamate could weaken the banking system.

Moreover, captives are able to generate profits at several different points in a typical customer transaction by manipulating sales prices, terms of credit, and other aspects of the customer-supplier relationship, possibly masking some of the costs the customer ultimately pays. And captives can more readily refurbish and resell any products their customers turn back or cannot pay off. While banks must sell the collateral they seize from bad loans in the same markets as captives do, many bankers are unable to complete that task efficiently and at low cost. Captive finance companies have established a solid foothold in the financial system and bankers must find new ways to work competitively with these giant financial firms.

Asset-Based Financing

Key URLs
The World Wide Web provides some guidance on analyzing and granting different types of business loans. For example, there are sites on lending to small businesses at **www.sba.gov/7alenders/** and the ABCs of Borrowing at **www. howtoadvice.com/ borrowing.** To learn more about asset-based borrowing and international lending see especially **www.factors.net** and **jolis.worldbankimflib. org/external.htm**.

An increasing portion of short-term lending in recent years has consisted of **asset-based loans**—credit secured by the shorter-term assets of a firm that are expected to roll over into cash in the future. Key business assets used for many of these loans are accounts receivable and inventories. The lender commits funds against a specific percentage of the book value of outstanding credit accounts or against inventory. For example, it may be willing to loan an amount equal to 70 percent of a firm's current accounts receivable (i.e., all those credit accounts that are not past due). Alternatively, it may make a loan for 40 percent of the business customer's current inventory. As accounts receivable are collected or inventory is sold, a portion of the cash proceeds flow to the lending institution to retire the loan.

In most loans collateralized by accounts receivable and inventory, the borrower retains title to the assets pledged, but sometimes title is passed to the lender, who then assumes the risk that some of those assets will not pay out as expected. The most common example of this arrangement is **factoring,** where the lender takes on the responsibility of collecting on the accounts receivable of one of its business customers. Because the lender incurs both additional expense and risk with a factored loan, it typically assesses a higher discount rate and lends a smaller fraction of the book value of the customer's accounts receivable.

Syndicated Loans (SNCs)

Key URL
If you would like to learn more about syndicated loans, see especially **www.federal reserve.gov/releases/ snc/default.htm**.

A **syndicated loan** normally consists of a loan package extended to a corporation by a group of lenders. These loans may be "drawn" by the borrowing company, with the funds used to support business operations or expansion, or "undrawn," serving as lines of credit to back a security issue or other venture. Lenders engage in syndicated loans both to reduce the heavy risk exposures of these large loans, often involving millions or billions of dollars in credit for each loan, and to earn fee income (such as facility fees to open a credit line or commitment fees to keep a line of credit available for a period of time).

Many syndicated loans are traded in the secondary (resale) market and usually carry an interest rate based upon the London Interbank Offered Rate (LIBOR) on Eurodollar deposits. Syndicated loan rates in recent years have generally ranged from 100 to 400 basis points over LIBOR, while the loans themselves usually have a light to medium credit quality grade and may be either short-term or long-term in maturity.

Because of the size and character of SNCs, federal examiners look at these loans carefully, searching for those that appear to be *classified credits*—that is, weak loans that are rated, in the best case, *substandard*, *doubtful* if somewhat weaker, or, in the worst case, an outright *loss* that must be written off. Interestingly enough, the majority of classified SNCs are held by nonbank lenders (such as finance and investment companies), which often take on subinvestment-grade loans in the hope of scoring exceptional returns.

17–5 Long-Term Loans to Business Firms

Term Business Loans

Term loans are designed to fund longer-term business investments, such as the purchase of equipment or the construction of physical facilities, covering a period longer than one year. Usually the borrowing firm applies for a lump-sum loan based on the budgeted cost of its proposed project and then pledges to repay the loan in a series of monthly or quarterly installments.

Term loans usually look to the flow of future earnings of a business firm to amortize and retire the credit. The schedule of installment payments is usually structured with the borrower's normal cycle of cash inflows and outflows firmly in mind. For example, there may be "blind spots" built into the repayment schedule, so no installment payments will be due at those times when the customer is normally short of cash. Some term loan agreements do not call for repayments of principal until the end of the loan period. For example, in a "bullet loan" only interest is paid periodically, with the principal due when the loan matures.

Term loans normally are secured by *fixed assets* (e.g., plant or equipment) owned by the borrower and may carry either a fixed or a floating interest rate. That rate is normally higher than on shorter-term business loans due to the lender's greater risk exposure from such loans. The probability of default or other adverse changes in the borrower's position is certain to be greater over the course of a long-term loan. For this reason, loan officers and credit analysts pay attention to several different dimensions of a business customer's term loan application: (1) qualifications of the borrowing firm's management, (2) the quality of its accounting and auditing systems, (3) whether or not the customer conscientiously files periodic financial statements, (4) whether the customer is willing to agree not to pledge assets to other creditors, (5) whether adequate insurance coverage will be secured, (6) whether the customer is excessively exposed to the risk of changing technology, (7) the length of time before a proposed project will generate positive cash flow, (8) trends in market demand, and (9) the strength of the customer's net worth position.

Revolving Credit Financing

A **revolving credit line** allows a customer to borrow up to a prespecified limit, repay all or a portion of the borrowing, and reborrow as necessary until the credit line matures. One of the most flexible of all business loans, revolving credit is often granted without specific collateral and may be short-term or cover a period as long as five years. This

Insights and Issues

form of business financing is particularly popular when the customer is highly uncertain about the timing of future cash flows or about the magnitude of his or her future borrowing needs. Revolving credit helps even out fluctuations in the business cycle for a firm, allowing it to borrow extra cash when sales are down and to repay during boom periods when internally generated cash is more abundant. Lenders normally will charge a *loan commitment fee* either on the unused portion of the credit line or, sometimes, on the entire amount of revolving credit available for customer use.

Loan commitments are usually of two types. The most common is a *formal loan commitment*, which is a contractual promise to lend up to a maximum amount of money at a set interest rate or rate markup over the prevailing base rate (prime or LIBOR). In this case, the lender can renege on its promise to lend only if there has been a "material adverse change" in the borrower's financial condition or if the borrower has not fulfilled some provision of the commitment contract. A second, looser form is a *confirmed credit line*, where the lending institution indicates its approval of a customer's request for credit, though the price of such a credit line may not be set in advance and the customer may have little intention to draw upon the credit line, using it instead as a guarantee to back up a loan obtained elsewhere. These looser commitments typically go only to top-credit-rated firms and are usually priced much lower than formal loan commitments.

One form of revolving credit that has grown rapidly in recent years is the use of *business credit cards*. Many small businesses today have come to depend upon credit cards as a *source of operating capital*, thus avoiding having to get approval for every loan request. Increasingly popular is *credit-card receivables financing* in which merchants receive cash advances and pay them off from their credit-card sales. Unfortunately, the interest rates charged usually are high and if a personal card is used, the business borrower winds up being personally liable for the business's debts.

Long-Term Project Loans

The most risky of all business loans are **project loans**—credit to finance the construction of fixed assets designed to generate a flow of revenue in future periods. Prominent examples include oil refineries, power plants, and harbor facilities. The risks surrounding such projects are large and numerous: (1) large amounts of funds, often several billion dollars' worth, are involved; (2) the project may be delayed by weather or shortage of materials; (3) laws and regulations in the region where the project lies may change in a way that adversely affects project completion or cost; and (4) interest rates may change, adversely affecting the lender's return on the loan or the ability of the project's sponsors to repay. Project loans are usually granted to several companies jointly sponsoring a large project. Due to their size and risk, project financings are often shared by several lenders.

Project loans may be granted on a *recourse basis*, in which the lender can recover funds from the sponsoring companies if the project does not pay out as planned. At the other extreme, the loan may be extended on a nonrecourse basis, in which there are no sponsor guarantees; the project stands or falls on its own merits. In this case, the lender faces significant risks and, typically, demands a high contract loan rate. Many such loans require that the project's sponsors pledge enough of their own capital to help see the project through to completion.

Concept Check

17–1. What special problems does business lending present to the management of a business lending institution?

17–2. What are the essential differences among working capital loans, open credit lines, asset-based loans, term loans, revolving credit lines, interim financing, project loans, and acquisition loans?

Loans to Support the Acquisition of Other Business Firms

The 1980s and 1990s ushered in an explosion of loans to finance mergers and acquisitions of businesses before these loans slowed as the 21st century opened. Among the most noteworthy of these acquisition credits are **LBOs**—*leveraged buyouts* of firms by small groups of investors, often led by managers inside the firm who believe their firm is undervalued in the marketplace. A targeted company's stock price could be driven higher, it is argued, if its new owners can bring more aggressive management techniques to bear, including selling off some assets in order to generate more revenue.

These insider purchases have often been carried out by highly optimistic groups of investors, willing to borrow heavily (often 90 percent or more of the LBOs are financed by debt) in the belief that revenues can be raised higher than debt-service costs. Frequently the optimistic assumptions behind LBOs have turned out to be wrong and many of these loans have turned delinquent when economic conditions faltered.

17–6 Analyzing Business Loan Applications

In many business loan situations the lender's margin for error is narrow. Often business loans are of such large denomination that the lending institution itself may be at risk if the loan goes bad. Moreover, competition for the best business customers tends to reduce the spread between the yield on such loans and the cost of funds that the lender must pay in order to make these loans. For most business credits, lenders must commit roughly $100 in loanable funds for each $1 earned after all costs, including taxes. This is a modest *reward-to-risk* ratio, which means that business lenders need to take special care, particularly with loans of large denomination and, therefore, large risk exposure. With such a small reward-to-risk ratio, it doesn't take many business loan defaults to seriously erode the lender's profits.

Most loan officers like to build several layers of protection around a business loan agreement to ensure return of loan principal and interest earnings by the end of the loan agreement. Typically, this requires finding two or three sources of funds the business borrower could draw upon to repay the loan. The most common sources of repayment for business loans are:

1. The business borrower's profits or cash flow.
2. Business assets pledged as collateral behind the loan.
3. A strong balance sheet with ample amounts of marketable assets and net worth.
4. Guarantees given by the business, such as drawing on the owners' personal property to backstop a loan.

Most commonly, if cash flows are inadequate the lender turns to assets whose value fluctuates with production in the economy. This suggests that lenders should diversify geographically and across different markets and different firms.

Each of the above sources of repayment involves an analysis of customer financial statements, especially balance sheets and income statements. Let's turn to these basic financial statements and look at them as a loan officer would.

Analysis of a Business Borrower's Financial Statements

Analysis of the financial statements of a business borrower typically begins when the lender's credit analysis department prepares an analysis of how key figures on the borrower's financial statement have changed (usually during the last three, four, or five years). An example of such an historical analysis for an oil and gas company, Black Gold, Inc., is shown in Table 17–1. It presents balance sheets for the last four years and income statements for the same time period.

Note that these financial statements include both dollar figures and percentages of total assets (in the case of the balance sheet) and total sales (in the case of the income statement). These percentage figures, often called *common-size ratios*, show even more clearly than dollar figures the most important financial trends experienced by a business loan customer. These percentage-composition ratios control for differences in size of firm, permitting the loan officer to compare a particular business customer with other firms and with the industry as a whole. The common-size ratios most often used to help analyze a business borrower's financial statements include the following:

Important Balance Sheet Composition Ratios	
Percentage Composition of Assets	**Percentage Composition of Total Liabilities and Net Worth**
Cash/Total assets	Accounts payable/Total liabilities and net worth (= total assets)
Marketable securities/Total assets	
Accounts receivable/Total assets	Notes payable/Total liabilities and net worth
Inventories/Total assets	Taxes payable/Total liabilities and net worth
Fixed assets, net of depreciation/Total assets	Total current liabilities/Total liabilities and net worth
Other (miscellaneous) assets/Total assets	
	Long-term debt obligations/Total liabilities and net worth
	Other liabilities/Total liabilities and net worth
	Net worth/Total liabilities and net worth

Important Income Statement Composition Ratios

**Percentage Composition of Total Income
(gross revenues or sales)**

Cost of sales/Sales
Gross profit/Sales
Labor costs (wages, salaries, and fringe benefits)/Sales
Selling, administrative, and other expenses/Sales
Depreciation expenses/Sales
Other operating expenses/Sales
Net operating profit/Sales
Interest expense on borrowed funds/Sales
Net income before taxes/Sales
Income taxes/Sales
Net income after taxes/Sales

Comparative analysis of changes in these ratios helps the loan officer determine any developing weaknesses in loan protection, such as decreases in assets that might be pledged as collateral or a reduction in earning power. For example, we can analyze the percentage composition statements showing assets, liabilities, and equity capital for Black Gold, Inc., as reported in Table 17–1. Based on these percentage composition statements, would Black Gold represent a good risk for the bank it has approached for a loan?

In this case Black Gold is asking for a $5 million working capital line of credit tied to a borrowing base of assets, in the guise of accounts receivable and inventory, in anticipation of a sharp rise in oil and gas prices. Black Gold currently owes $3.9 million to another bank with whom it has had a relationship for several years, but now the company has expressed unhappiness with its current banking relationship and wants to establish a new relationship. Sometimes a business customer's unhappiness springs from poor or inadequate service provided by its current financial-service provider; on other occasions, however, unhappiness with a banking relationship arises because the customer is in trouble and its current lender is simply trying to work its way out of a bad situation, either by demanding payment on current loans or by refusing to accommodate new credit requests. One of a loan officer's tasks is to find out as much as possible about a business customer's current lender relationships and why they are or are not working out.

Careful examination of Table 17–1 suggests the loan officer involved in this case would have several important questions to ask this customer. For example, Black Gold's net income after taxes and net income as a percentage of total net sales has been negative in two of the last four years. Its sales revenues have been essentially flat over the past four years, while the cost of goods sold, both in dollar terms and relative to net sales, has risen significantly over the past four years. Moreover, if this loan is to be secured by accounts receivable and inventory, the loan officer clearly has reason to be concerned, because the dollar amount and percentage of total assets of both of these balance sheet items have risen sharply. And the firm's short-term (current) liabilities have risen as well.

17–7 Financial Ratio Analysis of a Customer's Financial Statements

Information from balance sheets and income statements is typically supplemented by financial ratio analysis. By careful selection of items from a borrower's balance sheets and income statements, the loan officer can shed light on such critical areas in business lending as a borrowing customer's: (1) *ability to control expenses*; (2) *operating efficiency in using*

TABLE 17–1 Historical Analysis of the Financial Statements of Black Gold, Inc. (dollar figures in millions)

Black Gold's Balance Sheets Arrayed in a Spreadsheet

Balance Sheet Items	Most Recent Year Dollar Value	Percentage of Total	One Year Ago Dollar Value	Percentage of Total	Two Years Ago Dollar Value	Percentage of Total	Three Years Ago Dollar Value	Percentage of Total
Assets								
Cash	$ 1.0	3.6%	$ 1.3	4.5%	$ 1.7	5.7%	$ 2.2	6.9%
Marketable securities	0.5	1.8	0.8	2.8	1.0	3.3	——	0.0
Accounts receivable	8.3	29.6	7.4	25.5	6.2	20.7	4.1	12.8
Inventories	5.2	18.6	4.5	15.5	3.4	11.3	2.3	7.2
Total current assets	$15.0	53.6	$14.0	48.3	$12.3	41.0	$ 8.6	26.9
Fixed assets, gross	19.4	69.3	20.2	69.7	21.5	71.7	22.4	70.0
Less: Accumulated depreciation	10.1	36.8	9.2	31.7	8.0	26.7	5.1	15.9
Fixed assets, net	9.3	33.2	11.0	37.9	13.5	45.0	17.3	54.1
Other assets	3.7	13.2	4.0	13.8	4.2	14.0	6.1	19.1
Total assets	$28.0	100.0%	$29.0	100.0%	$30.0	100.0%	$32.0	100.0%
Liabilities and Equity								
Accounts payable	$ 1.3	4.6%	$ 1.2	4.1%	$ 0.8	2.7%	$ 1.0	3.1%
Notes payable	3.9	13.9	3.4	11.7	3.2	10.7	1.7	8.4
Taxes payable	0.1	0.4	0.2	0.7	0.1	0.3	0.8	2.3
Total current liabilities	$ 5.3	18.9	$ 4.8	16.6	$ 4.1	13.7	$ 4.5	14.1
Long-term debt	12.2	43.6	13.2	45.5	12.5	41.6	11.4	35.6
Other liabilities	0.0	0.0	0.4	−1.4	3.5	11.7	6.1	19.1
Total liabilities	$17.5	62.5%	$18.4	63.4%	$20.1	67.0%	$22.0	68.8%
Common stock	1.0	3.6	1.0	3.4	1.0	3.3	1.0	3.1
Paid-in surplus	3.0	10.7	3.0	10.3	3.0	10.0	3.0	9.4
Retained earnings	6.5	23.2	6.6	22.8	5.9	19.7	6.0	18.8
Total net worth	10.5	37.5%	10.6	36.6%	9.9	33.0%	10.0	31.3%

Black Gold's Income Statement

Income Statement Items	Most Recent Year Dollar Value	Percentage of Total	One Year Ago Dollar Value	Percentage of Total	Two Years Ago Dollar Value	Percentage of Total	Three Years Ago Dollar Value	Percentage of Total
Net Sales	$32.0	100.0%	$30.0	100.0%	$28.0	100.0%	$31.0	100.0%
Less: Cost of goods sold	18.0	56.3	16.0	53.3	15.0	53.6	14.0	45.2
Gross profits	$14.0	43.8	$14.0	46.7	$13.0	46.4	$17.0	54.8
Less: Selling, administrative, and other expenses	9.0	28.1	9.0	30.0	8.0	28.6	11.0	35.5
Less: Depreciation expenses	3.0	9.4	3.0	10.0	3.0	10.7	2.0	6.5
Net operating income	$ 2.0	6.3	$ 2.0	6.7	$ 2.0	7.1	$ 4.0	12.9
Less: Interest expense on borrowed funds	2.0	6.3	1.0	3.3	2.0	7.1	2.0	6.5
Net income before taxes	0.0	0.0	1.0	3.3	0.0	0.0	2.0	6.5
Less: Income taxes	0.1	0.3	0.3	1.0	0.1	0.4	0.2	0.6
Net income after taxes	($ 0.1)	(0.3)%	$ 0.7	2.3%	($ 0.1)	(3.6)%	$ 1.8	5.8%

resources to generate sales; (3) *marketability of product line*; (4) *coverage that earnings provide over financing cost*; (5) *liquidity position, indicating the availability of ready cash*; (6) *track record of profitability*; (7) *financial leverage* (or debt relative to equity capital); and (8) *contingent liabilities* that may give rise to substantial claims in the future.

The Business Customer's Control over Expenses

Factoid
Research suggests that business lending tends to follow the business cycle, rising during expansions and falling in recessions, perhaps adding to the severity of these cycles. One theory suggests this happens, in part, because credit standards fall over time as lenders forget previous bad loans.

A barometer of the quality of a business firm's management is how carefully it controls its expenses and how well its earnings—the primary source of cash to repay a loan in most cases—are likely to be protected and grow. Selected financial ratios, usually computed by credit analysts to monitor a firm's expense control program, include the following:

Wages and salaries/Net sales

Overhead expenses/Net sales

Depreciation expenses/Net sales

Interest expense on borrowed funds/Net sales

Cost of goods sold/Net sales

Selling, administrative, and other expenses/Net sales

Taxes/Net sales

A loan officer confronted with several of these expense-control measures for Black Gold, Inc., would probably have serious doubts about the firm's management quality and earnings prospects for the future, as shown in Table 17–2. Some of Black Gold's expense ratios—selling, administrative, and other expenses and taxes relative to net sales—have declined; however, the rest have either held steady or risen as a percentage of the firm's net sales. In fact, it is Black Gold's inability to reduce its overall expenses in the face of relatively flat sales that has caused its net earnings generally to decline over the past four years. The loan officer working on this case will need some highly convincing arguments from the customer to demonstrate that the firm's expense and earnings picture will improve.

Operating Efficiency: Measure of a Business Firm's Performance Effectiveness

Filmtoid
What 1991 film portrays Anthony Hopkins as a consultant working to improve the operating efficiency of a small family-owned shoe factory with some significant problems in operations and sales?
Answer: *The Efficiency Expert.*

It is also useful to look at a business customer's operating efficiency. How effectively are assets being utilized to generate sales and how efficiently are sales converted into cash? Important financial ratios here include:

Annual cost of goods sold/Average inventory (or inventory turnover ratio)

Net sales/Total assets

Net sales/Net fixed assets

Net sales/Accounts and notes receivable

$$\text{Average collection period} = \text{Accounts receivable} \div (\text{Annual credit sales} \div 360) \quad \textbf{(17–1)}$$

In the case of Black Gold, what do these efficiency ratios show? Clearly, as Table 17–3 reveals, some measures of Black Gold's efficiency show nothing conclusive, while others

TABLE 17–2
Expense-Control Ratios for Black Gold, Inc.

	Most Recent Year	One Year Ago	Two Years Ago	Three Years Ago
Cost of goods sold ÷ net sales	56.3%	53.5%	53.6%	45.2%
Selling, administrative, and other expenses ÷ net sales	28.1	30.0	28.6	35.5
Depreciation expenses ÷ net sales	9.4	10.0	10.7	6.5
Interest expense on borrowed funds ÷ net sales	6.3	3.3	7.1	6.5
Taxes ÷ net sales	0.3	1.0	0.4	0.6

TABLE 17–3
Efficiency Ratios for
Black Gold, Inc.

	Most Recent Year	One Year Ago	Two Years Ago	Three Years Ago
Inventory turnover ratio: Annual cost of goods sold ÷ average inventory	3.46×	3.56×	4.41×	6.09×
Average collection period: Accounts receivable ÷ (annual sales ÷ 360)*	93.4 days	88.8 days	79.7 days	47.6 days
Turnover of fixed assets: Net sales ÷ net fixed assets	3.44×	2.73×	2.07×	1.79×
Turnover of total assets: Net sales ÷ total assets	1.14×	1.03×	0.93×	0.97×

*360 days is used for ease of computation in calculating this ratio.

tell a story of deteriorating efficiency in the management of key assets, particularly accounts receivable. Moreover, *inventory turnover*—an indicator of management's effectiveness in controlling the size of the firm's inventory position—has shown a declining trend.[1]

The *average collection period,* or accounts receivable turnover ratio, for Black Gold reveals a disturbing trend. The collection period ratio reflects the firm's effectiveness in collecting cash from its credit sales and provides evidence on the overall quality of the firm's credit accounts. A lengthening of the average collection period suggests a rise in past-due accounts and poor collection policies. Clearly, this has happened to Black Gold: Its average collection period almost doubled during the past four years, rising from 47.6 days to 93.4 days. The loan officer would certainly ask why and what steps the firm was taking to bring the turnover of its receivables back into line.

The ratio measuring *turnover of fixed assets* indicates how rapidly sales revenues are being generated as a result of using up the firm's plant and equipment (net fixed assets) to produce goods or services. In this instance, Black Gold's fixed-asset turnover is rising, but there is little cause for comfort because the balance sheet in Table 17–1 shows the primary reason for rising fixed-asset turnover is a declining base of plant and equipment. The firm is either selling some of its fixed assets to raise cash or simply not replacing worn-out plant and equipment. Black Gold's management has asked for a $5 million line of credit in anticipation of increasing sales, but it is doubtful that the firm could handle these sales increases given its declining base of productive fixed assets. A similar trend is reflected in the turnover ratio for total assets, which is rising for the same reasons.

Marketability of the Customer's Product or Service

In order to generate adequate cash flow to repay a loan, the business customer must be able to market goods, services, or skills successfully. A lender can often assess public acceptance of what the business customer has to sell by analyzing such factors as the growth rate of sales revenues, changes in the business customer's share of the available market, and the *gross profit margin* (GPM), defined as

$$\text{GPM} = \frac{\text{Net sales} - \text{Cost of goods sold}}{\text{Net sales}} \qquad \textbf{(17–2)}$$

[1]In general, the higher a firm's inventory ratio, the better it is for lenders because this ratio shows the number of times during a year the firm turns over its investment in inventories by converting those inventories into goods sold. When the inventory turnover ratio is too low it may indicate poor customer acceptance of the firm's products or ineffective production and inventory control policies. Too high an inventory turnover ratio could reflect underpricing of the firm's product or inadequate stocks of goods available for sale, with frequent stockouts, which drives customers away.

TABLE 17–4
Gross and Net Profit
Margins of Black
Gold, Inc.

	Most Recent Year	One Year Ago	Two Years Ago	Three Years Ago
Gross profit margin (GPM)	43.8%	46.7%	46.4%	54.8%
Net profit margin (NPM)	−0.3	2.3	−3.6	5.8

A closely related and somewhat more refined ratio is the *net profit margin* (NPM):[2]

$$\text{NPM} = \frac{\text{Net income after taxes}}{\text{Net sales}} \qquad \textbf{(17–3)}$$

What has happened to the GPM and NPM of Black Gold, Inc.? Clearly, as revealed in Table 17–4, both GPM and NPM are on a downward trend. This trend tips off the loan officer to several actual or potential problems, including potentially inappropriate pricing policies, expense control problems, and market deterioration.

Coverage Ratios: Measuring the Adequacy of Earnings

Coverage refers to the protection afforded creditors based on the amount of a business customer's earnings. The best-known coverage ratios include:

$$\text{Interest coverage} = \frac{\text{Income before interest and taxes}}{\text{Interest payments}} \qquad \textbf{(17–4)}$$

$$\begin{array}{c}\text{Coverage of}\\ \text{interest}\\ \text{and principal}\\ \text{payments}\end{array} = \frac{\text{Income before interest and taxes}}{\left[\text{Interest payments} + \dfrac{\text{Principal repayments}}{1 - \text{Firm's marginal tax rate}}\right]} \qquad \textbf{(17–5)}$$

$$\text{Coverage of all fixed payments} = \frac{\begin{array}{c}\text{Income before interest, taxes,}\\ \text{and lease payments}\end{array}}{\text{Interest payments} + \text{Lease payments}} \qquad \textbf{(17–6)}$$

Note that the second of these coverage ratios adjusts for the fact that repayments of loan principal are *not* tax deductible, while interest and lease payments are generally tax-deductible expenses in the United States.

What has happened to Black Gold's coverage ratios? During the current year, Black Gold must pay back $930,000 of its long-term debt; it also owes $3.9 million in short-term notes payable. One year ago it paid back $1 million in long-term debt, while two and three years ago it paid back $1.1 million and $1.3 million in long-term obligations, respectively. As Table 17–5 shows, Black Gold's interest coverage is weak. Its earnings are barely adequate to cover interest payments, and once repayments of principal are thrown in, Black Gold's earnings are simply inadequate to cover both interest and principal payments. The firm must use less debt (but more owners' equity) to finance itself, find ways to boost its earnings, and lengthen its debt through restructuring so that current debt service payments are reduced. The loan officer should counsel this customer concerning these alternatives and suggest how the firm might strengthen its coverage ratios to increase its chances of securing a loan.

[2]The *gross profit margin* (GPM) measures both market conditions—demand for the business customer's product and how competitive a marketplace the customer faces—and the strength of the business customer in its own market, as indicated by how much the market price of the firm's product exceeds the customer's unit cost of production and delivery. The *net profit margin* (NPM), on the other hand, indicates how much of the business customer's profit from each dollar of sales survives after all expenses are deducted, reflecting both the effectiveness of expense control policies and the competitiveness of pricing policies.

TABLE 17–5
Coverage Ratios for
Black Gold, Inc.

	Most Recent Year	One Year Ago	Two Years Ago	Three Years Ago
Interest coverage	1.0×	2.0×	1.0×	2.0×
Coverage of interest and principal payments	0.29×	0.22×	0.32×	0.43×

Liquidity Indicators for Business Customers

Key URLs
The quality and
condition of
commercial loans made
in the United States are
periodically surveyed in
the Federal Reserve's
Senior Loan Officer
Opinion Survey (the
results are reported at
**www.federalreserve.
gov/boarddocs/
snloansurvey**) and the
FDIC's Regional
Outlook Survey at
**www.fdic.gov/bank/
analytical/regional**.

The borrower's liquidity position reflects his or her ability to raise cash in timely fashion at reasonable cost, including the ability to meet loan payments when they come due.[3] Popular measures of liquidity include:

$$\text{Current ratio} = \frac{\text{Current assets}}{\text{Current liabilities}} \quad \textbf{(17–7)}$$

$$\text{Acid-test ratio} = \frac{\text{Current assets} - \text{Inventory}}{\text{Current liabilities}} \quad \textbf{(17–8)}$$

$$\text{Net liquid assets} = \frac{\text{Current}}{\text{assets}} - \text{Inventory} - \frac{\text{Current}}{\text{liabilities}} \quad \textbf{(17–9)}$$

$$\text{Net working capital} = \text{Current assets} - \text{Current liabilities} \quad \textbf{(17–10)}$$

The concept of **working capital** is important because it provides a measure of a firm's ability to meet its short-term debt obligations from its holdings of current assets.

What has happened to Black Gold's liquidity position? The firm made substantial progress in building up its liquidity two years ago, when current assets covered current liabilities three times over. Since that time, however, Black Gold's current and acid-test ratios have dipped significantly (see Table 17–6). The only bright spots in the firm's liquidity picture are the recent expansion in its working capital of $9.7 million and its relatively stable net liquid asset position. However, when we examine the causes of this working capital gain, we discover that it has been brought about largely by selling off a portion of the firm's plant and equipment and through the use of debt. Neither of these events is likely to be well received by loan officers or credit analysts.

TABLE 17–6
Changes in Liquidity
at Black Gold, Inc.

	Most Recent Year	One Year Ago	Two Years Ago	Three Years Ago
Current ratio: Current assets ÷ current liabilities	2.83×	2.92×	3.00×	1.91×
Acid-test ratio: (Current assets − inventories) ÷ current liabilities	1.85×	1.98×	2.17×	1.40×
Working capital (= current assets − current liabilities)	$9.7 mil.	$9.2 mil.	$8.2 mil.	$4.1 mil.
Net liquid assets (= current assets − inventories − current liabilities)	$4.5 mil.	$4.7 mil.	$4.8 mil.	$1.8 mil.

[3]An individual, business firm, or government is considered *liquid* if it can convert assets into cash or borrow immediately spendable funds precisely when cash is needed. Liquidity is a short-run concept in which *time* plays a key role. For that reason, most measures of liquidity focus on the amount of *current assets* (cash, marketable securities, accounts receivable, inventory, prepaid expenses, and any other assets that normally roll over into cash within a year's time) and *current liabilities* (accounts payable, notes payable, taxes payable, and other short-term claims against the firm, including any interest and principal payments owed on long-term debt that must be paid during the current year).

Commercial lenders are especially sensitive to changes in a customer's liquidity position because it is through the conversion of liquid assets, including the cash account, that loan repayments usually come. Erosion in a firm's liquidity position increases the risk that the lender will have to attach the customer's other (less liquid) assets to recover its funds. Such a step can be time-consuming, costly, and uncertain in its outcome. If a lender ultimately decides to make a loan to Black Gold, it will almost certainly insist on covenants in the loan agreement requiring the firm to strengthen its liquid reserves.

We should note that liquidity can also have a "dark side." A business borrower with too many assets tied up in liquid form, rather than in income-producing assets, loses opportunities to boost returns. Excess liquidity invites dishonest managers and employees to "take the money and run." Clearly, a loan officer must be wary of extremes in performance and ask for explanations whenever performance extremes are found.

Profitability Indicators

The ultimate standard of performance in a market-oriented economy is how much net income remains for the owners of a business firm after all expenses (except stockholder dividends) are charged against revenue. Most loan officers will look at both pretax net income and after-tax net income to measure the overall financial success or failure of a prospective borrower relative to comparable firms in the same industry. Popular bottom-line indicators of financial success include

Before-tax net income ÷ total assets, net worth, or total sales
After-tax net income ÷ total assets, net worth, or total sales

How profitable has Black Gold been? Table 17–7 summarizes profitability trends for this oil and gas firm. Clearly, there is little cause for comfort for the loan officer handling this credit application. Black Gold's earnings began a long-term decline two to three years ago, and there is little evidence to suggest that a turnaround is in sight. The firm's management has predicted an upturn in sales, which *may* result in an earnings upturn. However, the loan officer must be satisfied that the prospects for recovery are truly bright. Of course, the loan might be granted if sufficient collateral were available that could be sold to recover the lender's funds. But most loan officers would find this a poor substitute for earnings and cash flow in repaying a loan.

The Financial Leverage Factor as a Barometer of a Business Firm's Capital Structure

Any lender is concerned about how much debt a borrower has taken on in addition to the loan being sought. The term *financial leverage* refers to use of debt in the hope the borrower can generate earnings that exceed the cost of debt, thereby increasing potential returns to a business firm's owners. Key financial ratios used to analyze any borrowing business's credit standing and use of financial leverage include:

$$\text{Leverage ratio} = \frac{\text{Total liabilities}}{\text{Total assets}} \qquad \textbf{(17–11)}$$

TABLE 17–7
Profitability Trends at Black Gold, Inc.

	Most Recent Year	One Year Ago	Two Years Ago	Three Years Ago
Before-tax net income ÷ total assets	0.0%	3.4%	0.0%	6.3%
After-tax net income ÷ total assets	−0.4	2.4	−0.3	5.6
Before-tax net income ÷ net worth	0.0	9.4	0.0	20.0
After-tax net income ÷ net worth	−1.0	6.6	−1.0	18.0

TABLE 17–8
Leverage Trends at
Black Gold, Inc.

	Most Recent Year	One Year Ago	Two Years Ago	Three Years Ago
Leverage ratio: Total liabilities ÷ total assets	62.5%	63.4%	67.0%	68.8%
Total liabilities ÷ net worth	1.67×	1.74×	2.03×	2.20×
Capitalization ratio: Long-term debt ÷ long-term debt plus net worth	53.7%	55.5%	55.8%	53.3%
Debt-to-sales ratio: Total liabilities ÷ net sales	54.7%	61.3%	71.8%	71.0%

Factoid
According to a recent
Federal Reserve survey,
what size business loan
carries the highest risk
rating—the smallest
loan, the largest loan, or
somewhere in between?
Answer: Somewhere in
between. The business
loan category bearing
the highest risk index
usually falls between
$100,000 and
$1 million—a moderate-
size business loan.

$$\text{Capitalization ratio} = \frac{\text{Long-term debt}}{\text{Total long-term liabilities and net worth}} \quad (17\text{–}12)$$

$$\text{Debt-to-sales ratio} = \frac{\text{Total liabilities}}{\text{Net sales}} \quad (17\text{–}13)$$

What has happened to Black Gold's leverage, or debt position? As shown in Table 17–8, Black Gold's leverage ratio has improved, with assets and net worth generally growing faster than debt. Moreover, its mix of long-term funding sources—debt and equity capital—has been relatively constant, while total liabilities have declined relative to sales. Much of the firm's recent funding has come from sources other than debt, such as depletion of fixed assets and a buildup in such current assets as accounts receivable and inventory. Table 17–9 summarizes the ratios that highlight Black Gold's current standing.

17–8 Comparing a Business Customer's Performance to the Performance of Its Industry

Key URLs
For detailed
information on how
industries are classified
today for economic and
financial analysis using
the Standard Industrial
Classification (SIC)
and North American
Industrial Classification
System (NAICS) codes
see especially the U.S.
Bureau of Labor
Statistics (**www.bls.
gov**) and the U.S.
Census Bureau (**www.
census.gov/epcd/www/
naics.html**).

It is standard practice among loan officers to compare each business customer's performance to the performance of the customer's entire industry. Several organizations work to aid loan officers in gathering industrywide data; two of the most famous are these:

Dun & Bradstreet Industry Norms and Key Business Ratios, which provides 14 business and financial ratios for industries containing over 18 million businesses for up to three years, including common-size balance sheets and income statements, dollar totals for sales and selected other accounts, and such key performance ratios as return on assets and net worth, turnover of accounts receivable and inventory, liabilities and fixed assets to net worth, and current assets to current liabilities. (See, for example, **www.bizminer.com**.)

RMA Annual Statement Studies, which assembles data provided by loan officers and their customers for over 640 industries (listed by their SIC and NAICS codes) from several different U.S. regions. Includes 16 common-size financial ratios based on the composition of the balance sheet and income statement, divides this information into six asset and sales size groups, presents average industry performance levels as well as upper and lower quartiles of performance, and is available to subscribers online in the form of industry profiles, and via CD Rom. (See **www.rmahq.org/Ann_Studies/asstudies.html**.)

Black Gold is classified as a member of the crude oil and natural gas extraction industry (SIC Code 1311 and NAICS code 211111). Generally, Black Gold's performance places it *below* industry standards in terms of several of the key performance ratios we have examined in the preceding sections. The loan officer would want to discuss with Black Gold's management the reasons for the firm's lagging performance and how management proposes to raise Black Gold's ranking within its own industry.

TABLE 17–9
Summary of Key
Financial Ratios
Showing Trends in
the Financial
Condition of Black
Gold, Inc.

Financial Ratio Categories and Key Ratio Measures	Values in Most Recent Year	Financial Ratios for Black Gold:		
		One Year Ago	Two Years Ago	Three Years Ago
Expense Control Measures				
Cost of goods sold/Net sales	56.3%	53.5%	53.6%	45.2%
Selling, administrative, and other expenses/Net sales	28.1	30.0	28.6	35.5
Depreciation expenses/Net sales	9.4	10.0	10.7	6.5
Interest expense on borrowed funds/Net sales	6.3	3.3	7.1	6.5
Taxes/Net sales	0.3	1.0	0.4	0.6
Operating Efficiency Measures				
Annual cost of goods sold/Average inventory	3.46×	3.56×	4.41×	6.09×
Average receivables collection period	93.4 days	88.8 days	79.7 days	47.6 days
Net sales/Net fixed assets	3.44×	2.73×	2.07×	1.79×
Net sales/Total assets	1.14×	1.03×	0.93×	0.97×
Marketability of Product or Service Measures				
Gross profit margin (GPM)	43.8%	46.7%	46.4%	54.8%
Net profit margin (NPM)	−0.3	2.3	−3.6	5.8
Coverage Measures				
Interest coverage	1.0×	2.0×	1.0×	2.0×
Coverage of interest and principal payments	0.29×	0.22×	0.32×	0.43×
Liquidity Measures				
Current assets/Current liabilities (current ratio)	2.83×	2.92×	3.00×	1.91×
Acid-test ratio (Current assets less inventories/Current liabilities)	1.85×	1.98×	2.17×	1.40×
Working capital (current assets less current liabilities)	$9.7 mil.	$9.2 mil.	$8.2 mil.	$4.1 mil.
Net liquid assets (current assets less inventories less current liabilities)	$4.5 mil.	$4.7 mil.	$4.8 mil.	$1.8 mil.
Profitability Measures				
Before-tax net income/Total assets	0.0%	3.4%	0.0%	6.3%
After-tax net income/Total assets	−0.4	2.4	−0.3	5.6
Before-tax net income/Net worth	0.0	9.4	0.0	20.0
After-tax net income/Net worth	−1.0	6.6	−1.0	18.0
Leverage or Capital Structure Measures				
Leverage ratio (Total liabilities divided by total assets)	62.5%	63.4%	67.0%	68.8%
Total liabilities/Net worth	1.67×	1.74×	2.03×	2.20×
Capitalization ratio (Long-term debt divided by long-term debt plus net worth)	53.7%	55.5%	55.8%	53.3%
Debt-to-sales ratio (Total liabilities divided by net sales)	54.7%	61.3%	71.8%	71.0%

Contingent Liabilities

Types of Contingent Liabilities

Usually not shown on customer balance sheets are other potential claims against the borrower that loan officers must be aware of:

1. Guarantees and warranties behind the business firm's products.
2. Litigation or pending lawsuits against the firm.

3. Unfunded pension liabilities the firm will likely owe its employees in the future.

4. Taxes owed but unpaid.

5. Limiting regulations.

These **contingent liabilities** can turn into actual claims against the firm's assets and earnings at a future date, reducing funds available to repay a loan. The loan officer's best move in this circumstance is, first, to ask the customer about pending or potential claims against the firm and then to follow up with his or her own investigation, checking government records, public notices, and newspapers. It is far better to be well informed than to repose in blissful ignorance. In a case like Black Gold, the loan officer would routinely check into contingent liabilities.

Environmental Liabilities

A new contingent liability that has increasingly captured lenders' concerns is the issue of possible lender liability for *environmental damage* under the terms of the Comprehensive Environmental Response, Compensation, and Liability Act and its Super Fund Amendments. These federal laws make current and past owners of contaminated property or of businesses located on contaminated property and those who dispose of or transport hazardous substances potentially liable for any cleanup costs associated with environmental damage. (Most states have enacted similar environmental damage and cleanup laws.) Other federal laws that establish liability for the creation, transportation, storage, and disposal of environmentally dangerous substances include the Resource Conservation and Recovery Act, the Clean Water Act, the Clean Air Act, and the Toxic Substance Control Act.

In 1990 a federal appeals court in the Fleet Factors case ruled that a lender could be held liable for cleanup of hazardous wastes spilled by a firm to whom it had loaned money if the lender was "significantly involved" in the borrower's decision making on how to dispose of hazardous wastes.[4] Faced with this and other court decisions, many lenders have felt compelled to scrutinize closely the pollution hazards of any property pledged as collateral upon which they might have the right to foreclose. In an effort to give lenders guidelines on how to evaluate environmental risks, the U.S. Environmental Protection Agency (EPA) issued a lender liability rule in 1992, defining a "security interest exemption" that creditors could take advantage of when taking possession of polluted property. The EPA guidelines state that a lender holding "indicia of ownership" (such as a deed of trust, lien, or mortgage) can be exempted from any environmental liability associated with the owner's property provided the lender takes certain steps. Lenders must not participate in the management of the borrower's property and must take action primarily to protect the credit they have extended rather than treating their interest in the borrower's property as a long-term investment. If the lender forecloses on polluted property, it must post that property for sale within 12 months after securing marketable title. A lender can require that: (*a*) a borrower perform an environmental assessment of his or her own property; (*b*) polluted property be cleaned up; (*c*) the lender be granted permission to inspect and monitor the borrower's property; and (*d*) a borrower comply with all environmental laws.

The Federal Deposit Insurance Corporation has issued guidelines to help federally supervised depository institutions develop an *environmental risk assessment program*. A senior officer inside each institution must be appointed to administer procedures for protecting against loss from environmental damage. Each depository institution is supposed

---

[4]See especially *United States v. Fleet Factor Corp.*, 901F2d 1550, and, for a similar decision, see *United States v. Maryland Bank & Trust Co.*, 632 F.Supp. 573.

to establish a training program for its staff, develop procedures for evaluating environmental risk present in loans collateralized by a customer's property, and install safeguards to shield the institution from environmental liability. A business borrower like Black Gold—an oil and gas company—would be carefully scrutinized for potential environmental liabilities.

Underfunded Pension Liabilities

Another contingent liability that may threaten Black Gold and other borrowing customers is underfunded pension plans. Under accounting rules promoted by the Financial Accounting Standards Board (FASB) and other agencies, borrowing customers may be compelled to record employee pension plan surpluses and deficits on their balance sheets rather than hiding them in footnotes. If projected pension-plan liabilities exceed expected funds sources, the result may be an increase in liabilities on a customer's balance sheet, threatening reductions in net worth and violation of loan covenants, allowing lenders to charge higher loan rates. Loan officers today must pay closer attention to the financial condition of borrowing customers' pension programs.

17–9 Preparing Statements of Cash Flows from Business Financial Statements

Besides balance sheets and income statements, loan officers like to see a third accounting statement from a business borrower—the **Statement of Cash Flows.** This statement, called for by the Financial Accounting Standards Board (FASB), is usually readily available from borrowers. It provides insights into how and why a firm's cash balance has changed and helps to answer several important questions: *Will the borrower be able to generate sufficient cash to support its production and sales activities and still be able to repay the lender? Why is the cash position of the borrower changing over time and what are the implications of these changes for the lender?*

The Statement of Cash Flows illustrates how cash receipts and disbursements are generated by operating activities, investing activities, and financing activities. Table 17–10 provides an illustration of the Statement of Cash Flows for Black Gold's most recent year prepared using the following format:

$$
\begin{aligned}
\text{Cash Flow by Origin} = \ & \text{Net Cash Flow from Operations} \\
& \text{(focusing upon the normal flow} \\
& \text{of production, inventories, and sales)} \\
& + \text{Net Cash Flow from Investing Activities} \qquad \textbf{(17–14)} \\
& \text{(focusing upon the purchase and sale of} \\
& \text{assets)} + \text{Net Cash Flow from Financing} \\
& \text{Activities (including the issuance of debt)}
\end{aligned}
$$

The most important of these activities are the *operations of a firm.* The operating cash flows may be identified using either a direct method or an indirect method. FASB recommends the direct method; however, the indirect method, which we will illustrate using Black Gold, Inc., is used more frequently. As introduced in Chapter 16 the traditional (direct) measure of operating cash flows is:

$$
\begin{aligned}
\begin{matrix} \text{Traditional} \\ \text{(Direct)} \\ \text{Operating} \\ \text{Cash Flow} \\ \text{Measure} \end{matrix}
& = \text{Net Cash Flow from Operations} + \text{Noncash Expenses} \\
& \quad \text{(measured on a cash, not an accrual, basis)} \\
& \\
& \qquad\qquad\qquad\qquad\qquad\qquad\qquad\qquad \textbf{(17–15)} \\
& = \text{Net Sales Revenue} - \text{Cost of Goods Sold} - \text{Selling,} \\
& \quad\ \text{General and Administrative Expenses} - \text{Taxes Paid in} \\
& \quad\ \text{Cash} + \text{Noncash Expenses (especially depreciation)}
\end{aligned}
$$

TABLE 17–10
Statement of Cash Flows for Black Gold, Inc. (figures in millions of dollars)

Most Recent Year	Source of Information
Cash Flows from Operations	
Net income (loss)	($0.1) *Most recent income statement (IS)*
Adjustments to Reconcile Net Income	
Add: Depreciation	$3.0 *Most recent income statement*
Changes in Assets and Liabilities	
Add: Decrease in other assets	$0.3 *Comparison of consecutive balance sheets (CBSs)*
Add: Increase in accounts payable	$0.1 *Comparison of consecutive balance sheets*
Subtract: Increase in accounts receivable	($0.9) *Comparison of consecutive balance sheets*
Subtract: Increase in inventories	($0.7) *Comparison of consecutive balance sheets*
Subtract: Decrease in taxes payable	($0.1) *Comparison of consecutive balance sheets*
Net Cash Flow from Operations	$1.6
Cash Flows from Investment Activities	
Purchase of new machinery	($1.3) *Acquisition cost (can be derived from CBSs after adjusting for all other changes)*
Redemption of marketable securities	$0.3 *Book value of securities sold (CBSs) + gains (IS) – losses(IS)*
Net Cash Flow from Investment Activities	($1.0)
Cash Flows from Financing Activities	
Increase in notes payable	$0.5 *Comparison of consecutive balance sheets*
Repayment of long-term debt	($1.0) *Comparison of consecutive balance sheets*
Repayment of other liabilities	($0.4) *Comparison of consecutive balance sheets*
Subtract: Dividends paid	$0.0 *Difference between net income (IS) and change in retained earnings (CBSs)*
Net Cash Flow from Financing Activities	($0.9)
Increase (decrease) in cash for the year	($0.3) *Sum of net cash flow from operations, investments, and financing activities. Entry should check with comparison of consecutive balance sheets.*

The income statement, which we associate with operations, is created using accrual rather than cash-basis accounting. The indirect method for calculating operating cash flows begins with net income from the income statement and shows the reconciliation of this figure to that of operating cash flows:

$$
\begin{aligned}
\text{Indirect Operating Cash Flow Measure} =\ & \text{Net Income} + \text{Noncash Expenses} + \text{Losses} \\
& \text{from the sale of assets} - \text{Gains from the sale of assets} \\
& - \text{Increases in assets associated with operations} \\
& + \text{Increases in current liabilities associated with} \\
& \text{operations} - \text{Decreases in current liabilities} \\
& \text{associated with operations} + \text{Decreases in current} \\
& \text{assets associated with operations}
\end{aligned}
$$

(17–16)

This equation begins with net income and adds back noncash expenses, such as depreciation. Then it adjusts for gains or losses from the sale of assets that are incorporated on the income statement in order to group them with investing activities. Finally, it adds all changes on the balance sheet that generate cash (i.e., decreases in accounts receivable, decreases in inventory, decreases in other assets, increases in accounts payable, and increases in accrued items) and subtracts all changes on the balance sheet that require cash (i.e., increases in accounts receivable, increases in inventory, increases in other assets, decreases in accounts payable, and decreases in accrued items). This process is illustrated as cash flows from operations for Black Gold in Table 17–10.

The second section of the Statement of Cash Flows describes inflows and outflows associated with the acquisition and disposition of assets used in operations. The cash flows associated with *investing activities* include all purchases and sales of securities and long-term assets, such as plant and equipment. While some notion of these activities can be gleaned from changes in marketable securities and fixed assets on consecutive balance sheets and gains and losses recorded on the income statement, the Statement of Cash Flows directs attention to actual funds needed or provided. Typically healthy, growth-oriented firms are investing in fixed assets to support operations. At the end of the most recent year, Black Gold wrote off $2 million in refinery equipment that was fully depreciated, but no longer serviceable. As a partial replacement they purchased equipment costing $1.3 million. While this investment in fixed assets required funds, Black Gold generated some $300,000 in funds by cashing in Treasury bills as they matured.

The third and final section of the Statement of Cash Flows reports *financing activities*. Cash inflows include the short- and long-term funds provided by lenders and owners, while cash outflows include the repayment of borrowed funds, dividends to owners, and the repurchasing of outstanding stock. In terms of cash inflows from financing activities, Black Gold increased notes payable by $500,000. Their cash outflows included the repayment of $1.4 million in long-term debt and other liabilities.

The Statement of Cash Flows in Table 17–10, compiled by the accountants at Black Gold, Inc., shows how Black Gold supported its production and delivery of oil and gas over the past year. The funds to support Black Gold's activities were generated by drawing down liquidity (cash and marketable securities), through short-term borrowings (accounts and notes payable) and by postponing the replacement of equipment. These sources of cash inflow suggest the company may be exhausting its liquidity and capacity to borrow, casting doubts regarding its ability to repay future borrowings.

Black Gold cannot continue deferring the replacement of assets. Claiming a noncash expense of $3 million for plant and equipment on their income statement, management wrote off $2.1 million of fully depreciated fixed assets while only purchasing the necessities for $1.3 million. The firm needs to develop *new* sources of funding (preferably through expanded sales and income) to remain viable in the long run. Black Gold's management must present a convincing argument to the loan officer on *how* the firm will improve its sales and earnings.

The cash outflows for Black Gold summarized in Table 17–10 reveal that funds amounting to $4.3 million were used to increase accounts receivable and inventories, purchase essential equipment, and repay various liabilities. The loan officer will examine closely the build-up of accounts receivable and inventories for quality and marketability because these assets can be hard to liquidate in a down market. On a brighter note, the $1.4 million that went to pay off long-term debt and other liabilities is a positive development. This reduction in debt helped to increase Black Gold's future borrowing capacity.

Pro Forma Statements of Cash Flows and Balance Sheets

It is useful not only to look at historical data in a Statement of Cash Flows, but also to estimate the business borrower's future cash flows and financial condition. Lenders often have the customer prepare these *pro forma* statements, and then credit analysts within the lending institution will prepare their own version of these forecasts for comparison purposes. Customers tend to overstate their forecasts of future performance while forecasts made by the lender's staff tend to be more conservative. Either way *pro forma* statements are, at best, an "educated guess" concerning the future.

Table 17–11 shows a *pro forma* balance sheet and Statement of Cash Flows for Black Gold, Inc. To no one's surprise, the firm has predicted a rosy future for its oil and gas operations. Net sales are forecast to increase 10 percent, resulting in positive net income of $100,000, while Black Gold's assets are predicted to climb from $28 to $31.8 million within the coming year. The predicted positive earnings would help to boost the firm's

TABLE 17–11 Pro Forma Balance Sheet and Statement of Cash Flows for Black Gold, Inc.
(figures in millions of dollars)

Items from the Balance Sheet	Actual Balance Sheet at End of Most Recent Year	Pro Forma Balance Sheet One Year from Now	Items from the Balance Sheet	Actual Balance Sheet at End of Most Recent Year	Pro Forma Balance Sheet One Year from Now
Asset items:			**Liabilities and net worth items:**		
Cash account	$ 1.0	$ 2.0	Accounts payable	$ 1.3	$ 1.4
Marketable securities	0.5	1.5	Notes payable	3.9	5.0
Accounts receivable	8.3	7.9	Taxes payable	0.1	0.5
Inventories held	5.2	4.8	Current liabilities	5.3	6.9
Current assets	15.0	16.2			
			Long-term debt obligations	12.2	12.0
Net fixed assets	9.3	10.3	Other liabilities	0.0	2.3
Other assets	3.7	5.3	Common stock outstanding	1.0	1.0
Total assets	$28.0	$31.8	Paid-in surplus	3.0	3.0
			Retained earnings	6.5	6.6
			Total liabilities and net worth	$28.0	$31.8

Pro Forma Cash Flows One Year from Now

Cash Flows from Operations		Cash Flows from Investment Activities	
Net income (loss)	$0.1	Purchase of new machinery	($4.0)
Adjustments to reconcile net income		Purchase of marketable securities	($1.0)
Add: Depreciation	$3.0	**Net cash flow from investment activities**	($5.0)
Changes in assets and liabilities			
Add: Decrease in accounts receivable	$0.4	**Cash flows from financing activities**	
Add: Decrease in inventories	$0.4	Increase in notes payable	$1.1
Add: Increase in accounts payable	$0.1	Repayment of long-term debt	($0.2)
Add: Increase in taxes payable	$0.4	Funds from other liabilities	$2.3
Subtract: Increase in other assets	($1.6)	Dividends paid	$0.0
Net cash flow from operations	$2.8	**Net cash flow from financing activities**	$3.2
		Increase (decrease) cash for the year	$1.0

Effect of the proposed loan: Black Gold proposes to pay off the $3.9 million note owed to its former bank with the $5 million it is requesting in new bank credit. If the loan is approved as requested, its cash account would rise by $1 million to $2 million and its notes payable account would increase by $1.1 million to $5 million, reflecting the amount owed the firm's new lender.

retained earnings account and thereby strengthen its equity capital. At the same time the cash account is forecast to return to its level of two or three years ago at $2 million by the end of the current year. For additional liquidity, the firm forecasts adding $1 million to its holdings of marketable securities and the less-liquid receivables and inventory accounts allegedly will be worked down (each by $0.4 million) through improved credit collection methods and better pricing and restocking policies.

Not only will the decline in plant and equipment be halted, Black Gold's management estimates, but also $4 million in new fixed assets will be added to replace obsolete facilities. According to Table 17–11, the firm is planning to expand its plant and equipment by $1 million. This would be accomplished by claiming a depreciation expense of $3 million, purchasing new assets of $4 million, while writing off the $3 million of fully depreciated assets that will be disposed of with neither gains nor losses accruing. Black Gold's management also plans to acquire other (miscellaneous) assets of $1.6 million, and pay off $200,000 of its outstanding long-term debt.

These cash outflows reportedly are to be covered by decreasing accounts receivable by $0.4 million, decreasing inventories by $0.4 million, increasing accounts payable by $0.1 million, increasing taxes payable by $0.4 million, increasing notes payable (to be provided by the lending bank) by $1.1 million, and increasing other (unspecified) liabilities by $2.3 million. Because the additional debt could weaken the lender's claim against this customer, the loan officer will want to find out exactly why and how this proposed additional debt capital would be raised and assess its possible adverse consequences.

What will make possible all these adventurous plans for restructuring and rebuilding Black Gold's assets and capital? As Table 17–11 shows in the notes payable account, the firm is relying heavily on its $5 million credit request from the bank to pay off its outstanding $3.9 million in short-term notes and to provide an additional $1.1 million in new cash to strengthen its assets and help fuel projected gains in its net income. Are these forecasts reasonable? That, of course, is the decision the loan officer must make. Experienced loan officers know that, in most cases, the customer is more optimistic and far less objective about the future than a lender can afford to be.

A key factor shaping this customer's future performance will be what happens to energy prices in the global market. The lender would be well advised to carry out a *simulation analysis* of this customer's future financial condition, assuming an array of different possible oil and gas prices and seeing what the consequences are for the firm's pro forma balance sheet, income statement, and statement of cash flows. Armed with this information, the loan committee can move toward a more satisfactory credit decision based on its assessment of the most likely future conditions in the global energy market.

The Loan Officer's Responsibility to the Lending Institution and the Customer

There is an understandable tendency on the part of many readers to look at the foregoing figures for Black Gold and say *no way*. This loan as requested does not appear to many analysts to have reasonable prospects for being repaid, given Black Gold's recent record of sales revenue, expenses, cash flow, and net earnings. But it is at this point that the credit analyst and the loan officer *may* part company. A loan officer must look beyond the immediate facts to the broader, longer-term aspects of a customer relationship. Denial of this loan request will almost certainly lose this customer's business (including any deposits the company may have placed with the lending institution) and probably lose the personal accounts of some stockholders and employees of Black Gold as well. Other firms in the same or related industries may also be discouraged from applying to this lender for coverage of their credit needs.

Lenders cannot stay in business for long by making bad loans of this size, but they also must be careful about flatly turning away large corporate accounts without at least exploring the possibilities for establishing *some* sort of customer relationship. That sort of policy soon leads to loss of market share and may ultimately damage bottom-line earnings. Many experienced loan officers argue that a better long-run loan policy is to *find some way to help a business customer* under terms the lender feels adequately protect its funds and reputation. This doesn't mean extending a loan where the risks appear unacceptable. Helping the customer may mean, instead, offering to provide noncredit services, such as cash management services, advice on a proposed merger, or assistance with a new security offering the customer may be planning.

Yet another possible option is a counteroffer on the proposed loan that is small enough and secured well enough to adequately protect the lender. In the case of Black Gold, Inc., the lender is confronted with a request for a $5 million credit line—an amount that is considerably more than the loan officer is likely to grant, given this customer's apparent financial and operating weaknesses. Suppose, however, that the loan officer, with the approval of the lender's loan committee, proposes the following alternative plan to this customer:

ETHICS IN BANKING AND FINANCIAL SERVICES

EARNINGS DECEPTION BY BORROWING BUSINESSES: WHAT SHOULD LOAN OFFICERS DO?

As the 21st century dawned, the credit markets were rocked by stories of corporate fraud and deception as several leading businesses inflated their earnings to attract capital and lower the cost of their borrowings. Many corporations, even those not committing outright fraud, have created their own earnings measures, reporting to lenders and the public such questionable numbers as "pro forma," "street," or "operating" earnings, while burying lower, but more generally accepted (GAAP) earnings measures in out of the way places in their reports. These "engineered" earnings figures often omit unfavorable items, inflating revenues and understating expenses.

Loan officers today must be especially conscious of earnings-inflation devices used by some of their largest customers. The well-trained loan officer today asks lots of questions about businesses' financial statements, including these:

- How exactly were earnings or income computed?
- What expense items have been excluded from earnings estimates and why?

- How are pension plan expenses and returns calculated?
- How are employee stock options (ESOPs) accounted for?
- How did your firm treat losses on assets, corporate restructuring charges, and other extraordinary expenses?

Recently several leading companies, such as General Motors, General Electric, Coca-Cola, and Procter & Gamble, have revised their reporting methods to include the expensing of employee stock options, more transparent treatment of pension plan obligations, and more conservative handling of extraordinary expenses. Unfortunately, many business borrowers still have not responded to the public and regulators' call for accurate and honest financial reports.

Note: See, for example, John B. Carlson and Erkin Y. Sahinoz, "Measures of Corporate Earnings: What Number Is It?" *Economic Commentary,* Federal Reserve Bank of Cleveland, February 1, 2003.

The lender will extend a $1.5 million line of credit for six months, with the line to be cleaned up at the end of that period. If all payments on this credit are satisfactorily made and there is no further deterioration in the customer's financial position, the lender will renew the credit line on a quarterly basis. Any drawings against the line will be secured by a lien against all unencumbered fixed assets of the firm, 70 percent of all accounts receivable that are current, and 40 percent of the value of all inventories held. The lender will be granted a first lien against any new fixed assets acquired by the firm. Interest payments will be assessed monthly. The customer agrees to hold a deposit with the lender equal to 20 percent of the amount of any actual drawings against the line and 5 percent of the amount of any unused portion of the line.

In addition, the customer agrees to file monthly reports on the status of sales, expenses, net income, accounts receivable, and inventory and to file quarterly audited balance sheet and income statements. Any changes in the management of the firm or any sales of plant and equipment, merger agreements, or liquidations must be approved in advance by the lender. The customer will maintain at least the current levels of the firm's leverage and liquidity ratios, and any significant deviations from the firm's projections or any significant changes in the firm's financial and operating position will be reported to the lender immediately. Any failure to conform to the terms of this agreement will make the loan immediately due and payable.

An agreement of this sort offers protection to the lender in a number of ways. For example, Black Gold has an estimated $2 million in unmortgaged fixed assets and plans to acquire an additional $1 million in new equipment. Added protection is provided by the conservative percentages of accounts receivable and inventory the lender would take as collateral and by the required balances (deposits) the customer would retain with the lender. In the event of a default on this loan, the lender could exercise its *right of offset* and take control of these deposits in order to repay the balance due on the loan. Interest must be paid monthly, which means the lender will recover a substantial portion of its expected interest income early in the loan's term, further reducing the lender's income risk associated with this credit. Any action by the customer or adverse change in the customer's position that leads to a violation of the loan agreement gives the lender legal grounds to take possession of the firm's assets pledged behind the loan and sell those assets to recover the loan's proceeds and any unpaid interest.

Black Gold may well decline this agreement, particularly because (*a*) it gives the customer much less money than requested ($1.5 million instead of $5 million), (*b*) the loan funds are offered for a shorter term than requested (six months instead of one year), and (*c*) the agreement places *many* restrictions on the freedom of Black Gold's management. But the key point is this: *If the customer says "no" to this proposal by the lender, it is the customer, not the lending institution, who is declining to establish a relationship.* The lender has demonstrated a willingness to help meet at least a portion of the customer's financing needs. Moreover, good lending policy calls for the loan officer to assure the customer that, *even if he or she turns down the lender's offer, the lending institution still stands ready at any future time to try to work with that customer to find a suitable service package that will satisfy both parties.*

The alert reader will note that we said nothing in the foregoing draft loan agreement about what *rate of interest* the loan should bear. The loan rate, too, can be shaped in such a way that it further protects and compensates the lender for any risks incurred. We turn finally to this loan pricing issue.

Concept Check

17–3. What aspects of a business firm's financial statements do loan officers and credit analysts examine carefully?

17–4. What aspect of a business firm's operations is reflected in its ratio of cost of goods sold to net sales? In its ratio of net sales to total assets? In its GPM ratio? In its ratio of income before interest and taxes to total interest payments? In its acid-test ratio? In its ratio of before-tax net income to net worth? In its ratio of total liabilities to net sales? What are the principal limitations of these ratios?

17–5. What are contingent liabilities and why might they be important in deciding whether to approve or disapprove a business loan request?

17–6. What is cash-flow analysis and what can it tell us about a business borrower's financial condition and prospects?

17–7. What is a pro forma statement of cash flows and what is its purpose?

17–8. Should a loan officer ever say "no" to a business firm requesting a loan? Please explain when and where.

17–10 Pricing Business Loans

Key URLs
Information on loan pricing techniques and statistics may be found at such sites as the Loan Pricing Corporation at **www.loanpricing.com** and Board of Governors of the Federal Reserve System's statistical releases on market interest rates at **www. federalreserve.gov/ Releases/H15/.**

One of the most difficult tasks in lending is deciding how to *price* a loan.[5] The lender wants to charge a high enough interest rate to ensure that each loan will be profitable and compensate the lending institution fully for the risks involved. However, the loan rate must also be low enough to accommodate the business customer in such a way that he or she can successfully repay the loan and not be driven away to another lender or into the open market for credit. The more competition the lender faces for a customer's loan business, the more it will have to keep the price of that loan in line with interest rates on similar loans available in the financial marketplace. Indeed, in a loan market characterized by intense competition, the lender is a price *taker*, not a price setter. With deregulation of financial services under way in many nations, deregulated competition has narrowed the profit margins many lenders are able to earn, making correct pricing of loans even more imperative today than in the past.

---

[5]This section is based upon Peter S. Rose's article [8], which appeared originally in *The Canadian Banker* and is used by permission of the publisher.

The Cost-Plus Loan Pricing Method

In pricing a business loan, management must consider the cost of raising loanable funds and the operating costs of running the lending institution. The simplest loan-pricing model assumes that the rate of interest charged on any loan includes four components: (1) the cost to the lender of raising adequate funds to lend, (2) the lender's nonfunds operating costs (including wages and salaries of loan personnel and the cost of materials and physical facilities used in granting and administering a loan), (3) necessary compensation paid to the lender for the degree of default risk inherent in a loan request, and (4) the desired profit margin on each loan that provides the lending institution's stockholders with an adequate return on their capital. A scheme of this sort is often called **cost-plus loan pricing.** Thus:

$$\begin{array}{c} \text{Loan} \\ \text{interest} \\ \text{rate} \end{array} = \begin{array}{c} \text{Marginal} \\ \text{cost of raising} \\ \text{loanable funds} \\ \text{to lend to} \\ \text{the borrower} \end{array} + \begin{array}{c} \text{Nonfunds} \\ \text{operating} \\ \text{costs} \end{array} + \begin{array}{c} \text{Estimated} \\ \text{margin to} \\ \text{compensate for} \\ \text{default risk} \end{array} + \begin{array}{c} \text{Desired} \\ \text{profit} \\ \text{margin} \end{array} \quad \textbf{(17–17)}$$

Each of these components can be expressed in annualized percentage terms relative to the amount of the loan.

For example, suppose a lender has a loan request from one of its corporate customers for $5 million (as in the Black Gold case discussed earlier in this chapter). If the lender must sell negotiable CDs in the money market at an interest rate of 5 percent to fund this loan, the marginal cost of loanable funds for this particular loan will be 5 percent. Nonfunds operating costs to analyze, grant, and monitor this loan are estimated at 2 percent of the $5 million request. The credit department may recommend adding 2 percent of the amount requested to compensate for default risk—the possibility that the loan will not be repaid on time. Finally, the lender may desire a 1 percent profit margin over and above the financial, operating, and risk-related costs of this loan. Thus, this loan may be offered to the borrower at an annual rate of 10 percent (= 5 percent + 2 percent + 2 percent + 1 percent).

The Price Leadership Model

One of the drawbacks of the cost-plus loan pricing model is its assumption that a lending institution accurately knows what its costs are. This is often not the case. Lenders today are usually multiproduct businesses that often face great difficulty in trying to properly allocate operating costs among the many different services they offer. Moreover, the cost-plus pricing method implies that a lender can price a loan with little regard for the competition posed by other lenders. For the vast majority of loans today this is simply *not* true. Competition will impact the lender's desired profit margin; in general, the more intense the competition, the thinner the profit margin becomes.

These limitations of the cost-plus approach led to a form of **price leadership** in the banking and financial-services industry, which began among leading money center banks more than 70 years ago. During the Great Depression of the 1930s, major commercial banks established a uniform base lending fee, the **prime rate,** sometimes called the *base* or *reference rate.* The prime rate is usually considered to be the lowest rate charged the most creditworthy customers on short-term loans. The actual loan rate charged any particular customer is determined by the following formula:

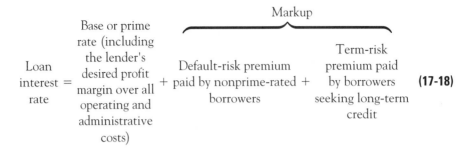

$$\underset{\substack{\text{Loan} \\ \text{interest} \\ \text{rate}}}{} = \underset{\substack{\text{Base or prime} \\ \text{rate (including} \\ \text{the lender's} \\ \text{desired profit} \\ \text{margin over all} \\ \text{operating and} \\ \text{administrative} \\ \text{costs)}}}{} + \overbrace{\underset{\substack{\text{Default-risk premium} \\ \text{paid by nonprime-rated} \\ \text{borrowers}}}{} + \underset{\substack{\text{Term-risk} \\ \text{premium paid} \\ \text{by borrowers} \\ \text{seeking long-term} \\ \text{credit}}}{}}^{\text{Markup}} \qquad \textbf{(17-18)}$$

For example, a medium-sized business asking for a three-year loan to purchase new equipment might be assessed an annual loan rate of 10 percent, consisting of a prime (or base) rate of 6 percent plus 2 percent for default risk and another 2 percent for term risk because of the long-term character of the loan. Longer-term loans are assigned a term-risk premium because lending over a longer period of time exposes the lender to more opportunities for loss than does an otherwise comparable short-term loan. Assignment of risk premiums is one of the most difficult aspects of loan pricing, with a wide variety of different risk-adjustment methods in use. Today computer models often monitor borrowers' adherence to the covenants attached to a loan and automatically adjust the risk premium and loan rate accordingly.

The risk premiums attached to loans are often referred to collectively as the *markup*. Lending institutions can expand or contract their loan portfolios simply by contracting or expanding their loan-rate markups. Many lenders prefer, however, simply to vary their loan rejection rates rather than changing either their base rate or their markups.[6]

In the United States today, the *prevailing prime rate* is considered to be the most common base rate figure announced by the majority of the 25 largest banks that publish their loan rates regularly. Prime rates used by other, generally smaller lending institutions often differ from the prevailing prime. For many years, the prime rate was changed only infrequently, requiring a resolution voted upon by each lending institution's board of directors. However, the advent of inflation and more volatile interest rates gave rise to a *floating prime rate*, tied to changes in such important money market interest rates as the 90-day commercial paper rate and the 90-day CD rate. With floating primes, major corporate borrowers with impeccable credit ratings might be permitted to borrow, for example, at a prime rate one-half a percentage point above the most recent commercial paper rate or the most recent four-week average CD rate.

Two different floating prime rate formulas were soon developed by leading money center banks: (1) the prime-plus method and (2) the times-prime method. For example, a borrowing corporate customer might be quoted a short-term *prime-plus-2* loan rate of 12 percent when the prime rate stands at 10 percent. Alternatively, this customer might be quoted a *1.2 times-prime rate*, that is,

Loan interest rate = 1.2 (prime rate) = 1.2 (10 percent) = 12 percent

[6]Charging high-risk borrowers the full risk premium is not always wise. Indeed, such a policy may increase the chances that a borrower will default on a loan agreement, resulting in the lender's earning a return on such a loan less than earned on prime-quality loans. For example, if an A-rated borrower is charged a prime rate of 6 percent and a high-risk borrower is assessed a loan rate of 12 percent, the second borrower may feel compelled to adopt high-risk business strategies with small chance of success in an attempt to meet such high loan payments. These high-risk business strategies may lead to default, sharply lowering the lender's actual return. This is why many lending institutions use *both* price (loan rate) and credit rationing (i.e., denying some loans regardless of price) to regulate the size and composition of their loan portfolios.

While these two formulas may lead to the same initial loan rate, as in the above example, they can lead to very different loan rates when interest rates change and the borrower has a floating-rate loan.

For example, in a period of *rising* interest rates, the times-prime method causes the customer's loan rate to rise faster than the prime-plus method. If interest rates *fall*, the customer's loan rate declines more rapidly under the times-prime method. For example, if the prime rate rises from 10 percent to 15 percent, the customer's loan rate in our example increases from 12 percent to 17 percent with the prime-plus method and from 12 percent to 18 percent with the times-prime method. However, if prime drops from 10 percent to 8 percent, the prime-plus method yields a 10 percent loan rate, while the times-prime approach yields only 9.6 percent.[7]

During the 1970s, the supremacy of the prime rate as a base for business loans was challenged by **LIBOR**—the London Interbank Offered Rate—on short-term Eurocurrency deposits, which range in maturity from a few days to a few months. As time has passed, more and more leading commercial lenders have switched to LIBOR-based loan pricing due to the growing use of Eurocurrencies as a source of loanable funds. A second cause was the spreading internationalization of the financial system, with foreign banks entering many domestic loan markets, including Canada and the United States. LIBOR offered a common pricing standard for all banks, both foreign and domestic, and gave customers a common basis for comparing the terms on loans offered by different lenders.

As an example of LIBOR-based pricing, we note that in 2006 leading international banks in London were quoting a three-month average LIBOR on Eurodollar deposits of 4.50 percent. Therefore, a large corporation borrowing short-term money for, say, 90 days might be quoted an interest rate on a multimillion dollar loan of

$$\begin{array}{l} \text{LIBOR-based} \\ \text{loan rate} \end{array} = \text{LIBOR} + \text{Default-risk premium} + \text{Profit margin}$$

(17-19)

$$= 4.50\% + 0.125\% + 0.125\% = 4.75\%$$

For longer-term loans stretching over several months or years the lender might add a term-risk premium to the above formula to compensate for the added risk of a longer-term commitment to its business customer.

Below-Prime Market Pricing

Further modifications to the prime or LIBOR-based loan pricing systems were made in the 1980s and 1990s when **below-prime pricing** became important. Many banks announced that some large corporate loans covering only a few days or weeks would be made at low money market interest rates (such as the Federal funds rate on domestic interbank loans) plus a small margin (perhaps one-eighth to one-quarter of a percentage point) to cover risk exposure and provide a profit margin.

Thus, if we can borrow Federal funds in today's market for 2.50 percent and a top-quality business customer requests a 30-day $10 million credit line, we may choose to make the loan at 2.75 percent (or 2.50 percent to cover the money market cost of borrowing + 0.25 percent markup for risk and profitability). The result is a short-term loan rate *below* the posted prime rate, diminishing the importance of prime as a reference point for business loans.

---

[7]Recent research by Dueker [6] and others suggests that the prime rate may be *asymmetric*—lenders tend to raise prime more readily than they lower prime. Thus, borrowers heavily dependent on banks for funds tend to pay higher loan rates than do borrowers that can tap the open market for funds. Bank-dependent borrowers, therefore, tend to be more vulnerable to business cycles.

Real Banks, Real Decisions

BANK LOAN TERMS FOR BUSINESS BORROWERS—WHAT FEDERAL RESERVE SURVEYS TELL US

The Federal Reserve System collects information on business loans granted by U.S. commercial banks and U.S. branches and agencies of foreign banks each quarter of the year. Recent surveys suggest that most business loans tend to have these characteristics:

1. Short maturities (under one year) rather than long maturities.
2. The more numerous short-term loans average about 30 days to maturity, with long-term (over-one-year) business loans approaching an average of about 50 months to maturity.
3. Fixed interest rates for shorter loans and floating interest rates for longer loans due to the latter's increased interest rate risk exposure.
4. Loan rates tied most often to the Federal funds interest rate, foreign money market rates (such as LIBOR), the prime rate, or other base rates.
5. Higher loan rates attached to longer maturity loans in order to compensate lenders for added term risk.
6. Higher loan rates on smaller denomination business loans (especially for loans under $1 million).
7. Loans carrying longer maturities or smaller denominations are more likely to be secured by collateral.

Recent research suggests that older firms, the longer the borrower–lender relationship, and the purchase of additional services from the same lender tend to result in lower loan rates or reduced chances of loan denial. Audited firms appear to pay somewhat lower loan rates than unaudited firms and business borrowers that successfully complete loan transactions often get lower loan rates on subsequent borrowings and usually get monitored less frequently.

Key URL
To learn about the Federal Reserve's quarterly survey of business lending, see **www.federalreserve.gov/releases/e2/**.

However, the prime rate continues to be important as a pricing method for smaller business loans, consumer credit, and construction loans. Thus, a two-tiered business loan market has emerged. Loans to small and medium-size businesses are often based on prime or some other widely recognized base rate, while large-denomination business loans increasingly are based on national and international (such as LIBOR) money market interest costs at the time the loan is made. The narrow margins (markups) on such loans have spurred wider use of loan participations, with banks more actively sharing their biggest loans, generating fee income, and moving at least a portion of these credits to lenders with lower funding costs.

Customer Profitability Analysis (CPA)

As lenders developed more comprehensive information systems to track their costs, a new loan pricing technique known as **customer profitability analysis** (CPA) appeared. CPA is similar to the cost-plus pricing technique discussed earlier, but comes at the pricing problem from a different direction. It begins with the assumption that the lender should take the *whole customer relationship*—all revenues and expenses associated with a particular customer—into account when pricing a loan. CPA rests on the following formula:

$$\text{Net before-tax rate of return to the lender from the whole customer relationship} = \frac{\begin{array}{c}\text{Revenue from} \\ \text{loans and other} \\ \text{services provided} \\ \text{to this customer}\end{array} - \begin{array}{c}\text{Expenses from} \\ \text{providing loans} \\ \text{and other services} \\ \text{to this customer}\end{array}}{\begin{array}{c}\text{Net loanable funds used in excess of this} \\ \text{customer's deposits}\end{array}} \quad \textbf{(17–20)}$$

Factoid
Which U.S. domestic interest rate is most commonly used to price business loans (measured by the dollar volume of business loans granted)?
Answer: The prime rate, followed by the Federal funds rate, according to recent Federal Reserve loan surveys.

Revenues paid by a borrowing customer may include loan interest, commitment fees, fees for cash management services, and data processing charges. *Expenses* incurred on behalf of the customer may include wages and salaries of the lender's employees, credit investigation costs, interest accrued on deposits, account reconciliation and processing costs and funds' acquisition costs. *Net loanable funds* are the amount of credit used by the customer minus his or her average collected deposits (adjusted for required legal reserves).

If the calculated net rate of return from the entire relationship with the customer is *positive*, the loan request will probably be approved, because the lender will be earning a premium over *all* expenses incurred (including a competitive rate of return to its shareholders). If the calculated net return is *negative*, the loan request may be denied or the lender may seek to raise the loan rate or increase the prices of other services requested by the customer in order to continue the relationship on a profitable basis. Customers perceived to be more risky are expected to return to the lender a higher calculated net rate of return. Customer profitability analysis (CPA) applied to the loan request of Black Gold, Inc., considered earlier, can be illustrated in the following example.

An Example of Annualized Customer Profitability Analysis

Problem A bank is considering granting a $1.5 million line of credit for six months to Black Gold, Inc., an energy company. Assuming Black Gold uses the full line and keeps a deposit equal to 20 percent of the credit line with the bank, the following revenues and expenses should result from dealing with this customer:

Sources of Revenue Expected to Be Supplied by This Customer	
Interest income from loan (12%, six months)	$ 90,000
Loan commitment fees (1%)	15,000
Fee for managing customer's deposits	45,000
Funds transfer charges	5,000
Fees for trust services and recordkeeping	61,000
Total annualized revenues expected	$ 216,000
Costs Expected to Be Incurred in Serving This Customer	
Deposit interest owed to the customer (10%)	$ 15,000
Cost of funds raised to lend this customer	80,000
Activity costs for this customer's accounts	25,000
Cost of funds transfers for this customer	1,000
Cost of processing the loan	3,000
Recordkeeping costs	1,000
Total annualized expenses	$ 125,000
Net Amount of the Bank's Reserves Expected to Be Drawn upon by This Customer This Year	
Average amount of credit committed to customer	$1,500,000
Less: Average customer deposit balances (net of required reserves)	−270,000
Net amount of loanable reserves committed to customer	$1,230,000

$$\begin{matrix} \text{Before–tax rate} \\ \text{of return over costs} \\ \text{from the entire} \\ \text{lender–customer} \\ \text{relationship} \end{matrix} = \frac{\text{Revenue expected} - \text{Cost expected}}{\text{Net amount of loanable funds supplied}}$$

(17–21)

$$= \frac{(\$216{,}000 - \$125{,}000)}{\$1{,}230{,}000} = 0.074 \text{ or } 7.4\%$$

Interpretation If the net rate of return from the entire lender–customer relationship is *positive*, the proposed loan is *acceptable* because all expenses have been met. If the calculated net rate of return is negative, however, the proposed loan and other services provided to the customer are not correctly priced as far as the lender is concerned. The greater the perceived risk of the loan, the higher the net rate of return the lender should require.

Earnings Credit for Customer Deposits

In calculating how much in revenues a customer generates for a lending institution, many lenders give the customer credit for any earnings received from investing the balance in the customer's deposit account in earning assets. Of course, it would be unwise to include the full amount of the customer's deposit in calculating any earnings from investing deposit money because a depository institution has to post legal reserve requirements, and a portion of the customer's deposit balance may consist of float (i.e., uncollected funds not yet available for use). Most depository institutions calculate the actual amount of *net investable funds* provided by a customer's deposit and the earnings credit for a customer using some version of the following formulas:

$$
\begin{array}{l}
\text{Net} \\
\text{investable} \\
\text{(usable)} \\
\text{funds for} \\
\text{the lender}
\end{array}
=
\begin{array}{l}
\text{Customer's} \\
\text{average} \\
\text{deposit} \\
\text{balance}
\end{array}
-
\begin{array}{l}
\text{Average} \\
\text{amount} \\
\text{of float} \\
\text{in the} \\
\text{account}
\end{array}
-
\left(
\begin{array}{l}
\text{Required} \\
\text{legal} \\
\text{reserves} \\
\text{behind} \\
\text{the deposit}
\end{array}
\times
\begin{array}{l}
\text{Net} \\
\text{amount of} \\
\text{collected} \\
\text{funds in the} \\
\text{account}
\end{array}
\right)
\quad \textbf{(17–22)}
$$

$$
\begin{array}{l}
\text{Amount of} \\
\text{earnings credited} \\
\text{to the customer}
\end{array}
=
\begin{array}{l}
\text{Annual} \\
\text{earnings} \\
\text{rate}
\end{array}
\times
\begin{array}{l}
\text{Fraction of the year} \\
\text{funds are available} \\
\text{from the deposit}
\end{array}
\times
\begin{array}{l}
\text{Net investable} \\
\text{(usable) funds}
\end{array}
\quad \textbf{(17–23)}
$$

For example, suppose a commercial customer posts an average deposit balance this month of $1,125,000. Float from uncollected funds accounts for $125,000 of this balance, yielding net collected funds of $1 million. If this is a checking account at a large bank, for example, the applicable legal reserve requirement will be 10 percent. After negotiation with the customer, the bank has decided to give this customer credit for an annual interest return from use of the customer's deposit equal to the average 91-day Treasury bill rate (assumed here to be 6.60 percent). In this instance, the customer's net usable (investable) funds and earnings credit will be:

$$
\begin{array}{l}
\text{Net investable} \\
\text{(usable) funds} \\
\text{for the bank}
\end{array}
= \$1{,}125{,}000 - \$125{,}000 - (.10 \times \$1{,}000{,}000) = \$900{,}000
$$

$$
\begin{array}{l}
\text{Amount of earnings} \\
\text{credit to this customer}
\end{array}
= 6.60 \text{ percent} \times \frac{1}{12} \times \$900{,}000 = \$4{,}950
$$

Therefore, in constructing a summary of revenues and expenses from all the lender's dealings with this customer, the lender would give the customer credit on the revenue side for $4,950 earned last month from investing the customer's deposits in earning assets.

The Future of Customer Profitability Analysis

Customer profitability analysis has become increasingly sophisticated. Detailed accounting statements showing sources of revenue and expenses from servicing each major customer have been developed. Often the borrowing company itself, its subsidiary firms, major stockholders, and top management are all consolidated into one profitability analysis statement so that the lender receives a comprehensive picture of the *total* customer relationship. The consolidation approach can determine if losses suffered from servicing one account are, in fact, made up by another account that is part of the same overall customer relationship. Automated CPA systems permit lenders to plug in alternative loan and deposit pricing schedules to see which pricing schedule works best for both customer and lending institution. CPA can also be used to identify the most profitable types of customers and loans and the most successful loan officers.

Concept Check

17–9.   What methods are used to price business loans?

17–10. Suppose a bank estimates that the marginal cost of raising loanable funds to make a $10 million loan to one of its corporate customers is 4 percent, its nonfunds operating costs to evaluate and offer this loan are 0.5 percent, the default-risk premium on the loan is 0.375 percent, a term-risk premium of 0.625 percent is to be added, and the

desired profit margin is 0.25 percent. What loan rate should be quoted this borrower? How much interest will the borrower pay in a year?

17–11. What are the principal strengths and weaknesses of the different loan-pricing methods in use today?

17–12. What is *customer profitability analysis?* What are its advantages for the borrowing customer and the lender?

Summary

In this chapter we have explored the many types of loans extended to businesses today. The key points in this chapter include the following:

- Business loans are often divided into *short-term* (under one year) and *long-term* (more than a year to maturity). A similar, but sometimes more meaningful classification divides these credits into *working capital loans*—short-term credits aimed principally at funding purchases of business inventories, meeting payrolls, paying taxes, and covering other temporary expenses—and *term loans*—typically employed to fund permanent additions to working capital or to purchase plant and equipment.

- There are numerous varieties of working capital and term loans, including *seasonal open credit lines* to deal with fluctuating demand for products and services during the year; *dealer financing* to cover the acquisition of appliances, equipment, and vehicles subsequently sold to customers; *asset-based loans*, which are backed by specific real and financial assets; *revolving credit*, which allows borrowings, paydowns, and reborrowings continually until the revolver's term expires; and *project loans* to construct new facilities.

- The evaluation of each business loan application usually involves *loan officers*, who contact and negotiate with the customer; *credit analysts*, who evaluate the customer's financial strengths and weaknesses; and a *loan committee* or *loan administrator*, who must ultimately approve or deny the requested loan.

- Among the more important credit evaluation techniques used today are (1) *composition analysis of borrower financial statements* (including the use of common-size balance sheets and income statements); (2) *financial ratio analysis* (including ratio measures of expense control, efficiency, coverage, profitability, liquidity, and leverage); and (3) actual and pro forma *statements of cash flows*.

- Several different methods for pricing business loans have appeared over the years, including *cost-plus* loan pricing, *price leadership* loan pricing, *below-prime loan pricing*, and *customer profitability analysis*. Many business loans today are priced directly off money market interest rates (such as LIBOR or the prevailing federal funds rate), with narrow profit margins reflecting intense competition.

- There is a growing trend toward pricing business credit based on the *total relationship* between lender and borrower (including all the services the customer purchases from the lender and the costs of all services provided) rather than pricing each requested loan independent of other services the customer uses.

Key Terms

self-liquidating loans, *544*
working capital loans, *545*
compensating deposit
balances, *545*
interim construction
loan, *545*
asset-based loans, *547*
factoring, *547*
syndicated loan, *547*

term loans, *548*
revolving credit line, *548*
project loans, *550*
LBOs, *550*
working capital, *557*
contingent liabilities, *561*
Statement of Cash
Flows, *562*

cost-plus loan pricing, *569*
price leadership, *569*
prime rate, *569*
LIBOR, *571*
below-prime pricing, *571*
customer profitability
analysis, *572*

Problems and Projects

1. From the descriptions below please identify what *type* of business loan is involved.

   a. A temporary credit supports construction of homes, apartments, office buildings, and other permanent structures.

   b. A loan is made to an automobile dealer to support the shipment of new cars.

   c. Credit extended on the basis of a business's accounts receivable.

   d. The term of an inventory loan is being set to match the length of time needed to generate cash to repay the loan.

   e. Credit extended up to one year to purchase raw materials and cover a seasonal need for cash.

   f. A security dealer requires credit to add new government bonds to his security portfolio.

   g. Credit granted for more than a year to support purchases of plant and equipment.

   h. A group of investors wishes to take over a firm using mainly debt financing.

   i. A business firm receives a three-year line of credit against which it can borrow, repay, and borrow again if necessary during the loan's term.

   j. Credit extended to support the construction of a toll road.

2. As a new credit trainee for Evergreen National Bank, you have been asked to evaluate the financial position of Hamilton Steel Castings, which has asked for renewal of and an increase in its six-month credit line. Hamilton now requests a $7 million credit line, and you must draft your first credit opinion for a senior credit analyst. Unfortunately, Hamilton just changed management, and its financial report for the last six months was not only late but also garbled. As best as you can tell, its sales, assets, operating expenses, and liabilities for the six-month period just concluded display the following patterns:

Millions of Dollars	January	February	March	April	May	June
Net sales	$48.1	$47.3	$45.2	$43.0	$43.9	$39.7
Cost of goods sold	27.8	28.1	27.4	26.9	27.3	26.6
Selling, administrative, and other expenses	19.2	18.9	17.6	16.5	16.7	15.3
Depreciation	3.1	3.0	3.0	2.9	3.0	2.8
Interest cost on borrowed funds	2.0	2.2	2.3	2.3	2.5	2.7
Expected tax obligation	1.3	1.0	0.7	0.9	0.7	0.4
Total assets	24.5	24.3	23.8	23.7	23.2	22.9
Current assets	6.4	6.1	5.5	5.4	5.0	4.8
Net fixed assets	17.2	17.4	17.5	17.6	18.0	18.0
Current liabilities	4.7	5.2	5.6	5.9	5.8	6.4
Total liabilities	15.9	16.1	16.4	16.5	17.1	17.2

Hamilton has a 16-year relationship with the bank and has routinely received and paid off a credit line of $4 to $5 million. The department's senior analyst tells you to prepare because you will be asked for your opinion of this loan request (though you have been led to believe the loan will be approved anyway, because Hamilton's president serves on Evergreen's board of directors).

What will you recommend if asked? Is there any reason to question the latest data supplied by this customer? If this loan request is granted, what do you think the customer will do with the funds?

3. From the data given in the following table, please construct as many of the financial ratios discussed in this chapter as you can and then indicate what dimension of a business firm's performance each ratio represents.

Business Assets		Annual Revenue and Expense Items	
Cash account	$ 10	Net sales	$680
Accounts receivable	95	Cost of goods sold	520
Inventories	108	Wages and salaries	61
Fixed assets	301	Interest expense	18
Miscellaneous assets	96	Overhead expenses	29
	610	Depreciation expenses	15
Liabilities and Equity		Selling, administrative, and other expenses	30
Short-term debt:		Before-tax net income	7
Accounts payable	83	Taxes owed	2
Notes payable	107*	After-tax net income	5
Long-term debt (bonds)	325*		
Miscellaneous liabilities	15		
Equity capital	80		

*Annual principal payments on bonds and notes payable total $55. The firm's marginal tax rate is 35 percent.

4. Conway Corporation has placed a term loan request with its lender and submitted the following balance sheet entries for the year just concluded and the *pro forma* balance sheet expected by the end of the current year. Construct a *pro forma* Statement of Cash Flows for the current year using the consecutive balance sheets and some additional needed information. The forecast net income for the current year is $217 million

with $65 million being paid out in dividends. The depreciation expense for the year will be $100 million and planned expansions will require the acquisition of $300 million in fixed assets at the end of the current year. As you examine the *pro forma* Statement of Cash Flows, do you detect any changes that might be of concern either to the lender's credit analyst, loan officer, or both?

Conway Corporation
(all amounts in millions of dollars)

	Assets at the End of the Most Recent Year	Assets Projected for the End of the Current Year		Liabilities and Equity at the End of the Most Recent Year	Liabilities and Equity Projected for the End of the Current Year
Cash	$ 532	$ 460	Accounts payable	$ 970	$1,023
Accounts receivable	1,018	1,210	Notes payable	2,733	2,950
Inventories	894	973	Taxes payable	327	216
Net fixed assets	2,740	2,898	Long-term debt obligations	872	931
Other assets	66	87	Common stock	85	85
			Undivided profits	263	373
Total assets	$5,250	$5,628	Total liabilities and equity capital	$5,250	$5,628

5. Morbet Corporation is a new business client for First Commerce National Bank and has asked for a one-year, $10 million loan at an annual interest rate of 7 percent. The company plans to keep a 5 percent, $2 million CD with the bank for the loan's duration. The loan officer in charge of the case recommends at least an 8 percent annual before-tax rate of return over all costs. Using customer profitability analysis (CPA) the loan committee hopes to estimate the following revenues and expenses which it will project using the amount of the loan requested as a base for the calculations:

Estimated Revenues:	**Estimated Expenses:**
Interest income from loan ?	Interest to be paid on customer's $2 million deposit ?
Loan commitment fee (1%) ?	Expected cost of additional funds needed to support the loan (3%) ?
Cash management fees (3%) ?	Labor costs and other operating expenses associated with monitoring the customer's loan (2%) ?
Trust services fees (2%) ?	Cost of processing the loan (1.5%) ?

a. Should this loan be approved on the basis of the suggested terms?

b. What adjustments could be made to improve this loan's projected return?

c. How might competition from other prospective lenders impact the adjustments you have recommended?

6. As a loan officer for Starship National Bank, you have been responsible for the bank's relationship with USF Corporation, a major producer of remote-control devices for activating television sets, DVDs, and other audio-video equipment. USF has just filed a request for renewal of its $10 million line of credit, which will cover approximately

10 1/2 months. USF also regularly uses several other services sold by the bank. Applying customer profitability analysis (CPA) and using the most recent year as a guide, you estimate that the expected revenues from this commercial loan customer and the expected costs of serving this customer will consist of the following:

Expected Revenues		Expected Costs	
Annual interest income from the requested loan (assuming a loan rate of prime + 1 percent, or 7% this month)	$700,000	Interest paid on customer deposits (5%)	$106,250
		Cost of other funds raised	475,000
		Account activity costs	19,000
Loan commitment fee (1%)	100,000	Wire transfer costs	1,300
Deposit management fees	4,500	Loan processing costs	12,400
Wire transfer fees	3,500	Recordkeeping costs	4,500
Fees for agency services	8,800		

The bank's credit analysts have estimated the customer probably will keep an average deposit balance of $2,125,000 for the year the line is active. What is the expected net rate of return from this proposed loan renewal if the customer actually draws down the full amount of the requested line? What decision should the bank make under the foregoing assumptions? If you decide to turn down this request, under what assumptions regarding revenues, expenses, and customer deposit balances would you be willing to make this loan?

7. In order to help fund a loan request of $10 million for one year from one of its best customers, Lone Star Bank sold negotiable CDs to its business customers in the amount of $6 million at a promised annual yield of 5.75 percent and borrowed $4 million in the Federal funds market from other banks at today's prevailing interest rate of 5.40 percent.

   Credit investigation and recordkeeping costs to process this loan application were an estimated $25,000. The Credit Analysis Division recommends a minimal 1 percent risk premium on this loan and a minimal profit margin of one-fourth of a percentage point. The bank prefers using cost-plus loan pricing in these cases. What loan rate should it charge?

8. Many loans to corporations are quoted today at small risk premiums and profit margins over the London Interbank Offered Rate (LIBOR). Englewood Bank has a $25 million loan request for working capital to fund accounts receivable and inventory from one of its largest customers, APEX Exports. The bank offers its customer a floating-rate loan for 90 days with an interest rate equal to LIBOR on 30-day Eurodeposits (currently trading at a rate of 4 percent) plus a one-quarter percentage point markup over LIBOR. APEX, however, wants the loan at a rate of 1.014 times LIBOR. If the bank agrees to this loan request, what interest rate will attach to the loan if it is made today? How does this compare with the loan rate the bank wanted to charge? What does this customer's request reveal about the borrowing firm's interest rate forecast for the next 90 days?

9. Five weeks ago, RJK Corporation borrowed from the commercial finance company that employs you as a loan officer. At that time, the decision was made (at your personal urging) to base the loan rate on below-prime market pricing, using the average weekly Federal funds interest rate as the money market borrowing cost. The loan was quoted to RJK at the Federal funds rate plus a three-eighths percentage point markup for risk and profit.

Today, this five-week loan is due, and RJK is asking for renewal at money market borrowing cost plus one-fourth of a point. You must assess whether the finance company did as well on this account using the Federal funds rate as the index of borrowing cost as it would have done by quoting RJK the prevailing CD rate, the commercial paper rate, the Eurodollar deposit rate, or possibly the prevailing rate on U.S. Treasury bills plus a small margin for risk and profitability. To assess what would have happened (and might happen over the next five weeks if the loan is renewed at a small margin over any of the money market rates listed above), you have assembled these data from a recent issue of the *Statistical Supplement to the Federal Reserve Bulletin*:

Weekly Averages of Money Market Rates over the Most Recent 5 Weeks					
Money Market Interest Rates	**Week 1**	**Week 2**	**Week 3**	**Week 4**	**Week 5**
Federal funds	3.72%	3.80%	3.69%	3.46%	3.46%
Commercial paper (one-month maturity)	3.55	3.63	3.53	3.43	3.40
CDs (one-month maturity)	3.54	3.58	3.50	3.40	3.35
Eurodollar deposits (three-month maturity)	3.58	3.56	3.60	3.43	3.38
U.S. Treasury bills (three-month, secondary market)	3.60	3.77	3.74	3.67	3.60

What conclusion do you draw from studying the behavior of these common money market base rates for business loans? Should the RJK loan be renewed as requested, or should the lender press for a different loan pricing arrangement? Please explain your reasoning. If you conclude that a change is needed, how would you explain the necessity for this change to the customer?

10. EFG Corporation has posted an average deposit balance this past month of $270,500. Float included in this one-month average balance has been estimated at $73,250. Required legal reserves are 3 percent of net collected funds. What is the amount of net investable (usable) funds available to the bank holding the deposit?

Suppose EFG's bank agrees to give the firm credit for an annual interest return of 3.75 percent on the net investable funds the company provides the bank. Measured in total dollars, how much of an earnings credit from the bank will EFG earn?

Internet Exercises

1. If you are a business lender and your assignment has recently been changed from making large corporate loans to small business lending—an area where you have almost no experience—you will want to become familiar with the Small Business Administration at **www.sba.gov/financing**. There you will find information about SBA loan programs. What is the Basic 7(a) Loan Program? How does this program benefit the lender?

2. As a small business lender, you have a customer that is an exporter and needs working capital on a short-term basis. Are there special loan programs available through the SBA that would be useful? See **www.sba.gov/financing**. What are the qualifications associated with the applicable loan program?

3. What is *factoring?* Visit **www.cfa.com** and click on the button, "What is asset based lending?" What types of factoring are described at this link? Describe three types of factoring arrangements.

4. Business lenders are made, not born. Visit **www.rmahq.org**. Click on the "About RMA" button. What is the objective of RMA (see FAQs)? Describe its eMentor product.

REAL NUMBERS FOR REAL BANKS

Assignment for Chapter 17

YOUR BANK'S OFFERINGS OF C&I LOANS TO SMALL AND LARGE FIRMS

In this assignment, we will be visiting your bank's Web site and exploring the types of loans offered to small businesses and large corporations. Terminology is not always consistent; hence, the descriptions become important in understanding a bank's offerings. Don't be intimidated when you encounter terms that are not familiar.

Part One: Small Business Loans

A. Visit your banking company's Web site. If you do not know the URL, use a search engine such as **www.google.com** or **www.alltheweb.com** to locate the Web site. Once you arrive at the site, look for small business services, lending in particular. Read everything you can about the instruments the bank offers the small business borrower, keeping in mind the basic types of C&I loans described in this chapter.

B. What types of short-term credit does the lender offer the small business customer? What types of long-term products are available?

C. Write approximately one page describing the loan products for the small business customer and assess the Web site's effectiveness in providing this information.

Part Two: Corporate Loans

A. Return to the home page for your banking company and look for corporate services. At this point, you are interested in instruments that will show up as C&I loans on your bank's balance sheet and that represent financing for the corporate customer. Read everything you can about the instruments offered to the large business borrower, once again keeping in mind the basic types of C&I loans described in this chapter. Web sites typically provide lots of information for corporate borrowers and often mix in other services with loan products. (Remember, fee-generating services are not the focus of this assignment.)

B. What types of short-term credit does the institution offer the corporate customer? What types of long-term products are available? Do you see any syndicated loans?

C. Write approximately one page describing the loan products for the large business customer and assess the Web site's effectiveness in providing this information.

5. What market interest rates are most widely used as base rates to price commercial loans? Go to **www.federalreserve.gov/releases/** and look at weekly releases of selected interest rates. What was the one-month Eurodollar deposit (London) rate for the latest week reported in this data source? What was the latest prime rate reported?

6. If you wanted to know more about the details of business loans, you might visit **www.loanpricing.com**. Go there and click on the link for the most recent U.S. lead arranger league tables. Who were the top three arrangers by volume? What were the volumes? Who were the top three arrangers by number of deals? How many deals did they do?

S&P Market Insight Challenge (www.mhhe.com/edumarketinsight)

STANDARD &POOR'S

1. In the S&P industry survey devoted to *banking*, loan quality is graphically portrayed using such account items as nonperforming assets, loss reserves, provision for loan losses, and net charge-offs. For an up-to-date graphic, click on the Industry tab in S&P's Market Insight, Educational Version. The drop-down menu you encounter supplies the subindustry groups labeled Diversified/Regional Banks. Upon selecting one of these subindustries you will uncover a recent S&P industry survey on banking, which you should download to examine the section, "Industry Trends." Print out the graphic illustration of loan quality that you find and describe and interpret recent loan-quality trends.

STANDARD &POOR'S

2. The biggest loan category, measured in dollars, for most money-center banks today is usually commercial and industrial (business) loans. Examining some of the leading banks for which Standard & Poor's Market Insight, Educational Version, provides data, reports, and stories, see if you can determine what major kinds of business loans these

banks typically grant. Do the banks differ in the make-up of the business loans they usually extend? Why is this so? Are the Insight banks active small business lenders? How do you know?

Selected References

For an exploration of recent trends in business lending, see especially:

1. Bassett, William F., and Egon Zakrajsek. "Recent Developments in Business Lending by Commercial Banks." *Federal Reserve Bulletin*, December 2003, pp. 477–492.
2. Carlson, John B., and Erkin Y. Sahinoz. "Measures of Corporate Earnings: What Number Is Best?" *Economic Commentary*, Federal Reserve Bank of Cleveland, February 1, 2003.
3. Craig, Ben R., William E. Jackson III, and James B. Thomson. "Are SBA Loan Guarantees Desirable?" *Economic Commentary*, Federal Reserve Bank of Cleveland, September 5, 2004, pp. 1–4.
4. Siems, Thomas F. "Supply Chain Management: The Science of Better, Faster, Cheaper." *Southwest Economy*, Federal Reserve Bank of Dallas, no. 2, March/April 2005, pp. 1, 7–12.

To discover more about the field of small business lending, see:

5. Samolyk, H. "Small Business Credit Markets: Why Do We Know So Little about Them?" *FDIC Banking Review* X, no. 2 (1997), pp. 14–32.

To learn more about business loan pricing techniques, please see:

6. Dueker, Michael J. "Are Prime Rate Changes Asymmetric?" *Review*, Federal Reserve Bank of St. Louis, September/October 2000, pp. 33–40.
7. Knight, Robert E. "Customer Profitability Analysis—Part I: Alternative Approaches toward Customer Profitability." *Monthly Review*, Federal Reserve Bank of Kansas City, April 1975, pp. 11–20.
8. Rose, Peter S. "Loan Pricing in a Volatile Economy." *The Canadian Banker* 92, no. 5 (October 1985), pp. 44–49.

For a discussion about assigning ratings for and evaluating business credit risk, see:

9. Gilbert, R. Alton. "Exposure of U.S. Banks to Problem Syndicated Loans." *Monetary Trends*, Federal Reserve Bank of St. Louis, December 2002.
10. Treacy, William F., and Mark S. Carey. "Credit Risk Rating at Large U.S. Banks." *Federal Reserve Bulletin*, November 1998, pp. 897–921.

To explore the factors businesses consider in choosing desired loan maturities, see:

11. Berlin, Mitchell. "Debt Maturity: What Do Economists say? What Do CFOs Say?" *Business Review*, Federal Reserve Bank of Philadelphia, First Quarter 2006, pp. 3–10.

www.mhhe.com/rose7e

Consumer Loans, Credit Cards, and Real Estate Lending

Key Topics in This Chapter

- Types of Loans for Individuals and Families
- Unique Characteristics of Consumer Loans
- Evaluating a Consumer Loan Request
- Credit Cards and Credit Scoring
- Disclosure Rules and Discrimination
- Loan Pricing and Refinancing

18–1 Introduction

Statesman, philosopher, and scientist Benjamin Franklin once observed: "If you would know the value of money go and try to borrow some." Over the past couple of generations millions upon millions of consumers (individuals and families) have tried to do just that—borrow money—in order to supplement their income and enhance their lifestyle. Apparently many have succeeded. Consumer debt is one of the fastest growing forms of borrowing money around the globe, reaching more than $10 trillion in volume in the United States alone as the 21st century began to unfold.

Just as consumer borrowing has become a key driving force in the financial marketplace today, so have banks choosing to make these loans. Bankers have emerged in recent decades to become dominant providers of credit to individuals and families, aggressively advertising their services through "money shops," "money stores," and other enticing sales vehicles. Of course, things didn't start out that way—for most of their history banks largely ignored household borrowers, allowing credit unions, savings associations, and finance companies to move in and capture this important marketplace, while banks concentrated on their business customers.

In part, the modern dominance of banks in lending to households stems from their growing reliance on individuals and families for their chief source of funds—checkable and savings deposits. Many households today would be hesitant to deposit their money in a bank unless they believed there was a good chance they would also be able to borrow from that same institution when they needed a loan. Then, too, recent research suggests that consumer credit is often among the most profitable services a bank can offer.

However, services directed at consumers can also be among the most costly and risky financial products that a financial firm sells because the financial condition of individuals and families can change quickly due to illness, loss of employment, or other family tragedies. Lending to households, therefore, must be managed with care and sensitivity to the special challenges they represent. Moreover, profit margins on many consumer loans have narrowed appreciably as leading finance companies like Household Finance and GMAC, key savings associations like Washington Mutual, and thousands of aggressive credit unions have grown to seriously challenge the dominance of banks in this field.

In this chapter we examine the types of consumer and real-estate-centered loans lenders typically make and see how they evaluate household loan customers. We also explore the broad dimensions of the enormously significant credit card market, which accounts for a major share of consumer loans today. In addition, the chapter examines the powerful role of regulation in the consumer financial-services field as federal and state governments have become major players in setting the rules that govern this important market. Finally, we examine the pricing of consumer and real estate loans in a financial-services marketplace where the battle for household borrowers has become intense and many institutional casualties are strewn along the way.

18–2 Types of Loans Granted to Individuals and Families

Several different types of consumer loans are available, and the number of credit plans to accommodate consumers' financial needs is growing in the wake of deregulation of financial institutions in the United States and in many other industrialized countries. We can classify consumer loans by *purpose*—what the borrowed funds will be used for—or by *type*—for example, whether the borrower must repay in installments or repay in one lump sum when the loan comes due. One popular classification scheme for consumer loans combines both loan types and loan purposes.

For example, loans to individuals and families may be divided into two groups, depending upon whether they finance the purchase of new homes with a *residential loan* (such as a home mortgage or home equity loan) or whether they finance other, nonhousing consumer activities through *nonresidential loans*. Within the nonresidential category, consumer loans are often divided into subcategories based on type of loan—*installment* loans (such as auto or education loans); *noninstallment* loans (such as a cash advance); and *revolving credit* loans (including the familiar credit-card loan). We will look at the nature of these consumer loan types more closely in subsequent sections of this chapter.

Residential Loans

Credit to finance the purchase of a home or to fund improvements on a private residence comes under the label of **residential mortgage loans.** The purchase of residential property in the form of houses and multifamily dwellings (including duplexes and apartment buildings) usually gives rise to a long-term loan, typically bearing a term of 15 to 30 years and secured by the property itself. Such loans may carry either a fixed interest rate or a variable (floating) interest rate that changes periodically with a specified base rate (such as the market yield on 10-year U.S. government bonds) or a national mortgage interest rate (for example, the Federal Home Loan Bank Board's average home mortgage yield). A commitment fee, typically 1 to 2 percent of the face amount of the loan, is routinely charged up front to assure the borrower that a residential loan will be available for a stipulated period. Although banks are the leading residential mortgage lenders today, several other important lenders in this market include savings associations, credit unions, finance companies, and insurance companies as well as the mortgage banking subsidiaries of financial holding companies.

Nonresidential Loans

In contrast to residential mortgage loans, nonresidential loans to individuals and families include installment loans and noninstallment (or single-payment) loans and a hybrid form of credit extended through credit cards (usually called revolving credit).

Installment Loans

Short-term to medium-term loans, repayable in two or more consecutive payments (usually monthly or quarterly), are known as **installment loans.** Such loans are frequently employed to buy big-ticket items (e.g., automobiles, recreational vehicles, furniture, and home appliances) or to consolidate existing household debts.

Noninstallment Loans

Short-term loans individuals and families draw upon for immediate cash needs that are repayable in a lump sum are known as *noninstallment loans*. Such loans may be for relatively small amounts—for example, $500 or $1,000—and include charge accounts that often require payment in 30 days or some other relatively short time period. Noninstallment loans may also be made for a short period (usually six months or less) to wealthier individuals and can be quite large, often ranging from $5,000 to $50,000 or more. Noninstallment credit is frequently used to cover the cost of vacations, medical care, the purchase of home appliances, and auto and home repairs.

Credit Card Loans and Revolving Credit

One of the most popular forms of consumer credit today is accessed via credit cards issued by VISA, MasterCard, Discover, and many smaller credit card companies. Credit cards offer their holders access to either installment or noninstallment credit because the customer can charge a purchase on the account represented by the card and pay off the charge in one billing period, escaping any finance charge, or choose to pay off the purchase price gradually, incurring a monthly finance charge based on an annual interest rate usually ranging from about 10 percent to 24 percent and sometimes more. Today approximately two-thirds of all credit cards have variable rates of interest.

Card companies find that *installment users* of credit cards are far more profitable due to the interest income they generate than are *noninstallment users*, who quickly pay off their charges before interest can be assessed. Banks and other card providers also earn discount fees (usually 1 to 7 percent of credit card sales) from the merchants who accept their cards. So rapid has been the acceptance of charge cards that close to two trillion are estimated to be in use today around the globe.

Credit cards offer *convenience* and a *revolving line of credit* that the customer can access whenever the need arises. Card providers have found, however, that careful management and control of their card programs is vital due to the relatively high proportion of delinquent borrowers and the large number of cards that are stolen and used fraudulently. There is evidence that significant economies of scale pervade the credit card field because, in general, only the largest card operations are consistently profitable. Nevertheless, credit card programs may survive for a considerable future period because of advancing technology that may give most cardholders access to a full range of financial services, including savings and payments accounts.

While the credit card market is heavily concentrated among a handful of leaders—VISA and MasterCard, in particular—new varieties of card plans, such as Citibank's AT&T Universal, are aggressively expanding to offer no-interest or low-interest programs to attract consumers willing to transfer their account balances from competing programs. However, once the no-interest or low-interest period ends, many card programs plan a

CREDIT CARDS: CAN EARNINGS BE PROTECTED IN A DECLINING MARKET?

The credit card market has seen better days. Consumers have been turning more toward debit cards, rather than credit cards, to make their purchases, avoiding expensive credit card balances. Many homeowners have turned from borrowings on their credit cards to home equity loans, using their homes as collateral to obtain cheaper credit with tax benefits. Moreover, leading card systems like VISA and MasterCard have been under attack in the courts over allegations that they have acted to restrain trade by prohibiting member institutions from accepting other card plans, such as American Express and Discover, or have been charging excessive fees without proper notice to their customers. Equally serious, U.S. government regulations have recently pressured card programs to tighten up their lending standards and disclose more fully to the public the terms of card usage.

With this assault from several different directions managers of card companies face a real dilemma: *where do we go from here?* One possible solution, which several companies adopted in 2005 and 2006, was to sharply increase minimum monthly payments and to raise fees for late payments and charges beyond the customer's credit limit. Other banks focused on diverting more of their resources to the markets for home equity loans, debit cards, smart cards, and affinity cards, appealing to special customer groups. Still other companies have looked overseas, especially to Europe and Asia where fewer families have cards and account balances are typically much lower. Most attractive to the largest banks, like HSBC, Citigroup, and the Royal Bank of Scotland, is China, where only about 1 percent of the 1.3 billion Chinese have credit cards, though China's market appears to be doubling in size every year.

If you were the manager of a credit card company, which way would you go and why?

jump in interest rates to 10 percent or higher. The purpose of this aggressive marketing effort is traceable to recently slowing growth in the credit card market.

New Credit Card Regulations

New credit card regulations appeared early in 2003 as the chief U.S. regulators of depository institutions—the Office of the Comptroller of the Currency, the Federal Reserve System, the Federal Deposit Insurance Corporation, and the Office of Thrift Supervision—moved to slow the expansion of credit card offers to customers with low credit ratings. Regulators expressed concern that many weak household borrowers were being carried on the books of credit card lenders for months even when their payments were woefully behind schedule. Some lenders allegedly had adopted the policy of liberalizing credit terms so that delinquent borrowers would continue to run up charges and fees with little hope of eventual repayment.

Indeed, there was evidence that some customers were charged high fees but asked to make low minimum payments, resulting in "negative amortization" of their debt. This meant that rather than paying down their debts, many troubled card customers found themselves owing still more over time due to late payment fees, over-credit-limit charges, and such. As the 21st century opened regulatory agencies warned lenders that federal examiners would begin looking for excessive use of fees and unreasonably liberal credit terms that appeared to "doom" low-credit-rated customers to making payments indefinitely without hope of ever retiring their debts. Regulators began to pressure lenders to make sure the majority of their credit card borrowers were set up in repayment plans that normally would result in complete repayment of balances owed within 60 months.

Debit Cards: A Partial Substitute for Credit Cards?

Debit cards—plastic cards that may be used to pay for goods and services, but not to extend credit—are today one of the fastest growing of all household financial services, substantially exceeding the recent growth of credit cards. Currently the credit card market is about triple the size of the debit card market, but debit cards are closing the gap. Among the leading firms offering these plastic substitutes for cash are First Data Corp. VISA USA Inc., and MasterCard International Inc.

Debit cards are a convenient method of paying *now* and a vehicle for making deposits into and withdrawals from ATMs. These cards are also used to facilitate check cashing and to establish a customer's identity. Close relatives of the debit card, especially popular in Europe today, are "smart cards" that carry balances that can be spent electronically in stores until the balance entered on the card is fully used up. Prepaid or niche cards, offered by such institutions as MasterCard International, VISA USA, and Comdata Corp., are emerging that, like smart cards, are preloaded with cash. One of the most common uses of these newer card types is by employers who can pay their employees by filling their cards with salary money each month or prepay employee travel expenses.

Debit cards enforce discipline on consumers who, when using such a card, must pay immediately without borrowing money. They save both customer and banker time and paperwork compared to the use of checks. Moreover, financial firms have found them to be an additional source of fee income with somewhat lower losses associated with default and theft than credit cards.

Rapid Consumer Loan Growth

Whatever their category, most types of consumer loans have grown explosively in recent years, fed by a growing economy and intense competition among consumer lenders. For example, household debt grew in the United States from less than 70 percent of family disposable income in 1985 to more than 100 percent of personal disposable income as the new century began to unfold. Home mortgage loan growth was the fastest of all consumer loan categories, rising from less than 45 percent of U.S. disposable personal income in 1985 to about two-thirds of that measure of household income nearly two decades later.

18–3 Characteristics of Consumer Loans

By and large, household lenders regard consumer loans as profitable credits with "sticky" interest rates. That is, they are typically priced well above the cost of funding them, but their contract interest rates often don't change readily with market conditions as do interest rates on most business loans, though flexible-rate consumer credit appears to be growing. This means that many consumer loans are exposed to significant interest rate risk. However, consumer loans are usually priced so high (i.e., with a large risk premium built into the loan rate) that market interest rates on borrowed funds and default rates on the loans themselves would have to rise substantially before most consumer credits would become unprofitable.

Why are interest rates so high on most consumer loans? One reason is that consumer loans are among the most costly and most risky to make per dollar of loanable funds of any of the loans that most lending institutions grant to their customers. Consumer loans also tend to be *cyclically sensitive*. They rise in periods of economic expansion when consumers are generally more optimistic about the future. On the other hand, when the economy turns down, many individuals and families become more pessimistic about the future and reduce their borrowings accordingly.

Household borrowings appear to be relatively *interest inelastic:* Consumers are often more concerned about the size of monthly payments required by a loan agreement than the interest rate charged (though, obviously, the contract rate on a loan influences the size of its required payments). While the level of the interest rate is often not a significant conscious factor among household borrowers, both education and income levels *do* materially influence consumers' use of credit. Individuals with higher incomes tend to borrow more in total and relative to the size of their annual incomes. Those households in which the principal breadwinner has more years of formal education also tend to borrow more heavily relative to their level of income. For these individuals and families, borrowing is often viewed as a tool to achieve a desired standard of living rather than as a safety net to be used only in emergencies.

Concept Check

18–1. What are the principal differences among residential loans, nonresidential installment loans, noninstallment loans, and credit card or revolving loans?

18–2. Why do interest rates on consumer loans typically average higher than on most other kinds of loans?

18–4 Evaluating a Consumer Loan Application

Character and Purpose

Key factors in analyzing any consumer loan application are the *character* of the borrower and the borrower's *ability to pay*. The lender must be assured that the borrowing customer feels a keen sense of moral responsibility to repay a loan on time. Moreover, the borrower's income level and valuable assets (such as holdings of securities or savings deposits) must be sufficient to reassure the lender that the customer has the ability to repay the loan with a comfortable margin for safety. For this reason, consumer lenders nearly always check with one or more national or regional **credit bureaus** concerning the customer's credit history. These institutions hold files on most individuals who, at one time or another, have borrowed money, indicating their record of repayment and credit rating.

Often the fundamental character of the borrower is revealed in the *purpose* of the loan request. Lenders often ask: Has the customer clearly stated what he or she plans to do with the money? Is the stated purpose of the loan consistent with the lender's loan policy? Is there evidence of a sincere intention to repay any funds borrowed? Some senior loan officers counsel new loan officers to visit with their customers, where this is practical, because such conversations often reveal flaws in character and sincerity that have a direct bearing on the likelihood of loan repayment. By asking the customer pertinent questions a lender often can make a better call on whether the customer's loan request meets the lender's quality standards.

Unfortunately, economic pressures encouraging automation in consumer lending have led most lenders to spend *less* time with the customer. Information gathering and loan evaluation increasingly are being turned over to computer programs. The result is that many consumer loan officers today know very little about the character traits of their customers beyond the information called for on a credit application, which may be faxed or telephoned in or sent via computer.

In the case of a borrower without a credit record or with a poor track record of repaying loans, a **cosigner** may be requested to support repayment. Technically, if the borrower defaults on a cosigned loan agreement, the cosigner is obligated to make good on the loan. However, many lenders regard a cosigner mainly as a psychological device to encourage repayment of the loan, rather than as a real alternative source of security. The borrower may feel a stronger moral obligation to repay the loan knowing the cosigner's credit rating also is on the line.

Income Levels

Both the *size* and *stability* of an individual's income are considered important by most lenders. They generally prefer the customer to report *net salary*, or *take-home pay*, as opposed to gross salary, and, with large loans, may check with the customer's employer to verify the accuracy of customer-supplied income figures and length of employment.

Deposit Balances

An indirect measure of income size and stability is the *daily average deposit balance* maintained by the customer, which the loan officer *may* verify with the depository institution involved. In some states lenders may be granted the **right of offset** against the customer's deposit as additional protection against the risks of consumer lending. This right permits the lender to call a loan that is in default and seize any checking or savings deposits the customer may hold in order to recover its funds. However, in many cases the customer must be notified at least 10 days in advance before this right is exercised, which can result in funds disappearing before the lending institution can recover any portion of its loan.

Employment and Residential Stability

Among the many factors considered by lenders is *duration of employment*. Many lenders are not likely to grant a sizable loan to someone who has held his or her present job for only a few weeks or months. *Length of residence* may also be considered because the longer a person stays at one address, the more stable his or her personal situation is presumed to be. Frequent changes of address can be a negative factor in deciding whether to grant a loan.

Pyramiding of Debt

Lenders are especially sensitive to evidence that debt is piling up relative to a consumer's income. *Pyramiding of debt*—where the individual draws credit at one lending institution to pay another—is frowned upon, as are high or growing credit card balances and frequent returned checks drawn against the customer's account. These items are viewed as indicators of the customer's money management skills. Customers lacking these basic skills may be unable to avoid taking on too much debt and getting themselves in serious trouble.

How to Qualify for a Consumer Loan

Are there ways to improve one's chances of getting a loan? One positive factor is *home ownership* or, for that matter, ownership of any form of real property, such as land or buildings. Even if such property is not posted as collateral behind a loan, it conveys the impression of stability and good money management skills. Having a telephone may also be a sign of stability and a low-cost way for the lender's collections department to contact the borrower in case of trouble. Another positive factor is maintaining *strong deposit balances*. Not only do above-average deposit levels suggest a financially disciplined individual determined to meet his or her obligations, but also the lender may be able to profitably use those deposits to fund other loans.

The most important thing to do, however, is to answer all the loan officer's questions truthfully. A lender may look for *inconsistencies* on a loan application as a sign the borrower is untruthful or, at best, forgetful. For example, a Social Security or personal ID number often reveals what geographic area a person comes from. Does the borrower's Social Security number match his or her personal history as indicated on the loan application? Are the borrower and his or her employer located at the addresses indicated? Is the amount reported as take-home pay the same as what the employer reports? Has the customer reported all debts outstanding, or does a credit bureau report reveal many unreported obligations the customer has forgotten or simply walked away from?

The Challenge of Consumer Lending

Consumer loans are not easy to evaluate. For one thing, it is often easier for individuals to conceal pertinent information bearing on the payout of a loan (such as their health or future employment prospects) than for most businesses (whose loan applications are frequently accompanied by audited financial statements). Moreover, a business firm usually can more easily adjust to ill health, injury, or financial setbacks than can individuals. The default rate on consumer loans usually is several times higher than that for many types of business loans. The key features of consumer loans that help lenders hold down potential losses are that most are small in denomination and often secured by marketable collateral, such as an automobile.

18–5 Example of a Consumer Loan Application

We can illustrate some of the most important types of information a consumer lender may gather and what these bits of information are designed to reveal by examining the sample loan application shown in Table 18–1. This is a credit application to finance the purchase of a new automobile, normally one of the more profitable and secure types of loans made by a consumer lending institution. The customer, J. P. Skylark, is trading in an aging used car in order to purchase a newer and more reliable vehicle. The trade-in value and down payment will cover nearly 20 percent of the purchase price, and the lender is asked to cover the remainder

TABLE 18–1

A Typical Consumer Loan Application

Credit application submitted by <u>J. P. L. Skylark V</u> on <u>December 1, this year</u> to First National Bank
Applicant's street address: <u>3701 Elm Street</u>
City of residence: <u>Orangeburg</u>   State and Zip Code: <u>CA 77804</u>
Purpose of the requested loan: <u>To purchase a newer car for personal and family use</u>
Desired term of loan: <u>5 years</u>
For auto loan requests, please fill in the following information:
Make: <u>Ford Taurus</u>
Model: <u>4-Door Sedan</u>   Vehicle identification no. <u>8073617</u>
The vehicle is equipped with: <u>Air conditioning, automatic transmission, power steering, disk brakes,</u>
<u>AM/FM stereo, disk player, automatic locks, tinted glass</u>
Vehicle to be traded in: <u>Chevrolet Monte Carlo</u>   Model: <u>4-door Sedan</u>
Age of trade-in vehicle: <u>8 years</u>   Vehicle identification no. <u>6384061</u>
Optional equipment on trade-in vehicle: <u>Air conditioning, automatic transmission, disk brakes,</u>
<u>power steering, AM/FM radio, tape player</u>
Details of the proposed purchase:

Purchase price quoted by seller:	$18,750
Cash down payment to be made:	$ 1,575
Value of trade-in vehicle:	$ 3,500
Total value put down:	$ 5,075
Unpaid portion of purchase price:	$13,675
Other items covered in the loan:	$ 650
Total amount of credit requested:	**$14,325**

Customer information:
Social Security no. <u>671-66-8324</u>   Birthdate: <u>2/21/75</u>
Time at present address: <u>10 months</u>   Phone no. <u>965-1321</u>
Previous home address: <u>302 W. Solar St., Casio City, California</u>

(Continued)

TABLE 18–1
Continued

How long at previous address: <u>1 year</u>

Driver's license no. and state: <u>A672435 California</u>   Number of dependents: <u>3</u>

Current employer: <u>Hometown Warehouse Co.</u>

Length of employment with current employer: <u>8 months</u>

Nature of work: <u>Drive truck, load merchandise, keep records</u>

Annual salary: <u>$30,000</u>   Employer's phone no. 963-8417

Other income sources: <u>Investments, Trust Fund</u>

Annual income from other sources: $2,000

Debts owed (including home mortgage): $103,000   Monthly debt <u>payments: $1,140</u>

Nearest living relative (not spouse): <u>Elsa Lyone</u>   Phone: 604-682-7899

   Address: <u>6832 Willow Ave., Amera, OK, 73282</u>

Does the applicant want the lender to consider spouse's income in evaluating this loan?

  <u>X</u> Yes _____ No

Spouse's current annual income: <u>$8,000</u>

Name of spouse's employer: <u>Dimmitt Savings and Security Association</u>

Occupation: <u>Secretary</u>   Length of employment: <u>8 months</u>

  The information I have given in this credit application is true and correct to the best of my knowledge. I am aware that the lender will keep this credit application regardless of whether or not the loan is approved. The lender is hereby granted permission to investigate my credit and employment history for purpose of verifying the information submitted with this credit application and for evaluating my credit status.

Customer's signature: J. P. Skylark

Date signed: 12/1/current year

(80 percent) of the automobile's price. The lending institution will take a *chattel mortgage* against the vehicle in order to gain the legal right to repossess if the loan is defaulted. As long as car prices remain fairly stable or increase, the lender's funds should be reasonably well secured.

However, character, stability, and adequate disposable income (not heavily burdened with debt obligations and taxes) are important components of any consumer loan request, and these elements raise serious questions about this particular credit request. Skylark has been at his present address for only 10 months and stayed at his previous address in another city for just one year. He has worked only eight months for his present employer. Many lenders prefer borrowing customers who have resided or worked in their market area for at least one year, often considered a sign of reliability.

The Skylarks' annual gross income is about average and, for both husband and wife, amounts to about $40,000 or about $32,000 in total take-home pay. The family has debt obligations amounting to $103,000 which appears to be high—about three times their take-home income—but includes their home mortgage loan. Most home mortgage lenders would find a debt to income ratio of two and one-half to three times not unusual by today's standards.

The monthly payments on this debt *are* on the high side, however, at just over $1,140 (including the home mortgage payment). Monthly debt payments already account for more than a third of monthly gross income, not counting the payments of $225 per month that the requested car loan will require. Many lenders prefer to see a required-monthly-payment-to-income ratio no more than 25 to 30 percent. However, the bulk of the family's debt and debt service payments are on their home and, in a reasonably strong local real estate market, the value of that home might provide adequate security for the lender. Moreover, the Skylarks seem to have adequate insurance coverage and hold at least some liquid financial

Factoid
Who are the two leading automobile lenders?
Answer: Commercial banks and finance companies.

investments in the form of stocks, bonds, and other securities. The loan officer's check with both Mr. and Mrs. Skylark's employers revealed that they both have good prospects for continued employment.

The Skylarks' loan application is for a reasonable purpose, consistent with this bank's loan policy, and the family's reported income high enough to suggest a reasonably strong

TABLE 18–2
Sample Credit Bureau Report

E-Z Credit Bureau Report on J.P.L. Skylark, SSN 671-66-8324
Credit bureau address: 8750 Cafe Street, San Miguel, CA 87513
607-453-8862
Credit items as of: 6/15/Current Year

Name of Creditor	Maximum Term Credit	Amount Owed	Outstanding Balance	Past Due	Monthly Payments	Status
Windcrest Deluxe Apts.	Six months	$ 610	$ 610	$610	$305	Past due
VISA	Open	$1,680	$1,540	$250	$125	Past due
MasterCard	Open	$1,435	$1,250	$176	$ 88	Past due
First State Bank of Slyvon	Six months	$ 750	$ 150	$150	$ 75	Past due
Kinney's Furniture Mart and Emporium	One year	$ 847	$ 675	—	$ 34	Current
First National Bank of Orangeburg	One year	$2,500	$ 675	—	$120	Current
Saint Barrio Hospital and Medical Clinic	Open	$ 160	$ 160	—	—	Charged off

TABLE 18–3
Statement of Denial, Termination, or Change on a Customer Credit Application

First National Bank

Statement to: <u>Mr. J. P. L. Skylark</u>
　　　　　　　Customer's Name

　　　　　　　<u>3701 Elm Street</u>　　　　　　<u>Orangeburg, CA 77804</u>
　　　　　　　Customer's residence address　 City　　　　State

Statement date: <u>6/18/current year</u>

Credit requested by customer: <u>$14,325, 5-year auto installment loan</u>

Action taken by the bank on the request: <u>Loan denied</u>

Unfortunately, the bank cannot approve the amount and terms of credit you have asked for as of the date indicated above. The reason(s) for our denial of your requested loan are: <u>Past-due loans.</u>

Our investigation of your credit request included a credit report from: <u>E-Z Credit Bureau, 8750 Cafe Street, San Miguel, CA 87513.</u> Federal law allows you to obtain, upon submission of a written request, a copy of the information that led to a denial of this credit request.

If you believe you have been discriminated against in obtaining credit because of your race, color, religion, sex, national origin, marital status, legal age, receipt of public assistance, or exercise of rights under the Consumer Credit Protection Act, you may apply to the principal federal regulatory agency for this bank, which is the Comptroller of the Currency, U.S. Treasury Department, Washington, D.C. 20219.

Please let me or other employees of our bank know at any time in the future if we can assist you with other services this bank offers. We value your business and would like to be of assistance in meeting your banking needs. Please consider submitting another loan request in the future if the situation that led to denial of this credit request improves.

Sincerely,

_____
　　　　　　　　　　　　　　　　　　　W. A. Numone
William A. H. Numone III
Senior Vice President
Personal Banking Division

Insights and Issues

THE KEY FUNCTION OF CREDIT BUREAUS IN CONSUMER LENDING DECISIONS

Credit bureaus—often called *credit-reporting agencies* (CRAs)—assemble and distribute to lenders the credit histories of millions of borrowers. The first CRAs operating in the United States go back to the 19th century and others emerged in Western Europe, Australia, and Canada at about the same time. Today CRAs receive close to 70 million data items daily from more than 30,000 lenders and provide more than 3 million credit reports a day. While there are many small CRAs, three agencies—Equifax, Experian, and Transunion—dominate the national financial marketplace in the United States.

The reports provided by CRAs provide lenders and others with:

a. *Personal identifying data* (name, old and new addresses, birth date, current and former employers, and Social Security number).

b. *Personal credit histories derived from data submitted by lenders* (including personal credit limits, loan balances, and payments records).

c. *Public information that may bear on each borrower's honesty and stability* (such as bankruptcy filings or court judgments against borrowers).

d. *The volume of inquiries from lenders and others about a borrower's credit status.*

CRAs provide valuable information to lenders in a society where borrowers move frequently and use extensive amounts of credit. They have made possible the rapid expansion of unsecured debt, encouraged borrowers and lenders to be more honest, increased competition in lending, and led to more efficient pricing of credit services by supplying timely information to lenders, employers, and others with a need to know.

At the same time CRAs have aroused considerable controversy that has led to a welter of new government regulations. They have a spotty record of protecting consumer privacy and have sometimes unintentionally leaked information that led to identity theft. Many credit files contain errors, often lacking credit limit information and overestimating open accounts and amounts owed. For their part CRAs have invested heavily in information technology and pledged to correct errors promptly. Federal rules require CRAs to set up a system of fraud alerts to aid ID theft victims.

In response leading CRAs are developing multiple new services, including account fraud monitoring, and, in some cases, loan term simulators to aid credit shoppers. These new services should help to expand and stabilize CRAs' revenues. (For a detailed discussion of credit bureaus see especially Robert M. Hunt, "A Century of Consumer Credit Reporting in America," Working Paper No. 05-13, Federal Reserve Bank of Philadelphia, June 2005.)

Key URLs

To find out more about the information credit bureaus provide consumer lenders you may wish to contact the 3 largest credit bureaus in the U.S. at **www.experian.com**, **www.equifax.com**, and **www.transunion.com**.

probability the loan would be repaid. Accordingly, the loan officer accepted their application and proceeded to check out the Skylarks' credit record. When the report from the *credit bureau* arrived on-screen minutes later, however, the loan officer saw very quickly that there was a serious problem with this application. Unfortunately, as shown in Table 18–2, the Skylarks had a mixed credit record, with at least five instances of delinquent or unpaid bills. The other debts were essentially as reported on the loan application with only minor discrepancies. At best, the loan officer would ask the Skylarks about these unreported debts, but more likely this loan request will simply be turned down due to an unacceptable credit record. The loan officer clearly would be justified in having doubts about this borrower's sense of judgment and responsibility in borrowing and repaying borrowed funds.

The Equal Credit Opportunity Act requires U.S. banks and selected other consumer lending institutions to notify their credit customers in writing when they deny a loan request. They must give *reasons* for the denial, and where a credit bureau report is used, the customer must be told where that credit bureau is located. This way the customer can verify his or her credit record and demand that any errors found in the report be corrected. Table 18–3 shows the credit denial report form given to the Skylarks and the reasons they were given on why their loan was turned down. In this case, the loan officer cited the customer's debts that remained past due and unpaid. A good feature of this particular denial form is that the customer is cordially invited to use other services at the lending institution and to reapply if his or her financial situation improves.

An acceptable consumer loan request will display evidence of (*a*) the stability of the borrower's employment or residence location; (*b*) the accuracy and consistency of information the borrower supplies; (*c*) the legitimacy of the borrower's purpose for borrowing money; and (*d*) the borrower's personal money management skills. It is when a household application is weak in one or two of these features that loan officers face tough decisions and increasingly today rely on objective credit scoring systems to make good lending decisions. The ultimate decision to accept or deny any particular loan request depends on the expected return and risk of that proposed loan relative to the expected returns and risks of other possible investments the lender might make and management's attitude toward risk.

18–6 Credit Scoring Consumer Loan Applications

Most lenders today use **credit scoring** to evaluate the loan applications they receive from consumers. In fact, major credit card systems, such as Master Card and VISA, use these systems routinely to evaluate their credit card applicants. Many insurance companies also use scoring systems today to help them evaluate new policyholders and the risks these prospective customers might present to the insurer.

Credit-scoring systems have the advantage of being able to handle a large volume of credit applications quickly with minimal labor, thus reducing operating costs, and they may be an effective substitute for the use of judgment among inexperienced loan officers, thus helping to control bad-debt losses. Many customers like the convenience and speed with which their credit applications can be handled by automated credit-scoring systems. Often the customer can phone in a loan request or fill out an Internet application, and in a matter of minutes the lender can dial up that customer's credit bureau report online and reach a quick decision on the customer's request (now within eight minutes, on average, for auto loan requests).

Key URL

You can learn more about credit scoring techniques by consulting Experian Scorex at **www. experian-scorex.com**.

Credit-scoring systems are usually based on discriminant models or related techniques, such as logit or probit analysis or neural networks, in which several variables are used jointly to establish a numerical score for each credit applicant. If the applicant's score exceeds a critical cutoff level, he or she is likely to be approved for credit in the absence of other damaging information. If the applicant's score falls below the cutoff level, credit is likely to be denied in the absence of mitigating factors. Among the most important variables used in evaluating consumer loans are credit bureau ratings, home ownership, income bracket, number and type of deposit accounts owned, and type of occupation.

The basic theory of credit scoring is that lenders and statisticians can identify the financial, economic, and motivational factors that separate good loans from bad loans by observing large groups of people who have borrowed in the past. Moreover, it assumes that the same factors that separated good from bad loans in the past will, with an acceptable risk of error, separate good from bad loans in the future. Obviously, this underlying assumption can be wrong if the economy or other factors change abruptly, which is one reason good credit scoring systems are frequently retested and revised as more sensitive predictors are identified.

Scoring systems usually select a few key items from a customer's credit application and assign each a point value (for example, from 1 to 10). Examination of a sample of consumer credit accounts might show that the factors in Table 18–4 were important in separating good loans (i.e., those that paid out in timely fashion) from bad loans (i.e., where repayment was seriously delayed or not made at all).

The highest score a customer could have in the eight-factor credit-scoring system that follows is 430 points. The lowest possible score is 90 points. Suppose the lender finds that, of those past-approved loan customers scoring 280 points or less, 40 percent (or 1,200) became bad loans that had to be written off as a loss. These losses averaged $600 per credit account, for a total loss of $720,000. Of all the good loans made, however,

TABLE 18–4
Predictive Factors
in an Example of a
Credit Scoring Model
and Their Point
Values

Factors for Predicting Credit Quality	Point Value
1. Customer's occupation or line of work:	
Professional or business executive	100
Skilled worker	80
Clerical worker	70
Student	50
Unskilled worker	40
Part-time employee	20
2. Housing status:	
Owns home	60
Rents home or apartment	40
Lives with friend or relative	20
3. Credit rating:	
Excellent	100
Average	50
No record	20
Poor	00
4. Length of time in current job:	
More than one year	50
One year or less	20
5. Length of time at current address:	
More than one year	20
One year or less	10
6. Telephone in home or apartment:	
Yes	20
No	00
7. Number of dependents reported by customer:	
None	30
One	30
Two	40
Three	40
More than three	20
8. Deposit accounts held:	
Both checking and savings	40
Savings account only	30
Checking account only	20
None	00

only 10 percent (300) scored 280 points or less under this scoring system. At $600 per loan, these low-scoring good loans amounted to $180,000. Therefore, if a loan officer uses 280 points as the *criterion score,* or *break point,* the lender will save an estimated $720,000 minus $180,000, or $540,000, by following the decision rule of making only those loans where the credit applicant scores higher than 280 points. If the lender's future loan-loss experience is the same, denying all loan applications scoring 280 points or less will reduce loss accounts by about 40 percent and reject just 10 percent of the good loan customers. Management can experiment with other criterion scores to determine which cutoff point yields the greatest net savings in loan losses for the institution's consumer credit program.

Let's suppose the lender finds that 280 points is indeed the optimal break point for maximum savings from loan losses. The lender's consumer credit history could be further analyzed to find out what influence the *amount of credit* extended to a customer has upon the lender's loan-loss experience. This lender might find that the point-scoring schedule shown in Table 18–5 results in the largest net savings from consumer credit losses.

TABLE 18–5
Point-Scoring
Schedule of Approved
Credit Amounts

Point Score Value or Range	Credit Decision
280 points or less	Reject application
290–300 points	Extend credit up to $1,000
310–330 points	Extend credit up to $2,000
340–360 points	Extend credit up to $3,000
370–380 points	Extend credit up to $4,000
390–400 points	Extend credit up to $6,000
410–430 points	Extend credit up to $10,000

Clearly, such a system removes personal judgment from the lending process and reduces the lender's decision time from hours to minutes. It does run the risk, however, of alienating those customers who feel the lending institution has not fully considered their financial situation and the special circumstances that may have given rise to their loan request. There is also the danger of being sued by a customer under antidiscrimination laws (such as the Equal Credit Opportunity Act) if race, gender, marital status, or other discriminating factors prohibited by statute or court rulings are used in a scoring system. Federal regulations allow the use of age or certain other personal characteristics as discriminating factors if the lender can show that these factors *do* separate, at a statistically significant level, good from bad loans and that the scoring system is frequently statistically tested and revised to take into account recent changes in actual credit experience. The burden of proof is on the lender to demonstrate that its credit scoring system successfully identifies quality loan applications at a statistically significant level.

Frequent verification and revision of a credit-scoring system are not only wise from a legal and regulatory point of view, but also mitigate the biggest potential weakness of such systems—their inability to adjust quickly to changes in the economy and in family lifestyles. An inflexible credit evaluation system can be a deadly menace to a lending institution's loan program, driving away sound credit requests, ruining the lender's reputation in the communities it serves, and adding unacceptably high risks to the loan portfolio.

The FICO Scoring System

The most famous of all credit-scoring systems currently in use is known as FICO, developed and sold by Fair Isaac Corporation. Fair Isaac's scoring system calculates scores for millions of consumers worldwide and provides these scores to credit bureaus, lending institutions, and individuals who file a request. Fair Isaac also provides programs for individuals and families that suggest how they can improve their FICO score and, thereby, gain access to more credit or access credit more cheaply. A FICO score simulator allows individuals to estimate what would happen to their FICO score if certain changes were made in their personal financial profile. Many borrowers check their FICO rating before they seek a large loan (such as a home mortgage) in order to assess their chances of getting approved and to make sure there are no errors in their record.

FICO scores range from 300 to 850, with higher values denoting less credit risk to lenders. An individual with a lower FICO score implies a lower probability of timely repayment if the lender should grant a loan and, therefore, a loan is less likely to be granted. However, all lenders do not adopt the same cutoff score for loan approval so that a good score for one lender may not be a good mark for another. It is an individual lender's decision.

While Fair Isaac provides the public only general information about its scoring systems, its credit scores are based on five different types of information (arrayed from most important to least important):

1. The borrower's payment history.
2. The amount of money owed.

Key URLs
To learn more about FICO credit scoring, see especially **www.fairisaac.com** and **www.myfico.com**. A competing system under recent development is Vantage Score at **www.vantagescore.com**.

CREDIT-SCORING SYSTEMS: PLUSES AND MINUSES

Credit scoring is a statistical device first developed about 50 years ago to objectively rank borrowers' likelihood of repaying a loan. In recent years credit-scoring models have become dominant tools in assessing the quality of borrowers seeking new credit cards, auto and home mortgage loans, and even loans to support businesses. Mortgage giants Fannie Mae and Freddie Mac have urged home mortgage loan originators to make greater use of these systems. Recent research suggests that credit-scoring technology has lowered loan delinquency rates 20 to 30 percent compared to lenders that use only loan officer judgment in making credit decisions. Moreover, scoring appears to increase borrower acceptance rates, lower loan processing costs, and result in faster credit decision making.

Credit-scoring systems use a variety of statistical techniques to calculate a prospective borrower's credit score, including multiple discriminant analysis and logistic regression. The factors used in predicting credit quality vary but there is a trend toward using more readily available data, such as items typically found in the average borrower's credit report. Examples include the number of credit lines the borrower has outstanding, the number of times a borrower has been 30 to 60 days late with payments, the number of inquiries creditors have made about a borrower's account, and the highest credit limit the customer currently has available from one or more lenders. However, system operators are very careful to avoid disclosing exactly what factors they consider.

Credit-scoring systems have been subject to great controversy almost from their beginnings. For example, it is alleged they tend to be biased against lower-income applicants and members of minority groups. They may exclude factors that might be more favorable to lower-income borrowers, such as length of time with the same employer or in the same residence. However, scoring systems tend to be objective and avoid "personality" clashes between lenders and borrowers.

3. The length of a prospective borrower's credit history.
4. The nature of new credit being requested.
5. The types of credit the borrower has already used.

Fair Isaac also indicates what elements of a borrower's background—especially age, race, color, sex, religion, marital status, employment history and salary, and residential location—are *not* considered in establishing a FICO score. It confines the list of factors considered in its credit scoring system to those items usually available in each customer's credit bureau report. FICO scores are recalculated as *new* information comes in.

Concept Check

18–3. What features of a consumer loan application should a loan officer examine most carefully?

18–4. How do credit-scoring systems work?

18–5. What are the principal advantages to a lending institution of using a credit-scoring system?

18–6. Are there any significant disadvantages to a credit-scoring system?

18–7. In the credit-scoring system presented in this chapter, would a loan applicant who is a skilled worker, lives with a relative, has an average credit rating, has been in his or her present job and at his or her current address for exactly one year, has four dependents and a telephone, and holds a checking account be likely to receive a loan? Please explain why.

18–8. What is FICO and what does it do for lenders? Why is this credit-scoring system so popular today?

18–7 Laws and Regulations Applying to Consumer Loans

Numerous laws and regulations limiting the activities of consumer lending institutions have been enacted during the past four decades. The principal federal laws fall into two broad groups: (1) **disclosure rules,** which mandate telling the consumer about the cost and other terms of a loan or lease agreement; and (2) **antidiscrimination laws,** which prevent categorizing loan customers according to their age, sex, race, or other irrelevant factors and denying credit to anyone solely because of membership in one or more of these groups. Many lenders view such rules as burdensome and out of step with technological and service innovations. They are a constant challenge to the enforcement powers of the regulatory community, which is burdened with numerous complaints and questions of interpretation. Yet, the flow of adequate financial information to consumers is vital in the wake of government deregulation of the financial sector, which has been accompanied by greater risk for both financial institutions and their customers.

Customer Disclosure Requirements

One of the most prominent pieces of federal legislation in the consumer services field is the **Truth-in-Lending Act,** passed in 1968 by the U.S. Congress and simplified in 1981 through passage of the Truth-in-Lending Simplification and Reform Act. The Federal Reserve Board has prepared Regulation Z to implement these laws. The express purpose of truth in lending is to promote informed use of credit among consumers by requiring full disclosure of credit terms and costs. Lenders must tell customers the annual percentage rate (APR, or actuarial, rate) on the loan requested, the amount of all finance charges, and, in the case of home mortgage loans, the required fees for approvals, closing costs, and other loan-related expenses.

Amendments to Truth in Lending in 1970 and 1974 gave rise to the Fair Credit Reporting Act and the Fair Credit Billing Act. The former expressly grants consumers access to their credit files, usually kept by credit bureaus. The **Fair Credit Reporting Act** authorizes individuals and families to review their credit files for accuracy and to demand an investigation and correction of any inaccuracies. The law requires a credit bureau to correct these inaccuracies promptly and to allow consumers to insert a brief statement of explanation for any damaging items displayed in the file. Moreover, it restricts access to consumer credit files, requiring an individual's written consent.

The **Fair Credit Billing Act** of 1974 permits consumers to dispute billing errors with a merchant or credit card company and receive a prompt investigation of billing disputes. The consumer may withhold payment on the disputed portions of a bill and cannot be reported as delinquent or forced to pay interest penalties until the dispute is settled. Any creditor who does not respond to a consumer's inquiry about a bill or, having responded, does not investigate and attempt to resolve the matter must ultimately forfeit the disputed charge (up to a maximum of $50). A 30-day notice to customers is required before a lender or merchant can alter credit charges or service fees.

The *Fair Credit and Charge-Card Disclosure Act* requires that customers applying for credit cards be given early written notice (usually before a credit card is used for the first time) about required fees to open or renew a credit account. Also, if a fee for renewal is charged, the customer must receive written notice in advance. The consumer must be told if there is any change in credit card insurance coverage or fees. These rules are designed especially for credit cards granted to customers following solicitations made by direct mail, by telephone, or through advertisements that reach the general public.

Finally, if a credit customer gets behind in his or her loan payments, the **Fair Debt Collection Practices Act** limits how far a creditor or collection agency can go in pressing that customer to pay up. For example, a bill collector is not allowed to "harass" a debtor or use misrepresentation to obtain information about or gain access to a debtor. Calls placed at unusual times or to a debtor's place of work are illegal if made without the debtor's permission; nor can a bill collector legally disclose the purpose of the call to someone other than the debtor. These debt collection rules are enforced in the United States by the Federal Trade Commission.

Outlawing Credit Discrimination

Access to credit is an essential ingredient of the good life for the average family today. Recognition of this fact led the U.S. Congress to outlaw discrimination in the granting of credit based on age, sex, race, national origin, religion, location of residence, or receipt of public assistance. The **Equal Credit Opportunity** Act prohibits lenders from asking certain questions of a customer, such as the borrower's age or race. (An exception is made for home mortgage loans so that the federal government can collect information on who is or is not receiving mortgage credit to determine if discrimination is being practiced in this vital loan area.) Also, the loan officer cannot ask about other income sources beyond wage and salary income unless the customer voluntarily supplies this information.

The **Community Reinvestment Act** (CRA) is designed to prevent a lender from arbitrarily marking out certain neighborhoods deemed undesirable and refusing to lend to people whose addresses place them in the excluded area. The CRA requires each lending institution to delineate the *trade territory* it plans to serve and to offer all of its services without discrimination to all residents in that particular trade territory. The lender's board of directors must review annually the definition of trade territory that management has chosen to see if it is still valid. Moreover, each lending institution's performance in making an affirmative effort to serve the financial-service needs of its trade territory is evaluated by federal examiners (known as a *CRA rating*). The regulatory authorities take a lender's CRA rating into account when it applies to establish a new branch office or close a branch, requests approval for a merger, or requests permission to offer new services.

In August 1989, Title XII of the Financial Institutions Reform, Recovery, and Enforcement Act required the federal banking agencies to *publish* the CRA ratings of depository institutions so their customers are aware of which lenders are providing broad-based support to their local communities. Each covered lending institution must place its CRA performance rating in a public file at its head office and in at least one office in each community the lender serves. This public file must be open for customers to inspect during regular business hours and the lender must provide copies to anyone requesting materials in the file.

CRA ratings are based on 12 "assessment factors" that examiners review when they visit a bank or other covered lender, including the lender's efforts to communicate with members of the local community concerning their credit needs, its participation in government-related housing programs, the geographic distribution of loans the lender has made, and any evidence of illegal credit discrimination. Federal examiners assign one of four different CRA ratings: outstanding (O), satisfactory (S), needs to improve (N), or substantial noncompliance (SN). A study by one of the authors [8] finds that banks receiving a grade of O—the highest CRA rating—periodically survey their employees who are active in the local community to be able to *document* their strong community involvement. Top-rated banks also frequently survey their customers to determine their perceptions about the quality of the bank's services and to keep up with changing customer service needs. Banks with the highest community service ratings often get involved in local affordable housing programs, hold seminars to counsel small businesses and new home buyers on how to apply for loans, and monitor the geographic distribution of their loans to make sure certain areas of the community are not systematically being shut out in their access to services.

Laws that supplement the provisions of the Community Reinvestment Act are the Home Mortgage Disclosure Act, the Fair Housing Act, and the Financial Institutions Reform, Recovery, and Enforcement Act. The former requires that mortgage lenders publicly disclose at least once a year the areas in urban communities where they have granted residential mortgage and home improvement loans. The Fair Housing Act prohibits discrimination in the sale, leasing, or financing of housing because of color, national origin,

ETHICS IN BANKING AND FINANCIAL SERVICES

IDENTITY THEFT CHALLENGES FINANCIAL INSTITUTIONS AND THEIR CUSTOMERS

The fastest rising financial crime against individuals today is *identity theft*—the deliberate attempt to make unauthorized use of someone else's Social Security number, credit card account numbers, or other personal data in order to fraudulently obtain money, credit, or other property. Millions have been victimized by this crime all over the globe. Moreover, unless an individual is alert virtually all of the time and aware of what's happening to their accounts, ID theft can be difficult to detect and costly to recover from.

It is also a big challenge to credit card companies and other financial-service providers who increasingly wind up "holding the bag" for customer losses. Recently the Federal Trade Commission estimated that the total cost to all U.S. businesses from identity theft was running close to $50 billion a year. Another study in New England suggested that close to 10 percent of consumers have switched banks in the wake of

widely publicized ID thefts, almost one-fifth stopped online shopping when reports of serious security breaches occurred, and close to half indicated they would be willing to move their accounts to another financial-service provider if they thought their accounts would be better protected from ID theft.

In an effort to encourage consumers to check their credit bureau reports more frequently, the U.S. Congress passed the Fair and Accurate Credit Transactions (FACT) Act in 2003, providing consumers the opportunity to order one free credit report annually from each of three nationwide credit bureaus—Equifax Inc., Experian, and TransUnion. Consumers are instructed to contact a central Web site, **www.annualcreditreport.com,** or call a toll-free phone number (1-877-322-8228), or send in a written request to the Annual Credit Report Request Service, P.O. Box 105281, Atlanta, Georgia 30348-5281. Credit reports may be requested from all three credit bureaus at the same time or spread out among the three over the period of a year.

race, religion, or sex. The Financial Institutions Reform, Recovery, and Enforcement Act requires lending institutions to report the race, sex, and income of all those individuals *applying* for mortgage loans so that federal regulators can more easily detect discrimination in home mortgage lending.

These laws do not tell lenders *who* should receive credit. Rather, they require each lending institution to focus on the facts pertinent to each individual loan application, case by case, and prevent lenders from lumping their customers into categories (such as by age, sex, or race) and making credit decisions solely on the basis of group membership.

Predatory Lending and Subprime Loans

One of the most controversial consumer credit practices today is **predatory lending**—an abusive practice among some lenders, often associated with home mortgage and home equity loans. This usually consists of granting **subprime loans** to borrowers with below-average credit records and, in the eyes of the regulatory community at least, charging excessive fees for these lower-quality loans. Subprime loans tend to go to borrowers with a record of delinquent payments, previously charged-off loans, bankruptcies, or court judgments to pay off.

Some predatory lenders may insist on unnecessary and expensive loan insurance in amounts well beyond what is needed to cover actual loan risk. Excessive loan insurance costs and higher interest rates may result in unaffordable payments for weak borrowers. This kind of abusive lending practice increases the chances that low-credit-rated borrowers will lose their homes.

In 1994 the U.S. Congress passed the Home Ownership and Equity Protection Act, aimed at protecting home buyers from loan agreements they couldn't afford to carry. Loans with annual percentage rates (APR) of 10 percentage points or more above the yield on comparable maturity U.S. Treasury securities and closing fees above 8 percent of the loan amount were defined as "abusive." When those high rates are charged, the consumer has a minimum of six days (three days before plus three days after a home loan closing) to decide whether or not to proceed with the transaction. If a credit-granting institution fails to properly disclose the costs and risks or includes prohibitive terms in a loan agreement, the borrower has up to three years to rescind the transaction, and creditors may be liable for damages.

Subprime lending is difficult to regulate. It can open the door to predatory lending practices. However, the subprime market also opens up opportunities for access to credit among those households who are unable to access credit in any other way.

Concept Check

18–9.   What laws exist today to give consumers fuller disclosure about the terms and risks of taking on
credit?

18–10. What legal protections are available today to protect

borrowers against discrimination? Against predatory
lending?

18–11. In your opinion, are any additional laws needed in
these areas?

18–8 Real Estate Loans

Depository institutions and finance and insurance companies, to name just a few financial institutions, make real estate loans to fund the acquisition of real property—homes, apartment complexes, shopping centers, office buildings, warehouses, and other physical structures, as well as land. Real estate lending is a field unto itself, possessing important differences from other types of loans. These credits may be either short-term **construction loans,** paid out within months as a building project is completed, or long-term mortgages that may stretch out 25 to 30 years in order to provide permanent financing for the acquisition or improvement of real property. Whatever their maturity, real estate loans have been one of the most rapidly growing areas of lending over the past decade, climbing at a double-digit growth rate and reaching nearly a third of all bank assets as the 21st century began. Unfortunately, such loans can be among the riskiest forms of credit extended to customers.

Differences between Real Estate Loans and Other Loans

Real estate loans differ from most other kinds of loans in several respects. First, the average size of a real estate loan is usually much larger than the average size of other loans, especially among consumer and small business loans. Moreover, certain mortgage loans, mainly on single-family homes, tend to have the longest maturities (from about 15 years to 30 years) of any loan made. Long-term lending of this sort carries considerable risk for the lending institution because many things can happen—including adverse changes in economic conditions, interest rates, and the financial and physical health of the borrower—over the term of such a loan.

With most other types of loans the projected cash flow or income of the borrower is most important in the decision to approve or deny a loan application. With real estate lending, however, the condition and value of the property that is the object of the loan are nearly as important as the borrower's income. In real estate lending, competent property appraisal is vitally important to the loan decision. Such appraisals must conform to industry standards and government regulations, particularly if it is likely the mortgage will be sold in the secondary market.

One such regulation is the Federal National Mortgage Association's requirement that any home mortgage loans FNMA purchases must come from borrowers whose monthly house payment (including loan principal and interest, taxes, and insurance) does not

Filmtoid

What 1989 film documentary reveals the negative effects the closure of a GM plant had on the property values in Flint, Michigan, and the inability of laid-off workers to meet debt obligations?

Answer: *Roger and Me.*

normally exceed 28 percent of their monthly gross income and the sum of whose regular monthly payments (including housing costs) does not exceed 36 percent of monthly gross income. The maturity of the home mortgage loan cannot be less than 10 years or more than 30 years, and the property must be appraised by a FNMA–approved appraiser. Fannie Mae's regulations also stipulate that the borrower's credit report cannot be more than 90 days old.

Changes in regulations and the shifting fortunes of different financial institutions have resulted in major changes in lenders granting mortgage loans. While banks often prefer to make shorter-term property loans (especially construction loans), the mortgage banking subsidiaries of financial holding companies now account for a major portion of all home mortgage loans. These subsidiary firms have strong market contacts and can usually resell any home mortgage loans they make in short order to long-distance mortgage lenders, such as life insurers, savings banks, or foreign investors. Mortgage subsidiaries usually establish short-term "warehouse lines" at other lending institutions in order to provide them with adequate funding to carry the mortgages they originate or buy until they sell those same loans to other investors.

Factors in Evaluating Applications for Real Estate Loans

In evaluating real estate loan applications loan officers must consider the following:

1. The amount of the down payment planned by the borrower relative to the purchase price of mortgaged property is a critical factor in determining how safe a mortgage loan is from the lender's point of view. In general, the higher the ratio of loan amount to purchase price, the less incentive the borrower has to honor all the terms of the loan because the borrower has less equity in the property. When mortgages reach 90 percent or more of the property's purchase price, mortgage insurance becomes important and the lender must place added emphasis on assessing the borrower's sense of responsibility.

2. Real property loans often bring in other business (such as deposits and future property-improvement loans) from the borrowing customer. Therefore, they should be viewed in the context of a *total relationship* between borrower and lender. For example, the lender might be willing to give a mortgage loan customer a somewhat lower loan rate in return for a pledge that the customer will use other financial services.

3. Home mortgage loans require the real estate loan officer to assess the following aspects of each credit application:

   a. *Amount and stability of the borrower's income*, especially relative to the size of the mortgage loan and the size of payments required.

   b. *The borrower's available savings and where the borrower will obtain the required down payment.* If the down payment is made by drawing down savings significantly, the customer has fewer liquid assets available for future emergencies, such as paying off the mortgage if someone in the family becomes ill or loses a job.

   c. *The borrower's track record in caring for and managing property.* If the mortgaged property is not properly maintained, the lender may not fully recover the loaned funds in a foreclosure and sale.

   d. *The outlook for real estate sales in the local market area in case the property must be repossessed.* In a depressed local economy with substantial unemployment, many homes and business structures are put up for sale often with few active buyers. The lender could wait a long time for recovery of its funds.

e. The outlook for market interest rates. While the secondary market for floating-rate mortgage loans has improved in recent years, fixed-rate home mortgages are still typically easier to sell.

During the 1970s and 1980s, severe problems appeared in the real estate loan portfolios of many home mortgage lenders. Several of the largest banks in the United States, for example, foreclosed on and sold commercial and residential properties at deeply discounted prices. In response to these problems, Congress enacted Title XI of the Financial Institutions Reform, Recovery, and Enforcement Act of 1989. Title XI requires the use of state-certified or licensed appraisers for real estate loans that come under the regulatory authority of the federal banking agencies. The four chief federal regulators of banks and thrifts have recently ruled that certified or licensed appraisals are required for most real estate loans that exceed $250,000 in amount. (Renewals of existing loans are generally exempt from specific appraisal requirements.) For smaller-denomination real estate loans, a lender must follow "prudent" evaluation standards and document in writing its valuation of any property that is the basis for a real estate loan, including the assumptions upon which estimates of property values are based.

Further tightening of standards and regulations surrounding real estate loans occurred when Congress passed the National Affordable Housing Act in 1990. This law and its supporting regulations require that applicants for mortgage loans must be given a disclosure statement indicating whether the servicing rights (i.e., the right to collect payments from the borrower) could be transferred to another institution that borrowers will have to deal with during the life of their loan. In an effort to reduce the loss of homes through foreclosure, Congress stipulated that lenders must tell borrowers delinquent in repaying their loans if the lender counsels home owners or knows of any nonprofit organizations that provide such counseling.

Concept Check

18–12. In what ways is a real estate loan unique compared to other kinds of bank loans?

18–13. What factors should a lender consider in evaluating real estate loan applications?

Home Equity Lending

In the United States, the 1986 Tax Reform Act opened up even wider the rapidly growing field of **home equity loans.** Under these credit programs, home owners whose residence has appreciated in value can use the *equity* in their homes—the difference between a home's estimated market value and the amount of the mortgage loans against it—as a borrowing base. Thus, if a home was purchased for $100,000 and has a $70,000 mortgage loan against it today and, due to inflation and growing demand for housing, its market value is now $150,000, the home owner will have a *borrowing base* of about $80,000 (i.e., $150,000 – $70,000). This base might be drawn upon as collateral for a loan to remodel the home, purchase a second home, or for some other legitimate purpose.

Two main types of home equity loans are in use today. The first is the *traditional home equity loan*—a closed-end credit covering a specific period of months and years and used mainly for home improvements. Traditional equity credits are normally repaid in equal installments, quarterly or monthly, and are most frequently secured by a second mortgage against the borrower's home. This lump-sum credit usually carries a fixed interest rate.

Many lenders have seized upon the home equity lending opportunity by offering consumers a second and newer type of home equity loan—*lines of credit against a home's borrowing base*. They usually determine the credit limit on these home equity lines by taking a percentage of the appraised value of the borrowing customer's home (say, 75 percent) and subtracting the amount the customer still owes on the existing loan. That is:

Appraised value of home	$150,000
Times percentage allowed	×75%
Equals percentage of home's appraised value	$112,500
Minus balance still owed on home mortgage	−70,000
Equals maximum credit line available to customer	$ 42,500

The maximum loan amount allowed may be adjusted based on the customer's income and debts plus his or her past repayment record with previous loans.

These credit lines can be used for any legitimate purpose, not just housing-related expenditures—for example, to purchase an automobile or finance a college education. Moreover, many home-equity credit lines are revolving credits—the customer can borrow up to the maximum amount of the loan, repay all or a portion of the amount borrowed, and borrow again up to the stipulated maximum amount any number of times until the credit line matures, usually within 1 to 10 years. Because home equity–based credit tends to be longer term and more secure, it often carries a lower loan rate and longer payout period, thus reducing the borrower's installment payments below the required payments on more conventional consumer loans. Traditional home equity loans normally are priced using longer-term interest rates, while home equity credit lines often have interest rates tied more closely to short-term rates, such as the prime rate. While normally carrying variable rates, some equity credit lines carry a fixed-rate option for a fee.

Home equity borrowers tend to be more affluent than the average homeowner. They report higher levels of personal income and more equity in their homes. Home equity borrowers also tend to be older customers with a longer period of home ownership and a longer record of employment. Most home equity customers are in their late 40s or older; many are in or approaching retirement and have substantially paid off their first home mortgage. Most equity loans are used to pay for home improvements, repay old loans, finance an education, fund vacations, or cover medical costs.

Loan officers need to exercise great care with home equity loan requests. For one thing, they rest on the assumption that housing prices will not decline significantly. Yet there is ample historical evidence that economic downturns and rising unemployment can flood local housing markets with homes for sale, depressing prices. While in most states a lender can repossess a home pledged as collateral for a loan, often the lending institution has difficulty selling the home for a price that recoups all its funds plus all the costs incurred in making and servicing the loan and taking possession of the collateral. There is also room to question the wisdom of using an appreciating asset, such as a house, to purchase an asset not likely to appreciate, such as an automobile, furniture, or appliances. Loan officers must exercise care in granting such credit requests, lending only a portion (perhaps no more than 60 or 70 percent in riskier markets) of the home's estimated equity value in order to allow an adequate cushion should real estate markets turn down.

Moreover, strict regulations at the federal level require lenders to put an interest rate cap on how high loan rates can go on floating-rate home equity loans. Lenders must provide their customers with information on all loan charges and risks under a required Truth in Lending Act disclosure statement. The consumer's overriding risk is that the lender would be forced to repossess his or her home. Not only does such an event destroy customer relationships and result in adverse publicity for the lending institution, but it may also saddle the lender with an asset that could be difficult to sell.

The Consumer Protection Act of 1988 prohibits a home equity lender from arbitrarily canceling a loan and demanding immediate payment. However, if the lender can show that the customer has committed fraud or misrepresentation, failed to pay out the loan as promised, or not kept up the value of the property involved, collection of the loan can be accelerated. The home equity loan customer, then, has little choice but to pay up or surrender the home that was pledged as collateral, unless protected by law.

The Most Controversial of Home Mortgage Loans: Interest-Only Mortgages

By the middle of the current decade nearly 70 percent of American families owned their own home and 30 percent of the value of U.S. households' assets came from their ownership of residential property. Not surprisingly, home mortgage credit has become the number one asset for many financial institutions.

Yet, recent soaring home prices have roused the concern of many mortgage lenders. The incredible housing boom of the past decade could become the "housing bust" of the new era. Fewer and fewer new home buyers seem able to afford the high-priced homes present in many parts of the United States and overseas. Many households are already deeply in debt as credit card balances approached record levels. How can households seeking new homes afford to buy them?

Clever mortgage bankers have quickly come up with an alternative—offering cash-strapped families an *interest-only adjustable mortgage loan* or **option ARM.** With this type of credit the home buyer is obligated to pay only the interest on his or her home loan for an initial period—for example, the first 10 years. Then after that initial time interval *both* principal and interest payments would have to be made until the loan was paid off. Unfortunately, some lenders failed to tell their clients that by paying only the interest on these new instruments, the principal payments would be much higher when these eventually came due because there would be a shorter time available to pay off their loan. To many observers interest-only loans resembled predatory lending against lower-income families.

Some mortgage bankers countered, however, that most families stay only a few years in any one home. A rough average is 7 to 8 years and then a new family moves in and takes out a new mortgage. Therefore, the interest-only loan customer may not stay in his or her home long enough to worry about a future sharp rise in his or her monthly home loan payments. However, what some mortgage bankers failed to convey was that a lack of repayment of principal meant that the family selling their home would gain little equity and might have a lot less money to make a down payment on their next home.

Equally problematic is the fact that most such loans carry an adjustable loan rate (though fixed-rate interest only home mortgages are on the rise). Therefore, in an environment of rising market interest rates many interest-only home borrowers face increased principal payments and higher interest payments down the road, raising the specter of possible bankruptcy or perhaps having to surrender their home. Mortgage lenders have learned that it's critically important to make sure their borrowing customer is fully informed about the *risks,* as well as the advantages, of any home mortgage contract in order to head off trouble for *both* home buyer and lender.

Key URL
Recently the U.S. Mortgage Bankers Association set up a consumer education site to help home buyers understand the terms of their home loans. See **www.homeloanlearning center.com.**

18–9 The Changing Environment for Consumer and Real Estate Lending

Powerful forces are reshaping the extension of credit to individuals and families today. For one thing, the population is *aging* rapidly in the United States, Japan, and other industrialized nations. As people grow older, they tend to make *less* use of credit and to pay down their outstanding debts. This suggests that the total demand for consumer credit per capita eventually may slow, forcing lenders to fight hard for profitable consumer loan accounts. Indeed, in the home equity credit line market there are already signs of slowing after several years of double-digit growth. Moreover, deregulation has brought more lenders into the consumer credit field. Financial institutions hoping to protect their revenues in this field will need to construct their fee schedules carefully and develop new marketing strategies.

A related trend in consumer lending—*point-of-sale loans*—also reflects changes going on in the population to whom lenders market their credit services. More loan customers today demand speed and convenience in the lending process. Many consumers want credit available instantly when they are making purchases rather than having to drive to a lending institution to request a loan. Many lenders today are offering *indirect loans* through dealers in autos, home appliances, and other big-ticket items.

The dealer prepares a credit agreement and phones or faxes the borrowing customer's information to the lender, seeking quick approval. Other lending institutions are offering *preapproval credit programs* where the customer phones in or mails credit information to the lender and gets approval for a loan before a purchase is made. In this instance the store or dealer where the customer makes a purchase can simply verify with the lending institution that a loan has already been approved.

These newer approaches reduce the need to enter a lending institution and result in more *indirect lending* at the point at which a sale is being made, rather than direct lending to the customer at the branch office of a lending institution. The result is greater convenience for the customer, but lenders must be alert to the added risks involved in making quick credit decisions and the possible loss of direct relationships with their customers, reducing opportunities to sell additional services.

18–10 A New Federal Bankruptcy Code Appears

Yet another powerful trend in consumer lending emerged recently as households in record numbers sought protection from their creditors under the U.S. bankruptcy code. Individuals filing bankruptcy petitions soared to well over a million annually as the 21st century opened, anticipating that a new, less forgiving bankruptcy code would soon become law. Most sought to have their debts completely erased, to literally "start over."

On April 20, 2005, President George W. Bush signed the Bankruptcy Abuse Prevention and Consumer Protection Act. The net effect of the new code is likely to make filing for bankruptcy more expensive and time-consuming than in the past, which, in turn, may discourage some consumers from taking on more debt and increasing their risk. Debtors seeking bankruptcy relief will be required to submit more personal information to the bankruptcy court (including payroll stubs and tax returns) and their attorney must verify the accuracy of the information submitted.

Consumers seeking debt relief must complete a U.S. Trustee–approved credit counseling program before becoming eligible to file for bankruptcy. The hope is that some consumers who would have filed may discover instead that a counselor-prepared repayment plan would better meet their needs. If the consumer still elects to seek bankruptcy protection he or she must complete an approved course on the principles of personal financial management before the court finally discharges their debts. This provision is designed to help debt-prone consumers avoid similar problems in the future.

A *means test*—an average of a debtor's past six months of "current monthly income"—determines whether an applicant must file under either Chapter 7 or Chapter 13 of the bankruptcy code. Under the old code most individuals filing for debtor relief went the Chapter 7 route, which wipes out all or most debts and allows them to start fresh. But the new code makes it harder to qualify for this preferred form of bankruptcy. In particular, people who earn more than their state's median household income must file under Chapter 13, which requires a court-approved repayment plan.

Overall, the new bankruptcy code is expected to reduce the cost of credit for the average family borrower, particularly if it reduces the incidence of bad loans. It may also slow the growth of credit card and installment loans as consumers become more cautious and shift more of their borrowing toward housing-related loans because a bankrupt's home may be protected from seizure by creditors depending upon the terms of state law.

Key URLs
For additional information concerning the new federal bankruptcy code see the Web site maintained by the U.S. Trustees' Office at **www.usdoj.gov/ust/eo/ust_org/about_ustp.htm**. For publications in the bankruptcy area, see **www.nolo.com/**.

18–11 Pricing Consumer and Real Estate Loans: Determining the Rate of Interest and Other Loan Terms

A financial institution prices every consumer loan by setting an interest rate, maturity, and terms of repayment that both lender and customer find comfortable. While many consumer loans are short term, stretching over a few weeks or months, long-term loans to purchase automobiles, home appliances, and new homes may stretch from one or two years all the way out to 25 or 30 years. Indeed, in some cases, such as with automobile loans, consumer loan maturities have been extended in recent years as higher product prices have encouraged lenders to grant longer periods of loan repayment so consumers can afford the monthly payments. A loan officer will usually work with a customer, proposing different loan maturities until a repayment schedule is found that, when taking into consideration the consumer's other obligations, fits current and projected household income. Competition among credit suppliers is also a powerful factor shaping consumer loan rates today. Where lenders face intense competition for loans, interest rates tend to be driven down closer to production costs.

The Interest Rate Attached to Nonresidential Consumer Loans

The Cost-Plus Model

Many consumer loans are priced off some base or cost rate, with a profit margin and compensation for risk added. For example, the rate on a consumer installment loan may be figured from the *cost-plus model:*

$$\begin{aligned}\text{Loan rate paid by the consumer} =\ &\text{Lender's cost of raising loanable funds} + \text{Nonfunds operating cost (including wages and salaries of lender personnel)}\\ &+ \text{Premium for risk of customer default} + \text{Premium for term risk with a longer-term loan} + \text{Desired profit margin}\end{aligned}$$

(18–1)

Lending institutions use a wide variety of methods to determine the actual loan rates they will offer to their customers. Among the more familiar methods for calculating consumer loan rates are the annual percentage rate (or APR), simple interest, the discount rate, and the add-on rate method.

Annual Percentage Rate Under the terms of the Truth-in-Lending Act, lenders must give the household borrower a statement specifying the **annual percentage rate (APR)** for a proposed loan. The APR is the internal rate of return (annualized) that equates expected total payments with the amount of the loan. It takes into account how fast the loan is being repaid and how much credit the customer will actually have use of during the life of the loan.

For example, suppose a consumer borrows $2,000 for a year, paying off the loan in 12 equal monthly installments, including $200 in interest. Each month the borrower makes a payment of $183.33 in principal and interest. The periodic interest rate may be found using a financial calculator or spreadsheet such as Excel and then annualized by multiplying it by the number of payment periods in a year in order to get the APR. You are looking for the periodic rate of return associated with 12 payments of $183.33 that have a present value (amount received at time of loan) of $2,000. The rate calculated is 1.4974 percent per month,[1] which equates to an APR of 17.97 percent (1.4974 × 12). Providing the APR allows borrowers to *compare* a particular loan rate with the loan rates offered by other lenders. Comparing loan rates encourages individuals to shop around for credit.

Key URL
To gather additional information on pricing consumer loans and determining customer loan payments, amortization rates, credit grades, and prepayment schedules see, for example, **www.hsh.com**.

For another APR example, suppose that you, as loan officer, quote your customer an APR of 12 percent on a one-year loan of $1,000 to be repaid monthly. The customer asks, *How much will I pay in finance charges under the terms of this loan?* To provide the answer to this question, you must determine the monthly payments for a 12-month (period) loan for $1,000 (present value) at a periodic interest rate of 1 percent (12%/12). Using a financial calculator or spreadsheet, you find that the monthly payment is $88.85.[2] The sum of all payments over the life of the loan is $1,066.20 (88.85 × 12) where $1,000 is the loan principal. The total finance charge to the customer is $1,066.20 − $1,000 = $66.20 over the life of the loan.

On the other hand, suppose the customer is told he or she must pay $260 in finance charges to get a $2,000 loan for 24 months. This means the consumer makes payments of $94.17 (2,260/24). What APR is this customer being quoted? The periodic rate for 24 monthly payments of $94.17 with a present value of $2,000 is 1.002 percent.[3] The APR is the periodic rate annualized (1.002 × 12) or 12.02 percent. Clearly, this customer is being quoted a 12 percent APR.

Simple Interest In various consumer markets around the globe use is frequently made of the so-called **simple interest method.** This approach, like the APR, adjusts for the length of time a borrower actually has use of credit. If the customer is paying off a loan gradually, the simple interest approach determines the declining loan balance, and that reduced balance is then used to determine the amount of interest owed.

For example, suppose the customer asks for $2,000 for a year at a simple interest rate of 12 percent in order to purchase some furniture. If none of the principal of this loan is to be paid off until the year ends, the interest owed by the customer is:

$$\text{Interest owed} = \text{Principal} \times \text{Rate} \times \text{Time} \qquad \textbf{(18–2)}$$

or

$$I = \$2,000 \times 0.12 \times 1 = \$240$$

At maturity the customer will pay the lender $2,240, or $2,000 in principal plus $240 in interest.

Now assume instead that the loan principal is to be paid off in four quarterly installments of $500 each. Total payments due will be:

First quarter:	$500 + $2,000 × 0.12 × 1/4 = $560
Second quarter:	$500 + $1500 × 0.12 × 1/4 = $545
Third quarter:	$500 + $1000 × 0.12 × 1/4 = $530
Fourth quarter:	$500 + $500 × 0.12 × 1/4 = $515
Total payments due:	$2,000 + $150 = $2,150

Clearly, with simple interest the customer saves on interest as the loan approaches maturity.

---

[1] Using a TI BAII plus financial calculator where N = 12, I/Y = ?, PV = 2,000, Pmt = − 188.33, and FV = 0, the periodic rate of return is 1.4974%.

[2] This is calculated using N = 12, I/Y = 1%, PV = 1,000, Pmt = ?, and FV = 0.

[3] 1.002 percent is obtained using N = 24, I/Y = ?, PV = −2,000, Pmt = 94.17, and FV = 0.

The Discount Rate Method   While most consumer loans allow the customer to pay off the interest owed gradually over the life of a loan, the **discount rate method** requires the customer to pay interest up front. Under this approach, interest is deducted *first*, and the customer receives the loan amount *less* any interest owed.

For example, suppose the loan officer offers a consumer $2,000 at a 12 percent loan rate. The $240 in interest ($2,000 × 0.12) is deducted from the loan principal; the borrower receives $2,000 minus $240, or $1,760. When the loan matures, however, the customer must pay back the full $2,000. The borrower's effective loan rate is $240/$1,760 or 13.6 percent.

The Add-On Loan Rate Method   One of the oldest loan rate calculation methods is the **add-on method.** Any interest owed is added to the principal amount of the loan before calculating the required installment payments. For example, if the customer requests $2,000 and is offered a 12 percent add-on interest rate and a repayment plan of 12 equal monthly installments, the total payments due will be $2,000 in principal plus $240 in interest, or $2,240. Each monthly payment will be $186.67 ($2,240 ÷ 12), consisting of $166.67 in loan principal and $20 in monthly interest. Because the borrower has only about $1,000 available during the year, on average, the effective loan rate is approximately two times 12 percent or 24 percent. Only if the loan is paid off in a single lump sum at the end will the add-on rate equal the simple interest rate.

Rule of 78s   A rule of thumb used to determine how much interest income a lender is entitled to accrue at any point in time from a loan that is being paid out in monthly installments is known as the **Rule of 78s.** This is particularly important when a borrower pays off a loan early and may, therefore, be entitled to a rebate of some of the interest charges. The Rule of 78s arises from the fact that the sum of the digits 1 through 12 is 78. To determine the borrowing customer's interest rebate from early repayment of an installment loan, total the digits for the months remaining on the loan and divide that sum by 78. For example, suppose a consumer requests a one-year loan to be repaid in 12 monthly installments, but is able to repay the loan after only nine months. This customer would be entitled to receive back as an interest rebate

$$\frac{1 + 2 + 3}{1 + 2 + \cdots + 11 + 12} \times 100 = \frac{6}{78} \times 100 = 7.69 \text{ percent} \qquad \textbf{(18–3)}$$

of the total finance charges on the loan. The lender is entitled to keep 92.31 percent of those finance charges.

Concept Check

18–17. What options does a loan officer have in pricing consumer loans?

18–18. Suppose a customer is offered a loan at a discount rate of 8 percent and pays $75 in interest at the beginning of the term of the loan. What net amount of credit did this customer receive? Suppose you are told that the effective rate on this loan is 12 percent. What is the average loan amount the customer has available during the year?

18–19. See if you can determine what APR you are charging a consumer loan customer if you grant the customer a loan for five years, payable in monthly installments, and the customer must pay a finance charge of $42.74 per $100.

18–20. If you quote a consumer loan customer an APR of 16 percent on a $10,000 loan with a term of four years that requires monthly installment payments, what finance charge must this customer pay?

Insights and Issues

CONSUMER LOAN RATES: RECENT SURVEYS AND WHAT THEY REVEAL

Recently the Federal Reserve Board began surveying banks and finance companies for the loan rates they quote as well as selected other loan terms for automobile loans and for personal credit. An example of the recent loan terms quoted on these different loan types is shown below.

Terms on Popular Consumer Loans
(Data for February 2005)

Type of Loan and Lending Institution	Average Annual Loan Rate (in percent)	Type or Characteristic of Loan	Survey Average Values
Commercial banks:		Average maturity of loans in months:	
48-month new car loan	6.86%	New car loans	59.1 mo.
24-month personal loan	12.01	Used car loans	57.9 mo.
Credit cards:		Loan-to-value ratios:	
All accounts	12.31	New car loans	89%
Accounts assessed interest	14.13	Used car loans	98
Auto finance companies:		Amount financed in dollars:	
New car loans	4.68	New car loans	$24,290
Used car loans	9.36	Used car loans	15,453

Source: Survey by the Board of Governors of the Federal Reserve System. See the *Federal Reserve Bulletin* for the latest survey results.

Surveying the table above reveals some interesting associations between consumer loan rates and other features of a consumer loan, such as maturity, cost, and risk. We notice, for example, that credit card loans, which are among the riskiest in terms of loan default and losses due to fraud, tend to carry the highest average interest rates. Automobile loans are generally cheaper than personal loans because auto loans are secured by marketable collateral—the automobile itself—whereas many personal loans are either unsecured or have collateral pledged that is more difficult to sell.

We note also that new car loan rates tend to be lower than used car loan rates. The newer the vehicle, the easier it generally is to sell should the borrower be unable to repay, and lenders find that new car owners tend to take better care of their vehicles.

Moreover, car rental companies have tended to keep their fleets for longer periods, so the supply of used cars has diminished. As a result, many used car loans are now extended for maturities that equal or exceed new car loan maturities, and lenders have been willing to extend a larger percentage of a used car's purchase price in the form of a loan.

Overall, there is evidence that consumers have recently become much more sensitive to differences in loan rates on different types of loans offered by different lenders. Indeed, even the smallest consumer borrowers with little financial education are now increasingly shopping around and learning to refinance everything from automobile, mobile home, and home mortgage loans to credit card obligations. The result is narrower spreads on consumer loans and greater consolidation among consumer lending institutions.

Interest Rates on Home Mortgage Loans

For nearly half a century, stretching from the Great Depression of the 1930s into the 1970s, most loans to finance the purchase of new homes were **fixed-rate mortgages (FRMs)**—that is, loans with a *fixed interest rate* that the borrower could rely upon. In the early 1970s, the pressure of inflation and more volatile interest rates gave rise to adjustable-rate home mortgage loans. Then in 1981, both the Comptroller of the Currency and the Federal Home Loan Bank Board authorized the offering of **adjustable-rate mortgages (ARMs)** for all federally chartered depository institutions and these flexible-rate loans, now amount to about a third of the new home loans granted each year.

The popularity of ARMs may be attributed to aggressive marketing of these loans by lenders seeking to make the yields on their earning assets more responsive to interest rate movements. Many lending institutions have offered teaser rates that are significantly below loan rates on FRMs. Because ARMs often carry lower initial interest rates than fixed-rate mortgages, they allow more families to qualify for a home mortgage loan. Some home mortgage lenders have offered *cap rates* on ARMs. For example, the lender may agree not to raise the loan rate more than two percentage points in any given year or more than five percentage points over the life of the loan, no matter how high other interest rates go.

Whether a customer takes out an FRM or an ARM, the loan officer must determine what the initial loan rate will be and, therefore, what the monthly payments will be. Each monthly payment on a home mortgage loan reduces a portion of the principal of the loan and a portion of the interest owed on the total amount borrowed. With the majority of mortgage loan contracts today, monthly payments early in the life of the loan go mainly to pay interest. As the loan gets closer to maturity, the monthly payments increasingly are devoted to reducing the loan's principal.

Loan officers and customers may determine if a mortgage loan is affordable by figuring the required monthly payment given the interest rate the mortgage lender proposes to charge. Such problems are applications of the time value of money that would usually be calculated using a financial calculator or spreadsheet. The formula for monthly payments is:

$$\text{Customer's monthly mortgage payment} = \frac{\text{Amount of loan principal} \times \left(\frac{\text{Annual loan rate}}{12}\right) \times \left(1 + \frac{\text{Annual loan rate}}{12}\right)^{t \times 12}}{\left[\left(1 + \frac{\text{Annual loan rate}}{12}\right)^{t \times 12} - 1\right]} \tag{18-4}$$

For example, the required monthly payment for a $50,000, 25-year mortgage loan calculated at the fixed rate of 12 percent is $526.61.[4] The total in payments over the life of the loan is $526.61 × 25 × 12 = $157,983. If you subtract the $50,000 in principal, you will find that the borrower will pay $107,983 in interest over the life of the loan. The actual monthly payment normally will vary somewhat from year to year even with an FRM due to changes in property taxes, insurance, and other fees that typically are included in each monthly payment.

In the foregoing example we calculated the required monthly payments on a fixed-rate mortgage. We can, of course, use the same method to calculate the required monthly payment on an adjustable rate mortgage loan by simply plugging in a new interest rate each time that interest rates change. For example, assume that, as in the previous FRM example, the initial loan rate for an ARM is also 12 percent. However, after one year (i.e., 12 monthly payments) has elapsed, the mortgage loan rate rises to 13 percent. In this case the customer's monthly payments would increase to $563.30:[5]

$$\text{Each monthly payment} = \frac{\$49,662.30 \times \left(\frac{0.13}{12}\right) \times \left(1 + \frac{0.13}{12}\right)^{24 \times 12}}{\left(1 + \frac{0.13}{12}\right)^{24 \times 12} - 1} = \$563.30$$

This example assumes that the loan rate increased to 13 percent beginning with the 13th monthly payment. Note that after one year the principal of the loan (which originally stood at $50,000) had dropped to $49,662.30 due to the monthly payments made during the first 12 months.[6] When considering whether or not to approve a customer's

[4]Using a financial calculator (TI Ball Plus), N = 25 × 12, I = 12%/12, PV = –50,000, PMT = ?, and FV = 0.
[5]Using the financial calculator once again, N = 24 × 12, I = 13%/12, PV = 49,662.30, PMT = ?, and FV = 0.
[6]The $49,662.30 is calculated using N = 24 × 12, I = 12%/12, PV = ?, PMT = 526.61, and FV = 0.

request for an adjustable-rate loan, the loan officer must decide whether a rise in interest rates is likely and whether the customer has sufficient budget flexibility and future earnings potential to handle the varying loan payments that can exist with an ARM.

Charging the Customer Mortgage Points

Home mortgage loan agreements often require borrowers to pay an additional charge up front called **points.** This extra charge is determined by multiplying the amount of the home mortgage loan by a specific percentage figure. For example, suppose the borrower seeks a $100,000 home loan and the lender assesses the borrower an up-front charge of two points. In this case the home buyer's extra charge would be

$$\begin{array}{c}\text{Dollar amount} \\ \text{of points} \\ \text{charged on} \\ \text{a home} \\ \text{mortgage} \\ \text{loan}\end{array} = \begin{array}{c}\text{Amount} \\ \text{of the} \\ \text{mortgage} \\ \text{loan}\end{array} \times \begin{array}{c}\text{Number} \\ \text{of points} \\ \text{charged} \\ \text{by the} \\ \text{lender}\end{array} = \$100,000 \times 0.02 = \$2,000 \qquad \textbf{(18–5)}$$

By requiring the borrower to pay something extra over and above the interest owed on his or her home loan, a lender can earn a higher effective interest rate. This extra yield can be found by deducting from the amount of the loan the dollar amount of points charged and by adding the dollar amount of points to the interest owed on the loan. In this instance the borrower has available for his or her use, not the full amount of the mortgage loan, but rather the loan amount *less* the points assessed by the lender.

Concept Check

18–21. What differences exist between ARMs and FRMs?

18–22. How is the loan rate figured on a home mortgage loan? What are the key factors or variables?

18–23. What are *points?* What is their function?

Summary

Lending to consumers has been among the most popular financial services offered by financial-service providers in recent years. Among the most important points discussed in this chapter are the following:

- Loans and other financial services extended to households represent one of the most important sources of financial-service revenues and deposits today as banks, credit unions, savings associations, and finance and insurance companies all compete aggressively for the consumer's account.

- Consumer credit represents an important supplement to business credit services, providing financial firms with a more diversified customer base and helping to reduce the exposure of lenders to the impact of business cycles when revenues expand and contract.

- Consumer lending presents special challenges to loan officers due to higher-than-average default rates related to the vulnerability of families to loss of employment, illness, and other adverse circumstances.

- The keys to successful consumer lending today center on the ability to process large volumes of credit requests quickly so the household borrower receives a fast decision from the lender. Automation has become a powerful force with the use of *credit-scoring systems* to mathematically evaluate each household's credit capacity and credit bureaus that give lenders quick access to consumer credit histories.

- Loans and other financial services sold to households have increasingly been shaped by federal and state laws and regulations designed to promote (*a*) fuller disclosure of contract terms and (*b*) greater fairness in the marketplace, outlawing discrimination on the basis of race, sex, religion, and other irrelevant factors. These rules serve to promote competition, encourage households to shop for credit, and, hopefully, lead to more informed household decision making.

- Real estate loans are most often directed at households seeking places to live. Real estate credit provides the financial resources to support the construction of homes, condominiums, apartments, shopping centers, office buildings, and other forms of real property. Banks and many of their competitors make both short-term mortgage credit (usually in the form of construction loans) and long-term mortgages available to businesses and households. Officers and staff of real estate lending institutions must have multiple skills in assessing property values, real estate law, and the extensive regulations that surround this field. More than any other type of loan, real-estate lending depends heavily on judging the value and outlook for a loan's collateral.

- Pricing consumer and real estate loans is challenging as several different techniques have emerged. With so many different methods available for calculating loan interest rates and other credit terms, confusion abounded for lenders and customers until the Truth in Lending Act was passed in the United States, requiring lenders to disclose the *APR* (annual percentage rate) that applies to a customer's loan, yielding a common standard to compare one proposed loan against another.

- A trend is unfolding today toward more *market-sensitive loan rates* in order to reduce interest rate risk on the part of consumer and real estate lenders, particularly in the home mortgage field where fixed-rate and adjustable-rate loans compete against each other for the customer's allegiance. In the case of adjustable-rate credit, loan officers must be especially careful in deciding whether a borrowing customer has sufficient budgetary flexibility to be able to adjust to variable loan payments, especially if interest rates are expected to rise during the life of a loan.

Key Terms

residential mortgage loans, 584
installment loans, 585
debit cards, 586
credit bureaus, 588
cosigner, 588
right of offset, 589
credit scoring, 594
disclosure rules, 597
antidiscrimination laws, 598
Truth-in-Lending Act, 598
Fair Credit Reporting Act, 598

Fair Credit Billing Act, 598
Fair Debt Collection Practices Act, 598
Equal Credit Opportunity Act, 599
Community Reinvestment Act, 599
predatory lending, 600
subprime loans, 600
construction loans, 601
home equity loans, 603
option ARM, 605
annual percentage rate (APR), 607

simple interest method, 608
discount rate method, 609
add-on method, 609
Rule of 78s, 609
fixed-rate mortgages (FRMs), 610
adjustable-rate mortgages (ARMs), 610
points, 612

Problems and Projects

1. The Childress family has applied for a $5,000 loan for home improvements, especially to install a new roof and add new carpeting. Bob Childress is a welder at Ford Motor Co., the first year he has held that job, and his wife sells clothing at Wal-Mart. They have three children. The Childresses own their home, which they purchased six months ago, and have an *average* credit rating, with some late bill payments. They have a telephone, but hold only a checking account with a bank and a few savings bonds. Mr. Childress has a $35,000 life insurance policy with a cash surrender value of $1,100. Suppose the lender uses the credit scoring system presented in this chapter and denies all credit applications scoring fewer than 360 points. Is the Childress family likely to get their loan?

2. Mr. and Mrs. Napper are interested in funding their children's college education by taking out a home equity loan in the amount of $24,000. Eldridge National Bank is willing to extend a loan, using the Nappers' home as collateral. Their home has been appraised at $110,000, and Eldridge permits a customer to use no more than 70 percent of the appraised value of a home as a borrowing base. The Nappers still owe $60,000 on the first mortgage against their home. Is there enough residual value left in the Nappers' home to support their loan request? How could the lender help them meet their credit needs?

3. Justin James has just been informed by a finance company that he can access a line of credit of no more than $28,000 based upon the equity value in his home. James still owes $105,000 on a first mortgage against his home and $25,000 on a second mortgage against the home, which was incurred last year to repair the roof and driveway. If the appraised value of James's residence is $197,500, what percentage of the home's estimated market value is the lender using to determine James's maximum available line of credit?

4. What *term* in the consumer lending field does each of the following statements describe?
   a. Plastic card used to pay for goods and services without borrowing money.
   b. Loan to purchase an automobile and pay it off monthly.
   c. If you fail to pay the lender seizes your deposit.
   d. Numerical rating describing likelihood of loan repayment.
   e. Loans extended to low-credit-rated borrowers.
   f. Loan based on spread between a home's market value and its mortgage balance.
   g. Method for calculating rebate borrower receives from retiring a loan early.
   h. Lender requires excessive insurance fees on a new loan.
   i. Loan rate lenders must quote under the Truth in Lending Act.
   j. Upfront payment required as a condition for getting a home loan.

5. Which federal law or laws apply to each of the situations described below?
   a. A loan officer asks an individual requesting a loan about her race.
   b. A bill collector called Jim Jones three times yesterday at his work number without first asking permission.
   c. Sixton National Bank has developed a special form to tell its customers the finance charges they must pay to secure a loan.
   d. Consumer Savings Bank has just received an outstanding rating from federal examiners for its efforts to serve all segments of its community.
   e. Presage State Bank must disclose once a year the areas in the local community where it has made home mortgage and home improvement loans.
   f. Reliance Credit Card Company is contacted by one of its customers in a dispute over the amount of charges the customer made at a local department store.

g. Amy Imed, after requesting a copy of her credit report, discovers several errors and demands a correction.

6. James Smithern has asked for a $3,500 loan from Beard Center National Bank to repay some personal expenses. The bank uses a credit-scoring system to evaluate such requests, which contains the following discriminating factors along with their associated point weights in parentheses:

Credit Rating (excellent, 3; average, 2; poor or no record, 0)

Time in Current Job (five years or more, 6; one to five years, 3)

Time at Current Residence (more than 2 years, 4; one to two years, 2; less than one year, 1)

Telephone in Residence (yes, 1; no, 0)

Holds Account at Bank (yes, 2; no, 0).

The bank generally grants a loan if a customer scores 9 or more points. Mr. Smithern has an average credit rating, has been in his current job for three years and at his current residence for two years, has a telephone, but has no account at the bank. Is James Smithern likely to receive the loan he has requested?

7. Jamestown Savings Bank, in reviewing its credit card customers, finds that of those customers who scored 40 points or less on its credit-scoring system, 35 percent (or a total of 10,615 credit customers) turned out to be delinquent credits, resulting in total loss. This group of bad credit card loans averaged $2,700 in size per customer account. Examining its successful credit accounts Jamestown finds that 12 percent of its good customers (or a total of 3,640 customers) scored 40 points or less on the bank's scoring system. These low-scoring but good accounts generated about $1,700 in revenues each. If Jamestown's credit card division follows the decision rule of granting credit cards only to those customers scoring more than 40 points and future credit accounts generate about the same average revenues and losses, about how much can the bank expect to save in net losses?

8. The Lathrop family needs some extra funds to put their two children through college starting this coming fall and to buy a new computer system for a part-time home business. They are not sure of the current market value of their home, though comparable four-bedroom homes are selling for about $410,000 in the neighborhood. The Van Nuys Federal and Merchants Savings Association will loan 80 percent of the property's appraised value, but the Lathrops still owe $242,000 on their home mortgage and a home improvement loan combined. What maximum amount of credit is available to this family should it elect to seek a home equity credit line?

9. San Carlos Bank and Trust Company uses a credit-scoring system to evaluate most consumer loans that amount to more than $2,500. The key factors used in its scoring system are as follows:

Borrower's length of employment in his/her present job:		Credit bureau report:	
		Excellent	8 points
More than one year	6 points	Average	5 points
Less than one year	3 points	Below average or no record	2 points
Borrower's length of time at current address:		Credit cards currently active:	
More than 2 years	8 points	One card	6 points
One to two years	4 points	Two cards	4 points
Less than one year	2 points	More than two cards	2 points
Borrower's current home situation:		Deposit account(s) with bank:	
Owns home	7 points	Yes	5 points
Rents home or apartment	4 points	No	2 points
Lives with friend or relative	2 points		

The Mulvaney family has two wage earners who have held their present jobs for 18 months. They have lived at their current street address for one year, where they rent on a six-month lease. Their credit report is excellent but shows only one previous charge. However, they are actively using two credit cards right now to help with household expenses. Yesterday, they opened an account at San Carlos and deposited $250. The Mulvaneys have asked for a $4,500 loan to purchase a used car and some furniture. The bank has a cutoff score in its scoring system of 30 points. Would you make this loan for two years, as they have requested? Are there factors not included in the scoring system that you would like to know more about? Please explain.

10. Ray Volkers wants to start his own business. He has asked his bank for a $25,000 new-venture loan. The bank has a policy of making *discount-rate* loans in these cases if the venture looks good, but at an interest rate of prime plus 2. (The prime rate is currently posted at 7 percent.) If Mr. Volker's loan is approved for the full amount requested, what net proceeds will he have to work with from this loan? What is the effective interest rate on this loan for one year?

11. The Robbins family has asked for a 20-year mortgage in the amount of $175,000 to purchase a home. At an 11 percent loan rate, what is the required monthly payment?

12. James Jones received an $8,000 loan last month with the intention of repaying the loan in 12 months. However, Jones now discovers he has cash to repay the loan after making just two payments. What percentage of the total finance charge is Jones entitled to receive as a rebate and what percentage of the loan's finance charge is the lender entitled to keep?

13. The Watson family has been planning a vacation to Europe for the past two years. Stilwater Savings agrees to advance a loan of $8,500 to finance the trip provided the Watsons pay the loan back in 12 equal monthly installments. Stilwater will charge an add-on loan rate of 6 percent. How much in interest will the Watsons pay under the add-on rate method? What is the amount of each required monthly payment? What is the effective loan rate in this case?

14. Joseph Key's request for a four-year automobile loan for $27,000 has been approved. Reston Center Bank will require equal monthly installment payments for 48 months. The bank tells Joseph that he must pay a total of $3,817 in finance charges. What is the loan's APR?

15. Kyle Bender has asked for a 30-year mortgage to purchase a home on Long Island. The purchase price is $465,000, of which Bender must borrow $375,000 to be repaid in monthly installments. If Kyle can get this loan for an APR of 7.75 percent, how much in total finance charges must he pay?

16. Mary Contrary is offered a $1,200 loan for a year to be paid back in equal quarterly installments of $300 each. If Mary is offered the loan at 8 percent simple interest, how much in total interest charges will she pay? Would Mary be better off (in terms of lower interest cost) if she were offered the $1,200 at 6 percent simple interest with only one principal payment when the loan reaches maturity? What advantage would this second set of loan terms have over the first set of loan terms?

17. Buck and Sue Rogers are negotiating with their local bank to secure a mortgage loan in order to buy their first home. With only a limited down payment available to them, Buck and Sue must borrow $225,000. Moreover, the bank has assessed them one and a half

points on the loan. What is the dollar amount of points they must pay to receive this loan? How much home mortgage credit will they actually have available for their use?

18. Dresden Bank's personal loan department quotes Lance Angelo a finance charge of $5.25 for each $100 in credit the bank is willing to extend to him for a year (assuming the balance of the loan is to be paid off in 12 equal installments). What APR is the bank quoting Lance? How much would he save per $100 borrowed if he could retire the loan in six months?

Internet Exercises

1. What is credit scoring? Visit **www.fairisaac.com** and look for an article by Jed Graham entitled, "After Nearly 50 Years, Fair Isaac Made Point." You will find it as an article listed under News. Describe this IT company's role in credit scoring.

2. How does the Web help a consumer loan officer determine a customer's credit rating and credit history? For an example, go to **www.experian.com** and see Business Services. What products and services does this firm have to offer the banker?

3. Go to **nt.mortgage101.com/partner-scripts/1038.asp** to find the meaning of such real estate lending terms as *adjustable-rate mortgage, points,* and *home equity credit.* Provide the definition for each of the above terms.

4. What methods and tools are available on the Web to aid in pricing consumer loans and real estate credit? See, for example, **www.financialpowertools.com**. Use the auto loan calculator to calculate the monthly payments on a 48-month car loan given that the purchase price is $23,000; the down payment is $1,200; the trade-in value of the customer's current vehicle is $5,000, but $4,000 is still owed; nontaxable fees are $40.00, sales tax is 7 percent, and the interest rate is 5 percent.

5. Why is regulation so important in the personal loan area? For some insights regarding this issue, visit **www.hud.gov** and **www.ffiec.gov**. At **www.hud.gov/groups/lenders. cfm** find the meaning of and concerns associated with *predatory lending.* At **www. ffiec.gov** determine the purpose of the Home Mortgage Disclosure Act (HMDA).

S&P Market Insight Challenge (www.mhhe.com/edumarketinsight)

1. Savings and loan associations have focused on home mortgage loans since their inception. For an up-to-date view of S&Ls' share of today's mortgage origination market, click the Industry tab in S&P's Market Insight. A drop-down menu reveals the subindustry category Thrifts & Mortgage Finance. By choosing this category you will be able to access the S&P Industry Survey on Savings and Loans. Please download this particular survey and explore the section entitled "Industry Trend." What is happening to the thrifts' share of mortgage originations? Can you explain why?

2. Who are the leading lending institutions in making credit available to consumers (individuals and families)? S&P's Market Insight contains a significant number of major household lenders, including Household International, Capital One Financial, and Bank of America. See if you can determine the ratio of consumer loans to total loans for each of these institutions and other leading household lenders on the Insight list. Why do the consumer loan to total loan ratios differ so much among these institutions? Do they also differ in the kinds of consumer loans they make? Why? What forms of risk does consumer lending present to these particular institutions?

REAL NUMBERS FOR REAL BANKS

Assignment for Chapter 18

YOUR BANK'S PROVISION OF CREDIT TO INDIVIDUALS AND FAMILIES

Chapter 18 explores consumer loans, credit cards, and real estate lending. In this assignment we look at how regulators categorize loans to individuals and families. We will use this information to evaluate the changing composition of your bank's retail loan portfolio across years and relative to other large banks.

Trend and Comparative Analysis

A. **Data Collection:** In the assignment for Chapter 16, we did a breakdown of gross loans and leases based on purpose.

Retail loans were allocated to either the real estate loan category or to the loans to individuals category. In this assignment we will go back to the SDI at **www3.fdic.gov/sdi/** and collect more detailed information on these loans. This entails using SDI to create a four-column report of your bank's information and peer group information across years. For Report Selection, you will access the Net Loans and Leases and 1–4 Family Residential Net Loans and Leases reports to collect percentage information as detailed below. Enter this data into the spreadsheet used for comparisons with the peer group as follows:

158	Loans to Individuals and Families	BHC	Peer Group	BHC	Peer Group				
159	Date	12/31/yyyy	12/31/yyyy	12/31/yyyy	12/31/yyyy				
160	Multifamily residential real estate								
161	1-4 family residential loans: Secured by first liens								
162	1-4 family residential loans: Secured by junior liens								
163	1-4 family residential loans: Home equity loans								
164	Credit cards and related plans**								
165	Other loans to individuals								

B. Use the chart function in Excel and the data by columns in rows 160 through 165 to create four pie charts illustrating the breakdown of loans to individuals and families. Your pie charts should include titles and labels. For instance, the pie charts for National City Corp (NCC) and the peer group for 12/31/05 are as follows:

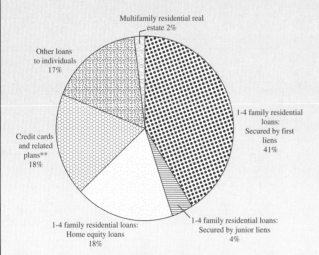

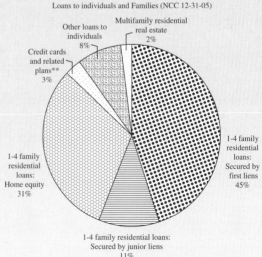

C. Write approximately one page about the types of loans your bank makes to individuals and families. Has the composition changed across time? How does the composition of your bank's retail loan portfolio compare to other very large banks (your peer group)? Can you make any inferences concerning credit risk and/or interest rate risk exposure? Use your pie charts as graphics and incorporate them in the discussion.

Selected References

For an analysis of the risks associated with consumer lending, see especially:

1. Aizcorbe, Ana M., Arthur B. Kennickell, and Kevin B. Moore. "Recent Changes in U.S. Family Finances: Evidence from the 1998 and 2001 Survey of Consumer Finances." *Federal Reserve Bulletin*, January 2003, pp. 1–32.

For an explanation of credit scoring and its impact on consumer lending, see:

2. Avery, Robert B., Raphael W. Bostic, Paul S. Calem, and Glenn B. Canner. "Credit Risk, Credit Scoring, and the Performance of Home Mortgages." *Federal Reserve Bulletin*, July 1996, pp. 621–648.
3. Mester, Loretta J. "What's the Point of Credit Scoring?" *Business Review*, Federal Reserve Bank of Philadelphia, September/October 1997, pp. 3–16.

To learn more about credit bureaus and their services, see especially:

4. Avery, Robert B., Paul S. Calem, and Glenn B. Canner. "An Overview of Consumer Data and Credit Reporting." *Federal Reserve Bulletin*, February 2003, pp. 48–73.
5. Avery, Robert B., Paul S. Calem, and Glenn B. Canner. "Credit Report Accuracy and Access to Credit." *Federal Reserve Bulletin*, Summer 2004, pp. 297–322.
6. Hunt, Robert M. "A Century of Credit Reporting in America." Working Paper 05-13, Federal Reserve Bank of Philadelphia, June 2005.

To examine recent trends in the credit card market and in the assumption of consumer debt, see:

7. Johnson, Kathleen W. "Recent Developments in the Credit Card Market and the Financial Obligations Ratio." *Federal Reserve Bulletin*, Autumn 2005, pp. 473–486.

For an explanation of the Community Reinvestment Act and its impact on banks and other lenders, see especially:

8. Rose, Peter S. "The Performance of Outstanding CRA-Rated Banks." *Bankers Magazine*, September–October 1994, pp. 53–59.

To examine consumer financial-service choices in an electronic era, see especially:

9. Anguelov, Christoslav E., Marianne A. Hilgert, and Jeanne M. Hogarth. "U.S. Consumers and Electronic Banking, 1995–2003." *Federal Reserve Bulletin*, Winter 2004, pp. 1–18.
10. Gerdes, Geoffrey R., Jack K. Walton II, May X. Liu, and Darrel W. Parke. "Trends in the Use of Payments Instruments in the United States." *Federal Reserve Bulletin*, Spring 2005, pp. 180–201.

To explore more fully the market for residential mortgages, see:

11. Emmons, William R., Mark D. Vaughan, and Timothy J. Yeager. "The Housing Giants in Plain View." *The Regional Economist*, Federal Reserve Bank of St. Louis, July 2004, pp. 5–9.
12. Feldman, Ron J. "Mortgage Rates, Home Ownership Rates, and Government-Sponsored Enterprises." *The Region*, Federal Reserve Bank of Minneapolis, 2005, pp. 5–23.
13. Li, Wenli, and Rui Yao. "Your House Just Doubled in Value? Don't Uncork the Champagne Just Yet!" *Business Review*, Federal Reserve Bank of Philadelphia, First Quarter 2006, pp. 25–34, **www.philadelphiafed.org**.
14. Gavin, William T. "Movin' On Up." *The Regional Economist*, Federal Reserve Bank of St. Louis, April 2006, pp. 11–13.

To learn more about the effectiveness of credit counseling in helping consumers better manage their debts, see especially:

15. Hunt, Robert M. "Whither Consumer Credit Counseling?" *Business Review*, Federal Reserve Bank of Philadelphia, Fourth Quarter, 2005, pp. 9–20.

www.mhhe.com/rose7e

PART SEVEN

Managing the Future in a Global Marketplace

Financial institutions not only must be profitable, but they also must grow to better serve their customers. Otherwise, they may face a buyout from competitors and simply disappear. Growth is also an indicator of how well their customer base is being served. Financial firms that grow at a substantial pace tend to have a satisfied base of customers.

However, there are many ways for a financial firm to grow. As we saw in Part One, Chapter 4, a financial-service provider can grow by developing and launching new customer-service facilities in both old and new markets, increasing customer convenience by building new offices, networks of ATMs, call centers, Internet services, and so on. Most financial firms grow and expand this way, particularly early in their history. However, an important alternative for achieving growth in the modern world is through *acquisitions and mergers*.

Prominent examples of the acquisition and merger route to expansion include the recent amalgamation of J. P. Morgan Chase Bank and Bank One and the combination of Bank of America with FleetBoston Financial Group, creating two of the largest banking firms in the United States and around the world with thousands of offices and other service facilities. Inside Asia recently we have seen Dai-Ichi Kangyo, Fuji, and the Industrial Bank of Japan come together in Mizuho Holdings to create one of the world's largest banks. There have been close to 10,000 mergers among banks and thrift institutions in the United States alone in recent decades and scores more in Asia and Europe.

As a result of these combinations most financial-service industries are experiencing massive *consolidation*—fewer but much larger financial-service providers all over the globe. Historically, most of these acquisitions and mergers have involved firms of the *same type* joining with one another. Banks buying banks, insurance companies gobbling up other insurance companies, and security firms going on the hunt to buy other security firms. But this too is rapidly changing as we saw way back in Part One. *Convergence* of different kinds of financial firms, one with another, has been well under way for at least a quarter century. Prominent examples include the recent acquisition of Household Finance, one of the world's leading consumer finance companies, by HSBC of London, one of the largest commercial banks on the planet. At the same time security firms and insurance companies have acquired depository institutions, finance companies, and other financial firms. These consolidations and convergences have been facilitated by more lenient regulations and the rapid economic recovery and growth of the economies of Asia and Europe along with continuing expansion in the Americas.

In theory, financial-service customers may benefit from these mergers and acquisitions because of lower costs from economies of scale and scope and lower risk from diversification. However, there are nagging questions today about the practical, as opposed to the theoretical, benefits of industry consolidations and convergences. We will explore that issue in the first of the chapters in this final part of the text.

Growth of financial firms has also been achieved by breaking out of narrower regional market areas, crossing national boundaries, and entering international markets, sometimes by merger and acquisition and sometimes by setting up completely new facilities in foreign lands. Certainly financial firms can more easily reach around the globe today, establishing electronic communications links with their customers in distant markets or by acquiring financial firms abroad and inheriting an established customer base. International expansion offers numerous potential benefits to financial-service firms, including greater geographic diversification to lower risk and greater capacity to stay abreast of the needs of their customers trading overseas.

Of course, international expansion is not without its challenges—new cultures, new languages, new regulations, and new monetary standards must all be dealt with. In short, expansion into foreign markets solves some problems and gives rise to new problems as we will see in the concluding chapter of the text. We will also explore the *future* of banking and financial services in the concluding sections of the final chapter, getting a glimpse of where financial firms appear to be headed in a rapidly changing, increasingly automated, and increasingly globalized financial-services marketplace.

CHAPTER NINETEEN

Acquisitions and Mergers in Financial-Services Management

Key Topics in This Chapter

- Merger Trends in the United States and Abroad
- Motives for Merger
- Selecting a Suitable Merger Partner
- U.S. and European Merger Rules
- Making a Merger Successful
- Research on Merger Motives and Outcomes

19–1 Introduction

In many nations around the globe a wave of mergers involving both large and small banks, securities firms, insurance companies, and other financial-service providers has been under way for decades. In the United States banking and financial services has consistently ranked in the top five of all industries in the number of merger transactions taking place each year. Since 1980 close to 10,000 mergers among U.S.-insured depository institutions have occurred, dramatically reshaping the financial-services industry and the services it supplies to the public.

These numerous marriages among financial-service institutions reflect the great forces of *consolidation* and *convergence* that have been dramatically reshaping the financial-services industry in the current era, driven by intense competition, the lifting of restrictive government rules (deregulation), and the continuing search for the optimal size financial-services organization that will operate at lowest cost with sufficient geographic and product-line diversification to reduce risk.

Our purpose in this chapter is to more fully understand the merger process among financial firms. We will explore the legal, regulatory, and economic factors that financial-service managers should consider before pursuing a merger or acquisition. We will examine the available research evidence on the benefits and costs of these corporate combinations for both investors and the public.

19–2 Mergers on the Rise

While mergers and acquisitions have swept through the entire financial-services sector in recent years, banking mergers and acquisitions have been the most numerous and widely publicized of these transactions. Many of these mergers sweeping through banking reflect lower legal barriers that previously prohibited or restricted expansion.

For example, in the United States both state and federal laws prohibited or restricted interstate banking in the United States until the 1980s, when new state laws allowing banks and bank holding companies to cross state lines appeared. Then, in 1994, the U.S. Congress passed the Riegle-Neal Interstate Banking Act, which permitted holding companies to reach for bank acquisitions nationwide. These new federal and state laws opened the floodgates to true nationwide banking for the first time in American history.

The merger wave in financial services received yet another legislative boost inside the United States when the Gramm-Leach-Bliley (GLB) Act of 1999 was passed (discussed in more detail in Chapters 2 and 3). The GLB law opened wide the arena for bank–nonbank financial-service combinations. It permits banks, insurance companies, and security firms to acquire each other, increasing opportunities for relatively large financial firms to diversify their product lines and reduce their dependence upon a limited menu of services. However, as Rhoades [17] and Pilloff [10] have observed, while GLB may offer the prospect of reducing U.S. financial firms' risk exposure, it doesn't appear to hold great promise for major improvements in operating efficiency among banks and other financial firms.

A massive merger wave involving leading banks, insurance companies, securities firms, and other service providers also swept through Europe during the 1990s and in the opening years of the 21st century, accompanying the expansion of the European Community (EC). Competition among European financial firms is becoming ever more intense, leading to continuing mergers and acquisitions, particularly in France, Germany, Italy, and Spain. However, financial-service mergers in Europe have slowed from time to time due to a slowing economy and European governments attempting to protect their home banks from acquisition by outsiders.

Asia and Japan followed Europe with a growing number of mergers involving mainly banks, insurers, and securities firms. These corporate combinations were being pieced together in an effort to shore up credit quality problems, fend off the ravages of deflation and sluggish economies, and compete with powerful U.S. and European banks expanding across the Asian landscape. Table 19–1 lists other examples of recent international banking and financial-service mergers.

In the United States a similar convergence and consolidation trend has brought banks into common ownership with security and commodity broker-dealer firms, finance companies, insurance agencies and underwriters, credit card companies, thrift institutions, and numerous other nonbank service providers. Prominent examples include Citicorp's 1998 merger with Travelers Insurance, Inc., creating one of the largest financial-service providers in the world (until Citicorp sold off its Travelers units early in the new century); Bank One's

Factoid
Where do most bank mergers take place in the United States?
Answer: In the southeastern United States (including such states as Alabama, Florida, Georgia, and the Carolinas).

TABLE 19–1
Recent Leading International Financial-Service Mergers and Acquisitions

Acquiring Institution	Acquired Institution	Year
UniCredito Italiano SpA	HVB Group AG, Germany	2005
Banco Santander Central Hispano	Abbey National, U.K.	2004
Mizuho Holdings, Japan	Dai-Ichi Kangyo, Fuji, and Industrial Bank, Japan	2001
HSBC Holdings, U.K.	Credit Commercial de France	2001
Banco Santander, SA, Spain	Banco de Estado, Brazil	2000
Deutsche Bank AG, Germany	Bankers Trust Company, U.S.	1999

Insights and Issues

CONSOLIDATION AND CONVERGENCE IN THE FINANCIAL SERVICES MARKETPLACE

Two of the dominant trends in the banking and financial services sector in recent years have been consolidation and convergence. *Consolidation* refers to a declining population of businesses in any one industry. Banking, security brokering, insurance, and several other financial-service industries have experienced this trend in recent years as they become dominated by fewer, but much larger businesses, largely through mergers and acquisitions. *Convergence,* on the other hand, refers to the movement of two or more industries toward each other, so that different firms wind up offering many of the same services. Convergence also often occurs through mergers and acquisitions as firms reach across industry boundaries to acquire business units with different service menus, though it can also take place through innovation and service diversification within an individual financial firm.

Listed below are some of the largest mergers among financial firms in recent years, some leading to *consolidation* and some to *convergence* of bank and nonbank firms:

Examples of Consolidating Mergers and Acquisitions in Banking	Examples of Converging Mergers and Acquisitions among Bank and Nonbank Firms
Dai-Ichi Kangyo Bank, Fuji Bank, and Industrial Bank of Japan combined into Mizuho Holdings Inc. in 2001 to form the world's largest bank.	Household Finance, a consumer-oriented finance company, was acquired by HSBC of London, one of the world's top five banks, in 2002.
J. P. Morgan Chase & Co. acquired Bank One, Chicago in 2004, creating the second largest U.S. bank	Allianz AG, one of the world's largest insurance companies, acquired Dresdner Bank, one of Germany's largest commercial banks, in 2001.

Key URLs

For information and data about the most recent bank mergers, see SNL Financial at **www.snl.com/bank/manda**. For information on nonbank financial service mergers see **www.snl.com/financial_SVC/manda** and **www.snl.com/insurance**.

acquisition of credit card leader First USA; and Summit Bancorp's purchase of the thrift institution, Collective Bankcorp. Moreover, after passage of the Gramm-Leach-Bliley Act in 1999, nonbank financial-service firms have gobbled up some banks on their own. One example is the acquisition of U.S. Trust Corporation, then the 12th largest commercial banking organization in New York, by security broker/dealer Charles Schwab Corporation of San Francisco. Table 19–2 lists some of the largest financial-firm mergers in U.S. history.

The current merger wave among financial-service industries is unlikely to end soon, and its effects will be long lasting. The public will be confronted in the future with fewer, but larger, financial-service organizations that will pose stronger competition for other financial firms not joining the acquisition and merger trend. In this chapter, we examine the nature, causes, and effects of mergers and acquisitions. We will look at the laws and regulations that shape these corporate combinations and the factors that are important in selecting a merger partner.

TABLE 19–2

Some of the Largest Financial-Service Mergers and Acquisitions in U.S. History

Acquiring Institution	Acquired Institution	Year
J. P. Morgan Chase, New York	Bank One, Chicago	2004
Bank of America, North Carolina	FleetBoston Financial, Mass.	2003
Chase Manhattan Corp, New York	J. P. Morgan & Co., New York	2000
Fleet Financial, Massachusetts	BankBoston Corp, Mass.	1999
Citicorp, New York	Travelers Group, California	1998
NationsBank, North Carolina	Bank of America, California	1998

19–3 The Motives behind the Rapid Growth of Financial-Service Mergers

As Table 19–3 illustrates, mergers usually occur because (1) the stockholders (owners) involved expect to increase their wealth (value per share of stock) or perhaps reduce their risk exposure, thus increasing their welfare; (2) management expects to gain higher salaries and employee benefits, greater job security, or greater prestige from managing a larger firm; or (3) *both* stockholders and management may reap benefits from a merger. There may be other motives as well. Let's take a closer look at some of the most powerful merger motives that appear to have been at work in recent years in the financial-services sector.

Profit Potential

To most authorities in the field the recent upsurge in financial-service mergers—averaging several hundred a year in the United States alone—reflects the expectation of stockholders that **profit potential** will increase once a merger is completed. If the acquiring organization has more aggressive and skillful management than the firm it acquires, revenues and earnings may rise as markets are more fully exploited and new services developed. This is especially true of interstate or international mergers where many new markets are entered, opening up greater revenue potential. Moreover, if the acquiring firm's management is better trained than the management of the acquired institution, the efficiency of the merged

TABLE 19–3   Possible Motives for Mergers and Acquisitions among Financial-Service Firms

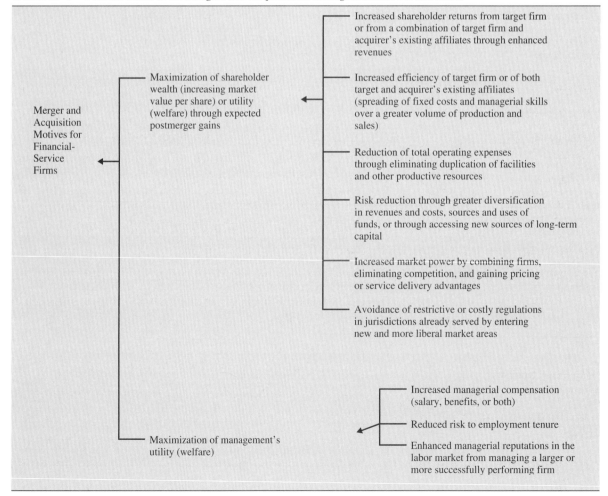

organization may increase, resulting in more effective control over operating expenses. Either way—through reduced expenses or expanded revenues—mergers *can* improve profit potential. Other factors held equal, the value of a merging firm's stock may rise, increasing the welfare of its stockholders.

Key URL
For a discussion of merger trends and how they are reshaping the financial-services business, see **www.innercitypress. org/bankbeat.html**.

One of the most dramatic examples of *profit potential* as a merger and acquisitions motive has been happening in China as the 21st century began to unfold. Several of the world's leading banks—for example, Citicorp, Bank of America, and J. P. Morgan Chase from the United States and HSBC Holdings and the Royal Bank of Scotland, both based in the United Kingdom—have been forecasting sharply increased revenues from carving out a portion of China's vast financial-services marketplace. With a population of over a billion, most of whom are "underbanked" but hold estimated savings of more than $1.5 trillion, China seems to offer enormous potential profitability from sales of credit cards, business loans, retirement plans, and insurance services.

Accordingly, the Bank of America invested close to $3 billion in the China Construction Bank in 2005, while HSBC purchased a sizeable share of the China Bank of Communications, the fifth-largest Chinese banking firm, in 2004. During the summer of 2005 the Royal Bank of Scotland, the world's sixth largest bank, announced the acquisition of a significant share of the Bank of China, that nation's second-largest banking firm and top foreign exchange trader. The invasion of China's banking industry by Bank of America is especially noteworthy because that huge U.S. bank has been rapidly approaching its maximum allowable share of the deposit market in the United States (10 percent under the terms of the Riegle-Neal Interstate Banking Act). Bank of America sees China as an alternative avenue for future market expansion and greater profit potential.

Risk Reduction

Alternatively, many merger partners anticipate reduced **cash flow risk** and reduced **earnings risk**. The lower risk may arise because mergers increase the overall size and prestige of an organization, open up new markets with different economic characteristics from markets already served, or make possible the offering of new services whose cash flows are different in timing from cash flows generated by existing services. For example, many European bank mergers in recent years (pursued by such leading banks as ABN AMRO and Verenigte Spaar-Bank) appear to have been motivated by the search for "complementarity" in services. Thus, a wholesale-oriented bank pursues a retail-oriented bank or a bank allies itself with an insurance company in an effort to broaden the menu of services offered the public, thereby reducing risk exposure from relying upon too narrow a lineup of services. Therefore, mergers can help to *diversify* the combined organization's sources of cash flow and earnings, resulting in a more stable financial firm able to withstand fluctuations in economic conditions and in the competitive environment of the industry.

Rescue of Failing Institutions

Filmtoid
What 1999 British film concludes with the ING Group of the Netherlands acquiring London's Barings Bank, which has gone "belly-up" due to the risk exposure of Nick Leeson's futures trading operation in Singapore?
Answer: *Rogue Trader.*

The failure of a company is often a motive for merger. For example, many bank mergers have been encouraged by the FDIC as a way to conserve scarce federal deposit insurance reserves and avoid an interruption of customer service when a depository institution is about to fail. One of the most prominent examples was the acquisition of First City Bancorporation of Texas in January 1993 by Chemical Bank of New York. In this case a well-managed and capital-strong banking company saw an opportunity to acquire substantial assets (nearly $7 billion) and deposits (close to $5 billion) with only a limited capital investment (less than $350 million). Following passage of the Garn–St Germain Depository Institutions Act (1982) and the Competitive Equality in Banking Act (1987), bank holding companies operating in the United States were allowed to reach across state lines to acquire failing banks and thrifts. Later, Congress voted to allow bank holding companies to acquire even healthy thrift institutions anywhere inside the United States, subject to regulatory approval.

Tax and Market-Positioning Motives

Many mergers arise from expected **tax benefits,** especially where the acquired firm has earnings losses that can be used to offset taxable profits of the acquirer. There may also be **market-positioning benefits,** in which a merger will permit the acquiring institution to acquire a base in a completely new market. For example, acquiring an existing financial firm, rather than chartering a new firm with new personnel, can significantly reduce the cost of positioning in a new market. Further expansion in the form of branching or future mergers can subsequently take place, with the most recently acquired bank as a base of operations. A good example of this merger motive is the 2003 acquisition of FleetBoston Financial Corp. in New England by Bank of America Corp., the latter seeking to purchase or open branches in numerous areas across the United States where there is strong market growth potential. The B of A/Fleet merger resulted in a single banking-facilities network of close to 6,000 branches and roughly 17,000 ATMs. Similar market-positioning objectives appeared to motivate the recent acquisitions of Golden West by Wachovia Corp. and North Fork Bancorp and Hibernia Corp. by Capital One.

These market-positioning mergers are likely to continue to move forward in the future as a result of passage of the Riegle-Neal Interstate Banking Act in the United States and recent banking directives issued by the European Economic Community to more freely allow banks and their competitors to cross state and national boundaries, make acquisitions, and purchase or establish new branch offices. Moreover, Germany's Commerzbank, ING Group of the Netherlands, and Allianz AG Holdings have recently bought sizeable ownership shares in Chinese and Korean banks to further position themselves in the developing financial markets of Asia, opening up potential new sources of revenue and earnings.

The Cost Savings or Efficiency Motive

Large-scale staff reductions and savings from eliminating duplicate facilities have followed in the wake of some of the largest mergers in the financial-services sector. For example, when insurer Allianz acquired Germany's Dresdner Bank in 2001, Dresdner's staff was cut by 8,000 (or about 16 percent of its labor force) in an effort to save money. The search for **cost savings** was also uncovered in a survey by Lausberg and Rose [13, 14] of the massive merger wave occurring in European banking during the 1980s and 1990s. Of the 107 European bank merger events examined, the single most important merger motivation was the desire to reduce operating costs, followed by a plan to diversify into new markets as part of an internationalization strategy.

We must be cautious about making too much of this efficiency or cost savings factor in explaining the recent rash of financial-services mergers, however. Most mergers are of the *market extension* type, which means the institutions involved don't overlap much or at all in terms of geographic area served. Thus, closing duplicate office facilities is less possible. In fact, to the surprise of many experts, branch offices are expanding in the banking industry, not contracting, even as the merger wave continues to unfold. For example, as Rhoades [17] points out, while the number of banks operating in the United States fell from about 14,400 in 1980 to less than 8,000 as the 21st century opened, the number of branch offices swelled to more than 70,000, and the number of ATMs soared even higher. What these numbers suggest is that some customers, especially households and smaller businesses, appear to demand a local banking connection. This limits how far financial-service managers can go in closing down what they feel is "unneeded" service space.

Mergers as a Device for Reducing Competition

Yet another possible explanation for hundreds, if not thousands, of recent mergers may be the wish to lower the degree of competition in the marketplace. When two competitors are allowed to merge, the public is served by fewer rivals for their business. Service quality may diminish, and prices and profits may rise. At least consistent with this merger explanation is the rapid rise in financial-services industry concentration under way all over the globe, including the United States nationally and in some American towns and cities. For example, as Rhoades [17] observes, the 100 largest U.S. banks jumped from just under 50 percent of total industry deposits in 1980 to more than 70 percent as the 21st century approached. While much less of an overall increase in concentration is evident in local markets, there are reports of greater concentration in the largest U.S. metropolitan areas and in some urban and rural communities. If true, there is the potential from this merger motive for damage to the public. More aggressive prosecution of the antitrust laws, as we will discuss later in this chapter, may need to be considered.

Mergers as a Device for Maximizing Management's Welfare

Some experts in this field see mergers as primarily driven by the interests of management. Managers are supposed to be the agents of a firm's stockholders, guiding the firm toward its goals for the stockholders' benefit. However, management may view a prospective acquisition as a way to increase salaries and employee benefits, lower the risk of being fired, and enhance managers' reputation in the labor market from working for a bigger firm. To the extent that managers reap these benefits at the expense of company stockholders an **agency problem** emerges. Higher management benefits can raise the merging firm's operating costs, lower its profits, and decrease returns to its shareholders. Many analysts see maximizing the welfare of management as one of the most important (and at times most perverse) of all merger motives.[1]

Other Merger Motives

Management may believe a merger will result in increased capacity for growth, maintaining the acquiring institution's historic growth rate. Moreover, a merger enables a lending institution to expand its loan limit to better accommodate large and growing corporate customers. This is particularly important in markets where the lender's principal business customers may be growing more rapidly than the lending institution itself (as noted by Peek and Rosengren [11]).

Mergers often give smaller institutions access to capable new management, which is always in short supply. For example, large banking firms recruit on college campuses and often hire through employment agencies in major metropolitan areas. Smaller, outlying banks have fewer market contacts to help find managerial talent, and they may not be able to afford top-quality personnel. The same is true of access to costly new electronic technology. For example, the merger of First Union Corp. of North Carolina and CoreStates Financial Corp. of Pennsylvania in 1998 appeared to be driven, in part, by CoreStates' need for upgraded computer systems to more efficiently handle its retail consumer accounts.

Merger Motives That Executives and Employees Identify

In a study by Prasad and Prasad [16], senior executives from 25 of the largest banking firms in the United States were asked what factors they consider in choosing target banks to acquire. The most prominent feature mentioned was *quality of management*. Several officers of leading banks said they preferred merger partners whose managements were compatible with their own. Other key factors mentioned in identifying desirable institutions to acquire were profitability (especially return on assets), efficiency of operations, and maintenance of market share.

---

[1] A dramatic example of managerial benefits from a merger appeared in 2006 when Capital One Financial Corp. proposed to buy North Fork Bancorp in order to gain access to an extensive branch office network in Connecticut, New Jersey, and New York. To sweeten the deal North Fork's top executives were promised close to $300 million in payouts and the company agreed to cover a portion of their tax bill in a so-called "tax gross up."

19–4 Selecting a Suitable Merger Partner

How can management and the owners of a financial firm decide if a proposed merger is good for the organization? The answer involves measuring both the costs and benefits of a proposed merger. Because the acquiring and acquired institutions may have different reasons for pursuing a merger, this is not an easy cost–benefit calculation. Even so, the most important goal of any merger should be to increase the *market value* of the surviving firm so that its stockholders receive higher returns on the funds they have invested. Stockholders deserve a return on their investment commensurate with the risks they have taken on.

For example, a merger is beneficial to the stockholders in the long run if it increases stock price per share. The value (price) of a financial firm's stock, like the stock of any other corporation, depends upon these factors:

1. The expected stream of future dividends flowing to the stockholders.
2. The discount factor applied to the future stock dividend stream, based on the rate of return required by the capital markets on investments of comparable risk.

Specifically,

$$\text{Market price per share of stock} = \sum_{t}^{\infty} \frac{D_t}{(1 + c)^t} \qquad \textbf{(19–1)}$$

where annual expected dividends per share are represented by D_t and c is the opportunity cost rate on capital invested in projects that expose investors to comparable risk. Clearly, if a proposed merger increases expected future stockholder dividends or lowers investors' required rate of return from the organization by reducing its risk, or combines the two, the financial institution's stock will tend to *rise* in price and its stockholders will benefit from the transaction.

How might a merger increase expected future earnings or reduce the level of risk exposure? One possibility is by *improving operating efficiency*—that is, by reducing operating cost per unit of output. A financial firm might achieve greater efficiency by consolidating its operations and eliminating unnecessary duplication. Thus, instead of two separate planning and marketing programs, two separate auditing staffs, and so forth, the merged institution may be able to get by with just one. Existing resources—land, labor, capital, and management skills—may be used more efficiently if new production and service delivery methods (such as automated equipment) are used, increasing the volume of services produced with the same number of inputs.

Another route to higher earnings is to enter new markets or offer new services via merger. Entry into new markets can generate *geographic diversification* if the markets entered have different economic characteristics from those markets already served. Alternatively, a merger may allow financial firms with different packages of services to combine their service menus, expanding the service options presented to their customers. This is *product-line diversification*. As we saw in Chapter 14, both forms of diversification tend to stabilize cash flow and earnings, presenting stockholders with less risk and perhaps increasing the market value of their stock. Ideally, merger-minded managers want to find an acquisition target whose earnings or cash flow is negatively correlated (or displays a low positive correlation) with the acquiring organization's cash flows.

For many financial-service managers, a major consideration in any proposed merger is its probable impact on the earnings per share (EPS) of the surviving firm. Will EPS improve after the merger, making the new combined institution's stock more attractive to investors? Stockholders of the firm being acquired are usually asking the same question: If we exchange our stock in the old institution for the stock of the acquiring firm, will our EPS rise?

Generally speaking, stockholders of both acquiring and acquired institutions will experience a gain in earnings per share of stock if (a) a company with a higher stock-price-to-earnings (P-E) ratio acquires a company with a lower P-E ratio and (b) combined earnings do not fall after the merger. In this instance, earnings per share will rise even if the acquired institution's stockholders are paid a reasonable premium for their shares.

For example, suppose the stockholders of Bank A, whose current stock price is $20 per share, agree to acquire Bank B, whose stock is currently valued at $16 per share. If Bank A earned $5 per share of stock on its latest report and B also earned $5 per share, they would have the following P-E ratios:

$$\text{A's P-E ratio} = \frac{\$20 \text{ price per share}}{\$5 \text{ earnings per share}} = 4$$

$$\text{B's P-E ratio} = \frac{\$16 \text{ price per share}}{\$5 \text{ earnings per share}} = 3.2$$

Suppose, too, that these two banks had, respectively, 100,000 shares and 50,000 shares of common stock outstanding and that Bank A reported net earnings of $500,000, while B posted net earnings of $250,000. Thus, their combined earnings would be $750,000 in the most recent year.

If the shareholders of Bank B agree to sell out at B's current stock price of $16 per share, they will receive 4/5 ($16/$20) of a share of stock in Bank A for each share of B's stock. Thus, a total of 40,000 shares of Bank A (50,000 Bank B shares × 4/5) will be issued to the stockholders of Bank B to complete the merger. The combined organization will then have 140,000 shares outstanding. If earnings remain constant after the merger, stockholders' earnings per share will be

$$\frac{\text{Earnings}}{\text{per share}} = \frac{\substack{\text{Combined} \\ \text{earnings}}}{\substack{\text{Shares of} \\ \text{stock outstanding}}} = \frac{\$750,000}{140,000} = \$5.36 \qquad \textbf{(19–2)}$$

which is clearly higher than the $5 per share that Bank A and Bank B each earned for their shareholders before they merged.

As long as the acquiring institution's P-E ratio is larger than the acquired firm's P-E ratio, there is room for paying the acquired company's shareholders at least a moderate **merger premium** to sweeten the deal. A merger premium expressed in percentage terms can be calculated from:

$$\substack{\text{Merger premium} \\ \text{(in percent)}} = \frac{\substack{\text{Aquired firm's} \\ \text{current stock} \\ \text{price per share}} + \substack{\text{Additional amount} \\ \text{paid by the acquirer} \\ \text{for each share of the} \\ \text{acquired firm's stock}}}{\text{Acquired firm's current stock price}} \times 100 \qquad \textbf{(19–3)}$$

For example, suppose that despite the difference in current market value between Bank A's and Bank B's stock (i.e., $20 versus $16 per share), Bank A's shareholders agree to offer

B's shareholders a bonus of $4 per share (i.e., a merger premium of [$16 + $4]/$16 = 1.25, or 125 percent). This means B's stockholders will exchange their stock for Bank A's shares with an **exchange ratio** of 1:1. Therefore, B's shareholders, who currently hold 50,000 shares in Bank B, will wind up holding 50,000 shares in Bank A. The combined organization will have 150,000 shares outstanding. If earnings remain at $750,000 following the merger, the consolidated banking organization will be able to maintain its earnings per share at the current level of $5 (i.e., $750,000/150,000 shares).

Unfortunately, paying merger premiums can easily get out of hand. Premiums ranging from 150 to 250 percent have sometimes emerged. High-premium deals often yield disappointing results for the stockholders of the acquiring firm long after these mergers are consummated.

In general, **dilution of ownership**—spreading the firm's ownership over more stockholders so that the average shareholder's proportion of firm ownership declines—results from offering the acquired firm's stockholders an excessive number of new shares relative to the value of their old shares. **Dilution of earnings**—spreading a fixed amount of earnings over more shares of stock so that the earnings per share (EPS) of the combined firm declines—will occur if the ratio of stock price to earnings (P-E) of the firm to be acquired is greater than the ratio of stock price to earnings (P-E) of the acquiring firm. The combined firm's EPS will fall below its original level. The amount of decrease is a function of the differential in price-earnings ratios of the two firms and the relative size of the two merging companies in terms of their total earnings.

The financial success of a merger, then, depends heavily on the comparative dollar amounts of earnings reported by the two participating organizations and their relative price-earnings ratios. For example, the immediate change in earnings per share from the merger of Bank A and Bank B depends on this ratio:

$$\frac{\text{Price per share of Bank A's stock}}{\text{Current net earnings of Bank A}} \div \frac{\text{Price per share of Bank B's stock}}{\text{Current net earnings of Bank B}} \qquad (19\text{--}4)$$

Of course, even if EPS goes down right after the merger, the transaction may still be worth pursuing if future earnings are expected to grow faster as a result of the acquisition. If significantly greater efficiency and cost savings result over the long run, the effects of paying a higher price (in new stock that must be handed over to the acquired institution's shareholders) will be more than made up eventually. Standard financial management practice calls for analyzing what will happen to the combined organization's EPS under different possible scenarios of future earnings and stock prices. If it takes too long to recover the cost of an acquisition according to the projected path of EPS, management of the acquiring institution should consider looking elsewhere for a merger target.

19–5 The Merger and Acquisition Route to Growth

Whatever its motives, each merger is simply a financial transaction that results in the acquisition of one or more firms by another institution. The acquired firm (usually the smaller of the two) gives up its charter and adopts a new name (usually the name of the acquiring organization). The assets and liabilities of the acquired firm are added to those of the acquiring institution.[2] A merger normally occurs after managements of the acquiring and

[2]Two or more firms may also *consolidate* their assets to form one institution, with all participating firms giving up their former identities to become parts of a larger organization. Consolidations are much less common in the financial services field than mergers, however.

acquired organizations have struck a deal. The proposed transaction must then be ratified by the board of directors of each organization and possibly by a vote of each firm's common stockholders.[3]

If the stockholders approve (usually by at least a two-thirds majority), the unit of government that issued the original charter of incorporation must be notified, along with any regulatory agencies that have supervisory authority over the institutions involved. For example, in the United States the federal banking agencies have 30 days to comment on the merger of two federally supervised banks and there is a 30-day period for public comments as well. Public notice that a merger application has been filed must appear three times over a 30-day period, at approximately two-week intervals, in a newspaper of general circulation serving the communities where the main offices of the banks involved are located. The U.S. Justice Department can bring suit if it believes competition would be significantly reduced after the proposed merger.

In deciding whether or not to merge, management and the board of directors of the acquiring firm often consider many characteristics of the targeted institution. The principal factors examined by most merger analysts fall into six broad categories: (1) the firm's history, ownership, and management; (2) the condition of its balance sheet; (3) the firm's track record of growth and operating performance; (4) the condition of its income statement and cash flow; (5) the condition and prospects of the local economy served by the targeted institution; and (6) the competitive structure of the market in which the firm operates (as indicated by any barriers to entry, market shares, and degree of market concentration).

In addition to the foregoing items, many acquirers will look at these factors as well:

1. The comparative management styles of the merging organizations.
2. The principal customers the targeted institution serves.
3. Current personnel and employee benefits.
4. Compatibility of accounting and management information systems among the merging companies.
5. Condition of the targeted institution's physical assets.
6. Ownership and earnings dilution before and after the proposed merger.

A thorough evaluation of any proposed corporate merger *before* it occurs is absolutely essential, as recent experience has shown.

19–6 Methods of Consummating Merger Transactions

Mergers usually take place employing one of two methods: (*a*) *pooling of interests* or (*b*) *purchase accounting*. For mergers begun before July 1, 2001, the Financial Accounting Standard Board (FASB) permitted use of the *pooling of interests* approach in which the merger partners merely sum the volume of their assets, liabilities, and equity in the amounts recorded just before their merger takes place. The result is a merged firm displaying a simple combined total of all the merger partners' assets, liabilities, and equity in one combined balance sheet. The income statement of the newly consolidated firm will reflect the income and expenses of both firms added together for the full period of time covered by the income and expense statement as though the merging businesses had been one company when the income statement began.

[3]In a purchase and assumption transaction, two-thirds of the shareholders of the acquired firm must approve; however, often no shareholder vote of approval is required by stockholders of the acquiring institution, nor is shareholder approval usually required when a firm engages in a partial liquidation of its assets (e.g., a bank or thrift institution selling some of its branch offices).

In contrast, under *purchase accounting* the firm to be acquired is valued at its purchase price and that price is added to the total assets of the acquirer. The purchase method requires that acquiring and acquired firms be handled on a different basis so it is important to know who is acquiring whom. The acquirer records the acquisition at the price paid to the stockholders of the acquired company, first valuing the acquired firm at market plus goodwill, if the acquisition price and market value are different.

Goodwill is an intangible asset usually arising from a merger transaction where the purchase price of the merger target is larger than the difference between the fair value of its assets minus any liabilities taken on. The Financial Accounting Standards Board (specifically, in FASB 142) labels goodwill as the "intangible synergies" of a combined firm resulting from a merger. As Carlson and Perli [20] observe, with the rapid pace of banking industry consolidation in recent years goodwill on bank balance sheets has exploded, growing at more than 30 percent annually to climb above 1 percent of total industry assets. While FASB used to require goodwill to be amortized (and, thus, gradually disappear) over its useful life (not to exceed 40 years), the Standards Board recently changed its mind and now goodwill need not be amortized as long as it doesn't become impaired due to deterioration in a merging company's financial strength. In contrast to the purchase accounting approach where goodwill *is* permitted, no goodwill is figured in when using the pooling of interests approach. However, after 2001 the pooling-of-interest method for merger accounting was eliminated for U.S. financial firms.

Another way to view the merger process is to determine exactly what the acquirer is buying in the transaction: assets or shares of stock. Mergers are generally carried out by using either (1) the purchase of assets or (2) the purchase of common stock. With the **purchase-of-assets method,** the acquiring institution buys all or a portion of the assets of the acquired institution, using either cash or its own stock. In purchase-of-assets mergers, the acquired institution usually distributes the cash or stock to its shareholders in the form of a liquidating dividend, and the acquired organization is then dissolved. With some asset purchase deals, however, the institution selling its assets may continue to operate as a separate, but smaller, corporation.

With the **purchase-of-stock method,** on the other hand, the acquired firm ceases to exist; the acquiring firm assumes *all* of its assets and liabilities. While cash may be used to settle either type of merger transaction, in the case of commercial banks regulations require that all but the smallest mergers and acquisitions be paid for by issuing additional stock of the acquirer. Moreover, a stock transaction has the advantage of not being subject to taxation until the stock is sold, while cash payments are usually subject to immediate taxation. Stock transactions trade current gains for future gains that are expected to be larger if everything goes as planned.[4]

The most frequent kind of merger among depository institutions involves **wholesale** (large metropolitan) **banks** merging with smaller **retail banks.** This lets money center banks gain access to relatively low-cost, less interest-sensitive consumer accounts and channel those deposited funds into profitable corporate loans. Most financial-firm takeovers are friendly—readily agreed to by all parties—although a few are *hostile*, resisted by management and stockholders. Not long ago in the acquisition of Irving Trust by Bank of New York, for example, the management and directors of Irving created obstacle after obstacle, legal and financial, to this corporate marriage before the courts finally cleared it to proceed.

---

[4]Merger transactions involving banks and other financial firms generally must be accounted for in accordance with Accounting Principles Board Opinion No. 16 (APB No. 16). The difference between the purchase price and the fair value of net assets acquired in mergers should be treated as an intangible asset in accordance with generally accepted accounting principles (GAAP).

19–7 Regulatory Rules for Bank Mergers in the United States

Mergers have transformed the banking industry perhaps more than any other financial-services industry. In this section we take a close look at government rules applying to bank mergers in the United States.

Two sets of rules generally govern the mergers of banks and other financial firms: (1) decisions by courts of law and (2) statutes enacted by legislators, reinforced by regulations. In the United States, for example, the Sherman Antitrust Act of 1890 and the Clayton Act of 1914 forbid mergers that would result in monopolies or significantly lessen competition in any industry. Whenever any such merger is proposed, it must be challenged in court by the U.S. Department of Justice.

Inside the United States the foundation law affecting the mergers and acquisitions of banks is the **Bank Merger Act of 1960.** This law requires each merging bank to request approval from its principal federal regulatory agency before a merger can take place. For national banks, this means applying to the Comptroller of the Currency for prior approval. For insured state-chartered banks that are members of the Federal Reserve System, the Fed's approval is required. Insured, state-chartered nonmember institutions must gain permission from the Federal Deposit Insurance Corporation.

Under the terms of the Bank Merger Act, each federal agency must give top priority to the **competitive effects** of a proposed merger. This means estimating the probable effects of a merger on the pricing and availability of financial services in the local community and on the degree of concentration of deposits or assets in the largest financial institutions in the local market. Thus, current merger laws in banking rest on three premises: (1) the *cluster of products* offered by a bank is the relevant product line to be considered in a merger or acquisition; (2) the relevant market to be concerned about, in most instances, is *local* (counties or metropolitan areas); and (3) the *structure* of the local market (usually measured by degree of concentration) is the principal determining factor in how much competition exists and how a merger might damage or aid competition. Where concentration is high—where the largest institutions control a dominant share of local deposits or assets—the risk of damaging competition is greater, and the merger is less likely to win regulatory approval unless the merging institutions agree to *divest* some of their affiliated banks and branches. For example, in 1992 Bank America was allowed to acquire Security Pacific Corp. only after agreeing to divest itself of 213 branch offices in five states, holding almost $9 billion in deposits.

Key URL
To learn more about law and regulation in the banking sector, see, for example, **http://library.findlaw.com/finance-and-banking/index.html**.

Moreover, the *trend* in concentration also comes under close scrutiny from the regulatory agencies. Markets that have recently experienced increasing concentration ratios or declining numbers of financial-service suppliers are less likely to see mergers approved than are markets where concentration is falling. Other factors that must be weighed include the financial history and condition of the merging institutions, the adequacy of their capital, their earnings prospects, strength of management, and the convenience and needs of the community to be served. Mergers with anticompetitive effects cannot go unchallenged by federal authorities unless the applicant can show that such combinations would result in significant **public benefits.** Among the possible benefits are providing financial services where none are conveniently available and rescuing a failing financial institution whose collapse would have damaging effects on the public welfare.

The federal supervisory agencies prefer to approve mergers that will enhance the financial strength of the institutions involved. Regulators repeatedly emphasize the need for improving management skills and strengthening equity capital. The existence of such laws and regulations creates a barrier for any merger that would lead to substantial changes in market share and market concentration, possibly damaging competition in the local market. This creates a dilemma for aggressive financial firms. Expansion-minded management and stockholders must distinguish proposed combinations that are likely to be challenged by government, resulting in expensive legal battles, from those that are likely to sail through with few problems. It should be noted that the large majority of merger applications filed—usually more than 90 percent—are approved. However, this high approval rate reflects a good deal of screening out of unacceptable mergers through informal conferences between merger-minded financial institutions and regulatory officials.

Justice Department Guidelines

To reduce legal uncertainties the U.S. Department of Justice issued formal guidelines for merger applicants in 1968. The initial **Justice Department Merger Guidelines** were quite restrictive. They required firms operating in markets judged to be highly concentrated, with only limited competition, to acquire primarily *foothold businesses* (i.e., those having a small or insignificant market share) or to enter such markets *de novo* (i.e., start a new firm). In June 1982, the Reagan administration authorized more liberal merger guidelines. These rules permitted combinations that would probably have been challenged by the Justice Department under the old guidelines. The Justice Department further modified its merger guidelines in 1992, including special guidelines for the mergers of banks and selected other financial institutions that we operate under today.

The degree of *concentration* in a market is measured by the proportion of assets or deposits controlled by the largest institutions serving that market. Presumably, if the largest firms control a substantial share of market assets or deposits, anticompetitive behavior (including collusive agreements) is more likely, resulting in damage to the public from excessive prices and poor service quality. The Justice Department guidelines require calculation of the **Herfindahl-Hirschman Index** (HHI) as a summary measure of *market concentration*. HHI reflects the proportion of assets, deposits, or sales accounted for by each firm serving a given market. Each firm's market share is squared, and HHI is calculated as the sum of squared market shares for all firms serving a specific market area. Thus, the Herfindahl-Hirschman index is derived from this formula:

$$HHI = \sum_{i=1}^{k} A_i^2 \qquad \textbf{(19–5)}$$

where A_i represents the percentage of market-area deposits, assets, or sales controlled by the *i*th financial firm in the market, and there are k financial firms in total serving the market. We note that the Herfindahl index reflects *both* the number of institutions in the market and the concentration of deposits, assets, or sales in the largest institutions and assigns heavier weight (by squaring each firm's market share) to those institutions commanding the biggest market share.

For example, suppose that a small local market contains four banks having the deposits and deposit market shares shown in the following table:

Deposits and Market Shares in Edgecroft County			
Name of Financial Firm	Deposits in Latest Annual Report	Market Shares of Total Deposits (A_i)	Square of Each Firm's Market Share (A_i^2)
First Security National Bank	**$245 million**	**50.8%**	**2,580.6**
Edgecroft National Bank	113 million	23.4	547.6
Lincoln County State Bank	69 million	14.3	204.5
Edgecroft State Bank and Trust Co.	55 million	11.4	130.0
Totals	$482 million	100.0%	3,462.7

In this case:

$$\text{HHI} = \sum A_i^2 = 3{,}462.7 \text{ points}$$

HHI may vary from 10,000 (i.e., 100^2)—a monopoly position, where the leading firm is the market's sole supplier—to near zero for unconcentrated markets. In theory, the smaller the value of HHI, the less one or a few firms dominate any given market and the more equally are market shares distributed among firms. The more nearly firms are equal in size, the more competitive the relevant market is assumed to be and the less likely is anticompetitive behavior.

Under Department of Justice guidelines, any merger that would (*a*) result in a post-merger HHI of less than 1,800 or (*b*) change the value of the HHI in the relevant market by less than 200 points would not likely be challenged by the Justice Department because, in the government's view, the merged firm would not gain enough market power to significantly damage public welfare. However, when a proposed merger appears to yield a Herfindahl index exceeding these guidelines (i.e., the HHI in the relevant market would be more than 1,800 and rise by more than 200 points), the Justice Department considers such a market "highly concentrated." Proposed mergers in highly concentrated markets may draw a Justice Department challenge in federal court unless the department's lawyers and economists find evidence of extenuating circumstances.

Consider the above example in which we calculated the market shares of banks serving Edgecroft County, where HHI equaled 3,462.7 points. According to the Justice Department's guidelines, Edgecroft would be a "highly concentrated market" (provided that Justice confined its definition of the relevant banking market to the local county itself and did not bring in surrounding areas that have more financial-service providers, as often happens where cities span several counties). The biggest bank in Edgecroft, First Security National, holds a 50.8 percent market share. First Security would have a difficult time gaining approval for a merger with any other Edgecroft bank. (The largest bank in the county is more than twice as large as its nearest competitor.)

Indeed, it would be difficult for *any* bank mergers to take place inside the Edgecroft market because of its highly concentrated status and because no matter which two of the four banks might wish to merge with each other, the resulting change in HHI would be relatively large. (As an example, if the two smallest banks merged, their combined market share would be 25.7 percent, which, when squared, is 660.5 points. The HHI for the market would climb more than 300 points, from 3,462.7 to 3,788.7, following this merger.) However, a bank outside the Edgecroft market might well be able to merge with one of the Edgecroft banks in what is known as a *market extension merger.* This would leave the local market's HHI unchanged and would not reduce the number of alternative suppliers of services to the public.

Extenuating circumstances are frequently considered in approving those mergers that lead to only moderate increases in market concentration. These mitigating factors may include the ease with which new firms can enter the same market, the conduct of firms already present in the market, the types of products involved and the terms under which they are being sold, and the type and character of buyers in the relevant market area.

In recent years the Justice Department has liberalized its standards for judging the anticompetitive effects of mergers. One device Justice has used to carry out this more liberal attitude is to include *nonbank financial institutions* in the calculation of some concentration ratios for local markets. Including at least a portion of the deposits held by savings and loans, credit unions, and other financial institutions in the total deposits of a local market area lowers the market share held by each bank. Thus, fewer financial-services mergers will appear to damage competition and more mergers will receive federal approval, other factors held equal. However, recent research suggests that in most local markets banks continue to be the principal financial-service provider to households and small businesses, especially for checking, savings, and credit services.

The Merger Decision-Making Process by U.S. Federal Regulators

U.S. bank regulatory agencies must apply the standards imposed by the Bank Merger Act and the Justice Department Merger Guidelines to *all* merger proposals. Each merger application is reviewed (*a*) by staff economists and attorneys working for the federal banking agencies to assess the potential impact of the proposed merger on competition and (*b*) by officials of the agencies' examination department to assess the merger's probable impact on the financial condition and future prospects of the banks involved.

The Bank Merger Act also requires the federal agency that is the merging banks' principal supervisor to assess the effect of the proposed merger on public convenience and the public's need for an adequate supply of financial services at reasonable prices. The agency involved must review the banks' records to determine if they have made an affirmative effort to serve all segments of the population in their trade area without discrimination. This assessment is required under terms of the Community Reinvestment Act (CRA), which forbids depository institutions from *redlining*—that is, marking off certain neighborhoods within their trade area and declining to extend financial services (especially credit) to residents of those neighborhoods.

19–8 Merger Rules in Europe

The formation of the European Union (EU) has resulted in a wave of mergers. Partly as a result, the European Commission—an executive body of the EU currently based in Brussels—has emerged as a key arbiter of mergers involving European businesses. Because the European Commission cannot break apart a merger after that combination has already occurred (unlike the U.S. Justice Department), the Brussels commission has been somewhat more aggressive than in the United States in denying some companies permission to merge if the proposed combination would lead to "collective dominance" in a given market.

The doctrine of *collective dominance* suggests that if a significant European market would become so concentrated as a result of a proposed merger that only about four firms would come to dominate that market, then the European Commission might well vote to block any further market concentration, even if non-European firms were involved. While, thus far, financial services in Europe do not appear to be as concentrated as are several other European industries, there is little question that a strong consolidation trend in financial services is under way in the EU and may soon lead to significant regulatory challenges. A prominent example was UniCredito Italiano's $20 billion bid for Germany's HUB Group AG in 2005—then Europe's largest cross-border financial services merger.

In 2002 the United States and the European Union agreed to work toward *joint review* of mergers involving multinational businesses in order to avoid conflicting merger decisions when a U.S. and a European firm propose to combine their ownership and resources. Subsequently, the EU's antitrust division announced that it wouldn't block mergers simply because competing firms might be harmed, but only if *consumers* might be damaged—a rule the United States generally follows under its antitrust laws.

19–9 Making a Success of a Merger

Many mergers simply do not work. A variety of factors often get in the way of mergers' success, including poor management, a mismatch of corporate cultures and styles, excessive prices paid by the acquirer for the acquired firm, a failure to take into account the customers' feelings and concerns, and a lack of strategic "fit" between the combining companies so that nothing meshes smoothly with minimal friction and the merged institution finds that it cannot move forward as a cohesive and effective competitor.

Recent experience has suggested a few helpful steps that improve the chances for a desirable merger outcome:

1. Acquirer, know thyself! Every financial-service company intent on growth through merger must thoroughly evaluate its own financial condition, track record of performance, strengths and weaknesses of the markets it already serves, and strategic objectives. Such an analysis can help management and stockholders clarify whether a merger would help to magnify each participating institution's strengths and compensate for its weaknesses.

2. Get organized for a detailed analysis of possible new markets to enter and institutions to acquire. Financial firms that are merger focused should create a management/shareholder team (including outside consultants, such as investment banking specialists) with the skills needed to successfully evaluate potential new markets and potential acquisitions.

   Favorable markets to enter typically show a track record of above-average, but stable growth in incomes and business sales, a somewhat older-than-average population with a high proportion of professional workers and business owners and managers, moderate to low inflation with stable currency prices, moderate competition, and a favorable regulatory environment that does not hinder expansion or the development of new services. Desirable institutional targets, on the other hand, show evidence of persistent earnings growth and market acceptance of the services they offer (as measured by the growth of assets and a rising market share), a strong capital base, facilities and equipment that are functioning well and are up to date, evidence of close control over operating costs, and complementary goals between acquiring and acquired institutions.

Key URL
Additional information about choosing the right merger target may be found at numerous Web locations, such as **www.yaledailynews. com/article.asp? AID=8420**.

3. Establish a realistic price for the target firm based on a careful assessment of its projected future earnings discounted by a capital cost rate that fully reflects the risks of the target market and target firm and reflects all prospective costs that will have to be met by the acquiring firm (such as closing or upgrading poorly located or inadequately equipped branch offices, replacing outdated or incompatible management information systems, educating inadequately trained staff to handle new services, and correcting salary disparities that may exist between the two merging organizations).

4. Once a merger is agreed upon, create a combined management team with capable managers from both acquiring and acquired firms that will direct, control, and continually assess the quality of progress toward the consolidation of the two organizations into a single effective unit.

5. Establish a reporting and communications system between senior management, branch and line managers, and staff that promotes rapid two-way communication of operating problems and ideas for improved technology and procedures so that employees feel involved in the merger, are convinced that effort and initiative will be rewarded, and believe they have a contribution to make toward the merger's ultimate success.

6. Create communications channels for both employees and customers to promote (*a*) understanding of why the merger was pursued, and (*b*) what the consequences are likely to be for both anxious customers and employees who may fear interruption of service, loss of jobs, higher service fees, the disappearance of familiar faces, and other changes. This may require setting up customer and employee "hot lines" to calm concerned people and give them the direction and assurances they seek.

7. Set up customer advisory panels to evaluate the merged institution's community image, service and marketing effectiveness, efforts to recognize loyal customers, pricing schedules, and general helpfulness to customers.

SELLING OFF BRANCH OFFICES TO GAIN APPROVAL FOR A MERGER: *DIVESTITURE*

For several decades now banks and thrift institutions that operate branch offices in local neighborhoods have sometimes been asked to *divest* themselves of some of their offices in order to secure regulators' approval for their proposed merger with other depository institutions. This type of request typically has come from such agencies as the U.S. Department of Justice, the Federal Reserve Board, the Comptroller of the Currency, and the Federal Trade Commission in an effort to promote competition.

For example, in a market dominated by three commercial banks, if two of them merge, all of their branches then become part of one banking firm. Consumers in that market now have only two banking alternatives. Worse still, in a given local neighborhood there may only be branch offices of the two merging institutions present which, after the merger, results in neighborhood residents having just one local service option.

Accordingly, in recent years several bank and thrift mergers have been approved by regulators only if some of the branch offices of the acquired depository institution are sold off to a third party. Examples of banks confronted with this divestiture decision have included BankAmerica Corporation in its merger with Security Pacific Corporation in 1992, NationsBank Corporation in its acquisition of Barnett Banks, Inc. in 1998, and Banc One Corporation in its acquisition of First Chicago NBD, also in 1998. In the BankAmerica–Security Pacific merger case, 187 branches were sold to other banks not involved in that merger.

What happened to the branch offices disposed of? Did they survive or did all of their depositors leave? A recent study by Pilloff [12] of the Federal Reserve Board finds that, in general, the branch offices disposed of did well. Initially, they faced a "runoff" around the time of their sale because some depositors apparently wanted to follow their old bank even after it was acquired by a larger institution, didn't trust the new owner of the branches, or perhaps used the occasion to make a change they may have been planning all along.

After the initial "runoff," growth in deposits resumed at a pace comparable to that of other branch offices. Interestingly, the larger the bank purchasing these branches, the faster the divested branches tended to grow, perhaps because larger depositories are more familiar to the public, offer more services, or manage their new offices more effectively. Overall, the *divestiture* requirement to promote competition appears to have worked reasonably well.

The foregoing steps, even if faithfully followed, do not promise successful mergers, but they will increase the probability that a merger will proceed smoothly and possibly achieve its goals.

Concept Check

19–4. What factors should a financial firm consider when choosing a good merger partner?

19–5. What factors must the regulatory authorities consider when deciding whether to approve or deny a merger?

19–6. When is a market too concentrated to allow a merger to proceed? What could happen if a merger were approved in an excessively concentrated market area?

19–7. What steps that management can take appear to contribute to the success of a merger? Why do you think many mergers produce disappointing results?

19–10 Research Findings on the Impact of Financial-Service Mergers

What is the track record of mergers involving banks and other financial firms? What impact do they have on the public and stockholders? A number of studies over the years have addressed these questions. In general, the results are mixed—some positive and some negative effects. Other challenging problems—such as establishing a solid base in a new market—are often resolved successfully through the merger route, however.

The Financial and Economic Impact of Acquisitions and Mergers

Do mergers always increase profits? Do they result in clear benefits for stockholders of merging financial-service companies? For many mergers the answers to these two questions appear to be "no" at worst and "not necessarily" at best.

A substantial number of studies suggest that, on average, there are no statistically significant differences in profitability between financial firms pursuing merger strategies versus firms that are not merger active. Acquiring financial firms are usually not more profitable (and often less profitable) than the firms they acquire. However, there is some evidence that acquired financial-service companies are often significantly less profitable than nonmerging institutions serving the same markets. Perhaps the reason for this last finding is that stockholders and managements of acquiring financial firms *believe* they can improve the performance of the companies they have targeted for merger. Unfortunately this belief in postmerger gains is often *not* justified. Another possible explanation for mediocre postmerger profit results may be the sizeable premiums acquirers often wind up paying shareholders of acquired firms.[5]

When interstate banking became legal in the United States during the 1980s and 1990s many industry analysts thought that interstate acquisitions would surely yield positive results for shareholders and improved performance overall, especially because these interstate transactions had been prohibited for so long. Once again, research findings were mixed, though generally favorable. Stockholders of interstate banking companies and shareholders of firms they acquired frequently scored positive abnormal returns when these acquisitions were first announced. Moreover, in the wake of these interstate combinations some studies found evidence of postmerger earnings gains, improved cost control, higher employee productivity, and more rapid growth. However, there was also evidence from the earliest interstate acquisitions that market shares and profitability were little different after large interstate banks bought out smaller banking firms across state lines.[6]

Factoid

Do mergers seem to improve firm performance? Not according to the Federal Reserve Bank of San Francisco, which finds only that, in some instances, operating costs are lowered when banks merge. See especially **www.frbsf. org/econrsrch/ workingp/wp99-10.pdf**.

Concept Check

19–8. What does recent research evidence tell us about the impact of most mergers in the financial sector?

19–9. Does it appear that most mergers serve the public interest?

Do the managers of financial firms involved in mergers generally regard their efforts as successful? A survey by Rose [9] of nearly 600 U.S. bank mergers asked that very question of the CEOs involved. Overall, no more than two-thirds of the merging institutions believed they had fulfilled their merger expectations. For example, in only about half the cases did profits, growth, market share, or market power actually increase and risk and operating costs fall. Roughly one-third of those seeking more qualified management apparently did *not* find it. However, CEOs at a majority of these merging institutions (at least 80 percent) believed their banks' capital base had improved and they were now more efficient.

Unfortunately, there are absolutely *no* guarantees any merger will be successful, just as there is never any guarantee for any other type of capital investment. A study by Rose [5] of 572 U.S. acquiring banking institutions, purchasing nearly 650 other banks, found a nearly *symmetric distribution* of earnings outcomes from mergers—roughly half registering positive earnings gains and about half displaying negative earnings results. Among those institutions

[5]See especially the studies on mergers and profitability by Pettway and Trifts [4] and Rose [9].
[6]See, for example, Goldberg and Hanweck [2], Millon-Cornett and Tehranian [3], and Spong and Shoenhair [7].

experiencing positive earnings gains, lower operating costs, greater employee productivity, and faster growth appeared to account for at least a portion of the greater earnings achieved. Moreover, part of the higher postmerger returns seemed to be related to increases in post-merger market concentration. This latter outcome suggests that, in some cases, the public may be paying higher prices for services than would prevail in less concentrated (more competitive) markets. If so, regulatory agencies need to take a closer look at proposed mergers for possible evidence of adverse changes in the competitive climate.

Finally, an extensive study on an international scale by Amel, Barnes, Panetta, and Salles [1], published by the Federal Reserve Board, examined the effects of mergers among banks, insurance companies, and securities firms in leading industrialized countries. They found that mergers and acquisitions in the financial sector often seemed to yield operating cost savings (economies of scale), though only for relatively small firms. However, there was little evidence of substantial cost reductions among larger financial firms or of improvements in management quality.

Public Benefits from Mergers and Acquisitions

In what ways does the *public* benefit from mergers? Generally research has found few real benefits from the public's perspective. For example, a survey by Rose [8] asked the CEOs of merging U.S. banks whether there had been any increase in hours of operation in order to provide the public with better access to services. Fewer than 20 percent reported any increase in hours of operation. About one-third changed their pricing policies, but the most common change was a price *increase* following a merger, particularly in checking-account service fees, loan rates, deposit interest rates, and safe-deposit box fees. Research generally finds that financial firms absorbed in a merger change their prices, sooner or later, to match those of the acquiring organization.

One factor that appears to keep price increases following mergers under *some* control at least is *population migration*. For example, loan and deposit interest rates tend to be more favorable for customers in areas where substantial numbers of households and businesses are relocating and, because of this movement, are compelled to seek out new providers for the financial services they need. Unfortunately, the majority of businesses and households move infrequently and usually to a nearby location, generally keeping their working relationship with the same financial firms. This fact of life appears to give merging institutions more latitude to raise prices and limit competition.

On the positive side there is *no* convincing evidence that the public has *suffered* from a decline in service quality or in service availability flowing from most mergers. And there is some evidence that bank failure rates decline in the wake of merger activity. Moreover, crossing state lines seems to be somewhat effective in helping to stabilize asset and equity returns, reducing the chances of insolvency and resulting in lower operating costs. Some smaller businesses may suffer a bit if their principal bank is acquired and they don't yet have a relationship with the new owners (unless they have the clout and flexibility to switch service providers).

Finally, there may be an unexpected procompetitive aspect to merger activity. A recent study by Seelig and Critchfield [18] explores an apparent connection between bank and thrift mergers inside a given market area and an increase in charters to form *new* depository institutions in that same market. In short, mergers and acquisitions tend to stimulate *de novo* entry, suggesting, perhaps, that new competitors are more likely to appear in those markets where merger activity appears to be changing the balance of power. No one is exactly sure why this increase in new financial-firm entry occurs—perhaps mergers anger some customers who quickly look around for new service providers or maybe mergers lead to cost cutting, including firing some employees who then start up new financial firms to challenge their former employers. Whatever the reasons, mergers and acquisitions usually have multiple outcomes and generate a mixture of winners and losers.

Summary

Mergers and acquisitions of financial firms have been a major vehicle for change in the financial-services industry for many decades. This chapter has explored these key points regarding the merger and acquisition process in financial services:

- Mergers and acquisitions in the financial-services field have absorbed thousands of depository institutions, securities firms, insurance companies, finance companies, and other financial firms in recent years. Among the driving forces behind these corporate combinations are changes in legislation and regulation, intense competition, and the continuing search for greater operating efficiency and reduction of risk exposure.

- Mergers in the banking industry, in particular, have been powerfully influenced by changing legislation and regulation as governments around the world have moved to loosen the rules governing the financial marketplace. In the United States the passage of the Riegle-Neal Interstate Banking Act opened up the possibility of nationwide banking through mergers and acquisitions. Subsequently, the Gramm-Leach-Bliley Act permitted merger combinations among banks, security firms, and insurance companies. Parallel financial-service mergers and acquisitions unfolded at about the same time in Europe as the European Union established a common currency and financial system.

- While government deregulation has opened up substantial opportunities for financial-service mergers, key economic and financial forces have encouraged the managers and owners of financial firms to take advantage of these new opportunities. Among the powerful economic and financial forces at work has been the movement of customers to distant markets, encouraging financial firms to expand in order to follow and retain those customers. Moreover, mergers and acquisitions have proven to be a less expensive route for expansion than has the creation of new financial firms or the construction of chains of new branch offices. Finally, the possibility of risk reduction through the processes of geographic diversification (expansion into new market areas) and product-line diversification (expansion into new types of services) has lured many financial-service managers to seek out promising acquisition targets.

- Despite recent deregulation, significant government rules still surround the merger process. A prominent example in the United States is the Bank Merger Act which stipulates that proposed mergers involving banking firms must be approved or denied by each institution's principal federal regulatory agency—the Comptroller of the Currency for national banks, the Federal Deposit Insurance Corporation for U.S.-insured banking firms not members of the Federal Reserve System, or the Federal Reserve for state-chartered banking companies that have established membership in the Federal Reserve System.

- Merger laws in the United States require the Department of Justice (DOJ) to evaluate the competitive effects of any proposed merger. The Department can file suit in federal court to stop any proposed merger that, in its judgment, would have an adverse impact on competition, thereby harming the public interest.

- Mergers and acquisitions are capital investment decisions and, as such, must be carefully examined for their potential economic benefits and costs. If the expected returns are less than the minimum returns sought by each firm's stockholders, the proposed transaction is not likely to be pursued unless other mitigating factors intervene. The key to successful mergers among financial firms involves carefully assessing the strengths and weakness of both the acquirer and the proposed acquisition target and designing a strategy to maximize any synergies that may emerge once the merger is under way.

- Current research on the impact of mergers among financial-service providers comes to very mixed conclusions. While most mergers appear to be profitable, many are either unprofitable or fall disappointingly short of their premerger objectives. Moreover, the majority of cases offer meager evidence of public benefits. For example, service charges and fees often rise, rather than fall, following the completion of a merger transaction. However, the menu of financial services offered to the public frequently increases once a merger or acquisition takes place.

Key Terms

profit potential, 626
cash flow risk, 627
earnings risk, 627
tax benefits, 628
market-positioning
benefits, 628
cost savings 628
agency problem, 629
merger premium, *631*

exchange ratio, 632
dilution of ownership, 632
dilution of earnings, 632
purchase-of-assets
method, 634
purchase-of-stock
method, 634
wholesale banks, 634
retail banks, 634

Bank of Merger Act
of 1960, 635
competitive effects, 635
public benefits, 635
Justice Department
Merger Guidelines, 636
Herfindahl-Hirschman
Index, 636

**Problems
and Projects**

1. Evaluate the impact of the following proposed mergers upon the *postmerger earnings per share* of the combined organization:

   a. An acquiring bank reports that the current price of its stock is $20 per share and the bank earns $6 per share for its stockholders; the acquired bank's stock is selling for $17 per share and that bank is earning $5 per share. The acquiring institution has issued 200,000 shares of common stock, whereas the acquired institution has 100,000 shares of stock outstanding. Stock will be exchanged in this merger transaction exactly at its current market price. Most recently, the acquiring bank turned in net earnings of $1,200,000 and the acquired banking firm reported net earnings of $300,000. Following this merger, combined earnings of $1,600,000 are expected.

   b. The financial firm to be acquired is currently earning $14 per share, and its acquirer is reporting earnings of $12 per share. The acquired firm's stock is trading in today's market at $27 per share, while the acquiring firm's stock exchanges today for $24 per share. The acquired institution has 75,000 shares outstanding; the acquiring institution, on the other hand, has issued 80,000 shares of common stock. The combined organization is expected to earn $900,000; before the merger, the acquired firm posted net earnings of $400,000 and the acquiring firm tallied net earnings of $600,000.

2. Under the following scenarios, calculate the *merger premium* and the *exchange ratio*:

   a. The acquired financial firm's stock is selling in the market today at $10 per share, while the acquiring institution's stock is trading at $16 per share. The acquiring firm's stockholders have agreed to extend to shareholders of the target firm a bonus of $5 per share. The acquired firm has 30,000 shares of common stock outstanding, and the acquiring institution has 50,000 common equity shares. Combined earnings after the merger are expected to remain at their premerger level of $1,250,000 (where the acquiring firm earned $1,000,000 and the acquired institution $250,000). What is the postmerger EPS?

   b. The acquiring financial-service provider reports that its common stock is selling in today's market at $25 per share. In contrast, the acquired institution's equity shares are trading at $20 per share. To make the merger succeed, the acquired firm's shareholders will be given a bonus of $1 per share. The acquiring institution has 120,000 shares of common stock issued and outstanding, while the acquired firm has issued 40,000 equity shares. The acquiring firm reported premerger annual earnings of $850,000, and the acquired institution earned $150,000. After the merger, earnings are expected to decline to $900,000. Is there any evidence of dilution of ownership or earnings in either merger transaction?

3. The Goldmore metropolitan area is presently served by five depository institutions with total deposits as follows:

	Current Deposits
Goldmore National Bank	$840 million
Goldmore County Merchants Bank	600 million
Commerce National Bank of Silverton	395 million
Rocky Mountain Trust Company	200 million
Security National Bank and Trust	107 million

Calculate the Herfindahl-Hirschman Index (HHI) for the Goldmore metropolitan area. Suppose that Rocky Mountain Trust Company and Security National Bank propose to merge. What would happen to the HHI in the metropolitan area? Would the U.S. Department of Justice be likely to approve this proposed merger? Would your conclusion change if the Goldmore County Merchants Bank and the Rocky Mountain Trust Company planned to merge?

4. Space Savings Association has just received an offer to merge from Courthouse County Bank. Space's stock is currently selling for $58 per share. The shareholders of Courthouse County agree to pay Space's stockholders a bonus of $10 per share. What is the merger premium in this case? If Courthouse County's shares are now trading for $85 per share, what is the exchange ratio between the equity shares of these two institutions? Suppose that Space has 10,000 shares and Courthouse County has 30,000 shares outstanding. How many shares in the merged firm will Space's shareholders wind up with after the merger? How many total shares will the merged company have outstanding?

5. The city of Gertrude is served by three banks, which recently reported deposits of $230 million, $180 million, and $65 million, respectively. Calculate the Herfindahl index for the Gertrude market area. If the second and third largest banks merge, what would the postmerger Herfindahl index be? Under the Department of Justice guidelines discussed in the chapter, would the Justice Department be likely to challenge this merger?

6. In which of the situations described in the accompanying table do stockholders of both acquiring and acquired firms experience a gain in earnings per share as a result of a merger?

	P-E Ratio of Acquiring Firm	P-E Ratio of Acquired Firm	Premerger Earnings of Acquiring Firm	Premerger Earnings of Acquired Firm	Combined Earnings after the Merger
A.	5	3	$ 750,000	$425,000	$1,200,000
B.	4	6	$ 470,000	$490,000	$ 850,000
C.	8	7	$ 890,000	$650,000	$1,540,000
D.	12	12	$1,615,000	$422,000	$2,035,000

7. Please list the steps you believe should contribute positively to success in a merger transaction in the financial-services sector. What management decisions or goals? On average, what proportion of mergers among financial firms would you expect would be likely to achieve the goals of management and/or the owners and what proportion would likely fall short of the mergers' objectives? Why?

Internet Exercises

1. You are interested in the mergers and acquisitions that are reshaping the financial services industry. Visit **www.innercitypress.org/bankbeat.html** and you will get more recent news than you want to read in one sitting. If you are using Internet Explorer, click Edit button, then use the Find command to look for the word *merger*. What are the newsworthy merger announcements?

REAL NUMBERS FOR REAL BANKS
Assignment for Chapter 19

A LOOK AT YOUR BANK'S USE OF MERGERS FOR EXPANSION

The overall number of BHCs and banks is decreasing due to consolidation within the industry and convergence across different financial-services industries. In this assignment we will examine the history of your bank in the context of mergers and acquisitions. With mergers and acquisitions, the acquisition may take place through the BHC or one of its subsidiary banks.

An Examination of How Your Bank Evolved

A. You will need to go back to your informational spreadsheet created in Chapter 2 and view the names of the banks listed as part of your BHC. You will want to check the history of the BHC and each bank. Go to the National Information Center at **www.ffiec.gov/nic/pubweb/nicweb/nichome.aspx** and click on the "Top 50" BHC link. Focus on all mergers occurring since January 1, 2000. Collect information on your BHC and each bank within your BHC, who acquired whom and when, noting the state of the target institution.

B. Choose one or more acquisitions and search for press releases on your BHC's Web site.

C. Focusing on the chosen acquisition, go to a search engine such as **www.alltheweb.com** and do a news search.

D. Using the data you found and the press releases and any news articles collected, compose several paragraphs describing your BHC's acquisitions and providing inferences concerning your BHC's merger strategy. Remember to reference your sources of information.

2. *Consolidation* refers to a declining population of businesses in any one industry. Visit **www.financialservicesfacts.org/financial/**, click the Financial Services Industry Button, and explore the link for mergers. Discuss the number of financial-service mergers by industry.

3. *Convergence* refers to the movement of two or more industries over time toward each other, resulting in different firms offering many of the same services. Visit **www.financialservicesfacts.org/financial/** and explore the link on convergence. How do the service offerings of large banks compare with securities firms? How do banks compare with insurance firms?

4. Which ingredients appear to be associated with a successful merger or acquisition? Go to **www.snl.com/bank/manda/** and read everything available on the SNL merger model. What are the important factors?

5. Which ingredients appear to be associated with a successful nonbank financial-services merger or acquisition? Go to **www.snl.com/financial_svc/manda/** and read one of the latest merger and acquisition stories from the M&A story archives. What are the important factors?

S&P Market Insight Challenge (www.mhhe.com/edumarketinsight)

STANDARD &POOR'S

1. The banking and thrift industries have been in a consolidation mode—fewer but larger companies—for years. Recent information concerning acquisitions and mergers in these industries may be found using the Industry tab in S&P's Market Insight, Educational Version. A drop-down menu displays such industry groups as Diversified Banks, Regional Banks, and Thrifts & Mortgage Finance. By choosing these particular industry groups you will be able to find the S&P Industry Survey on Banking as well as the survey covering savings and loans. Please download both of these industry surveys and explore the parts labeled "Industry Profile" and "Industry Trends." Please describe the most recent trends in mergers and discuss their underlying motivations.

STANDARD &POOR'S

2. Please examine closely the list of bank holding companies, investment banking or security/broker dealer firms, finance companies, and life and property/casualty insurers listed on S&P's Market Insight, Educational Version. Which of these companies have engaged in a significant merger or acquisition within the past three years? Which have

been acquired themselves within that time span by a bank or nonbank business? (Prominent examples include Citigroup, HSBC Holdings PLC, Bank of America, Salomon Smith Barney, Aetna Life and Casualty, and Household International among many others on the Insight list.)

STANDARD &POOR'S

3. As this chapter relates, business mergers and acquisitions, including those in the financial sector, frequently result in disappointing financial and operating performance. Can you cite any examples in the financial-services group of firms on Standard & Poor's Market Insight experiencing disappointing postmerger or postacquisition performance? What reasons can you cite for the disappointing performance results?

Selected References

For analyses of how mergers and acquisitions may affect the performance of financial firms, please see:

1. Amel, Dean, Colleen Barnes, Fabio Panetta, and Carmelo Salles. "Consolidation and Efficiency in the Financial Sector: A Review of the International Evidence." *Finance and Economics Discussion Series*, Study 2002–47, Board of Governors of the Federal Reserve System, Washington, DC, 2002.

2. Goldberg, L. G., and G. A. Hanweck. "What Can We Expect from Interstate Banking?" *Journal of Banking and Finance* 12 (1988), pp. 51–67.

3. Millon-Cornett, M., and H. Tehranian. "Changes in Corporate Performance Associated with Bank Acquisitions." *Journal of Financial Economics* 31 (1992), pp. 211–234.

4. Pettway, Richard, and J. W. Trifts. "Do Banks Overbid When Acquiring Failed Banks?" *Financial Management* 14 (Summer 1985), pp. 5–15.

5. Rose, Peter S. "The Distribution of Outcomes from Corporate Mergers: The Case of Commercial Banking." *Journal of Accounting, Auditing and Finance* X, no. 2 (March 1995).

6. Rose, Peter S. "The Diversification and Cost Effects of Interstate Banking." *Financial Review* 31, no. 2 (May 1996), pp. 431–452.

7. Spong, Kenneth, and J. D. Shoenhair. "Performance of Banks Acquired on an Interstate Basis." *Financial Industry Perspectives*, Federal Reserve Bank of Kansas City, December 1992, pp. 15–23.

The following studies focus especially upon merger regulations and laws:

8. Rose, Peter S. "Improving Regulatory Policy for Mergers: An Assessment of Bank Merger Motivations and Performance Effects." *Issues in Bank Regulation* 9, no. 3 (Winter 1987), pp. 32–39.

9. Rose, Peter S. "The Impact of Mergers in Banking: Evidence from a Nationwide Sample of Federally Chartered Banks." *Journal of Economics and Business* 39, no. 4 (November 1987), pp. 289–312.

For an analysis of the scope of merger activity in the financial sector of the United States, see especially:

10. Pilloff, Steven J. *Bank Merger Activity in the United States, 1994–2003*. Staff Study 176, Board of Governors of the Federal Reserve System, Washington, DC, May 2004.

For a review of the public interest aspects of financial-service mergers, see:

11. Peek, Joe, and Eric S. Rosengren. "Have Borrower Concentration Limits Encouraged Bank Consolidation?" *New England Economic Review*, Federal Reserve Bank of Boston, January/February 1997, pp. 37–47.

12. Pilloff, Steven J. "What's Happened at Diversified Bank Offices? An Empirical Analysis of Antitrust Divestitures in Bank Mergers." *Finance and Economics Discussion Series*, Federal Reserve Board, no. 60, Washington, DC, 2002.

www.mhhe.com/rose7e

For a discussion of planning for mergers, see these studies:

13. Lausberg, Carsten, and Peter S. Rose. "Merger Motives in European Banking: Results of an Empirical Study." *Bank Archive* 43, no. 3 (1995), pp. 177–186.

14. Lausberg, Carsten, and Peter S. Rose. "Managing Bank Mergers." *Bank Archive* 45 (June 1997), pp. 423–427.

15. Pilloff. Steven J. "Multimarket Contact in Banking." *Review of Industrial Organization* 14 (March 1999), pp. 163–182.

16. Prasad, Rose M., and S. Benjamin Prasad. "Strategic Planning in Banks: Senior Executives' Views." *International Journal of Management* 6, no. 4 (December 1989), pp. 435–441.

17. Rhoades, Stephen A. *Bank Mergers and Banking Structure in the United States, 1980–98.* Staff Study 174, Board of Governors of the Federal Reserve System, Washington, DC, August 2000.

For an analysis of the possible impact of merger activity on the chartering of new banks and on the profitability, efficiency, and shareholder wealth of merging banks, see:

18. Seelig, Steven A., and Tim Critchfield. "Merger Activity as a Determinant of De Novo Entry into Urban Banking Markets." Working Paper 2003–01, Federal Deposit Insurance Corporation, Washington, DC, April 2003.

19. Rhoades, Stephen A. *A Summary of Merger Performance Studies in Banking, 1980–93, and an Assessment of the "Operating Performance" and "Event Study" Methodologies.* Staff Study 167, Board of Governors of the Federal Reserve System, Washington, DC, July 1994.

For a discussion of the rules regarding the treatment of goodwill in mergers between financial firms, see, for example:

20. Carlson, Mark, and Roberto Perli. "Profits and Balance Sheet Developments at U.S. Commercial Banks in 2002." *Federal Reserve Bulletin*, June 2003, pp. 243–270.

International Banking
and the Future
of Banking
and Financial Services

Key Topics in This Chapter

- Types of International Banking Organizations
- Regulation of International Banking
- Foreign Banking Activity in the United States
- Services Provided by International Banks
- Managing Currency Risk Exposure
- Challenges for International Banks in Foreign Markets
- The Future of Banking and Financial Services

20–1 Introduction

Banks were not only among the first financial institutions to appear in history but also were among the first financial firms to venture into international markets and offer their services in distant locations. The first banks were located principally in global trading centers around the Mediterranean, including Athens, Cairo, Jerusalem, and Rome, aiding merchants in financing shipments of raw materials and goods and exchanging one nation's coin for that of another to assist travelers. Much later, during the colonial period of American history, foreign banks based in Europe entered the Americas and met a large share of the financing needs of American businesses.

United States banks established a significant beachhead in Europe and elsewhere around the globe as the 20th century opened. This was followed by a dramatic expansion in the 1950s and 1960s as U.S. banks set up branch offices, subsidiaries, and joint ventures with local firms in hundreds of foreign markets. This period of foreign expansion was directed mainly at the commercial centers of Western Europe, the Middle East, and South and Central America. During the 1970s and 1980s American banks expanded their presence around the Pacific Rim, especially in Japan, Hong Kong, and Singapore. American, European, and Japanese multinational banks played a key role in investing the huge amounts of funds flowing to petroleum producers as world oil prices

Key URLs
To stay abreast of developments in international banking around the globe financial managers often consult such sources as the Bank for International Settlements at **www. bis.org** and the World Bank and International Monetary Fund libraries at **jolis.worldbank imflib.org/external.htm**.

rose. American banks were also called upon to help finance the huge trade deficits that the United States has incurred in purchasing a growing number of goods and services from abroad.

For a time, the torch of leadership in international banking passed to the Japanese, whose banks established strong beachheads in London, New York, and other financial centers around the globe. At the same time, growth of international banking firms in the United States and Western Europe slowed markedly. Intensified competition, spurred on by deregulation among the governments of Great Britain, the United States, and other leading nations and by significant advances in communications technology, forced many international financial firms to reduce their physical presence in foreign markets in order to cut operating expenses. Moreover, many of their principal credit customers, especially nations like Argentina and Brazil, were experiencing serious problems, fueling the retrenchment of international banking around the globe.

As the 21st century approached, leadership in financial services passed once again to American and European banks and many of their nonbank financial-service competitors, led by such giants as Citigroup, Bank of America, HSBC, UBS, J. P. Morgan Chase, Barclays PLC, ING Group, and Deutsche Bank. These banking giants began to carve out a major share of the rapidly developing Asian markets, especially China, thus circling the globe. International financial services today continue to be vitally important sources of revenue and earnings for leading financial firms around the world.

In this chapter we take a close look at the organizational forms, services, problems, and challenges facing large international banking and financial-service organizations today.[1]

20–2 Types of International Banking Organizations

Filmtoid
What 2001 action film starring John Travolta and Halle Berry concludes with the transfer of billions of dollars to a Credit Suisse account in a Grand Cayman branch as a result of cyber crime meeting the fight against terrorism?
Answer: *Swordfish*.

In their pursuit of business around the world, banks use a wide variety of *organizational structures* to deliver services to their customers (as illustrated in Exhibit 20–1).

Representative Offices

The simplest organizational presence for a bank active in foreign markets is the **representative office**—a limited-service facility that can market the services supplied by the home office and identify new customers but does not take deposits or book loans. These offices supply support services both to the parent bank and its customers.

Agency Offices

Somewhat more complete than the representative office is an **agency office,** which in many jurisdictions does not take deposits from the public, but extends commitments to make or purchase loans, issues letters of credit, provides technical assistance and advice to customers, administers their cash accounts, and assists with customer security trading.

Branch Offices

The most common organizational unit for most international banks is the **branch office,** normally offering a full line of services. Foreign branches are *not* separate legal entities, but merely the local office that represents a single large financial-service corporation. They can accept deposits from the public subject to regulations of the country where they are located and may escape some of the rules for deposit taking faced by branches of the same bank in its home country. For example, the branch offices of U.S. banks overseas do not have to post legal reserve requirements or pay FDIC insurance fees on the deposits they accept abroad.

---

[1]Portions of this chapter are based on Peter S. Rose's article in *The Canadian Banker* [2] and are used with the permission of the publisher.

EXHIBIT 20–1
Types of International
Banking
Organizations
and Facilities

International Banking Service Options

Subsidiaries

When an international bank acquires majority ownership of a separate, legally incorporated foreign bank, the foreign bank is referred to as a **subsidiary.** Because a subsidiary possesses its own charter and capital stock, it will not necessarily close down if its principal owner fails. Similarly, a subsidiary can be closed without a substantial adverse effect on the international bank that owns it (as happened in the Philippines when a subsidiary of New York's Citicorp closed several years ago). Subsidiaries may be used instead of branches because local regulations may prohibit or restrict branching or because of tax advantages. Also, many international banks prefer to acquire an existing firm overseas that already has an established customer base.

Joint Ventures

A bank that is concerned about risk exposure in entering a new foreign market, lacks the necessary expertise and customer contacts abroad, or wishes to offer services prohibited to banks alone may choose to enter into a **joint venture** with a foreign financial firm, sharing both profits and expenses.

Edge Act Corporations

Edge Acts are domestic U.S. companies owned by a U.S. or foreign bank, but located outside the home state of the bank that owns them. These subsidiary corporations are limited primarily to international business transactions. Federal legislation passed at the end of World War I permitted banks large enough to post the required capital to apply for Edge Act charters from the Federal Reserve Board.

Agreement Corporations

These business corporations are subsidiaries of a bank organized under Section 25 of the Federal Reserve Act. Agreement corporations must devote the bulk of their activities to serving international customers, similar to Edge Act corporations.

IBFs

An **international banking facility (IBF)** is a creation of U.S. banking regulations, first authorized by the Federal Reserve Board in 1981. IBFs are computerized account records that are not part of the domestic U.S. accounts of the bank that operates them. They must be domiciled inside U.S. territory and focus upon international commerce. Deposits placed in an IBF are exempt from U.S. deposit reserve requirements and deposit insurance fees. IBFs may be operated by either U.S.-chartered banks or by banks foreign to the United States.

Shell Branches

In order to escape the burden of regulation, many international banks have established special offices that merely record the receipt of deposits and other international transactions. These **shell branches** may contain little more than a desk, a telephone, fax machine, and computer where deposits from the worldwide Eurocurrency markets are booked to avoid deposit insurance assessments, reserve requirements, and other costs incurred when a domestic bank accepts deposits. Many international banks have operated shell branches for years in such attractive offshore locations as the Bahamas and the Grand Cayman Islands.

Export Trading Companies (ETCs)

In 1982, the U.S. Congress passed the **Export Trading Company Act** (ETCA), which allowed U.S. banking firms and Edge Act corporations to create **export trading companies** (ETCs). According to Federal Reserve regulations, these specialized firms must receive over half their income from activities associated with exporting goods and services from the United States. An ETC can offer such services as export insurance coverage, transportation and warehousing of salable products, trade financing, and research into markets abroad.

Concept Check

20–1. What organizational forms do international banks use to reach their customers?

20–2. Why are there so many different types of international organizations in the financial institutions' sector?

20–3 Regulation of International Banking

International banking activities are closely regulated by both home and host countries all over the globe. However, a strong trend today is toward deregulation of banking and the related fields of securities brokerage and securities underwriting. An increasing number of nations today recognize the necessity of coordinating their regulatory activities so that eventually all financial firms serving international markets will operate under similar rules, called *harmonization*.

Goals of International Banking Regulation

International banking activities are regulated for many of the same reasons that shape domestic banking regulations. There is an almost universal concern for *protecting the safety of depositor funds*, which usually translates into laws and regulations restricting risk exposure and rules specifying minimum amounts of owners' equity capital to serve as a cushion against operating losses. Regulations frequently limit nonbanking business activities to avoid excessive risk taking and criminal activity, as in the famous Bank of Credit and Commerce International (BCCI) case in the early 1990s. Then, too, to the extent international banks can create money through lending and deposit-creating activities, international banking activity is regulated to *promote stable growth in money and credit* in order to avoid threats to economic health in individual nations.

However, many international banking regulations are unique to the international field itself—they don't apply to most domestic banking activity. For example, *foreign exchange controls* prohibit the export of domestic currency in order to protect a nation against loss of its foreign currency reserves, which might damage its prospects for repaying international loans and purchasing goods and services abroad. Another instance would be rules that *restrict the outflow of scarce capital* that some governments see as vital to the health of their domestic economies. There is also a strong desire in many parts of the world to *protect domestic financial institutions and markets from foreign competition*. Many countries prefer to avoid international entanglements and excessive dependence on other countries for vital raw materials and other goods and services. This isolationist philosophy often leads to outright prohibition of outsiders from entry.

U.S. Banks' Activities Abroad

American banks operate large numbers of agencies, branches, and other service facilities in overseas markets. According to data provided by the Federal Reserve Board—the chief regulator of both U.S. bank activities overseas and foreign bank activities inside the United States—there were 71 U.S. chartered banks operating 768 full-service branch offices in foreign markets by the end of 2005. When U.S. banks' foreign subsidiaries and other international facilities were combined with their full-service branches more than 100 American banks held nearly a trillion dollars in assets and almost $900 billion in deposits through their overseas offices.

Loans extended to foreigners and foreign deposits received by U.S.-based international banks were concentrated most heavily in Europe (especially in Great Britain, Germany, and Switzerland), in Asia (particularly in China and Japan), and in the Caribbean (especially in the Bahamas and the Cayman islands). These areas of the world represented the richest sources of loan demand, deposit growth, and fee income for America's multinational banking firms.

Expansion and Regulation of Foreign Bank Activity in the United States

Key URLs
Two of the chief sources of international banking statistics today are the Bank for International Settlements at **www.bis.org/publ** and the Federal Reserve System at **www.federalreserve.gov**.

In recent years foreign bank expansion inside the United States has been about as extensive as American banks reaching abroad. Foreign banking entities have sought solid footholds inside U.S. territory for decades, attracted by the huge size of the common market formed by the 50 states, the economic and political stability inside the United States, and the migration of foreign banks' own customers toward the Americas (e.g., foreign-owned auto and electronic firms setting up manufacturing plants on American soil).

By year-end 2005 183 foreign banks headquartered in 54 different countries operated close to 300 agency, branch, and representative offices as well as other financial-service facilities inside the United States. In addition, foreign banks held an ownership (equity) interest of at least 25 percent in about 70 U.S. commercial banks. The U.S. offices of foreign banks accounted for 18 percent (or about one-fifth) of the total assets held by all U.S. banks combined.

Foreign banks operating in the United States are controlled by more than 200 corporate families, led by such international giants as Barclays and HSBC of Great Britain, Credit Lyonnais from France, and Germany's Deutsche Bank. Most of these foreign-owned facilities are based in New York with substantial additional units centered in San Francisco, Los Angeles, Chicago, and Atlanta. These facilities are examined at least once every 18 months by U.S. federal and state regulators to determine if they pose substantial risks to the American banking system.

Recently foreign bank expansion in the United States has slowed somewhat, especially in the years following the 9/11 terrorist tragedy. Some of the slowdown has been traceable to slower growth in the world economy, particularly in Europe. Then, too, government deregulation of domestic U.S. banking has permitted American financial firms to be more aggressive competitors and recapture some of the market share they had previously lost to foreign financial firms.

The International Banking Act of 1978

The expansion of foreign banking activity inside America's borders led to strong pressure on the U.S. Congress by domestic banking groups and, eventually, to passage of the **International Banking Act** (IBA) of 1978—the first major federal law regulating foreign bank activity in the United States. The IBA's key components included:

- It required branches and agency offices of foreign banks to secure federal licenses for their U.S. operations.
- It restricted foreign branching within the United States, requiring each bank to designate a home state and follow that state's branching rules just as American banks had to do.
- It stipulated that deposits accepted at the U.S. branch or agency offices of foreign banks holding $1 billion or more in consolidated assets are subject to legal reserve requirements determined by the Federal Reserve Board.
- It made U.S. branches of foreign banks eligible for deposit insurance under stipulated conditions and granted them access to certain Federal Reserve services, such as the ability to borrow from the Federal Reserve banks.

The Foreign Bank Supervision Enhancement Act of 1991

Key URL
To learn more about the activities of foreign banks in the United States see, for example, the Institute of International Bankers at **www.iib.org**.

On December 19, 1991, Congress amended the IBA with passage of the **Foreign Bank Supervision Enhancement Act.** This law placed tighter controls on foreign bank operations in the United States. Applications from foreign banks to expand their U.S. banking activities must be approved by the Federal Reserve Board. Service offerings of foreign banks are basically limited to the same list of banking services that U.S. national banks are permitted to offer. Moreover, no foreign bank can accept retail deposit accounts of less than $100,000 from the public unless it first obtains insurance coverage from the FDIC. Any foreign bank desiring to acquire more than 5 percent of the voting shares of a U.S. bank company must first seek Federal Reserve Board approval.

The Federal Reserve must also review how thoroughly foreign banks are supervised by their home countries. If the Fed determines that regulation of a foreign bank by that bank's home nation is inadequate, it can deny that foreign bank permission to establish a branch, agency, or representative office inside United States territory or to start or acquire any U.S. subsidiary firms. Moreover, the Fed can terminate the operations of a foreign bank if it finds that bank has violated U.S. laws, engaged in unsafe or unsound banking practices, or is not being operated in a manner consistent with the public interest. The 1991 law empowered the Fed to examine the U.S. offices and affiliates of *any* foreign bank and stipulated that the Fed must be notified a minimum of 30 days in advance if a foreign bank wishes to close any of its U.S. offices.

New Capital Regulations for Major Banks Worldwide

Key URL
To learn more about the Russian banking system see, for example, the Web site of the Russian Federation's Central Bank at **www.cbr.ru/eng**.

The spread of international banking coupled with international debt problems soon led to new regulatory standards for the capital that international banks must hold as a buffer against risk. First, in November 1983, the U.S. Congress passed the **International Lending and Supervision Act,** which required federal regulatory agencies to prepare capital and lending rules for U.S.-supervised banks. The 1983 law required American banks to restrict the size of fees charged for rescheduling payments on loans made overseas in order to avoid excessive burdens on debtor countries, report their foreign loan exposures to bank examiners, and hold adequate reserves to protect depositors against possible losses on foreign loans.

Soon after these rules were implemented, negotiations began between the United States and other leading nations to determine if international cooperation in banking regulation was possible. Finally, on July 15, 1988, representatives of 12 nations announced an agreement in Basel, Switzerland, on common bank capital standards.

RUSSIAN BANKING: RECOVERY AND RENEWAL

The Russian banking system experienced the equivalent of a Chernobyl nuclear meltdown in 1998. Hundreds of banks failed and thousands of depositors lost confidence in the banking system, many stashing their cash in the proverbial "cookie jar" rather than risking the loss of still more of their savings. If this were not enough, another crisis appeared in 2004 as several banks closed and depositors lined up demanding their funds, while the Bank of Russia rushed to inject liquidity into the system.

Today the Russian banking system has several problems: too many banks (about 1300), too much government control, too little public trust, too few business loans, and a general lack of quality employee training. However, a *new* banking system continues to evolve out of the ashes of the old as aggressive managers pursue what remains of a potentially lucrative market, especially among young adults, many of whom have high-paying jobs and need credit and an efficient way to pay for their purchases (including credit and debit cards). New banking market leaders have emerged, such as Alfa Bank, MDM Bank, and Rosbank as well as Citibank from the United States. There is also an expansion of customer-service facilities under way, including new branch offices, more ATMs, and the growing use of online banking. Russia's great size and "underbanked" population appear to offer great marketing opportunities for international banks.

The **Basel Agreement,** as we saw earlier in Chapter 15, called for all banks to achieve a minimum total-capital-to-total risk-adjusted assets ratio of 8 percent. The announced purpose of the Basel Agreement was twofold: (1) to strengthen international banks, thereby strengthening public confidence in them; and (2) to remove inequalities in regulation between nations that contribute to competitive inequalities between their banks. In the wake of the Basel Agreement, many leading banks announced plans to raise new capital and sell off assets to improve their capital positions. Most recently a second phase of the Basel Agreement has appeared, requiring leading international banks to develop risk models to determine their individual risk exposures and capital needs.

Concept Check

20–3. What are the principal goals of international banking regulation?

20–4. What were the key provisions of the U.S International Banking Act of 1978 and the International Lending and Supervision Act of 1983?

20–5. Explain what the Basel Agreement is and why it is so important.

20–4 Services Supplied by Banks in International Markets

Customers active in foreign markets require a wide variety of services, ranging from credit and the execution of payments to the provision of marketing assistance (see, for example, Table 20–1). The variety of services international banks and their strongest competitors offer has expanded significantly in response to evolving customer needs and intense international competition.

Making Foreign Currencies Available to Customers

International banks supply foreign currency—**FOREX**—to their customers. Many customers require sizable quantities of spendable currencies to pay for imported goods and raw materials, to purchase foreign securities, and to complete mergers and acquisitions.

TABLE 20–1
Key Customer
Services Offered by
International Banks

Key Elements of The International Bank Service Menu	
Supplying foreign currencies to customers	Supplying long- and short-term credit and credit guarantees
Hedging against foreign currency risk	Payments and cash management services
Security underwriting for corporations	Savings or thrift instruments
Hedging against interest rate risk	Foreign marketing assistance for customers

Other customers may receive large amounts of foreign currency or foreign-currency–denominated deposits from businesses and individuals abroad who buy their products or purchase their securities. These foreign funds must be exchanged for domestic currency and deposits to help the customer meet his or her own cash needs. International banks routinely hold working balances of those foreign currencies most in demand.

Top Trading Firms
Operating in Today's
Global Currency
Markets

Citigroup, Inc.	UBS Warburg	J. P. Morgan Chase & Company
Deutsche Bank AG	Morgan Stanley Group	Goldman Sachs Group, Inc.
Credit Suisse-First Boston Corp.	ABN AMRO Bank	HSBC Holdings PLC

Recently there has been a sharp increase in FOREX trading activity among leading commercial and investment bank dealers due to volatility among leading currencies, especially the U.S. dollar, the pound, and the euro. Trading volume now exceeds a trillion dollars a day and is climbing, making this market one of the largest on the planet. Somewhat unique is the recent upsurge in *proprietary trading* where dealers speculate on trends in the prices of selected currencies. Revenues from currency trading seem to behave somewhat differently than revenues from other services, frequently improving while other markets are down. However, bid-ask spreads among dealers have narrowed substantially in today's marketplace, which favors high-volume trading businesses.

Hedging against Foreign Currency Risk Exposure

Customers who deal with large amounts of foreign currencies look to international banks for protection against *currency risk*—the potential for loss due to fluctuations in currency prices (exchange rates). But customers are not the only ones who face currency risk; international banks themselves must deal with currency risk.

Currency risks arise most often in international banking when (*a*) making foreign-currency–denominated loans to customers, (*b*) issuing foreign-currency–denominated IOUs (such as deposits) to raise new funds, (*c*) purchasing foreign-issued securities, or (*d*) trading in foreign currencies for a bank's own currency position as well as the currency needs of its customers. The *net exposure* of a bank or its customers to fluctuations in currency values can be determined from the following equation:

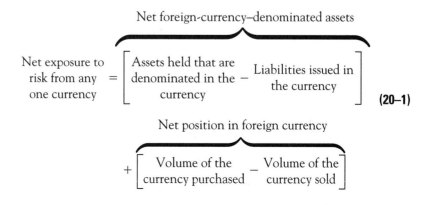

Insights and Issues

THE JAPANESE FINANCIAL SYSTEM STILL FACES BIG PROBLEMS

The Japanese financial system is one of the largest in the world with more than a thousand depository institutions (including banks and cooperatives), nearly a hundred insurance companies, and well over 200 securities firms. But despite its great size and complexity the Japanese system continues to struggle after more than a decade of faltering consumption and investment spending, rising unemployment, price deflation, and deterioration in the viability of many of its financial institutions.

Desperate to find effective countermeasures to these problems the Bank of Japan pushed key domestic interest rates down toward zero in an effort to stimulate borrowing and spending and set in motion an economic recovery. As the 21st century began to unfold some signs of recovery began to appear, though Japan still has a long way to go.

These economic and financial problems have been especially perplexing because more than a decade ago the Japanese system was the envy of the world. Its economy was characterized by surging property values and a massive balance of payments surplus with the rest of the world, which couldn't get enough Japanese cars, TVs, and other electronic devices. A high domestic savings rate fueled massive Japanese investment abroad, including the acquisition of huge amounts of U.S. property. By the late 1980s at least 16 of the world's top 20 banks were Japanese.

All of these positive trends were turned around during the 1990s and early in the 21st century. Japanese stocks fell to less than a quarter of their peak values, while land prices plummeted to a third of their earlier heights. These massive declines led to the collapse of hundreds of bank and nonbank firms, which were pulled down by the combined assault of bad loans, falling stock and real estate prices, and rapidly eroding capital cushions. Because many Japanese banks hold a huge volume of corporate stock associated with loans to their borrowing customers and also have large amounts of "paper" capital in the form of estimated future tax credits, they have relatively weak defenses against economic adversity. Moreover, Japanese banks seem to attract somewhat riskier borrowers than do competing foreign banks. This risk-exposure problem appears to be exacerbated by weak marketplace disciplining of Japanese bank behavior (in part, because most deposits are fully covered by insurance).

In need of more capital to offset loan losses several of Japan's leading banks have pulled back somewhat from international banking activities and declared themselves to be domestic banking firms once again. Pleas for government help in the form of injections of new bank capital led the Japanese government to become proactive in using taxpayer funds to shore up the domestic financial system. Financial firms receiving aid had to pledge to make fundamental changes in their operations and financing, including cleaning up bad loans and searching for new sources of private capital.

At the same time, the Japanese government began borrowing heavily to flood the economy with liquidity and shore up depressed stock and bond markets. The Bank of Japan purchased the depressed stock of some Japanese companies from the banks that held these shares. In the wake of these expensive measures to rescue Japan's economy, the nation's public debt mushroomed to over 100 percent of its GDP.

Troubled Japanese banks have been asked to scale back their overseas ventures in hopes of shoring up the domestic supply of credit. However, in today's open international economy this has had the effect of transferring some of Japan's problems to other nations, especially in Asia. On the other side of the coin, however, if the Japanese economy continues to recover as the 21st century unfolds, it will not only greatly strengthen the domestic banking system, but it will also help recapitalize much of the remainder of Asia and foster economic growth there and in other parts of the world.

Key URL
To learn about the Japanese banking and financial system, see especially **www.zenginkyo.or.jp/en/index.html**.

An international bank or bank customer with a *positive* net exposure in a given foreign currency—that is, whose net foreign-currency–denominated assets plus its net foreign-currency position is greater than zero—is said to be *net long* in that particular currency. This condition may arise because the bank or its customer has more foreign-currency–denominated assets than liabilities, has purchased more of a foreign currency than it has sold, or both. If the foreign currency involved declines in value relative to the value of the domestic currency, the bank or its customer will suffer a loss due to its net long position in that particular currency.

For example, suppose J. P. Morgan Chase holds assets denominated in euros of 100 million and liabilities of 60 million. Its euro purchases in the most recent period amounted to 50 million while its euro sales reached 40 million. This represents an exposure to fluctuations in the exchange value of euros of:

Net exposure to risk from a position in euros
= (100 million euros − 60 million euros) + (50 million euros − 40 million euros)
= + 50 million euros

Should the euro decline in value relative to U.S. dollars, for example, J. P. Morgan would experience a loss from its sizeable net long position in euros unless offset by the use of currency hedging tools, such as currency futures or options. On the other hand, a bank or bank customer may have a *negative* net exposure in a given foreign currency, indicating that its net foreign-currency–denominated assets plus net foreign-currency position is less than zero. This may occur because the bank's or the customer's liabilities in a given foreign currency are greater than its assets denominated in that same currency, or the volume of the currency sold exceeds the amount purchased or both. In this instance the international bank or its customer is said to be in a *net short* position in that particular currency. If the currency involved increases in value against the international bank's or customer's home currency, a loss will occur in a net short position. In general, the more volatile a currency is, the greater the possibility for scoring gains or for experiencing losses from any given currency position.

Research evidence (see, for example, Hopper [9]) suggests that currency exchange rates are not consistently predictable and show no reliable connection to such fundamental factors as money supply growth and output in different countries—two forces that finance theory suggests should help to explain relative currency-price movements. Accordingly, international banks typically employ a wide variety of currency-hedging techniques to help shelter their own and their customers' risk exposure. The most widely used of these currency-risk management techniques include forward contracts, currency futures and option contracts, currency warrants, and currency swaps.

Forward Contracts

For example, international banks may use **forward contracts,** in which a customer anticipating a future need to make currency purchases will work through the bank to negotiate a contract calling for the delivery of currency at a stipulated price on a specific future date. On the other hand, customers expecting to *receive* currency will often seek out contracts to sell that currency at a prespecified price. Because the price is set at the opening of a forward contract, the customer is protected from currency risk no matter which way currency prices go. If the customer is uncertain of the future date and the amount of currency involved, the international bank may provide an *option forward contract,* in which the customer receives the right, but not the obligation, to deliver or take delivery of specific currencies on a future date at an agreed-upon exchange rate.

Currency Futures Contracts

An increasingly popular alternative to the forward contract among banks and their customers is a **currency futures contract**. These contractual agreements promise delivery of stipulated currencies at a specified price on or before a terminal date. The two basic futures contract types are long hedges and short hedges.

Long hedges in currency futures are designed to protect an international bank's customer from increases in the price of the currency the customer must eventually acquire. They are particularly useful for *importers*, because payment for goods received often must be made in the foreign exporter's home currency, and a rise in the exchange rate between the exporter's home currency and the importer's home currency can quickly eliminate any profit on the sale of goods. Under a long hedge contract, the customer pledges to take delivery of currency at contract maturity for price X. If currency prices subsequently rise, the customer can go back to the currency futures market and sell similar currency futures contracts at the new higher price, Y. This cancels out the customer's obligation to take delivery of currency and, at the same time, generates a trading profit on each contract equal to the price difference $(Y - X)$ less any commission charged and taxes. Profits made on currency futures help to offset any loss that arises when the customer must actually acquire the currency and pay for the imported goods.

Alternatively, many international customers, especially those *exporting* goods, find *short-hedge* futures contracts useful. These agreements require the customer to pledge delivery of a stipulated currency at a guaranteed price, X, to a counterparty on the maturity date. If currency prices subsequently fall, the customer can enter the futures market again on or before the first contract's maturity date and buy similar contracts at the lower price, Y, thus eliminating the responsibility to deliver currency. A profit is earned on each contract first sold and then bought equal to $X - Y$ (minus taxes and transactions costs).

Other Tools for Reducing Currency Risk

The Development of Currency Options

The **currency option** gives a buyer the right, though not the obligation, to either deliver or take delivery of a designated currency or foreign-currency–denominated futures contract at a set price any time before the option expires. Thus, unlike the forward market, where delivery must take place on a certain date, actual delivery may not occur in the option market. Currency options include both spot and futures options.

Exchange-traded currency options on futures contracts have been growing rapidly in recent years. These contracts depend for their value on the underlying futures contract, which in turn depends on the price of the currency itself. When the price of a currency rises, the nearest-term currency futures contract also rises in price. An international bank holding sizable assets denominated in that currency can reduce the risk of loss from falling currency spot prices by selling currency futures or by buying put options or selling call options for that same currency.

Call currency options give their holder the right to purchase currency or currency futures contracts at a fixed price any time before the option expires. *Put* currency options represent the right to sell currency or currency futures contracts at a specified price on or before the published expiration date. For example, a call on euro futures contracts at a strike price of $0.92 gives the buyer of this call option the right to buy a contract calling for delivery of euros at a price of $0.92 to the buyer. If the market price of euro futures climbs above $0.92 per euro, the call option is said to be "in the money," and its buyer will exercise his or her option and take delivery of euro futures contracts at a price of $0.92. On the other hand, if euro futures stay below a strike price of $0.92, the call option will go unexercised because the buyer of the call can purchase futures contracts more cheaply in the market; in this case, the call option would be "out of the money." Generally, a put option is needed to protect against a fall in currency prices, whereas call options protect against loss from rising currency prices.

The advantage of the currency option is that it limits downside risk but need not reduce upside profits. The purchase price of a currency option is normally low enough to permit even small firms to participate in currency-hedging activities.

Currency Swaps

Finally, currency risk can be reduced with **currency swaps.** A currency swap is a contract between two parties—often two borrowers who have borrowed money denominated in different currencies—to exchange one currency for another and thereby help reduce the risk of loss as currency prices change. For example, suppose a U.S. corporation (Company A) has received a loan denominated in pounds and will need pounds when it must make payments on its loan. A's swap partner is Company B—the *counterparty* to the currency swap. B is based in Great Britain but has a loan in dollars from a U.S. bank. Clearly, Company A has easy access to dollars but needs pounds when its loan payments come due, while Company B has easy access to pounds but needs dollars to make its loan payments. Under the terms of a straight currency swap B pays out pounds to A and receives, in turn, dollars from Company A when loan payments must be made. (See Exhibit 20–2.)

What's the great advantage of a currency swap? It makes it easier and more efficient for a borrower to tap the international financial markets for loanable funds, borrowing through whatever type of currency-denominated loan results in the best deal. Another advantage, unlike so many other currency risk-hedging tools, is that currency swaps can be set up to cover long periods of time (stretching into years, if necessary) as opposed to other risk-hedging tools, like futures and options, which generally have short horizons. Moreover, while other hedging tools are often highly standardized in form and, therefore, rigid and inflexible, a currency swap can be tailored to conform to the two swap partners' specific needs.

For an international bank currency swaps offer several advantages:

• International banks are heavy borrowers in a variety of foreign currencies and can enter into swap contracts to reduce their own currency risk exposure.

• International banks can generate fee income by arranging currency swaps for their customers, serving as a swap dealer and ensuring that either or both swap partners fulfill the terms of their contract, serving as a swap guarantor.

The swap market has become one of the largest financial markets in the world. It has helped thousands of businesses and governments hedge risk and given some of the world's largest central banks a new instrument to trade in and help shape money and credit conditions in order to strengthen their home nations' economies. Thus, swap contracts have become a global financial instrument, fostering trade, managing risk, and assisting policymakers.

Supplying Customers with Short- and Long-Term Credit or Credit Guarantees

International banks are the leading source of credit for multinational corporations and many governmental units at home and abroad. They provide both short- and long-term financing for the purchase of raw materials and for meeting payrolls, constructing buildings, and other important projects.

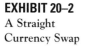

EXHIBIT 20–2
A Straight
Currency Swap

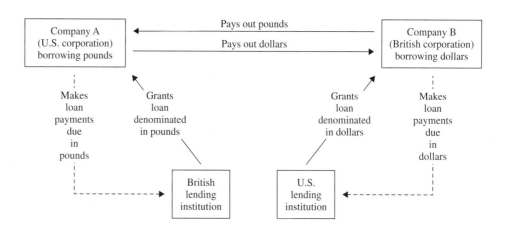

Note Issuance Facilities

Most international bank loans are short-term business credits carrying floating interest rates usually tied to some international base rate. The most popular rate of this type is LIBOR, the London Interbank Offer Rate on borrowings of short-term Eurodollar deposits between banks. Increasingly in recent years, however, international banks have provided *credit guarantees* for their customers' borrowings in the open market. One of the most popular is the **note issuance facility (NIF).** NIFs are primarily medium-term credit agreements between international banks and their larger corporate and governmental customers. The NIF customer is authorized to periodically issue short-term notes, each of which usually comes due in 90 to 180 days, over a stipulated period (such as five years). International banks pledge to either buy up any notes not bought by other investors or to grant supplemental loans. In most cases, the customer's notes are in large denominations (e.g., $1 million U.S. or larger).

Europaper

International banks have also played a key role in the **Eurocommercial paper (ECP)** market, where multinational corporations raise short-term credit covering weeks or months. This short-term loan market is centered in London's financial district and has attracted international banks and nonfinancial corporations as investors. While most ECP borrowers are based outside the United States, a growing cadre of U.S. companies whose credit ratings are not strong enough to crack the U.S. commercial paper market or who need to sell longer-maturity paper are successfully placing their notes in the Europaper market. A recent spur to this market has come from financial deregulation in Japan, which permits Japanese bank affiliates abroad to underwrite international commercial paper, while both Japanese and non-Japanese firms have recently been allowed to issue and buy yen-denominated commercial paper. International banks are heavy buyers of ECPs for themselves and their investing customers and are also among the leading sellers of ECP issues.

Issuing and Managing Depository Receipts

A related form of assistance that international banks provide domestic and foreign customers is the issuance of **depository receipts (DRs).** A DR is a negotiable instrument representing an ownership interest in the stock or debt securities of a foreign company or other foreign institution. This instrument usually arises when a broker purchases securities issued by a foreign entity and delivers them to a custodian who, in turn, instructs a depository bank to issue DRs representing the securities.

Depository receipts are usually denominated in a leading international currency—most prominently the U.S. dollar but also in euros today. This transformation into dollars or euros makes it easier for a foreign borrower to sell its securities in the global marketplace. To date DRs have been issued representing companies in more than 70 countries.

When the borrowing company issuing securities approves of such an arrangement the DR is said to be "sponsored" by the issuer. However, a broker can simply choose to package *any* foreign securities that might be of interest to international investors and request a bank to issue and distribute DRs without the approval of the issuing company, resulting in an "unsponsored" DR. Today sponsored DRs are generally popular with investors while unsponsored DRs appear to be fading due, in part, to lack of control. Quality sponsored DRs that meet the rules often trade on major securities exchanges.

One of the principal attractions of depository receipts for international investors is the *absence of currency risk*. For example, through an American depository receipt (ADR) the value of a foreign security is literally converted into U.S. dollars. Another advantage is that international investors can *geographically diversify* their portfolios and thereby reduce country risk. Moreover, an investor usually can recover his or her funds more quickly by liquidating a DR than by attempting to sell a foreign-issued security.

ETHICS IN BANKING AND FINANCIAL SERVICES

ETHICS IN LENDING: THE CHINESE LOAN MARKET

The Chinese banking industry is one of the world's largest and most complex, embracing large state-owned banks (such as China Construction Bank and the Industrial and Commercial Bank), thousands of bank branch offices, smaller regional banks, and local credit cooperatives as well as more than 200 offices representing banks from nearly 40 nations. Indeed, the People's Republic of China today represents one of the most promising markets on the planet for making loans and providing other financial services.

The rapid industrialization of China's economy, coupled with the migration of millions of Chinese workers from the countryside into higher-paying city jobs, has led to soaring growth in business and consumer loans. Unfortunately some of these loans have been accompanied by scandal and poor management.

In the past Chinese banks were often compelled by government to support projects that did not meet the discipline of the private marketplace. Frequently local government officials had more pervasive influence over the decisions of loan officers in thousands of bank branches scattered across China than did senior bank management. Local bank offices often granted loans on the basis of political connections, not based on expected profitability. The result was that the banking system became one of the real problem areas in China's economy, while the industrial sector became plagued with overproduction.

As the Chinese banking system opens itself up to foreign investors in the new century these damaging practices seem to be fading somewhat. Increasingly, new managers with training in foreign banks and business schools are coming home to China and taking over. Written loan policies and risk assessment software are gradually replacing older lending methods. Moreover, paralleling many leading U.S. banks, Chinese bankers are centering more major lending decisions at bank headquarters where skilled loan officers decide what loans to approve.

Meanwhile, leading international banks see great potential in China's financial-service markets. Already Citigroup from the United States and HSBC and Standard Chartered from the United Kingdom have branch offices in China, while Bank of America has a strategic alliance with China Construction Bank. Other international banks, such as the Royal Bank of Scotland and Merrill Lynch, are not far behind. Bank managers from America and Europe see profit opportunities not only in making new loans to Chinese businesses and consumers, but also in packaging China's troubled loans into pools and selling claims against those pools to international investors.

Supplying Payments and Thrift (Savings) Instruments to International Customers

Payments Services

International banks are essential to the functioning of global commerce through the offering of *payments and thrift instruments*. Not only do they provide foreign currencies for a customer making cash payments overseas, but they also issue and accept drafts in payment for purchases of goods and services across national borders. These irrevocable commitments of an international bank to pay may be in the form of *sight drafts*, due and payable upon presentation, or *time drafts*, payable only on a specific future date, usually just long enough for goods to be shipped to another country. Time drafts usually arise when an importer requests its bank to issue a *letter of credit*, guaranteeing that the bank will pay an exporter of goods if the importer fails to do so. The exporter may then draw through one of its correspondent banks a bill for payment, which is presented to the importer's bank for acceptance and eventual payment. International banks also issue traveler's checks denominated in foreign currencies and will wire funds anywhere a customer designates.

Savings (Thrift) Services

International banks encourage *thrift*—short-term and long-term savings—by their customers. Most of these savings instruments are certificates of deposit (CDs)—interest-bearing receipts for funds deposited in a bank. While CDs were developed to be fixed-rate savings instruments, a sizable portion carry floating interest rates tied to movements of a specific

Factoid
Which do you suppose
is biggest—the revenue
from loans held at the
foreign offices of U.S.
banks or the interest
expense on the deposits
held at these foreign
offices? **Answer:** They
are often close in
amount but deposit
interest has often
outstripped loan
revenue at U.S banks'
foreign offices in recent
years, quite unlike the
situation inside the
United States where
loan revenue received
usually outstrips deposit
interest paid out to
customers.

base rate (such as LIBOR). Each day, major international banks post CD rates for the most popular deposit maturities, posting higher or lower rates depending on their need for funds.

The tremendous success of this bank funds-raising instrument led to an expansion of the CD concept around the world in the form of the EuroCD, a deposit sold in million-dollar units, first in London and eventually reaching all major financial centers. Today, most EuroCDs are issued by branches of the largest U.S., Japanese, Canadian, European, and British clearing banks. Large-denomination EuroCDs traded in the interbank market are often called *tap CDs*, while packages of smaller-denomination EuroCDs sold to a wide range of investors are called *tranche CDs*. While most Eurodollars are fixed-rate deposits, floating-rate CDs (FRCDs) and floating-rate notes (FRNs) are also issued to protect investors and borrowers against interest rate risk. These flexible-rate investments tend to be medium- to long-term in maturity, ranging from about 1 year to about 5 years in the case of FRCDs and up to about 20 years for FRNs, with the attached interest rates typically adjusted every three to six months to reflect current market conditions.

Underwriting Customer Note and Bond Issues in the Eurobond Market

The development of note issuance facilities (NIFs) by international banks, discussed earlier, is but one example of the growing role of international banks in *underwriting new securities issues* in the open market. Another example is the **Eurobond market,** where borrowers issue bonds outside their home country. One reason for the growth of such a market was the increasing number of U.S. corporations, led by firms the size of Ford Motor Co. and Campbell Soup Co., that decided to tap Eurobonds to fund their overseas ventures. When U.S. interest rates rise, even purely domestic firms may find that Eurobond borrowings look cheaper by comparison. Leading international banks active in this market include Lloyds Bank PLC, J. P. Morgan Chase, and Citigroup. In an effort to broaden the market's appeal for the future, recent innovations have appeared. Among them are debt securities denominated in European currency units (ECUs), representing currencies issued by various European countries.

Protecting Customers against Interest Rate Risk

International banks help protect their customers against *interest rate risk*—the risk of loss due to adverse interest rate movements. Rising interest rates can increase a customer's borrowing cost and threaten to erode the profit margin on investment projects supported by borrowing. Conversely, an international bank's customer may suffer a loss in the event interest rates fall if the customer's funds are placed in investments with floating interest yields or in other short-maturity investments that must be renewed at lower interest rates. Similarly, a customer with a fixed-rate loan fails to benefit from lower market interest rates unless steps are taken to cover that eventuality.

Interest-Rate Swaps

International banks can help their customers limit interest rate risk exposure by arranging **interest-rate swaps.** As described in Chapter 8, these contractual agreements require each party to pay at least a portion of the interest bill owed on the other party's loan. Not only can interest-rate swaps reduce interest expense for each party, but they also permit each swap partner to more accurately balance cash inflows generated by its assets with cash outflows traceable to its liabilities.

Interest-Rate Caps

International banks also limit the interest-rate risk exposure of borrowing customers by imposing caps (maximum rates) on a customer loan in return for a fee. For example, the customer requesting a $100 million loan with an interest rate based on LIBOR may ask for an 8 percent interest-rate cap so that a rise in market interest rates does not send the loan rate above 8 percent. Such caps transfer interest rate risk from the borrowing customer to the international bank and often carry a stiff fee to compensate the bank for its added risk exposure.

Financial Futures and Options

International banks are also active in assisting their customers with trading in financial futures and option contracts. For example, if the customer faces substantial loss from a *rise* in interest rates, then a *short* futures hedge (as described in Chapter 8) can be used to offset any loss due to a higher loan rate; alternatively, a *put* option could be employed. The prospect of customer losses from *falling* interest rates, on the other hand, could be hedged through a *long* (or buying) futures hedge or through the use of a *call* option.

Helping Customers Market Their Products through Export Trading Companies

An increasingly popular device for aiding customers to sell their goods abroad is the *export trading company* (ETC), developed originally by the Japanese. ETCs research foreign markets, identify firms in those foreign markets that could distribute products, and then provide or arrange the funding, insurance, and transportation needed to move goods to market. While larger manufacturers often have extensive foreign trading operations, thousands of smaller firms have not maximized their opportunities in export markets, in part due to a lack of adequate market research and few contacts abroad.

Inside the United States ETCs have been developed by leading money center banks and by several smaller regional and community banks. Leading U.S. institutions launching ETCs at various times include Bank of America, Bankers Trust Co. (now affiliated with Deutsche Bank), J. P. Morgan Chase Corp., Citigroup, and Fleet Boston (now part of Bank of America). Despite widespread interest, however, the growth of export trading activity via ETCs based in the United States has been somewhat disappointing. To be sure, external developments have played a major role in limiting ETC activities, particularly the difficulties many less-developed countries have faced in finding resources to pay for imports from the United States and in servicing their international debt. Lack of management experience with the ETC form and lack of distribution channels and market data from abroad have proven to be major hurdles, especially for smaller banks.

Concept Check

20–6. Describe the principal customer services supplied by international banks serving foreign markets.

20–7. What types of risk exposure do international banks strive to control in order to aid their customers?

20–8. What is an NIF? A DR?

20–9. Of what benefit might NIFs and DRs be to international banks and their customers?

20–10. What are ETCs? What services do they provide and what problems have they encountered inside the United States?

20–11. What do the terms *Europaper* and *Eurobonds* refer to? Why are these instruments important to international banks and to their customers?

20–12. What types of tools have international banks developed to help protect themselves and their customers against currency and interest rate risk? How does each tool accomplish its purpose?

Key URLs
What trends are reshaping international banking today and in the future? See, for example, **www.bis. org/review** and **www. lacefinancial.com**.

U.S. banks have also complained of heavy capitalization requirements, regulatory limits on credit extended from banks to their ETC affiliates, and legal restrictions on the proportion of income that must come from exporting activities. For example, at least 51 percent of ETC income must come from U.S. exporting activities, and a U.S. international bank can invest no more than 5 percent of its consolidated capital in an ETC nor lend more than 10 percent of its capital to its own ETC.

20–5 Challenges for International Banks in Foreign Markets

Growing Customer Use of Securities Markets to Raise Funds

All banks—both domestic and international banking firms—today face an ongoing challenge to their business—namely growing competition from securities markets and securities dealers for the fund-raising needs of their customers. When many international loans developed severe repayment problems during the 1980s and 1990s, many international banks withdrew substantial resources from the global credit markets. Securities houses were quick to seize this opening and provide a conduit for borrower offerings of notes and bonds in the Eurocurrency markets. Later, large insurance companies, finance companies, and other nonbank financial institutions joined the competition to attract borrowers away from banks and assist them in their access to the open market to sell securities and raise new capital. While international banks have purchased many of these securities themselves, they have been forced to settle for slower growth in their credit-providing business, with smaller earnings margins on the credit they do extend to international borrowers.

Whether international banks can regain or even maintain their share of the global business credit market depends on current and future regulations that control their risk-taking worldwide, changing public attitudes regarding the safety and soundness of these multinational institutions, and the aggressiveness of their principal competitors in the international marketplace—securities dealers, insurance firms, and finance companies—who are also intent on widening their shares of the lucrative international corporate financing market. Indeed, several of the world's largest securities dealers (such as Merrill Lynch, Nomura Securities, Goldman Sachs, and Lehman Brothers), insurance companies (such as Allianz, AXA, Prudential, and Swiss Reinsurance), and finance companies (such as GE Capital and Household Finance—an affiliate of HSBC Holdings in Great Britain) have grown and expanded their service menus to compete with many of the globe's biggest banks. Challenged as never before, international banks today must work hard to find new sources of revenue and capital to meet the potent competition posed by other financial-service institutions—for example, by selling their superior ability at credit evaluation, at packaging loans and securities for resale, and at issuing credit guarantees in support of their customers' financial-service needs.

Developing Better Methods for Assessing Risk in International Lending

International Loan Risks

The greatest source of risk for most international banks lies in granting foreign loans. Foreign lending is generally more risky than domestic lending because information sources overseas are often less reliable than those at home, it's easier to monitor a loan made nearby rather than one made thousands of miles away, and the court systems needed to enforce contracts and conduct bankruptcy proceedings are often absent in the international arena. This form of risk is often called *country risk*. A related type of risk, usually called *sovereign risk*, occurs when a foreign government takes actions that interfere with repayment of an international loan, such as by repudiating all foreign debt, appropriating private property, or suspending loan payments to conserve the home government's foreign exchange reserves. The result is that financial institutions choosing to lend abroad must analyze *both* the individual borrower and the country and government where the borrower resides.

Possible Solutions to Troubled International Loans

Troubled foreign loans, like problem domestic loans, may be *restructured* so that a new loan agreement is put together to replace the old loan agreement. The new loan may assesses the borrower a lower interest rate and grant a longer maturity until final payment in return for a restructuring fee. The net cost (*concessionality*) to the lender is usually measured by the difference in present value of the original loan versus the (usually lower) present value of the newly restructured loan. Alternatively, a troubled loan can be sold in the secondary market for international loans that has grown up since the early 1980s and is centered around commercial banks and security dealers in New York and London. Many international banks have found buyers for discounted foreign loans among large corporations, other banks, and wealthy investors seeking speculative investments with the potential for high return. Selling international loans removes these credits from the balance sheet, provides funding for new assets, and may raise the value of the selling bank's stock.

Still another method used to deal with troubled international credits is to write off all or a portion of a foreign loan, recognizing that loan as a probable loss. The result is a credit against taxes that, in effect, shares the loan loss between the international bank's shareholders and the government.

Another alternative is for international banks to accept *exit bonds* in lieu of loan repayments. These debt securities are typically valued below the loans they replace and usually require lower or longer-term debt-service payments. Exit bonds may be backed by government securities or other acceptable collateral. For example, during the 1990s the U.S. Treasury Department announced plans to sell zero-coupon U.S. government bonds to Mexico at prices below their market value in order to support a refinancing agreement worked out between the government of Mexico and leading international banks. Mexico could use these bonds, issued as part of the Brady Plan, to pay off exit bonds issued to international banks lending to that nation. Other nations, including Argentina, Brazil, and the Philippines, converted some of their loans into Brady bonds bearing longer maturities and lower interest rates than the original loans. These swaps of Brady bonds for international loans were frequently supported by the central bank of the country where the borrower resides, providing a quality loan guarantee.

In most cases, a *combination* of remedies for troubled international loans has been used. The package of remedies may include restructuring delinquent loans and rescheduling their interest and principal payments, supplemental financial support by the International Monetary Fund (IMF) and other international agencies, stimulation of exports, and reduction of imports by indebted nations in an effort to buy time so these countries can move toward debt retirement and a stronger domestic economy.

International Loan Risk Evaluation Systems

There is little argument today with the proposition that banks engaged in international lending need to develop improved methods for analyzing the quality and soundness of international loans before they are made and better methods for monitoring borrower performance after loans are granted. Several risk evaluation systems are in use today.

For example, the *checklist approach* lists economic and political factors believed to be correlated with loan risk, such as military conflicts, balance-of-payments deficits, and rising unemployment. Comparative weights may be applied to each factor on the list, or all may be equally considered in the international loan evaluation process. The weights may take the form of statistical or mathematical probabilities, leading to the calculation of an index value for default risk. Changes in the index then become part of an early warning loan evaluation system. The listed items may be supplemented by field reports from bank personnel with first-hand knowledge of the debtor country.

An alternative approach, which uses expert opinion, is the *Delphi method*. Business analysts, economists, and experts in international law are assembled, and their separate, independently derived risk evaluations of a country are compiled and shared with each member of the expert panel. Panel members are then given an opportunity to revise their earlier assessments of a country's risk exposure. The final report is prepared as a consensus view of an individual country's risk exposure.

One serious problem with both of these approaches is *timeliness*. Significant changes in default-risk exposure may occur well before any of the calculated indexes or group opinion surveys pick it up. More recently, advanced statistical methods (including discriminant analysis) have been applied to country risk problems. Linear modeling techniques have been constructed that attempt to classify international loans into those that will be successfully repaid versus those that will require debt rescheduling or will be defaulted outright based upon preselected predictor variables.

Among the most popular predictor variables to measure the risk exposure of loans to a particular country are growth of the domestic money supply (an indicator of possible future inflation and currency devaluations), the ratio of real investment to gross domestic product (which measures a nation's future ability to be productive), the ratio of interest and debt amortization payments to total exports (which compares required debt payments to the principal source for generating foreign exchange reserves to repay debt—a nation's exports), and the ratio of total imports to a nation's foreign exchange reserves (which measures a country's spending abroad relative to the availability of its foreign exchange reserves to pay for that spending). However, controversy has continued to swirl around the usefulness of these advanced statistical models due to delays in the reporting of data, the importance of hard-to-capture random events (such as labor strikes or political revolutions), and instability over time in the relative importance of the different predictor variables used in country-risk models.

Recently published country-risk indicators have become popular aids for bank loan officers trying to evaluate an international loan. One such widely used indicator is the *Euromoney Index*, published by *Euromoney* magazine. *Euromoney*'s country-risk index is based upon a variety of economic and political variables, including access to financing sources, credit ratings, and the international borrower's default history. A second popular indicator of country risk today is the *Institutional Investor Index* (III), published by *Institutional Investor* magazine. The III is derived from a survey of loan officers from multinational banks and other institutions who submit their rankings of each nation as to its probability of default.

Finally, one of the newest and most comprehensive country-risk indicators is provided by the *International Country Risk Guide* (ICRG), developed in 1980 to assess the probability of a successful venture in a particular marketplace around the globe. The ICRG supplies political, economic, and financial risk ratings and an overall composite rating (between 0 and 100) for 140 countries monthly and also prepares one- and five-year risk forecasts for the period ahead. A nation's composite rating is based on 22 factors, including government stability, corruption, ethnic and religious tensions, quality of bureaucracy, per-capita gross domestic product (GDP), real GDP growth, annual inflation rate, foreign debt as a proportion of GDP, and the stability of exchange rates. Users of this country-risk index are granted access to the underlying data so they can assign their own risk weights, if need be, in order to reach a credit decision.

Factoid
Which nation today seems to promise both the most rapid economic growth but also the greatest barriers to foreign bank entry? **Answer:** The Peoples' Republic of China.

Key URLs
For an analysis of risks and opportunities across different regions of the globe, see **www.euro money.com**; **www. institutionalinvestor. com**; and **www.icrg online.com**.

Insights and Issues

THE EXPANDING EUROPEAN UNION (EU) AND ITS IMPLICATIONS FOR INTERNATIONAL BANKERS

The unification of Europe has been a lengthy historical drama, following centuries of political and economic turmoil. A key milestone in the decades-long process of establishing the European Union (EU) took place in 1992 when the Maastricht Treaty on European Union was adopted. Among the most controversial of its provisions was a call for the creation of a single currency; a common central bank; and the integration of foreign policies, judicial and legal systems, and domestic affairs. Maastricht set in motion rules for each nation to become a member state of the European Community (EC), provided it could jump over the tough hurdles Maastricht laid down.

Initially, in January 1999, 11 nations joined the European Union (EU), establishing the *euro* as the Union's common currency, and creating a national banking system led by a new European Central Bank. The 11 nations forming the initial common monetary system (later expanding to 12 nations) included Austria, Belgium, Finland, France, Germany, Ireland, Italy, Luxembourg, the Netherlands, Portugal, and Spain. Eventually other nations—such as Denmark and the United Kingdom—that made up the original European Union formed under the Maastricht Treaty are expected to join the new common money and credit system. Moreover, several other nations inside Europe and on its fringes have applied to join the EU, including the Czech Republic, Cyprus, Estonia, Hungary, Latvia, Malta, Lithuania, Poland, Slovakia, Slovenia, and Turkey.

Perhaps the greatest consequence of the EU for international bankers is the creation of a single banking market. The new European *single banking market* is shaped by several guiding rules that govern all member states:

A. Each member country will keep its own regulatory agencies and will be the chief supervisor of banks headquartered in its territory, no matter how far these banks extend into other EU member states.

B. While regulatory rules may differ, all member states must maintain minimal regulatory standards so that banks from each country face a level playing field and will not have a strong incentive to leave a European nation with tough rules and migrate to another with more lenient rules.

C. The principle of "national treatment" generally applies: regardless of what EU member country a bank uses as its headquarters, when it enters a new EU state, it is subject to the same rules as domestic banks operating there. An individual EU member state can impose restrictions on international banks entering its territory, but its own banks then may be subject to the same restrictions. The principle of national treatment gives nations a powerful incentive to keep regulations as simple and equal as possible.

D. The principle of "mutual recognition" was also adopted by selected nations. A nation can allow an entering foreign bank to continue offering the same services it is allowed to offer in its home country even if domestic banks are not allowed to do so. This principle tends to give foreign banks a competitive edge over domestic banks if there are great differences in rules from nation to nation.

E. Under the Second Banking Directive of 1993, the term *banking* was defined in one way across the whole EU so that all European banks can offer a common set of services (*universal banking*). These common services include deposit taking; lending; financial leasing; payments services; guarantees and credit commitments; trading in money market instruments, currencies, financial futures, options, and other interest-bearing or interest-rate hedging instruments; aiding issuers of new securities; advising on acquisitions and mergers; brokering funds; supplying portfolio advice, management services, and safekeeping services; and providing credit references.

F. All EU states agree to a *single passport* so that any international bank from a member nation can conduct business in any other member nation in whatever form it views as giving it the best advantage, including the possibility of setting up a new branch or subsidiary firm or possibly merging with another bank.

G. All EU states must offer some form of deposit insurance, which may be government run or supervised, as in Belgium, Finland, France, and Italy, or privately owned, as in Austria, Germany, Ireland, Luxembourg, the Netherlands, Portugal, and Spain. Depositors of failed banks must be reimbursed within three months. A member nation may establish an insurance system where insurance fees are assessed against all banks and funds are accumulated to deal with future bank failures (as in the United States) or a different system could be adopted where member banks are assessed charges only after a failure occurs.

H. All banks within the EU are to have identical capital standards that mirror the Basel International Capital Standards (discussed more fully in Chapter 15) in order to avoid giving some EU banks significant advantages over others.

I. No EU bank is permitted to loan to a single client more than 25 percent of its capital, a provision designed to ensure that each bank has a diversified loan portfolio with limited risk exposure.

Overall, research studies suggest that competition has increased and at least some banking services now seem to be available at lower prices. However, many steps still need to be taken to level the playing field throughout the EU, particularly in such areas as taxation, governmental subsidies, labor laws, and excess capacity in the banking industry. Moreover, several European nations have shown a tendency to protect their domestic businesses from foreign takeover.

Adjusting to New Market Opportunities Created by Deregulation and New International Agreements

International financial markets are passing through dramatic change as deregulation in one nation after another and international treaties open up new financial service opportunities. Inside the United States the federal government moved in 1994 to allow nationwide acquisitions of American banks by holding companies to open up the opportunity for interstate branch banking. Five years later, the U.S. Congress voted to permit banks, insurance companies, and security dealers to acquire each other through the creation of financial holding companies (FHCs). These same privileges were extended to foreign banks, making the United States a more attractive market for expanding international banks, security dealers, insurance companies, and other global financial-service providers.

Opportunities Created by NAFTA and CAFTA

In November 1993 the U.S. government gave final approval to the North American Free Trade Agreement (NAFTA), setting in motion a gradual opening up of Mexico's financial system to outside entry by financial-service firms from Canada and the United States. The Mexican financial marketplace has become attractive for entry from outside the country because Mexico's financial firms have not moved aggressively to serve such important customer groups as small businesses and households. In contrast, leading banks in Canada and the United States have benefited from NAFTA because Mexico's restrictions on foreign banks' market share recently have been lifted. International investors are now free to be a part of the Mexican financial system through the direct acquisition of existing financial firms or through the establishment of foreign-owned subsidiaries. Meanwhile, member nations of NAFTA are considering expansion to include Chile and other countries, creating still more opportunities for leading international banks.

Also centered upon the Americas is the Central American Free Trade Agreement (CAFTA), approved by the U.S. Congress in 2005. Central America is the second biggest U.S. export market in the Americas after Mexico, especially for agricultural products and fabrics. CAFTA calls for the gradual lowering of trade barriers between the United States, Guatemala, El Salvador, Honduras, Nicaragua, Costa Rica, and the Dominican Republic. Proponents of this newest trade agreement argue that it will increase living standards, improve trade volume, enhance the availability of financial services and capital investment in Central America, and reduce illegal immigration into the United States.

Opportunities in the Expanding European Community

An even larger and more challenging expansion opportunity lies in the continuing integration of the European Union (EU) and the opening up of Eastern Europe and nations from the former Soviet Union to privatization and free markets. By 2006 there were 25 nations in the EU, with Bulgaria and Romania expected to join in 2007 and Croatia and Turkey negotiating possible future membership. Trade barriers within the EU are due for further reduction and eventual elimination as the 21st century continues to unfold. EU supporters boast of great marketing potential for sales of financial services because of a combined population of more than 370 million, significantly larger than that of the United States.

However, marketing success across Europe demands a significant local presence throughout the area. Merely setting up a financial firm on the continent without building a local network of financial-service distributors seems to carry little chance of long-term success, particularly in wresting market share from established European-owned competitors and from leading U.S. and Canadian financial firms that have had a significant presence there for many years.

Insights and Issues

INDIA'S FINANCIAL-SERVICES MARKETPLACE

Like China, India represents a tremendous opportunity for international financial firms if these institutions can break through domestic barriers, mainly due to its population of roughly a billion people, rapid economic growth, high gross savings rate, and growing need for auto and home loans and credit cards. However, entry by foreign banks into the retail market is largely restricted in an effort to allow India's state-owned banks to strengthen themselves against foreign competition. The foreign leader is Citigroup with close to 40 branches, though India's leading domestic banks operate hundreds of branches. Foreign finance companies (notably GE Finance) and investment banks (such as Merrill Lynch, Goldman Sachs, and Barclays) appear to have made substantial inroads due to the pressing need of many Indian corporations for new capital. At the same time Citigroup, ABN AMRO, HSBC Holdings, and other foreign companies have become active supporters of India's rapidly expanding micro lending industry in which millions of very small loans are made to individual entrepreneurs trying to escape poverty.

Factoid

Which Asian nation has the greatest number of separately incorporated commercial banks relative to the size of its population?
Answer: Taiwan with more than 50 different banking companies.

Opportunities in Asia as Barriers Erode

Finally, perhaps the most promising geographic area for future expansion is Asia, especially such rapidly growing nations as China, India, Hong Kong, Indonesia, South Korea, Thailand, and Vietnam. The huge populations of these countries represent business opportunities of historic proportions for those international financial-service providers positioned to take advantage of them. Moreover, the cultural and legal barriers that have prevented Asia's consumers and businesses from buying financial products popular in the Western World—such as credit cards, life insurance policies, and retirement plans—appear to be eroding as several international banks have moved aggressively to establish strong toeholds with these financial products in the Asian marketplace.

One example of this foreign "invasion" of Asian Markets is J. P. Morgan's recent successful effort to secure licenses in order to trade in China's national monetary unit, the yuan, on behalf of foreign businesses seeking deals inside China. Moreover, China is committed under a recently signed agreement with the World Trade Organization (WTO) to allow foreign banking firms to sell a full menu of services throughout that nation as 2007 approaches. Already such leading financial firms as Citigroup, HSBC Holdings, Standard Chartered Bank of Great Britain, and the Carlyle Group in the United States have purchased significant interests in China, Korea, and neighboring Asian nations in preparation for lower entry barriers into one of the world's largest commercial and consumer markets.

Concept Check

20–13. This chapter focuses on several major problem areas that international banks must deal with in the future. What are these problem areas?

20–14. What different approaches to country-risk evaluation have international banks developed in recent years?

20–15. What different regions around the globe today appear to offer the greatest opportunities for expansion for international banks? Why do you think this is so?

20–6 The Future of Banking and Financial Services

As we end this book it seems appropriate to peer briefly into the *future*, to try to anticipate where the financial-services industry may be headed. No one knows for sure what the fate of this vital service industry will be, but we can at least make some "educated guesses" based on what we have learned from the pages of this text.

HOW BANKERS KEEP TRACK OF GLOBAL EVENTS

Today there are numerous sources of data on international markets and institutions that bankers can use to stay up to date and make critical decisions. Prominent examples include:

The Economist, Economist Newspaper Limited in London (**www.economist.com**)

The Banker, London (**www.thebanker.com**)

Euromoney, London (**www.euromoney.com**)

Institutional Investor (**www.institutionalinvestor.com**)

BusinessWeek (**www.businessweek.com**)

Scotiabank Group, *Global Economic Research* (**www.scotiabank.com**)

US-ASEAN Business Council, Washington, D.C. (**www.us-asean.org**)

U.S. International Trade Commission, Washington, D.C. (**www.usitc.gov**)

Office of the U.S. Trade Representative, Washington, D.C. (**www.ustr.gov**)

World Bank, *World Development Report,* Washington D.C. (**www.worldbank.org**)

International Monetary Fund, *World Economic Outlook,* Washington, D.C. (**www.imf.org/external**)

Board of Governors of the Federal Reserve System, *International Finance Discussion Papers,* Washington, D.C. (**www.federalreserve.gov/pubs/ifdp**)

Federal Reserve Bank of San Francisco, *Pacific Basin Notes and Economic Letter* (**www.frbsf.org**)

Federal Reserve Bank of St. Louis, *International Economic Trends* (**research.stlouisfed.org/publications**)

Convergence

Some future trends seem fairly obvious. As we saw in Chapters 1–4, 14, and 19 banking all over the globe is *converging* with other financial-service industries. Institutions like Citibank of New York operate security broker/dealer firms, while security dealers like Merrill Lynch operate banks. Insurance companies such as Axa and MetLife own and operate their own banks, while giant universal banks like Deutsche Bank sell insurance. Despite some recent setbacks this convergence trend seems likely to continue (though probably at a somewhat slower pace) as bankers and their closest competitors continue to invade each other's territory and grow in both size and diversity.

Consolidation

As we saw repeatedly in earlier chapters, financial-service firms are also *consolidating* into fewer, but much larger, service providers all over the globe. This trend, whose roots go back nearly a century, seems to be continuing. For example, U.S. banking's 100 largest firms hold more than 90 percent of the industry's total assets, and the European and Japanese banking industries are even more concentrated in a handful of huge banks than is presently the case in the United States. Many experts see this consolidation trend as a map of the industry's future—eventually all the big fish will gobble up all the little ones and banking and financial services will become exclusively an ocean dominated by giants.

Are these two powerful trends in financial services—*convergence* and *consolidation*—really *inevitable* for the future?

Not necessarily! For example, the consolidation trend appears to be slowing in the early years of the new century. There are still in excess of 7,000 U.S. banks and thousands more in Europe and Asia, most of them small. While the industry population continues to decline, the rate of decline has definitely slowed. Some experts believe this is due to a lack of good acquisition targets—the best targets, allegedly, have already been bought out. Others suggest, however, that there is still a profitable niche for many small financial-service providers.

Moreover, as Citigroup's recent sloughing off of its ownership interest in two Traveler's Insurance affiliates suggests, the surge toward giant multiservice companies has also slowed somewhat. Banking today is highly profitable, but bankers have discovered that not all financial-service companies are as profitable as they are and do not necessarily make good partners to pursue. Moreover, larger and more diverse companies are more difficult to manage successfully than are smaller, more sharply focused financial firms.

Survival of Smaller Community Financial-Service Institutions

Thus, the "small fry"—financial firms of a few hundred million to perhaps a few billion dollars in asset size, centered in a single community, with a relatively narrow menu of services (such as loans, credit cards, deposits, and investment advice)—may well survive. Research evidence accumulated over several decades suggests that economies of scale in financial services are relatively *modest*. Small and moderate-size community-oriented financial firms don't need to grow very big before they reach the point of lowest production cost per unit of service. A financial-service firm that has reached its most efficient size can compete with *anyone*, even with the giants of the industry.

Indeed, smaller community banks have been able to maintain their share of the industry's population and their returns to stockholders despite intense competition from industry giants. They remain a viable business model as reflected by their sustained profitability and the continued chartering of new financial firms each year. They possess unique strength in personalized lending to small businesses and households and often possess superior knowledge of their customers.

Reaching the Mass Media

Where the small fry may struggle—and some *will* continue to disappear—is on the revenue side of the business, advertising to attract customers. Only a firm with nationwide or global service capacity normally can make efficient use of the mass media. It is the largest financial firms who tend to be the most aggressive advertisers, reaching out over the Internet, through cell phones, and on television networks to fight for sales. Industry leaders like Wells Fargo and Bank of America are using their branch offices as sales-focused "stores," each with a similar appearance and each intent on selling their clients as many different services as possible. Also, it is the largest financial firms who are best able to follow an increasingly mobile population and retain their customers who may be migrating into distant markets.

Can the smallest, community-oriented financial-service providers find a way to contend effectively with mass advertising and aggressive sales practices? That remains to be seen, though the Internet and the telephone are open to all in an electronic world where headquarters' location doesn't matter the way it used to for many products. Moreover, the continuing expansion of smaller suburban communities may well continue to provide a platform for smaller financial firms to compete successfully, even against the industry's leaders.

Invasion by Industrial and Retailing Companies

One of the great imponderables for the future is how effectively conventional financial firms will be able to stand up against aggressive nonfinancial companies (including, for example, General Electric, GM, Target, etc.). These firms have been chipping away at banking's market share for decades. And waiting in the wings *may* be, perhaps, one of the toughest nonfinancial competitors of them all—the largest retailer on the planet, Wal-Mart, with thousands of neighborhood stores.

American and Japanese banking laws, as well as the rules followed by many other nations, erect walls to separate nonfinancial firms from financial-service providers. These legal barriers have been erected to protect financial firms from ruinous affiliations with more risky ventures. For example, banks affiliated with industrial firms and retail chains might make cut-rate, unprofitable loans to their parent company or transfer their losses from an industrial or retail firm to the affiliated bank, threatening it with collapse. However, these laws can never be strong enough to stop all those who search for loopholes and who want to be in the financial-services industry in the worst way.

The Wal-Mart Challenge

The biggest distributor of groceries and other household goods, Wal-Mart, has recently explored several avenues for expanding its current beachhead in the financial-services industry. For example, when 1999 rolled around Wal-Mart attempted to purchase a savings bank in Oklahoma until the Gramm-Leach-Bliley (GLB) Act closed the door on that avenue. Today Wal-Mart is taking a serious look at states that issue industrial bank charters because in 1987 the U.S. Congress okayed the ownership of industrial banks by any type of business. (Industrial banks are similar to small finance companies, credit unions, and savings banks, offering small loans and deposits and issuing credit cards.) Wal-Mart *may* be attempting to follow the lead of several other huge companies—notably American Express, GM, GE, Merrill Lynch, and Target—that had previously received industrial bank charters and set up banking operations, though Wal-Mart has declared that it is not interested in setting up a nationwide branch banking system even if it is eventually awarded an industrial bank charter.

Nevertheless, Wal-Mart seems to be increasing its financial-service menu through its affiliate, Wal-Mart Financial Services. It already sponsors credit card and money transfer programs, marketed to its customers in high volume and at characteristically low prices. Couldn't Wal-Mart do the same thing with business and consumer loans through its thousands of retail outlets? with insurance policies? with sales of stocks, bonds, and mutual funds?

Currently the world's leading retailer invites selected financial-service providers to rent space in its retail stores and has pursued joint financial-services arrangements with GE Consumer Finance, SunTrust Banks, and MoneyGram. These programs would seem to represent one more step in moving Wal-Mart into the role of a major player in the global financial-services marketplace. After all, what could be more convenient than buying groceries, hardware, clothing, jewelry, and hundreds of other products under the same roof as loans, credit cards, deposits, and insurance policies, all marketed at bargain-basement prices?

Might this trend mixing industry and commerce with financial services be damaging, even devastating, to smaller community banks and credit unions? Indeed, this *may* be banking and financial services' biggest challenge for the future as more and more commercial and industrial companies scramble to plant their feet firmly in financial services. The financial sector is an industry vital to the public interest, but one that faces drastic structural and technological changes. It will be fascinating to watch the future unfolding story of the financial-services marketplace as it reaches out to better serve millions of businesses, individuals, and families, spanning continents and bringing together cultures and resources from all over the globe.

Concept Check

20–16. In looking at the future of the banking and financial-services industry does it appear likely that the powerful trends of *convergence* and *consolidation* will continue into the future? Why or why not? Is this likely to occur at the same pace as in the past?

20–17. What appears to be the future of *community banking?* What significant threats does community banking seem to face?

20–18. Are banking and commerce—financial *and* nonfinancial firms—on a collision course for the future? What challenges do companies like Wal-Mart pose for small community banks? For the largest financial firms? For regulation? For ongoing efforts to maintain a safety net to protect the public's deposits and preserve public confidence in the financial system?

Summary

In this chapter we have explored the development of international banking and the many services that financial firms offer in international markets today. Among the key points covered in the chapter are the following:

- International banking has been practiced for centuries in the Middle East and Western Europe as bankers emerged to provide business loans and exchange currencies to aid merchants and foreign travelers. Within the past century U.S., European, and, more recently, Japanese and Asian banks have grown to play leading roles on the international scene, competing with security dealers, insurance companies, and other nonbank providers to reach across national borders.

- In order to expand abroad, international banks and many of their closest competitors have used a wide variety of different organizational forms. Examples include *representative offices* (which facilitate the flow of information between financial firms and their overseas customers), *agencies* (which provide selected financial services such as credit and cash management), *branch offices* (which offer many of the same services that an international bank's home office provides), and *affiliated companies* and *joint ventures* (which often supply key supporting services such as insurance, marketing, and security trading). Frequently the different organizational forms are used to avoid burdensome regulations in a particular country.

- International banking services today include supplying foreign currencies, providing hedging services to deal with currency and interest-rate risk, supplying credit and credit guarantees to fund trade and capital expansion, helping customers tap the Eurocurrency and Eurobond markets to raise new capital, supplying cash management services, and providing assessments of foreign marketing opportunities.

- The *regulation* of international banking and financial services remains a powerful force shaping global finance and trade. Nations vary greatly in the scope and content of their laws and regulations surrounding the financial-services sector. The managers of internationally focused financial firms have often taken advantage of these regulatory discrepancies between nations, entering those markets where regulation is less of a burden (referred to as *regulatory arbitrage*).

- One of the most significant regulatory trends is *government deregulation* among leading industrial nations, giving international financial firms more latitude to expand abroad. Prominent examples include passage of the Gramm-Leach-Bliley (GLB) Act in the United States, allowing banks to combine with insurance and securities firms, and the opening of a common financial system in Europe, facilitating mergers within the European financial sector.

- Recently *international regulatory cooperation* among nations has become more common so that all financial firms may eventually face the same set of rules. One of the best examples is the Basel Agreement, enforcing common capital standards among the world's leading banks.

- Nevertheless, serious problems confront the international financial-services sector today due to the inherent risks in this field. Foreign expansion often presents financial-service providers with new government restrictions; new credit, currency, and interest-rate risks; new cultural standards and practices; and less quality information upon which to base business decisions than often is available in domestic markets. New emerging trade blocs and more open economies in Europe, North America, and Asia are creating new marketing opportunities today, but also major new challenges for international financial-service providers.

- Finally, whether international or domestic in scope, banks and other financial firms continue to undergo substantial change, led by *consolidation* and *convergence* trends that are resulting in fewer, larger, and more diverse financial-service providers. Yet, numerous smaller financial firms continue to operate, compete, and remain profitable in many nations around the globe, principally because they successfully keep their production costs comparatively low. However, a significant challenge to the future of *both* large and small financial-service firms is powerful retail and manufacturing companies entering or threatening to enter the financial marketplace, intensifying competition and narrowing profit margins.

Key Terms

representative office, 650
agency office, 650
branch office, 650
subsidiary, 651
joint venture, 651
Edge Acts, 651
international banking facility (IBF), 651
shell branches, 652
Export Trading Company Act, 652

export trading companies, 652
International Banking Act, 654
Foreign Bank Supervision Enhancement Act, 654
International Lending and Supervision Act, 654
Basel Agreement, 655
FOREX, 655
forward contracts, 658

currency futures contract, 658
currency option, 659
currency swaps, 659
note issuance facility (NIF), 661
Eurocommercial paper (ECP), 661
depository receipts (DRs), 661
Eurobond market, 663
interest-rate swaps, 663

Problems and Projects

1. Pacific Trading Company purchased Canadian dollars yesterday in anticipation of a purchase of electric equipment through a Canadian supply house. However, Pacific was contacted this morning by a Japanese trading company that says equipment closer to its specifications is available in 48 hours from an electronics manufacturer in Osaka. A phone call to Pacific's bank this morning indicated that another of the bank's customers, a furniture importer located in San Francisco, purchased a comparable amount of yen in order to pay for an incoming shipment from Tokyo, only to discover that the shipment will be delayed until next week. Meanwhile, the furniture company must pay off an inventory loan tomorrow that it received 30 days ago from Toronto-Dominion Bank.

   Which of the instruments described in this chapter would be most helpful to these two companies? Construct a diagram that illustrates the transaction you, as an international banker, would recommend to these two firms to help solve their current problems.

2. Art's Sporting Goods has ordered a shipment of soccer equipment from a manufacturer and distributor in Munich. Payment for the shipment (which is valued at $3.5 million U.S.) must be made in euros that have changed in value in the last 30 days from .8198 euros/$ to .8419 euros/$. If this trend is expected to continue, would you as Art's banker recommend that this customer use a currency futures hedge? Why or why not?

3. Pinochio Corporation will import new wooden toys from a French manufacturer this week at a price of 200 euros per item for eventual distribution to retail stores. The current euro–dollar exchange rate is .8538 euros per U.S. dollar. Payment for the shipment will be made by Pinochio next month, but euros are expected to appreciate significantly against the dollar. Pinochio asks its bank, Southern Merchants Bank, N.A., for advice on what to do. What kind of futures transaction could be used to deal with this problem faced by Pinochio? Futures contracts calling for delivery of euros

next month are priced currently at .8769 euros per dollar and are expected to be priced next month at .8376 euros per dollar.

4. Watson Hardware Corporation regularly ships tools to the United States to retail outlets from its warehouse in Stuttgart, Germany. Its normal credit terms call for full payment in U.S. dollars for the hardware it ships within 90 days of the shipment date. However, Watson must convert all U.S. dollars received from its customers into euros in order to compensate its local workers and suppliers. Watson has just made a large shipment to retail dealers in the United States and is concerned about a forecast just received from its local bank that the U.S. dollar–euro exchange rate will fall sharply over the next month. The current euro–U.S. dollar exchange rate is 0.81 euros per dollar. However, the local bank's current forecast calls for the exchange rate to rise to .86 euros per dollar, so that Watson will receive substantially less in euros for each U.S. dollar it receives in payment. Please explain how Watson, with the aid of its bank, could use currency futures to offset at least a portion of its projected loss due to the expected change in the euro–dollar exchange rate.

5. Johanna International Mercantile Corporation has made a $15 million investment in a stamping mill located in northern Germany and fears a substantial decline in the euro's spot price from $1.21 to $1.15, lowering the value of the firm's capital investment. Johanna's principal U.S. bank advises the firm to use an appropriate option contract to help reduce Johanna's risk of loss.

   What currency option contract would you recommend? Explain why the contract you selected would help to reduce the firm's currency risk.

6. Ebi International Bank of Japan holds U.S. dollar-denominated assets of $416 million and dollar-denominated liabilities of $479 million, has purchased U.S. dollars in the currency markets amounting to $166 million, and sold U.S. dollars totaling $14 million. What is Ebi's *net* exposure to risk from fluctuations in the U.S. dollar relative to the bank's domestic currency? Under what circumstances could Ebi lose if dollar prices change relative to the yen?

7. Suppose that Canterbury Bank has a net short position in U.S. dollars of $8 million, dollar-denominated liabilities of $115 million, U.S. dollar purchases of $268 million, and dollar sales of $173 million. What is the current value of the bank's dollar-denominated assets? Suppose the U.S. dollar's exchange value rises against the pound. Is Canterbury likely to gain or lose? Why?

Internet Exercises

1. Why are banks more prone to cross national borders today and even span continents to acquire other financial-service providers? Visit the Institute of International Bankers Web site at **www.iib.org**. Click on the Institute's Annual Global Survey covering the activities of more than 40 countries. Choose a country of interest to you and read the synopsis at the end of the survey. What are some key issues for your country?

2. You want some current news on international banks. Visit **www.newsnow.co.uk** and use the newsfeed to locate banking topics within business and finance news. Read an article from a country other than the United States. What were the major issues discussed in this article?

3. Suppose you want some detailed information about central banks outside the United States. Visit **www.bis.org/cbanks.htm**. What is the URL for the central bank of the European Union? Hong Kong? Thailand?

4. To get an idea of the internationalization of some of our large banks, visit Citigroup's Country Web site at **www.citigroup.com/citigroup/global/index.htm.** Describe its presence in Morocco, Saudi Arabia, and Finland.

Assignment for Chapter 20

YOUR BANK'S USE OF FOREIGN OFFICES

Chapter 20 explores the services and issues involved with foreign banks operating in the United States and U.S. banks operating abroad. One way that U.S. banks can operate abroad is through foreign offices. This chapter describes the different types of offices, and they will be the focus of this assignment. First we will collect and examine the data to see how foreign offices affect our BHC's balance sheet. Then we will look at the number, types, and location of foreign offices associated with the BHC you have chosen.

Part One: Trend and Comparative Analysis of the Contribution of Foreign Offices to Your BHC's Report of Condition

A. **Data Collection:** In this assignment we return to the SDI at **www3.fdic.gov/sdi/main.asp** and collect data from the net loans and leases and total deposits reports. This entails using SDI to create a four-column report of your bank's information and the peer group information across years. You are to collect the two items listed below and enter this data into the spreadsheet for peer-group comparisons.

B. Write one paragraph about the contributions of foreign offices to operations. Has your BHC focused more or less attention on foreign offices? Has your BHC moved into foreign markets using offices more or less than other very large banks (your peer group)?

Part Two: How Your BHC Used Foreign Offices to Expand Internationally

A. Go to the FDIC's Institution Directory at **http://www3.fdic.gov/idasp/,** and do a search for your bank holding company (BHC) using the BHC ID. This search will produce a list of bank and thrift subsidiaries. If you click on the active

certificate links, additional information will appear and you will be able to pull up a current list of offices for that bank. At the bottom of the list of all offices associated with that bank you'll find information on location, codes identifying the type of office, and the date foreign offices were established. You will want to focus your attention on the number of foreign offices, their types, and their locations. Collect this information for each bank belonging to the bank holding company you have chosen.

B. Compose several paragraphs discussing your banking company's expansion internationally and evaluate their strategy to expand or not.

STANDARD &POOR'S

S&P Market Insight Challenge (www.mhhe.com/edumarketinsight)
S&P's Market Insight, Educational Version has a number of foreign bank and financial-service firms listed in its inventory of financial-service providers. Examples include Mitsubishi Financial Group, HSBC Holdings PLC, and Barclays PLC, among others represented in the Insight collection. Most of these foreign financial corporations have a solid presence in the United States, the European Community, Japan, and selected Asian markets. Which are significantly represented in all four of these areas of the globe? With what financial services? What advantages might this bring to those financial firms with the broadest global representation?

Selected References

To examine the activities of U.S. banks in international markets, see, for example:

1. Federal Deposit Insurance Corporation. "The Globalization of the U.S. Banking Industry." *FDIC Outlook*, Washington, DC, Summer 2005, **www.fdic.gov/bank.analytical/regional/ro20052q.**

www.mhhe.com/rose7e

2. Rose, Peter S. "The Quest for Funds: New Directions in a New Market." *The Canadian Banker* 94, no. 5 (September/October 1987), pp. 46–55.

For an analysis of Japanese banking and its expansion into international markets, see:

3. Cargill, Thomas. "Japan Passes Again on Fundamental Financial Reform." *FRBSF Economic Letter,* no. 2002-28, Federal Reserve Bank of San Francisco, September 2002.
4. Cox, W. Michael, and Jahyeong Koo. "Miracle to Malaise: What's Next for Japan?" *Economic Letter,* Federal Reserve Bank of Dallas, vol. I, no. 1 January 2006, pp. 1–8, **www.dallasfed.org**.
5. Glick, Reuven. "Financial Issues in the Pacific Basin Region." *FRBSF Economic Letter,* no. 2002-38, Federal Reserve Bank of San Francisco, December 2002.
6. Japanese Bankers Association. *Japanese Banks 2005.* Zenginkyo, Tokyo, Japan, 2005, **www.zenginkyo.or.jp**.
7. Rose, Peter S. *Japanese Banking and Investment in the United States: An Assessment of Their Impact upon U.S. Markets and Institutions.* New York: Quorum Books, 1991.

For an analysis of banking and financial problems in Europe and Asia, see:

8. Alm, Richard. "Five Years of the Euro: Successes and New Challenges." *Southwest Economy,* Federal Reserve Bank of Dallas, July/August 2004, pp. 13–18.
9. Hopper, Gregory P. "What Determines the Exchange Rate: Economic Factors or Market Sentiment?" *Business Review,* Federal Reserve Bank of Philadelphia, September/October 1997, pp. 17–29.

For a look at China, its emerging economy, and financial institutions sector, see:

10. Cox, W. Michael, and Jahyeong Koo. "China: Awakening Giant." *Southwest Economy,* Federal Reserve Bank of Dallas, Issue 5 (September/October 2003), pp. 1–8.
11. Higgins, Patrick, and Owen F. Humpage. "The Chinese Renminbi: What's Real. What's Not." *Economic Commentary,* Federal Reserve Bank of Cleveland, August 15, 2005, pp.1–4.

To take a closer look at the future of the banking and financial-services industries, see especially:

12. Blair, Christine E. "The Future of Banking in America: The Mix of Banking and Commerce." *FDIC Banking Review,* Federal Deposit Insurance Corporation, 16, no. 4 (2004), pp. 97–120.
13. Craig, Valentine V. "The Future of Banking in America: The Changing Corporate Governance Environment." *FDIC Banking Review,* Federal Deposit Insurance Corporation, 16, no. 4 (2004), pp. 121–135.
14. Poole, William. "Wal-Mart Application Focuses Spotlight on Industrial Loan Companies." *The Regional Economist,* Federal Reserve Bank of St. Louis, April 2006, p. 3.

DICTIONARY OF BANKING AND FINANCIAL-SERVICE TERMS

A

account party   The customer who requests a standby letter of credit from a bank or other lender of funds.

add-on method   A procedure for calculating a consumer's loan rate in which interest is assessed on the full principal of an installment loan.

adjustable-rate mortgages (ARMs)   Loans against real property whose interest rate periodically adjusts to changes in market interest rates.

affiliated banks   Banks whose stock has been acquired by a holding company.

agency offices   International banking offices that provide credit and other nondeposit services.

agency problems   An issue that often arises in acquisitions and mergers when management pursues these transactions for management's benefit rather than the benefit of the stockholders.

agency theory   An explanation of the risk-taking behavior of individuals and institutions that focuses on the parties to a principal–agent contract in which any agent may seek to optimize his or her position at the expense of the principal(s) involved.

agricultural loans   Credit extended to farm and ranch operations to assist in planting and harvesting crops and to care for and market livestock.

American depository receipt (ADR)   A receipt issued by a U.S. bank that makes it easier for a foreign business borrower to sell its securities in the United States.

annual percentage rate (APR)   Interest rate on a loan that the U.S. Truth and Lending Act requires to be quoted to a household consumer seeking a loan.

annuities   An investment product sold by many financial firms today in which the customer invests his or her savings under the terms of a contract that promises a stream of income in the future (either fixed or variable in amount).

antidiscrimination laws   Laws that prevent the grouping of loan customers into categories according to their age, sex, race, national origin, location of residence, religious affiliation, or receipt of public assistance and that prohibit the denial of a loan to anyone solely because of membership in one or more of these groups.

asset-based loans   Loans secured by a business firm's assets, particularly accounts receivable and inventory.

asset conversion   A strategy for meeting liquidity needs in which liquid reserves are stored in readily marketable assets that can be quickly converted into cash.

asset-liability management   The process of decision making to control a financial institution's exposure to interest rate risk.

asset management   A management strategy that regards the volume and mix of a financial firm's sources of funds as determined largely by the wishes of its customers and calls for management to concentrate on controlling assets, rather than on managing liabilities, in order to meet liquidity needs and other goals.

asset utilization   The ratio of total operating revenues to total assets, measuring the average yield on assets.

assignments   A form of loan sale in which ownership of a loan is transferred to the loan buyer who then has a direct claim against the borrower.

ATMs   Automated teller machines through which a customer can access his or her deposit account, make loan payments, or obtain information and other services.

available funds gap   The difference between current and projected credit and deposit flows that creates a need for raising additional reserves when the gap is negative or for profitably investing any excess reserves that may arise when the gap is positive.

B

balanced liquidity management   The combined use of both asset management and liability management to cover liquidity needs.

bank   The financial intermediary that offers the widest range of financial services—especially credit, savings, and payment services—and performs the widest range of financial functions of any business firm in the economy.

bank discount rate   The method by which yields on Treasury bills and other money market securities are calculated using par value and a 360-day year to determine the appropriate discount rate or yield.

bankers' acceptance   A bank's written promise to pay the holder of the acceptance a designated amount of money on a specific future date.

bankers' banks   Regional service firms, often created as joint ventures by groups of banks and other financial firms, in order to facilitate the delivery of certain customer services, such as the rapid transfer and investment of customer funds and the execution of orders to buy or sell securities.

bank holding company   A corporation chartered for the purpose of holding the stock (equity shares) of one or more banks.

Bank Holding Company Act   U.S. law that brought bank holding company organizations under comprehensive federal regulation.

Bank Merger Act of 1960   A law passed by the U.S. Congress that requires each merging bank to notify its principal federal regulatory agency of a pending merger and requests federal approval before the merger can be completed.

Bank of Japan   The central bank of Japan, chartered to control inflation and stabilize the Japanese economy.

Basel Agreement   A negotiated agreement between bank regulatory authorities in the United States, Canada, Great Britain, Japan, and eight other nations in western Europe to set common capital requirements for banks under their jurisdiction.

Basel I   The first official agreement between the United States, Belgium, Canada, France, Germany, Italy, Japan, the Netherlands, Sweden, Switzerland, the United Kingdom, and Luxembourg, formally approved in Basel, Switzerland, in 1988 and imposing common minimum capital requirements on banks headquartered in these countries.

Basel II   The version of the Basel accord on bank capital requirements designed to succeed Basel I, permitting banks to employ their own internal risk-assessment methods and calculate their own minimum capital requirements as well as mandating periodic stress testing to estimate the impact of changing market conditions on each bank's financial position.

basic (lifeline) banking   Low-cost deposits and other services that are designed to meet the needs of customers of limited means.

below-prime pricing   Interest rates on loans set below the prevailing prime rate, usually based on the level of key money market interest rates (such as the current market rate on Federal funds or Eurodollar deposits).

beneficiary   The party who will receive payment under a financial guarantee if certain events occur, such as default on a loan.

board of directors   The committee elected by the stockholders to set policy and oversee the performance of a bank or other corporation.

Board of Governors   The center of authority and decision making within the Federal Reserve System; the board must contain no more than seven persons, each selected by the president of the United States and confirmed by the U.S. Senate for a term not exceeding 14 years.

branch banking   An arrangement in which a bank offers a full range of services from multiple locations, including a head office and one or more branch offices.

branch offices   Full-service units operated by a business that is headquartered in another location.

business risk   The probability that the economy will turn down into a recession, with reduced demand for loans, deposits, and other products and services.

C

call risk   The danger that an investor in loans or securities will experience a lower-than-expected rate of return due to the issuer of the loans or securities calling in these instruments and retiring them early before they reach maturity.

CAMELS rating   A system that assigns a numerical rating to a depository institution based on examiner judgment regarding its capital adequacy, asset condition, management quality, earnings record, liquidity position, and sensitivity to market risk.

capital   Long-term funds contributed to a bank or other financial institution primarily by its owners, consisting mainly of stock, reserves, and retained earnings.

capital market instruments   Investment securities that reach maturity over periods longer than one year.

capital risk   The probability that a financial institution or one of its borrowing customers will fail, exhausting its capital.

cash   This term is one of the six Cs of credit, which loan officers should review in any loan application, referring to the generation of income or cash flow by a borrowing customer.

cash flow   Often measured by the net income plus noncash expenses (such as depreciation) of a business loan customer.

cash flow analysis   An analytical approach to measuring the volume and composition of cash inflows and cash outflows experienced or expected by a borrowing customer.

cash flow risk   The danger that cash flows may fluctuate widely due to economic conditions, service mix, and other factors; a merger may help to reduce this risk by combining organizations and service packages that have different cash flow patterns over time.

cash management services   A service in which a financial firm agrees to handle cash collections and cash disbursements for a business firm and to invest any temporary cash surpluses in interest-bearing securities until those funds are needed.

certificate of deposit (CD)   An interest-bearing receipt for the deposit of funds in a bank or thrift institution for a specified period of time.

charter of incorporation   A license to open and operate a bank or other business, issued either by the commission of the state where the firm is to be located or by the Comptroller of the Currency (for federally chartered banks) inside the United States.

clearing balances   Deposits held with the Federal Reserve banks by depository institutions to help clear checks for payment and collection and that allow the depository institutions using Federal Reserve services to earn interest credits on these balances in order to help offset the cost of Fed services.

collateral   A borrower's possession of adequate net worth, quality assets, or other items of value that give added support to his or her ability to repay a loan.

commercial and industrial loans   Credit granted to businesses to help cover purchases of inventory, plant, and equipment and to meet other operating expenses.

commercial paper   Short-term, unsecured IOUs offered to investors in the money market by major corporations with the strongest credit ratings.

commercial paper market   Market where short-term notes with maturities ranging from three or four days to nine months are traded, issued by well-known banking and nonbanking companies for the purpose of raising working capital.

common stock   Type of capital measured by the par value of all common equity shares outstanding that pays a variable return to its owners after all expenses and other claims are met.

Community Reinvestment Act   Federal law passed in 1977 requiring covered depository institutions to make "an affirmative effort" to serve all segments of their trade territory without discrimination.

compensating deposit balances   Required deposits a customer must keep with a lender as a condition for getting a loan.

competitive effects   The aspect of a merger or acquisition between two or more financial institutions that will have an impact on interfirm rivalry, either reducing or increasing competition in the markets served by the firms involved; this impact of a merger or acquisition is, under current federal law, the most important factor federal regulatory agencies must weigh in deciding to approve or deny any proposed acquisitions or mergers.

Competitive Equality in Banking Act   Legislation that authorized recapitalization of the Federal Savings and Loan Insurance Corporation to deal more effectively with failing savings and loan associations, required depository institutions to provide more information to their customers on when credit is given for deposited funds, and placed a moratorium on the creation of nonbank banks and the offering of insurance, securities, and real estate services by banks operating inside the United States.

compliance risk   Uncertainty as to whether a financial firm is engaging in behavior or taking actions not consistent with current laws, industry rules, or regulations.

Comptroller of the Currency (or Administrator of National Banks)   The federal government agency, a part of the U.S. Treasury Department, that awards charters for new national banks in the United States and also supervises and regularly examines all existing national banks.

conditional pricing   Establishing minimum-size account balances and charging a lower or even zero fee if the customer's deposit balance climbs *above* that required minimum but a higher fee if the average balance falls *below* the required minimum amount.

conglomerates   Corporations that bring together a wide variety of different businesses and product lines under common ownership.

consolidating mergers   Acquisitions of firms in the same industry as the acquiring firm.

construction loans   Short-term loans designed to fund the building of new structures and then be paid off and replaced with a longer-term mortgage loan once the construction phase of the project has ended.

contingent liabilities   Debt obligations that will not come due unless certain events occur, such as borrower default or the exercise of product warranties.

contingent obligation   A financial instrument whose issuer pledges to pay if certain events (such as default on a loan) occur; for example, federal deposit insurance is a contingent obligation of the government, payable if a depository institution fails.

convergence   The bringing together of firms from different industries to create conglomerate firms offering multiple services.

converging mergers   Businesses reaching across industry boundaries to acquire a different type of firm.

convexity   The rate of change in an asset's price or value varies with the level of interest rates or yields.

core capital   Permanent capital, consisting mainly of common stock, surplus, retained earnings, and equity reserves.

core deposits   A stable and predictable base of deposited funds, usually supplied by households and smaller businesses, that is not highly sensitive to movements in market interest rates but tends to remain loyal to the depository institution.

corporate bonds   Debt securities issued by private corporations with original maturities longer than five years.

corporate governance   The network of relationships between a corporation's board of directors and members of its management team that help to define who has control over what issues and who makes pivotal decisions within the organization.

corporate notes   Debt securities issued by private corporations with original maturities of five years or less.

correspondent banking   A system of formal and informal relationships among large and small depository institutions established to facilitate the exchange of certain services, such as the clearing of checks and the exchange of information.

cosigner   A person obligated to support the repayment of a loan by a borrower who either has no credit record or has such a poor track record of repaying loans that he or she cannot get a loan without the support of the cosigner.

cost-plus deposit pricing   Charging customers for the full cost or a significant portion of the total cost of any deposit services they use.

cost-plus loan pricing   Figuring the rate of interest on a loan by adding together all interest and noninterest costs associated with making the loan plus margins for profit and risk.

cost savings (efficiency)   A motivation for mergers that rests on the possibility that by combining two or more institutions together, overall operating expenses will be reduced, creating the possibility of a rise in net income for the combined (merged) institution.

credit availability risk   The possibility that lenders may not have the funds to loan or be willing to accommodate every qualified borrower when credit is requested.

credit bureau   A business firm that keeps data files on people who have borrowed money, indicating their previous record of loan repayments.

credit default swaps   Financial agreements that permit a lender to protect itself against credit (default) risk by receiving compensation from a counterparty to help offset excessive loan losses or excessive fluctuations in loan revenue.

credit derivatives   Financial contracts that are designed to protect a lending institution against loss due to defaults on its loans or security holdings.

credit enhancement   A contract in which a financial institution promises to back up the credit of another firm.

credit life insurance   An insurance policy that guarantees repayment of a loan if a borrower dies or is disabled before his or her loan is paid off.

credit option   An agreement between a lending institution and an option writer that is designed to protect a lender against possible loss due to declines in the value of some of its assets or to prevent a significant rise in borrowing costs should the borrower's credit rating be lowered or other events occur that result in higher fund-raising costs.

credit risk   The probability that the issuer of a loan or security will fail and default on any promised payments of interest or principal or both.

credit risk models   Analytical tools, including computer programs, designed to assess the level of default risk associated with a loan customer seeking to borrow funds or the default-risk exposure of a whole portfolio of loans or other assets.

credit scoring   The use of a discriminant equation to classify loan applicants according to the probability of their repaying their loans, based on customer characteristics, such as their credit rating or length of employment.

credit swap   A financial contract designed to reduce the risk of default on loans by having two lending institutions exchange a portion of their expected loan payments with each other.

credit unions   Nonprofit depository institutions that make loans to and accept deposits only from their members who must share a common bond (such as working for the same employer).

crime risk   The danger of fraud, embezzlement, robbery, or other crimes that could result in loss for a financial institution.

currency exchange   Trading one form of currency (such as dollars) for another (such as euros or pesos) in return for a fee; one of the first services offered when the banking industry began centuries ago.

currency futures contract   Agreement between a buyer and a seller of foreign currencies that promises delivery of a stipulated currency at a specified price on a specific date in the future.

currency option   Contract giving the option holder the right, but not the obligation, to deliver or take delivery of a specific currency at a set price on or before the contract's expiration date.

currency swaps   Agreements between two or more parties who need to borrow foreign currency that help to protect each of them against changes in currency prices by agreeing to exchange payments denominated in different currencies.

customer privacy   Protecting the personal information that customers supply to their financial-service providers so that customers are not damaged by the release of their private data to outside parties.

customer profitability analysis   A method for evaluating a customer's loan request that takes into account all revenues and expenses associated with serving that particular customer and calculates an expected net return over all costs incurred from serving the customer.

customer relationship doctrine   The management strategy whose first priority is making loans to all those customers who meet the lender's quality standards and from whom positive earnings are expected.

D

demand deposit   Checking account services that permit depositors to write drafts in payment for goods and services that the depository institution involved must honor immediately upon presentation.

de novo **bank**   A newly chartered banking corporation.

Depository Institutions Deregulation and Monetary Control Act   Law passed in the United States in 1980 requiring that federal interest rate ceilings on deposits sold to the public be phased out so that deposit interest rates could more closely reflect prevailing market conditions; it also authorized the offering of NOW accounts throughout the United States, which pay an explicit interest return to the customer and have third-party payment powers.

depository receipt (DR)   A receipt issued by a domestic bank or other financial firm making it easier for a foreign firm to sell its securities to domestic investors.

dilution of earnings   Spreading a fixed amount of earnings over additional shares of stock so that the earnings per share flowing to existing stockholders declines, as in the case when a merger results in excessive shares being issued to the stockholders of the acquired firm.

dilution of ownership   The degree to which the proportionate share of ownership held by the current owners of a firm is reduced when additional equity shares are issued to new stockholders or to the shareholders of a firm that is being acquired.

disclosure rules   Laws and regulations that mandate telling the consumer about financing costs and other essential terms of a loan or lease agreement, deposit contract, or other financial service.

discount brokerage services   A service designed to assist customers with purchases and sales of securities at relatively low brokerage fees.

discounting commercial notes   The process of making loans to local merchants who use IOUs received from their customers as collateral.

discount rate method   The procedure used to assess interest on a loan in which interest is deducted up front at the beginning of the loan and the customer receives for his or her use the full principal of the loan less the interest assessed.

discount window   Department within each Federal Reserve bank that lends legal reserves to eligible institutions for short periods of time.

dual banking system   A system of banking regulation in which both federal and state authorities have significant regulatory powers and supervisory responsibilities over the activities of banks.

duration   A present-value weighted measure of the maturity of an individual security or portfolio of securities in which the timing and amount of *all* cash flows expected from the security or portfolio of securities are considered.

duration gap   The difference between the duration of an institution's assets and the duration of its liabilities.

duration gap management   A strategy or technique used by the management of a financial institution to achieve a desired spread between the duration of its assets and the duration of its liabilities in order to control the institution's interest-rate risk exposure.

E

earnings risk   The danger that earnings may fluctuate widely due to changes in economic conditions, demand for services, mix of services offered, or other factors; a merger between two or more organizations may dampen this form of risk by bringing together different revenue sources with different cash flow patterns over time.

economies of scale   Cost savings achieved when a firm expands in size and becomes more efficient in using productive resources to produce goods and services.

economies of scope   Employing the same management, staff, and facilities to offer multiple products or services, thereby helping to reduce the per-unit cost of production and delivery of goods or services.

Edge Acts Subsidiary companies of a banking organization that must devote the majority of their activities to transactions involving international trade and commerce; establishment of these subsidiaries must be approved by the Federal Reserve Board.

efficiency An indicator of how well management and staff have been able to keep the growth of revenues and income ahead of rising operating costs.

Equal Credit Opportunity Act Legislation passed by the U.S. Congress in 1974 that prohibits lenders from asking certain questions of a borrowing household customer, such as his or her age, race, or religion, and from denying a loan based solely upon a credit applicant's age, race, religion, ethnic origins, receipt of public assistance, or similar characteristics.

equipment leasing services The purchase of equipment on behalf of a customer in order to lease the equipment to that customer in return for a series of lease payments.

equity commitment notes Type of bank capital in the form of debt securities that is repayable only from the future sale of bank stock.

equity multiplier The ratio of total assets to total equity capital.

equity reserves Type of capital representing funds set aside for contingencies such as losses on assets, lawsuits, and other extraordinary events, as well as providing a reserve for dividends expected to be paid out to stockholders but not yet declared and a sinking fund to be used to retire stock or debt capital instruments in the future.

Eurobond market An institution that brings together sellers of bonds issued outside their home country and interested buyers in one or more other nations.

Eurocommercial paper (ECP) Short-term notes issued by multinational corporations and sold to investors in one or more countries that permit these corporations to borrow funds for a few days, weeks, or months.

Eurocurrency deposit Deposits denominated in a currency different from the currency of the home country where they are created.

events of default A section contained in most loan agreements listing what actions or omissions by a borrower would represent a violation of the terms of the agreement and what action the lender is legally authorized to take in response.

exchange ratio The number of shares of stock in the acquiring firm that stockholders of the acquired firm will receive for each share they hold.

exchange risk The probability of loss because of fluctuating currency prices in international markets.

expense preference An approach to the management of a firm in which managers draw upon the resources of the firm to provide them with personal benefits (such as lavish offices, country club memberships, etc.) not needed to produce and sell products, thereby raising the cost of production and reducing returns to the firm's owners; an agency cost problem in which the interests of the managers of a firm take precedence over the interests of its owners.

Export-Import Bank A lender of funds created by the U.S. government to aid with export-import financing and to make loans that support the development of overseas markets.

export trading companies (ETCs) Organizational devices to aid customers in selling their goods abroad, particularly the products of smaller businesses, by creating a subsidiary firm to help with foreign marketing and the financing of exports.

Export Trading Company Act Law passed by the U.S. Congress in 1982 that allowed U.S. banks to make direct investments in export trading companies to help their U.S. business customers sell goods and services abroad.

F

factoring Sale of the shorter-term assets of a business firm that are expected to roll over into cash in the near term, such as accounts receivable and inventory, in order to raise more working capital.

Fair Credit Billing Act Law enacted by the U.S. Congress in 1974 that permits consumers to dispute alleged billing errors committed by a merchant or credit card company and requires that consumers receive a prompt investigation of any billing disputes under penalty of forfeiture of at least a portion of the amount billed.

Fair Credit Reporting Act Law that authorizes U.S. consumers to review their credit records, as reflected in the files of a credit bureau, for accuracy and to demand the investigation and correction of any inaccuracies.

Fair Debt Collection Practices Act Law passed by the U.S. Congress limiting how far a creditor can go in pressing a loan customer to pay up.

FDIC Improvement Act A law passed by the U.S. Congress in 1991 to recapitalize the Federal Deposit Insurance Corporation and exercise closer regulation over troubled depository institutions.

federal agency securities Marketable notes and bonds sold by agencies owned by or started by the federal government, such as the Federal National Mortgage Association (FNMA) or the farm credit agencies.

Federal Deposit Insurance Corporation (FDIC)   The U.S. government agency that guarantees the repayment of the public's deposits in U.S. banks and thrifts up to a maximum of $100,000 and assesses insurance premiums that must be paid by depositories offering federally insured deposits.

Federal funds market   A domestic source of reserves in which a depository institution can borrow the excess reserves held by other institutions; also known as *same-day money* because these funds can be transferred instantaneously by wire from the lending institution to the borrowing institution.

Federal Open Market Committee (FOMC)   Composed of the members of the Federal Reserve Board and the presidents of the Federal Reserve banks, the FOMC sets money and credit policies for the Federal Reserve System and oversees the conduct of open market operations, the Federal Reserve's chief policy tool.

Federal Reserve Bank   A quasi-public U.S. institution created in 1913 by the Federal Reserve Act that provides financial services, such as check clearing, to depository institutions in the region served by each individual Federal Reserve Bank.

Federal Reserve System   The federal agency that serves as a "lender of last resort" for depository institutions in need of temporary loans and is charged by the U.S. Congress to monitor and control the growth of money and credit and stabilize credit market conditions and the economy.

fiduciary relationship   An agreement between a financial institution and its customer in which the institution becomes responsible for managing the customer's funds or other property.

finance companies   Financial institutions that extend credit to businesses and individuals, either through direct loans or through purchasing accounts receivable from their customers, and raising loanable funds principally through borrowing in the money and capital markets.

financial advisory services   A range of services that may include investment advice, the preparation of tax returns, and help with recordkeeping; business customers often receive aid in checking on the credit standing of prospective customers unknown to them and assistance in evaluating marketing opportunities abroad.

financial boutiques   Financial-service companies that offer a limited set of services to selected customer groups.

financial futures   Contracts calling for the delivery of specific types of securities at a set price on a specific future date.

financial guarantees   Instruments used to enhance the credit standing of a borrower in order to help lower the borrower's credit costs by pledging to reimburse a lender if the borrower fails to pay.

financial holding companies (FHCs)   Corporations that control one or more financial institutions and, perhaps, other businesses as well; under the terms of the Gramm-Leach-Bliley Act of 1999 banks, insurance companies, security dealers, and selected other financial firms may be acquired and brought under common ownership through a financial holding company organization.

financial institution loans   Both long- and short-term credit extended to banks, insurance companies, and other financial institutions.

Financial Institutions Reform, Recovery, and Enforcement Act   U.S. law passed in 1989 that authorized bank holding companies to acquire healthy savings and loan associations and restructured the FDIC, dividing its insurance fund into a Bank Insurance Fund (BIF) to cover U.S. commercial bank deposits and a Savings Associations' Insurance Fund (SAIF) to insure the deposits of U.S.-based savings and loan associations and other thrifts.

fixed-rate mortgages (FRMs)   Loans against real property whose rate of interest does not change during the life of the loan.

Foreign Bank Supervision Enhancement Act   U.S. law, passed in 1991, giving the Federal Reserve Board greater regulatory powers over foreign banks operating in the United States, including the power to close a foreign bank's U.S. facilities if found to be inadequately supervised or operated in an unsafe manner.

FOREX   Foreign currencies and foreign-currency—denominated deposits offered by international banks to aid their customers who trade and travel abroad.

forward contracts   Agreements that can be used when a customer anticipates a future need to acquire foreign currency or expects to receive foreign currency; a financial institution negotiates a contract with another party on behalf of its customer, fixing the price at which currency is exchanged and specifying a date on which the currency will be delivered.

full-service branch   A branch office that offers all or most of the same services that the firm's head office also offers.

full-service interstate banking   The establishment of banks or bank branches across state lines by individual banking organizations that offer a complete menu of banking services.

Funds-Flow Statement   A financial statement that shows where funds have come from and how they have been used over a specific time period.

funds gap The difference between current and projected credit and deposit flows that creates a need for raising additional reserves or for profitably investing any excess reserves that may arise.

funds management Combining asset and liability management strategies in order to achieve a financial institution's goals and meet its liquidity needs more effectively.

G

Garn–St Germain Depository Institutions Act A U.S. deregulation law, passed in 1982, that permitted thrift institutions to become more like commercial banks in the services they could offer and allowed all federally regulated depository institutions to offer deposits competitive with money market mutual fund share accounts.

geographic diversification Spreading out credit accounts and deposits among customers located in different communities, regions, or countries in order to reduce the overall risk of loss to a bank or other financial institution.

Glass-Steagall Act Law passed by the U.S. Congress in 1933 that legally mandated the separation of commercial and investment banking, imposed interest rate ceilings on bank deposits, authorized the creation of the Federal Deposit Insurance Corporation, and granted federally chartered banks the power to branch throughout a state, provided that state grants similar powers to its own state-chartered banks.

Gramm-Leach-Bliley (Financial Services Modernization) Act A U.S. federal law approved in 1999 permitting common ownership of banks, securities firms, and insurers through financial holding companies or subsidiaries if well capitalized and well managed and granted regulatory approval.

H

hedge funds Private partnerships that sell shares to only a limited group of investors in order to invest in a wide variety of assets and derivative instruments in the hope of achieving exceptional returns regardless of the direction the market subsequently moves.

Herfindahl-Hirschman Index A summary measure of market concentration used by the U.S. Justice Department, in which the assets of each firm serving a given market are squared and the squared market shares of all firms are then summed to derive a single index number reflecting the degree of concentration of assets in the largest firms.

holding period yield (HPY) A rate of discount bringing the current price of a security into line with its stream of expected cash inflows and its expected sale price at the end of the investor's holding period.

home equity loans Credit extended to an individual or family on the basis of the spread or gap between the estimated market value of a home and the amount of mortgage loans outstanding against the property.

I

inflation risk The probability that the prices of goods and services (including the interest rate on borrowed funds and the cost of personnel and other productive resources) will rise or that the value of assets will be eroded due to rising prices, lowering the expected return on invested capital.

installment loans Credits that are repayable in two or more consecutive payments, usually on a monthly or quarterly basis.

in-store branches Branch offices located in a grocery store or other retail outlet.

insurance policies Contracts that guarantee payment if the customer dies, becomes disabled, or suffers loss of property or earning power.

interest-rate cap Ceiling interest rate imposed on a loan designed to protect the borrower from an unacceptable rise in the interest cost of that loan.

interest-rate collar A combination of an interest-rate cap and an interest-rate floor; puts brackets around the movement of a loan rate so that it cannot rise above the cap or fall below the floor.

interest-rate floor Minimum interest rate below which the interest cost of a loan normally cannot fall, thus protecting the lender from additional lost revenue if market interest rates move lower.

interest-rate option A contract that either (1) grants a holder of securities or loans the right to place (put) those instruments with another investor at a specified exercise price before the option expires or (2) allows an investor to take delivery of securities or other financial instruments (call) from another investor at a specified price on or before the option's expiration date.

interest rate risk The probability that rising or falling interest rates will adversely affect the margin of interest revenues over interest expenses or result in decreasing the value of net worth.

interest-rate swaps Agreements that enable two different borrowers of funds to aid each other by exchanging some of the most favorable features of their loans; usually the two participating institutions exchange interest rate payments in order to reduce their borrowing costs and better balance their inflows and outflows of funds.

interest sensitive   An asset or liability item that can be repriced as market interest rates change.

interest-sensitive gap management   Management techniques that usually require a computer analysis of the maturities and repricing opportunities associated with interest-bearing assets, deposits, and money market borrowings in order to determine when and by how much a financial institution is exposed to interest rate risk.

interim construction loan   Secured short-term lending to support the construction of homes, apartments, office buildings, shopping centers, and other permanent structures.

internal capital growth rate   The rate of growth of net earnings that remain inside a firm rather than being paid out to its stockholders; this growth rate depends on a firm's return on equity and its dividend policies.

International Banking Act   Law passed by the U.S. Congress in 1978 that brought foreign banks operating in the United States under federal regulation for the first time; it required foreign banking offices taking deposits from the public to post reserve requirements and allowed them to apply for federal deposit insurance coverage.

international banking facility (IBF)   Computerized account records that are kept separate from a U.S. bank's domestic accounts and that keep track primarily of international transactions.

International Lending and Supervision Act   Law passed by the U.S. Congress in 1983 that requires U.S. banks to hold stipulated minimum amounts of capital and that sets standards for making, evaluating, and restructuring overseas loans.

Internet banking   The offering of information and selected services through the World Wide Web by banks and other financial-service firms.

Internet service sites   Computer files or pages set up on the World Wide Web to advertise services or offer selected service options to Web users.

investment banking   A financial firm that underwrites new stock and bond issues and provides financial advice to corporate and governmental clients.

investment banking services   A bank's offer to underwrite a corporate or institutional customer's securities in order to aid that customer in raising funds.

investment products   Sales of mutual funds, annuities, and other nondeposit instruments offered through a bank's service delivery facilities, either with the aid of an affiliate or offered by an unrelated financial services company but sold through the bank's service outlets.

J

joint venture   Cooperative service production and delivery between banks or between banks and nonbank firms in order to provide a wider array of customer services at a profit.

Justice Department Merger Guidelines   Standards for evaluating the impact of a proposed merger on the concentration of assets or deposits in a given market area; the Justice Department uses these standards to help it decide whether to sue to block a proposed merger that might damage competition.

L

lagged reserve accounting (LRA)   An accounting system begun by the Federal Reserve in 1984 for calculating each depository institution's legal reserve requirement, in which the reserve computation and reserve maintenance periods for transaction deposits are not exactly the same.

LBOs (leveraged buyouts)   Contractual agreements in which a company or small group of individual investors purchases a business or buys a portion of a business firm's assets with heavy use of debt and relatively little equity capital and relies on increased earnings after the business is taken over to retire the debt.

legal reserves   Assets that by law must be held behind deposits or other designated liabilities; in the United States, these assets consist of vault cash and deposits at the Federal Reserve banks.

legal risk   Uncertainty in earnings or returns due to actions taken within the legal system, such as lawsuits or court judgments impacting a financial firm.

letter of credit   A legal notice in which a financial institution guarantees the credit of one of its customers who is borrowing from another institution.

liability management   Use of borrowed funds to meet liquidity needs, in which a financial institution attracts the volume of liquidity it needs by raising or lowering the rate of interest it is willing to pay on borrowed funds.

LIBOR   The London Interbank Offered Rate on short-term Eurodollar deposits, which is used as a common basis for quoting loan rates to corporations and other large borrowers.

life and property casualty insurers   Firms selling risk protection to their customers in an effort to offset financial losses related to death, ill health, negligence, storm damage, and other adverse events.

life insurance policies   Contracts that promise cash payments to beneficiaries when the death of a policyholder occurs.

life insurance underwriters   Companies that manage the risks associated with paying off life insurance claims and collecting premium payments from life insurance policyholders.

liquid asset   Any asset that meets three conditions: (1) price stability, (2) ready marketability, and (3) reversibility.

liquidity   Access to sufficient immediately spendable funds at reasonable cost exactly when those funds are needed.

liquidity gap   The amount by which the sources and uses of liquidity do not match.

liquidity indicators   Certain bellwether financial ratios (e.g., total loans outstanding divided by total assets) that are used to estimate liquidity needs and to monitor changes in liquidity position.

liquidity risk   The probability that an individual or institution will be unable to raise cash precisely when cash is needed at reasonable cost and in the volume required.

loan commitment agreements   Promises to provide credit to a customer in the future, provided certain conditions are met.

loan option   A device to lock in the amount and cost of borrowing for a designated time period by allowing a customer to borrow at a guaranteed interest rate, regardless of any subsequent changes in market interest rates, until the option expires.

loan participation   Agreement under which a lender will share a large loan with one or more other lenders in order to provide the borrower with sufficient funds and reduce risk exposure to any one lending institution.

loan review   A process of periodic investigation of all outstanding loans to make sure each loan is paying out as planned, all necessary documentation is present, and loan officers are following the institution's loan policy.

loan sales   A form of investment banking in which the lender trades on his or her superior ability to evaluate the creditworthiness of borrowers and sells some of the loans the lender has made to other investors who value the lender's expertise in assessing credit quality.

loans to individuals   Credit extended to households to finance the purchase of automobiles and appliances, medical and personal expenses, and other household needs.

loan strip   The sale of a portion of a large loan for a short period of time, usually for a period less than the loan's remaining time to maturity.

loan workouts   Activity within a lending institution that focuses on delinquent loans and that tries to develop and implement strategies designed to recover as much as possible from troubled borrowers.

M

market-penetration deposit pricing   Offering high interest rates (often well above current market levels) or charging low or zero customer fees in order to bring in as many new deposit customers as possible.

market-positioning benefits   A motive for conducting a merger between two or more firms, in which the firms involved anticipate gaining access to important new markets not previously served or securing a stronger foothold in markets currently served.

market risk   The potential for loss due to rising or falling interest rates; the danger that changing interest rates may force a financial institution to accept substantial losses on any assets that must be sold or acquired or on any funds that must be borrowed or repaid.

maturity gap   The difference between the average maturity of a financial-service firm's assets and the average maturity of its liabilities.

McFadden-Pepper Act   Legislation passed by the U.S. Congress in 1927 that allowed national banks to branch within the city where they are headquartered if the laws of the state involved do not forbid such branches.

member bank   A commercial bank that has joined the Federal Reserve System and is subject to its rules and regulations; includes all national banks as well as state-chartered banks that elect to join the Federal Reserve System.

merchant banks   Banks that often provide not only all the consumer and commercial services a regular bank provides but also offer credit, investment, and consulting services in an attempt to satisfy all the financial service needs of their clients; usually these banks invest a substantial share of their own equity capital in a customer's commercial project.

merger premium   A bonus offered to the shareholders of a firm to be acquired, consisting of an amount of cash or stock in the acquiring institution that exceeds the current market value of the acquired firm's stock.

minority interest in consolidated subsidiaries   Partial ownership interest that a financial firm holds in other business firms.

monetary policy   A central bank's primary job, which involves making sure that the financial system functions smoothly and that the supply of money and credit from that system contributes to the nation's economic goals.

money market deposit accounts (MMDAs)   Short-maturity deposits having a term of only a few days, weeks, or months and on which the offering depository institution can pay any competitive interest rate over designated short intervals of time; these deposits also have limited checking account powers.

money market instruments   Investment securities that reach maturity within one year and are noted for their low credit risk and ready marketability.

money position manager   Managerial position that is responsible for ensuring that the institution maintains an adequate level of legal reserves to meet its reserve requirements as set by law and also has access to sufficient quantities of reserves to accommodate customer demand and meet other cash needs.

mortgage-backed bond   A debt instrument representing a claim against the interest and principal payments generated by a pool of mortgage loans.

mortgage banking companies   Financial-service firms that acquire mortgage loans for eventual resale to longer-term lenders (e.g., insurance companies and pension funds).

multibank holding companies   A type of holding company that holds stock in more than one bank.

municipal bonds   Debt obligations issued by states, cities, counties, and other local governmental units.

mutual funds   Investment companies that attract savings from the public and invest those funds in a pool of stocks, bonds, and other financial instruments, with each saver receiving a share of the earnings generated by the pool of financial instruments.

N

National Credit Union Administration   A federal regulatory agency set up during the 1930s as a result of passage of the Federal Credit Union Act in the United States to charter and supervise federal credit unions.

negotiable CD   A type of interest-bearing deposit that may be sold to other investors in the secondary market any number of times before it reaches maturity.

net interest margin   The spread between interest income and interest expense divided by either total assets or total earning assets.

net liquidity position   The difference between the volume of liquid funds available and the demand for liquid funds.

net profit margin   The ratio of net income after taxes divided by total operating revenues.

networking   The sharing of facilities for the movement of funds and financial information between financial-service providers.

nonbank banks   Financial-service firms that either offer checking account services or grant commercial loans, but not both.

noninterest margin   The spread between noninterest income and noninterest expenses divided by total assets or total earning assets.

note   A written contract between a borrowing customer and a lender describing the responsibilities of both parties.

note issuance facility (NIF)   A medium-term credit agreement between an international bank and its larger corporate and governmental credit customers, where the customer is authorized to periodically issue short-term notes, each of which usually comes due and is retired in 90 to 180 days, over a stipulated contract period (such as five years), with the bank pledging to buy any notes the customer cannot sell to other investors.

NOW accounts   Savings deposits against which a customer can write negotiable drafts (checks) but that reserve the depository institution's right to insist on prior notice before the customer withdraws his or her funds.

O

Office of the Comptroller of the Currency   See Comptroller of the Currency.

Office of Thrift Supervision   A federal regulatory agency inside the U.S. Treasury Department that is authorized to charter and supervise thrift institutions, including savings and loan associations and savings banks.

open market operations (OMO)   Purchases and sales of securities—in most cases, direct obligations of the government—that are designed to move reserves and interest rates toward levels desired by a central bank (such as the Federal Reserve System).

operational (transactional) risk   Uncertainty surrounding a financial firm's earnings or rate of return due to failures in computer systems, management errors, employee misconduct, floods, hurricanes, and similar events.

opportunity cost   Forgone income that is not earned because idle funds have not been invested in earning assets; also, the yield available on the next best alternative use of an individual's or institution's funds.

option ARM   Home mortgage loan that allows the borrower to pay a reduced amount the first few years (such as paying interest only) and then requires larger payments (including principal) in the later years.

organizational forms   The structure of operations, facilities, and personnel within a bank or other financial firm that enables it to produce and deliver financial services.

P

participation loans   Purchases of loans by a third party, not part of the original loan contracts.

passbook savings deposits   Accounts sold to household customers in small denominations along with a small booklet or computer statement showing the account's current balance, interest earnings, deposits, and withdrawals.

People's Bank of China   The central bank of China, directing that nation's money and credit policies.

pledging   Backing deposits owed to the federal government and local units of government by requiring the financial institutions holding those deposits to hold designated high-quality (low-risk) assets (usually government securities of various types) that could be sold to recover government funds if the depository institution fails.

point-of-sale (POS) terminals   Computer equipment in stores to allow electronic payments for goods and services.

points   An up-front fee often charged a borrower taking on a home mortgage, which is determined by multiplying the loan amount by the number of percentage points assessed the borrower.

portfolio diversification   Spreading out credit accounts and deposits among a wide variety of customers, including many large and small businesses, different industries, and households in order to reduce the lender's risk of loss.

portfolio immunization   An interest-rate hedging device that permits a financial institution to reduce loss in the value of its assets or in the value of its net worth due to changing interest rates by equating the average duration of its assets to the average duration of its liabilities.

portfolio shifting   Selling selected securities, often at a loss, to offset taxable income from other sources and to restructure a financial firm's asset portfolio to one that is more appropriate for current market conditions.

predatory lending   Granting loans to weaker borrowers and charging them excessive fees and interest rates, increasing the risk of their defaulting on those loans.

preferred stock   Type of capital measured by the par value of any shares outstanding that promise to pay their owners a fixed rate of return or (in the case of variable-rate preferred) a rate determined by an agreed-upon formula.

prepayment risk   A risk carried by many securitized assets in which some of these assets (usually loans) are paid off early and the investor receiving those prepayments may be forced to reinvest the prepaid funds at lower current market yields, resulting in a lower than expected overall return from investing in securitized assets.

price leadership   A method for setting loan rates that looks to leading lending institutions to set the base loan rate.

primary capital   The sum of total equity capital, the allowance for possible loan losses, mandatory convertible debentures, and minority interests in consolidated subsidiaries, minus intangible assets other than purchased loan-servicing rights.

prime rate   An administered interest rate on loans quoted by leading banks and usually set by a vote of each bank's board of directors; the interest rate that the public usually thinks is the best (lowest) rate for loans and that a bank quotes to its biggest and best customers (principally large corporations).

product-line diversification   Offering multiple financial services in order to reduce the risk associated with declining revenues and income from any one service offered.

profitability   An important indicator of performance, it represents the rate of return a financial firm or other business has been able to generate from using the resources at its command in order to produce and sell services.

profit potential   A motive for carrying out a merger, in which the shareholders of either the acquiring firm, the acquired firm, or both anticipate greater profits due to greater revenues or lower operating costs after the merger is completed.

project loans   Credit designed to finance the construction of fixed assets associated with a particular investment project that is expected to generate a flow of revenue in future periods sufficient to repay the loan and turn a profit.

property-casualty insurance policies   Contracts that pledge reimbursement of policyholders for personal injuries, property damage, and other losses incurred in return for policyholder premium payments.

public benefits   Aspect of a merger or holding-company acquisition application in which merging or acquiring financial firms must show how the transaction will improve the quality, availability, or pricing of services offered to the public.

public need   One of the criteria used by governmental agencies to determine whether a new bank, branch, or other financial service unit should be approved for a charter, which focuses on whether or not an adequate volume and variety of financial services are available conveniently in a given market area.

purchase-of-assets method   A method for completing a merger in which the acquiring institution buys all or a portion of the assets of the acquired organization, using either cash or its own stock to pay for the purchase.

purchase-of-stock method   A method for carrying out a merger in which the acquired firm usually ceases to exist because the acquiring firm assumes all of its assets and liabilities.

R

real estate brokerage services   A service that assists customers in finding homes and other properties for sale or for rent.

real estate loans   Credit secured by real property, including short-term credit to support building construction and land development, and longer-term credit to support the purchase of residential and commercial structures.

relationship pricing   Basing fees charged a customer on the number of services and the intensity of use of those services that the customer purchases.

Report of Condition   A depository institution's balance sheet, which lists the assets, liabilities, and equity capital (owners' funds) held by or invested in the depository institution at any single point in time; reports of condition must be filed periodically with regulatory agencies.

Report of Income   A depository institution's income statement, which indicates how much revenue has been received and what expenses have been incurred over a specific period of time; reports of income must be filed periodically with regulatory agencies.

representative office   The simplest organizational presence for an international bank in foreign markets, consisting of limited-service facilities that can market services supplied by the home office and identify new customers but usually cannot take deposits or make decisions on the granting of loans.

repurchase agreement (RP)   A money market instrument that involves the temporary sale of high-quality assets (usually government securities) accompanied by an agreement to buy back those assets on a specific future date at a predetermined price or yield.

reputation risk   Uncertainty associated with publicity that a financial firm may attract or changing public opinion regarding a firm's behavior and performance.

reserve computation period   A period of time established by the Federal Reserve System for certain depository institutions over which the daily average amounts of various deposits are computed to determine each institution's legal reserve requirement.

reserve maintenance period   According to federal law and regulation, a period of time spanning two weeks, during which a depository institution must hold the daily average amount of legal reserves it is required by law to hold behind its deposits and other reservable liabilities.

residential mortgage loans   Credit to finance the purchase of homes or fund improvements on private residences.

restrictive covenants   Parts of a loan agreement, specifying actions the borrower must take or must not take for a loan agreement to remain in force.

retail banks   Consumer-oriented banks that sell the majority of their services to households and smaller businesses.

retail credit   Smaller-denomination loans extended to individuals and families as well as to smaller businesses.

retirement plans   Financial plans offered by various financial institutions that accumulate and manage the savings of customers until they reach retirement age.

revolving credit line   A financing arrangement that allows a business customer to borrow up to a specified limit, repay all or a portion of the borrowing, and reborrow as necessary until the credit line matures.

Riegle-Neal Interstate Banking and Branching Efficiency Act   Federal law passed in 1994 that permits bank holding companies to acquire banks nationwide and authorized interstate branching and mergers beginning June 1, 1997.

right of offset   The legal authority of a lender that has extended a loan to one of its customers to seize any checking or savings deposits the customer may hold with the lender in order to recover the lender's funds.

ROA   Return on total assets as measured by the ratio of net income after taxes to total assets.

ROE   Return on equity capital invested in a corporation by its stockholders, measured by after-tax net income divided by total equity capital.

Rule of 78s   A method for calculating rebates of interest payments to be returned to a customer if a loan is retired early.

S

safekeeping   A financial institution's practice of holding precious metals, securities, and other valuables owned by its customers in secure vaults.

Sarbanes-Oxley Accounting Standards Act   Federal law passed in the United States in 2002 designed to prohibit public companies from publishing false or misleading financial reports and creating an accounting standards board to oversee the practices of the accounting and auditing professions.

savings and loan associations   Depository institutions that concentrate the majority of their assets in the home mortgage loan area and rely mainly on savings deposits as their principal source of funding.

savings deposits   Interest-bearing funds left with a depository institution for a period of weeks, months, or years (with no minimum required maturity under U.S. regulations).

secondary capital   The sum of all forms of temporary capital, including limited-life preferred stock, subordinated notes and debentures, and mandatory convertible debt instruments not eligible to be counted as primary capital.

Securities and Exchange Commission   A federal oversight board created by the Securities and Exchange Act of 1934 that requires public companies to file financial reports and disclose relevant information about their financial condition to the public and to prevent the issuance of fraudulent or deceptive information in the offering of new securities to the public.

securitization   Setting aside a group of income-earning assets and issuing securities against them in order to raise new funds.

securitized assets   Loans placed in an income-generating pool against which securities are issued in order to raise new funds.

security brokerage   Offering customers a channel through which to buy or sell stocks, bonds, and other securities at low transactions cost instead of having to go through a security broker or dealer.

security brokers and dealers   Financial firms engaged in buying and selling stocks, bonds, and other securities on behalf of their customers and providing underwriting services for new issues of stocks and debt securities as well as financial advice regarding market conditions and other financial matters.

security underwriting   A service provided by investment banks to corporate and governmental customers in which new securities issued by a customer are purchased by the investment bank and sold in the money and capital markets in the hope of earning a profitable spread.

self-liquidating loans   Business loans, usually to support the purchase of inventories, in which the credit is gradually repaid by the borrowing customer as inventory is sold.

service differentiation   Creating perceptions in the minds of customers that a particular financial firm's services are of better quality, are more conveniently available, or differ in some other significant way from similar services offered by competitors.

servicing rights   Rights retained by a lender selling a loan in which the lender continues to collect interest payments from the borrower and monitors the borrower's compliance with loan terms on behalf of the purchaser of the loan.

shell branches   Booking offices located offshore from the United States that record international transactions (such as taking deposits) and escape many regulatory restrictions that limit the activities of domestic offices.

simple interest method   A method for calculating the interest rate on a loan that adjusts for the declining balance on a loan and uses a formula, principal times interest times time, to determine the amount of interest owed.

sources and uses of funds method   Approach developed for estimating liquidity requirements that examines the expected sources of liquidity (for a bank, principally its deposits) and the expected uses of liquidity (principally its loans) and estimates the net difference between funds sources and uses over a given period of time in order to aid liquidity planning.

Sources and Uses of Funds Statement   Financial reports on a business customer showing changes in assets and liabilities over a given period of time.

standby letter of credit (SLC)   Popular type of financial guarantee in which the issuer of the letter guarantees the beneficiary of the letter that a loan he or she has made will be repaid.

state banking commissions   Boards or commissions appointed by governors or legislators in each of the 50 states that are responsible for issuing new bank charters and supervising and examining state-chartered banks.

state insurance commissions   Regulatory bodies created by state law in each of the 50 U.S. states that regulate life and property/casualty insurance companies selling their policies to the public in an effort to ensure adequate service at reasonable cost.

Statement of Cash Flows   A financial report often constructed by credit analysts or by borrowing customers that shows a prospective borrower's sources of cash flowing in and flowing out and the actual or projected net cash flow available to repay a loan or other obligation.

stockholders   The owners of a business who hold one or more shares of common and/or preferred stock issued by their corporation and elect its board of directors.

strategic risk   Variations in earnings or rates of return due to longer-range business decisions or a financial firm's responses to changes in the business environment.

stripped security   A debt security whose promised interest payments and promised repayments of principal are separated from each other; each of these promised payment streams becomes the basis for issuing new securities in the form of interest-only (IO) and principal-only (PO) discount obligations.

structure of funds method   Method of estimating liquidity requirements that depends on a detailed analysis of deposit and loan customers and how the levels of their deposits and loans are likely to change over time.

subordinated debentures (or notes)   Type of capital represented by debt instruments whose claim against the borrowing institution legally follows the claims of depositors but comes ahead of the stockholders.

subprime loans   Credit granted to borrowers whose credit rating is considered to be weak or below average, often due to a prior record of delinquent payments, bankruptcy, or other adverse developments.

subsidiary   A corporation operated by international banks that is used to sell bank and nonbank services overseas and is often set up or acquired because bank branch offices may be prohibited in some foreign markets or because of tax advantages or other factors.

super NOWs   Savings accounts that usually promise a higher interest return than regular NOW accounts but often impose restrictions on the number of drafts (checks) or withdrawals the depositor is allowed to make.

supplemental capital   Secondary forms of capital, such as debt securities and limited-life preferred stock, that usually have a definite maturity and are not, therefore, perpetual funding instruments.

surplus   Type of capital representing the excess amount above each share of stock's par value paid in by stockholders when they purchased their shares.

sweep accounts   Contracts executed between a depository institution and some of its deposit customers that allow the institution to transfer funds (usually overnight) out of the customers' checking accounts into their savings deposits or into other types of deposits that do not carry legal reserve requirements.

syndicated loan   A loan or line of credit extended to a business firm by a group of lenders in order to reduce the credit risk exposure to any single lending institution.

synthetic CDOs   Financial instruments based on pools of derivatives, usually issued to help guard against defaults on corporate bonds.

T

tax benefits   Ways to save on a potential tax obligation by investing in tax-exempt earning assets, incurring tax-deductible expenses, or accruing income losses that help offset taxable income from loans or other income sources.

tax swapping   A process in which lower-yielding securities may be sold at a loss that is deductible from ordinary taxable income, usually to be replaced by securities bearing more favorable returns.

term loans   Credit extended for longer than one year and designed to fund longer-term business investments, such as the purchase of equipment or the construction of new physical facilities.

thrift deposits   Accounts whose principal purpose is to provide an interest-bearing outlet for customer savings— that is, a place for the customer to store liquid purchasing power at interest until needed.

Tier 1 capital   Core capital for a banking firm that includes common stock, undivided profits, selected preferred stock and intangible assets, and minority interest in subsidiary businesses.

Tier 2 capital   Supplemental long-term funds for a bank, including allowance for loan and lease losses, subordinated debt capital, selected preferred stock, and equity notes.

time deposits   Interest-bearing accounts with stated maturities, which may carry penalties in the form of lost interest earnings or reduction of principal if early withdrawal occurs.

transaction deposit   A deposit service in which checks or drafts against the deposit may be used to pay for purchases of goods and services.

Treasury bill   A direct obligation of the U.S. government that must mature within one year from date of issue.

Treasury bonds   The longest-term U.S. Treasury debt securities, with original maturities beyond 10 years.

Treasury notes   Coupon instruments issued by the U.S. government, with original maturities from more than 1 year to a maximum of 10 years, which promise investors a fixed rate of return.

trust services   Management of property and other valuables owned by a customer under a contract (the trust agreement) in which the bank serves as trustee and the customer becomes the trustor during a specified period of time.

Truth-in-Lending Act   Law passed by the U.S. Congress in 1968 that promotes the informed use of credit among consumers by requiring full disclosure of credit terms and costs.

Truth-in-Savings Act   Law passed by the U.S. Congress in 1991 that requires depository institutions to fully disclose the prices and other terms offered on deposit services so that customers can more easily compare deposit plans offered by different service providers.

U

underwriting   Buying new securities from the businesses that issued them and attempting to resell those securities at a profit to other investors.

underwriting property/casualty insurance risks
Companies that attempt to profit from collecting policyholder premiums that exceed cash outflows to pay off policyholder claims for injuries and damages.

undivided profits   Type of capital representing net earnings that have been retained in the business rather than being paid out as dividends to the stockholders.

Uniform Bank Performance Report (UBPR)   A compilation of financial and operating information, periodically required to be submitted to federal banking agencies, which is designed to aid regulators and financial analysts in analyzing a U.S. bank's financial condition.

unit banks   Banks that offer the full range of their services from one office, though a small number of services (such as taking deposits or cashing checks) may be offered from limited-service facilities, such as drive-up windows and ATMs.

USA Patriot Act   Federal law passed in the United States in the fall of 2001 requiring selected financial institutions to verify the identity of customers opening new accounts and to report any suspicious activities (especially those possibly related to terrorism) to a division of the U.S. Treasury Department.

V

value at risk (VaR) models   A statistical framework for measuring an asset portfolio's exposure to changes in market prices or market rates of interest over a given time period, subject to a given probability level.

virtual banks   Banking firms chartered by federal or state authorities to offer financial services to the public exclusively online.

W

warranties   A section within a loan agreement in which a borrower affirms to the lender that the information he or she supplies is true and correct.

wholesale banks   Large metropolitan banks that offer financial services mainly to corporations and other large institutions.

wholesale lenders   Lending institutions that devote the bulk of their credit portfolios to large-denomination loans extended to corporations and other relatively large business firms and institutions.

working capital   The current assets of a business firm (consisting principally of cash, accounts receivable, inventory, and other assets normally expected to roll over into cash within a year); some authorities define working capital as equal to current assets minus current liabilities.

working capital loans   Loans that provide businesses with short-term credit lasting from a few days to one year and that are often used to fund the purchase of inventories in order to put goods on shelves or to purchase raw materials.

Y

yield curve   A graphic picture of how interest rates vary with different maturities of securities as viewed at a single point in time.

yield to maturity (YTM)   The expected rate of return on a debt security held until its maturity date is reached, based on the security's purchase price, promised interest payments, and redemption value at maturity.

Page numbers followed by n indicate notes.

Imperial Chemical Industries PLC	www.ici.com
Independent Community Bankers of America	www.ibaa.org
Inflation-Linked.com	www.inflation-linked.com
Inner City Press	www.innercitypress.org
Innovative Interfaces, Inc.	www.iii.com
Institute of International Bankers	www.iib.org
Institute of Islamic Banking and Insurance	www.islamic-banking.com
Insurance Information Institute	www.iii.org
International Country Risk Guide	www.icrgonline.com
International Monetary Fund	www.imf.org
International Swaps and Derivatives Association, Inc.	www.isda.org
Internet Fraud	www.internetfraud.usdoj.gov
InternetNews.com	www.internetnews.com
InvestingInBonds.com	www.investinginbonds.com
Investment Company Institute	www.ici.org
iMoneyNet	www.imoneynet.com
The Investment FAQ	www.invest-faq.com
Investopedia	www.investopedia.com
InvestorGuide	www.investorguide.com
InvestorWords.com	www.investorwords.com
Japanese Bankers Association	www.zenginkyo.or.jp/en/
KeyBank	www.key.com
LACE Financial Corp.	www.lacefinancial.com
LaSalle Bank	www.lasallebank.com
Lehman Brothers	www.lehman.com
Lendertraining.com	www.quick-start.net
The Library of Economics and Liberty	www.econlib.org
Loan Pricing Corporation	www.loanpricing.com
MarketWatch, Inc.	www.marketwatch.com
Markit Group	www.markit.com
MerchantConnect	www.merchantconnect.com
Merrill Lynch & Co.	www.ml.com
Moody's KMV	www.moodyskmv.com
Morningstar, Inc.	www.morningstar.com
Mortgage 101	www.mortgage101.com
Mutual Fund Investor's Center	www.mfea.com
myFico	www.myfico.com
National Association for Bank Security	www.banksecurity.com
National Association of Credit Management	www.nacm.org
National Association of Insurance Commissioners	www.naic.org
National Bankers Association	www.nationalbankers.org
National Banking Network, Inc.	www.nbn-jobs.com
National Credit Union Administration	www.ncua.gov
National Venture Capital Association	www.nvca.org
New York State Banking Department	www.banking.state.ny.us
Nexus Generations	www.nexusgenerations.com
Nolo	www.nolo.com
The Office of Thrift Supervision	www.ots.treas.gov
Olson Research Associates, Inc.	www.olsonresearch.com
Onecle	www.contracts.onecle.com